D0889728

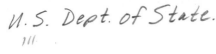

**Foreign Relations of the
United States, 1964–1968**

Volume XXXI

South and Central America; Mexico

Editors	David C. Geyer
	David H. Herschler
General Editor	Edward C. Keefer

United States Government Printing Office
Washington
2004

DEPARTMENT OF STATE PUBLICATION 11152

OFFICE OF THE HISTORIAN

BUREAU OF PUBLIC AFFAIRS

For sale by the Superintendent of Documents, U.S. Government Printing Office
Internet: bookstore.gpo.gov   Phone: toll free (866) 512-1800;   DC area (202) 512-1800
Fax: (202) 512-2250 Mail: Stop SSOP, Washington, DC 20402-0001

ISBN 0-16-072318-3

Preface

The *Foreign Relations of the United States* series presents the official documentary historical record of major foreign policy decisions and significant diplomatic activity of the United States Government. The Historian of the Department of State is charged with the responsibility for the preparation of the *Foreign Relations* series. The staff of the Office of the Historian, Bureau of Public Affairs, under the direction of the General Editor, plans, researches, compiles, and edits the volumes in the series. This documentary editing proceeds in full accord with the generally accepted standards of historical scholarship. Official regulations codifying specific standards for the selection and editing of documents for the series were first promulgated by Secretary of State Frank B. Kellogg on March 26, 1925. These regulations, with minor modifications, guided the series through 1991.

A new statutory charter for the preparation of the series was established by Public Law 102–138, the Foreign Relations Authorization Act, Fiscal Years 1992 and 1993, which was signed by President George Bush on October 28, 1991. Section 198 of P.L. 102–138 added a new Title IV to the Department of State's Basic Authorities Act of 1956 (22 USC 4351, *et seq.*).

The statute requires that the *Foreign Relations* series be a thorough, accurate, and reliable record of major United States foreign policy decisions and significant United States diplomatic activity. The volumes of the series should include all records needed to provide comprehensive documentation of major foreign policy decisions and actions of the United States Government. The statute also confirms the editing principles established by Secretary Kellogg: the *Foreign Relations* series is guided by the principles of historical objectivity and accuracy; records should not be altered or deletions made without indicating in the published text that a deletion has been made; the published record should omit no facts that were of major importance in reaching a decision; and nothing should be omitted for the purposes of concealing a defect in policy. The statute also requires that the *Foreign Relations* series be published not more than 30 years after the events recorded. The editors are convinced that this volume, which was compiled in 1994–1997, meets all regulatory, statutory, and scholarly standards of selection and editing.

Structure and Scope of the Foreign Relations Series

This volume is part of a subseries of volumes of the *Foreign Relations* series that documents the most important issues in the foreign policy of the 5 years (1964–1968) of the administration of Lyndon B. Johnson. The subseries presents in 34 volumes a documentary record of major foreign policy decisions and actions of President Johnson's administration. This volume documents U.S. policy toward South and Central America, and Mexico.

Focus of Research and Principles of Selection for Foreign Relations, 1964–1968, Volume XXXI

The editors of the volume sought to include documentation illuminating the foreign policymaking process of the U.S. Government, emphasizing in particular the highest level at which policy on a given subject was determined. The documents selected include memoranda and records of discussions that set forth policy issues and show decisions or actions taken. The focus is on the development of U.S. policy and on major aspects and repercussions of its implementation rather than on the details of policy execution.

The volume features eleven bilateral and two regional compilations, demonstrating the breadth of the U.S. Government's relations with the countries of South and Central America. Many of the bilateral compilations document the Johnson administration's responses to a series of crises: the 1964 Panama Canal flag incident; the 1964 coup d'etat in Brazil; the 1964 Presidential election in Chile; the 1966 coup in Argentina; the 1967 hunt for Ernesto "Che" Guevara in Bolivia; the 1968 coups in Peru and Panama. The bilateral compilations also show how the administration tried to address more fundamental problems: the Panama Canal treaty negotiations; the insurgencies in Ecuador, Peru, and Venezuela; the authoritarian regimes in Brazil and Argentina; the continuation of covert political support in Bolivia and Chile; economic assistance to Brazil, Colombia and Chile; the protection of American business interests in Venezuela, Argentina, Peru, and Chile. The Latin America regional compilation emphasizes the broader themes of the administration's policy in the hemisphere: the Alliance for Progress; the threat of Cuban subversion; the Punta del Este conference. This regional compilation also highlights how personalities affected policymaking, especially the working relationship between President Johnson and Assistant Secretary of State Thomas Mann. The Central America regional compilation examines how the United States exercised its influence in the region, from elections in Costa Rica and Guatemala to authoritarian regimes in Honduras and Nicaragua. Given subsequent events, including the assassination of Ambassador Gordon Mein in August 1968, the compilation also emphasizes the U.S. response to the escalation of violence between the insurgents and the Government in Guatemala.

The volume's principal focus is on the President, since Lyndon Johnson made the major foreign policy decisions during his administration. The editors sought to document his role as far as possible. Although the foreign policy record of the Johnson administration is voluminous, only the most important internal discussions between

Johnson and his advisers were documented. The record of Johnson's involvement as well as that of Secretary of State Rusk in the policy process often had to be pieced together from a variety of sources.

Editorial Methodology

The documents are presented chronologically according to Washington time or, in the case of conferences, in the order of individual meetings. Memoranda of conversation are placed according to the time and date of the conversation, rather than the date the memorandum was drafted.

Editorial treatment of the documents published in the *Foreign Relations* series follows Office style guidelines, supplemented by guidance from the General Editor and the chief technical editor. The source text is reproduced as exactly as possible, including marginalia or other notations, which are described in the footnotes. Texts are transcribed and printed according to accepted conventions for the publication of historical documents in the limitations of modern typography. A heading has been supplied by the editors for each document included in the volume. Spelling, capitalization, and punctuation are retained as found in the source text, except that obvious typographical errors are silently corrected. Other mistakes and omissions in the source text are corrected by bracketed insertions: a correction is set in italic type; an addition in roman type. Words or phrases underlined in the source text are printed in italics. Abbreviations and contractions are preserved as found in the source text, and a list of abbreviations is included in the front matter of each volume.

Bracketed insertions are also used to indicate omitted text that deals with an unrelated subject (in roman type) or that remains classified after declassification review (in italic type). The amount of material not declassified has been noted by indicating the number of lines or pages of source text that were omitted. Entire documents withheld for declassification purposes have been accounted for and are listed by headings, source notes, and number of pages not declassified in their chronological place. The amount of material omitted from this volume because it was unrelated to the subject of the volume, however, has not been delineated. All brackets that appear in the source text are so identified by footnotes.

The first footnote to each document indicates the document's source, original classification, distribution, and drafting information. This note also provides the background of important documents and policies and indicates whether the President or his major policy advisers read the document. Every effort has been made to determine if a document has been previously published, and, if so, this information has been included in the source footnote.

Editorial notes and additional annotation summarize pertinent material not printed in the volume, indicate the location of additional documentary sources, provide references to important related documents printed in other volumes, describe key events, and provide summaries of and citations to public statements that supplement and elucidate the printed documents. Information derived from memoirs and other firsthand accounts has been used when appropriate to supplement or explicate the official record.

Advisory Committee on Historical Diplomatic Documentation

The Advisory Committee on Historical Diplomatic Documentation, established under the *Foreign Relations* statute, reviews records, advises, and makes recommendations concerning the *Foreign Relations* series. The Advisory Committee monitors the overall compilation and editorial process of the series and advises on all aspects of the preparation and declassification of the series. Although the Advisory Committee does not attempt to review the contents of individual volumes in the series, it does monitor the overall process and makes recommendations on particular problems that come to its attention.

The Advisory Committee has not reviewed this volume.

Declassification Review

The Information Response Branch of the Office of Information Programs and Services, Bureau of Administration, Department of State, conducted the declassification review of the documents published in this volume. The review was conducted in accordance with the standards set forth in Executive Order 12958 on Classified National Security Information and applicable laws.

The principle guiding declassification review is to release all information, subject only to the current requirements of national security as embodied in law and regulation. Declassification decisions entailed concurrence of the appropriate geographic and functional bureaus in the Department of State, other concerned agencies of the U.S. Government, and the appropriate foreign governments regarding specific documents of those governments. The final declassification review of this volume, which began in 1997 and was completed in 2003, resulted in the decision to withhold 12 documents in full, excise a paragraph or more in 10 documents, and make minor excisions of less than a paragraph in 52 documents.

On the basis of the research conducted in preparing this volume and as a result of the declassification review process described above, the Office of the Historian is confident that the documentation and editorial notes presented here provide a substantially accurate account of the major decisions and actions that constituted U.S. foreign policy toward South and Central America (and Mexico) during the Johnson administration.

Acknowledgements

The editors wish to acknowledge the assistance of officials at the Lyndon B. Johnson Library of the National Archives and Records Administration, especially Regina Greenwell and Charlaine Burgess, who provided indispensable assistance in the process of research. The editors also wish to acknowledge the assistance of historians at the Central Intelligence Agency, especially Gerald Haines. Dallas Lindgren of the Minnesota Historical Society provided important documentation from the papers of former Vice President Hubert Humphrey.

W. Taylor Fain, Jeffrey Soukup, David H. Herschler, and David C. Geyer collected the documentation for the volume. Under the general supervision of General Editor Edward C. Keefer, David Herschler selected and edited the documents on Panama and Bolivia; David Geyer selected and edited the documents in the remaining compilations. David Geyer also prepared the lists of names, sources, and abbreviations. Vicki E. Futscher and Rita M. Baker did the copy and technical editing and Susan C. Weetman coordinated the final declassification review. Max Franke prepared the index.

Marc J. Susser
The Historian
Bureau of Public Affairs

August 2004

Johnson Administration Volumes

Following is a list of the volumes in the *Foreign Relations* series for the administration of President Lyndon B. Johnson. The titles of individual volumes may change. The year of publication is in parentheses.

Contents

Sources

Sources for the Foreign Relations Series

The Foreign Relations statute requires that the published record in the *Foreign Relations* series include all records needed to provide comprehensive documentation on major U.S. foreign policy decisions and significant U.S. diplomatic activity. It further requires that government agencies, departments, and other entities of the U.S. Government engaged in foreign policy formulation, execution, or support cooperate with the Department of State Historian by providing full and complete access to records pertinent to foreign policy decisions and actions and by providing copies of selected records. Many of the sources consulted in the preparation of this volume have been declassified and are available for review at the National Archives and Records Administration.

The editors of the *Foreign Relations* series have complete access to all the retired records and papers of the Department of State: the central files of the Department; the special decentralized files ("lot files") of the Department at the bureau, office, and division levels; the files of the Department's Executive Secretariat, which contain the records of international conferences and high-level official visits, correspondence with foreign leaders by the President and Secretary of State, and memoranda of conversations between the President and Secretary of State and foreign officials; and the files of overseas diplomatic posts. All of the Department's indexed central files for these years have been permanently transferred to the National Archives and Records Administration (Archives II) at College Park, Maryland. Many of the Department's decentralized office (or lot) files covering this period, which the National Archives deems worthy of permanent retention, have been transferred or are in the process of being transferred from the Department's custody to Archives II.

The editors of the *Foreign Relations* series also have full access to the papers of President Johnson and other White House foreign policy records. Presidential papers maintained and preserved at the Presidential libraries include some of the most significant foreign affairs-related documentation from the Department of State and other Federal agencies including the National Security Council, the Central Intelligence Agency, the Department of Defense, and the Joint Chiefs of Staff.

Department of State historians also have access to records of the Department of Defense, particularly the records of the Joint Chiefs of Staff and the Secretaries of Defense and their major assistants.

Sources for Foreign Relations, 1964–1968, Volume XXXI

In preparing this volume, the editors made extensive use of the most authoritative source on President Johnson's policies on South and Central America: the Presidential papers and other White House records at the Lyndon B. Johnson Library. Within the National Security File, the Agency Files, including files on the Alliance for Progress, the Country Files, the file of Memos to the President, the National Security Council Meetings Files, and the files of Walt Rostow were particularly useful. The Thomas C. Mann Papers, especially records of his telephone conversations with Johnson, were also valuable in revealing the politics behind the President's policies.

Due to the efforts of the Johnson Library, Department of State historians have full access to the audiotapes of President Johnson's telephone conversations. Johnson frequently discussed the details of his foreign policy, including South and Central America, with his key advisors: Secretary of State Rusk, Secretary of Defense McNamara, Special Assistants to the President Bundy and Rostow, Assistant Secretary of State Mann, and senior members of Congress. As such, the tape recordings provide an unparalleled perspective on decision-making often missing in more formal documentation. The editors transcribed numerous tape recordings specifically for this volume; these transcripts are printed both as documents and in the annotation.

The records of the Department of State were also indispensable in documenting President Johnson's role in South and Central America. Although the President made the important decisions, the Department of State was primarily responsible for the development, coordination, and implementation of the administration's policy in the region. The editors of this volume relied heavily upon the Department's "subject-numeric" central files, which contain the essential telegrams, memoranda, correspondence, and other records of U.S. diplomacy. The editors also mined the materials found only in the Department's "lot" files, including the office files of Assistant Secretaries Thomas Mann, Lincoln Gordon, and Covey Oliver, and other records maintained by the Bureau of Inter-American Affairs. Additional high-level documentation was found in the files of the Department's Executive Secretariat, including the records of the Senior Interdepartmental Group, the Special Group (Counter-Insurgency), the conference files, and Secretary Rusk's memoranda of telephone conversations.

The Central Intelligence Agency provides Department of State historians access to intelligence documents from records in its custody and at the Presidential libraries. The CIA's History Staff, part of the Center for the Study of Intelligence, arranged and facilitated the research for this volume, pursuant to a May 1992 memorandum of understanding.

In compiling this volume, the editors reviewed a wide array of intelligence materials—both operational and analytical in nature—on South and Central America. In addition to the sources cited above, these materials included the files of the Directors of Central Intelligence John McCone and Richard Helms, the CIA Registry of National Intelligence Estimates and Special National Intelligence Estimates, the Directorate of Plans, and the Western Hemisphere Division. The editors found important documentation on the meetings of the Special Group/303 Committee in the files of the National Security Council and the Department of State's Bureau of Intelligence and Research. The records of the weekly meetings between representatives of the Bureau of Inter-American Affairs and the Central Intelligence Agency also yielded valuable information on the day-to-day decision-making on intelligence matters.

Almost all of this documentation has been made available for use in the *Foreign Relations* series thanks to the consent of the agencies mentioned, the assistance of their staffs, and especially the cooperation and support of the National Archives and Records Administration.

The following list identifies the particular files and collections used in the preparation of this volume. The declassification and transfer to the National Archives of these records is in process. Many of the records are already available for public review at the National Archives.

Unpublished Sources

Department of State, Washington

Central Files. See National Archives and Records Administration below.

Lot Files. For other lot files already transferred to the National Archives and Records Administration at College Park, Maryland, Record Group 59, see National Archives and Records Administration below.

INR/IL Historical Files
> Files of the Office of Intelligence Coordination, containing records from the 1940s through the 1980s, maintained by the Office of Intelligence Liaison, Bureau of Intelligence and Research including: ARA/CIA Weekly Meetings File, ARA Country Files, Latin America Files, LAPC Action Minutes, Special Group Files, 303 Committee Files, 303 Committee Special Files

National Archives and Records Administration, College Park, Maryland

Record Group 59, Department of State Records

Subject-Numeric Central Files. The following are the principal files consulted for this volume.

AID(AFP): economic assistance under the Alliance for Progress
AID(AFP) 3 ECOSOC–IA: conferences of the Inter-American Economic and Social Council
AID(US) 5: U.S. economic assistance, laws and regulations
AID(US) ARG: U.S. economic assistance to Argentina

AID(US) 7 ARG: U.S. economic assistance to Argentina, program operation and termination
AID(US) 8 ARG: U.S. economic assistance to Argentina, grants and technical assistance
AID(US) 9 ARG: U.S. economic assistance to Argentina, loans
AID(US) 10 BOL: U.S. economic assistance to Bolivia, supporting assistance
AID(US) BRAZ: U.S. economic assistance to Brazil
AID(US) 9 BRAZ: U.S. economic assistance to Brazil, loans
AID(US) CHILE: U.S. economic assistance to Chile
AID(US) 8 CHILE: U.S. economic assistance to Chile, grants and technical assistance
AID(US) 9 CHILE: U.S. economic assistance to Chile, loans
AID(US) 9 COL: U.S. economic assistance to Colombia, loans
AID(US) 8–5 ECUADOR: U.S. economic assistance to Ecuador, health and sanitation
AID(US) 9 ECUADOR: U.S. economic assistance to Ecuador, loans
AID(US) 15–8 ECUADOR: U.S. economic assistance to Ecuador, PL 480 commodity sales
    for foreign currency
AID(US) 8–8 GUAT: U.S. economic assistance to Guatemala, community development
    and social welfare
AID(US) 9 PERU: U.S. economic assistance to Peru, loans
AID(VEN) VIET S: Venezuelan economic assistance to South Vietnam
DEF 9 ARG: Argentine military personnel
DEF 1–1 BRAZ: military contingency planning for Brazil
DEF 6 BRAZ: Brazilian armed forces
DEF 12–5 BRAZ–US: procurement and sale of armaments from the U.S. to Brazil
DEF 12 CUBA: Cuban armaments
DEF 6 IA: inter-American armed forces
DEF 1 LA: military policy, plans and readiness in Latin America
DEF 1–1 PAN: military contingency planning for Panama
DEF 1 PERU: military policy, plans and readiness in Peru
DEF 12–5 PERU: procurement and sale of armaments to Peru
DEF 11 US: U.S. military research and development
DEF 19–8 US–ARG: U.S. military assistance to Argentina, equipment and supplies
DEF 19–8 US–BRAZ: U.S. military assistance to Brazil, equipment and supplies
DEF 19 US–PERU: U.S. military assistance to Peru
DEF 19–8 US–PERU: U.S. military assistance to Peru, equipment and supplies
DEF 19–3 US–VEN: U.S. military assistance to Venezuela, organizations and conferences
DEF 19–4 US–VEN: U.S. military assistance to Venezuela, agreements
E 1 BRAZ: general economic policy, plans and programs in Brazil
ECIN 3 CACM: Central American Common Market, organizations and conferences
ECIN 3 LA: economic integration in Latin America, organizations and conferences
ECIN 3 LAFTA: Latin American Free Trade Agreement, organizations and conferences
FN 14 BRAZ: Brazilian servicing of public debt
FN 1 COL: general financial policy and plans in Colombia
FN 16 COL: Colombian revenue and taxation
FN 10 IMF: International Monetary Fund, foreign exchange
FN 17 PERU: money and currency in Peru
FN 10 PERU/IMF: International Monetary Fund, foreign exchange in Peru
FN 6–1 VEN: bank credit and loans in Venezuela
FN 10 VEN: foreign exchange in Venezuela
FN 11 VEN: investment guarantees in Venezuela
FSE 12 BRAZ: electric power in Brazil
FT 23 MEX: Mexican customs administration
INCO COPPER 17: copper trade
INCO COPPER CHILE: copper in Chile
LAB 11 CHILE: wages, hours and working conditions in Chile
LEG 7 KENNEDY: visits of Senator Robert F. Kennedy

OAS 5–2: Organization of American States, charter and constitution
OAS 8–3: Organization of American States, secretariat
ORG 7 ARA: visits of officials from the Bureau of Inter-American Affairs
ORG 7 S: visits of the Secretary of State
ORG 7 VAUGHN: visits of Assistant Secretary Jack H. Vaughn
PER 2–1: personnel, general reports and statistics
PER Cole, Charles W.: personnel matters relating to Ambassador Charles W. Cole
PER Mein, John Gordon: personnel matters relating to Ambassador John Gordon Mein
PET 15 ARG: industrial organization and control of petroleum in Argentina
PET 15–2 ARG: nationalization and expropriation of petroleum in Argentina
PET 6 PERU: petroleum companies in Peru
PET 15 PERU: industrial organization and control of petroleum in Peru
PET 15–2 PERU: nationalization and expropriation of petroleum in Peru
PET 15 US: industrial organization and control of petroleum in the U.S.
PET 17–2 US: imports of petroleum to the U.S.
PET 1 US–VEN: U.S.-Venezuelan general policy and plans on petroleum
PET 17 US–VEN: U.S.-Venezuelan trade of petroleum
PET 17–2 US–VEN: U.S.-Venezuelan imports of petroleum
PET 2 VEN: general reports and statistics on petroleum in Venezuela
PET 6 VEN: petroleum companies in Venezuela
PET 12 VEN: production and consumption of petroleum in Venezuela
PET 15 VEN: industrial organization and control of petroleum in Venezuela
PET 17–1 VEN: exports of petroleum from Venezuela
PET 17–2 VEN: imports of petroleum to Venezuela
POL ARG: Argentine political affairs
POL 15 ARG: Argentine Government
POL 15–1 ARG: Argentine head of state, executive branch
POL 15–5 ARG: Argentine constitution
POL 16 ARG: recognition of Argentina
POL 23–9 ARG: rebellion and coups in Argentina
POL ARG–US: U.S.-Argentine political relations
POL 1–1 ARG–US: U.S. contingency planning and coordination for Argentina
POL 1–1 BOL: contingency planning and coordination for Bolivia
POL 7 BOL: visits and meetings with Bolivian leaders
POL 8 BOL: neutralism and non-alignment of Bolivia
POL 14 BOL: Bolivian national elections
POL 15 BOL: Bolivian Government
POL 15–1 BOL: Bolivian head of state, executive branch
POL 16 BOL: recognition of Bolivia
POL 23 BOL: internal security and counter-insurgency in Bolivia
POL 23–7 BOL: infiltration, subversion, and sabotage in Bolivia
POL 23–9 BOL: rebellion and coups in Bolivia
POL 30 BOL: Bolivian defectors and expellees
POL BOL–US: U.S.-Bolivian political relations
POL 1–1 BRAZ: contingency planning and coordination for Brazil
POL 2 BRAZ: general reports and statistics on Brazil
POL 7 BRAZ: visits and meetings with Brazilian leaders
POL 15 BRAZ: Brazilian Government
POL 15–1 BRAZ: Brazilian head of state, executive branch
POL 15–3 BRAZ: Brazilian judiciary
POL 23–5 BRAZ: Brazilian laws and regulations
POL 23–9 BRAZ: rebellion and coups in Brazil
POL 29 BRAZ: political prisoners in Brazil
POL BRAZ–US: U.S.-Brazilian political relations

POL 1 BRAZ–US: general policy and background on U.S.-Brazilian political relations
POL 7 BRAZ–US: visits and meetings between U.S. and Brazilian leaders
POL 32–1 BR GU–VEN: territory and boundary disputes between Venezuela and British Guiana
POL 19 BR HOND: Colonial Government of British Honduras
POL BR HOND–GUAT: British Honduran-Guatemalan political relations
POL CHILE: Chilean political affairs
POL 1–1 CHILE: contingency planning and coordination for Chile
POL 7 CHILE: visits and meetings with Chilean leaders
POL 12 CHILE: Chilean political parties
POL 12–3 CHILE: Chilean political parties, meetings and conferences
POL 14 CHILE: Chilean national elections
POL 15–1 CHILE: Chilean head of state, executive branch
POL 18–1 CHILE: Chilean provincial, municipal and state government elections
POL 23–9 CHILE: rebellion and coups in Chile
POL CHILE–US: U.S.-Chilean political relations
POL 17 CHILE–US: Chilean diplomatic and consular representation in the U.S.
POL COL: Colombian political affairs
POL 14 COL: Colombian national elections
POL 23 COL: internal security and counter-insurgency in Colombia
POL 7 COSTA RICA: visits and meetings with Costa Rican leaders
POL 14 COSTA RICA: Costa Rican national elections
POL 15 COSTA RICA: Costa Rican Government
POL 15–1 COSTA RICA: Costa Rican head of state, executive branch
POL 23–9 COSTA RICA: rebellion and coups in Costa Rica
POL COSTA RICA–US: U.S.-Costa Rican political relations
POL CUBA: Cuban political affairs
POL 6 CUBA: Cuban people, biographic data
POL 23–7 CUBA: infiltration, subversion and sabotage in Cuba
POL 33–3 CZ: international canals, Panama Canal Zone
POL 15 ECUADOR: Ecuadorian Government
POL 15–1 ECUADOR: Ecuadorian head of state, executive branch
POL 17 ECUADOR: Ecuadorian diplomatic and consular representation
POL 23–3 ECUADOR: internal security forces and organizations in Ecuador
POL 23–9 ECUADOR: rebellion and coups in Ecuador
POL ECUADOR–US: U.S.-Ecuadorian political relations
POL 7 EL SAL: visits and meetings with Salvadoran leaders
POL GUAT: Guatemalan political affairs
POL 2 GUAT: general reports and statistics on Guatemala
POL 14 GUAT: Guatemalan national elections
POL 23 GUAT: internal security and counter-insurgency in Guatemala
POL 23–8 GUAT: demonstrations, riots and protests in Guatemala
POL 23–9 GUAT: rebellion and coups in Guatemala
POL 1 GUAT–US: general policy and background on U.S.-Guatemalan political relations
POL 32–1 GUAT–UK: territory and boundary disputes between the UK and Guatemala
POL 1–2 HOND: basic policies, guidelines and directives on Honduras
POL 12 HOND: Honduran political parties
POL 14 HOND: Honduran national elections
POL 15–1 HOND: Honduran head of state, executive branch
POL 18–1 HOND: Honduran provincial, municipal and state government elections
POL 23–9 HOND: rebellion and coups in Honduras
POL HOND–US: U.S.-Honduran political relations
POL 1 HOND–US: general policy and background on U.S.-Honduran political relations
POL 3 IA: Inter-American organizations and alignments

POL 3 IA SUMMIT: organizations and alignments relating to the inter-American summit meeting
POL 7 IA: visits and meetings with inter-American leaders
POL 7 IA SUMMIT: inter-American summit meeting
POL 1 LA–US: general policy and background on U.S.-Latin American political relations
POL 7 MEX: visits and meetings with Mexican leaders
POL 15–1 MEX: Mexican heads of state, executive branch
POL 23–8 MEX: demonstrations, riots and protests in Mexico
POL MEX–US: U.S.-Mexican political relations
POL 33–1 MEX–US: river boundaries between the U.S. and Mexico
POL 7 NIC: visits and meetings with Nicaraguan leaders
POL 14 NIC: Nicaraguan national elections
POL 15–1 NIC: Nicaraguan head of state, executive branch
POL 23–8 NIC: demonstrations, riots and protests in Nicaragua
POL 23–9 NIC: rebellion and coups in Nicaragua
POL PAN: Panamanian political affairs
POL 2 PAN: general reports and statistics on Panama
POL 14 PAN: Panamanian national elections
POL 15 PAN: Panamanian Government
POL 15–1 PAN: Panamanian heads of state, executive branch
POL 23–8 PAN: demonstrations, riots and protests in Panama
POL 33–3 PAN: international canals, Panama
POL PAN–US: U.S.-Panamanian political relations
POL 33–3 PAN–US: U.S.-Panamanian political relations, Panama Canal
POL 7 PAR: visits and meetings with Paraguayan leaders
POL PAR–US: U.S.-Paraguayan political relations
POL PERU: Peruvian political affairs
POL 2 PERU: general reports and statistics on Peru
POL 15–1 PERU: Peruvian head of state, executive branch
POL 15–2 PERU: Peruvian legislature
POL 16 PERU: recognition of Peru
POL 23 PERU: internal security and counter-insurgency in Peru   ·
POL 23–7 PERU: infiltration, subversion and sabotage in Peru
POL 23–9 PERU: rebellion and coups in Peru
POL 23–10 PERU: travel control in Peru
POL 29 PERU: political prisoners in Peru
POL 33–4 PERU: Peruvian territorial waters
POL PERU–US: U.S.-Peruvian political relations
POL 12 UR: Uruguayan political parties
POL 15 UR: Uruguayan Government
POL 23–9 UR: rebellion and coups in Uruguay
POL 1 UR–US: general policy and background on U.S.-Uruguayan political relations
POL 1 US: U.S. general policy and background
POL 7 US: visits and meetings by U.S. leaders
POL 7 US/HARRIMAN: visits and meetings by W. Averell Harriman
POL 15–1 US/JOHNSON: visits and meetings by Lyndon B. Johnson
POL 17 US–BRAZ: U.S.-Brazilian diplomatic and consular representation
POL 17 US–ECUADOR: U.S.-Ecuadorian diplomatic and consular representation
POL 17–1 US–ECUADOR: acceptability and accreditation of U.S.-Ecuadorian diplomatic and consular representation
POL 17 US–PERU: U.S.-Peruvian diplomatic and consular representation
POL US–VEN: U.S.-Venezuelan political relations
POL VEN: Venezuelan political affairs
POL 1 VEN: general policy and background on Venezuela

POL 7 VEN: visits and meetings with Venezuelan leaders
POL 14 VEN: Venezuelan national elections
POL 15 VEN: Venezuelan Government
POL 15–1 VEN: Venezuelan head of state, executive branch
POL 23 VEN: internal security and counter-insurgency in Venezuela
POL 23–8 VEN: demonstrations, riots and protests in Venezuela
POL 23–9 VEN: rebellion and coups in Venezuela
POL 33–4 VEN: Venezuelan territorial waters
POL 33–4 VEN–CUBA: territorial waters between Cuba and Venezuela
PPB 3: press and publications, organizations and conferences
PPB 9 BRAZ: press relations and activities in Brazil
SOC 12–1 BRAZ: religion in Brazil
TEL PERU: telecommunications in Peru

Lot Files

ARA Files: Lot 68 D 385

> Subject and country files of the Bureau of Inter-American Affairs, 1964–1966, including minutes and policy documents on the Latin American Policy Committee, 1964.

ARA Files: Lot 70 D 295

> Subject and country files of the Office of the Assistant Secretary of State for Inter-American Affairs, 1965–1967

ARA Files: Lot 68 D 93

> Files of Lincoln Gordon: subject files as Ambassador to Brazil, 1961–1966; subject, country, and chronological files as Assistant Secretary of State for Inter-American Affairs, 1966, including staff assistants' files

ARA Files: Lot 70 D 150

> Subject and country files of the Office of the Assistant Secretary of State for Inter-American Affairs, 1967

ARA Files: Lot 72 D 33

> Country files and chronological files of the Bureau of Inter-American Affairs, 1967–1969

ARA Files: Lot 74 D 467

> Country files, chronological files, subject files, and staff assistants' files for Assistant Secretaries of State for Inter-American Affairs, Covey Oliver and Charles Meyer, 1967–1971

ARA/APU/A Files: Lot 66 D 243

> Subject and chronological files of the Office of Argentine, Paraguayan, and Uruguayan Affairs on Argentina, 1964, including correspondence with the Embassy in Buenos Aires

ARA/APU/A Files: Lot 69 D 87

> Subject files of the Office of Argentine, Paraguayan, and Uruguayan Affairs on Argentina, 1964–1967

ARA/APU/U Files: Lot 67 D 468

> Subject files of the Office of Argentine, Paraguayan, and Uruguayan Affairs on Uruguay, 1964

ARA/BC/B Files: Lot 70 D 443
Political subject files of the Office of Bolivian-Chilean Affairs on Bolivia, 1961–1967

ARA/BR Files: Lot 66 D 418
Subject files of the Office of Brazilian Affairs, 1962–1964

ARA/CEN Files: Lot 69 D 515
General subject files of the Office of Central American Affairs, 1967

ARA/CEN/G Files: Lot 68 D 464
Subject files of the Office of Central American Affairs on Guatemala, 1966

ARA/CEN/G Files: Lot 70 D 75
Subject files of the Office of Central American Affairs on Guatemala, 1967

ARA/CEN/H Files: Lot 67 D 46
Subject and chronological files of the Office of Central American Affairs on Honduras, 1964

ARA/CEN/H Files: Lot 70 D 59
Subject files of the Office of Central American Affairs on Honduras, 1967–1968

ARA/CEN/BH Files: Lot 69 D 528
Subject files of the Office of Central American Affairs on British Honduras, 1966–1967

ARA/CV Files: Lot 67 D 622
Subject and chronological files of the Office of Colombian-Venezuelan Affairs on Colombia, 1965

ARA/CV/C Files: Lot 69 D 407
Subject and chronological files of the Office of Colombian-Venezuelan Affairs on Colombia, 1966

ARA/EP/E Files: Lot 70 D 247
Political subject files of the Office of Ecuadorian-Peruvian Affairs on Ecuador, 1967

ARA/EP/E Files: Lot 70 D 478
Political subject files of the Office of Ecuadorian-Peruvian Affairs on Ecuador, 1968

ARA/EP/P Files: Lot 67 D 566
Subject files of the Office of Ecuadorian-Peruvian Affairs on Peru, 1955–1964

ARA/EP/P Files: Lot 72 D 101
Subject files of the Office of Ecuadorian-Peruvian Affairs on Peru, 1959–1968

ARA/EP/P Files: Lot 70 D 139
Subject files of the Office of Ecuadorian-Peruvian Affairs on Peru, 1966–1967

ARA/IRG Files: Lot 70 D 122
Meeting and subject files of the Interdepartmental Regional Group for Inter-American Affairs, 1966–1968

ARA/IPA Files: Lot 69 D 537
Files of the Office of Inter-American Political Affairs on the meeting of American Presidents at Punta del Este in 1967

ARA/LA Files: Lot 66 D 65
    Country files of Assistant Secretary of State for Inter-American Affairs Thomas
    Mann, 1964

ARA/MEX Files: Lot 69 D 377
    Subject files of the Office of Mexican Affairs, 1966

ARA/MEX Files: Lot 71 D 188
    Files of the Office of Mexican Affairs on Presidential visits and inaugurations,
    1958–1967

ARA/NC Files: Lot 72 D 235
    Official correspondence of the Director of the Office of North Coast Affairs,
    1964–1970

ARA/NC/V Files: Lot 66 D 469
    Subject files of the Office of North Coast Affairs on Venezuela, 1965

ARA/NC/V Files: Lot 69 D 19
    Subject files of the Office of North Coast Affairs on Venezuela, 1968

ARA/OAS Files: Lot 70 D 272
    Files of the Office of the US Representative to the Council of the Organization of
    American States on the meeting of American Presidents at Punta del Este in 1967

ARA/PAN Files: Lot 66 D 329
    Subject files of the Office of Panamanian Affairs, 1963–1964

ARA/PAN Files: Lot 75 D 457
    Files of the Office of Panamanian Affairs on the Panama Canal treaty negotiations,
    1964–1973, including position papers, memoranda, and correspondence to and from
    the President

ARA/SR/PAN Files: Lot 73 D 216
    Files of the Special Representative for Interoceanic Canal Negotiations; historical
    documents on the Panama Canal treaty negotiations, 1961–1968

ARA/SR/PAN Files: Lot 73 D 286
    Files of the Special Representative for Interoceanic Canal Negotiations; historical
    documents on the Panama Canal treaty negotiations, 1964–1967

Conference Files: Lot 67 D 586
    Collection of documentation on international conferences abroad attended by the
    President, Secretary of State, or other U.S. officials, September 1966–April 1967

Conference Files: Lot 68 D 453
    Collection of documentation on international conferences abroad attended by the
    President, Secretary of State, or other U.S. officials, May 1967–January 1968

Conference Files: Lot 69 D 182
    Collection of documentation on international conferences abroad attended by the
    President, Secretary of State, or other U.S. officials, 1968

E/OR/FSE Files: Lot 69 D 76
    Subject, country, and chronological files of the Office of Fuels and Energy, Bureau
    of Economic Affairs, 1963–1965

E/OR/FSE Files: Lot 70 D 54
Subject, country, and chronological files of the Office of Fuels and Energy, Bureau of Economic Affairs, 1965–1966

Katzenbach Files: Lot 74 D 271
Files of Under Secretary of State Nicholas deB. Katzenbach, 1966–1969

Lima Embassy Files: Lot 69 F 191
Classified central subject files of the US Embassy in Lima, 1966

Lima Embassy Files: Lot 71 F 154
Subject case files of the US Embassy in Lima on the International Petroleum Company, 1962–1968

Lima Embassy Files: Lot 73 F 100
Classified personal files of Ambassador J. Wesley Jones, 1965–1971

Official Visit Chronologies: Lot 68 D 475
Collection of documentation on international conferences abroad attended by the President, Secretary of State, or other U.S. officials, 1967

OPR/FAIM/IS Files: Lot 81 D 121
Files maintained by the Foreign Affairs Management Center, Information Services Division, for congressional investigations on Chile, the International Telephone and Telegraph Corporation, and the Central Intelligence Agency

Rusk Files: Lot 72 D 192
Files of Secretary of State Dean Rusk, 1961–1969, including texts of speeches, miscellaneous correspondence files, White House correspondence, chronological files, and memoranda of telephone conversations

Senior Interdepartmental Group Files: Lot 70 D 263
Master file maintained by the Executive Secretariat on the meetings and decisions of the Senior Interdepartmental Group, 1968–1969

Special Group (CI) Files: Lot 70 D 258
Master file maintained by the Executive Secretariat on the meetings and decisions of Special Group (Counter-Insurgency), 1963–1966

U. Alexis Johnson Files: Lot 90 D 408
Chronological files of Deputy Under Secretary of State U. Alexis Johnson, including his date books, 1961–1976

Lyndon B. Johnson Library, Austin, Texas

National Security File
Agency File
Country File
Walt W. Rostow Files
Intelligence File
International Meetings and Travel File
Memos to the President
Name File
National Security Council Histories

National Security Council Meetings File
National Security Action Memorandums
Situation Room File
Special Heads of State Correspondence
Subject File

Special Files
President's Daily Diary
Recordings and Transcripts of Telephone Conversations and Meetings

Personal Papers
George Ball Papers
Tom Johnson's Notes of Meetings
John McCone Memoranda of Meetings with the President
Thomas C. Mann Papers
John Wesley Jones Papers
Dean Rusk Appointment Books

White House Central Files
Cabinet Papers
Confidential File
Subject File

Minnesota Historical Society

Hubert H. Humphrey Papers
Vice Presidential Files, Foreign Affairs General Files

Central Intelligence Agency

DCI Files: Job 80–B–01285A
Files of the Directors of Central Intelligence John McCone and Richard Helms in-
cluding: McCone Memos for the Record, McCone Meetings with President Johnson,
McCone Telephone Calls, Helms Chronological File as DDP and DDCI

DO Files: Job 80–01690R, Job 90–1156R
Files of the Western Hemisphere Division (Latin America Division), Directorate of
Plans (Directorate of Operations)

DO Files: Job 90–347R
Files of the Directorate of Plans

DDO/IMS Files: Job 78–03041R, Job 78–5505, Job 78–06423A, Job 88–01415R
Files of the Directorate of Plans

O/DDI Registry: Job 79–R01012A
Files of the Office of the Deputy Director of Intelligence

National Security Council

Johnson Administration Intelligence Files

303 Committee Files
   Minutes
   Subject Files

Washington National Records Center, Suitland, Maryland

Record Group 59, Records of the Department of State

E/CBA/REP Files: FRC 72 A 6248
   Current Economic Developments

Record Group 84, Records of the Foreign Service Posts of the United States

Guatemala City Embassy Files, 1966: FRC 71 A 2420
   Subject files of the U.S. Embassy in Guatemala, 1966

Santiago Embassy Files, 1964: FRC 69 A 6507
   Subject files of the U.S. Embassy in Chile, 1964

Record Group 330, Records of the Office of the Secretary of Defense

OSD Files: FRC 69 A 7425
   Decimal files of the Office of the Secretary of Defense, 1964

OSD Files: FRC 70 A 1266
   Decimal files of the Office of the Secretary of Defense, 1965

OSD Files: FRC 72 A 2468
   Decimal files of the Office of the Secretary of Defense, 1967

OSD Files: FRC 73 A 1250
   Decimal files of the Office of the Secretary of Defense, 1968

OASD/ISA Files: FRC 64 A 7425
   Official top secret and secret files of the Secretary of Defense, Deputy Secretary of Defense, and their special assistants, 1964

OASD/ISA Files: FRC 68 A 306
   Secret files of the Office of the Assistant Secretary of Defense for International Security Affairs, 1964

OASD/ISA Files: FRC 68 A 4023
   Top Secret files of the Office of the Assistant Secretary of Defense for International Security Affairs, 1964

OASD/ISA Files: FRC 70 A 3717
   Decimal files of the Office of the Assistant Secretary of Defense for International Security Affairs, 1965

National Defense University, Fort McNair, Washington, D.C.

Maxwell Taylor Papers

Published Sources

Ball, George W. *The Past Has Another Pattern.* New York: W.W. Norton, 1982.

Berle, Beatrice Bishop and Travis Beal Jacobs, eds. *Navigating the Rapids, 1918–1971: From the Papers of Adolf A. Berle.* New York: Harcourt Brace Jovanovich, 1973.

Beschloss, Michael, ed. *Taking Charge: The Johnson White House Tapes, 1963–1964.* New York: Simon & Schuster, 1997.

Bird, Kai. *The Chairman: John J. McCloy, the Making of the American Establishment.* New York: Simon & Schuster, 1992.

Califano, Joseph A., Jr. *The Triumph and Tragedy of Lyndon Johnson: The White House Years.* New York: Simon & Schuster, 1991.

Humphrey, Hubert H. *The Education of a Public Man: My Life and Politics.* Garden City, New York: Doubleday, 1976.

Johnson, Lyndon B. *The Vantage Point: Perspectives of the Presidency, 1963–1969.* New York: Holt, Rinehart and Winston, 1971.

Jorden, William J. *Panama Odyssey.* Austin, Texas: University of Texas Press, 1984.

Larsen, Stanley R. and James L. Collins. *Allied Participation in the Vietnam War.* Washington, D.C.: Department of the Army, 1975.

Martin, Edward M. *Kennedy and Latin America.* Lanham, Maryland: University Press of America, 1994.

McPherson, Harry. *A Political Education: A Journal of Life with Senators, Generals, Cabinet Members and Presidents.* Boston: Little, Brown and Company, 1972.

National Archives and Records Administration. *Public Papers of the Presidents of the United States: Dwight D. Eisenhower.* U.S. Government Printing Office: Washington.

———. *Public Papers of the Presidents of the United States: John F. Kennedy.* U.S. Government Printing Office: Washington.

———. *Public Papers of the Presidents of the United States: Lyndon B. Johnson.* U.S. Government Printing Office: Washington.

Ryan, Henry Butterfield. *The Fall of Che Guevara: A Story of Soldiers, Spies, and Diplomats.* New York: Oxford University Press, 1998.

Schlesinger, Arthur M., Jr. *Robert Kennedy and His Times.* Boston: Houghton Mifflin, 1978.

U.S. Department of State. *American Foreign Policy: Current Documents.* Washington: U.S. Government Printing Office.

———. *Bulletin, 1964–1968.* Washington, 1964–1968.

United States Senate, Committee on Government Operations, Subcommittee on Foreign Aid Expenditures. *United States Aid in Action: A Case Study.* Washington: U.S. Government Printing Office, 1966.

Walters, Vernon A. *Silent Missions.* Garden City, New York: Doubleday, 1978.

Abbreviations

AALAPSO, Afro-Asian-Latin American Peoples' Solidarity Organization
ABC, American Broadcasting Company
ACDA, Arms Control and Disarmament Agency
AD, Acción Democrática (Democratic Action), Venezuelan political party
ADDP, Assistant Deputy Director for Plans, Central Intelligence Agency
AFL–CIO, American Federation of Labor–Congress of Industrial Organizations
AFP, Alliance for Progress
AID, Agency for International Development
AID/OPS, Agency for International Development, Office of Public Safety
AID/W, Agency for International Development/Washington
AIFLD, American Institute for Free Labor Development
AMFORP, American and Foreign Power Company
ANAPO, Alianza Nacional Popular (Popular National Alliance), Colombian political party
ANZUS, Australia, New Zealand, and the United States
AP, Associated Press
APRA, Alianza Popular Revolucionaria Americana (American Popular Revolutionary Alliance), Peruvian political party
ARA, Bureau of Inter-American Affairs, Department of State
ARA/APU, Bureau of Inter-American Affairs, Office of Argentine, Paraguayan, and Uruguayan Affairs
ARA/BC, Bureau of Inter-American Affairs, Office of Bolivian-Chilean Affairs
ARA/BR, Bureau of Inter-American Affairs, Office of Brazilian Affairs
ARA/CEN, Bureau of Inter-American Affairs, Office of Central American Affairs
ARA/CV, Bureau of Inter-American Affairs, Office of Colombian-Venezuelan Affairs
ARA/EP, Bureau of Inter-American Affairs, Office of Ecuadorian-Peruvian Affairs
ARA/LA, Bureau of Inter-American Affairs, Department of State; Bureau for Latin America, Agency for International Development
ARA/MEX, Bureau of Inter-American Affairs, Office of Mexican Affairs
ARA/NC, Bureau of Inter-American Affairs, Office of North Coast Affairs
ARA/OAP, Bureau of Inter-American Affairs, Office of Central American and Panamanian Affairs
ARENA, Aliança Renovadora Nacional (National Renewal Alliance), Brazilian political party
ARMA, Army Attaché
AV, aviation

BA, Buenos Aires
BG, British Guiana
BOB, Bureau of the Budget

CA, Central America
CABEI, Central American Bank for Economic Integration
CACM, Central American Common Market
CAS, Controlled American Source
CASP, Country Analysis and Strategy Paper
CCC, Commodity Credit Corporation (Farm Service Agency of the Department of Agriculture)
CEA, Council of Economic Advisers

CGT, Comando Geral dos Trabalhadores (General Command of Workers), Brazil
Chicom, Chinese Communist
CI, counter insurgency
CIA, Central Intelligence Agency
CIAP, Comité Interamericana de la Alianza para el Progreso (Inter-American Committee on the Alliance for Progress)
CINC, Commander-in-Chief
CINCLANT, Commander-in-Chief, Atlantic
CINCSO, Commander-in-Chief, Southern Command
CINCSTRIKE, Commander in Chief, Strike Force
COAS, Council of the Organization of American States
COIN, counter insurgency
COMIBOL, Corporacion Minera de Bolivia (Bolivian Mining Corporation)
COMUSARSO, Commander, US Army, Southern Command
COPEC, Companïá de Petróleos de Chile (Chilean Petroleum Company)
COPEI, Comité de Organización Politica Electoral Independiente (Committee of Independent Electoral Political Organization), Venezuelan political party
CORFO, Corporación de Fomento de la Producción (Production Development Corporation), Chile
COS, Chief of Station
CPSU, Communist Party of the Soviet Union
CS, Clandestine Service (Central Intelligence Agency); o-chlorobenzalmalononitrile (a dispersal agent or tear gas)
CST, Central Standard Time
CT, Country Team
CY, calendar year

DAO, Defense Attaché Office
DATT, Defense Attaché
DCI, Director of Central Intelligence
DCM, Deputy Chief of Mission
DDCI, Deputy Director of Central Intelligence
DDP, Deputy Director for Plans, Central Intelligence Agency
Deptel, Department of State telegram
DF, Frente Democrática (Democratic Front), Chilean electoral alliance
DIA, Defense Intelligence Agency
Dissem, dissemination
DOD, Department of Defense
DOD/ISA, Department of Defense, Office of the Assistant Secretary for International Security Affairs
DR, Dominican Republic

E, Bureau of Economic Affairs, Department of State; Escudos
EA, Bureau of East Asian and Pacific Affairs, Department of State
ECOSOC, Economic and Social Council
Emb, Embassy
Embtel, Embassy telegram
Esso, Standard Oil of New Jersey
EST, Eastern Standard Time
EUR, Bureau of European and Canadian Affairs, Department of State
Exdis, Exclusive Distribution
Eximbank, Export-Import Bank of the United States

FAA, Foreign Assistance Act of 1961
FALN, Fuerzas Armadas de Liberación Nacional (Armed Forces of National Liberation), Venezuela
FAO, Food and Agriculture Organization, United Nations
FAR, Fuerzas Armadas Rebeldes (Rebel Armed Forces), Guatemala
FBI, Federal Bureau of Investigation
FDP, Fuerza Democrática Popular (Popular Democratic Force), Venezuelan political party
FND, Frente Nacional Democrático (Democratic National Front), Venezuelan political party
FonMin, Foreign Minister
FRAP, Frente de Acción Popular (Popular Action Front), Chilean electoral alliance
FSB, Falange Socialista Boliviana (Bolivian Socialist Falange), Bolivia
FTN, Frente Nacional (National Front), Colombian Government coalition
FY, fiscal year
FYI, for your information

G, Deputy Under Secretary of State for Political Affairs
G/PM, Office of the Deputy Assistant Secretary of State for Politico-Military Affairs
GATT, General Agreement on Tariffs and Trade
GN, Guard Nacionale
GNP, Gross National Product
GOA, Government of Argentina
GOB, Government of Bolivia; Government of Brazil
GOC, Government of Chile; Government of Colombia
GOCR, Government of Costa Rica
GOE, Government of Ecuador
GOG, Government of Guatemala
GOH, Government of Honduras
GOM, Government of Mexico
GON, Government of Nicaragua
GOP, Government of Panama; Government of Peru
GOU, Government of Uruguay
GOV, Government of Venezuela

HEW, Department of Health, Education, and Welfare

IA, Inter-American; Institutional Act (Ato Institucional)
IADB, Inter-American Development Bank
IA-ECOSOC, Inter-American Economic and Social Council
IAF, Inter-American Force
IAPF, Inter-American Peace Force
IBRD, International Bank for Reconstruction and Development (World Bank)
IBWC, International Boundary and Water Commission
IDA, International Development Association
IDB, Inter-American Development Bank
IMF, International Monetary Fund
INDAP, Instituto de desarrollo agropecvario (Institute of Agricultural Development)
INR, Bureau of Intelligence and Research, Department of State
INR/DDC, Bureau of Intelligence and Research, Deputy Director for Coordination
INR/RAR, Bureau of Intelligence and Research, Office of Research and Analysis for American Republics
IPC, International Petroleum Company
IRG, Interdepartmental Regional Group
IRG/ARA, Interdepartmental Regional Group for Inter-American Affairs
ITT, International Telephone and Telegraph Corporation

JBUSMC, Joint Brazil–United States Military Commission
JCS, Joint Chiefs of Staff

L, Office of the Legal Adviser, Department of State
LA, Latin America; Bureau for Latin America, Agency for International Development
LAFTA, Latin American Free Trade Association
LAPC, Latin American Policy Committee
LASO, Latin American Solidarity Organization
LBJ, Lyndon Baines Johnson
LDC, less developed country
Limdis, Limited Distribution
LME, London Metals Exchange
LSD, landing ship, destroyer

M, Under Secretary of State for Economic Affairs; Under Secretary of State for Political Affairs
MAP, Military Assistance Program
MAS, Military Assistance Sales
MDAP, Mutual Defense Assistance Program
MFM, Meeting of Foreign Ministers
MILGP, Military Group
MIR, Movimiento de la Izquierda Revolucionaria (Movement of the Revolutionary Left), Venezuela
MLN, Movimiento de Liberación Nacional (National Liberation Movement), Guatemala
MMT, Military Mobile Training Team
MNR, Movimiento Nacionalista Revolucionario (National Revolutionary Movement), Bolivia
MNRI, Movimiento Naciondista Revolucionario de Izqierda (Revolutionary Party of the National Left), Bolivia
MOD, Minister of Defense
MOIP, Mandatory Oil Import Program
MPC, Moviemento Popular Christiano (Popular Christian Movement), Bolivia
MRL, Movimiento Revolucionario Liberal (Liberal Revolutionary Movement), Colombia

NATO, North Atlantic Treaty Organization
NCG, National Council of Government, Uruguay
NCO, non-commissioned officer
NIE, National Intelligence Estimate
NIH, National Institutes of Health
Nodis, No Distribution
Noforn, No Foreign Distribution
NSA, National Security Agency
NSAM, National Security Action Memorandum
NSC, National Security Council
NU, National Union Party, Panama

OAS, Organization of American States
OARS, other American Republics
ODECA, Organization of Central American States
OECD, Organization for Economic Cooperation and Development
OEO, Office of Economic Opportunity
OEP, Office of Emergency Planning
OPR/LS, Office of Operations, Language Services Division, Department of State
OSD, Office of the Secretary of Defense

PCB, Partido Comunista Boliviano (Bolivian Communist Party)
PCB, Partido Comunista Brasileiro (Brazilian Communist Party)
PCV, Partido Comunista Venezolano (Venezuelan Communist Party)
PDC, Partido Democrático Cristiana (Christian Democratic Party), Chile
Petrobrás, Petróleo Brasileiro, S.A., national petroleum company of Brazil
PGT, Partido Guatemalteco del Trabajo (Guatemalan Labor Party)
PID, Partido Institucional Democrático (Democratic Institutional Party), Guatemala
PL, Public Law
PLN, Partido Liberacion Nacional (National Liberation Party), Costa Rica
PLN, Partido Liberal Nacionalista (Nationalist Liberal Party), Nicaragua
POL, petroleum, oil, lubricants
POLAD, Political Adviser
PR, Partido Radical (Radical Party), Chile
PR, Partido Revolucionario (Revolutionary Party), Guatemala
PRA, Partido Revolucionario Auténtico, (Authentic Revolutionary Party), Bolivia
PRI, Partido Revolucionario Institucional (Institutional Revolutionary Party), Mexico
PRIN, Partido Revolucionario de la Izquierda Nacional (Revolutionary Party of the Nationalist Left), Bolivia
PSD, Partido Social Democrático (Social Democratic Party), Brazil
PTB, Partido Trabalhista Brasileiro (Brazilian Labor Party)

ref, reference
reftel, reference telegram
rpt, repeat

S, Office of the Secretary of State
SEATO, Southeast Asia Treaty Organization
Secto, series indicator for telegrams from the Secretary of State while away from Washington
septel, separate telegram
SIG, Senior Interdepartmental Group
SNIE, Special National Intelligence Estimate
SPEU, Special Police Emergency Unit, Peru
S/S, Executive Secretariat, Department of State
S/S–S, Executive Secretariat Staff, Department of State
SUDENE, Superintency for the Development of the Northeast, Brazil

TDY, temporary duty
TOAID, series indicator for communications to the Agency for International Development
Tosec, series indicator for telegrams to the Secretary of State while away from Washington

U, Under Secretary of State
UCRP, Unión Cívica Radical del Pueblo (Peoples' Radical Civic Union), Argentine political party
UDN, Uniäo Democrática Nacional (National Democratic Union), Brazilian political party
UK, United Kingdom
UN, United Nations
UNCTAD, United Nations Conference on Trade and Development
UNGA, United Nations General Assembly
URD, Unión Republicana Democrática (Democratic Republican Union), Venezuelan political party

USCINCSO, Commander-in-Chief, Southern Command
USA, United States Army
USAID, Agency for International Development
USG, United States Government
USIA, United States Information Agency
USIS, United States Information Service
USSR, Union of Soviet Socialist Republics
USUN, United States Mission to the United Nations
UTC, Unión de Trabajadores de Colombia (Union of Colombian Workers)

WH, White House
WHD, Western Hemisphere Division, Directorate of Plans, Central Intelligence Agency

YPFB, Yacimientos petrolíferos fiscales bolivianos, (Bolivian National Oilfields)

Persons

Ackley, H. Gardner, Chairman of the Council of Economic Advisers November 1964–March 1968

Adair, Charles W., Jr., Ambassador to Panama from May 6, 1965

Adams, Robert W., Chief of the Political Section of the Embassy in Mexico until February 1964; Deputy Assistant Secretary of State for Inter-American Affairs to March 1965; Special Assistant to the Under Secretary of State for Economic Affairs March 1965– May 1966

Agüero Rocha, Fernando, leader of the Partido Conservador Tradicionalista in Nicaragua; Union Nacional de Oposición candidate for President, February 1967

Ailes, Stephen, Under Secretary of the Army until January 28, 1964; Secretary of the Army until June 30, 1965

Alemán, Roberto, Special Panamanian Representative, United States–Panama Relations (after April 1965 Inter-Oceanic Canal Negotiations), from November 1964

Alessandri Rodríguez, Jorge, President of Chile until November 4, 1964

Allen, Ward P., Director, Office of Regional Political Affairs (after June 1965 Office of Inter-American Political Affairs), Bureau of Inter-American Affairs, Department of State, and Alternate U.S. Representative on the Council of the Organization of American States until October 1967

Allende Gossens, Salvador, Senator (PSP, Chile); FRAP candidate for President, September 1964; President of the Chilean Senate from December 1966

Alsogaray, Alvaro C., Argentine Ambassador at Large July–September 1966; Argentine Ambassador to the United States October 1966–September 1968

Alsogaray, Major General Julio R., (later Lieutenant General), Commander of the First Army Corps in Argentina in June 1966; Head of the Military Household; Commander-in-Chief of the Army December 1966–August 1968

Anderson, Robert B., Special U.S. Representative, U.S.–Panama Relations (after April 1965 Inter-Oceanic Canal Negotiations) from April 1964

Arenales Catalán, Emilio, Foreign Minister of Guatemala from July 1966

Arias Espinosa, Ricardo M., Panamanian Ambassador to the United States October 1964–January 1968

Arias Madrid, Arnulfo, former President of Panama; leader of the Panameñista Party; Panameñista candidate for President, May 1964; National Union candidate for President, May 1968; President of Panama October 1–October 12, 1968

Arosemena Gómez, Otto, President of Ecuador November 16, 1966–September 1,1968

Balaguer, Joaquín Videla, President of the Dominican Republic from July 1, 1966

Ball, George W., Under Secretary of State until September 30, 1966; U.S. Permanent Representative to the United Nations June 26–September 25, 1968

Barall, Milton, special assistant to the Assistant Secretary of State for Inter-American Affairs, Deputy U.S. Representative to the Inter-American Economic and Social Committee, and Alternate U.S. Representative on the Inter-American Committee on the Alliance for Progress, May 1964–July 1966

Barneby, Malcolm R., Deputy Director, Office of Ecuadorian-Peruvian Affairs, Bureau of Inter-American Affairs, Department of State, September 1964–October 1965; Director until June 1967

Barnes, Donald F., interpreter in the Language Services Division, Office of Operations, Department of State

Barr, Joseph, Under Secretary of the Treasury April 29, 1965–December 22, 1968; thereafter Secretary of the Treasury

Barrientos Ortuño, General René, Vice President of Bolivia August–November 1964; leader of the military junta in Bolivia November 5, 1964–May 26, 1965; Co-President of Bolivia May 26, 1965–January 5, 1966; President of Bolivia from August 6, 1966

Barrios, Gonzalo, Venezuelan Minister of Interior March 1964–November 1966; thereafter Secretary General of Acción Democrática; AD candidate for President December 1968

Belaunde Terry, Fernando, President of Peru until October 3, 1968

Belcher, Taylor G., Director, Office of West Coast Affairs, Bureau of Inter-American Affairs, Department of State, until February 1964

Bell, David E., Administrator of the Agency for International Development until July 31, 1966

Bell, John O., Ambassador to Guatemala until August 26, 1965

Bennett, W. Tapley, Jr., Ambassador to the Dominican Republic until April 13, 1966

Berle, Adolf A., former Assistant Secretary of State and Ambassador to Brazil; emeritus professor of law, Columbia University; chairman of the board, Twentieth Century Fund

Berlin, Lawrence H., Deputy Director, Office of Ecuadorian-Peruvian Affairs, Bureau of Inter-American Affairs, Department of State, from March 1967

Bernbaum, Maurice M., Ambassador to Ecuador until January 14, 1965; Ambassador to Venezuela from February 4, 1965

Betancourt, Rómulo, President of Venezuela until March 11, 1964

Bloomfield, Richard J., Director, Office of Ecuadorian-Peruvian Affairs, Bureau of Inter-American Affairs, Department of State, October 1967–July 1968

Bohlen, Charles E., Deputy Under Secretary of State for Political Affairs from February 11, 1968

Bosch, Juan, former President of the Dominican Republic

Boster, Davis E., special assistant to the Assistant Secretary of State for Inter-American Affairs January 1964–April 1965

Bowdler, William G., Deputy Coordinator of Cuban Affairs, Bureau of Inter-American Affairs, Department of State, until April 1965; member of the National Security Council staff until September 1968; Ambassador to El Salvador from September 26, 1968

Boyd, Aquilino Edgardo, Panamanian Permanent Representative to the United Nations

Breen, John R., Deputy Director, Office of Development Planning and Programs, Bureau of Inter-American Affairs, Department of State, January 1967–July 1968; thereafter Director, Office of Central American Affairs

Brewin, Roger C., Officer-in-Charge of Bolivian Political Affairs, Office of Bolivian-Chilean Affairs, Bureau of Inter-American Affairs, Department of State, June 1964–August 1966

Brezhnev, Leonid I., General Secretary, Central Committee, Communist Party of the Soviet Union from October 1964

Briz(z)ola, Leonel, former Governor of Rio Grande do Sul; Congressman (PTB-Guanabara) until April 1964; brother-in-law of President Goulart

Broderick, William D., Deputy Director, Office of Bolivian-Chilean Affairs, Bureau of Inter-American Affairs, Department of State, July 1966–August 1968

Broe, William V., Chief of the Western Hemisphere Division, Directorate of Plans, Central Intelligence Agency, from June 1965

Bronheim, David, Deputy U.S. Coordinator of the Alliance for Progress July 1965–July 1967

Brown, Aaron S., Ambassador to Nicaragua until May 3, 1967

Bulhões, Otávio Gouvéia de, Brazilian Minister of Finance April 1964–March 1967

Bundy, McGeorge, Special Assistant to the President for National Security Affairs until February 28, 1966

Bunker, Ellsworth, U.S. Representative on the Council of the Organization for American States January 29, 1964–November 7, 1966; Ambassador at Large November 8, 1966–April 11, 1967

Burnham, Linden Forbes Sampson, Prime Minister of British Guiana December 1964–May 1966; thereafter Prime Minister of Guyana

Burrows, Charles R., Ambassador to Honduras until June 28, 1965; Director, Office of Central American Affairs, Bureau of Inter-American Affairs, Department of State, November 1965–July 1968

Burton, Ralph J., Director, Office of Brazilian Affairs, Bureau of Inter-American Affairs, Department of State, until March 1965

Busby, Horace, Jr., Special Assistant to the President until October 1965

Caldera Rodríguez, Rafael, founder and leader of the Comité de Organización Política Electoral Independiente, Venezuela; COPEI candidate for President December 1968; thereafter President-elect of Venezuela

Califano, Joseph A., Jr., General Counsel, Department of the Army, until March 1964; Special Assistant to the Secretary of Defense until July 1965; thereafter Special Assistant to the President

Calle Restropo, Diego, Colombian Finance Minister, February 1964–March 1965

Campos, Roberto de Oliveira, former Brazilian Ambassador to the United States; Brazilian Minister of Planning and Economic Cooperation April 1964–March 1967

Carlson, Reynold E., Ambassador to Colombia from September 16, 1966

Carrillo Flores, Antonio, Mexican Ambassador to the United States until November 1964; Foreign Minister of Mexico from December 1, 1964

Carter, Albert E., Deputy Director of Coordination for Intelligence and Research, Bureau of Intelligence and Research, Department of State, until December 1965

Carter, Lieutenant General Marshall S., USA, Deputy Director of Central Intelligence until April 28, 1965; thereafter Director of the National Security Agency

Castello Branco, General Humberto de Alencar, Chief of Staff of the Army in Brazil until April 1964; President of Brazil April 15, 1964–March 15, 1967

Castro, Raul H., Ambassador to El Salvador October 3, 1964–July 17, 1968; Ambassador to Bolivia from August 1, 1968

Castro Ruz, Fidel, Premier of Cuba

Cater, S. Douglass Jr., Special Assistant to the President July 1965–October 1968

Chamorro Cardenal, Pedro Joaquín, owner and publisher of *La Prensa* in Nicaragua; coordinator of the Union Nacional de Oposición during the 1967 Presidential campaign

Chase, Gordon, member of the National Security Council staff until January 1966

Chayes, Abram J., Legal Adviser, Department of State, until June 27, 1964

Chiari Junior, Roberto Francisco, President of Panama until October 1, 1964

Christian, George E., Special Assistant and Press Secretary to the President from February 1967

Clark, Edward W., Director, Office of Panamanian Affairs, Bureau of Inter-American Affairs, Department of State, August 1964–June 1968

Clifford, Clark M., Secretary of Defense from March 1, 1968

Cline, Ray S., Deputy Director for Intelligence, Central Intelligence Agency, until January 1966; thereafter Special Assistant to the Director for Central Intelligence

Coerr, Wymberley deR., Ambassador to Uruguay until January 22, 1965; Ambassador to Ecuador February 4, 1965–October 7, 1967

Cole, Charles W., Ambassador to Chile until September 27, 1964

Collins, V. Lansing, Director, Office of Central American and Panamanian Affairs (after March 12, 1964, Office of Panamanian Affairs), Bureau of Inter-American Affairs, Department of State, until August 1964

Costa e Silva, General Arturo da, Chief of the Brazilian Army Department of Production and Works until April 1964; Brazilian Minister of War April 1964–June 1966; ARENA candidate for President, October 1966; President of Brazil from March 15, 1967

Costa Méndez, Nicanor, Foreign Minister of Argentina from July 5, 1966

Cottrell, Sterling J., Deputy Assistant Secretary of State for Inter-American Affairs until February 1964; Special Adviser to the Special U.S. Representative, U.S.-Panama Relations, May 1964–April 1965; Deputy Chief of Mission, Embassy in Venezuela, until April 1967

Crimmins, John H., Coordinator of Cuban Affairs, Bureau of Inter-American Affairs, Department of State, until January 1966; Ambassador to the Dominican Republic from June 27, 1966

Crowley, John J., Jr., Officer-in-Charge of Venezuelan Affairs, Office of Colombian-Venezuelan Affairs (after May 1966 Officer-in-Charge of Venezuelan Political Affairs, Office of North Coast Affairs), Bureau of Inter-American Affairs, Department of State, August 1964–August 1966; thereafter Deputy Chief of Mission, Embassy in Ecuador

De Gaulle, Charles, President of France

De la Rosa, Diógenes, Special Panamanian Representative, U.S.-Panama Relations (after April 1965 Inter-Oceanic Canal Negotiations) from November 1964

De Lavalle, Juan Bautista, Peruvian Representative to the Council of the Organization of American States until February 1968; also Chairman of the General Committee on the Council of the Organization of American States until November 1964

Delvalle, Max, First Vice President of Panama October 1964–September 1968; rival President of Panama March 25–October 1, 1968

Denney, George C., Jr., Deputy Director of the Bureau of Intelligence and Research, Department of State

Dentzer, William T., Jr., Director, Office of Bolivian-Chilean Affairs, Bureau of Inter-American Affairs, March 1964–August 1965; Director, AID Mission in Peru, until September 1968

Díaz Ordaz, Gustavo, PRI candidate for President, July 1964; President of Mexico from December 1, 1964

Dillon, C. Douglas, Secretary of the Treasury until March 31, 1965

Dirksen, Everett M., Senator (Republican–Illinois); Senate Minority Leader

Dreyfuss, John T., Officer-in-Charge of Argentine Political and Development Affairs, Office of Argentine, Paraguayan, and Uruguayan Affairs, Bureau of Inter-American Affairs, Department of State, December 1965–August 1968

Duke, Angier Biddle, Chief of Protocol, Department of State, until January 20, 1965

Dungan, Ralph A., Special Assistant to the President until September 1964; Ambassador to Chile November 24, 1964–August 2, 1967

Durán Neumann, Julio, Senator (PR, Chile); DF candidate for President, September 1963–March 16, 1964; PR candidate for President from April 5, 1964

Eaton, Samuel D., Deputy Director, Office of Colombian-Venezuelan Affairs (after May 1966 Office of North Coast Affairs), Bureau of Inter-American Affairs, Department of State, April 1965–July 1966; Special Assistant to the Assistant Secretary of State for Inter-American Affairs July 1966–August 1967

Echandi Jiménez, Mario, former President of Costa Rica

Eisenhower, Dwight D., former President of the United States

Eisenhower, Milton S., President of Johns Hopkins University until June 1967; Special Adviser on Latin American Affairs from December 1967

Eleta Almaran, Fernando, Foreign Minister of Panama October 1964–September 1968

Ensor, Andrew F., Chief, Fuels and Energy Division, Office of International Resources, Bureau of Economic Affairs, Department of State, later Director, Office of Fuels and Energy, to 1966

Evans, Allan, Deputy Director for Research, Bureau of Intelligence and Research, Department of State

Figueres Ferrer, José, former President of Costa Rica

FitzGerald, Desmond, Deputy Chief of the Western Hemisphere Division for Cuban Affairs, Directorate of Plans, Central Intelligence Agency, until March 1964; Chief of the Western Hemisphere Division March 1964–June 1965; Deputy Director for Plans until July 1967

Fitzgerald, John F., Deputy Coordinator of Cuban Affairs, Bureau of Inter-American Affairs, Department of State, May 1966–July 1967; thereafter Coordinator

Ford, Gerald R., Representative (Republican–Michigan); House Minority Leader from January 1965

Foster, William C., Director of the Arms Control and Disarmament Agency

Fowler, Henry H., Secretary of the Treasury April 1, 1965–December 23, 1968

Fowler, James R., Deputy U.S. Coordinator of the Alliance for Progress from August 1967

Frank, Richard A., Assistant Legal Adviser for Inter-American Affairs, Department of State, November 1966–September 1968

Freeman, Fulton, Ambassador to Colombia until February 1964; Ambassador to Mexico from March 4, 1964

Freeman, Orville L., Secretary of Agriculture

Frei Montalva, Eduardo, Senator (PDC, Chile); PDC candidate for President, September 1964; President of Chile from November 4, 1964

Friedman, Alvin, Deputy Assistant Secretary of Defense for International Security Affairs (Far East and Latin America) 1964–1966

Fulbright, J. William, Senator (Democrat–Arkansas); Chairman of the Senate Foreign Relations Committee

Gardner, James R., Deputy Director of Coordination for Intelligence and Research, Bureau of Intelligence and Research, Department of State, from December 1965

Gaud, William S., Deputy Administrator of the Agency for International Development February 1964–August 2, 1966; thereafter Administrator

Gestido, Oscar, President of Uruguay March 1–December 6, 1967

Glaessner, Philip J. W., Deputy Assistant Administrator for Capital Development, Bureau for Latin America, Agency for International Development; from March 12, 1964, also Director, Office of Capital Development, Bureau of Inter-American Affairs, Department of State

Goodpaster, Lieutenant General Andrew J., USA, Assistant to the Chairman of the Joint Chiefs of Staff until July 1966; Director, Joint Staff, August 1966–March 1967

Gordon, A. Lincoln, Ambassador to Brazil until February 25, 1966; Assistant Secretary of State for Inter-American Affairs and U.S. Coordinator of the Alliance for Progress March 9, 1966–June 30, 1967

Goulart, João Belchior Marques, President of Brazil until April 2, 1964

Greenfield, James L., Deputy Assistant Secretary of State for Public Affairs until September 1964

Gruening, Ernest, Senator (Democrat–Alaska)

Guerrero Gutiérrez, Lorenzo, President of Nicaragua August 3, 1966–May 1, 1967

Guevara de la Serna, Major Ernesto "Che," Cuban Minister of Industry until 1965

Harriman, W. Averell, former Governor of New York; Under Secretary of State for Political Affairs until March 17, 1965; thereafter Ambassador at Large

Hartman, Arthur A., special assistant to the Deputy Secretary of State and staff director, Senior Interdepartmental Group, from August 1967

Haya de la Torre, Raúl Víctor, founder and leader of the Alianza Popular Revolucionaria Americana (APRA) and the Partido Aprista Peruano

Helms, Richard, M., Deputy Director for Plans, Central Intelligence Agency, until April 28, 1965; Deputy Director of Central Intelligence April 28, 1965–June 30, 1966; thereafter Director of Central Intelligence

Henderson, Douglas, Ambassador to Bolivia until August 7, 1968

Herbert, Ray, Deputy Chief of the Western Hemisphere Division, Directorate of Plans, Central Intelligence Agency until June 1965

Herrera Lane, Felipe, President of the Inter-American Development Bank

Hickenlooper, Bourke B., Senator (Republican–Iowa)

Hill, John Calvin, Jr., Deputy Chief of Mission, Embassy in Venezuela, until April 1965; thereafter Director, Office of Colombian-Venezuelan Affairs (after May 1966 Office of North Coast Affairs), Bureau of Inter-American Affairs, Department of State

Hornig, Donald F., Special Assistant to the President for Science and Technology

Hoyt, Henry A., Director, Office of Argentine, Paraguayan, and Uruguayan Affairs, Bureau of Inter-American Affairs, Department of State, January 1964–May 1965; Ambassador to Uruguay May 6, 1965–December 16, 1967

Hughes, Thomas L., Director of the Bureau of Intelligence and Research, Department of State

Humphrey, Hubert H., Senator (Democrat–Minnesota) and Senate Majority Whip until December 29, 1964; Vice President of the United States from January 20, 1965; Democratic candidate for President, November 1968

Hurwitch, Robert A., First Secretary of the Embassy in Chile July–September 1964

Illia, Arturo Umberto, President of Argentina until June 28, 1966

Illueca, Jorge E., Special Panamanian Representative, U.S.–Panama Relations (Panama Canal Treaty negotiations) April–November 1964

Iribarren Borges, Ignacio, Foreign Minister of Venezuela from March 11, 1964

Irwin, John N., II, Special U.S. Representative for Inter-Oceanic Canal Negotiations April 1965–July 1967

Jagan, Cheddi B., Prime Minister of British Guiana until December 1964

Jenkins, Walter W., Special Assistant to the President until October 1964

Jessup, Peter, member of the National Security Council staff; executive secretary of the 5412 Special Group (after June 2, 1964, the 303 Committee)

Johnson, General Harold K., USA, Chief of Staff, U.S. Army

Johnson, Lyndon B., President of the United States

Johnson, U. Alexis, Deputy Under Secretary of State for Political Affairs until July 12, 1964 and November 1, 1965–October 9, 1966

Johnson, W. Thomas, Jr., Assistant Press Secretary to the President September 1966–September 1968; thereafter Deputy Press Secretary to the President

Johnston, James D., staff assistant to the Assistant Secretary of State for Inter-American Affairs January 1964–April 1965; staff assistant to the Under Secretary of State for Economic Affairs until September 1966

Johnston, James R., Officer-in-Charge of Nicaraguan Political and Economic Affairs, Office of Central American Affairs, Bureau of Inter-American Affairs, Department of State, June 1966–May 1968; also Officer-in-Charge of British Honduran Political and Economic Affairs February–December 1966

Jones, J. Wesley, Ambassador to Peru

Jones, James R., Assistant to the President February 1965–January 1968; thereafter Deputy Special Assistant to the President

Jova, Joseph John, Deputy Chief of Mission in Chile until May 1965; Ambassador to Honduras from June 7, 1965

Karamessines, Thomas, Assistant Deputy Director for Plans, Central Intelligence Agency, until July 1967; thereafter Deputy Director for Plans

Katzenbach, Nicholas deB., Attorney General September 4, 1964–September 30, 1966; thereafter Under Secretary of State

Kennedy, Robert F., Attorney General until September 3, 1964; Senator (Democrat–New York) January 1965–June 6, 1968

Khrushchev, Nikita S., Soviet Premier until October 15, 1964

Kilday, Lowell C., Officer-in-Charge of Ecuadorian Political Affairs, Office of Ecuadorian-Peruvian Affairs, Bureau of Inter-American Affairs, Department of State, August 1967–November 1968

Killoran, Thomas F., U.S. Consul General in San Pedro Sula September 1964–July 1966; Officer-in-Charge of Guatemalan Political and Economic Affairs, Office of Central American Affairs, Bureau of Inter-American Affairs, Department of State, August 1966–February 1968; thereafter Deputy Director, Office of Central American Affairs

King, Colonel J. C., USA (retired), Chief of the Western Hemisphere Division, Directorate of Plans, Central Intelligence Agency, until March 1964

Kitchen, Jeffrey C., Deputy Assistant Secretary of State for Politico-Military Affairs until July 1967

Kohler, Foy D., Deputy Under Secretary of State for Political Affairs November 29, 1966–December 31, 1967

Komer, Robert W., member of the National Security Council staff until October 1965; Deputy Special Assistant to the President for National Security Affairs October 1965–March 1966; acting Special Assistant to the President for National Security Affairs, March 1966; thereafter Special Assistant to the President until January 1967

Koren, Henry L. T., Deputy Director for Coordination, Bureau of Intelligence and Research, Department of State, September 1965–June 1966

Korry, Edward M., Ambassador to Chile from August 23, 1967

Kosygin, Alexei N., Soviet Premier from October 15, 1964

Krebs, Max V., Deputy Chief of Mission in Guatemala from August 1967

Krieg, William L., Director, Office of Argentine, Paraguayan, and Uruguayan Affairs, Bureau of Inter-American Affairs, Department of State, from May 1965

Kruel, General Amaury, Commander of the Second Army in Brazil until August 1966

Kubisch, Jack B., Chief of the Economic Section, Embassy in Brazil, and Director of the AID Mission until January 1965; Director, Office of Brazilian Affairs, Bureau of Inter-American Affairs, Department of State, from March 1965

Kubitschek, Juscelino, former President of Brazil

Lacerda, Carlos, Governor of Guanabara, Brazil, until December 1965

Lang, William E., Deputy Assistant Secretary of Defense for International Security Affairs (Africa and Foreign Military Rights) 1965–1966, then (Africa, Latin America, and Foreign Military Rights)

Leandro Mora, Reinaldo, Venezuelan Minister of Interior from November 1966

Lechín Oquendo, Juan, General Secretary of the Mine Workers' Federation in Bolivia until May 1965; also Vice President of Bolivia until May 1964

Leddy, John M., Assistant Secretary of State for European and Canadian Affairs from June 16, 1965

Leitão da Cunha, Vasco, Foreign Minister of Brazil April 1964–December 1965; Brazilian Ambassador to the United States January 1966–June 1968

Leonhardy, Terrence G., Director, Office of Mexican Affairs, Bureau of Inter-American Affairs, Department of State, September 1964–December 1967

Leoni Otero, Raúl, President of Venezuela from March 11, 1964

Lewis, Samuel W., member of the National Security Council staff from September 1968

Linowitz, Sol M., U.S. Representative on the Council of the Organization of American States, the Inter-American Economic and Social Committee, and the Inter-American Committee on the Alliance for Progress from October 13, 1966

Little, Edward S., special assistant to the Secretary of State until May 1965

Lleras Restropo, Carlos, National Front (Liberal Party) candidate for President, May 1966; President of Colombia from August 7, 1966

López Arellano, Colonel Oswaldo, later General, leader of the military junta in Honduras until June 6, 1965; thereafter President of Honduras

López Mateos, Alfonso, President of Mexico until December 1, 1964

Lord, Peter P., Officer-in-Charge of Colombian Affairs, Office of Colombian-Venezuelan Affairs (after May 1966 Officer-in-Charge of Colombian Political Affairs, Office of North Coast Affairs), Bureau of Inter-American Affairs, Department of State, July 1964–August 1966; Officer-in-Charge of Venezuelan Political Affairs until June 1967

Lowenfeld, Andreas F., Assistant Legal Adviser for Economic Affairs, Department of State, until August 1965; thereafter Deputy Legal Adviser

Magalhães Kelly, Juracy Montenegro, Brazilian Ambassador to the United States July 1964–September 1965; Brazilian Minister of Justice and the Interior October 7, 1965–January 14, 1966; Foreign Minister of Brazil until March 15, 1967

Magalhães Pinto, José de, President of the União Democrática Nacional; Governor of Minas Gerais, Brazil, until December 1965; Congressman (ARENA-Minas Gerais) from November 1966; Foreign Minister of Brazil from March 15, 1967

Manatos, Mike N., Administrative Assistant to President Johnson

Mann, Thomas C., Assistant Secretary of State for Inter-American Affairs and U.S. Coordinator of the Alliance for Progress January 3, 1964–March 17, 1965; Under Secretary of State for Economic Affairs until May 31, 1966; President of the Automobile Manufacturers Association from 1967

Manning, Robert J., Assistant Secretary of State for Public Affairs to July 31, 1964

Mansfield, Michael J., Senator (Democrat–Montana); Senate Majority Leader

Margolies, Daniel F., Director, Office of East Coast Affairs (after March 12, 1964, Office of Colombian-Venezuelan Affairs), Bureau of Inter-American Affairs, Department of State, until May 1965

Marks, Leonard H., Director of the United States Information Agency September 1, 1965–December 6, 1968

Martin, Edwin M., Assistant Secretary of State for Inter-American Affairs until January 2, 1964; Ambassador to Argentina January 29, 1964–January 5, 1968

Mayobre, José Antonio, Venezuelan Minister of Mines and Hydrocarbons from January 1967

Mazzilli, Pascoal Ranieri, President of the Brazilian Chamber of Deputies until February 1965; Acting President of Brazil April 2–15, 1964

McCone, John A., Director of Central Intelligence until April 28, 1965

McNamara, Robert S., Secretary of Defense until February 29, 1968

McNaughton, John T., Assistant Secretary of Defense for International Security Affairs July 1, 1964–July 19, 1967

McPherson, Harry C., Jr., Deputy Under Secretary of the Army for International Affairs until August 1964; also Special Assistant to the Secretary of the Army for Civilian Functions March–August 1964; Assistant Secretary of State for Educational and Cultural Affairs August 23, 1964–August 14, 1965; thereafter Special Counsel to the President

Meeker, Leonard C., Legal Adviser of the Department of State from May 18, 1964

Mein, John Gordon, Deputy Chief of Mission, Embassy in Brazil, until August 1965; Ambassador to Guatemala September 1, 1965–August 28, 1968

Méndez Montenegro, Julio César, PR candidate for President, March 1966; President of Guatemala from July 1, 1966

Mercado Jarrin, Brigadier General Edgardo, Foreign Minister of Peru from October 1968

Meyer, Cord, Jr., Chief, Covert Action Staff, Directorate of Plans, Central Intelligence Agency, until July 1967; thereafter Assistant Deputy Director for Plans

Molina Silva, Sergio, Chilean Minister of Finance from November 1964
Mora Otera, José A., Secretary General of the Organization of American States until May 1968
Moreno, Miguel J., Jr., Panamanian Representative to the Council of the Organization of American States until September 1964; also Panamanian Ambassador to the United States April–September 1964
Morgan, Thomas E., Representative (Democrat–Pennsylvania); Chairman of the House Foreign Affairs Committee
Morris, Patrick F., Director, Office of Bolivian-Chilean Affairs, Bureau of Inter-American Affairs, Department of State, November 1965–September 1968
Morse, Wayne L., Senator (Democrat–Oregon); Chairman of the Subcommittee on American Republics Affairs, Senate Foreign Relations Committee
Moscoso, Teodoro, U.S. Representative to the Inter-American Economic and Social Committee and the Inter-American Committee on the Alliance for Progress, and Special Adviser to the Assistant Secretary of State for Inter-American Affairs, January–May 1964
Moyers, Bill D., Special Assistant and Press Secretary (from July 1965) to the President to February 1967

Nitze, Paul H., Deputy Secretary of Defense from July 1, 1967
Nixon, Richard M., former Vice President of the United States; President-elect of the United States from November 5, 1968

O'Brien, Lawrence F., Special Assistant to the President until November 1965
Oduber Quirós, Daniel, Foreign Minister of Costa Rica until January 1965; PLN candidate for President, February 1966
Oliver, Covey T., Ambassador to Colombia May 1, 1964–August 29, 1966; Assistant Secretary of State for Inter-American Affairs and U.S. Coordinator of the Alliance for Progress July 1, 1967–December 31, 1968
O'Meara, General Andrew P., USA, Commander-in-Chief, U.S. Southern Command, until February 22, 1965
Onganía, Lieutenant General Juan Carlos, Commander-in-Chief of the Army in Argentina until November 1965; President of Argentina from June 28, 1966
Orlich Bolmarcich, Francisco José, President of Costa Rica until May 8, 1966
Ovando Candía, General Alfredo, Commander-in-Chief of the Armed Forces in Bolivia; Co-President of Bolivia May 26, 1965–January 5, 1966; President of Bolivia January 5–August 6, 1966

Pacheco Areco, Jorge, President of Uruguay from December 6, 1967
Palmer, Donald K., Director, Office of Regional Economic Policy, Bureau of Inter-American Affairs, Department of State, January 1964–August 1965; thereafter Deputy Assistant Secretary of State for Inter-American Affairs (Economic Policy)
Pastor de la Torre, Celso, Peruvian Ambassador to the United States until October 1968
Paz Estenssoro, Victor, President of Bolivia until November 4, 1964
Peralta Azurdia, Colonel Enrique, President of Guatemala until July 1, 1966
Pérez Alfonso, Juan Pablo, former Venezuelan Minister of Mines and Hydrocarbons
Pérez Guerrero, Manuel, Venezuelan Minister of Mines and Hydrocarbons until January 1967
Perón, Juan Domingo, former President of Argentina
Peterson, Lawrence L., Deputy Director, Office of North Coast Affairs, Bureau of Inter-American Affairs, Department of State, from August 1968
Pinilla Fábrega, Colonel José María, President of Panama from October 13, 1968
Pistarini, Major General Pascual Angel, later Lieutenant General, Commander-in-Chief of the Army in Argentina November 1965–December 1966; also Argentine Minister of Defense July–September 1966

Poats, Rutherford M., Deputy Administrator of the Agency for International Development from May 1967

Porter, General Robert W., Jr., USA, Commander-in-Chief, U.S. Southern Command, from February 22, 1965

Pryce, William T., staff assistant to the Assistant Secretary of State for Inter-American Affairs January 1964–April 1965

Raborn, Vice Admiral William F., Jr., USN (retired), Director of Central Intelligence April 28, 1965–June 30, 1966

Read, Benjamin H., Special Assistant to the Secretary of State and Executive Secretary, Department of State

Reedy, George E., Special Assistant and Press Secretary (from March 1964) to the President until July 1965

Resor, Stanley R., Under Secretary of the Army April 5–July 7, 1965; thereafter Secretary of the Army

Ribeiro, General Jair Dantas, Brazilian Minister of War until April 1, 1964

Richardson, Ralph W., Officer-in-Charge of Chilean Affairs, Office of West Coast Affairs (after March 12, 1964 Office of Bolivian-Chilean Affairs), Bureau of Inter-American Affairs, Department of State, until September 1964

Rielly, John, Assistant to the Vice President from January 1965

Robles Méndez, Marco Aurelio, National Liberal Party candidate for President, May 1964; President of Panama October 1, 1964–October 1, 1968

Rockefeller, David, President and Chairman of the Executive Committee of Chase Manhattan Bank; Director of the Council on Foreign Relations; head of the Business Group for Latin America (from 1965 the Council for Latin America)

Rogers, William D., Deputy U.S. Coordinator of the Alliance for Progress until June 1965

Rostow, Eugene V., Under Secretary of State for Political Affairs from October 14, 1966

Rostow, Walt W., Counselor and Chairman, Policy Planning Council, Department of State, until March 31, 1966; also U.S. Representative to the Inter-American Economic and Social Committee and the Inter-American Committee on the Alliance for Progress May 1964–March 1966; Special Assistant to the President from April 1, 1966

Rowan, Carl T., Director of the United States Information Agency February 27, 1964–July 10, 1965

Rowell, Edward M., Officer-in-Charge of Honduran Affairs, Office of Central American and Panamanian Affairs (after March 12, 1964, Office of Central American Affairs), Bureau of Inter-American Affairs, Department of State, until April 1964

Rusk, Dean, Secretary of State

Russell, Richard B., Senator (Democrat–Georgia); Chairman of the Senate Armed Services Committee

Saccio, Leonard J., Deputy Chief of Mission, Embassy in Argentina, from July 1965

Salans, Carl F., Assistant Legal Adviser for Inter-American Affairs, Department of State, June 1965–March 1967; thereafter Deputy Legal Adviser

Salinger, Pierre E. G., Special Assistant and Press Secretary to the President until March 1964

Samudio Avila, David, Panamanian Minister of Finance October 1964–December 1967; Liberal Party candidate for President, May 1968

Sánchez Gavito, Vicente, Mexican Representative to the Council of the Organization of American States until February 1965

Sanders, Irving L., Officer-in-Charge of Uruguayan Political Affairs, Office of Argentine, Paraguayan and Uruguayan Affairs, Bureau of Inter-American Affairs, Department of State, from August 1967

Sanders, Terry B., Jr., Director, Office of Panamanian Affairs, Bureau of Inter-American Affairs, Department of State, from September 1968

Sanjines-Goytia, Colonel Julio, Bolivian Ambassador to the United States from May 1965

Sanz de Santamaría, Carlos, Chairman of the Inter-American Committee on the Alliance for Progress

Sapena Pastor, Raúl, Foreign Minister of Paraguay

Sause, Oliver L., Jr., Director, Office of Central American Affairs, Bureau of Inter-American Affairs, Department of State, March 1964–November 1965

Sayre, Robert M., Director, Office of Mexican Affairs, Bureau of Inter-American Affairs, Department of State, until April 1964; member of the National Security Council staff until April 1965; Deputy Assistant Secretary of State for Inter-American Affairs April 1965–July 1968; Ambassador to Uruguay from July 24, 1968

Schlesinger, Arthur M., Jr., Special Assistant to the President until March 1, 1964

Schultze, Charles L., Director of the Bureau of the Budget June 1, 1965–January 29, 1968

Scott, Joseph W., Deputy Director for Coordination, Bureau of Intelligence and Research, Department of State, until July 1964

Seidenman, Neil A., interpreter in the Language Services Division, Office of Operations, Department of State

Sessions, Edson O., Ambassador to Ecuador from August 1, 1968

Sevilla Sacasa, Guillermo, Nicaraguan Ambassador to the United States; also Nicaraguan Representative to the Council of the Organization of American States; Dean of the Diplomatic Corps, Washington

Shankle, A. Perry, Officer-in-Charge of Chilean Political Affairs, Office of Bolivian-Chilean Affairs, Bureau of Inter-American Affairs, Department of State, from January 1967

Sharp, Frederick D. III, Deputy Director, Office of Inter-American Security Affairs, Bureau of Inter-American Affairs, Department of State, August 1966–June 1968; thereafter Director

Shumate, John P., Jr., Officer-in-Charge of Peruvian Political Affairs, Office of Ecuadorian-Peruvian Affairs, Bureau of Inter-American Affairs, Department of State, from July 1967

Siracusa, Ernest V., Deputy Chief of Mission, Embassy in Peru

Sloan, Frank K., Deputy Assistant Secretary of Defense for International Security Affairs (Regional Affairs) until 1965

Smith, Bromley K., Executive Secretary of the National Security Council staff

Smith, James F., Officer-in-Charge of Ecuadorian Development Affairs, Office of Ecuadorian-Peruvian Affairs, Bureau of Inter-American Affairs, Department of State, May 1966–April 1968

Snow, William P., Ambassador to Paraguay until June 15, 1967

Solís, Galileo, Foreign Minister of Panama until September 1964

Solomon, Anthony M., Deputy Assistant Secretary of State for Inter-American Affairs (Economic Policy) until April 1965; Acting Assistant Secretary of State for Economic Affairs April–May 1965; Assistant Secretary of State for Economic Affairs from June 1, 1965

Somoza Debayle, General Anastasio, Commandant of the National Guard in Nicaragua; PLN candidate for President, February 1967; President of Nicaragua from May 1, 1967

Somoza Debayle, Luis, former President of Nicaragua

Sorensen, Theodore C., Special Counsel to the President until February 29, 1964

Sowash, William B., Deputy Director, Office of Central American Affairs, Bureau of Inter-American Affairs, Department of State, July 1964–September 1965

Starzel, Robert F., staff assistant to the Assistant Secretary of State for Inter-American Affairs July 1967–July 1968

Stedman, William P., Jr., Chief of the Economic Section, Embassy in Peru, and Deputy Director, AID Mission, September 1966–July 1968; thereafter Director, Office of Ecuadorian-Peruvian Affairs, Bureau of Inter-American Affairs, Department of State

Steins, Kenedon P., Officer-in-Charge of Guatemalan Affairs, Office of Central American Affairs, Bureau of Inter-American Affairs, Department of State, April 1964–August 1966

Stevenson, Adlai E., U.S. Permanent Representative to the United Nations until July 14, 1965

Stewart, C. Allen, Ambassador to Venezuela until November 28, 1964

Stoessel, Walter J. Jr., Deputy Assistant Secretary of State for European Affairs September 1965–July 1968

Stroessner, General Alfredo, President of Paraguay

Sullivan, Leonor K., Representative (Democrat–Missouri); Chairman of the Panama Canal Subcommittee, House Merchant Marine and Fisheries Committee

Taylor, General Maxwell D., USA, Chairman of the Joint Chiefs of Staff until July 1, 1964

Taylor, Vice Admiral Rufus L., USN, Deputy Director of Central Intelligence from October 13, 1966

Tejera París, Enrique, Venezuelan Ambassador to the United States; also Venezuelan Representative to the Council of the Organization of American States until April 1966; chairman of the Inter-American Peace Committee (Panama Crisis) January–April 1964

Telles, Raymond, Ambassador to Costa Rica until February 19, 1967

Thomas, Charles H., II, staff assistant to the Assistant Secretary of State for Inter-American Affairs May 1965–March 1966

Thompson, Llewellyn E., Ambassador at Large until December 26, 1966; also Acting Deputy Under Secretary of State for Political Affairs July 1964–October 1965

Tomic Romero, Radomiro, Senator (PDC, Chile); Chilean Ambassador to the United States April 1965–March 1968

Torrijos Herrera, Lieutenant Colonel Omar, Secretary of the General Staff of the Panamanian National Guard in October 1968; thereafter Colonel, Chief of Staff of the National Guard

Trejos Fernández, José Joaquín, National Unification Party candidate for President, February 1966; President of Costa Rica from May 8, 1966

Trueheart, William C. Deputy Director for Coordination, Bureau of Intelligence and Research, Department of State, from June 1967

Tuthill, John W., Ambassador to Brazil from May 27, 1966

Tyler, William R., Assistant Secretary of State for European and Canadian Affairs until May 18, 1965

Udall, Stewart, Secretary of Interior

Vaky, Viron P., Deputy Assistant Secretary of State for Inter-American Affairs August– December 1968; Acting Assistant Secretary of State for Inter-American Affairs from January 1969

Valdés Subercaseaux, Gabriel, Chilean Foreign Minister from November 1964

Valencia, Guillermo León, President of Colombia until August 7, 1966

Valenti, Jack J., Special Assistant to the President until May 1966

Vallarino, Colonel Bolívar, later General, Commandant of the Panamanian National Guard until October 1968

Vance, Cyrus R. Secretary of the Army until January 20, 1964; Deputy Secretary of Defense until June 30, 1967

Van Reigersberg, Fernando A., interpreter in the Language Services Division, Office of Operations, Department of State

Vásquez Salas, Jorge, Foreign Minister of Peru September 1965–September 1967

Vaughn, Jack Hood, Ambassador to Panama April 8, 1964–February 27, 1965; Assistant Secretary of State for Inter-American Affairs and U.S. Coordinator of the Alliance for Progress March 22, 1965–February 28, 1966; thereafter Director of the Peace Corps

Velasco Alvarado, General Juan, Commanding General of the Army and Chief of the Armed Forces Joint Command in Peru from 1967; President of the Revolutionary Government of the Armed Forces of Peru from October 4, 1968

Velasco Ibarra, José María, President of Ecuador from September 1, 1968

Villeda Morales, Ramón, former President of Honduras

Walters, Colonel Vernon A., later Brigadier General, USA, U.S. Army Attaché in Brazil until June 1967

Warner, Leland W., Jr., Officer-in-Charge of Honduran Political and Economic Affairs, Office of Central American Affairs, Bureau of Inter-American Affairs, Department of State, August 1966–June 1968

Warnke, Paul C., Assistant Secretary of Defense for International Security Affairs from August 1, 1967

Watson, W. Marvin, Jr., Special Assistant to the President February 1965–April 1968

Webster, Bethuel M., U.S. mediator in dispute between Guatemala and the United Kingdom over the status of British Honduras (Belize) October 1965–September 1968

Weissman, H. Andre, Deputy Director, Office of Brazilian Affairs, Bureau of Inter-American Affairs, Department of State, until November 1965

Wheeler, General Earle G., USA, Chairman of the Joint Chiefs of Staff from July 3, 1964

Whiteman, Marjorie M., Assistant Legal Adviser for Inter-American Affairs, Department of State, until June 1965

Wiggins, Guy A., Officer-in-Charge of Guatemalan Political and Economic Affairs, Office of Central American Affairs, Bureau of Inter-American Affairs, Department of State, from February 1968

Williams, G. Mennen, Assistant Secretary of State for African Affairs until March 23, 1966

Williams, Murat W., Deputy Director for Coordination, Bureau of Intelligence and Research, Department of State, September 1964–June 1965

Williams, William L. S., Deputy Director, Office of Bolivian-Chilean Affairs, Bureau of Inter-American Affairs, Department of State, July 1964–July 1966

Wilson, Donald M., Deputy Director of the United States Information Agency until August 1, 1965

Wilson, Henry H., Jr., Administrative Assistant to the President until May 1967

Wilson, James Harold, Prime Minister of the United Kingdom from October 17, 1964

Wolfe, Gregory B., Director, Office of Research and Analysis for American Republics, Bureau of Intelligence and Research, Department of State, August 1964–August 1968

Woodward, Robert F., Special Adviser, Office of Inter-Oceanic Negotiations, Bureau of Inter-American Affairs, Department of State, May 1965–July 1967

Yerovi Indaburú, Clemente, President of Ecuador March 29–November 16, 1966

Zavala Ortiz, Miguel Ángel, Foreign Minister of Argentina until June 28, 1966

Zúñiga Augustinius, Ricardo, leader of the Partido Nacional in Honduras; Secretary of Government in Honduras until June 1965; thereafter Minister of the Presidency

South and Central America; Mexico

Regional

1. Editorial Note

At a White House reception for Latin American representatives on November 26, 1963, President Johnson announced that relations within the Western Hemisphere would be "among the highest concerns of my Government." Acknowledging that the Alliance for Progress had its share of problems, Johnson pledged to "improve and strengthen the role of the United States," thereby making the program a "living memorial" to the late-President Kennedy. (*Public Papers of the Presidents of the United States: Lyndon B. Johnson, 1963–64*, Book I, pages 6–7) In a December 3 memorandum for the President, Director of Central Intelligence McCone addressed an important aspect of this pledge to "improve and strengthen" the Alliance: personnel. Citing "our recent conversations" on the subject, McCone observed that the Alliance had become so "deeply enmeshed in administrative problems" that no man "could be expected to take over the responsibilities of directing the program, overcome the obstacles that would confront him, and give the program the forward motion you desire." What the administration needed was a "special assistant" to the President or a "special deputy to the Secretary of State," a man "with the experience to envision the program, the stature to speak with conviction with all the Latin American countries and who additionally holds the complete respect of the Congress." McCone recommended former Secretary of the Treasury Robert B. Anderson for the job with Thomas C. Mann, then Ambassador to Mexico, assuming the role of administrator. (Johnson Library, National Security File, Agency File, Alliance for Progress)

Anderson evidently declined the appointment, forcing the President to consider other candidates for the top position, including Mann himself. (Ibid., Recordings and Transcripts, Transcript of telephone conversation between President Johnson and Robert Anderson, December 5, 1963, 2:14 p.m.) In a telephone call to Mexico City on December 9 Johnson offered Mann the position as "kind of an Undersecretary" of State for Latin America—an offer that, he suggested, should not be refused. (Ibid., Transcript of telephone conversation between President Johnson and Thomas Mann, December 9, 3:30 p.m.) Mann arrived in the United States on December 10 and met the President at the White House the following day. (Ibid., President's Daily Diary) On December 14 Johnson announced that Mann had agreed to "undertake the coordination and direction of all policies and programs of the U.S. government, economic, social, and cultural, relating to Latin America." Johnson later announced that Mann would exercise this role not only as the Assistant Secretary of State for Inter-American Affairs—a position he had held during the second Eisenhower administration—but also as Special Assistant to the President and United States Coordinator of the Alliance for Progress. (*Public Papers of the Presidents of the United States: Lyndon B. Johnson, 1963–64*, Book I, pages 56, 65, 88) To accommodate Mann's appointment, Assistant Secretary Edwin M. Martin was appointed Ambassador to Argentina, and Teodoro Moscoso, the former U.S. Coordinator of the Alliance, was named to represent the United States on the Inter-American Committee on the Alliance for Progress (CIAP). Mann assumed his new responsibilities on January 3, 1964.

---

2.   **Telephone Conversation Between President Johnson and the Assistant Secretary of State for Inter-American Affairs (Mann)**[1]

Washington, February 19, 1964, 11:32 a.m.

President: Tom?

Mann: Yes, sir?

President: Are we going to call in these Latin American ambassadors for the Alliance for Progress meeting?

Mann: Yes sir, we have it tentatively scheduled for about the 15th.

President: About the 15th?

Mann: Of March.

President: That's the American ambassadors in this Hemisphere.

Mann: Well, it's a number of things. We thought we would have a ceremony at the Pan American Union, you would—

---

[1] Source: Johnson Library, Recordings and Transcripts, Recording of telephone conversation between President Johnson and Thomas Mann, Tape F64.13, Side B, PNO 4. No classification marking. This transcript was prepared in the Office of the Historian specifically for this volume. A memorandum of this telephone conversation, prepared in Mann's office, is ibid., Papers of Thomas C. Mann, Telephone Conversations with LBJ, January 4, 1964–April 30, 1965.

President: Yeah, but I'm talking about, we're inviting to come to Washington the American ambassadors in this Hemisphere.

Mann: Oh, yeah, the American. I thought we would do that at the same time.

President: That's what I'm saying.

Mann: And combine that—we got a budgetary problem, but I think we can find the money—and get them all up here at that time and make a big shindig, and launch your Alliance program with a good speech.

President: All right. Now what is that? The anniversary of the Alliance?

Mann: It's the third anniversary of Kennedy's—

President: Announcement of it?

Mann: Yeah.

President: Third anniversary of Kennedy's announcement of the Alliance.

Mann: And it's also the occasion for creating the, launching this new CIAP, this inter-American thing with Santamaría.

President: It's also the occasion for the launching of this CIAP—

Mann: CIAP thing—

President: Santamaría's the head of. Colombia. What do you call that? The Wise Men? Is that what they're called?

Mann: No, that's a different group. I would call this the Inter-American Alliance for Progress Committee.

President: The Inter-American Alliance for Progress Committee. That's made up of five people?

Mann: It's made up of seven people, counting Santamaría, the President.

President: Seven, counting Santamaría, the President. They raised hell about us not giving him enough attention here. I don't know how much more we could give him. We had him in here, and we had him, had his picture made and everything else. I couldn't put him on my knee and bounce him.[2]

Mann: I think he was happy and I hadn't even heard of any criticism on that.

President: Well, I did. I saw the papers, said that we ignored him, and paid no attention to him and so forth, didn't emphasize it enough. Your *New York Times* sources over there.

---

[2] Carlos Sanz de Santamaría arrived in Washington on February 3 for consultation with Department of State and AID officials. No evidence was found to indicate when Sanz visited the White House or to identify the newspaper that criticized his reception.

Mann: Well, he had a little press conference, and I heard him, and after, as he came out of your office. It was all very complimentary to you personally and to the Alliance, and—

President: Have you talked to Admiral today? Has he sawed off any more pipe down there?[3]

Mann: [Laughter] I haven't talked to him today.

President: Anything, is everything all right in Guantanamo?

Mann: Everything's going fine.

President: Did you read your *New York Times* State Department on Cuba this morning? And how you screwed up things good?[4]

Mann: Well, I'll give you some bright stories. I had an hour and a half yes—

President: The answer is "no," I guess, to my question.

Mann: Sir?

President: I guess the answer is—

Mann: No. [Laughter]

President: All right. Read it on the second page this morning, 'cause you have to know what they're saying about you.

Mann: I read that. Let me give you some bright news.

President: All right.

Mann: Yesterday, I spent an hour and a half before the House Subcommittee on Latin American Affairs. I think that the Republicans were happy. This morning, I spent another hour, just at random in the Congress. We talked largely about Panama, and they asked for additional meetings, and it went very well. So we're working hard on the Hill like you want us to, and I think we're going to make a lot of progress up there. I don't know what you can do with some of these left wing fellows and two or three newspapers. I think—

President: Why in the hell don't you tell that guy that you all leak to over there all the time, the State Department—you got one named Szulc and one named Raymont, is it?

Mann: That's right, and a guy named Kurzman.

President: —and—that you all work like a sieve to—why don't you say: "Now you and Herbert Matthews[5] didn't handle this Cuban

---

[3] Admiral John D. Bulkeley, commander of the Guantanamo Naval Base. For documentation on the Guantanamo water supply incident, see the compilation on Cuba in *Foreign Relations, 1964–1968*, volume XXXII.

[4] Reference is to an article by Max Frankel criticizing the administration's decision to reduce assistance to 5 of the 19 countries that maintained trade with Cuba. Information on the decision is ibid.

[5] Tad Szulc and Henry Raymont, correspondents, and Herbert L. Matthews, editor, of *The New York Times*. Dan Kurzman was a foreign correspondent with *The Washington Post*.

situation in such an excellent fashion yourself. Now for God's sakes give me a little chance. I just been here two months. Let me, give me a little chance to retrieve some of the work you all did"?

Mann: [Laughter] I'll try that line on them. Okay, sir.

President: I think that we got to get something to show that we got better feeling and more respect in the Hemisphere than ever before. So you better propagandize some folks along that line. And I guess that we can have a dinner for the ambassadors from America, the ambassadors from the Hemis—our ambassadors to the Hemisphere, their ambassadors to us, and probably the OAS ambassadors.

Mann: And the seven people in CIAP ought to all be there, I think, and maybe even the ten Wise Men, if we could.

President: Well, what would that be? 65? 70?

Mann: That would run you close to 70 or 80.

President: Well, but the wives, you see, 140. Can't take care of 125. We'll try to give a dinner like that for them.

Mann: All right. Wonderful. And I—

President: I want you to dance with some of those short, fat women again. Old Mennen Williams was the only guy that delivered for me last night. Salinger went home.[6]

Mann: [Laughter] I'm the worst dancer, but—

President: Larry O'Brien.

Mann: —I'll even do that for you, Mr. President.

President: Well, all right. Anything else now on Panama?

Mann: No, everything's quiet down there. The [unintelligible] aren't going to do much until we get back from Los Angeles.[7] I had a talk with Sánchez Gavito this morning and told him to keep everything buttoned down until we got back.

President: I don't think we're going to do anything until after that election down there.

Mann: I doubt it myself.

President: I wouldn't encourage them much. I think we're doing all right. Just let them have that problem: they did the invading and they did the aggression. And let's see how they—I'm not one that believes that a fat Communist is better than a lean one.

Mann: No, I'm not. I think we're going to have to have a lot of steady nerves on some of these problems.

---

[6] According to the President's Daily Diary, Johnson held a White House reception, February 18, for members of the House of Representatives. (Johnson Library)

[7] Johnson and Mann were in Los Angeles February 20–23 for meetings with President López Mateos of Mexico.

President: I sure would. And I would, though, have a planning group awful busy with the World Bank, and the Export-Import Bank, and the Alliance for Progress, and the health organizations, and the 480's. And I see now we're trying to figure out how to give Mexico some food. And I saw in one of the briefing papers that she wanted water, and we might not be able to give her water, but we could give her food. I don't know. I don't want to be giving away, but I'd damn sure have some things on my Santa Claus list, and coordinate them and then when I did something, I'd make them, I'd have a quid pro quo.

Mann: Well, that's what we've been—

President: I think that you have turned a flop in Mexico. I think you've got them where instead of confiscating everything now, they're trying to promote private enterprise, aren't they?

Mann: That's our hope, and they're drifting in that direction. They do have a lot of problems, have to stay with this thing day by day, but I'm not pessimistic about Mexico. They've got a good President coming in, and—

President: What other places in the Hemisphere have you got problems? Argentina? Brazil?

Mann: Mr. President, this Hemisphere is in worse shape than I've seen it in 20 years. We've got problems in Bolivia right now. The cabinet—Paz is the only man there that can hold things together—and his whole cabinet is splintering in all directions because they want to be president four years from now.

President: Well, can we get in there and do something to help him before it goes to hell?

Mann: We're working on that this morning, and we're coming up with some ideas on that. We've got a possible revolt and military, against the military fellow in Honduras.

President: Yeah, Honduras.

Mann: We're watching that. We got Peru and Argentina about to expropriate oil properties. Brazil is sick. Goulart is irresponsible. Nearly everywhere we look we have problems, but I'm sort of optimistic. I think what we did in Panama and Guantanamo is going to help us a lot in the Hemisphere. We need time, we need about—

President: Why don't you try to sell this *New York Times* on the problem that you need help, and that this thing you picked up, pretty sick, and that you can't do it just by being a floor mop and you've got to have a little steel in your spine. If you don't they'll shove you to death. They'll be like a country dog. And see if you can't get *The Washington Post* and *New York Times* to quit taking the line they are.

Mann: I'm going to try it, but those fellows are basically hostile to everything you believe in, Mr. President.

President: OK.

Mann: The guys that write the stories are. You know I spent, I had lunch over with the whole staff of *The Washington Post*, and they, in essence, this same pitch. And I was told later that Mrs. Graham[8] after the lunch said that they ought to give us time to see what we could do. What you have is a half a dozen very far left wing guys like Kurzman, who are pretty stupid people really. They don't know anything about Latin America, they don't speak the language, never been there, but they're full of theories. And these guys are crusaders, and how you deal with a crusader is, I think, the toughest problem of all. But I think we're going to have to work on Mrs. Graham.

President: Mrs. Graham doesn't have any authority; she won't exercise it. She claims she's the best friend I got, and they murder me every day. That Friendly[9] runs that paper.

Mann: Well, let me talk to Manning and see if we can't plot something out. I'll get together with him, and see if we, do the most effective thing we can.

President: I think you ought to lay the groundwork and say that now we, we need some help on American policy, and we don't think that you're doing your God-damned country a bit of good, and we wish you'd try to help us a little.

Mann: All right, sir.

President: OK. Bye.

Mann: Bye.

---

[8] Katharine M. Graham, president of the Washington Post Company.

[9] Alfred Friendly, managing editor of *The Washington Post*.

3.   Memorandum for the Record[1]

Washington, February 19, 1964.

SUBJECT

Cuba Meeting—Wednesday, February 19, 1964[2]

PARTICIPANTS

The Attorney General; General Taylor; Director McCone; Ambassador Bunker; Deputy Secretary Vance; Under Secretary Fowler; Deputy Under Secretary Johnson; Assistant Secretary Mann; Assistant Secretary Behrman; Acting Director Wilson; Special Assistant Califano; Desmond FitzGerald: John Crimmins; McGeorge Bundy; Ralph Dungan; Gordon Chase

The group discussed the problem of OAS action resulting from the Cuban arms cache discovery. [3] (State's staff paper of February 19 is attached.)[4]

1. *Timing and Form*—The OAS investigating team is expected to submit its report to the C/OAS on about February 24.[5] Mr. Mann said that while the Venezuelans are anxious to get an MFM under way as soon as possible, we want to slow up the pace. Among other things, we want to give the public some time to digest the OAS report; also, we can use the time to work the corridors and have as many OAR's as possible on our wave-length by the time of the meeting. Mr. Mann

---

[1] Source: Johnson Library, National Security File, Country File, Cuba, OAS Resolution (Arms Cache), Vol. II, Memos, 11/63–9/64. Secret; No Distribution. Drafted by Chase on February 22.

[2] On February 18 Rusk called Mann to discuss the upcoming meeting: "The Sec said he thought Bundy believed the Cabinet people should be there but the Sec said he thought it was something which should be worked out beforehand. The Sec said he thought it should be discussed below the Cabinet level. He said when you got it to the Cabinet level, it didn't lift it to Cabinet level but brought it back into the seminar business. Mann said he would talk to Bundy." (National Archives and Records Administration, RG 59, Rusk Files: Lot 72 D 192, Telephone Calls 2/11/64–2/29/64)

[3] On November 28, 1963, the Venezuelan Government announced it had discovered a large arms cache on the coast of the Paraguaná Peninsula; that an internal investigation had determined that the arms were of Cuban origin, intended for use in a guerrilla operation to seize power in Caracas before the Presidential elections of December 1; and that evidence against Cuba would be presented to the OAS, thereby justifying retaliatory measures under the Inter-American Treaty of Reciprocal Assistance, the so-called "Rio Treaty" of 1947. Regarding the initial response to the discovery of the arms cache, see *Foreign Relations, 1961–1963*, vol. XII, Documents 169–171. For text of the Rio Treaty, see 4 Bevans 559 or Department of State *Bulletin*, September 21, 1947, pp. 565–567.

[4] Attached but not printed.

[5] The report was submitted to the COAS and made public on February 24. At a news conference on February 27 Rusk said that the report should lead the OAS to act in such a way that Castro would clearly understand that subversion "will not be acceptable in the hemisphere." (Department of State *Bulletin*, March 16, 1964, p. 408)

added that the odds are presently better than even that we will get involved with either an extended or a brief MFM.

2. *Corollary to the Monroe Doctrine*—Mr. Mann, noting that Castro is probably going to be with us for some time, said that we ought to think seriously about doing something fairly drastic to prevent further Cuban subversion. He suggested that we add a paragraph to our draft OAS resolution which will warn Castro that if he continues with his subversion, we will retaliate with force under the Rio Treaty. Such a paragraph will do two things: *First,* it will make clear to the Russians and Cubans that we regard subversion as "armed aggression." Given time to digest this message the Russians may be encouraged to control Castro. *Second,* it will provide a juridical umbrella for any future forceful retaliation we have to take. The group went on to discuss the Mann proposal at some length.

(a) General Taylor wondered whether this doctrine could have world-wide application.

(b) The Attorney General, in the first instance, expressed doubt on several scores. *First,* how do you define subversion? *Second,* subversion is hard to prove even when, on rare occasion, we have the evidence; for every witness we could find to support a charge of subversion, Castro would come up with four who would say there was no subversion. *Third,* retaliation by force is no simple matter; our decision-making experience of October, 1962 made this clear. Finally, time-lag is a problem; the arms cache occurs and three months later, after the research is completed, we retaliate—this is somewhat unrealistic. Alexis Johnson wondered how we know if a particular act of subversion is Castro-inspired.

(c) Mr. Bundy said that, generally speaking, the Mann proposal has merit and noted that it represents a thickening and variation of the "Kennedy Doctrine", expressed in President Kennedy's Miami speech of November 18.[6] He added, however, that we should be careful about how much we thicken the Doctrine in the context of the arms cache discovery; our response must be appropriate to the crime. Generally speaking, we should keep the language of the resolution general and flexible and not tie ourselves down to a particular course of action in the event of further Castro subversion. But even general and flexible

---

[6] On November 18, 1963, in an address before the Inter-American Press Association in Miami President Kennedy announced the so-called Kennedy Doctrine: "The American States must be ready to come to the aid of any government requesting aid to prevent a take-over linked to the policies of foreign communism rather than to an internal desire for change. My country is prepared to do this. We in this hemisphere must also use every resource at our command to prevent the establishment of another Cuba in this hemisphere." (*Public Papers of the Presidents of the United States: John F. Kennedy, 1963,* pp. 872–877)

language will be useful; it will probably serve as a deterrent of sorts and will tend to put the President in a stronger position if and when we do have to resort to forceful action. Mr. Bundy added that we should continue to explore and study the "eye for an eye" doctrine.

(d) The group agreed that we should try to get "warning-type" language into the OAS resolution. If we succeed, it will strengthen our juridical position; if we fail, we lose little and may even gain politically. The group further agreed that the language should be cognate to a possible Presidential statement on the same subject to the U.S. public and to a stern, private warning to the Russians that Cuban subversion could lead to a very dangerous situation. In the latter regard, Mr. Bundy thought that, if we do the job right, the Russians may well take us seriously.

(e) The Attorney General said that we had to concern ourselves not only with preventing the export of subversion from Cuba but also with the problem of responding in the event "another Cuba" occurs in Latin America. Mr. Bundy said that a study last spring indicated that it was extremely difficult to plan for this sort of eventuality which can come in innumerable shapes and sizes, not all of which clearly call for a U.S. response. At the request of the group, he agreed to distribute copies of the study.[7] Mr. Bundy added that it might also be worthwhile to study our capabilities to respond (e.g. a "snuff-out" force).

3. *Surveillance Involving Force*—The group generally did not favor an OAS resolution which calls for a surveillance system involving the stopping and searching of selected vessels on the high seas (the "force" option). The measure would not be very effective and would probably give us as much trouble as it would give Castro. On the other hand, a resolution which calls for a surveillance system involving the stopping and searching of vessels in territorial waters (the "non-force" option) appears to be the appropriate response to the arms cache issue. Also, with such language as an umbrella, we can work out measures whereby U.S. forces can assist other OAR's in their territorial waters.

General Taylor dissented; he favored the "force" option. It would act as a deterrent to the Cubans and would give us a reprisal capability.

4. *Cuban Reaction*—The group agreed that, in response to OAS charges, the Cubans will take the public line that the OAS ought to investigate U.S. overt and covert aggressions against Cuba. The Cubans have already started peddling this line.

---

[7] Reference is presumably to a May 25, 1963, memorandum from Bundy to the President printed in *Foreign Relations*, 1961–1963, vol. XII, Document 167. Bundy distributed copies of the memorandum to Robert F. Kennedy et al. on February 21, 1964. (Ibid., Document 168, footnote 3)

5. *Proclaimed List*—The group agreed that we should consider laying a basis in the OAS for possible proclaimed list action. Mr. Bundy noted that it would be nice if other OAR's took proclaimed list action also. It would not only make the measure more effective in impeding Free World commercial ties with Cuba, but would also demonstrate to the Free World that the U.S. is not alone in its concern over Cuba. Mr. Fowler added that the proclaimed list action should be prospective and should not include the freezing of assets.

One stumbling block to a proclaimed list is the Soviet Bloc dimension—i.e. can we blacklist Free World firms which trade with Cuba while not blacklisting Soviet Bloc organizations which trade with Cuba? Mr. Johnson and Mr. Behrman felt that this appeared to be an impossible hurdle. Messrs. Bundy, Mann, and Fowler felt that the apparent inconsistency was bearable; in this regard, Mr. Fowler noted that we expect more from our friends than our enemies.

6. *Salability of a Tough OAS Resolution*—Mr. Mann felt that with careful planning and great determination, we may well be able to get a tough resolution out of the OAS. The group then discussed the consequences of getting beaten in the OAS; Mr. Bundy noted that going in tough and getting licked may not be so unbearable from certain points of view.

Mr. Bundy pointed out that we should be under no illusions about the coming OAS action. As tough as our resolution may be, the chances are very good that we will still be living with Castro some time from now and that we might just as well get used to the idea. At the same time, we should probably continue our present nasty course; among other things, it makes life a little tougher for Castro and raises slightly the poor odds that he will come apart and be overthrown.

7. *Venezuelan Leadership and Noise-Level*—The group agreed that while the Venezuelans should publicly lead the fight, we will have to give them plenty of support. In this regard, USIA is geared up to do an intensive selling job in Latin America if it is deemed desirable; the U.S. Government will have to determine the size and shape of the noise-level to be produced during the period which follows the submission of the OAS report.

GC

4.   Memorandum for the Record[1]

Washington, February 21, 1964.

SUBJECT

Cuba Meeting—Friday, February 21, 1964

PARTICIPANTS

The Attorney General; General Taylor; Ambassador Bunker; Ambassador
Stewart; Deputy Secretary Vance; Deputy Under Secretary Johnson; Special
Assistant Califano; Acting Director Wilson; Ward Allen; John Crimmins;
Desmond FitzGerald; McGeorge Bundy; Gordon Chase

The group met to follow up their discussion of February 19 regarding OAS action resulting from the Venezuelan arms cache discovery. (Attached is a copy of the discussion paper.)[2]

1. *The Venezuelan Position*—After a status report by Mr. Allen, the group discussed the Venezuelan position.

(a) Ambassador Stewart said that the Venezuelans are prepared to take very strong Rio Treaty action, up to and including invasion; they are especially anxious to quarantine Cuba's export of subversion. He went on to admit, however, that the capability of the Venezuelan Foreign Office to sell a tough OAS resolution to other Latin American countries is not great. We will have to do a major share of the selling.

(b) Ambassador Stewart said that the Venezuelans might agree to a surveillance system whereby U.S. ships could shadow suspect vessels into Venezuelan waters. He had some doubts as to whether or not the Venezuelans would allow us to seize a suspect vessel in territorial waters; they might, if it were clear that Venezuelan forces could not arrive at the scene in time to make the seizure themselves.

2. *Surveillance System*—With the exception of General Taylor, the group favored the "non-force" option. Mr. Vance favored the "non-force" option because it is a more flexible system. Mr. FitzGerald noted that the arms shipment to Venezuela was a deviation from Castro's normal mode of procedure; he is unlikely to ship arms in the future. General Taylor commented that we should be clear that neither the "force" nor the "non-force" surveillance system will be very effective. He likes the "force" option because it gives us a reprisal capability.

---

[1] Source: Johnson Library, National Security File, Country File, Cuba, OAS Resolution (Arms Cache), Vol. II, Memos, 11/63–9/64. Secret; No Distribution. Drafted by Chase on February 27.

[2] Attached but not printed.

The group agreed that the OAS resolution should include language which will allow us to search suspect vessels and aircraft for subversives as well as for arms.

3. *Economic Sanctions and Warning to Castro*—The group agreed that the OAS language should be as general as possible in encouraging OAS countries to take action against Free World traders who deal with Cuba. General language is more likely to get OAS approval. The group agreed that, in warning Cuba that it had better not continue its subversion, the OAS language should also be general and flexible.

4. *Noise-Level*—The group agreed that a high noise-level in Latin America will be needed to obtain a tough OAS resolution. At the same time, it is desirable to keep the noise-level low in the U.S.

The general shape of the noise-level we want to get across is that Cuba is not solely a U.S. problem, but is a genuine Hemispheric problem. A confident but outraged Hemisphere is banding together to take further measures against Castro. The arms cache incident is a grave demonstration of what we have been saying for some time.

5. *Action Items*—The group agreed that a series of actions should be taken:

(a) The State Department should write a fresh draft of the OAS resolution and send it to Palm Beach to the Secretary so that the Secretary might get the President's approval in principle.[3]
(b) State should explore the problem of how the OAS meeting ties in with the Alliance for Progress meeting in March. This situation must be handled carefully.
(c) Mr. Chase should write a paper by February 24 which discusses the action against Cuba we want the OAS to take, and the results we expect to achieve by getting the OAS to take such action. Mr. Chase should clear his paper with Mr. Crimmins.

6. *USIS Film*—The group watched a USIS film about the arms cache, which will be shown on TV in Latin America. The general consensus was that it is a very convincing piece of work.

GC

---

[3] Rusk was in Palm Springs, California, February 20–23 for a meeting between President Johnson and President López Mateos of Mexico.

5.   Telegram From the Department of State to Secretary of State Rusk in Palm Springs, California[1]

Washington, February 22, 1964, 4:15 p.m.

Tosec 13. For the Secretary from Alexis Johnson.

1. Text working draft OAS Resolution contained immediately following telegram[2] represents outcome two White House meetings chaired by Bundy and attended by Attorney General, Vance, General Taylor, State (Johnson, Bunker and Amb. Stewart), USIA and CIA. Mann and Commerce and Treasury representatives participated first meeting.

2. Text developed ad referendum to you and, if you approve, for you to seek approval of the President to use text as basis for further discussions with Venezuela with view arriving at agreed text which they would take as basis for initiating soundings of OARs.

3. Following is background of critical parts of resolution:

a. Article 2, warning:

We wanted here to seek umbrella for possible future unilateral action and at same time provide ourselves maximum flexibility with respect nature our response to further Castro actions. Judgment is that it will be most difficult to get two-thirds vote for this blank check and we would be prepared negotiate back from this initial position. This article places emphasis on future action and is not designed provide basis for response of general OAS concern in instant case. Concept is also to provide basis of expressed OAS concern for considering approaches to Soviet Union urging they exercise restraint on Castro.

b. Article 3, surveillance:

We examined closely the question of an alternative which would permit search and seizure, involving the use of force, of OAS member states flag vessels (including Cuba), *on the high seas*. There was agreement that this alternative would not do anything more in a practical sense (i.e., in stopping arms shipments) than the language in the above draft and would be much more difficult to get agreement on. Wish to note that under either method chances actual apprehension of vessels carrying arms or subversives not good, and in fact it is doubtful Castro will revert at least for some time to technique used exceptionally in Venezuelan operation. Therefore, effect this article essentially psychological. It would be viewed as a further tightening measure, and

---

[1] Source: National Archives and Records Administration, RG 59, Central Files 1964–66, POL 23–8 VEN. Secret; Limdis. Drafted by Crimmins and U. Alexis Johnson, cleared by Allen, and approved by U. Alexis Johnson.

[2] Telegram Tosec 14 to USDel Palm Springs, February 22. (Ibid.)

the fact no further arms shipments occurred could be interpreted as result establishment surveillance system.

c. Article 6 on economic measures:

After examining variants, which included recommendation specifically calling for "proclaimed list" action by member states, we agreed on generalized formula presented in draft. This language does not commit us or others (who we estimate would be reluctant go so far) to establishment "proclaimed list", but would provide basis for such additional action and measures by us and other OAS countries as we may decide to take to discourage free-world trade with Cuba.

4. White House meetings produced following additional conclusions:

a. Aggrieved party, Venezuela, which is prepared propose strong measures, should float draft resolution, with US prepared move in firm support Venezuelan initiative. So long as possible, US should not be in lead.

b. USIA would proceed with large-scale effort in Latin America through its Latin American outlets to publicize Investigating Committee report (which is to be released 24th). (USIA is distributing dramatic non-attributed TV show on report.) Decision based conviction that high noise level effort needed in order develop Latin American support for even a minimum package.

c. On US domestic side, issue should be placed in low key, with no major statements coming out of Washington. Basic theme US public position would be that, as we have consistently maintained, US itself not threatened by Cuba; real Cuban threat is subversion directed against Latin America; therefore problem is one for entire hemisphere, particularly for the Caribbean basin countries directly threatened; and action to meet threat must be decided upon in common.

d. We should withhold decision on whether issue should be handled in Meeting of Foreign Ministers or in COAS acting provisionally as Organ Consultation until we have clear idea of Latin American lineup on action to be taken.

Text conclusions Investigating Committee also being transmitted septel.[3]

Foregoing also discussed with George Ball. I will be available in Dept after 10 a.m. Sunday for telcon if you desire.[4]

Ball

---

[3] Telegram Tosec 15 to USDel Palm Springs, February 22. (Ibid.)

[4] Rusk called U. Alexis Johnson on February 23 to report his decision "to check out the draft resolution further with the lawyers before he shows it to the President." (Memorandum from Chase to Bundy, February 24; Johnson Library, National Security File, Country File, Cuba, OAS Resolution (Arms Cache), Vol. II, Memos, 11/63–9/64)

6.   Draft Paper Prepared by Gordon Chase of the National Security Council Staff[1]

Washington, February 24, 1964.

*OAS Action on Venezuelan Arms Cache—U.S. Objectives and
   Expectations*

The following is a discussion of the action against Cuba we want the OAS to take as a result of the discovery of the Cuban arms cache in Venezuela. It is also a discussion of the results we expect to achieve by getting the OAS to take such action.

1. *U.S. Cuban Policy in General*—The bare minimum objective of our Cuba policy is a Cuba which poses no threat to its neighbors and which is not a Soviet satellite. In moving towards this objective we have rejected the options of unprovoked U.S. military intervention in Cuba and of an effective, total blockade around Cuba—primarily because they would risk another US/USSR confrontation. Instead, we are engaged in a variety of unilateral, bilateral, and multilateral actions and pressures, both offensive (e.g. economic denial and covert programs) and defensive (e.g. counter-subversion program) which stop short of invasion or blockade.

It is not at all clear that these measures short of military intervention/blockade will lead to our minimum objective. About the most that can be said is that we appear to be moving in the right direction. A tough, nasty, but no invasion/blockade policy, as opposed to a softer policy, is most likely to protect the Hemisphere from Castro's aggressive intentions and probably lays the best groundwork for bringing about any of the eventualities which would constitute a removal of the Soviet satellite from the Hemisphere—such as an overthrow of the Castro regime or a Soviet decision to quit Cuba. From a domestic political viewpoint, a tough but no invasion/blockade policy, fortuitously, is one policy which the American people appear prepared to support at this time.

2. *The Opportunity Afforded by the Arms Cache Discovery*—While the discovery, four months ago, of three tons of Cuban arms is not considered to be sufficiently provocative to lead us to risk a US/USSR

---

[1] Source: Johnson Library, National Security File, Country File, Cuba, OAS Resolution (Arms Cache), Vol. II, Memos, 11/63–9/64. Secret. Chase forwarded the draft paper to Bundy under cover of a February 24 memorandum in which he noted the draft was cleared by John Crimmins and asked if Bundy wanted it circulated to the participants of the Friday meeting. No record of Bundy's response or a final version of the paper has been found.

confrontation and to take decisive action against Cuba via military intervention/blockade, the discovery of the arms cache does provide us with an excellent opportunity to make further progress in tightening up and extending our present policy towards Cuba. In working towards this end we must be careful to move in those areas where we want to move, and not necessarily in those areas where false logic would appear to dictate that we move. For example, since the crime is a matter of arms, it does not necessarily follow that we must do something flashy and expensive (politically and financially) about arms, especially since our best estimate is that the likelihood of further significant arms shipments from Cuba is small.

In taking advantage of the arms cache discovery and the concomitant OAS attention, there are two areas in which we can profitably move with energy in the shoring up and extension of our isolation policy and in the strengthening of our anti-subversion program.

3. *Further OAS Action to Isolate Cuba*—Appropriate OAS action on the arms cache issue can take us a long way in our effort to shore up and extend our present isolation policy. Specifically, the following is what we want:

(a) We want the OAS resolution, in flexible and general language, to provide a basis for possible unilateral U.S. action to reduce Cuban/Free World commercial relations (e.g. the drastic measure of a proclaimed list); more importantly, we want the resolution to encourage as many OAR's as possible to join us in our effort. At present, one of the major obstacles to our efforts in the field of economic denial is the non-OAS Free World argument that the U.S. is the only country in the Western Hemisphere which is really concerned about Cuba. To counter this argument, we must demonstrate clearly that the Hemisphere regards Cuba as a threat, that the Hemisphere supports the isolation policy, that the Hemisphere looks with disfavor upon traders who do business with Castro, and that the Hemisphere intends to take appropriate action against such traders.

If we fail in this effort to get OAS support, we will probably be faced with a continuation of the serious deterioration which has already begun with respect to our economic denial program. On the other hand, if we succeed in our effort, the chances are considerably enhanced that we will be able to break the growing Cuban/Free World commercial ties. Assuming we can get appropriate OAS language and follow up, it is conceivable that the U.S., Colombia, Venezuela, Nicaragua, Guatemala, Honduras, Salvador, Paraguay, Costa Rica, Dominican Republic, and Ecuador will all take some kind of action (not necessarily the same in each country) which will make it clear to Free World traders that they can't have it both ways and that they must choose between Cuba, with a population of 6,000,000, and selected OAS countries whose populations total about 230,000,000. In selling this proposal to the OAR's we will point out, inter alia, that they will not be forced to sacrifice much in real terms since there will be relatively few Free World traders who will ultimately choose the Cuban market in such circumstances. Indeed, only Cuba will be seriously hurt.

Assuming the OAS passes a resolution which meets this problem, we will be in a position to follow it up immediately by proposing to willing OAR's that they meet with us to devise means of implementing the OAS decision—e.g. the circulation of lists of Free World Cuban traders among OAS countries.

(b) We want the OAS resolution to encourage further steps within the Hemisphere to isolate Cuba. First, we want the remaining five OAS countries which maintain diplomatic and consular relations with Cuba to sever such relations. Such a step will be dramatic evidence of Cuba's isolation and to some extent will hinder Cuba's subversive operations by denying Cuba the use of its overseas missions for this purpose. Importantly, it will be a clear sign to other Free World countries that the Hemisphere, expressing itself through the OAS, feels strongly about Cuba. It will also be a heavy psychological blow to Castro who has tried persistently and energetically in the past several months to establish "normal" relations with many Free World countries. Second, we want the suspension of all trade (except food and medicines) between Cuba and the OAR's. While trade between Cuba and the OAR's is small, such action will again demonstrate Cuba's isolation and OAS solidarity on the matter of Free World trade with Cuba. Third, we want a general call to Free World countries to cooperate with us in our effort.

4. *Further OAS Action to Counter Castro/Communist Subversion*—Appropriate OAS action on the arms cache issue can also take us a long way in our effort to strengthen our counter-subversion program. Specifically, the following is what we want:

(a) We want the OAS resolution, in flexible and general language, to warn Castro that the OAS will not stand by idly if he continues his subversive efforts. This resolution will be cognate with a possible Presidential statement along similar lines to the U.S. public and with a stern, private warning to the Russians that Cuban subversion is leading to a highly dangerous situation. Hopefully, such a resolution will have two main results. First, it will deter Castro from further subversive actions; among other things, the Russians may find it in their interest to control Castro more closely. Second, it will provide a juridical umbrella for and pre-position the OAS and/or the U.S., to use force against Cuba in the future if it is deemed desirable to do so.

(b) We want the OAS resolution to call for the establishment of a surveillance system which will permit the stopping and searching in territorial waters of all vessels suspected of carrying arms and sub-versives; a similar air surveillance system will also be established. While there are some negative aspects to such a resolution (few, if any, arms will be found), there are good reasons for having it. First, since an arms cache is involved, we must, at a minimum make a bow to-wards the problem of controlling arms shipments. Also, the resolution will be viewed as a tightening measure, and the fact that no further arms shipments occur can be interpreted as a result of the establish-ment of a surveillance system. Second, it will possibly deter Castro somewhat from sending men and arms to Latin America. Third, it will provide a peg on which to hang closer and more effective bilateral co-operation which may be called for in the future. For example, the U.S. and Venezuela may want to work out an arrangement whereby U.S. vessels can enter Venezuelan waters to assist in the seizure of a sus-pect vessel. Fourth, while it will give us an instrument to harass Cas-tro marginally, it has no significant escalation implications.

(c) We want the OAS resolution to call for the suspension of all air and sea communications between Cuba and OAS countries—ie. that ships and aircraft of OAS countries will not go to Cuba, that Cuban aircraft and ships will not be permitted in OAS country ports or air-fields and that ships and aircraft of non-OAS countries will not be al-lowed to stop at an OAS country port or airfield if proceeding enroute to or from Cuba. This action will have some most desirable effects. It will considerably increase Cuba's difficulties in exporting subversives, especially if the Cuba/Mexico air-link is cut. In addition, it will prob-ably be effective in reducing even further the number of Free World ships which still call at Cuban ports.

(d) We want the OAS resolution to encourage further steps within the Hemisphere to counter Castro/Communist subversion. We want a condemnation of the Castro regime for its aggressive acts against Venezuela. Also, we want a renewed call for alert against Castro/Com-munist subversion and an endorsement of the Lavalle Committee rec-ommendations outlining specific measures on control of travel, funds, and propaganda for subversive purposes.

5. *Priority Listing of U.S. Objectives*—The following is a summary listing of the major actions we want. They are listed in order of their im-portance in furthering the objectives of present U.S. policy towards Cuba.

(a) OAS words and action to stop the rapid deterioration in our economic denial program.

(b) Warning to Castro regarding future subversive action, with the threat of meaningful retaliation.

(c) Breaking of air and sea communications with Cuba.

(d) Breaking of diplomatic and consular relations.

(e) Establishment of a surveillance system.

It should be noted that the actions most important to us may not be the most difficult to get. For example, the economic sanctions may not be as difficult to get as the breaking of diplomatic relations.

6. *Tactics*—It is impossible to predict how many of the above mentioned actions we will get until we have an opportunity to publicize the arms cache issue and to reconnoiter the OAS landscape. Our general objective is to obtain as much of the total package as possible. To this end, our tactics will include the following elements.

(a) To the extent possible, we will keep Venezuela in the lead. We will be close behind the Venezuelans, however, supporting them with great determination and energy.

(b) A high noise-level will be needed in Latin America to obtain our objective. To this end, the USIA will proceed with a large scale effort to publicize the investigating committee's report.

(c) A fairly high noise-level will be desirable in non-OAS Free World countries to gain their acceptance of OAS decisions, particularly in the economic field. The general theme we will convey is that a confident but outraged Hemisphere is banding together to take further measures against Cuba. We have been telling the truth all along about the Cuban threat to Latin America and the arms cache discovery proves it. As appropriate, we will distribute the USIS film to non-OAS Free World countries.

(d) Domestically, the arms cache issue will be played in low-key. The general theme will be that the U.S. is not directly threatened and the real Cuban threat is subversion directed against Latin America. While we intend to aid the Hemisphere as much as possible in the fight against Cuban subversion, the control of subversives is and must necessarily be primarily the responsibility of the target countries.

A low-key posture in the U.S. will be very difficult to maintain if an MFM is scheduled in Washington. Therefore, if an MFM is to be held, we will consider carefully whether or not it should be held elsewhere.

7. *Practical Results*—Assuming we are entirely successful in obtaining all the OAS action we want, we must be clear as to what the practical results will be, and what they will not be.

(a) There will not be an immediate overthrow of the Castro regime and an immediate and complete cessation of Castro/Communist subversion in Latin America.

(b) There will be a juridical umbrella for the use of force against Cuba in the future, if deemed desirable.

(c) There will be, at a minimum, a delay in an upswing of the Cuban economy.

(d) There will be an increased burden placed on the Soviets to support the Cuban economy.

(e) There will be a further political isolation of Castro. Psychologically, this will wound Castro deeply.

(f) There will be a substantial impediment put in the way of Castro/Communist subversive activities in Latin America.

Gordon Chase[2]

---

[2] Printed from a copy that bears this typed signature.

---

7. **Paper Prepared by the Assistant Secretary of State for Inter-American Affairs (Mann)**[1]

Washington, February 25, 1964.

I would like a re-examination of paragraph two of the draft resolution with a view to determining whether the lawyers can strengthen this paragraph under either of the two following separate theories:

1. UN Article 51 says in substance that nothing in the Charter affects the right of individual or collective self-defense in the case of armed attack.

I recall that in the past some people have construed this article to limit the right of self-defense to cases in which there has been an armed attack. I seem to recall that there is respectable authority (McDougal of Yale)[2] which takes the opposite view, i.e., that the inherent right of individual or collective self-defense is not so limited. If the second line of authorities are followed we could simply have the resolution declare in substance that in the event of a situation comparable to the Venezuela one, the American States would have the right to resort to the use of armed force, individually or collectively, in the exercise of their inherent right of self-defense.

2. Why can't we capitalize on the fact that there has been an aggression by Cuba against Venezuela which falls within the purview of Article 6 of the Rio Treaty? More specifically, why can't we have this paragraph invoke the sanctions of Article 8 of the Rio Treaty (which include

---

[1] Source: National Archives and Records Administration, RG 59, ARA/LA Files, 1964: Lot 66 D 65, Venezuelan Arms Cache. Limited Official Use. Copies were sent to Dungan, Sorensen, Chayes, Whiteman, Bunker, Allen, and Crimmins.

[2] Myres S. McDougal, professor of law at Yale University.

the use of armed force) and then suspend the actual use of armed force—suspend the pushing of the button—on some theory such as, for example, the repetition of the same kind of aggression against another country? If the answer to the second question is that we cannot make the future employment of armed force dependent on some future event, then why can't we invoke and simply suspend in an effort to give the United States a clear right to act in the future without specifying future contingencies?

The trouble with paragraph 2 of the present draft is that it adds nothing to our existing legal rights to act in the future—nothing to our existing rights under the Rio Treaty. What we should be seeking is to capitalize on the Venezuelan situation so as to improve our legal posture.[3]

---

[3] Chase explained in a February 26 memorandum to Bundy that "the Secretary and Tom Mann want the wording strong enough so that it gives the U.S. a release in order to act unilaterally, if necessary. Abe Chayes, however, takes the position that the present wording (which will be tough enough to sell in the OAS) does not give us that release." (Johnson Library, National Security File, Country File, Cuba, OAS Resolution (Arms Cache), Vol. II, Memos, 11/63–9/64) Chayes offered new language for the second paragraph in a February 28 memorandum to Mann that "would provide a firmer legal basis for future individual or collective action against Cuba than the present draft." (National Archives and Records Administration, RG 59, ARA/LA Files, 1964: Lot 66 D 65, Venezuelan Arms Cache)

---

8.   Memorandum From the Assistant Secretary of State for Inter-American Affairs (Mann) to Secretary of State Rusk[1]

Washington, March 2, 1964.

SUBJECT

Draft OAS Resolution Re Cuban Aggression Against Venezuela

Attached for your approval is a draft OAS resolution dealing with the recent aggression by Cuba against Venezuela.[2] If, as we anticipate,

---

[1] Source: National Archives and Records Administration, RG 59, ARA/LA Files, 1964: Lot 66 D 65, Cuba 1964. Secret. Drafted by Mann and cleared by Chayes subject to several points concerning the second paragraph of the draft resolution. In a March 2 memorandum to Mann, Chayes warned that "legal arguments will be made by the opponents of the paragraph, both in and out of the OAS, against my view that this paragraph provides a legal basis for future individual or collective action." He also emphasized "the risks in using substantial international political capital to obtain approval of this paragraph when the result may be both to expose a major division within the OAS and to stimulate immediate demands for U.S. armed intervention against Cuba." (Ibid.)

[2] Attached but not printed.

this draft is acceptable to Venezuela, it would be presented as a Venezuelan rather than a United States initiative. We would, however, have to support it strongly in order to obtain the necessary two-thirds majority.

The draft resolution would do the following: (1) condemn Cuba for its aggression against Venezuela; (2) authorize in advance the taking of necessary measures individually and collectively, including the use of force, against Cuba if it commits aggression of comparable gravity against another American state; (3) recommend that the American governments cooperate in establishing systems of air, sea and land surveillance to prevent clandestine shipment of arms and men from Cuba to their countries; (4) require break in diplomatic and consular relations, suspension of all trade except in food and medicines, and suspension of all air and sea transportation except for humanitarian reasons; (5) provide an umbrella for unilateral action to further the trade embargo; (6) call upon free-world countries to take measures to help the American governments in their efforts to isolate Cuba; and (7) reaffirm the COAS recommendations on measures to counteract Castro-communist subversion. By far the most meaningful part of the resolution is paragraph 2.

Even if we succeed in getting the two-thirds majority for the resolution as a whole there is a possibility that both Mexico and Brazil, perhaps joined by others, would refuse to go along. By committing ourselves to strong support of this resolution we would be accepting not only the risk of a division in the OAS family but the possibility that the countries opposing would refuse to be bound by the two-thirds majority. To some extent these risks can be minimized by working quietly with Venezuela, in advance of setting a date for the OAS meeting, to obtain firm agreement with 13 countries to support a particular resolution. This preliminary work should be done so that we can know in advance what will come out of the OAS meeting.

There is a good chance—provided we take in the beginning strong and decisive leadership in favor of a resolution of this kind—of obtaining the thirteen votes needed for a two-thirds majority under the Rio Treaty.

The critical problem involves paragraph 2 of the resolution. This paragraph in effect says that in the event there should be another aggression by Cuba against an American Republic similar to the recent aggression against Venezuela, the United States would have advance Rio Treaty authorization to move militarily against Cuba itself without the need for calling another OAS meeting. On the other hand, it would, however, leave the United States free to make this decision in the light of all the circumstances existing at the time. It should be noted, of course, that if evidence comes to light of further Cuban aggression and intervention in other American states, the paragraph will give strong impetus to those seeking prompt, decisive military action against the Castro regime. Pressures for action can be expected to be all the greater during an election year.

We should not support this kind of provision unless we are prepared to follow through. The hope is that the risk of escalation in case of United States military action against Cuba would be decreased by saying to the USSR, in essence, immediately after the proposed OAS action, that they should either take the necessary steps to prevent Castro from engaging in further adventures of a subversive character in other American Republics or, if they cannot control Castro, to disengage. Obviously, others are better able than I to judge this aspect of the problem.

The other operative paragraphs in the draft resolution will by themselves have significant beneficial effects, but it is not expected that they will be decisive in bringing about an overthrow of Castro in the foreseeable future. They may, however, constitute good trading material for getting a two-thirds vote on paragraph 2.

If the draft resolution is satisfactory, I recommend that we try to meet with the President today or tomorrow to obtain his approval. Then we will be in a position to send it to President Betancourt who is awaiting our views on the measures which should be taken before initiating consultations.[3]

---

[3] According to Rusk's Appointment Book he met Mann and Chayes on March 3, at 9:37 a.m. (Johnson Library) Although no substantive record of the meeting was found, a notation on this memorandum indicates that the draft was "overtaken." On March 2 Rusk briefed the President on the draft resolution: "Our big problem there is how far to go in relation to the number of votes we'll get, but we got a good strong resolution, and we think [if] the Venezuelans float that, we can do work in capitals, and come up with a pretty good result on that." (Johnson Library, Recordings and Transcripts, Recording of telephone conversation between President Johnson and Dean Rusk, March 2, 1964, 11:35 a.m., Tape F64.15, Side B, PNO 1) An uncorrected transcript of the conversation is ibid.

9.   Summary Record of the 523rd Meeting of the National
     Security Council[1]

Washington, March 5, 1964, 4:55–5:30 p.m.

*Secretary McNamara's Mission to Vietnam; OAS Action on Venezuelan
     Arms Cache*

[Omitted here is discussion of Secretary McNamara's trip to South
Vietnam.]

2.   OAS Action on Venezuelan Arms Cache

Secretary Rusk said that as a result of the proof of Cuban efforts
to subvert the government of Venezuela by shipping arms into that
country, we must take stronger action against Cuba than any we have
taken so far. He summarized the attached paper, "OAS Action Against
Cuba," and the draft resolution which it contains.[2] He made two points:

a. There is some question as to whether we can get a two-thirds
vote in the OAS for the resolution. Venezuela will not be voting.

b. Paragraph 2 of the resolution is a warning to Cuba. It does not
mean that if another incident such as the Venezuelan arms cache occurred, we would be forced to act against Cuba.[3]

Assistant Secretary Mann commented that the Latin American
states go along with us, as they did in the missile crisis, when the U.S.
appears ready to use military measures, but there is strong domestic
pressure in the various Latin American countries opposing lesser actions against Cuba. Elections in the various Latin American countries
make this problem more difficult. Unless we find out by prior questioning that the Latin American states will support a meaningful OAS
resolution, we should oppose the convening of the OAS on this issue.[4]

---

[1] Source: Johnson Library, National Security File, NSC Meetings, Vol. 1, Tab 4. Secret. Drafted by Bromley Smith. The time of the meeting is from the President's Daily
Diary. (Johnson Library) The first item of record, "Secretary McNamara's Trip to South
Vietnam," is printed in *Foreign Relations, 1964–1968*, vol. I, Document 71. FitzGerald also
drafted an account of the meeting, portions of which are cited in footnotes below.

[2] Attached but not printed.

[3] According to FitzGerald: "He [Rusk] said that paragraph 2 as drafted is designed
as a blank check for OAS or individual member action in the event of further Cuban aggression; that it does not require U.S. action but does constitute a solemn warning both
to Castro and the Soviet Union. He pointed out that if we go all out to get this resolution and fail it will have unfortunate effects." (Memorandum for the Record, March 6;
Central Intelligence Agency, DCI (McCone) Files, Job 80–B01285A, Meetings with President Johnson)

[4] On this point, FitzGerald wrote: "The Secretary of State pointed out that Venezuela
is taking a very hard position, i.e. talking about an invasion of Cuba. The President said
that it seemed to him that this would only stir things up."

The President said we should begin now to find out how the Latin American states feel toward this resolution and then decide what we should do. Let the Venezuelans begin the sounding out, we will support them, and when we know who would support us, we could make a firm decision.

Secretary Dillon expressed his concern about paragraph 2 which he felt was very strong and might force us to act. He suggested that the draft resolution be changed from "should be taken" to "authorizes the member states to take action" in the event that the government of Cuba continues its aggression against other American states.[5] The President agreed to the suggested change.

Mr. Mann said that paragraph 2 gives us jurisdictional authority to move troops in the event of further Cuban subversion actions without going back to the OAS for approval. Secretary Rusk doubted that the OAS would give us this kind of a blank check.

Mr. Mann said we would have to twist arms to get the required thirteen votes for the resolution. What we are looking for is authority in advance from the OAS to act quickly and unilaterally. The issue today is not armed warfare but subversion. The UN Charter talks only of armed aggression, and Article 6 of the Rio Treaty defines aggression somewhat broadly. What we need to meet the existing situation is authority such as stated in paragraph 2.

The President agreed that we should try to get advance authority so that we do not have to go back to the OAS in the event of another action by Castro.

In response to Mr. Bundy's question, Mr. Chayes, as the State Department Legal Adviser, pointed out the legal differences between the statement approved at Punta del Este[6] and paragraph 2 of the resolution.

The President suggested that we say this is what we did at Punta del Este and this is what we should now have authority to do so that we can act in an emergency. We should find out how far the Latin American states will go.

---

[5] FitzGerald's memorandum reads: "Mr. Bundy agreed with Secretary Dillon's point. Governor Stevenson asked whether under this resolution, in the event of new aggressions by Castro, a meeting of the OAS would have to be held prior to action. He was advised that, although a meeting would be held, action could be taken at once without recourse to such a meeting."

[6] Reference is to paragraph 3, Resolution II, Final Act of the Eighth Meeting of Consultation of Ministers of Foreign Affairs, Punta del Este, Uruguay, January 22–31, 1962. (Department of State Bulletin, February 19, 1962, pp. 278–282) Documentation on the meeting is in Foreign Relations, 1961–1963, vol. XII, Documents 136–145.

Ambassador Thompson said the resolution created a problem. The Russians would read the resolution to mean that we are no longer committed not to invade Cuba if there is a repetition of an act such as the shipment of arms to Venezuela by Cuba.[7]

Mr. Mann pointed out that our technique would involve convincing Venezuela to accept our draft as their own and do the sounding out with the other Latin American states as if it were their resolution. The Speaker asked what we would do if we failed to sell the resolution. Mr. Mann repeated his view that we should not call an OAS meeting if we could obtain approval of only a mushy resolution.

Mr. Bundy called attention to the problem involved in paragraph 4 of the resolution calling for the suspension of trade and the suggestion that U.S. shipments of lard to Cuba be allowed. The President saw nothing inconsistent.

Mr. Bundy expressed grave doubts about the wisdom of obtaining support of about thirteen small states if the six large states opposed the resolution. Secretary Rusk said the small countries threatened by Castro are important. The big Latin American states are far away from the threat, and, therefore, consider the threat less important, but we have a responsibility to protect the small nearby threatened countries.

Mr. Mann summarized his understanding that he was authorized to proceed to find out what countries would support the draft resolution.[8]

Bromley Smith[9]

---

[7] FitzGerald wrote: "Mr. Bundy pointed out that this pledge was always subject to Cuba's good behavior and that we would indeed expect the Soviets to help in maintaining that good behavior."

[8] On this point FitzGerald wrote: "The President said to move ahead with the present resolutions and to have the State Department canvass OAS members concerning the acceptability of these resolutions and report back to him." (Ibid.)

[9] Printed from a copy that bears this typed signature.

---

10.   Editorial Note

On March 16, 1964, the Johnson administration began a concerted effort to reaffirm the ideals of the Alliance for Progress while establishing its own policy on Latin America. At noon that day the President delivered a major address before an audience of U.S. and Latin American diplomats. The ceremony, held at the Pan American Union, marked the third anniversary of the Alliance as well as the inauguration of the Inter-American Committee on the Alliance for Progress (CIAP). Although Johnson noted that the program owed much to the "vision" of his predecessor, he vowed that U.S. support for the Alliance would not diminish in the wake of Kennedy's assassination. As a sign of his personal interest, the President declared that the recent appointment of Thomas C. Mann "reflects my complete determination to meet all the commitments of the United States to the Alliance." (*Public Papers of the Presidents of the United States: Lyndon B. Johnson, 1963–64*, Book I, pages 381–384) The same day the Department of State announced that Mann would assume direct responsibility for economic assistance to Latin America as an Assistant Administrator of the Agency for International Development. To allow Mann the freedom to exercise full authority in Latin American affairs, the relevant operations in both agencies would be reorganized, merging the Bureau for Latin America (AID) with the Bureau of Inter-American Affairs (State). (Department of State *Bulletin*, April 6, 1964, page 540)

March 16 was also the first of a 3-day conference for U.S. Ambassadors and AID mission directors in Latin America. Mann had summoned these officials to Washington for consultation on the administration's policy, in particular, the Alliance for Progress. Most of the conference, which included sessions on regional as well as bilateral affairs, was considered off-the-record. Nevertheless, the day after the conference ended, *The New York Times* published an account of a closed session in which Mann allegedly suggested abandoning Kennedy's policy to deter Latin American dictators. The article, written by Tad Szulc, reported that Mann had emphasized the difficulty in classifying political leaders as either "good" or "bad," citing, for example, such authoritarian presidents as Adolfo López Mateos of Mexico, Víctor Paz Estenssoro of Bolivia, and Alfredo Stroessner of Paraguay. According to Szulc, Mann argued that the administration should be guided by practical not moral considerations: promoting economic growth while protecting U.S. business interests; and avoiding intervention in internal affairs while continuing to oppose communism. Senators Hubert H. Humphrey (D–Minnesota) and Wayne Morse (D–Oregon) were reported to have reacted to Mann's remarks by insisting that the United States "fight for the preservation of democracy in Latin America as part of the Alliance." (*The New York Times*, March 19, 1964)

The Johnson administration reacted swiftly to *The New York Times* article. In a telephone conversation with Mann and President Johnson the morning of March 19, McGeorge Bundy mentioned "the trouble about that Szulc piece." The discussion continued as follows:

"Mann: Well, I'm going to do something on that.
"Bundy: I assumed you would be going to.

"Mann: Yeah, we're going to do something on that. This is also very distorted.

"Bundy: I have no doubt of it. [Laughter] That I—the time Szulc writes a straight story will be the news.

"Mann: I talked both to [Senator Ernest] Gruening and to Morse this morning and they're not worried about it.

"Bundy: Good. Well, I guess that—just a moment—anything else, sir?

"President: Do we have some Ambassador you reckon is talking to Szulc or do you have enough Departmental people in there doing it?

"Mann: I think a lot of this—I think this came from, probably from somebody in the AID side of the Department, but I can't be sure. We had a big group and you don't get—If you don't talk about these things and you don't have any coordination, the Bureau doesn't function. You talk, then they distort. But this is a gross distortion of what I said on—I said essentially the same thing that Morse said: that we were in favor of democracy—

"President: I hope you let him know that before he makes a speech.

"Mann: I've already called him. I've already called him, and he said he does know that. I called Gruening too. They're both not worried about it. I'm going to have a talk about the whole problem, which is a very complex problem, but this is just a [unintelligible] job as I've ever—slanted, distorted—

"President: OK, my friend." (Johnson Library, Recordings and Transcripts, Recording of telephone conversation among President Johnson, Thomas Mann, and McGeorge Bundy, March 19, 1964, 11:27 a.m., Tape F64.18, Side A, PNO 4) The portion of the conversation printed here was prepared in the Office of the Historian specifically for this volume.

Later that afternoon Richard I. Phillips, press spokesman for the Department, issued the following statement: "United States devotion to the principles of democracy is an historical fact. United States policy toward unconstitutional governments will as in the past be guided by the national interest and the circumstances peculiar to each situation as it arises." (Circular telegram 1730, March 19; National Archives and Records Administration, RG 59, Central Files 1964–66, POL 1 US) In spite of this denial, the position attributed to Mann by The New York Times soon became known in the press as the "Mann Doctrine."

11.   National Security Action Memorandum No. 297[1]

Washington, April 22, 1964.

TO

The Secretary of State
The Secretary of Defense
The Administrator, Agency for International Development

SUBJECT

Latin American Military Aid

The President has today approved determinations with regard to military aid to Latin America.

In administering these funds and planning future programs, the President wishes to insure that our policies, MAP and otherwise, are directed toward the following general objectives:

1. Military expenditures by the host country which are consistent with and proportionate to expenditures for social and economic development.

2. The maintenance of a military establishment in the host country which is realistic in terms of our estimate of its potential missions.

3. The establishment of elite units which might be used in U.N. peace-keeping assignments.

4. Continued emphasis on civic action and internal security missions, the latter to be realistically defined.

5. Definition of a clear relationship between military internal security missions and police functions and a rational pattern of U.S. funding for same.

6. Emphasis in training and by other means on the role of the military in a modern democratic society.

7. Avoidance of sophisticated and expensive prestige equipment in our grant or sale programs except where specifically justified. In this connection, host country purchase from other sources of non-essential prestige equipment is to be actively discouraged.

The President desires, by 1 August 1964, a brief analysis and report on the military situation in each country and the changes, if any, to which our policies are being directed. These reports should measure the existing situation against the above general objectives and other

---

[1] Source: Johnson Library, National Security File, Country File, Latin America, Vol. II, 6/64–8/64. Confidential.

relevant factors. The reports should be prepared under the general direction of the Assistant Secretary for Latin American Affairs with the cooperation of other agencies.[2]

McGeorge Bundy

---

[2] In a July 28 memorandum to Bundy, Sayre explained that the reports had encountered difficulty within the bureaucracy, and suggested extending the deadline to September 1. Bundy agreed. (Ibid.)

---

12. Telephone Conversation Between President Johnson and the Assistant Secretary of State for Inter-American Affairs (Mann)[1]

Washington, May 5, 1964, 6:45 p.m.

[Omitted here is discussion of a proposal to send Attorney General Robert F. Kennedy to Chile.]

President: What do you think about the Szulc article this morning?[2]

Mann: [Laughter] Those fellas are really on a vendetta, you know. They've got their knives out, and it's the most biased reporting I've ever seen. If I were outside of government—the American election and so forth—I would answer in proper Texan style. But I'm not in a position to get into a donnybrook right now, because I think it might be disruptive.

President: How are we doing—

---

[1] Source: Johnson Library, Recordings and Transcripts, Recording of telephone conversation between President Johnson and Thomas Mann, Tape F64.26, Side A, PNO 4 & 5. No classification marking. This transcript was prepared in the Office of the Historian specifically for this volume. An informal memorandum of the conversation, prepared in ARA, is ibid., Papers of Thomas C. Mann, Telephone Conversations with LBJ, January 4, 1964–April 30, 1965.

[2] The article reported that Teodoro Moscoso had resigned from the Inter-American Committee on the Alliance for Progress in order to return to private life in Puerto Rico. Szulc wrote: "His resignation comes at a time of growing disillusionment in Latin America and among Latin-American officials of the Alliance in Washington over present conduct of the program by the United States. The consensus in those quarters is that the program as conceived by President Kennedy no longer exists, and that Washington seems to have returned to its unilateral approach to problems of the hemisphere." (*The New York Times*, May 5)

Mann: What do you think I should be doing about this?

President: How are we doing in Latin America in your judgment?

Mann: Oh, I think we're making good progress. We're making good progress, better than I think anybody could have hoped for. The Brazilian development. Colombia's going well—I just got a report today from [unintelligible]: everybody's happy, the President's very delighted, happy the way everything's going. The Mexicans are happy—I got a message today from López Mateos. Central America's going good. Chile and Brazil have problems. But this is the bleeding-heart, left wing group; they're just mad.

President: Well, now what are we doing to hurt them?

Mann: I don't know, but any [laughter]—Well, I think it's pretty hard to figure out a way to hurt them effectively. I think we're getting a broader base with the press, a better understanding, but these two *New York Times* twins are [unintelligible]. I don't think they like anything that's happened since November 22nd. And it's pretty hard to convince them. I haven't figured out a way to gag them yet.

President: Do they ever come talk to you?

Mann: Oh, I see them occasionally. I haven't seen them lately. I'm not sure it's a good idea to see them because you start to talk, they've made up their mind.

President: Where do they get their stuff? Schlesinger?

Mann: I would think so. I would think there and in this club of left-wing reporters.

President: Do you have any people leaking it on you over in the Department?

Mann: Well, I—Yes, we've had two or three that we think are out now and we've got only one left, and I think maybe Moscoso. I only have one guy that I don't trust, and I think he—

President: I'd get rid of him.

Mann: Well, we're going to. We're going to—I already told him.

President: The quicker, the better.

Mann: Yes, sir.

President: Now, what did Moscoso—why did he quit?

Mann: Well, this I don't know. I had a very friendly telegram from him today saying that he didn't expect this news to break so soon, he had expected to talk to me and to you—but I don't really trust him myself. I'm not sure what he hopes to—

President: OK.

Mann: OK.

President: You call me in the morning.

Mann: I'll call.[3]

---

[3] According to the President's Daily Diary Mann attended an afternoon meeting on May 6 between the President and the Panamanian Ambassador. (Johnson Library) No record has been found, however, to indicate whether Mann telephoned Johnson in the morning—or later in the day.

---

13.   Memorandum for Record[1]

Washington, May 11, 1964, 4:45 p.m.

SUBJECT

Memorandum of Conversation in the Cabinet Room Monday, May 11, 4:45 p.m.

PRESENT WERE

The President
Ambassadors or Chargé d'Affaires of the Latin American Republics
Dr. Carlos Sanz de Santamaria (head of CIAP)
Acting Secretary George Ball
Ambassador Duke
Mr. McGeorge Bundy
[Assistant Secretary Mann]

The President opened the meeting by offering a welcome to the Ambassadors who were seated around the Cabinet table. He said that this group of advisers might well be more effective than his regular Cabinet, and he then read or paraphrased the attached statement.[2] At the close of his statement the President announced that he was proposing the appointment of The Honorable Walt W. Rostow to replace Mr. Teodoro Moscoso as the American Representative on CIAP. The President initially asked that this announcement be kept private,

---

[1] Source: Johnson Library, National Security File, Agency File, Alliance for Progress. Secret. No drafting information appears on the memorandum. Bundy wrote "OK" on it. The meeting was held in the Cabinet Room.

[2] Not found. During a telephone conversation Johnson had asked Mann to prepare a "page" for the meeting. Mann replied: "All right. I think the scenario is that you're going to open up with a couple of things. We've primed two or three of them to set the right tone." Both men agreed that this might avoid a "gripe session," which would inevitably leak to the press. (Ibid., Recordings and Transcripts, Recording of telephone conversation between President Johnson and Thomas Mann, May 11, 12:50 p.m., Tape F64.26, Side B, PNO 3)

because he had not had a chance to discuss it with Mr. Rostow, who was airborne—but while he was making the announcement, Acting Secretary Ball was called to the telephone and reported that Mr. Rostow had accepted the President's proposal. The announcement was greeted with obvious pleasure by the Ambassadors.

The first reply to the President's remarks came from Dr. Sanz de Santamaria, who described his recent swing through Central America. He said that he conceived of CIAP as a political motor for the promotion of the Alliance. He had found a very affirmative response in every country from Mexico to Panama. All were trying to do their part. He particularly praised the efforts of coordination of the Central American nations. He believed that they had made great progress in integration, and that their effort compared favorably with the achievement of the European nations over a similar period of time.

Dr. Sanz said that he made it a practice to emphasize that the Alliance for Progress was not simply another name for AID, and that AID was merely one agency for the work of the Alliance, and that indeed the Alliance must never be conceived of as an effort by the U.S. alone.

Dr. Sanz reported that in some countries he found that the people were not yet interested in the Alliance. The Governments and the larger business interests were actively engaged, but the Alliance had a need for the people as a whole and for political action.

Dr. Sanz reported that he had repeatedly been asked whether he himself believed in the Alliance for Progress and that his standard answer had been a strong "Yes." He has explained that he had talked to President Johnson, Secretary Rusk, and Secretary Mann, and he knew of their own personal commitment to the Alliance, commitments reemphasized again by this meeting.

Dr. Sanz praised the appointment of Walt Rostow. He said that this was a very intelligent appointment which would be received with favor in Latin America and he emphasized the importance of this appointment in the light of the very great service which Teodoro Moscoso had rendered to the Alliance.

Dr. Sanz said that it was his practice to discuss needed improvements frankly both with the U.S. officials and with officials in Latin America. He was proud that in Mexico he had been invited to speak as if he were a Mexican. He had done so, and he believed that much could be accomplished in both directions by this kind of candor. He believed that in the case of the U.S. there was a need for the reduction of red tape, and for an ability to make decisions promptly even if the decision was negative.

The President asked if Mr. Mann found it difficult to say "No," and Mr. Mann promptly defended himself, while agreeing that the criticism offered by Dr. Sanz was justified.

Dr. Sanz said in conclusion that he was asked in Latin America why the U.S. insisted on a development program when the U.S. itself had never had such a program. Dr. Sanz said that his answer was that it was not the United States but the Latin American countries themselves which had requested such programs, and that when resources were limited and choice was necessary, it was entirely natural that a lending or granting agency would need to know how a given proposal fitted into the general program of the country concerned.

The President said that Dr. Sanz had made a very constructive statement. We agreed with it, and the President could say that however long he was in the White House, he was going to be at work on the Alliance. There was not a man living that cared more than he did, and no one more competent to work for the Alliance than Tom Mann. The President agreed that there was too much red tape and he believed it could be cut down. We were going to act for the Alliance and we were glad to have the help in this work of such men as Dr. Sanz.

The next speaker was Dr. Francisco R. Lima of El Salvador. He spoke briefly and made four points: (1) that at Geneva there was a significant difference between the hopes of the Latin American countries and the position of the United States delegation; his Government hoped that the U.S. could take a more sympathetic position;[3] (2) that the assignment of sugar quotas was a matter of the greatest importance to Latin American countries, and that his Government hoped for part of the Cuban quota. The President interjected that his Government was not alone. (3) That coffee prices should go up, and that the housewife should be brought to accept the need for higher coffee prices. The President interjected that producers always had believed in high prices, but that consumers were not so easily persuaded. (4) That concern with the U.S. balance of payments was interfering with relations between the U.S. and countries of the Hemisphere.

At the President's request, Ambassador Mann replied briefly to Ambassador Lima saying that sugar quotas were under careful review, that the U.S. expected to pass legislation supporting the coffee agreement, and that in cases where transactions having a very minor effect on the balance of payments were impeded by restrictions growing out of this problem, it should be possible to make arrangements that would prevent delay or obstruction on this account.

---

[3] Reference is to the United Nations Conference on Trade and Development (UNCTAD), which met in Geneva, March 23–June 16.

Ambassador Correa of Ecuador emphasized the concern of his country with the fate of the IDA legislation.[4] The President responded by saying that this was one of the many great problems we have this year, that we were working very hard on it and that we were worried about it too, and that he proposed to discuss it with the Legislative Leadership. The President telephoned on the spot to Mr. Lawrence O'Brien and asked for an up-to-date report on the legislative account. A little later in the meeting he received a telephone answer from O'Brien's office and reported to the meeting that the current estimate was that there would be 215 votes in the House for the measure, which would probably be just enough.

The Ambassador of Uruguay remarked that trade also was very important, that we should work at the increase of trade as a part of the whole program, and that we were not yet working on it as we should.

Acting Secretary Ball, in response, emphasized the concern of the U.S. with the expansion of trade and, with a reference back to the earlier comments of Ambassador Lima, he remarked that there was real hope for progress in the UNCTAD meeting in Geneva during the last five weeks of hard work. He himself hoped that there would be answers that would not be too disappointing to the assembled group.

Mr. Ball pointed out that we face a real problem in framing our policy on tariff preferences. This was a problem on which we ought to work together. The U.S. has to trade with all the world, and if the U.S. should introduce tariff preferences specifically for Latin America, we would be one step further along on the road toward the creation of a series of closed trading systems, in place of the traditional target of a single world-wide open system.

The President said that we ought to list some of our common interests and work on them some more. He reemphasized his conviction that the Latin American future was the American future, that "your welfare is our welfare."

The Ambassador of Chile remarked that some of the criticism which the Alliance for Progress was now receiving was the result of understandable impatience. In order to launch the Alliance for Progress we had set it at a very high pitch, and the things said at the beginning may have made the overall task seem easier than in fact it is.

The President entirely agreed with this point and said that in his view we had indeed started off on a very high pitch and that we must now show leadership in getting the real difficulties better understood.

---

[4] Reference is to a bill authorizing an increase in the U.S. contribution to the International Development Association, a World Bank affiliate. The House approved the legislation on May 13; the President signed the bill into law on May 26. (78 Stat. 200)

The Ambassador of Chile continued that we had nevertheless accomplished a good deal, although there was a natural tendency for each of us to suppose that he was doing everything and that the other fellow wasn't doing enough. The President agreed, remarking that is his experience the other fellow always thought it was the President of the United States who wasn't doing his part. The Ambassador of Chile replied that in the U.S. press it always appeared that it was the U.S. that was doing the work and no one else was doing enough. The Ambassador recognized that we all had bureaucratic problems. He thought that CIAP was a good way of meeting responsibility, but that it had taken too long to get organized. Nevertheless, most of our countries had prepared or were preparing development programs, and programs for tax reform and agrarian reform, and while we should not relax, we need not feel frustrated either. The Latin American countries were doing better. The weakest point was in the private sector. The conditions for a perfectly stable private sector were very complex, and in his judgment only two countries in the world could meet all the desired standards: the U.S. and Switzerland. He did not think Latin American countries could turn Swiss overnight. The Ambassador felt that Latin America faced a heavy requirement for political and social reform, and such programs commit governments and they have to go on forward with them.

The Ambassador pointed out that annual debate of public funds available for the Alliance put the whole case in suspense and created an element of doubt and concern.

The Ambassador of Venezuela conveyed the apologies of President Betancourt.[5]

The President concluded the meeting by emphasizing the need for optimism and enthusiasm in supporting the Alliance. He remarked that if you want to lose an election all you have to do is predict that you will lose it. If you want to lose a baseball game, all you have to do is announce your doubts. The President believed that we had come a long way and we should emphasize our success and do all that we can to create the appearance of success as well, since the appearance would reinforce the reality. The President reemphasized his complete confidence in Secretary Mann, who was going to be the one "Jefe" here in Washington for the Alliance. The Ambassadors should think of him as a friend, that if they would work with us we would keep at the improvement of the Alliance. But if we should predict its failure, the Congress would make it a failure. The program was surrounded by outsiders who liked to criticize and editors who looked for diplomats

---

[5] Bundy inserted the following phrase by hand: "for his inability to attend the meeting in response to the President's invitation."

whom they might quote in a critical vein, and the President believed it of great importance that we should do our best to build up the Alliance, not tear it down.[6]

---

[6] After the meeting the President invited the participants to the East Room, where he delivered an address and signed 12 loan agreements under the Alliance for Progress. Earlier that afternoon Johnson discussed the address with Mann: "I think we need some facts in there about what we've done the last 6 months. We ought to know if we've done anything worthwhile, in the achievements, and we ought to point them out, not defensively but rather positively, so that we can show that we haven't been asleep, and—This damn Schlesinger is going all over the world denouncing us. I saw a cable yesterday, it had been circularized to everybody, about how our whole policy on Latin America had changed, and how we'd abandoned the Alliance. And so I think we ought to answer him by saying: 'We're building this big waterworks here, and we're doing this road here, and we're doing this here—all this has been done in the last 90 days.'" (Johnson Library, Recordings and Transcripts, Recording of telephone conversation between President Johnson and Thomas Mann, May 11, 12:19 p.m., Tape F64.26, Side B, PNO 2) For text of Johnson's remarks, see *Public Papers of the Presidents of the United States: Lyndon B. Johnson, 1963–64*, Book I, pp. 677–681.

---

14.   Memorandum From Secretary of State Rusk to President Johnson[1]

Washington, May 19, 1964.

SUBJECT

    OAS Action Against Cuba

Recommendation:

With reference to the NSC decision of March 5 to seek support for a resolution which, inter alia, would authorize future use of force against Cuba in the event of further subversion, I recommend that you now authorize the Department to agree to the milder alternative along the lines of the enclosed,[2] in view of the impossibility of obtaining the necessary two-thirds' support for a stronger text and in view of the de-

---

[1] Source: National Archives and Records Administration, RG 59, Central Files 1964–66, POL CUBA. Secret. Drafted by Allen and approved by Bunker.

[2] Attached but not printed.

sirability of obtaining as broad support as possible for any action to be taken.[3]

Discussion:

Consultations undertaken by the Venezuelans and ourselves with the other American Republics on the March 5 text have shown considerable opposition to the "blank check" concept in paragraph 2 under which, as you recall, the OAS would not authorize the use of force against Cuba at any time in the future without going back to the OAS, should there be a repetition elsewhere of the type of subversive campaign Castro undertook against Venezuela last fall. From the point of view of public opinion both at home and abroad, it seems to us highly desirable that there be as broad support as possible for some meaningful action against Cuba, including, if possible, Mexico's vote. Therefore we believe it desirable to revise the basis of the idea involving the possible use of force to one of individual and collective self-defense and embody this concept in a separate resolution on which we have some hope for virtually unanimous agreement. The other provisions of the March 5 draft concerning surveillance around Cuba, severance of diplomatic and economic relations, suspension of air and surface transportation and appeal to other free world countries for cooperation, would then be put in one or more separate resolutions, but would be in the form of recommendations rather than as binding decisions as provided in the earlier draft.

The revised draft would still offer the advantages of clearly establishing the doctrine that Castro-type subversive activities constitute "aggression" and that, under the right of self-defense, some action could be taken by us in support of an aggrieved state at its request in the future without awaiting recourse to the OAS.

Dean Rusk[4]

---

[3] A note on the memorandum indicates this recommendation was "approved by the President at lunch with Secretary 5/19/64." According to the President's Daily Diary Johnson met his Tuesday Luncheon group—Rusk, McNamara, and Bundy—on May 19 at 1 p.m. (Johnson Library) No substantive record of the meeting has been found. The Department circulated the revised text of the draft resolution on May 21, pending Venezuelan approval. (Circular telegram 2171; National Archives and Records Administration, RG 59, Central Files 1964–66, POL 23–8 VEN) The Venezuelan Government subsequently agreed to the proposed revision, but continued to insist on taking action at a meeting of Foreign Ministers rather than the OAS Council. (Circular Telegram 2214, May 28; ibid.)

[4] Printed from a copy that indicates Rusk signed the original.

15. **Telephone Conversation Between President Johnson and the Assistant Secretary of State for Inter-American Affairs (Mann)**[1]

Washington, May 26, 1964, 1 p.m.

President: Tom?

Mann: Yes, sir?

President: I have been looking at the amount obligated by the Alliance program and it's quite disturbing. It's only about 60 percent of what they've appropriated.

Mann: Uh huh.

President: And I thought that I better talk to you and the Director of the Budget and see if we can't get something done that will get that money obligated, because you don't, Passman's[2] just going to take it away from us.

Mann: Well, I think—We testified up there the other day where we're going to have it all obligated by the end of the fiscal year, but I'll check on it again to make sure.

President: Well, they estimate that they're going to do it faster, but I just think you ought to call in some people there and approve some loans.

Mann: Well, we'll do that.

President: You know what you got now? You got May the 15th, 59 percent of the Alliance loans obligated.

Mann: Well, I think it may be higher than that right now.

President: Well, this was May the 15th, 59 percent.

Mann: Yeah.

President: April the 30th, you only had 45 percent.

Mann: Yeah, we got a slow start.

President: Now, they estimate that they're going to get up there, maybe 90 some-odd percent. But if you get it the last month, he's going to start hearings on it in the next few days and he's going to look at what you got now. And everyday that you wait you just cost you

---

[1] Source: Johnson Library, Recordings and Transcripts, Recording of telephone conversation between President Johnson and Thomas Mann, Tape F64.27, Side A, PNO 6. No classification marking. This transcript was prepared in the Office of the Historian specifically for this volume. An informal memorandum of this conversation, prepared in ARA, is ibid., Papers of Thomas C. Mann, Telephone Conversations with LBJ, January 4, 1964–April 30, 1965.

[2] Congressman Otto E. Passman (D–Louisiana), chairman of the Foreign Operations Subcommittee of the House Appropriations Committee.

money. And I'm not going to fight for it if they don't go on spending when they got it.

Mann: All right. I got it. We'll spend it. I'll make sure we get it all obligated.

President: Let's get another ceremony and sign some more and let's get those ambassadors in here in another month.

Mann: All right.

President: Get them back. You get with Rostow and you all get some plan and some new ideas and some new programs that we can announce for some of the rest of them. And sometime in the next 30 days let's get them back in.

Mann: Will do.

President: All right.

Mann: OK.[3]

---

[3] Mann forwarded a memorandum to the President on June 15 in which he reported that 80 percent of the funds appropriated for the Alliance for Progress had already been obligated; the remainder would be committed within 1 month. (Johnson Library, National Security File, Agency File, Alliance for Progress, Vol. I) No evidence has been found that Johnson invited the Latin American Ambassadors to the White House for a second signing ceremony for the Alliance.

---

16.   **Telephone Conversation Between President Johnson and the Assistant Secretary of State for Inter-American Affairs (Mann)[1]**

Washington, June 11, 1964, 7:05 p.m.

Mann: I just got back from the Hill talking to Cooley about sugar with Charlie Murphy.[2]

---

[1] Source: Johnson Library, Recordings and Transcripts, Recording of telephone conversation between President Johnson and Thomas Mann, Tape F64.31, Side B, PNO 5 and Tape F64.32, Side A, PNO 1 & 2. No classification marking. This transcript was prepared in the Office of the Historian specifically for this volume. Although the President's Daily Diary indicates that Johnson placed the call, the tape does not include a salutation. (Johnson Library) The recording otherwise appears to document the entire conversation. An informal memorandum of the conversation, prepared in ARA, and incorrectly dated June 12, is ibid., Papers of Thomas C. Mann, Telephone Conversations with LBJ, January 4, 1964–April 30, 1965.

[2] Representative Harold D. Cooley (D–North Carolina) and Charles S. Murphy, Under Secretary of Agriculture.

President: What are our problems now? You got the Kubitschek problem in Brazil. What are the hot ones? You got an election in Chile.

Mann: We got an election in Chile in September.

President: All right.

Mann: We got this Foreign Ministers meeting which will probably take place in July on this Cuban, Venezuelan accusation against Cuba.

President: Are you, have you got that worked out where you're going to get the kind of resolution that you want?

Mann: Well, we're going to get, I think, a fairly good one. We're having trouble with Mexico; Chile, because of its elections in September, probably going to vote against it; but we think that Brazil and Argentina will come along. We've been working on, haggling over words. Bunker's working on it almost full time. I was talking, when you called, with the Mexican about it. Trying to get him to—

President: Who do you talk to? Who do you mean, the Mexican?

Mann: Sánchez Gavito.

President: Yeah.

Mann: He's their OAS ambassador.

President: Is he pretty difficult?

Mann: No, he's on our side, but he's having trouble at home because of politics down there. Their basic problem is Lombardo Toledano and Cárdenas and trying to keep the party from splitting.[3] It's an internal problem with them. They're fiddling with words that everybody can live with and—

President: When does that come up?

Mann: We think the first, within the first—it will be after the elections which in Mexico, which I believe are, it's on a Sunday, I think the 6th of July, the 5th of July.

President: Any question about the Mexican election?

Mann: No, no, there's no question at all there. They've had some disturbances—you know the Commies are growing up in Mexicali, that's a serious problem for us, Mr. President—but I think we're making progress.

President: How—Did you get Hayden[4] to agree to what you want to do on that water?

---

[3] Vicente Lombardo Toledano, founder and leader of the Partido Popular Socialista (PPS), and Lázaro Cárdenas, former President of Mexico (1934–1940), who remained active on the left wing of the Partido Revolucionario Institucional (PRI).

[4] Senator Carl T. Hayden (D–Arizona).

Mann: We're still waiting for word from him, but the Secretary is going to see him again tomorrow.

President: He told me, Hayden told me, yesterday that he had agreed to go along with the State Department.

Mann: Well, I think what he's doing is waiting on some kind of a political commitment from your office about the central Arizona project.

President: That's right, but he told me he'd agreed to go along with you all on the other one. I want to be sure it's satisfactory before I agree with him.

Mann: Well, I think maybe that's where we are, that's the last word I had at noon today, that—I'll talk to the Secretary about it in the morning if I may—

President: You be positive about that and tell him that he already told me he'd go with the Secretary. The Secretary ought to tell him that the President says that "you told him you're going with us."

Mann: I think he may infer back: "Yes, but this is a package deal, and whereas—"

President: He never has made it conditional that way, never has put it on that basis. He's just said: "I've already helped you, now you help me."

Mann: All right. Well let me—I'll see the Secretary in the morning. I'll tell him that it's not conditional and—

President: No. No, that's right. I'm trying to—

Mann: We have a lot of potential problems. For example, Uruguay has five presidents, as you know, and they're just in a hell of a mess because they can't manage their affairs very well; their growth rate is now down below their birth rate. The Kubitschek thing is bad. We'll get some flak on that for two weeks, but the general trend, we think—after June 15 they can no longer do this, the law, their power to designate new people, expires then. We are urging them to set up an appeals procedure for Kubitschek and all of the others, so they'll have a chance to be, for their day in court, to be heard. There'll be charges against them and so forth—I don't think it will get anywhere—but I would think the Brazilian thing would get better starting in about two weeks. I think it will look pretty good in thirty days.

President: You got any more hot spots?

Mann: We've got lots of headaches.

President: What's happening in the Dominican Republic?

Mann: Well, they just reached an agreement with the Monetary Fund, and we're now negotiating with them on trying to get them to take the self help measures that they have to take. They've got lots of problems. It takes them 7 cents—which is absurd—to produce sugar, and the world price is now around 5 and futures are about 4.5. So they have to fire a lot of people, and get more efficient, and increase agricultural production. And they've got to find a way to hold elections. And we've come to—some of them are really, Mr. President, are, you wonder sometimes whether they're capable of governing themselves. But things are moving along pretty well. We've got problems nearly everywhere. Costa Rica's in trouble. Their, they claim there's a 35 percent loss of foreign exchange in their coffee exports and, I think it's sugar, and we're going to work on that because the President will be up here to see you and we'll fill you in on that before he gets here. Panama is rocking along. They haven't started talking yet but they will resume the next week. Illueca,[5] I think, is coming in on Monday back from Panama.

President: What do we hear from our Ambassador down there?[6] Is he doing all right?

Mann: think he's done a fine job, and you made a good selection, I say that without qualification. He's exercised good judgment, he's been calm, and he's been tough when he had to be tough. He'll be up this week. By the way—early next week—we'll have about seven ambassadors. You said you wanted to meet with them. Any time next week you're ready, we'll send about seven over there.

President: Yeah. All right. You just stay after Jack, make him give you a date, just hound him every day, 'cause we just—The ones that raise the most hell get the most sugar.

Mann: All right. [laughter] I'll stay on the phone—

President: You're too good and too nice. So you just, you just give him hell. Just tell him every day, you got to call him the next day and get your date so you'll know what you're doing—

Mann: All right, will do.

President: And then you get me a briefing paper so I can tell me what I can say to them. And—what can I say that we've done in this Hemisphere now that's improved the situation? What have we got that we can point to with pride besides pointing to with alarm?

Mann: Well, we're going to send you over a memo with, it's in preparation now, on the Alliance side.[7] Where we're weaker than any other place, Mr. President, is on trade. AID thing is going good, as you know, thanks to you. We'll hear more complaints, I think, on trade,

---

[5] Jorge Illueca, principal Panamanian representative in the negotiations to revise the Panama Canal Treaty.

[6] Jack Hood Vaughn.

[7] See footnote 3, Document 15.

about sugar and coffee and things that they need to live, to sell in order to live. But I think on the whole that—

President: Can we say that these 6 months are better than the last 6 months before we came in?

Mann: I think we can. I believe—

President: Well, how or why are they better? How are they better now than they were—

Mann: Let me give you about twelve points on the AID side, and we'll scratch around and find some other general points on—

President: From March though, if you're just making a general statement, from March to November, the period in November to now, what's the difference?

Mann: All right. Let us think about that.

President: I guess we'll say Brazil, Brazil, say that's the best thing, isn't it?

Mann: No, I was thinking of things you could say.

President: No, no, I'm just talking about in my own mind.

Mann: Oh, well, the Panama thing went very well, Mr. President. The Guantanamo thing has gone well. The whole Cuban thing, in my opinion, has gone well.

President: The Brazil thing went all right.

Mann: Brazil is the most important thing outside of Cuba that's happened in the last 20 years in Latin America—in spite of the difficulties, in spite of the excesses, and there have been excesses, stupidities, the pendulum swung too far back and now we've got to push it back toward the center. We're going to win this election in Chile, things look good, we've done a hell of a lot of work on that. And—

President: Now, what have you got? A Communist running?

Mann: Well, we have a socialist running with Communist support, but the Communists are stronger than the socialists, and if he wins we think the Commies, he'll be a prisoner of the Commies, cause they're much, much better organized and much more disciplined.

President: What about our candidate? He's not the incumbent is he?

Mann: No, our can—the candidate we hope will win is a Christian Democrat, and he's being supported by the conservatives, the liberals, and, of course, the Christian Democrats, which is a new party. We're not telling anybody this, but we've been taking polls, and even allowing for inaccuracies, the margin of inaccuracies, it looks pretty good. Frei, the Christian Democrat, comes up with 52 percent; Allende, the Communist-socialist candidate, with 36; and a third candidate, who represents the Radical Party—which is not radical at all, but it's more anti-clerical, which we're keeping in the race so, because we think all of his votes would go to Allende—he's running about 7 percent; and the other 5, I think it's 5 remaining, 5 or 6 percent undecided. So we're not doing bad, we've picked up a lot of steam in the last, a lot of support for Frei in the last 6 weeks.

President: What are our danger spots?

Mann: Well, that's the—

President: Chile election?

Mann: That's the biggest one, I would say, with the fact of the Communist element in it.

President: And the Dominican—

Mann: The overflights over Cuba.

President: What in the world can we do to minimize that? We can't go around them. We can't circle the island. We got to go over it. And—

Mann: I think we'll get, I'm hoping we'll get some good resolutions, which would be very helpful on the domestic front, and also of real value to us.

President: Is trade going up much between the British and the Cubans?

Mann: Well, it has in terms of British exports to Cuba, and French exports.

President: They told me when they were here that they'd been 55 million, they'd cut them to five, but they'd be up on account of the buses. Now what, how much are they up to?

Mann: Well, what really happened, I don't have the figures in my head, but I know it's up quite a bit, Mr. President, because they've been buying all this sugar, and they've got these, Cuba's got the convertible currencies to buy anything they want. I think it's about two hundred million dollars a year that Castro made last year, and we expect him to make about the same this year as a result of the increased price of sugar. Now sugar prices are dropping, this is a very temporary phenomenon, sugar prices are dropping and he's just, he's not going to have the money to buy this kind of stuff much longer. So I don't think that the prognosis, the medium and long term prognosis, is bad. It's good.

President: You getting any reports of the things inside Cuba? What's happening?

Mann: Well, not really anything new that—

President: Is there any dissatisfaction?

Mann: Yes, we figure about 25 percent of the people—the job holders, the office holders, especially the young people in the country who are better off than they ever were before—are totally in favor of Castro. We think he can count on about 25 to 30 percent of the people. We think there are about 25 to 30 percent of the people who are opposed to him, and the middle ground there, the 40 to 50 percent, are just sort of apathetic. And that's the way it's been for the last year or so, and there isn't much change in that, because his hard core of support is built around the people who hold jobs.

President: Would you say that our economic isolation policy has been a complete failure?

Mann: No, sir. I think it's been largely successful. I—

President: How? When the French and British are all trading with him?

Mann: Well, he's had these dollars and they've sold him some things, and that's hurt us. But on the, if—the alternative would be to let the bars down and let them extend credits and that sort of thing. And we've been very successful in keeping this limited to a number of isolated transactions. And this is a hell of a lot better than taking him into our bosom.

President: How are we going to get rid of him?

Mann: It's going to take some time.

President: Well—

Mann: I think it's going to have to come from—I really don't think that, unless somebody kills Castro, or he dies, or the army is split in the very top command where they turn on him, the army especially, that the people themselves can get rid of him. As long as that army is loyal to him, he's going to be there until he dies. And when he dies, nobody knows what's going to happen, because he's got the same power to mesmerize people that Hitler had, and we doubt that anybody else has got, can project this same kind of image. The only other way to knock him off would be to go in there with force from the outside, and this could happen, either as a result of our reactions to his shooting at our planes that are doing this photographic stuff, or as a result of collective action which we're working on in this Venezuelan thing, whereby he tries again what he did in Venezuela, and if at that time you decide you want authority, the legal basis to go in, and you want to go in, I think we could get it. The main objective we hope to get out of this meeting is to say that subversion, communist subversion, is an aggression which is not an armed attack within the meaning of article six of the Rio Treaty, get them to accept that, so that if we have another act of subversion, we'll have a good legal basis of going to the OAS and saying now you agreed that this was the law, and here are the facts, and this is what we ought to do. Because the biggest problem, as you know, that we had in the Bay of Pigs, was this doubt on the part of the lawyers and others that we had any right in international law to do anything, and we hope to clear that up considerably.

President: So that for the subversion by importing arms to other countries to be considered aggression, that would justify our moving.

Mann: That's what we—if he does it again. But we would have to go to the OAS and prove the facts. They didn't want to give us a blank check.

President: Well, you've got a statement there, say I ought to say at a press conference that I don't intend to invade Cuba, just as Kennedy didn't.

Mann: Well, sir, if I were you, I wouldn't make a statement like that, because who can tell what's going to happen tomorrow? Suppose he shoots tomorrow and—

President: Well they say Khrushchev is saying that he hadn't seen us repeat Kennedy's pledge and we ought to do it.

Mann: Well, I would send, I wouldn't make a public statement, I'd have the Secretary of State say that if he behaves himself, doesn't commit any aggressive acts against other Republics, and doesn't shoot at any of our planes, or doesn't give us cause to do anything, that everything's going to be all right in terms of war and peace.

President: You tell, in the morning you call Mac Bundy, he's not here, but you call him, and tell him I was talking to you last night, and you'd like to know what he'd propose to say in that statement and then you tell him why you don't think it ought to be done.

Mann: All right.

President: Now, what's the problem in Uruguay?

Mann: Well, Uruguay. They have this silly political system, Mr. President, where they've got five presidents of the country and, I think, it's seven mayors of Montevideo, the capital city, and it's a little tiny place, and graft and corruption is growing. They have an executive that's almost paralyzed because there isn't any one president. The people are beginning to talk about the need for strong leadership, but nobody's done anything about it yet. And in the meantime their expenses are too high, they're paying too much, they're spending more than they're earning on social security and a number of other things, and just having a hell of time making ends meet. And the result of this is a deterioration in confidence, the private sector is not investing in job-producing industries, and production is not going up. They actually had a slight decrease in their national GNP rate last year as compared with a fairly high birth rate, I think about two and a half per cent. And we are going to—[1 second sanitized by the Johnson Library under the donor's deed of gift]—a skull session to see what it is we can do—

because I see this one coming in some months ahead—and what it is we can do to get that economy rolling again. But when you have to work with five heads, a five-headed animal, a government, it isn't always very easy to do, because they don't, they fight like cats and dogs between themselves, they can't agree on anything. That's a major problem. We've got these, the possibilities of oil expropriations in Argentina and in Peru, but we think we've got those dampened down in Peru. We may have trouble in Argentina though, and it may come this month.

President: What are they going to do? Expropriate some of our oil companies?

Mann: It won't be an expropriation. It will be a compensation for the amount of money they put in, which will satisfy some of the companies. Those that invested a lot of money and didn't find oil, near as I can find out, they would be happy to get their money back. Then you have other companies like Standard of Indiana and Tennessee Gas and, I think, Cities Service, those three, made an investment and hit it pretty big, and they're not about to think about, they're not about to be satisfied with just getting their money back. So I told the Minister of Defense of Argentina the other day that we would not buy that, we thought the Hickenlooper Amendment would apply, and his reply was that they could not renegotiate those contracts. I suggested they might sit down and do whatever's fair and reasonable. He said they couldn't do that, it was too hot a political issue, but they could go through a procedure of opening this to bids, putting the concessions, the oil fields, up for bids, and then making the terms and conditions so that the same companies that own them now would end up owning them. Now this looks like to me it's gonna be hard to do, and we decided this morning that I would call in these three companies and talk to them directly, and get their ideas, the ones who would be hurt the worst. I think Standard of Jersey and that crowd are going to be happy about it, but the others are not, and I think you can't, can't, without those guys.

President: Who's that? Standard and Tennessee Gas?

Mann: I think Tennessee Gas, Cities Service and Standard Oil of Indiana are the ones who would be hurt the worst if they didn't get—if they tried just to return their investments with interest. And I don't think we can buy that, because if you apply that formula to Venezuela, where we have four billion dollars in assets, they'll try to go back and say: "Well, you've already recovered your initial investment, so you ought to get out." We have to be very careful about the precedent.

President: These damn coal men are really murdering me, because we don't give them some of this substantial increase. They think that we ought to quit adding, importing that Venezuela oil all the time. Can we do anything like that?

Mann: Mr. President, I think there's too much oil coming in from Canada. Their production—I worked out this exemption, overland exemption thing, about 4 years ago.[8] We had a deal with them at that time that they would ship us in about 50,000 barrels a day mostly in the Pugent Sound area, and they're now up to over 300,000 barrels a day or around there, especially in Humphrey's state. I have to talk to Marlin[9] about this. The Venezuelans are getting awfully nervous about this. The Ambassador was in to see me yesterday protesting.

President: What am I going to do about coal though if you and Marlin take all the God-damned oil that Canada and Venezuela produce? I've got all my people here that's starving in these coal areas?

Mann: Well, we'll have a look at the coal industry. I think they're doing pretty good. I'd like to look at the figures, I—

President: No, they're not. They're in here this week, all of them, and just saying "you cost us 4,000 jobs by raising the oil quota on residuals."[10] And I'm going to appoint a committee, put you on it with McNamara, and make them redo it and do something for coal. We ought to help some of the people of West Virginia and Pennsylvania and Illinois, as well as help the people of Venezuela and Canada. I don't mean just help them to the exclusion but give them some help.

Mann: Well, I'd rather give them help any place except at Venezuela's cost. Maybe we can do, maybe we can find something in the Near East or something. Let us look at it, and see what we can do.

President: OK. All right. Bye.

Mann: Thank you.

---

[8] Mann was Assistant Secretary of State for Economic Affairs in April 1959 when the United States agreed to give Canada and Mexico an "overland exemption" to the oil import program. For documentation on that program, see *Foreign Relations, 1958–1960*, vol. IV, pp. 579–594, 608–609.

[9] Marlin E. Sandlin, chairman of the Pan American Sulphur Company, Houston, Texas.

[10] The Johnson administration amended the oil import regulation on March 6, raising the maximum level for residual fuel oil to the eastern United States (District I). (29 F.R. 3200, 3207) The President attended a National Coal Policy meeting on June 5 to discuss the concerns of the coal industry, including representatives from management, labor, and transportation. (President's Daily Diary; Johnson Library)

17.   **Memorandum From the President's Special Assistant for National Security Affairs (Bundy) to President Johnson**[1]

Washington, June 16, 1964.

SUBJECT

Staff Assistance in Latin America

Walter Jenkins has told me of your quite proper concern over the Sunday *Star* story about Bob Sayre joining my staff.[2] The story, which must have come from some State Department gossip, is a damaging distortion of a move which was made to deal with a real problem. That problem is that Ralph Dungan and Tom Mann really have not communicated easily together, so that Latin American business has kept coming through my desk.[3] I was either doing things myself or playing liaison officer between the two of them. This I just did not have time enough to do without help, so about six weeks ago I told Ralph that I thought we ought to add to the NSC staff a relatively junior officer (like Dave Klein for European affairs) who would be available to us here, and who would be acceptable to Tom Mann, too. I should add in candor that both Ralph and I knew that this arrangement would in fact reduce his direct involvement in Latin American affairs, although I told him that I for one would be glad to have him continue to keep a hand in when he felt like it.

Sayre was recommended by Crockett[4] and Mann for this job, and while I was wary at first, I found him very good in our interview, and I found that Ralph had a very high opinion of him. He has been over

---

[1] Source: Johnson Library, National Security File, Memos to the President, McGeorge Bundy, Vol. V. No classification marking.

[2] The article reported that Sayre had assumed responsibility for Latin American affairs at the NSC and suggested that he would be "much more closely oriented to the State Department view of events" than Dungan and Richard M. Goodwin had been under President Kennedy. (*Washington Star*, June 14, 1964)

[3] Bundy also raised the communication problem with the President on April 14, citing criticism that would result if Dungan left, i.e. "another good White House man goes west." Johnson replied that his standing in the public opinion polls was such that "Ralph's leaving me wouldn't hurt me really politically." (Johnson Library, Recordings and Transcripts, Recording of telephone conversation between President Johnson and McGeorge Bundy, April 14, 1964, 12:50 p.m., Tape F64.23, Side B, PNO 1) In an April 28 memorandum to Bundy, Chase warned of a possible consequence if Dungan departed: "I, for one, do not favor Tom Mann's implied proposal that White House/State contact take place solely or substantially through his office (it probably bothers Tom somewhat that he does not now control everything that ARA says to the White House)." (Ibid., National Security File, Country File, Latin America, Vol. I, 11/63–6/64)

[4] William J. Crockett, Deputy Under Secretary of State for Administration.

here for several weeks now, and he has already proved his value in a number of ways. The most conspicuous example is Tom Mann's speech on our recognition policy.[5] Because of his friendly relations with Mann and his own sensitive eye for the politics of the matter, Sayre was able to get amendments made which made that speech entirely safe at home and successful in Latin America.

I have spoken to Ralph about this unsatisfactory story, and neither he nor I think it is something we should make an issue over, since it was way on the inside of a Sunday paper. Of course, Tom Mann himself is a Special Assistant to the President, but de facto he is now working with our staff in the same way that other Assistant Secretaries do.

Unfortunately, there does exist a real—but manageable—problem of Ralph's own state of mind. I have told Walter Jenkins that in my own judgment the best thing we can do for Ralph is to make it clear to him that he will be in line for one of the jobs he wants after the election, if all goes well. The two things which he has in mind are the Ambassadorship to Chile and a relatively senior U.S. appointment at the World Bank.[6] He is highly qualified for either one, in my judgment. Meanwhile, I am doing all that I can to keep in good harness with him, given the difficult fact that as long as Tom Mann is No. 1 on Latin America, it simply will not be practicable for Ralph to play the role there which he had in the last administration.

McG. B.

---

[5] Mann delivered the speech, "The Democratic Ideal in Our Policy Toward Latin America," on June 7 at the University of Notre Dame. (Department of State *Bulletin*, June 29, 1964, pp. 995–1000)

[6] Dungan was eventually appointed Ambassador to Chile; see Document 271.

18.   **Memorandum From Robert M. Sayre of the National Security Council Staff to the President's Special Assistant for National Security Affairs (Bundy)[1]**

Washington, June 23, 1964.

SUBJECT

Meeting with President and U.S. Ambassadors to Latin America

Mr. Mann believes the meeting between the President and six of our Ambassadors in Latin America went well because:

1. The group includes two or three of our best Ambassadors in Latin America and
2. The Ambassadors were prepared to discuss *general* trends and prospects, and raised specific country problems to illustrate the general trend.

I would add a third point—that in three of the countries (Brazil, Panama, and the Dominican Republic), there are active and serious issues in which our own interests and security are deeply involved.

The President received in his night reading material before the meeting a brief status report on the Alliance, a few lines of biography on the Ambassadors with whom he was not well-acquainted, and three or four sentences on the current situation in each of the six countries concerned.[2] During the meeting, the President asked each Ambassador what he regarded as the key problems in his country and the Hemisphere, and what he thought should be done about them. Most of the talking from the Ambassadors' side was done by Lincoln Gordon (Brazil), Jack Vaughn (Panama), and W. Tapley Bennett (Dominican Republic), in each of whose country we have some pretty tough problems.

The President had an oral briefing by Mr. Mann on the Alliance for Progress a few days before the meeting.[3] The extent to which this

---

[1] Source: Johnson Library, National Security File, Country File, Latin America, Vol. II, 6/64–8/64. Confidential. According to the President's Daily Diary the meeting was held in the Cabinet Room, June 18, 12:10–1:10 p.m. The attendees included: the President, Lincoln Gordon, Jack Vaughn, W. Tapley Bennett, Aaron Brown, Covey Oliver, John Bell, Tom Mann, Ralph Dungan, Robert Adams, Anthony Solomon, and William Rogers. (Johnson Library)

[2] A report prepared by Sayre that fits this description was forwarded to Bundy under cover of a June 18 memorandum. (Ibid., National Security File, Country File, Latin America, Vol. II, 6/64–8/64)

[3] Evidently a reference to the telephone conversation between Johnson and Mann on June 11; see Document 16.

may have contributed to the meeting with the Ambassadors is hard to say.

Although no specific effort was made to brief either the President or the Ambassadors concerned, each had fairly well in mind the general problems in the area. The Department has just completed an intensive review of Brazil's debt situation, and the requirements for financial assistance in which Ambassador Gordon participated fully. The same is true in Panama and the Dominican Republic, although we are not as far along in either country toward decisions as we are in Brazil.

RMS

---

19.   **Information Memorandum From the President's Special Assistant for National Security Affairs (Bundy) to President Johnson**[1]

Washington, June 26, 1964.

SUBJECT

OAS Resolution on the Cuban Arms Cache in Venezuela

1. A meeting of OAS Foreign Ministers (MFM), probably lasting three or four days will start in Washington on July 21 to consider action against Cuba on the Venezuelan arms cache issue. The following is meant to bring you up to date.

2. The OAS countries are likely to discuss and take action on the following three resolutions when they meet on July 21.

(a) *Resolution I recommends* that member states cooperate in surveillance to detect the subversive movements of men and arms between Cuba and Latin America. The resolution also *recommends* that OAS countries, which still maintain diplomatic and air relations with Cuba, break such relations. It goes on to *require* member states to suspend all sea and commercial relations (except food and medicines) with Cuba.

We can live with this resolution and there is a very good chance that it can be passed with a strong majority; at present, only Chile and

---

[1] Source: Johnson Library, National Security File, Country File, Cuba, OAS Resolution (Arms Cache), Vol. II, Memos, 11/63–9/64. Confidential. According to a June 25 memorandum from Chase to Bundy this information memorandum was drafted by Chase. (Ibid.)

Mexico, both of which have domestic political problems, are opposed. It is quite possible, moreover, that, by the date of the MFM, Mexico may change its mind and decide to abstain or, conceivably, to vote favorably.

(b) *Resolution II* issues the warning and establishes the principle that the OAS regards subversion as aggression and that future acts of Cuban subversion will trigger an immediate OAS meeting to agree on measures to be taken against the guilty party. The resolution goes on to say that the above OAS procedure does not limit the right of the victim of such aggression and the right of other states, at the victim's request, to take appropriate measures inherent in the right of individual or collective self-defense.

As the resolution now stands, we can live with it and can probably get a substantial majority to vote favorably (e.g. all but Chile and probably Mexico). However, we may get some heat at the MFM to weaken the resolution in two ways. First, most of the OAR's would like to generalize the warning language so that it pertains to subversion by both the left *and* right. We prefer the language to pertain more sharply to Cuba—so Cuba will feel the heat directly and unequivocally and so there will be no chance (although already unlikely) that the resolution will be turned against us because of our own "rightist" subversive activities against Cuba. *Second,* Chile would like to limit the right of individual and collective self-defense in the event of subversive aggression. We and most other OAR's oppose the Chilean position.

(c) *Resolution III* urges non-OAS Free World countries to cooperate with the OAS in its economic denial program against Cuba. It also recommends that OAS countries take necessary measures to achieve non-OAS Free World cooperation in this area. This resolution should pass easily. At present, there seems to be little opposition.

3. If we get the three resolutions as they now stand, with the majorities which we now estimate, we will have done fairly well. While we will *not* be able to point to an imminent overthrow of the Castro regime and to a complete cessation of Castro–Communist subversion in Latin America, we will be able to point to some movement towards a number of intermediate objectives, achieved without excessively straining the unity of the OAS.

First, Cuba will be further isolated. The break in the remaining commercial and sea relations and further possible diplomatic breaks, at a minimum, will hurt Castro psychologically. *Second,* the spread of Cuban subversion will be impeded. The warning resolution might inhibit Castro's will to spread subversion while the establishment of a surveillance system and the isolation measures will make it physically somewhat more difficult to move subversive men, funds, and arms between Cuba and Latin America. *Third,* the warning resolution will give us some juridical basis for and pre-position the OAS to use force against future Cuban subversion, if it is deemed desirable to do so. *Fourth,* Cuba's economic difficulties will be increased marginally by the break in commercial and sea relations with the OAS. To the extent we decide to use Resolution III as a lever, multilaterally if possible, on non-OAS Free World countries to reduce commercial relations with Cuba, Cuba's economic difficulties will be further increased. *Fifth,* the economic burden to the Soviet Union will be increased marginally—to the extent that we can continue to force Cuban commercial activities into abnormal, uneconomic channels.

McG. B.

---

20.   Memorandum of Conversation[1]

Washington, July 16, 1964, 6:50 p.m.

SUBJECT

Prospects for Adoption of Venezuelan Resolution at OAS Foreign Ministers' Meeting

PARTICIPANTS

The Secretary
Assistant Secretary Mann
Ambassador Bunker
Mr. Daniel Margolies (ARA:CV)
Dr. Iribarren, Venezuelan Foreign Minister
Ambassador Tejera-Paris, Venezuelan Ambassador

1. Position of Mexico and Chile

The Foreign Minister expressed the intention to modify the first resolution by making certain measures, e.g. breaking of diplomatic relations and severance of air traffic, mandatory rather than discretionary.

The Secretary said that there were two questions involved: first, whether there were enough votes for the adoption of the resolution with the mandatory provisions and second, whether the consequences

---

[1] Source: National Archives and Records Administration, RG 59, Central Files 1964–66, POL 3 IA. Confidential. Drafted by Margolies and approved in S on July 29. The time of the meeting is taken from Rusk's Appointment Book. (Johnson Library)

of adopting the resolution as proposed by the Foreign Minister would be in the best interest of the hemisphere.

The Secretary said, and Mr. Mann confirmed, that both Chile and Mexico were adamantly opposed to the Venezuelan proposal for mandatory language. It appeared likely that their strategy would be to take the resolution up paragraph by paragraph, registering their opposition to the points which they opposed, which would without any doubt include the requirement for the break in diplomatic relations. There was a possibility that Mexico, at any rate, would abstain when the entire resolution was voted on.

The Secretary said that if the resolution were adopted with mandatory language, this would confront Mexico and Chile with the necessity of complying with the resolution, or of taking issue with the OAS. Given the depth of feeling on this issue in both countries, it was possible that this could lead to an open break between them and the rest of the American system.

The Secretary said that he thought that it would be desirable to weigh carefully the consequences that might ensue from such a development, both with respect to the future of the American system and with respect to the impact on opinion at home.

Mr. Mann said that he thought that the mandatory language proposed by the Foreign Minister would be well received in the United States. He added that his experience with Mexico had persuaded him that the Mexicans did not respond well to pressure, but were open to reason. He thought it very possible that if left to their own discretion the Mexican Government would voluntarily break relations with Cuba, as the Brazilians have recently done, after the new President took office at the end of the year.

The Secretary said that his principal concern was the situation in Chile. He would have been able to face the risks with equanimity last January. However, with the Chilean elections so close, it was possible that the OAS action could play into the hands of the Communists in Chile and damage the election prospects of Frei. He thought that this required very careful consideration.

The Secretary said that he thought it would be well for both to talk with the Chilean Foreign Minister and the Mexican delegation. He planned to ask the Chileans whether they might take some constructive step toward accomplishing the objective sought, such as downgrading the level of their representation.

The Venezuelan Foreign Minister said that Venezuela had a serious domestic problem that he would like to emphasize. His government was committed publicly to seeking mandatory language in the resolution. If they backed down, it would be regarded at home as retreat. The Communists had recently renewed their terrorist campaign of bombing and shootings in Venezuela because of the OAS meeting. If the Venezuelan Government appeared to retreat before such conduct, it would invite further terrorist conduct.

The Venezuelans expected the OAS to do something about Cuban aggression. If the OAS failed to take effective action, this would discredit the Leoni administration and discredit the OAS in Venezuela.

The Secretary said that he felt that the OAS had made much progress on the Cuban issue since 1960. He thought that the resolution, even if certain sanctions were recommended rather than required, would represent further progress. He noted in particular that the second resolution would be a major advance in dealing with Cuban aggression in the future and would have a deterrent effect.

The Foreign Minister said that he did not share the Secretary's view on the second resolution. Assistant Secretary Mann said that he would explain our position in detail at a later time.

The Secretary said that a possibility to be considered was that of taking action in two stages. At the current meeting, certain sanctions could be recommended, and the OAS Council could be instructed to review compliance and to report to the Foreign Ministers at a subsequent meeting at which time mandatory language could be approved if considered appropriate. This would allow for an interval of several months during which the Chilean election would be over and the new Mexican Administration would take office. He said this was not advanced as a U.S. Government position but as an idea to be considered.

2. Line Up of Votes

The Foreign Minister said that he considered fourteen votes necessary to satisfy the two-thirds requirement. Ambassador Bunker said the precedents supported the view that only thirteen were required, and promised to furnish the Foreign Minister with a memorandum explaining the position.

The Foreign Minister said that he thought there were at least thirteen votes in favor of his position for mandatory requirements:

1. Guatemala
2. Honduras
3. Costa Rica
4. Panama
5. El Salvador
6. Nicaragua
7. Dominican Republic
8. Ecuador
9. Colombia
10. Bolivia
11. Peru
12. Paraguay
13. Brazil

Assistant Secretary Mann said that our information on Bolivia was different and Bolivia appeared to be opposed. The Foreign Minister said his report on Brazil was based on the Brazilian Foreign Minister's recent statement to the press.

3. *Publicity*

The Secretary said that he favored keeping the meeting of the Foreign Ministers private, without the press and television, so that they could better arrive at a satisfactory solution. The Foreign Minister agreed.

4. *Conclusion*

The Secretary congratulated the Foreign Minister on Venezuela's impressive showing of courage and support of the democratic process in the December elections.

He said that he believed it would be useful to reflect further on what had been discussed, to take further soundings and meet again soon to continue the discussion.[2]

---

[2] The Secretary met Iribarren on July 20. Iribarren reported that his government could not budge on mandatory sanctions and President Leoni had instructed him to ask that the United States support Venezuela on this issue. Rusk said that Iribarren "could rest assured that the United States Government would support the Venezuelan position." (Memorandum of conversation, July 20; National Archives and Records Administration, RG 59, Central Files 1964–66, POL 3 IA)

---

21. Memorandum From the President's Special Assistant for National Security Affairs (Bundy) to President Johnson[1]

Washington, July 20, 1964.

SUBJECT

Your meeting July 21, 6 p.m., with heads of Latin American delegations

You are receiving the heads of the Latin American delegations to the Foreign Ministers meeting on Cuba on July 21 at 6 p.m. All of these delegations are headed by Foreign Ministers, except Mexico and the

---

[1] Source: Johnson Library, National Security File, Country File, Cuba, OAS Resolution (9th MFM), Vol. V, 7/64–8/64. Confidential. According to a July 14 memorandum from Sayre to Bundy this memorandum was drafted by Sayre. (Ibid., Latin America, Vol. II, 6/64–12/64)

Dominican Republic, which will be represented by their OAS Ambassadors. We have discouraged the Dominican Foreign Minister, Donald Reid Cabral, because he is a Chief of State, and we would have had to treat him accordingly. The Mexican Foreign Minister, Jose Gorostiza, is not coming because Mexico has been in a minority and he didn't want to take a public beating in his first international meeting.

The meeting will also include Secretary Rusk, Tom Mann, Ambassadors Bunker and Duke, Senators Morse and Hickenlooper, Congressmen Selden and Mailliard, Secretary General of the OAS Mora, and myself.

Our suggestion is that during this reception you should talk informally with the Foreign Ministers in somewhat the way that you have with the Latin American Ambassadors. The group has been kept small for this purpose. Since you already talked on Latin American problems, our suggestion is that you might give them a general review of the world situation, and Horace Busby is putting some suggested remarks into final form.[2] The experts think that such a review would be welcomed by the Foreign Ministers, and that they would find it flattering to hear your views on the world. If you agree, the prepared remarks could be made available to the press through George Reedy, together with some background comment.

These prepared remarks do not contain any argumentation on Cuba because we think the Foreign Ministers would regard this as undue pressure before they begin their deliberations. At the same time, it is entirely proper that you should informally state your own views in a private session, and we would plan to make it clear in backgrounding that you had done so, since we do not want the Republicans to be able to claim that you are uninterested in the resolution. In such informal remarks we suggest that you may want to make the following points which Tom Mann and Dean Rusk are already making in their discussions with the delegates:

1. Venezuela has been the victim of aggression and we should support her.
2. We should not do anything at this meeting that would give Cuba or the Soviet Union an impression that we have lessened our resolve to defend the Hemisphere against aggression.
3. Therefore we should adopt a strong and substantial resolution.

The present line-up on the Cuban resolution is reasonably hopeful. The Venezuelans are insisting on a mandatory break in relations and air service with Cuba, and eleven other Latin American countries share this view. Both on the merits and for political reasons we do not want to be against the Venezuelans, who are very firm on this issue.

---

[2] The remarks prepared by Busby have not been found.

Argentina, Brazil, and Bolivia are debating this issue of mandatory sanctions, but we think they will probably agree. That would give
us 15 votes in favor of a resolution on Cuba at least as strong as the
one you have already reviewed.

The Mexicans, however, are said to be bitter about the possibility
of being forced to suspend relations and air service. They regard this
move as a sanction against Mexico, not Cuba, and they are likely to
carry Chile and perhaps Uruguay with them.

Haiti will try to blackmail us, but will probably vote on our side
because we have two-thirds without her.

This picture is not perfect, and Tom Mann had hoped in particular for a less troublesome Mexican reaction, but I do not think we
should try to second-guess him from the White House at this stage. I
will try to have an up-to-the-minute account for you tomorrow before
the meeting.[3]

McG. B.[4]

---

[3] Although no substantive record of the meeting has been found, according to a
memorandum for the record by W.Y. Smith it was discussed at the daily White House
staff meeting on July 22: "At the soiree between the President and certain Latin American ambassadors yesterday the Mexican ambassador [to the OAS, Vicente Sánchez Ga-
vito] misbehaved a bit. There was informal agreement before him that nothing would
be said on the OAS resolution on Cuba, now under discussion by the OAS Foreign Ministers. The Mexican ambassador, however, made an impassioned plea for a resolution
that the Mexicans could live with. The President handled the matter expertly, making
some bland reply. Secretary Rusk stepped in and said that the resolution was the subject for discussion later, not at the meeting then underway." (Memorandum for the record,
National Defense University, Maxwell Taylor Papers, Chairman's Staff Group, Box 25)

[4] Printed from a copy that bears these typed initials.

**22.   Memorandum From Robert M. Sayre of the National
Security Council Staff to the President's Special Assistant for
National Security Affairs (Bundy)**[1]

Washington, July 23, 1964.

At the OAS meeting this morning, Argentina came out strongly
against Cuba, but at the same time said that the action taken should

---

[1] Source: Johnson Library, National Security File, Country File, Cuba, OAS Resolution, Vol. V (9th MFM), 7/64–8/64. Confidential.

be a matter of conviction with each American Republic. The Foreign Minister said Argentina had already resolved what it would do—it has broken relations, etc., but did not want to vote a resolution that would give other countries troubles. How Argentina will come out is hard to say; its position this morning was not helpful. The military members of the Argentine delegation are most unhappy with their Government's position. State's Director Argentine Affairs[2] continues of the view that the Argentine Government will have to get in line or face the prospect of being tossed out by the military as it was in 1962, when it failed to agree at Punta del Este.

Haiti said it would vote with the majority on sanctions, but a double-cross is possible. The Haitian Foreign Office put the heat on Ambassador Timmons to get approval of an export license for T–28's in the same conversation about Haiti's support on Cuba.

Brazil is working with our delegation, and is ready to go down the line with us. Counting Haiti, there are 13 votes lined up with us. Rusk discussed with the President at lunch, a telegram to President Paz to get Paz to instruct his Foreign Minister to vote with us.[3] Peru says it will vote with the majority, but it is also still talking like Argentina.

Chile, Mexico and Uruguay are opposed to sanctions, and unlikely to change their minds.

RMS

---

[2] Henry A. Hoyt.

[3] Although no substantive record of this discussion has been found, the President approved the telegram to Paz. (Telegram 49 to La Paz, July 23; National Archives and Records Administration, RG 59, Central Files 1964–66, POL 23–8 VEN) Rusk also called Ambassador to Bolivia Douglas Henderson to emphasize the importance of Bolivia's vote: "Sec asked what time he [Henderson] would see Pres Paz and Henderson said 4:15. Sec asked him to do his very best; this could make quite a lot of difference. Sec said we could get very good result if Henderson was successful. Sec. asked the Amb to phone us after his interview." (Rusk to Henderson, July 24, 2:50 p.m.; ibid., Rusk Files: Lot 72 D 192, Telephone Calls 7/1/64–8/5/64) No record of a return call from Henderson has been found. The subsequent reply from Paz was non-committal. (Telegram 121 from La Paz, July 25; ibid., Central Files 1964–66, POL 23–8 VEN)

23.   Summary Record of the 536th Meeting of the National Security Council[1]

Washington, July 28, 1964, 12:15 p.m.

Ninth Foreign Ministers Meeting; Cyprus, Mainland China

Secretary Rusk reported on the recent meeting of the Foreign Ministers of the Organization of American States, which was convened to deal with Cuban subversion in this Hemisphere, especially the shipment by Cuba of arms to Venezuela. Secretary Rusk summarized the Resolution adopted by the Foreign Ministers. The major advance is the agreed definition of "subversion" as "aggression". Secretary Rusk made the following points:

1. The United States did not press Mexico to break its air link to Cuba because this is the last remaining airline operating between Havana and the mainland.

2. The clause in the Resolution calling on non-OAS States to join with States in the Hemisphere in taking measures against Cuba is of major importance.

3. Chile, Uruguay and Bolivia may comply with the Resolution and break relations with Cuba. What Mexico will do remains in doubt.[2]

4. An important achievement was to handle discussion in the meeting so that it did not become a United States versus Latin America contest. Emphasis was kept on the threat to Venezuela arising out of the shipment of arms by Cuba.

5. The United States avoided arm-twisting.

6. We hope the message contained in the Resolution will get through to Castro, as the Punte del Este Resolution did not.

---

[1] Source: Johnson Library, National Security File, NSC Meetings, Vol. 2, Tab 9, 7/28/64. Top Secret. The time of the meeting is from a memorandum dictated by McCone on July 29. According to McCone, Rusk "forecast that the resolution will have an important effect on Castro and intimated, but did not express, the thought that there would be a change in Castro's attitude as a result of the resolution. He [Rusk] seemed highly satisfied with the resolution." (Ibid., John McCone Memoranda, Meetings with the President, 1/4/64–4/28/65) President Johnson, who joined the discussion at 12:46 p.m., may have missed the Secretary's report on the OAS resolution, which was first on the agenda. (Ibid., President's Daily Diary)

[2] Although Mexico refused to sever its ties to Cuba, the other countries later announced suspension of relations in accordance with the OAS resolution: Chile (August 11), Bolivia (August 21), and Uruguay (September 8).

7. The meeting was a success from our point of view. It was impossible to obtain unanimous agreement on the Resolution but Brazil, contrary to earlier meetings, played a constructive role.[3]

[Omitted here is discussion on Cyprus and Laos.]

Bromley Smith[4]

---

[3] The final act of the meeting of Foreign Ministers, including the text of the OAS resolution, is in Department of State *Bulletin,* August 10, 1964, pp. 179–184.

[4] Printed from a copy that bears this typed signature.

---

24.   National Intelligence Estimate[1]

NIE 80/90–64   Washington, August 19, 1964.

COMMUNIST POTENTIALITIES IN LATIN AMERICA

Foreword

The purpose of this estimate is to review, with respect to each Latin American country:[2]

(a) The internal conditions which favor or hinder Communist political or subversive activities.

(b) The strengths, capabilities, and policies of indigenous Communist elements, and the policies of their overseas patrons (the USSR, Communist China, or Cuba).

(c) The strengths and capabilities of the internal security forces.

These matters are reviewed in 21 annexes, each relating to one of the countries under consideration. These annexes are introduced by a summary estimate in general terms.

---

[1] Source: Central Intelligence Agency, Job 79–R01012A, O/DDI Registry. Secret; Controlled Dissem. According to a note on the cover sheet this estimate was prepared in the Central Intelligence Agency with the participation of the intelligence organizations of the Departments of State and Defense and the NSA and FBI. The United States Intelligence Board concurred in this estimate on August 19.

[2] Excluding Cuba, but including British Guiana and Surinam. The current estimate with respect to Cuba is NIE 85–64, "Situation and Prospects in Cuba," dated 5 August 1964. [Footnote in the source text; for text of NIE 85–64, see *Foreign Relations, 1964–1968,* Vol. XXXII, Document 281.]

The Estimate

1. Each of the 21 countries under consideration has its own distinctive character and internal situation. Each is exceptional in some respect. The appropriate annex should therefore be consulted as regards the situation in any particular country.[3]

2. Throughout Latin America there is a rising popular demand for radical change in existing conditions—economic, social, and political. The intensity of this demand varies from country to country and within most countries. Backwardness is not in itself a spur to revolution, but rising consciousness of deprivation is. Nowhere as yet is this demand explosive, but the longer it is frustrated and suppressed the more likely it is to become so. The direction that political change may take remains open. It could as well be democratic or Peronist[4] as Communist. But everywhere the rising demand for change is accompanied by an intensification of nationalistic emotions. Because the predominent foreign presence in the region is that of the US, Latin America ultranationalism has a predominantly anti-Yankee character.

3. This situation manifestly offers a fertile field for Communist political and subversive activity. Communists have been working to exploit it for about 40 years. Their efforts have been hindered by countervailing factors, most notably by the ignorance and apathy of the masses, by the existence of strong non-Communist leftist movements in some countries, and by the strongly anti-Communist attitude of the military, who still exercise ultimate political authority in almost all countries.[5] But the rising demand for revolutionary change, only partly

---

[3] As an indication of the range of variation within the region, consider the following extreme cases:

Area (sq. mi.): Brazil, 3,300,000; El Salvador, 8,000. Population: Brazil, 78,000,000; Surinam, 335,000. Density: Haiti, 420 per sq. mi.; Surinam, 6. Literacy: Uruguay, 88 percent; Haiti, 10 percent. GNP: Brazil, $14.4 billion; Surinam, $101 million. Per capita: Chile and Venezuela, over $700; Haiti, $71.

Three countries have predominantly white populations: Costa Rica (98%), Argentina (97%), and Uruguay (90%). Nine are predominantly *mestizo*: Paraguay (95%), Honduras (90%), Chile (88%), El Salvador (78%), Panama and Venezuela (70%), Nicaragua (68%), Colombia (57%), and Mexico (55%). Five have large, generally unassimilated Indian populations: Bolivia (55%), Guatemala (54%), Peru (50%), Ecuador (40%), and Mexico (30%). The Dominican Republic is predominantly mulatto (70%); Haiti is almost 100% Negro. The populations of Brazil, British Guiana, and Surinam are too variegated to permit classification in these terms. [Footnote in the source text.]

[4] That is, an authoritarian regime catering to nationalistic and working class interests. [Footnote in the source text.]

[5] The anti-Communist attitude and effectiveness of the military have been most recently demonstrated in Venezuela and Brazil. But there is another side to this coin. In times not long past, such military figures as Arbenz, Batista, and Pérez Jiménez found it convenient to use known Communists in order to undermine democratic opposition, in some cases to longterm Communist advantage. [Footnote in the source text.]

a result of Communist agitation, will operate to ultimate Communist advantage—unless the Communists are forestalled by fundamental reforms carried out by strong and stable non-Communist regimes.

4. We doubt that present efforts to reform Latin American society will have any fundamental effect over the short run in most countries. Rapid population growth will continue to press upon the limited resources available for consumption and capital investment. Thus the pace of economic and social development is not likely to be rapid enough to satisfy the rising expectations of the masses. The unwillingness or inability of traditional political parties and institutions to provide effective remedies will continue to enhance the appeal of charismatic leaders disdainful of the slow pace of evolutionary reform, and will afford the Communists recurrent opportunities to associate themselves with popular political and revolutionary movements.

5. Communism in Latin America is preponderantly an urban phenomenon. The Communists have made little impression on the rural masses, the bulk of the population, principally for want of contact and opportunity. In recent years, however, they have begun to make special efforts to reach and organize the peasantry, notably in Mexico, Peru, Chile, and Brazil.

6. Among the urban Communists there are two sorts with generally different characteristics: i.e., labor leaders and intellectuals. The Communist leaders with labor backgrounds tend to be older men, pragmatic, calculating (i.e., "opportunistic"), predisposed toward political organization and action reinforced by politically-motivated strikes and mass demonstrations. The Communist intellectuals, on the other hand, tend to be doctrinaire revolutionaries, at least verbally addicted to revolutionary violence, although they have little or no contact with the masses whom they would lead to revolution. This last consideration hardly deters the student element in this category, who tend to be highly "adventuristic."

7. In Latin America organized labor is composed largely of skilled workmen who enjoy a privileged status and are more interested in differentiating themselves from the masses than in leading the masses to revolution. This factor has limited the appeal of communism among industrial workers. By and large, the Communists have not been successful in their efforts to gain control of organized labor. Nevertheless, they have been able to gain strong influence or control in some unions, and to use this labor leadership to exert political influence, or to make expedient deals with power seekers or power holders. Often, however, Communist "control" of important labor organizations reflects only their skill in political machinations. In such cases they cannot rely on the rank-and-file to follow their lead when a direct economic interest is not evident.

8. The Communists' most striking success has been among middle class students and intellectuals. These are the people most acutely aware of the shortcomings of the societies in which they live and most impatient to transform them. They are well aware of the powers of resistance of the vested interests and consider existing democratic institutions ineffectual as a means of achieving rapid and radical reform. They are attracted to communism by its promise to cut this Gordian Knot, and by the expectation of being able to play an important role in the new dispensation. Even the non-Communist intellectuals tend to think in terms of a Marxist analysis of the situation—i.e., to attribute national shortcomings to "federal" class rule and to "Yankee imperialism."

9. In many Latin American countries the Communists are much divided amongst themselves, by personal factionalism, ideological sectarianism, and disputes over tactics. From the beginning there has been a general division between those who would pursue a "hard" line—immediate revolutionary violence—and those who prefer a more expedient "soft" line—patient organization and agitation in preparation for an eventual revolution. A generation ago this difference was expressed in terms of Trotskyism and Stalinism. Trotskyist elements still survive in many Latin American countries. Nowadays, however, essentially the same difference tends to be defined in terms of the Sino-Soviet controversy, or of the influence of Fidel Castro.

10. For purposes of analysis, it is possible to distinguish between the attitudes of the USSR, Communist China, and Castroist Cuba toward revolution in Latin America, but the reservation must be made in advance that these distinctions are blurred in practice and are not universally applicable. The essential point is that Communist action in Latin America depends on the willingness of indigenous individuals to act, at whatever personal risk they are disposed to accept, and consequently on their own tactical and doctrinal predilections. The USSR, Communist China, and Cuba can incite, encourage, advise, and render some degree of clandestine aid from the outside; the decision to act, and in what manner, is local and personal. The CPSU does exercise a measure of control over the established Communist party organizations, but the "Chinese" and "Cuban" factions are merely obtaining ideological justification and material support where they can find it, for actions which they are moved to take for their own reasons. They are not under Chinese or Cuban control.

11. The Soviet leaders, and the Communist parties responsive to them, certainly desire to exploit every opportunity to impair US interests in Latin America and to reduce US influence there. To those ends they have worked to stimulate already existing tendencies toward anti-US nationalism and to identify the US with the unsatisfac-

tory status quo. But the Soviets almost certainly regard the Latin American Communist parties as presently incapable of seizing and holding power in their respective countries—and as not surely subject to Soviet control if they should do so. Thus, in the Soviet view, Communist seizure of power in Latin America remains a distant objective, not a present potentiality. An intermediate Soviet objective is to facilitate the coming to power of nationalistic regimes disposed to turn to local Communists and to the USSR for support in their defiance of "Yankee imperialism."

12. The Soviets generally prefer to pursue their objectives in Latin America by political means. On the international plane, this means Soviet cultivation of good relations with selected incumbent governments through offers of trade and aid, and Soviet encouragement of an independence in foreign policy verging toward neutralism. In domestic politics, it means Communist party pursuit of legal recognition and of collaboration with other parties in popular fronts, as in Chile. But the Soviets and local Communists also consider it imperative to prevent the success of any democratic reform movement in Latin America. To this end, the Communists have collaborated on occasion with the most ruthless dictatorships and have sought by violence to frustrate democratic reformist regimes, as in Venezuela.

13. The Chinese and their ideological adherents scorn Soviet "opportunism" in Latin America and hold that revolutionary ends can be achieved only by revolutionary violence. But the Chinese are not "adventuristic." They too recognize that the Communist revolution in Latin America is a distant objective, to be patiently prepared for, not an immediate potentiality. As a practical matter, the Chinese are more interested in gaining the adherence of the Latin American Communist parties for their own immediate purposes in their present struggle with the Soviets for the leadership of the international Communist movement. But the Latin American enthusiasts for the Chinese line are considerably less sophisticated about this matter than are the Chinese. They take their Chinese texts literally because they are themselves motivated toward early violent action.

14. The Cubans, like the Chinese, advocate violent revolution, but they are more "adventuristic." They hold that their own experience proves that even a premature and abortive revolutionary attempt would be a positive contribution to the cause, in that it would provoke regressive measures which would arouse the population against the government and so hasten the day of the successful revolution. This idea has appeal for undisciplined and "adventuristic" elements who want immediate action. Castro's efforts to foment revolutionary action in Latin America have suffered severe setbacks during the past year—e.g., the reverses suffered by the FALN in Venezuela and by Leonel Brizola in Brazil. Nevertheless, he will continue to provide training

and other aid to potential revolutionaries in anticipation of future opportunities.[6]

15. Factional conflicts among pro-Soviet, pro-Chinese, and pro-Cuban elements have tended to disrupt and discredit the Communist movement in Latin America. Nevertheless, all seek in one way or another to destroy the position of the US in Latin America and eventually to revolutionize the continent. All three Communist lines can be pursued simultaneously in a given country, thus catering to diverse disaffected elements. Moreover, these distinctions do not always apply. The USSR approves of violent resistance operations in countries in which political action is impossible, as has been the case in Venezuela, although Cuba is the active agent in such cases. (The USSR has a strong presence in the Cuban agency charged with fomenting and supporting such operations.) On the other hand, Communist China and Cuba pursue a primarily political approach in countries such as Mexico, where that is obviously the more expedient course.

16. On the basis of a country by country review, the Communists' chances for gaining control of any Latin American country in the foreseeable future seem slight.[7] Yet the same could validly have been said of Cuba in 1957. There is a real danger inherent in the situation, and that danger will persist for at least a generation.

17. The danger in Latin America results less from the Communists' ability to convert people to communism than from the ability of a few dedicated Communists to exploit for their own purposes the widespread tendency toward anti-US nationalism. Both the traditional order and the potential democratic order are under sharp attack by radical ultranationalists as well as by Communists. Many of these ultranationalists also seek dictatorial power, for the gratification of personal ambitions, but also in order to transform their societies without hindrance by vested interests. By their appeal to nationalistic emotions, they can gain a wider acceptance in Latin America than can the Communists. But an ultranationalist regime could become Communist through dependence on the aid of local Communists and of the USSR

---

[6] In 1963 about 4,600 Latin Americans visited Cuba, of whom most presumably received some formal indoctrination. Several hundred probably received training in the techniques of guerrilla warfare and urban terrorism. [Footnote in the source text.]

[7] Possible exceptions are British Guiana and Chile. If the Jagan regime is still in power when British Guiana becomes independent, the Communists would be likely to gain control of that country. The forthcoming election on the basis of proportional representation is designed to unseat Jagan, but the possibility of his winning cannot be excluded. If FRAP should win the presidential election to be held in Chile in September 1964, which is at least possible, the Communists would gain great influence in the government, but not immediate control of it. [Footnote in the source text.]

in its defiance of "Yankee imperialism." This is in some part the explanation of what happened in Guatemala under Arbenz and in Cuba under Castro. The significance of the local Communist parties in this context is that they provide a continuity of organization and purpose unusual in Latin American political life and a link with the USSR as a world power believed to be able to provide aid and protection in the event of a hostile confrontation with the US.

[Omitted here are Annexes A through U.]

---

25.   **Memorandum From the President's Special Assistant for National Security Affairs (Bundy)**[1]

Washington, October 26, 1964.

MEMORANDUM FOR

  Secretary of State
  Secretary of Defense
  Administrator, Agency for International Development

SUBJECT

  Study of U.S. Policy Toward Latin American Military Forces

The report of September 2, 1964 on NSAM 297 has been reviewed.[2] The Department of Defense is requested to undertake to draft a new U.S. strategy for dealing with Latin American military forces.

Specific proposals should be studied for such changes in U.S. policies and programs of military assistance and other military-associated programs, projected over the next five years, as may be necessary to carry out the new strategy. The basic strategy objective should be the restructuring of Latin American military establishments to relate country force levels, defense budgets and military capabilities as closely as possible to the domestic resources available for military purposes and

---

[1] Source: Johnson Library, National Security File, National Security Action Memorandums, NSAM No. 297. Secret.

[2] The report, prepared by the Department of State, is ibid. Bundy evidently chaired an interagency meeting to review the report on October 19. In an October 19 memorandum Sayre briefed Bundy on the meeting, explaining that the agencies could not agree on the proper use of military assistance for internal security. (Ibid.) No substantive record of the meeting has been found.

to realistic current and potential security threats, with dominant emphasis on the internal security threat. The study should assess the political feasibility of achieving any such restructure in the context of the Latin American political scene and the possible contribution which might be made to achieving the strategy objectives by regional institutions, such as the OAS or IADB.

The study should include, but not be limited to, an examination of the following points:

1. A critical analysis of how Latin American military forces should be restructured in order to provide them with an increased capability to respond more effectively to internal security threats.

2. Whether, and the extent to which, the concept of hemispheric defense remains valid as a mission for Latin American forces and as a basis for U.S. military assistance in Latin America.

3. The current role of Latin American military forces in civic action with a view to determining whether military or civilian organizations provide the better channel for socially and economically desirable projects.

4. The utility of the Latin American military conscription system as a means of providing security forces and of absorbing excess labor.

5. How to identify, develop, equip, train and insure the availability of select units for OAS/UN peacekeeping assignments.

6. The proper balance between the roles of military and police units in maintaining internal security.

7. The feasibility of a shift in U.S. military assistance to increasing reliance upon credit sales instead of grants.

8. The feasibility of developing cooperative logistic arrangements and common-use training facilities on either a bi-lateral or regional basis among Latin American countries, including possible U.S. participation.

9. The contribution of U.S. military training programs to the education of Latin American military officers on the role of the military in a democratic society, on the effect of military expenditures on economic and social programs of the country, and on the need for continuing adjustment and reorganizations of military forces to meet current security threats.

The study should analyze disproportionate military expenditures, identified in the report of September 2, 1964 on NSAM 297, and the reasons for them, and propose specific measures for their reduction which are likely both to be politically feasible and to increase the effective utilization of available resources.

It is requested that the study and your recommendations, which should be drawn up in consultation with the Department of State and the NSC staff, be submitted by 1 February 1965.[3]

McGeorge Bundy

---

[3] DOD submitted a draft report on January 12, 1965. (Washington National Records Center, OSD/ISA Files: FRC 330 70 A 3717, Latin America 1965, 320.2) Sayre later explained that there was disagreement on the utility of the draft report. According to Sayre, the report was "directed at how our military policy should be financed and not at what the military policy should be," leading JCS and State to take "sharp issue" with its conclusions. Rostow considered the report a "pedestrian" effort. While trying to remain neutral, Sayre insisted that the NSC "wanted a study which outlined a policy, not a financing arrangement." (Memorandum from Sayre to Bundy, March 8, 1965; Johnson Library, National Security File, Name File, Sayre Memos) For a summary of the final report, see Document 29.

---

26.   Circular Telegram From the Department of State to Certain American Republic Posts[1]

Washington, February 12, 1965, 1:47 p.m.

1479. In late 1964 President Castello Branco invited President Johnson to visit Rio de Janeiro. Subsequently other Latin American Chiefs of State have also extended invitations to President Johnson.

President Johnson has suggested to President Castello Branco that in view of pressures on time of all Presidents, this might be good opportunity for all ten Presidents of South America and President Johnson to have informal meeting without agenda under circumstances which would permit each President to exchange views with every other President. GOB has welcomed this suggestion and has requested US to inform governments of nine South American republics of US proposal.

Precedents for group meetings of this kind include meeting of all Chiefs of State of Inter-American system in Panama in 1956 and President Kennedy's meeting with Presidents of Panama and five Central American countries in 1963.

---

[1] Source: National Archives and Records Administration, RG 59, Central Files 1964–66, POL 3 IA. Confidential; Immediate; Exdis. Drafted by Mann; cleared by Sayre, Adams, Weismann, Read, and Chief of Protocol Lloyd N. Hand; and approved by Mann. Sent for action to the Embassies in Argentina, Bolivia, Chile, Colombia, Ecuador, Paraguay, Peru, Uruguay, and Venezuela.

Plans are that Presidents would arrive Rio April 28 or early morning 29th. April 29 and April 30 would be used for informal conversations without agenda by each President with other Presidents present on any topics of hemisphere or world interest which Presidents wished to discuss. Purpose of meeting would be to permit Presidents to become better personally acquainted with each other and with each other's views rather than to have more formalized type of meeting. All discussions would be off the record.

Our thoughts are that similar meeting could be held with Chiefs of State in Middle America later this year or in 1966.

We hope other Presidents will share our view that such a meeting would be useful and have been authorized by GOB to state that invitations will be extended by President Castello Branco to all South American Chiefs of State who wish to attend.

Please inform President or Foreign Minister of foregoing and report reaction soonest.

Information addressees should take no action at this time.[2]

Ball

---

[2] On February 24 Mann raised the proposed trip with the President, particularly in light of unauthorized newspaper accounts. Mann suspected that the leak had come from "Latin American diplomats in Washington who were always anxious to talk to the press." The President wondered if the trip could be postponed; "the more he thought about it the more he felt it would be taking a lot of chances and not accomplishing much." Johnson suggested "that the Secret Service could say that they did not think now was a good time for the President to be traveling around. He did not think it would be good for a doctor to make the statement, but he thought that the Secret Service could." (Johnson Library, Papers of Thomas C. Mann, Telephone Conversations with LBJ, January 14, 1964–April 30, 1965) On March 7 the Department reported that "new developments in the international scene, particularly in Viet Nam, have made it necessary for President Johnson to defer consideration of possible visits to this hemisphere." (Telegram 836 to Buenos Aires, et al., March 7; National Archives and Records Administration, RG 59, Central Files 1964–66, POL 3 IA) At 8 p.m. the same day two Marine Battalion Landing Teams, the first American combat troops in Vietnam, arrived to defend the air base at Danang.

---

27. Editorial Note

On February 19, 1965, President Johnson nominated Thomas C. Mann as Under Secretary of State for Economic Affairs and Jack Hood Vaughn as Assistant Secretary of State for Inter-American Affairs. In recommending his successor, Mann told the President that Vaughn had done a "superior job" as Ambassador to Panama and had enough of a "liberal image" that "he might even be able to convert Schlesinger." Mann also said that Secretary of State Rusk had given "no objection" to the appointment. (Memorandum of telephone conversation, January 26; Johnson Library, Papers of Thomas C. Mann, Telephone Conversations with LBJ, January 14, 1964–April 30, 1965) Mann later told the President that "we had to build up Vaughn to the Latin American Ambassadors so they will think of him as the boss and let Mr. Mann work behind the scenes." (Memorandum of conversation, February 24; ibid.) In a meeting with Rusk on March 18, Director of Central Intelligence McCone criticized the choice, warning that "much of the good work accomplished in the last year or year and a half would be undone by Vaughn unless he was given very strong supervision and guidance by Rusk, Ball and Mann." According to McCone: "Rusk indicated he had nothing to do with the appointment, inferred, but not mentioned, that the appointment was made by the President." (Memorandum for the record, Central Intelligence Agency, DCI (McCone) Files, Job 80–B01285A, Memos for the Record) Vaughn was confirmed by the Senate on March 9 and assumed his new responsibilities on March 22. For additional documentation on the Vaughn and Mann appointments, see *Foreign Relations, 1964–1968,* volume XXXIII.

---

28.   Memorandum for the Record[1]

Washington, April 8, 1965.

SUBJECT

> Minutes of the Meeting of the Special Group (CI) 2:00 p.m., Thursday, April 8, 1965

PRESENT

> Governor Harriman, Mr. McCone, General Wheeler, Mr. Komer, Mr. Gaud vice Mr. Bell, Mr. Wilson vice Mr. Rowan, Mr. Friedman vice Mr. Vance
>
> General Anthis, Messrs. Adams, FitzGerald, Engle and Maechling were present for the meeting

---

[1] Source: National Archives and Records Administration, RG 59, Special Group (CI) Files: Lot 70 D 258, 3/18/65–4/15/65. Secret. Drafted by C.G. Moody, Jr., Executive Secretary of the Special Group (CI).

1. Counterinsurgency Intelligence Summary

Special CIA Review of Latin America:

Mr. McCone began by saying that he wished to express as emphatically as possible the dangers in Latin America that require positive, concerted and prompt action. He reviewed the Latin American section in the summary[2] and called the attention of the Group to recent statements out of Moscow for increased activity in Latin America naming the countries Venezuela, Colombia, Guatemala, Honduras, Paraguay and Haiti as immediate targets for wars of liberation.[3] He said that there is evidence that a policy decision has been made to conduct a more aggressive campaign not only in Latin America, but everywhere, though he only wished to address the Latin American situation today.

Mr. McCone then briefed the Group on background information on this evidence and said that increased activity in certain designated target areas would be difficult if not impossible for some of the governments to handle. He stated that he is of the opinion that the Communist's planning in most Latin American countries is still in an embryonic stage and might be handled by small but skillfully trained organizations. He said that plans in each country must be developed to fit particular situations. He asked Mr. Desmond FitzGerald to outline a suggested approach to the problem.

Mr. FitzGerald explained that the counterinsurgency problem can be broken down into the three following phases:

Phase 1. In the earliest stages of insurgency, the subversion phase, the use of basic intelligence from successful penetrations to gain information, frustrate or hamper.

Phase 2. In the later and more violent terrorist stage, the use of intelligence in conjunction with local police forces who are trained to use the information. In this connection, security within police forces poses the greatest problem in Latin America in utilization of sensitive data.

Phase 3. In the more overt guerrilla and terrorist stage, the employment of military forces plus all other capabilities, especially communications and intelligence to permit rapid response by security forces.

---

[2] Reference is to a CIA Intelligence Memorandum, "Developments in Countries on the Counterinsurgency List," April 7. (Ibid.)

[3] Reference is to the Conference of Representatives of Latin American Communist Parties, which met in Havana, November 1964; the communiqué of the conference was published in *Pravda*, January 19, 1965. The Conference endorsed a number of proposals in the struggle against "imperialism," including: "To render active support to those who are at present being subjected to brutal reprisals, such as, for instance, the Venezuelan, Colombian, Guatemalan, Honduran, Paraguayan and Haitian fighters." (*Current Digest of the Soviet Press*, Vol. XVII, No. 3, February 10, 1965, pp. 15–16)

To bridge the gap between Phase 2 and Phase 3 a small strike force must be provided which can be broken into small groups. Preferably this should be police. Such a force has been recommended for Peru and it will be air transportable. Mr. FitzGerald said that the Peruvians need air support for this plan and it probably will have to be provided by the U.S. Mr. McCone pointed out that this Special Police unit will be trained in counterinsurgency.

In response to the Chairman, Mr. FitzGerald said that the plan has been discussed with Peruvian officials, but would be raised again upon Ambassador Jones' return this weekend because the Peruvians have a new Chief of Staff who was not in on the previous discussions. AID has agreed to finance this particular plan.

Mr. Friedman suggested that this concept should be used in all Latin American countries. Mr. FitzGerald replied that country-by-country treatment was preferable since each country had special internal political problems which affected their capabilities. Mr. McCone said that if we do decide to go forward with this plan, Peru could be used as the pilot plan. In replying to a question on funding, Mr. Gaud answered that there should be no problem, but each country would have to be studied separately to determine what is needed.

Mr. McCone suggested an action memorandum from the Chairman of the Special Group (CI), or an NSAM may ultimately be desirable. He emphasized that everyone's support is needed. Mr. Komer stated that there is no doubt that the evidence indicates widespread activity and preventive measures should be taken now because the price is cheaper early in the game. The Chairman and Mr. FitzGerald both offered examples showing that few people in these countries including high government officials are aware of the Havana Conference of November 1964 or the *Pravda* statements, and suggested that psychological warfare is not receiving proper attention. Mr. FitzGerald pointed out that one of the main problems in creating security forces is that whenever a regime is toppled, the security forces are the first to be thrown out; this has had the effect of requiring constant retraining. General Wheeler stated he was in agreement with what had been said but felt we may be neglecting the source of much of the infection, Cuba itself. The Chairman agreed and asked Mr. Komer to advise Mr. McGeorge Bundy of the feelings of the Special Group on this score.

Mr. FitzGerald pointed out to the Group that U.S. military personnel in Venezuela are not permitted to accompany local forces into combat areas. This limits their capability to observe and take corrective action. The Group discussed the advisability of a high-level approach to the Venezuelan Government on the seriousness of this limitation.

After hearing Director McCone's presentation on new Communist insurgency effort in Latin America, *the Special Group (CI) called for a full-scale review of this problem by the agencies concerned. To this end the Group proposed that the Latin American Ad Hoc Working Group analyze: (a) the intensified threat arising out of decisions at Havana Conference in November 1964; (b) the effectiveness of current CI programs addressed to this problem—intelligence, police, military aid, economic aid, psychological warfare and counter-propaganda, and (c) ways of stepping up U.S. and local efforts to cope with the threat on a country-by-country basis. The Latin American Working Group should report to CI Group by 1 June 1965, but may do so earlier on a country-by-country basis.*[4]

The Group also endorsed the CIA/AID proposal for a special airborne police unit to be tried out on an experimental basis in Peru and asked that the Latin American Working Group comment as soon as possible on the feasibility of this proposal for other Latin American countries.[5] *It was further agreed that USIA would be represented on the Ad Hoc Working Group.*

[Omitted here is discussion of a report on Public Safety Programs.]

C. G. Moody, Jr.
Executive Secretary
Special Group (CI)

---

[4] No evidence was found that the Latin American Ad Hoc Working Group completed a full-scale review of counterinsurgency.

[5] Regarding the airborne unit, the so-called Special Police Emergency Unit (SPEU), see Document 471.

---

29. Memorandum From Secretary of Defense McNamara to the President's Special Assistant for National Security Affairs (Bundy)[1]

Washington, June 11, 1965.

SUBJECT

Study of U.S. Policy Toward Latin American Military Forces

In response to your memorandum of October 26, 1964 on the above subject,[2] I am forwarding herewith a study prepared in the Department

---

[1] Source: Johnson Library, National Security File, Country File, Latin America, Vol. III, 1/65–6/65. Secret.

[2] Document 25.

of Defense proposing a new strategy for dealing with Latin American military forces.[3]

The basic recommendations of the study are: (1) to initiate in FY 67 a gradual, selective and controlled phasedown of MAP matériel grants extending over two three-year periods: (a) FY 67–69—maintenance, overhaul items; (b) FY 69–71—investment items, and (2) concurrently to place increasing emphasis on credit sales, local defense production and better budgetary planning and programming by Latin American military establishments in a major effort to bring their forces more into line with domestic resources and with a realistic appraisal of the security threat. The proposal would include provision of matériel grants for emergency purposes to meet foreign exchange inadequacies or for political reasons on an ad hoc basis when specifically justified.

The views of the Department of State, AID and the JCS have been sought and fully considered in drawing up this paper. However, it has not been possible to reconcile the differing views with the result that not all of the conclusions and recommendations of the study are concurred in by other agencies.

The principal objections of the Joint Chiefs of Staff are: (1) to the threat analysis, which they believe understates the insurgency problem, and (2) to the relatively minor military importance the study attaches to the future anti-submarine warfare requirements in South American waters. An extract of their views is enclosed as a separate memorandum.[4]

The views of the Department of State are also enclosed in a separate memorandum.[5] While the Department of State accepts most of the conclusions of the study, they reject the above basic action recommendations. They acknowledge that the proposals are sound in principle and desirable of attainment, but believe that action should be delayed until some indefinite time in the future. Their fundamental reason is that to embark on such a course of action would be disruptive of U.S. influence in these countries and might tend to alienate the military forces on whom the Alliance for Progress must depend to maintain stability in the area.

In the light of these comments, I recommend that the new strategy proposed in this study be regarded as a long-term goal, but one which must be approached without a rigid time frame.

---

[3] Dated February 25; attached but not printed.

[4] Undated; attached but not printed.

[5] Reference is to a letter from Vaughn to McNaughton, March 29, attached but not printed.

Under our present MAP guidance we have been undertaking:

(1) A systematic effort to induce Latin American MAP recipients, to the extent feasible, to gradually assume the maintenance burden, e.g. spare parts and overhaul, now being borne by the MAP, and
(2) The development of integrated grant-credit packages of military assistance designed to provide maximum leverage in (a) holding down external military procurement of the Latin American armed forces to agreed upon levels and (b) directing their procurement toward realistic security requirements.

I believe that our best course of action is to continue these efforts, concentrating on prudent management of the MAP rather than upon the initiation of a new strategy.

In the meanwhile, the enclosed study provides a useful basis upon which to measure our progress toward accomplishment of the long-range goals of our Military Assistance Program in Latin America.[6]

Robert S. McNamara

---

[6] For additional discussion of U.S. policy toward Latin American military forces, see Document 65.

---

30.   Action Memorandum From the Assistant Secretary of State for Inter-American Affairs (Vaughn) to Secretary of State Rusk[1]

Washington, August 4, 1965.

SUBJECT

Celebration of Fourth Anniversary of Charter of Punta del Este (Alliance for Progress) August 17, 1965

We have previously avoided a major celebration of the anniversary of the Charter of Punta del Este because the statistics provided no basis for celebration. The figures for 1964 are good, however, and prospects for 1965 are as good or better. But more important, the Alliance needs a psychological shot-in-the-arm and the personal imprint of the President. It is erroneously charged that we are neglecting the

---

[1] Source: National Archives and Records Administration, RG 59, Central Files 1964–66, AID(AFP). Confidential. No drafting information appears on the memorandum.

social aspects of the Alliance. Some Latins assert the Alliance died with Kennedy; others that our Dominican policy overshadows it.[2]

Mr. Sayre discussed this problem with the President on July 23 when he accompanied Ambassador Dungan. The President asked Mr. Sayre to send over a proposal.[3]

We assume we could not get the President to make a trip to Latin America now because of Vietnam. In any event, I would be reluctant to recommend it, because of the security problems associated with it.

The President should kick if off in Washington. He has already taken the first step by the loan signing ceremony at the White House on July 29 with the Central Americans.[4] We have in mind a "social justice" address at the White House. The President has offered a trip on the *Sequoia*. After thinking this over, I have concluded that a boat trip does not do what we want, but would take as much of the President's time. The *Sequoia* cannot accommodate the 33 OAS and White House Ambassadors. Moreover, we get little, if any, publicity. If a White House ceremony does not appeal to the President, we might consider something as unique as a luncheon at Monticello, Jefferson's home. Jefferson was the exponent for all the things we want the President to emphasize—individual liberty, social justice, higher education, modernization of agriculture, etc.

Recommendation:

That you sign the memorandum (Tab B) to the President.[5]

---

[2] On April 27 the President sent U.S. Marines to the Dominican Republic to protect American lives in the midst of civil war. He later claimed that action was necessary to prevent the establishment of a Communist dictatorship. In response to criticism that he had acted unilaterally, the President dispatched Ambassador at Large Harriman and a team of high-level officials to Latin America for consultation.

[3] According to the President's Daily Diary Johnson met Dungan and Sayre on July 23, 2:55–3:43 p.m. (Johnson Library) Although no substantive record of the meeting has been found, a note attached to this memorandum reports that the President asked the two men "for ideas on how to revitalize the Alliance." (Note from Read to Rusk, August 4; National Archives and Records Administration, RG 59, Central Files 1964–66, AID(AFP))

[4] Reference is to a $35 million AID loan to the Central American Bank for Economic Integration. For text of the President's remarks upon signing the agreement, see *Public Papers of the Presidents of the United States: Lyndon B. Johnson, 1965*, Book II, pp. 809–811.

[5] There is no indication of Rusk's approval on the memorandum, but a copy of the signed memorandum to the President is in the National Archives and Records Administration, RG 59, Central Files 1964–66, AID(AFP). During the signing ceremony on August 17 at the White House Johnson emphasized several elements to strengthen the Alliance, including: stabilizing the price of such basic commodities as coffee, cocoa, and sugar; and promoting economic integration in the region by reducing tariff barriers. (*Public Papers of the Presidents of the United States: Lyndon B. Johnson, 1965*, Book II, pp. 884–889)

31. Memorandum of Telephone Conversation[1]

Washington, August 27, 1965, 1:30 p.m.

PARTICIPANTS

Mr. Mann
The President

The President called and said he wanted a real good announcement written this afternoon he can put out on Monday[2] which would say that he has been devoting a good deal of personal interest and attention to our relations with our good neighbors in this Hemisphere; that since he became President he has consulted with not only the people in the State Department that are experienced in this field but with the Congressional leaders and with the private sector and labor leaders and with the educators and former officials—Burley [*Berle*], Eisenhower and others who have served in official functions; that he has exchanged views and visits with some of the Presidents and officials of the nation and the Hemisphere, but the heavy workload has kept him from seeing them as much as he likes. He has met all the Ambassadors, OAS and Latin America, and that he has asked Dr. Milton Eisenhower, President of Johns Hopkins, who has served the Government for many years with distinction, an authority in this field, has written in this field and travelled in Latin America and advised him on this matter, to plan some visits to Latin America, and that he would hope that in the next few days that he would make his first one—his itinerary would be announced later, and a somewhat longer visit made in the next few weeks and perhaps others.[3] That he will be accompanied by a staff of experts in the economic and political fields—get out of military angles as much as possible—and that he will be consulting regularly with the Department officials in the next few days. Be sure to bring in when he says expert some of his ideas and dreams that went into the Act of Bogota, subsequently reaffirmed and implemented in the Alliance, but give him some good credits for his ideas and dreams. Also that his stuff was copied by the Kennedys and he had no recognition, this means more to us than to them.

---

[1] Source: Johnson Library, Papers of Thomas C. Mann, Telephone Conversations with LBJ, May 2, 1965–June 2, 1966. No classification marking. Drafted by Viola Emrich (M).

[2] August 30.

[3] Eisenhower agreed to this arrangement earlier that afternoon. (Johnson Library, Recordings and Transcripts, Recording of telephone conversation between President Johnson and Milton Eisenhower, August 27, 12:25 p.m., Tape 6508.10, PNO 7)

The President said to build him as a real patriot. He asked Mr. Mann to touch base with Morse, say that earlier in the year he asked Eisenhower, Fulbright went to Brazil, asked Vaughn to visit some places;[4] he said he had told Morse on two or three occasions to visit any countries he wanted. He said to ask Dr. Morgan and Selden,[5] touch base with them and say we want them to go if they want to; don't tell him just ask. In the past, off-the-record, has asked Eisenhower to go and asked them to go, not on the same trips but individually to any countries they want to. He said to make it a good announcement and get Watson[6] to put it on his wire tomorrow.

Mr. Mann asked when would he want to make it. The President said the Secretary is coming down for dinner tomorrow night and Mr. Mann can send it by him, he will leave by Noon. He said he thought he would make it Sunday, quick as he can before Bobby is on every front page.

The President said to say in the announcement that he has asked Fulbright and other members of the Latin American Committees, he has Secretary Vaughn down there now, and give him the biggest title— Ambassador at Large if need be. Make a good announcement that will make the Latins happy. He said he wants to go to Mexico first, and told Mr. Mann he would call Flores[7] and tell him that the President is sending an emissary and turn out for him and talk up everything for Mexico, sugar and everything else and put on a big show for him. The President said he would check it with his President and by Tuesday or Wednesday of next we would hear from him.

The President said we didn't want to get to Brazil, we are out of Brazil, he would say Mexico or two others. He said Mr. Mann could talk to Flores pretty quick and see if he likes it, while the Sugar Bill is up would be a good time. He said that Milton Eisenhower could have a good welcome and show good relations and could reflect it in this country.

Mr. Mann asked if Flores would be too many, and the President said no, should be at least three days on the plane, one place a day. Mr. Mann suggested perhaps one in Central America and one in Panama.

---

[4] Fulbright headed the Senate delegation that accompanied high-level U.S. officials on a trip to Brazil in early August. (Department of State *Bulletin,* August 23, 1965, p. 332) Vaughn left on August 20 for a 2-week trip to Latin America, including stops in Mexico, El Salvador, Panama, Ecuador, Bolivia, Chile, and Peru. For Vaughn's report to the President on the trip, see ibid., October 4, 1965, pp. 548–549.

[5] Congressmen Thomas E. Morgan (D–Pennsylvania), Chairman of the House Committee on Foreign Affairs, and Armistead I. Selden, Jr. (D–Alabama).

[6] W. Marvin Watson, Jr.

[7] Antonio Carrillo Flores, Mexican Foreign Minister.

The President said to make it sound good and mention his ideas and dreams, Act of Bogota, and talk to him this afternoon and select the countries. He said to get Oliver in, and to get it to him without question, he wants it tomorrow. He said to salute it big.[8]

[8] The President left Washington on August 27, his 58th birthday, to spend the weekend at his Ranch in Texas. (Johnson Library, President's Daily Diary) Before Rusk arrived the following afternoon, *The New York Times* reported that Senator Robert F. Kennedy was planning to visit South America in November. (*The New York Times*, August 28, 1965) The Johnson administration apparently decided against announcing its own plans for Milton Eisenhower. No evidence has been found that Eisenhower visited Latin America as the President's personal emissary in 1965.

32. Memorandum of Telephone Conversation[1]

Washington, November 4, 1965, 4:45 p.m.

PARTICIPANTS

Mr. Vaughn
Governor Harriman

Governor Harriman said that he had talked to Bobby Kennedy about a couple of things before he left and he had mentioned having a good talk with JV, and seemed quite happy about it. JV said that Kennedy had seemed quite rough.[2] In reply Harriman stated that Kennedy was a wonderful fellow but it was hard for him to get readjusted—that he felt things were just not as good as they used to be. JV mentioned that Kennedy had three specific points, which bother him and on which he felt he must speak out—

1) D.R. (Harriman interupted to say that he thought Kennedy wrong in his views on the D.R. and had told him so)
2) Policy in Peru—and
3) Recent developments in Brazil.

On the last point JV mentioned that Kennedy thought we should stop aid and Harriman remarked that this was "crazy." Harriman then explained that Kennedy had asked him to keep in touch and he

[1] Source: National Archives and Records Administration, RG 59, ARA Files, 1965–67: Lot 70 D 295, Inner Office Memoranda, November 1965. No classification or drafting information appears on the memorandum. A copy was sent to Sayre.

[2] For an account of the meeting between Kennedy and Vaughn, see Arthur M. Schlesinger, Jr., *Robert Kennedy and His Times*, pp. 693–694.

(Harriman) felt that Dungan and Linc Gordon could do Kennedy some good. Continuing, Governor Harriman said that his interest was to be sure Kennedy was constructive—rather than destructive—because he "has so much steam," and asked if there was anything he could do in the way of communicating with him. JV and Harriman discussed further the things Kennedy would probably say in LA—he will probably say that we were wrong in the D.R. but that he is willing to forget the past and talk about the future. It was agreed that Kennedy was not as bad as Fulbright but that he would talk and would "raise this hell in Brazil" (Harriman). The Governor asked what Kennedy planned to do in Argentina and JV said that he wouldn't do anything since we are so far on the way of resolving the oil problem. Chile?—he wouldn't say anything. Venezuela?—no, the main problem there is oil and he feels it is too complicated for him to go into. Harriman asked if Kennedy really planned to talk against our policy in Peru and JV replied that he would express his view that we should stick to the Alliance for Progress objectives and not work with the oil companies. Harriman expressed hope that Linc Gordon could get to him on Brazil but JV said most likely Kennedy would be asked about Brazil before he gets there.

Going to another subject, Governor Harriman asked if Chile was going to show up at Rio and JV said that chances are that they will be going—the question mark being Venezuela. Harriman said that he thought Venezuela would follow Chile—JV said no, that they would not go because they did not have diplomatic relations.[3] As to U.S. policy on the Brazilian situation JV stated that the Second Institutional Act contained 32 different authoritarian steps the President could take and we felt it best to wait and see what he chose to do before making any statement of condemnation. Harriman said that it was his understanding that Castello Branco took these steps to appease his military and JV said "yes, he did."

Returning to the subject of Kennedy's trip Harriman asked JV if he planned to write to any of the Ambassadors and JV said he was going to discuss this with the Secretary. Harriman suggested that a letter be sent Linc Gordon and Ralph Dungan—Dungan and Kennedy are friends and this might be helpful. Thought it advisable to let the Ambassadors know the mood Kennedy was in. Governor Harriman again stated that he would do anything he could to help in corralling Kennedy and asked JV to mention this to the Secretary.[4]

---

[3] Although a Chilean delegation attended the Rio conference, Venezuela refused to send a delegation; in accordance with the Betancourt doctrine, the Leoni administration had suspended diplomatic relations with Brazil after the coup d'état of March–April 1964.

[4] According to the Secretary's Appointment Book Vaughn met Rusk on November 8 (10:40 a.m.); the two men also attended a briefing session for the Rio Conference on November 9 (3 p.m.). (Johnson Library) No substantive record of either meeting was found.

33. Memorandum From William G. Bowdler of the National Security Council Staff to President Johnson[1]

Washington, November 17, 1965, 5:30 p.m.

SUBJECT

Visits by Secretary Rusk and Senator Robert Kennedy to Latin America

The main developments in our Latin American relations this past week have centered on the visits of Secretary Rusk and Senator Robert Kennedy to several Latin American countries. Ellsworth Bunker brought you up-to-date on the Dominican picture yesterday.[2] The only other significant development is that of President Frei's reported decision to put an end to the copper strike, now in its fourth week. This may involve military intervention in the mines.

Secretary Rusk's trip. Secretary Rusk's brief visits to Venezuela, Argentina and Uruguay, on his way to the Rio Conference, went very well.[3] The Communists and extreme leftists carried out some of their usual propaganda and pyrotechnic stunts but these did not directly affect the Secretary, except for one incident in Montevideo.

In Venezuela, the Secretary had a useful talk with President Leoni on the world situation. Leoni gave him a full airing of Venezuela's complaints over our oil import restrictions. This was to be expected. As we told you last night, the Venezuelan Foreign Minister misread part of their conversation as an invitation by you to President Leoni to visit the United States. This may have been a deliberate attempt to display U.S. support for Venezuela, despite its decision not to attend the Rio meeting.

The visit with the Argentines was particularly cordial. President Illia showed special interest in the Vietnam problem and expressed support for our position. He stressed the necessity for the Latin American countries to promote the objectives of the Alliance for Progress and to rely on self-help measures. He reported that he had already spoken to the Chilean and Uruguayan Presidents about the Alliance along these lines, and planned to continue the dialogue with other Presidents. Secretary Rusk compared notes with the Argentine Foreign Minister on

---

[1] Source: Johnson Library, National Security File, Country File, Latin America, Vol. IV, 3/65–8/66. Secret.

[2] According to the President's Daily Diary Johnson met Bunker twice on November 16. (Johnson Library) For a memorandum from Bunker to the President, November 15, see *Foreign Relations, 1964–1968,* vol. XXXII, Document 144.

[3] The Secretary's itinerary in South America was: Venezuela (November 13–14); Argentina (November 15–16); Uruguay (November 16); Brazil (November 16–24); and Paraguay (November 24). Rusk was chairman of the U.S. Delegation to the Second Special Inter-American Conference, which met in Rio de Janeiro, November 17–30.

key issues at the Rio meeting and found a large measure of agreement. Secretary Rusk was so encouraged by his talks with the Argentine President and Foreign Minister and by what his economic team found on Argentine self-help measures, that he has asked that we consider moving ahead with some assistance projects being held in abeyance pending Argentine self-help performance and satisfactory settlement of the termination of the oil company contracts.

Secretary Rusk was in Montevideo for only three hours. An otherwise productive round of talks with President Beltran and Foreign Minister Vidal Zaglio was marred by an incident at an unscheduled wreath-laying ceremony. A 25-year old man broke through police lines and managed to get close enough to the Secretary to spit at him, but did not hit him.

Senator Kennedy's trip. Senator Kennedy has visited Peru, and today completes his tour in Chile.[4] From press and Embassy reports, the Peruvian visit was quite successful. Large, enthusiastic crowds turned out to meet him, and he was not the target of any anti-U.S. demonstrations. On the touchy issue of nationalization of the International Petroleum Company (IPC), he took a correct public position, despite his sharp disagreement with the Administration's position on the handling of the IPC case with the Peruvian Government. He said that this is a matter for the Peruvian people to decide. He also acknowledged that under international law, a country is within its right to expropriate foreign property, *provided* it makes prompt, adequate and effective compensation.

After his departure from Lima, two pro-nationalization magazines carried accounts of what he is alleged to have said on the IPC case at a private party. No one from the Embassy was present, so we do not have an official account. The thrust of these stories is that he, in effect, encouraged nationalization, pointing out that other Latin American countries had done this before without any significant long-term damage to their relations with the U.S. He is also alleged to have made some unflattering references to the Rockefeller family (IPC is an ESSO holding) and to have said that the Peruvian Ambassador in Washington advised him not to mention the IPC problem. This latter remark is already causing the Ambassador some trouble at home.

Ambassador Jones brought these stories to Kennedy's attention in Santiago and he has authorized a statement reaffirming his public position on expropriation and describing the use of remarks he made in a private conversation as "an irresponsible distortion of my position." The text of the statement is at Tab A.[5]

---

[4] Kennedy's itinerary in South America was: Peru (November 10–13); Chile (November 13–18); Argentina (November 18–20); Brazil (November 20–30); and Venezuela (November 30–December 1).

[5] Attached but not printed.

So far we have only press reports on Kennedy's five-day visit to Chile. He seems to have received a warm public reception, without incident, except in his speaking engagements with university groups. The themes he has stressed—e.g., the importance of the Alliance for Progress, praise for Frei's revolution-in-liberty program, the vital role which young people have to play—have gone over well and created no problems for him or for us.

He seems to have been adroit in handling questions about the Bay of Pigs and our action in the Dominican Republic. The press reports that he described our Dominican intervention as a mistake, but he has taken strong issue with questioners who cast our intervention as "American imperialism". The press has him saying more than he should about changes in his program in Brazil resulting from recent events there. The Brazilian Embassy has informally protested to State over his alleged remarks.

At the University in Santiago, a group of extremists tried to prevent him from speaking. Opposing students shouted them down. At Concepcion, he ran into stronger opposition as "pro-Communist" students used eggs and stones and saliva to disrupt his talk. The larger projectiles reportedly did not hit him, but he was spat upon.

We will have a more complete and accurate report of the Chilean leg of the journey as soon as the Embassy reports are received.[6]

WGB

---

[6] The Embassy reports on Kennedy's trip were transmitted in: telegram 751 from Lima, November 11; telegram 761 from Lima, November 13; telegram 670 from Santiago, November 19; telegram 747 from Buenos Aires, November 23; telegram 1351 from Rio de Janeiro, December 2; and telegram 602 from Caracas, December 1. (All in National Archives and Records Administration, RG 59, Central Files 1964–66, LEG 7 KENNEDY)

34.   **Telegram From the Embassy in Brazil to the Department of State**[1]

Rio de Janeiro, November 30, 1965, 2315Z.

1329. For the Secretary from Harriman.

The Final Act of the Conference was signed today with considerable enthusiasm.[2] Carrillo Flores spoke for the conference members, underlining progress in the social and economic fields. Throughout the conference he has been far more cooperative than previous Mexican ministers.

Chairman Leitao concluded the session with a brief, businesslike speech summarizing the real achievements of the conference. In addition, he returned to Castello Branco's theme of collective security and the need to equip the OAS with means for dealing with the new kind of threat we face today, namely, aggression by subversion. He handled skillfully the question of new members by expressing the hope that Canada, Trinidad, and Jamaica would soon join the organization and suggested that they be welcomed by acclamation. All, including the Guatemalan, clapped enthusiastically. This I believe satisfies the assurances you gave to the Jamaica and Trinidad representatives who can now report to their governments that conference expressed unanimous welcome if they indicated desire to join.[3]

The Economic and Social Act was approved without a dissenting voice. The Latinos agreed to a series of actions which they themselves are to take to promote development by self help and particularly by mutual assistance. They were not looking solely towards Uncle Sam, but with new emphasis on self help and particularly mutual aid among Latin Americans. Jack Vaughn and Walt Rostow deserve much credit in helping to hammer out the principles agreed to. Recalling the inestimable value of mutual assistance in Europe in Marshall Plan days, all this appeals to me as being a major forward step.

On the political side, the guidelines to the preparatory committee for the amendment of the charter on organization went along without much hitch except for the paragraph on the responsibilities that might

---

[1] Source: National Archives and Records Administration, RG 59, Central Files 1964–66, POL 3 IA. Confidential; Immediate; Limdis. Passed to the White House.

[2] The text of the first two resolutions of the Final Act, a proposal to amend the OAS Charter and the Economic and Social Act, are in Department of State *Bulletin*, December 20, 1965, pp. 996–1001. The full text of the Final Act, which included 30 resolutions, is in *The OAS Chronicle*, February 1966, pp. 5–29.

[3] All three countries eventually joined the OAS: Trinidad and Tobago (1967), Jamaica (1969), Canada (1990).

be assigned to the council "relative to the maintenance of peace and the peaceful settlement of disputes", a phrase proposed by Guatemala and passed by split vote in committee one. Our delegation felt since it had been included we should stick to those who had supported it, and not give in to the soft group. After some rather heated discussion, the paragraph was approved 12 to 1 with 6 abstentions. Some appeared to be afraid that "maintenance of peace" was a first step to a peace force. Nevertheless, the whole section was unanimously approved.

There have been, however, a few reservations attached to the final document.

The resolution on human rights was constructive and the resolution on consultation prior to recognition of governments resulting from coups was innocuous.

Old hands here say that there was greater consensus and less argument than usual, and a good spirit of confidence in the progressive steps taken, particularly those relating to integration, mutual aid and area development.

The discordant note was the rigidities of countries such as Peru, Chile, Uruguay in the field of peaceful settlements. The majority, however, recognized that the long-festering disputes must be got out of the way if there is to be real economic integration and mutual aid. Peru's failure to get Lima as a conference site was a lesson to the conference, and the conference was profoundly impressed by our recent settlements with Panama and Mexico.

President Johnson's proposal to extend the duration of the Alliance has been warmly received and was frequently referred to with appreciation.[4] There is no doubt your own week of consultation here had a highly salutary influence and your parting statement set the tone for the conference. The effective teamwork of the delegation could not have been better and the assistance of efficient Embassy was invaluable.

Gordon

---

[4] Rusk read the President's message to the delegates, including the following passage: "Recognizing that fulfillment of our goals will require the continuation of the joint effort beyond 1971, I wish to inform the Conference—and through you, your respective governments—that the United States will be prepared to extend mutual commitments beyond the time period foreseen in the charter of Punta del Este." (*Public Papers of the Presidents of the United States: Lyndon B. Johnson, 1965,* Book II, pp. 1123–1124) The text of the Secretary's address to the conference, November 22, is in Department of State *Bulletin,* December 20, 1965, pp. 985–995.

35.   **Memorandum From the Deputy Director for Coordination, Bureau of Intelligence and Research (Koren) to the Director (Hughes)**

Washington, January 11, 1966.

[Source: Department of State, INR/IL Historical Files, ARA–CIA Weekly Meetings, 1966–1967. Secret. 4 pages of source text not declassified.]

36.   **Editorial Note**

[*text not declassified*]

37.   **Memorandum of Telephone Conversation Between President Johnson and the Under Secretary of State for Economic Affairs (Mann)**[1]

Washington, January 17, 1966, 11:05 a.m.

The President said that they had been giving a lot of thought to making Jack Vaughn the Peace Corps Administrator to succeed Shriver.[2] He did not know whether Vaughn would be interested, but what would we do if he were?

Mr. Mann said he did not know. The President said we needed someone with a liberal image who could get rid of this crowd. Mr. Mann said he thought it would be a good move for Jack and good for the President, because Mr. Mann thought Bobby K. had his knife sharpened for Mr. Vaughn and perhaps Morse and a couple of others also. Mr. Mann said he thought they fully intended to cut Vaughn down in

---

[1] Source: Johnson Library, Papers of Thomas C. Mann, Telephone Conversations with LBJ, May 2, 1965–June 2, 1966. No classification or drafting information appears on the memorandum.

[2] R. Sargent Shriver was also Director of the Office of Economic Opportunity.

66. The President agreed and asked about Ambassador Gordon. Mr. Mann said he thought he would be as good as the President could get. He has some lines out to the left—he belonged to the left three years ago. He came in with Kennedy. Mr. Mann said he thought that Berle and Gordon had been on an advisory committee to the President[3] and had had a lot to do with the Alliance and the liberal image, so presumably this would stand him in good stead. Mr. Mann said on the other hand, Gordon is a determined guy, but all good people are. He has his own views and he sticks to them.

The President asked about his loyalties. Mr. Mann said he did not think he had any strong ones to Kennedy but that he did not consider Kennedy his enemy. The President asked what Ambassador Gordon had reported about the Kennedy visit down there and Mr. Mann said he would have to look this up.[4]

The President asked if Mr. Mann thought that Vaughn would go for this. Mr. Mann said he did not know but he thought he could help talk him into it. The President asked who we would put in Brazil and Mr. Mann said he did not know. The President mentioned Berle, but Mr. Mann said no, he was too old, too contentious and too arrogant. He thought he would talk down to the Brazilians.

The President told Mr. Mann to think about who we could put in there. He asked if Oliver would do it instead of coming home. Mr. Mann said Oliver was a Spanish type. He said he would think about it and call the President back. The President said to call him back in an hour.[5]

---

[3] Adolf A. Berle served as the chairman of two task forces on Latin America, November 1960–July 1961; Gordon was a member of both.

[4] See footnote 6, Document 33.

[5] In that telephone conversation with the President, at 12:10 p.m., Mann reported that "he had done a little looking around and he thought that the choice of Gordon for ARA would be the best the President could do." Mann expected that Vaughn would agree to the proposed change; he also suggested several candidates to replace Gordon in Rio. (Johnson Library, Papers of Thomas C. Mann, Telephone Conversations with LBJ, May 2, 1965–June 2 1966) Johnson called Vaughn at 1:50 p.m. and received a call at 3:14 p.m. from Gordon in Cambridge, Massachusetts. (Ibid., President's Daily Diary) One hour later the President announced that Vaughn would replace Shriver as Director of the Peace Corps. (*Public Papers of the Presidents of the United States: Lyndon B. Johnson, 1966*, Book I, pp. 24–25) After meeting Gordon the next morning Johnson announced his nomination as Assistant Secretary. (Ibid., p. 26) Gordon took office on March 9. On May 22 John W. Tuthill was appointed to succeed Gordon as Ambassador to Brazil.

38.   National Intelligence Estimate[1]

NIE 80/90–66   Washington, February 17, 1966.

INSURGENCY IN LATIN AMERICA[2]

The Problem

To estimate the character of the insurgency threat in Latin America, and the prospects over the next few years.[3]

Conclusions

A. There has been a rash of insurgencies in Latin America since Castro's triumph in Cuba in 1959, but only a few have developed much virulence. The more active ones, in Venezuela, Guatemala, Peru, and Colombia, have either lost ground or gained little over the past year.

B. The growth of Latin American insurgencies has been hindered by the disunity of extremist groups, the want of willing martyrs, and the failure to attract much popular support. It has also been contained by the counteraction undertaken by the governments involved, with substantial US support.

C. Insurgencies tend to prosper along one of two lines: the largely unhampered expansion of a guerrilla campaign, as in Cuba, or the exploitation of a sudden upheaval, as in the Dominican Republic in 1965. Thus the prospects for a particular insurgency are likely to depend less on its initial strength than on the disabilities of the government which may prevent effective counteraction. The danger of insurgency is probably greater in some chronically unstable countries not now plagued by insurgent activity, such as Bolivia or Haiti, than in a country like Venezuela, where the government is moving effectively against an active insurgency and, to an extent, against the underlying social tensions.

---

[1] Source: Central Intelligence Agency, Job 79–R01012A, O/DDI Registry. Secret; Controlled Dissem. According to a note on the cover sheet this estimate was prepared in the Central Intelligence Agency with the participation of the intelligence organizations of the Departments of State and Defense, and the National Security Agency. The United States Intelligence Board concurred in this estimate on February 17. The estimate supplements NIE 80/90–64 (Document 24).

[2] Excluding Cuba, for which the current estimate is NIE 85–65, dated 19 August 1965. [Footnote in the source text; for text of NIE 85–65, see Foreign Relations, 1964–1968, vol. XXXII, Document 305.]

[3] By insurgency we mean the systematic use of violence to overthrow or undermine the established political and social order. We exclude military coups d'état, endemic banditry, and spontaneous disorder. [Footnote in the source text.]

D. In this context, the inherently unstable political situations in the following countries render them vulnerable to the rapid development of insurgency: Bolivia, the Dominican Republic, Ecuador, Guatemala, Haiti, Honduras, and Panama.

[Omitted here is the Discussion section of the estimate.]

---

39.   Memorandum From Secretary of State Rusk to President Johnson[1]

Washington, May 3, 1966.

SUBJECT

OAS Charter Amendments

Background

1. At the OAS Conference in Rio last November, it was unanimously agreed that the Charter of the OAS should be amended in three respects:

(a) To improve the structure of the organization by holding annual meetings of Foreign Ministers and in other respects;
(b) To strengthen the capacity of the organization to assist in the peaceful settlement of disputes among member countries; and
(c) To incorporate as treaty obligations the basic principles of the Alliance for Progress, including self-help and mutual assistance to accelerate economic and social progress. It was made clear that mutual assistance included actions by the Latin Americans for one another as well as actions by the United States.

2. A special OAS Committee met in Panama in late February and March of this year to draft Charter amendments in accordance with the decisions of Rio. Substantial agreement was reached on the matters of structure and peaceful settlement of disputes, but there was disagreement between the Latin American and United States delegations regarding the economic and social chapters. We believed that the Latin American proposals were unnecessarily elaborate, and that they might involve treaty commitments to aid and trade policies which would be

---

[1] Source: Johnson Library, National Security File, Memos to the President, Walt W. Rostow, Vol. 2. Confidential. No drafting information appears on the memorandum. Rostow forwarded the memorandum to the President on May 4.

opposed by the Senate as an unacceptable infringement on Congressional prerogatives. We, therefore, reserved our position, indicating that further consultations were required with the Senate on the basis of which we would offer counter-proposals. We stated, however, that the United States Government stands by the basic principles of the Economic and Social Act of Rio, and that our differences related only to the appropriate form for incorporation of these principles into treaty language.

3. After Assistant Secretary Gordon returned from Buenos Aires in early April,[2] a revised draft was prepared and presented to the Latin American Subcommittee of the Senate Foreign Relations Committee. It was discussed at length on April 25 with about 12 members of Senator Morse's subcommittee. Senator Fulbright participated as Chairman of the full Committee.

4. On Monday afternoon, May 2, Senators Fulbright and Morse, together with Senators McCarthy, Aiken and Carlson met again with Assistant Secretary Gordon. Senator Morse, speaking for the group stated that it was the Committee's considered opinion that commitments to mutual assistance, even with the safeguards contained in the State Department's draft, should not be incorporated into treaty obligations, but should be left to normal legislative action. The Senators recognized that Article 26 of the present Charter (adopted in 1948) does include a broad commitment to economic cooperation. The discussion made it clear that their objection to going further is related to concerns arising from the Vietnamese situation and generally from concern about the breadth of international commitments of the United States. All efforts to persuade them that the Western Hemisphere situation differs from others, in view of our long-standing special relations within this Hemisphere and the collective security engagements under the Inter-American Treaty of Reciprocal Assistance (Rio treaty) of 1947, proved unavailing.

5. We have prepared a revised draft of the relevant articles which removes the qualified undertaking "to extend mutual assistance", thereby meeting the central objection of the Committee. In an effort to keep faith with the understandings of Rio and to avoid a potential major setback in the climate of inter-American relations, we have drawn from the present Article 26 and then tied the use of resources under that Article to the self-help commitments and other provisions

---

[2] Gordon went to Buenos Aires in late-March for the fourth annual meeting of the Inter-American Economic and Social Council. For text of his remarks before the Council, March 29, see Department of State *Bulletin,* May 9, 1966, pp. 738–746. Gordon's report on the outcome of the meeting is in telegram 1470 from Buenos Aires, April 2. (National Archives and Records Administration, RG 59, Central Files 1964–66, AID (AFP) 3 ECOSOC–IA)

of the Alliance for Progress. Even this proposal will probably be regarded by the Latin Americans as a significant retreat from the Rio agreements; but we believe that it might barely suffice to bridge the gap. Anything less would not do so.

6. Enclosure 1[3] contains in parallel columns (1) the "Panama Draft" on mutual assistance as approved by all the Latin American Delegations, (2) the draft submitted to the Senate Committee and opposed by them, and (3) the new proposed draft, the first article of which is identical with Article 26 of the present Charter.

7. Enclosure 2 contains in parallel columns the entire chapter on economic standards (1) as approved by the Latin American Delegations at Panama, and (2) as contained in the United States counterproposals submitted to the Senate Committee.

8. The problem of timing is very tight. The Buenos Aires conference of Foreign Ministers to approve Charter amendments is now scheduled for July 30. To meet this date the OAS Council must submit its report by May 31. We do not want to maintain the present Buenos Aires schedule unless agreement on assistance among all the Member Governments can be reached before May 31. Assistant Secretary Gordon leaves Friday morning for Central America and Chile and hopes to discuss this matter on his trip. Any significant slippage in the Buenos Aires schedule would affect adversely the proposed Presidential Summit Meeting.

Alternative Courses of Action

(Linc Gordon and I would welcome the opportunity of a few minutes' discussion with you on these alternatives at your earliest convenience.)[4]

1. We can proceed to negotiate the revised language without further consultation with the Senate. In this case, we should inform them that we have taken their basic point into account and are seeking to negotiate the new language which would be given to them.

2. We could take the revised proposals back for further discussions with the Senate Committee at the State Department level. In the present frame of mind of key members, this would run the risk that they would object on the ground that the proposed Article 7 gives a

---

[3] Both enclosures are attached but not printed.

[4] No decisions are recorded on the memorandum. According to the President's Daily Diary Johnson met Rusk and Gordon on May 5 to discuss the proposed amendments to the OAS charter. (Johnson Library) Although no substantive record of the meeting has been found, the administration apparently proceeded on the basis of the first alternative.

broader construction to the existing obligation under Article 6, and constitutes in spirit, if not in form, a commitment to mutual assistance.

3. The new proposals (or a return to something stronger) could be discussed with the Senators with your own participation.

Dean Rusk

---

40.   Memorandum From the President's Special Assistant (Rostow) to President Johnson[1]

Washington, May 27, 1966.

SUBJECT

Frontiers of South America

On January 31, 1966, you requested that I undertake urgently a preliminary assessment of the potentialities of developing the frontiers of South America.

I attach a summary report and seven appendixes.[2] In addition, there is included a special report developed by the Department of the Army's Engineer Agency for Resources Inventories.[3]

These represent the present state of thought and knowledge in the town. They have been assembled to provide a foundation for future systematic work. None can be regarded as definitive.

In compiling the data and writing the report, I have received the whole-hearted support of every element in the government with interest in and knowledge of the problem:

Agency for International Development
Department of Agriculture
Department of Commerce
Department of Interior
Department of the Army
National Aeronautics and Space Agency.

---

[1] Source: Johnson Library, National Security File, National Security Action Memorandums, NSAM No. 349. Confidential.

[2] The report was prepared by the Department's Policy Planning Council in May 1966; attached but not printed. Rostow was chairman of the Council until April 1, when he succeeded Bundy as Special Assistant to the President.

[3] Dated February 14; attached but not printed.

This is, I believe, the first time this problem has been systematically examined in our government. It is evident that there is much more for us all to learn; and my first recommendation is that, under Linc Gordon's leadership, work on this problem be made a continuing account and that the various agencies capable of making a contribution continue to expand and refine their knowledge on a coordinated basis. A working party operating under the Latin American IRG might perform this function.

In addition, CIAP should set up a working group that would regularly engage the IBRD, IDB, AID, and the OAS in this field.

What emerges of substance may be briskly summarized as follows:

1. South America is at a stage of historical evolution where the further development of its frontiers can contribute to food production, a widening of markets, regional integration, and the settlement of various bilateral disputes.

2. A rational program for exploiting these frontiers must be geared to other aspects of South American development, with careful attention to the comparative benefits to be derived from intensive investment in existing areas as opposed to extensive investment in expanding the frontiers. The opening of the South American frontiers has an important role to play in the region's future; but it is not a panacea.

3. There are four major complexes which comprise the bulk of the frontier regions of South America capable of rational economic exploitation from the present forward.

—The Darien Gap area of Panama and Colombia;
—The Andean Piedmont, running in an irregular narrow belt for 3,000 miles from the Venezuelan border through Colombia, Ecuador, Peru, to the Santa Cruz region of Bolivia;
—The Campo Cerrado area, east and south of the Amazon basin;
—The Gran Chaco and Gran Pantanal region covering portions of Bolivia, Paraguay, Brazil and Argentina.

There are special further potentialities in the tropical flood plains of the Amazon; the Guayana region of Venezuela and British Guiana; the linking of Buenos Aires to the whole region south of Rio–Sao Paulo; and the River Plate drainage system.

The character of all these regions are briefly sketched in the report.

4. There is little prospect in sight for the economic exploitation of the vast Amazon–Orinoco basin unless the proposal for making it a lake (by damming the rivers) should prove feasible.

5. As the survey of seventy-four projects under way or envisaged indicates (Appendix I), there is now a great deal of activity focused on the opening up of the frontiers; and it is generally following a rational

pattern. The task for policy in Latin America is to make the expansion of the frontiers more effective and purposeful.

6. A political point of some importance: the opening up of these frontier regions could, in a number of South American countries, strengthen the sense of nationhood and contribute to political and social stability. Moreover, notably in the Andean Piedmont, but elsewhere as well, the laying out of roads and organized settlements is a significant element in preventing the possibilities of Communist insurgency.

7. Detailed recommendations are set out in Part Four of the attached summary report. Briefly, they are:

—The Darien Gap complex be urgently examined as a whole, notably in the light of our Panamanian negotiations. Its various elements have been hitherto treated separately.

—We maintain a policy of selective but continued support for roadbuilding in each of the four countries engaged in opening up the Andean Piedmont. (The report isolates the road segments judged most rational for the next phase.)

—We assign specific responsibility to Linc Gordon quietly to explore the possibility of exploiting work on multinational projects to ease or settle the major outstanding bilateral quarrels in South America.

—We clarify our minds on the economics of frontier settlement in the light of recent experience and establish Alliance for Progress policies based on this review. No serious agreed guidelines now exist.

—We examine urgently on an interdepartmental basis, perhaps under the aegis of the SIG, the security and other problems involved in a systematic use of orbital remote-sensor measurement of land and geological formations in South America, providing you with a report. These methods could accelerate rapidly mineral discovery and exploitation, notably in the Andes.

—We intensify our support for your proposal, via CIAP, for accelerated development of chemical fertilizer production in Latin America.

—We set up both within the CIAP framework and within the U.S. Government continuing systematic work on the development of the South American frontiers.

—CIAP should consider this summer (after the report on multinational projects by the Development and Resources Corporation, headed by David Lilienthal) the publication of materials that would dramatize what is going forward in this field and its potentialities for Latin American development and integration.

—We re-examine (with full attention to our balance of payments position) our present policy on local cost financing of development projects with a view to permitting financing of local costs of certain infrastructure projects as part of an over-all program for opening frontier areas.

If further detailed examination of this study makes sense to you, I recommend that an NSAM be issued assigning responsibility for the task to State—specifically to Linc Gordon. A suggested draft NSAM for your approval is at Tab A.[4]

You may wish to weave into your statements on Latin America passages indicating an awareness of the frontier development going forward, its potentialities, and your support for it. A possible draft is at Tab B.[5]

Should you (or the Vice President) visit Latin America, you may wish to visit certain selected frontier areas as well as the conventional cities.[6]

Walt

---

[4] Attached but not printed. In NSAM No. 349, May 31, the President instructed the Department to report on development of the South American frontier. (Johnson Library, National Security File, National Security Action Memorandums, NSAM No. 349) Progress reports, dated February 14, 1967, July 2, 1967, and March 25, 1968, are ibid.

[5] Attached but not printed. The President approved the draft statement. In a speech marking the fifth anniversary of the Alliance for Progress, August 17, Johnson referred to development of the inner frontier: "The eastern slopes of the Andes, the water systems of the Gran Pantanal River Plate, and Orinoco, the barely touched areas of Central America and of Panama—these are just a few of the frontiers, which, this morning, beckon to us." (*Public Papers of the Presidents of the United States: Lyndon B. Johnson, 1966,* Book I, pp. 824–829)

[6] A handwritten note by the President at the end of the memorandum reads: "Good. L"

---

41. Memorandum From the President's Special Assistant (Rostow) to President Johnson[1]

Washington, October 15, 1966, 12:30 p.m.

SUBJECT

Our Program for the OAS Summit

Secretary Rusk in the attached memorandum[2] requests your approval of general guidelines for our negotiators on Summit preparations.

---

[1] Source: Johnson Library, National Security File, Memos to the President, Walt W. Rostow, Vol. 14. Secret. A copy was sent to Moyers.

[2] Memorandum from Rusk to the President, undated; attached but not printed. A copy, dated October 14, is in the National Archives and Records Administration, RG 59, Central Files 1964–66, POL 7 IA SUMMIT.

The guidelines are based on a Summit program which has substantial inter-agency concurrence except for the budgetary implications. Because of the difference, Secretary Rusk is not asking that you make a decision on this aspect until you can review the Summit price tag in the light of the total aid request for FY 1968.

These guidelines provide adequate interim direction for the preliminary multilateral preparatory work which will take place during the next 6–8 weeks.

The Summit Deal

We are asking the Latins to:

—integrate their economies and sharply reduce tariffs.
—revamp their antiquated agricultural and educational systems.
—work with us in promoting private investment.

It will take courage for the Latin American Presidents to take their countries down this uncharted path.

To induce them to step off into the dark and break past the obstacles, a substantial U.S. "carrot" will help. Expanded economic assistance is our part of the deal.

The guidelines will enable our negotiators to explore:

—how far the Latins are prepared to go.
—how much inducement must we offer to make them take the jump.

Based on their findings, you can decide on the specific proposals.

Our Present Summit Program

It is *designed to begin meeting now serious social and political problems we see coming in the decade ahead* from population increase, growing urban unemployment and continued backwardness of agriculture. The main elements are:

1. Latin American Economic Integration

The broadened, more competitive market that can result from more rapid *economic integration is the single, most promising move that Latin America can take* to accelerate growth and reduce future foreign aid needs.

We would expect the Latin Americas to agree *to a concrete plan for automatic reduction of intra-zonal tariffs and non-tariff barriers;* a commitment to adopt reasonable external tariffs, declining as their economies strengthen; competitive investment and internal trade policies; and reasonable access to the region for foreign investment.

You, in turn, would announce at the Summit our readiness to support this effort by *expanding our contribution to the Inter-American Bank's*

Fund for Special Operations (IDB/FSO). This would involve increasing the U.S. contribution in the three fiscal years 1968–70 from the present level of $250 million per year to $300 million, with an indication that if additional funds are required, we would consider further replenishment of the FSO.

The *IDB would agree to set aside a stated amount* of the new resources to:

a. *finance sound multinational projects* in support of economic integration and development of "inner frontiers" (e.g., roads, flood control, hydroelectric power, irrigation, communications).

b. *assist countries with temporary adjustment problems* resulting from rapid integration (e.g., balance of payment difficulties, affected industries and workers, export financing for intra-Latin American trade).

2. Higher Alliance Targets: Primarily Agricultural and Education

Annual per capita growth rates in Latin America *should increase* from the 2.5% level realized in 1964 and 1965 *to 4–6%*. Economic integration will help. But also *basic to the objective are more dynamic agricultural sectors and broader access to higher quality education.*

The type of across-the-board programs and self-help we have in mind are described in the guidelines paper (Enclosure 1 of the Rusk memo).[3] In addition to remedial measures for the more common deficiencies, the programs include some exciting new ideas such as establishing two or three regional centers of excellence in science and engineering in Latin America.

At the Summit *you would announce an increase* in AID bilateral assistance in these two fields *of up to $200 million per year* for 5 years.

3. Stimulate Private Investment

There are *two proposals for increasing U.S. investment in Latin America* under favorable conditions which State has advanced but *on which full inter-agency agreement has not been reached.* They are:

a. an imaginative idea for *expansion of AID risk guarantees* developed by Tony Solomon.

b. the negotiation with the Latin Americans of an agreed *investment code* to encourage use of modern technology and provide for coordination of foreign investment with development plans.

---

[3] Attached but not printed.

Budgetary Implications of the Package (Linc Gordon's estimates *not* concurred in by AID or BOB)

For *FY 1968* the *implications* are

	Appropriation	*Expenditure*
	(in millions)	
Economic Integration (replenishment of the IDB/FSO over the planned level of $250 million)	$50	$5
Increased Bilateral Aid for Agriculture and Education	$200	$50
Total	$250	$55

For the four-year period beyond FY 1968:

—Replenishment of the FSO will continue for 2 years at $50 million per year.

—Requirements for bilateral assistance in agriculture and education will not exceed $200 million per year and may be less, depending upon allocation of IDA funds to Latin America.

The Original Package

Linc Gordon's original Summit proposals[4] had three elements which have been deleted or diluted. They added a zest to the program which is now lacking.

1. Separate Integration Fund

As an inducement to the Latin Americans to take the plunge on integration he proposed a *separate* Latin American Integration Fund to handle adjustment assistance and a Multinational Projects window at the IDB to finance such projects. We would contribute up to $300 million to the fund and $500 million to the IDB for multinational projects, both over a five-year period.

Joe Fowler took sharp exception to these proposals and countered with the idea of using the Bank's FSO and increasing our contemplated annual contribution to the FSO by $50 million for the next three years. Linc reluctantly went along with this.

I think the Treasury formula dilutes the "carrot" aspect of the proposals to such a degree that much of its value as an inducement for prompt Latin American action is lost. We need more flexibility in negotiating with the Latins on integration.

---

[4] As contained in a draft memorandum to the President, undated; attached but not printed.

2. Expanded Risk Guarantee Program

The Solomon proposal is to:

—expand the program in six basic fields: iron and steel, chemicals, fertilizers, pulp and paper, petro-chemicals, automobiles.
—cover up to the legal maximum of 75% of each investment, and relax the 100% tieing requirement.
—require the U.S. investor to offer for sale up to 51% of the stock of his company to Latin American purchasers within a fixed number of years after the start of the project (e.g., 15–20 years) and reinvest a percentage of his profits while he still held a controlling interest.

The proposal is encountering heavy going in Treasury and Commerce on balance of payments grounds and the advisability of conditioning guarantees to the mandatory offer of stock sales after a fixed period and to required profit reinvestment. I am not convinced by:

—the balance of payments argument because Latin America does not leak to Europe, or
—the preoccupation with conditioning of guarantees since the investor is free to decide whether or not he wants to accept them.

3. Limited Untieing of Procurement

To accommodate Latin American criticism to "tied" aid, Linc proposed extending procurement eligibility for Alliance financing to include Latin America. It would apply, in effect, to manufactured products, mostly capital goods. This is largely a gesture—but symbolically a meaningful one for the Latin Americans—because they produce few such goods on competitive terms. State estimates that over an initial three-year period the procurement might reach $15 million.

The Treasury objection is on balance of payments grounds. Since the proposal is largely cosmetic, Linc dropped it from the package. I think it bears closer examination.

My Reaction to the Program

It goes to the heart of what the Latins must do and only Presidents can take the political decisions required. It is, therefore, of Presidential stature.

If the Latins are willing to start down the track we propose, the bargain to help them financially is a good one.

The portions of Linc's original package which have not prospered are "carrot" which we may have to use to get the Latins to accept the deal. They should be held in reserve.

Recommendation

That you approve the guidelines proposed by Secretary Rusk, with the understanding that you wish to review at a later date each of the three aspects of Linc Gordon's original proposals not adequately covered in the Summit program as it now stands.[5]

Approve

Disapprove

Speak to me

Walt

---

[5] Although the memorandum does not record the decision, Bromley Smith subsequently reported that the President approved this recommendation—"with the understanding that no decisions or commitments are to be made with respect to additional United States assistance without prior referral to him along with a firm indication of what the Latin Americans are prepared to do." (Memorandum from Smith to Rusk, October 19; National Archives and Records Administration, RG 59, Central Files 1964–66, POL 7 IA SUMMIT)

---

42.   Memorandum From the President's Special Assistant (Rostow) to President Johnson[1]

Washington, November 30, 1966, 9:30 a.m.

Mr. President:

This broad agenda on Latin America was drafted yesterday by Gordon, Linowitz, and Bill Bowdler. It is worth reading as a quick summary of the Latin American situation.

For your talks on Saturday,[2] I suggest the following simpler agenda.

1. *Linowitz's trip to Central America.* (Linowitz)
2. *Preparations and Prospects for the Summit meeting.* (Gordon)
3. *Implications of the Summit for U.S. Policy.* (Gordon)

---

[1] Source: Johnson Library, National Security File, Memos to the President, Walt W. Rostow, Vol. 15. Confidential. The President was at his ranch, November 19–December 9 and December 16–January 2.

[2] December 3; the meeting was evidently held aboard Air Force One during a brief trip on December 3 to Ciudad Acuña, Mexico, where Johnson inspected construction of the Amistad Dam and met informally with President Diaz Ordaz. According to the President's Daily Diary Johnson "went to a back cabin of the plane and was not seen in the front again until after landing." (Johnson Library) Passengers on the flight included Rusk, Gordon, Linowitz, and Rostow. Tom Johnson reported that "the President spent much of the flight in conversation with Secretary Rusk." (Memorandum from Johnson to Marie Fehmer, December 3; ibid.) No substantive record of the meeting was found.

For your information, Latin Americans' preparations for the Summit are now going rather well. We have put ourselves in the position where we do not have to decide what add-ons to the Alliance for Progress we shall make until we can see how seriously the Latin Americans are prepared to move forward. Our Latin American experts are thinking in terms of an add-on of perhaps $200,000, partially through the IDB, which would put additional resources into international projects and integration, on the one hand, agriculture and education, on the other.

W. W. Rostow[3]

Attachment

AGENDA

For Gordon–Linowitz–Rostow Talks With the President

1. General Political Situation

a) 1966 has been a banner election year: Costa Rica, Guatemala, Bolivia, Dominican Republic, Colombia, Brazil, Peru, Uruguay.

b) Except for the Argentine setback, representative democracy has been considerably strengthened through the electoral process and with it the promise of greater political stability.

c) Soft spots continue to be: Haiti, Ecuador, Dominican Republic, Guatemala, Panama.

d) So-called "arms race" centering around recent subsonic aircraft purchases by Argentina, Chile, and Venezuela is a real—but exaggerated—problem.

2. General Economic Situation

a) Most encouraging trend is that the hemisphere is moving out of the economic crisis stage and can now increasingly devote its attention and energies to development.

—All the major countries have passed the economic crisis stage; the ones still caught in it are small countries: Ecuador, Uruguay, Haiti, Dominican Republic, Panama.

—The new political and economic stability is fostering:

—institutional reform;
—steady increase in tax revenues;
—greater attention to development planning;
—more diversification;

---

[3] Printed from a copy that bears this typed signature.

—increase in important private investment projects;

—movement toward Latin American economic integration.

b) But the base for this progress is still fragile:

—problems of inadequate exports;

—inflationary pressures remain;

—rise in population;

—impact of any deflationary trend in the US and Europe;

—growing urban unemployment;

—backwardness of agriculture.

c) The Alliance for Progress at a crossroads:

—has had another year of solid accomplishments, although we will fall short of 2.5% GNP per capita;

—but economic and social progress must be accelerated if the present gains are to be consolidated;

—Alliance goals and requirements which the President will wish to keep in mind as he reviews the FY 1968 budget.

3. *Special Issues*

a) *Summit Preparations:*

—Status of OAS work;

—Status of our preparations;

—Linowitz trip to Central America;

—Projected Gordon–Linowitz trip to South America, following which they wish to report to the President on Summit prospects and obtain his approval of time and place for the Summit and of our program and its budget implications.[4]

b) *Dominican Republic*

—Political polarization process and what we propose to do to arrest it.

—Present economic situation and outlook for 1967.

---

[4] Gordon and Linowitz toured Latin America for consultation on the OAS summit and reported to the President on December 19. (Johnson Library, President's Daily Diary) The President gave Senator Mike Mansfield (D–Montana) the following account of the meeting: "They've covered most of the countries—I think all but a couple of them, Ecuador and Bolivia—and they're pleased with the situation generally. They're particularly pleased with Carrillo Flores and Diaz Ordaz and what they said to them and so forth. They think that the summit's going to come off in good shape. They pretty well got an agenda, pretty well agreed upon, pretty well decided that it's not going to be a place to express your envies or jealousies or to demagogue or campaign." (Ibid., Recordings and Transcripts, Recording of telephone conversation between President Johnson and Mike Mansfield, December 20, 12:16 p.m., Tape F6612.05, Side A, PNO 4)

c) *Haiti*

—Duvalier has weathered another crisis, but the situation remains explosive.

—Status of our contingency planning.

d) *Panama Negotiations*

—Status of the negotiations.

—Outlook for negotiations of satisfactory treaties with the Robles Government.

e) *Visits by Latin Americans*

—President Frei.

—President-elect Costa e Silva.

f) *Amistad Dam Visit*

—Scenario.

—Themes for remarks.

---

43.   Memorandum From William G. Bowdler of the National Security Council Staff to the President's Special Assistant (Rostow)[1]

Washington, January 17, 1967.

Walt—

Hal Hendrix[2] is right about the Presidential image in Latin America, although I think he may overstate it.

Goodness knows, the President has paid more personal attention to Latin America than probably any other President—the record of speeches, ceremonies, lunches, dinners, visits, boat rides, special delegations, personal letters, congratulatory messages, funeral planes, etc., is ample evidence.

These are his principal image problems:

—He does not project the sparkling intellectual image of Kennedy—young, scholar, pretty wife, small children, Catholic, etc.—which so appeals to the Latins.

---

[1] Source: Johnson Library, National Security File, Agency File, Alliance for Progress, 9/1/66 (1 of 2). Secret.

[2] Harold V. Hendrix was Latin American correspondent with the Scripps Howard Newspaper Alliance.

—He had the distasteful—but necessary—job of sending troops into the DR and of fighting the nasty war in Vietnam with all the "egghead" criticism that it has brought.

—A very personal observation—I have for some time detected a growing cynicism among AID and USIA personnel toward the Alliance and the President which translates itself into lack of drive and imagination.

What I would do about it:

—The Summit meeting and the trip is the single most important thing the President can do.

—A trip by Lynda later on this year would project an image of youth, charm, good looks and stylishness.

—One or more taped television interviews with carefully chosen, well-known Latin American newsmen in the President's office, with a trip around the White House; the same might be done on the distaff side. (Len Marks should be able to arrange these.)

—A Coordinator for the Alliance for Progress separate from the Assistant Secretary of State, but who will naturally work closely with him. The Alliance needs a figure of prestige who is close to the President and who can devote time travelling around visiting projects, conferring with Latin officials and instilling enthusiasm into our rank and file. The Assistant Secretary is too busy running the show back here to do the necessary missionary work the Alliance requires. The economics of the Alliance is in good hands—what it needs is a spiritual leader who will mirror the President. The change of the guard in ARA provides the opportunity to do this.[3]

—Len Marks needs to get the word to his staff in Latin America not to miss a chance to weave in the LBJ image in their operations.

---

[3] Reference is to the upcoming departure of Gordon, who had accepted the presidency of Johns Hopkins University. On January 20 Johnson called Senator Fulbright to discuss Gordon's replacement: "I want to get a good man that can move forward and be progressive; and I have nobody to reward, as you know, in the State Department and never have had; and I've just looked at them, and I'm telling you the Foreign Service from the Latin American standpoint is awfully weak. As a matter of fact, it's weak everywhere, Bill." (Johnson Library, Recordings and Transcripts, Recording of telephone conversation between President Johnson and J. William Fulbright, January 20, 5:30 p.m., Tape F67.03, Side A, PNO 1) On May 24 Johnson announced the nomination of Covey T. Oliver, Ambassador to Colombia, to be Assistant Secretary. Oliver was confirmed by the Senate on June 8 and took office on July 1.

—It might be useful to have the AID and USIA directors in the South American countries congregate in Venezuela at the end of the President's trip for him to give them a pep talk.[4]

WGB

---

[4] Rostow wrote the following instructions to Bowdler on the memorandum: "Go and have a talk with Len Marks about this problem & your suggestions." Bowdler noted on March 4 that this was "done."

---

44. Memorandum From the President's Special Assistant (Rostow) to President Johnson[1]

Washington, February 10, 1967.

SUBJECT

Your 6:00 p.m. Appointment with Secretary Rusk on OAS Summit Preparations

Secretary Rusk wishes to discuss what he should say about the Summit meeting at Buenos Aires in view of the wide inter-agency disagreement on what our part of the Summit deal should be.

The Summit Deal

We are asking the Latin Americans to:

—take the plunge on economic integration;
—modernize their agricultural and educational systems;
—forego expensive military equipment.

These steps involve tough political decisions. What we are prepared to do to help is critical to their willingness to take the decisions. The success of the Summit hinges on this interplay.

Linc Gordon and Sol Linowitz have recommended this package as our part of the deal:

1. Express willingness to ask Congress for up to $300 million for Latin American integration adjustment assistance, to be contributed over a period of years and on a matching basis after the Latin American Common Market treaty is negotiated.

---

[1] Source: Johnson Library, National Security File, International Meetings and Travel File, Inter-American Summit Meeting, Vol. III. Secret. A notation on the memorandum indicates the President saw it.

2. Approve asking Congress in this session for an *authorization and appropriation* in FY 1968 of $300 million for replenishment of the Inter-American Development Bank Fund for Special Operations, i.e., $50 million more than you have already approved for *authorizing* legislation for FY 1968.

3. Indicate an intention to ask Congress to increase our Alliance for Progress assistance for education and agriculture by $100 million in FY 1968 (it is already in the budget) and (an average of $200 million for the following four years, dependent on demonstrated need and adequate self help).

4. Consider modifying tying arrangements for our capital project loans (but not program loans) to permit hemisphere-wide procurement after the Latin Americans negotiate a Common Market Treaty. This would shift the tying from the present individual country basis to a regional basis. The balance of payments effects would not be appreciable.

A table on how the costs of this package would be spread out over the next five years is at Tab A.[2]

Views of Other Agencies

Treasury—Joe Fowler opposes Recommendations 1 and 4 of the package. I don't believe he is sympathetic toward economic integration. He feels that if integration adjustment assistance is necessary, the Inter-American Bank should handle it, and by increasing our contribution (as per Recommendation 2) we would meet our responsibilities. On Recommendation 4, he agrees that the balance of payments effect will probably be small, but he fears adverse psychological effects on our balance of payments posture.

AID—Bill Gaud is strongly opposed to Recommendation 3. He fears that an increase of this dimension in the Alliance will most likely result in the Congress granting it *at the expense* of other areas.

BOB—Charlie Schultze prefers not to mention a specific amount for integration adjustment assistance in Recommendation 1. On paragraph 2, he favors seeking authorization only in this session, leaving the issue of whether to seek a supplemental appropriation this year or next January to be decided later.

My Views and Recommendation

Latin America stands at a crossroads. Over the next few years population increase, growing urban unemployment and agricultural

---

[2] Not attached, but the table is attached to another copy of this memorandum. (Ibid.)

backwardness could, at present rates of modest growth, lead to new social crises and political extremism. If the Latin American Presidents are willing to establish a Common Market and make a major effort to boost agriculture and improve education, the region during the 1970's could attain a level of "take-off" for self-sustained growth which would promote social and political stability and dependence on US public financing.

The issue boils down to whether you wish to exploit this historic moment to get the Latin Americans to move boldly on integration, and thereby put your stamp on it, or whether you prefer to let nature take its course. The pressure of events can be expected to move the Latins gradually toward integration over the next 15–20 years. And we can take our chances on the present rate of growth under the Alliance keeping the hemisphere a step ahead of social and political troubles.

I favor the Gordon–Linowitz package because:

—I believe you should take advantage of the historic moment.

—If we make our part of the deal any less, I doubt whether the Latins will be willing to make the commitments we want.

—The package is so structured that financial commitments on integration and the untying of aid will not come into play for another 18–24 months after the Latins have negotiated their Common Market Treaty.

—The FY 1968 budget already provides for the $100 million for agriculture and education for the coming fiscal year. By the time FY 1969 rolls around, the Vietnam situation hopefully will not represent the current drain and permit a further modest increase in the Alliance for Progress assistance.[3]

Walt

---

[3] According to the President's Daily Diary the meeting on OAS summit preparations was evidently rescheduled for February 11 (Johnson Library); see Document 45.

45.   Memorandum of Meeting[1]

Washington, February 11, 1967.

PARTICIPANTS

The President
Secretary Rusk
Assistant Secretary of State Lincoln Gordon
U.S. Ambassador to the Organization of American States Sol Linowitz
Mr. Walt Rostow
Mr. William Bowdler

Secretary Rusk opened the meeting by explaining the nature of the two conferences he would be attending in Buenos Aires,[2] i.e., approval and signature of OAS Charter amendments and preparation for the OAS Summit.

On the Summit meeting he described what we expected the Latin Americans to do in negotiating a Common Market. We would help them by contributing $300 million over a period of years for integration adjustment assistance after they negotiated a treaty. The Secretary mentioned that the Europeans might be persuaded to contribute the remaining $125 million which we made available to the European Monetary Agreement members.

Mr. Gordon pointed out that the $123.5 million left was being considered for possible use in supporting a world-wide agricultural diversification fund. We need a decision on which project it should be used for, assuming we can get the Europeans to relinquish their claim. The President asked Secretary Rusk and Mr. Rostow where the $125 million should be put. They both recommended the Latin American Common Market. The President told them to proceed on this basis.

Secretary Rusk next brought up the replenishment of the IDB/FSO (Inter-American Development Bank Fund for Special Operations). The President asked whether any or all of the $300 million contemplated

---

[1] Source: Johnson Library, National Security File, NSC Histories, OAS Summit Meeting 4/67, Chron. 4/1/66–3/13/67. Secret. Drafted by Bowdler. A copy was sent to Rostow. The memorandum indicates the meeting began "at approximately 1:00 p.m." and was held in the President's office.

[2] Reference is to the Third Special Inter-American Conference and the Eleventh Meeting of Consultation of Ministers of Foreign Affairs of the American Republics, held in Buenos Aires, February 15–27 and February 16–26, respectively. Documentation on both is in the National Archives and Records Administration, RG 59, Conference Files, 1966–72: Lot 67 D 586, CF 122 through CF 133; and the Johnson Library, National Security File, International Meetings and Travel File, Third Special IAC and Eleventh MFM Bilateral Papers, 2/67. Also see Document 46.

was in the FY 1968 budget. A quick check with Budget Bureau Director Schultze revealed that none had been included. Following further discussion of the amounts required by our Summit package and the inter-agency disagreement on its elements, the President said that he wanted Congressional approval before he made a commitment of the magnitude contemplated. He directed that a joint resolution be prepared, separate from the AID bill, which would place the Congress behind the Summit offer. Secretary Rusk could test the willingness of the Latin Americans at Buenos Aires to assume the commitments we want. If he finds a basis for the Summit, then we can use the time between the Buenos Aires meeting and the Summit to put the joint resolution through.

WGB

---

46.   Telegram From the Embassy in Argentina to the Department of State[1]

Buenos Aires, February 19, 1967, 0312Z.

3192/Secto 26. Eyes Only for the President and Acting Secretary from Secretary.

We have now reached the point where the opinions of all countries are in and it is possible to report general agreement that there should be a summit conference and, indeed, that a failure to hold one would have a very negative effect throughout the hemisphere. I have seen all the FonMins personally and have encountered only the friendliest reactions to you and to the US. There is general understanding of the burdens we are carrying these days and real appreciation for the personal attention which you have given to Latin American affairs and to the Alliance for Progress despite your many other problems.

As far as the ministers are concerned the fact that I am remaining over the weekend has been accepted as a compliment contrasted with the notion that my departure before the end of the conference is somehow a "walk out."[2]

---

[1] Source: National Archives and Records Administration, RG 59, Central Files 1967–69, POL 3 IA. Secret; Nodis.

[2] Rusk headed the U.S. delegation in Buenos Aires until February 21, when he was replaced by Ambassador at Large Ellsworth Bunker.

I have tried to be very realistic with my Latin colleagues about what they should expect from the US. On the subject of integration I have insisted that this is their decision. I have emphasized that if they were to move toward integration because of the possibility of modest amounts of help from the US they would move for the wrong reasons and integration efforts could not succeed. They understand fully that we must consult with the Congress before making commitments and that, in such consultations, we must have specific information on what our friends in Latin America really intend to do. We cannot have them come up with some meaningless phrases involving the word "integration" and expect that we will come forward with substantial additional assistance. It would take the Congress only ten minutes to prick any such bubble and ask for specifics. Somewhat to my surprise, I am beginning to feel (after a full day's discussion today) that they really are quite serious about integration. They seem to recognize that rapid modernization will pass them by unless they enlarge their markets among themselves and open up the possibilities provided by the internal American market for US and the enlarged European Common Market.

Again in the direction of realism I have stated quite simply that they must compete with the rest of the world for private investment, that private investment cannot be commanded by US or anyone else but must be attracted by them, and that if they fail to attract it they cannot expect the same investments to come through the public sector at the taxpayer's expense.

I have also tried, in personal conversations with ministers, to remind them that a meeting of Presidents is an informal meeting at the highest political level and is not an occasion to resolve every trivial issue which twenty governments might have in mind. Some of the nervousness about the need for "adequate preparation" arises from an unrealistic view of what Presidents will do when they get together. You will not wade through stacks of black boots but will share your political and other problems with each other and give direction to the grand strategy of the hemisphere. My impression is that the FonMins will greatly simplify the recommendations they make to their Presidents. From our own point of view, it seems to me that the principal benefit to come from a summit meeting is the enlistment of public interest in the hemisphere, in the successes and prospects of the Alliance for Progress and in your own personal commitment to what happens to ordinary men and women. Our own people have been hearing almost nothing else but Viet-Nam, President de Gaulle and China, and hemispheric affairs have dropped somewhat into the background. We will need this public attention as a defense against Congressional assaults on the Alliance for Progress.

Outstanding among the FonMins have been Mexican, Chilean, Argentine, Brazilian and Colombian colleagues. It is a great relief to find Chile in a cooperative mood and I have no doubt this reflects the growing personal relations between you and President Frei. Tony Carrillo has been a stalwart friend.

I have emphasized in talks that we are not pressing for a summit meeting if there is any reluctance on their part. Their response has been one of alarm that we might lose interest. I think they realize that they are competing for the attention of the American people with many other problems and that it is in their interest to find a way to dramatize hemispheric cooperation.

I have tried to keep our Congressional delegation involved as much as possible although private meetings of ministers have limited their participation. They came, understandably enough, with considerable skepticism about whether the Latin Americans really mean business on integration. It is a skepticism which I myself shared. But if our Latin friends demonstrate that they mean business and are prepared to take some additional tangible steps, I think our Congressional friends will be both surprised and impressed.

We have had press backgrounders every day since my arrival and I will try to have a wrap up with them before I depart for Washington.[3]

Rusk

---

[3] For texts of the resolution of the Eleventh Meeting of Consultation of Ministers of Foreign Affairs of the American Republics and the final act of the Third Special Inter-American Conference, see Department of State *Bulletin,* March 20, 1967, pp. 473–476. The amendment of the OAS Charter—the so-called Protocol of Buenos Aires—was adopted on February 27, becoming effective 3 years later upon ratification of two-thirds of the member states.

47.   Memorandum From the President's Special Assistant (Rostow) to President Johnson in Texas[1]

Washington, March 6, 1967.

SUBJECT

Meeting the Latin American Experts on the Summit

I met yesterday at my home for lunch with Milton Eisenhower, Adolf Berle, Tom Mann, Jack Vaughn, Linc Gordon and Sol Linowitz to discuss the Latin American Summit.

We had a useful three-and-a-half hour session reviewing the Summit package and joint resolution, discussing the focus of your speech at the Summit and examining some new ideas which you might advance.

These are the highlights:

—All thought that the Summit package was well structured to get at the root of Latin America's basic development problems.

—All agreed that time was running short in Latin America and the moment for decisive action was now. The Summit offered a historic opportunity for the Latin Americans to make the necessary political commitments and for you to redefine US policy.

—All agreed that we should encourage the Latin Americans to move rapidly down the path of economic integration as the single, most important step they can take to speed up the development process and transform economic and social situations. Our help should be closely geared to their performance.

—Milton Eisenhower stressed that the Summit gave you the chance to dramatize at the highest level that our relation with the Latin Americans is that of junior partner and that while money is important and we will help, it can only be a supplement to their own commitment and action.

—Adolf Berle focused on the trade issue, pointing out that if meaningful help for the LDC's does not come from the Kennedy Round negotiations, we may have to think in terms of extending regional preferences for Latin America.

---

[1] Source: Johnson Library, National Security File, International Meetings and Travel File, Inter-American Summit Meeting, Vol. II. Confidential. The memorandum is an uninitialed copy; a handwritten note indicates that it was "sent via wire to Ranch." According to the President's Daily Diary, Johnson was at his Ranch in Texas, March 2–6. (Ibid.)

—Jack Vaughn observed the need to come to grips with the birth rate and the urban slum problem, but all recognized the difficulties in doing anything meaningful at the Summit in these two areas.

On themes for your Summit speech:

—Milton Eisenhower suggested that in emphasizing economic integration you point to the dramatic shift in policy which this represents for us. Historically, we have discouraged it. Only in the last ten years has our thinking shifted. You would be the first President to give it a major thrust forward.

—Adolf Berle said you should point to the progress made in recent years in strengthening democracy and getting governments to work for the people as never before.

—Both Eisenhower and Berle urged that you stress that the US is not in the business of building empires but wants to help others in this hemisphere, and elsewhere, to build up themselves. Berle had an excellent quote from Seneca about there being no possibility of lasting friendship except between equals.

In the realm of new ideas, the group thought we should examine these areas:

—speeding up a satellite communications system for Latin America;

—help in promoting educational TV;

—development of research libraries on microfilm;

—cooperation in development of "food from sea" resources;

—development of protein concentrates for child-feeding programs; and

—computerized access to information, perhaps drawing on NIH's development of an electronic library in medicine.

---

48. Memorandum From the President's Special Assistant (Rostow)[1]

Washington, March 7, 1967.

MEMORANDUM FOR

Secretary Rusk
Under Secretary of the Treasury Barr
AID Administrator Gaud
Budget Director Schultze

---

[1] Source: Johnson Library, National Security File, NSC Histories, OAS Summit Meeting, Chron. 4/1/66–3/13/67. Confidential.

SUBJECT

Meeting with the President on OAS Summit Preparations on March 1, 1967[2]

So that the participants in the meeting will have the same understanding of the decisions made by the President, I recapitulate them as follows:

1. *Standby resources for integration adjustment assistance*

The President approved obtaining Congressional support for the United States providing standby resources through the IDB to be matched by the Latin Americans for integration adjustment assistance to facilitate the transition to a fully functioning Latin American Common Market once appropriate steps have been taken by the Latin Americans toward progressive establishment of such a Market. The President agreed that in discussions with Congress an order of magnitude figure of ¼ and ½ billion dollars, to be furnished over a period of years (probably not beginning until 1970), could be used.

Under Secretary Barr observed that Congressman Reuss is not in favor of economic integration and can be expected to oppose adjustment assistance. The President asked Secretary Barr and Ambassador Linowitz to speak with Congressman Reuss in the light of the Buenos Aires meeting decisions.

2. *Replenishment of the IDB/FSO*

The President directed that authorization for 3 years and appropriation of $300 million for the first year be sought during the current session of Congress.

3. *Additional Alliance for Progress assistance for education and agriculture*

The President agreed to increase Alliance for Progress assistance for education and agriculture by $100 million in FY 1968 (it is already in the budget) and an average of $200 million for the following four years, dependent on demonstrated need and self-help.

He expressed a preference for obtaining a specific Congressional commitment for the full amount, but agreed to be guided by what Congressional leaders think should be done about the Summit package price tag in the Joint Resolution. (See paragraph no 5.)

In response to Budget Director Schultze's observation that a substantial portion of the increase for education and agriculture would

---

[2] According to the President's Daily Diary, Johnson held a meeting on March 1, 5:42–6:50 p.m., "to discuss plans for Latin American Summit meeting." The attendees included Rusk, Sayre, Linowitz, Gaud, Rostow, Bowdler, Under Secretary of the Treasury Joseph W. Barr, and Deputy Assistant Secretary of the Treasury for International Affairs Winthrop Knowlton. (Ibid.) No other record of the meeting was found.

necessarily be for projects with a high local cost component, the President said that he understood this and wanted the funds to be made available for sound projects in the two sectors with this understanding.

4. *Modification of tying arrangements for capital project loans to permit hemisphere-wide procurement*

The President agreed to modify tying arrangements in our loan policy toward Latin America with respect to project, but not program or local cost, lending to permit hemisphere-wide procurement after the Latin Americans begin major steps toward a Common Market and with subsequent tying to the US through the Special Letter of Credit procedure.

Under Secretary Barr asked that Treasury's opposition to the modification be recorded.

5. *Joint Resolution on the Summit*

The President reviewed and approved the Joint Resolution (copy attached)[3] and directed that consultation on the Resolution begin right away. The process should be started with the Congressional delegation that went to the Buenos Aires meeting: Senators Smathers and Hickenlooper, and Congressmen Selden and Mailliard. Senator Mansfield should be contacted next. Further action will depend on the advice obtained from these contacts. The President is prepared to meet with the Congressional leadership if this is desirable and necessary.

The President also directed that State brief the Council for Latin America on the resolution and get them to sell it to key Congressional members such as Dirksen, Hickenlooper and Ford. In response to Ambassador Linowitz's inquiry as to whether he would be willing to receive the Council for Latin America group when they meet in Washington next week, the President replied that he would if he were in town.

With respect to the text of the draft joint resolution, the President accepted Secretary Rusk's recommendation that the paragraph on Europe be deleted.

The President expressed a preference for including a global cost figure for the Summit package in the final operative paragraph. He thought the Congress would also want to specify what it was agreeing to and would not be satisfied with amounts expressed only in hearings. But he agreed that Congressional leaders should be sounded out on this point. He is prepared to go the way they recommend.

WR

---

[3] Attached but not printed.

49.   Telephone Conversation Between President Johnson and the Representative to the Council of the Organization of American States (Linowitz)[1]

Washington, April 4, 1967, 8:35 a.m.

President: Sol, how are you?

Linowitz: I'm fine, Mr. President.

President: I was talking to Morse this morning. I think the best way now that we've got this thing in shape where we ask the Congress to consult with us and to give us their views on what we should do in regard to this program that we brought back from the Foreign Ministers meeting. The House has expressed themselves and the Senate has said that they do not want to do anything that would go beyond saying that they would consider considering it. That's about the best way I can read that resolution. It just says we'll give consideration to consideration.[2]

Linowitz: Yes, sir. There were only nine men in that Senate who said that.

President: Yeah, but they're the ones that are leading it, and they have more—We couldn't get anything but a zero on our end of it. They wouldn't either stand up or—So I told Morse that I thought that he ought to talk to Mansfield who is out in Montana and hold it up until he comes back.

Linowitz: Yes. He's not due back till the end of the week though.

President: And I had much rather see it just—I don't see anything to be gained by bringing it out and having a mean debate. I don't think that—

Linowitz: I agree.

---

[1] Source: Johnson Library, Recordings and Transcripts, Recording of telephone conversation between President Johnson and Sol Linowitz, Tape F67.11, Side A, PNO 1. No classification marking. This transcript was prepared in the Office of the Historian specifically for this volume.

[2] In a special message to Congress on March 13, President Johnson presented a proposal to increase support to the Alliance for Progress and asked Congress to show its support by approving a joint resolution before the Punta del Este conference. (*Public Papers of the Presidents of the United States: Lyndon B. Johnson, 1967*, Book I, pp. 318–324. Although the House approved a modified version, the Senate Foreign Relations Committee rejected the resolution on April 3, opting instead for its own resolution by a vote of 9–0. A spokesman for the administration subsequently called the Senate resolution "worse than useless." The President went to Punta del Este without a formal expression of Congressional support. (*Congressional Quarterly Almanac, 1967*, pp. 331–333)

President: I don't think that you can get anywhere that way. And I think then we—It will destroy our ability to make any real commitment, but we can see how far they want to go.

Linowitz: Yes, sir. The only question, sir: there was talk of the possibility of getting the committee to reconsider. Do you think that—

President: I don't believe they'll do that. Fulbright's an adamant man and I do not believe we can beat the chairman of the committee any more than you can beat the President on who he's going to appoint as his appointments secretary. He's just got that authority, and he's got that position, he's got that power. And this is a gesture to the Congress that a President would ask them to express themselves. Most Presidents don't ask them—they've done it two or three times—but it's generally they go on and make a commitment and treaty and send it up and negotiate without any resolutions or anything. Now if they don't want to be consulted, I think our public position can be: we sought to consult them, we were ready to put on our hearings. We'll know next time if we submit something, we ought to submit it by putting the amount in it and asking just for an authorization. And I thought that if we'd bring Tom Mann and Jack Vaughn and Adolph Berle and Milton Eisenhower and David Rockefeller and all these folks in for the hearings that we've been having up there—just arguing back and forth, and they could give the positive aspects of it—I would have thought that it would have been better, but our people didn't think so. So—

Linowitz: Did you know that I put that actually to both Morse and Hickenlooper and both of them said that it would be a mistake.

President: Yes. Well—

Linowitz: So—I think they were wrong. I agree with you, sir, that it would have been helpful to build us a stronger record.

President: Yeah, then they could have—Fulbright couldn't have said that we hadn't had a hearing and we didn't, we hadn't presented our case. Well anyway, I don't want us to get crossways, so I have told Mike Manatos to try to talk to Mansfield, so you ought, you and Macomber[3] ought, to get with Mike. I think the best thing to do is leave it in the committee and just say: "Well the House acted on it; the Senate chose not to go further than to say that they'd give us consideration." Now we don't need a resolution for that.

Linowitz: That's right.

President: If they pass it, it won't have any more effect on the conference or on me than it would to just stay in the committee and then it would have to go to conference committee.

---

[3] William B. Macomber, Jr., Assistant Secretary of State for Congressional Relations.

Linowitz: At the press conference yesterday I read the latter part of your message in which you talked about your having the executive authority to do this but you wanted to go having first consulted with the Congress—and that's exactly what you did.

President: Yeah. Well, now we've done that.

Linowitz: The record is clear.

President: We've done it. So I would try then to get a hold of our friends or talk to Morse and anyone else on the committee that would be friendly, I guess Hickenlooper—

Linowitz: Yes, sir.

President: And just say: "Now it appears to us we don't have the votes without a big fight. The President wanted to consult with the Congress. He has. They've had a chance to express themselves, the committee's expressed itself, and it says in effect it doesn't want to do anything." So we'll just leave it there. We'll go on to the conference, if they don't bomb us out down there. I've been very concerned about that. I don't like these intelligence reports I read about them.[4]

Linowitz: Well, you know, sir, that we've been in close touch and—On the assumption that you'll be arriving at 11 in the morning: there isn't any problem that anybody can foresee before you get out of Montevideo and to Punta del Este. I agree with you that this action they've taken—you notice they did that to the Brazilians too. It's just troublemakers who are hoping, I think, exactly what is happening will happen: that is people will begin to get a little worried about it. I think these, the people there don't, the Communists there don't want to have this conference. They think it's not going to do them any good, and I think they've—We probably will get more of this, a few here and there. But from what I can gather—and I've been in touch with Hoyt down in Montevideo and I've talked to the Uruguayans here on a regular basis—if we work it as we are now planning, arriving around 11—because I guess Frei is coming in at noon and you're coming in at 11—we'll be out of there and into Punta del Este before the lunch hour and before any of these people are even around. So I think that's going to work out all right. We're at least keeping an eye on it, sir.

President: Good. I would do that. I told them to take whatever people they needed. They want to borrow some military people to [wear] civilian clothes over there. And I sure think we ought to watch that very, very carefully.

---

[4] A recent intelligence assessment judged that "the risk to President Johnson during the course of this trip will be slight—though greater than was the case with his visit to Mexico a year ago." (SNIE 98–67, "Security Conditions in Uruguay," March 23; Central Intelligence Agency, Job 79–R01012A, O/DDI Registry)

Linowitz: Yes, sir, I agree.

President: I think that they can cause a Nixon incident[5] very easy. And I heard a lot of ambassadors—I don't know, at least their personal opinion, but I heard a lot of them at the Ranch this week[6] say awful nice things about what you're doing, and you evidently have a very good rapport with them and understanding with them.

Linowitz: Well, I do. I wish I had done better for you up at the Senate.

President: Well, we just can't do that. That's not you; that's not you and I don't think it's me. I think Fulbright is very unhappy because he wasn't Secretary of State, and he was this way with President Kennedy, and I had to nurse him all during the Bay of Pigs. I had him down and worked with him because he couldn't, and then he took the position that we ought to bomb Cuba out, just the opposite of what he's doing now.

Linowitz: Well, I can't help the feeling that I let you down there, sir.

President: No, no. Not at all. No, we just haven't got that situation. And I think that this will have rather serious repercussions on our whole aid program. My judgment is they just don't have the votes there for aid this year. That's what I'm afraid of. I think yours is the most popular of all, and if you can't get them to commit on yours, why I don't know what's going to happen with the others.

Linowitz: I think that's true. There's one other thing, sir. I do, upon reflection, I do believe that Fulbright has chosen the worst possible place at which to take his stand.

President: Yes, I do too.

Linowitz: I just think that this was—if we could have picked a battleground, an issue on which we could say "this is how we ought to proceed, this is what we've done, this is a case we can make"—I don't think we could have picked it better than this one, and that's the one he chose to make an issue on.

President: That's right. Now how do we get that line drawn over the country?

Linowitz: Well, I'm meeting with Max Frankel of *The New York Times* in about 20 minutes. What I'm trying to do is, I've been doing

---

[5] Reference is to Richard M. Nixon's trip to South America, April–May 1958, when demonstrators in Lima and Caracas showered the Vice President with spit and stones. For documentation on the trip, see *Foreign Relations, 1958–1960*, vol. V, pp. 222–248.

[6] On April 1 Johnson hosted a barbecue at his Texas Ranch for Latin American Ambassadors to the United States and the OAS, and other guests. (Johnson Library, President's Daily Diary)

constantly is, at least getting to these people. I know that Walt talked to *The New York Times* yesterday. I was on the phone yesterday with Punch Sulzberger,[7] and the editorial today is pretty good—not as good as it ought to be, but it's pretty good. And I'm just trying to get this around to the news people so that they see this in the context. I had a good chance to talk to Scotty Reston[8] before he took off. I hoped he was going to do a piece on consultation, but this is exactly what these people up on the Hill have been talking about and that no President has ever done more to give advance consultation for a meeting than what you did in this case, and for that you get blamed. I've been trying to do this with the people across. [*sic*] I was going to go on "Meet the Press" this Sunday, but I can't, of course, because they're going to have this strike again, but I'm trying it anyway, sir.

President: Well, I think that's very good and I think that's quite important. I think you ought to point out to Frankel that this barbecue thing was not a great elaborate deal that he pictured yesterday. He said five hundred people, four or five hundred people: we had a hundred and four, I think.

Linowitz: Hell, he was down there. I saw him at the press briefing yesterday and I said: "where did you get your nose count?"

President: [Laughter] And he had it very elaborate, and very outlandish, almost like a bribe, and then winding up, I thought, that way, slap-happy stuff. I thought it was a little ugly, his article. But anyway, I think that we ought to say that we have tried to consult with them, the House has given us their opinion, and Fulbright and his group have said in effect that they don't want us to make any overtures to Latin America in this regard at this time until the Latin Americans act and then they want to take a look at it in the light of their action. Now that's the effect of what they've said. So we will go, and we will listen, and that was what I told Walt to say in his backgrounder. He did, but didn't quite get it over. I read it. The impression we've got to leave is to play this thing down as much as we can. We did that with Guam and we did it with Manila.[9] But they play it up, and they boost it, and they say "Great Big Elaborate Conference." Then when nothing really shocking comes out of it, then they say it's a failure. Now that's what they'll do again, so you better start Frankel off and say: "Now I want you to keep these notes, so when the conference is over, you won't say we misled you. We're going there as we did in the Manila Conference,

---

[7] Arthur O. Sulzberger, publisher and president of *The New York Times*.

[8] James B. Reston, associate editor of *The New York Times*.

[9] Reference is to two conferences on Vietnam in Manila (October 1966), and Guam (March 1967).

not to run it, not to ram something down their throat. The future of Latin America depends largely upon the Latins themselves; and we're going to be an interested brother, sitting there, hearing their reports, and getting their recommendations; and we're not going to try to force anything down them. We're not going to try to press anything upon them. We would have liked to have been able to have said that 'if you will do these various things that you talk about doing, then we will support you to this extent.' But the Congress doesn't want to do that, and we're not going to be angry about it, not going to fight about it, not going to get into any personal brawls about it, not going to mention anybody's name. We're just going to make it clear that we can't say what we want to say, what we had intended to say, but we will come back, and we will point out what they say, and then submit our recommendations again." But let's play it down just as much as we possibly can, and say to him that we're just going to be a good listener.

Linowitz: May I just say, sir, two things. First, if I might suggest, I think it's awful important not to convey the suggestion that you didn't have, and that you don't have, full authority to speak as President on what you would like to do when you get there, and that this isn't interfering at all with that. What you had hoped to do was to go down there and say "not only I but the Congress gives you this assurance." That all you can do now is say "this is what I would like to have accomplished, but, of course, I'll have to go back and see if Congress will go along with me." Is that appropriate to say that that's the difference in the two?

President: Yes. Yes. Yes.

Linowitz: Because it seems to me, that one of the things that the aginners may now try to do is say this has cut off, or tried to cut off, your own executive authority, which is nonsense. And that's the other side that troubles me a little bit, that the "worse than useless" phrase has created the impression that it's really put a damper onto your authority to go there and do whatever you think is right. And I just think that would be inconsistent too.

President: OK. All right.

Linowitz: OK, sir.

50.   Memorandum of Conversation[1]

US/MC–14   Punta del Este, Uruguay, April 11, 1967, 6 p.m.

SUBJECT

    Cuban Subversion in Venezuela

PARTICIPANTS

United States	Venezuela
President Johnson	President Leoni
Mr. Walt Rostow	Sr. Ignacio Iribarren Borges,
Assistant Secretary Gordon	Foreign Minister of Venezuela
Assistant Secretary Solomon	
Mr. Neil A. Seidenman, Interpreter	

The President assured President Leoni that we are equally concerned with Venezuela about the matter of communist aggression. We have been gratified by Venezuela's actions against Cuba. We support Venezuela's position against Cuba in the OAS. We believe that measures against Cuba by the OAS need even more tightening up. We would also hope that Venezuela will have suggestions for further moves in this direction. We will welcome all the noise that Venezuela can make about Cuba in the OAS.

President Leoni mentioned the assassination of the brother of Minister Iribarren Borges.[2] He said that Venezuela has evidence that points to Cuban responsibility for this act, including material that has come to them in print from Havana. Venezuela intends to make a case against Cuba on this score in the OAS. Before initiating this action, Venezuela is carefully examining all of the details involved, inasmuch as it wishes to gather sufficient and convincing evidence and consult with President Johnson and the State Department as well as with the governments of other member countries. Venezuela wants to proceed in this way, so that whatever decision is taken—and Venezuela itself will not

---

[1] Source: National Archives and Records Administration, RG 59, Central Files 1967–69, POL 7 IA–SUMMIT. Confidential. Drafted by Seidenman and approved in the White House on April 28. The memorandum of conversation is part 3 of 3; for parts 1 and 2, see Documents 540 and 541. According to George Christian, the meeting was held at Leoni's residence in Punta del Este. (Press statement, April 11; Johnson Library, President's Daily Diary) President Johnson attended the Punta del Este Conference April 11–April 14.

[2] Dr. Julio Iribarren Borges, former Director of Social Security, was assassinated on March 3.

be asking for any specific decision—it will be on a unanimous basis, if this is possible.

The President reiterated his desire to cooperate with the Venezuelans in the work of facing the trials they are going through. He reiterated our support for Venezuela's cause in the OAS against Cuba, which he said he hoped they would pursue with aggressiveness; we want to be of help in the matter of military equipment if we can—because we don't want Venezuela to have to wait one minute to chase the communists.[3]

---

[3] For further discussion of this matter, see Document 541.

---

51.   Memorandum of Conversation[1]

Punta del Este, Uruguay, April 13, 1967, 1 p.m.

SUBJECT

U.S. Policy Regarding the Alliance for Progress

PARTICIPANTS

United States
President Lyndon B. Johnson
Assistant Secretary Gordon
Assistant Secretary Solomon
Deputy U.S. Coordinator David Bronheim
Mr. Fernando A. Van Reigersberg, Interpreter

Ecuador
President Otto Arosemena
Minister of Industries and Commerce Galo Pico Mantilla
Minister of Finance Jose Federico Intriago Arrata

Responding to a question by Arosemena as to why the suggestions he had proposed in his speech before the Presidents at the

---

[1] Source: National Archives and Records Administration, RG 59, Central Files 1967–69, POL 1 US. Confidential. Drafted by Reigersberg and Fisher on April 18 and approved in the White House on April 26. The memorandum is part 4 of 4. The full text of all four parts is in telegram 182377 to Quito, April 26. (Ibid.)

Plenary Session that afternoon[2] had not been approved and accepted, President Johnson stated that he had not wanted to get into the debate himself, since he felt that the Summit Conference document had been sufficiently well-prepared in advance and therefore satisfactory to all. He felt that the Latin Americans themselves should express their own views and that the American President should listen to their comments without actively participating in the debate. He assured President Arosemena that he would do everything possible to help the Latin American countries, but that his own position and internal problems should be understood by everybody. One difficulty is to try to convince people in the lower income brackets in the U.S. that they must contribute to foreign aid. Once this is achieved, it becomes very difficult to convince them that they should continue supporting assistance to Latin America when one of its presidents says that loans from the United States are tendered under unacceptable conditions. American taxpayers communicate frequently with their Congressional representatives, and if dissatisfied, make their views known in no uncertain terms. At the present time, the Foreign Aid Bill is the most unpopular piece of legislation facing the Congress.

The President said he had hope that the Latin American presidents would give him arguments which he could use to convince members of Congress of the importance of aid to Latin America. In his own speech, he had promised assistance in such fields as educational television, marine research, research on production of fish concentrates for food, and promotion of science and technology. The United States had increased its contribution to the Alliance for Progress by 35% in the last three years, but a recent request for additional funds had been turned down in Congressional Committee. He repeated that he needed arguments to try to change the views held by some United States Senators who appeared to be as difficult to convince as was the President of Ecuador, but that tonight he had fewer arguments to get the Foreign Aid Bill passed than he had twenty-four hours ago. U.S. press headlines tonight would probably make things more difficult and would probably compel the President of the United States to go back to his country able only to tell his people that in spite of everything it is still a moral obligation to support foreign aid.

---

[2] Arosemena suggested that the Alliance for Progress must adjust to meet the economic realities of 1967; the terms required for assistance were unacceptable—the borrowing country was forced to contribute funds "above its capacity." Arosemena also questioned why the United States "should be so concerned with democracy in a noble but distant country such as Viet Nam," when democracy was so obviously in need of support in Latin America. An English translation of Arosemena's address is ibid., ARA/EP/E Files: Lot 70 D 247, POL 3 Summit Conference.

The President discussed the historical background of the Summit Conference, indicating that while initially he had been reluctant to attend, he felt that his presence here would give new thrust to the Alliance for Progress. What really disappointed him was that, after being told in Washington that he was trying to do too much for the Latin Americans, in Punta del Este some had said that he was doing too little.

President Arosemena stated that he was very pleased to have met President Johnson personally, and that he felt that he was a different man from the kind of person Latin America thinks he is. He had felt that the President was a very human, practical, and compassionate man who faced many problems and many difficulties. It was not Ecuador's intention to cause any difficulties for anyone. He suggested that Latin Americans must get to know President Johnson as he had and that many American Senators, including Senator Fulbright, should come to Latin America so that they could share the burden which was now carried solely by President Johnson. He further stated that people in the United States erroneously feel that Latin Americans do not pay enough taxes, while the Ecuadorean Government collects as many taxes as possible; if it collected any more, it might destroy the country.

After referring to the cost of the war in Viet Nam, to the increase in Alliance for Progress funds, and to his attempt to get more public and private funds channelled toward Latin America, the President emphasized that both he and the Ecuadorean President really worked for the same objectives, namely, to help the poor and hungry people.

President Arosemena said that he wanted to help, but that he had to face problems in his own country. He stated that he wanted President Johnson to go back to the United States with the support and backing of 300 million Latin Americans, and that this could be achieved easily by just adding two or three sentences to the Presidential Declaration. He stated that no U.S. monetary commitments would be necessary, and that the inclusion of these two or three phrases would give President Johnson the unanimous support of Latin America. He added that the Latin American presidents were really on his side, although they did not have the courage to come out and say so. He felt that, if he would sign the present Declaration, he would not be able to go back to Ecuador because his people consider the document a step backward from the Punta del Este Charter. While President Johnson had proved to him that the Alliance for Progress had been more vigorous in the last three years and had provided more funds than in any previous period, unfortunately, Latin America was not aware of this; the people did not know this, and they should be told.

President Arosemena asked President Johnson to help gain approval for adding a couple of sentences to the document so that he too could defend the Declaration as a worthwhile document. He suggested that the President could justify these additions before United States Senators by pointing out the advantages of preventing a popular upheaval rather than have to put one down after it got started, and also by the fact that United States loans are not really gifts, but rather down payments on an insurance policy aimed at protecting the hemisphere against communism and avoiding having the United States face a "gigantic Cuba" south of its borders.

The President once more referred to the highlights of his speech and to his personal pledge to assist the Latin American countries. He noted that the schools, classrooms, roads, highways and bridges that have been built are physical evidence that much is being done.

Assistant Secretary Gordon stated that every President and Foreign Minister attending the meeting agreed that the program for the future was a step forward and not a step backward from the Alliance.

The President said he could not understand how the programs which he had outlined in his speech could be interpreted as stagnation. He suggested that the President of Ecuador should consider a hypothetical situation in which Ecuador would have to assist the poor people of the United States, and in which after taxing humble Ecuadoreans heavily to obtain the assistance to send to the United States, the Americans would express their dissatisfaction and their President would say in a public meeting that assistance from Ecuador was insufficient, was slow because of red tape, and therefore was unacceptable.

President Arosemena stated that all he wanted was a slight change in the document and asked the President whether two sentences from his speech to the Summit Conference could be included in the final Declaration. This would satisfy Ecuador's requirements and provide for unanimity.

The President answered that he did not know whether the other Presidents would agree to such a procedure, and since the pertinent sentences were not then available, the matter should be discussed further between President Arosemena and Assistant Secretaries Gordon and Solomon. Assistant Secretary Gordon said he would be unavailable due to a conflicting meeting and it was agreed Assistant Secretary Solomon would meet President Arosemena later.[3]

---

[3] According to an attached handwritten note, much of the last paragraph was inserted by Solomon, reflecting his "annoyance at having been saddled by LG[ordon] with the dirty work." (Fitzgibbons to Carroll Brown, April 24; ibid.) No record of Solomon's meeting with Arosemena has been found.

52.   Circular Telegram From the Department of State to All American Republic Posts[1]

Washington, April 17, 1967, 7:44 p.m.

176889. Subject: Summit Assessment. From Gordon.

1. Following is our summary assessment of Summit outcome. We will send you full sets of Summit documents[2] as soon as possible.

2. Ultimate results of Summit decisions will not be known for number of years and will depend upon degree of implementation of actions agreed at Summit. However, we consider Summit meeting and Declaration signed there definite successes. Our reasons follow.

a. When President Johnson agreed a year ago to join with Latin American leaders to explore proposed Summit meeting, we saw meeting as opportunity for:

(1) Agreement on a few significant, concrete actions which, building on experience and achievements of first years of Alliance for Progress, could result in needed accelerated economic and social advances in future.

(2) Re-emphasis on cooperative approach, under which Latin American initiative and self-help would be stressed at same time that U.S. would reassure Latin America on its concern and assistance.

(3) Strengthening of personal relations among leaders of Hemisphere.

b. Substantive content of Declaration of Presidents of America signed at Punta del Este,[3] which is result of long and painstaking preparatory process in which every signatory government (except Trinidad and Tobago) was deeply involved, goes beyond what might reasonably have been expected a year ago. It includes:

(1) A stronger, broader, and much more specific Latin American commitment to a Common Market than seemed likely when process began.

---

[1] Source: National Archives and Records Administration, RG 59, Central Files, 1967–69, POL 7 IA SUMMIT. Confidential; Priority. Drafted by Eaton, cleared by Sayre, and approved by Gordon.

[2] The documentary record of the Punta del Este Conference is ibid., Conference Files, 1966–1972: Lot 67 D 586, CF 151 through CF 162; Washington National Records Center, RG 59, ARA/IPA Files, FRC 71 A 6682, Item 31, Meeting of American Presidents—1967; ibid., ARA/OAS Files, FRC 71 A 6682, Item 50, Meeting of American Presidents—1967; and Johnson Library, National Security File, International Meetings and Travel File, Punta del Este, 4/12–14/67.

[3] For text of the declaration, see American Foreign Policy: Current Documents, 1967, pp. 673–685, or Department of State Bulletin, May 8, 1967, pp. 712–721. Arosemena refused to sign the declaration, the only attending Latin American head of state to so refuse.

(2) Increased attention to multinational projects which will facilitate integration.

(3) Increased emphasis and better focus on two lagging but key sectors of the development process—agriculture and education.

(4) A special emphasis on science and technology which grew stronger as the preparatory process progressed, and culminated in a commitment to an Inter-American Science Program including several specific points.

(5) A useful (although not as strong as we had hoped for at one stage) statement on limitation of military expenditures.

(6) From the U.S., most importantly, (a) agreement to increased assistance in support of the greater Latin American efforts; and (b) in a major new trade policy departure, willingness to consult carefully within the U.S. and with other industrialized countries on generalized trade preferences, for limited time periods, by all industrialized countries in favor of all developing countries.

c. As stated above, all signatory governments (except Trinidad and Tobago) were deeply involved in preparatory process and final Declaration is truly inter-American document.

d. Personal relationships developed among Presidents during Summit were in almost all cases very satisfactory and should be helpful in future.

3. While reactions of other delegations to Summit varied in degree, all but Ecuador seemed agree that meeting had on balance been clear success. President Frei was most categorical and emphatic in so stating. President Diaz Ordaz made statement which probably most nearly expressed consensus when he said that while all might have wanted more from Summit, negotiators had achieved what was possible, and what they had achieved was a substantial advance. Arosemena's negative position was not supported by any other Latin American President.

4. Press reaction to the Summit from within the U.S. has been strikingly and almost uniformly favorable. From reports we have had thus far, press reaction from Latin America has been uneven, perhaps reflecting to considerable extent lack of understanding of full meaning of decisions reached at Summit. In particular, many Latin journalists apparently failed to appreciate significance President Johnson's statement on point 2(b)(6) above.

5. The job now before all the OAS Members is to follow up on the Summit decisions with sustained action. In some fields, notably economic integration, the lead must be taken by Latin America. In others, such as trade and the regional science and technology efforts, we shall be working jointly with them or, as in the case of preferences, following up ourselves with the other industrialized countries. In the expanded programs in agriculture, education, and health, the next steps should come from the national Latin American authorities concerned. The same is true on elimination of unnecessary military expenditures.

In the whole process of implementation, we should maintain the attitude of urgency set forth in the President's April 13 speech,[4] and make clear that we view the Summit objectives as serious undertakings.

6. You may draw on the foregoing assessment as you deem useful in both official and private contacts.

Rusk

---

[4] For text of the speech, see *Public Papers of the Presidents of the United States: Lyndon B. Johnson, 1967*, Book I, pp. 446–449. For other statements made during the conference, see ibid., pp. 442–446 and 449–451.

---

53. Memorandum From the President's Special Assistant (Rostow) to President Johnson[1]

Washington, May 12, 1967.

Mr. President:

The Venezuelan security forces report that they have captured a guerrilla infiltration force coming from Cuba. They claim 12 prisoners (4 of whom are Cuban), the boat and outboard motor in which they landed, US $10,000 in 50 dollar bills, and quantities of ammunition and other supplies. Interrogation of the prisoners reveals that another landing from Cuba can be expected in the next few days.

CIA is trying to verify these reports. If the information is fully borne out, there will be a strong—if not stronger case—for OAS action against Cuba than there was following the discovery of the Cuban arms cache in Venezuela in 1963. The 1963 incident led to the Meeting of Foreign Ministers in July 1964 which applied diplomatic and economic sanctions against Castro.

The resolution of the Foreign Ministers also contained this warning:

"To warn the Government of Cuba that if it should persist in carrying out acts that possess characteristics of aggression and intervention against one or more of the member states of the Organization, the member states shall preserve their essential rights as sovereign states by the use of self-defense in either individual or collective form, which could go so far as resort to armed force, until such time as the Organ

---

[1] Source: Johnson Library, National Security File, Country File, Venezuela, Vol. III, 12/66–12/68. Secret.

of Consultation takes measures to guarantee the peace and security of the hemisphere."[2]

If the case is an airtight one, we may find the Venezuelans moving in the OAS for action pursuant to this warning.[3]

Walt

---

[2] For full text of the resolution, see *American Foreign Policy: Current Documents, 1964*, pp. 328–334, or Department of State *Bulletin*, August 10, 1964, pp. 181–182.

[3] The President wrote the following instruction at the bottom of the memorandum: "Why don't we provide leadership quietly now. L"

---

54.   Memorandum From William G. Bowdler of the National Security Council Staff to the President's Special Assistant (Rostow)[1]

Washington, May 15, 1967.

Walt—

I met this morning with State and CIA to review the latest information on the Cuban landing in Venezuela and to see how we can provide some "quiet leadership".

The facts in the case are as I described them in staff meeting this morning, except that CIA thinks the second rubber raft foundered and did not make it back to the mother ship.

The Embassy reports that the Venezuelans are more aroused over this incident than during the arms cache in 1963.[2] All major Venezuelan parties have publicly condemned the Cubans and called for a vigorous response. Only a small centrist party and the far left have withheld comment. The incident must be acutely embarrassing to the Venezuelan Communist Party which has been trying to resume the "via pacifica" line.

As of this afternoon, the Venezuelan OAS Delegation had taken no action to call for a meeting of the OAS Council to ask for collective action. This probably means that the Venezuelans are still debating whether to move in the OAS or the UN.

---

[1] Source: Johnson Library, National Security File, Country File, Cuba, Bowdler File, Vol. II, 2/66–7/67. Confidential.

[2] In telegram 6016 from Caracas, May 14. (National Archives and Records Administration, RG 59, Central Files 1967–69, POL 23–7 CUBA)

In considering the forum for OAS action and the measures which might be taken, the group concluded:

1. The only forum where meaningful obligatory action could be taken is a Meeting of Foreign Ministers under the Rio Treaty. This was the body which acted in 1963–64.

2. The OAS Council, under the special authority given to it by the 1962 MFM, could investigate the incident and make recommendations to governments. But this is an untried authority and it is doubtful whether the governments would want to use it in this case.

3. Use of armed force against Cuba—to blockade Cuban ports, to intercept and search Cuban ships on the high seas, or to overthrow Castro—is out of the question.

4. The measures which might be considered are:

—to condemn the Castro regime for its continued intervention.

—to establish a blacklist (OAS would do this) of trading and shipping entities and vessels which engage in significant new transactions with Cuba and agree that:

(1) no governmental contracts be awarded to listed entities;
(2) listed vessels be denied governmental or government-financed cargos;
(3) OAS member countries apply any other restrictions against the listed entities and vessels which their laws permit, and
(4) require commercial concerns in OAS member countries to observe the blacklist in their operations.

—to call to the attention of those governments supporting AALAPSO Cuba's aggressive activities and ask them to withdraw their support of the Organization.

—to press Mexico to break all ties with Castro.

State is putting the foregoing into a memo for Secretary Rusk[3] to get his reaction and views on how to proceed. The Secretary may bring this subject up at the Tuesday luncheon.[4]

WGB

---

[3] Bowdler forwarded the Department memorandum to Rostow on May 16, noting that "it parallels what I put in my memo to you yesterday." (Memorandum from Bowdler to Rostow, May 16; Johnson Library, National Security File, Venezuela, Vol. III, 12/66–12/68)

[4] May 16; no substantive record of the meeting has been found.

55.   Memorandum From the President's Special Assistant (Rostow) to President Johnson[1]

Washington, May 17, 1967.

SUBJECT

Venezuelan Case Against Cuba

The Venezuelan Foreign Minister yesterday announced President Leoni's decision to call for a Meeting of Foreign Ministers (MFM) to consider the problem of Cuban support for guerrilla movements in the hemisphere. The Venezuelans have as yet taken no formal action in the OAS. Their OAS Ambassador has been recalled to Caracas. We assume that he will return with orders to ask the OAS Council to convoke an MFM.

Yesterday Ambassador Bernbaum spoke with President Leoni and Foreign Minister Iribarren. He found them both concerned over what further meaningful action can be taken to punish Castro short of use of armed force against Cuban territory. Bernbaum's reports are attached.[2]

You will recall that the 1964 MFM approved mandatory sanctions: break in diplomatic relations and suspension of trade and sea transportation. All have complied except Mexico.

State is taking a look at possible additional measures:

Through the MFM

1. A strong comdemnation of the Castro regime.

2. An OAS blacklist of trading and shipping entities and vessels which engage in significant transactions with Cuba.

3. Authorization for OAS member states, acting individually and collectively, to stop and search Cuban flag ships (or ships without flag) in the Caribbean suspected of acting as mother ships for Cuban-sponsored infiltration teams.

Outside the MFM

1. Prevail upon Mexico to comply with the 1964 MFM decision and break all diplomatic and economic ties with Cuba.

---

[1] Source: Johnson Library, National Security File, Country File, Venezuela, Vol. III, 12/66–12/68. Secret. A notation on the memorandum indicates the President saw it.

[2] Transmitted in telegrams 6069 and 6070 from Caracas, May 16 and 17; attached but not printed. Also in the National Archives and Records Administration, RG 59, Central Files 1967–69, OAS 5–2 and POL 23–7 CUBA, respectively.

2. The United States and Latin American countries having relations with the Soviet Union to impress upon the Soviets the gravity of continued promotion of subversion by Castro.

The blacklist and stop-and-search measures raise many serious problems which need careful analysis before we sign on. State is engaged in this analysis.

In the meantime—as you will see from Bernbaum's cable—we continue to help the Venezuelans as you promised President Leoni we would.

Walt

---

56. **Memorandum From William G. Bowdler of the National Security Council Staff to the President's Special Assistant (Rostow)**[1]

Washington, May 31, 1967.

SUBJECT

Venezuelan Case Against Cuba

Yesterday I learned that the Venezuelans were about to make a formal request for an MFM to consider the Cuban case.

In checking with ARA I found that they still had not sorted out where they wanted to go because of differences inside the Bureau and with E and EUR. I told Sol Linowitz and Bob Sayre that they had better alert Foy Kohler—whom the Secretary had tapped to follow up on this one—and ask him to resolve the differences. Getting the Secretary into an MFM without knowing where we are headed is a helluva situation.

Kohler met this morning with Solomon, Stoessel, Covey Oliver, Linowitz, Sayre and Bernbaum.[2] I participated.

These are the highlights of the meeting:

1. Sol reported that the Venezuelans are determined to proceed with a call for an MFM under Art. 39 of the OAS Charter—probably

---

[1] Source: Johnson Library, National Security File, Country File, Venezuela, Vol. III, 12/66–12/68. Secret.

[2] Kohler convened the meeting "as a follow-up to the Secretary's instruction" that "he [Kohler] work out a coordinated Department position." (Memorandum for file, May 31; National Archives and Records Administration, RG 59, ARA Files, 1967–69: Lot 72 D 33, Venezuelan Complaint (Cuba))

today. They claim practically unanimous support for the convocation, but do not have the faintest idea where they want to come out beyond appointing a group to collect all the evidence on Cuban intervention.

2. Kohler noted that we are now committed to an MFM and must proceed on this basis.

3. It was agreed that we could support these measures in the MFM which would find generally wide acceptance among the Latin Americans:

a. Condemnation of Cuba for its aggressive activity.

b. Better enforcement of existing OAS sanctions approved in July 1964.

c. A renewed appeal for cooperation by friendly non-member countries in restricting trade and shipping with Cuba, and a call on countries actively supporting Cuba (the Soviets, etc.) to reassess their position in the light of Cuban subversion.

d. Action by all OAS Members to deny bunkers and government cargoes to ships in the Cuban trade. The US is already taking this action.

e. Improvement of surveillance and intercept especially in the Caribbean, search, and seizure of suspicious Cuban and unidentified vessels within a 12-mile zone, permitted under international convention, and search and seizure of such vessels outside the 12-mile zone if there is specific information of subversive intent warranting such action.

4. A sixth measure was discussed at great length: an OAS blacklist of firms trading with Cuba to which OAS member governments would deny government contracts. Tony Solomon was strongly opposed on general trade policy grounds and the ineffectiveness of the measure. EUR endorsed this view. Covey Oliver favored the measure in the form of an MFM recommendation (not mandatory) as symbolic support for Venezuela. Kohler took it under advisement and to discuss with Secretary Rusk.[3]

5. Kohler made a strong point of the need for the Latin Americans to take the initiative in convincing the Europeans that they should restrict trade with Cuba. It was agreed that one action the MFM might take is to select 3 or 4 prominent and effective Latin American Foreign Ministers to go to Europe to discuss the Latin American concern over mounting Cuban intervention and the desire of the OAS for the European governments to curtail their assistance to Castro, particularly in credit guarantees and Iberia's flights to Cuba. If the Europeans re-

---

[3] Kohler reached a decision before meeting Rusk: "I have mulled this matter over since that [May 31] meeting, trying to lean over backwards to understand the frustrations of ARA and of the Latin American countries. However, I have reluctantly come to the conclusion that the proposed economic sanction is not feasible." (Memorandum of record, June 1; ibid., ARA Files, 1967: Lot 70 D 150, Cuba, 1967)

sponded to this initiative, fine. If not, the OAS might consider a recommendatory blacklist.

6. As things now stand, this seems to be the sequence of contemplated action:

a. Venezuela will ask that the MFM be convoked initially *at the ambassadorial level* to appoint a committee to make a study of Cuban intervention in Venezuela, and other places (e.g., DR, Colombia, Bolivia, Guatemala) if the governments so request.

b. The study when completed would be presented to the MFM *at the ministerial level.*

c. The MFM would:

—denounce Cuba for its continued intervention.

—call upon the Europeans to cooperate with the measures approved by the MFM against Cuba in 1964.

—appoint a committee of Foreign Ministers to go to Europe to explain OAS concern and OAS desire for their cooperation in restricting assistance to Castro as long as he continues to promote subversion.

d. Depending upon the response of the Europeans, the MFM would reconvene. If their response is affirmative, no additional OAS action would be taken. If negative, the MFM might:

—apply the blacklist.

—deny bunkering facilities to ships calling at Cuba.

WGB

---

57. Memorandum From the President's Special Assistant (Rostow) to President Johnson[1]

Washington, June 1, 1967.

SUBJECT

Venezuelan Case Against Cuba

The Venezuelans today asked for an early Meeting of Foreign Ministers (MFM) to consider their complaint against Cuba.

---

[1] Source: Johnson Library, National Security File, Country File, Venezuela, Vol. III, 12/66–12/68. Confidential. A notation on the memorandum indicates the President saw it.

The convocation is under the OAS Charter rather than Rio Treaty. The essential difference is that a Charter MFM is limited to *recommendations,* while a Rio Treaty MFM normally takes *mandatory measures.*

Venezuela chose the OAS Charter track because it can count on almost unanimous support for convocation. This is not the case if they moved under the Rio Treaty.

The OAS Council meets on Monday, June 5, to act on the Venezuelan request. The first step will be to convoke the MFM at the ambassadorial level. A Committee will then be appointed to go to Venezuela (and other countries which have cases against Cuba) to examine all the evidence. The MFM at the ministerial level will meet after the Committee completes its report.

Venezuela has no clear picture of what it wants the MFM to recommend. Part of its difficulty is that there is little more that can be done against Castro of an effective nature short of armed force, which is out of the question. Another problem is the general unwillingness of the larger Latin American countries to apply additional economic pressure against countries trading with Cuba.

State is still sorting out what meaningful collective action can be taken. What is needed is a keener sense by the Latin Americans that Cuban subversion is a common problem and that *they* should be taking the lead in: (1) publicizing Cuban interventionist activities, (2) bringing pressure on the Western Europeans to curtail their trade with Cuba; (3) forcing the Soviet bloc to define its position and (4) strengthening their internal security forces to liquidate the guerrillas at the incipient stage. What is called for, in effect, is a collective security self-help effort by the Latins.

We will be trying to move them in this direction, making clear that they can count on our shield against overt Cuban military action and our support in developing their security capabilities.

Walt

58. Memorandum of Conversation[1]

Washington, June 2, 1967, 10 a.m.

SUBJECT

Cuban Intervention in Venezuelan Affairs—OAS

PARTICIPANTS

The Secretary
Mr. Foy D. Kohler—G
Mr. Anthony M. Solomon—E
Ambassador Maurice M. Bernbaum

Following a discussion of Venezuela's petroleum problem, the Secretary turned to the question of the U.S. position in the OAS on Venezuela's complaint against Cuba.

Mr. Kohler said that he had come to the conclusion that the idea presented by ARA for the establishment of a list of firms doing business with Cuba to be utilized by the member states of the OAS in denying government contracts to such firms was not feasible. It was his impression based on Mr. Solomon's views that the potential costs to U.S. policy and U.S. interests were too great to justify the limited benefits which might be derived.

The Secretary then asked whether this would apply to the blacklisting of vessels touching at Cuban ports. Mr. Solomon said this was not a point at issue since such action was already taken by the USG and would merely represent a generalization of our policy. He explained that our policy involved the denial to such vessels of bunkering facilities in U.S. ports as well as government cargoes.

The Secretary then referred to OAS action involving the search of suspicious vessels outside territorial waters. He suggested in this connection the desirability of establishing a Caribbean Security Committee made up of countries bordering the Caribbean Sea. He thought that this would involve specifically the countries directly threatened by Cuban intervention without involving the South American countries more remote from the scene as well as Mexico. It was agreed in the ensuing discussion that this would have the great advantage of creating an organization which could facilitate and implement search procedures.

Ambassador Bernbaum then outlined a program which had been discussed the previous evening by Ambassador Linowitz, Ward Allen

---

[1] Source: National Archives and Records Administration, RG 59, Central Files 1967–69, POL 23–7 CUBA. Confidential. Drafted by Bernbaum and approved in S on June 5.

and others interested in the problem and which had been described earlier in the morning to Robert Sayre. This provided for the following measures:

1. An OAS denunciation of Cuban aggression in strong language.
2. Strong criticism of Soviet responsibility through assistance to Cuba making its actions possible and appealing to the Soviet Union to assist in solving this problem.
3. An appeal to friendly countries to assist in the efforts of the OAS countries to protect themselves against Cuban aggression by not encouraging or facilitating trade with that country.
4. The establishment of a high level committee, possibly made up of a selected group of foreign ministers to visit the European countries concerned and possibly the Soviet Union to make known the Latin American concern over the problem and to request collaboration. The results of this trip would be reported back to the MFM. In addition there might be behind the scenes agreement on the action by all OAS Chiefs of State to call in the Ambassadors of the European countries, Soviet Union, Canada and Japan to emphasize the appeal made in the OAS Resolution.

Further steps to be taken by the OAS would be applied in the event of the failure of the mission during its talks in Europe and other areas and would be the subject of further action by the OAS upon the submittal of their report. At that time there would be taken up various punitive measures such as (1) Generalization of U.S. policy toward vessels touching at Cuban ports to the other OAS countries; (2) The pressure on Spain to discontinue its air services to Cuba; and (3) Other appropriate and feasible measures.

Mr. Kohler said that he agreed with this program, particularly in the sense of making known to the Soviet Union the concerted feeling of the OAS countries. He felt that the Latin Americans had been far too weak and delicate in their approaches to the Soviet Union which he thought would be far more sensitive to such pressure than they apparently thought. He also agreed on the desirability of a widespread publicity campaign to make known the Latin American position.

The Secretary thought that this kind of program including the establishment of a Caribbean Security Committee would be useful. He did not, however, want the OAS action to be of such a nature as to create the impression that the United States was about to embark on an important punitive program against Cuba. He thought that we already had too many problems in our basket at the present time for such a policy to be adopted now. It seemed to him that a policy of this nature could be envisaged after a few more crises involving Cuba. The Secretary also wanted to know whether the proposed action by the Chiefs of State would be mentioned in the Resolution. Ambassador Bernbaum said that this might best be done behind the scenes. The Secretary agreed. He then asked whether the Ambassadors concerned would be called in by the Presidents en masse or individually. Ambassador Bernbaum thought that this might best be done individually. The Secretary then said that since a decision of this kind would involve President Johnson he thought it best for him to consult with the President before giving the green light. He wondered whether it might be possible for President Johnson to be exempted from this requirement by utilizing language such as "the highest feasible levels". Ambassador Bernbaum said that Foreign Ministers in Latin America did not have the prestige and weight of the Secretary of State and that it might therefore be desirable to arrange for the Chiefs of State in Latin America to do the job leaving the way open for the Secretary of State to do it in Washington. This produced some laughter and was left at that.

---

59.   Telegram From the President's Special Assistant (Rostow) to President Johnson in Texas[1]

Washington, June 24, 1967, 1939Z.

CAP 67582. As you requested, I had a good meeting this morning with CIA, State and DOD on the whole guerrilla problem in Latin America.

This is the boxscore:

Country by Degree of Urgency	Number of Active Guerrillas	Hard Evidence of Cuban Involvement
Bolivia	60–100	Yes: Cuban military officers among ranks, arms and training.
Guatemala	300	Yes: Arms deliveries via Mexico.
Venezuela	400	Yes: Arms, training, Cuban military personnel captured during infiltration mission, Cuban admission of operation.
Colombia	800	Yes: But only training in Cuba.
Dominican Republic	dormant	Yes: Training, funds and special agents.
Ecuador	dormant	Yes: But only training in Cuba.
Peru	dormant	Yes: But only training in Cuba.

---

[1] Source: Johnson Library, National Security File, Country File, Latin America, Vol. VI, 6/67–9/67. Secret.

To understand these figures it is necessary to appreciate that each organized guerrilla can tie up 10–20 government soldiers. We do better in Viet-Nam only because of airpower, mobility, firepower, etc. These are some further insights into the situation in each country:

Bolivia:

We have put Bolivia on top of the list more because of the fragility of the political situation and the weakness of the armed forces than the size and effectiveness of the guerrilla movement. The active band numbers probably 50–60 but may run up to 100. CIA believes that "Che" Guevara has been with this group. There are indications that six other bands, totalling 100–200 men may be organizing in other parts of the country. President Barrientos is hard pressed in coping with the active band. If other fronts were successfully opened, the situation could get out of hand. The 17-man mobile training team we have in Bolivia expects to have another ranger battalion trained by September 1.

The active movement has 8 top Bolivian Communist Party leaders in it who were trained in the Soviet Union. The owner of the farm which the guerrillas used as their training camp belongs to a man (Roberto Peredo) who visited Moscow in 1966. We know of six Cuban military officers in this band. We also know that they have radio contact with Cuba using the same procedures taught by the Soviets.

Guatemala:

The guerrillas are divided into two organizations. The FAR—250 men—has the backing of Castro. Last summer when President Mendez Montenegro took over, the guerrillas were making steady progress. With the death of FAR leader Turcios and strong pressure by the Guatemalan military. The guerrillas have been scattered and are on the defensive.

In September 1966, Mexican authorities uncovered an arms smuggling channel to Guatemalan insurgents. Documents found showed that over 4000 weapons had been sent. A Cuban Embassy officer was caught red handed passing money to the smugglers.

Venezuela:

This is Cuba's primary target. After 1963 the guerrilla movement came to a virtual standstill while the Venezuelan Communist Party debated whether to pursue the peaceful or violent approach. The party split and Douglas Bravo led the activist faction into resumed guerrilla activity. Since mid-1966 his group (150–250 men) and the MIR group (100 men) have stepped up their campaign. Leoni responded by organizing 9 new ranger battalions which we are helping to train and equip.

Soviet-manufactured AK–13 weapons have been captured in Venezuela from guerrillas known to have landed from Cuba in July

1966. The boat and motors used are known to have come from Cuba. In May 1967 a Cuban/Venezuelan group landed from a Cuban fishing vessel. The Venezuelans escaped into the mountains, but two Cubans were captured and two killed.

Colombia:

There are two guerrilla units operating, one responsive to Cuba and the other to the USSR. After a long inactive period, they resumed operations last February. So far the operations have consisted of sporadic hit-and-run raids. The Colombian armed forces, which are well-trained and disciplined, are putting pressure on them. President Lleras has moved quickly to improve intelligence collection, strengthen coordination between services and mount social programs in guerrilla areas. There is no Cuban presence in Colombia, but there is hard evidence of Colombians being trained in Cuba. The guerrillas do not represent an immediate threat to Lleras.

Dominican Republic:

There are no active guerrillas although there are indications that the Communist MPD and 14th of June Movement would like to open a front. The Dominican armed forces are keeping a close watch on their activities. Balaguer has given strong support to our efforts to help him develop special anti-guerrilla units. In recent months Dominican authorities have obtained documents from Cuban-trained agents showing that Cuba is furnishing money and training for guerrilla activities.

Ecuador and Peru:

Cuba tried to start guerrilla activities in these two countries about two years ago. The movements were quickly put down, but they remain as potential trouble spots. Cuba continues to train nationals from both countries.

I have collected a full folder of background material which you may want to review.

I told my working group to make a careful review of what we were now doing in each country and meet with me again in one week to discuss additional measures which we might take to strengthen the anti-guerrilla capabilities of these countries.[2]

W.W.R.

---

[2] According to a June 24 note, the President told Jim Jones to "hold this, I want to talk to him [Rostow] about this tomorrow." (National Archives and Records Administration, RG 59, ARA Files, 1967: Lot 70 D 150, Latin America Miscellaneous 1967) Rostow was in the delegation that met Johnson on June 25 for the second Glassboro meeting with Soviet Premier Alexei N. Kosygin. (Johnson Library, President's Daily Diary) No evidence was found indicating whether Johnson talked to Rostow about Cuban subversion at Glassboro.

60.   Editorial Note

President Johnson raised the issue of Cuban subversion in Latin America at the Glassboro Summit with Soviet Premier Alexei N. Kosygin. According to the official record of the afternoon session on June 25, 1967, the President said "he wished to inform Mr. Kosygin of an extremely important matter. He said we had direct evidence of Cuba's encouragement of guerrilla operations in seven Latin American countries. This was a form of aggression and was dangerous to peace in the Hemisphere as well as in the world at large. He pointed out that Soviet-manufactured arms coming from Cuba had been seized in Venezuela in July 1966 and in May 1967, with seven Cubans having been captured in this latter incident. He also wished to point out that on March 13 of this year, Castro openly stated his support for this type of activity. The Government of Venezuela had stated its determination to put an end to such operations. Our Ambassador to the OAS and some of his colleagues from the Organization were now investigating in Venezuela the evidence of those activities. The President emphasized that he therefore strongly felt that Castro should be convinced to stop what he was doing. Mr. Kosygin did not comment on this statement." (National Archives and Records Administration, RG 59, Central Files 1967–69, POL 7 US) For the complete memorandum of conversation, see *Foreign Relations, 1964–1968*, volume XIV, Document 235.

That evening Johnson gave former President Eisenhower the following account of this discussion with Kosygin: "[I] told him there were 6 or 7 hot spots; that they're using Soviet material, Cuba was; that we caught a bunch of them the other day in Venezuela; that they were giving us hell in the Dominican Republic, and Haiti, and Bolivia, and half a dozen places; that this is a very serious matter, Soviet equipment and Castro-trained people." Johnson said Kosygin "ought to realize that we thought this was very serious and we were going to have to take action—the OAS was going to take action." The President then asked Kosygin for a response. According to Johnson's account, Kosygin "said he couldn't comment now, but he was leaving for Cuba tomorrow, and he would bear these things in mind in talking to them. Acted like he was a little upset with Castro. Didn't say so." (Johnson Library, Recordings and Transcripts, Recording of telephone conversation between President Johnson and Dwight D. Eisenhower, June 25, 1967, 9:44 p.m., Tape F67.13, Side A, PNO 1) An uncorrected transcript of the conversation is ibid.

**61.   Memorandum From the President's Special Assistant
(Rostow) to President Johnson**[1]

Washington, July 6, 1967.

Mr. President:

I had another good round yesterday with Covey Oliver and other members of the inter-agency working group on Cuban subversion in Latin America.[2]

This time we examined the adequacy of current DOD, CIA and AID/Public Safety (police) programs in the seven countries with active or potential insurgency movements.

Our conclusions were:

Bolivia

This is our most serious problem, not because of the size of the guerrilla movement, but the weakness of the security forces and fragility of the political situation. Given Bolivia's limited capacity to assimilate our assistance, we should for now:

—press forward with the training of a second Ranger Battalion, and develop an intelligence unit to work with the Battalion.
—expand our police program in rural areas.
—start contingency planning for dealing with a situation which Barrientos can no longer control.

Colombia

President Lleras Camargo is concerned and working for better coordination and action by his security services. We have good on-going military, intelligence and police programs. We agreed that:

—DOD would review equipment needs of the armed forces in the light of CINCSO's recommendations.
—Covey Oliver would consider a modest expansion of the rural police program.

Dominican Republic

With the full cooperation of Balaguer and the armed forces, we have made good progress in our internal security programs. No additional measures by us are necessary. It would help if Balaguer got rid of his thuggish Chief of Police. Covey Oliver will ask John Crimmins to make the pitch.

---

[1] Source: Johnson Library, National Security File, Country File, Latin America, Vol. VI, 6/67–9/67. Secret. A notation on the memorandum indicates the President saw it.

[2] A memorandum of the meeting, drafted by Bowdler, is ibid.

Ecuador

There is no active insurgency, but this is a good time to help the Ecuadoreans improve their grossly deficient rural police. Covey Oliver will work out an expanded program with AID/Public Safety.

Guatemala

Mendez Montenegro has tackled the insurgency problem with energy and has accomplished a good deal. He has welcomed our assistance and we have responded with additional help on the military and police side. Our present programs look about right. A modest increase in our rural police program is warranted and Covey Oliver will pursue this.

Peru

There is no active insurgency. The security forces have demonstrated their ability to handle insurgent bands in the past. Our current programs are adequate.

Venezuela

We have done what Leoni asked you for at Punta del Este: to expedite delivery of equipment for 9 new Ranger battalions. [*1½ lines of source text not declassified*] Additional support for the National Guard (police) in rural areas is needed and Covey Oliver will work this out with AID/Public Safety.

Another decision reached by the group is that henceforth Covey Oliver will organize a group (probably the same people who attended yesterday)[3] which will meet on a regular basis to:

—keep a close watch over Cuban insurgency trends throughout the hemisphere.
—review individual country situations and requirements.
—expedite decisions on increased assistance, as necessary.

As a starter Covey Oliver will write each Ambassador to impress upon him the importance which you attach to alertness to internal security requirements and communicating needs to Washington in a timely way.[4]

From the review which I have made, I am convinced that at the present level of insurgency in Latin America, the important elements of the equation are:

1. For the most part, the institutional base for internal security in Latin America is primitive. The opportunities we have to build it up

---

[3] Documentation on the IRG/ARA Counter-Insurgency Subgroup is in the National Archives and Records Administration, RG 59, IRG/ARA, 1966–68: Files: Lot 70 D 122.

[4] Copies of the letter and subsequent replies are ibid., ARA Files, 1967–69: Lot 72 D 33, Military/Security Policy.

vary with the local officials in power. We must be alert to every chance given us to advance the building process.

2. If the President of the country is concerned over the problem and willing to act, the armed forces will back him and, with our assistance, they can produce impressive results. This has been the case in Guatemala. We hope to repeat it in Bolivia.

3. The cost to us in furnishing "preventive medicine" assistance is small, but our Ambassadors and their country teams must understand the key importance of "preventive medicine" and exploit every opportunity which presents itself.

4. The "Establishment" in Washington must be geared to keeping a continuous review of the problem and acting quickly on assistance requirements.

Walt

---

62.   **Memorandum From the President's Special Assistant (Rostow) to President Johnson**[1]

Washington, September 7, 1967, 11:30 a.m.

SUBJECT

Asuncion Meeting on Latin American Economic Integration[2]

Bill Bowdler met with Covey Oliver and his Latin American Common Market experts to review the results of the Asuncion meeting which the press has reported as a failure.

Two things emerged:

—until we have a fuller picture of what took place at the LAFTA (South American countries, plus Mexico) session, where we do not have observer status, it is premature to draw conclusions about the lack of success at Asuncion and what country was responsible.

—despite inability of LAFTA to reach agreement on the first try on certain key issues, interest in the economic integration movement

---

[1] Source: Johnson Library, National Security File, Country File, Paraguay, Vol. I, 1/64–8/68. Confidential. A notation on the memorandum indicates the President saw it.

[2] A joint meeting of the Latin American Free Trade Association and the Central American Common Market was held in Asuncion August 28–September 2. Additional documentation on the meeting is in the National Archives and Records Administration, RG 59, Central Files 1967–69, ECIN 3 LA, ECIN 3 LAFTA, and ECIN 3 CACM.

has *not* slackened and the timetable agreed at Punta del Este has *not* been irretrievably upset.

The Asuncion Goals

We had hoped the Asuncion meeting would agree on three major issues:

—programmed tariff reductions among LAFTA members.

—preparations by LAFTA members for a common external tariff.

—mechanism for joint LAFTA–CACM exploration of gradual merger into a Latin American Common Market.

Up until the last two days of the meeting, it seemed that agreement would be reached on the first two points based on a compromise formula which would give the poorest countries (Bolivia, Ecuador and Paraguay) free access to the markets of all the other LAFTA members in five years.

At the last moment, Peru asked to receive similar treatment as the poor countries. The other LAFTA members balked, and Peru's continued refusal to drop its request worked as a veto. This, in turn, seems to have triggered a veto by Paraguay of other decisions relating to programmed tariff cuts and preparations for a common external tariff.

We do not know why Peru took this inflexible position. It had not been enthusiastic about a common market from the start, and recent financial problems probably compounded its fears about competition from other countries. Significantly, none of the big three—Argentina, Brazil, Mexico—opposed the concession to the poor countries. They would have been harder to turn around than Peru.

The Asuncion Round in Perspective

Disappointing as the results were, it is important to look at the Asuncion round in perspective:

—the meeting showed that most of the LAFTA countries are prepared to move rapidly toward a common market.

—LAFTA gave its blessing to the formation of an Andean subregional group (Venezuela, Colombia, Ecuador, Peru, Bolivia and Chile) which plans to reduce trade barriers among themselves at a faster pace than provided in the President's timetable.

—at the joint LAFTA–CACM meeting the Foreign Ministers agreed to recommend annual meetings to consider acceleration of execution of the Punta del Este decisions and decided to establish a Coordinating Committee to study on a priority basis five key aspects of the merger of the two groups.

—the Meeting of Presidents envisaged an 18-month period or more for the Latin Americans to negotiate all the specific arrangements leading toward a common market.

—LAFTA members, while disappointed at the inability to reach agreement on all issues, do not look upon the meeting as a failure. This is reflected in public statements by the Argentine and Colombian Foreign Ministers.

—the European economic integration movement faced several complex negotiating sessions before basic obstacles were removed.

What Needs to be Done

To keep the momentum of the movement going, two things must be done:

—get Peru turned around.

—have the LAFTA Foreign Ministers renew negotiations as rapidly as possible, preferably before the second quarter of 1968 which they have set for their next meeting.

Among the opportunities we will have to use our influence with the LAFTA group are:

—the Meeting of Foreign Ministers in Washington on September 22–23 to consider Venezuela's complaint against Cuba.

—the World Bank and Fund meetings in Rio de Janeiro in mid-September. Tony Solomon and Don Palmer (Covey Oliver's Common Market man) will attend.

—a special CIAP meeting in Rio at the end of September to consider the financial aspects of economic integration.

—Tony Solomon is going to Peru after the Rio Bank–IMF meeting to address a group of Peruvian businessmen. He will speak on the advantage of economic integration. He will also be able to talk to Belaunde about the Peruvian attitude.

—We may help Peru overcome its integration fears by supporting the Andean subregional group, with necessary adjustment assistance if they take specific action cutting tariffs among themselves.

Before deciding how to use these opportunities, we need a full reading of what took place at the LAFTA meeting. State has asked our Embassies for this assessment.[3]

Walt

---

[3] The President wrote the following instructions on the memorandum: "Let's follow these carefully & keep me informed. L"

63.   **Telegram From the President's Special Assistant (Rostow) to President Johnson in Texas**[1]

Washington, September 7, 1967, 2151Z.

CAP 67764. This lively memorandum to me from Covey Oliver on counterinsurgency developments in Latin America will give you some satisfaction.

"As you know, we and the Latinos have our ups and downs in the counterinsurgency business. But I want to call to your attention an unusual series of successes which have taken place in three Latin American countries during the past few weeks. They are particularly significant in that they follow close on the heels of the militant and optimistic pronouncements by Castro and his fellow Latin American revolutionaries at the recent Havana meeting of the Latin American Solidarity Organization (LASO).

1. Bolivia:

A. An important cache of passports, signal plans and other documents was discovered by a Bolivian Army element. Inter alia, the documents provide solid evidence that Che Guevara earlier this year was in Bolivia operating with the guerrillas.

B. On August 31, a Bolivian Army patrol executed an imaginative and sophisticated ambush of the guerrilla rearguard, killing several key Cubans and Bolivians, and taking prisoner a knowledgeable Bolivian who is cooperating well under interrogation.[2]

2. Venezuela:

In early August, Venezuelan police learned that the principal action arm of the Communist subversives in Caracas was a 50-man terrorist unit called Strategic Sabotage Command. Since that time, the unit has been 'decapitated.' The commander was captured and his four lieutenants killed in a series of police raids. A roundup of the lower echelons is now underway.

3. Nicaragua:

On August 12 the Guardia Nacional began a sweep of an area of north central Nicaragua on the basis of fragmentary reports of guerrilla training camps. Insurgent basecamps were located and we estimate that in a subsequent series of firefights at least 14 Castro-oriented

---

[1] Source: Johnson Library, National Security File, Country File, Latin America, Vol. VI, 6/67–9/67. Secret. James R. Jones, Assistant to the President, wrote the following note on the telegram: "9–7–67. Sent copy to Christian & he might leak it."

[2] Documentation on the subsequent capture and death of Ernesto "Che" Guevara de la Serna is in Documents 170–173.

guerrillas were wiped out. The survivors are reported fleeing the area on an 'every-man-for-himself' basis.

The situation in Guatemala continues to improve, while in Colombia there have been no significant contacts between government forces and insurgents recently.

All in all, while one swallow doesn't make a summer, August 1967 has been a vintage month for the COIN forces in Latin America."

---

64. Memorandum From the President's Special Assistant (Rostow) to President Johnson[1]

Washington, September 25, 1967, 4 p.m.

SUBJECT

OAS Meeting of Foreign Ministers[2]

On all counts, the OAS Meeting of Foreign Ministers went well, within the limits of what we thought possible.

The basic resolution was approved 20 to 0, with Mexico abstaining.

The resolution has all the points which the Venezuelans and we originally sought (copy attached):[3]

—a strong condemnation of Cuba for acts of aggression in Venezuela and Bolivia.

—a request to free world countries to restrict their trade with Cuba and a recommendation to OAS members that they press this request individually or collectively.

—an expression of serious concern to the Communist countries that their support of Castro stimulates his subversive activities, and a recommendation to OAS members that they make joint or individual representations to manifest this concern.

---

[1] Source: Johnson Library, National Security File, Subject File, Organization of American States, Vol. II. Secret. A notation on the memorandum indicates the President saw it.

[2] The final plenary sessions of the Twelfth Meeting of Consultation of the Ministers of Foreign Affairs of the Organization of American States were held in Washington September 22–24. Documentation on the meeting is ibid., International Meetings and Travel File, Ministers of Foreign Affairs, 9/22–24/67; and National Archives and Records Administration, RG 59, Conference Files, 1966–1972: Lot 68 D 453, CF 212 and CF 213.

[3] Attached but not printed. For an excerpt of the Final Act, see *American Foreign Policy: Current Documents, 1967*, pp. 648–652; the text of the final act of the meeting, including the "basic resolution," is in Department of State *Bulletin*, October 16, 1967, pp. 493–498.

—a call upon governments supporting the Afro-Asian-Latin American People's Solidarity Organization to withdraw their support of the organization because it fosters subversion.

—a recommendation to OAS Governments not to use ships in the Cuban trade and deny them bunkering facilities.

—a call on OAS Governments for tighter controls over subversive activities.

At Congressman Selden's request, Secretary Rusk tried to get in the notion of the OAS Secretariat keeping a list of private firms trading with Cuba, but this did not prosper.

In the separate resolution, sponsored by Chile, Venezuela and Colombia, it was agreed to call attention in the UN to Cuba's subversive activities. Mexico went along with this decision.

The resolutions will not topple Castro but they provide OAS-sanctioned levers for pressuring our European friends and Soviet bloc countries to put the heat on him. Now we must get the Latins to pull these levers. Covey Oliver is working on this.

The resolutions also give Venezuela strong moral support which will be helpful to President Leoni domestically. To the extent that Cuba becomes a political issue here over the next 13 months, the resolution will help to show that we have been active in mobilizing additional collective action to squeeze Castro.

We may well find that Castro will persist in his guerrilla activities, despite getting his fingers burned. This raises the question of what further action can be taken to deter Castro. Bill Bowdler and I were discussing this over the weekend. We concluded that the next step might be measured retaliation by the aggrieved state against Cuba. There is authority for this in the 1964 resolution. Many aspects need to be sorted out. We plan to use the IRG–SIG mechanism to assess the advisability of this course.

Walt

65.   Record of Discussion and Decisions of 22nd Meeting of the Senior Interdepartmental Group[1]

Washington, September 28, 1967.

PRESENT

Under Secretary of State, Chairman
Deputy Secretary of Defense
General Johnson for the Chairman, JCS
Admiral Taylor for the Director of Central Intelligence
Director, United States Information Agency
Administrator, Agency for International Development
Under Secretary of the Treasury
Under Secretary of Agriculture
The Special Assistant to the President, Mr. Walt W. Rostow
The Deputy Under Secretary of State for Political Affairs
The Staff Director

Ambassador Foster, ACDA
Mr. Oliver, Chairman IRG/ARA
General Orwat, JCS
Mr. Lang, ISA

[Omitted here is discussion of future agenda suggestions and the status of talks on the nuclear non-proliferation treaty.]

3. US Regional Policy Toward Latin American Security Forces

A. Summary of Discussion

The Chairman of IRG/ARA introduced the subject with a brief review of the report itself and its current status.[2] He mentioned the ACDA dissent and the fact that, owing to time pressures, staffing by the Services had not yet been completed.[3] He listed the main reappraisals and

---

[1] Source: National Archives and Records Administration, RG 59, S/S–SIG Files: Lot 70 D 263, SIG/RA #22, 10/2/67, Future Agenda Suggestions. Secret.

[2] The report, approved by IRG/ARA on September 20, recommended that the United States carry out its "commitment to cooperate with the larger South American countries in obtaining jet fighter aircraft of the F–5 type in 1969–70 to replace jet fighter aircraft in existing inventory. It is recognized that air combat support could be performed by less sophisticated jets but that for primarily political reasons we are prepared to see the five large South American countries receive these aircraft." (Ibid., SIG Agenda: #22—9/28/67)

[3] In a September 23 memorandum to the SIG Acting ACDA Director Alexander argued that the United States "should continue to resist pressure from the Latin American countries for supplying supersonic military aircraft." (Johnson Library, National Security File, Agency File, SIG, 22nd Meeting, 9/28/67, Vol. 2) In an October 20 memorandum to Katzenbach, Chairman Wheeler reported that, subject to several reservations, the JCS generally supported the paper, including the proposal to provide F–5 aircraft to the larger South American countries. (Ibid.)

reformulations of policies contained in the report. He noted that the Navy wished to give further consideration to the specific lines of action (page 20) suggested for navies in the area. On the sale of F–5s, to which the ACDA dissent was addressed, he pointed out that this kind of question had been raised at each of the previous plateaus of air force re-equipment—T–5 to 600 mph and now to near supersonic.

The Chairman stated his view that this policy paper should be considered a general re-statement of our present policies with some new emphasis, but that SIG should not give approval to the paper in all its details. Gen. Johnson summed up his view that the general thrust of the policy was good and a simple adjustment would probably meet the one criticism noted. (He mentioned that a paper 36 months in preparation[4] should not have to be staffed in five days.)

Mr. Barr explained his difficulty in presenting the case for arms sales to Latin America in his recent Congressional appearances. He welcomed the detailed statement and reasoning behind US objectives and thought these would be useful to him in the future, although he foresaw continued opposition on the Hill. Some important and influential leaders saw our activities in this field as only aiding military dictatorships. Others on the SIG thought opinion was less opposed in the Armed Services and Foreign Relations and Foreign Affairs Committees.

Mr. Gaud thought that, leaving the F–5 problem aside, the other policies would win support in the Congress. Gen. Johnson suggested that Gen. Porter had good relations on the Hill and would be willing to help with any Congressman who might benefit from a first hand view of the practical problems in this area.

Mr. Rostow summed up the case to be made as follows: the military play an important role in the countries which is not well understood; they can be a force for progress; and we do have some leverage through equipment modernization. Therefore, we should aim to guide the military leadership toward support of democratic institutions, toward the right military tasks, toward a reduced share of GNP for military purposes and toward keeping the modernization impulse in line

---

[4] In a September 28 memorandum to Oliver, Sayre explained that the report was a late response to NSAM No. 297: "One of the first things I did when assigned to the White House in 1964 was to get McGeorge Bundy to ask for a study and an agreed U.S. security policy for Latin America. Defense and State appointed a study group which worked for six months. It produced a study which DOD/ISA considered satisfactory, but State, JCS and CINCSO refused to accept it. It was finally sent to the White House for information. Primarily because of the Dominican crisis, but also because DOD/ISA preferred the ad hoc system which it controlled, we have made progress slowly." (National Archives and Records Administration, RG 59, ARA/IG Files: Lot 70 D 122, U.S. Regional Policy Toward L.A. Security Forces—1967)

with US interest as against outsiders (e.g., the French). A strong case can be made using such examples as Venezuela and Peru.

Mr. Foster agreed that the policy paper was a good one but maintained that the F–5 sales were contrary to it. He queried whether the "commitments" mentioned in the paper circulated by Mr. Oliver were in fact definitive. Mr. Rostow cited the letter to the Brazilian President and Ambassador Tuthill's authorized oral remarks.[5] Gen. Johnson said he had no knowledge of the letter but on his recent trip to Brazil he was left in no doubt by his Brazilian hosts that they considered we had a commitment to sell F–5s and that they expected the authorization for talks with Northrop to come shortly after October 1. Mr. Foster also recalled the Punta del Este recommendation on arms limitation but Mr. Nitze thought the Latin Americans would consider F–5 purchases as "necessary expenditure" in the terms of the resolution.

Mr. Foster thought the Foreign Relations Committee particularly would take the line that we aren't holding down the appetites. Mr. Oliver thought a good case could be made that we are. On a comparative basis Latin America's military expenditures were smaller than those of other areas on military expenditure and of those sums only a small part went for matériel. The Latin American forces were in many cases used more as CCC-type camps and, said Gen. Johnson, for vocational training. The Chairman said that the comparative element should be added to the IRG/ARA paper.

The Chairman thought we had delayed the sale as long as feasible but we were now faced with imminent Mirage sales. Gen. Johnson pointed out that F–5 deliveries would not be made before 1969, whereas the Mirage was available now.

Mr. Gaud described the special case of Peru, where we must make a decision on a program loan with conditions—no Mirage purchases, sound economic policies, no higher defense expenditure, but agreement to F–5 purchases. He concluded, as did Mr. Rostow, that a Peruvian purchase of Mirage aircraft could result in Congressional retaliation on the Alliance for Progress. Mr. Rostow stressed the importance of President Belaunde's position and the consequences for him of our failure to comply with the request for F–5s. If pressed too far by us and by his military, Belaunde might denounce AID entirely, to the great damage of the Alliance, to American policy, and to the President of the United States.

Mr. Gaud and others stated their firm belief that the matter had to be discussed with Congressional leaders before action is taken or we would run a serious risk of equally strong reaction against *our* sale of F–5s.

---

[5] See Document 230.

B. Decisions and Next Steps

(1) The Chairman summarized the general agreement of members to continued development and implementation of the following guidelines for US action:

(a) Increasing Latin American military role in internal defense;
(b) Attempting to enhance OAS/UN peacekeeping role of L.A. military forces;
(c) Continued "go slow" on more sophisticated equipment; and
(d) Re-examining US military presence.

(2) SIG agreed that the "general thrust" of the policy was good and its objectives were generally approved subject to possible changes as the JCS complete their staffing.

(3) SIG further agreed that the State–Defense Study Group should not consider themselves bound in any way by this document but should be free to reexamine these policies in their review of broader area policies.

(4) On the F–5 sales, SIG agreed that we must proceed but that it was essential to inform Congressional leaders prior to final action with the Latin American countries. The Chairman of IRG/ARA was requested to prepare a detailed, step-by-step plan for dealing with the sales of F–5s to all the countries in question and including the tactics to be used domestically.

C. Suggestions for Further Follow-Up

(1) Should we study the actual influence of the Latin American military and also analyze what groups are represented in forces today? (IRG/ARA—Admiral Taylor suggested Major Gen. Roland del Mar would be a good person to conduct such a study. The Chairman also suggested the Rand Corporation.)

(2) The Chairman asked that the projected State–Defense study on Latin America consider the following:

(a) Multilateral programs to influence Latin American military;
(b) Possible pooling of sophisticated equipment (helicopters, interceptor boats) (General Johnson mentioned the Army Regional Assistance Command);
(c) Mr. Gaud's suggestion to relate aid to increasing use of resources on economic development as an indirect way to hold down defense expenditure.[6]

---

[6] In April 1968 Ambassador Edwin M. Martin submitted the joint State–Defense study, entitled "Latin America: A Recommended U.S. National Strategy." The SIG discussed the Martin study at its meetings on May 2 and June 13. At the latter meeting, Katzenbach directed that the Country Teams consider the study "in their policy/program planning and development." (National Archives and Records Administration, RG 59, S/S–SIG Files: Lot 70 D 263, SIG/RA #41, 6/26/68, Chairman's Summary at Discussion and Decision)

(3) Gen. Johnson requested preparation of a SIG discussion on how to give useful guidance to American military officers in their contacts with Latin American military leaders (State–G/PM to prepare paper for SIG discussion and action).

AA Hartman
Staff Director

---

66. Special National Intelligence Estimate[1]

SNIE 80/90–2–68   Washington, January 29, 1968.

PROBABLE CONSEQUENCES OF A REFUSAL BY THE US TO
SELL F–5 AIRCRAFT IN LATIN AMERICA

The Problem

To estimate how US interests in Latin America would be affected by a US refusal to sell F–5s to certain Latin American countries.

Note

Recent US foreign aid legislation (the Conte–Long and Symington amendments)[2] directs the President (a) to deny grants or credits to certain countries for the purchase of "sophisticated weapons systems;" (b) to withhold economic aid from such countries in an amount equivalent to the cost of such equipment purchased by them; (c) to terminate

---

[1] Source: Johnson Library, National Security File, Agency File, SIG, 29th Meeting, 1/9/68, Vol. 3. Secret; Controlled Dissem. According to a note on the cover sheet this estimate was prepared in the Central Intelligence Agency with the participation of the intelligence organizations of the Departments of State and Defense and the National Security Agency. The United States Intelligence Board concurred in this estimate on January 29. Hartman circulated copies of the estimate to SIG members on January 29. (Ibid.)

[2] Reference is to two amendments to the Foreign Assistance Act of 1961 (as amended), one sponsored by Representatives Silvio O. Conte (R–Massachusetts) and Clarence Long (D–Maryland), the other by Senator Stuart Symington (D–Missouri). The Conte–Long amendment required the President to withhold economic assistance to any "under-developed country" that used military assistance to acquire sophisticated weapons systems. The provision did not apply to Greece, Turkey, Iran, Israel, Taiwan, the Philippines, and Korea, or to any country that the President specifically exempted on the basis of national security. (81 Stat. 937 and 81 Stat. 940) The Symington amendment stipulated that the President terminate development loans and PL–480 assistance to any country that made military expenditures "to a degree which materially interferes with its development." (81 Stat. 459)

economic aid to such countries if unnecessary military expenditures are materially interfering with economic development; (d) to use the US voting power in the Inter-American Development Bank to deny any loan which might assist in the acquisition of "sophisticated or heavy" military equipment.[3] The full text of these amendments is set forth in the Annex.

For the purposes of this estimate, we have assumed a determination that such weapons as the F–5 and Mirage 5 jet aircraft are "sophisticated weapons systems" within the meaning of the Acts.

Conclusions

A. A number of Latin American countries, having put off replacement of obsolescent military equipment for some years, are determined to undertake early procurement of particular items. They see an especially urgent requirement for jet aircraft, and the governments of Argentina, Brazil, Chile, Peru, and Venezuela have received recent assurances from US officials that the F–5 will be made available. If the US now refuses to provide F–5s, resentment in these countries will be strong. Some or all of them would almost certainly decide to acquire Mirage jets. They would also shift to greater reliance on European countries for the supply of other types of military equipment, and perhaps for military training as well.

B. Denial of the F–5s would be regarded in Latin America as but one part of a change in US policy—a change centered on the use of economic aid as a lever to restrict military expenditures. Most Latin Americans would consider this an affront to their national pride and an unwarranted interference by the US in their internal affairs; their reactions would be intense and adverse. US relations with the governments and the military establishments of major Latin American countries would suffer. The US would encounter increasing difficulty in obtaining cooperation under the Alliance for Progress and in the Organization of American States.

C. The loosening of ties with the Latin American military would endanger joint programs in specialized training and counterinsurgency, sharply increase US problems in carrying out contingency planning,

---

[3] The SIG discussed the impact of the Conte–Long and Symington amendments on foreign assistance to Latin America at its meeting on January 9, and Katzenbach approved the suggestion for further consultation with Congress. He also asked Helms to prepare "an assessment of the political costs in Latin America of a withdrawal of the F–5 offer." (Record of discussion, January 18; National Archives and Records Administration, RG 59, S/S–SIG Files: Lot 70 D 263, SIG/RA #29, 1/1/68, Strategy for Cyprus Settlement)

and make it more difficult and expensive for the US to maintain facilities for space ventures and nuclear detection.[4]

D. Those Latin American governments which responded to the denial of F–5s by arranging to purchase Mirages or other "sophisticated" jet aircraft would then run the risk of curtailment or termination of US developmental aid. In this event, the effect on their economies would vary considerably: in Argentina and Venezuela, for example, they would not be severe; in Brazil, Chile, and Peru they would be more serious. In several of the major countries, there would be internal political effects, reenforcing existing tendencies toward more assertive nationalism and sharper anti-US attitudes.

E. Damage to US relations with Latin America from such developments would be severe and would persist for some time. How long relations remained clouded, and how widely such effects would spread through Latin America, would depend on many broader political and economic factors and on the general world situation.[5]

[Omitted here are the Discussion section and Annex of the estimate.]

---

[4] Mr. Thomas L. Hughes, The Director of Intelligence and Research, Department of State, believes that this paragraph overstates both the existing advantages of our Latin American military relationships and the potential jeopardy to them. [Footnote in the source text.]

[5] The implementation of the Conte–Long and Symington amendments, particularly in Latin America, was discussed at SIG meetings on January 25 and February 15. (National Archives and Records Administration, RG 59, S/S–SIG Files: Lot 70 D 263, SIG/RA #30 & SIG/RA #31) The subject was also discussed at an NSC meeting on February 7 in which the President agreed to send Oliver to Latin America, including a stop in Peru to raise the F–5 issue with President Belaúnde. A record of the NSC meeting is in *Foreign Relations, 1964–1968,* vol. IX, Document 73.

---

67.   Action Memorandum From the President's Special Assistant (Rostow) to President Johnson[1]

Washington, February 5, 1968, 5 p.m.

SUBJECT

Measures to Invigorate the Form and Substance of Our Activities in Latin America

---

[1] Source: Johnson Library, National Security File, Country File, Latin America, Vol. VII, 1/68–2/68. Secret.

You asked for ideas to dramatize our Latin American policy. I suggest the following:

Measures Demonstrating High-level US Interest

1. *Special Message to the Inter-American Cultural Council.* Dr. Eisenhower and Dr. Hornig leave for Venezuela on February 13 to attend a special meeting of the Inter-American Cultural Council. The Council will pass on programs for carrying out the OAS Summit decisions in education and science and technology. I suggest you send a special message, with emphasis on the possibilities of satellite ETV. I have asked Dr. Hornig and Doug Cater to prepare a draft.

Approve[2]

Disapprove

Call me

2. *Trip by the Vice President.* To demonstrate our interest in economic integration and in opening the inner frontiers of South America, the Vice President could make a 3-week tour, visiting primarily projects related to development of the heartland of the continent: road building, hydroelectric plants, colonization, community development, cooperatives. Covey Oliver, Bill Gaud (who hasn't been to Latin America except to Punta del Este) and perhaps some Congressman should go with him. They would dramatize these two distinctly Johnsonian dimensions of the Alliance for Progress: integration and multinational projects.

Approve[3]

Disapprove

Call me

---

[2] The President approved the first five measures, adding the handwritten instructions noted in footnotes below.

[3] Johnson wrote: "check Pickets, Parades etc." Rostow later explained the instruction as a "careful check of the security aspects." (Memorandum from Rostow to Read, February 7; Johnson Library, National Security File, Country File, Latin America, Vol. VII, 1/68–2/68) Humphrey left for Latin America on March 31 and was in Mexico City that evening when Johnson announced that he would neither seek nor accept the nomination of the Democratic Party for reelection. (*Public Papers of the Presidents of the United States: Lyndon B. Johnson, 1968–69,* Book I, pp. 469–476) After signing Protocol II to the Treaty of Tlatelolco, Humphrey returned to the United States on April 1. (Hubert H. Humphrey, *The Education of a Public Man,* pp. 358–360) The Treaty for the Prohibition of Nuclear Weapons in Latin America was signed by 14 Latin American countries at Tlatelolco on February 14, 1967; see *Foreign Relations, 1964–1968,* vol. XI, Document 226.

3. *Invite Presidents to the Opening of Hemisfair.* Hemisfair officials could invite the Presidents of participating countries to the opening of the Fair. As part of their visit to San Antonio, you could invite them to the Ranch.

Approve

Disapprove

Call me

4. *Visits of Latin American Presidents.* You have the President of Paraguay, Alfredo Stroessner, scheduled for March. For the remainder of the year you could have:

President Leoni of Venezuela. He was invited for January but could not make it. State is proposing July.
President Lleras of Colombia. He is going to Europe this spring and would like to stop in the US.
President Balaguer of the Dominican Republic. He will have finished half of his term on July 1.

The Amistad Dam will be ready for dedication in September. You could join President Diaz Ordaz for that ceremony.

Approve[4]

Disapprove

Call me

5. *Interview with Selected Latin American Newsmen.* An interview with a group of carefully selected, prominent Latin American reporters would give you good exposure in Latin America. You could make it an informal, personal affair by having the interview in your office and taking the newsmen on a tour of the White House. This could be filmed by USIA for the newsmen and played all over Latin America. You could use the interview to project your vision of an economically integrated Latin America with the benefits that this would bring to the entrepreneur as well as the average citizen. State and USIA have developed a plan for bringing such a group of newsmen to the US, using Hemisfair as the cover.

Approve

Disapprove

Call me

---

[4] Johnson wrote: "plus 2 or 3 others." The following Latin American Presidents visited the United States in 1968: Stroessner of Paraguay (March), Trejos Fernandez of Costa Rica (June), Barrientos Ortuño of Bolivia (July), and Diaz Ordaz of Mexico (December).

5. [*sic*] *More Direct Contact by Covey Oliver with Latin Americans.* Covey has just finished a highly successful, two-week swing through Central America and Panama. He plans to travel to Peru, Chile, and Brazil, starting this week. A Taveras Dam loan signing ceremony in the Dominican Republic in March is another possibility. On these trips he tries to reach the people through TV, press conferences and public appearances in places outside the capital. His mastery of Spanish and natural empathy are a great asset.[5]

Our OAS–CIAP man should also be doing some missionary work of this nature, but he lacks the language and substantive knowledge of country problems and what CIAP might do to dramatize the Alliance. Nevertheless, if you reject proposal 2 above, he could tour the inner frontiers and be photographed on the modern roads, at dams, gas pipelines, etc. in the interior.

Measures to Give New Thrust to the Alliance for Progress

1. *Restructure CIAP.* CIAP is not giving leadership to the Alliance. The Chairman tends too much towards private diplomacy and does not exert enough firm, imaginative, public leadership. Our man is not feeding him ideas and pushing him for action behind the scenes. There is a serious structural weakness—7 *part-time* members cannot do the job of policy direction, country review, and performance follow-up that is required. It is politically impossible to replace the present members, but a few more *full-time* members with imagination and drive could be added. The new men are needed to translate the Summit directives into specific courses of action, determine priorities and, through close personal contact, persuade governments to move accordingly. Bill Bowdler has prepared a proposal for restructuring CIAP which he is taking up with Covey and Sol. We are shooting to get this done at the Inter-American Economic and Social Council meeting in June.

We can also expect more dynamism from a new OAS Secretary General if Galo Plaza is elected.

2. *New US Executive Director on the IDB.* Related to our leadership in CIAP is leadership in the Inter-American Bank. The Bank is assuming a larger role in the Alliance. Last year annual investments by the Bank reached the half billion mark. It did more dollar lending than our entire AID program in Latin America. My hunch is that the Congress will increasingly want to funnel assistance through the multilateral lending institutions, so the IDB's role in the Alliance is likely to increase. This makes it most important that we have a top-flight pro as US Executive Director

---

[5] Johnson underlined the last two sentences of this paragraph and wrote: "good give us all he can take."

who knows how to work with Latins while protecting our interests—especially since our top man on the Bank management is not effective. I know you are considering this matter. You have in Ray Sternfeld—the present US alternate—the man who can do that kind of job. I strongly recommend that you name him. (Tom Mann and Joe Barr agree.)

Approve

Disapprove[6]

Call me

3. *Modernize our Military and Security Relations with Latin America.* The pattern of these relationships was established during World War II and the years immediately thereafter. They are outdated. There is too much emphasis on bilateral programs with us and an excessive paternalism on our part. As we have done in the economic field, we should get the Latins to think more of military and security policy in collective terms and in relationship to economic and social goals. New instruments of inter-American cooperation are needed to replace the present antiquated—and stigmatized—ones. Bob Sayre has prepared a strategy for doing this which Nick Katzenbach has approved and is now awaiting the concurrence of Secretary McNamara.

4. *Three Additional Measures Contingent on Future Developments.* These measures of high impact for Latin America are contingent on future developments:

a. *Untying of AID for the Western Hemisphere, when* our balance of payments situation permits.
b. *Granting of Trade Preferences to Latin America, if* the Europeans continue their preferences for Africa and do not go along with further temporary worldwide tariff cuts for the LDCs.[7]
c. *A New Program to Open South America's Inner Frontiers More Rapidly,* after the heavy expenditures in Vietnam decrease.

Walt

---

[6] This option is checked.
[7] The President checked measures 4b and 4c.

68.   Memorandum From William G. Bowdler of the National Security Council Staff to President Johnson[1]

Washington, March 1, 1968.

SUBJECT

Covey Oliver's Trip to Venezuela, Bolivia, Peru and Colombia

The trip was a highly successful venture from the standpoint of public relations and personal contacts. On the substantive side, Covey achieved a considerable measure of understanding of the need for co-operative action to meet a crisis situation in Haiti and for a new mechanism for discussing and defining Latin America's military role and equipment needs. Covey was unable, however, to get President Belaunde to reduce military expenditures by any meaningful amount or to postpone purchase of unnecessary military equipment. Covey will be sending you a full report.[2] Here are the highlights:

Inter-American Cultural Conference

The meeting approved programs to carry out the Summit directives in education, science and technology. The Latin Americans pledged sufficient funds to finance, with our matching contribution, a $16-million effort the first year.

Venezuela

President Leoni would like to visit Washington, but it seems doubtful that he can do so this year.

The security forces have made great strides in the past four years with our help. I visited the police Central Command Center and the Armed Forces Joint Operations Center and was impressed by their organization and skill. The ten Venezuelan Ranger Battalions, for which you authorized fast delivery of equipment, are all in the field. Insurgency has not been eliminated but is at one of its lowest points in years.

Bolivia

The visit gave President Barrientos a boost and us the opportunity to examine Bolivia's economic situation at first hand. The economic outlook is generally good, but Barrientos faces a temporary budget

---

[1] Source: Johnson Library, National Security File, Latin America, Vol. VI, 10/67–4/68. Confidential. According to telegram CAP 80618 from Rostow to the President, March 1, the President saw the memorandum. (Ibid., Name File, Bowdler Memos)

[2] Rostow forwarded Oliver's report to the President on March 5. (Ibid., Country File, Latin America, Vol. VI, 10/67–4/68)

problem resulting largely from increased expenditures from the counter-guerrilla effort and the drop in tin prices. He is prepared to trim his budget and impose new revenue measures but still needs modest assistance from us.

Liquidation of the Guevara guerrillas has given the Bolivians pride and much needed self-confidence. The security situation looks reasonably good. I was impressed by dedication and quality of our country team in La Paz. The AID Mission is particularly impressive.

Peru

Covey did not get very far with President Belaunde on reducing the share of the budget for military expenditures or postponing the acquisition of additional military equipment. Belaunde is the prisoner of a strong-minded military, an opposition-controlled Congress bent on currying the military's favor and his own weakness as a political leader. Peru is one case where the Symington–Conte–Long amendments clearly apply. But this would probably provoke a crisis of confidence in Peru which would end up with the military ousting Belaunde. Rather than make a formal finding of applicability, it is better to turn the faucet on bilateral assistance to a trickle.

Despite our problems on aid, it is evident that there is vitality in the Peruvian economy. Control of insurgency is good. These factors make Peruvians pass off our curtailment of aid with a shrug of the shoulders.

Colombia

President Lleras was pleased to get your invitation to make a visit. He accepts, leaving the dates to be worked out. From his conversation with Covey Oliver and what we know of Lleras' performance during the past 18 months, it is clear that Lleras is a rare combination—for Latin America—of good executive, smart politician, knowledgeable economist, and statesman with a broad grasp of hemispheric and world problems. He is getting the Colombian economy back on its feet. With a smart mix of force and economic assistance he is making steady headway in curbing insurgency.

WGB

69.   Memorandum of the 583rd Meeting of the National Security Council[1]

Washington, March 6, 1968, noon.

THOSE PRESENT

The President
The Vice President

State
Secretary Rusk
Deputy Under Secretary Bohlen
Assistant Secretary Oliver
Deputy Assistant Secretary Sayre

Defense
Secretary Clifford
Under Secretary Nitze

JCS
General Wheeler

Treasury
Secretary Fowler

CIA
Director Helms

USIA
Director Marks

WH
W. W. Rostow
B. K. Smith
Tom Johnson
W. G. Bowdler

Assistant Secretary Oliver opened the discussion on Latin America by reporting on his appearance this morning before Senator Morse's Latin American Subcommittee. He said he had been "well and tolerantly" received with no grilling on the arms buildup in Latin America.

On the Latin American paper before the NSC,[2] Assistant Secretary Oliver singled out three issues:

(1) the problem of keeping up the momentum of the Alliance for Progress if the Alliance appropriation were cut a second year in a row.

---

[1] Source: Johnson Library, National Security File, NSC Meetings, Vol. V, 3/6/68, Inter-American Objectives and Problems. Secret. No drafting information appears on the memorandum. The meeting took place in the Cabinet Room, and according to the President's Daily Diary it began at 12:46 p.m. (Johnson Library)

[2] A copy of the paper is attached to a memorandum from Paul C. Warnke, Assistant Secretary of Defense for International Security Affairs, to McNamara, March 5. (Washington National Records Center, OSD Files: FRC 330 73 A 1250, Latin America 1968, 0–092)

(2) the drop in Latin American trade in 1967 which amounted to 6%, or $600 million.

(3) some—though exaggerated—backsliding on economic integration since the Summit.

Reporting on his trips to Central America and four South American countries, Mr. Oliver made these points:

(1) The Central American Common Market (CACM) is going through a difficult adjustment period. The members are considering restrictive measures which would undo the progress made by CACM. We should shift the emphasis of our assistance away from bilateral aid and toward adjustment assistance tied to the strengthening of CACM institutions.

(2) As the Mexican Foreign Minister has suggested, we should place more emphasis on physical integration to encourage economic integration.

(3) During the South American tour, he launched the idea of a periodic meeting of Ministers of Defense as a way of getting the Latin Americans to focus more realistically on their military requirements.

(4) In his conversation with Belaunde, he achieved limited success in getting the promise of a memorandum explaining projected military expenses for 1968, but he received no assurances with respect to postponement of additional military equipment.

The President gave these directives:

(1) that a task force be established to make a detailed study of existing national road systems in Latin America and how they might be linked up. He indicated a willingness to give his support to findings of the task force.[3]

(2) that top level officers responsible for managing our Latin American affairs make a special effort to visit Latin America and engage in other activities demonstrating our continued, high-level interest in the area.

[Omitted here is discussion of other subjects.]

---

[3] The President subsequently said that the study might be expanded to include air transportation and communications. [Footnote in the source text.] On April 5 Johnson approved a State Department plan to promote the task force proposal in Latin America. (Memorandum from Rusk to the President, April 4; National Archives and Records Administration, RG 59, Central Files 1967–69, POL 3 IA SUMMIT)

70.   National Intelligence Estimate[1]

NIE 80/90–68   Washington, March 28, 1968.

THE POTENTIAL FOR REVOLUTION IN LATIN AMERICA

Note

This estimate treats the question of revolutionary development in Latin America more broadly and over a longer period of time than has been customary in previous estimates.

There are many defensible definitions of the word *revolution*, and many traditional applications of that word to events in Latin America, where in the past 40 years there have been more than a hundred successful *golpes*, insurrections, and other violent or irregular changes of government. Our subject here is not simply the sudden overthrow of regimes but the pressures in Latin America for fundamental change. In an effort to assess the potential effects of those pressures, we define revolution as *a series of developments which, in a relatively short time, produces profound and lasting change in a nation's political, economic, and social institutions.* Among other movements to bring about such change, we survey the current status and future prospects of the several Communist insurgencies.

Some of the judgments we reach in this paper are quite specific and apply to the next year or two. Some, considerably more general, pertain to the next four or five years. Still others describe emerging trends which will be felt in the area over more than a decade.

Conclusions

A. The focus of attention in most discussions of this subject has been on insurgency movements supported by Castro. Such movements are still active in three countries: Colombia, Guatemala, and Venezuela. In all three cases they are relatively small, have attracted little sympathy among the local populace, and are encountering strong responses by the security forces. In no case do insurgencies pose a serious short-run threat to take over a government, though they are troublesome, difficult to deal with, and likely to remain an unsettling factor on the political scene.

---

[1] Source: Central Intelligence Agency, Job 79–R01012A, O/DDI Registry. Secret; Controlled Dissem. According to a note on the cover sheet this estimate was prepared in the Central Intelligence Agency with the participation of the intelligence organizations of the Departments of State and Defense and the National Security Agency. The United States Intelligence Board concurred in this estimate on March 28. The estimate superseded NIEs 80/90–64 and 80/90–66 (Documents 24 and 38).

B. Even over a much longer period, we do not believe that these, or similar insurgencies which may become active, will be the main engine of revolution in Latin America. The factors and forces which bring revolutions will be more complicated and will vary widely from country to country in form and character.

C. Because discontent has not yet become organized and acute, and because there is a lack of appealing radical leadership, revolution seems unlikely in most Latin American countries within the next few years. Over a longer period, however—certainly within the next decade—we see conditions developing throughout the area which will be much more conducive to revolution. Whether and when these conditions actually produce revolutionary changes will depend upon fortuitous combinations of factors within individual countries.

D. The establishments which now control the seven largest Latin American countries (Brazil, Mexico, Argentina, Colombia, Peru, Venezuela, and Chile) are much stronger than any proponents of revolutionary violence. Though the government of such a country might be displaced during the next year or two, the change almost certainly would not be revolutionary. In Chile, the government which comes to power in 1970 may follow revolutionary policies. In a number of the smaller countries, there is greater likelihood of a sudden overthrow of government and also more chance that a revolutionary government might come to power. (See Annex B for a discussion of six smaller countries which are particularly lacking in stability.)

E. Elements on the political left will be in the forefront of most future revolutionary movements, but we do not believe that the Communist organizations in Latin America have, or will develop, the strength to play the central role. We do not rule out the possibility that they might attempt on their own to seize power in one or more countries, but we think it far more likely that they would make common cause with other stronger revolutionary elements, settling temporarily for an influential voice in a new government and hoping to progress from there.

F. While we do not conclude that Castro-style insurgency is of no importance, we do believe that the forces which undertake future revolutions will develop and operate primarily in the cities. They will require—or wish to have—mass support, and such support will be more readily obtainable in the cities than in the countryside. The influx of people from countryside to city in Latin America is striking, and most of it swells the population of the slums. In 1940, there were five Latin American metropolitan areas with more than one million residents; in 1960, there were nine. We estimate that in 1970 there will be 18, and in 1980, 26.

G. The inhabitants of these urban slums—and particularly the young people born in them—will, we think, provide a key source of revolutionary raw material. The source of revolutionary leadership will vary from country to country; the personal qualities of the individuals will be of much more importance than the class or profession they represent. Some may be from the military—perhaps younger officers or noncommissioned officers; others from the Catholic priesthood; others from the university-intellectual community; and still others from new versions of existing political parties.

H. Varied as they may be in other respects, we believe that revolutionary movements will have one important common feature: a nationalistic, independent attitude with strong overtones of anti-US sentiment.

[Omitted here are the Discussion section, Annex A, and Annex B of the estimate.]

71.   Action Memorandum From the President's Special Assistant (Rostow) to President Johnson[1]

Washington, June 6, 1968, 2:15 p.m.

SUBJECT

Offer of Integration Adjustment Assistance to the Andean Subregional Group

In the memorandum at Tab A,[2] Under Secretary Katzenbach requests authorization to explore with the governments of the Andean Subregional Group (Bolivia, Chile, Colombia, Ecuador, Peru and Venezuela) a United States loan of up to $25 million for adjustment assistance to industries affected by formation of an Andean Common Market.

This group of six middle-size countries is now considering a treaty establishing a common market. The private sector in three (Venezuela, Ecuador and Peru) is nervous about adverse effects of rapid integration and are pressuring their governments to delay the treaty.

A year after Punta del Este it is clear the Latin American Common Market is more likely to come through a series of subregional groups than the merger of the Central American (CACM) and South Ameri-

---

[1] Source: Johnson Library, National Security File, Country File, Latin America, Vol. VIII, 9/68–10/68, 2 of 2. Confidential.

[2] Tab A is a May 29 memorandum from Katzenbach to the President; attached but not printed.

can (LAFTA) blocs, as contemplated at Punta del Este. That is why the action of the Andean Group is the most promising development on economic integration since the Summit.

The last-minute opposition of the private sector in some Andean countries threatens establishment of this subregional common market. By offering to join in establishing adjustment assistance, we may help the governments overcome this resistance. No loan would be made unless this objective is assured.

The key issue in making an adjustment loan offer is the tying arrangement. State argues that we will maximize our chances of getting governments to move if we follow the formula we use in the Inter-American Bank—our dollars could be used only to purchase goods and services in the United States, in the country of the user, or from other members of the Andean Group. This is also the formula we use in our loans to the Central American Integration Bank. (We allow this flexibility in Latin America because a large proportion of Latin foreign exchange eventually comes back to the US, even if it is not directly tied to US purchases.)

Secretary Fowler raises three issues on the State proposal (Tab B):[3]

1. *He takes sharp exception to the tying formula.* He wants the dollars tied to 100% US procurement, as we do in our bilateral aid loans. To do otherwise, he says, would undermine your January 1 balance-of-payments program and subsequent directive to AID to tighten up on balance-of-payments aspects of its operations.

2. *He questions the wisdom of immobilizing $25 million of scarce FY 1969 funds.* He thinks $25 million should be an upper limit and it should be used for adjustment assistance *and* capital financing.

3. *He wants the Inter-American Bank to be associated with integration lending proposals.* He recalls that in considering adjustment assistance for the Latin American Common Market prior to the Summit, Treasury took the line that the IDB should manage the adjustment fund.

These are my comments on Secretary Fowler's points:

1. The State tying formula would be a significant sweetener which would improve the odds on moving the proposal forward. The balance-of-payments impact would be minimal and at least a year in the future. The State tying arrangement would not weaken your January 1 program[4] because it would not cause substantial outflow nor

---

[3] Tab B is a June 1 memorandum from Fowler to the President; attached but not printed.

[4] Reference is to the President's statement on January 1 outlining a "Program on Action to Deal with the Balance of Payments Problem." (*Public Papers of the Presidents of the United States: Lyndon B. Johnson, 1968–69,* Book I, pp. 8–13)

introduce a new principle in balance-of-payments policy. AID's ability to achieve its new outflow targets would not be impaired. The targets will still be met.

2. AID would not automatically immobilize $25 million of FY 1969 funds. AID wants to talk to the Andean group about our joining with them in setting up an adjustment fund. The $25 million is only a ball-park figure. There would be no obligation of funds until a concrete loan proposal is worked out—based on the Andean Common Market coming into operation on terms satisfactory to us—and your approval under the new commitments procedure obtained.

3. Inter-American Bank Association with the Andean group can be explored when we discuss the loan with the Andean governments. I would not make the IDB association an absolute condition.

I recommend you decide this one in favor of State, in the understanding that the amount of our loan offer will be flexible and participation of the Inter-American Bank will be examined further if the Andean countries are interested in the proposal.

Walt

1. Authorize offering Andean Group adjustment assistance loan up to $25 million

Yes

No

Call me[5]

2. On the tying formula, approve:

the formula we use with IDB

the restrictive formula recommended by Secretary Fowler

---

[5] The President checked this option. No indication of the President's subsequent decision appears on this memorandum. In an October 23 memorandum to the President Rostow noted: "Last June you authorized State to explore with the six governments a possible AID loan of as much as $25 million for 'adjustment assistance'." Johnson subsequently approved a proposal to proceed with the loan, even though several countries, including Venezuela, Peru, and Ecuador, appeared reluctant to join the subregional group. (Johnson Library, National Security File, Country File, Latin America, Vol. VIII, 9/68–10/68, 2 of 2)

Central America

72. Memorandum From the Assistant Secretary of State for Inter-American Affairs (Mann) to the Under Secretary of State for Political Affairs (Harriman)[1]

Washington, February 6, 1964.

SUBJECT

Honduras—Possible Coup

REF

Agenda for Special Group (CI) for Friday, February 7[2]

Pressure in Honduras for removal of Ricardo Zúñiga A., Secretary General to Chief of Government Col. Lopez, has grown so rapidly in the past month, that unless he leaves the scene peacefully, there could be a counter-coup within the next two weeks.

Lopez depends completely on Zúñiga who runs the government. Zúñiga, as Lopez' personal adviser since 1956, has engineered Lopez' career to the present point in which Lopez hopes to become constitutional president. Lopez will not let Zúñiga go unless forced to by a united demand from the Army.

Today only the last Infantry Battalion and the newly formed Special Tactical Force (each numbering about 600 men and located just outside Tegucigalpa) stand between Lopez and a counter-coup. Lopez personally commands the Special Tactical Force through an executive officer whose support for Zúñiga is increasingly questionable. The commander of the 1st Battalion, Maj. Juan Melgar, is supposedly fanatically loyal to Lopez and has supported Zúñiga. However, Zúñiga secretly came to the United States in the last week of January, and in the last four days there have been reports that Melgar may be weakening in his resistance to pleas from his military colleagues to join them in evicting Zúñiga.

If Zúñiga leaves the government, Lopez would almost certainly be replaced by a civilian-military junta, though if the change were accomplished through a palace coup rather than an open revolt, Lopez might remain as head of the junta.

---

[1] Source: National Archives and Records Administration, RG 59, ARA/CEN/H Files, 1964: Lot 67 D 46, POL 1, General Policy. Secret; Noforn. Drafted by Rowell.
[2] Not found.

Without Zúñiga, Lopez probably would lose some of his presidential ambition, and those persons who oppose a military candidacy would have more influence. Opponents of a Lopez candidacy include a number of military officers as well as the Liberal Party (deposed in last October's coup) and major elements of the Nationalist Party (principal civilian allies of the present military government). The armed forces will almost certainly take a preconstitutional non-partisan attitude once Lopez is no longer a serious presidential contender.

Although much of the Army's antagonism toward Zúñiga is a spontaneous response to Zúñiga's high-handed operations, the Liberal Party, especially Jorge Bueso Arias, has contributed substantially to the plotting. Bueso is very competent, anti-communist, and was Finance Minister under deposed President Villeda Morales.

The leader of the military plotters is Defense Minister, Chief of Air Force, Lt. Col. Armando Escalon. Escalon is very competent and anti-communist, but his was one of the bitterest anti-U.S. voices during the period of non-recognition last fall (October 3 to December 14, 1963).[3]

The communists would welcome any change away from the present military government, though they are not involved in the present Liberal-Army scheming. The communists have begun to seize control of the MIL, an uncoordinated group of lower-level Liberal terrorists not countenanced by the Liberal leaders. The MIL began to function in December, 1963.

A junta government probably would have much more Liberal participation than does the present government, and thus would receive broader labor and Liberal backing. This would reduce the strength of the MIL. Thus, chances of a peaceful transition to generally accepted civilian representative government in 1965 are much better under a junta, especially if military partisanship declines. The increased civilian participation would improve the efficiency of the transition government as well.

---

[3] Colonel López Arellano overthrew President Villeda Morales on October 3, 1963. The Kennedy administration initially refused to recognize the new government, choosing instead to recall Ambassador Burrows on October 6 for "consultation," thereby suspending normal diplomatic relations. For documentation on the coup in Honduras and the initial U.S. response, see *Foreign Relations, 1961–1963*, American Republics, Microfiche Supplement, Honduras. The Johnson administration agreed to recognize the new government on December 14, 1963, but only after receiving "public assurances of respect for civil liberties, freedom of action for political parties, and that international obligations will be fulfilled." By that time, the López administration had also announced that elections for a constituent assembly would be held in February 1965. (Department of State *Bulletin,* December 30, 1963, p. 624) For a detailed account of these events, see Edward M. Martin, *Kennedy and Latin America,* pp. 125–141.

The anti-Zúñiga forces now believe they have gone too far to quit. As long as Zúñiga stays out of Honduras, there is a good chance that there will be only a palace coup. This would avoid bloodshed or extremism, and would add to the possibility that Lopez and the junta would resolve the conflict by exiling both Escalon and Zúñiga as ambassadors. Many of the military officers who are working against Zúñiga do not like the prospect of having Escalon as the new head of the junta.

If Zúñiga returns to Honduras soon, the plotters probably will resort to open revolt. Whether they win or lose, there will be some bloodshed and new openings for communist subversion. If they win, the United States will be faced with a not-too-friendly Escalon. If they lose, there probably will be a series of jailings and other repressive measures which will force large numbers of Liberal Party members and organized laborers into open alliance with the communists in the MIL.

Conclusions:

1. United States interests are best served by the earliest possible removal of Ricardo Zúñiga from his present influential position in Honduras.

2. A palace coup is much more to our interest than an open revolt in Honduras.

3. Therefore, the Honduran situation is most favorable to the United States the longer Zúñiga stays out of Honduras.[4]

---

[4] In a memorandum to Mann, February 4, Collins suggested that the Special Group (CI) consider detaining Zúñiga in the United States "to improve the chances for a peaceful alteration of government in Honduras." (National Archives and Records Administration, RG 59, ARA/CEN/H Files, 1964: Lot 67 D 46, General Policy) The minutes of the Special Group meeting have not been found. The Latin American Policy Committee also met to discuss the situation in Honduras, in particular, ways in which to "effect a non-violent transition to representative civilian government." On February 6 the LAPC approved a plan of action for the remainder of 1964, including the following proposal: "Seek ways to reduce the influence of Ricardo Zúñiga A." (Airgram CA–7933 to Tegucigalpa, February 10; ibid., Central Files 1964–66, POL 1 LA–US) In a telephone conversation with President Johnson, February 19, Mann mentioned the possibility of a another coup in Honduras; see Document 2.

73.   Memorandum of Conversation[1]

Washington, June 30, 1964, 11:30 a.m.

SUBJECT

> U.S.–Costa Rican Relations

PARTICIPANTS

> *U.S. Side*
> The President
> Assistant Secretary Mann
> Ambassador Telles
>
> *Costa Rican Side*
> Francisco Orlich, President of Costa Rica
> Daniel Oduber Quirós, Minister of Foreign Affairs
> Ambassador Gonzalo J. Facio
> Mario Quirós Sasso, Minister of the Presidency
> Mr. Eduardo Lizano, Economic Advisor
> Mr. Fidel Tristan, Economic Advisor

After speaking privately together, President Johnson and President Orlich joined members of the United States and Costa Rican delegations in the Cabinet Room. President Johnson said that President Orlich had raised two matters, first, a ten million dollar commitment which President Kennedy made during his visit to Costa Rica[2] and, second, the attitude of the United States towards the activities in Costa Rica of the two Cuban exile groups headed respectively by Mr. Ray and Mr. Artime. The President asked Mr. Mann to comment on these two points.

Mr. Mann indicated that he was not aware of any unfulfilled ten million dollar commitment to Costa Rica but he would look into this

---

[1] Source: National Archives and Records Administration, RG 59, Central Files 1964–66, POL COSTA RICA–US. Secret. Drafted by Mann and approved by the White House on July 11.

[2] President Kennedy visited Costa Rica in March 1963 to attend a conference of the Central American Presidents. In a meeting at the Embassy on March 20 Orlich asked Kennedy for financial aid, including budgetary assistance. No evidence was found to suggest that Kennedy gave any commitment other than an assurance "that he would look into this matter." A memorandum of the conversation is in *Foreign Relations, 1961–1963*, American Republics, Microfiche Supplement, Costa Rica.

and speak with the Costa Rican officials later on.[3] He said that it was understood that Costa Rica, because of the volcano and the drop in the production of coffee and other export crops, might need help. We would be glad to look into this on the basis of concrete projects as we wished to be cooperative. Regarding Ray and Artime, Mr. Mann stated that since last September no raids had been staged from U.S. territory because of President Kennedy's decision to avoid the risks of having Cuban exiles attack, from a U.S. base, ships of various nationalities. Mr. Mann stated that the United States was not participating in the activities of Mr. Artime and Mr. Ray which might be based in other countries. Mr. Mann said that he did not know a great deal about the activities of these two exile groups but he gathered that Mr. Artime might be somewhat more responsible than Mr. Ray. President Orlich ventured the opinion that the more responsible of the two was Mr. Ray. Mr. Mann indicated that we did recognize that the two Cuban exile leaders were trying to help Cuba return to freedom and we sympathized with their objective.

President Orlich in reply to a question by President Johnson said that the Alliance for Progress had been working more efficiently during the last few months. Mr. Mann explained some of the administrative steps that had been taken to make the Alliance machinery operate more speedily.

---

[3] In a July 1 memorandum for Rusk, Mann confirmed that Kennedy had "made no such commitment." "It was clear yesterday," Mann explained, "that President Orlich himself did not know what he would ask of President Johnson when he walked into the meeting." (National Archives and Records Administration, RG 59, Central Files 1964–66, POL 7 COSTA RICA) Orlich discussed the issue of financial assistance in meetings with Rusk on July 1 at 10 a.m. and Mann immediately thereafter. Memoranda of conversation for the two meetings are ibid., POL 15–1 COSTA RICA, and POL 7 COSTA RICA, respectively.

---

74.   Editorial Note

On October 13, 1964, Ambassador Burrows recommended a plan for political action in Honduras to February 1965, the month scheduled for elections to the constituent assembly. Burrows suggested that the United States identify candidates "with the necessary qualifications" for the Honduran presidency, while diminishing the influence of such "irreconcilables" as Ricardo Zúñiga. (Telegram 177 from Tegucigalpa; National Archives and Records Administration, RG 59, Central Files

1964–66, POL 23–9 HOND) On October 17 Assistant Secretary Mann indicated "general agreement" with the proposal, but with a cautionary note: "We do not think it would be wise for the Embassy to become identified with any particular candidate or candidacy nor do we believe that Embassy should oppose any particular candidate." (Telegram 137 to Tegucigalpa; ibid.) The Latin American Policy Committee (LAPC) tried to resolve the issue at its meeting on November 4, when it approved a revised plan of action for Honduras. Although avoiding direct support for specific candidates, the committee recommended that the U.S. "use every influence available, both to the Country Team and to Washington, to reduce the influence of Ricardo Zuniga." (Airgram CA–4918, November 5; ibid., POL 1–2 HOND)

On December 23 Mann and Deputy Assistant Secretary Adams discussed the Zúñiga problem with Desmond FitzGerald, Chief of the Western Hemisphere Division of the Central Intelligence Agency. According to a record of the meeting: "FitzGerald referred to the Honduran Government as possibly the worst in Honduras' history and [1 line of source text not declassified]. Agreeing the Government is bad, Adams doubted that President Lopez would 'become a sort of Cincinnatus and retire.' Also he wondered whether it was worthwhile at this late date to try to get rid of Zuniga. He said he would consult with the desk officer and report back." (Memorandum from Carter to Hughes, December 23; Department of State, INR/IL Historical Files, ARA–CIA Weekly Meetings, 1964–1965)

On February 16 Zúñiga and the Nationalist Party won a majority of the seats to the Constituent Assembly. According to Adolf A. Berle, who served as an official observer, the elections were "very suavely stolen." (Letter from Berle to Mann, March 3; National Archives and Records Administration, RG 59, Central Files 1964–66, POL 14 HOND) Three months later, Assistant Secretary Vaughan approved a proposal to reduce Zúñiga's influence, although a final decision was delayed to allow the Ambassador-designate, Joseph John Jova, time to discuss the issue further with other Embassy officials. (Memorandum from Broe to Vaughan, June 5; Department of State, INR/IL Historical Files, Latin America Files, 1965) No evidence has been found to indicate whether the proposal was, in fact, implemented. The policy to "reduce the influence of Ricardo Zuniga," however, was retained in the subsequent plan of action for Honduras, which was approved by the LAPC in September 1965. (Airgram CA–2964 to Tegucigalpa, September 14; National Archives and Records Administration, RG 59, Central Files 1964–66, POL 1 HOND–US)

75.   Memorandum From the Deputy Assistant Secretary of State
       for Inter-American Affairs (Sayre) to the President's Special
       Assistant for National Security Affairs (Bundy)[1]

Washington, June 12, 1965.

As you know the President asked for task force reports on
Guatemala, Bolivia and Colombia.[2]

As I mentioned in a meeting at the White House while I was still
on your staff,[3] ARA had set up a committee to study the counter-
insurgency problem in several countries. When I returned to ARA, the
first country I tackled was Guatemala. We had three or four meetings
with Defense, CIA, USIA and State participating. The actions outlined
on page 6 are essentially those proposed by the Ad Hoc Committee,
but they have been brought up to date.

The assessment is current.

As I understand it what the President wants to know is the current situation and what the United States should be doing to help maintain and improve the situation. I believe the attached paper provides
this information but would appreciate your reaction as to whether you
consider it adequate.

Mr. Vance thought we should also go into all the contingencies
should the present Peralta government fall. I would agree that we
should do this if we thought that the government would fall within
the immediate future. However, the situation in Guatemala is such that
we do not anticipate any sudden or violent change down there in the
near future, that is, the next 60 or 90 days. Accordingly, my own feeling is that an attempt to determine contingencies at this time would
not be a very profitable exercise. We have, however, asked CIA to come
up with a list of all the leading personalities in the political arena in
Guatemala with an indication of their political complexion. As soon as
this is done and discussed with us here in State, it would become an
annex to the attached paper.

---

[1] Source: Johnson Library, National Security File, Country File, Latin America, Vol.
III, 1/65–6/65. Secret.

[2] The President asked Mann on June 5 to set up a task force "to develop plans for
what we do in Guatemala, Colombia and Bolivia." "We should have a special task force
on top of it with the best names," Johnson said, "and be prepared in advance instead of
waiting until they are shooting at us." (Memorandum of conversation, June 5, 12:10 p.m.;
ibid., Papers of Thomas C. Mann, Telephone Conversations with LBJ, May 2, 1965–June
2, 1966)

[3] Sayre returned to ARA in May 1965 after serving 1 year as the Latin American
expert on the National Security Council staff.

Colombia and Bolivia are slightly different stories. On Colombia especially, I think we will want to give serious consideration to contingencies. We are working on those papers and hopefully will have them to you next week.

In the meantime, after you have looked over the Guatemala paper I would appreciate an indication from you that we are heading in the right direction.[4]

RMS

REPORT ON GUATEMALA

Assessment of Current Situation

A. *Political*

The present regime began governing after the overthrow of Ydigoras with a fairly broad degree of public support. It was avowedly an interim government and announced that it would return to constitutionality and free elections as soon as feasible. In 1964, a time table was announced which called for the promulgation of a constitution in March 1965 and elections to be held within six months from that date. A Constituent Assembly was formed consisting of most important middle-of-the-road parties. The regime inspired confidence among the business community for a considerable period and was helped in this regard by a fairly vigorous campaign to reduce the grosser aspects of corruption so evident in the Ydigoras government.

Over the past twelve months, however, the regime has gradually lost a part of its original support. This loss has been caused primarily by Peralta's failure to adhere to the original time-table for return to constitutional government and uncertainty over his intentions. The promised constitution was not promulgated in March, and until recently there had been growing indications that Peralta intended to seek to perpetuate his regime until at least 1967. In this atmosphere, an important left-of-center political party (PR, headed by Mario Mendez-Montenegro), which, with the government's PID and the right-of-

---

[4] According to a June 22 memorandum from Vaughn to the Secretary, Bundy advised the Department on June 18 that the report on Guatemala would satisfy "current requirements provided biographic data were included." Vaughn also wrote: "In general, Ambassador Bell regards the situation in Guatemala as reasonably satisfactory over the short term (the next two to three months). We are not as optimistic about Guatemala as the Ambassador, but we do not regard the situation so serious as to require contingency planning." (National Archives and Records Administration, RG 59, Central Files 1964–66, POL 23 GUAT) The Department officially forwarded the report to Bundy on June 18, noting that the biographical information would be sent at a later date. (Memorandum from Read to Bundy, June 18; ibid., POL 2 GUAT)

center MLN, was participating in the Constituent Assembly, has resigned in a bloc from the Assembly and is now in full opposition, because the Assembly refused to prohibit leaders of past coups from being presidential candidates.

There have been severe strains within the two parties remaining in the Constituent Assembly because of political maneuvering by several potential presidential candidates attempting to get Peralta's official sanction as the government candidate for future elections. The resulting progressive deterioration has given rise to fears that splits within the middle-of-the-road parties, and within the military itself, might even lead to civil war, creating a vacuum which could be exploited by trained communist minorities.

The situation has been ameliorated by a resolution passed by the Constituent Assembly on June 9. This resolution has fixed the following timetable for the country's return to constitutional rule: 1) promulgation of the constitution on September 15; 2) convocation of presidential and congressional elections on October 1, with the elections to be held within six months from that date; 3) installation of the new congress on June 1, 1966; 4) inauguration of the new president, vice president and supreme court justices on July 1, 1966. Shortly before this resolution, Peralta was quoted in a press interview with the *New York Times* to the effect that he would not seek to be elected President, but he has not made a public statement to this effect.[5]

Even though this new timetable differs substantially from that originally set forth, it probably will have the immediate effect of reducing current tensions. It will not, however, eliminate the political maneuverings among the two major parties and may still result in dissatisfaction among other moderate parties if, for example, it becomes clear that Peralta will not permit the PR to conduct an electoral campaign, or if he excludes other moderate left-of-center parties, such as the Christian Democrats, from participation in the electoral process. The government's intentions in this regard, however, can only be determined over the next several months.

Taking advantage of the political uncertainties which have prevailed, there have been several rumors of coups and one serious attempt at a coup against the Peralta government by non-communist elements. The most serious was one planned by Roberto Alejos, a strong supporter of former President Ydigoras. Alejos, presently in exile in Miami, claimed to have a number of supporters among the military in Guatemala, planned to transport arms and Cuban mercenaries from

---

[5] According to *The New York Times,* June 3, Peralta said: "I will absolutely not be a candidate for the Presidency."

Miami to Guatemala during May. His plans were thwarted due to close coverage of his activities by Customs and other U.S. enforcement agencies and the sizeable quantity of arms he accumulated were seized by U.S. enforcement officials.[6]

B. Economic

Indecision in the political field has been matched by indecision in the business of government. The Peralta regime, despite its effectiveness in reducing corruption, has been unable to take any affirmative decisions in the economic and social fields which would have contributed to progress and to reduction of counter-insurgency problems. Government investment programs have stagnated. No AID loans of any consequence have been completed since installation of the Peralta government two years ago. Several loans have been authorized by AID and one loan from the Export-Import Bank has been approved for negotiation, but U.S. representatives have, up to date, been unable to penetrate the suspicion and apathy of Guatemalan officials and complete negotiations on these loans. Neither the AID loans nor the proposed EXIM loan differ in their provisions from loans which have been concluded with all the other countries in Latin America.

This inability to come to terms on international loans in support of the government investment program is not a problem unique with U.S. agencies, and the Guatemalan attitude cannot be attributed solely to suspicion of North American motives. The Inter-American Development Bank has also had its difficulties in working with the GOG. Although the IDB has concluded negotiations on several loans, the rates of disbursement on these loans have been abnormally slow due to GOG inaction. It seems clear that lack of action in the economic field fundamentally results from the unwillingness or inability on the part of some members of the government to make effective decisions.

Fortunately, the governmental shortcomings have been somewhat offset by a vigorously expanding private sector. Exports have continued to climb significantly and there has been a substantial shifting away from dependence on coffee over the last three years due to the emergence of cotton as an important export commodity. There has also been a substantial increase in exports to Guatemala's partners in the C.A. Common Market, consisting primarily of light manufactures and processed agricultural products. Under the impetus of increasing exports and private investment activity, Guatemalan GNP has risen by

---

[6] The initiative in this matter evidently came from Ambassador Bell, who urged the U.S. Government to move quickly against Alejos. (Telegram 965 from Guatemala City, May 27; National Archives and Records Administration, RG 59, Central Files 1964–66, POL GUAT)

over 6% per year over the last 2 years. Current prospects are that it will continue to increase at this rate.

Despite improved exports, rapidly rising imports have resulted in a continued deficit on current account. Since much of the increase in imports has been financed by supplier credits from the U.S., Guatemalan foreign exchange reserves have continued to rise. Immediate foreign exchange difficulties have thus far been avoided, but repayment of supplier credits and short-term debts contracted with private banks in the U.S. will all create a strain over a somewhat longer period.

The major determinant of Guatemala's immediate economic future however is whether or not the business sector will continue to have confidence in the stability of the government. In the absence of confidence in the future, foreign exchange reserves could rapidly disappear, as they did immediately before the overthrow of Ydigoras.

Guatemalan inability to maintain an effective public investment program has also seriously affected the ability of economic assistance programs to focus on some of the social problems and basic causes of the country's backwardness. A phenomenon of this backwardness is the sprawling city slums in Guatemala City on which urban terrorism feeds. Community development efforts in the countryside although given lip service by the government are almost non-existent or couched in such grandiose terms as to be impossible of fulfillment. The government appears to feel no need for urgent action in areas of social reform.

C. Internal Defense

For the past several years there have been small bands of guerrillas in Guatemalan eastern hill country which have engaged in isolated raids and occasional political assassinations. The Government has been unable to eliminate these groups although sporadically aggressive patrol activity by the military has succeeded in keeping them somewhat off balance. The guerrillas, headed by Yon Sosa, former Guatemalan army officer, are financed from Cuba and have been conducting their activities independently of the regular Guatemalan Communist Party structure (PGT).

In recent months there have been reports of attempts to coordinate terrorist activities between the PGT and the Yon Sosa guerrillas and turn the attention of both groups to urban rather than rural activities. The extent to which this coordination of efforts has been achieved is uncertain but in any event there has been a significant increase in urban terrorism.

In January there was an attempted assassination of the Chief of the U.S. Army Mission and the USAID motor pool in Guatemala City was burned to the ground. In February, terrorists in Guatemala City, who had intended to assassinate Peralta, threw grenades at a crowd of people and into a Guatemalan Army truck causing several casualties. As an immediate effect of this action, a state of siege was imposed by the Peralta government.

Since imposition of the state of siege, terrorists on March 20 assassinated a police officer who had a reputation as a terrorist, on March 25 threw a grenade at an Army truck which bounced off in the street and killed a girl, and on March 31 machine-gunned a Guatemalan Army building and planted bombs around the city causing several casualties.

On May 2, the U.S. Consulate was sprayed with machine-gun fire and bombs were thrown elsewhere in the city. At noon, May 21, the Vice Minister of Defense was assassinated near his home. On June 7, approximately 7 bombs were exploded in different parts of the city, including the residences of the Brazilian and Nicaraguan Ambassadors, the latter in an apparent protest against the action of these two countries in sending troops to the Dominican Republic.

CAS reports have continued to give strong indication of communist intentions to take direct action against U.S. personnel and installations. As a result of this, security in U.S. Government installations has been increased sharply. The Marine Corps complement in the Embassy has been more than doubled and emergency radio and telephone communications facilities have been installed to increase the alert capability.

The Guatemalan military forces have sufficient training and equipment to counter isolated hit-and-run raids by guerrillas in the rural areas. There are several units in a fair state of readiness, including an airborne infantry company which could be airlifted to severe trouble spots should actions develop beyond the capability of local military commanders. One reason the Guatemalan military forces are not more effective against the guerrillas is the inadequacy of their information and patrol systems. More coordinated effort between police and military efforts should be sought. Another reason is the general attitude of the rural population as a result of the military tendency to behave like an army of occupation in the areas they visit.

In an effort to change their image, the military have engaged in active and fairly successful civic action programs throughout the country. Unfortunately, very few of these programs have been located in areas of rural guerrilla activity.

The qualified success of the military in the rural areas is not matched by security force capabilities within the city. There are substantial elements of the national police force located in Guatemala City but their training and equipment are relatively poor. More importantly there has been no clear definition of the roles of the police and military in counter-insurgency operations either in the cities or in rural areas.

Efforts to improve the police have been hampered by the same lack of GOG ability to make decisions evident in political and economic fields. Current levels of assistance to the police through AID/OPS programs amount to $276,000 of which $100,000 is for U.S. technical advisors. The current level of MAP financing for support of military forces is $1.3 million. Despite indications that the U.S. was prepared to consider increased assistance to the police, the Government of Guatemala has so far not responded affirmatively.

The existence of urban terrorism and guerrilla activities will not in themselves cause the overthrow of the Peralta government if there is no major deterioration of the political and economic situation. Nevertheless, the evidence of increasingly coordinated efforts among the two extremist groups, and the increasing number of urban terrorist actions indicate that an effective organization is being created. Vigorous measures are required to reduce its potential for damage and to weaken its ability to seize on a deteriorating situation should one develop.

Action Recommendations

The Latin American Ad Hoc Inter-Agency Group on Counter-Insurgency has been reviewing in detail the situation described above. It has come to the obvious conclusion that one of the key impediments to the development of a counter-insurgency program in Guatemala is ineffective government leadership and the unwillingness of the Peralta government to make decisions involving the economic, political and social development of the country.

The actions set forth below, which the group has sent as an instruction to the Country Team,[7] will be inhibited by this overriding problem. To the extent that the Country Team can move forward on such action, however, the following steps should be taken:

I. Political

1. Undertake to convince Peralta, other members of his government and responsible leaders of the moderate, nonextremist political parties that it is in Guatemalan interests for the government to press forward now with a broad range of programs directed towards national progress and development.

2. In low key, undertake in various ways, including direct personal conduct, to make known to Peralta the U.S. view that early

---

[7] Airgram CA–12888 to Guatemala City, June 2. (Ibid., POL 23 GUAT)

return to constitutional government is essential and emphasizing the U.S. concern that failure to move in this direction enhances the possibility of subversion or civil war.

3. Encourage Peralta to permit all "middle-of-the-road" political parties to present candidates for the presidency.

4. Discreetly strengthen moderate political parties by all feasible means.

5. Discreetly support selected moderate politicians as a potential leadership resource in the event of a breakdown or sharp deterioration of the present situation.

II. Economic

1. Complete negotiations on outstanding AID loans as soon as possible waiving minor provisions which the present Government of Guatemala can use as an excuse for its inability to make decisions.

2. Consider the possibility of financing slum clearance and related projects in Guatemala City in an attempt to reduce the major subversion potential represented by urban discontent.

3. Explore the possibility of U.S. financing of additional mobile health units to be concentrated in guerrilla-threatened rural areas.

4. Consider the possibility of initiating community development programs, particularly in guerrilla-threatened areas.

III. Internal Defense

1. Continue to push for an expanded Public Safety program to enable the police to deal more effectively with insurgency problems, with primary emphasis on urban areas but also including rural activities.

2. Consider the creation of a special group within the police force to deal with counter-insurgency.

3. Urge that there be a clear definition of the roles of the police and military in counter-insurgency operations.

4. Examine the attitudes of the rural population toward Guatemalan security forces and the possibility of more effective training of such forces to improve civilian/security-forces relationships.

5. To the extent feasible, urge the expansion of civic action programs in threatened areas coordinating with AID programs which may be developed.

76.   **Action Memorandum From the Assistant Secretary of State for Inter-American Affairs (Vaughn) to the Under Secretary of State (Ball)[1]**

Washington, July 22, 1965.

SUBJECT

U.S. Position on Mediation Request in British Honduras Dispute

Discussion

The Governments of Guatemala and the United Kingdom formally requested the United States Government on July 6, 1965 to move beyond its role of good offices in the UK–Guatemala dispute over British Honduras and to serve as a mediator in the dispute either solely or in conjunction with other governments to be mutually agreed upon. This request was the outcome of informal talks held in London during the last week of June between representatives of the Governments of Guatemala, the United Kingdom, and British Honduras. These talks, as well as the round of talks which preceded them in May in Miami, were arranged through the good offices which the U.S. Government has been extending to the U.K. and Guatemala since 1963, shortly after the long-standing dispute over British Honduras (or Belize) led to the rupture of diplomatic relations between those two governments. Having received informal notice from both sides that the London talks would probably lead to a request for U.S. Government mediation, the Department unsuccessfully attempted to ward off such a request by informing both sides, prior to the London talks, that the USGovt would prefer not to mediate but would be willing, on request, to suggest prominent foreign (non-U.S.) private citizens as mediators. Our position was dictated by our desire to avoid the onus of a settlement which is bound to be unpopular with one side or the other and particularly so with Guatemala. The possible adverse reaction to direct USG mediation by Mexico, which also has a claim to part of British Honduras, has been another consideration.

Following receipt of the request for U.S. Government mediation, Embassy Guatemala strongly urged the Department to accede (Embtel 13, July 6, Tab A).[2] AmConsul Belize endorsed Embassy Guatemala's

---

[1] Source: National Archives and Records Administration, RG 59, Central Files 1964–66, POL 32–1 GUAT–UK. Confidential. Drafted by Steins on July 21; cleared by Shullaw, Reis, and Salans. Sayre initialed for Vaughn. Another copy indicates that the memorandum was also cleared by Leonhardy and Sause. (Ibid.)

[2] Not attached. (Ibid., POL BR HOND–GUAT)

recommendation (Belize No. 3 of July 13, Tab B).[3] The British Government is believed to desire a favorable U.S. response primarily to ensure continuation of the search for a solution which will enable it to withdraw from British Honduras. Embassy Mexico recommended that, if the USGovt were to undertake the mediation, prior consultation should be carried out with the GOM because of Mexico's own historic claim to part of British Honduras (Embtel 63, July 7, Tab C).[4] Embassy Mexico believes GOM would not object to mediation by a prominent U.S. private citizen, but recommends that announcement of the appointment of a mediator be made, not by the U.S. Government, but by the UK and the GOG, to minimize the appearance of official U.S. participation (Embtel 143, July 15, Tab D).[5] Mr. Meeker, in a memorandum of July 12 (copy attached, Tab E)[6] suggested that the Department be responsive to the request but attempt, at least for the time being, to keep to a minimum the U.S. Government association with the mediation by offering to suggest a prominent U.S. private citizen or citizens as mediator(s).

Recommendation

With the concurrence of EUR and of L, I recommend that the Department reply to the UK and GOG request by offering to suggest to them a prominent U.S. private citizen or citizens to serve as mediator. I further recommend that, if the answer of the UK and GOG to this offer is affirmative, ARA and L be authorized together to begin discreet, informal exploratory soundings with appropriate U.S. private citizens.[7]

---

[3] Not attached. (Ibid., POL 32–1 GUAT–UK)

[4] Not attached. (Ibid., POL BR HOND–GUAT)

[5] Not attached. Reference should be to telegram 142 from Mexico. (Ibid.)

[6] Not attached. Reference is in error; the memorandum from Meeker to Vaughn and Leddy is dated July 13. (Ibid., POL 32–1 GUAT–UK)

[7] Ball approved this recommendation on July 24.

77.   **Telegram From the Embassy in Guatemala to the Department of State**[1]

Guatemala City, August 2, 1965, 1508Z.

64. For the Secretary from Ambassador. I am very much concerned that we appear to be on point rejecting request made jointly on July 6, 1965 by Governments of Guatemala and Great Britain to extend our good offices further in matter of Belize-British Honduras dispute and accept function of mediator either alone or (if we prefer) in association with other states. Deptel 48 of July 30 indicates that this is likely.[2] Only reason for such refusal known to me is set forth Deptel 23 July 13[3] where indicated: "We remain reluctant assume direct responsibility for settlement which likely be unpopular, at least with GOG."

I have sought in several messages to point out reasons why I thought in our interests to respond affirmatively to the request. (Embtels 13 July 6, 26 July 15[4] and 53 July 29.[5]) For past two years Guatemalan Govt has sought find way out this political problem which has been source both trouble and political exploitation for nearly a century. British Govt which two yeas ago had no confidence in Guatemalan sincerity is now persuaded thereof. No comparable opportunity to reach peaceful solution has existed during last hundred years. If not seized upon and cultivated not likely again to recur.

I have reluctantly come to conclusion that GOG will conclude it cannot accept mediation through private citizens; thus if we refuse to serve as mediators we may find that effort will collapse or be abandoned. GOG has gone very far in effort to demonstrate its readiness to work to solve its political problem but it feels it needs the help and reassurance that having USG as USG can give and which private citizens cannot. This reflects fact that however much USG is criticized from time to time GOG believes and believes that its citizens believe in basic fairness of US and that chances getting adequate face-saving formulas out of mediation are better with prestige and moral influence of USG involved. This may not be entirely reasonable and I may not explain it very clearly but I am convinced that with USG acceptance of role we have excellent chance resolving problem in manner safeguarding interests of all, and that if we turn down request, we face

---

[1] Source: National Archives and Records Administration, RG 59, Central Files 1964–66, POL 32–1 GUAT–UK. Confidential; Immediate; Limdis. Passed to the White House.

[2] Not printed. (Ibid.)

[3] Not printed. (Ibid., POL BR HOND–GUAT)

[4] Neither printed. (Ibid., and POL 32–1 GUAT–UK, respectively)

[5] Telegram 53 from Guatemala City is dated July 28. (Ibid.)

likelihood that such action will destroy or negate progress so painfully made over past two years. Responsibility for this undesirable result would be ours.

Obviously fact of GOG desire for USG as USG implies that we would have to accept some responsibility for results of mediation. As I have pointed out, it could not be exclusive since the GOG would have to have freely accepted any proposals, but it is true that we might be faced with share of any onus that arose out of mediation. If we assume this was considerable, (which I do not believe it would be) would this be a very big price to pay for a successful resolution of dispute? If mediation fails, we are only where we began.

We do not shirk our responsibilities when they have reached points of critical danger, as in Viet-Nam and in Dominican Republic, and certainly our investments and our risks there are major. What is required in Belize is a minor investment of brain power employment and lots of patience and determination. If we turn down request and Belize becomes the focus of infection later as it could very well become, we will surely regret having been timid.

I do not understand how we can justify denial of joint request of two allied powers to serve as friendly mediator in effort to solve dispute between them. I respectfully urge that this matter be reconsidered at highest level.

Bell

---

78. Memorandum From the Acting Assistant Secretary of State for Inter-American Affairs (Sayre) to Secretary of State Rusk[1]

Washington, August 6, 1965.

SUBJECT

   Mediation of British Honduras Dispute

Discussion

We have endeavored to avoid a direct role in the United Kingdom–Guatemala talks on Belize because of our desire to avoid the onus of

---

[1] Source: National Archives and Records Administration, RG 59, Central Files 1964–66, POL 32–1 GUAT–UK. Confidential. Drafted by Sowash on August 5 and cleared by Leddy and Meeker. A notation on the memorandum indicates that Rusk saw it.

a settlement which may well be unpopular, particularly in Guatemala, where the weakness of the Government's claim is in inverse proportion to the emotional appeal of the issue. The possible adverse reaction to direct USG mediation from Mexico, which also has a claim to part of British Honduras, has been another consideration. The British and Guatemalan Governments, however, formally requested direct U.S. Government mediation on July 6 either solely or in conjunction with other Governments to be mutually agreed upon.

On July 24, the Under Secretary approved a proposal that the USG adopt a more responsive attitude by offering to suggest the name of a prominent U.S. private citizen or citizens to serve as mediator(s) (Tab A).[2] Apprised of this position informally, Ambassador Bell requested that you review this decision (Tab B—Emb. Guatemala telegram 64).[3] He urges direct U.S. Government mediation.

It has been the position of ARA that the U.S. should avoid pursuing a role in which we would be charged in Guatemala with responsibility for the loss of Belize. We have explored the possibility of a tripartite governmental mediation but the Legal Adviser's Office believes this procedure to be unwieldy and we are inclined to agree. Moreover, under such a procedure we might well have the U.S. representative casting the decisive vote on questions on which the other two mediators were divided and thus reap as much onus as if we had undertaken the mediation by ourselves.

We see advantages in suggesting a prominent American citizen as mediator in a private capacity, although we recognize that, in practice, the distinction between an American acting in a private capacity or in a governmental capacity may not be great. The onus for an unpopular settlement in either case may rest on the USG. Despite this risk, we recognize that an opportunity now exists to settle the long-standing dispute. On balance therefore, we believe that we should respond to the British and Guatemalan requests, in the sense that we are prepared to arrange for a mediation effort by suggesting the names of a prominent American citizen or citizens to serve as the mediator but leaving open the question of the private or governmental character of the mediator. We would be prepared in subsequent discussions with the UK and Guatemala to agree to direct USG mediation if we find this to be necessary to get the mediation underway. EUR and L concur.

---

[2] Document 76.

[3] Document 77.

Recommendations:[4]

That you authorize a reply to the United Kingdom and Guatemalan Governments' request which offers to suggest the name of a prominent U.S. citizen or citizens to undertake the mediation.

That you authorize direct mediation by the U.S. Government in the event this is required.

---

[4] Although the memorandum does not record the decision, the Secretary evidently approved both recommendations. Rusk authorized the delivery of diplomatic notes in Guatemala and London indicating his "readiness to propose the name of a prominent and distinguished citizen or citizens of the United States to undertake the mediation of this dispute." (Telegram 75 to Guatemala City and London, August 18; National Archives and Records Administration, RG 59, Central Files 1964–66, POL 32–1 GUAT–UK) The Department subsequently conceded the issue of direct mediation by appointing Bethuel M. Webster, a New York City lawyer and former member of the Permanent Court of Arbitration, as mediator with ambassadorial rank. (Telegram 174 to Guatemala City, October 20; ibid.)

---

79.   Memorandum From the Assistant to the Vice President (Rielly) to Vice President Humphrey[1]

Washington, September 14, 1965.

SUBJECT

Your Meeting with Daniel Oduber

Daniel Oduber is making his final trip to Washington before the Presidential election scheduled to take place on February 6, 1966. He is here to mobilize all possible outside support for the government and to the extent possible for the party during this critical election period.

The electoral race in Costa Rica has changed considerably since his last visit and his left of center Populista party now faces the opposition of a united conservative front. Our independent assessments indicate that though he will have strong competition, he is still expected

---

[1] Source: Minnesota Historical Society, Hubert H. Humphrey Papers, Vice Presidential Files, Foreign Affairs General Files, Meeting with Daniel Oduber, September 15, 1965. Secret; Sensitive. Oduber also met Humphrey on April 15 to discuss, among other issues, "the Presidential campaign in Costa Rica next year." (Memorandum from Rielly to Humphrey, April 14; ibid., Meeting with Daniel Oduber and Amb. Facio of Costa Rica, 4/15/65) No substantive record of the meeting has been found.

to win. The current estimate is that he will carry about 54 percent of the vote, although an estimated swing vote of 100,000 votes could alter this outcome.

Oduber contends that it is not sufficient merely to win the election but to win by a sufficiently large majority so that the new president will have in the Assembly a working majority sufficiently large to put through the needed constitutional changes. This would require getting about 60 percent of the vote, as constitutional amendments require approval by two-thirds vote of the legislature. To effect basic structural reforms in the economy and the society it is necessary to change the constitution.

The government is encountering economic problems which could have a direct bearing on the election. A two million dollar repayment to the Ex-Im Bank falls due sometime late this year. The Costa Rican Government would like to get it rolled over for six months or so so they can have that money available for other purposes during this period. Secondly, the government must raise electricity rates by 12 percent before the election if it is to meet requirements set down by a previous World Bank loan. It is doubtful that the World Bank will consider delaying this. However, the Ex-Im loan repayment could easily be rolled over if it is considered important to do so here in Washington.

The Costa Ricans are also seeking to expedite the disbursements under a 7½ million dollar project loan approved earlier. They would like to have part of the remaining 4 million dollars disbursed ahead of schedule so as to permit them to have funds to meet the government payroll for the rest of the year. Apparently there is some possibility they will default on the government payroll unless they get some external assistance—which would be disastrous politically.

I believe the Costa Ricans may be operating under the assumption that external funds might be available for the *election campaign itself.* They argue that much of the 1.5 million dollars that is being spent by the conservative opposition comes from outside the country, namely from the Somozas in nearby Nicaragua. Therefore they consider it legitimate for them to accept funds from outside of the country. A check with the appropriate people here reveals great reluctance to get involved in this contest, as it does not involve any left-wing threat. Most everyone in Washington agrees that it is desirable from the U.S. point-of-view for Oduber to win, but it is not considered appropriate to actively intervene as the conservative opposition is not considered a threat to U.S. interests.

As a practical matter, I believe you could say something to Dean Rusk, who is a friend and a great admirer of Oduber, about the U.S. Government doing all it can to help him. Rusk could pass the word both to Ex-Im and to AID to do everything they can to cooperate with the Costa Rican Government. With a word from Rusk both Ex-Im and AID would grant the roll-overs and the advance disbursements.[2]

Whether you would want to raise with Rusk the question of additional aid, I am not sure. It would take a strong push from the White House to get final approval on this. On the basis of his knowledge of previous elections in the hemisphere (Venezuela, Chile, Dominican Republic), I believe Daniel may be making some false deductions about what is available.[3]

---

[2] Although no evidence has been found that he spoke to Rusk, Humphrey evidently asked the Export-Import Bank to refinance construction of the Pan-American Highway in Costa Rica. In an October 12 telephone conversation Vaughn discussed the project with president of the Bank, Harold Linder, complaining of a "rather exotic process trying to pin down what the White House wants on Costa Rica." Linder explained that the loan had been refinanced three times, but thought that "something could be arranged to get at what the White House had in mind." (National Archives and Records Administration, RG 59, ARA Files, 1965–67: Lot 70 D 295, Inner Office Memoranda, October 1965)

[3] Humphrey met Oduber on September 15. According to a draft memorandum of conversation, Oduber said that he needed outside assistance "for his campaign to be really successful," charging that his opponent had already received support from the Somoza family and a local television station owned by the American Broadcasting Company. Humphrey maintained that "liberal people up here should have an interest in the outcome of this election," and agreed to enlist "some labor friends of his." The Vice President promised that "he would have his lawyer and confidante, Max Kampelman, look into this matter and see what the possibilities are." Humphrey also said that he would ask Kampelman to "get word to the ABC people that they are discriminating against a candidate whose program is favorable to the United States." (Minnesota Historical Society, Hubert H. Humphrey Papers, Vice Presidential Files, Foreign Affairs General Files, Meeting with Daniel Oduber, September 15, 1965)

---

80.   Memorandum of Conversation[1]

San José, September 21, 1965.

SUBJECT

Current Presidential Campaign

PARTICIPANTS

José Joaquin Trejos Fernandez, Presidential Candidate, National Unification Party
Mario Echandi, Former President of Costa Rica
Ambassador Telles

---

[1] Source: National Archives and Records Administration, RG 59, Central Files 1964–66, POL 14 COSTA RICA. Confidential. Drafted by Willis and Sedgwick. The meeting was held at the home of Edmundo Gerli. Forwarded as an enclosure to airgram A–151 from San José, September 28.

Echandi started off a discussion of the election campaign by remarking that he was seriously concerned by the increasing amount of violence at campaign rallies and stated that during his Presidency (1958–1962) there had been no such problem. At the same time, Echandi also made it clear to me that he sees no likelihood of an attempted golpe, although he remarked that one could never predict the behavior of "irresponsible" elements in Costa Rica. Likewise he did not seem concerned that campaign violence might lead to a possible assassination attempt, planned or otherwise, on either candidate saying that it was out of keeping with the Costa Rican character.

Echandi mentioned again to me a favorite grievance of his regarding the U.S.—the fact that President Kennedy, during his original speech on the Alliance for Progress, had mentioned José Figueres.[2] Both Trejos and Echandi alleged that the U.S. Government through "bad advisors in Washington", and PLN candidate Daniel Oduber, as a deliberate effort, have tried to create the impression that the Alliance in Costa Rica is somehow the property of the National Liberation Party and that the benefits which Costa Rica receives from the Alliance are due to PLN efforts. Echandi asserted that Vice President Humphrey has befriended Oduber and that the latter is conveying the impression that without a PLN Government, the Alliance would not operate in Costa Rica. Trejos and Echandi both suggested that this impression could be countered by a public statement from me to the effect that the Alliance is politically neutral.

I replied that no political party in Costa Rica (or in any other Latin American country) has a monopoly on the Alliance, which is politically neutral, and that the U.S. is ready to cooperate with any freely elected government in this country. I recalled that during the Echandi Government, the U.S. had provided a great deal of assistance. I said that our only interest is that the 1966 elections be carried out in the best Costa Rican democratic tradition and assured them that once the Costa Rican people have elected a government we will support it. I also reminded Echandi that I had taken various steps to help ensure free elections in 1962 and told him how I had insisted then and have now on the strict neutrality of all Embassy personnel. As for Oduber's relationship with Mr. Humphrey, I commented that Oduber has probably made a considerable effort to cultivate Mr. Humphrey, but that Mr.

---

[2] Reference is to President Kennedy's address at a White House reception for members of the Diplomatic Corps from Latin American Republics on March 13, 1961, in which he formally announced the formation of the Alliance for Progress. The speech included the line: "In the words of Jose Figueres, 'once dormant peoples are struggling upward toward the sun, toward a better life.'" (*Public Papers of the Presidents of the United States: John F. Kennedy, 1961*, p. 172)

Humphrey would certainly not assist in Oduber's campaign and further neither the Vice President nor any other U.S. Government official will extend any financial interest to either candidate. Regarding a public statement, I countered that any such statement would have to be carefully thought out, especially as to context and timing, but that I would be glad to consider it.

Referring to Trejos' recent speech in which he had alleged U.S. Government favoritism toward the PLN, I said that, given the widespread pro-U.S. attitudes in Costa Rica, any statement which might be construed by the Costa Rican public as being anti-U.S. might well prove to be counterproductive. Echandi replied, rather heatedly, that "Costa Ricans would never tolerate U.S. involvement in Costa Rican affairs". I quickly made the point that the U.S. was not involving itself in the Costa Rican elections and that it was apparent that we were not doing so. Both Echandi and Trejos agreed with me. Trejos then stated that he regards himself as a great friend of the U.S., but that he still had the impression that Embassy was attempting to "seek out" and "consult" Oduber. I said that the source of Trejos' misunderstanding should not be difficult to dispel, since it must have arisen when two AID technicians were invited to attend a recent meeting at the Planning Office at which Oduber was also present; a fact of which they had no knowledge before the meeting. I said that this, of course, had placed the AID people in an awkward position, but that there was nothing they could do about it except to proceed with their presentation of facts; there was, of course, no "consultation" with Oduber. I then told Trejos that we would be glad to give him a full briefing on the AID program, or on any other U.S. program that might interest him at any time, as we had "absolutely nothing to hide." I assured him that if he should ever be disturbed about any aspect of U.S. policy that I would attempt to explain it to him and if it should prove that the Embassy or I were in the wrong that I would do my best to correct it. Trejos seemed pleased at the invitation and said he would take up my offer at the first opportunity.

The conversation turned to other matters and I brought up the subject of the CIAP tax mission and asked Trejos his opinion of this effort to achieve an improved system of taxation in Costa Rica. The candidate replied that he was fully aware of the mission and thought that it would be "helpful", and was in favor of technical assistance in connection with the Costa Rican tax program.

81. **Memorandum From William G. Bowdler of the National Security Council Staff to the President's Special Assistant for National Security Affairs (Bundy)**[1]

Washington, November 18, 1965.

SUBJECT

Costa Rican Election

At your request I have looked into the Costa Rican electoral picture. This is what I have found:

1. *Essential Facts*

The election is scheduled to take place on February 6, 1966. It is a general election, covering the Presidency, Legislative Assembly and Municipal Councils.

The principal candidates are Daniel Oduber Quiros of the Partido Liberacion Nacional (the party now in power) and Jose Trejos Fernandez, representing a coalition of opposition groups (Partido Republicano, Partido de Union Nacional, and Partido Union Republicana Autentica).

The Presidential inauguration is scheduled for May 8, 1966.

2. *The Candidates*

Full, up-to-date biographic sketches of the two Presidential candidates are at Tab A.[2] They are staunch democrats. Both are friendly to the United States and can be expected to work closely with us. Both have the right orientation on the communist threat, although Oduber's views are better known because of his role in the OAS on this issue. The principal difference seems to be one of background and political outlook. Trejos comes from a prominent and well-to-do family. He is described as a "moderate conservative". Oduber comes from a modest background and is clearly left of center.

3. *The Outlook*

The campaign is just beginning to get under way in earnest. The reporting is scanty, so it is hard to get a very clear picture of issues and trends. This is being corrected.

The Embassy last month expressed the view that Oduber had a "reasonable edge" over Trejos, but declined making any firm prediction

---

[1] Source: Johnson Library, National Security File, Country File, Costa Rica, Vol. I, 4/64–10/68. Secret; Sensitive. Bundy wrote the following note on the memorandum: "Bill: Good, this makes sense to me."

[2] Attached but not printed.

on the probable outcome.[3] Ambassador Telles in a recent letter reported that Oduber was still favored to win.[4]

State/INR last August did a roundup on the elections (Tab B).[5] Their estimate was that the race would be close but that Oduber had an edge. The INR Costa Rican analyst has recently come back from a trip to Costa Rica. He states that the August estimate is still valid, with Oduber's chances slightly improved. He found Trejos to be a lackluster campaigner and Oduber the same old spell-binder.

4. Degree of U.S. Assistance

No USG assistance has been given to Trejos.

[*1 paragraph (7 lines of source text) not declassified*]

[*less than 1 line of source text not declassified*] Oduber has been in touch with AFL–CIO leaders. [*2 lines of source text not declassified*] Oduber has informed [*less than 1 line of source text not declassified*] that Victor and Walter Reuther invited [*1 line of source text not declassified*], to go to Detroit about November 1 to pick up funds for the political campaign. We have no further details on this.

5. My Recommendation

I think we can live quite comfortably with either candidate. Our interests would be better served, however, by an Oduber victory. He would give Costa Rica progressive, left-of-center leadership more closely attuned to the aims of the Alliance for Progress. He would have the support of a single party. Trejos would be leader of an unstable coalition, with all the problems that this could bring.

I do not think that we should choose sides to the extent of bankrolling Oduber. [*less than 1 line of source text not declassified*] He knows that we are pulling for him—Jack Vaughn told him so, and I imagine the Vice President conveyed the same impression. The AFL–CIO seems to be helping him out. [*3½ lines of source text not declassified*]

WGB

---

[3] In airgram A–179 from San José, October 12. (National Archives and Records Administration, RG 59, Central Files 1964–66, POL 14 COSTA RICA)

[4] Not found.

[5] Dated August 16; attached but not printed.

82.   Memorandum From William G. Bowdler of the National
Security Council Staff to the President's Special Assistant for
National Security Affairs (Bundy)

Washington, December 9, 1965.

[Source: Johnson Library, National Security File, Country File,
Costa Rica, Vol. I, 4/64–10/68. Secret; Sensitive. 1 page of source text
not declassified.]

83.   Memorandum From William G. Bowdler of the National
Security Council Staff to the President's Special Assistant for
National Security Affairs (Bundy)

Washington, December 15, 1965.

[Source: Johnson Library, National Security File, Country File,
Costa Rica, Vol. I, 4/64–10/68. Secret; Sensitive. 1 page of source text
not declassified.]

84.   Memorandum From the President's Special Assistant for
National Security Affairs (Bundy) to President Johnson[1]

Washington, December 17, 1965, 3:30 p.m.

SUBJECT

Deepening Crisis in Guatemala

1. Recent reports from our Embassy and CIA sources in Guatemala
indicate that President Peralta's position has deteriorated and that a
military coup may be attempted prior to December 20.[2]

---

[1] Source: Johnson Library, National Security File, Memos to the President, McGeorge
Bundy, Vol. XVII. Secret. A notation on the memorandum indicates the President saw it.

[2] As reported in CIA Intelligence Memorandum, [text not declassified]; ibid., Country File, Guatemala, Vol. I, 3/64–1/66. A memorandum from Vaughn to Rusk, December 10, closely following the language of the CIA memorandum, is in the National
Archives and Records Administration, RG 59, Central Files 1964–66, POL 23–9 GUAT.

2. The leader of the coup is Col. Miguel Angel Ponciano, candidate for President of the minority, rightist Movement for National Liberation (MLN). Ponciano suspects that Peralta is working to insure the election of another candidate. The elections are scheduled for March 6, 1966. Ponciano is trying to develop enough support among military commanders to overthrow Peralta.

3. Embassy officers met with Ponciano on Tuesday and told him that we strongly favor return to constitutionality via the scheduled elections. He made quite clear that the issue is Peralta's suspected support of another candidate. He said in effect that either Peralta stops interfering in the elections, or he must go. He claims that he would remove only Peralta and his cousin and that elections would be held on schedule. What is clear is that Ponciano wants to count the ballots on March 6.[3]

4. The danger in this situation is that an attempted coup may split the military, lead to protracted fighting and play into the hands of the Communists. We have instructed Ambassador Mein to convey a strong warning against a coup to Ponciano.[4] At the same time, we want him to urge Peralta, in his own interest, to request OAS supervision of the elections with a visit now by OAS Secretary General Mora or OAS Council Chairman Penna Marinho (Brazil).[5] Such a proposal might give Peralta some insurance and could not do any of us any harm. He is seeing Peralta today and will afterwards lean hard on Ponciano.

5. This is *not* at present a Dominican Republic situation, but it may easily require some energetic diplomatic pressures in order to prevent real deterioration via military civil war.

6. We are following developments closely. State, DOD and CIA are doing some contingency planning.[6]

McG. B.

---

[3] As reported in telegram 373 from Guatemala City, December 14. (Ibid., POL 23–8 GUAT)

[4] Instructions transmitted in telegram 279 to Guatemala City, December 15. (Ibid., POL 23–9 GUAT)

[5] As suggested in telegram 277 to Guatemala City, December 15. (Ibid., POL 23–8 GUAT)

[6] The Department forwarded a report on its contingency plans in a December 27 memorandum to Bundy. The report reflected the recommendations of the LAPC, and considered a number of contingencies, including Situation A, in which Guatemala continues "more or less as it is from now to the elections." In this event, the Department recommended that the U.S. maintain its course of: a) providing assistance for the counterinsurgency effort; b) keeping in touch with presidential candidates and other leaders; and c) "making clear at every opportune moment to Peralta and to all conspirators that we favor not a coup but elections on schedule." (Ibid., POL 2 GUAT)

85. **Memorandum From William G. Bowdler of the National Security Council Staff to the President's Special Assistant for National Security Affairs (Bundy)[1]**

Washington, December 21, 1965.

SUBJECT

Guatemalan Situation

The December 20 target date passed with no coup in Guatemala. According to [*less than 1 line of source text not declassified*] reports,[2] the new date is December 22.

Ambassador Mein saw President Peralta last Friday (Tab A).[3] He found him relaxed and confident that he could deal with any coup attempt. He seemed fully aware of Col. Ponciano's doings and completely uninterested in our approaches to Ponciano. Mein seems to share a good deal of Peralta's confidence—more than I think he should. Much to my annoyance, Mein did not raise with Peralta the desirability of an OAS presence. He believes it would be a mistake to suggest it. (Tab B)[4] Peralta in his present frame of mind would probably have said "no," but it would be interesting to sound him out and start him thinking along these lines. Mein is scheduled to see coup leader Ponciano tomorrow.[5]

Our approaches to President Schick and "Tachito" Somoza in Nicaragua seem to have paid off. Latest CIA reports indicate Somoza has stopped supporting plotters working for the overthrow of Peralta and Echandi in Costa Rica.[6]

WGB

---

[1] Source: Johnson Library, National Security File, Country File, Guatemala, Vol. I, 3/64–1/66. Confidential.

[2] None found.

[3] Tab A, telegram 380 from Guatemala City, December 18, is attached but not printed. Another copy is in the National Archives and Records Administration, RG 59, Central Files 1964–66, POL 14 GUAT.

[4] Tab B, telegram 377 from Guatemala City, December 16, is attached but not printed. In the telegram Mein argued that the suggestion would "only cause resentment," since Peralta had repeatedly maintained that the elections would be free, i.e. without interference from either the government or the army. (Also ibid.)

[5] In his account of the meeting, Mein reported that Ponciano was "not as vehement in his comments on Peralta," but had warned "that there would be serious trouble in Guatemala if March elections are not free." (Telegram 391 from Guatemala City, December 22; ibid., POL 23–9 GUAT)

[6] Echandi was a former President of Costa Rica; the current President was Francisco Orlich Bolmarich. Documentation on U.S. efforts to discourage General Somoza from interfering in Costa Rica and Guatemala is ibid., POL 23–9 COSTA RICA. A handwritten note by McBundy on the memorandum reads: "Thanks."

86.   Telegram From the Embassy in Guatemala to the Department of State[1]

Guatemala City, January 4, 1966, 2:50 p.m.

412. For the Secretary and Assistant Secretary Vaughn.

1. This message is in response to Secretary's request, when I called on him in September prior to my departure for Guatemala,[2] for reports every 3 or 4 months on local situation. Beginning of new year and completion of third month since presentation credentials (September 22) would seem good time for such review.

2. Principal factors in present situation are:

(A) Elections of President, Vice President, entire Congress, and all municipal authorities are scheduled for March 6, and the electoral campaign is expected to get into full swing this month;

(B) Terrorist activities have increased in last two months. There have been four known kidnappings of leading businessmen, with over $250,000 paid in ransom, several other threats and extortion efforts by the terrorists and possibly others taking advantage of the situation, and several murders.

(C) The regime's failure to solve some of the country's problems, the three-year period in return to constitutionality, and the regime's apparent inability to deal with the terrorist threat, have led to general loss of confidence in the government and to a deterioration of Peralta's personal standing and prestige.

(D) The military appear to be divided not only in their support of Peralta, but, which could be more serious in the long run, between the younger and older officers since the former see the latter standing in their way of further advancement.

(E) There are several groups, both civilian and military, plotting against the regime, and a general expectancy that a coup will be staged before March. The reasons for feeling a coup might be necessary vary, depending on the plotters, from those who sincerely feel Peralta no longer capable of handling the situation to those who simply would like to get into power and some military who enjoy the status quo and would like to see it continued.

---

[1] Source: National Archives and Records Administration, RG 59, Central Files 1964–66, PER 2–1. Secret. Also in Washington National Records Center, RG 84: FRC 71 A 2420, Guatemala Embassy Files, 1966, POL Guatemala, Jan–June 1966.

[2] According to Rusk's Appointment Book, Rusk briefly met Mein on August 31, 1965, the day before Mein received his nomination. (Johnson Library) No substantive record of the meeting was found.

(F) The economic situation has deteriorated during the last few months, with the prospect of an economic crisis during the first half of the year if remedial steps are not taken. The terrorist activities have resulted in the flight of some capital, but more importantly is the almost complete cessation of new investments and a general slow-down in business. The business and industrial groups have panicked as a result of terrorist activities, and this of course is having its effect on the economy.

3. In this situation Peralta's attitude and thinking is of key importance. All indications, as reflected in his public statements and to me in private, are that he believes he has complete control of the situation, that the military are united in support of the government, and that the elections will be held as scheduled and the timetable for return to constitutionality adhered to. He says the military are prepared to cope with any situation that might arise, and he therefore tends to minimize the seriousness of the terrorist threat or the possibility of a coup against his regime. There is no reason to doubt his ability to handle any political problem, unless the military are more divided than would seem to be the case, but there is reason for serious concern as to his determination and ability to handle the terrorist situation. We are helping in the security field as requested by Peralta.

4. Notwithstanding all the rumors of possible coups against the regime, present indications are that the elections will probably be held as scheduled, unless (a) Peralta and the military decide that for security or any other reason they should be postponed, or (b) the Constituent Assembly should feel that it would not be in the best interests of the country to continue the electoral campaign and would persuade Peralta to serve as president for a fixed period. Peralta is so committed to the elections, however, that in either case, especially (a), he might prefer to step down as a point of honor rather than see the timetable altered. The danger of action against the regime would seem to be greater in March, after the elections, rather than during the next two months. If the campaign and the elections are reasonably free, that is, free of any interference by the government or attempt of the regime to impose a candidate, there might not be any problem provided the military are willing to accept the results of the polls. If the elections are not free, however, or the regime attempts to impose a candidate, we might find not only segments of the population but also some of the military taking matters in their own hands. That would obviously lead to a very nasty situation, and one which the Communists and others would tend to seize for their own purposes. It could also raise some very difficult problems for us.

5. This raises of course the question of our posture and what we should do to assure a smooth transition to a constitutional system. It

is clearly in our interest that free elections be held and that a constitutional government assume power. Our ability to exercise any positive influence is limited, however, especially since we have very little leverage with the present regime. I believe our policy during the next six months should be as outlined below, and that while planning ahead we must move only one step at a time:

(A) To do what we can so that the elections are held on schedule. We have and are continuing to let it be known that in our opinion the elections should be held, that they should be free, and that any attempt to overthrow the regime could play into the hands of the Communists and could therefore have serious repercussions not only for Guatemala but also for the rest of the hemisphere.

(B) To assure to the extent we can acceptance of the results of free elections. The three candidates are mediocre, and do not inspire any great confidence, but we should be able to work with any one of them.

(C) Support the new government when it comes into power on July 1, to enable it to meet the problems of the country, and to avoid any need for it to rely on the extremists for support. This last consideration would be especially true if the PR candidate, which is supported by the left, should win.

6. I regret that the situation does not permit a more optimistic report.

7. I have shown this message to CAS and DATT and they have indicated their concurrence.

Mein

---

87.   Memorandum From William G. Bowdler of the National Security Council Staff to President Johnson[1]

Washington, March 5, 1966, 9 a.m.

SUBJECT

Elections in Guatemala

Guatemala is scheduled to hold general elections tomorrow. Whether they will bring tranquility or turmoil cannot be forecast with

---

[1] Source: Johnson Library, National Security File, Memos to the President, Robert W. Komer, Vol. XXI. Secret. A notation on the memorandum indicates the President saw it.

certainty. Much depends on the returns and whether the Guatemalan people accept them as a reasonably fair expression of popular will. Communist-dominated subversive groups are waiting on the wings to exploit discontent.

Despite protestations that the voting will be unhindered and the ballot counting honest, President Peralta has shown partiality during the campaign for the PID party which his regime created, whose standard-bearer is Juan de Dios Aguilar. The other two candidates—Professor Julio Mendez of the moderately left of center PR party and Col. Miguel Ponciano of the extreme right MLN party—are already protesting the government's partiality. Peralta has not wanted OAS observers. But there will be a large press representation on hand, some 25 reporters from the U.S.

Our Embassy's estimate is that none of the three candidates is sufficiently strong to win an absolute majority.[2] If this happens, the new Congress which takes office on May 5 must select the President from the two receiving the most votes. We expect considerable political maneuvering during this period (assuming an immediate post-election blow-up does not materialize) accompanied by political unrest. The guerrillas and other elements of the extreme left are awaiting election results and popular reaction thereto before deciding the course which they will follow. If popular disturbances materialize, we can anticipate their adding fuel to the fire in a bid to get a revolutionary situation started.

In recent months we have tried to help the Peralta Government improve its capabilities for dealing with rural and urban insurgency. The Guatemalans were slow in responding to our offers of assistance. Last week they acted. AID and DOD have done a good job in getting equipment and experts down there to help them.[3]

Unless the election results produce a more violent popular reaction than can be foreseen at the present time, the Guatemalan security forces can probably cope with the situation. As a precautionary step, Linc Gordon met yesterday afternoon with his interdepartmental Latin American Policy Committee to review the general situation and the contingency plans.

WGB
RWK[4]

---

[2] Transmitted in telegrams 566 and 594 from Guatemala City, February 15 and 24. (Both National Archives and Records Administration, RG 59, Central Files 1964–66, POL 14 GUAT)

[3] On February 25 the Embassy reported that Peralta had requested emergency assistance for his counter-insurgency campaign. The United States shipped equipment to the Guatemalan army on March 1; a team of military advisers, and supplies for the Guatemalan police, arrived shortly thereafter. (Memorandum from Burrows to Sayre, March 14; ibid., ARA/CEN/G Files, 1966: Lot 68 D 464, DEF 19 GUAT)

[4] Komer initialed below Bowdler's typed signature and initials.

88.   Memorandum From William G. Bowdler of the National Security Council Staff to President Johnson[1]

Washington, March 10, 1966, 5 p.m.

SUBJECT

Guatemalan Situation

Latest reports from Guatemala indicate that there are certain civilian and military elements strongly opposed to the moderate PR party of Julio Mendez, who are trying to pressure President Peralta to annul the elections or step aside and let a successor do it. At this point we don't know how strong these elements are.

Ambassador Gordon Mein spoke with Peralta this morning about these reports. Peralta tended to dismiss them and expressed his determination not to alter the schedule for return to constitutionality. When Ambassador Mein asked him whether Mendez and the PR would be allowed to take office should they be elected, he was less definite, saying that the election would not be final until the Congress has selected a President from the two leading candidates in May.[2]

Ambassador Mein and his staff yesterday and today have made the rounds of the party candidates, certain business and military leaders, and President Peralta, to convey to them our strong desire to see the results of the elections fully respected and our extreme distaste with any effort to alter or annul them.

I think it might strengthen Ambassador Mein's efforts to prop up Peralta's determination to stay in power—and at the same time disincline him to tamper with the election results—if he were able to convey to Peralta that the "White House" would like to see the results fully respected and power transferred peacefully, and offering U.S. cooperation and support in his efforts to achieve this. An ounce of prevention now may be worth more than a pound of cure later.[3]

---

[1] Source: Johnson Library, National Security File, Country File, Guatemala, Vol. II, 1/66–11/68. Secret; Sensitive. A notation on the memorandum indicates the President saw it.

[2] As reported in telegram 666 from Guatemala City, March 10. (National Archives and Records Administration, RG 59, Central Files 1964–66, POL 14 GUAT)

[3] Komer wrote in the margin next to this paragraph. "Mr. President, this is tricky but it is *oral*, and if it did leak it would sound like a good noise, not a bad one. On balance I'm for it."

Attached is a suggested statement which the Ambassador in his discretion could use *orally* in making this pitch to Peralta.[4] I would like to have your authorization to send this to Ambassador Mein. Linc Gordon concurs in this step.[5]

WGB

Approve message

Prefer not to send message

See me

---

[4] Attached but not printed.

[5] Although the memorandum does not record the President's decision, the Department proposed that Mein deliver the message to Peralta on the Secretary's behalf. (Telegram 460 to Guatemala City, March 11; National Archives and Records Administration, RG 59, Central Files 1964–66, POL 14 GUAT) Mein replied that the proposed message was "not necessary at this time" since an agreement had been "reached and signed last night by representatives of military, PR and PID providing for orderly transfer of power if PR wins elections which is generally assumed to be the case." (Telegram 675 from Guatemala, March 12; ibid.) An election tribunal later certified that the PR had won a majority of seats in congress, clearing the way for Méndez' elevation to the presidency. (Memorandum from Rostow to the President, April 5; Johnson Library, Memos to the President, Walt W. Rostow, Vol. I)

---

89.   National Intelligence Estimate[1]

NIE 82–66   Washington, June 24, 1966.

PROSPECTS FOR STABILITY IN GUATEMALA

The Problem

To estimate the situation in Guatemala and the prospects for stability over the next year or two.

---

[1] Source: Central Intelligence Agency, Job 79–R01012A, O/DDI Registry. Secret; Controlled Dissem. According to a note on the cover sheet this estimate was prepared in the Central Intelligence Agency with the participation of the intelligence organizations of the Departments of State and Defense, the National Security Agency, and the Atomic Energy Commission. The United States Intelligence Board concurred in this estimate on June 24.

Conclusions

A. The staying power of the new, moderate-left government of Méndez will depend primarily on its relationship with the Guatemalan military. The military leaders, recalling the Communist surge to power in the early 1950s, may tend to overreact to any administration appointments or policy moves which they regard as favorable to the far left. Méndez, a proud and somewhat sensitive man, is likely to become restive over such circumscription of his powers.

B. In our view, his chances of maintaining himself in power through 1966 are good. During this period he will have the opportunity to improve his ties with military leaders and the economic elite, but probably this would require the sacrifice of some of the reform measures he favors. The Communist guerrilla bands, although not capable of taking power, are strong enough to carry out terrorist campaigns that could keep the government under heavy pressure from the military. These campaigns might be used to justify military intervention if the right and the military leadership became dissatisfied with Méndez' conduct of his administration.

C. In view of the economic, social and political problems which will confront Méndez beyond 1966, we are not confident that he will survive in office through the next two years. His administration's chances for accomplishing much, either in reform or in significant economic growth and development, will depend heavily upon whether it accepts substantial outside assistance—with its attendant obligations—and uses it effectively.

[Omitted here is the Discussion section of the estimate.]

---

90.   **Letter From the Ambassador to Nicaragua (Brown) to the Director of the Office of Central American Affairs (Burrows)**[1]

Managua, January 7, 1967.

Dear Chuck:

In our recent letters we have been discussing various aspects of possible results of General Somoza's mounting drive for power, and threats and predictions of the "chaos" which will allegedly ensue

---

[1] Source: National Archives and Records Administration, RG 59, ARA/CEN Files: Lot 69 D 515, POL Nicaragua—1967. Secret; Official–Informal.

because of mass refusal to accept the election results.[2] We have been reporting the evidence of communist and extreme leftist preparations and even early attempts to take advantage of any disorder, and the separate but equal concerns of the government and anti-communist opposition about the communist potential for trouble. Rumors are, as you know, endemic in these countries, and right now many of them have to do with plots and plans of the various protagonists. I heard from one of our locals yesterday, for example, that there is a street story to the effect that the Acting Chief of the Guardia, General Montiel, is planning a pre-election golpe designed to forestall serious trouble on or after Election Day. I'm told it is said that he would establish a junta militar in place of the present constitutional government, put General Somoza in charge of the junta and clamp down on everything for two or three years, just to keep the peace which Nicaragua needs. So it goes, but this is by way of introducing the report to you of a plot which for once has come directly to our attention by means of one of the self-styled plotters. This scheme has not yet, as far as we know, become the subject of gossip, and it appears to have at least some of the earmarks of more probability and/or gravity than many of the others.

An approach was made recently to one of our officers by a young Nicaraguan lawyer named Morales, who is known for his solid anti-Somoza record over several years and for his membership in, and association with leaders of, the Social Christian Party. Morales has no communist connections. According to Morales, the participants in the plot are some Social Christians and some officers of the National Guard, who are quietly joining forces for a golpe against the authorities, in order to prevent General Somoza's election and to seize power before the communists can take advantage of the disorders which will accompany the election. The event is supposed to take place on January 22 when Agüero is holding a rally in Managua and the President and the Somozas are in Leon for the Liberal candidate's demonstration in that city. Morales was probing for an indication of our attitude toward such a golpe. He was of course given a healthy slug of our hands-off treatment. Nonetheless, he has wanted to keep the line open to us. We shall see most discreetly what more we can find out.

The plot is more detailed than I have given you in the barebones description above, which I think includes enough of the essential elements to give you another example of what may be going on under the surface. My own view is that the plot is almost certain to be discovered, if it has not already come to the attention of the GON. Even if it isn't, I find it difficult to believe that it will be successful. In any

---

[2] For background on the elections, see Document 91.

event, our information so far is half-baked indeed, and depends entirely on the word of one (half-baked?) informant. We also wanted you to have this information at this stage so that we might lay some sort of basis for what might come out of it.

The next episode of the Perils of Pauline will be shown on this same screen.

Sincerely,

Aaron

---

91.   **Information Memorandum From the Director of the Office of Central American Affairs (Burrows) to the Assistant Secretary of State for Inter-American Affairs (Gordon)**[1]

Washington, January 10, 1967.

SUBJECT

Nicaraguan Election Campaign and Prospects

With the Nicaraguan elections less than one month away (February 5), I think you will be interested in Ambassador Brown's assessment of the situation, including the post-election role of the opposition. Summarized below are views he has expressed to me in recent letters, responding to some provocative communications from me.

General Somoza, the front-running candidate of the government party, could win a free election, although it might be close. Nevertheless, the Somoza tactic is apparently to build up a large majority, by fair means or foul. Opposition candidate Fernando Aguero, as well as many others in his camp, cannot believe that Aguero could lose in a free election. Aguero is the kind who, when he does lose, would be inclined to lead a resistance movement. However, in view of his proved ineptness as an organizer and leader, as well as the probable reluctance of his supporters to risk their current prosperity in a turmoil that might lead to revolution, Aguero is unlikely to have much success in any post-election efforts.

---

[1] Source: National Archives and Records Administration, RG 59, Central Files 1967–69, POL 14 NIC. Confidential. Drafted by James R. Johnston. Another copy indicates that the memorandum was cleared by Sayre. (Ibid., ARA/CEN Files: Lot 69 D 515, POL Nicaragua—1967)

For many years the opposition, including its spokesmen in the United States, has been making dire predictions of calamity to come, in an attempt to frighten the United States into "doing something about General Somoza". In fact, only a massive stroke by the United States could have dissuaded Somoza from his candidacy, and there would have been little support in the United States Government for such a move.

General Somoza seems to have the Nicaraguan armed forces, the Guardia Nacional, behind him for a long time to come. Instead of heaping abuse on the Guardia Nacional, the opposition is appealing to it with blandishments promising a better deal under Aguero, and is actually shouting "Viva la Guardia Nacional!"

Although serious trouble is not expected in Nicaragua, if it does occur, we could not stop it if we tried. In any case, maybe a little revolution would in the long run not really harm our interests. Even discounting reports from prejudiced sources to the effect that General Somoza is in ill health and is emotionally unstable, there is other evidence, varying in degree of realiability, which indicates that once in office he may not be equal to his aspirations. In Ambassador Brown's own words, "The wondering eyes of the world may sooner or later see Anastasio Somoza explode and fall apart into little pieces, as he finds himself forced to take measures which may war with one part of his nature, as he finds that Nicaragua will not move as fast as he thinks it must under his peerless leadership, as he does not get the hemisphere's recognition of his deeds and good intentions, etc."[2]

All this does not mean that the first months of 1967 will pass with general tranquillity, but Nicaragua is expected to stagger through them without major disorder.

---

[2] The sentence is in a letter from Brown to Burrows, December 23, 1966. (Ibid., ARA/CEN/N Files: Lot 69 D 528)

92.   Memorandum From the President's Special Assistant (Rostow) to President Johnson[1]

Washington, January 23, 1967.

SUBJECT

Nicaraguan Situation

The rioting which broke out in Managua yesterday was a deliberate provocation by opposition candidate Fernando Aguero to gain at least a delay in the February 5 general elections and, if possible, intervention by the US or OAS.

In a speech to his followers, Aguero called upon the Nicaraguan National Guard to join him in overthrowing the Somozas. (General "Tachito" Somoza is the Government's candidate.) He then led a demonstration through the city. A clash between the demonstrators and the National Guard occurred, leading to an extensive street fight. A CIA estimate as of midnight placed casualties at 16 dead, 66 wounded.

Aguero and his entourage took refuge in Managua's largest hotel in the center of the city. The National Guard has the hotel surrounded. Through the night, there was sporadic sniping at the National Guard, but the Government seems to be firmly in control. CIA reports that the Government has authorized two priests to enter the hotel to talk to Aguero.

Ambassador Brown reports that to his best knowledge, no Americans have been hurt. Some 20 United States citizens are in the besieged hotel. Brown has asked Nicaraguan authorities to exercise extreme care in any action against Aguero so that the lives of Americans and other foreigners will not be endangered.

Walt

---

[1] Source: Johnson Library, National Security File, Country File, Nicaragua, Vol. I, 12/63–12/68. Confidential. A notation on the memorandum indicates the President saw it.

93.   Editorial Note

On the evening of January 22, 1967, several Embassy officers tried to reach the Americans held hostage at the Gran Hotel in downtown Managua; others tried to reach the leader of the Nicaraguan National Guard. Both attempts were unsuccessful. After failing to contact interim President of Nicaragua Lorenzo Guerrero Gutiérrez, Ambassador Brown managed to express "grave US concern" to the President's press secretary. The press secretary called back to report that President Guerrero and General Somoza were fully aware of the gravity of the situation, particularly since the lives of Americans and other hotel guests were at stake and assured Brown that, contrary to reports the Embassy had received, the National Guard was not firing into the hotel. (Telegram 1065 from Managua, January 23, 0514Z; National Archives and Records Administration, RG 59, Central Files 1964–66, POL 23–9 NIC)

In the early hours of January 23 the Embassy began to receive appeals to intervene in the hotel siege. Ambassador Brown received such a call from opposition leader Fernando Agüero. The Embassy initially responded to these appeals by stating that "the action requested would constitute foreign intervention into Nicaraguan affairs." (Telegram 1066 from Managua, January 23, 0740Z; ibid.) Several hours later the Nicaraguan Government allowed the Papal Nuncio and the Auxiliary Bishop of Managua to approach Agüero in an attempt to negotiate a "peaceful evacuation beleaguered inmates, especially foreign guests." (Telegram 1067 from Managua, January 23, 1145Z; ibid.) When the two prelates proved unable to mediate a settlement, the Nicaraguan Government recommended that the Embassy assume the initiative. Ambassador Brown sent a team of senior officers to "persuade Aguero importance immediate release hostages, pointing out obvious impact his continued control over them will have on his American friends." (Telegram 1068 from Managua, January 23, 1330Z; ibid.) After 2 hours of negotiation, the team returned empty-handed. (Telegram 1073 from Managua, January 23, 1640Z; ibid.) Meanwhile the Department, although agreeing with the decision to intervene on behalf of the American hostages, expressed its concern that the "GON seems to be shifting burden to Embassy and USG." The Department instructed the Embassy to "make unmistakably clear to GON that we regard GON responsible for safety of Americans." (Telegram 123306 to Managua, January 23, 11:23 a.m.; ibid.)

Before the Embassy could remind the Nicaraguan Government of its responsibilities, a summons arrived from Agüero. He wanted the Embassy to deliver a message to the Guerrero administration, containing his terms to resolve the stalemate. The Embassy agreed to deliver the message "without taking any responsibility for promoting conditions laid down." (Telegram 1077 from Managua, January 23, 2157Z; ibid.) Following further negotiations, with the Embassy acting as intermediary, Agüero and his followers agreed to evacuate the hotel, thereby releasing the hostages. (Telegram 1078 from Managua, January 23, 2227Z and telegram 1085 from Managua, January 23, 2330Z; both ibid.)

94.   Telegram From the Embassy in Nicaragua to the Department of State[1]

Managua, January 24, 1967, 2120Z.

1105. Subject: President Guerrero's Comments on January 22–23 Events.

1. I called on President Guerrero this morning in order attempt evaluate his morning-after attitude and to get across two points to him categorically and officially.

2. I opened conversation by congratulating President on GON's contribution to resolution very difficult and dangerous situation at Gran Hotel yesterday. Guerrero replied that GON had of course been extremely concerned. There were those, he went on, who wanted to take the toughest kind of line of action, and "today some of us are being criticized for having been too lenient in letting those people go unscathed." But, he added, he was confident GON was right. If hotel had been conclusively attacked there would have been much more blood shed on both sides, and of course GON had to think about safety of Americans and other foreigners in hotel. Guerrero said he was most grateful for our Embassy's help in making this possible.

A. *Comment:* There is little doubt that there were hardliners within GON circles, possibly headed by General Somoza, who were ready and anxious give National Guard its head to clean up situation ruthlessly. But we are also confident that it was Luis Somoza, President himself and most of other GON leadership who were responsible for

---

[1] Source: National Archives and Records Administration, RG 59, Central Files 1967–69, POL 23–9 NIC. Confidential; Immediate. Repeated to USCINCSO for POLAD, Guatemala City, Panama City, San José, San Salvador, and Tegucigalpa and passed to the White House, DOD, CIA, USIA, and CIA.

moderate solution which was reached. They were not of course unaware that eyes of world and especially the US was on them.

3. Guerrero's reference to Embassy's role gave me opening for first of points I wanted make. I said I wanted to make absolutely clear to him that in our passages back and forth yesterday between Aguero group in hotel and GON safety of endangered Americans was uppermost in our minds. As far as messages we carried between two sides and the agreement in all its details which was ultimately reached were concerned, he should understand that we were acting merely as agents, without responsibility for any of the arrangements. I said it was like two Nicaraguans talking to each other over a telephone line which we provided. We tried to make this abundantly clear to both sides during course of negotiations yesterday, but I wanted to re-emphasize it today. President said of course GON understood this and was most appreciative our undertaking do what we did. Other governments who had citizens in hotel also, he added, should also be grateful to US. Finally he said many moderates in opposition had called him during course of yesterday urging him to negotiate directly with Aguero and it was great satisfaction to him be able tell them that talks were going on successfully through our medium.

A. *Comment:* Since there are bound to be many critics on both sides who will and probably are now attacking agreement which permitted hotel evacuation, I thought I should make above disclaimer of responsibility for content of agreement at highest level GON as soon as possible, in event there any doubt. Besides, it happens to be quite true. We will make same point again with opposition when we have chance.

4. I then made other point I had in mind based on fact that when Aguero and other leaders (Pasos, two Chamorros, Rivas and Frixione) emerged from hotel last night they suddenly entered my well identified official car which had been used all day take Embassy team back and forth. This was of course without any pre-arrangement our part or expectation they might do so since they were supposed proceed to homes on their own responsibility. DCM Engle, who in charge of Embassy team at hotel was horrified and considered forcing them out of car. But he quickly and correctly concluded that to do so in such public place and in front of many foreign and domestic newsreel and other photographers would create most unpleasant scene, to say the least, and consequences could not be foreseen. Therefore they drove off in Ambassador's car and were taken to their homes. I explained to President exactly how this happened. Guerrero brushed the incident aside and said it made no difference at all. He added that what really annoyed him was what the oppositionists had done after they got home. Aguero for example made a grandstand play by visiting hospitals, and he and other oppositionists held "drunken fiestas" in celebration.

Guerrero said he thought this in extremely poor taste so shortly after so many innocent people had been killed and wounded.

A. This incident will hopefully not loom large as an issue, but I thought I should attempt convince President of truth which is that Aguero and company took outrageous advantage of us in this instance. Morning news broadcasts apparently have not specifically identified car in which they left. This connection government representative at Hotel Arostegui was eye-witness.

5. I concluded conversation by remarking that I hoped all would go well from now on. Guerrero said he shared my hope and added that he trusted that Department of State had been and would be kept fully informed of developments as they occurred. I said he could count on that. Guerrero then said that he knew that Senator Kennedy had made a statement yesterday[2] which was very critical of the GON, calling for OAS action of some kind, etc. I replied that if there was such a statement I had not seen it but perhaps Senator's comment had been based largely on events of Sunday rather than peaceful conclusion of Gran Hotel crisis yesterday. President mildly reaffirmed hope that US Government would be completely informed and understanding. I said we would do our best.

A. *Comment:* Again, there is little doubt that course which events took yesterday afternoon was considerably influenced image-building considerations, certainly on part GON and perhaps also to some degree on part opposition. Dominican experience was in many people's minds, and Luis Somoza at least is ever most alert to his family's public relations.

6. *Comment:* We will attempt further analysis as we make further contacts. President did not mention election prospects and I had concluded I should not raise matter at this stage. Probably each side going make public claims "great victory" for themselves. If Kennedy statement has not been sent us, please transmit soonest for our info.

Brown

---

[2] In telegram 125185 to Managua, January 25, the Embassy forwarded the full text of the statement, in which Senator Robert F. Kennedy urged the OAS Human Rights Commission to investigate the situation in Managua and called for a meeting of the OAS Council "to determine what steps would be appropriate in the event that the violence continues." (Ibid.)

95.   Telegram From the Embassy in Nicaragua to the Department of State[1]

Managua, February 10, 1967, 2100Z.

1286. Subject: Significance of Somoza's Election for US.

1. General Somoza's election is now a reality, two weeks after the heavy suppression of the opposition leadership's attempt provoke intervention and/or forestall election and overthrow government. Review of what this all means in terms US policy and tactics, short and long term, seems desirable soon as possible, because of its potential effect network our relationships, including our aid programs. Small and large decisions on many aspects US-Nicaraguan relationships cannot long be postponed. My evaluations and suggestions set forth herein are supplement to commentary we have provided as developments occurred. Department's views from its vantage point will be most helpful.

2. Depending somewhat on how GON handle Pedro Joaquin Chamorro[2] and other prisoners, and whether GON exercises retaliation on Aguero and other opposition leaders still at large (other than severe election drubbing), events of Jan 22–23 and subsequent pre-election period may be allowed fairly quickly and smoothly recede into history as just another in series of foolish opposition attempts overthrow Somoza-controlled regimes by violence with accompanying bloody, heavy-handed, somewhat confused methods employed by GON restore order and keep constitutional forms in operation. Aguero's move on Jan 22 and course GON followed during Jan 22–Feb 4 period have unquestionably added to Nicaraguan pot large residue bitterness which would not otherwise be there now, but in long-run I wonder if period will not widely be regarded, here and in outside world, merely as additional hard evidence firm Somoza determination maintain control Nicaragua by any means, and advance proof of many people's fears and expectations of character of General Somoza's forthcoming administration.

---

[1] Source: National Archives and Records Administration, RG 59, Central Files 1967–69, POL 14 NIC. Confidential.

[2] In telegram 1138 from Managua, January 26, the Embassy reported that Chamorro had been arrested without a warrant, an apparent violation of the Gran Hotel agreement that held that "constitutional and ordinary legal procedures would remain in force since state of siege not imposed." (Ibid., POL 23–9 NIC) In a meeting with Ambassador Brown on January 31, former President Luis Somoza explained: "We decided after Gran Hotel evacuation that we ought pick up at least one big one. Pedro Joaquin gave us our chance when he organized street disorder which took place subsequently." Somoza denied that Chamorro had been seriously mistreated, although "guard did shove him around with his rifle butt." (Telegram 1220 from Managua, February 1; ibid., POL 23–8 NIC)

3. Somoza's election last Sunday had of course long been accepted as inevitable by all observers and probably by almost all Nicaraguans (Aguero's attempt make holding of election impossible is good indication his own expectation). We still maintain belief that Somoza would have won in fairest and most honest election because of liberal party's traditional power base plus organization, program, hard work and money. Nevertheless, many pro-Somoza election irregularities have been proved by our own observation on election day, tending to confirm opposition charges of hundreds more. Creeping processing (if that is the most expressive word) of election returns can only indicate further Somoza machine manipulation in order show the world a landslide victory. Aguero's antics Jan 22 and later probably contributed to diminishing his vote, because they led to GON control measures which prohibited opposition build up to civic campaign climax and also perhaps because the outbreak of violence drove some oppositionists to abstain or even to vote for Somoza as leader party of "peace, order and progress." My own preliminary guess is that Luis Somoza has been author, producer and director of show that has been played last few weeks, with his candidate-brother and other liberal leaders more or less willing go along with his tactics. His objects may have included keep control, maintain conservative party as principal and traditional opposition rival to Liberal Party, let Aguero destroy himself for future PCT leadership, martyrize Pedro Joaquin Chamorro temporarily so that he can knock off Aguero when he gets out of jail (although Aguero will presumably still be strong enough so that both will go down fighting), and let a relatively moderate opposition leadership emerge which will safely represent the other half or so of the elite. In meantime internal struggle for power within PCT might help give new president some breathing-spell and chance get administration off to relatively unhampered start.

4. It is no news that an administration headed by General Somoza will add elements of instability, tension and probable violence to the Nicaraguan scene which were not present during the later years of Luis Somoza's presidency nor the Schick–Guerrero interregnum. Although he bore the family name and was his father's direct heir, Luis Somoza loosened the reins and largely because of his personal qualities and achievements gained some measure of opposition acceptance. Nicaragua flourished and breathed even more freely during the past four years. The problem inherent in General Somoza's presidency, made somewhat more insoluble by recent events, is that the opposition will never give him the benefit of the doubt. He has intelligence and might even show some statesmanship if left alone and given a chance. Strong probability, however, is that he will not be and the troubles which are likely to come will be just those suited to bring out the worst in his personality. He will have some problems getting and

keeping an able group of collaborators, even if he tries. As far as the non-Communist opposition is concerned, there will probably be five years of varying degrees of grumbling, lashing out in anger, subversive plotting, uneasiness and unrest leading to sporadic outbreaks of violence of one kind or another, etc., with some Communist potential waiting in wings take advantage of any turmoil which might be produced. All this is notwithstanding General Somoza's plus factors: a majority of "the people" who are hoping he will help Nicaragua advance in peace, a prosperous but basically fragile economic and fiscal outlook, and guidance and assistance of his brother and some trained and able government servants.

5. Inevitable problem for us is how to live with this situation and move toward our objectives. To exemplify just one set of problems on the horizon, Somoza and his administration are going to come to us with fresh economic assistance ideas, and some will no doubt be good ones worthy of our support. If we continue to do business as usual in this field of our endeavors we will have to face the stings of an obstreperous group of oppositionists, probably a minority, it is true, but still one which is quite capable of loudly berating us with the old charges that the US is thus helping Somozas line their pockets and stay in power. I think that with luck, a Somoza who was not being too obvious in taking advantage of us and with a lot of fervent persuasion we could eventually turn away such charges locally. I am not as qualified to estimate chances in the US of successfully braving press comment to effect that we again "embracing militarist dictators" and so on. I would hope that we can somehow find it possible to work constructively and safely with the Somoza administration, building on what we have already accomplished in the economic assistance area. There are several other segments of our bilateral relationships which can be similarly or more troublesome.

6. I have no bright ideas or solutions, supposing as I do that we shall have to wait a little longer to see how things go. I do urge however that we receive as soon as possible an indication of the Department's current views on "Somozaland." Foregoing are preliminary comments re implications for US relationships with Nicaragua of recent developments. We hope to come up later with some specific suggestions re US stance.[3]

Brown

---

[3] In telegram 139655 to Managua, February 17, the Department suggested a careful review of military and economic assistance programs "to ensure that they continue to conform with basic U.S. strategy of encouraging and supporting sound economic, social and political development of country, including progressive evolution of representative democracy." (Ibid., POL 1 US)

96.   Telegram From the Embassy in Nicaragua to the Department of State[1]

Managua, February 15, 1967, 0045Z.

1313. Subject: General Somoza Asks for a Chance.

1. I lunched alone with General Somoza today at his invitation. His purposes were evidently try feel me out as to our general attitude toward him and forthcoming administration and give me his views on events since Jan 22, his poor public relations in US, intransigence of opposition and Communist menace. Following are few highlights. Memo of conversation follows by pouch.[2]

2. Somoza said he deeply disturbed about attitude American press toward himself and family. He had tried help correspondents get well rounded view Nicaragua, but they persisted in lambasting his family as cruel dynasty. Made specific reference *Newsweek* article (Managua 1293)[3] and hoped Department could somehow teach them some history. I remarked that he indeed has public relations problem, that adverse press image will die hard and then only if deeds are eventually persuasive to impartial observers.

3. Though he did not once suggest Aguero and other opposition leaders are Communists, Somoza said Aguero hoped by abortive coup attempt Jan 22 to bring about intervention. Communists used him in attempt implement detailed plot destroy capital. Aguero was mistaken in thinking he had support US and others in hemisphere, but on January 23 manner Gran Hotel evacuation arranged inevitably helped encourage him and Pedro Joaquin Chamorro to further excesses. Street fracas January 25 proved this and gave excuse for jailing Chamorro. On this score I told General that if he critical our part evacuation as encouraging Agueristas, he might like know we receiving criticism from other side too. He admitted he understood but some others did not.

---

[1] Source: National Archives and Records Administration, RG 59, Central Files 1967–69, POL 15–1 NIC. Confidential. Repeated to USCINCSO, Guatemala, San Salvador, San José, Tegucigalpa, and Panama.

[2] Forwarded as an enclosure to airgram A–220 from Managua, February 18. (Ibid.)

[3] In telegram 1293 from Managua, February 11, the Embassy reported that recent press accounts had stung the Nicaraguan Government, including a *Newsweek* article in which an Embassy officer allegedly admitted: "we got the wrong number in 1932", when the elder Somoza was elevated to head the National Guard, "and to this day we're trying to live it down." (Ibid.)

4. Somoza went on at length and kept doubling back to theme that conservatives are incorrigible in sniping at GON and free election in which will of people demonstrated. Fundamentally what they were doing was running down their own country in eyes of outside world, and this would hurt them as much as the liberals, by affecting investment climate and business. I said that many people now are over-excited, expressed hope tempers would calm and spoke of virtues of concept of compromise which vital to practice democracy here or anywhere else. Somoza said rich conservatives are not going to like him because he is going to make them pay their taxes and thus prove to world that Nicaragua loyal member Alliance for Progress. Nicaragua has tremendous possibilities which will be realized if he is given a chance.

4. *Comment:* Above brief summary gives impression much more give and take our conversation than actually occurred. In true Somoza style he did most of talking in rich and confident detail, and my few remarks were interjected to take advantage his cordial and apparently receptive attitude. Chiefly I tried give impression friendly listener who hopes Nicaragua will continue thrive in every way. Underneath surface General Somoza seemed wary and alert for any indications our pre-campaign and pre-election personal relationship had changed. As usual he tried hard make good impression, without showing much if any humility, and yet seemed to be seeking almost desperately the understanding of his best friends the Americans.[4]

Brown

---

[4] On February 15 the Embassy reported that Somoza planned to visit the United States in March. (Telegram 1312 from Managua; ibid., POL 7 NIC) The Department instructed the Embassy to discourage the visit, "since persons he might expect to see in Department will be out of the country." (Telegram 138358 to Managua, February 16; ibid.) The Department also recommended against a White House appointment, arguing that "the President and other United States officials concerned with Latin American affairs are so involved in Summit preparations" that an appointment "would not be appropriate." (Memorandum from Read to Rostow, March 14; ibid.) The President met Somoza at the White House for a half hour on April 6 and introduced him to Rusk and McNamara before a Cabinet meeting. (Johnson Library, President's Daily Diary) The Department later explained that the meeting had been arranged "on very short notice when President found he had few minutes available to receive Somoza unofficially and informally." (Telegram 171222 to Managua, April 7; National Archives and Records Administration, RG 59, Central Files 1967–69, POL 7 NIC)

97.   Special National Intelligence Estimate[1]

SNIE 83.3–67   Washington, October 12, 1967.

POLITICAL PROSPECTS IN NICARAGUA OVER THE NEXT YEAR OR SO

Conclusions

A. President Anastasio Somoza is in uncertain health, but the chances are better than even that he will remain alive and active during the period of this estimate. He is not likely to alter the basic lines of Nicaraguan foreign policy, though his regime may become somewhat more authoritarian, and the incipient friction in his relations with the US is likely to grow.

B. In the event of Somoza's death within the next year or so, members of the country's inner political circle—from the Somoza family, other propertied interests, the Nationalist Liberal Party (PLN), and the National Guard—would probably work for a constitutional succession with excellent prospects of success. The resulting government would probably be more flexible in domestic policy and easier for the US to deal with.

C. If, however, Somoza became incapacitated but remained active enough to insist on continuing in office, or if he undertook a series of ill-advised, disruptive moves and then died, the sequence of events would be more unsettling. We regard these contingencies as possible but not probable.

[Omitted here is the Discussion section of the estimate.]

---

[1] Source: Central Intelligence Agency, Job 79–R01012A, O/DDI Registry. Secret; Controlled Dissem. According to a note on the cover sheet this estimate was prepared in the Central Intelligence Agency with the participation of the intelligence organizations of the Departments of State and Defense and the National Security Agency. The United States Intelligence Board concurred in this estimate on October 12.

98.   Memorandum From the Director of the Office of Central
American Affairs (Burrows) to the Assistant Secretary of
State for Inter-American Affairs (Oliver)[1]

Washington, October 12, 1967.

SUBJECT

Your Meeting Today with Mr. Broe of CIA[2]

CIA appears to feel more strongly than we do at this time with respect to certain threatening aspects of the Guatemalan situation. The Agency in recent briefings for key officials of the U.S. Government has stated that President Mendez of Guatemala has abdicated all power to the military and is himself in the hands of extreme rightists.

Our own analysis of the situation is that Mendez has allowed the military great latitude in their activities, but that the situation is not out of hand. Mendez agrees in principle with the need to eliminate communist and insurgent elements by clandestine means, but at the same time recognizes the danger to his administration of the counter-terrorists, who include among their targets certain members of the majority Partido Revolucionario, as well as some labor and peasant leaders and intellectuals.

Our Embassy in Guatemala now feels that with the relative success of the GOG in dealing with the insurgency problem, the continued activities of the counter-terrorist organizations could lead to a loss of popular support for the Mendez Government and the creation of a coup climate. I agree with this assessment. We are, in effect, at a crucial point: Mendez could lose control of the situation, but it does not appear that he has. Ambassador Mein feels that the Minister of Defense is both loyal to Mendez and in control of the Army and that he has done an effective job of preventing a confrontation between the Army and the Partido Revolucionario.

If the opportunity arises, you might wish to determine on what basis the CIA has decided that Mendez has lost control. I should like to add as a footnote that Mendez never really gained full control over events in Guatemala; he has no power base and as a result has been forced to attempt to balance opposing factions and satisfy divergent interest groups. In this he has been successful and we have reason to believe he can prevent a serious deterioration in the political climate. His style, however, will continue to be one of compromise rather than self-assertion.

---

[1] Source: National Archives and Records Administration, RG 59, ARA/CEN/G Files: Lot 70 D 75, POL 15–1 Head of State, Guatemala 1967. Confidential. Drafted by Killoran.

[2] No substantive record has been found of the October 12 meeting between Oliver and Broe.

**99.   Information Memorandum From the Acting Assistant
Secretary of State for Inter-American Affairs (Sayre) to
Secretary of State Rusk**[1]

Washington, January 17, 1968.

SUBJECT

Terrorist Assassination in Guatemala of U.S. MILGP Commander and Chief of
Navy Section[2]

The Guatemalan Government has declared a "State of Alert." The
Guatemalan Minister of Defense believes that a strong reaction is necessary to the pattern of Communist terrorist activities which has developed in the last few days in order to demonstrate that the Government has control of the security situation. He therefore intends to make
a maximum effort and has taken personal charge of the investigation
of the assassination of the two U.S. military officers.

The Guatemalan President has extended written condolences to
Ambassador Mein.

From the information available to me I would tentatively conclude:
a) that the assassination is part of a pattern of Communist terrorist activities in Guatemala; b) the assailants knew that the occupants of the
car were U.S. military personnel and c) there is no reason for believing at this time that U.S. personnel in other countries in Latin America will be objects of such attacks. With respect to this last point, however, the Communists have now "broken the ice" on assassination of
U.S. personnel in Latin America.

All of the available information indicates that the Country Team
was fully alert to the possibility of terrorist attacks; however, there is
a press indication that the terrorists were able to set up the assassination because the MILGP Commander was following a routine pattern
of travel between his Headquarters and home. If so, this would be contrary to instructions from the Department which required Country

---

[1] Source: National Archives and Records Administration, RG 59, ARA Files: Lot 72
D 33, Guatemala. Confidential. No drafting information appears on the memorandum.

[2] The White House Situation Room forwarded a brief account of the incident to
President Johnson on January 16: "Two members of our military mission in Guatemala
City were killed and one was wounded when the car in which they were riding was machine gunned shortly before noon this morning. Col. John Webber, Jr., the Commander
of the U.S. Guatemala Military Group, was killed outright, and Lt. Comdr. Ernest Monroe died shortly after the attack from his wounds. The identity of the assassins is not
known, but it is suspected that they were members of the Rebel Armed Forces, a Communist guerrilla organization." (Johnson Library, National Security File, Country File,
Guatemala, Vol. II, 1/66–11/68)

Teams to assure that their top personnel varied their pattern of activity sufficiently in going to their offices, departing for lunch, and going home at night so that it could not be regarded as routine. We will be checking this point out with Ambassador Mein.

I will also be sending a round-up message on the situation in Guatemala to all of our Ambassadors, who were instructed yesterday to review their security procedures.

I understand that Ambassador Mein has discussed with Assistant Secretary Oliver the latter's planned visit to Guatemala today. At present, Ambassador Mein recommends and Oliver agrees that Oliver should proceed according to schedule. However, Ambassador Mein desires to review the situation this morning and discuss it with Oliver before a final decision is made. Ambassador Mein has a message prepared giving the rationale and his recommendations which he will transmit to the Department this morning.[3]

---

[3] In telegram 2854 from Guatemala, January 17, the Embassy recommended that Oliver proceed as planned since canceling the visit "might be interpreted by President [Méndez] and others as indication that we wavering in our support of government at very difficult time." (National Archives and Records Administration, RG 59, Central Files 1967–69, ORG 7 ARA)

---

100.   Letter From the Ambassador to Guatemala (Mein) to the Assistant Secretary of State for Inter-American Affairs (Oliver)[1]

Guatemala City, February 27, 1968.

Dear Covey:

Your letter of February 6[2] reached me on February 12, when I was having to devote a great deal of time to personnel reductions. The

---

[1] Source: National Archives and Records Administration, RG 59, ARA Files: Lot 72 D 33, Guatemala. Secret; Official–Informal.

[2] Attached but not printed. Oliver reported that the assassinations of Webber and Monroe led the Interdepartmental Regional Group for Inter-American Affairs (IRG/ARA) to "explore the underlying causes of such dramatic incidents to determine whether the U.S. should take some action." The IRG/ARA had discussed a number of suggestions, but sought the Ambassador's "advice on what we might do to induce the Guatemalan Army to put an end to its clandestine operations." "What bothers us at this end," Oliver explained, "is the growing concern in the U.S. about the violence in Guatemala and the feeling that we are associated with a repressive regime."

questions raised by your letter and by the IRG/COIN decisions are of such importance that I did not want to give you a hasty reply. Our recommendations on personnel reductions are in, and we are now tackling the CASP. The points raised in your letter and those we must consider in the preparation of the CASP are so closely related that I wanted to be sure that my reply not only represented my own analysis and recommendations, but also that it did not reflect views contrary to those of the other members of the Country Team as they will be included in the CASP.

Let me say in the first place that I appreciate the opportunity to comment. We have not been sent officially any details of the IRG/COIN meeting, although through informal channels we have been sent IRG/ARA/COIN Action Memorandum No. 9[3] containing the decisions taken at the January 31 meeting. Parenthetically, I would like to suggest that some machinery be established for sending IRG documents to the field. They would be very helpful. At its meeting on January 31, the IRG/COIN decided (a) that diplomatic and military approaches should be made to the Guatemalan Government to induce it to end its counter-terrorist activities, and (b) to approach the President of Mexico and ask for suggestions regarding the Guatemalan situation, and whether he would be willing to take any initiatives with the Guatemalan Government toward remedying this situation. Your letter only touched on the first point, but, and I trust you do not object, I would like to comment on both aspects of the IRG/COIN paper.

The situation in Guatemala is, as you say, an extremely complex one. It is further complicated at the present time by extensive, and more often than not erroneous reporting by an uninformed press in the United States, and also by the apparent acceptance as "gospel" in some quarters of statements regarding Guatemala by a couple of frustrated priests. I am sure it is also complicated by the present frame of mind of the people in the U.S., the frustrations over Viet-Nam, and the general attitude toward the administration. I find the IRG/COIN decisions, to the extent they represent Washington thinking, very disturbing and can only hope that my comments, our reporting, and the CASP will help to clarify the picture and to place recent developments in their proper context so that any action we might take will not reflect only a negative posture but will direct itself to the real problem, and will be of help to the Guatemalan Government in its counter-insurgency activities.

It is very difficult to predict what lies ahead. That there will be further acts of terrorism and counter-terrorism is generally accepted.

---

[3] Dated February 6. (National Archives and Records Administration, RG 59, ARA/IG Files: Lot 70 D 122, IRG/ARA/COIN Action Memos)

The unanswered questions in everyone's mind are who, when, where and why. The apparent open break between the PGT and the FAR is likely to lead to increased terrorism since not only has the PGT been a moderating force, as hard as it might be to believe that there has been any moderation, but the degree of force to be used is the very issue which has led to the break. We do not know yet whether all the elements of the FAR have broken with the PGT, but we do know that at least one large group has done so and that its plans include further assassinations, robberies, terrorism, etc. It is a fact of life, therefore, that terrorism will continue to be a part of the Guatemalan scene, at least for the immediate future. There is little the Guatemalan Government or its security forces can do to prevent terrorist actions, and since it is well nigh impossible to know when and where the terrorists will strike, it is extremely difficult to take measures to prevent or meet such strikes. The only remedy, therefore, seems to be constant vigilance and to handle each incident as it occurs, while at the same time searching out the terrorists in the hope of eventually eliminating the problem. This is what the Guatemalan security forces are attempting to do. It is a very difficult problem which requires unpleasant, and at times unpalatable, remedies, and which cannot be just wished away.

We should not lose sight of the fact that the Guatemalan Government is fighting not only for the survival of the present administration but also for its very existence as an institution, and that what is at stake for the Guatemalans is what we and others are fighting for in Viet-Nam and other parts of the world. The proclaimed objective of the PGT and of the FAR, whether together or separately, is to take over Guatemala and to establish a communist regime. The difference between the two groups is primarily one as to methods. Thus challenged it is only natural that not only the government, but the people also, react in defense of their institutions, as deficient or ineffective as they may be, and of their way of life. This is what is taking place and the counter-terrorist actions taken by the security forces have, up to now, the backing and tacit approval of the people.

There is one aspect of the IRG/COIN position that I find not only disturbing but also puzzling. We have for some time, certainly since I arrived in Guatemala, been concerned over the internal situation, the guerrillas in Zacapa and Izabal, possible support from Cuba, and so forth, and in the early days with the government's failure to recognize the problem and its apparent inability to take any corrective action. The record will show that during the Peralta Administration, and since Mendez Montenegro came to power on July 1, 1966, we have urged the government and the security forces to take measures to eliminate the guerrilla problem. The insurgency situation has been one of our great concerns in Guatemala, and many of our actions and programs have been directed specifically at getting the government to move and then in supporting it once it began its counter-insurgency actions. We have had special groups visit us to study the situation, and we have directed a large part of our Military Assistance and Public Safety programs to this problem. The Guatemalan Armed Forces finally launched their campaign against the guerrillas in Zacapa and Izabal in October 1966. The campaign was successful, so that today there are no organized guerrilla units in that area. The surviving guerrillas either left the country or moved to other sections of the country, with many of them coming to Guatemala City to join forces with their urban comrades. The terrorists in the city today are the same elements which were operating earlier in the mountains, led by the same persons, and with the same objectives they had before, that is, to create chaos and eventually take power. Their method of operation may be different, that is, terrorism, assassinations, bombs, etc. rather than encounters between units in the field, but otherwise there is no change.

I am puzzled, therefore, by what appears to be a change in Washington thinking. While the campaign was going on in the mountains we gave it our blessing, but once the center of action shifted to the capital we seem to view the matter in a different perspective. We seem to be saying that the campaign in the mountains was "counter-insurgency", and therefore necessary if the democratic institutions were to survive, while the campaign in the city against the same forces is "repressive action", and therefore wrong. I frankly fail to see the difference.

This does not mean that we should approve or command all that is being done or all the methods that are being used. We don't. We must, however, view the matter in its true perspective and in the Guatemalan context. The Guatemalan Government, and its security forces, is determined to overcome the threat posed by the PGT/FAR and the only way it can apparently do so, certainly in its own eyes, is by searching out and eliminating the terrorists and the guerrillas. Economic and social reforms, as necessary and urgent as they are, will help to weaken whatever popular appeal the guerrillas might have among the lower classes but they will not in themselves meet the immediate problem created by the terrorists. The terrorists are not reformists who would put down their arms if the government undertook social and reform measures, but rather are men who have but one goal, namely, the assumption of power.

Unless I misread the information coming out of Washington, there appears to be a view held by some that the terrorists are reacting to the action of the security forces—that counter-terrorism breeds terrorism—and that if the security forces cease their activities there will be no more terrorism. (This reminds me a little of the debate in the States over the bombing of North Viet-Nam.) To a certain extent this is true, since the greater the pressures against the terrorists the more likely they are to react, and some of their recent activities would seem to indicate that they have been acts of desperation. This does not mean, however, that the terrorists would have been inactive, since that is not in their nature and in line with their program. I am sure the security forces would be very happy to put a stop to their actions if they could be assured that the PGT/FAR would cease all violence. As mentioned earlier, the terrorists have the initiative in that no one knows exactly where or when they will strike next, so that if the situation is to be resolved by means other than force the terrorists must either stop their activities or be prepared to come to terms with the security forces. The President tried on at least two occasions in the early days of his administration to find a peaceful solution to the problem but he was rebuffed each time by the PGT/FAR.

The ideal situation would be, of course, for the government to depend on the courts for the enforcement of the law and the application of justice. The court system in Guatemala is not only antiquated but the quality of the judges is very low. The security forces feel they cannot rely on the courts for the administration of justice, and, unfortunately, some of their recent experiences have not served to reassure them. The judges are not only often incompetent, but they are in many cases corrupt, and responsive to pressures and threats. Also, the entire judicial process makes it very difficult to prosecute anyone apprehended. There are no prosecuting attorneys as we know them, and often the only accusing officer and witness is the policeman who happened to arrest the defendant. The case of the guerrilla Obregon killed in the city last Friday, February 23, is a good illustration of this point. Obregon was captured by the police early in 1967, along with several others, including the sister of the guerrilla leader Turcios. The members of the group were tried and found guilty but released on appeal. The speculation at the time was that the appellate judge had been threatened and had, therefore, decided to release the prisoners. Rogelia Cruz Martinez, whose death triggered the mid-January incidents, is another case in point. She was being held for a traffic violation, but the threats received by the judge from the FAR were such as to lead him to release her. There have been other similar cases. The Congress begins this week debate on a bill revamping the entire judicial system. Maybe this will help in the long run, but it provides no alternative for the present.

I must apologize for going to such great length before answering the question posed by the IRG/COIN, that is, what might we do to induce the Guatemalan Army to put an end to its clandestine operations. I would answer the question as follows:

1. In my opinion we should not seek to influence the Guatemalan Army "to put an end" to its clandestine operations. Not only do they believe the method being followed is correct, but since they are

dealing with a subversive movement it would be difficult to suggest a substitute. We have not been able to think of a more effective method. An approach by us to the Guatemalans would not produce the intended results since they would, undoubtedly, tell us that they have no alternative, that they must eliminate the enemy, and that they would, therefore, have to continue their counter-terrorist activities. It would, therefore, be a non-productive effort on our part. In addition to being foredoomed to failure, it would also weaken whatever influence we might be able to exert for moderation.

2. Any suggestion by us that the Army put an end to its clandestine operations would more than likely be misunderstood, not only by the Army, but by the President and other political leaders as well. As discussed earlier, the security forces have been successful thus far in their counter-insurgency operations, as the very reaction of the terrorists would indicate, and for us to suggest to them at a time when they have the enemy on the defensive that they should let up could be interpreted by them to mean that we have changed our position, that we no longer support the government, and that we disapprove of its security measures. There would even be those who, maliciously or otherwise, would interpret our approach as an indication that we no longer opposed the cause of the guerrillas. That may sound ridiculous, but it would not be unlikely. Some could even go so far as to speculate that what they might interpret as a change of position on our part had been motivated by the Maryknoll incident, and was simply an effort by us to save the lives of those involved.

3. We should also not deceive ourselves by thinking that if the security forces put an end to their clandestine activities the problem will disappear. At least since 1963 the communist insurgents have engaged in widespread acts of terrorism throughout Guatemala, and the government's entrance into the clandestine counter-insurgency field in late 1966 was a reaction to the communist terror; an effort to find an effective means to contain a threat which had not been contained within the existing legal framework of law enforcement. If the armed forces should cease their counter-insurgency activities before the situation is brought under control the guerrillas and terrorists would not only continue but would, undoubtedly, intensify their efforts since they would be able to operate more freely. Such freedom would probably also result in a more rapid reorganization of the FAR guerrilla force and a corresponding increase in the insurgency threat to the government. This could also lead to an eventual open confrontation between the PGT/FAR and the extreme rightists, which would not only be nasty, but which would pose some real issues for us. It should not be overlooked that one of the reasons which led the armed forces to organize the clandestine groups, and to use them in counter-insurgency, was the threat by the extreme right in the early days of the present adminis-

tration that if the government did not move against the communists the right would. The actions taken by the armed forces, including its clandestine operations, have served to remove this issue from the political arena.

4. This does not mean that there is nothing we can do. We have on several occasions, and when supported by information available to us, pointed out to the Minister of Defense, and to others, that they might be contemplating action against innocent or mistakenly-identified individuals. We have also suggested to the Army that it exercise stricter control over the special unit of the National Police engaged in locating and eliminating FAR elements. Also, we have suggested that if the security forces feel it necessary to carry out summary executions in certain cases that they bury the bodies rather than leave them to be found, which produces a bad psychological effect, and creates an impression abroad that blood is flowing in the streets of Guatemala and that bodies are appearing everywhere. This poses a problem for the security forces, however, since they must continually show the public that they are moving effectively against the guerrillas and terrorists, and one way to do so is to leave the bodies of known communists where they will be found, identified by the families, and the events reported in the press. We should continue to urge moderation, which is probably the only effective thing we can do at the present time, and we will, of course, continue to do this.

I realize this still leaves the problem of public and Congressional concern over the situation in Guatemala unanswered, but I am afraid we are going to have that problem as long as the situation here remains as it is, and as long as the press in the U.S. continues to report mostly the negative aspects of developments in Guatemala. Judging from the reports I see, the press these days seems to be interested only in terrorists, guerrillas, and so on, or in issues which can be played up as anti-administration or anti-U.S. foreign policy. There seems to be no ready answer to this specific problem, except to present the facts as we see them, and to let the facts speak for themselves, while at the same time pressing for moderation, and, if possible, an early solution to the insurgency problem in Guatemala.

With reference to the suggestion that we approach the President of Mexico, I am of two minds. In the first place, the suggestion reflects a tendency which has always bothered me of calling upon others to help us when we can probably do the job ourselves, or before we have even tried. In this instance we have not discussed the matter with the Guatemalan Government, and yet we are considering asking for help from Mexico. Also, if we are going to approach a third party for help, why Mexico? Mexico, contrary to what we might think, does not have much influence with the Guatemalans, so that an approach by them on this issue would probably not be productive. The other Central American Governments would have greater influence than Mexico, but even that would be minimal. On the other hand, maybe an approach by the Mexican President, should he agree to make one, might be helpful in that it would give the Guatemalans one more opportunity to seek Mexican Government cooperation in establishing more effective control to prevent the smuggling of arms across the border and the travel by Guatemalan insurgents through Mexico to Cuba, Prague and other points behind the curtain. The Guatemalans believe that their problems with the insurgents would be more manageable if the Mexican authorities were more cooperative. If the Guatemalans are correct in their estimate, and if the President of Mexico is willing to use his good offices, it might therefore be a fruitful exercise.

In your letter you raised the question of a trip to Washington to discuss this problem. I frankly have no desire to go to Washington at this time, but your letter and recent communications from Chuck Burrows lead me to believe that it might be a good thing to do. It might be helpful to sit down with those working on Guatemala and to discuss not only the situation as we see it, but also to get a better understanding of some of the questions being raised in Washington. As to timing, I would prefer to wait until we have our CASP well underway, since our discussions in the preparation of that document are basic to any fruitful discussions I might have in Washington. Unless there is some urgency from the Department's standpoint I would prefer, therefore, to go some time in the latter part of March. I will write Chuck Burrows about this, and, if you agree, plan to go up at that time.[4]

Best personal regards.

Sincerely,

Gordon

---

[4] Oliver continued the discussion of Guatemalan security in a letter to Mein, March 8: "There was no thought here that you suggest to the Guatemalan Government that it stop its efforts to eliminate guerrilla activity either in the campo or the city. The distinction we were seeking to make (and in re-reading my letter, I see that this distinction was not made clearly) was between discriminate and non-discriminate activities." "What has bothered us," Oliver emphasized, "is the physical elimination of a rather large number of persons who appear to have no political coloration, or could not by a reasonable definition be called Communists." (Ibid., ARA Files: Lot 72 D 33, Guatemala)

101. Memorandum of Conversation[1]

Washington, March 13, 1968.

SUBJECT

Security Situation, Terror and Counter-Terror in Guatemala

PARTICIPANTS

For Guatemala
Col. Rafael Arriaga, Guatemalan Defense Minister
Col. Laugerud, Deputy Chief of Staff, Guatemalan Army
Col. Ponciano, Embassy of Guatemala Attaché

For the U.S.
Covey T. Oliver, Assistant Secretary for Inter-American Affairs
Charles R. Burrows, Country Director, Central American Affairs
Robert Starzel, ARA
Guy A. Wiggins, ARA/CEN/G

General Robert Porter, CINC, South Command
Robert F. Corrigan, Political Adviser CINCSO, Panama

Mr. Oliver began the substantive conversation by asking Col. Arriaga to summarize the security situation in Guatemala.

Col. Arriaga replied that he was directing the counter-terrorism campaign, which he justified as necessary to preclude right-wing reaction against the Government of Mendez Montenegro. The Government of Guatemala had been unjustly criticized for this campaign in the press. He was, therefore, much concerned and wanted to know how it could prevent newspapers (i.e., *Miami Herald*), from printing false stories about it. The Maryknoll fathers, particularly the Melvilles and Blase Bonpane, knew only people on the far left in Guatemala. That is, they did not know anyone but the poor, so could not give an honest interpretation of events. *Life* magazine, which had printed three hostile articles, was not interested in the attractive aspects of Guatemala, but only in reporting how the army was protecting extreme right-wing terrorism.

Col. Arriaga then turned to the subject of the assassination of Col. Webber, whom he described as a man who understood the Latin temperament and was almost a Latino himself. Col. Webber, he said, had understood the situation in Guatemala.

At this point General Porter arrived, accompanied by Mr. Robert Corrigan. The conversation turned briefly to Panama and Col. Arriaga

---

[1] Source: National Archives and Records Administration, RG 59, Central Files 1967–69, POL 23 GUAT. Confidential. Drafted by Wiggins on March 20.

asked if the political crisis there did not portend a coup by the extreme left. Mr. Corrigan explained that it did not, and that the extreme left was not involved in the crisis.

Mr. Oliver reviewed the conversation for the new arrivals and pointed out to Col. Arriaga that informed public opinion in the U.S., including congressional opinion, took the view that there was too much violence from the right in Guatemala.

In reply, Col. Arriaga cited the bazooka attack of March 7 on the counter-insurgency force barracks at Cipresales. This bloody attack which, he said, left two dead and 30 wounded did not get as much attention from the press as the killing of one or two leftists by the right-wing. Similarly the press always backed up statements by Castro claiming that the CIA was behind every anti-communist movement in Central America. Ambassador Burrows interjected that O'Leary of the *Washington Star* would like to talk to Col. Arriaga and it might be useful for him to do so.

Mr. Oliver reiterated U.S. sympathy with Guatemala's problems but asked, with all due respect to the good intentions of the Mendez Montenegro Government, if it could not do more to help the campesinos. He cited the army's civic action program and suggested that this was the type of activity that should be stepped up to help the newspapers give the other side of the government's story. He reminded his guest that his impressions were not based on press reports alone but also on other sources.

Reverting to the question of the press, Col. Arriaga said the security forces had finally hit upon a way of making sure their story was told correctly. When they captured two university students who set fire to two department stores in Guatemala City they obtained the students' confessions on tape and played the tape to the reporters, who "printed the story exactly right this time".

Mr. Oliver reminded him that we still had a serious public relations problem; right-wing terrorist groups were killing indiscriminately and many innocent people were losing their lives. This was making thoughtful people in the U.S., including members of the judiciary, question the present tendency of the Mendez Montenegro Government. Arriaga countered that 90% of the casualties were inflicted by the leftists.

Mr. Oliver reiterated that it was most important for us to collaborate on positive programs to improve the lot of the people, so that the press would have something to concentrate on other than violence. Col. Arriaga did not have an opportunity to respond before the meeting ended.

102.   Memorandum From Viron P. Vaky of the Policy Planning Council to the Assistant Secretary of State for Inter-American Affairs (Oliver)[1]

Washington, March 29, 1968.

SUBJECT

Guatemala and Counter-terror

I made the points in the attached memorandum in a private conversation I had with Ambassador Mein yesterday prior to the IRG meeting.[2] These views are based on my experience as DCM in Guatemala and upon a close following of events since I left.[3] They are the product also of extended reflections on the situation and my experience there. As I told Ambassador Mein I feel somewhat like Fulbright says he felt about the Tonkin Gulf resolution—my deepest regret is that I did not fight harder within Embassy councils when I was there to press these views. I can in any case understand quite well how easy it is to be complacent or rationalize things.

Because I do feel so very strongly about the problem, I felt compelled to repeat these points to you with the hope they may receive a hearing.[4]

---

[1] Source: National Archives and Records Administration, RG 59, ARA/CEN/G Files: Lot 74 D 26, POL 23, Internal Security, Jan–March 1968, Guatemala. Secret. Vaky did not initial the memorandum. According to marginalia on the memorandum it was seen by Oliver, Sayre, and Burrows. A handwritten note, evidently from Vaky, reads: "This is a response based on my conversation with INR/RAR."

[2] At the IRG/ARA/COIN meeting on March 28 Ambassador Mein analyzed the problems and policies of the Guatemalan Government, including the status of the counterinsurgency campaign. According to the record of the meeting, Sayre indicated concern about the Guatemalan Government's response to insurgency and terror; he noted that the element of counter-terror in this response had adverse repercussions in Congress and public opinion in the United States; and he questioned the effectiveness of counter-terror as a doctrine. In conclusion he thought the Country Team should assess whether counter-terrorism was "necessary to cope with the insurgency and terror problems, and, if yes, submit specific recommendations for making the counter-terror campaign more palatable. If no, the U.S. Government should inform key Guatemalan officials that unless the counter-terror campaign is stopped or substantially modified, the USG will have to reassess its assistance to Guatemala." (IRG/ARA/COIN Action Memo No. 10, April 4; ibid., ARA/IG Files: Lot 70 D 122, IRG/ARA/COIN Action Memos)

[3] Vaky was Deputy Chief of Mission in Guatemala July 1964–August 1967.

[4] No written response to the memorandum has been found.

Attachment

GUATEMALA AND COUNTER-TERROR

The Guatemalan Government's use of "counter-terror" to combat insurgency is a serious problem in three ways:

a) The tactics are having a terribly corrosive effect on Guatemalan society and the nation's political development;

b) they present a serious problem for the U.S. in terms of our image in Latin America and the credibility of what we say we stand for;

c) the problem has a corrosive effect on our own judgments and conceptual values.

A. Impact on the Country

Counter-terror is corrosive from three points of view:

1. *The counter-terror is indiscriminate,* and we cannot rationalize that fact away. Looking back on its full sweep one can cite instances in which leftist but anti-Communist labor leaders were kidnapped and beaten by the army units; the para-military groups armed by the Zacapa commander have operated in parts of the northeast in war-lord fashion and destroyed local PR organizations; people are killed or disappear on the basis of simple accusations. It is argued that the "excesses" of the earlier period have been corrected and now only "collaborators" are being killed. But I question the wisdom or validity of the Guatemalan Army's criteria as to who is a collaborator or how carefully they check. Moreover, the derivative violence of right-wing vigilantes and sheer criminality made possible by the atmosphere must also be laid at the door of the conceptual tactic of counter-terror. The point is that the society is being rent apart and polarized; emotions, desire for revenge and personal bitterness are being sucked in; the pure Communist issue is thus blurred; and issues of poverty and social injustice are being converted into virulent questions of outraged emotion and "tyranny." The whole cumulative impact is most unhealthy.

It is not true, in my judgment, that Guatemalans are apathetic or are not upset about the problem. Guatemalans very typically mask their feeling with outward passivity, but that does not mean they do not feel things. Guatemalans have told me they are worried, that the situation is serious and nastier than it has ever been. And I submit that we really do not know what the campesinos truly feel.

2. *Counter-terror is brutal.* The official squads are guilty of atrocities. Interrogations are brutal, torture is used and bodies are mutilated. Many believe that the very brutal way the ex-beauty queen was killed, obviously tortured and mutilated, provoked the FAR to murder Colonel Webber in retaliation. If true, how tragic that the tactics of "our side" would in any way be responsible for that event! But the point is

that this is a serious practical political problem as well as a moral one: Because of the evidence of this brutality, the government is, in the eyes of many Guatemalans, a cruel government, and therefore righteous outrage, emotion and viciousness have been sucked into the whole political situation. One can argue about the naivete of the Maryknoll priests, but one should not discount the depth of the emotion and the significance of the reaction. One can easily see there how counter-terror has blurred the question of Communist insurgency and is converting it into an issue of morality and justice. How fortunate for us that there is no charismatic leader around yet to spark an explosion.

   3. *Counter-terror has retarded modernization and institution building.* The tactics have just deepened and continued the proclivity of Guatemalans to operate outside the law. It says in effect to people that the law, the constitution, the institutions mean nothing, the fastest gun counts. The whole system has been degraded as a way to mobilize society and handle problems. Our objectives of helping Guatemala modernize are thus being undermined. The effect of the money we put into civic-action and the pilot program in the northeast is, in my personal opinion, more than offset by the effect of the counter-terror. The value to the nation's political development of Mendez completing his term is probably already gone.

B. The Image Problem

   We are associated with this tactic in the minds of many people, and whether it is right or wrong so to associate us is rapidly becoming irrelevant. In politics just as important as the way things are is the way people *think* things are. In the minds of many in Latin America, and, tragically, especially in the sensitive, articulate youth, we are believed to have condoned these tactics, if not actually to have encouraged them. Therefore our image is being tarnished and the credibility of our claims to want a better and more just world are increasingly placed in doubt. I need hardly add the aspect of domestic U.S. reactions.

C. U.S. Values

   This leads to an aspect I personally find the most disturbing of all—that we have not been honest with ourselves. We *have* condoned counter-terror; we may even in effect have encouraged or blessed it. We have been so obsessed with the fear of insurgency that we have rationalized away our qualms and uneasiness. This is not only because we have concluded we cannot do anything about it, for we never really tried. Rather we suspected that maybe it is a good tactic, and that as long as Communists are being killed it is all right. Murder, torture and mutilation are all right if our side is doing it and the victims are Communists. After all hasn't man been a savage from the beginning of time so let us not be too queasy about terror. I have literally heard these arguments from our people.

Have our values been so twisted by our adversary concept of politics in the hemisphere? Is it conceivable that we are so obsessed with insurgency that we are prepared to rationalize murder as an acceptable counter-insurgency weapon? Is it possible that a nation which so reveres the principle of due process of law has so easily acquiesced in this sort of terror tactic?

I cannot, from my own personal experience in Guatemala and what I have seen since, honestly say to myself that the Guatemalan military have any reason to believe that we really are opposed to this tactic. I honestly think that on the contrary they believe we have accepted and encouraged it—even though we have pro forma remonstrated against excesses. We have talked to them to be sure, but not very insistently, and the image the Guatemalan military man gets from his total contact with the U.S. and U.S. advisors at all levels is very much a mixed bag. It betrays, I am afraid, intentionally or unintentionally, acquiescence and condonment.

Counter-terror is, in short, very wrong—morally, ethically, politically from the standpoint of Guatemala's own interest and practically from our own foreign policy point of view.

D. What To Do?

I am frankly not sanguine we can stop counter-terror. But one thing we can do is be honest with ourselves and admit to ourselves that there is a problem, and that counter-terror *is* wrong as a counter-insurgency tactic. I just do not think we have done that.

Beyond that there are three things to do:

a) The record must be made clearer that the United States Government opposes the concept and questions the wisdom of counter-terror;

b) the record must be made clearer that we have made this known unambiguously to the Guatemalans; otherwise we will stand before history unable to answer the accusations that we encouraged the Guatemalan Army to do these things;

c) most importantly, we should put our thinking caps on and devise policies, aid and suggestions that can make counter-terror unnecessary. It is argued that if we can remonstrate strongly to the Guatemalans, they will say we encouraged them to go ahead and now what do we suggest? It is a good question, and we should ask ourselves that. If counter-terror is justified by Guatemalans in terms of the weakness of the legal system, is there nothing we can do to help and prod them on legal reforms? Is there nothing we can do to make them stop the brutality of torture and mutilation? Is there nothing we can do to help them develop philosophical concepts of institutions and a legal system? I know that primitive violence has gone on a long time in Guatemala and elsewhere. Do we just throw up our hands and accept all of its wrongness as long as it is also "effective" (and will history's verdict say it was "effective" in Guatemala)? If, in fact, the GOG pleads weakness in the conventional security apparatus, is that not precisely what our assistance and counsel is for—to help them perfect conventional, legal law enforcement?

If the U.S. cannot come up with any better suggestion on how to fight insurgency in Guatemala than to condone counter-terror, we are in a bad way indeed. But most of all, even if we cannot dissuade them, we owe it to ourselves to come to terms with our values and judgments and take a clear ethical stand.

103. Action Memorandum From the Assistant Secretary of State for Inter-American Affairs (Oliver) and the Legal Adviser (Meeker) to Acting Secretary of State Katzenbach[1]

Washington, March 29, 1968.

SUBJECT

British Honduras Mediation

Discussion

In November of 1965 the United States agreed, at the request of the Governments of Guatemala and the United Kingdom, to mediate their dispute over British Honduras. On the Department's recommendation the President appointed Bethuel M. Webster as the United States Government mediator.

Ambassador Webster has met with representatives of the two parties and British Honduras many times during the last two years. These discussions have centered on the conclusion of a settlement under which British Honduras would become independent but would have close ties with Guatemala. We have now reached a point where further negotiations are unlikely to resolve the remaining differences between the parties. We believe, therefore, that the time has come when the

---

[1] Source: National Archives and Records Administration, RG 59, Central Files 1967–69, POL 32–1 GUAT–UK. Confidential. Drafted by Frank and McCormack; concurred in by Webster, Salans, Burrows, Wiggins, and Shullaw. Originally addressed to the Secretary; the word "Acting" was subsequently inserted by hand. According to Rusk's Appointment Book he was in Washington on March 29 but left the next day for Wellington, New Zealand, to attend SEATO and ANZUS meetings. (Johnson Library)

United States should present to the parties the proposed treaty worked out by Ambassador Webster, which we believe represents a fair solution to the dispute and would provide constructively for the future of British Honduras.

The British and British Hondurans are considering calling a constitutional convention in London this summer to prepare for British Honduran independence in early 1969—even without settlement of the dispute with Guatemala. It is important that they and the Guatemalans have an opportunity to give consideration to our proposals for settling the dispute before the first public steps toward independence are taken. The claim to sovereignty over the territory of British Honduras is an emotional issue in Guatemala, and the Guatemalans may react strongly when the United Kingdom moves toward granting independence.

The proposed treaty (attached)[2] embodies many of the suggestions made by the parties during their meetings with Ambassador Webster. They have reviewed and commented on earlier drafts. The treaty provides that British Honduras would obtain its independence from the United Kingdom by the end of 1970 (Article 1); that Guatemala would have access to the Caribbean through British Honduras (Article 2); that Guatemala may use free-port areas in British Honduras (Article 3); and that certain common service facilities would be integrated where feasible (Article 5). A joint authority would be established to take jurisdiction over these matters and others of mutual concern in the economic field (Article 9); the United States would appoint the seventh member of the authority if Belize and Guatemala cannot agree on a candidate. The British would make a financial contribution of $3 million to the joint authority which could be used, inter alia, to help construct a road connecting British Honduras and Guatemala. (This road is of importance to the Guatemalans since they believe the United Kingdom has an unfulfilled obligation, resulting from an 1859 agreement, to build such a road.) The treaty establishes a basis for British Honduras' joining the Central American Common Market if it should decide to do so (Article 10), and for British Honduras' joining the OAS (Article 13 (4)). It also provides for consultation and cooperation between Guatemala and British Honduras in internal security (Article 12), foreign policy (Article 13), and external defense (Article 14).

The treaty does not satisfy Guatemala's demands for control over British Honduras' defense and foreign affairs and for the construction, by the United Kingdom, of a $40 million road in Guatemala. The treaty would, in general, be acceptable to the British and the Government of British Honduras; it is likely to be opposed, for political reasons, by

---

[2] Attached but not printed.

the opposition party in British Honduras and by other elements of the population who deeply distrust Guatemala.

We believe that it would be desirable for you to present the proposed treaty to the British and Guatemalan Ambassadors. We suggest your doing so on April 11 in Washington with Ambassador Webster present. If you agree, we will prepare a talking paper for the occasion.

Recommendation

That you agree to present the United States' proposed treaty in the British Honduras mediation to the British and Guatemalan Ambassadors on April 11.[3]

---

[3] Katzenbach approved this recommendation on April 4. Rusk met separately with the Guatemalan and British Ambassadors on April 18, presenting each with a copy of the draft treaty and an accompanying diplomatic note. (Telegram 149198 to Guatemala, April 18; National Archives and Records Administration, RG 59, Central Files 1967–69, POL 32–1 GUAT–UK) At a meeting in Washington on April 23 Guatemalan Foreign Minister Arenales told Rusk that the draft treaty was unacceptable to his government although he "would be able to sell treaty easier in Guatemala if he had prestige of being President of UNGA." (Telegram 151804 to Guatemala, April 23; ibid.) On June 18 the Department received a diplomatic note indicating that the U.K. Government also found the draft unacceptable. (Telegram 193917 to Guatemala, June 29; ibid.)

---

104. Telegram From the Embassy in Honduras to the Department of State[1]

Tegucigalpa, April 2, 1968, 2330Z.

1943. For Assistant Secretary Oliver. Ref: Tegucigalpa 1917,[2] 1941,[3] 1942.[4]

1. I am deeply disturbed by manner in which municipal elections have been carried out particularly in view of relative optimism which

---

[1] Source: National Archives and Records Administration, RG 59, Central Files 1967–69, POL 18–1 HOND. Confidential; Limdis.

[2] In telegram 1917 from Tegucigalpa, April 1, the Embassy reported that unofficial election returns indicated a "crushing defeat" for the Liberal Party. (Ibid.)

[3] In telegram 1941 from Tegucigalpa, April 2, the Embassy assessed general reaction to the municipal elections, concluding that the Honduran public had reached a consensus that the results were "so lopsided as to beg the question of free electoral process." (Ibid.)

[4] In telegram 1942 from Tegucigalpa, April 2, the Embassy reported on Liberal reaction to the "fraudulent elections." (Ibid.)

we had come to feel regarding conciliatory atmosphere and the position of non-partisanship of president and of the armed forces.

2. The lopsided election results are an incitement to the liberals to look for unconstitutional solutions and at same time are an embarrassment to the Nationalist Party, to the GOH, to President Lopez and, frankly, to the United States. Zuniga and his close associates did their work not wisely but too well. Had he limited himself to bribery, use of government transportation and other facilities for Nationalist voters, this would have been not laudable perhaps but at least understandable and, in the local context, acceptable. The use of repressive gangster methods has, however, created a very bad effect. The Nationalists, moreover, would probably have made a very respectable showing without need resort to violence and bloodshed.

3. The question already being asked (and one which we must ask ourselves) is what is to be the reaction of the U.S. Government and specifically of this Embassy to elections which were so palpably un-Alianza and un-Punta del Este in procedures. As an illustration of how seriously this is viewed, Minister of Economy Acosta Bonilla came to see me at lunch time April 1 unannounced and without chauffeur. He foresaw grave harm to the laboriously built improved image of the GOH abroad with possible difficulties obtaining alliance loans as well as increasing trouble and potential disturbances domestically unless something is done at once to remedy situation. He said the only way this can be done is if President Lopez promptly declared the most controversial of the electoral districts null and called for re-elections in those places, accompanied by an announcement that he would dismiss Zuniga as person solely responsible for the elections. He urged that I see the President and press this course on him. (We must recognize, of course, that Acosta has his own axe to grind.) In meantime, he said, public opinion closely watching Embassy and he recommended we avoid taking any actions which might give impression we support Zuniga or more unpleasant aspects of Lopez government. (Sandoval subsequently told the DCM[5] that he so disturbed with Zuniga's manipulations that he considering offering his resignation to President and specifically asked whether there would be a change in U.S. economic assistance policy towards Honduras.)

4. Today I saw President and stressed to him our fear that handling of election had been real step backward for Honduras, for his government, and for his own prestige. I urged him to find some way to restore conciliatory climate which had been so encouraging. Lopez seemed tense and disturbed at events and said he feared that he had

---

[5] Jean M. Wilkowski.

now lost confidence of Liberals and any possibility they might participate in government. He spoke of possibility of repeat elections in six or seven most controversial municipalities, was critical of Zuniga and even touched on possibility of Zuniga absenting himself from country for a couple of months. While I frankly doubt latter will happen, Lopez' attitude at least seems constructive and he was regretfully aware of damage which had been done to Honduras' image abroad.

5. At noon today Zuniga came to the residence at this [*his*?] request. I found him nervous and full of self-justification. In same snow job he is probably giving President he claimed poor Liberal showing was "a Liberal plot to embarrass government" and claimed Nationalist success largely due to hard work, good organization, and expenditure large sums of money for bribery as well as pork barrel. He expressed suitable distaste for intimidation and atrocities which he admitted had occurred in two departments and which he said would be investigated. I told him that regardless his rationalization, elections had done great harm to Honduras both here and abroad and would certainly make our task more difficult.

6. I recognize that memories can be short here and the adverse reactions may evaporate in a few weeks. I sincerely hope so. In the meantime I request the Department's authorization to return to Washington for a few days' consultation at my discretion if it appears that this is most appropriate way to make known our concern over situation.

Jova

---

105. Telegram From the Department of State to the Embassy in Honduras[1]

Washington, April 4, 1968, 2338Z.

142043. Ref: Tegucigalpa 1943.[2]

1. Department shares your distress at manner in which elections were carried out and your concern re possible consequences. However, before a final determination is made of the necessity for consultation

---

[1] Source: National Archives and Records Administration, RG 59, Central Files 1967–69, POL 18–1 HOND. Confidential; Immediate; Limdis. Drafted by Warner, cleared by Burrows, and approved Sayre.

[2] Document 104.

you may wish to consider the following factors that have occurred to Department:

1. We believe it important that Lopez be persuaded to decide for himself to take steps to redress the situation. If such actions were taken following your return from hurried consultation, it would be apparent to practically all Hondurans that Lopez acted only under severe U.S. pressure.

2. On the other hand, if you returned from Washington and nothing happened, it probably would be interpreted as evidence U.S. acceptance of repression.

3. It seems to us that you now even more than before offer only possible channel of communication between Lopez and Liberals. Your presence and influence may well be only calming factor in this highly volatile situation.

4. Your departure with its obvious implication of disapproval of Sunday's happenings could tempt Liberals to greater militancy.

2. Above considerations lead us to believe it may be advisable that you remain in Tegucigalpa and continue your attempt convince Lopez that it is to his advantage to assuage Liberal outrage. Nullification of elections in five to ten municipalities where violations of electoral laws and spirit of democracy were most flagrant and announcement of date for new voting would be important to show Liberals that Lopez seeking meet them half way. We also believe that Lopez' idea of sending Zuniga on mission outside Honduras would be helpful in giving passions time to cool. In your conversations with Lopez you may wish to tell him of Department's deep concern and hope that he will take immediate steps to restore confidence of Honduran people and rest of world in GOH dedication to democratic principles. If it later becomes evident that Lopez unwilling to act to restore situation, we will consider bringing you to Washington for longer period (sixty to ninety days).

Katzenbach

**106. Memorandum From the Director of the Office
of Central American Affairs (Burrows) to the Deputy
Assistant Secretary of State for Inter-American
Affairs (Sayre)[1]**

Washington, April 12, 1968.

SUBJECT

Zuniga and what to do about him

Our Country Team in Tegucigalpa and we have given some thought to the possibility and desirability of using such influence as we have to bring about the removal of Zuniga from the Government of Honduras. The Ambassador and the Country Team have heretofore ruled out such action for the following reasons:

1. The Government does function, however haltingly, and Zuniga has been believed a key element in that limited functioning.

2. Were we to press for Zuniga's ouster and succeed, we had no idea who might succeed him and what might be the consequences of the change (we still do not know).

3. Were we to attempt to unseat Zuniga and fail, we would lose almost all our influence with Lopez and the GOH.

These considerations are still valid, but the apparent brutality and chicanery employed to make a farce of the March 31 municipal elections necessitate a new review of the question, especially since it is quite possible that Zuniga acted deliberately to sabotage any possible conciliation between the GOH and the Liberals. The review should consider, in addition to the questions outlined above, the following:

1. If Zuniga remains, how much further deterioration is to be expected in the political situation? Is violence probable?

2. What effect will a complete Liberal break with the government have on economic and social development?

3. If the U.S. does decide to work for Zuniga's removal what leverage have we?

---

[1] Source: National Archives and Records Administration, RG 59, ARA/CEN/H Files: Lot 70 D 59, Honduras 1968, POL 14 Elections. Confidential.

a. External Assistance

Although I believe that the degree of leverage available to us because of A.I.D. programs is often exaggerated, it is one source of pressure. The near certainty that we will receive a formal request for assistance in providing the infrastructure for the projected pulp and paper complex does provide a leverage not ordinarily present. However, if we use this leverage in an attempt to unseat Zuniga we will not be able to use the same leverage to try to obtain more self-help measures from the GOH in the development field. Further, we would need the firm support of the World Bank and the IDB to make this leverage effective.

b. U.S. Private Investment

We might be able to convince the Hondurans (Lopez, that is) that unless Zuniga is removed to permit more stable and effective government we would find it difficult to encourage potential U.S. investment.

c. U.S. Influence Over Honduran Opinion

A very large number of Hondurans are accustomed to looking to the U.S. for guidance. Measures that would clearly show our disapproval of the elections (and by implication of Zuniga) probably would have a strong effect. They might well lead Army leaders and others to conclude that Zuniga must go and to press Lopez to this end.

In this connection, it has been suggested that the Ambassador and Country Team might be instructed to maintain an attitude of cold correctness toward Zuniga while exhibiting increased friendship and approval for Acosta Bonilla and Sandoval. This course might be useful, but might also backfire. On balance, I think it would not accomplish too much. Unless we decide to try to "get" Zuniga, there is little to be gained by angering him (and probably Lopez).

4. If Zuniga goes will the Lopez government survive?

Although the loyalty apparently is to Lopez there is a possible danger that the confusion that would be created by Zuniga's removal and Lopez' own lack of ability for the day-to-day operation of the government might lead the Army to feel that a change is needed. Furthermore, Zuniga's own performance in keeping this government on top of all potential threats should not be underrated.

I believe that unless the government takes some action to assuage the Liberals' bitterness and to some extent redress the electoral injustices we should seriously contemplate attempting to procure Zuniga's removal. I would think that if by the latter part of April the situation has not improved, Ambassador Jova should be brought to Washington for protracted consultation and discussion of the procedure we should follow with regard to Zuniga.[2]

<hr>

[2] In an April 16 memorandum to Sayre, Burrows recalled that Zúñiga had recently invited "an Embassy officer to his home and in a 90-minute conversation quite explicitly admitted his deliberate sponsorship of the violence and fraud attending the March 31 elections." It appears that Zúñiga wanted to tell the United States: "I am number 1 in Honduras and neither you nor anyone else can do anything about it." "The validity of such confidence on Zuniga's part," Burrows concluded, "is something that should be considered carefully before we decide to 'go for broke' to obtain his removal." (Ibid.) According to the Embassy's account of the meeting: "Zuniga said it was he who pushed Lopez into power, made him what he is and now does the real work of governing. He enigmatically implied that Lopez' presence was now not indispensable." (Telegram 1994 from Tegucigalpa, April 9; ibid., Central Files 1967–69, POL 12 HOND)

<hr>

107. Airgram From the Embassy in Honduras to the Department of State[1]

Tegucigalpa, April 24, 1968.

A–321. Subject: The President and the Zúniga Problem.

1. In my conversation with President López on April 19 I pushed him further on the Zúniga problem than any time previously. He attempted to make the point that his conscience was clear as he considered himself apolitical, had received the Liberal leaders openly and cordially in the pre-election period and had given strict orders for the Armed Forces to play a non-partisan role. I told him that while it was well known that he himself was apolitical, he could not separate his own role as President from that of Zúniga, his most intimate

<hr>

[1] Source: National Archives and Records Administration, RG 59, Central Files 1967–69, POL 15–1 HOND. Secret; Limdis. Drafted by Jova on April 23. Jova forwarded the airgram to Sayre under cover of an April 23 letter in which he wrote: "Frankly, I am increasingly convinced that while the survival of the Government is important to stability and development, our interests would be much better served if we could eliminate Zúniga from the picture." Jova explained that, "in accordance with the Department's desires I have tried to act as a channel between the Liberals and the President and to help bring about a reduction of tensions. This is very difficult under present circumstances, and you will note from the attached airgram as well as from our telegrams that we have been drawn into a considerably more active role than is traditional. While in Honduras it is almost impossible for the American Embassy to remain uninvolved, even here this has its dangers." (National Archives and Records Administration, RG 59, ARA Files: Lot 74 D 467, Honduras 1968)

collaborator and "Prime Minister" who was at the same time the admittedly real leader of the Nationalist Party and the organizer of the electoral process. I stressed to the President the very real usefulness of his apolitical stance as one of the true unifying forces in the country. I urged that he not let this be eroded. The President replied that he has even considered resigning as his patience with the politicians has grown even thinner, but fears that this would solve nothing and might plunge the country into real chaos. I urged that he forget thoughts of resigning but instead play his full role as President.

2. I pointed out that the very fact that the President had received the Liberals may in itself have led to their persecution as Zúniga had himself told us that he considered this as a threat to himself. When the President later remarked that his door continued open to the Liberal leaders and that he was willing to receive them at any time, I queried him whether this might not cause trouble with Zúniga who, we understood, wished that contacts with the Liberals be carried out through him. The President reacted rather sharply to this, replying that Mr. Zúniga had nothing to do with this matter, this did not concern him, and that he as President was free to see the Liberals when and as he wished.

3. In another portion of the conversation the President referred to Zúniga as he has in the past as merely his assistant and collaborator and one who could be dispensed with at will. To that I replied that, while Zúniga had previously wielded power as in effect the President's private secretary and closest collaborator, he now, as a result of the municipal elections, had unquestionably emerged as a political power in his own right and as a consequence we understood his attitude had changed and had become considerably more domineering. I told the President that I recognized how useful Zúniga had been to him, and the fact that as a private secretary their interests were in large part mutual. Zúniga's interests as a political power now, however, might not coincide with the President's own interests and I suggested that the President examine very carefully to what extent their interests coincided and to what extent they diverged in order that he might be guided accordingly. Certainly their interests had not coincided in regard to the municipal elections and in this instance it had not been the President's interests which had been served. . .

4. The President not only took my various references to Zúniga in good grace but seemed to agree. In fact, I noted on his part an attitude which bordered on the hostile towards Zúniga and it may be that his recognition of the divergency of their interests is growing. We must not forget that others, including Mrs. López, are pressing him on this divergency. It may also have been significant that in reply to my query he suggested that I not mention to Zúniga the memorandum prepared

by former President Villeda Morales which I had handed him.[2] On this occasion he said that this should remain between the two of us, "If you tell Zúniga the whole town will know in no time."

5. I think it is obvious that the differences between these two men are growing and the President may even have begun to fear him. (Could this be why he is starting a new military unit to serve under his personal command as a "Presidential Guard"?) I know that Mrs. López is in a very depressed state, is increasingly anti-Zúniga, and told the Archbishop that her husband has lost prestige and power to "that man" and that she has no hope left for the future. (This admittedly is an emotional woman's view.) Certainly the confirmation of Zúniga as the "political master of the country" as a result of the election has increased the alarm and the jealousy of various other Nationalist leaders and perhaps of some of the military. Nevertheless, it is very possible that the President would find it difficult (perhaps more so than we know) to take action against Zúniga and will continue living with a situation to which he has become accustomed and which in many respects has been useful (and even profitable) to him. On the other hand, [*less than 1 line of source text not declassified*] received indications [*less than 1 line of source text not declassified*] that it would not be impossible for the President to drop Zúniga were this to his interest (see enclosure A).[3]

6. In any case, my conversations with the President should make it clear to him that, contrary to what we sometimes believe Zúniga has led him to think, the American Embassy is not supporting Mr. Zúniga in his present office and would be prepared to work directly with the President toward a more conciliatory type of government at any time the President might wish.

Jova

---

[2] Not found.

[3] Attached but not printed.

108. Memorandum of Conversation[1]

Bogota, April 25, 1968, 12:15 p.m.

SUBJECT

Current Political Conditions in Honduras

PARTICIPANTS

Roberto Ramirez, President, Central Bank of Honduras
Manuel Acosta Bonilla, Honduran Minister of Economy
Covey T. Oliver, Assistant Secretary of State for Inter-American Affairs

During the course of the Plenary Session of the IDB Governors on April 24, Minister Acosta requested an opportunity for Ramirez and him to talk with Mr. Oliver, topic unspecified. When the conversation was held, Acosta opened on the above subject and did most of the talking. No other subjects arose.

Minister Acosta said that the recent municipal elections in Honduras had not been conducted with complete honesty on the part of the Nationalist Party and that, although the Honduran military had been kept scrupulously out of the elections by the President, the resulting bitterness had badly divided the country. He mentioned specifically the estrangement of the labor unions.

Minister Acosta expressed the concern that if Vice President Zuniga prevails in his drive for greater power within the government of Honduras, the result will be a dictatorship. The Minister explained that Ambassador Jova had made clear the bad reaction in Washington to the latest elections but that the President is blind to Zuniga's faults and does not comprehend the seriousness of the problem. At the same time, the Minister confided that there are strong elements within the GOH which desire the ouster of Zuniga.

Mr. Oliver asked about the possible motivations of Zuniga and Minister Acosta replied that Zuniga simply wants to control the government. At the present time he stands in the way and is a bottleneck to all im-

---

[1] Source: National Archives and Records Administration, RG 59, Central Files 1967–69, POL 14 HOND. Confidential. Drafted by Starzel on April 29. The meeting was held at the Hotel Tequendama. Oliver forwarded the memorandum with a letter to Jova on April 30, in which he suggested: "In view of my discussion with Acosta Bonilla you may have different ideas now about an approach to oust Zuniga. If so, we would like to hear them." (Ibid., ARA Files: Lot 74 D 467, Honduras 1968) Jova replied by reiterating his position on Zúñiga's removal, with an important qualification: "López must be brought to desire it himself." (Letter from Jova to Oliver, May 7, transmitted in telegram 2254 from Tegucigalpa, May 9; ibid., Central Files 1967–69, POL 12 HOND)

portant programs. In the case of fulfilling the requirements of the IMF Standby for curtailing excessive government costs, Zuniga continues to run his Ministry in defiance of the demands of the Minister of Economy.

Mr. Oliver asked if there were solutions to the problem, such as holding new elections. The Minister doubted the possibility of doing this, saying that the only answer was to confront the President with the problem and cure his myopia towards Zuniga. Mr. Oliver then asked if there was any outside help which could be used to persuade the President, suggesting both the outgoing and incoming OAS Secretaries General. Acosta discounted these but thought President Somoza might be helpful. However, he believed that Ambassador Sevilla Sacasa was probably the best man, as he is both a close friend of President Lopez and a highly respected figure as well. The possibility of contact at the Central American Meeting of Presidents was also discussed, the advantage there being that Somoza might offer counsel without causing public notice of their contact.

Mr. Oliver asked if it might settle tensions if the President brought more Liberals into his government. Acosta thought that most Liberals would refuse to associate with the present government, and he doubted that there could be any such workable coalition. On this note, he also remarked that while many of the "exaltados Liberales" were leaving the country or merely throwing up their hands in frustration, the Communists are planning to take advantage of the worsening situation.

The Minister commented that President Lopez may believe that Ambassador Jova is acting on his own and siding with the Liberals. Also, there is a belief that Washington may not see the situation as the Ambassador does. Mr. Oliver praised the Ambassador's reporting and assured the Minister that Washington is as concerned about the situation as the Ambassador is. Mr. Oliver then asked what serious consequences would arise from the removal of as powerful a figure as Zuniga, referring as he did to Colombian President Valencia's removal of General Ruiz Novoa in 1964. Both Acosta and Ramirez agreed that Zuniga is really without power, that his only source of strength is that the people at many levels view him as the shadow of the President. That notwithstanding, Zuniga has no support from either political party (except from "la basura"), the military, or labor. Mr. Oliver remarked that Zuniga is then "not a power but a symbol of power." Acosta agreed and noted that Ambassador Jova understands this well.

Going back to an earlier general reference of Acosta's, Mr. Oliver called up the possibility of a visit to Washington by President Lopez, noting that we would have difficulties with this in the United States. Acosta nodded his understanding and said that the President would be delighted to come, that he has already made official visits to Nicaragua, Costa Rica and Mexico, and that he went to Punta del Este.

Mr. Oliver closed stating that he would consider calling Ambassador Jova to Washington for consultations, briefing Ambassador Sevilla Sacasa on the issue and the role he might play. There was brief discussion of the possibility of Presidents Lleras and Trejos being useful, but it was agreed they would not be so at this time.[2]

---

[2] Jova returned to Washington for consultation in early June, and participated in an IRG/ARA meeting on June 5, to consider the Zúñiga problem. (Telegram 173654 to Tegucigalpa, May 30; ibid., POL 1 HOND–US) An action memorandum records the decision as follows: "To the extent feasible the USG should work to achieve its objectives in Honduras through power centers other than Minister of the Presidency Ricardo Zuniga. We should avoid giving the impression that the USG favors Zuniga or is building up his image. We should not become involved in pressing for Zuniga's ouster, but if internal pressures for his removal build up in Honduras, the USG may be able to use its influence discreetly to help nudge him out." (IRG/ARA Action Memo No. 49, June 7; ibid., IRG/ARA Files: Lot 70 D 122, IRG/ARA Action Memos, 1968)

---

109. Summary of the Discussion and Decisions at the 37th Senior Interdepartmental Group Meeting[1]

Washington, May 16, 1968.

PRESENT

 Under Secretary of State, Chairman
 Deputy Secretary of Defense
 General Brown for the Chairman, Joint Chiefs of Staff
 The Director of Central Intelligence
 Mr. Poats for the Administrator, Agency for International Development
 The Director, United States Information Agency
 Mr. Bowdler for the Special Assistant to the President
 Under Secretary for Political Affairs
 Deputy Under Secretary for Political Affairs
 SIG Staff Director

 Ambassador Mein, Guatemala
 JCS—General Orwat
 ISA—Mr. Lang; Mr. Earle
 State—Mr. Oliver; Mr. Ruser

---

[1] Source: National Archives and Records Administration, RG 59, S/S–SIG Files: Lot 70 D 263, SIG/RA No. 37, 5/14/68, Latin America. Secret. No drafting information appears on the summary; it was prepared on May 24 and approved by Katzenbach on May 27.

The SIG, at its 37th meeting, considered the situation in Guatemala. Following are highlights of Ambassador Mein's presentation and the ensuing discussion.

Statement of Positions

The purpose of the meeting was to review the strategy toward Guatemala proposed in the Country Team's Country Analysis and Strategy Paper (CASP) for FY 70.[2] The IRG/ARA, reviewing the CASP, had found itself at variance with the Country Team's conclusions and recommendations.[3]

Ambassador Mein, summarizing the CASP's recommendations, said the Country Team had considered three alternative strategies toward Guatemala.

—To continue the present strategy of supporting the Mendez regime, and develop United States programs more or less along present lines;

—To put the Mendez regime on notice that we would have to cut back our programs unless it moves faster on economic and social reform;

—To offer a substantial increase in our aid effort as an inducement to more rapid reform.

The Country Team was proposing continuation of our present strategy—albeit with certain changes in emphasis. It had discarded the third alternative essentially because it understood that budget stringencies would preclude a substantial increase in assistance. It had concluded that the second alternative—a strategy of pressure—was both unwise and undesirable. Mendez, with all his shortcomings, was preferable to any alternative now in sight. Should he be replaced, the next government would be either a purely military or a rightist military-civilian regime. Mendez was committed to reform to the extent politically feasible and was well aware of our position. It was not in our interest to threaten Mendez with withdrawal of our support.

---

[2] The FY 1970 CASP for Guatemala was transmitted as an enclosure to airgram A–35 from Guatemala, March 22. (Ibid., Central Files 1967–69, POL 1 GUAT–US)

[3] At its meeting on April 26 the IRG/ARA "unanimously agreed that the basic U.S. strategy toward Guatemala proposed by the Country Team in its FY 1970 Country Analysis and Strategy Paper (CASP) would not meet U.S. objectives generally for the hemisphere or specifically for Guatemala." As an alternative, the IRG proposed a strategy in which the U.S. Government would increase assistance to Guatemala if the Méndez administration agreed to promote economic development and social reform. The strategy included the following: "If Mendez is unwilling to move on the basis of our proposal, we should then reduce our aid on all three fronts (economic, police and military) to minimal levels." (IRG/ARA Action Memo No. 38, April 29; ibid., S/S–SIG Files: Lot 70 D 263, SIG/Memo No. 64, 5/3/68, IRG/ARA Decision on Basic US Strategy Toward Guatemala)

Assistant Secretary Oliver reported that the IRG/ARA, in contrast to the Country Team's conclusions, had unanimously recommended in favor of a combination of the Embassy's second and third alternatives—a strategy of pressure, combined with an offer of increased assistance in return for accelerated self-help efforts. We should encourage Mendez to mount a reform program and be prepared to review our assistance effort in light of the regime's performance.

In the discussion, it was noted that there had recently been considerable criticism in the United States press concerning repressive measures by the Guatemalan Government and our apparent association with them. The United States Government was in a difficult position supporting a regime which appeared to carry out—or tolerate—a campaign of counter-terror against its political opponents. Our military assistance program and AID's public safety program, in particular, were politically vulnerable. The United States public, not aware of our limited leverage on Guatemala, misinterpreted these programs as evidence of our support for the status quo.

Resilience of the Regime

There was a consensus that the resilience of the regime, its capacity to undertake reform, was the key issue as between the opposing views.

Ambassador Mein said that in his judgment Mendez' freedom of action continued to be severely circumscribed both by political factors and by available resources. The politically dominant forces in the country remain opposed to significant reforms.

The IRG/ARA view, on the contrary, was that, following the events of March 28,[4] Mendez was now in a much stronger position. He, therefore, would be able to make a start on carrying out the measures necessary for Guatemala's development.

A third view was that we should not focus entirely on the capacity of the government but also on the attitude of Guatemala's socio-economic establishment. Since 1954, this power structure had remained essentially unchanged: land-owning groups, some business interests, some elements of the army. The Mendez government would be unable to undertake significant reforms without at least the acquiescence of these groups. We should attempt to engage these groups in a dialogue in an effort to persuade them to accept such a program.

---

[4] On March 28 Méndez fired three high-level military officers: the Minister of Defense, the Commander of the Zacapa Military Brigade, and the Commander of the Honor Guard Brigade. (Memorandum from Bowdler to Rostow, March 28; Johnson Library, National Security File, Country File, Guatemala, Vol. II, 1/66–11/68)

United States Objectives

Ambassador Mein underlined his belief that survival of the duly elected Mendez government, followed by an orderly transfer of power in 1970, should be the primary United States objective—even if Mendez should have to sacrifice major reforms during the remainder of his term. Survival of an elected government—this would be the third such government to survive since 1821—would set an important precedent, which would benefit the development of viable democratic institutions in Guatemala.

In the discussion, the question was raised whether, if the government was in fact so heavily dependent upon tolerance by the power structure, its survival really made that much difference from the United States point of view.

Another view was that a head-on confrontation with the regime—and all the risks attached to such an approach—made in any case little sense, given the regime's limited room for maneuver. This issue was really not one of how far we were willing to go in risking the regime's survival but whether Mendez and the United States could persuade the power structure to accept a measure of reform.

Mendez' Regime Performance

Ambassador Mein stressed his disagreement with the estimate that the Mendez regime had been a standstill administration. There had been significant progress, although not as much as we would have liked to see and probably not as much as Mendez could have accomplished. In assessing Mendez' accomplishments, we should keep in mind that the Mendez administration had started from scratch. Progress under the previous military regime had been negligible.

In this connection, the Ambassador recalled that the United States had proposed 26 projects to the new government in late 1966; 24 of these had been accepted by the Mendez government. The large loan pipeline ($70 million) was mainly in IBRD, IDB, and CABEI financed projects; the AID pipeline was quite modest.

Other Guatemalan achievements were:

—sound monetary fiscal policies;
—little labor unrest;
—considerable progress under the northeast rural development program;
—encouragement of private enterprise and private foreign investment (e.g., negotiations with International Nickel were virtually completed).

In the important field of tax legislation, the government in 1967 had increased the land tax and it now hoped to get the Guatemalan Congress to approve AID's property tax development loan, which would result in a substantial increase in tax revenues. The Ambassador considered prospects for this loan favorable although he conceded that there remained considerable opposition.

It was acknowledged that this loan, if authorized, could be an important step towards a more equitable sharing of the tax burden by the land-owning classes of Guatemalan society.

Rightist Counter-Terror

As regards the counter-insurgency situation, Assistant Secretary Oliver noted that the existence of rightist counter-terrorist groups was a major source of concern to the IRG/ARA.

Ambassador Mein said that he shared this concern and had raised this matter with Mendez on several occasions. The President had not conceded any excesses in the clandestine counter-insurgency operations.

Equally important, since removal of the three generals, there had, in fact, been no new incidents. The clandestine units of the national police had been dissolved. Activity of the clandestine army groups had been curtailed. Victims of the counter-terror were, in fact, overwhelmingly leftist subversives and sympathizers.

United States Leverage

Ambassador Mein said we should recognize that our influence and leverage were, in fact, very limited. There remained residues of resentment related to the events of 1954. There also was some resentment related to the rather large United States presence. Nationalism was a force to be reckoned with in our policy.

The question was raised whether the threat of withdrawal of our aid, even if taken seriously, was likely to give us much leverage. Our present program, in fact, was a modest one. Included in it were a prospective educational loan and some $3 million in technical assistance, to which we probably attached greater importance than the Guatemalan leadership. The military assistance program was less than $2 million.

A contrary view was that we presumably would extend our approach to IDB activities, which are of considerably greater magnitude. A United States veto on IDB loans would undoubtedly be rather painful to the regime.

Ambassador Mein said that Mendez was fully aware of our views. Threats to withdraw the remaining program would not be helpful. Our dissatisfaction with Guatemalan self-help efforts was reflected in the fact that no loan agreements, excepting the educational loan, were pending at this time. He strongly urged that we proceed with the educational loan, which had been under discussion for more than a year and which tried to deal with one of Guatemala's basic requirements.

Desirable Reform Steps

The discussion showed that there was essential agreement on the steps we would like the Mendez government to take.

The steps identified were:

—tax reform;
—a rural development program;
—educational reform and development;
—cessation of the counter-terror;
—freedom of activity for progressive democratic groups.

As regards political reform, Ambassador Mein suggested that this was not much of an issue. The only important democratic political group now denied freedom was the Christian Democrats. This matter was now in court and there was not too much for us to do at this time.

Mr. Oliver said there was an issue of whether to use economic aid as lever for political reform or whether to relate political reform exclusively to our MAP and public safety programs. ARA came out in favor of the more moderate of these two approaches.

Role of Milgroup

The Chairman raised the question of whether and how we could use our Milgroup to encourage a democratic political orientation in the Guatemalan armed forces.

The observation was made that there was some risk in our military personnel entering the political dialogue of their host country. The Guatemalan military was no longer a major obstacle to reform. Its officer corps was increasingly drawn from the middle classes. Many of these officers had received training in the United States.

As regards AID's public safety program, indoctrination in democratic political processes and the importance of orderly judicial procedures were an important element of the training program at the International Police Academy in Washington. We could not, of course, be sure how much of this training Guatemalan police officials were able to sustain, confronted as they were with political cross pressures in their jobs back home.

Ambassador Mein said that the Guatemalan military academy's curriculum was being adjusted to modern conceptions of the role of the military. It now includes a political science course. Our military training program envisages sending young military men to public and private universities in this country. In the coming year four Guatemalan officers would be brought to this country for this purpose.

The Chairman concluded that the personal and professional contacts of our Milgroup—as well as AID's public safety officers—were an asset we should be sure to use fully. It was important that our people speak up in all their contacts with Guatemalans and vigorously express their viewpoint on the value of democratic and orderly judicial processes.

Conclusion

There was a consensus that we should make a serious effort at a dialogue with the Mendez government and the Guatemalan establishment on the requirements for modernization. In this dialogue we should not threaten withdrawal of our already limited program, as this might merely weaken the Mendez government's position. Conversely, however, we should use the offer of additional aid as an inducement to obtain a commitment by the government—and acceptance by the establishment—to a meaningful reform and development program.

Action Summary

The Chairman directs:

1. That the Country Team, in cooperation with the IRG/ARA:

a. develop, in more specific terms, elements of a development program which the United States would support, and specific performance in the fields of tax reform, agricultural development and educational reform expected from the Mendez government in connection with such a program.

b. develop a plan for a dialogue with elements of the Guatemalan social-economic power structure for the purpose of assisting the Mendez government in obtaining their acquiescence or endorsement for a stepped up reform/development program.

2. That, after this preliminary work is completed, the Ambassador, supported by ARA/LA, commence a formal dialogue with President Mendez and his government on the requirements for accelerated development, offering an increased level of United States assistance in return for increased self help efforts.

3. That, drawing on its preparatory work, the Country Team undertake a systematic effort at a dialogue with the Guatemalan power structure on the need for accelerated development.

4. That the Milgroup continue using its contacts for the purpose of encouraging a democratic political orientation in the Guatemalan armed forces.

5. That all elements of the Country Team continue to emphasize the importance we attach to democratic processes, freedom of expression for democratic political forces, and orderly judicial procedures.

6. That ARA, in due course, report on the results of these efforts.[5]

Approved:

Nicholas deB Katzenbach
Chairman
Senior Interdepartmental Group

---

[5] The Department forwarded the action summary on May 30 and instructed the Embassy to submit first "its recommendations for implementing 1a and 1b above, for IRG/ARA review." (Telegram 173821 to Guatemala, May 30; National Archives and Records Administration, RG 59, Central Files 1967–69, AID(US) 8–8 GUAT) In airgram A–581 from Guatemala, September 7, the Embassy submitted its recommendations, including the following explanation: "The airgram was drafted by Ambassador Mein and reviewed by him with members of the Country Team thoroughly prior to his tragic and untimely death on August 28. The only changes made since then are minor ones which he had discussed with the Country Team and authorized on the morning of August 28." (Ibid., POL 1 GUAT–US) In a memorandum to Katzenbach, October 14, Oliver reported that the IRG/ARA judged that "the airgram constitutes compliance with the SIG directive." (Johnson Library, National Security File, Agency File, SIG, 37th Meeting, 5/16/68, Vol. 5)

---

110. Information Memorandum From the President's Special Assistant (Rostow) to President Johnson[1]

Washington, June 3, 1968.

SUBJECT

Visit of Costa Rican President Trejos—June 4–5, 1968

The visit of President Trejos gives you the opportunity to stress democracy and development under the Alliance for Progress. Costa Rica gets high marks on both. It has one of the longest traditions of stable, democratic government in the hemisphere. It also has a good record of meeting Alliance goals in education, health, agriculture and industry.

Your participation in the visit is limited to the welcoming ceremony, a half hour office visit and a state dinner—all on Tuesday, June 4. The welcoming statement and toast, which were sent to you at the Ranch, are designed to give maximum emphasis to the democracy and development themes.

---

[1] Source: Johnson Library, National Security File, Country File, Costa Rica, President Trejos Fernandez Visit, 6/68. Confidential.

On the official call, there are no outstanding issues in our relations which require decision at the Presidential level. Our intelligence is that President Trejos is not likely to raise bilateral issues, leaving that for his accompanying Ministers to discuss with State and AID. I attach a memorandum from Under Secretary Katzenbach with talking points (Tab A)[2] which you might use in your conversations with President Trejos. You will want to mention his consistent support on Vietnam.

There is one point not covered in the Katzenbach memorandum which President Trejos is likely to mention: his pet project of a highway from San Jose to the Caribbean port of Limon and modern port facilities. He regards this as the single most important contribution to Costa Rican development at this stage. The World Bank and the Central American Bank are interested in financing the project. What remains is to work out the details. If he raises the subject, I recommend you tell him you know about the project, and agree on its importance.

Our record of assistance to Costa Rica is good. It has received $188.7 million under the Alliance in loans and technical assistance. For FY 1969, another $6.7 million is earmarked, subject to Congressional action on the AID Bill and Costa Rican self-help measures.[3]

Walt

---

[2] Dated May 31; attached but not printed.

[3] Johnson met Trejos in the Oval Office, on June 6 at 12:25–1:10 p.m. (Johnson Library, President's Daily Diary) A memorandum of conversation is ibid., National Security File, Country File, Costa Rica, Vol. I, 4/64–10/68. At his Tuesday luncheon meeting later that afternoon, Johnson gave the following brief assessment: "The Trejos meeting was a good one. They have some population problems and are not too happy about all the conditions placed on World Bank loans." (Ibid., Tom Johnson's Notes of Meetings)

---

111.   Editorial Note

In late May 1968 President Johnson proposed visiting Central America as part of a trip to demonstrate his interest in the Western Hemisphere, including stops in Colombia and Brazil. (Memorandum from Rostow to the President, May 25; Johnson Library, National Security File, Memos to the President, Walt W. Rostow, Vol. 79) Although the plans for South America subsequently fell through, the White House announced on July 1 that Johnson had accepted an invitation to attend a meeting at the headquarters of the Organization of Central American States (ODECA) in San Salvador. (Ibid., President's Daily

Diary) The President arrived in San Salvador on July 6; later that day, he participated in a "working session" with the Central American Presidents, addressing such issues of common concern as regional economic integration. On July 7 Johnson toured several sites in El Salvador, including a primary school named in his honor. Before returning to Washington on July 8 he escorted Presidents Somoza, Trejos, López, and Méndez to their respective countries, attending a brief ceremony upon arrival at each airport.

The Embassy in San Salvador considered the visit to Central America an "unqualified" success: "This was probably the greatest event this little country has ever experienced and US-Salvadoran relations will benefit for years to come. Of more significance, the President's demonstrated and expressed personal interest in Central American regionalism and integration cannot help but give a big shot in the arm to this concept." (Telegram 2268 from San Salvador, July 8; National Archives and Records Administration, RG 59, Central Files 1967–69, POL 7 EL SAL) For Johnson's remarks during the trip, see *Public Papers of the Presidents of the United States: Lyndon B. Johnson, 1968–69*, Book II, pages 780–800; and Department of State *Bulletin*, July 29, 1968, pages 109–121) Documentation on the visit is also in the Johnson Library, National Security File, International Meetings and Travel File, Central America; ibid., Hemisfair and Central America, 7/68; National Archives and Records Administration, RG 59, Conference Files: Lot 69 D 182, CF 305 through CF 308; and ibid., Central Files 1967–69, POL 7 EL SAL.

112.   Minutes of Cabinet Meeting[1]

Washington, July 10, 1968, 12:10 p.m.

The President opened the meeting of the Cabinet at 12:10 p.m.

He began with a brief summary of the week-end trip to Central America (see attached outline). After completing his formal report, the President said:

"I would say there is no problem in Central America that money and resources cannot cure. But the problems are many, and they are

---

[1] Source: Johnson Library, Cabinet Papers, July 10, 1968. Confidential. According to the President's Daily Diary, Johnson met with the Cabinet, July 10, 12:10–1:15 p.m. The first item on the agenda was the President's report on his trip to Central America. (Johnson Library)

great. There is a great deal to do in education, in health, in housing, in transportation and communication.

"When all these problems are solved, we can expect to see a better life for all the people of this hemisphere, and we can expect to see greatly expanded trade between our country and all these nations.

"The trip was well worth the weekend. Never—not even on the last night of a campaign, surrounded by my closest friends—have I experienced such a warm spirit of affection and hospitality.

"Minor incidents—paint throwing and so forth—were really unimportant, negligible occurrences on this trip. Every place we went, there were thousands of people applauding the United States and applauding the President. They appeared to me about as friendly as any people could be.

"We received the same kind of welcome when we visited each country's airport, to drop off their Presidents.

"All in all, it was a good weekend. Now I hope that AID and USIA and the other agencies will follow up this effort, and help these Central American countries as they have helped other countries.

"My most vivid impression is that there is so much to do—and so little time to do it."

Attachment I

OUTLINE FOR THE PRESIDENT'S REPORT TO THE CABINET ON HIS RECENT CENTRAL AMERICAN TRIP[2]

A. *Purpose of the Trip*

1. To show United States support for economic integration in Central America.

2. To dramatize the success of the Central American Common Market as an example for other areas of the hemisphere and world of what can be accomplished through regional cooperation.

3. To rally increased effort to expand the quantity and quality of education.

B. *Direct Accomplishments*

1. The meeting took place at a critical time when the Central Americans faced important adjustment problems in the Common Market; morale was sagging.

---

[2] The outline was drafted by Rostow on July 9 as "Talking Points on the Central American Trip." (Ibid., Cabinet Papers)

2. My trip to review their achievements and problems with them and offer increased US support recharged their confidence and determination.

3. Before I arrived, *they made a frank assessment of their accomplishments,* which are impressive:

—almost 700% increase in intraregional trade;
—an average annual growth in GNP of 6%, although it has slowed down in the past 2 years;
—a 65% increase in investment;
—a 50% increase in expenditures for education;
—effective regional institutions under dynamic, young leadership.

But more importantly, they also measured how much more needs to be done:

—in education, housing, health and population control;
—in diversifying and increasing exports;
—in linking the countries with better roads and telecommunications;
—in perfecting the Common Market institutions.

4. They agreed to redouble their efforts in these fields.

5. They committed themselves to ratify the protocol imposing a 30% surtax on exports—an essential first step.

C. *Important Follow-Up*

1. The trip convinced me more than ever before that the road to peace and progress lies through regionalism and subregionalism in Central America.

2. Central America can be made a microcosm for this process which will be a challenge and stimulus for other areas to follow.

3. I am impressed by the material gains I saw and the human talent available. I saw this particularly in the educational field symbolized by the LBJ School in a poor neighborhood and in the San Andres Normal School which will house the Instructional Television pilot project for Central America.

4. But as I drove through the streets and countryside and saw thousands of children and young people, I realized how much more needs to be done quickly in schooling, housing, health and jobs.

I am asking Walt Rostow to work with Secretary Rusk and Bill Gaud in organizing a working group to bring together resources in private industry, the universities and government to spur a major development effort in Central America.

A *Political Side-Benefit*

1. For the past 13 months relations between Honduras and El Salvador had progressively deteriorated as both sides refused to exchange prisoners seized in a border dispute area.

2. The increased bitterness between the two countries was also poisoning Common Market cooperative relations.

3. My trip prompted the two sides to work out a quick solution announced on the eve of my arrival.

---

113.   **Memorandum From the Assistant Legal Adviser for Inter-American Affairs (Frank) to the Assistant Secretary of State for Inter-American Affairs (Oliver), the Legal Adviser (Meeker), and the Deputy Assistant Secretary of State for Inter-American Affairs (Vaky)[1]**

Washington, August 2, 1968.

SUBJECT

British Honduras Mediation

On June 29, 1968 the Department, in accordance with a decision made by Ambassadors Oliver and Webster and Mr. Meeker, informed our posts that we would terminate the British Honduras mediation and our active participation in the dispute, and would so inform the parties to the dispute in writing.[2]

Ambassador Mein has suggested that we not abandon our role as mediator and that we continue our participation through diplomatic channels rather than through Ambassador Webster.[3] Further suggestions have been made that we end the mediation without sending a note, and/or inform the Guatemalans of our willingness to remain involved and of our sympathy for their position.

The issue is whether we should overturn the previous decision, i.e. (1) whether we should terminate the mediation; (2) if so, how we should terminate the mediation; and (3) whether we should inform the Guatemalans of our sympathy and willingness to remain involved.

I strongly believe that we should end the mediation, that we should do so in writing, and that we should make no commitments vis-à-vis further participation in the dispute, for the following reasons:

---

[1] Source: National Archives and Records Administration, RG 59, Central Files 1967–69, POL 32–1 GUAT–UK. Confidential. Copies were sent to Webster and Killoran.

[2] In telegram 193917 to Guatemala, London, and Belize; attached but not printed.

[3] In telegram 5715 from Guatemala, July 25. (National Archives and Records Administration, RG 59, Central Files 1967–69, POL 32–1 GUAT–UK)

1. Ambassador Mein suggests that the parties can reach agreement. I believe it is now quite evident that *a solution will not be found in the foreseeable future*—because of Arenales' reaction to the mediator's proposal, Mendez Montenegro's disinterest in the dispute, the politics and emotions in British Honduras manifested after the treaty was published, and the British unwillingness to resolve the dispute with a large cash settlement.

2. A solution will only come with time, when the reality of an independent British Honduras is recognized in Guatemala and when the British Hondurans, as masters of their own affairs, realize the need to make concessions. These events will occur more quickly *if the parties are looking to themselves rather than to the United States for an answer.*

3. *The United States can no longer fill a useful role as a neutral third party.* We are not needed to facilitate contact and communication between the parties. We do not have fresh ideas. The parties seem unprepared to have a solution "imposed" on them by the USG, as has been shown by the unanimous objection to the US treaty.

4. *Becoming involved in Arenales' machinations leaves us dangerously exposed.* Arenales has told us he wishes to reduce British influence in British Honduras. He has told the British he wishes to reduce US influence in Central America. He has told both of us that he believes the best solution would be the *bribery* of either Price or Goldson.

5. By following the recommended course of action, *we can always re-enter the discussions* and consideration of the dispute if we find it would later be in our interest. This flexibility is preferable to a commitment to participation, when significant events will soon occur, e.g., BH constitutional conference and independence.

6. The British Honduras issue is not of major concern to either the Guatemalan public or to the President of Guatemala at the present. It is possible this dispute could die a natural death. However, if we remain involved and mislead the Guatemalans by showing support or sympathy, *we could induce Guatemalan politicians to make the claim a political issue—it could sprout like, and reach the proportions of, the Venezuela–Guyana dispute.* Rather than nipping this at the bud, we would be assisting in creating an unfortunate situation calling for later reaction.

7. Only Arenales (for personal reasons) and a handful in Guatemala are concerned with the dispute. Mendez Montenegro has shown little interest in assuming the risks of a settlement or in using the issue for political purposes. *I believe the Government of Guatemala would not object* if we terminate the mediation and dampen rather than encourage Arenales.

8. *Ending the mediation in an oral or equivocal fashion,* especially when extrapolated in Guatemala City, will result in the *Guatemalans misreading our position,* in Arenales believing the Treaty was a Webster

rather than a US proposal, and in our diplomatic missions becoming more involved—subjectively involved.

In conclusion, I recommend that we send notes to the British and Guatemalans as outlined in paragraph three of the attached cable. If you believe it advisable, we could always console the Guatemalans although we should do so without any implication that we would support any further efforts of theirs to gain control of British Honduras, to prevent British Honduras from becoming independent, or to inflame the British Honduras issue in Guatemala.[4]

---

[4] An attached handwritten note of August 3 indicates that Meeker agreed that the United States should "deliver notes & cut this off clean." The issue of U.S. mediation in the British Honduras was resolved on September 12, when the Department informed the U.S. Embassies in Guatemala City and London of its conviction that "in balance it is now in best interests US formally end its role as mediator." (Telegram 236943 to Guatemala City and London, September 12; ibid., POL 19 BR HOND) Identical diplomatic notes to this effect were delivered to the Guatemalan and British Embassies in Washington on September 20. (Telegram 242405 to London and Guatemala City, September 20; ibid.)

---

114.   Telegram From the Embassy in Guatemala to the Department of State[1]

Guatemala City, August 28, 1968, 2310Z.

Guatemala Critic. The following has been passed USIB agencies.

1. Following details re death Ambassador Mein obtained from Embassy chauffeur and Dr. Salvador Ortega, who was on scene:

1500 Ambassador returning toward Embassy in official limousine, along with driver. Proceeding north along Avenida Reforma, between 12th and 13th streets, Zone 10.

1502 Green car, possibly 64 Buick, overtook limousine on left, forcing it to curb, grazed left front fender. Small red truck stopped immediately behind limousine, blocking it. Young man, dressed olive-green fatigues, armed submachine gun, emerged from green car, ordered chauffeur and Ambassador step out. Driver stepped out of car, but

---

[1] Source: National Archives and Records Administration, RG 59, Central Files 1967–69, PER Mein, John Gordon. Confidential; Flash; Limited Office Use. This telegram repeats a telegram originally sent from the Embassy to the Director of the National Security Agency.

Ambassador opened right rear door and began run back in direction south, protected by car.

Armed youth ran to left rear fender of car, shouted halt, while driver green car said "Shoot him, kill him." Youth fired burst 5–8 shots, Ambassador fell about 12–15 yards behind limousine. Green and red cars fled.

Embassy driver ran to Ambassador, was immediately joined by Dr. Ortega who happened have been driving some twenty yards behind limousine, had witnessed whole incident. Dr. Ortega says Ambassador was killed instantly, probably by bullet through back which cut aorta.

2. GOG authorities investigating, more follows.

Krebs

---

115. Information Memorandum From the Acting Assistant Secretary of State for Inter-American Affairs (Vaky) to Secretary of State Rusk[1]

Washington, August 29, 1968.

SUBJECT

Assassination of Ambassador Mein

The Guatemalan Government has reacted quickly to the assassination of American Ambassador John Gordon Mein, who was shot down in the streets of the capital yesterday afternoon while attempting to escape from would-be kidnappers. Last night President Mendez Montenegro declared a state of siege. A curfew was imposed and the frontiers sealed. The security forces have rounded-up suspected left-wing extremists and are conducting a house-to-house search for the assassins. Five suspects have been arrested, but as yet no firm leads have developed.

The Castro-oriented Rebel Armed Forces (FAR), the organization that killed Colonel Webber and Commander Munro of the U.S. Military Group last January, has just claimed responsibility for the assassination. A bulletin issued by the FAR states that Ambassador Mein was killed in reprisal for the arrest by Guatemalan security forces of a

---

[1] Source: National Archives and Records Administration, RG 59, ARA Files: Lot 74 D 467, Guatemala, 1968. Drafted by Wiggins and cleared by Killoran.

top terrorist, Carlos Francisco Ordonez Monteagudo. This bulletin appears to confirm the belief that the FAR intended to kidnap the Ambassador and hold him in exchange for their imprisoned leader. So far the GOG has managed to suppress the bulletin.

The assassination has evoked an outpouring of messages of sorrow and condolence from official and private Guatemalans. President Mendez Montenegro has energetically condemned the killers and the Guatemalan Congress has called for three days of mourning. Hundreds of visitors called at the funeral home where the Ambassador's remains are lying to pay their respects. They included President and Mrs. Mendez, members of the cabinet, the Supreme Court, and a congressional contingent which came at midnight directly from the session at which they approved the imposition of a state of siege. Similar widespread expressions of sorrow are being reported by our embassies in other Central American countries.

Our diplomatic and consular posts in Latin America have been requested to fly the United States flag at half-staff in respect to the memory of Ambassador Mein.

Ambassador Mein's remains will be brought to Washington by an airplane provided by the White House. Interment will take place at the Rock Creek Cemetery on Saturday morning,[2] at an hour not yet fixed.

---

[2] August 31.

---

116.   Telegram From the Embassy in Guatemala to the Department of State[1]

Guatemala City, September 4, 1968, 2110Z.

6306. Subj: Death of Ambassador: Preliminary Political Assessment. Ref: (A) Guatemala Critic;[2] (B) Guatemala 6220, 6221; (C) Guatemala 6238, 6264.[3]

---

[1] Source: National Archives and Records Administration, RG 59, Central Files 1967–69, PER Mein, John Gordon. Secret; Priority; Limdis.

[2] Document 114.

[3] Telegrams 6220, 6221, 6238, and 6264 from Guatemala City, August 29, 29, 30, and 31, respectively, reported developments in the investigation of the Ambassador's assassination. (National Archives and Records Administration, RG 59, Central Files 1967–69, PER Mein, John Gordon)

1. While it may yet be too early attempt full analysis significance and repercussions assassination, following is effort summarize current status from our viewpoint. Must be recognized that significant reactions to event this magnitude are slow in developing here, and shock effect has not yet worn off. Hence, assessment such reactions at this point necessarily tentative, speculative, and subject later correction. Nonetheless, status summary may be useful in maintaining congruence of views between post and Dept.

2. Facts of Case.

There are no significant changes or additions to details reported Guatemala Critic message Aug 28. Other witnesses have confirmed all essential details related by Embassy driver with exception items such as make of green car (one witness who observed incident from point some 60 yards away, across center strip Avenida Reforma, believes green vehicle may have been 1968 model Chevy II) and number assailants involved (other witnesses state three men were in green car, as many as five in small red Japanese back-up car. Consensus is that three of assailants fled scene on foot when green and red car fled rapidly immediately following shooting).

3. Status of Investigation.

Witnesses have been intensively questioned by authorities for clues, descriptions, etc. GOG security forces have published flyer with pictures 6 (six) suspects, requesting public report any trace these individuals. Flyer scattered over city by helicopter Sept 1. While there have been continuing house-to-house searches, we have no word any evidence found directly connected to murder. Military patrols, roadblocks, area searches, etc., also being conducted, but technique of GOG security forces seems be more pinpointed "rifle" tactic than indiscriminate "shotgun" approach so often used previously. We are satisfied GOG actually making every effort within its power apprehend culprits, and that lack of success to date due intrinsic difficulty of problem rather than to any lack of will or effort.

4. Motivation for Assassination.

All available indications, analysis modus operandi, known facts and projections point to validity and authenticity FAR statement (Guatemala 6220, 6221) as to motive and character of crime. This explanation fits all known facts: none other does. In summation, we think following is motivation story: important FAR leader Camilo Sanchez was captured by GOG security forces night of Aug 24–25. In fear he would be made talk with disastrous results to FAR, his comrades planned abduct Ambassador as hostage for release of Camilo. Probable that FAR unit seized first clear opportunity to make attempt, which happened be afternoon Aug 28. When Ambassador appeared be escaping them, FAR gunman fired. (We simply do not know whether

FAR intent was eliminate Ambassador in any case, but it would appear live hostage would be more useful to them, hence we believe intent was abduct Ambassador live, hold him at least until Camilo released to them.)

5. Consequences, Short Term.

(A) On violence: We note FAR statement threatens further measures in aid of Camilo. Presumably such measures would be other similar terrorist acts against local and foreign representatives or symbols of authority. While security measures already taken would make any such attempts more difficult to accomplish, we recognize FAR still has capabilities for additional terrorism of this kind. Under present conditions, FAR may find kidnapping of another hostage too difficult to undertake. In frustration, they might turn to indiscriminate hit-and-run bombings, machine-gunnings, etc. as they have done in past. It also possible that, at least during remainder state of siege, terrorists will go underground, attempt hide, flee country or in any case keep very quiet. Again, this has been pattern after similar major incidents. They prefer not confront GOG security forces when latter engaged in major "offensive" such as present one, but rather to lie low preserving organization and individuals intact for resumption when heat is off. This, however, is rational pattern—loss of Camilo to GOG may prove sufficient stimulus for FAR act in irrational, unpredictable ways including renewed terrorism despite security forces' offensive. FAR may believe it must make its threat (in statement) credible by further terrorism: this would probably take form attempted assassinations or kidnapping prominent personalities.

(B) On stability of GOG: We see no evidence to date of any threat to stability GOG as result this incident. Military establishment remains loyal to regime, fulfilling constitutional role, there are no indications discontent among military with such role. We have heard of no coup-type plotting (and state of siege has, of course, legally suspended all political activity). There is considerable hand-wringing and talk of the "shame" visited on Guatemala by this murder—but this is analogous in tone to similar expressions heard in US after magnicides there. As of moment, we would say that incident has either had no measurable effect on GOG stability or that such stability has been enhanced in some degree by unanimity and uniformity of reaction among all vital sectors repudiating senseless violence of which this crime is result.

6. Consequences—Longer Term.

Effect of assassination on stability over longer term will depend essentially on whether or not subversives resume terrorism. If they do, GOG is prepared resume counter-insurgent (including extra-legal, if necessary) measures. This could again result in high level of violence which is intrinsically dangerous to stability. Should be recalled that in

March–August period, relative calm was possible because of decision by subversives to temporarily suspend their terrorism while they reorganize, in wake of GOG decision suspend offensive extra-legal COIN measures. Since subversives are capable again initiating terror, tranquility is not wholly within power of GOG to determine—it must necessarily react to insurgent-initiated violence even if consequences that violence include stagnation in development, economic deterioration and intrinsic political instability. GOG's primary objective remains—survival.

7. Murder of Ambassador has also produced great outpouring from all sectors of expressions sympathy, friendship, respect, admiration for him personally, and for country he so ably represented. Granting that this is in part natural reaction of emotional Latins, there is nonetheless evidence of a great reservoir of goodwill toward the United States remaining here.[4]

8. [*less than 1 line of source text not declassified*] and DAO concur.

Krebs

---

[4] At a meeting in the Cabinet Room on September 9, the Secretary briefed the President and Congressional leaders on the "tragic loss of Ambassador Mein, who was one of our best ambassadors—the first time in our history we've had an ambassador assassinated." After providing details of the assassination and subsequent investigation, Rusk reported that President Méndez "clearly is popular in the country" and "the military actually are loyal to the constitutional government in Guatemala at the present time." "Despite the danger to some of our own people," he concluded, "we're not basically disturbed about the possibility the Communists could take over Guatemala." (Johnson Library, Recordings and Transcripts, Recording of a meeting in the Cabinet Room, September 9, 1968, 5:45–7:24 p.m., Tape FC003, Part 1 of 3)

---

117. Memorandum of Conversation[1]

SecDel/MC/1   New York, October 3, 1968, noon.

SECRETARY'S DELEGATION TO THE TWENTY-THIRD SESSION
OF THE UNITED NATIONS GENERAL ASSEMBLY
New York, September–October 1968

SUBJECT

Secretary's Talk with the Honduran Vice President, Foreign Minister, and White House Ambassador

---

[1] Source: National Archives and Records Administration, RG 59, Central Files 1967–69, POL HOND–US. Confidential. Drafted by Cates and approved by S on October 5.

PARTICIPANTS

US	Honduras
The Secretary	Vice President Ricardo Zuniga
Mr. John M. Cates, Jr., USUN	Foreign Minister Tiburcio Carias Castillo
	Ambassador Midence (Washington)

Zuniga opened saying he had a message of friendship from the President of Honduras, to which the Secretary replied referring to Mr. Johnson's enjoyment with his visit to Honduras.[2]

The Honduran presentation began with a review of the economic difficulties, and also of the progress recently made, in Honduras. As part of the development program, tax reforms had been introduced, in accordance with the protocol of San Jose, growing out of the Central American Common Market. The taxes were on luxury items outside of general public use. However, after the tax had been introduced in San Jose, Costa Rica, and thus supported by, and with the full knowledge of, the Secretary General of the Confederation of Workers, FESESITLE, FESISTRAN and SITRATERCO, public unrest had followed, charges being made that the tax reform would affect the standard of living of the workers by increasing their cost of living. This argument was seized upon by the opposition party (Liberals) union with a segment of the business community.

After a certain number of civil disturbances, the Minister said, one Celio Gonzalez was arrested. It developed that he was actually the leader of certain political interests, a Deputy in the opposition Liberal Party, that were allied with employer interests in a plan to overthrow the Government. The activity of this capital-labor coalition against the Government was limited to the San Pedro Sula area. Although they declared a general strike for the whole country it was not approved by all unions and it only took hold in San Pedro. The Honduran Government became concerned when the opposition announced that it had found allies in its cause against the Government, and that one of its allies was the United States. Despite claims on the part of the opposition that the U.S. was supporting its cause, the U.S. Embassy had not publicly denied the charges and this silence on the part of the U.S. Embassy allowed the idea that the U.S. was involved to grow. Mr. Johnson of United Fruit had obtained a denial from the State Department in a phone call to Washington after Celio Gonzalez had told him of U.S. support for the strike. This type of denial was not enough. Belief in U.S. support for the opposition actually came to be a stimulant to the opposition forces. The Minister pointed out that it put the Honduran Government in a very difficult position when a diplomatic

---

[2] Reference is to President Johnson's brief and informal visit to Honduras on July 8.

representative of a friendly country was believed to give aid to the Government's local opposition.

The Secretary noted that the U.S. Government's relations were with the Government of Honduras and that these relations were friendly and correct; that the U.S. maintained the practice of not interfering in the internal affairs of Honduras and had no intention of interfering in the future.[3] He noted that in many countries people in opposition parties liked to claim U.S. support. However, he pointed out that there was a big difference between what people said the U.S. was doing and what it was actually doing. The Secretary stated that if any U.S. representative had done anything that departed from our policies and practices, he wanted to be informed. He noted, however, that the U.S. cannot accept responsibility for words that someone else had put in its mouth. He then asked the Minister what Honduras wanted the U.S. to do.

Vice President Zuniga then reported details on the alleged activities of Mr. Mike Hammer, a member of the staff of the Institute for Free Labor Development in Latin America. He said that Mr. Hammer had come from El Salvador to deal with Mr. Johnson of the United Fruit Company. Mr. Hammer as well as others are reported to have told Mr. Johnson that the U.S. and AID favored the strike and the opposition to the Government. Mr. Zuniga said that Mr. Hammer had been aided by the American Consul in San Pedro Sula[4] having lived in his house, used his car, and operated out of the U.S. Consulate as his headquarters in working with the opposition strikers.

The Secretary said that he would investigate the matter at once and that the U.S. had no intention of making difficulties for Honduras.

The Minister then said that the real interest of Honduras is to have constructive friendly relations with the U.S. but that these relations may be frustrated by local diplomats whose views do not conform to both governments' official interests.

The Secretary reiterated that there is a great difference between what the U.S. does and what someone says we do.

The Minister then commented, however, that it was easy for the opposition to exploit the failure of the U.S. to deny charges against it and that U.S. contacts with the opposition had made people suspicious. The Minister stated that the U.S. Ambassador himself requested that the President of Honduras grant interviews to the opposition party leaders, thus giving the impression of U.S. backing.

---

[3] According to a note attached to the memorandum, this sentence was inserted by S/S.

[4] Herbert D. Swett.

The Secretary reiterated that he would investigate the situation thoroughly.[5]

Following the departure of the Secretary, Vice President Zuniga and Ambassador Midence sought out the Reporting Officer to fill in, between them, details on the rather general presentation given formally to the Secretary.

Mike Hammer, they said, works for the Institute which is under the sponsorship of AID and thus is viewed as a U.S. agency. When he came to San Pedro Sula, he was at home in the Consulate and was taken around by the Consul more or less as a protege. It is important to realize that the head of the strikers, Celio Gonzalez, is not only a labor man but a Deputy in Congress for the opposition party and that his interest was not the betterment of the strikers but the overthrow of the Government. Midence pointed out that Gonzalez had been the leader in the Honduran legislature of a move to criticize the U.S. for its intervention during the Dominican crisis, implying that the return to power of the opposition party would result in weakening the close Honduran-U.S. working relations. Zuniga reiterated that the real complaint from the Honduran Government was that the U.S. Embassy does not deny rumors of U.S. implication in opposition maneuvers. In the public opinion, Zuniga said, the American Ambassador is fighting against the Honduran Government.

Another example of the U.S. interference on the side of the opposition was seen in a visit to Honduras by Andrew McClellan, AFL/CIO representative. McClellan had come to visit a project developed by the Syndicato del Centro for giving land to various unions for housing, etc. The Union was seeking financial support from the AFL/CIO. However, according to Zuniga, the American Ambassador advised Mr. McClellan against the project on the grounds that the particular Honduran union did not deserve the loan from AFL/CIO because the union was in favor of, and too friendly towards, the present Honduran Government. Mr. McClellan subsequently advised the Honduran labor leaders that the AFL/CIO was refusing the loan on the advice of the U.S. Embassy. The labor leaders then wanted to issue a condemnation of this interference by the U.S. Ambassador but the GOH stopped them. Zuniga said he would be glad to have these labor leaders come to Washington to corroborate this story.

Comment: The presentation was extremely confusing with all three persons sometimes talking at the same time. The Foreign Minister was somewhat embarrassed by bothering the Secretary at a moment like this with a matter which appeared so trivial. The details of alleged U.S.

---

[5] In a December 2 memorandum to Rusk, Oliver reported that the allegations had been fully investigated and were without foundation. (National Archives and Records Administration, RG 59, ARA/CEN/H Files: Lot 70 D 59, Honduras 1968, POL 1 General)

interference and the exact request for U.S. rectification of the situation were difficult to identify. According to Midence, most of the information put before Secretary Rusk on October 3 had already been given to Assistant Secretary Oliver. The main purpose of the Vice President's interview with the Secretary was apparently to make clear on a personal basis the Honduran Government's deep concern and to make sure that the "U.S. did something."

The Hondurans were critical of two former U.S. officers in Honduras: Robert White, whose departure, Midence said, had been requested by the GOH, and Thomas Killoran, alleging that these officers' reports had to be taken "with a grain of salt."

Midence made a particular point of saying that the full political implications of the situation had not been spelled out for Assistant Secretary Oliver in their meeting last week[6] nor had the names of the American individuals whom the Hondurans felt had been working against their interests been exposed. He and Vice President Zuniga also emphasized that this matter was being handled only by the Foreign Ministry and themselves.

Ambassador Midence at the end made it clear that in his opinion Mr. Killoran was the villain of the piece, as far as the Hondurans were concerned, and could not be expected to give a correct account of the events.

One thing was clear: the Hondurans are badly rattled about what they consider American interference to aid the opposition party and took special care to send to Washington and New York their Vice President to impress upon Secretary Rusk the seriousness of the situation.

As to what action the Hondurans really believed Secretary Rusk should take, the Hondurans, after repeated questions by the reporting officer, suggested that the American Ambassador should be warned of the serious consequences of the continued interference of his officers, and indeed of himself, for the safety of the present Honduran regime, and for the future of Honduran–U.S. relationships. Elaborating on the theme, they requested that the American Ambassador "normalize his activities" so that he does not lend support to the aims of the opposition and become an unwitting instrument of the opposition. This would mean, they said, that the Ambassador follow a "more correct policy" and be "more distant". The Hondurans apparently do not wish a public denial by the U.S. (the possibly fatal consequences of this were suggested by the Secretary and subsequently by the Reporting Officer) but they do wish to be sure that the U.S. Embassy in Honduras "gets the word."

---

[6] Oliver met Carías and Midence on September 23; a memorandum of the conversation is ibid.

118.   Letter From the Ambassador to Honduras (Jova) to the Assistant Secretary of State for Inter-American Affairs (Oliver)[1]

Tegucigalpa, October 11, 1968.

Dear Covey:

I deeply appreciated your good letter of October 7[2] and the patience you have shown in going into all the details. I can only start off by saying that it is ironic that the thrust of their complaints is against me personally. To be frank, one of my concerns during the strike crisis was that I might be considered by the Department as showing too much bias in favor of the Government in what did seem to me from the beginning to be an ill-conceived strike that had political motivations.

I do wish to thank the Secretary and you personally for the confidence you have expressed in me, both in your letter and in your conversations with Carías and Zúniga. Carías, of course, is not returning until around October 21. Zúniga is back, however, but I have not seen him. I have been told by others that he is in an extremely good mood. As a matter of tactics, it is important to know whether Zúniga himself asked for my removal or did he make that poor Foreign Minister take the lead? I agree with your analysis of the essential weakness of Midence, but can quite see him enjoying playing a role which includes "big time politics" and currying favor with Zúniga, on whom, of course, he is entirely dependent for his job.

I did not speak directly with the President during the strike as at that time I felt there was no need for this as he was extremely busy and I was in touch at least three times a day with Zúniga and an equal number of times with Acosta Bonilla. There was, as a review of the cables will show, no lack of communication with the Government on my part during that period. I have, however, subsequently seen the President on three separate occasions at public gatherings, the last time only yesterday. He has gone out of his way to seek me out, has been very cordial and readily assented when I expressed the hope of seeing him to discuss the strike and post-strike situation. I hope this interview comes off, but Zúniga may stop it.

This should provide the President a good opportunity to make any points he may desire concerning any doubts he personally may have

---

[1] Source: National Archives and Records Administration, RG 59, Central Files 1967–69, POL HOND–US. Confidential; Eyes Only.

[2] Not found. The letter evidently related the Honduran complaints against Jova as outlined in Document 117.

regarding the Embassy/Consulate activities and should also provide me with a better feel for what his own opinions are towards us and towards me personally. I should be able to write you a more conclusive letter as to what might then be our best follow-up response to the GOH after I have had such an opportunity to speak with the President.[3]

As to the purpose behind Carías' request and Zúniga's intent, I fully agree with your own analysis. Certainly Zúniga's own position with López and within the Government had been weakened somewhat by the events succeeding the March 31 election and even by his apparent victory in that election. The changes in the Cabinet and in other areas of the Government strengthened the so-called economic group which had been his "enemies" (you will recall your own April 25 conversation in Bogota with Acosta Bonilla)[4] and eliminated various Zúniga henchmen, particularly within the Supreme Court. Zúniga and his wife were not appearing at social events at which the President was present and as recently as September 4 at a party at the home of the President of the Congress, President López held forth at length and with considerable vehemence on how badly served he was by his immediate staff, how poor the coordination was within the Government and how his own commitments to Liberals and others were undermined by his immediate collaborators for their own political ends. While he did not mention Zúniga by name, all present afterwards commented that he was the obvious target.

The strike, however, served at least for the time being to change this atmosphere. It has apparently strengthened Zúniga and has drawn together all of the Government, including Acosta Bonilla and Zúniga as well as the military. I can thus well understand the reports that Zúniga has returned from Washington and his high level meetings in a mood of self-confidence and good humor. The Liberal Party has in effect been pulverized as a result of the March 31 election and its own foolishness and has a long road ahead to pull itself together; the unions have been "put in their place" and for the time being at least their energies must be devoted to internal matters and to rebuilding their strength; the alliance between the unions and the business community of the north coast has been shattered and several individual members of the business community (including Gabriel Mejia) feel cowed, with a fear that their business interests will be made to suffer; the Church is already passively pro-Government while its pro-labor and campesino members have received a warning through the expulsion of the Jesuits Alberdi and Carney.

---

[3] Jova met López on October 14. Jova enclosed a memorandum of the conversation with an October 15 letter to Oliver in which he reported: "I have heard locally that having failed to get me recalled Zúniga is now attempting to discredit my reputation by circulating vicious fabrications about my personal conduct." (National Archives and Records Administration, RG 59, Central Files 1967–69, POL HOND–US)

[4] Document 108.

(Although the latter has been readmitted at our instance, stiff conditions have been placed on his activities.) This does leave relatively untouched the only other traditional "power center" of Honduras, i.e. the U.S. Embassy, and it now appears that it is our turn.

In fact, "our turn" began some time ago, perhaps the moment Zúniga felt the López Government was firmly installed, and I think it would be illuminating for Chuck Burrows to tell you of some of the harassments he encountered in his later days as Ambassador and also on some of his subsequent visits here. I think there is no doubt that Zúniga has always regarded the American Embassy as a check or monitor on his undemocratic and unsavory operations and thus a potential enemy of the regime. Zúniga probably looks upon U.S. military and economic assistance as a source of competing rather than supporting political power and in his mind the Embassy is thus his own potential enemy if not the regime's. In addition to an element of native paranoia which he seems to have, I think it is only fair to recollect that it was long our policy to keep López from coming to power, and I believe that John Dreier, when Ambassador to the OAS, came here in 1957 on a special mission to dissuade López from running.

Since I have been here, while my own relationships on the surface have appeared very good, the Embassy as an institution and individual officers, specifically Bob White, have repeatedly been targets for attack and subject for complaint. While Bob White's actual departure from here was due to other reasons, I am sure that Zúniga in his own mind takes credit for it as he made a special trip to Washington to raise this matter in early June of this year. My own request for Joe Then's departure, you will recall, was also based largely on allegations which, although they seem well founded, were made by Zúniga. You will also recall that his deep suspicions of me arose when, at the Department's bidding, I tried to act as a channel between the Liberals and the President and tried to bring about a reduction in tension following on the March 31 elections. It was at this time that you considered sending an emissary such as Sevilla-Sacasa to insure that President López realized that I was not acting on my own but in accordance with the Department's instructions.

I am pretty sure that my own difficulty dates from that time and that Zúniga is now ready for bigger game than White and Then. Certainly there was nothing done or said by me during the current strike which would justify even a mild complaint, let alone a request for my removal. The Consulate at San Pedro Sula was in a more unenviable position, being right in the thick of things. I daily preached caution to our Consul, and I think that he capably played out a difficult role of keeping communications open and at a most difficult time. The activities of the visiting AIFLD representative, Mike Hammer, may admittedly have been somewhat injudicious until brought under control by the Consul. But even in his case his actions were more subject to misinterpretation than to actual wrongdoing, and when I found out about them I on my own apologized to Zúniga for his activities and he returned to San Salvador as the strike finished.

I appreciate the Secretary's suggestion that it might be wise to send a senior Inspector to Tegucigalpa. Much as I would welcome such a visit, I am inclined to feel that it might, as you suggested, serve to undercut my position here at this time. I should point out that in addition to the telegraphic traffic, which was copious, we kept fairly complete records of our telephonic conversations with the Consulate in San Pedro Sula, with some of the Government authorities, and with the Department. Thus rather than to send an Inspector here at this time, I would suggest my sending up our file of telegrams, letters, and memoranda of conversation, as well as memos prepared for me by the Consul covering his activities and those of the AIFLD representative. This material should permit someone on your staff or in the Inspection Corps to reconstruct the situation here in a satisfactory manner. Should, after this, there be questions still unanswered, it would then always be possible to send someone down.

I shall look forward to writing you again after I have had a further chance to sound out the President. In the meantime, I appreciate the position you have taken that if the Government of Honduras desires my removal it would have to formally indicate that I am persona non grata. At the moment I am inclined to agree with your thesis that this was something of a fishing expedition on the part of Zúniga,[5] and one which may require no significant follow-up on our part. I can assure you, however, that should I at any time find that my presence here is in fact a hindrance to the carrying out of satisfactory relations with this country, I shall be the first to suggest a move.[6]

With warm personal regards,

Sincerely yours,

John

---

[5] Jova added the following handwritten footnote: "the slimiest of characters!"

[6] In a letter to Oliver on October 18 Jova reported that López had been able "to 'reestablish communications' between Zúniga and myself." In a meeting on October 18 Zúñiga denied that it had been his intention to have Jova recalled, blaming instead "those dummies Carías and Midence," who had misinterpreted and exceeded his instructions during their visit to the United States. Zúñiga pleaded that "we work together closely for the development of Honduras and good relations between our countries." Although he assured Oliver that "this 'crisis' has been overcome," Jova suggested that the time had come for a change: "I suppose it is only logical that I will be leaving here shortly after the new administration takes over. By that time I will be approaching my 4th anniversary and I would say that even in the best of circumstances that is long enough in a place like this." (National Archives and Records Administration, RG 59, Central Files 1967–69, POL HOND–US) Jova left Honduras on June 21, 1969; 2 weeks later he was appointed U.S. Representative to the Organization of American States.

119. National Security Action Memorandum No. 371[1]

Washington, October 18, 1968.

TO

Secretary of State
AID Administrator
Secretary of Commerce
Secretary of Agriculture
Secretary of the Treasury

SUBJECT

Central American Export Development Program

At my recent meetings with the Presidents of Central America we agreed on the critical importance of accelerating growth and diversification of exports from the Central American countries to both U.S. and third country markets. A series of follow-up meetings among officials of the Central American Common Market, U.S., and Central American officials, and prominent members of the U.S. private sector, reinforce my conviction that it is important to maintain momentum toward a solution of these problems. Accordingly I have approved the initiation of a Central American Export Development Program to be organized at the regional and country levels to insure participation of all elements necessary to exploit successfully Central America's export potential.

The U.S. Coordinator of the Alliance for Progress is charged with the responsibility for organizing the program, and in particular for establishing effective administrative arrangements to link key groups from the U.S. government and private sector to public and private authorities in Central America.

All U.S. Departments and Agencies should, to the maximum possible extent, assist the Coordinator to make this program a success.

Lyndon B. Johnson

---

[1] Source: Johnson Library, National Security File, National Security Action Memorandums, NSAM No. 371. Limited Official Use. Rostow forwarded the NSAM to the President as an attachment to an October 17 memorandum in which he noted: "Covey Oliver and his staff have cooperated fully on this effort and share our conviction about its importance. Nonetheless, to make sure no momentum is lost, I think it important formally to record your continuing interest and endorsement for this program. The attached NSAM, which has been cleared with both Bill Gaud and Covey Oliver, would achieve this objective. I recommend that you sign it." (Ibid.)

120. Special National Intelligence Estimate[1]

SNIE 82–68   Washington, December 19, 1968.

INSURGENCY AND INSTABILITY IN GUATEMALA

The Problem

To assess the prospects over the next several years for the insurgency in Guatemala in the context of the country's continuing political, economic, and social problems.

Conclusions

A. The persistent insurgency by a small number of leftist extremists is a particularly troublesome manifestation of Guatemala's chronic political instability. Nonetheless, the insurgency, now in its ninth year, has survived rather than flourished. The insurgents, though able to carry out dramatic acts of urban terror, have had little success in gaining adherents in the countryside. Much of the energy of the insurgent movement has been squandered on internal dissidence and factionalism.

B. We believe it unlikely that the insurgency, now at a low ebb, will expand greatly, at least for several years to come. Over the next year or so, the insurgents will probably attempt to keep the pressure on the government through sporadic terrorism, including acts against US officials. Their apparent motive is to provoke the replacement of President Méndez by a repressive military regime in the hope that it would cause the people to rally to the insurgency.

C. There are some indications that Fidel Castro is planning to increase his support of the Guatemalan insurgency, perhaps to the point of dispatching a small force of guerrillas now undergoing training in Cuba. Such foreign assistance might increase the insurgency's capacity for violence and terror, and thus increase its disruptive effect. But it would probably not enhance the insurgents' overall prospect for seizing power.

D. Since early 1968, Méndez has increased his control over Guatemalan security forces and sharply reduced the bloody and often indiscriminate counter-terrorism through which they and right-wing vigilantes were combating the insurgents. The President's freedom of

---

[1] Source: Central Intelligence Agency, Job 79–R01012A, O/DDI Registry. Secret; Controlled Dissem. According to a note on the cover sheet this estimate was prepared in the Central Intelligence Agency with the participation of the intelligence organizations of the Departments of State and Defense and the National Security Agency. The United States Intelligence Board concurred in this estimate on December 19.

action, however, still is limited, and he is unlikely to undertake basic reforms or any other actions that would coalesce the military and the political right generally against him. Though the security forces have been able to keep the rural insurgency from getting out of hand, they suffer from a variety of disabilities, including weak leadership and poor and uncoordinated intelligence. The latter disability in particular puts them at a disadvantage in coping with urban terrorism.

E. The basic political and social problems of Guatemala are not caused by the insurgency, and they would persist even if it collapsed. Even if the insurgents were to achieve their interim objective of provoking the establishment of a harsh military dictatorship, they would in our view benefit little, at least in the short run. Over the longer period, the actions of such a regime might increase the prospects for the emergence of a more vigorous revolutionary movement; but we cannot know at this point what role, if any, the current insurgents and their sometime allies among Guatemalan Communists would have in such a movement.

[Omitted here is the Discussion section of the estimate.]

Argentina

121. Telegram From the Department of State to the Embassy in Argentina[1]

Washington, June 20, 1964, 3:53 p.m.

1259. Following are Department's current views on oil problem.[2] Would appreciate your comments:

1. About eight months have gone by since the contracts were annulled. While we have received during this time vague generalized assurances from Illia about fair solutions Argentine Government has in fact made no concrete proposals about how companies' contractual rights are to be restored or respected or, in the alternative, for prompt adequate and effective compensation. The alleged decision to intervene some or all of the properties on an interim or permanent basis prior to some kind of mutually satisfactory arrangement may not be decisive but it further complicates situation.

2. We have asked that Legal Adviser's latest opinion re Hickenlooper Amendment[3] be sent to you by separate telegram (Deptel 1257).[4] Question remains in both legal and political terms of how much longer we will be justified in saying that the GOA has not failed for a reasonable period of time to take appropriate steps to discharge its obligations under international law, and that the GOA is in fact operating in good faith in the oil problem.

We would assume that the answer to this question will depend on what happens hereafter and particularly on our estimate of Illia's will and ability to overrule extremists in his government.

The fact that legal rights to claim eventual compensation have not been impaired will have little effect in preventing application of Hickenlooper Amendment if steps taken by GOA from here on out are not "appropriate".

---

[1] Source: National Archives and Records Administration, RG 59, Central Files 1964–66, PET 15 ARG. Confidential; Immediate. Drafted by Mann; cleared by Harriman, Ensor, and Meeker; and approved by Rusk.

[2] On November 15, 1963, the Illia administration issued a decree annulling the contracts of foreign oil companies operating in Argentina. For documentation on the decree, and the response of the U.S. Government, see *Foreign Relations, 1961–1963*, vol. XII, Documents 199–202.

[3] The amendment stipulated that the President suspend assistance to any country that expropriated the property of U.S. citizens or corporations without proper compensation. (76 Stat. 260)

[4] Dated June 19. (National Archives and Records Administration, RG 59, Central Files 1964–66, PET 15 ARG)

3. Mann's conversation with MOD Suarez here week before last[5] gave us no ground for optimism although he was described as one of the "moderates". Suarez said in effect that annulment of the contracts was final, that "renegotiation" was a word which could not be used, and that a process of "open bidding" would be necessary.

4. Suarez talked about returning the investments with interest as if this would be a satisfactory formula. Mann tried to disabuse him but is not sure he succeeded. The essence of our position must be, it seems to us, that if the contracts are to remain annulled then either a new arrangement must be made or the companies should be compensated for the fair value of the contractual rights which they had. Those companies which risked their capital and found little or no oil and gas might be pleased to pick up a windfall by having their money returned but we fail to see why they are entitled to it. On the other hand, those which found substantial quantities of oil are entitled to more than the mere return of investment. Without trying to decide what is fair value in a particular case, it seems to us that it is essential that we have this general principle clearly in mind because on it rests very large oil investments in Venezuela, the Near East and elsewhere.

5. This raises the question of whether there is not a danger that Argentina will settle with one or more of the unsuccessful investors on the basis of return of investment and then become politically frozen on this formula which we assume we could not accept here. Would appreciate your comments on this point.

6. This is one of the reasons we thought it would be prudent for the U.S. Government to have a general review of the situation with the Argentine Government. You could best decide with which officials the matter should be raised. But if there are no talks USG runs the risk of becoming prisoner of developments which could seriously affect our relations with Argentina and in which we did not play a role. We worry, in a word, about leaving relations entirely to discussions between private oil companies and the Argentine Government. This does not mean that we would assume authority to speak for the companies about details of particular settlements. It does mean we should be free to influence the companies to accept what we consider to be a fair settlement if one can be arrived at.

7. On the question of the application of the Hickenlooper Amendment, if worst comes to worst we are giving thought here to quietly cutting back on aid, including military aid, without a formal invocation of the Amendment. We could leave a token program or programs going as proof that we have not applied sanctions and if pushed by press justify

---

[5] Mann met Suárez on June 4 at a dinner hosted by Secretary of Defense McNamara. (Telegram 1208 to Buenos Aires, June 5; ibid.) The principal points made by the Argentine Minister of Defense are summarized in telegram 1267 to Buenos Aires, June 23. (Ibid.)

in an off-the-record way the cut-back on the ground of failure of Argentina to take self-help measures or some other line. There would seem to be ample ground for this in current Argentine budgetary deficit, inflationary pressures, etc. Would appreciate your opinion on this assuming we can obtain support for this procedure in Congress as we think we have chance of doing. The companies Mann has talked to here seem to be fully aware of the disadvantages to them of formally applying the Amendment and the importance of keeping doors open and playing for time.

8. We are of course conscious of the political pressures on Illia and of the risk of a golpe regardless of what is done about the oil problem. Our concern is heightened by the apparent failure of the GOA to realize there is any connection between a settlement of oil problems and its avowed need for further private investment and outside financial and economic assistance. Interview with Illia appearing N.Y. Times today would seem further emphasize Illia's lack of reality.[6] We also have in mind the possible effect on the Chilean elections of applying the Amendment to Argentina.

Since time would appear to be of the essence you should therefore promptly convey to the Argentine Government in the way you deem most appropriate that while the USG has hoped that the Argentine Government and the companies would be able to arrive at a satisfactory agreement oil problem is not one simply between companies and Argentine Government. It involves very basic inter-governmental relations between Argentina and US. Therefore, before any final decision and action by Argentine Government on oil question USG would wish to review whole question with Argentine Government with view to working out solution under which either new agreements are negotiated or just compensation provided. In this connection, you should make very clear that any formula for returning to companies merely their investment costs plus interest could not constitute proper compensation.[7]

Rusk

---

[6] Reference is apparently to Illia's comment that "the door is open to foreign investments," even though Argentina was preparing to "move into American oil field operations." (New York Times, June 20, 1964, p. 29)

[7] In its reply the Embassy commented that the "adverse impact of oil actions on foreign public and private investment is not now [an] important factor in Argentine thinking." "What it comes to is US public funds." (Telegram 2064 from Buenos Aires, June 22; National Archives and Records Administration, RG 59, Central Files 1964–66, PET 15 ARG) The Department subsequently decided to withhold such public funds by refusing to sign an amendment to the Silo loan, an AID agreement to assist grain storage in Argentina. Mann initially explained that this action was taken "pending further study of questions of self-help and effect of annulment of oil contracts, particularly the former." (Telegram 1288 to Buenos Aires, June 26; ibid.) Three weeks later, however, Mann gave Rusk a different explanation: "we are delaying signature because of the oil question." (Memorandum from Mann to Rusk, July 20; ibid., POL 15–1 ARG)

122. Action Memorandum From the Assistant Secretary of State for Inter-American Affairs (Mann) to Acting Secretary of State Harriman[1]

Washington, November 25, 1964.

SUBJECT

Oil Contract Problem in Argentina

I bring the oil situation in Argentina to your attention at this time because we cannot foresee a satisfactory settlement in the near future and because of the following two factors: 1) The failure to reach an agreement on the oil contract problem would probably bring the Hickenlooper Amendment into the picture again when our Congress reconvenes. As you know, we have dealt with this matter so far by slowing down or stopping our aid without the formal invocation of the Hickenlooper Amendment;[2] we continue to believe that this is the most effective way to handle this problem. 2) Argentina may soon seek large-scale financial assistance from us, as well as from the Europeans and from the international financial institutions for an Economic Development Plan which the GOA hopes to present after the first of the year. Argentina has tried to separate the oil situation and its probable request for international financial assistance. Obviously, this cannot be done. The oil contract problem bears not only on our ability to be of any assistance (Hickenlooper Amendment) but also on Argentina's balance of payments and budget situation and on its ability to inspire confidence in both foreign and domestic investors.

Although there has been little progress during the last three months toward a settlement of the oil contract problem in Argentina,

---

[1] Source: National Archives and Records Administration, RG 59, Central Files 1964–66, PET 15–2 ARG. Confidential. Drafted by Hoyt on November 23 and concurred in by Ensor and Lowenfeld.

[2] In late July, Mann drafted an action memorandum for AID Administrator Bell, justifying the "slow down" policy and outlining a plan for its execution. (Ibid., ARA/APU/A Files: Lot 69 D 87, PET 15–2, Airgrams, etc., 1964) In a July 31 letter Mann asked Martin for comment. (Ibid., ARA/LA Files: Lot 66 D 65, Argentina 1964) In response on August 15, Martin agreed questioning only certain "points of emphasis and marginal issues of pace." (Ibid., Central Files 1964–66, AID(US) ARG) After a meeting with Senator Hickenlooper on August 12, Mann expedited implementation of the policy. Congress clearly felt, he reported, that the "time has come for United States to stand up for validity of contracts and of treaties of all kinds." (Telegram 194 from Buenos Aires, August 19; ibid., AID(US) 8 ARG) In an October 5 letter to Martin, Hoyt explained that the memorandum to Bell was no longer necessary: "Tom's telegram 194 of August 19 gave you the answer that we were going to continue with the slowdown program." (Ibid., ARA/APU/A Files: Lot 66 D 243, Correspondence—Hoyt Letters)

it is possible that developments during the next months may again bring this question into prominence. During the past few days, there have been reports that a settlement is about to be reached with one of the Argentine companies whose contract was annulled (ASTRA) and that the GOA would then attempt to use the formula adopted in this case as a basis for settlement with some of the foreign companies. We will not know the opinion of the companies until they have actually been presented with a concrete proposal. Much would probably depend upon the amounts offered and whether the interest rate covers potential or real profits.

While an attempt may be made to reach a settlement at this time with some of the companies, we are inclined to doubt that any satisfactory solution will be reached prior to the Argentine congressional elections in March of next year and maybe not even then. We believe the GOA continues to consider this question largely on the basis of its political rather than its economic aspects and is not convinced as yet that a settlement with the foreign companies will gain any votes in the March elections. There seems to be some growing realization within the GOA that the oil question will have a direct bearing on an Argentine request for external financial assistance which the GOA is likely to request early next year. But, there is not sufficient evidence to indicate that these realists have effectively gained the upper hand within the Argentine Government over the more nationalistic group which is opposed to a settlement of the oil question.

Several of the oil companies seem to be prepared to wait for a settlement until after the March elections, feeling that time is on their side. They believe the Argentine Government needs the foreign companies in order to produce sufficient oil to maintain self-sufficiency and that pressures will grow on the GOA to reach a settlement and thus avoid the loss of foreign exchange through the importation of oil. However, the case of each company differs as does the extent of their optimism and some will find it very difficult to convince their stockholders that they should continue discussions after the end of this year.

The U.S. oil companies have become concerned over some recent indications that the Argentine Government may be counting on a more favorable attitude within the U.S. Government toward the oil contract annulments now that our own elections are over. We have informed the companies as well as some Argentines that any such fallacious reasoning is entirely unwarranted and that we continue to be just as much concerned over a settlement of this problem as we were before. Nevertheless, we can expect there will be some continued Argentine thinking along this line and perhaps some attempts to try and convince us that now we should not be concerned with the fate of the oil companies.

Recommendation

That we continue our present "slow-down" policy with respect to aid for Argentina and try through this device to avoid the formal application of the Hickenlooper Amendment while at the same time achieving its objectives.

Also, that we avoid further comment to the Argentines on the oil question. We have made clear many times our concern and the fact that failure to settle this problem affects our ability to cooperate as fully as we would like with Argentina. In my opinion, a more effective policy is to now let the Argentines learn through experience that our cooperation will be limited if the oil problem is not settled.[3]

---

[3] Harriman approved this recommendation.

---

123.   Memorandum of Conversation[1]

SecDel/MC/44   New York, December 19, 1964, 5 p.m.

SECRETARY'S DELEGATION TO THE NINETEENTH SESSION
OF THE UNITED NATIONS GENERAL ASSEMBLY
New York, December 1964

SUBJECT

    Effect of Hickenlooper Amendment on Argentine Silo Loan Application

PARTICIPANTS

    U.S.   *Foreign*
    The Secretary   Foreign Minister Zavala Ortiz
    Mr. Irwin (Reporter)   Ambassador Ruda
    Mr. Von Reigersburg (Interpreter)

Foreign Minister Zavala launched into a long and detailed presentation of the effect of the Hickenlooper Amendment on recent

---

[1] Source: National Archives and Records Administration, RG 59, Central Files 1964–66, AID(US) ARG. Confidential. Drafted by Irwin on December 21 and approved in S on December 24. The meeting was held at the Waldorf Towers. The memorandum is part II of III.

Argentine applications for a $25 million loan for wheat storage silos. He said that the Argentine Minister of Economy had met Assistant Secretary Mann at the recent ECOSOC meetings in Lima.[2] The Minister stated that Mr. Mann had told the Minister of Economy that the Hickenlooper Amendment would prevent favorable action by the U.S. on the silo loan applications, and that subsequent meetings with Assistant Secretary of Agriculture Murphy confirmed Mr. Mann's statement.

Mr. Zavala said that the GOA was taken completely by surprise by this information because Ambassador Martin had been urging the GOA to complete the loan applications as quickly as possible. He said that the GOA did not understand why military aid was not similarly affected. He also referred to conversations with the Secretary and Mr. Mann at the 9th Meeting of the OAS Consultative Group [where] the silo loan had been discussed but no mention was made then of the possible applicability of the Hickenlooper Amendment. He said that the GOA understood that since the problem between the GOA and the oil companies was under study in the courts and since some companies had made out of court settlements the oil issue would not affect the silo loan. He expressed the hope that the oil cases would be settled soon.

Mr. Zavala said that had the U.S. oil companies been Argentine in nationality, they, too, would have been concerned with the wasteful exploration methods used. He said his country had lost a great fortune in gas revenues because of the companies' actions.

The Foreign Minister said he deeply regretted this situation, and emphasized what he called the unfair, heavy press campaign against Argentina in both Europe and the U.S. and cited *The Washington Post*. He deplored the possibility that the companies might be able to exert undue influence on the U.S. Government saying that the U.S. should not permit its excellent relations with Argentina to be jeopardized by the opinions of private companies. He pointed out that the lack of silos would force the price of Argentine wheat to drop because the perishable product could not be held back from the market.

The Secretary thanked Foreign Minister Zavala for his observations. He said that he regretted that he was not fully informed on the details of the problem of the silos, because recently he had been so heavily preoccupied with United Nations and NATO matters. The Secretary said that it is not the desire nor the intent of the U.S. to apply any U.S. law in an arbitrary or discriminatory manner. The Secretary agreed that private firms should not have undue influence on the foreign relations of nations. He assured the Foreign Minister that

---

[2] Mann met Minister of Economy Pugliese in Lima on December 8; a report on the conversation was transmitted in telegram 685 from Lima, December 8. (Ibid., AID(US)9 ARG)

Argentina had a large reservoir of friendship in the U.S., and said there is no campaign here against the Argentine Government.

The Secretary said he wished personally to study the silo issue, and offered to send an appropriate official to New York to discuss it with the Foreign Minister.

Foreign Minister Zavala regretted that he was returning to Buenos Aires December 20 directly from New York.

The Secretary replied that he wished to be able to speak constructively on the matter, and said that he would send the Foreign Minister a personal letter explaining the situation after he had made a careful review.[3] He inquired whether the Foreign Minister had had an opportunity to talk with Mr. Mann concerning the matter during the OAS meetings.

Foreign Minister Zavala replied that he had been so busy with OAS matters that he had not, although he said he had referred to the subject briefly with Mr. Hoyt at the airport in Washington December 19.[4] He expressed his personal pleasure that the Secretary had not participated in the decision and said that he had told President Illia that he has great faith in the Secretary as a friend of Latin America and Argentina. The Foreign Minister said he had just concluded visits to the Central American nations where he had declared Argentina's faith in the U.S., and told their officials that Argentina supported the U.S. in a common cause. He said he plans to make a similar visit to Africa later this year in this common interest. He said that the silo incident is embarrassing both at home and abroad, especially when the press points out that the U.S. is making large loans to Brazil and Chile. The Minister said that, as everyone knows, Argentina inherited a heavy budgetary deficit, but that this year it has been able to meet salaries, has made payments on some debts, has met its international organization dues, has not made new loans and has not sought to refinance old ones.

Foreign Minister Zavala then referred briefly to trade relations and suggested that it might be time to study bilateral trade relations between the two countries. He suggested a joint committee be established without publicity.

The Secretary expressed the hope that forthcoming GATT negotiations will help ease matters. He said that we believe our efforts to

---

[3] Rather than send a personal letter, the Secretary asked Martin to deliver an oral message to Zavala, indicating that the matter had been "pursued and studied" as promised. Rusk also accepted Martin's suggestion that "basic discussions of overall economic policies be left for Minister Economics and possibly President," i.e., not the Foreign Minister. (Telegram 659 to Buenos Aires, January 8; ibid., PET 15 ARG)

[4] A memorandum of the conversation between Zavala and Hoyt is ibid., POL ARG–US.

lower trade barriers across the board on a most favored nation basis would be particularly advantageous to Latin America, especially to Argentina. The Secretary said he would also comment on this trade issue in his letter to the Foreign Minister. He suggested that Argentina take another look at trade opportunities in the U.S. because it might uncover some hitherto overlooked markets.

Foreign Minister Zavala concluded with the plea that the silo issue is more than a matter of dollars or law, but rather a "spiritual" issue between two friends, a matter of trust. The relations of the two countries could be seriously damaged, he said, by attitudes or actions reflecting distrust. The moral effect would be more damaging than the economic effect of not getting the silos.

---

124.   National Intelligence Estimate[1]

NIE 91–65   Washington, June 9, 1965.

PROSPECTS FOR ARGENTINA

The Problem

To assess the situation in Argentina, and to estimate the prospects for the Illia administration through the congressional elections scheduled for the spring of 1967.

Conclusions

A. During its nearly two years in office, the Illia administration has achieved for Argentina the longest period of political stability in its recent history, but has failed to develop a strong base of popular and congressional support. During the same period the Argentine economy has experienced a recovery, but only to the level it had achieved in 1961. The Illia administration has failed to cope effectively with inflationary pressures or to make headway with the measures required to promote balanced economic growth. (Paras. 7–30)

---

[1] Source: Central Intelligence Agency, Job 79–R01012A, O/DDI Registry. Secret; Controlled Dissem. According to a note on the cover sheet this estimate was prepared in the Central Intelligence Agency with the participation of the intelligence organizations of the Departments of State and Defense and the National Security Agency. The United States Intelligence Board concurred in this estimate on June 9.

B. The March 1965 congressional elections marked the return of the Peronists as a major legitimate political force. The trend toward a political polarization around the Illia administration and the Peronist opposition will probably develop further in the congressional and gubernatorial elections in 1967. (Paras. 12, 34)

C. To avert a Peronist landslide in the 1967 elections, President Illia will have to act more vigorously to create an attractive political alternative to Peronism. We believe it unlikely that he can do so. Alternatively, he will have to devise some way to restrict Peronist participation in the election. This would, of course, frustrate the endeavor to reintegrate the Peronists into the normal political system. The reaction of the die-hard Peronists would be violent, but could almost certainly be contained. (Paras. 34, 37)

D. The Argentine military remain the only element capable of overthrowing the government. The officers now in control of the military establishment would prefer to preserve the constitutional regime. However, the military leadership in general has been antagonized by the frustration of its desire for Argentina to play a leading role in the OAS peacekeeping force in the Dominican Republic. Some officers who have long regarded the Illia administration as weak and ineffectual are now less disposed than ever to make due allowance for its political handicaps. Whether the Argentine military will overthrow the Illia administration within the period of this estimate remains highly uncertain, depending almost entirely on their own estimate of the developing situation in Argentina. (Paras. 33, 38–40)

E. If the military should conclude that the Peronists under extremist leadership were likely to prevail in the 1967 elections, they would first urge upon the government the necessity of restricting Peronist participation in the elections. If not satisfied in that respect, they would almost certainly intervene to impose their will, or to prevent or annul the elections. (Para. 41)

F. Most Peronist leaders recognize that the movement is on probation in its resurgence into the national political arena. If, during the next year or so, the Peronist leadership, or some elements of it, should establish a reputation for reasonableness and moderation, some of the military might come to discriminate between "good" Peronists and "bad" Peronists and to tolerate the former. Thus a Peronist electoral victory under moderate leadership might precipitate a division among the military, with some calling for immediate counteraction and others seeking to preserve the constitutional regime at least until the presidential election in 1969. In such a case, a period of recurrent military crises, like that which occurred in 1962–1963, might ensue. (Paras. 32, 42)

G. The Argentine Communist Party is the largest in the Western Hemisphere (60,000–65,000 members), but is not an influential political force. The Communists and Castroists have no significant subversive potential in Argentina except insofar as they may be able to act in conjunction with a mass reaction of frustrated and embittered Peronists. (Paras. 18, 35)]

[Omitted here is the Discussion section of the estimate.]

---

125.   **Memorandum From the President's Special Assistant for National Security Affairs (Bundy) to President Johnson**[1]

Washington, October 19, 1965, 7 p.m.

SUBJECT

Aircraft for Argentina

Last May, DOD, with Secretary McNamara's approval, reached an understanding with the Argentine Ministry of Defense for the sale of 50 of our Navy A–4B aircraft to help them modernize their Air Force. Our offer to help the Argentines came after we learned that they were considering bids for very expensive French planes. We did not want French influence in the Argentine Air Force. Since the Argentines were determined to acquire fighters, we wanted to see them do it at a price more nearly commensurate with their ability to pay. (The French "Mirage" fighter costs 2 to 3 times more than the A–4B.) Another consideration was the desire to maintain standardization of Latin American military equipment with ours.

The Argentines have reached agreement with the Douglas Aircraft Corporation on cost of modification and overhaul of the aircraft and now are ready to conclude the necessary credit agreements with us.

In our 1966 Military Assistance Program for Latin America, there is an item for $2.5 million in grant assistance to Argentina for spare parts and support equipment for use in connection with the A–4B's. Use of MAP grant funds for training and support assistance has been standard practice in the Latin American area and is designed to help the recipient government maintain and obtain maximum use of its equipment.

In view of your desire to review commitments of this nature, I wanted to obtain your authorization before Defense proceeds to

---

[1] Source: Johnson Library, National Security File, Memos to the President, McGeorge Bundy, Vol. 16. Confidential.

formalize the transaction. I recommend that you authorize me to tell Defense that they may go ahead.

McG. B.

Proceed with the transaction[2]
Hold up for further review

---

[2] The President checked this option.

---

126. Telegram From Secretary of State Rusk to the Department of State[1]

Rio de Janeiro, November 17, 1965, 0320Z.

Secto 11. For Ball from Secretary. I am convinced after my talks with Illia, Foreign Minister, and economic team that it is time for us to begin to move forward with Argentina.

They have proceeded with oil negotiations in good faith.[2] So far as I can see the Hickenlooper amendment is not now being violated in letter or in spirit. The oil companies including PanAm are making profits and repatriating them.

In terms of self-help the Argentines have taken significant steps to increase tax collections which have risen 74 percent over last year, they have produced a serious development plan; they have the respect of the IBRD and IAB and are actively negotiating project loans with them; they are entering a period of crucial confrontation with Peronist unions in an effort to hold wage increases to 15 percent in the next round.

They believe—and I agree—1966 may be the crucial year to demonstrate that stabilization and growth are compatible.

And I am not unmindful of the 1967 Argentine elections and the various matters in which I shall wish to have the collaboration of the Foreign Minister in the months ahead.

---

[1] Source: National Archives and Records Administration, RG 59, Central Files 1964–66, POL ARG–US. Confidential; Exdis. Rusk was in Buenos Aires, November 15–16, for meetings with the Illia administration; he then proceeded to Rio de Janeiro for the Second Special Inter-American Conference.

[2] In a November 18 memorandum to Mann, Sayre reported that Argentina has recently settled with five American oil companies, leaving two with outstanding contracts. (Ibid., ARA/APU/A Files: Lot 69 D 87, PET 4—Agreements)

In all our conversations there was no whining. But they feel they have now created the basis for a new relation with us. What they want to know is what we are prepared—and what we are not prepared—to do in Argentina over the next year.

Specifically, as I understand it, there are the following issues:

1. The Ex-Im loan for the four Boeings. The domestic airlines operate at a deficit. There is a decent hope that their international flights can be made profitable if they get the Boeings. We understand that the British made yesterday an offer of UC–10's for immediate delivery. They would be less economical than the Boeings. For quite narrow reasons of U.S. interest I am inclined to believe this loan should be urgently completed. Would you inform Linder.[3]

2. The three loans for which funds have been committed and which simply await our action. I believe we should move in one or more of these promptly.

3. The housing loan which was held up awaiting legislation and then withdrawn. The legislation has now gone through. We should carefully consider if we cannot move in this field of considerable political and social importance.

4. Assistance in debt roll-over. I am told they will require debt and other adjustments of something like $100 million in 1966. Against the background of a favorable IMF report and U.S. support they seek a further European roll-over early in 1966. We should begin staff work now to see what can be done, if their performance continues to improve.

Neither the position of our bilateral relations nor their actual self-help performance yet justify full steam U.S. support. But would you look into the best ways to put some coal in the furnace promptly.[4]

Rusk

---

[3] Harold F. Linder, president and chairman of the Export-Import Bank.

[4] Ball replied that the Department was "in general agreement" with the Secretary's analysis but that action on the silo and housing loans would require "special strong presentation at highest level because of potential effect on U.S. balance of payments." (Telegram Tosec 46 to Rio de Janeiro, November 18; National Archives and Records Administration, RG 59, Central Files 1964–66, POL ARG–US) Martin later complained that the Embassy had heard "noises" from Washington which were not in keeping with the Secretary's telegram from Rio. The Deputy Chief of the AID Mission in Argentina, for example, had recently reported that the "attitude in AID/LA was quite negative on reactivating housing loan which was canceled last June." (Letter from Martin to Vaughn, December 21; ibid. AID(US) 7 ARG)

127.   Telegram From the Embassy in Argentina to the Department of State[1]

Buenos Aires, June 4, 1966, 1813Z.

1836. From Ambassador.

1. I find myself very puzzled about what might happen to Illia government. Week ago qualified local observers were noting increased tranquility and improved atmosphere for seeking political rather than military solutions to Argentina's problems. Yesterday was generally agreed to have been most tense since Illia government took office with B.A. full of rumors of all sorts of dramatic events, all pointing in one way or another toward disappearance of Illia government, and all as of this morning unfulfilled. [*less than 1 line of source text not declassified*] reports also alarmist but many of them are from golpe-slanted sources.

2. During week several events took place which, added to others which have occurred over past several weeks, provide basis for this changed atmosphere, though no one of them was of major importance. This combination of disturbing developments gave ammunition to active golpistas, largely civilian, who are impatiently seeking to create situation which military will consider justifies removal of government. Long expected economic and political chaos or collapse of government has not materialized and crisis over March 67 elections may be avoided and is in any case some months away. Hence these frantic efforts to provide chaos through rumor and to pressure military into action which government cannot overlook and which might lead to confrontation in which military will be forced to use their power.

3. While some military leaders share this impatience, Ongania and to lesser extent Pistarini, will make decision. Basically I believe Ongania would prefer not to move but is profoundly unhappy about state of country twelve years after Peron was overthrown and about performance of this government. Therefore careful plans for takeover have been drawn up by military in cooperation civilian experts. He may have concluded move inevitable but if so I believe he will prefer wait for situation in which he can justify action as clearly necessary and in national interest and can avoid charge military manuevered into action by civilian golpista intrigues with their variety of good and bad motives. He is very close mouthed and I doubt if more than two or three

---

[1] Source: National Archives and Records Administration, RG 59, Central Files 1964–66, POL 15 ARG. Secret; Immediate. Repeated to Lima for Gordon and passed to the White House and USIA.

people, if that many, know what he thinks about situation as of today. We are trying to find out but I am doubtful of success. He is well informed on U.S. Government position.

4. If military moves believe there will not be armed opposition though may be a few resignations in armed forces. Nor will there be serious civilian disorder. However, short period in power may see considerable strains as proponents of golpe, both civilian and military, have varying motivations and policy conflicts could soon become serious.

5. I am convinced that Illia will fight his removal to end. His skill at this should not be underestimated. Some of his colleagues are apt to be less cool and determined. Already there is considerable increase in activity and flexibility in economic field though no major shifts have occurred. President has held unprecedented series of long meetings over past three weeks with economic team and with ministries responsible for various areas of social and economic development. Wednesday[2] he met for four hours with Pugliese and economic team and yesterday for another several hours. His veto action on dismissal law was strong and basically sound. Thursday Labor Minister Sola made radio speech which attacked general strike called for June 7 in stronger terms than old-timers here remember any labor minister to have used. At the same time Sola has resumed dialogue with labor confederation (CGT). Government has persuaded leaders to call off tenday national teachers' strike scheduled to start June 6. Currently there are rumors that President will in few days intervene Tucuman provincial government and University of B.A. Both measures military have urged.

6. Nevertheless, situation is sufficiently fragile that it is at mercy of accidents. Our radio and newspaper contacts and trustworthy personal friends feel nothing will happen now and that there is good chance of Illia staying until can be seen whether he can satisfy military on March election issue. This will come to head in September–December period. But, without knowing directly what Ongania and Pistarini think, this must remain a guess. Parenthetically, Ongania and wife attended large buffet supper given at Residence May 26 for Philadelphia Orchestra, ate at small table with Cantilo, UCRP President of Industrial Bank, gave President Illia an abrazo, and was quite cordial with me and other Embassy acquaintances.

---

[2] June 1.

7. Pouched today contingency paper on which we have been working for some weeks.[3]

Martin

---

[3] On June 4 the Embassy forwarded a plan that considered a number of contingencies, including Situation F, in which the "present government is removed and replaced by a military junta which rules by decree." In this event, the Embassy recommended consultation with other Latin American countries on the understanding that recognition would be withheld until the new regime promises to honor its international commitments, to respect civil liberties, and to hold free elections; U.S. recognition only after a majority of the "important Latin American countries" have taken similar action; suspension of all economic and military assistance until recognition; and a public statement that the United States regrets "that a country of this hemisphere has left the constitutional path" and will "wait and see what the implications may be with respect to US–Argentine relations and Argentine cooperation in the OAS and in the Alliance for Progress." (Airgram A–950 from Buenos Aires; National Archives and Records Administration, RG 59, Central Files 1964–66, POL 1–1 ARG–US)

---

128.   Telegram From the Department of State to the Embassy in Argentina[1]

Washington, June 7, 1966, 12:02 p.m.

1363. For Ambassador from Gordon.

1. I am of course aware your strenuous efforts to make known both generally and to key Argentine figures our position of strong opposition to coup against Illia Government and our support for continuous Constitutional Government in Argentina. However, I raise question whether most if not all of those actively pushing for golpe—and perhaps key figures such as Ongania and Pistarini—may believe we are making "the expected noises" and that, after a brief hiatus, we would continue business as usual with an Argentine de facto government should the coup against Illia actually materialize.

2. Your contingency paper has not yet arrived. Meanwhile, in view of fact that as stated in your telegram 1836[2] "the situation is sufficiently fragile that it is at the mercy of accidents," I would like to have your views on the desirability and feasibility of making absolutely clear to

---

[1] Source: National Archives and Records Administration, RG 59, Central Files 1964–66, POL 15 ARG. Secret; Immediate; Nodis. Drafted by Dreyfuss and Krieg on June 6 and approved by Gordon and Ball.

[2] Document 127.

those likely to be key figures in future developments that we would not be able easily to cooperate with a de facto government that had ousted constitutional Illia administration. If you agree, an approach might be made to Ongania, Pistarini, Julio Alsogaray and/or such others as you may suggest along following lines:

A. Express concern over most recent spate coup rumors and approaches by golpistas who purport express attitude Military High Command and Ongania that coup inevitable and will be carried out.

B. Point out that we are currently engaged in planning cooperative programs with GOA—both in military and economic fields—and that we feel continuance constitutional government and political stability necessary for us move ahead with these plans. Our opposition to coup is not merely philosophical opposition to rupture constitutionality and democratic process, but also strongly based on belief that military coup would be serious setback to Argentina's economic and political development. Moreover, congressional and public reaction in U.S. would be such as to limit severely if not make impossible U.S. cooperation.

FYI. As you know MAP is subject strong criticism encourages coups. Thus Argentine coup could lead to amendment to pending legislation forbidding military assistance to de facto governments or at most elimination MAP entirely. End FYI.

C. If it seems desirable to be more explicit, you could mention that among the significant joint projects currently under consideration are the five-year MAP/MAS Program (approx. $42 million grant and $67 million credit) and a loan for expansion Somisa facilities ($100 million approximately). Our ultimate decisions on these projects would have to be taken in light of circumstances then prevailing, including climate of congressional and public opinion in U.S. A breach of constitutionality would clearly create extremely unfavorable atmosphere. Debt rescheduling would also be prejudiced.

D. A golpe would clearly rule out B.A. as site for OAS Conference.

E. A military government offers certain superficial advantages in terms of action over present civilian administration, whose errors of omission and commission, chiefly the former, are easy to point out. However, it is our view that institutional instability constitutes a serious obstacle to foreign investment, which is in turn essential to economic development. Stability is perhaps more important in this regard than efficiency. There is considerable doubt in our minds that a military government, which would not have organized public support, would in fact be able to carry out the economic program needed to put country on its feet or that such gains as were made would not be swept away as soon as civilian government was restored. This is reenforced by possible instability flowing from fallings-out among coup leaders once constitutional structure swept away.

F. We continue to hope that coup can be avoided and that Argentina will show that degree of maturity which is expected of such a highly cultured, sophisticated country.

3. Please classify reply Nodis.

Ball

---

129.   Telegram From the Embassy in Argentina to the Department of State[1]

Buenos Aires, June 8, 1966.

1866. From Ambassador for Assistant Secretary Gordon. Reftel: Deptel 1363.[2]

1. Appreciate sense and spirit of your thoughtful message in reftel.

2. My immediate reaction is that approach you suggest likely to have only limited value for two reasons.

A. There is considerable indirect evidence that many military have convinced themselves that in removing Illia government they would be fulfilling basically identical role in Argentina that armed forces performed in Brazil in ousting Goulart. I am aware how different two situations really are and of our official view of legality of transfer of power there, but fact that new Brazilian regime harps on its revolutionary character has easily led local military to regard any differences of legal form that may be required here as only ones of form and to believe that they would be acting with identical spirit of renovation, of anti-communism, anti-corruption, anti-inefficiency and of unreserved support for pro-Western foreign policy. They have followed closely US aid to Brazil since Goulart departure and press here has publicized, perhaps excessively, enthusiasm of US investors for new regime in Brazil.

Hence indications of so different a US response are I fear being received either with considerable incredulity or as last example in long

---

[1] Source: National Archives and Records Administration, RG 59, Central Files 1964–66, POL 15 ARG. Secret; Immediate; Nodis. No time of transmission appears on the telegram.

[2] Document 128.

history of US favoritism toward Brazil over Argentina, already a subject of considerable current comment here. It is not easy to convince them that, so far as treatment by US would be distinct, the difference would stem from quite different situations in two countries preceding change in government.

B. I have met considerable comment that no foreigner can understand depth of Argentine national frustration and of desire that country get moving to catch up on 35 wasted years. Therefore they feel that regardless of effect on external opinion of actions, they must make decisions and take actions necessary to initiate this process. They refer to it as deeply felt private problems which only Argentines can understand or solve. In this sense I think they have looked longingly at successes of Castelo Branco, at Franco's progress in Spain in recent years and at de Gaulle success in France as showing what an intelligent authoritarian regime of the sort they plan to have can accomplish.

There is evidence that belief that only Argentina can solve basic problems of Argentina, a nationalistic attitude with a considerable history, it widely shared, even outside golpe circles. We must move cautiously to insure net positive result.

3. There are two points of lesser importance to be made:

A. Belief is spreading, with considerable justification, that favorable evolution Argentine trade surplus so far this year will make refinancing avoidable, so this reference not particularly helpful point.

B. Also believe military would consider OAS meeting in BA of some importance to prestige of Illia government but of no significance to Argentine nation in finding solutions to many grave problems with which they believe it to be confronted and with which they purport to be wholly preoccupied.

4. Wish to note that in June issue of respectable *Look*-type magazine called *Atlantida* there is article on coup plans which gives some purported details about three plans. With respect to that of Army General Staff it states, "The opposition of the United States is expected and it is estimated that the opposition of the White House 'to the new form of government will be of a duration of no less than 6 months.'" Part in single quotes claims to be from text of plan. This and other evidence which has reached us lead us to believe that US position is not only known but understood to be more than "pro forma."

5. Given these negative factors and possible exploitation of our initiative by golpistas to arouse nationalist sentiments, I am not disposed to seek out Ongania, whom I believe to be decisive figure in implementing plans as now drawn up by military, to convey this message now but to see if occasion may arise naturally or wait until there is clearer evidence of crystallization of program for golpe action

justifying taking risk of charge of interventionism. There is of course other possibility that more impatient and incautious military figures may seek or find opportunity to create situation in which he is forced to move outside contingencies now foreseen by him in order to maintain prestige and/or unity of armed forces. In this latter case our position has only remote chance of influencing course of events for potential instigators such pressure play are so emotionally committed that US representations to them would be counter productive. This position does not preclude Embassy military and other officials following line you propose, with exclusion points mentioned in paragraph 3 above in conversations where they may use it without giving appearance of taking initiative. There will, we think, be such opportunities in days ahead.

6. Suggest it might help remove any possible belief in Argentine military circles that at least Pentagon supported golpe idea that we keep running into from time to time, if senior Pentagon army officer could find occasion to make contrary clear to General Shaw who is member Ongania group.[3] Could base remarks not on intelligence reports but on public comments by you and by Embassy here, as to tension in Argentina.

7. Leak, attributable to legislative source, if to anyone, that consideration being given to requiring cutting off military aid to de facto governments might be of minor value in situation here though again possibly counter-productive. However, I should think such an inflexible provision would be so harmful to US interests generally that we would want to take no initiative which would appear in any way to endorse it. Therefore, I do not recommend that such leak be attempted. To best of my recollection no sanction of even as much as six months for this reason has ever been enforced.

8. Our basic line here has been that US could contribute best to maintenance legality by helping in such small ways as available to us in improving GOA's performance record. Still believe this more likely be profitable than necessarily somewhat imprecise predictions of future consequences, though vagueness, diffusiveness, illogicality and deviation from facts characteristic of golpista rationale is most discouraging. Hard to pinpoint issues which are in fact crucial to them.

---

[3] General Shaw was approached on June 14 by General William P. Yarborough, the Assistant Deputy Chief of Staff for Special Operations, Department of the Army, who indicated that a coup d'état in Argentina "could affect our assistance programs, including those concerned with military." According to Yarborough's account, Shaw "implied clearly though subtly his belief that interruption US assistance would not be great disaster for Argentina." (Telegram 1405 to Buenos Aires, June 15; National Archives and Records Administration, RG 59, Central Files 1964–66, POL 15–5 ARG)

Even with this qualification, however, believe we must continue do what we can on positive side. For example:

A. While IBRD decision will help, believe evidence of US willingness to consider help for Somisa also valuable because of army interest in plant and in development heavy industry. Project could not go forward without Illia's full backing, which it now has, on domestic and foreign financing. Therefore any sign of progress helps government. However, statement by Pugliese in present political atmosphere will be heavily discounted and carry far less weight than US release. Urge reconsider.

B. Also would help if could be some evidence of action on AIFLD housing loan. With proper handling here, US approval could improve atmosphere in some circles.

C. Shortcuts to permit earlier action than would result from normal procedures on release of silo fund loans also could help. Our recommendations went to Washington in TOAID A–531 of June 7.[4]

D. We are working hard with some prospects of success to shortcut usual bureaucratic delays and secure early announcement of decrees approving new large investments by Ford and Dupont.

E. We are also feeling our way toward making recommendations to Illia government in several fields outside area of direct US interest or involvement, though political factors at moment, including within UCRP, are so fluid and complex that this is not simple.[5]

Martin

---

[4] Not found.

[5] Martin reported on June 15 that the Embassy had received information that the military would give the Illia administration "time to produce concrete results," possibly as late as September. The Ambassador concluded that the situation had improved enough to allow his departure the following day for a vacation in the United States. (Telegram 1908 from Buenos Aires, June 15; National Archives and Records Administration, RG 59, Central Files 1964–66, POL 23–9 ARG) The Department cabled its concurrence. (Telegram 1406 to Buenos Aires, June 16; ibid.)

---

130. Editorial Note

On June 14, 1966, Félix Elizalde, head of the Argentine National Bank, called on Special Assistant to the President Rostow to discuss the recent Argentine proposal for a summit meeting of Latin American Presidents. Elizalde delivered an oral message from President Illia in which he maintained that "Latin America appeared to be coming into a rare moment of political stability." He "wryly noted," however, "that Argentina appeared to have somewhat changed its status" since late-March, when Illia first issued his invitation for the summit. Rostow asked Elizalde "how seriously he took the military coup rumors coming from Argentina." Elizalde explained that "the problem came to rest on the elections of 1967. He thought Illia could hold the line until then but some of the military were looking for excuses to move earlier. The key task was to have non-Peronists win the elections of 1967." Rostow asked what the United States could do to help. Elizalde replied that two projects needed immediate attention, the Somisa steel mill and the El Chocón hydroelectric plant. The former—"a symbol of independence in Argentina and an important installation for the military"—required AID cooperation with the Export-Import Bank; the latter was under consideration at the World Bank. (Memorandum of conversation, June 17; National Archives and Records Administration, RG 59, Central Files 1964–66, POL 7 IA) According to a note for Rusk, June 20, President Johnson instructed the State Department to "follow through" on Elizalde's request "to assist President Illia to keep the Argentine military in line." (Ibid.)

---

131.   Telegram From the Embassy in Argentina to the Department of State[1]

Buenos Aires, June 28, 1966, 0640Z.

1981. Subj: Reported Fall of Illia Government (report number eight).[2]

1. At 0200, based on many sources but not officially confirmed, commanders-in-chief of armed forces have taken over as junta or provisional government. Reports also state that Ongania will be declared provisional president at 0700.

---

[1] Source: National Archives and Records Administration, RG 59, Central Files 1964–66, POL 23–9 ARG. Confidential; Immediate. Repeated to DIA and USCINCSO and passed to the White House, DOD, CIA, USIA, NSA, and CINCLANT for POLAD.

[2] In telegram 1974 from Buenos Aires, June 27, the Embassy reported that the Commander in Chief of the Army, Pascual Angel Pistarini, had ordered the arrest of Carlos Augusto Caro, Commander of the Second Army Corps. (Ibid.) The Embassy continued to follow developments, subsequently predicting the "imminent fall of Illia government." (Telegram 1980 from Buenos Aires, June 28; ibid.) For an account of events leading to the coup, see Document 134.

2. Report from Army G–2 source is that President Illia's resignation was demanded and received.[3]

3. Troops now surround War Ministry. Troops not in evidence outside presidency. City quiet.

4. Assuming military take-over now or about to be accomplished fact, have instructed all Embassy MilGroup and U.S. agencies personnel to desist until further notice from formal contact with Argentine authorities. Military mission personnel having offices in ministries will either report at Embassy or (lower echelons) stay at home. All other personnel will report at Embassy as usual.

5. Await instructions. No further reports until 0700.

Saccio

---

[3] The Embassy later reported that Illia had not yet resigned but agreed to leave the Presidential palace, and Onganía was to be "installed as new President some time this morning." (Telegram 1983 from Buenos Aires, June 28; ibid.)

---

132. Telegram From the Department of State to the Embassy in Argentina[1]

Washington, June 28, 1966, 9:44 a.m.

1451. Ref Embtel 1981.[2]

1. Department approves your action cutting off overt and official contact with Argentine authorities by all US representatives. You should maintain this posture until further instructions. Do not take any action vis-à-vis de facto authorities that could imply recognition or continuance official relations. However, discreet informal contact with de facto authorities, their spokesmen and intelligence sources for purpose obtaining information and learning of their plans should take place at your discretion.

---

[1] Source: National Archives and Records Administration, RG 59, Central Files 1964–66, POL 23–9 ARG. Confidential; Flash. Repeated to USCINCSO. Drafted by Dreyfuss and Sayre; cleared by Gordon, Martin, and Andreas F. Lowenfeld (L); and approved by Ball. At 9 a.m., Gordon read the text of the telegram to Rostow and asked if President Johnson would like to clear it. (Ibid., ARA Files: Lot 68 D 93, Telephone Conversations January 1966–December 1966) There is no indication on the telegram that the President cleared it.

[2] Document 131.

2. In response any press inquiries, you may state you keeping Washington fully informed, that US Government carefully studying developing situation, that you have no instructions as yet bearing on future relations between US and Argentina, and that any USG announcement on policy in new situation will be made in Washington.

3. At noon briefing today we intend state we greatly concerned over displacement democratic government and rupture constitutional processes in OAS member state, that we are following developments carefully, and we are reviewing programs now in progress or planned for Argentina in light developing situation. In keeping with international practice in such cases, diplomatic relations are suspended. We will be consulting with other OAS members in accordance Resolution XXVI of 1965 Rio Conference.[3] If you have any comment send Flash message.[4]

4. Further instructions will follow on AID and military assistance programs. Your immediate recommendations on these and other ongoing programs would be appreciated.[5]

5. Department appreciates Embassy's alert reporting of last night's activities and events and looks forward to continued up-to-the minute reports of developments.

Ball

---

[3] Resolution XXVI of the Final Act of the Second Special Inter-American Conference recommended that member states consult before recognizing a de facto government, giving consideration to: whether a foreign country was involved in the overthrow of the old regime and whether the new regime promised to hold free elections, to honor its international obligations, and to respect human rights. After consultation, each country was free to decide whether to maintain diplomatic relations.

[4] The Chargé d'Affaires ad interim, Leonard J. Saccio, responded: "I realize dilemma USG faced with but Department should take into consideration bare faced take over of constitutional democratic government by military with no justification. I recommend that some element of condemnation be indicated in Department statement through use of stronger language." Saccio also suggested that the Department announce the immediate recall of the AID mission director and the military group chief. (Telegram 1986 from Buenos Aires, June 28 (1530Z); National Archives and Records Administration, RG 59, Central Files 1964–66, POL 23–9 ARG) The official statement, delivered at the noon briefing, did not reflect the Embassy's suggestions. (Department of State *Bulletin,* July 25, 1966, p. 124)

[5] The Embassy recommended action in accordance with Situation F of the contingency plan (see footnote 3, Document 127), including: a) suspension of all economic and military assistance; b) immediate recall of the AID mission director and the military group chief; and c) cancellation of all official travel to Argentina. (Telegram 1988 from Buenos Aires, June 28; National Archives and Records Administration, RG 59, Central Files 1964–66, POL 23–9 ARG) Although it agreed to cancel official travel to Argentina, the Department declined to recall any members of the Country Team and would only report that "careful consideration is being given to economic and military assistance during period of nonrecognition." (Telegram 1460 to Buenos Aires, June 29; ibid.)

133. Memorandum From the President's Special Assistant (Rostow) to President Johnson[1]

Washington, June 28, 1966, 11 a.m.

SUBJECT

Argentine Situation

The latest reports from Buenos Aires indicate that the Army has arrested President Illia and removed him from the Presidential Palace.

Where he will be taken is not known at this juncture. There are three likely possibilities:

1. detained on Martin Garcia island in the River Plate estuary.
2. put across the border in Uruguay.
3. sent to the United States to join his wife who is hospitalized in Houston.

This unjustified military coup is a serious setback to our efforts to promote constitutional government and representative democracy in the hemisphere. It will be necessary to re-examine our whole policy toward Argentina.[2] This process will be carried out through the IRG–SIG mechanism starting at noon today. The OAS may also have to shift the site of the Foreign Ministers Meeting on OAS Charter amendment scheduled to open on August 29 in Buenos Aires.

State this morning sent the attached cable to our Embassy in Buenos Aires with guidance on official contacts and dealings with the press.[3] In paragraph 3 it gives the press line which State is going to follow on the coup. The line is the correct one for the time being.

Walt

---

[1] Source: Johnson Library, National Security File, Country File, Argentina, Vol. II, 9/64–2/67. Confidential. A copy was sent to Moyers. Another copy indicates that the President saw the memorandum. (Ibid., Memos to the President, Walt W. Rostow, Vol. 7)

[2] Rostow inserted the following handwritten comment at this point in the margin: "Mr. President: This is Bill Bowdler. I wish to add a word of caution when you have a moment." According to the President's Daily Diary Johnson called Rostow at 11:42 a.m. (Johnson Library) No substantive record of the conversation has been found.

[3] Document 132.

134.   Telegram From the Department of State to Secretary of State Rusk in Australia[1]

Washington, June 28, 1966, 3:18 p.m.

Tosec 60. Argentine Sitrep No. 1.

1. Argentina's military forces, headed by Army Commander-in-Chief Pascual Pistarini, ousted President Arturo Illia in a sudden move last night. Retired CINC Juan Carlos Ongania, who is highly respected by diverse civilian groups as well as in military circles, is likely to be called upon by a junta composed of commanders of three services to head new provisional government. There has been no violence.

2. Early in June there had been a spate of rumors of this possible move by the military in association with various civilian groups, who accused the Illia Administration of indecisiveness in the face of the nation's economic and social problems and of being incapable of averting a Peronist victory in congressional and gubernatorial elections scheduled for early 1967. Statements by Illia over the past two weeks promising to take steps to assuage the military's discontent had appeared to calm the situation and buy the President some breathing space.

3. The spark that ignited the coup was a dinner held last week at which Secretary of War Eduardo Castro Sanchez and II Corp Commander Carlos Augusto Caro, both strongly constitutionalist and pro-Illia, met with several Peronist leaders. Pistarini yesterday relieved Caro of his command, accusing him of endangering the unity of the armed forces by dabbling in politics outside approved channels. He also said Castro Sanchez was unacceptable to the army and demanded his resignation, as well as that of the rest of the Cabinet. Illia countered by attempting to remove Pistarini from his position, bringing on the sudden confrontation that resulted in Illia's ouster.

4. The coup, as it developed, does not appear to be what most military and civilian coup planners had hoped for, as they had intended eventually to lead a "national revolution," to save the country from the "inept" Illia regime. The current move, however, has the earmarks of an old fashioned military power play and will not attract the popular

---

[1] Source: National Archives and Records Administration, RG 59, Central Files 1964–66, POL 23–9 ARG. Confidential; Immediate. Repeated to DOD, USCINCSO, CINCLANT, and all ARA posts except Kingston, Port-of-Spain, and Georgetown. Drafted by Dreyfuss, cleared by Krieg, and approved by Sayre. Rusk was in Canberra June 25–July 2 to attend meetings of the SEATO and ANZUS Councils.

support the military leaders had hoped for, although there is little likelihood of concerted violent popular opposition.

5. Foregoing is for your background information.

Ball

---

135.   Memorandum From the President's Special Assistant (Rostow) to President Johnson[1]

Washington, June 29, 1966, 7 p.m.

SUBJECT

Our Policy Toward Argentina

Linc Gordon, through the IRG/ARA mechanism, has done a careful analysis of our political, military, economic and cultural relations with Argentina and come up with specific recommendations for continuing or suspending elements of on-going programs until diplomatic relations are resumed. The attached memorandum from George Ball contains these recommendations.[2] It is a first-class job, which, incidentally, shows that the IRG/SIG mechanism can be made to work promptly and effectively.

What the memorandum proposes is a delicately balanced package which permits as much of our present programs to continue consistent with the automatic break in diplomatic relations. The dividing line is essentially official contacts: what can be carried forward without dealing officially with the new military government should proceed and what requires official contact should be held in abeyance. This puts us in a correct posture with respect to the other OAS countries while we consult on recognition without antagonizing the new Argentine government.

With respect to recognition, this must await formation of the new government, a definition of the policies it intends to pursue, a request for recognition and consultation with the other OAS governments. This may take 2–3 weeks. As George Ball suggests, we should seek the usual assurances regarding acceptance of international obligations, as well

---

[1] Source: Johnson Library, National Security File, Country File, Argentina, Vol. II, 9/64–2/67. Secret.

[2] Attached but not printed.

as respect for civil liberties and an early return to constitutional government, before recognizing. But we should not take too rigid a position on the scheduling of elections which might preclude recognition if we did not get the commitment.

I recommend your approval.

William Bowdler[3]

Approve[4]

Disapprove

Speak to me

---

[3] Bowdler signed for Rostow.
[4] The President checked this option.

---

136. Telegram From the Embassy in Argentina to the Department of State[1]

Buenos Aires, June 30, 1966, 2341Z.

2027. For Assistant Secretary Gordon. Subject: Private Conversation with General Alsogaray.

1. Conversation took place in office of Alvaro Alsogaray under conditions outlined in Embtel 2019.[2] No one else present. Statement in three parts: 1. Why the golpe took place, 2. What the new government proposes to do, 3. The structure of the new government.

2. Stated that he and others had been working on the matter for some months. Illia government had been great hope that problems of the country would be solved. However it began to make mistakes. The first was the cancellation of the oil contracts which not only hurt investors but the country; communism, the lack of order, the severe

---

[1] Source: National Archives and Records Administration, RG 59, Central Files 1964–66, POL 15 ARG. Secret; Immediate; Limdis. Received in the Department on June 30 at 9:17 p.m.

[2] Telegram 2019 from Buenos Aires, June 30 (1507Z), reported that the head of the military household, General Julio Alsogaray, had indirectly requested a private meeting with the Chargé d'Affaires. Saccio proposed to accept the invitation on the condition that he "need only listen and make no comment." (Ibid., DEF 9 ARG) The Department cabled its concurrence. (Telegram 1465 to Buenos Aires, June 30, 12:27 p.m.; ibid.)

worsening of the economy, political maneuverings, corruption, all caused great concern. Every attempt was made to get the government to meet these problems, however, nothing was done, suggestions were made. All that happened was a calling of cabinet meetings out of which issued nothing of constructive nature. The opening of dialogue with all sectors, calling on the cardinal, these are things that should have been done as a matter of course. No date had been fixed for the golpe. It had been generally agreed that action would have to be taken in October or December because of oncoming March elections unless of course the government took affirmative and satisfactory action to solve the problems of the country. It was obvious that the military had to work clandestinely; the press picked this up; the government reacted; the vicious circle was started. The military was forced to act because its integrity was being challenged—(the activities of General Caro and Secretary of War Castro Sanchez).

3. What the new government proposes to do. The eventual goal to create a democratic system of three or four parties. This could be accomplished only sometime in the future after the basic problems of the country are solved. (He did not say how long this would take or use the term "years", but clearly indicated that such a development was well in the future.) In the past, under the political system in effect there were but two choices, the bad and the worse, the Radicales or the Peronistas. The experience of the country proved that democratic political system could not successfully solve the problems of the country. It is not going to be easy to solve the economic problems of the country. He expected that the economy would continue to go down in the near future then hopefully, once the new government was able to restore confidence, Argentine investors would withdraw their funds from the Swiss and American banks and investments and foreign interests would begin to invest. The new government will strive to establish a modern economy of free enterprise taking full account of social obligations. It would not be a 19th century free enterprise type, but akin to that which exists as example, in Western Germany. The constitution still reigns; liberties will be guaranteed; free press will be allowed to continue. However if, for example, former government officials attempt to attack present government, measures will have to be taken. A full social security system will be established assuring pension, unemployment benefits, benefits to mothers, the whole gamut. The labor unions will be regulated; employer-employee relations determined, but political activity by unions will be prohibited. Outrageous demands on the part of labor, such as in the case of the longshoremen, who get six times regular pay for working at night—Buenos Aires is the most expensive port in the world—will not be tolerated. State enterprises will be put on paying basis.

4. Peronism. Peronism as a political movement will not be permitted. All political activity will be prohibited, Peronism included. The

belief in Peronism is deep in the people but this will be taken into account through proper labor and social welfare provisions to satisfy legitimate needs.

5. Foreign Relations. Argentina is a member of the Western world. It is so by nature not by convenience. The U.S. is a friend; this too is by nature and not by convenience. Great Britain is an old client and an important market. With Spain, Argentina has special ties of origin. (No mention was made of USSR, satellite countries or ChiCom.) As to the countries immediately bordering Argentina, the border matters with Chile will have to be settled. The establishment of a special relationship with Uruguay, Paraguay and Bolivia, because of Argentina's size and potential, would be the "rector" of these three countries. (Alsogaray repeated the word "rector" searching for something better to express his meaning. It was clear that he considered these three countries would be within the sphere of influence of Argentina.)

6. I asked Alsogaray to repeat what he said about Chile. It was clear that he was not comfortable in doing so. Obvious that there is a question in his mind propriety of the present solution. I persisted and asked whether the settlement of this problem would be along present lines. He ducked the question again. In this exchange he mentioned England and the Islands (Malvinas).

7. He returned to the question of the economy again describing it as a modern economy of free enterprise with full regard to social obligations. He mentioned no specific measures that the new government would undertake, however he said it was clear that it would need assistance from outside sources. No mention was made of military assistance.

8. Structure of Government. There will be five ministries: Interior, Economy and Labor, Defense, Justice, and Foreign Relations. Fifteen secretariats will operate under the five ministries. Most of these will be under Economy and Labor with Interior having charge of Education as well as its usual functions. The three services will be under defense. The five ministries with the president will constitute the executive cabinet, the national cabinet will include the ministries and the secretariats.

9. Except for the exchange on Chile, Alsogaray's statement was frank and open. Because of the nature of the meeting I did not ask many questions except to bring him out on the subject of the guaranty of liberties, the program in the field of labor and of course, Chile.

Saccio

137.   Telegram From the Embassy in Argentina to the Department of State[1]

Buenos Aires, June 30, 1966, 1720Z.

2020. Subject: Recognition of Ongania Government.

1. Embassy realizes others have experienced, as Country Team has here, feelings of repugnance over military overthrow of constitutional government of Illia.

A) There was no real justification for move, and pretext was flimsy.

B) It was a long premediated power play which left in its wake no semblance of constitutionality.

C) Alliance for Progress received serious blow.

D) Effect on public opinion in US, Latin America and elsewhere is bound to blacken Argentina's image abroad.

2. Cool analysis, however, results in recognition of following.

A) Illia government not only unpopular but object of attack by all sectors and even within own party.

B) There is no turning back.

C) Ongania, of all Argentine military, is most prestigious, respected, and capable.

D) If there were plebiscite Ongania would probably win, even over Peron.

E) There has been no counter-action to golpe. Public mood has been one of apathy toward events and expectancy and wishfulness toward future.

F) Ongania regime would probably not only meet all conditions for recognition (except assurance of early elections), but be firm anti-Communist partner of free world in OAS, UN, and other international bodies.

G) Argentina still plays important role in achievement US objectives such as projects Clear Sky and Skin Diver[2] and in OAS and UN.

---

[1] Source: National Archives and Records Administration, RG 59, Central Files 1964–66, POL 16 ARG. Secret; Priority; Limdis. Received in the Department on July 1 at 11:10 a.m. Passed to the White House, DOD, CIA, USIA, NSA, and CINCLANT for POLAD.

[2] In telegram 1472 to Buenos Aires, June 30, the Department instructed the Embassy to discontinue negotiations for Clear Sky, a project to monitor Soviet compliance with the Limited Test Ban Treaty of August 1963, until the restoration of diplomatic relations. (Ibid.) The Department determined, however, that Skin Diver, a "military scientific flight operation" could continue. (Telegram 1460 to Buenos Aires, June 29; ibid., POL 23–9 ARG)

H) Other members of hemisphere will undoubtedly be recognizing Ongania government in short order.

3. Embassy's recommendation is that, after decent interval during which US consults with fellow members of OAS, we recognize Ongania government. We should, however, be neither first nor last.[3]

Saccio

---

[3] In telegram 1186 to Buenos Aires, July 2, the Department forwarded the text of the administration's recognition policy as contained in the IRG paper (see Document 135). The Department also instructed the Embassy to convey the message that diplomatic relations would be restored if the Onganía administration issued a public statement testifying to its commitment to democracy and civil liberties. (National Archives and Records Administration, RG 59, Central Files 1964–66, POL ARG–US)

---

138.   Telegram From the Embassy in Argentina to the Department of State[1]

Buenos Aires, July 5, 1966, 2333Z.

64. Subj: Private Conversation With Alvaro Alsogaray. Ref: Buenos Aires 44.[2]

1. Civil and Human Rights. Alsogaray stated that it had been the intention from the very beginning (in the planning stage) that none of the civil rights be infringed except as absolutely necessary in the political field. The constitution is still in effect and will continue in effect. The top level of the court system had to be changed for political reasons as well as for corruption but the courts remain intact and will continue as before. Though the provincial intervenors have the power to remove individual members of the highest court in the provinces, very few have been removed. No ad hoc committees of investigation have been established. There have been no political arrests. The unions stand

---

[1] Source: National Archives and Records Administration, RG 59, Central Files 1964–66, POL 23–9 ARG. Secret; Immediate; Limdis. Passed to the White House, DOD, CIA, USIA, NSA, and CINCLANT for POLAD.

[2] Telegram 44 from Buenos Aires, July 5, reported the upcoming "talk" with Alvaro, brother of General Julio Alsogaray. (Ibid.) The Department suggested that Saccio explain the U.S. position on recognition, particularly with regard to democracy and human rights. The Department provided the following guidance: "You should not imply that we will refuse recognition if these points not covered but stress that public commitments along these lines would be most helpful with respect public and congressional opinion in this country." (Telegram 1713 to Buenos Aires, July 5; ibid., POL 16 ARG)

as they were before. Where there had been arrests as in the case of Ricardo Illia and Mayor Rabanal, the others have been immediately turned over to the courts for adjudication. Unless there is an attack against the revolution, there will be no change in the rights of the people. The press will continue to be free. All that the revolution planned to do is to make minimum changes necessary to resolve the political situation. In a democracy people have the right to change by voting against the administration in power. In Argentina this meant Peronists as the only [garble—alternative?]. This could not be permitted. Even the Peronistas knew this as proven by their acceptance of the revolution. Alsogaray referred to the Peronist labor leaders acceptance of invitation to Ongania's swearing in.

2. Elections in the Future. The plan of revolution and the present intention is to solve the basic problems of the country so that it can operate eventually as a viable democracy. It is hoped that in time there will be created a democratic system of a limited number of parties instead of the hundreds that existed before. However, the government does not intend to fix a date or commit itself to a time as to when elections will be held. This was mistake that was made before since once a time is fixed the government cannot accomplish anything; everybody becomes a politician. Besides problems in the economic area are extremely difficult to resolve in a democracy. However, there is no question about the intent of this government to work for a democratic system. In fact, outside of the political, none of the basic institutions of the country will be modified.

3. International Economic Policy. It is the intention of the government to move toward a free enterprise system. (Instead of elaborating on this, Alsogaray referred to our conversation in March, stating that I was fully cognizant with his theories and that these would all obtain in the new government.) The oil contracts problem will be resolved; Argentina will sign investment guarantee agreement. The exchange rate will be freed but not immediately. Ongania determined to proceed carefully. This was not a problem that could be resolved today. Many factors had to be taken into consideration. He, Alsogaray, will be given the job of coordinating all international economic relations, working with the Minister of Economy and the Foreign Ministry. He has already had conferences with the new Minister of Economy and after similar conferences with the Foreign Minister and President, he will take off on a quick review of the situation in Western Europe and the U.S. Come September he will start the negotiations on behalf of his government.

4. International Relations. Argentina will be a close partner of the U.S. on all questions involving free world and hemisphere. There will be no hesitance on part of Argentina in joining the U.S. in the solution of hemispheric problems. There will be no holding back as in the case

of the Dominican Republic. However, as to Vietnam, Argentina will not send troops to assist the South Vietnamese. If there is any action in this sphere by the UN or other international body, Argentina will support the U.S.

5. In outlining these policies Alsogaray made clear that though he was speaking with intimate knowledge of the previous plans of the revolution and the present thinking, he could not make any authoritative statements. He did say that the government would be issuing public statements on these matters and that they would be coming out probably next week or the week after. I asked him specifically about whether a statement would be made on the subject of future elections. He wasn't sure of this but he assured me that he was reporting correctly the thinking of the new government. On foreign policy, para 4 above, he referred to his conversation with Ongania yesterday as authority for his statements. One reason he gives for the delay in making public statements on policy was that the revolution was planned for later in the year. With a smile he said that they had to respond to the counter golpe of the government.

6. I do not intend to pursue suggested talk with FonMin Costa Mendez unless he persists, knowing that I have already talked to the Alsogarays. Regardless of their views, I believe latter have been frank and sincere. Do not think it wise to appear to be checking their statements unless Department feels it would be valuable to get a more "official" statement on future elections. Not likely that I will be successful or that it will be useful in view of the nature of their justification.[3]

Saccio

---

[3] After this meeting Saccio recommended recognition of the new government by July 9, the national holiday and sesquicentennial of Argentina's independence. "Delay beyond July 9," he explained, "runs risk of damaging long-term U.S. interests with respect to Argentina, since it starts to build up incomprehension and resentment." (Telegram 62 from Buenos Aires, July 5, 2331Z; ibid.) The Department replied that recognition by July 9 would be impossible without a declaration of the regime's democratic intentions. A public statement by an authorized spokesman that was similar to the private assurances of Alvaro Alsogaray could provide the basis for immediate consultation, possibly resulting in recognition by July 9. (Telegram 1872 to Buenos Aires, July 6; ibid.)

139. Telegram From the President's Special Assistant (Rostow) to President Johnson in Texas[1]

Washington, July 7, 1966, 5:48 p.m.

CAP 66481. Subject: Argentine Recognition. Acting Secretary Ball requests standby authorization to recognize the Ongania government.[2]

The classical criteria for recognition (i.e., general control of the country and pledge to honor international obligations) have been met. We are still awaiting public affirmation of the OAS criteria: respect for human rights, peaceful settlement of disputes, and eventual return to constitutional government.

Secretary Ball would use the standby authorization this way:

1. If the government makes a public statement on the OAS criteria prior to July 9, we would recognize promptly.
2. If the statement is not forthcoming, we would delay recognition for several more days after July 9.

Our Embassy in Buenos Aires is now in contact with the new Foreign Minister through a trusted intermediary.[3] We relayed our desire for an affirmative public statement on the OAS criteria. He replied that he personally has no difficulty with the criteria, except for the election criterion which he believes can be handled by appropriate wording. (We would not stick on the establishment of an early date for elections.) He is trying to get President Ongania to make the statement before July 9.

Through the Chileans, Colombians, Peruvians, and Uruguayans we are seeking to bring additional pressure on Ongania for an early statement.

I recommend that you grant the standby authorization in the understanding that I will call you before recognition is extended to:

A. Report on the nature of the Argentine statement.
B. Obtain your approval of our announcement of recognition.[4]

---

[1] Source: Johnson Library, National Security File, Country File, Argentina, Vol. II, 9/64–3/67. Secret. According to an attached note, the telegram was originally a memorandum drafted by Bowdler and revised by Bromley Smith. President Johnson was at his ranch in Texas June 30–July 11. (Johnson Library, President's Daily Diary)

[2] Reference is to a memorandum from Ball to the President, July 7, attached but not printed.

[3] The Embassy reported on the initial use of this channel in telegrams 79 and 80 from Buenos Aires, July 6. (National Archives and Records Administration, RG 59, Central Files 1964–66, POL ARG–US)

[4] There is no indication on the telegram that the President approved this recommendation.

140.   Information Memorandum From the President's Special Assistant (Rostow) to President Johnson[1]

Washington, July 9, 1966.

SUBJECT

Argentine Situation

The Ongania Government is not expected to make a helpful public statement over the weekend on respect for human rights, peaceful settlement of border disputes and eventual elections.

The Argentine Foreign Minister late yesterday sent word to the Embassy that

—the question of elections is difficult and requires careful study and precise definition.

—there is no problem on human rights and peaceful settlement and this will be made clear "in forthcoming actions and statements" (no time indicated).

—he fully understands that the U.S. is not laying down conditions for recognition.

—he regrets that our suggestion for a public statement now could not be adopted.[2]

In the balance of a public statement, we will put off recognition until sometime next week. More than half of the Latin American countries are with us in holding up on recognition. Those who have recognized are: Bolivia, Brazil, Chile, Mexico, Paraguay, Peru and Uruguay.

WGB[3]

[1] Source: Johnson Library, National Security File, Country File, Argentina, Vol. II, 9/64–3/67. Confidential. A copy was sent to Bill Moyers. The memorandum was "sent by wire" to the LBJ Ranch.

[2] As reported in telegram 125 from Buenos Aires, July 8. (National Archives and Records Administration, RG 59, Central Files 1964–66, POL 15 ARG)

[3] Bowdler initialed the memorandum for Rostow.

141.   Memorandum From Secretary of State Rusk to President Johnson[1]

Washington, July 12, 1966.

SUBJECT

Recognition of the Argentine Government

Recommendations:

1. That you approve the enclosed telegram which would authorize our Chargé in Buenos Aires to deliver a note to the Argentine Government at noon on July 14, which would constitute an act of recognition.[2]

2. That you also approve the text of a proposed press release, herewith enclosed.[3]

Background:

The Argentine military overthrew the Illia Government on June 28. Subsequently, General Juan Carlos Onganía, former Commander-in-Chief of the Argentine Army, was sworn in as President.

We have been consulting with the Latin Americans since the overthrow of the Illia Government under Resolution XXVI which was approved at the Rio Conference in November 1965. We also indicated informally to the Argentine authorities that public statements on the points contained in Resolution XXVI, plus a commitment on peaceful settlement of disputes, would facilitate recognition by the United States. We added the point on peaceful settlement after the Chileans expressed concern to us over Argentine statements which the Chileans interpreted as forecasting trouble between Argentina and Chile on their boundary disputes.

---

[1] Source: National Archives and Records Administration, RG 59, Central Files 1964–66, POL 16 ARG. Confidential. Drafted by Sayre and cleared by Krieg. Original forwarded as an attachment to a memorandum from Rostow to the President, July 13. (Johnson Library, National Security File, Country File, Argentina, Vol. II, 9/64–2/67)

[2] Attached but not printed. The instructions were eventually sent as telegram 2885 to Buenos Aires, July 14. (National Archives and Records Administration, RG 59, Central Files 1964–66, POL 16 ARG)

[3] Attached but not printed. For text of the press release, see Department of State *Bulletin*, August 1, 1966, p. 184. The President approved both recommendations. A note attached to this memorandum explains, however, that recognition had to be rescheduled due to an apparent delay in the bureaucratic process. The Department subsequently authorized delivery of the official note of recognition for July 15 at noon. (Telegram 7529 to Buenos Aires, July 14; National Archives and Records Administration, RG 59, Central Files 1964–66, POL 16 ARG)

In the note from the Argentines requesting recognition they explicitly stated their intention to respect their international obligations. A speech by General Ongania on July 9[4] has statements in it which apparently were intended to respond to our concern about respect for human rights (Paragraph 2b of Resolution XXVI) and about pacific settlement of disputes. Chile had recognized the Ongania Government on July 8.

The significant omission is any statement on elections. Argentine authorities have indicated to the Brazilians and us that it would be very difficult at this time to make any definite statement on return to constitutional democracy. However, Martinez Paz, the new Minister of the Interior, told the press on July 9 that the Government would stay in power as long as necessary to create a climate conducive to the exercise of representative democracy.

Mr. Gordon discussed the recognition problem on July 8 with Senators Fulbright and Morse. The former felt we should be in no hurry to recognize; the latter made no comment but his public statement on the Military Assistance Program bill suggests that he will again charge the Administration with "walking out on democracy" if we do recognize. Mr. Sayre has discussed it with Senator Hickenlooper and Congressman Selden. He also briefed Boyd Crawford, Chief of the House Foreign Affairs Committee Staff, who stated he would inform Dr. Morgan. All three felt that we had no other choice but to recognize the new government. With the exception of Senator Morse all of them expressed reservations on resumption of economic and military assistance. Senator Hickenlooper went further and questioned whether we should carry out any commitments we have made on economic and military assistance to Argentina until Argentina fulfills its contractual obligations; for example, the oil problem.

Eight Latin American countries have already recognized the Argentine Government (Bolivia, Brazil, Chile, Haiti, Mexico, Paraguay, Peru and Uruguay). With the exception of Venezuela and, just possibly, Colombia, the other Latin American countries are awaiting our decision and will probably recognize at about the same time. Japan, Spain and all of the NATO countries have recognized.

We have traditionally tried to maintain diplomatic relations with all of the members of the OAS. We also give considerable weight to the views of the Latins. In addition, the United States has important interests in Argentina and Argentina is one of the major countries in the OAS system. We cannot exercise any significant influence in Argentina unless we maintain relations with the authorities.

Dean Rusk

---

[4] Attached but not printed. The Embassy also forwarded excerpts of the speech in telegram 143 from Buenos Aires, July 11. (Ibid., POL 15 ARG)

142.   Telegram From the Department of State to the Embassy in Argentina[1]

Washington, July 21, 1966, 7:12 p.m.

12800. Ref: Buenos Aires 219.[2]

1. U.S. policy toward Argentina for balance of 1966 will be to observe plans, policies, and executive skill of new government with view to developing longer range policy early in 1967 in light of experience accumulated in interim period.

2. Attitude toward GOA should be friendly but reserved. We wish Argentine people well and want to further economic and social development in line with principles of Alliance for Progress, but are not yet certain to what extent policies of new government will make our collaboration possible or what form new GOA may want assistance to take. We expect new authorities may need some time to familiarize themselves with their work and develop own ideas regarding our existing programs.

3. U.S. will observe its commitments to Argentina, in accordance normal international practice and international law. Commitments made with Argentina prior to the change of government must still be considered in effect, unless Congress approves amendments now pending to Foreign Assistance Act which would require termination of assistance.[3]

A. Economic Assistance

4. AID projects which are already under way pursuant to existing agreements should be continued unless the new authorities object. If in any instance Embassy/USAID believes any programs we have agreed to carry out should be suspended, reduced or altered, Department should be notified promptly with reasons.

---

[1] Source: National Archives and Records Administration, RG 59, Central Files 1964–66, POL ARG–US. Confidential. Repeated to USCINCSO. Drafted by Krieg; cleared by Pringle, Sternfeld, Salans, Gaud, Lang, and Sayre; and approved by Gordon.

[2] The Embassy submitted its recommendations for U.S. policy once diplomatic relations were restored in telegram 100 from Buenos Aires, July 8. Telegram 219 from Buenos Aires, July 18, requested the Department's comments. (Both ibid.)

[3] Reference is to several proposals to modify the Foreign Assistance Act of 1966, in particular, an amendment offered by Senator Jacob K. Javits (R–New York), that would suspend assistance to any member of the OAS that "came into power by the unconstitutional overthrow of a freely elected, constitutional, democratic government." (Telegram 6406 to Buenos Aires, July 13; ibid., POL 16 ARG) Although the administration eventually defeated the proposal, Congress adopted an amendment sponsored by Senator J. William Fulbright (D–Arkansas) that set a ceiling of $85 million per fiscal year for military assistance and sales to Latin America, not including support for military training or the Inter-American Peace Force in the Dominican Republic. (80 Stat. 803)

5. Initiation of new projects during interim period is not contemplated. Department does not desire to encourage discussion of possible new projects during the interim period and suggests that any proposals from the GOA be heard without commitment.

6. In an intermediate area between firm commitments and new undertakings lie those projects which have been under intensive discussion during recent months but which have either lapsed or on which agreements have not been perfected. Grain storage project and Central Housing Bank project fall in this category. In these cases, Embassy/USAID should await Argentine initiatives and report them with recommendations to Department–AID/W.

B. Military Assistance

7. Deliveries where there are contractual obligations will be observed. Until Congress acts on foreign aid legislation, we plan to hold deliveries on approved and funded grant program even though Argentines may have already been informed of them. Our present disposition (assuming satisfactory outcome on foreign aid legislation) would be to proceed with items such as spare parts, but continue withhold delivery on major end items such as armored personnel carriers until we can (a) assess fully US Congressional and public opinion on military assistance and (b) review five-year grant credit program. Country Team members should not convey foregoing policy to Argentine authorities but limit their comments on requests for military assistance to stating (a) Congress is now considering foreign aid legislation, and (b) requests will be referred to Washington for consideration and decision.

8. Training programs including MMTs and normal MILGP personnel movements should proceed according to plan.

9. Visits of General or Flag rank officers not assigned to Argentina should be deferred if possible. Suggest prior referral to State/Defense for decision in each case.

10. Department is aware foregoing does not cover all contingencies but desires supply requested interim guidance. Washington agencies studying assistance programs further and would appreciate your raising such additional policy questions as you deem pertinent.

11. DOD implementing instructions re training and rotation MILGP personnel to be issued promptly. Will be followed shortly by instructions on contractual obligations.

Rusk

143.   Memorandum of Conversation[1]

Washington, July 30, 1966, 10:30 a.m.

PARTICIPANTS

The Secretary
Dr. Alvaro Alsogaray, Ambassador-at-Large of Argentina
Mr. Carlos A. Quesada Zapiola, Argentine Chargé d'Affaires
Mr. Angel R. Caram, Argentine Financial Counselor
ARA—Assistant Secretary Gordon
LS—Mr. F. A. VanReigersberg

Mr. Alsogaray opened the meeting by repeating the reasons for the recent Argentine revolution which he had already given to Mr. Gordon in a previous meeting,[2] stressing that the two immediate causes were the rapid deterioration of the Argentine economy and its move towards socialism as well as the imminent threat of a Peronista victory at the polls. He added that while no one had wanted the revolution, it had become inevitable since the Argentine people are as afraid of a Peronista return as the German people would be of a return of Hitler. He then explained the objectives of the revolution, which in the political field would be to re-establish the bases for representative democracy (although the date for a "return to democracy" could not yet be announced in order to avoid renewed plotting on the part of politicians) and the transformation of the present "semi-collective system" into a free enterprise system. The Argentine revolution is only beginning its work but its leaders are optimistic as to its future because Argentine labor and even the Peronistas have not come out against it yet. Nevertheless, the Ongania Administration expects to face some difficulties in the future as stern economic measures and anti-inflationary policies are adopted. He described the external debt situation as good and pointed to the internal budgetary deficit as one of the main economic problems which the new administration wants to tackle from the outset. The scandalous situation of the national railroads will be the first item of business which the Government will face since "100,000 men cannot be allowed to paralyze a country of 22 million." In the field of petroleum, the Government will allow both domestic and foreign

---

[1] Source: National Archives and Records Administration, RG 59, Central Files 1964–66, POL ARG–US. Confidential. Drafted by VanReigersberg and approved in S on August 4. The time of the meeting is from the Secretary's Appointment Book. (Johnson Library) A brief account of the meeting was forwarded to the Embassy on August 1 in telegram 19146. (National Archives and Records Administration, RG 59, Central Files 1964–66, POL ARG)

[2] Gordon met Alsogaray on July 28; a memorandum of the conversation is ibid., POL 23–9 ARG.

companies to explore the Argentine subsoil although no general law will be passed to cover all such companies and the activities of each foreign company will be regulated on a case by case basis. Furthermore, the new administration is prepared to go ahead with the last stages of the negotiations leading up to an investment guaranty agreement with the United States which should attract foreign investors.

The Secretary stated that he was well aware of the importance of Argentina in the world today and what happened in Argentina had a bearing on every other country in this hemisphere. He indicated that the U.S. Government regretted the steps that had to be taken in Argentina a few weeks ago since it had hoped that the Argentine military and civilian authorities would have been able to work out their differences without the necessity of a coup. Nevertheless, it was important to look towards the future and not allow this disappointment to color relations between the countries. He noted that one positive element resulting from the coup was the respect for General Ongania's personal qualities in most of the Latin American countries and the United States, and he could only express the hope that the General would act on the basis of those qualities and that his colleagues would permit him to do so. He stated that Ambassador Martin would return to Buenos Aires in two weeks and that he would keep in close touch with the Argentine Government, trying to repair some of the damage that had been done and to work constructively with a view toward the future. With regard to the philosophy of private enterprise, the Secretary indicated that while the United States firmly believes in it, he hoped that Argentina would fully consider the changing role of private enterprise both in this country and in Western Europe. He deplored the fact that in a number of countries private enterprise had not caught up with the 20th Century, noting that in the United States, for instance, the "robber barons" of the 19th Century had been superceded by the socially aware businessmen of the 20th Century with a strong sense of public responsibility. He expressed the hope that Argentina would move in the direction of modern capitalism. The Secretary also noted that American businessmen are constantly being told that the U.S. Government expects them to uphold the same standards of public responsibility abroad as in this country.

Mr. Alsogaray stated that he was well aware of the need for a greater sense of public responsibility on the part of Argentine businessmen and indicated that the present Argentine administration wants to model the country's economy on the basis of the European version of enlightened capitalism, which he described as a "socially aware market economy."

The Secretary stated that recent events in Argentina have affected the lives of every country in this hemisphere. He stated that the United

States therefore has a problem now which it did not have two months ago and that a number of Senators and U.S. organizations had attacked the U.S. Government because of its recognition of the Ongania administration. He expressed the hope that Argentina would keep in mind that other hemispheric countries have problems of their own and that it would follow a policy of moderation and restraint, especially in the OAS. He added that the next MFM had become a "problem" although the United States would have preferred that it had not become a problem and that now it was up to Argentina to show understanding for the position of its sister republics. The Secretary stated that Argentina could adopt one of two alternatives with regard to the next MFM. Firstly, it could decide that the site of the meeting was a nonnegotiable issue and therefore disregard the wishes of other countries, or else it could take the initiative and by so doing increase the prestige of its government all over the hemisphere by indicating that it is willing to accept a solution that would receive the backing of the majority of the hemispheric countries.

Ambassador Alsogaray stated that in his meeting with Mr. Gordon he had discussed this problem at length and that he was well aware of domestic problems both in the U.S. and in other hemispheric countries. He said that he would get in touch with his Foreign Minister and with General Ongania right away and that he would explain the situation to them and advise them to refrain from adopting a tough line on hemispheric matters. He insisted, however, that it would not be easy for the Government to explain any softening of its attitude to the Argentine people. Ambassador Alsogaray then referred to the matter of economic relations and stated that a number of organizations in Washington were awaiting instructions from the State Department to go ahead with their studies of assistance programs for Argentina which had been paralyzed for some time. He asked the Secretary to intercede on his country's behalf so that even though decisions might not be taken, the examination and study of these problems might continue in order to avoid any delays or slow-downs.

The Secretary stated that Mr. Gordon would look into the matter. In response to a question from Mr. Gordon, Ambassador Alsogaray stated that Argentina was in favor of stepping up the process of Latin American economic integration although the present administration had not devised any new policies on the matter. He knew that General Ongania and Economics Minister Salimei supported integration, both on a hemispheric and on a bilateral basis, especially with Brazil and Chile, and that they were also interested in reducing tariffs.

The Secretary stated that there was one additional item he wanted to bring up to which increasing attention will have to be given in the next months and that was the matter of the worldwide food situation in the next 10 years. He stated that all food-producing countries will be facing growing markets over the next decade and that purchasing countries will face increasing difficulties both in increasing their domestic production and in paying for food imports. Therefore there is a great need for increasing efficiency on the part of the producing countries and for offering food to potential buyers under terms which they can meet. He added that Argentina, the United States, Canada and Western Europe may also have to find a way to set up food and fertilizer reserves in the case of future emergencies. He indicated that in spite of an increasing production of wheat in the United States, our present reserves were somewhat below what was considered a prudent level. Therefore the matter would have to be given increased international attention in the next months and years and there might be a need for looking at the situation both on a worldwide and on a hemispheric level.

---

144. Information Memorandum From the Assistant Secretary of State for Inter-American Affairs (Gordon) to Secretary of State Rusk[1]

Washington, February 6, 1967.

SUBJECT

Military Assistance to Argentina

When the United States resumed relations with the Argentine Government on July 15, 1966, it was decided that the United States would carry out existing commitments. We resumed disbursements on existing AID loans, but have entered into no new ones.

We are applying the same standards on loans through the Eximbank, IBRD, and IDB as we would on any other Latin American countries.

We have not as yet resumed military assistance. It was decided in June 1966 that we would not do so for at least six months, and then only after a full review of our relations. As you know, Ambassador Martin was here in January and Defense and State reviewed the military assistance issue in detail.[2]

---

[1] Source: National Archives and Records Administration, RG 59, ARA Files, 1967: Lot 70 D 150, Argentina, 1967. Confidential. No drafting information appears on the memorandum. Also sent to Katzenbach. A notation indicates that Rusk saw the memorandum.

[2] Memoranda to Gordon from Dungan, Martin, and Sayre, January 12, 12, and 19, respectively, debating whether to resume military assistance to Argentina, are ibid.

In summary we agreed:

1. The FY 1966 grant program should be carried out as it had been agreed with Argentina before the coup. The program includes armored personnel carriers.

2. The FY 1967 grant program should be carried out but with a substantial reduction which is more than proportional to the cut taken by most other Latin American countries. Controversial items such as armored personnel carriers were shifted from grant to sale. Other major items of a non-controversial nature such as C–130 cargo aircraft would be provided on a credit or cash basis.

3. Tanks which Argentina sought to purchase before the coup would not be provided on any basis.

4. Two destroyers authorized by the Congress would be loaned or sold to Argentina.[3]

I have consulted with the House Foreign Affairs Subcommittee on Latin America which raised no significant objections to the proposed course of action. I talked to Senator Javits who said he understood our position, but could not modify his own position as reflected in the Javits Amendment. Mr. Sayre and I have talked to Carl Marcy and Pat Holt,[4] respectively, but my several efforts to agree on a time for consultation with the Morse Subcommittee[5] have been unsuccessful. Pat Holt informs me that it would not be possible to arrange for consultation before the end of February given the absence of Committee members in Mexico until February 15 and my absence at the Buenos Aires meetings. I believe that we should now proceed on the FY 1966 and FY 1967 programs.

As you are aware, our future policy on military assistance to Argentina and Latin America in general is under review.

---

[3] In telegram 134762 to Buenos Aires, February 10, the Department informed the Embassy of these decisions. (National Archives and Records Administration, RG 59, Central Files 1967–69, DEF 19–8 US–ARG) According to a note attached to this memorandum, Rusk approved the telegram without reading it.

[4] Carl Marcy, chief of staff, and Pat Holt, staff member, of the Senate Committee on Foreign Relations.

[5] Senator Wayne Morse (D–Oregon), was chairman of the Subcommittee on American Republics Affairs of the Senate Committee on Foreign Relations.

145.   Telegram From the Department of State to the Embassy in Argentina[1]

Washington, April 28, 1967, 11:46 a.m.

184026. 1. Following is Memorandum of Conversation between Presidents Johnson and Onganía, at the San Rafael Hotel, Punta del Este, April 13, 1967 at 6:30 p.m. Present at the meeting were: President Johnson, Mr. Walt W. Rostow, and Assistant Secretary Solomon for the United States; and President Onganía, Foreign Minister Costa Mendez and two unidentified persons for Argentina.[2]

2. *Argentina's Political Situation*

President Onganía apologized for monopolizing the conversation, but said that it was important for President Johnson to get a panoramic view of Argentina's situation from the lips of the Argentine President.

3. President Onganía said that after the experience of two decades of difficulties, it had become necessary for his country to undertake what he called the "Argentine Revolution". The Argentine Revolution called for the elimination of political parties, within the framework of a democratic system. As proof of the existence of a democratic system in Argentina, he could mention freedom of the press and freedom for the individual. For example, there was a better application of justice at the present time than before June 28, 1966. In addition, there was no state of siege, and there had been nothing but peace and tranquility in his country during the ten months of his government.

4. President Onganía went on to say that the main problem that Argentina faced was the existence of an archaic governmental structure which has the task of governing a modern country. This archaic governmental structure had proved to be unable to utilize the human resources of the country as they should be used. In his conception, the function of the government was to provide guidance and supervision to the individual and to private enterprise so that the latter could go about the process of developing the country. He added that he was convinced that Argentina's main problem is political and not economic.

5. President Onganía went on to say that in the first stage of the Argentine revolution it would be necessary to systematize the government's machinery. The second stage called for a reorganization of

---

[1] Source: National Archives and Records Administration, RG 59, Central Files 1967–69, POL 15–1 US/Johnson. Confidential; Priority. Drafted by Barnes and Dreyfuss on April 18, cleared by Solomon and Rostow, and approved by Sayre.

[2] According to the President's Daily Diary the meeting lasted from 6 to 7 p.m.; one of the "unidentified" participants was the Minister of Trade and Industry, Angel A. Solá. (Johnson Library)

the entire community, including its material, spiritual, and intellectual values, so that Argentina could become what it should be.

6. *Argentina's Economic Situation*

President Onganía said that his government had taken a series of important steps in the economic field, with a view to reducing inflation, which was growing at a 30% per year rate. These steps required the business and labor sectors to contain their aspirations, but were necessary to reduce the rate of inflation which was strangling the nation's economy.

7. President Onganía said that his government, by making adjustments in the current budget, had reduced the projected deficit from $1 billion to $400 million. One of the items that had been taking up a large share of the budget was government-owned enterprises, especially railroads. His government planned to establish a higher degree of rationality in the management of these enterprises, and eventually to shift surplus personnel to more productive sectors. This same process would be applied to government personnel.

8. President Onganía said that there is one area in which the economy as a whole could be reactivated, and that is housing, as there was a deficit of 1,500,000 units in his country. In this endeavor, Argentina would need outside assistance.

9. President Onganía also said that Argentina wants to increase its exports, especially in non-traditional goods. He added that this does not mean neglect of beef exports, since his country had built up its reserves of beef cattle, and is now ready to go into the world market again. In that connection, Argentina is worried about the lack of progress on a world meat agreement in the Kennedy Round, although it had been assured of the support of the United States in this connection. President Johnson at this point observed that the Kennedy Round meat group discussions were *not* promising.

10. President Onganía said that his country is putting to good use the IDB loan for agriculture, and that he is convinced of the need of bringing the benefits of technology, specifically electricity, to the rural areas.

11. Of equal importance to the problem of housing is the need to begin the Chocon-Cerro Colorado project, which is a multi-faceted development effort.

12. President Johnson said that he and his government were impressed with the economic steps that had been taken in Argentina under President Onganía's direction and that he was a great supporter of rural electrification.

13. *Arms*

President Johnson said that it is important that the Latin American countries not embark on an arms race, and that he hoped that

President Onganía would provide leadership to the rest of Latin America in this matter.

14. President Onganía replied that his country does not aspire to have large weapons, rockets, or anything like that, but that at the present time the Argentine Armed Forces do not even have a minimum level of equipment. He said that it is important that the military vocation of the Latin American countries not be twisted, and that the Armed Forces of the Latin countries should not become mere national police forces.

15. *Summit Conference*

President Johnson said that he hoped that President Onganía would make a clear statement on the success of the Summit Conference, to counterbalance the effect that the statements of the Ecuadorean President might have on the American public and Congress.[3]

Rusk

---

[3] See Document 51.

146.　National Intelligence Estimate[1]

NIE 91–67　　　　　　　　　　　　　　Washington, December 7, 1967.

ARGENTINA

The Problem

To consider the nature of Argentina's basic problems, the character and actions of the Onganía administration, and the prospects for significant economic and political progress over the next four or five years.

Conclusions

A. President Onganía is bent on retaining power as long as necessary to revive the country's economy and, when that is accomplished,

---

[1] Source: Central Intelligence Agency, Job 79–R01012A, O/DDI Registry. Secret; Controlled Dissem. According to a note on the cover sheet this estimate was prepared in the Central Intelligence Agency with the participation of the intelligence organizations of the Departments of State and Defense and the National Security Agency. The United States Intelligence Board concurred in this estimate on December 7.

to tackle its political maladies. The government has given priority to a sustained attack on the most serious economic aberrations; it has meanwhile suspended politics as usual, ordered all the political parties dissolved, and put off indefinitely any attempt to come to grips with the country's most divisive political problem—Peronism.

B. Onganía's administration has, for the most part, avoided repressive actions, and, in the conduct of its business, it appears more civilian than military. Most Argentines, though not enthusiastic about him, seem quite willing to wait and see how his government performs. We believe that Onganía will continue to hold power over the next year or so.

C. The administration has initiated a complex economic program designed to achieve both financial stabilization and economic development. It has sharply reduced the power of organized labor and has taken positive action to reduce budget deficits, increase production, and control inflation. These measures have attracted considerable official and private financial and technical support from abroad. Over the next year or two we look for additional progress in budgetary reforms, in stabilization measures, and in some aspects of development.

D. Over the longer run—the next four or five years—we doubt that the regime can continue to keep Argentine political problems on the shelf. We think Onganía will have great difficulty in holding cohesive civilian support behind his program, and as time passes his military backing is likely to become less solid. These factors will complicate any attempts by Onganía to come to grips with the Peronist problem. Further, we do not believe that even over this longer period of time Argentina will establish a representative system of government capable of reaching a consensus on policies and tactics for dealing with its social and economic problems.

E. We believe, nonetheless, that the government will make considerable progress in reducing the impact of fluctuating harvests and commodity prices on annual growth rates. Broader economic success, however, will depend on the government's ability to maintain continuity in its policies and to retain public confidence in their durability over a number of years. We believe that the government's chances of remaining in power over this longer run are considerably better than even, but we are less confident that it will be able to adhere firmly to a successful economic policy.

F. Onganía's anti-Communist leanings will continue to be a force for close cooperation with the US. Among the issues which could adversely affect US-Argentine relations would be a refusal by the US to carry out what the Argentine military establishment regards as a commitment to assist in the modernization of its armed forces.

[Omitted here is the Discussion section of the estimate.]

Bolivia

147. Editorial Note

Covert financial assistance was a key element of U.S. foreign policy toward Bolivia during the Johnson Presidency. CIA documents have characterized the overall goals of the U.S. Government's covert action programs in Bolivia during this period as follows:

"The basic covert action goals in Bolivia are to foster democratic solutions to critical and social, economic, and political problems; to check Communist and Cuban subversion; to encourage a stable government favorably inclined toward the United States; and to encourage Bolivian participation in the Alliance for Progress. The main direction and emphasis of C[overt] A[ction] operations is to force Communists, leftists, and pro-Castroites out of influential positions in government, and to try to break Communist and ultra-leftist control over certain trade union, student groups, and campesino organizations."

Covert action expenditures in Bolivia between fiscal year 1963 and fiscal year 1965 were as follows: FY 63—$337,063; FY 64—$545,342; and FY 65—$287,978. The figure for FY 65 included funds to influence the campesino movement, for propaganda, to support labor organizations, and to support youth and student groups. The FY 66 program also allocated funds to support moderate political groups and individuals backing General Barrientos for President.

When he took office in November 1963 President Johnson inherited a longstanding U.S. Government policy of providing financial support for Bolivian political leaders. The policy was intended to promote stability in Bolivia by strengthening moderate forces, especially within the National Revolutionary Movement (MNR) itself, which had a strong left wing under the leadership of Juan Lechin Oquendo, General Secretary of the Mine Workers' Federation.

In August 1963 the 5412 Special Group approved a covert subsidy to assist the MNR to prepare for the presidential elections scheduled for May 1964. The Special Group agreed in March 1964 that the MNR receive additional financial support. Paz won the election; Lechin (who had been Vice President under Paz) left the government and founded a rival leftist party.

On November 4, 1964, the new Vice President, General René Barrientos Ortuño (MNR), led a successful military coup d'etat, forcing Paz into exile. In February 1965 the 303 Committee authorized a financial subsidy to the MNR under Barrientos (who was aware of U.S. financial support to the MNR) to help establish an organizational base for the presidential election scheduled for September. In May 1965 Barrientos responded to growing labor unrest by arresting and deporting Lechin and postponing the election. The 303 Committee, which considered a recommendation to support Barrientos as the best available candidate, agreed in July 1965 and March 1966 to authorize additional funds for MNR propaganda and political action in support of the ruling Junta's plans to pacify the country and hold elections to establish a civilian, constitutional government.

When the presidential election was finally held in July 1966, Barrientos won easily, and officials concerned with the covert operation concluded that the objectives of the program—the end of military rule and a civilian, constitutional government whose policies would be compatible with those of the United States—had been accomplished.

148.   Memorandum Prepared for the Special Group[1]

Washington, March 10, 1964.

SUBJECT

> Increase of Subsidy Provided to the Bolivian Government to support its Covert Action Projects designed to break the power of the National Revolutionary Movement of the left (MNRI) and the Communist Party of Bolivia (PCB)

REFERENCE

> Special Group action taken on 8 August 1963

1. *Background:* On 8 August 1963, the Special Group approved a request to provide a covert subsidy in the amount of [*1 line of source text not declassified*] to take the necessary covert actions to overcome the emergency situation which existed in Bolivia at that time and, once the situation normalized, to enable Paz to consolidate his control. In late December, the United States Ambassador and the CIA [*less than 1 line of source text not declassified*] requested an additional sum of [*2 lines of source text not declassified*] to wrest control of labor organizations away from Juan Lechin Oquendo, the MNRI, and the PCB. On 8 January 1964, the CIA [*less than 1 line of source text not declassified*] discussed the request for additional funds with Assistant Secretary

---

[1] Source: Department of State, INR/IL Historical Files, 5412 Special Group Meetings, S.G.114, March 12, 1964. Secret; Eyes Only.

Edwin W. Martin,[2] and it was mutually agreed that an increase in the subsidy was justified.[3] The United States Ambassador was informed that Special Group approval would be requested at the earliest possible date.

2. *Accomplishments:* The first [*less than 1 line of source text not declassified*] provided [*less than 1 line of source text not declassified*] the following major accomplishments:

a. Eliminate Communist control over the National Campesino Federation.

b. Meet the necessary expenses in connection with the establishment of the new anti-left Confederation of Bolivian Workers (COB).

c. Provide support to democratic elements in an effort to unseat extremist leaders in the teachers, chauffeurs, and printers unions.

d. Break the power of the Communists over the Railroad Confederation and subsequent congresses of the flour, construction, and factory workers unions.

3. *Recommendation:* That the Special Group approve an increase [*less than 1 line of source text not declassified*] to the authorized subsidy being provided to the Bolivian Government. The requested funds are available within [*less than 1 line of source text not declassified*] authorized budget.[4]

---

[2] As of January 3 Thomas Mann was Assistant Secretary of State for Inter-American Affairs.

[3] A discussion of this plan is contained in a January 9 memorandum prepared by J.C. King, Chief of the Western Hemisphere Division in CIA (DDP). (Central Intelligence Agency, Job 80–01690R, Directorate of Operations, Latin America Division, WH/1/Bolivia, [*file name not declassified*])

[4] The recommendation was endorsed by Assistant Secretary of State for Inter-American Affairs, Thomas C. Mann, on March 10. (Department of State, INR/IL Historical Files, 5412 Special Group Meetings) According to minutes of the March 12 meeting, the Special Group approved the recommendation. (Ibid., Bolivia, 1962–1980)

149.   **Memorandum From the Executive Secretary of the Department of State (Read) to the President's Special Assistant for National Security Affairs (Bundy)[1]**

Washington, May 28, 1964.

SUBJECT

The May 31 Elections in Bolivia

Government Party in Transition

When President Paz decided that it was time for the Bolivian revolution to enter a new, "constructive," development phase, internal stresses in the governing National Revolutionary Movement (MNR) which had grown over the years since 1952 were intensified. These tensions were brought to the breaking point late last year by United States pressure on the Government to carry out reforms in the state-owned tin mines, since these reforms tended to undercut the power base of leftist Vice President Lechin, his followers in the MNR, and the Communists who support him.[2] The result was Lechin's expulsion from the MNR, and his own candidacy against Paz for election to the Presidency on May 31.

In April, former President Siles (1956–1960) returned from his ambassadorial post in Spain to reenter politics as a champion of party unity (presumably under his leadership). He advocates the return of Lechin and other splinter elements to the MNR. Paz has resisted this, and so far opposition groups have been unable to unite against him.

Military Appear Loyal to Paz

Former Air Force Chief Rene Barrientos is Paz' vice presidential running mate. He was involved in a plot to overthrow Paz earlier this

---

[1] Source: Johnson Library, National Security File, Country File, Bolivia, Vol. I, Memoranda, December 1963–July 1964. Secret. According to a State Department copy, this memorandum was drafted by Nicholas V. McCausland (ARA), cleared by Henry E. Mattox (INR) and Allen D. Gordon (AID), and approved by Deputy Assistant Secretary of Inter-American Affairs Robert W. Adams. (National Archives and Records Administration, RG 59, Central Files 1964–66, POL 14 BOL)

[2] In particular, the United States pressed for better financial management of the Bolivian tin mines. The issue was discussed in a meeting between President Kennedy and President Paz on October 23, 1963; see *Foreign Relations*, 1961–1963, American Republics and Cuba, Microfiche Supplement.

month but now seems to have abandoned his anti-Paz activities.[3] Paz believes the military high command is loyal and able to control sporadic violence by the opposition as well as any further attempts by Barrientos or Siles to use middle and junior grade officers to advance their personal ambitions. President Paz has declared that the elections will be held on May 31 even though all of the opposition parties which had presented presidential candidates have announced their intention to abstain.

Implications for the United States

Negative Factors

Instability in the months following the elections is very likely. There will be continuing resistance within the party and outside it to the course Paz has set, especially to his close association with the United States and the Alliance for Progress. Lechin, Siles, and other opposition leaders will probably continue to plot a coup d'etat since they do not believe the way to power is open to them by constitutional means; and Paz' decision to succeed himself poses the question of personal as distinct from party dictatorship. If, on election day, Paz is the only candidate as now seems likely, the validity of his claim to a popular mandate will be suspect.[4]

Positive Factors

Paz seems committed to Bolivia's economic and social development under the Alliance for Progress. Now outside the government party, Lechin is in a less advantageous position to obstruct Government efforts to rehabilitate the state-owned tin mines and in other ways to strengthen Bolivia's economy. Nevertheless, Paz' government inevitably will have further clashes with the Lechin and Communist-led miners if it is determined to carry out its rehabilitation program. If Paz is resolute, however, our aid policy should begin to show dramatic

---

[3] Information on Barrientos' role in the alleged coup plot is in telegrams 575 to La Paz, May 4; 1515 from La Paz, May 16; and 1547 from La Paz, May 25. (All ibid.) On May 15 Lieutenant Colonel Edward J. Fox, Jr., the Air Attaché in La Paz, met with Barrientos at the Bolivian's request to discuss relations with Paz. Fox told Barrientos to "use his head for something other than a hat rack. He [Barrientos] agreed and stated that he would get with the program and even though he would lose many Paz-haters, he would positively support Paz." (Department of the Army cable IN 293440, May 18; Central Intelligence Agency, Job 90–1156R, Directorate for Operations, Latin America Division, [file name not declassified])

[4] The Embassy in La Paz reported Paz's victory in the Presidential election in telegram 1580, June 1. (National Archives and Records Administration, RG 59, Central Files 1964–66, POL 14 BOL)

results in the near future and forces of political instability may be weakened.

Benjamin H. Read[5]

---

[5] Printed from a copy that indicates Grant G. Hilliker signed for Read above Read's typed signature.

---

150. Memorandum From Gordon Chase of the National Security Council Staff to the President's Special Assistant for National Security Affairs (Bundy)[1]

Washington, October 28, 1964.

SUBJECT

Bolivia

I talked briefly to Bill Dentzer, the Office Director for Bolivian/ Chilean Affairs, about the current goings-on in Bolivia. Here are some points of interest.

1. Bill said that the present disturbances can be characterized as a popular reaction to repressive government. The students are a big factor in this reaction.[2] Much of the leadership for the disturbances is coming from the Falangists (a leftist but tolerable party) and the Communists.

2. I asked Bill what the disturbances could leave in their wake.[3] He described the following alternatives:

(a) Paz could stay on. This looks like the most likely alternative; Paz seems to be keeping the support of the military.

---

[1] Source: Johnson Library, National Security File, Country File, Bolivia, Vol. II, Memoranda, July–November, 1964. Secret.

[2] The Embassy reported on the student demonstrations and their political implications in telegram 426 from La Paz, October 24, suggesting that the demonstrations were in part a response to the shooting of a student in Cochabamba, and in part by the climate of political agitation and discord between Paz and the military. (National Archives and Records Administration, RG 59, Central Files 1964–66, POL–8 BOL)

[3] A separate assessment of the political unrest in Bolivia, which focused on the prospects for a military coup, is in an October 29 memorandum from Lieutenant General Alva R. Fitch, Deputy Director of the Defense Intelligence Agency, to Secretary of Defense McNamara. (Washington National Records Center, OSD Files: FRC 330 68A 306, Bolivia 000.1, 1964)

Bill went on to say that, while Paz is not particularly popular with the people, they probably like him "best." The people see no clear alternative and, under Paz, they at least get less instability.

(b) The military could capitalize on the present disturbances and take over the government. The leader of a military government could be Barrientos, but it could also be someone else; in this regard, it should be noted that Barrientos is not all that popular with the military.

Bill does not regard a military takeover as highly likely; however, it is in the ball park.

(c) Paz could get killed and there could be a state of anarchy for a while, followed by some sort of coalition. Bill feels this is not a likely alternative.

(d) Bill said that the possibility of a Communist takeover is nil. The Communists do not have enough popular following or acceptability. In addition, the military is violently opposed to them.

Bill went on to say that the main threat that the Communists pose is that, in a state of instability or transition, other parties will be looking around for support. In such a situation, the Communists, while not being able to take over the country, will be in a position to exert significant influence.

3. The upshot seems to me to be that there is little likelihood of something happening in Bolivia which we cannot live with. Given our "druthers," however, we would probably just as soon see the disturbances end with Paz still in the saddle.

GC

---

151.   Telegram From the Department of State to All American Republic Posts[1]

Washington, November 4, 1964, 9:22 p.m.

836. Subject: Bolivia. President Paz Estenssoro has fled the country and arrived in Lima with his family afternoon November 4. Gen-

---

[1] Source: National Archives and Records Administration, RG 59, Central Files 1964–66, POL 23–9 BOL. Secret; Priority. Drafted by William L.S. Williams and Roger Brewin (ARA/BC) and approved by Adams. Also sent to Paris for TOPOL.

eral Ovando Candia, Commander-in-Chief of the armed forces, announced today the formation of a military junta which he would head, but full junta has not been named.[2] General Suarez, Army Commander, announced he was a member. The situation is extremely fluid, reports indicating the possibility that Vice President Barrientos and Ovando may vie for the leadership of the military government, possibly through force.[3] There is thus some uncertainty regarding the unity of the armed forces as well as over the relationship of Communist-led miner militia to army units in Oruro, leading mining center. The relationship of pro-Communist workers in La Paz to the junta is also uncertain. Fighting between pro-Paz militia and the Army broke out November 4, but has subsided. Sporadic rioting and sacking of buildings continues, however. The military possess only a limited capacity to preserve public order.[4]

We are principally concerned by the extent of Communist power in the country and the possibility that in the developing situation the Communists may gain control of the government. Our overriding objectives in the present situation, therefore, are to prevent the collapse of authority, civil war and a Communist takeover, and to protect U.S. lives and property. We have no present intention of recognizing any group which may be contending for power, and would wish at appropriate time to consult with other American governments this subject. We are, however, endeavoring to maintain informal contact with the military

---

[2] A November 4 situation report from Mann to the Special Group (Counter-Insurgency) indicated that the coup began when pro-Barrientos commanders of the Ingavi Regiment in La Paz rebelled early on November 3. By late evening military garrisons in all major cities except La Paz had joined the Barrientos cause. When the army high command in the capital told Paz that the army would no longer support him in office, the President fled. (National Archives and Records Administration, RG 59, ARA Files: Lot 70 D 443, Political Affairs and Relations, 1964, Pol 23, Internal Defense Plan)

[3] In a conversation with Bolivian Ambassador Enrique Sanchez de Lozada on November 4, Mann expressed the view that "it was not at all clear who was in control." (Memorandum of conversation; ibid., Central Files 1964–66, POL 15 BOL) Reporting in telegram 496 from La Paz, November 4, Henderson indicated that "Ovando claim to government has no color of constitutionality while Barrientos' does," and that Barrientos had referred to the Bolivian Government as "his government." Following a demonstration at the presidential palace that day, Ovando allowed Barrientos to assume leadership of the junta while he took on the position of commander in chief of the armed forces. (Ibid., POL 23–9 BOL)

[4] Two separate reports prepared on November 5, one by the Central Intelligence Agency ([text not declassified]), and one by the Defense Intelligence Agency, provide details on the political situation and prospects in Bolivia resulting from establishment of the military junta. Both reports projected that the newly established junta would maintain the pro-U.S. position of the Paz government. (Johnson Library, National Security File, Country File, Bolivia, Vol. II, Memoranda, July–November 1964)

leaders and Barrientos with a view toward learning their intentions and the likely orientation of a successor government.[5]

In discussing the Bolivian situation with officials of other American governments you may in your discretion say that the U.S. government supported the constitutional government of Bolivia until it fell and that just prior to his departure President Paz through his foreign minister conveyed to our ambassador his thanks for the support and assistance we had given him during recent crisis.

For Lima, Buenos Aires, Santiago, Rio de Janeiro, Caracas: Embassies should make special effort brief appropriate officials because situation might arise in which we would wish consult on urgent basis on situation and attitude toward successor government.

Rusk

---

[5] The Department instructed the Embassy in La Paz to "take every appropriate action to ensure continuation of a non-communist Barrientos government during this interim period." It stated that the Barrientos government should be encouraged to consolidate and strengthen itself by reaching a political truce with key non-Communist parties and leaders in order to ensure a Lechin defeat in future elections, which "should be scheduled for such time as Barrientos or other non-communists are confident they can win." (Telegram 267 to La Paz, November 4; National Archives and Records Administration, RG 59, Central Files 1964–66, POL 15 BOL)

---

152. Memorandum From Acting Secretary of State Harriman to President Johnson[1]

Washington, December 3, 1964.

SUBJECT

Recognition of New Bolivian Government

---

[1] Source: Johnson Library, National Security File, Country File, Bolivia, Vol. III, Memoranda. December 1964–September 1965. No classification marking. The Department of State copy indicates it was drafted by Brewin (ARA) on December 2. (National Archives and Records Administration, RG 59, Central Files 1964–66, POL 16 BOL) The following handwritten note is at the bottom of this memorandum: "Mr. President: Rusk, Mann, and I concur—the plan is to deal with this in State Department—from press point of view. McG.B." Sayre recommended the President concur in a December 3 covering memorandum to Bundy. (Johnson Library, National Security File, Country File, Bolivia, Vol. III, Memoranda, December 1964–September 1965)

Recommendation:

I recommend that the United States recognize the military junta headed by General Barrientos as the government of Bolivia, and that our Embassy in La Paz be instructed to acknowledge the junta's note of November 7 requesting recognition.[2]

Background:

President Paz of Bolivia fled the country on November 4 and a military junta headed by former Vice President Rene Barrientos was installed on November 5. The new regime is in control of the country, has encountered no resistance, has reestablished constitutional liberties, and has reiterated its intentions to hold elections. Barrientos and his principal advisers have privately pledged that communist influence will be reduced and eventually eliminated, and that they will not reestablish relations with Cuba or Czechoslovakia. While the new government may not be able to fulfill completely all of its assurances, unless we resume normal relations with the Barrientos government, the possibilities for communist influence and chaos increase. Congressional leaders have been consulted and concur that recognition is desirable and U.S. performance on existing aid commitments should be resumed. The AFL–CIO has been reassured on labor rights by recent actions of the new government. The Barrientos government has been recognized by seven countries in Latin America, by most of the NATO powers, and by others including India, Japan, Israel, and the Republic of China.

W. Averell Harriman

---

[2] The President approved the recommendation.

153.   Memorandum Prepared for the 303 Committee[1]

Washington, January 29, 1965.

SUBJECT

Provide Support to [*less than 1 line of source text not declassified*] and the Popular Christian Movement in Bolivia

1. Summary

It is proposed to provide in appropriate stages the total sum of [*2 lines of source text not declassified*]. Barrientos, due to his popularity and power position, appears to have the best chance for organizing behind him a national consensus which would provide the needed unity to proceed with the development of Bolivia. [*less than 1 line of source text not declassified*] this sum of money will expedite and help other negotiations currently being undertaken by the Embassy and the AID program. Barrientos has requested U.S. Government help in his election campaign. [*2 lines of source text not declassified*] The Embassy in La Paz, the Department of State, and the CIA all concur that in the present circumstances the best possibility for stability in Bolivia is the ascendency to the Presidency of Barrientos with a return to constitutionality. It is important that he have a strong organizational base in order to bring in with him a Congress which would be cooperative. This proposal has been fully coordinated with and concurred in by Ambassador Henderson and Assistant Secretary Mann.[2]

---

[1] Source: Department of State, INR/IL Historical Files, 303 Committee Special Files, January–June 1965. Secret; Eyes Only.

[2] Acting Deputy Under Secretary for Political Affairs Llewellyn E. Thompson concurred on February 3, but according to a February 5 handwritten note by Murat W. Williams (INR): "In approving this paper Ambassador Thompson remarked that he thought the whole question of this type of support in elections should be reviewed on a general basis. A distinction must be drawn between action to check communism and other activities in internal political affairs." (Memorandum from Mann to Thompson; ibid.) At a January 6 meeting of CIA and ARA officials Mann had suggested that, in response to a request for financial aid, "Barrientos should be told we do not like to intervene in an election of this nature, however if it were a 'matter of Bolivian independence,' we might do something." Mann thought it was time for Bolivia "to stand on its own feet." (Memorandum from Carter to Hughes, January 8; ibid., ARA/CIA Weekly Meetings, 1964–1965) A message was sent to La Paz apparently turning down Barrientos' request for financial aid, but with a proviso that the question could be reopened if events made it necessary. (Draft message to La Paz with handwritten note by Carter, January 14; ibid., Bolivia, 1962–1980)

2. Problem

a. To strengthen the organizational base of General Barrientos within all sectors of the population through aid to his newly organized political vehicle—the Popular Christian Movement. This movement will be used to make inroads into the crucial areas where the communists and leftist followers of Juan Lechin are strongest, thus undercutting their natural support.

b. To indicate to General Barrientos that the U.S. government is in support of him personally and of his efforts to create the conditions for stability and unity which are essential for the return to constitutional government.

3. Factors Bearing on the Problem

a. Background

(1) Because of the constitutional provision that anyone holding public office must resign from that office 180 days prior to an election, General Barrientos must step down from the Junta in order to run for the office of the presidency. General elections have been called for September 1965. When Barrientos does step down he will no longer have access to the facilities of the government such as air transport, vehicles, and even government funds. Thus he is seeking an alternate source of funding for his campaign. He [1 *line of source text not declassified*] provided a detailed budget of his requirements to establish his organizational base. He also provided a statement of his principles and program together with a listing of the individuals who would constitute his top command.

(2) [8½ *lines of source text not declassified*]

(3) Barrientos is a long standing friend of the United States. He received a good portion of his military training in the United States. He was Air Attaché to Washington, attended American University, and is a close friend of many high officials in the United States Government.

[Omitted here is further discussion of the proposal.]

4. Coordination

This proposed activity has been fully coordinated with and approved by the U.S. Ambassador, Assistant Secretary Thomas Mann, and has been discussed in detail with appropriate officials of the Department of State.

5. Recommendation

That the 303 Committee approve the covert subsidization of the Popular Christian Movement which will be the vehicle [1 *line of source text not declassified*] upon which to effect a return to constitutional government in Bolivia. The total sum requested for this program is [*less than 1 line of source text not declassified*].[3]

---

[3] The 303 Committee approved the recommendation by a vote by telephone on February 5. (Memorandum from Williams to Mann, February 16; ibid.) According to a February 10 memorandum [*text not declassified*] to ARA, Barrientos was informed on that date of the decision and of the U.S. Government view "that relations between sovereigns should be based upon dignity and mutual respect rather than financial considerations; but in order to dispel any doubts" in Barrientos' mind "of our attitude toward him, his request was approved as a one-shot affair." (Ibid.) Privately the [*text not declassified*] assessment of the operation was more positive, pointing out that "the risk of exposing U.S. participation in the MPC program is probably worth taking, especially if the operation helps to unify the country, reduces political turmoil, and helps Bolivia along the road to economic and social progress. The exposure of U.S. participation would, undoubtedly, be embarrassing, but it probably would not lead to serious repercussions." (Memorandum from FitzGerald to Helms, March 3; Central Intelligence Agency, Job 80–01690R, Directorate of Operations, Latin America Division, WH/Bolivia, [*file name not declassified*])

---

154. Telegram From the Embassy in Bolivia to the Department of State[1]

La Paz, March 29, 1965, 6 p.m.

966. At President's request, had four hour interview at his home with him and MinEconomy Berdecio March 28. Barrientos in apparent good health, disposition good, not suffering much pain from wound. (From other reports we understood Barrientos had been extremely anxious and depressed that wound might have caused permanent nerve damage. Since securing medical advice that no permanent damage will result, his attitude has improved remarkably. We are now reasonably sure wound not self-inflicted, though many politicians choose to believe it was.)

Barrientos said wished to inform me of fundamental change of policy and tactics to be followed by him and entire junta. In extended meeting night of March 27, well into morning March 28, junta agreed

---

[1] Source: National Archives and Records Administration, RG 59, Central Files 1964–66, POL 15 BOL. Secret; Limdis. Repeated to USSOUTHCOM for POLAD.

it imperative armed forces remain united to protect their existence.[2] This required that Barrientos resign as candidate, which he agreed to do. Also required that Ovando stop flirting with political parties, which Ovando agreed to do. Junta would henceforth devote itself to substantive governmental accomplishments.

President explained logic of new position by admitting that his efforts to get political parties work together had failed. His efforts increase his own popularity had also failed. Since a political solution through conciliation not possible, a solution would have to be imposed. This means junta will remain in power for indefinite period, devote itself to governing effectively, without trying to win favor of all sectors of population. Admitted has made error in neglecting economic issues while trying achieve political compromises, but said he now could not be criticized for having failed try achieve political consensus.

Political and economic issues are, under the new "tough line," to be faced forthrightly. For instance, if miners give trouble, GOB will go in and seize mines. Army is now in process taking over refineries in face of YPFB strike. Said Communists active in sabotaging economy, and GOB would deal with them forcefully, though would not make indiscriminate arrests or use documents mentioned Embtel 957.[3] Juan Lechin Oquendo of PRIN is apparently to be among junta's first targets for neutralization. Barrientos said junta would do whatever necessary to get country straightened out and on road to recovery.

President said trouble could ensue as result implementation new policy and junta would need military support.[4] He argued that best method of avoiding a shooting situation is for armed forces present formidable appearance. Simplest way in his view would be through

---

[2] In a meeting between State and CIA representatives in Washington on March 31 FitzGerald remarked that although Barrientos and Ovando "don't like each other, the truth is they are necessary to each other and recognize it." Ovando and Barrientos "say harsh words about each other from time to time, but often have a beer together at night." (Memorandum from Carter to Hughes, April 2; Department of State, INR/IL Historical Files, ARA/CIA Weekly Meetings, 1964–1965)

[3] In telegram 957 from La Paz, March 26, the Embassy reported that the junta planned to arrest "300 Communists and leftists" and exile them to Paraguay as political asylees. The documents in question were three letters from the Italian Communist Party to Lechin regarding $25,000 that it allegedly sent him." (National Archives and Records Administration, RG 59, Central Files 1964–66, POL 15 BOL)

[4] At the same March 31 meeting between State and CIA officials (see footnote 2 above), Vaughn remarked: "You don't have to go down many notches economically in Bolivia to be at the disaster point." Vaughn said that "we have been hard, we have demanded performance in return for aid. He questioned, however, whether Barrientos can deliver." The group decided to send an observer to Bolivia to "give Barrientos advice on current economic and political problems—particularly the question of whether or not to have elections, as scheduled." (Memorandum from Carter to Hughes, April 2; Department of State, INR/IL Historical Files, ARA/CIA Weekly Meetings, 1964–1965)

use armored personnel carriers. Felt they would so intimidate possible demonstrators that bloodshed could be avoided. Barrientos added that junta does not trust most of police officer corps, thus could not rely on police to handle serious public order problems.

I limited my response to Barrientos to saying I would present his request to Washington, but at same time warned him APCS are not type of equipment which provided Latin America through MAP under current policy. (Country Team recommendations will follow.)[5] Also, while assuring him US wants to assist his government, asked him realize that our requesting performance of GOB before extending further assistance was not evidence of plot against junta. He agreed that four months had been lost with little or no performance, and our position not unreasonable.

Much of this extended conversation spent reviewing major economic issues such as COMIBOL, budget, railroads, Lloyd. Barrientos assured me he now prepared come to grips with these issues. Conversation also included some observations political scene, in which Barrientos said he less concerned by Falange plotting, believed Falange being led on by PRIN. He expressed some reservations about Siles and MNR as troublemaking element, and indicated he felt political parties largely limited their activities to conspiracy.

Comment: On March 28 ARMA found great relief expressed by general staff officers that divisive forces pressing on junta had been eliminated, a reaction which would tend confirm new line taken by Barrientos and junta. Believe we can expect a few more decisions from junta on economic and administrative problems. Though Barrientos may have lost some ground by having to agree to withdraw as candidate, he remains as junta president and could reconsider candidacy if public clamor for him became intense. Apparently junta has made no decision on further postponement elections at this time.

Henderson

---

[5] Not further identified.

---

155.   Editorial Note

On May 24, 1965, the Department of State reported to the White House that the military junta headed by General Barrientos had committed Bolivian armed forces against the miners in the state-owned tin mining enterprise, COMIBOL. The purpose of this action was to remove labor union leaders, "who are to a large extent either communist or far leftist, and practically all of whom are opposed to the Government of Barrientos," and who "have resisted reform and sabotaged the rehabilitation program" initiated by the junta to reduce labor costs and improve the ability of the government to manage the mines in order to ensure further U.S. assistance to COMIBOL. The report noted that although the junta "undertook its action without U.S. commitments for assistance, it has hoped for such aid." (Department of State Background and Situation Report, as of 1400, May 24, attached to memorandum from Read to McGeorge Bundy, May 24; National Archives and Records Administration, RG 59, Central Files 1964–66, POL 23–9 BOL)

Barrientos had requested such assistance, including arms, so he could move into the mines. The request was considered on May 19 at the weekly meeting of ARA and CIA representatives. According to ARA's record of this meeting, prepared on May 20, FitzGerald asserted that providing arms to Barrientos to move into the mines "would make us 'strike breakers,' and 'this we can't do.'" Sayre responded: "I think you're right on the arms question. I think we're really not going to finance it." A handwritten note in the margin, apparently made by Denney, said: "but we did!" (Memorandum from Carter to Hughes, Denney, and Evans, May 20; Department of State INR/IL Historical Files, ARA/CIA Weekly Meetings, 1964–1965)

The Department informed Ambassador Henderson that AID had authorized approximately $1.8 million in "special financial support for planned military intervention in COMIBOL mines." (Telegram 644 to La Paz, May 26; National Archives and Records Administration, RG 59, Central Files 1964–66, POL 23–9 BOL) The Department authorized Ambassador Henderson "to commit all funds requested and communicate this to GOB." In addition, the Department instructed Henderson to look into arranging for emergency military supplies and equipment, including ammunition and planes. (Telegram 624 to La Paz, May 24; ibid.)

Also on May 24 General Ovando signed, on his own initiative, cease-fire agreements with student and labor leaders representing the tin miners. Under the terms of the agreements, Ovando would halt troop movements on the mines and withdraw troops from the mines already occupied, while the workers agreed to return to work. The government and the miners were to negotiate their differences. This action, according to a Central Intelligence Agency report of May 26 ([*document number not declassified*]), "was a direct violation of junta policy and determination to follow through with military operations to gain control over the tin mines." As a result, the report indicated, "the military government of General Rene Barrientos is in serious danger of collapse." The report continued, "an assessment of those forces attempting to oust him reveals that a successor government would probably permit Communists and extreme leftists to consolidate and increase their power." (Johnson Library, National Security File, Bolivia, Vol. III, Memoranda, December 1964–September 1965) The report was forwarded on May 26 to McGeorge Bundy by CIA Deputy Director for Intelligence Ray Cline.

On May 27, with indications that Barrientos and Ovando were near an open split, Ovando became co-President of the junta along with Barrientos with both men having the right to exercise authority of commander-in-chief over the armed forces. According to a May 28 Department of State Situation Report, "Barrientos earlier had told our Ambassador that he intended to elevate Ovando to the co-Presidency in order to 'keep an eye on him.'" The report continued:

"We believe that relations between Ovando and Barrientos, never notably good, have now reached their nadir, though their differences are again momentarily plastered over. A split between the two would divide the Armed Forces, whose ability to act as a stabilizing anti-communist influence over the near and longer term would be drastically diminished. We have instructed our Embassy to continue exerting every reasonable effort to prevent such a split, and that such efforts should be from a posture of neutrality as between the two men. A senior United States officer, who served in Bolivia for four years and is closely acquainted with both Barrientos and Ovando, will leave the United States for Bolivia Friday evening [May 28]. He will emphasize to both men the paramount importance which the highest levels of the United States Government attach to the preservation of the unity of the Bolivian Armed Forces."

The report was forward to the White House under cover of a memorandum from Read to McGeorge Bundy on May 28. (National Archives and Records Administration, RG 59, Central Files 1964–66, POL 23–9 BOL)

156.   Memorandum From the Executive Secretary of the
Department of State (Read) to the President's Special
Assistant for National Security Affairs (Bundy)[1]

Washington, June 5, 1965.

SUBJECT

Bolivia: Visit of Lieutenant Colonel Paul Wimert to La Paz

Lietenant Colonel Wimert arrived in La Paz on May 29 and departed on June 2, arriving back in Washington on June 3 in the afternoon. His talks with Generals Barrientos and Ovando are reported in
Exdis telegrams Numbers 1222 and 1227[2] from the Embassy and in [1
line of source text not declassified].[3]

Assistant Secretary Vaughn and other officers have talked with
Wimert since his return. We believe that he carried out his assignment
fully in keeping with the instructions he was given, and chances are
fair that there will not be a split in the Bolivian Government in the immediate future. Both Generals Barrientos and Ovando have been made
unmistakably aware that the United States Government attaches the
greatest importance to the complete unity of the Military Junta and of
the Armed Forces in Bolivia. A Bolivian mission now in Washington[4]
has discussed in credible terms the relationships between Barrientos
and Ovando and it has given assurances that they must and will keep
together.

Wimert's presence in La Paz was reported in today's New York
Times, the source being Bolivian. We are treating the article as inaccu-
rate, as it is in a number of respects, and explaining, if asked, that
Wimert was in La Paz in preparation for his imminent assignment to
Santiago as Army Attaché.

On the basis of his talks and observations, Colonel Wimert believes
that civilians and military alike realize the necessity of Presidents

---

[1] Source: Johnson Library, National Security File, Country File, Bolivia, Vol. III,
Memoranda, December 1964–September 1965. Secret.

[2] Dated May 31 and June 1. (National Archives and Records Administration, RG
59, Central Files 1964–66, POL 7 US)

[3] Dated May 30 and May 31. (Ibid., POL 1 BOL; and Johnson Library, National Security File, Country File, Bolivia, Vol. III, Cables, December 1964–September 1965)

[4] A record of meetings of the Bolivian mission with Vaughn on June 3 and Mann
on June 4 was transmitted in telegram 670 to La Paz, June 7. The main points of the mission's presentation were a request for immediate U.S. assistance to allow Bolivia to increase its armed forces by 10,000 to maintain security in cities where the army occupied
the mines, to improve the image of the armed forces, and to provide funds for social and
road projects so that surplus miners could be hired. (National Archives and Records Administration, RG 59, Central Files 1964–66, POL BOL–US)

Barrientos and Ovando sticking together. He says that General Ovando can be classified as a "conniver" who has always been known to play various parties against one another, and that Ovando has not been making key decisions and is not as forceful as Barrientos. He has, however, a fair knowledge of economic problems and government administration. General Barrientos, Wimert thinks, would best be described as a "can-doer", perhaps too impetuous, and not given to thinking out the entire problem. According to Wimert, Barrientos has matured and is becoming more aware of the economic problems of the country, and believes that the Junta now has to stop shooting and come up with positive programs, especially in the mines, to give the people something in return for having supported the Junta.

Wimert's characterizations of the two men coincide with our own, but our problem will be to shape and make realistic the Junta's generalized desires to move forward on the socio-economic front.

Hawthorne Mills[5]
Executive Secretary

---

[5] Hawthorne Mills signed for Read above Read's typed signature.

---

157. Memorandum From the Executive Secretary of the Department of State (Read) to the President's Special Assistant for National Security Affairs (Bundy)[1]

Washington, June 19, 1965.

SUBJECT

Report on Bolivia

Enclosed is a report on Bolivia prepared by the Latin American Policy Committee during the past two weeks. The Committee, chaired by State, includes representatives of DOD, AID, CIA and USIA. The report outlines actions that are now underway and that will be carried out during the next thirty to sixty days. Such actions are designed to prevent possibility of serious political, economic and social disturbances in Bolivia.

---

[1] Source: Johnson Library, National Security File, Country File, Bolivia, Vol. III, Memoranda, December 1964–September 1965. Secret.

In our estimate, Bolivia is now in the process of making a promising, albeit precarious, transition. The Department deems the situation sufficiently serious, however, to warrant the preparation of contingency plans.[2] A draft plan has been prepared and will be considered by the Latin American Policy Committee during the coming week, prior to its scheduled transmittal to your office on June 25.[3] In addition, [*less than 1 line of source text not declassified*] is preparing biographic data on Bolivians who have or could assume key roles in the government. This biographic data will be forwarded to you on completion.

The Department's Director of Bolivian and Chilean Affairs departed for La Paz June 17 to discuss implementation of the enclosed report with the Ambassador and the Country Team.[4]

Benjamin H. Read[5]

---

[2] In a telephone conversation with President Johnson on June 5, McNamara stated that he was "worried" about a blowup in Bolivia. (Ibid., Recordings and Transcripts, Recording of telephone conversation between President Johnson and McNamara, Alpha Series, June 5, 1965, 4:50 p.m., Tape 6506.01, PNO 4) In a telephone conversation earlier that afternoon, Johnson told Mann that "he wanted to have a Task Force composed of high level people from CIA, State, Defense," to develop contingency plans for Guatemala, Colombia, and Bolivia. The President said "he would like to have a Task Force which meets regularly and to which he could look for advice and information." (Ibid., Mann Papers, Telephone Conversations with LBJ, May 2 1965–June 2, 1966) On June 8 Helms reported that Vance said he was going to phone Vaughn and "have him proceed immediately to set up a task force or task forces to develop contingency plans on Colombia, Guatemala and Bolivia." (Central Intelligence Agency, DCI Files, Job 80–B01285A, Helms Chrono as DDP and DDCI)

[3] Transmitted to Bundy on June 24, the paper provides extensive coverage of seven possible contingencies for Bolivia. These included assassination of Barrientos, of Ovando, forced removal of either Barrientos or Ovando by pressures applied by the other, the onset of a political crisis in which the United States would be required to side with Barrientos or Ovando, Communist-supported disorder erupting in Bolivia and threatening the lives and property of non-combatants, non-Communist political elements seeking to topple the Junta by an armed coup, or fighting erupting between the Barrientos and Ovando factions in the Bolivian military. In general the plan recommended supporting Barrientos, if possible, and seeking peaceful means—through unilateral and multilateral channels (such as the OAS)—to disarm any crisis. Direct use of U.S. forces was recommended only in the case of a Communist-supported coup, and only with close consultations with key OAS members. (National Archives and Records Administration, RG 59, Central Files 1964–66, POL 1–1 BOL)

[4] Dentzer reported on his impressions about Bolivia based on his trip in a June 25 memorandum to Vaughn. (Ibid., POL 15 BOL)

[5] Initialed for Read in an unidentified hand.

Enclosure

BOLIVIA

Introduction

This paper considers the short-term outlook for Bolivia and United States actions over the next 30 to 60 days. It has been approved in substance by the Latin American Policy Committee.

[Omitted here are a "Background" section on political events leading up to the crisis in Bolivia's mines and a "Current Developments" section dealing with the events of May and early June 1965.]

Aims and Outlook

Our short-term aim is to take advantage of GOB willingness to bring stability to the mining areas, in order to gain what progress we can for COMIBOL and the increased political stability for Bolivia which could grow out of successful action. This is the first time in more than a decade, and perhaps the last time for a long while, that a Bolivian government has a chance to bring law and order to the mines. We seek to attain these ends, however, without unduly jeopardizing the status quo, since any change now in the situation which finds the Armed Forces in power could have unpredictable consequences. We also seek to achieve these goals without decreasing the financial incentive for the government to take a variety of actions which would improve the development and long-term stability of the country. With the expulsion or voluntary exile of many communists and extreme leftists, and the split within the PCB, communist influence is now weaker than it has been for some time. To keep the extreme left from regaining its organized base in the mines, GOB policies affecting them must be sound and workable. Meanwhile, with no viable alternative to the Junta now on the Bolivian political scene, the principal danger to the Junta lies from within; Barrientos and Ovando must be given strong encouragement to stick together. These are the principal problems lying immediately ahead. Beyond that are our longer-term goals. These involve getting the Armed Forces to retire from running the government before they fail, seriously damage their influence, or are torn asunder. To accomplish this, a viable political alternative to the Junta government must be present within a year or so. That alternative may be General Barrientos as a civilian candidate for the Presidency, especially if the mine rehabilitation scheme goes well.

The entry of government troops into the potentially most rebellious mines on June 11 and 12 without bloodshed was a great victory for the government. If the Junta successfully completes the operations in which it is now engaged, its prestige will be greatly enhanced. If something goes wrong, that is, if it stops now or fails in the attempt—and we do not think the Junta is out of the woods yet—its claim to the reins of government will be jeopardized and it will face bloody skirmishes with its enemies. We are cautiously optimistic that the Barrientos–Ovando relationship will hold together for a while. We do not think anything has happened to change the underlying causes of differences between the two; they both reached the brink and, looking over it, retreated from it; realizing that the abyss below represented, in all likelihood, a suicidal split in the Armed Forces and the removal from the Bolivian scene of the only force for order and stability, given present political and economic conditions. Their relations probably will come under more intense strain, as the COMIBOL reorganization progresses, and the question of whether and when to call for elections becomes again a divisive issue for the Junta. Elections originally were called for May, postponed until September, delayed until October, and most recently postponed indefinitely.

Action Agenda

The following special actions are underway to carry out U.S. objectives:

1. Economic

a. Advice to the GOB, directly from Embassy/USAID and through the Triangular Operation's Advisory Group, on COMIBOL policy and operations. U.S. financial and recruiting assistance to obtain competent non-Bolivian nationals to manage individual mines.

b. Undertake a $1 million P.L. 480 Title IV wheat program to stock COMIBOL commissaries with cheap flour for the miners.

c. Prepare special projects, as requested by the recent GOB mission to the U.S., which increasingly can absorb unemployed miners and which manifest GOB and U.S. desire to assist the mining areas. Embassy/USAID to make initial recommendations by June 17.

2. Internal Security

a. Report by CINCSO and the MilGroup in La Paz by June 16 on whether Bolivian force levels should be increased, whether additional needs for military hardware exist, and whether the discipline and reliability of the Armed Forces can be improved by any short-term measures.

b. Insure stepped-up delivery of the two T–28D aircraft is arranged for June 17.

c. Improve GOB capacity to deter and control riots through the supply of a limited number of personnel-carrying armored cars.

d. Encourage the GOB to intensify its drive to collect weapons from the miners and to insure their destruction so that they do not get back into circulation.

3. Political

a. Reiterate through various channels to key leaders the importance attached by the U.S. to Junta unity.

b. Continue discussions with governments of countries adjoining Bolivia on the significance of developments there to the hemisphere and to their national interest.

c. Seek to influence union elections and developments, including action by American trade union contacts.

d. Increase through all official U.S. sources the quality and quantity of political biographic data on individuals who may become important in the near future.

e. Complete contingency plans to deal with possible emergencies.

---

158.   Memorandum Prepared for the 303 Committee[1]

Washington, July 13, 1965.

SUBJECT

Expansion of Political Action Program in Bolivia

REFERENCE

Memorandum dated 29 January 1965[2]

1. Summary

It is proposed to expand up to [*less than 1 line of source text not declassified*] already approved on 5 February 1965, and [*less than 1 line of source text not declassified*] more to be used upon exhaustion of the original sum) for propaganda and political action in support of the ruling Bolivian military junta's plans to pacify the country and eventually hold elections to establish a constitutional government. This support would be designed (a) to promote an eventual transfer of power to a

---

[1] Source: Department of State, INR/IL Historical Files, 303 Committee Special Files, July–December 1965. Secret; Eyes Only. This is a revised version of a draft prepared in the CIA on June 7. (Ibid., 303 Committee Files, c. 21, June 25, 1965)

[2] Document 153.

government more stable than the present provisional military regime and potentially capable of meeting the country's pressing problems; (b) to bolster the junta's unity and stability through discreet aid to political groups and key individuals who will support continuation of the regime and of the required power balance within it for as long as may be necessary or desirable, as instruments for the achievement of U.S. policy objectives in Bolivia, and (c) to provide levers with which the two co-presidents of the junta, Generals Rene Barrientos and Alfredo Ovando, can be restrained from ill-judged or precipitate action that might split the Bolivian armed forces and plunge the country into political and economic chaos. The present proposal has a much broader purpose than that presented last January as regards ultimate objectives, and differs chiefly in the amount of funds now required because of changed circumstances, the mechanisms to be used, and the variety and scope of activities to be funded. It is possible that further expenditures may later become necessary, but specific requirements cannot yet be accurately predicted in view of the highly fluid Bolivian situation. This proposal has the concurrence of Embassy La Paz, the Department of State, and CIA.[3] Implementation will be [1 line of source text not declassified] in coordination with Ambassador Henderson in the field and with appropriate officers of the Department of State in Washington.

2. Problem

a. To help create the conditions for an orderly transfer of power to a constitutional government which would have reasonable prospects for stability.

b. To maintain in the meantime the stability of the junta government through aid to political groups and individuals who will support

---

[3] The June 7 draft proposal occasioned considerable discussion before and after its preparation. When FitzGerald stated at a June 2 meeting of representatives of the ARA and CIA that it might be an ideal time to "give [less than 1 line of source text not declassified] a little covert support," Denney replied that "it seems like a waste of money to me." (Memorandum from Carter to Hughes, Denney, and Evans, June 4; Department of State, INR/IL Historical Files, ARA/CIA Weekly Meetings, 1964–1965) At the June 25 meeting of the 303 Committee the draft proposal was criticized by the participants because it openly supported Barrientos. There was a difference of opinion expressed concerning the relative merits of Barrientos and Ovando and the risk, according to Deputy Secretary of Defense Cyrus Vance, that supporting one over the other could cause a "ruinous civil war." The 303 Committee agreed to postpone decision on the proposal pending further study. (Ibid., 303 Committee Files, c. 22, July 26) The revised July 13 proposal reflected a U.S. policy decision, according to Sayre, "to encourage moderate and responsible civilian political organizations looking to the time when pressure will greatly increase on the junta to make concessions to the desire of political groups to participate in the government or to hold elections." (Memorandum by Sayre, July 7; National Security Council 303 Committee Files, Subject Files, Bolivia, 1962–1980) This memorandum was addressed to the Acting Deputy Under Secretary (Thompson) and was marked "not sent."

continuation of the present regime until the orderly transfer of power can take place, which may not occur for a year or two.

3. Factors Bearing on Problem

a. Background

(a) The present situation in Bolivia is different from that prevailing at the time the referenced memorandum was prepared and approved. The chief new developments have been (1) the failure of Barrientos' effort to have himself elected president quickly and the indefinite postponement, announced on 7 May 1965, of the national elections previously scheduled for October of this year; (2) the mid-May decision of the junta to carry out drastic reforms in the operation of the state mining corporation known as COMIBOL, including the use of force to extend governmental authority to the mining areas; (3) the subsequent arrest and deportation to Paraguay of the extreme leftist labor leader and politician Juan Lechin and later of other troublemakers of the far left; (4) the ensuing increased tensions and stresses within governmental, military and political circles, heightened by public disturbances which occurred during the last half of May and (5) the naming on 26 May of Ovando as co-president of the junta.

(2) The present co-presidential arrangement is regarded as essentially unstable over the long term. There appears to be strong sentiment within the junta in favor of keeping Ovando from ousting Barrientos and vice-versa, since any such move by either might irreparably damage the solidarity of the armed forces and split them into irreconcilable factions. This could in turn destroy both the junta's ability to govern and public acceptance of the military establishment. The regime would rapidly collapse under those circumstances. The Embassy and the CIA [less than 1 line of source text not declassified] believe that such a collapse would entail passage of the political initiative to extremist groups of both the Right and the Left, with a high probability that a prolonged period of chaotic civil disturbance and/or civil war would ensue.

(3) The Popular Christian Movement (MPC), regarded in January 1965 as the main vehicle for the promotion of Barrientos' presidential candidacy, has come to play a definitely secondary role. It lacks political sophistication and good leadership, and has remained essentially a rural, peasant organization without substantial appeal to urban elements of the population. In view of this and of the indefinite postponement of elections, the MPC is no longer considered adequate as the primary focus of the political action program although it remains a useful instrument for mobilizing peasant support. Of the [less than 1 line of source text not declassified] approved on 5 February 1965, [less than 1 line of source text not declassified] had been expended as of the end of

June 1965, directly for MPC organizational, propaganda, and administrative expenses and indirectly for related support to the regime.

(4) The essential factors in the present situation lead to the conclusion that the present regime should continue, as the only apparent feasible alternative for the time being to chaos and the eventual dominance of extremist groups, pending the holding of elections and installation of a constitutional government. There are strong feelings among junta members as well as subordinate officers of the armed forces in favor of the indefinite maintenance of military pre-eminence in Bolivia, as insurance against a resurgence of the sentiment that resulted in the downgrading of the military establishment during the 12-year tenure of the National Revolutionary Movement (MNR). Coupled with this is a realization that strong-arm tactics are not enough and that the military must work to establish broadly-based support—passive if not active—for its chosen role. There are political elements also which appear willing to back the military for the time being, by non-opposition if not by any overt act, lest a worse fate befall them. The U.S. Government's role should accordingly be that of encouraging the emergence of a national consensus along these lines. It will be necessary to provide covert support to these individuals and groups that can be mobilized behind U.S. policy objectives, since overt action, or even inaction, on the part of the U.S. which appeared to favor one faction or another would imperil the unity of the regime.

(5) The fluidity of the situation in the country makes it impossible at this time to identify all elements to be aided through covert channels. [*11 lines of source text not declassified*] There will necessarily be flexibility in the extent of the covert funding to be provided each of these and other groups, in view of the rapidity with which Bolivian events tend to move.

b. Origin of Requirement

[*1 paragraph (6 lines of source text) not declassified*]

c. Pertinent U.S. Policy Considerations

Bolivia needs a moderate and effective government. There is neither a single party nor a likely combination of parties capable of forming a viable government with which we could cooperate. Hence, for the present, there is no acceptable alternative to the junta, and there may be none for a year or more. The unity of the armed forces is the key factor in the continued strength of the government. The armed forces could be split by the rivalry of Barrientos and Ovando, both of whom desire to be the constitutional president. Meanwhile there is increased maneuvering among civilian parties and groups who are looking toward the time when they can play a more meaningful role in governmental affairs. In the long run there must be a civilian government, and we should encourage the growth of conditions which will make this possible. As the civilian political situation unfolds we should identify that group which gives promise of being most viable politically and most energetic in attacking developmental problems, and give it our support. Under present circumstances we must carefully assess the relative strengths of Barrientos and Ovando as well as other leaders. We are inclined to favor Barrientos at this time, but we must not antagonize Ovando, about whose orientation and motivations we should know more, by playing favorites in such a way as to set Ovando against us or to cause him to bring his differences with Barrientos to a head.

[Omitted here is additional discussion of the proposal.]

4. Coordination

This proposal has been coordinated with and approved by the U.S. Ambassador in La Paz and has been discussed in detail with appropriate officials of the Department of State.

5. Recommendation

That the 303 Committee approve the covert political action program outlined above. The total sum requested at this time is [*less than 1 line of source text not declassified*], of which [*less than 1 line of source text not declassified*] is covered by a previous approval. [*less than 1 line of source text not declassified*][4]

---

[4] The recommendation was endorsed by Thompson on July 19. (Ibid., 303 Committee Files, c. 23, August 9, 1965) In a July 21 memorandum to McGeorge Bundy, Executive Secretary of the 303 Committee Peter Jessup indicated that "both State and Vance have approved" the proposal and wrote "I have no magic formula either and recommend working along with Barrientos as the only semi-competent available." Bundy initialed his approval. (National Security Council, 303 Committee Files, Subject File, Bolivia) The 303 Committee approved the recommendation on July 26. (Memorandum for the Record, July 27; ibid.) At the request of Ambassador Henderson, the 303 Committee on March 28, 1966, approved a request for [*text not declassified*] additional funding to strengthen the political coalition backing Barrientos in the upcoming election, with the stipulation that such requests would "be frowned upon" in the future. (Memorandum from Koren to Gordon, March 28; Department of State, INR/IL Historical Files, 303 Committee Special Files, January–June 1966). The CIA paper, February 26, proposing the extension of the political action program is ibid., c. March 28, 1966)

159. Letter From the Ambassador to Bolivia (Henderson) to the Assistant Secretary of State for Inter-American Affairs (Gordon)[1]

La Paz, May 31, 1966.

Dear Linc:

The short run Country Team objective in the domestic political field has been to foster the circumstances in which elections can be held. In this effort, we have held no brief for, and we have tried to avoid identification with any particular candidate.

The Armed Forces must eventually transfer power. This can be done by violence, or by elections.

The civilian political parties must eventually accept responsibility for governing the country, and for engaging in political activities, as contrasted with quasi-military activities. This can only come about by holding elections.

We have used our resources to further this objective of elections, both with the Junta, and with the leaders of the political parties (with the sole exception of the extreme left). We have encouraged the Junta to stand firm on the date of elections, once chosen; and have encouraged political leaders to take a positive attitude towards the elections.

Any slate of candidates for the Presidency must include Barrientos, both because he is willing to fight to be included, and because he has genuine popular support. He can be eliminated by physical violence, or by political chicanery, but as long as he lives, he will return to the fight. He could also lose at the polls, although at present writing this seems unlikely, but in that event, the new government would face a formidable opposition.

Since Barrientos is a necessary element to holding elections, *but not because he is our "chosen candidate"*, we have used some of our resources with him. He will not be an easy president to deal with, and his regime may not live out its term. Much will depend on his cabinet, and the degree of influence individual ministers are able to exercise. But if there are to be elections, he has to be there, and we have to deal with him.

Elections with Barrientos as the sole candidate, however, with the major traditional political parties abstaining, would increase the probabilities of post-election instability. The Falange would certainly abstain if their candidates were running only against Barrientos. We,

---

[1] Source: National Archives and Records Administration, RG 59, ARA Files: Lot 70 D 443, Def 19, Military Assistance, 1966. Secret; Official–Informal.

therefore, encouraged Andrade to take a chance (he didn't really need much persuasion) in order that the MNR (as still the major political force in the country, even though presently divided) would be represented at the polls. This has caused the Junta and the Armed Forces some serious doubts, since they regard the MNR, however represented, as their mortal enemy (shades of 1946 and 1952).

The Andrade candidacy, and some behind-the-scenes maneuvering, (and, modestly, our own conversations with Falange leaders) has now brought the Falange into the campaign. The conditions are therefore present for a (relatively) meaningful election.

Some flies, of course, remain in the ointment, this being Bolivia. If the Junta plays too many tricks on Andrade, he will either throw his support to a unified MNR, or be discredited. In either case, the hand of the more extreme elements of the MNR will be strengthened, and Bolivia will face a prolonged period of civil unrest.

It is one thing to win an election in Bolivia, it is quite another to govern this country. Any administration needs an organization with workers everywhere; a political philosophy responsive to popular demand however imperfectly expressed; and skill in the arts of government. The MNR, disregarding for the moment its present plight, could muster these elements. Barrientos' present political coalition can not, although he has personal charisma and political flair. The Falange has few assets in this respect, and would quickly polarize the political scene.

This means to me that after the election will come a period of political jockeying for new, more meaningful alignments. We hope that this jockeying will be in purely political terms, and that violence can be avoided. But uncertainty and a certain amount of boiling and bubbling cannot be avoided.

Finally, there is always the enigma of Ovando. We know very little certainly about him. We do know that he is unlikely to precipitate a showdown; that he is a master of devious maneuver; that he puts the unity of the Armed Forces above everything else; that he avoids imposing a decision (which has resulted in vacillation and indecision on many trying occasions); and that he has told us on a number of occasions that Barrientos must be a candidate for the Presidency, against moderate opponents, naming Andrade of the MNR and Romero of the Falange.

This leads us to conclude that Ovando now wants elections, with Barrientos winning. He could then retire with glory, to command a unified Armed Forces, free from the divisive threat of Barrientos, and thus control the only real unified force in the country. If Barrientos succeeds in governing the country for four years, he will have resolved at least some of the sticky problems which now confront the government, and

Ovando could easily succeed him. If Barrientos does not do what the Armed Forces thinks he should do, Ovando could remove him, although this would always be dangerous, both to the Armed Forces, and to the country.

If we are wrong, and Ovando intends to out-maneuver Barrientos, we will have little chance to anticipate his move. We have, therefore, been careful to keep a clear channel to Ovando, too.

I hope you concur, at least in major outline, in our strategy.[2] I would be pleased to have your comments.

Sincerely,

Doug

---

[2] In a June 3 memorandum to Morris commenting on Henderson's letter, Williams wrote that this strategy was approved months ago and confirmed more recently in a 303 Committee paper. He went on to indicate that he was "puzzled that at this late hour, thirty days before the elections in Bolivia, the Ambassador should ask Mr. Gordon if he approves a strategy which we have been pursuing for many months." (Ibid.)

---

160.   Memorandum From the President's Special Assistant (Rostow) to President Johnson[1]

Washington, July 1, 1966.

SUBJECT

Bolivian Elections

Bolivia holds a national election on Sunday.

It is *not* an interesting contest. The government candidate—General Rene Barrientos, who has headed the military junta for the past 18 months—is almost certain to win.[2] The opposition is weak and divided. As many as four of the six opposition parties may pull out of the race at the last minute. There may be some violence. The OAS is sending observers, which should provide some stability and help reduce the traditional electoral manipulations.

---

[1] Source: Johnson Library, National Security File, Country File, Bolivia, Vol. IV, Memoranda, January 1966–December 1968. Confidential.

[2] Results of the Bolivian election, in which Barrientos won handily, are reported in airgram CA–219 to all ARA posts except Caracas, July 8, 1966. (National Archives and Records Administration, RG 59, Central Files 1964–66, POL 14 BOL)

The best that can be said for the elections is that it will serve to put Bolivia back in the ranks of constitutional government—in form, if not in substance.

W. W. Rostow[3]

---

[3] Printed from a copy that bears this typed signature.

---

161. Memorandum Prepared for the 303 Committee[1]

Washington, July 15, 1966.

SUBJECT

Results of the Political Action Program for Bolivia[2]

REFERENCES

A. Memorandum for the 303 Committee Subject: "Provide Support to [*less than 1 line of source text not declassified*] and the Popular Christian Movement in Bolivia," dated 29 January 1965[3]
B. Memorandum for the 303 Committee Subject: "Expansion of Political Action Program in Bolivia," dated 13 July 1965[4]
C. Memorandum for the 303 Committee Subject: "Additional Financial Support for Political Action Program in Bolivia," dated 26 February 1966[5]

---

[1] Source: National Security Council, Files of the 303 Committee, Subject File, Bolivia. Secret; Eyes Only. A handwritten notation on this memorandum reads: "Distributed to members of 303 Committee for information on 21 July 1966. Not reflected in 303 Minutes."

[2] William V. Broe, chief of the Western Hemisphere Division of the Deputy Directorate of Plans, briefly summarized the covert action program for Bolivia in a July 15 memorandum to Helms: "With the election of Rene Barrientos as President of Bolivia on July 3, 1966 this action was brought to a successful completion." Broe continued, "in view of President-elect Barrientos' arrival in Washington next week, it might be appropriate to remind the Committee of [*less than 1 line of source text not declassified*] actions undertaken with Committee approval in Bolivia." (Department of State, INR/IL Historical Files, Bolivia, 1962–1980) A separate undated briefing memorandum on [*text not declassified*] support for Bolivian Presidential candidate Barrientos was forwarded by the CIA to Rostow on July 14 (Johnson Library, National Security File, Intelligence Files, Guerrilla Problems in Latin America) under cover of a memorandum from Broe to Jessup. (Ibid., National Security File, Memos to the President, Walt W. Rostow, Vol. VIII) On July 16 Rostow provided President Johnson a copy of this briefing memorandum, with the following note: "This is to explain why General Barrientos may say thank you when you have lunch with him next Wednesday, the 20th." (Ibid.)

[3] Document 153.

[4] Document 158.

[5] Not printed. (Department of State, INR/IL Historical Files, 303 Committee Files, c. 35, March 28) Also see footnote 4, Document 158.

1. Purpose of the Political Action Program

The referenced memoranda, the most recent of which was approved by the 303 Committee on 28 March 1966, concerned a political action program for Bolivia. The purpose of this [*less than 1 line of source text not declassified*] program was through covert means to ensure the orderly transfer of power via elections to a civilian, constitutional government whose policies would be compatible with those of the United States by:

(1) Providing covert financial assistance to the groups supporting the candidacy of General Barrientos.

(2) Providing covert financial encouragement to opposition groups who might otherwise abstain and endanger the legitimacy of the elections.

(3) [*3 lines of source text not declassified*]

2. Results of the Political Action Program

The objectives of this program have been accomplished. A new political party was built to provide the platform for General Barrientos. This base was reinforced by a coalition of already existing parties. Despite many internal stresses, this pro-Barrientos complex was held together during the crucial pre-electoral period by [*1½ lines of source text not declassified*] covert financial support. At the same time covert financial assistance was given to [*less than 1 line of source text not declassified*] a rival party to ensure its participation in the elections. In addition, a [*less than 1 line of source text not declassified*] subsidy payment was made to [*less than 1 line of source text not declassified*] a second important opposition party which was considering withdrawing from the electoral process. When these two most important opposition parties would not abstain from elections, three other groups made [*less than 1 line of source text not declassified*] entries into the race, with the result that the election contest took place between the Barrientos coalition and five opposition slates.

The combination of providing money and covert guidance to [*less than 1 line of source text not declassified*] contending parties changed the political climate from a volatile, conspiratorial atmosphere with little discussion of peaceful resolution through elections to a full fledged electoral atmosphere with the traditional violence and conspiracy thrust into the background.

While the very final count of the elections is not in at this writing, it can be said that General Barrientos has won by the impressive majority of about 60% of the vote in an election praised by OAS observers as democratic and honest. [*2 lines of source text not declassified*] The inauguration on 6 August 1966 will mean the end of 21 months of military rule and the beginning of what hopefully will be a four-year term of office for the desired civilian, constitutional government.

3. Prognosis

It is obvious that the recent election of this government is but the first step towards establishing political stability in Bolivia. Much depends on the political acumen of Barrientos himself, who is faced with the task of manipulating and maneuvering the many divergent political forces which now may be expected to turn their energies to toppling him. The military, suppressed since 1952 by the previous regime, has obtained another taste of power during the past 21 months, and although its announced intention is to withdraw from politics, this may be only temporary. The opposition parties will not want to depend on honest elections in 1970 and can be expected to begin the anti-government scheming which is endemic to Bolivian politics. The economic problems continue to be as serious and extensive as ever. In summary, while the above described political action program has returned Bolivia to a constitutional government headed by a popular president, the prognosis whether Barrientos can last out his term of office must be one of cautious optimism.

---

162. Memorandum of Conversation[1]

Washington, July 21, 1966, 5:30 p.m.

SUBJECT

Visit of General Rene Barrientos Ortuno, President-elect of the Republic of Bolivia.

---

[1] Source: National Archives and Records Administration, RG 59, Central Files 1964–66, POL 7 BOL. Confidential. Drafted by Patrick F. Morris (ARA/BC) and approved in S on July 27. The meeting was held in Rusk's office immediately following a meeting between Barrientos and Gordon that focused on the status of negotiations with the Export-Import Bank, the delay in U.S. disbursements for a loan for COMIBOL, and U.S. supplying Bolivia with helicopters under the MAP program. (Ibid.)

President-elect Barrientos visited Washington July 19–23, in a private capacity, primarily to address the International Platform Association, a public speaking group, on July 22. He had lunch with President Johnson at the White House on July 20 and according to the President's Daily Diary, there was an exchange of gifts, followed by luncheon in the State Dining Room at 1:50 p.m. (Johnson Library) No further record of discussions has been found. In telegram 7236 to La Paz, July 14, the Department had instructed the Embassy to inform Barrientos not to expect substantive discussions nor concessions during his trip. (National Archives and Records Administration, RG 59, Central Files 1964–66, POL 7 BOL)

PARTICIPANTS

> The Secretary
> Gen. Rene Barrientos Ortuno, Pres.-elect of Bolivia
> Jaime Berdecio, Minister of National Economy—Bolivia
> Julio Sanjines, Ambassador of Bolivia
> Lincoln Gordon, Assistant Secretary—ARA
> Douglas Henderson, Ambassador—La Paz
> Patrick F. Morris, Country Director—BC

The Secretary opened the meeting by congratulating the President-elect on his successful electoral campaign. He indicated that he and President Johnson had followed developments in Bolivia with a great deal of interest and were happy to see a return to a constitutional government in that country. He said that General Barrientos' election victory was impressive.

General Barrientos thanked the Secretary and said that Bolivia was a democratic country; that he had won the election but now he had to win at successfully governing his country. He said that Bolivia made common cause with the United States in upholding the democratic processes, improving economic conditions and in countering communism.

The Secretary asked the General what he considered his three most important problems. The General answered that the first was tin; Bolivia must increase its production and at the same time must receive adequate prices for the tin it sells. The second most important concern of his Government is transportation; Bolivia must construct a road network so as to integrate the national territory. The General and Ambassador Henderson described to the Secretary the road projects which were either under way or under consideration for United States assistance. General Barrientos said that the third area of importance was the connecting of Bolivia with outside world by better means of transport. He said that on his way to the United States he had stopped in Peru and talked to President Belaunde about the necessity for a road from the Peruvian port of Ilo to the Bolivian border near Lake Titicaca. He said the Peruvians have agreed to request assistance from the Inter-American Development Bank to construct this road. He said that this road was of primary importance for Bolivia.

The Secretary then asked about Bolivia's food production capacity. He wanted to know whether Bolivia was dependent upon large food imports or whether it was comparatively self sufficient. It was explained to the Secretary that a large segment of the indigenous population lived from subsistence agriculture with potatoes as a staple; that in recent years Bolivia had become self-sufficient in rice and sugar, but that it was a net importer of wheat and wheat products.

The Secretary then asked about educational problems. Ambassador Henderson explained that the United States Government was assisting the Bolivians in defining their educational needs through a contract with Ohio State University.

General Barrientos explained that there was a need for technical education especially in the agricultural sector since campesinos who were taught to read and write but who were not taught how to be better farmers usually became migrants to the cities. He said it was absolutely necessary to educate the campesino in practical agriculture so that they would stay on the land.

The Secretary asked about health problems and was informed that tuberculosis and silicosis were serious problems in the country especially in the high lands. The high incidence of tuberculosis was related to malnutrition. It was also explained that the anti-malaria campaign begun initially by the Rockefeller Foundation in 1949 has been very successful, continuing under the Bolivian Government with some assistance from the United States.

The Secretary asked General Barrientos about the kind of cabinet he thought he would have. The General answered that he hoped to have a competent cabinet composed of men dedicated to the solution of the nation's problems. He said he hoped to avoid choosing representatives of various political groups in order to satisfy partisan demands. He said that he realized that he would have problems with the political groups by doing this but that his main interest was in satisfying the people, not political parties.

The Secretary said that President Kennedy set an example by choosing people on the basis of their reputations. He said that he did not know personally practically anybody in his first cabinet except his brother Robert Kennedy who became Attorney General.

The Secretary then asked about Bolivia's relations with its neighbors. The General answered that Bolivia was on good terms with all of the neighboring countries with the exception of Chile. He said that there was a very deep feeling that Bolivia should have access to the sea.

The Secretary asked whether or not joint economic projects developing contiguous border areas might not be an indirect way of lessening tensions so that an eventual solution could be worked out.

Ambassador Henderson asked General Barrientos whether some kind of regional development wasn't the answer. General Barrientos responded that the northern part of Chile was very poor; that regional development projects would only improve the economic condition of that area and would make Chile more determined to keep it than it is now.

The Secretary said that accelerated economic growth in border areas have proved to be one way of lessening the possibility of border problems. He used the Saar region as a specific example.

General Barrientos said that he thought the Bolivian situation was different since Bolivia was seeking access to the sea.

Ambassador Sanjines then described a plan of providing Bolivia with a port within an enclave of ten square kilometers between the present cities of Tacna and Arica. He said he did not believe that there was need for a corridor from Bolivia to the sea, if Bolivia could have a port on the ocean which was duly recognized as Bolivian territory, this would be sufficient. He said with air transport becoming more and more important such an enclave was sensible since one would be able to take off from La Paz and land on Bolivian territory on the Pacific Ocean.

The Secretary suggested that such a port might be multi-national or perhaps an Alliance for Progress port.

The Bolivian Ambassador insisted that the only way that Bolivia would be interested was if the Bolivian flag would fly over the territory.

The Secretary concluded the meeting by emphasizing President Johnson's dedication to the Alliance for Progress and his specific interests in agriculture, education and health. He said that the President had a passion for performance; that he was interested not in just words but deeds. He wanted to see concrete accomplishments under the Alliance as the result of United States assistance as well as the result of the efforts of the various countries themselves.

---

163. Editorial Note

On March 16, 1967, the Embassy in La Paz reported that President Barrientos had personally informed Ambassador Henderson that two guerrilla suspects had been detained by Bolivian authorities and, upon interrogation, had admitted association with a group of 30 to 40 guerrillas "led by Castroite Cubans" and other foreigners. The suspects reportedly mentioned that Che Guevara was leader of the guerrilla group, but they had not seen him. Barrientos urgently requested U.S. communications equipment to enable the Bolivian Government to locate reported guerrilla radio transmitters. Henderson made no commitments beyond a promise to look into what the United States could do. (Telegram 2314 from La Paz, March 16; National Archives and Records Administration, RG 59, Central Files 1967–69, POL 23–9 BOL)

A year earlier there were intelligence reports that Che Guevara was in South America, but U.S. analysts found little supporting evidence. In a March 4, 1966, memorandum concerning rumors of Guevara's presence in Colombia, FitzGerald noted that "penetrations of insurgent groups had revealed no indication of Guevara's presence in any of these groups." (Central Intelligence Agency, DDO/IMS, Operational Group, Job 78–5505, Area Activity—Cuba) Further analysis by the Agency identified seven conflicting rumors of Guevara's whereabouts. A March 23, 1966, memorandum prepared in the Western Hemisphere Division noted that Guevara's usefulness had been reduced to his ability as a guerrilla, and that "with his myth he is ten feet tall; without it, he is a mortal of normal stature." Under the circumstances, the Agency concluded:

"... it is not believed justifiable to divert considerable amounts of time, money and manpower to an effort to locate Guevara. It is considered far more important to use these assets to penetrate and monitor Communist subversive efforts wherever they may occur, since Guevara's presence in an area will not affect greatly the outcome of any given insurgent effort." (Ibid.)

On March 24, 1967, the Embassy in La Paz reported that Barrientos met with the Deputy Chief of Mission on March 23 to advise him that the guerrilla situation had worsened and that this deterioration caused him increasing concern. Barrientos believed the guerrilla activity was "part of a large subversive movement led by Cuban and other foreigners." He pointed out that Bolivian troops in the area of guerrilla activity were "green and ill-equipped," and reiterated his urgent request for U.S. assistance. The Embassy told Barrientos that "our military officers were working with the Bolivian military to ascertain facts relating to requirements." (Telegram 2381 from La Paz, March 24; National Archives and Records Administration, RG 59, Central Files 1967–69, POL 23–9 BOL) Two U.S. military assistance advisory group officers reported that on March 23 guerrillas had ambushed a 22-man Bolivian Army patrol near Nancuahazu, prompting the Embassy to report to the Department on March 27: "There is now sufficient accumulation of information to bring Country Team to accept as fact that there is guerrilla activity in area previously mentioned, that it could constitute potential security threat to GOB." (Telegram 2384 from La Paz, March 27; ibid.)

In a 90-minute meeting with Ambassador Henderson on March 27, Barrientos appealed for direct U.S. budgetary support for the Bolivian armed forces to meet the "emergency and one in which Bolivia was 'helping to fight for the U.S.'" In reporting this discussion to the Department, Henderson observed:

"I suspect that Barrientos is beginning to suffer some genuine anguish over the sad spectacle offered by the poor performance of his armed forces in this episode; i.e., an impetuous foray into reported guerrilla country, apparently based on a fragment of intelligence and resulting in a minor disaster, which further tended to panic the GOB into a lather of ill-coordinated activity, with less than adequate professional planning and logistical support." Henderson continued, "pressed by his military he may seek resort to the lobbying talents of Ambassador Sanjines in Washington in an effort to end-run proper channels of communication with U.S. authorities." (Telegram 2405 from La Paz, March 29; ibid.)

On March 29, the CIA reported that two guerrillas captured by the Bolivian Army had furnished information that the guerrilla movement "is an independent, international operation under Cuban direction and is not affiliated with any Bolivian political party. The Agency had received information about the development of other guerrilla groups in Bolivia. "Should these other groups decide to go into action at this time, the Bolivian Government would be sorely taxed to cope with them" in addition to the Cuban-backed group. (Memorandum from [*name not declassified*] to the Chief, Western Hemisphere Division, March 29; Central Intelligence Agency, DDO/IMS, Job 88–01415R, [*file name not declassified*])

On March 31, the Department responded to Henderson's concerns: "We have no evidence 'end runs' being attempted here." The Department instructed the Embassy in La Paz:

"You may at your discretion inform Barrientos that we most reluctant consider supporting significantly enlarged army, either thru provision additional material or thru renewal budget support. We fully support concept of providing limited amounts of essential material assist carefully orchestrated response to threat, utilizing to maximum extent possible best trained and equipped troops available. Should threat definitely prove greater than capacity present forces, Barrientos can be assured U.S. willingness consider further assistance." (Telegram 166701 to La Paz, March 31; National Archives and Records Administration, RG 59, Central Files 1967–69, POL 23–9 BOL)

Also on March 31, the Department informed U.S. posts in neighboring countries to Bolivia that the current plan "is to block guerrilla escape then bring in, train and prepare ranger-type unit to eliminate guerrillas." The Department also indicated that the United States was considering a special military training team (MTT) "for accelerated training counter guerrilla force." (Telegram 16641 to Buenos Aires, et al., March 31; ibid.)

On May 11 Rostow reported to President Johnson that "CIA has received the *first credible report that 'Che' Guevara is alive* and operating in South America." The information had come from interrogation of guerrillas captured in Bolivia. "We need more evidence before concluding that Guevara is operational—and not dead, as the intelligence community, with the passage of time, has been more and more inclined to believe." (Memorandum from Rostow to Johnson, May 11; Johnson Library, National Security File, Country File, Bolivia, Vol. IV, Memoranda,

January 1966–December 1968) According to the CIA report, May 10, Che Guevara told [*text not declassified*] that he had come to Bolivia "in order to begin a guerrilla movement that would spread to the other parts of Latin America." (CIA Information Cable TDCS 314/06486–67; ibid.)

---

164.   Memorandum From the President's Special Assistant (Rostow) to President Johnson[1]

Washington, June 23, 1967.

Mr. President:

This is what is going on with guerrillas in Bolivia:

Last March 24 Bolivian security forces were ambushed in a remote area of southeastern Bolivia as they were investigating reports of a guerrilla training camp. Since then 6 other skirmishes have been fought. The Bolivian forces have come off poorly in these engagements, losing 28 of their men to 2 or 3 known rebels killed.

Interrogation of several deserters and prisoners, including a young French communist—Jules Debray—closely associated with Fidel Castro and suspected of serving as a Cuban courier, strongly suggests that the guerrillas are Cuban-sponsored, although this is hard to document. There is some evidence that "Che" Guevara *may* have been with the group. Debray reports seeing him. A highly sensitive source [*less than 1 line of source text not declassified*] reports a recent statement by Brezhnev that Guevara is in Latin America "making his revolutions".[2]

Estimates of the strength of the guerrillas range from 50 to 60 men. It appears that they were flushed out while still in a preliminary training phase and before they intended to open operations. Despite this,

---

[1] Source: Johnson Library, National Security File, Country File, Bolivia, Vol. IV, Memoranda, January 1966–December 1968. Secret; Sensitive. The memorandum indicates President Johnson saw it.

[2] In a June 4 cable to President Johnson, Rostow noted that "CIA believes that 'Che' Guevara has been with this group." He also indicated that "we have put Bolivia on top of the list more because of the fragility of the political situation and the weakness of the armed forces than the size and effectiveness of the guerrilla movement." (Ibid., Latin America, Vol. VI, June–September 1967) The CIA received information, reportedly based on a document written and signed by Che Guevara, in which the revolutionary stated that "revolt started in Bolivia because wide-spread discontent there and disorganization army." ([*text not declassified*] Central Intelligence Agency, DDO/IMS Files, [*file name not declassified*])

they have so far clearly out-classed the Bolivian security forces. The performance of the government units has revealed a serious lack of command coordination, officer leadership and troop training and discipline.

Soon after the presence of guerrillas had been established, we sent a special team and some equipment to help organize another Ranger-type Battalion. On the military side, we are helping about as fast as the Bolivians are able to absorb our assistance. The diversion of scarce resources to the Armed Forces could lead to budgetary problems, and our financial assistance may be needed later this year.

The outlook is not clear. The guerrillas were discovered early before they were able to consolidate and take the offensive. The pursuit by the government forces, while not very effective, does keep them on the run. These are two pluses.

At their present strength the guerrillas do not appear to pose an immediate threat to Barrientos. If their forces were to be quickly augmented and they were able to open new fronts in the near future, as now rumored, the thin Bolivian armed forces would be hard-pressed and the fragile political situation would be threatened. The hope is that with our help Bolivian security capabilities will out-distance guerrilla capabilities and eventually clear them out.

State, DOD, and CIA are following developments closely.[3] As I mentioned, Defense is training and equipping additional forces. CIA has increased its operations.

The Argentines and Brazilians are also watching this one. Argentina is the only other country with a military mission in La Paz. Close military ties between Argentina and Bolivia are traditional. The Argentines have also furnished military supplies to the Bolivians.

W. W. Rostow[4]

---

[3] A June 14 memorandum prepared by the CIA focused on Cuban sponsorship of the Bolivian guerrillas and the failure of the Bolivian Government to meet the insurgency threat. (Johnson Library, National Security File, Intelligence File, Guerrilla Problem in Latin America)

[4] Printed from a copy that bears this typed signature.

165.   Memorandum of Conversation[1]

Washington, June 29, 1967.

PARTICIPANTS

Ambassador of Bolivia
Julio Sanjines-Goytia

Mr. William G. Bowdler

At the invitation of the Bolivian Ambassador, I went to his residence this afternoon to discuss the Bolivian situation.

Most of the one-hour conversation was a monologue by the loquacious Ambassador describing the background to the Barrientos administration and the present political situation. Toward the end of the conversation, he got around to the two points he had on his mind.

The first was increased external assistance. I asked him what specifically he had in mind. He replied that he was not thinking of budgetary support since Bolivia had passed that stage and was proud of its accomplishment. I then asked him what type of project assistance he had in mind. On this he was very vague, saying that we should send a special mission from Washington to study what additional projects might be started to further Bolivia's development.

The question in which he was most interested—and obviously the main purpose for the invitation—was to ask for our help in establishing what he called a "hunter-killer" team to ferret out guerrillas. He said this idea was not original with him, but came from friends of his in CIA. I asked him whether the Ranger Battalion now in training were not sufficient. He said that what he has in mind is 50 to 60 young army officers, with sufficient intelligence, motivation and drive, who could be trained quickly and could be counted on to search out the guerrillas with tenacity and courage. I asked him whether such an elite group would not cause problems within the army and perhaps even political problems between Barrientos and his supporters. The Ambassador said that these problems could be minimized by rotating a fixed number of the team back into the army at regular intervals. The rotation system would have the added benefit of bringing a higher degree of professionalism into the officer ranks of the army. I told him that his idea may have merit, but needs further careful examination.

---

[1] Source: Johnson Library, National Security File, Country File, Bolivia, Vol. IV, Memoranda, January 1966–December 1968. Secret. Prepared by Bowdler. Copies provided to Rostow and Sayre.

Before leaving, I told him that I had seen reports that Bolivia might be considering declaring a state of war against Cuba. I asked him whether he had any information to substantiate these reports. He expressed complete surprise and strong opposition, pointing out that such action would expose Bolivia to international ridicule. He speculated that these reports might have been planted by Cuban exiles. He said that some Cubans had approached him along this line and there may well be Cuban exiles in Bolivia who are doing likewise with other Bolivian officials. I told him that I also thought that this action would be a serious mistake not only because of the light in which it would cast Bolivia, but also because of the serious legal and practical problems which would arise from being in a state of war with Cuba.

Upon departing, he said he appreciated having the opportunity to talk frankly with me and expressed the desire to exchange views on his country from time to time. I told him I would be happy to do this whenever he thought it useful.

WGB

166. Editorial Note

In a July 5, 1967, memorandum to Special Assistant Walt Rostow, William Bowdler of the National Security Council Staff summarized the current U.S. military training role in Bolivia: "DOD is helping train and equip a new Ranger Battalion. The Bolivian absorption capacity being what it is, additional military assistance would not now seem advisable. [3 lines of source text not declassified]" Bowdler recommended that "a variable of the Special Strike Force acceptable to the Country Team be established. It might be part of the new Ranger Battalion." (Johnson Library, National Security File, Intelligence File, Guerrilla Problem in Latin America) The Country Team objections were transmitted in telegram 2291 from La Paz, May 24. The team stated that a strike force would be viewed by the Bolivians as a "magical solution" and a "substitute for hard work and needed reform." (National Archives and Records Administration, RG 59, Central Files 1967–69, POL 23 BOL)

At 4:30 p.m. on July 5 Rostow, Bowdler, and Peter Jessup met in the Situation Room of the White House with representatives of the Department of State including Assistant Secretary of State Covey Oliver, Deputy Assistant Secretary Robert Sayre, and Ambassador Henderson, with William Lang of the Department of Defense, and Desmond FitzGerald and William Broe of the Central Intelligence Agency. The group agreed that a special strike force was not advisable because of the Embassy's objections. They decided that the United States should "concentrate on the training of the Second Ranger Battalion with the preparation of an intelligence unit to be part of the Battalion." They also agreed to look into expansion of the rural police program, prepare contingency plans to cover the possibility of the insurgency getting beyond the control of Barrientos and the Bolivian armed forces, and suggested that Barrientos might need $2–5 million in grant or supporting assistance in the next 2 months to meet budgetary problems resulting from the security situation. (Memorandum of meeting; Johnson Library, National Security File, Country File, Latin America, Vol. VI, June 1967–September 1967) The gist of these decisions was relayed to the President in the context of a broader policy for counterinsurgency in Latin America; see Document 61.

U.S. efforts to support the counterinsurgency program in Bolivia against Cuban-led guerrillas followed a two-step approach. To help overcome the deficiencies of the Bolivian Army, a 16-man military training team of the U.S. Special Forces was sent to Bolivia to support the Bolivian Second Ranger Battalion in the development of anti-guerrilla tactics and techniques. The United States also provided ammunition, rations, and communications equipment on an emergency basis under MAP and expedited delivery of four helicopters. (Paper by W.D. Broderick, July 11; National Archives and Records Administration, RG 59, ARA Files: Lot 70 D 443, POL 23–4, 1967, IRG Counter-Insurgency Subgroup) A July 3 memorandum prepared by the CIA reads: "Although original estimates were that the battalion would not be combat ready until approximately December 1967, the MILGROUP now believes that this date can be advanced to mid-September 1967." (Central Intelligence Agency, Job 88–01415R, DDO/IMS, [file name not declassified])

As the training of the Ranger battalion progressed, weaknesses in its intelligence-collecting capability emerged. The CIA was formally given responsibility for developing a plan to provide such a capability on July 14. (ARG/ARA/COIN Action Memo #1, July 20; National Archives and Records Administration, RG 59, ARA Files: Lot 70 D 122, IRG/ARA/COIN Action Memos) The planned operation was approved by the Department of State, CINCSO, the U.S. Ambassador in La Paz, Bolivian President Barrientos and Commander-in-Chief of the Bolivian Armed Forces Ovando. A team of two instructors arrived in La Paz on August 2. In addition to training the Bolivians in intelligence-collection techniques, the instructors—[text not declassified]—planned to accompany the Second Ranger battalion into the field. Although the team was assigned in an advisory capacity, CIA "expected that they will actually help in directing operations." The Agency also contemplated this plan "as a pilot program for probable duplication in other Latin American countries faced with the problem of guerrilla warfare." (Memorandum for the Acting Chief, Western Hemisphere Division, August 22; ibid.)

167.   Memorandum From the President's Special Assistant (Rostow) to President Johnson[1]

Washington, September 5, 1967, 3:30 p.m.

SUBJECT

Insurgency in Bolivia

During the past few days there have been two significant developments in Bolivia's efforts to deal with communist guerrillas:

1. Bolivian security forces have discovered caches of documents belonging to the guerrillas. These include passports, identity cards, codes and photographs. The documents have been turned over to us for analysis.[2] A preliminary reading from CIA shows rather conclusively that "Che" Guevara travelled to Bolivia via Spain and Brazil in late 1966 using false documents.[3] The other passports and ID cards are expected to give the identity of additional Cubans active in the Bolivian guerrilla movement. I will send you the CIA report as soon as received.

2. After a series of defeats at the hands of the guerrillas, the Bolivian armed forces on August 30 finally scored their first victory—and it seems to have been a big one. An army unit caught up with the rearguard of the guerrillas and killed 10 and captured one, as against one soldier killed. Two of the dead guerrillas are Bolivians and the rest either Cubans or Argentines. CIA believes that several of the captured false passports they are now analyzing may have been used by the Cubans to get to Bolivia.

The Bolivians want to use the information on "Che" Guevara in the trial of Regis Debray, a young French Marxist intellectual, who is close to Fidel Castro and strongly suspected of being on a courier mission when he was caught in guerrilla territory in Bolivia last April. It is not in our interest, or the Bolivians', to have the U.S. appear as the sole authenticating agent for the documents. Tomorrow in the 303 Committee we will consider how best to handle the authenticating aspect.

The victory of the Bolivian army over the guerrillas should do much to bolster the morale and determination of the Bolivian troops

---

[1] Source: Johnson Library, National Security File, Country File, Bolivia, Vol. IV, Memoranda, January 1966–December 1968. Secret. The memorandum indicates the President saw it.

[2] As reported in telegram 408 from La Paz, August 25. (National Archives and Records Administration, RG 59, Central Files 1967–69, POL 23–7 BOL)

[3] This information was based on an early CIA assessment of the documents captured by Bolivian anti-guerrilla forces in late August. ([text not declassified] Central Intelligence Agency, DDO/IMS Files, [file name not declassified])

and their officers. The second Bolivian Ranger battalion which we have been training since June will give them added capability to pursue the guerrillas. The new unit will go into operation late this month.

Walt

---

168.   Memorandum From the President's Special Assistant
(Rostow) to President Johnson[1]

Washington, September 6, 1967, 1:30 p.m.

SUBJECT

Documents Relating to Cuban Intervention Captured in Bolivia

CIA's interim technical report on the guerrilla documents found by Bolivian security forces in early August, 1967 is attached.[2]

The report focuses on the evidence pertaining to "Che" Guevara. The other material is still being analyzed. The documentation on Guevara—two passports, identity cards, health certificates and snapshots—show the following:

—the two passports bearing different names carry the same photograph and fingerprints.

—the fingerprints are identical to examples of prints of Guevara furnished to CIA [*less than 1 line of source text not declassified*] in 1954 and [*less than 1 line of source text not declassified*] in 1965.

—a CIA photo comparison analyst is of the opinion that the photographs are "most probably" photographs of Guevara in disguise.

—the passports show that Guevara most likely travelled legally from Madrid to Sao Paulo, Brazil at the end of October, 1966, and from there to La Paz on November 3, although the documents do not indicate arrival in La Paz.

—certain snapshots of what looks like Guevara in the jungle give no evidence of a montage.

---

[1] Source: Johnson Library, National Security File, Country File, Bolivia, Vol. IV, Memoranda, January 1966–December 1968. Secret. The memorandum indicates the President saw it.

[2] Not attached. The undated report was a preliminary technical analysis of the documentation and other material found in five caches in various parts of Bolivia in early August. The material included 21 different passports, 5 Bolivian internal documents, photographs, notebooks, maps, and 7 reels of magnetic recording tape. The report contained an inventory of the materials. (Department of State, INR/IL Historical Files, 303 Committee Files, c. 58, September 8, 1967)

These findings lead to a strong presumption that Guevara arrived in Bolivia last November, but they are still short of conclusive proof. The CIA report does not draw conclusions at this stage.

In furnishing us the documents, the Bolivians asked that we give them the results of our analysis so they could use the information in the impending trial of Regis Debray—the young French Marxist intellectual who is known to be close to Fidel Castro. He was arrested in Bolivian guerrilla territory last April after having entered the country clandestinely.

We do not want to become this closely involved with the Debray trial, which has already become a cause celebre in France. The nature of the evidence is such that it can be attacked as fabrication. Exclusive US analysis will add credibility to the almost inevitable charge that CIA planted the material. Debray, echoed by the French press and the Communist propaganda mill, is already claiming CIA and FBI involvement.[3]

To get around these problems, the 303 Committee has decided that we should tell the Bolivians to surface the documents and request the assistance of several governments in analyzing them. This could include Argentina where Guevara was born, Peru, Guatemala and Mexico where he resided; Uruguay, whose passport he used; and Brazil through which he travelled enroute to Bolivia. We would, of course, also cooperate. By broadening the analysis base, we narrow our exposure and enhance credibility of the evidence.[4]

Walt

---

[3] In an August 24 memorandum to Oliver, James R. Gardner (INR/DDC) had urged that the Department be prepared to address charges by Debray of CIA involvement: "Normally the Department and CIA have taken the line that we should neither confirm nor deny charges about CIA activities even though in some cases the temptation to deny is strong. (The Secretary has asked, incidentally, that in no case should such a denial be made without consulting him if there is any chance whatever that such a denial might later be exposed as false or misleading.)" (Ibid., Bolivia, 1962–1980) INR was aware "that CIA agents have participated in some of the Debray debriefings." (Memorandum from Gregory B. Wolfe (INR/RAR) to Hughes, August 23; ibid.)

[4] The 303 Committee decided this on September 8. (Minutes of September 8 meeting of the 303 Committee, September 12; ibid., 303 Committee Files, c. 58, 9/8/67)

169. National Intelligence Estimate[1]

NIE 92–67   Washington, September 14, 1967.

THE SITUATION IN BOLIVIA

The Problem

To estimate the situation in Bolivia and the probable impact of the present insurgency on it, over the next year or so.

Conclusions

A. The present insurgency in Bolivia is organized and supported by Cuba. Its seriousness lies in the possibility that the insurgents may eventually provide a rallying point for many disaffected elements which hitherto have been unable to coalesce. The threat posed is more a function of the inherent fragility of Bolivia's political, economic, and social structure than of the insurgents' own strength and capabilities.

B. Over the next year or so, there is little chance that the insurgents will be able to bring about the overthrow of the Barrientos regime, but it is also unlikely that the regime will be able to stamp out the insurgency.

C. A prolongation and expansion of the insurgency would impose severe financial and psychological strains on Bolivia, greatly hindering the economic development and social amelioration that are essential to the achievement of stability in that country. Defense costs for a protracted guerrilla war would add heavily to the already serious deficit in the national budget, would further limit public investment, and would threaten the government's stabilization program. In these circumstances, Barrientos would become increasingly dependent on US aid. Although eager to obtain technical and material military aid, he would be extremely reluctant to sanction a military intervention in force by the already concerned neighboring states or by the OAS.

D. If the government's counterguerrilla operations are protracted and unsuccessful, that would encourage other disaffected elements to undertake more active opposition to the government. It would also seriously damage the morale of the military. In these circumstances, the tenure of the Barrientos regime would become precarious.

[Omitted here is the Discussion section of the estimate.]

---

[1] Source: Central Intelligence Agency, Job 79–R01012A, O/DDI Registry. Secret; Controlled Dissem. According to a note on the cover sheet this estimate was prepared in the Central Intelligence Agency with the participation of the intelligence organizations of the Departments of State and Defense and the National Security Agency. The United States Intelligence Board concurred in this estimate on September 14.

170.   Editorial Note

A significant counterinsurgency program was a key element of U.S. foreign policy toward Bolivia. The United States undertook in 1967 to help train and equip a Bolivian Ranger battalion as part of Bolivia's counterinsurgency program aimed at Cuban-led guerrilla forces. In addition to military training and advice provided by a Green Beret team, the interagency Regional Group for Inter-American Affairs, which viewed the Bolivian program as a pilot program for other Latin American countries faced by guerrilla insurrections, approved in July 1967 the assignment of a team to provide intelligence and technical support to the battalion. The Bolivian Ranger battalion tracked down the guerrillas in October 1967. CIA contract personnel assigned to the Bolivian battalion as advisors unsuccessfully attempted to prevent the execution of Cuban leader Ernesto "Che" Guevara by the Bolivian military. These advisors provided on-scene reports of the execution to Washington. After Guevara's death and the end of the danger from Cuban-led insurgency, U.S. officials responsible for coordinating covert activities took note of these actions in Bolivia as evidence of the excellent U.S.-Bolivian cooperation which supported efforts to acquire detailed intelligence on Cuban-sponsored insurgency throughout Latin America.

171.   Memorandum From Director of Central Intelligence Helms[1]

Washington, October 11, 1967.

MEMORANDUM FOR

The Secretary of State
The Secretary of Defense
Mr. Walt W. Rostow
Assistant Secretary of State for Inter-American Affairs

SUBJECT

Capture and Execution of Ernesto "Che" Guevara

---

[1] Source: Johnson Library, National Security File, Country File, Bolivia, Vol. IV, Memoranda, January 1966–December 1968. Secret. A copy of the memorandum in CIA files indicates it was drafted by W.V. Broe and [name not declassified] in the Western Hemisphere Division and approved by Thomas H. Karamessines, Deputy Director for Plans. (Central Intelligence Agency, DDO/IMS, Operational Group, Job 78–06423A, U.S. Government—President)

1. You are aware of the published accounts concerning the death of Ernesto "Che" Guevara which were based in essence on the Bolivian Army press conference on 10 October attributing Guevara's death to battle wounds sustained in the clash between the Army and the guerrillas on 8 October 1967.[2] Guevara was said to be in a coma when captured and to have died shortly thereafter, the heat of battle having prevented early or effective treatment by Bolivian soldiers.

2. [1 line of source text not declassified] contrary information from [less than 1 line of source text not declassified] the Bolivian Second Ranger Battalion, the army unit that captured Guevara. According to [less than 1 line of source text not declassified] Guevara was captured on 8 October as a result of the clash with the Cuban-led guerrillas. He had a wound in his leg, but was otherwise in fair condition.[3] He was questioned but refused to give any information. Two Bolivian guerrillas, "Willy" and "Aniceto," were also captured.

3. At 1150 hours on 9 October the Second Ranger Battalion received direct orders from Bolivian Army Headquarters in La Paz to kill Guevara. These orders were carried out at 1315 hours the same day with a burst of fire from an M–2 automatic rifle.[4] [less than 1 line of source text not declassified] was an eye witness to Guevara's capture and execution.

Richard Helms[5]

---

[2] On October 9 Rostow informed President Johnson the "tentative information" that the Bolivian unit trained by the U.S. "got Che Guevara," but that information was inconclusive and based primarily on press reports from Bolivia. (Johnson Library, National Security File, Country File, Bolivia, Vol. IV, Memoranda, January 1966–December 1968)

[3] According to the text of a message sent by [text not declassified] on the scene, Guevara's fate would be decided on October 9 by the highest Bolivian military authorities. "I am managing to keep him alive," he reported, "which is very hard." ([telegram number not declassified]; Central Intelligence Agency, DDO/IMS Files, [file name not declassified])

[4] In an October 11 memorandum informing President Johnson of the killing of Che Guevara, Rostow remarked: "I regard this as stupid, but it is understandable from a Bolivian standpoint, given the problems which the sparing of French Communist and Castro courier Regis Debray has caused them." Rostow pointed out that the death of Che Guevara would have a strong impact in discouraging further guerrilla activity in Latin America. He also noted: "It shows the soundness of our 'preventive medicine' assistance to countries facing incipient insurgency—it was the Bolivian 2nd Ranger Battalion, trained by our Green Berets from June–September of this year, that cornered and got him." (Johnson Library, National Security File, Country File, Bolivia, Vol. IV, Memorandum, January 1966–December 1968) On October 13 Rostow informed Johnson of confirmation that Che Guevara was dead. (Ibid.)

[5] Printed from a copy that indicates Helms signed the original.

172.   Memorandum From Director of Central Intelligence Helms[1]

Washington, October 13, 1967.

MEMORANDUM FOR

   The Secretary of State
   The Secretary of Defense
   Mr. Walt W. Rostow
   Assistant Secretary of State for Inter-American Affairs

SUBJECT

   Statements by Ernesto "Che" Guevara Prior to His Execution in Bolivia

1. Further details have now been obtained from [*less than 1 line of source text not declassified*] who was on the scene in the small village of Higueras where Ernesto "Che" Guevara was taken after his capture on 8 October 1967 by the Bolivian Army's Second Ranger Battalion.[2]

2. [*less than 1 line of source text not declassified*] attempted to interrogate Guevara on 9 October 1967 as soon as he got access to him at around 7 a.m. At that time "Che" Guevara was sitting on the floor in the corner of a small, dark schoolroom in Higueras. He had his hands over his face. His wrists and feet were tied. In front of him on the floor lay the corpses of two Cuban guerrillas. Guevara had a flesh wound in his leg, which was bandaged.

3. Guevara refused to be interrogated but permitted himself to be drawn into a conversation with [*less than 1 line of source text not declassified*] during which he made the following comments:

   a. *Cuban economic situation:* Hunger in Cuba is the result of pressure by United States imperialism. Now Cuba has become self-sufficient in meat production and has almost reached the point where it will begin to export meat. Cuba is the only economically self-sufficient country in the Socialist world.

   b. *Camilo Cienfuegos:* For many years the story has circulated that Fidel Castro Ruz had Cienfuegos, one of his foremost deputies, killed because his personal popularity presented a danger to Castro. Actually the death of Cienfuegos was an accident. Cienfuegos has been in

---

[1] Source: Johnson Library, National Security File, Country File, Bolivia, Vol. IV, Memoranda, January 1966–December 1968. Secret. Copies of this memorandum in CIA files indicate that it was drafted by Broe and [*name not declassified*] in the Western Hemisphere Division and approved by Karamessines. (Central Intelligence Agency, DDO/IMS, Operational Group, Job 78–06423A, U.S. Government—President)

[2] A full account of the capture and death of Che Guevara is in CIA Intelligence Information Cable [*telegram number not declassified*], October 12. (Central Intelligence Agency, DDO/IMS Files, [*file name not declassified*])

Oriente Province when he received a call to attend a general staff meeting in Havana. He left by plane and the theory was that the plane became lost in low-ceiling flying conditions, consumed all of its fuel, and crashed in the ocean, and no trace of him was ever found. Castro had loved Cienfuegos more than any of his lieutenants.

c. *Fidel Castro Ruz:* Castro had not been a Communist prior to the success of the Cuban Revolution. Castro's own statements on the subject are correct.

d. *The Congo:* American imperialism had not been the reason for his failure there but, rather, the Belgian mercenaries. He denied ever having several thousand troops in the Congo, as sometimes reported, but admitted having had "quite a few".

e. *Treatment of Guerrilla Prisoners in Cuba:* During the course of the Cuban Revolution and its aftermath, there had been only about 1,500 individuals killed, exclusive of armed encounters such as the Bay of Pigs. The Cuban Government, of course, executed all guerrilla leaders who invaded its territory. . . . (He stopped then with a quizzical look on his face and smiled as he recognized his own position on Bolivian soil.)

f. *Future of the Guerrilla Movement in Bolivia:* With his capture, the guerrilla movement had suffered an overwhelming setback in Bolivia, but he predicted a resurgence in the future. He insisted that his ideals would win in the end even though he was disappointed at the lack of response from the Bolivian campesinos. The guerrilla movement had failed partially because of Bolivian Government propaganda which claimed that the guerrillas represented a foreign invasion of Bolivian soil. In spite of the lack of popular response from the Bolivian campesinos, he had not planned an exfiltration route from Bolivia in case of failure. He had definitely decided to either fall or win in this effort.

4. According to [*less than 1 line of source text not declassified*] when Guevara, Simon Cuba, and Aniceto Reynaga Gordillo were captured on 8 October, the Bolivian Armed Forces Headquarters ordered that they be kept alive for a time. A telegraphic code was arranged between La Paz and Higueras with the numbers 500 representing Guevara, 600 meaning the phrase "keep alive" and 700 representing "execute". During the course of the discussion with Guevara, Simon Cuba and Aniceto Reynaga were detained in the next room of the school house. At one stage, a burst of shots was heard and [*less than 1 line of source text not declassified*] learned later that Simon Cuba had been executed. A little later a single shot was heard and it was learned afterward that Aniceto Reynaga had been killed. When the order came at 11:50 a.m. from La Paz to kill Guevara, the execution was delayed as long as possible. However, when the local commander was advised that a helicopter

would arrive to recover the bodies at approximately 1:30 p.m., Guevara was executed with a burst of shots at 1:15 p.m. Guevara's last words were, "Tell my wife to remarry and tell Fidel Castro that the Revolution will again rise in the Americas." To his executioner he said, "Remember, you are killing a man."[3]

5. At no time during the period he was under [*less than 1 line of source text not declassified*] observation did Guevara lose his composure.

Dick[4]

---

[3] The [*text not declassified*] on site, reporting on Guevara's execution, indicated that "it was impossible keep him alive." ([*telegram number not declassified*] October 10; ibid., [*file name not declassified*])

[4] Printed from a copy that indicates Helms signed the original.

---

173. Memorandum From the President's Special Assistant (Rostow) to President Johnson[1]

Washington, October 14, 1967, 12:30 p.m.

SUBJECT

"Che" Guevara

Attached is a memorandum from Dick Helms describing the detention and execution of "Che" Guevara.[2]

CIA has also obtained [*less than 1 line of source text not declassified*] messages sent from Havana to "Che" in January and February 1967 showing that the Bolivian guerrilla movement was a Cuban show designed to spark a movement of "continental magnitude".[3] Several high ranking members of the Bolivian Communist Party were called to Havana to convince them that it would be an error to present the Bolivian operation as a national movement. These messages also indicate

---

[1] Source: Johnson Library, National Security File, Country File, Bolivia, Vol. IV, Memoranda, January 1966–December 1968. Secret; Sensitive; Eyes Only. The memorandum indicates Johnson saw it.

[2] Document 172.

[3] According to information provided to the CIA, Che Guevara stated that the ultimate purpose of the insurgency in Bolivia was to "create a Viet Nam out of South America." ([*telegram number not declassified*] Central Intelligence Agency, DDO/IMS Files, [*file name not declassified*])

that the French pro-Castro communist theoretician Jules Debray was sent to Bolivia to contact "Che" Guevara in late February. He was arrested in March.

[less than 1 line of source text not declassified] we gather that Cuban officials accept the fact that "Che" is dead and may be trying to recover the body. The communist-leaning President of the Chilean Senate, Salvador Allende, has sent a message to President Barrientos asking for the remains. This request, and one by the family,—"Che's" brother went to Bolivia to claim the body—probably led Barrientos to make the announcement that "Che" had been cremated. The Bolivians do not want an independent autopsy to show that they executed "Che" and they are intent on not permitting the remains to be exploited by the communist movement.

The death of "Che" and Debray's dramatic public reversal of plea from innocent to guilty in the court case represents a serious blow to Castro. Both his leading guerrilla fighter and guerrilla theoretician have fallen in Bolivia. We do not know how he will react. Against the possibility that he might try to recoup lost prestige by some dramatic act against United States interests in Latin America—such as bombing of one of our Embassies or kidnapping of diplomatic personnel— we have instructed our missions to be on the alert and take necessary precautions.[4]

Walt

---

[4] This instruction was transmitted in telegram 54210 to all ARA posts, October 14; it also instructed the posts to refrain from any statements in which the United States takes credit for defeat of the Cuban-led insurgency in Bolivia. (National Archives and Records Administration, RG 59, Central Files 1967–69, POL 6 CUBA) In an October 10 memorandum Broe wrote that the defeat of the guerrillas and killing of Che Guevara in Higueras "not only wiped out the guerrillas active in Bolivia, but also probably uprooted a Cuban-directed guerrilla network which was destined to spread throughout Latin America." (Broe to the Deputy Director for Plans, October 10; Central Intelligence Agency, Job 88–01415R, DDO/IMS Files, [file name not declassified]) The CIA prepared a report on Cuban Subversive Policy and the Bolivian Guerrilla Episode, May 1968, that was forwarded to President Johnson on June 11, 1968, with the following comment by Helms: "This detailed study gives an insight into the doggedness with which Communist Cuba pursues its revolutionary aims in Latin America." (Johnson Library, National Security File, Country File, Cuba, Vol. IV, Bowdler File, 1965–1968)

174. Memorandum Prepared for the 303 Committee[1]

Washington, November 22, 1967.

SUBJECT

Exploitation of Residual Relationships Developed During the Political Action Program for Bolivia

REFERENCE

Memorandum for the 303 Committee, Subject: "Results of the Political Action Program for Bolivia," dated 15 July 1966[2]

1. Summary

Reference memorandum reported the successful conclusion of a political action program for Bolivia. This program, approved by the 303 Committee on 5 February 1965, culminated approximately 18 months later in an orderly transfer of power via elections to a civilian, constitutional government and inauguration of President Rene Barrientos on 6 August 1966. [10½ lines of source text not declassified]

2. Current Status

[6 lines of source text not declassified] This effort which was responsive to the IRG/ARA/COIN Action Memorandum number one dated 20 July 1967,[3] entailed the dispatch to the area of guerrilla operations, by the Agency, of a highly professional and well equipped team using Bolivian Government cover. [4½ lines of source text not declassified] It so effectively improved the intelligence capability of the Bolivian Second Ranger Battalion that elements of that unit acting on field acquired intelligence were able within a matter of days to establish contact with the main force of guerrillas and on 8 October 1967 eliminate all but six of the insurgents. Ernesto "Che" Guevara was among those who lost their lives. Clean up operations are continuing.

[3 lines of source text not declassified] Specifically they were used to prevent the summary executions of Ciro Roberto Bustos, Jules Regis Debray and other guerrilla captives, and subsequently to arrange for their interrogation by experienced [less than 1 line of source text not declassified] interrogators. It was through information provided by

---

[1] Source: Department of State, INR/IL Historical Files, 303 Committee Files, c. 63, December 1, 1967. Secret; Eyes Only.

[2] Document 161.

[3] See Document 166.

Bustos that the Bolivian Army was able to recover documents and matériel cached by the insurgents. These were later used in the Bolivian presentation to the meeting of Foreign Ministers where Foreign Minister Guevara Arce surfaced participation of Ernesto "Che" Guevara in the guerrilla operations.

[1 paragraph (2 lines of source text) not declassified]

3. *Future Plans*

[1 paragraph (3 lines of source text) not declassified]

4. *Coordination*

Assistant Secretary Oliver and Ambassador Henderson concur with the continuance of these operational relationships.[4]

5. *Recommendation*

It is recommended that the 303 Committee note and endorse this activity.[5]

---

[4] Oliver recommended approval in a memorandum to Kohler on November 29. (Department of State, INR/IL Historical Files, 303 Committee Files, c. 63, December 1, 1967) This approval elicited criticism, however, from within INR and ARA. In a memorandum to Trueheart on November 30, Gardner remarked: "we learn that CIA sent a CI team to Bolivia in August of this year, under Bolivian Government cover, [text not declassified]. I would have supposed that this matter was preeminently fit for 303 consideration." (Ibid.) [text not declassified]

[5] The 303 Committee approved the recommendation at its December 1 meeting. (Ibid.)

---

175.   Letter From the Ambassador to Bolivia (Henderson) to the Assistant Secretary of State for Inter-American Affairs (Oliver)[1]

La Paz, January 5, 1968.

Dear Covey:

As you know from your discussions with Bolivian Foreign Minister Guevara Arce and Foreign Minister Romero Loza, the GOB

---

[1] Source: National Archives and Records Administration, RG 59, Central Files 1967–69, POL 23–7 BOL. Confidential; Official–Informal.

budget problem threatens the capacity of Bolivia to resist extremist subversion and move the country forward on its longer term development effort which I see as the best insurance against successful future subversion.

My approach to the threat of subversion has been the policy spelled out in our meetings last July. Acting on the understanding reached in our discussion at the White House with Walt Rostow, I have taken those measures which were necessary to insure the stability and continuance of the Barrientos Administration. At the same time, I have avoided precipitous, unnecessary military and/or financial aid which would have tended to reduce pressure on the GOB to look primarily to its own resources for dealing with the guerrilla/subversion threat.

Within this approach, I have carefully weighed the desirability and timing of extraordinary aid. As we agreed last July, when I felt the time had come for such aid, I would so advise you. I am convinced that this time has now come and request your support in obtaining immediate approval for $5,000,000 in supporting or similar aid for meeting this budget crisis.

Throughout the struggle against Che Guevara and his guerrilla movement, this Mission has used its influence and resources to eliminate this threat to Bolivia and hemisphere-wide stability. The immediate success of this policy is apparent, but it has left the GOB with a legacy of problems which I consider we must help the GOB resolve. The budget crisis is part of the legacy.

At the beginning of 1967, the GOB faced an uncovered budget deficit, after permissible borrowing from the Central Bank under the IMF ceiling, of about $7,000,000. My Country Team and I felt that this deficit was manageable by the GOB itself and put pressure on the GOB to accelerate measures for generating new revenues and for basic institutional reforms in its fiscal and budgetary practices. However, the injection of Che and his guerrillas changed this picture radically: Not only did the uncovered deficit double largely because of direct and indirect GOB expenditures required to meet the threat but revenue generating and reform measures were postponed in large part to avoid disaffecting key political groups.

Today, the Bolivian Government faces an uncovered deficit of between $12,000,000 and $15,000,000 which, under the IMF ceiling, cannot be met through borrowing from the Central Bank. Bolivia has pursued a policy of monetary stabilization since 1956 and has accepted the guidance of the IMF in carrying out this policy. Without raising questions here about the appropriateness of some IMF guidelines, I am convinced that violating the IMF ceiling and suspending the stand-by would create a most serious crisis in confidence and could lead to political and economic consequences which could pose as immediate a threat to Bolivian stability as Che did.

It seems to me to be incumbent upon us to take those actions, through financial and other assistance, which will prevent the emergence of conditions propitious to extremist subversion, particularly since some Cuban Communist elements and organized supporters still survive and there are, as you know, credible if inconclusive reports of guerrilla planning and training by pro-Chinese Communists.

In seeking this $5,000,000 aid—preferably in the form of Supporting Assistance, given the underlying political reasons for the problem itself and for responding to it—I am asking for an extraordinary injection of resources above the presently planned level of project spending. I continue to endorse the development strategy spelled out in our program documents, but I recognize that this strategy is seriously endangered if the recurring imbalance in GOB revenues and expenditures is not overcome.

As a result, this $5,000,000 request is not intended to be a one-shot palliative but part of a long-term strategy to help the GOB develop and install sound fiscal policies and institutional competence to administer these policies. The Country Team has been working on this approach for several years and on the basis of experience gained, can be expected to continue to press effectively for performance.

In view of the magnitude of the Bolivian problem and the need for sufficient leverage to accomplish the results we have in mind, we are developing a package of additional assistance over three years of about $7–$8 million beyond the $5 million now requested. We are satisfied that funding for this package can be provided from future PL 480 generations rather than additional dollar inputs. Our analysis of existing project commitments plus permissible counterpart drawdowns under the IMF ceiling have convinced us that the initial $5 million needed now cannot be provided from local currencies at our disposal.

The strategy will be presented to Mr. Richard Richardson for his analysis and evaluation when he arrives in mid-January. My Country Team and I are looking forward to discussions with him which can facilitate my negotiating with the Bolivians and expedite the processing of this extraordinary aid package.

Let me reiterate my concern for immediate action. In the framework of our discussions last July, this extraordinary $5,000,000 aid is required now to bolster the capability of the GOB to meet the aftereffects of the anti-guerrilla operation and to insure its capacity to move forward sound fiscal and development policies. The political climate, as reflected already to you by Ministers Guevara and Romero, requires prompt response by us if we are to retain our capacity to influence the course of political, military and economic events here, and not piddle away the goodwill we might have generated—and then later have to do the operation at greater cost.[2]

With best personal regards and my best wishes for 1968.

Sincerely,

Doug

---

[2] In a January 10 response to Henderson, Oliver stated that Henderson had "definitely corroborated my hunches." Oliver indicated that "once decisions are made we ought to move very fast." (Ibid.)

---

176.   Information Memorandum From the President's Special Assistant (Rostow) to President Johnson[1]

Washington, June 26, 1968, 6:20 p.m.

SUBJECT

The Barrientos Visit and Economic Assistance

Bolivia had a $7 million deficit in 1967 and may have an additional $10 million in 1968. The deficits are due principally to a drop in tin prices, the cost of putting down the Guevara guerrillas, a decline in revenues from the nationalized mines, and delay in implementation of planned revenue measures.

The Bolivians asked us for budgetary help last year, and Covey Oliver reluctantly agreed to continue them on the dole (they were supposed to come off on January 1, 1968) provided they took self-help measures to cover part of the deficit. The deal worked out after months of negotiations has these elements:

1. *The US* would authorize a $4.5 million supporting assistance loan for budget support in 1968 and approve standby authority to use up to $9 million in 1969 and 1970 from PL 480 local currency generations.

2. *The Bolivians* would implement fiscal reform measures; increase revenues by 25% in 1968; reduce 1968 spending by 12% under planned levels; establish tighter controls over free spending autonomous agencies; and continue IMF drawing eligibility.

---

[1] Source: Johnson Library, National Security File, Country File, Bolivia, President Barrientos Visit. Confidential. The memorandum indicates that President Johnson saw it.

By late May, the loan was on the verge of being signed.[2] The Bolivians had taken all the self-help measures except the key revenue-raising 10% import surtax, but seemed ready to do that. Then President Barrientos ran into some political flak with students, teachers and military plotting. He did not want to increase political tensions with the surtax, so postponed action until he had the situation well in hand. But after taking care of his troubles, he continued to delay.

From some of our special intelligence, we have the distinct impression the delay is related to Barrientos' visit to the Ranch. We suspect his advisers have told him that by talking to you, he can probably get the budget support money without imposing the surtax. He may also think he can get you to move three development loans (roads, community development, aviation) which AID is holding back until Bolivia gets its financial house in order because each calls for a sizeable local contribution.

AID has told the Bolivians that the FY 1968 SA money must be obligated by June 30 or it lapses, and the prospects for FY 1969 money are most uncertain. Ambassador Henderson reports that even these facts of life have not persuaded them to move on the surtax.

Unless the Bolivians have a change of heart between now and Sunday,[3] President Barrientos may try to use the Ranch visit to engage in substantive talks.[4] We will try to discourage this.

In reviewing the background, Bill Bowdler concludes that AID's insistence on self-help measures is justified from an economic standpoint, but it does not give due weight to political factors. Bill thinks we should hold firm on the import surtax, but be more forthcoming on the three development loans since they would help to sugar-coat the surtax for Bolivian public opinion.[5]

Walt

---

[2] Details of the proposed U.S. aid package to Bolivia were transmitted in telegram 167959 to La Paz, May 21. (National Archives and Records Administration, RG 59, Central Files 1967–69, AID (US) 10 BOL) Further negotiations in La Paz on the loan agreement were reported in telegram 5287 from La Paz, June 25. (Ibid.)

[3] June 30.

[4] According to the President's Daily Diary of July 5, Johnson met with President Barrientos at the LBJ Ranch in Johnson City, Texas, from 1:23 to 2:29 p.m. A State luncheon followed. (Johnson Library) No memorandum of conversation of the Johnson–Barrientos meeting has been found. A White House press statement on July 5 indicates that in the discussion Barrientos "underlined the efforts that this government had made to create an environment of political and social stability as well as loyalty to democratic process." (Ibid., National Security File, Country File, Bolivia, President Barrientos Visit)

[5] On June 28 the President approved Oliver informing the Bolivian Finance Minister that if they put through the import surcharge, the United States "would move right" with budget support and project loans. The President would not raise the issue with Barrientos. (Ibid.)

177.   Action Memorandum From William G. Bowdler of the National Security Council Staff to President Johnson[1]

Washington, July 30, 1968, 4 p.m.

SUBJECT

Letter from President Barrientos

The Bolivian Embassy has delivered to State a long letter (Tab B)[2] from President Barrientos thanking you for the invitation to the Ranch and discussing issues he did not have time to take up with you while there.

The issues boil down to:

—recognition of Bolivia's contribution to hemispheric security by eliminating "Che" Guevara.

—Bolivia's willingness to cooperate in physical integration, but it also desires access to the sea.

—a request that GSA make its 3-month suspension of tin sales indefinite.

—United States approval of a loan to moderate Bolivia's airports and airline.

At Tab A is a suggested reply prepared by State.[3] It compliments President Barrientos on his decision to work toward greater economic integration (i.e., Andean Common Market and the River Plate Basin Development) and his success in dealing with the Guevara guerrillas. On bilateral economic matters, the letter avoids getting into specifics because we do not know what use President Barrientos might make of it. He knows that since the Ranch visit, two loans (roads and agricultural cooperatives) have been approved, and the airport-aircraft loan will be completed when details on the down payment are worked out. We cannot agree to an indefinite suspension of GSA tin sales, but the letter makes clear we will consult fully with Bolivia on any significant actions we might contemplate taking.

I recommend you sign the letter.[4]

WGB

---

[1] Source: Johnson Library, National Security File, Special Heads of State Correspondence, Bolivia, March 1, 1968. Confidential.

[2] A Department of State translation is attached but not printed. The Barrientos letter, July 8, was sent from New York. (Ibid.)

[3] Attached but not printed. The draft was prepared in the Department of State and transmitted to the White House on July 24, along with the Department's translation of the Barrientos letter, under a covering memorandum from Read. (Ibid.)

[4] The signed letter to Barrientos is ibid.

178.   Information Memorandum From William G. Bowdler of the National Security Council Staff to President Johnson in Texas[1]

Washington, August 2, 1968, 3:30 p.m.

SUBJECT

Political Crisis in Bolivia

President Barrientos is facing the most serious political crisis of his two years in office. It stems from the publication of the "Che" Guevara diary, a copy of which was surreptitiously furnished to Fidel Castro by someone in Bolivia.[2]

Since the diary was kept under lock and key by the Army, the finger pointed there, bringing into question the loyalty and discipline of the Armed Forces. This produced a political chain reaction of protest by opposition groups, a police crackdown, threats of strikes and student disturbances, unrest in the Armed Forces, and finally, replacement of the civilian cabinet with a mediocre military one.[3]

In the midst of all this, Barrientos' Interior Minister Antonio Arguedas took off for Chile where he announced that he had been the one that passed the Guevara diary to Castro. The circumstances of his "fleeing" Bolivia, his public statements, and his desire to come to the United States rather than go to Cuba which has been desperately trying to get him, all cast serious doubt on the bona fides of the Arguedas story.[4] It sounds to me as though he agreed to be the scapegoat for his old friend Barrientos in order to take the heat off the restive Armed Forces. Incidentally, Arguedas is due to arrive in the United States on Saturday, August 4.

---

[1] Source: Johnson Library, National Security File, Country File, Bolivia, Vol. IV, January 1966–December 1968. Confidential. The memorandum indicates it was received at the LBJ Ranch August 3 at 11 a.m.

[2] The Embassy at La Paz reported publication of the Che Guevara diary in *Presencia* on July 9. (Telegram 5629 from La Paz, July 10; National Archives and Records Administration, RG 59, Central Files 1967–69, POL 6 CUBA)

[3] On July 19 the Embassy in La Paz reported that "public criticism of armed forces for leak of Che Guevara diary has dragged their prestige to new low, putting irresistible pressure on them to find scapegoat." (Telegram 5812 from La Paz; ibid., POL 15–1 BOL)

[4] At a meeting of the Interdepartmental Regional Group for ARA, the group concluded that the Barrientos government was in serious danger from a military coup and danger from students and labor should he prorogue the Congress. The Group agreed it was in U.S. interest for Barrientos to remain in power. They recommended the U.S. Ambassador persuade Barrientos to return to a civilian cabinet and maintain a functioning Congress. (National Archives and Records Administration, RG 59, ARA Files: Lot 70 D 122, IRG/ARA Action Memos, 1968)

Barrientos still confronts a difficult situation at home. The shift to a military cabinet has not really satisfied the Armed Forces and is being severely criticized by civilian elements. Fearing a congressional investigation of the diary episode if he allows Congress to convene on August 6, Barrientos seems inclined to delay its opening. There are also indications that ambitious officers in the Army would like to use the crisis to dump Barrientos.

Ambassador Henderson talked to Barrientos yesterday about our interest in seeing him complete his constitutional term. He gave him our impression that allowing Congress to convene on schedule and going back quickly to a civilian cabinet would help him hold to this objective. Barrientos agreed, but was vague on the timing.

So far, Barrientos has weathered the storm and probably has a better than even chance to see it through. Given the internal nature of his problems, there is little we can do but give him continued moral support. This we are doing. It is definitely in our interest that he remain in power, because it is doubtful that anyone else could make as good a showing in managing that difficult country.[5]

WGB

---

[5] [text not declassified]

---

179. Information Memorandum From the Acting Assistant Secretary of State for Inter-American Affairs (Vaky) to Secretary of State Rusk[1]

Washington, August 19, 1968.

SUBJECT

Bolivia—Former Minister of Government Returns, Makes Accusations Against CIA

Former Bolivian Minister of Government Arguedas returned to La Paz on August 17. At press conferences held upon his arrival and again later in the day, Arguedas ascribed his action of providing the Guevara diary to Castro to his desire to rid Bolivia of "imperialism", as exemplified by the activities of the CIA. Arguedas claimed that he had been

---

[1] Source: National Archives and Records Administration, RG 59, Central Files 1967–69, POL 30 BOL. Secret; Sensitive. The date is handwritten on the memorandum.

recruited by the CIA in 1965, and provided considerable information on names of CIA personnel and their alleged activities in recent years in Bolivia.[2]

Embassy La Paz believes that Arguedas' anti-CIA line may have been ordered by President Barrientos to place the onus of the diary scandal on the U.S., thereby diverting attention from the GOB's shortcomings.[3]

Possible ramifications of this development are several:

1) Greatly increased press attention here to CIA "activities".
2) Possible public demonstrations against our Mission in Bolivia.
3) Possible intensification by radical student and labor groups of agitation against the GOB (a minor demonstration occurred in La Paz on August 16, but was easily broken up).
4) This raises the question of U.S.–Barrientos relationships if the Embassy's belief is correct.

Regarding (1) above we are planning, at least for the time being, to adhere to our usual policy of declining comment on accusations about the CIA, no matter how absurd such accusations are.

Regarding point (2) above, our most recent information is that La Paz is calm. The Embassy has taken security precautions.

Regarding point (3), we continue to believe that the GOB can weather local threats as long as support from the military is forthcoming. The Barrientos–Military relationship, while uneasy since the onset of the diary scandal, is not yet at a point where military support seems likely to be withdrawn.

On point (4), it is too early to predict the effects of this incident on our relationship with Barrientos. We will be evaluating this question over the next few days.

Action Taken: I have instructed Ambassador Castro (who is in San Salvador making his protocolary goodbyes there) to delay his arrival in Bolivia (scheduled for August 20 but not yet announced publicly) for a few days. The Ambassador will return here for further consultations. This action is in accordance with the recommendation of Embassy La Paz which believes demonstrations against Ambassador Castro are likely if he arrives at the height of the present crisis.

---

[2] The Arguedas affair was the subject of a meeting on August 19 at the Department of State between CIA and representatives of INR and ARA. (Memorandum from William C. Trueheart (INR/DDC) to Hughes and Denney; Department of State, INR/IL Historical Files, ARA/CIA Weekly Meetings, 1968–1969) A separate record of this meeting, dated August 20, was prepared by the CIA. (Ibid., Latin America General, 1967–1968)

[3] On August 22, in summarizing the Arguedas affair for President Johnson, Rostow reported: "At first, it appeared Arguedas and Barrientos were in league to make the CIA a scapegoat and deflect from themselves some of the criticism over the Guevara diary episode. But in an August 20 press conference, Barrientos defended Bolivia's relations with the US and condemned Cuba as the real threat." (Johnson Library, National Security File, Country File, Bolivia, Vol. IV, Memoranda, January 1966–December 1968)

180. Memorandum From Director of the Bureau of the Budget Zwick to President Johnson[1]

Washington, December 21, 1968.

SUBJECT

Proposed P.L. 480 Program for Bolivia

Bill Gaud and Orville Freeman request your approval to negotiate a *$6.8 million P.L. 480 sales agreement with Bolivia* for wheat/wheat flour and tobacco.[2] Repayment will be in dollars over twenty years with 5 percent down. There will be no currency use payment under the Purcell amendment since no additional currency is needed at this time.

Last June, AID authorized a $4.5 million Supporting Assistance loan to Bolivia as the initial budgetary support for an 18-month fiscal reform and stabilization program jointly developed among AID, the IMF, and the Government of Bolivia. This P.L. 480 agreement will constitute AID's major 1969 resource input for Bolivia and as such *forms an important continuing element in the fiscal reform program.*

The local currency proceeds from this agreement will be earmarked on a standby basis for budget support in CY 1969 should the need arise. Thus, *the P.L. 480 agreement should eliminate the need for additional Supporting Assistance funds.* If the need for budget support does not arise, the proceeds will be used in the agricultural sector.

State/AID has determined that Bolivia's resources are not being diverted to unnecessary military expenditures to a degree which materially interferes with its development and that neither U.S. development assistance nor P.L. 480 sales proceeds are being diverted by Bolivia to military purposes.

Because this P.L. 480 agreement will support and reinforce the fiscal reform program and will substitute for dollar assistance, *I recommend that you approve negotiation of the agreement.*[3]

Charles J. Zwick

---

[1] Source: Johnson Library, National Security File, Country File, Bolivia, Vol. IV, Memoranda, January 1966–December 1968. Confidential.

[2] Attached, but not printed.

[3] The approve option is checked. Rostow appended a handwritten note to a December 24 memorandum to Johnson recommending approval of the package, indicating: "Final approval by telephone, 27 December, 1968." (Johnson Library, National Security File, Country File, Bolivia, Vol. IV, Memoranda, January 1966–December 1968)

Brazil

181. Memorandum From the Director of the Office of Brazilian Affairs (Burton) to the Assistant Secretary of State for Inter-American Affairs (Mann)[1]

Washington, January 8, 1964.

SUBJECT

The Position of the Military in Brazil

Regarding your query on the above at the noon inter-agency meeting (the meeting on the contingency paper)[2] today, may I offer the following comment.

I believe that it is reasonably clear that a substantial proportion well in excess of a majority among the military officers in Brazil are heavily oriented toward the maintenance of orderly democratic processes. However, I do not think that there has been up to now any really substantial capability or will to mount a coup to overthrow Goulart. The military already had one unhappy and unsuccessful experience in attempting to disrupt orderly democratic processes when they unsuccessfully tried to block Goulart's succession to the presidency in 1961 and had to settle for a parliamentary arrangement which was subsequently discredited and abandoned. In this sense, I think that there has been a lot of confused thinking on the subject of a deteriorating military capability to overthrow Goulart. I submit that this capability has been deteriorated and ineffective since the ill-fated fiasco of 1961, even before Goulart understandably started making appointments and promotions to protect himself against similar future actions.

---

[1] Source: National Archives and Records Administration, RG 59, ARA/BR Files: Lot 66 D 418, DEF—Defense Affairs, 1964. Confidential. Drafted by Burton.

[2] The parenthetical comment was handwritten by Burton. An inter-agency group met on January 8 to consider a draft contingency plan for Brazil; no substantive record of the meeting has been found. The draft, prepared in ARA/BR, addressed four contingencies: Extreme Leftist Revolt; Democratic Revolt Against Excesses of Regime; Removal of Goulart by Constructive Forces; and Gradual Extreme Leftist Takeover. It recommended that the United States avoid association with "rightist coup plottings," although covert contact with such groups was necessary for intelligence collection and "the exercise of a moderating influence, where appropriate." In the event of an "interim military takeover," the United States should assume a "constructive friendly attitude" while pressing for a "quick return to constitutional democratic processes." ("A Contingency Plan for Brazil," December 11, 1963; ibid., Central Files 1961–63, POL 23–9 BRAZ)

On the other hand, the military can be a restraining force against extremists and undemocratic excesses. I think it is generally recognized that the Army Attaché in Brazil, Colonel Walters, feels most strongly that Goulart is bringing about a political erosion in the military. Yet, Colonel Walters just last August acknowledged to me that if Goulart attempted to move toward dictatorship in violation of the constitution, there would, at the very least, be shooting. While Goulart has shown a great penchant for generating acute political tension and crisis at periodic intervals, past history indicates a considerable tendency on his part to retreat and compromise—to avoid ultimate explosion. For this reason the military should be viewed as a potential politically strong restraining force against Goulartist undemocratic excesses. Our chief worry should be that the military might be confused and immobilized by continuing slick and subtle political maneuverings by Goulart.

I might add that there is in the military a very considerable reservoir of good will toward the United States and sympathy toward U.S. objectives and policy; evidence of this erupted in many quarters at the time of the Cuban missile crisis. *For this reason and because of the considerations set forth above we have taken the position that the cultivation of the Brazilian military has high political importance and we have therefore, for example, pushed forward a program of defense lending for C–130's.*[3]

I believe that the above is a reasonably accurate reflection of the thinking of Ambassador Gordon, except that he might possibly speak with more vigor in view of past difficulties and delays we had to surmount before we got implementation of his C–130 recommendations.

I understand that you have recently been exposed to various opinions on the Brazilian military in connection with a recent general discussion of military assistance. This memorandum is intended to be responsive to such comment as well as to the question you raised on the contingency paper.

Please let me know if there is any additional information you would like on the subject of the military in Brazil.

---

[3] Negotiations on the sale of C–130 aircraft to Brazil were completed in June, when the Brazilian Air Minister signed a memorandum of understanding. (Telegram 2799 from Rio de Janeiro, June 10; ibid., DEF 12–5 BRAZ–US)

182. Notes of Meeting Between the Ambassador to Brazil (Gordon) and the Assistant Secretary of State for Inter-American Affairs (Mann)[1]

Washington, January 22, 1964.

Goulart—Childish and erratic. Apparently tries to keep an inch or two windward. Does not believe he is a commie. Very tolerant of commies because they are useful to him. More a follower of Vargas and Peron. Personable demagogue.

Possibility of a Goulart coup followed by an eventual commie takeover.

Brizola is Goulart's brother-in-law, has a radio station, former Gov. of Rio Grande do Sul. Now a Congressman from Rio where he got a big vote. Demagogue more than an intellectual type. Has said he would like to be the Fidel Castro of Brazil. Schilling is his chief advisor who is a member of Communist Party.

Miguel Arrais, Gov. of Pernambuco. Wife is commie and he could be. Shrewd—eligible for Presidency.

Carlos Lacerda (48)—Gov. of Guanabara. No. one anti-commie. One of ablest in country. Brilliant. Was newspaper publisher. Good administrator. Would make good President—under attack for being pro-American.

Adhemar de Barros (63)—Still Gov. of Sao Paulo, a key power. Steals but is on our side. Says he will run but could not be elected. Ideal ticket would be Lacerda–de Barros.

Meneghetti, Gov. of Rio Grande do Sul. (Around 65) Older but good. Some iron but not vigorous.

Nei Braga—Gov. of Parana, south of Sao Paulo and most rapidly growing state in Brazil. Good population with lots of drive. Around 40 years and head of Christian Democratic Party. Anti-Communist and not always outspokenly so. Catholic new dealer. Possible V.P. choice.

---

[1] Source: National Archives and Records Administration, RG 59, ARA/LA Files, 1964: Lot 66 D 65, Brazil 1964. Confidential. Drafted by Mann. These notes were typed in ARA from an attached set of Mann's handwritten notes. Gordon was in the United States for consultation January 20–February 10. At an interagency debriefing on January 23 Gordon argued that the United States need intervene only if the Brazilian armed forces were divided: "If this split were not to occur, a coup from either the right or left with armed forces support would be over before the U.S. could exercise any significant influence." (Memorandum for the record from Robert J. Hill, Jr., January 24; Washington National Records Center, OASD/ISA Files: FRC 330 68 A 306, Brazil 334–703, 1964)

In Middle

Magalhaes Pinto (high 50's). Gov. of Minas Gerais. Has presidential ambitions. Plays both sides. Technically in UDN but in minority group which would bolt if Lacerda nominated. Difficult to say how able. But is smarter than Goulart.

Carvalho Pinto. Former Gov. of Sao Paulo and Finance Minister. Able, good administrator but provincial who does not understand finance. Honest and puritanical. Sometimes plays to left. Dark horse presidential possibility.

Trend against Kubitschek, and in favor of Lacerda. But election nearly two years away.

Power Centers

Army

Church (weak and divided)

Industrial and Financial Community (Sao Paulo, Rio and Belo Horizonte in that order)

Labor—Official part built by Vargas run by commies or Goulart partisans.

Important to keep alive the Alliance for Progress idea in Brazil.

1. Burton has piece of paper of loans. About 27 in project loans.
2. Maybe handle PL 480
3. IDB
4. World Bank
5. FRINGE—Peace Corps, etc.

---

183.   Telegram From the Embassy in Brazil to the Department of State[1]

Rio de Janeiro, February 21, 1964, 6 p.m.

1761. 1. Goulart received me Thursday[2] afternoon for one hour responding my request early in week for renewal contact after my recent Washington trip. He was in good mood, appearing pleased with generally favorable reaction his Wednesday night speech.

---

[1] Source: National Archives and Records Administration, RG 59, Central Files 1964–66, FN 14 BRAZ. Confidential; Limdis.

[2] February 20.

2. I handed him original and translation Mrs. Kennedy letter of thanks,[3] which he said would publish. He then questioned me at some length about U.S. political scene, expressing great interest in strength of President Johnson's position and expressing hope he might at some time meet President Johnson informally. Said he was still thinking of European trip in April or May and wondered whether he might pass through Texas on way back. This was in tone vague conversation rather than a pointed inquiry, and he emphasized that no definite travel plans yet made, since they would require Congressional leave.

3. He then asked about prospects for early OECD response.[4] I replied hoped not later than Monday[5] and possibly sooner. I expressed concern that statement his Wednesday speech had over anticipated successful results when negotiation not yet started, to which he replied had to put best foot forward and had had personal message from de Gaulle indicating latter's disposition cooperate. I also remarked that he had singled out reference to prospective fifty million dollar German aid projects, which were much less than we had done in recent years, to which he replied that structure of speech intended show recent actions to strengthen relations with various countries, beginning with December exchange of letters with President Johnson.[6]

4. Apropos of de Gaulle, I mentioned with some asperity reported statements visiting French Gaullist deputies on General's ideas building up economic relations with LA to help "free LA from excessive dependence on U.S." I left with Goulart memorandum[7] showing Brazilian trade with U.S. ten times that with France, relative amounts of Brazilian coffee bought by two countries, absence of tariffs and taxes on our part. Also pointed out that Brazil is receiving half its wheat from U.S. practically as gift. This led to general discussion de Gaulle's motivations and notions world leadership, during which I emphasized costliness world leadership under present conditions, weakness French resource base, and tendency to exploit nuisance value with being able back up by positive acts. I said that if de Gaulle would lead Common Market to abandon taxes and discriminations against LA trade, this would really mean something, but vague talk of blocs based on Latin affinities should be viewed skeptically. This seemed to leave considerable impression on Goulart.

---

[3] Not found.

[4] Reference is to the negotiations to reschedule Brazil's foreign debt coordinated by the Organization for Economic Cooperation and Development in Paris. Documentation on the negotiations is in the National Archives and Records Administration, RG 59, Central Files 1964–66, FN 14 BRAZ.

[5] February 24.

[6] For text of the letters, see *Public Papers of the Presidents of the United States: Lyndon B. Johnson, 1963–64*, Book I, pp. 81–83.

[7] Not found.

5. He asked me about Guantanamo and Panama problems, on which I gave him straight forward factual background.

6. Cuba–Venezuela dispute reported separately.[8]

7. AMFORP problem reported separately.[9]

8. He said looking forward to McCloy visit and thought Hanna case could have constructive solution.[10]

9. I then remarked on growing Washington concern at increasingly open and favored Communist influence in Brazil, saying this now much greater even than when Attorney General saw him December 1962. He replied with defense legalization PCB, saying he genuinely believed this would reduce their infiltration in and influence in other parties and would demonstrate their small real strength in contrast highly organized noise they were able to make. I asked how he could justify idea legalizing. Replied Prestes'[11] trip excellent way reducing receptivity PCB in Brazil, comparable to Prestes' Senate statement in 1946 that he would side with Russia if Russia and Brazil in opposite sides of a war. Moreover, he said, Communists and allies are now divided into three groups. There is the Brizola group, largest in popular support but very radical in policies, wanting violent overthrow regime now. There was the Chinese-Cuban group, also violent but relatively small. Then there was the orthodox Moscow group, by far the best disciplined, which was taking a very moderate line corresponding within Brazil to Khrushchev's moderate international line in relation to U.S.

10. I said that Washington preoccupation went beyond question legalization PCB, and was especially great at Communist strength in Petrobras, communications, key labor unions, Ministry of Education, etc. Long-term strategy was to get power, and if short-term tactics change from moderation to violence, was there not a most serious dan-

---

[8] Goulart questioned how "a small boatload of arms" could be considered an "invasion" and recommended that the OAS consider "some form of mild sanction proportional to the crime." (Telegram 1759 from Rio de Janeiro, February 21; National Archives and Records Administration, RG 59, Central Files 1964–66, DEF 12 CUBA)

[9] Reference is to ongoing negotiations to expropriate holdings of the American and Foreign Power Company (AMFORP) in Brazil. In his conversation with Gordon, Goulart raised specific problems associated with the AMFORP subsidiary in Vitória, suggesting that responsibility for its management be transferred to the state. (Telegram 1760 from Rio de Janeiro, February 21; ibid., FSE 12 BRAZ)

[10] On February 29 John J. McCloy, then a partner at the New York law firm of Milbank, Tweed, Hadley, and McCloy, met Goulart in Rio de Janeiro to discuss the status of the M.A. Hanna Mining Company. For a secondary account of the meeting, see Kai Bird, *The Chairman: John J. McCloy, the Making of the American Establishment,* pp. 550–553.

[11] Luís Carlos Prestes, leader of the Moscow-oriented Partido Comunista Brasileiro (PCB). A PCB delegation met Soviet officials at the Kremlin on February 9. (*New York Times,* February 10, 1964)

ger of paralyzing country unless concessions were made to Communist taste. He replied you may stop worrying about that. There was a test when Petrobras unions wanted to launch general strike when two Petrobras directors were discharged, but Goulart had opposed them and they had not struck. (If price of this was Osvino's appointment as President Petrobras, I remain dubious as to who won.) He went on to say, however, that he thought it was good for reactionary elite of country to believe that left had such power, since this might prove only way of getting them to accept basic reforms. He then launched into lengthy disquisition on reforms, saying they were indispensable and that blindness of Brazilian elite to their necessity was incredible. Said eight thousand peasants wanting land had appeared in Governador Valadares in Minas, and even if half of these Communists and other outsiders, other half remained a serious problem for which practical solution must be found and efforts to suppress through arming land owners or police or army action would not do. Moreover, he said, no reforms can be considered basic unless they amend constitution. A basic reform must be reflected in revision of nation's basic constitutional document. He intended to keep on with his fight, and the reactionaries would see that he would win. He ended the disquisition by saying "they will give— they will give".

11. As conversation was ending, he said he noted that I was probably going to Washington in March for Ambassadors meeting on Alliance for Progress widely reported in morning press. I said this not yet definite, but purpose would be consideration how make AFP more effective. I said Washington perplexed at his apparent prejudice against AFP. He replied had no prejudice, but felt reformulation was essential. Said best way of doing this would be meeting of all Western Hemisphere Presidents, in which new ideas would not come simply from U.S. but as common ideas to which all LA countries would be committed because they had participated in formulation.

12. *Comment:* General tone conversation, including apparent desire reasonable settlement Vitoria problem, more forthcoming attitude on AMFORP in general, welcome for McCloy's prospective visit beginning March, and enthusiastic appreciation our role on debt rescheduling problem, appeared reflect real change his attitude toward U.S. over last few months, giving me impression that idea radical break in favor line-up with Russia which he had entertained last August was now abandoned. This is quite likely reflection Russian indications that they are in no position to assume heavy commitments to Brazil. On domestic front, on other hand, I read both in and between lines disposition to take extreme risks, through stimulation sporadic violence in countryside, mass meetings, strikes, etc. to force constitutional amendments for basic reforms. I increasingly suspect that major reform he is seeking is vote for illiterates in hope this will spell death knell for

Lacerda candidacy. This bodes very ill for domestic tranquillity here in coming months.[12]

Gordon

---

[12] On February 19 Gordon discussed the situation in Brazil with Lacerda, who reportedly felt "slighted because of very long interval since our last talk." Gordon told Lacerda that some distance was necessary to avoid "so obvious a public relationship as to make him appear a favorite son of U.S." Lacerda believed that the chances of a coup d'état, either for or against Goulart, were "negligible." He feared, however, that Goulart would "register millions of illiterates under guise of adult illiteracy," thereby throwing the presidential election in October 1965. (Telegram 1773 from Rio de Janeiro, February 24; National Archives and Records Administration, RG 59, Central Files 1964–66, POL 15 BRAZ)

---

184.   Telegram From the Embassy in Brazil to the Department of State[1]

Rio de Janeiro, March 18, 1964, 7 p.m.

2002. For Ambassador Gordon. Examination of latest phase of crisis (ushered in by March 13 rally and President's message to Congress) leads us to conclusion that there are dangerous elements present which have not previously existed—even at previous high-water mark of state of siege episode.[2]

---

[1] Source: National Archives and Records Administration, RG 59, Central Files 1964–66, POL 15–1 BRAZ. Secret; Priority; Limdis. Repeated to Brasilia and Sao Paulo. Gordon was in Washington March 13–22 for consultation and the conference of U.S. Ambassadors and AID Mission Directors to Latin America.

[2] On October 4, 1963, Goulart asked Congress for a 30-day state of siege to restore order in the midst of general political unrest, including rumors of an impending coup d'état. Goulart withdrew the request 3 days later in the face of widespread opposition. On March 13, 1964, Goulart addressed a mass rally in Rio de Janeiro organized by the General Command of Workers (CGT). Earlier in the day the President had issued a decree to seize "underutilized" land within certain federal jurisdictions. At the rally Goulart signed a decree to expropriate all privately owned oil refineries. The next day, after signing a measure on rent control, Goulart called on Congress to amend the constitution as a means to promote other "basic reforms," including the legalization of the Communist Party. In response to the President's campaign, the opposition organized its own mass rallies, including the "March of the Family with God for Liberty" in Sao Paulo on March 19.

In broad terms, essentially new elements of current situation which increase criticalness are as follows:

1. There is general realization that Goulart has finally "defined himself". This commitment (which seems much firmer and more explicit than anything Goulart has come up with in past) has thus far received sustained support of left as whole—including Brizola, PCB, various other groups and subgroups. Only small Amazonas group (CPB) has attacked Goulart's new position. While same sort of coalescing of elements of left took place at time of state of siege, obvious and disturbing difference is that they then opposed President whereas they now support him.

2. This phase of crisis, unlike predecessors, thus far appears to be sustained push. Momentum of new Goulart offensive shows none of usual signs of let-up (e.g. rumors of dissention among left, back-offs by President, etc.).

3. While success or failure of October fiasco seems to have been—intentionally or not—geared to attempt on Lacerda, no such problematic wild card exists in current drive which seems carefully planned and appears to contain provisions for substantial flexibility in likely event that favorable Congressional action on President's proposals not forthcoming.

4. Following factors bear on what Goulart might do in this case: (1) Goulart in various contacts has given impression that he does not necessarily expect Congress to accede to demands set forth in presidential message; (2) Goulart now appears to be sure enough of his power position to be willing to consider by-passing Congress (without necessarily closing that body); President's confidence seems to be based at least partially on CGT threat of general strike if impeachment action started, CGT virtual ultimatum to Congress to act on proposals of presidential message by April 20, rumored possible declaration of military ministers in support of Goulart's proposals, etc.; (3) among welter of rumors, two stand out which have unusual persistence and ring of authenticity: First, that if Congress does not act on request, Goulart will "decree" plebiscite on basic reforms, and second, that Goulart will continue to flood market with series of decrees (e.g. paper import monopoly, expropriation of petroleum distribution industry, etc.). Aside from probability or otherwise Goulart will actually take these steps, psychological effect on public of rumored impending action is very definitely such as to lead to continued high pitch of crisis.

5. Opposition—so far at least—has definitely not effectively coalesced position. There seems to be some individual and/or small group reflex reaction (talk about impeachment, Congressional withdrawal to Sao Paulo, etc.) but efforts to coordinate unified position in face of threat have not materialized. (Lacerda's appeal to Adhemar and

Juscelino to form common front has resulted in somewhat ridiculous poses of "I've always been a democrat; what's new?" instead of any real cooperation.)

In view of above factors, we somewhat apprehensive that (1) if rapid deterioration of situation continues and (2) if opposition does not somehow rally, substantial amount of ground may be lost irrevocably. This leads us to wonder what actions within framework short term policy paper[3] U.S. could take at this time to keep opposition from becoming overly demoralized in face of Goulart drive.

One suggestion we have for your consideration at present is as follows:

1. Discrete press leaks originating in Washington which clearly demonstrate concern of USG over recent turn of events in Brazil.

2. In view of fact that you are staying over after general departure of other LA Ambassadors from Washington, might it not be useful to have this played up as "extra and special consultation necessary in light of Brazilian situation."

Incidentally, our contacts with U.S. business community in last few days have shown that most, if not all, view situation with alarm.

Brazilian business reaction appears similar, dollar on free market having gone from 1460 to 1640 in last two days, while stock market has dropped sharply (Embtel 2001).[4]

CAS concurs.

Mein

---

[3] For text of the "Proposed Short Term Policy Paper—Brazil," September 30, 1963, see *Foreign Relations*, 1961–1963, vol. XII, Document 240.

[4] Telegram 2001 from Rio de Janeiro, March 18. (National Archives and Records Administration, RG 59, Central Files 1964–66, POL 2 BRAZ)

185.   Memorandum From Gordon Chase of the National Security Council Staff to the President's Special Assistant for National Security Affairs (Bundy)[1]

Washington, March 19, 1964.

SUBJECT

Chiefs of Mission Conference—Brazil and Chile

I attended a few sessions of the Chiefs of Mission Conference. One of the more interesting included discussions by Ambassadors Gordon and Cole about the situations in Brazil and Chile.

Brazil

1. Ambassador Gordon said that the *economic* situation in Brazil is terrible. Inflation was 80% last year and 50% the year before; prospects for this year are even worse. In addition, there is stagnation— a decline in net per capita income for the first time since the 1930's. This stagnation results from a downward trend in the rate of foreign investment (partly attributable to an unfortunate law on profit remittances), and from a downward trend in the rate of domestic investment (largely attributable to inflation and a lack of confidence in the future). About the only bright spot is the foreign exchange position, which is improved because of good coffee prices.

2. The only thing worse than the economic situation is the *political* situation. Goulart is an incompetent, juvenile delinquent, who represents a minority of Brazilians. In the short run, he seems intent merely on survival. In the long run, he would probably like a Peronista-type revolution, with a lot of corruption at the top and support from the working classes.

A Communist takeover is conceivable. Brizola and Goulart are rivals who often work with each other; it is hard to tell how much. But there are mitigating factors. Though a rabble-rouser, Brizola is not very smart and not a good leader. In general, the leadership of the extreme left seems divided.

The majority of voters are upset. They would like to throw out Goulart. Also, the military, which traditionally stays out of government, and which traditionally is anti-Communist, is having its patience sorely tried. But the leadership of the opposition is divided and it has neither

---

[1] Source: Johnson Library, National Security File, Country File, Latin America, Vol. I, 11/63–6/64. Secret.

the power nor the capacity to eject Goulart; furthermore, it would be difficult to give the opposition this power and capacity. Generally speaking, the policy of the opposition is to try to keep the ship of state afloat in this very fluid situation until next year's elections. In this regard, the two likely successors look pretty good. Kubitschek is spotty but, on the whole is O.K. Lacerda would be excellent.

3. There are bright spots in the federal structure which, in Brazil, is meaningful because the states have real power. Generally speaking, the leadership in the states is first-class. Of the 22 governors, only one is really bad, three are poor, ten are good, and eight are excellent.

4. U.S. policy has the following elements in it:

(a) Like the Brazilian opposition, we hope the ship of state can stay afloat until the elections.

(b) We try to take advantage of the loose, sprawling, multiple nature of Brazil to encourage the constructive forces which reflect the majority of the people. Our PL 480 program, project aid, and the Alliance for Progress help to demonstrate that, in the job of bringing about change, there is a viable alternative to violent revolution.

The AID director from Brazil[2] made the point that many people in Washington feel that we should stand off from Brazil until the Brazilians behave. This would be tragic because it does not take into account the fact that Brazil is a multiple society and that there are many segments who are with us and whom we should not ignore.

(c) Our relations with the Brazilian military are good. This is very important.

(d) We have a friendly audience for USIS activities; in this regard the Embassy has a "truth squad" which attempts to answer false charges against the U.S.

Efforts with students in Brazil have been made, but there is still a long way to go. This is a crucial field in Latin America and, by and large, we have left it to our enemies. We need more student exchanges, more books, more pamphlets, etc. We must make the case for the democratic alternative. An IMF stabilization program and foreign investment are not good enough; they do not capture the imagination.

---

[2] Jack B. Kubisch.

(e) In view of the civil war possibilities, the Embassy has done contingency planning.[3]

[Omitted here is discussion on Chile, see Document 249.]

GC

---

[3] In telegram 1805 from Rio de Janeiro, February 27, Gordon reported completing a review of "possible lines of covert action related to situation described in Burton draft contingency paper" (see footnote 2, Document 181) and suggested that the Special Group meet on March 19 to consider his recommendations. (National Archives and Records Administration, RG 59, Central Files 1964–66, DEF 1–1 BRAZ) The Special Group, however, did not meet while Gordon was in Washington. (Department of State, INR/IL Historical Files, Special Group Files, Meetings) In a March 14 letter to Mann, Frank K. Sloan reported that Gordon had expressed reservations about a military contingency plan prepared in DOD and "will discuss the subject while in Washington next week." (National Archives and Records Administration, RG 59, Central Files 1964–66, POL 1–1 BRAZ) No record of the meeting has been found. A copy of the DOD paper, "Précis of Contingency Plan for Brazil," is in the Washington National Records Center, OASD/ISA Files: FRC 330 64 A 7425, Brazil 381, 1964.

---

186.   Telegram From the Embassy in Brazil to the Department of State[1]

Rio de Janeiro, March 26, 1964, 8 p.m.

2084. Please pass White House.

1) It has been reported by press that second Army Commander Kruel recently told Goulart that he could not assure security of President if latter attended planned May 1 rally in Sao Paulo. On this basis, it is widely believed that Kruel's ouster as second army commander may be imminent.

Comment: If Goulart were to try to remove Kruel from second army command it is not certain that he would go quietly. Efforts have recently been made both by Adhemar and democratic military leaders to secure Kruel's adherence to opposition side.

---

[1] Source: National Archives and Records Administration, RG 59, Central Files 1964–66, POL 15–1 BRAZ. Secret; Priority; Exdis. Passed to White House. The telegram is based in part on information reported independently by the U.S. Army Attaché, Vernon A. Walters. According to Walters the conspirators had agreed on seven grounds that could trigger a revolt. When they appealed for U.S. assistance, however, Walters explained that he had "no authority to discuss such matters." Walters noted that he had "passed information on to Ambassador who is taking matter up at highest levels." (Telegram DISC D–20 from Rio de Janeiro to the Department of the Army, March 26; ibid., POL 23–9 BRAZ)

2) On March 20 Army Chief of Staff Humberto Castello Branco sent letter to generals and other officers of army headquarters and subordinate units (i.e. most senior officers other than those in major commands) analyzing current situation in country and strongly upholding army's traditional role as a non-partisan defender of democratic institutions. Letter (of which [*less than 1 line of source text not declassified*] has acquired copy) is anti-Communist and by obvious implication anti-Goulart, condemning, for example, unattributed intentions of closing Congress and calling Constituent Assembly.

Comment: Castello Branco, who is perhaps Brazil's most energetic, courageous and responsible army general on active service, is reported by ARMA [*less than 1 line of source text not declassified*] recently to have agreed to lead democratic resistance group in military. In his letter he is assuming this leadership and throwing his own very considerable prestige against Goulart in direct challenge to latter.

3) According [*less than 1 line of source text not declassified*], WarMin Jair currently in hospital for gall bladder operation learned of letter only on March 24, on eve his operation. He was furious and almost called off operation. According ARMA, who got it from Army Chief Surgeon, Jair recovering well but under any hypothesis will be away from work for at least 30 days.

4) According ARMA, who has obtained copies of documents in question, leaders of Democratic Military Group are sending by safe-hand to officers sympathetic to their cause throughout Brazil 3 questionnaires, which are in reality instructions telling them how to put their units in readiness to resist undemocratic moves by President and/or left. Second "questionnaire" which is intended only for most trustworthy officers, suggests that responsibility for giving signal for action against regime should be vested in single senior officer.

Comment: This single senior officer will presumably be understood to be General Castello Branco.

General Comment: While above mentioned events are encouraging in showing better leadership and new elements of organization among democratic military resistance group, they also obviously introduce short-term factors of instability into situation.

Gordon

187.   Telegram From the Ambassador to Brazil (Gordon) to the Department of State[1]

Rio de Janeiro, March 28, 1964.

[*telegram number not declassified*]. The following is [*telegram number not declassified*] transmitted at the request of Ambassador Gordon:

Personal from Ambassador Gordon. Please pass immediately to Sec. State Rusk, Assistant Secretary Mann, Ralph Burton, Sec. Defense McNamara, Assistant Sec. Defense McNaughton, General Maxwell Taylor, CIA Director John McCone, Col. J.C. King, Desmond FitzGerald, White House for Bundy and Dungan, pass to Canal Zone for General O'Meara. Other distribution only by approval above named.

1. Since returning to Rio 22 March I have canvassed Brazilian situation thoroughly with key civilian and military staff members here, convoking Sao Paulo and Brasilia Post Chiefs to assist and also making selected contact with some well informed Brazilians.

2. My considered conclusion is that Goulart is now definitely engaged on campaign to seize dictatorial power, accepting the active collaboration of the Brazilian Communist Party, and of other radical left revolutionaries to this end. If he were to succeed it is more than likely that Brazil would come under full Communist control, even though Goulart might hope to turn against his Communist supporters on the Peronist model which I believe he personally prefers.

3. The immediate tactics of the Goulart palace guard are concentrated on pressures to secure from the Congress constitutional reforms unattainable by normal means, using a combination of urban street demonstrations, threatened or actual strikes, sporadic rural violence, and abuse of the enormous discretionary financial power of the federal government. This is being coupled with a series of populist executive decrees of dubious legality and an inspired rumor campaign of other decrees calculated to frighten resistance elements. Especially important in this connection is the ability of the President to weaken

---

[1] Source: National Archives and Records Administration, RG 59, Central Files 1964–66, POL 23–9 BRAZ. Top Secret; Immediate; Exdis. Received in the Department at 8:01 p.m., March 27. Bundy received an advance copy of this telegram on March 27. (Johnson Library, National Security File, Country File, Brazil, Vol. II, 3/64) The next morning Bundy briefed the President on "a very disquieting message" from Gordon: "We will have a recommendation for you, I think, on the wire. It's a standby problem, but it might explode, he says, anytime in the next month or so, day to day or month to month." (Johnson Library, Recordings and Transcripts, Recording of telephone conversation between President Johnson and Bundy, March 28, 1964, 9:30 a.m. CST, Tape F64.21, Side A, PNO 1) The President was at his Ranch in Texas, March 26–31.

resistance at the state level by withholding essential federal financing. The government is also subjecting radio and TV outlets to a partial censorship, increasing the use of the National News Agency and requisitioning broadcast time for its reformist propaganda, and making thinly veiled threats against the opposition press. The purpose is not in fact to secure constructive social and economic reforms, but to discredit the existing constitution and the Congress, laying a foundation for a coup from the top down which might then be ratified by a rigged plebiscite and the rewriting of the constitution by a rigged Constituent Assembly.

4. I do not wholly discard the hypothesis of Goulart's being frightened off this campaign and serving out his normal term (until January 31, 1966) with proper presidential elections being held in October, 1965. This would still be the best outcome for Brazil and for the United States if it can happen. Goulart's commitments to the revolutionary left are now so far-reaching, however, that the chances of achieving this peaceful outcome through constitutional normalcy seem a good deal less than 50–50. He may make tactical retreats to tranquilize the opposition again, as he has in the past. There are some signs that this has happened in the past few days, as a result of the 19 March massive opposition street rally in Sao Paulo, the declared hostility of the governors of several major states, and warnings and rumblings within the officer corps, especially of the army. But past experience shows that each tactical retreat leaves considerable ground gained and the next advance goes further than the previous one. With his time running out and the candidates for the succession getting actively into the field, Goulart is under pressure to act faster and with less calculation of the risks. Misgovernment is also accelerating the rate of inflation to a point threatening economic breakdown and social disorder. A desperate lunge for totalitarian power might be made at any time.

5. The Goulart movement, including its Communist affiliates, represents a small minority—not more than 15 to 20 percent of the people or the Congress. It has systematically taken control of many strategic points, however, notably Petrobras (which under the decree of March 13 is now taking over the five remaining private oil refineries not already under its control), the Department of Posts and Telegraphs, the trade union leadership in oil, railroads, ports, merchant shipping, the newly formed rural workers' associations, and some other key industries, the military and civil households of the presidency, important units of the Ministries of Justice and Education, and elements in many other government agencies. In the armed forces, there are a number of far leftist officers, who have been given preferment and key assignments by Goulart, but the overwhelming majority are legalist and anti-Communist and there is a modest minority of long-standing right-wing coup supporters. The left has sought to weaken the armed forces through subversive organization of the non-commissioned officers and

enlisted personnel, with significant results especially in the air force and navy.

6. I undertook in March 21 talk with Secretary Rusk[2] to appraise the strength and spirit of the resistance forces and the circumstances that might trigger internal violence and showdown. I find that since the Goulart-syndicalist street rally in Rio on March 13 there has been a radical polarization of attitudes. Political and public leadership in crystallizing overt support for the constitution and Congress, for reforms only within the constitution, and for rejection of communism, has come from a group of governors: Lacerda of Guanabara, Adhemar de Barros of Sao Paulo, Meneghetti of Rio Grande do Sul, Braga of Parana, and (somewhat to my surprise) Magalhaes Pinto of Minas Gerais. They have been fortified by the clear declaration of ex-President Marshal Dutra and the nomination acceptance speech of Kubitschek. The huge pro-democratic rally in Sao Paulo March 19, largely organized by women's groups, has provided an important element of mass popular showing, which reacts favorably in turn on Congress and the armed forces.

7. There is a reciprocal interdependence of action between Congress and the armed forces. Congressional resistance to illegal executive actions and to unwarranted presidential demands for constitutional change depends on the conviction that the members will have military coverage if they take a stand. The legalist tradition of the armed forces is so strong that they would desire, if at all possible, congressional coverage for any action against Goulart. The action of Congress is therefore one major key to the situation.

8. While a clear majority of Congress mistrusts Goulart's purposes and scorns his evident incompetence, the present consensus of anti-Goulart congressional leaders is that an absolute majority of the lower house cannot now be mustered for impeachment. They also oppose a move of Congress away from Brasilia as tending to undercut their already tarnished prestige, although they would keep open a dramatic retreat to Sao Paulo or elsewhere as a last resort in a near civil war or open civil war situation. They are presently focussing on the approval of some mild reform measures as one way of countering Goulart's anti-Congress campaign, and considering other more affirmative means of showing resistance. They are most unlikely to vote a plebiscite law, a delegation of powers, legalization of the Communist Party, votes for illiterates, or other political changes sought by Goulart.

---

[2] According to Rusk's Appointment Book, he met Mann, Gordon, Burton, King, and FitzGerald at 10:02 a.m., March 21. (Johnson Library) No substantive record of the meeting has been found.

9. By all odds the most significant development is the crystalliz-ing of a military resistance group under the leadership of Gen. Hum-berto Castello Branco, Army Chief of Staff. Castello Branco is a highly competent, discreet, honest, and deeply respected officer who has strong loyalty to legal and constitutional principles and until recently shunned any approaches from anti-Goulart conspirators. He has asso-ciated with him a group of other well placed senior officers and is now assuming control and systematic direction of the widespread but hith-erto loosely organized resistance groups, military and civilian, in all areas of the country.

10. Castello Branco's preference would be to act only in case of ob-vious unconstitutional provocation, e.g., a Goulartist move to close Con-gress or to intervene in one of the opposition states (Guanabara or Sao Paulo being the most likely ones). He recognizes, however (as do I) that Goulart may avoid such obvious provocation, while continuing to move toward an irreversible fait accompli by means of manipulated strikes, financial undermining of the states, and an executive plebiscite—in-cluding voting by illiterates—to back up a Bonapartist or Gaullist-type assumption of power. Castello Branco is therefore preparing for a pos-sible move sparked by a Communist-led general strike call, another ser-geants' rebellion, a plebiscite call opposed by Congress, or even a ma-jor governmental countermove against the democratic military or civilian leadership. In these cases, political coverage might have to come in the first instance from a grouping of state governors declaring them-selves the legitimate Government of Brazil, with congressional en-dorsement following (if Congress were still able to act). It is also possi-ble that Goulart might resign under pressure from solid military opposition, either to flee the country or to lead a "populist" revolu-tionary movement. The possibilities clearly include civil war, with some horizontal or vertical division within the armed forces, aggravated by the widespread possession of arms in civilian hands on both sides.

11. Unlike the many previous anti-Goulart coup groups who have approached us during the past two and one half years, the Castello Branco movement shows prospects of wide support and competent lead-ership. If our influence is to be brought to bear to help avert a major dis-aster here—which might make Brazil the China of the 1960s—this is where both I and all my senior advisors believe our support should be placed. (Secretaries Rusk and Mann should note that Alberto Byington[3]

---

[3] According to Adolf A. Berle, Byington, a Brazilian businessman, had been work-ing to forestall a "Goulart dictatorship" and "bought on his own credit a shipload of oil to make sure the Brazilian Navy would be able to function." (Diary entry, April 2, 1964; Beatrice Bishop Berle and Travis Beal Jacobs, eds. *Navigating the Rapids, 1918–1971: From the Papers of Adolf A. Berle,* pp. 788–789)

is working with this group.) We hold this view even should Castello Branco be relieved as Army Chief of Staff.

12. Despite their strength in the officer corps, the resistance group is concerned about the adequacy of arms and the possible sabotage of POL supplies. Within the coming week, we will be apprised of their estimates of needed arms through contact between ARMA and Gen. Cintra, righthand man of Castello Branco. POL needs would include the navy fuel now being sought by Byington together with motor fuel and aviation gasoline.

13. Given the absolute uncertainty of timing of a possible trigger incident (which could occur tomorrow or any other day); we recommend (a) that measures be taken soonest to prepare for a clandestine delivery of arms of non-US origin, to be made available to Castello Branco supporters in Sao Paulo as soon as requirements known and arrangements can be worked out. Best delivery means now apparent to us is unmarked submarine to be off-loaded at night in isolated shore spots in state of Sao Paulo south of Santos, probably near Iguape or Gananeia. (b) This should be accompanied by POL availabilities (bulk, packaged, or both may be required), also avoiding USG identification, with deliveries to await outbreak active hostilities. Action on this (Deptel 1281)[4] should proceed forthwith.

14. The above two actions might suffice to secure victory for friendly forces without any overt US logistical or military participation, especially if politically covered by prompt US recognition our side as legitimate GOB. We should, however, also prepare without delay against the contingency of needed overt intervention at a second stage and also against the possibility of Soviet action to support the Communist-leaning side. To minimize possibilities of a prolonged civil war and secure the adherence of large numbers of band-wagon jumpers, our ability to demonstrate commitment and some show of force with great speed could be crucial. For this purpose and in keeping with our Washington talks March 21, one possibility appears to be the early detachment of a naval task force for maneuvers in south Atlantic, bringing them within a few days' steaming distance of Santos. Logistical supplies should meet requirements specified in CINC South Brazil contingency Plan (USSCJTFP–Brazil)[5] reviewed here March 9.

---

[4] Telegram 1281 to Rio de Janeiro, March 26, reported: "Defense providing list of materials required and other data on POL tanker action we discussed with you. Urgently awaiting your on-scene assessment of total situation as basis for moving ahead on this and on shaping next steps vis-à-vis Brazil." (National Archives and Records Administration, RG 59, Central Files 1964–66, POL 2 BRAZ)

[5] Reference is apparently to "US Southern Command Contingency Plan," undated. (Johnson Library, National Security File, Country File, Brazil, Vol. III, 4/64)

Carrier aircraft would be most important for psychological effect. Marine contingent could perform logistical security tasks set forth CINC South Plan. We would welcome advice soonest on this or alternative methods meeting objective described above.

15. We recognize problem uncertain duration of need these forces in area. With near-daily crises of varying intensity here, however, and violence ready to become epidemic through rural land invasion, clashes of rival Communist and democratic street meeting, or general strike efforts, and with programmed crescendo of Goulart actions with special commitment to "having achieved basic reforms" by August 24 (tenth anniversary of Vargas suicide), real danger exists of eruption civil war at any time. Only convincing sign of latter would be clean sweep of extremists from military and civilian palace guard. Current episode of rebellious sailors demonstrates fragility of situation and possible imminence of showdown.

16. We are meanwhile undertaking complementary measures with our available resources to help strengthen resistance forces. These include covert support for pro-democracy street rallies (next big one being April 2 here in Rio, and others being programmed), discreet passage of word that USG deeply concerned at events, and encouragement democratic and anti-Communist sentiment in Congress, armed forces, friendly labor and student groups, church, and business. We may be requesting modest supplementary funds for other covert action programs in near future.

17. I also believe that it would be useful, without entering into detail, for Sec State or Presidential press conference response to indicate concern at reports of economic deterioration and political restlessness in Brazil and importance to future of hemisphere that Brazil, true to its deep-rooted democratic and constitutional traditions, will continue its economic and social progress under representative democracy. We recommend such statement in next few days.

18. This message is not an alarmist or panicky reaction to any one episode. It reflects the joint conclusions of the top Embassy staff based on a long chain of actions and intelligence information which convince us that there is a real and present danger to democracy and freedom in Brazil which could carry this enormous nation into the Communist camp. If this were a country of less strategic importance to the U.S.—both directly and in its impact on all Latin America—we might suggest a further period of watchful waiting in the hope that Brazilian resistance unaided would take care of the problem. We believe that there is substantial likelihood that it may do so, given the basic sentiments and attitudes of the majority of the people and the strength of organized democratic sentiment especially in the southern half of the country. The power of Goulart and the presidency to sap and undermine

resistance is so great, however, that our manifest support, both moral and material and even at substantial cost, may well be essential to maintain the backbone of the Brazilian resistance. No loss of time can be afforded in preparing for such action. The alternative of risking a Communist Brazil appears unacceptable, implying potentially far greater ultimate costs in both money and lives.

188. Memorandum of Conversation[1]

Washington, March 28, 1964.

SUBJECT

    Brazil

PARTICIPANTS

    Alexis Johnson, Robert Adams, Ralph Burton, Gen. Goodpaster, Gen. Crawford, Richard Helms, Desmond FitzGerald, J.C. King, McGeorge Bundy, Gordon Chase

The group discussed the situation in Brazil with particular reference to Ambassador Gordon's message of March 27, 1964 (copy attached).[2]

1. *General*—The group agreed that it would be preferable if we could waffle through to the next election. However, this is obviously not the primary consideration; we don't want to watch Brazil dribble down the drain while we stand around waiting for the election.

The group discussed the present situation vis-à-vis Goulart and the Brazilian military. It is not at all clear when and at what point we can expect the military to act against the regime. Mr. Bundy said that the shape of the problem is such that we should not be worrying that the military will react; we should be worrying that the military will not react. Mr. Adams thought that the military would certainly react if Goulart started firing any of the plotting army commanders. The group

---

[1] Source: Johnson Library, National Security File, Country File, Brazil, Vol. II, Cables, 3/64. Top Secret; No Distribution. Another copy of the memorandum indicates it was cleared by Bundy. (Memorandum from Chase to Bundy, March 30; ibid.) The meeting was held at the White House. FitzGerald also drafted an account of the meeting, portions of which are summarized in footnotes below.

[2] Document 187.

agreed that, in any event, all the plotters in Brazil should react on the same signal.[3]

Mr. FitzGerald wondered whether we will have a problem in deciding when to move in favor of the anti-Goulart forces; how far will we have to let Goulart go? Others felt that this would not be a serious problem; there would be plenty of signals we could act on.

2. *Ambassador Gordon's Request*—The group discussed Ambassador Gordon's requests for action by Washington.

(a) *Submarine Delivery of Arms*—The group agreed that this was a puzzling request. Mr. Johnson wondered why the Brazilian Army would need a drop of this relatively small size; the military must have plenty of arms.

(b) *Petroleum*—The group agreed that the request for POL was legitimate. Noting that the 2nd Army in the Sao Paulo area is the most likely to be anti-Goulart, [1½ *lines of source text not declassified*]. This would be used if an anti-Goulart move takes place. It was noted that the Army must have the ability to march from Sao Paulo to take over Rio; such action, by the way, would probably end the fight.

(c) *Task Force*—The group questioned Ambassador Gordon's request for the early detachment of a naval task force for maneuvers in the South Atlantic. Mr. Bundy noted that ". . . the punishment doesn't seem to fit the crime . . .". Gen. Goodpaster also did not clearly understand how this particular move would be helpful to the anti-Goulart forces at this time.

(d) *Public Statement*—The general consensus was that there should not be a high-level public statement of concern about the deteriorating situation in Brazil. The group went on to discuss the possibility of stimulating an appropriate editorial in the *N.Y. Times* or *The Washington Post*. The group agreed, however, that this would have to be handled carefully since the editorial could easily come out in an unsatisfactory way (e.g., "Once again, the State Department has misunderstood the deep revolutionary forces in Latin America . . .").

(e) *Belo Horizonte Meeting*—The group agreed that we are better off to let the Belo meeting go on on April 21, and then do what we can

---

[3] According to FitzGerald "there was considerable discussion concerning the need on the part of the anti-Goulart plotters to come to agreement concerning the nature of Goulart actions which would trigger a revolt. Mr. Burton referred to a recent State cable from Ambassador Gordon in which seven possible triggers were mentioned. It was pointed out that Goulart has the capability of weakening the conspiracy by dismissing or reassigning certain of the key military members of the conspiracy. There was some speculation as to whether such dismissals would result in counter-action by the conspirators." (Memorandum for the record, March 28; National Security Council, 303 Committee Files, Subject Files, Brazil)

to make it a flop. Mr. FitzGerald noted that if we try to stop the meeting and are successful, the meeting might be held in a place where our capabilities for making it a flop are not as great as they are in Belo.

3. *Action Items*—The group agreed that the following action should be taken:

(a) [*4 lines of source text not declassified*]

(b) Mr. Burton will explore the possibility of getting the *N.Y. Times* to publish a satisfactory editorial calling attention to the situation in Brazil; among other things, he will try to determine what the *N.Y. Times* has said about Goulart in the past. Mr. Bundy will explore the possibility of getting an appropriate editorial from *The Washington Post*.[4]

(c) State will send a cable to Ambassador Gordon which, inter alia, will say (a) that we are taking action with respect to petroleum; (b) that we are still not clear as to the rationale behind the Ambassador's requests for a submarine drop and for a task force appearance; (c) that we want the Ambassador to review our economic and financial relations with Brazil and give us his recommendation on action we should take; and (d) that we question the desirability of a high-level public statement at this time. The cable will also instruct Ambassador Gordon to keep a high level of security in his contact with anti-Goulart forces. We don't want to hamper him in making contact, but want him to use a cut-out. Above all, we don't want to turn off our hearing aids.[5]

GC

---

[4] Although *The Washington Post* did not print an "appropriate editorial," *The New York Times* published the following assessment: "The political situation is close to chaos. President Goulart is a curious combination of stubbornness and weakness. He has proved in recent years that he loves power, needs power and will do almost anything to hold on to it." (*New York Times*, March 31, 1964, p. 34)

[5] [*text not declassified*] (Memorandum for the record, March 28; National Security Council, 303 Committee Files, Subject Files, Brazil)

189.   Telegram From the President's Special Assistant for National
       Security Affairs (Bundy) to President Johnson in Texas[1]

Washington, March 28, 1964.

CAP 64100. To Colonel Connell for the President from Bundy. Following two messages are: first, a long and important message from Ambassador Gordon, and a summary of a response which we are making.

Text of Gordon Message:[2]

After interdepartmental consultation with DOD, JCS, State and CIA, we are drafting an answer[3] which in substance will do the following:

1. Inform Gordon that neither submarine landing nor carrier task force sounds right to us and ask for further elaboration of their thinking.

2. Tell him that we think key problem in event of Army action is supply and are actively preparing a covert capability for rapid supply in this field.

3. Ask Gordon to review our economic and financial relations with Brazil and recommend any desirable actions in the light of gathering crisis.

4. Instruct him to insure highest degree of security consistent with effective communication to anti-Goulart elements.

5. Question advisability of early strong public statement here. Instead we are exploring possibility of generating active press comment against Goulart since this strengthens his opponents without setting up USG as target of his demagoguery.

6. Make plain that fundamentally we share Gordon's concern that he can rely on us for effective action if worst comes to worst.

---

[1] Source: Johnson Library, National Security File, Country File, Brazil, Vol. II, 3/64. Top Secret; Priority. No time of transmission appears on the telegram; it was received by the White House Army Signal Agency at 6:56 p.m. Printed from a draft copy that includes Bundy's minor handwritten revisions. A note indicates that the copy sent to the President was "retrieved and destroyed."

[2] Document 187. Although the text does not appear here, a copy of the telegram was forwarded to the President. A handwritten note indicates the copy was returned to Dungan on March 30.

[3] See Document 190.

190.   Telegram From the Department of State to the Ambassador to Brazil (Gordon)[1]

Washington, March 28, 1964.

1. Steps being taken to provide tanker service for POL requirements as estimated here. Our estimate based on 30 day supply MO gas for Sao Paulo forces for both combat and movement as far as Rio or Porto Alegre, AV gas for 40 squadron 1½ hour sorties, and navy special and diesel fuel for 30 days. Hope to advise you fully of detailed implementation within few days.

2. Exploring with other agencies additional courses of action recommended in your report but awaiting word from you on logistic support required. In this connection, while not desirous of disrupting needed contacts or normal ARMA activities, hope you and ARMA or other key staff can avoid direct contact with military plotters. Leave to your judgment but suggest that [2 *lines of source text not declassified*].

3. To what purposes would armaments offloaded from submarine be put? How critical would small shipment this kind be to success of main military thrust? Questions also arise here about feasibility furnishing unmarked or non-US origin arms without these later being attributed to US covert operation.

4. Would not Brazilian military be able to provide military protection in Sao Paulo–Santos areas for logistic support? If so, why is there any need for stand-by US naval units or follow-up military participation? Doubtful we can provide plausible cover for naval operation.

5. Would appreciate more detail on status of Castello Branco operation and on estimated alignment and relative effectiveness, actual or potential, of officers and key elements in the four armies and other armed forces; also degree likelihood various possible Goulart actions which would trigger their resistance. To what extent would such estimates be affected by (a) Congressional support or non-support (b) differing degrees gubernatorial action?

6. Reply to your query on coffee tax or blocking coffee receipts in preparation and will advise by April 1. How does your assessment affect debt negotiations? Should we abandon, slow down or otherwise modify debt negotiating strategy to avoid strengthening Goulart's prestige? Should we hold up approval or announcement of AID loans? Are

---

[1] Source: Johnson Library, National Security File, Country File, Brazil, Vol. II, 3/64. Top Secret. Drafted by Adams and Burton. Printed from a draft copy of the telegram. A typewritten note indicates that it was "cleared in substance at a White House meeting."

other non-military measures desirable further to polarize situation to Goulart's disadvantage?

7. Statement by President or Secretary not believed desirable at this time.

---

191. Telegram From the Ambassador to Brazil (Gordon) to the Department of State[1]

Rio de Janeiro, March 29, 1964.

Personal from Ambassador Gordon. Please pass immediately to Secretary of State Rusk, Assistant Secretary Mann, Ralph Burton, Secretary Defense McNamara, Assistant Secretary Defense McNaughton, General Maxwell Taylor, CIA Director John McCone, Colonel J.C. King, Desmond FitzGerald, White House for Bundy and Dungan, pass to Canal Zone for General O'Meara. Other distribution only by approval above named.

1. Since my message on Friday,[2] effects of Navy crisis have substantially worsened the overall situation and possibly shortened the time factors. The replacement of Navy Minister Silvio Mota by a superannuated left-wing Admiral, Paulo Mario Cunha Rodrigues, reliably reported to have been proposed by Communist leaders and the CGT, the retention of Aragao as Marine Commandant, and the total amnesty for the rebellious sailors and Marines, are all body blows to the morale of the officer corps of all three services and are apparently frightening many congressmen. (We expect more light on latter point from Brasilia Monday.)[3] The worst feature of the episode is that the tactical moves by the palace Friday afternoon were directed hour by hour by a close-knit group composed mainly of Communists. Left-wing group now talking openly about new advances beginning with "cleaning out the Army".

---

[1] Source: Johnson Library, National Security File, Country File, Brazil, Vol. II, 3/64. Top Secret. Printed from a draft copy of the telegram. It was forwarded to the White House on March 30. (Memorandum from Helms to Bundy, March 30; ibid.)

[2] Document 187. The Navy crisis began on March 24 when the Navy Minister, Sílvio Mota, imprisoned six leaders of the sailors' association for political activities. On March 25 the sailors' association responded with a rally in the Guanabara metalworkers' building, refusing to leave until a new minister released their comrades. After negotiating for 3 days Goulart accepted the sailors' terms, forcing Mota's resignation.

[3] Telegrams 127, 128, and 129 from Brasilia, March 30, reported on Congressional reaction to events surrounding the Navy crisis. (Johnson Library, National Security File, Country File, Brazil, Vol. II, 3/64)

Resistance forces, both military and civilian, seeking recover from unexpected setback and consulting feverishly on future courses of action.

2. Re para 2 of reference,[4] will transmit bill of goods as soon as available. I have had no direct contact with military plotters. My definite judgement is that ARMA must continue intelligence contacts for which he uniquely qualified, but that any operational contacts will become responsibility of [*less than 1 line of source text not declassified*].

3. Re para 3 of Saturday's message[4] purpose of unidentified arms made available soonest and if possible pre-positioned prior any outbreak of violence could be manifold, depending on unforeseeable development of events. Could be used by para-military units working with democratic military groups, or by friendly military against hostile military if necessary. Immediate effect, which we stress, would be bolster will to resist and facilitate initial success. Given Brazilian predilection joining victorious causes, initial success could be key to side on which many indecisive forces would land and therefore key to prompt victory with minimal violence. Risk of later attribution to US Government covert operation seems minor to us in relation positive effects if operation conducted with skill, bearing in mind that many things we don't do are being regularly so attributed.

4. Re paragraph 4 of Saturday's message, my purpose in paragraphs 14 and 18 of Friday's message was to make clear that in civil war type situation our ability show force promptly in response appeal from politically recognized democratic side might be crucial determining factor in early victory that side. I well understand how grave a decision is implied in this contingency commitment to overt military intervention here. But we must also weigh seriously the possible alternative, which I am not predicting but can envisage as real danger of defeat of democratic resistance and communization of Brazil. We did not intend naval operation to be covert, and overt maneuvers in South Atlantic could be healthy influence.

5. Re para 5 of Saturday's message recent ARMA [*less than 1 line of source text not declassified*] reports cover much of this ground. We will continue studying and reporting regularly on these questions, especially possibility and consequences initiative of group of governors without prior Congressional coverage.

6. Re para 6 of Saturday's message, I see no present point in foot-dragging on debt negotiations or hold action on AID loans, unless preceded by some clear indication of United States government concern with basic problem of Brazilian political regime. No one expects action on debts until a month hence anyway. In case of AID projects of direct

---

[4] Document 187.

interest to clearly democratic elements, such as Cemat, we believe approvals and announcements should continue. We shall evaluate each case as it arises in light of political effects at the time. If we later reach point of wanting to suspend aid publicly, which would be especially dramatic if wheat included, more appropriate time would be in response more obvious political developments than have yet occurred and which would probably include direct attacks on our economic interests. On this subject I await eagerly your April 1 advice on coffee penalties.

7. What is needed now is a sufficiently clear indication of United States government concern to reassure the large numbers of democrats in Brazil that we are not indifferent to the danger of a Communist revolution here, but couched in terms that cannot be openly rejected by Goulart as undue intervention. I am cancelling my trip programmed to Alagoas and Bahia Monday through Wednesday, sending Kubish to represent me, and this cancellation will convey some measure of concern. Our discreet, informal contacts with friendly Brazilians also help. Nothing that we here can do, however, will be nearly as influential as a high-level Washington statement. Press reports at home on the navy crisis surely could serve as a peg for such statement.

8. I therefore reiterate recommendation in para 17 of Friday's message. In light developments described para 1 this message, earliest possible action would achieve optimum results.

---

192. **Telegram From the Army Attaché in Brazil (Walters) to the Department of the Army**[1]

Rio de Janeiro, March 30, 1964.

ARMA saw General Cintra at 2400 hours local Sunday.[2] He had just come from meeting of resistance movement to Goulart and said it had been decided to take action this week on a signal to be issued later. Response to Castello Branco document from Second Army

---

[1] Source: Johnson Library, National Security File, Country File, Brazil, Vol. II, Cables, 3/64. Secret. Repeated to DIA, CINCSO, and COMUSARSO. No time of transmission appears on the copy printed here which is an information copy sent from the JCS and received at the White House at 7:12 p.m., and includes a handwritten note from Bromley Smith: "Linc Gordon asked that all who received his messages see this one from our army attaché."

[2] March 29.

Commander General Kruel fully satisfactory. Kruel stated that he agreed one hundred percent with document and considered himself released from any obligation to Goulart by reasons of latter's recent actions. Kruel added that if relieved as Second Army Commander he would not turn over command. Cintra said that when Castello Branco is relieved as Chief of Staff early this week he will immediately issue denunciation to nation. Helicopter has been laid on to move Castello Branco, Gen Cordeiro de Farias[3] and Marshal Dutra out of Rio and on to Sao Paulo when movement is imminent. Cintra indicated that he and BGEN Syseno Garmento will remain in Rio de Janeiro. BGEN Moniz de Aragao will operate in Rio Vila Militar. Movement in Vila Militar will begin from bottom up and plans have been made to neutralize key units believed to be favorable to Goulart and leftists. Cintra said that central command of movement would initially be in Sao Paulo. Arrangements have been made with navy and air force for joint action. BGEN Souto Malan proceeding this morning to Porto Alegre with full instructions for Maj Gen Adalberto Pereira dos Santos there in command of Sixth Inf Div and next senior officer to Third Army Commander. Cintra confident of Minas Gerais Garrison and said Governor Magalhaes Pinto of that state eager for move. Total movement may be triggered by meeting of democratic governors in Porto Alegre on Wednesday.[4] Day not yet decided for initiation of movement. Cintra seemed confident of success.

Major Moraes Rego leaves in morning for Recife carrying instructions for Fourth Army Commander Justino Alves Bastos. *Comment:* While this may be only talk ARMA has never seen Cintra as assured and positive. ARMA expects to be aware beforehand of go signal and will report in consequence. If opposition intends to do something this is time. Cintra stated flatly move would occur during coming week barring overriding reason for postponement as further waiting would only help Goulart.[5]

---

[3] Reference is to the following military leaders: Osvaldo Cordeiro de Farias, former Armed Forces Chief of Staff; Eurico Gaspar Dutra, former President of Brazil (1946–1951); Siseno Sarmento, Chief of Staff to Costa e Silva; and Augusto César Moniz de Aragão.

[4] April 1.

[5] Walters gave the following account in his memoirs: "I told the Ambassador [Gordon] on Sunday, March 30, that all of my information pointed to an imminent action by those Brazilian officers who feared that further delay would create an irreversible situation. I told the Ambassador that I felt the provocation the plotters had been awaiting had just been given by the President [Goulart] in seeking to disrupt the discipline, unity and hierarchy of the armed services." (*Silent Missions,* p. 386) At 7 p.m. (EST), Gordon reported: "Conviction is spreading here also that showdown will result from current sequence of events. We think critical point could come soon, perhaps even in next day or so." (Telegram 2116 from Rio de Janeiro, March 30; National Archives and Records Administration, RG 59, Central Files 1964–66, POL 23–9)

193.   Telephone Conversation Between Secretary of State Rusk and President Johnson[1]

March 30, 1964, 9:35 p.m.

Rusk:—Mann and group here, including CIA, on this Brazilian situation.[2] The crisis is coming to a head in the next day or two, perhaps even over night. There is a snowballing of resistance to Goulart and therefore the thing may break at any moment. The armed forces, the governors, particularly in populated states of the east coast, seem to be building up real resistance there. I would like to send a message to Linc Gordon. I'd like to read it to you, if I may, and then also indicate that I've asked Bob McNamara to get some tankers ready for some POL supplies and things of that sort.

[Rusk reads a draft of Document 194.]

Rusk: Now the situation is that—

President: Are you through with the message?

Rusk: Yes.

President: What you—

Rusk: Now, the situation basically is that there is a very substantial build-up of resistance to Goulart. Now, if the governors of the key states of the east coast, such as Minas Gerais and Sao Paolo, and all those heavily populated states of the east coast who are anti-Goulart, should join together with the armed forces who are stationed in those key states, then I think this may be something that we will have to go along with and get in touch with. And we need to get Linc Gordon's fundamental judgment. I tell him that this is the principle judgment that he has got to make in which he will earn his pay. He's got to tell us his best judgment as to whether this is an opportunity which will

---

[1] Source: Johnson Library, Recordings and Transcripts, Recording of telephone conversation between President Johnson and Rusk, Tape F64.21, Side B, PNO 1. No classification marking. Rusk was in Washington; the President was in Texas. According to the President's Daily Diary, Rusk placed the call. (Johnson Library) The beginning of the conversation was not recorded. This transcript was prepared in the Office of the Historian specifically for this volume.

[2] Rusk met at 6 p.m. with Mann, Burton, U. Alexis Johnson, Adams, and Ball; the meeting was joined in progress by Greenfield, Bundy, Noland, and FitzGerald. (Johnson Library, Rusk Appointment Book) They met to draft instructions to Ambassador Gordon in Rio de Janeiro and were still meeting when the telephone conversation between Rusk and Johnson began. During the discussion a decision was reached to have a Navy task force commence moving as quickly as possible. The CIA representatives' suggestion that this task force "include an LSD loaded with a barge containing appropriate arms and ammunition, in case of a semi-clandestine arms drop, was accepted. Secretary McNamara was advised of this decision." (Memorandum for the record by FitzGerald, March 31; Central Intelligence Agency, Job 78–03041R, [*file name not declassified*])

not be repeated, and which, if not taken now, will give Goulart a chance to undermine his opposition, and take Brazil down the road to a Communist dictatorship. This message that I have read to you does not commit you in any way, it simply, basically asking him for information, to give him a certain atmosphere of our attitude here—

President: The effect though, what it says is get somebody legitimate and get him substantial and don't let it go Communist.[3]

Rusk: That's right. And I talked to Bob McNamara to lay on some tankers to get some POL supplies and other things on the way. And also General O'Meara has been ordered by Bob McNamara to come to New York, to Washington tonight to talk about contingency plans that might be needed in this situation. So I would like just to send off this in effect advisory telegram to Linc Gordon, our Ambassador, to see whether by morning or during the day tomorrow that we might want to make a decision here as to how we move in this situation.

President: Sure.

Rusk: That's all right?

President: That sounds good. That's fine.

Rusk: Now I have also, we had an unfortunate accident today. The House Foreign Affairs Committee put out a report on, that included some references to Brazil, a report that was prepared last January, that included a reference to the fact that we did not expect an early Communist takeover in Brazil.

President: Was prepared January '64?

Rusk: That's right. Now I, background has impressed people tonight to have them say that a high State Department official said that the situation in Brazil had deteriorated in the meantime, since that report was issued, that we are deeply concerned about the prospects for representative and constitutional democracy in Brazil. Because if this report had gone down, goes down to Brazil without some sort of a correction, Goulart might take this as a blessing for the things he's trying to do. So without any direct quote of you or me, I did do some backgrounding to try to counteract one or two sentences in this report, for its, because of its impact in Brazil tomorrow morning.

President: All right.

[Omitted here is discussion of Panama.]

Rusk: Right. Now, except for this Brazilian matter, I can call you early in the morning. There's nothing here other than Brazil that would pull you back to Washington tomorrow rather than Wednesday. But I

---

[3] According to FitzGerald, Rusk said that "the President instructed him that under no circumstances should Brazil be allowed to go Communist."

think this Brazilian matter just could blow over night, and I'll be in touch with you about it, so that you can make your plans.

President: Fine. Call me, if not I'll be coming back on Wednesday, but I'll come any time I need to.[4]

Rusk: Oh, fine. Thank you, Mr. President.

President: Bye.

Rusk: Bye.

---

[4] The President later told Reedy that Rusk "expects something could happen tonight. So I rather expect we ought to go on back to Washington as soon as we can without being emergency. I don't see anything to be gained to be in Johnson City with the Hemisphere going Communist." (Johnson Library, Recordings and Transcripts, Recording of telephone conversation between President Johnson and Reedy, March 30, 1964, 9:35 p.m. CST, Tape F64.21, Side B, PNO 2)

---

194. Telegram From the Department of State to the Embassy in Brazil[1]

Washington, March 30, 1964, 9:52 p.m.

1296. For Ambassador from Secretary.

US policy toward Brazil is based upon our determination to support in every possible way maintenance of representative and constitutional government in Brazil free from continuing threat of dictatorship from the left erected through a Goulart/Brizzola manipulation. It is of great importance that there be a preemption of the position of legitimacy by those who will oppose communist and other extremist influences. It is highly desirable, therefore, that if action is taken by the armed forces such action be preceded or accompanied by a clear demonstration of unconstitutional actions on the part of Goulart or his colleagues or that legitimacy be confirmed by acts of the Congress (if it is free to act) or by expressions of the key governors or by some other means which gives substantial claim to legitimacy.

With respect to US support capabilities, we can act promptly on financial and economic measures. With regard to military assistance logistic factors are important. Surface vessels loaded with arms and ammunition could not reach southern Brazil before at least ten days.

---

[1] Source: National Archives and Records Administration, RG 59, Central Files 1964–66, POL 23–9 BRAZ. Top Secret; Flash; Nodis. Drafted and approved by Rusk.

Airlift could be provided promptly if an intermediate field at Recife, or other airfields in northeast Brazil capable of handling large jet transports, is secure and made available. In ambiguous situation it may be difficult for us to obtain permission for intermediate stops from other countries such as Peru.

You should ask your own service attachés, without consulting Brazilian authorities just yet, to prepare recommendations on types of arms and ammunition most likely to be required in light of their knowledge of the situation.

In fast moving situation we are asking all of our posts in Brazil to feed Washington continual flow of information on significant developments their areas and to stay on 24-hour alert.

At this particular moment it is important that US Government not put itself in position which would be deeply embarrassing if Goulart, Mazzilli, Congressional leaders and armed forces leadership reach accommodation in next few hours which would leave us branded with an awkward attempt at intervention. However, every disposition here is to be ready to support those elements who would move to prevent Brazil from falling under an authentic dictatorship of the left heavily infiltrated or controlled by the communists. Obviously, in a country of over 75 million people, larger than continental United States, this is not a job for a handful of United States Marines. A major determination by the authentic leadership of Brazil and a preemption of the position of legitimacy are the greatest possible importance. We will not, however, be paralyzed by theoretical niceties if the options are clearly between the genuinely democratic forces of Brazil and a communist dominated dictatorship.

As we see problem tonight, the greatest danger may well be that Goulart will be able to pull back enough within next day or two to confuse situation, blunt edge of key incipient conservative military action, and gain more time to paralyze those elements who could resist a Communist infiltrated authoritarian regime. Fragmentary reports reaching here tonight suggest that anti-Goulart forces may be developing a certain momentum. Our big problem is to determine whether this presents an opportunity which might not be repeated. In this case we would wish to make a major decision as to whether and by what means we might give additional impetus to forces now in motion consistent with considerations expressed above. No judgment you have been required to make will compare to this in earning the pay of an underpaid Ambassador.

Rusk

195. **Telegram From the Embassy in Brazil to the Department of State**[1]

Rio de Janeiro, March 31, 1964, 9 a.m.

2121. Pass White House, OSD, JCS, CINCSOUTH, CIA.

[*less than 1 line of source text not declassified*] has just received word from [*less than 1 line of source text not declassified*] that "balloon has gone up" in Minas Gerais and that revolt against Goulart government expected to start in Sao Paulo in about two hours. We have no confirmation. No details available at this point other than report General Mourao Filho is in command. (Mourao Filho is Commander 4th Military Region with headquarters in Juiz de Fora.)[2]

Gordon

---

[1] Source: National Archives and Records Administration, RG 59, Central Files 1964–66, POL 23–9 BRAZ. Secret; Flash; Limdis. Repeated Immediate to Brasilia, Sao Paulo, and Recife. Received in the Department at 7:12 a.m., and passed to White House, CIA, JCS, OSD, and CINCSO.

[2] At 10 a.m., the CIA confirmed that "an anti-Goulart revolutionary movement has actually started in Minas Gerais and that Mourao Filho is leading an unspecified number of troops toward Rio de Janeiro from Juiz de Fora." ([*telegram number not declassified*], March 31; Johnson Library, National Security File, Country File, Brazil, Vol. II, 3/64)

---

196. **Editorial Note**

At 9:46 a.m. on March 31, 1964, Secretary of State Rusk called Assistant Secretary Mann to discuss the emerging coup d'état in Brazil: "Sec said M might want to get someone to put together task force of 3–4 to start working on post coup emergency assistance for Brazil. They discussed the confusing situation; don't know how much is true. Sec suggested M's calling President to keep him informed. M said he would prefer after the 11 am meeting; there would be much more to say." (National Archives and Records Administration, RG 59, Rusk Files: Lot 72 D 192, Telephone Calls 3/20/64–4/9/64) Later that morning Rusk chaired an interagency meeting on Brazil. (Johnson Library, Rusk Appointment Book) In addition to Rusk, the participants included Secretary of Defense McNamara, Chairman of the Joint Chiefs of Staff Taylor, Lieutenant General O'Meara, and Director of Central Intelligence McCone. (Message for Embassy Rio, March 31; ibid., National

Security File, Country File, Brazil, Vol. II, 3/64) Other scheduled attendees were Under Secretary Ball, Deputy Under Secretary Johnson, Mann, Deputy Assistant Secretary Kitchen, Special Assistant to the President Bundy, Lieutenant General Goodpaster, Assistant Secretary of Defense McNaughton, Deputy Assistant Secretary of Defense Sloan, and Deputy Director of Central Intelligence Helms. (National Archives and Records Administration, RG 59, U. Alexis Johnson Files: Lot 90 D 408, Date Books, 1964) After briefings on the latest developments and U.S. support capabilities, the agenda called for consideration of possible military and political action, including the dispatch of a naval task force, oil tankers, and an airlift of ammunition to Brazil. (Johnson Library, National Security File, Country File, Brazil, Vol. II, 3/64) No substantive record of the discussion at the meeting has been found.

The Joint Chiefs of Staff met on March 31 to review a revised contingency plan for Brazil, USCINCSO Contingency Plan 2–61. Talking points for the meeting recommended that the JCS deploy a naval task force toward Brazilian waters but defer any decision on whether to provide "covert delivery of arms to the Castello Branco Group." In the event of civil war in Brazil, however, the United States should "be prepared unilaterally to deliver arms and other material support on an overt basis, employing any available means, to the faction whose victory would best serve U.S. interests." (Washington National Records Center, OASD/ISA Files: FRC 330 69 A 7425, Brazil) No substantive record of the meeting has been found.

Deputy Assistant Secretary Solomon also chaired an inter-agency task force on March 31, which met to consider economic assistance to Brazil, on the assumption that a "democratically-inclined pro-Western group" came to power. The task force recommended that the "most effective form of assistance" would be for creditor nations to participate in a voluntary, 3-month moratorium on payment toward Brazil's debt. (Memorandum from Weismann to Burton, March 31; National Archives and Records Administration, RG 59, ARA/BR Files: Lot 66 D 418, AID, 1964) The Department forwarded the "preliminary views" of the task force to the Embassy for further comment. (Telegram 1316 to Rio de Janeiro, April 1; ibid., Central Files 1964–66, FN 14 BRAZ)

197.   Telegram From the Embassy in Brazil to the Department of State[1]

Rio de Janeiro, March 31, 1964, 1 p.m.

2125. For Secretary from Ambassador. Deptel 1296.[2]

1. I warmly welcome reftel. Things moving very quickly with apparently reliable reports military movements in Minas Gerais fully backed by Governor Magalhaes Pinto and state police. As of noon, no clear indications corresponding action Sao Paulo or other states.

2. I have taken action to get to key governors' message on vital importance color of legitimacy, stressing desirability political coverage by majority Congress if that humanly possible. My intermediaries are inquiring how governors' group proposes handle critical question mantle of legitimacy and position as defenders of constitution, both in immediate and in subsequent actions, if congressional coverage not available.[3]

3. Most urgent logistical problem is motor and aviation gasoline in event normal supplies become unavailable to friendly forces. Local Esso contact states only Avgas tanker en route is Petrobras vessel, and he knows of no Mogas in South Atlantic. Immediate action set this in motion is in order. We are developing recommendations on possible arms and ammunition requirements.

4. Goulart's Monday night speech to sergeants,[4] which was ending when you telephoned, looks like last straw. He made appropriate verbal bows to constitution and legality, to church, and to green and yellow nationalism rather than red models, but this was transparent disguise for active support of subversion in NCO's and psychological warfare against officer corps, as well as Congress, press, and foreign and domestic business groups. While dictating this, I received reliable report that Kubitschek phoned Goulart this morning to declare his open opposition and has so stated to press.[5]

---

[1] Source: National Archives and Records Administration, RG 59, Central Files 1964–66, POL 23–9 BRAZ. Top Secret; Nodis; Flash. Received in the Department at 12:21 p.m. and repeated at 6:23 p.m. to the White House for Bundy, OSD for McNamara, and CIA for McCone only. (Johnson Library, National Security File, Country File, Brazil, Vol. II, 3/64)

[2] Document 194.

[3] Gordon's instructions are in telegrams 96 to Belo Horizonte, 235 to Brasilia, and 101 to Sao Paulo. (All March 31; National Archives and Records Administration, RG 59, Central Files 1964–66, POL 23–9 BRAZ)

[4] March 30; an account of the speech was transmitted in telegram 2120 from Rio de Janeiro, March 31. (Ibid., POL 23–8 BRAZ)

[5] See footnote 2, Document 203.

5. After deducting sixty-four dollars from my pay, my present judgment is that this might not be last opportunity, but well might be last good opportunity to support action by anti-Goulart group which still occupies large proportion strategic military commands and direction state-level forces in cohesive region states accounting for over half population and all industry. I believe your major decision should be in affirmative and will be preparing recommend means giving resistance forces additional impetus.

6. Your background briefing statement supplementing House Committee Report was very well played here in press and serves immediate purpose desired by my recommendations for some public expression interest and concern.[6]

Gordon

---

[6] Mann told Rusk earlier that the Brazilian Chargé d'Affaires had complained about the press reports, predicting that he would receive "protest instructions." Mann asked how the press spokesman should handle the incident at the noon briefing and "it was agreed he should say in view of the situation we are making no official comment and are following the situation closely. Sec said if Linc thinks we cannot get away with that, we will take another look. They agreed we should play for time; maybe tomorrow we could talk." (Mann to Rusk, March 31, 11:20 a.m.; National Archives and Records Administration, RG 59, Rusk Files: Lot 72 D 192, Telephone Calls 3/20/64–4/9/64)

198.　Telegram From the Department of State to the Embassy in Brazil[1]

Washington, March 31, 1964, 2:29 p.m.

1301. For your personal information only, the following decisions have been taken in order be in a position to render assistance at appropriate time to anti-Goulart forces if it is decided this should be done.

---

[1] Source: National Archives and Records Administration, RG 59, Central Files 1964–66, POL 23–9 BRAZ. Secret; Flash; No Distribution. Drafted by Adams and approved by Ball. The Department later informed Gordon of several corrections to the telegram; they are in footnotes below. (Telegram 1305 to Rio de Janeiro, March 31; ibid.) The JCS instructions implementing the decisions outlined in the telegram, which were also in accordance with USCINCSO Contingency Plan 2–61, are ibid. The JCS assigned the code name "Brother Sam" to the operation. (Telegram 5591 from JCS to CINCLANT, March 31; ibid.)

1. Dispatch of US Navy tankers bearing POL from Aruba, first tanker expected off Santos between April 8 and 13; following three tankers at one day intervals.[2]

2. Immediate dispatch of naval task force for overt exercises off Brazil. Force to consist of aircraft carrier (expected arrive in area by April 10), four destroyers, two destroyer escorts, task force tankers (all expected arrive about four days later).[3]

3. Assemble shipment of about 110 tons ammunition, other light equipment including tear gas[4] for mob control for air lift to Sao Paulo (Campinas). Lift would be made within 24 to 36 hours upon issuance final orders and would involve 10 cargo planes,[5] 6 tankers, and 6 fighters.

Unloading of POL by US Navy tankers (item 1) and dispatch of airlift (item 3) would require further development politico-military situation to point where some group having reasonable claim to legitimacy could formally request recognition and aid from us and if possible from other American Republics. Dispatch of tankers from Aruba and of naval task force does not immediately involve us in Brazilian situation and is regarded by us as normal naval exercise.

Rusk

---

[2] In telegram 1305 this sentence was replaced as follows: "Dispatch of U.S. Navy tankers bearing POL from Aruba, first tanker expected off Santos April 13; following three tankers at one day intervals."

[3] The sentence was replaced as follows: "Force to consist of aircraft carrier and two guided missile destroyers (expected arrive in area by April 10), four destroyers, task force tankers (all expected arrive about four days later)."

[4] The words "tear gas" were replaced with the phrase "CS agent".

[5] "10 cargo planes" was corrected to read "6 cargo planes".

199. Telephone Conversation Among the Under Secretary of State (Ball), the Assistant Secretary of State for Inter-American Affairs (Mann), and President Johnson[1]

March 31, 1964, 3:38 p.m.

President: Hello?

Ball: Hello? Oh, Mr. President, this is George Ball.

President: Yes, George.

Ball: Tom Mann is on with me.

President: Hi, Tom.

Mann: Hi.

Ball: A quick run-down of the situation in Brazil. We had a meeting this morning with Bob McNamara and Max Taylor and General O'Meara, who's come up overnight. And we decided, on the basis of the information that had come in this morning, to go ahead and start a naval task force out but with no commitment so that it will be steaming down in that direction. It couldn't get into the area before April 10th and in the meantime we can watch the developments and see whether it should go on or not. But it could be done in a way that doesn't create any kind of public stir. The second thing is: I've located some navy tankers in Aruba, and the big thing that they're going to need if they have a successful revolt down there, at some point probably, is some gasoline, both for motor vehicles and for the aviation. The tankers are going to be loaded, but again they can't be down there till around April the 8th to the 13th. But this is a precautionary move that we're taking. Third is: they're getting together a shipment of ammunition, but this will have to wait before we start moving it because it will probably have to be moved by plane and that can only be done after the situation is clarified and we would, clearly decide to make a commitment in the situation. Now, what is actually happening on the field is very confused. We've just had a teletype con-

---

[1] Source: Johnson Library, Recordings and Transcripts, Recording of telephone conversation among President Johnson, Ball and Mann, Tape F64.21, Side B, PNO 3. No classification marking. Ball and Mann were in Washington; the President was in Texas. This transcript was prepared in the Office of the Historian specifically for this volume. Before telephoning the President, Ball called Rusk: "B said he and Mann were thinking of calling the President and wondered if the Sec had. Sec had not. Sec asked if there was anything new after the call to Rio. B said not much; it is quite fluid, indefinite; Minas seems to be in revolt. Sec asked if Linc were playing it carefully. B mentioned the cable that went out." (March 31, 3:31 p.m., National Archives and Records Administration, RG 59, Rusk Files: Lot 72 D 192, Telephone Calls 3/20/64–4/9/64) Ball's account of both conversations is in the Johnson Library, Papers of George W. Ball, Brazil, 3/30/64–4/21/66.

versation with Linc Gordon in Rio.[2] It seems clear that the state just north of Rio, which is Minas Gerais, is in revolt. Both the army and the civilian authorities of the state seem to be acting together and the army has apparently moved in and authorities blocked the road from Rio so that the First Army in Rio couldn't move up and stop the revolt. We're waiting for some clarification of the situation in Sao Paulo, which is the key to the matter. There has apparently been no movement in Sao Paulo but there is some expected at almost any moment and we should know within the next few hours what's happening. The hope there would be that the Second Army would move and block the road from Rio down and isolate Rio. And in the meantime they have drafted an impeachment, in Congressional circles, of Goulart, but there has been no action taken on it. But they've listed all the offenses against the constitution which they allege. And there is a lot of bickering around to see what could be done presumably in the way of forming some kind of a rump civilian government which would have a claim to legitimacy. The anti-Goulart government—governors are apparently going to meet Wednesday[3] and, on the basis of the information that Gordon has, there is a significant number of the governors who are prepared to move against Goulart, about 9 of them altogether, which is a very impressive number.

President: How many do they have?

Ball: The total number of states there is about, how many altogether? Nineteen.

President: Twenty?

Ball: No, 21 they tell me, but these are the big ones, these are the important states. Now, we have instructed Gordon not to make any more contact with the Brazilians until we see how the situation develops. I think there has to be some more movement in Sao Paulo to make sure that this thing is going to move, since we don't want to get ourselves committed before we know how the thing is going to come out. He feels that on the basis of the momentum that's been started so far that it can wait for 12 hours before anything has to be, or overnight, before we have to take any decision on whether we should or shouldn't move. And I think that we can see the developments and then make a judgment on it. I gather you're planning on coming back [unintelligible] tonight.

President: Yeah, I'll be in there about 8:30.

---

[2] The text of the teletype conversation (2:30 p.m.) is ibid., National Security File, Country File, Brazil, Vol. II, 3/64.

[3] April 1.

Ball: Right. We may have another meeting this afternoon with Mc-Namara,[4] but in any event we'll be changing the information, but I did want you to know that—

President: I think we ought to take every step that we can, be prepared to do everything that we need to do, just as we were in Panama, if that is at all feasible.

Ball: Right. Thank you, Mr. President. We're canvassing all the possibilities to make sure we're not—

President: I'd put everybody that had any imagination or ingenuity in Gordon's outfit, or McCone's, or you all's, or McNamara's, and we just can't take this one, and I'd get right on top of it, and stick my neck out a little.

Ball: Right.

Mann: Well, we're doing that.

Ball: Well, this is just our own feeling about it, and we've gotten this well organized I think now, I wanted you to know—[5]

President: All right. [Omitted here is a short discussion of Panama.]

---

[4] In a telephone conversation at 4 p.m., Ball briefed McNamara on the situation in Brazil. The two men agreed that "nothing further could be gained at this time so the 5:00 meeting scheduled for today was canceled." (Johnson Library, Papers of George W. Ball, Brazil, 3/30/64–4/21/66) Rusk held a meeting on Brazil at 5 p.m. (National Archives and Records Administration, RG 59, U. Alexis Johnson Files: Lot 90 D 408, Date Books, 1964) No substantive record of the meeting has been found.

[5] Bundy called Ball at 6:40 p.m. to explain that "the President would prefer to be brought up to date on the Brazil situation in the morning unless there was some reason for a meeting tonight." (Johnson Library, Papers of George W. Ball, Brazil, 3/30/64–4/21/66) In a March 31 memorandum to the President, Bundy and Dungan reported that they would be kept informed by the Situation Room and would notify the President of any developments. (Ibid., National Security File, Memos to the President, McGeorge Bundy, Vol. I)

200.   Memorandum From the Special Assistant to the Assistant
Secretary of State for Inter-American Affairs (Boster) to the
Special Assistant to the Secretary of State (Little)[1]

Washington, April 1, 1964.

SUBJECT

Brazil

In two conversations last night and this morning with U.S. correspondent Jules DuBois, the anti-Goulart Governor of Guanabara, Carlos Lacerda, asked that word be gotten to Mr. Mann "that it was extremely important for the U.S. not to interfere by making any statement
whatsoever."

Mr. Mann has asked that you convey this message to the Secretary and suggests that, if he agrees, you might also convey this to the
White House. Mr. Mann agrees that it is extremely important that we
(the U.S. Government) stay in the background and not make any statements that might damage the forces friendly to us in Brazil.

---

[1] Source: National Archives and Records Administration, RG 59, ARA/LA Files:
Lot 66 D 65, Brazil 1964. Confidential. Drafted by Boster. Copies were sent to Manning,
Adams, Burton, and S/S. The memorandum indicates that Rusk saw it.

---

201.   Teleconference Between the Department of State and the
Embassy in Brazil[1]

April 1, 1964, 1500Z.

Sec 1

Ball, Adams and Burton will be at 1500Z teleconference here. Same
rules as yesterday.[2] All messages considered Secret and Exdis.

---

[1] Source: Johnson Library, National Security File, Country File, Brazil, Vol. II, 3/64.
Secret; Exdis. According to Rusk's Appointment Book, Rusk met Ball and U. Alexis Johnson at 10 a.m. for the teleconference to Rio. (Ibid.)

[2] The Department stated the rules as follows: "During telecon request you number
conference items sequentially preceded by geographic indicator 'Rio'. Dept will number
sequentially preceded by 'Sec'." (Telegram 1299 to Rio de Janeiro, March 31; National
Archives and Records Administration, RG 59, Central Files 1964–66, POL 2 BRAZ)

Sec 2

Secretary also present this end.

Sec 3

Secretary requests brief situation report as of this hour.

Sec 4

A. Briefly, what is situation at this hour?

B. What is present attitude first army?

C. Where is Kubitschek at present? Did you meet with him last night?

D. Will the momentum continue on the anti-Goulart side without some covert or overt encouragement from our side?

Sec 5

Any signs of hostility toward American personnel?

Sec 6

Are fourth army and Rio Grande do Sul supporting Goulart?

Sec 7

On our Sec 6 change "fourth army" to "third army."

Sec 8

Have any leaders of rebellion pressed you for overt support? Would overt indication our support play into Goulart's hands at this moment?

Sec 9

We have nothing further here. Do you have anything further?

Sec 10

If you have nothing further we terminate conference. Thanks very much.

Rio

Ambassador Gordon, Minister Mein, Mr. Gresham present.

This is Ambassador Gordon.

Rio 1

Hard news is that Kruel and second army as well as Alves Bastos and fourth army in Pernambuco have declared for rebellion. Fourth army has taken over Governor's palace in Recife.

Favorable rumors include:

A. Second army past Rezende on border Sao Paulo state of Rio and moving toward this city. Expected arrive some time this late afternoon.

B. Possible joining of rebellion by first army forces sent toward Minas last night.

[C.] Stories inside Agencia Nacional that high command officer corps resolved not to fight rebellion.

D. Refusal Gen Oromar Osorio of Vila Militar to permit marines to arrest Lacerda who still barricaded in Guanabara Palace.

Unfavorable rumors are:

A. That Brizola forces have occupied all Rio Grande do Sul radio stations.

B. That third army in far south loyal to Goulart and moving north against Sao Paulo.

Congress awaiting military resolution of events and appears disposed legitimize whatever emerges.

Navy friends tell us of effort to get three destroyers and submarine out of Guanabara Bay. Not yet successful. If successful may need diesel fuel for sub.

CGT has called general strike on nationwide basis but without visible effects in Sao Paulo. This ends Rio 1.

Rio 2.

Garble above refers to report from navy friends that they trying to send three destroyers and one submarine out of Guanabara Bay.

Above replies to Sec 3. On Sec 4 para B has been very hard get intelligence on first army. Ministry of War completely shut off from access and surrounded by tanks and armored cars. Agencia Nacional rumors reported above purport to come from inside phone messages but we unable confirm at this time.

I met Kubitschek at 2115 and drafted message which apparently not sent during last night's confusion. Essence was much less complacency re outcome than yesterday morning[3] and wonderment that Sao Paulo had not yet moved. This now overtaken by events with Kruel and Adhemar statements and actual move by second army. Kubitschek said that move from Sao Paulo would be critical to success and if rebellion smothered Goulart would be on high road to dictatorship.

We discussed legitimacy problem which he thought would be readily cared for by Congress if military balance favorable. He had seen Goulart in midafternoon and pleaded with latter to save mandate by making clean break with CGT and Communists but Goulart said this would be sign of weakness which he could not afford.

Momentum now clearly gathered and for these hours does not need special encouragement from US.

---

[3] In a conversation with James Minotto, staff member to the Senate Appropriations Committee, Kubitschek said that "for practical purposes situation all over. There was going to be successful coup against Goulart, resistance to which would be general strike lasting two or three days. Workers, however, would go back to work when they got hungry." Kubitschek also reported that he told Goulart that "he was breaking with him since President following course which would lead to turning country over to Communists." (Telegram 2126 from Rio de Janeiro, March 31; ibid., POL 23–9 BRAZ)

Have just learned that Kubitschek conversation report was sent last night as Embtel 2134.[4]

Flash [*less than 1 line of source text not declassified*] has just received report from usually reliable source that General Jair has sent note to Goulart saying he is breaking with him and will urge army troops loyal to him, Jair, to unite and join forces with Kruel. If this is true it should have profoundly favorable influence on outcome.

Re Sec 5 there are no such signs of hostility.

Re Sec 6 we have only unfavorable rumor re third army reported above.

Sec 7 is last received from you. This ends Rio 2.

Rio 3

Except for Adhemar and some of his fellow Paulistas who continue talking unclearly about arms needs and possible desirability of show of naval force there has been no pressing for overt support. I do not consider Paulista approaches as serious or responsible. At this moment overt indication our support would be a serious political error which would play into Goulart's hands. We shall of course continue focussing on this question hourly as situation evolves. This ends Rio 3.

Rio 4

Sec 8 received and answered by Rio 3. This ends Rio 4.

Rio 5

Nothing more now. This terminates teleconference.

---

[4] Dated April 1. (Ibid.)

---

202. Memorandum for the Record[1]

Washington, April 1, 1964, 11:15 a.m.

SUBJECT

Meeting at the White House 1 April 1964
Subject—Brazil

---

[1] Source: National Security Council, 303 Committee Files, Subject Files, Brazil. Secret. Drafted by FitzGerald. The time of the meeting is taken from the President's Daily Diary. (Johnson Library) FitzGerald also drafted a longer version of the memorandum, which included the discussion of Panama and Cuba. (Central Intelligence Agency, DCI (McCone) Files, Job 80–B01285A, Meetings with the President, 1 Jan–30 Apr 64)

PRESENT

> The President
>
> State Department: Secretary Rusk, Under Secretary Ball, Deputy Under Secretary Johnson, and Mr. Ralph Burton
>
> Defense Department: Secretary McNamara, Deputy Secretary Vance, General Taylor and General O'Meara
>
> White House Staff: Messrs. Bundy, Dungan, Moyers, and Reedy
>
> CIA: The Director, Colonel King and Mr. FitzGerald

1. The meeting commenced with a briefing on the latest intelligence reports by Colonel King including items from the 10 o'clock telecon between State and Ambassador Gordon.[2] Matters seemed to be more favorable to the insurgents than they had been the previous evening, particularly in view of indications that General Kruel is moving Second Army troops to the Sao Paulo border.

2. Secretary Rusk said that Ambassador Gordon was not advocating U.S. support at this time. Only the Paulistas had requested such aid and this without definition. Ambassador Gordon, with whom the Secretary agreed, believes that it would be wrong at this stage to give Goulart an anti-Yankee banner.

3. Secretary Rusk referred to a "leak" the evening before regarding the movement of a Naval task force to the area of northern Brazil. (General Taylor said that there was not actually a leak but that it appeared to be a deduction by newsmen based on knowledge that a special meeting of the Joint Chiefs took place.) It was agreed that newspaper queries concerning the Naval movement would be treated routinely and that it would not be shown as a contingency move having to do with Brazil.

4. Secretary Rusk commented that the reporting from Brazil was excellent and endorsed the statement of facts presented by Colonel King.

5. Secretary McNamara reported on the status of the task force. It sailed this morning and would be in the vicinity of Santos by the 11th of April. The arms and ammunition are now being assembled for airlift in New Jersey and the airlift would take 16 hours from the time of decision. As to POL, the earliest Navy tanker, diverted from the Aruba area, would be in place on the 10th or 11th of April. There is, however, a Norwegian tanker chartered by Esso in the South Atlantic loaded with the necessary motor and aviation gasoline. It is headed for Buenos Aires and should arrive there on the 5th or 6th of April. It was decided that [3 lines of source text not declassified]. This should be done as soon as possible.

---

[2] Document 201.

(Messrs. Bundy and Dungan, following the meeting, said that they had taken exception to the Navy's order to its task force which had placed the movement clearly within the contingency plan for Brazil. They felt that this was an unnecessary security hazard.)

D

Deputy Chief, WH (Special Affairs)

203.   Teleconference Between the Department of State and the Embassy in Brazil[1]

April 1, 1964, 2030Z.

For Ambassador.

Our request for teleconference at 2030Z today grows out of decision at White House this morning that we have regular daily teleconferences with you in view of high value placed on information obtained by this means previously.

If impossible for you to be present each time DCM entirely satisfactory. Ordinarily DOD and CIA representatives will also be present this end with Ball, or U A Johnson and Mann.

Suggest 1500Z, 1900Z and 2300Z for times of teleconference tomorrow.

Suggest you send telecon message in advance each teleconference to be available at start of conference here with situation report covering any significant developments under following headings referred to by number and letter.

---

[1] Source: Johnson Library, National Security File, Country File, Brazil, Vol. II, 3/64. Secret; Exdis. A handwritten note indicates that "Ball gave essence of this to the President by phone." According to the President's Daily Diary, Ball called Johnson at 3:52 p.m. (Johnson Library) No substantive record of the conversation has been found. Ball briefed the Secretary at 3:53 p.m.: "B said Gordon thinks it is all over. B reported on his talk with Rio. Sec said we should look into the question of recognition; perhaps if Mazzilli succeeds, there is no question. B will get Chayes working on it. B said we were still working on getting POL down there, since we could not be sure of the situation." (National Archives and Records Administration, RG 59, Rusk Files: Lot 72 D 192, Telephone Calls 3/20/64–4/9/64)

1. Military Situation

(A) Developments in each of four armies
(B) Action by air force or navy
(C) Shifts in allegiance of key military forces or officers
(D) Possible or actual independent moves by non-coms or enlisted
(E) Other

2. Logistic Situation

(A) Adequacy of POL, armaments, ammo, other military supplies
(B) Need for US logistic support action
(C) Other

Sec 1

Teleconference—Washington–Rio.

Treat all messages Secret and Exdis.

Conferees here are UA Johnson, Adams, McNaughton (DOD) and Col. King (CIA). Who is at your end and did you get our advance?

Sec 2

Your 2147 and Brasilia 133 received.[2] Do you have anything further on Goulart resignation?

End Sec 2.

Sec 3

Undersecretary Ball now present.

End Sec 3.

Sec 4

Re POL Norwegian tanker *Finnanger* under Esso charter carrying Avgas and Mogas en route Buenos Aires will be off Santos on or about 7 April. If diversion required instructions must be given 6 April.

There is also Tidewater ship *J Paul Getty* carrying 500,000 barrels bunker fuel scheduled arrive Rio 5 April. Another Tidewater vessel carrying same amount bunker fuel due arrive Santos 9 April.

Re para 1 JANAF msg J–9[3] we perceive no way get diesel fuel off Rio until arrival MSTS tankers 13 April.

End Sec 4.

Sec 5

Re last sentence Rio 1, we have a special task force here now at work several days on economic and financial assistance, emergency relief, etc. and are prepared promptly to act on your recommendations.

---

[2] Telegram 2147 from Rio de Janeiro, April 1, forwarded unconfirmed reports that Goulart had resigned. (Ibid., Central Files 1964–66, POL 15–1 BRAZ) Telegram 133 from Brasilia, April 1, reported that Goulart had evidently flown to Brasilia to "confer with congressional leaders." (Ibid., POL 23–9 BRAZ)

[3] Dated April 1. (Ibid.)

End Sec 5.

Sec 6

Nothing further here now. Would appreciate flash wrap-up report tonight about four hours from now. Would be prepared gather for another telecon tonight if you consider desirable. Otherwise will telecon with you at 1500Z tomorrow.

Will reply Rio 6 by cable tonight.

CCN line 1 wrap-up.

End Sec 6

This is Ambassador Gordon.

Rio 1

We believe it is all over with democratic rebellion already 95 percent successful. First army solidly in favor and at 1640 Gen Ancora[4] ordered cessation military action against rebels. Ancora and Kruel meeting at 1800 in Rezende. First army command to be assumed by Gen Costa e Silva, strongly democratic. Still awaiting formal announcement but we believe Goulart has already or is just about to resign. Mazzilli would then take over on interim basis as provided in constitution. Castello Branco states no need US logistical support. Radio stations in Rio all now in friendly hands state Goulart has resigned but Brigadeiro Mello[5] of air force states this not yet true.

Still some concern at possible civil strife in Porto Alegre, Recife and on limited scale perhaps here too, as well as problem left leaning groups in marines and other scattered groups armed forces. Reaction labor unions still uncertain. We have begun staff work on possible needs for internal security help, financial stabilization etc. No word yet on Congressional reactions. Goulart arrived Brasilia 1430 Brasil time. This ends Rio 1.

Rio 2

Have received your Sec 1 and 2 and 3. I am accompanied here by Mein and Gresham. Have you received my Rio 1?

End Rio 2.

Rio 3

Have just received [less than 1 line of source text not declassified] indicating that Goulart may be planning to stay in Brasilia and look for some kind of compromise political solution. My first reaction is that this would be most difficult to achieve, given momentum of anti-Goulart movement.

---

[4] Armando de Morais Âncora, former commander of the First Army, was appointed Minister of War following the resignation on April 1 of Jair Dantas Ribeiro; he was replaced the next day by Artur Costa e Silva.

[5] Francisco de Assis Correia de Melo, Air Force Chief of Staff.

Regarding your advance message, some of it is obsolete but we can meet teleconference times suggested and will also be guided by your format in wrap-up report tonight.

This ends Rio [3].

Rio 4

Sec 4 recd. Possibility Petrobras sabotage cannot yet be wholly discounted and we should keep these tankers coming until situation clarified. End Rio 4.

Rio 5

Do you have any other questions for us now? End Rio 5.

Rio 6

Sec 5 is good news. Would appreciate summary your thinking these points. End Rio 6.

Rio 7

We have nothing further now. If you do not, should we terminate? End Rio 7.

Rio 8

Sec 6 recd. Will act accordingly. Presently doubt need for further telecon tonight but will give advance warning if desired. Confirm 1500Z tomorrow. End Rio 8.[6]

---

[6] Bundy called the President at 4:30 p.m., explaining that, in light of Gordon's report, it would not be necessary to reconvene that day to discuss Brazil. Johnson agreed to schedule a meeting of the National Security Council for the following morning. (Johnson Library, Recordings and Transcripts, Recording of telephone conversation between President Johnson and Bundy, April 1, 1964, 4:30 p.m., Tape F64.22, Side A, PNO 3) Bundy later explained to Rusk that the NSC meeting, although "more for show than for use," would allow the participants to "wrap up on Brazil." (April 1, 6:37 p.m.; National Archives and Records Administration, RG 59, Rusk Files: Lot 72 D 192, Telephone Calls 3/20/64–4/9/64)

---

204. Editorial Note

On April 2, 1964 (12:25 a.m. EST), the Embassy Office in Brasilia reported that President Goulart had left Brasilia by airplane. Although he might land first in Porto Alegre, reliable congressional sources indicated that Goulart was flying to Montevideo. Meanwhile a special joint session of Congress was meeting to declare that Goulart had fled the country, that the presidency was vacant, and that Paschoal Ranieri Mazzilli, formerly President of the Chamber of Deputies, was now

Acting President of Brazil. (Telegram 137 from Brasilia; National Archives and Records Administration, RG 59, Central Files 1964–66, POL 15–1 BRAZ) At 3:05 a.m. EST, the Embassy Office reported that the President of the Senate, Auro de Moura Andrade, had declared that the presidency was vacant—in spite of an official statement that Goulart was merely "absent in Rio Grande do Sul." Shortly thereafter, Mazzilli took the oath of office at Planalto, the presidential palace in Brasilia. (Telegram 138 from Brasilia, April 2; ibid.)

Under Secretary of State Ball, who was monitoring the situation from Washington, described his role in subsequent events:

"At three o'clock in the morning I was down at the Department, which was normal in any crisis. Rusk was away somewhere. As I mentioned, crises always seemed to occur when I was Acting Secretary. I don't know why. Finally, on the strong urging of our ambassador down there who was [Lincoln Gordon], I sent a telegram which had the effect of, in effect, recognizing the new government. Goulart wasn't quite out of the country, and I was taking a chance. But it worked out beautifully and was very effective. It was the kind of thing that marked a period to the end of Mr. Goulart. But the President was furious with me, the only time he was ever really angry with me, I think. Why hadn't I let him know? Why did I do this without letting him know? I said, 'It was three o'clock in the morning, Mr. President.' He said, 'Don't ever do that again. I don't care what hour of the morning it is, I want to know. I'm not saying what you did wasn't right, but after this I want to know.' Thereafter I never hesitated." (Johnson Library, Transcript, George W. Ball Oral History Interview #2, July 9, 1971, pages 39–40; see also George W. Ball, *The Past Has Another Pattern*, page 429)

The telegram described by Ball has not been found.

---

205.   Teleconference Between the Department of State and the Embassy in Brazil[1]

April 2, 1964, 1500Z.

Sec 1

Participants in Washington:

Under Secretary Geo. Ball; Deputy Under Secretary U.A. Johnson; Mr. Burton; Mr. Sloan (DOD)

---

[1] Source: Johnson Library, National Security File, Country File, Brazil, Vol. II, 3/64. Secret; Exdis.

Sec 2

NSC meeting here 1700Z on Brazil. Do you have statement to suggest for White House or State Department and your view as to what level we should play this. We do not want to tie President on prematurely.

End Sec 2.

Sec 3

MAP civic action and military spare parts cargoes are on ships *Del Sud* arriving Rio 8 April, *Del Mundo* arriving Recife 3 April, *Mormon Hawk* arriving Rio 10 April and *Del Sol* arriving Recife 13 April. Will presume you have no objection to cargo being landed unless you advise otherwise.

End Sec 3.

Sec 4

Who likely to be FinMin in Mazzilli government? What will be chances for a serious effort to put financial affairs in order during next 30 days of political campaigning?

End Sec 4.

Sec 5.

What is your assessment of Mazzilli? Is he apt to stand for election at end of constitutional 30 day period? Who are other likely contenders for presidency?

End Sec 5.

Sec 6

Since Naval task force will not be approaching northern Brazilian waters until April 4 we are not now planning to take any action turn it back for another 24 hours unless you think otherwise.

End Sec 6.

Sec 7

Share your concern that Mazzilli election be fully constitutional and approve action you have taken. We can avoid statement here until you think it desirable in light situation there. However, would appreciate soonest your draft for message from the President to Mazzilli for despatch at such time as you recommend. If you believe that additional White House or Department statement would be desirable I would also appreciate your recommendations on text.

End Sec 7.

Sec 8

Four Navy tankers in loading and movement process. Schedule of arrivals in Santos area and description of loading on each ship will be sent you immediately. We concur they should continue. Will advise further on recall of Task Force.

End Sec 8.

Sec 9

We have nothing further here. Do you?

Please be sure to have sitrep sent to us 30 minutes in advance of 1900Z telecon, since Ball and others will be briefing Senate Foreign Relations Committee at 2000Z.

All messages in telecon should be considered Secret and Exdis.

End Sec 9.

Sec 10

Ref Rio 7.

Yes we will work out wider distribution here.

All right to send sitrep by telegram for wider distribution provided no reference made therein to covert operations or US military activities.

End Sec 10.

[Omitted here is text of Situation Report as of 1100 hours.]

Rio 2

This is Ambassador Gordon. I am troubled about questionable juridical situation surrounding early morning installation of Mazzilli as Acting President. Declaration by Congress and Senate President Moura Andrade that presidency vacant was not backed by congressional vote. Supreme Court President did preside over swearing in of Mazzilli but it was not backed by Supreme Court vote. If Goulart leaves Brazil without permission from Congress he automatically forfeits office under Article 85 of Constitution. In absence of that, however, I believe it most desirable that Congress legitimize situation by some sort of vote and that this be done before Pres Johnson send any telegram to Mazzilli.

I have so advised Dean in Brasilia and he is seeking out various congressional leaders in order impress on them importance from international viewpoint of clear congressional legitimation. Will report results as soon as available.

New subject is Navy Task Force described Deptels 1301 and 1305.[2] I believe this should now be recalled with avoidance any showing in Brazilian waters or public information of its having been despatched. Navy tankers on other hand should be kept heading this way until oil supply situation clarified. If Brizola led resistance movement in RGS[3] does not evaporate, POL may be needed there. Also morning radio reports indicate that large Duque de Caxias refinery here still under

---

[2] Document 198 and footnote 2 thereto.

[3] Rio Grande do Sul.

Commie control and they preventing operation. On other hand smaller local Manguinhas refinery apparently operating about half capacity. Sabotage danger Petrobras refineries cannot yet be discounted. Please inform types and quantities POL contained Navy tankers referred para 1 Deptel 1301. This ends Rio 2.

Rio 3

Sitrep was sent as advance material and supplemented by my Rio 1.

Did you receive this? We would like brief time to reflect on question White House or State Dept statement. Preferring if possible to hold off until situation in RGS and prospects congressional action referred Rio 2 are clearer. How much time can you give us before some sort of statement may be unavoidable? [End Rio 3.]

Rio 4

ARMA just returned from seeing Castello Branco who reports whole country quiet except Porto Alegre. There Brizola still in control having claimed deposition of Meneghetti. Army troops from STA Maria, RGS Parana and STA Catarina are moving on Porto Alegre. Gen Joao Costa COMDR parachute unit was with Castello Branco planning airborne attack if necessary. Navy units going to lagoon and Guaiba estuary to complete action against Porto Alegre. Goulart still there as is Assis Brasil.[4] Fico gave up in Brasilia and some arrests being made.

Chief of Cabinet to War Minister Costa e Silva is very pro US Brig Gen Siseno Sarmento.

Castello Branco states ADM Aragao is not under arrest, contrary previous reports, but is being sought. Brig Teixeira likewise. Jurema is confirmed as under arrest.

Further on petroleum. Osvino Alves is reported under arrest this morning. Supply situation could become serious or critical within three or four days since Petrobras supplies have been sharply reduced in last ten days. Rationing in Sao Paulo with service stations held to 30 percent of normal supplies. Belo Horizonte stocks requisitioned for military use. Confusion Petrobras and Fronape their tanker organization. Oil company representatives have been summoned to Navy Ministry for meeting at 1400 local time. [End Rio 4.]

Rio 5

Reply to Sec 3 is that we have no objection to landings in Rio and Recife.

---

[4] Reference is to Argemiro Assis Brasil, Chief of the Casa Militar; General Nicolau Fico, Army Commander in Brasilia; Admiral Cândida Aragão, Commander of the Marines; Brigadier Francisco Teixeira, Commander of the Third Air Zone; Abelardo Jurema, Minister of Justice; and Osvino Ferreira Alves, President of Petrobras.

Reply to Sec 4 not yet known or indicated. My purely personal hunch is that leading Paulista banker such as Gastao Vidigal would be good prospect. Any new FinMin obviously faces gravest problems but we cannot yet see political situation sufficiently clearly to answer second question.

Reply to Sec 5 is that Mazzilli is man of clearly moderate orientation and skillful legislative tactician but unlikely have great executive force or vigorous policy ideas. Policies would have to come from cabinet members. He is likely to look to capable and highly respected names for cabinet.

Reply to Sec 6 was given in Rio 2. We believe Task Force but not tankers should be recalled soonest.

This ends Rio 5.

Rio 6

Will send draft message President Johnson to Mazzilli this afternoon. Also other drafts if indicated. Will also send sitrep in ample time for 1990Z teleconference. On handling of our sitreps do you want us to send appropriate material as regular telegrams for wider Washington distribution or can you arrange that for us? This ends Rio 6.

Rio 7

On last point above it would help us if you could handle wider Washington distribution of necessary material since we feel heavily loaded here. This ends Rio 7.[5]

---

[5] Ball briefed the President on the situation in Brazil at 10:40 a.m. After reviewing the teleconference with Gordon, Ball explained "that we will probably not have a recognition problem because this will be the same government and this will avoid the recognition of a new government. We will treat this government as a continuation of the old one." (Johnson Library, Papers of George W. Ball, Brazil, 3/30/64–4/21/66)

206.   Summary Record of the 525th Meeting of the National Security Council[1]

Washington, April 2, 1964, noon.

U.S. Policy Toward Brazil and Other General Topics

CIA Director McCone gave a briefing from prepared notes[2] on the following items:

[Omitted here is discussion of unrelated items.]

e. *Brazil*—Colonel King was asked to review the latest information from Brazil. Most of his facts came from a teleconference between the State Department and Ambassador Gordon in Rio (copy attached).[3] He reported that Goulart and his brother-in-law, Brizola, had left Rio for Porto Alegre. Military resistance has ended everywhere except in Porto Alegre, where there may be fighting later if Goulart's supporters choose to resist Brazilian forces now moving on the city. Secretary Ball reported that last night's action by a minority of the Members of the Brazilian Congress who declared the office of the Presidency vacant and named the President of the Congress, Mazzilli, as President was of doubtful legality. This doubt will remain as long as Goulart is in Brazil or until he formally resigns. The Brazilian Constitution contains no provision to oust a President. While we do not wish to cast doubt on the legitimacy of Mazzilli as President, we do not wish formally to accept a government which the Brazilian courts may later decide is illegal. Mazzilli can hold office for thirty days during which time the Congress elects a President to hold office until the national election scheduled for 1965.

The President pointed out that Mazzilli was not in a very strong position if only 150 out of over 450 Congressmen voted him into office. Under Secretary Ball replied that while it was true that a minority of Congressmen had acted to put Mazzilli in office, the legal situation would be improved as soon as Goulart resigned or went into exile.

The President asked whether there were any pockets of resistance remaining. General Wheeler said that Goulart has relatively little military force loyal to him. One regiment and possibly a cavalry unit have not yet given up to the rebels.

---

[1] Source: Johnson Library, National Security File, NSC Meetings File, Vol. I, Tab 6, 4/2/64, US Policy Toward Brazil. Secret. Drafted by Bromley Smith.

[2] McCone's record of the meeting, including the notes for his briefing on Brazil, is in the Central Intelligence Agency, DCI (McCone) Files, Job 80–B01285A, Meetings with President Johnson.

[3] Document 205.

The President asked what happens next. General Wheeler replied that the Brazilian army would move on the pockets of resistance and clear them out. He indicated that the Second Army would move into Porto Alegre to overcome any units still supporting Goulart.

Secretary Rusk commented that it was more important to the Brazilians than to us to achieve a legitimate transfer of power. The domestic situation in Brazil would be improved if a new government could be legitimized quickly.

The President asked why the Congress shouldn't meet to make Mazzilli the legal President pro tem. Secretary Rusk replied that Ambassador Gordon was using the resources available to him to encourage Brazilian legislators to do just this. Under Secretary Ball noted that there would be no problem of U.S. recognition of the new government because we would merely continue our relations with the President.

Secretary Rusk said that all we could do today would be to sit and wait. He said that the U.S. Navy task force proceeding toward Brazil should continue until we receive further information from Brazil.

Secretary McNamara recommended that the task force continue southward. It is now near Antigua and can be turned around tomorrow if the situation continues to improve. It will still be a long way from Brazil.[4]

[Omitted here is discussion of unrelated items.]

The President asked what we were doing in Cuba to make it "just a nuisance." Following the laughter, Secretary Rusk commented that if Brazil turned out the way it appears to be going, there would be a beneficial effect on the Cuban problem and on the political situation in Chile.

Bromley Smith[5]

---

[4] In a telephone conversation the next morning, McNamara and Rusk agreed that it was time to "turn that task force around." McNamara said that he would do so "after talking to the President." (National Archives and Records Administration, RG 59, Rusk Files: Lot 72 D 192, Telephone Calls 3/20/64–4/9/64) The JCS issued the instructions recalling the task force at 11:30 a.m. (Telegram 5644 from JCS to CINCLANT, April 3; ibid., Central Files 1964–66, POL 23–9 BRAZ)

[5] Printed from a copy that bears this typed signature.

207.   Editorial Note

In a teleconference on April 2, 1964 (4 p.m. EST), Ambassador Gordon reported that Army Chief of Staff Castello Branco had just confirmed that "democratic forces" were in full control of Rio Grande do Sul, thereby eliminating the last pocket of military resistance. When a radio station announced shortly thereafter that former President Goulart had arrived in Montevideo, Gordon relayed the news with the salutation: "Cheers!" (Johnson Library, National Security File, Country File, Brazil, Vol. II, 3/64) At 5 p.m. EST, the Embassy reported that Congress was not interested in a formal vote transferring power to the new government, preferring a fait accompli to "new juridical arguments." The Embassy therefore recommended "proceeding forthwith with dignified LBJ public telegram" of congratulations to Acting President Mazzilli. (Telegram 2162 from Rio de Janeiro, April 2; National Archives and Records Administration, RG 59, Central Files 1964–66, POL 23–9 BRAZ) Gordon reiterated this recommendation in a teleconference at 6 p.m., "despite continued uncertainty whereabouts Goulart." After discussion among Secretary Rusk, Under Secretary Ball, and Deputy Under Secretary Johnson, the Department gave its tentative approval: "If you are satisfied that message from President Johnson to Mazzilli would not be premature and would not be interpreted as interference in internal affairs we are prepared to recommend to the President its prompt issuance this evening." Gordon replied: "Since country now completely pacified and in hands democratic forces with congressional support even though no formal vote, I cannot see how message could be construed as interference. Since prospects congressional vote now seem minimal, I believe that the sooner we act the better." (Johnson Library, National Security File, Country File, Brazil, Vol. II, 3/64) President Johnson approved the message, which the White House released later that evening. The text of the message is in *Public Papers of the Presidents of the United States: Lyndon B. Johnson, 1963–1964*, Book I, page 433.

208.   Summary Record of the 526th Meeting of the National Security Council With the Congressional Leaders[1]

Washington, April 3, 1964, 2 p.m.

Various Subjects

The President opened the meeting with the Congressional Leaders by saying that his purpose was to bring them up to date on recent developments. Various Council members would report on current situations. He first called on Secretary Rusk for a summary of developments in Brazil.[2]

Secretary Rusk summarized our relations with Goulart, including Goulart's discussion with President Kennedy, and later, in Rio, his discussion with the Attorney General.[3] Despite our efforts to persuade Goulart to follow a democratic reform program, and despite our efforts to support the Brazilian economy by making large loans, Goulart had moved toward the creation of an authoritarian regime politically far to the left. The current revolt in Brazil was not the traditional "golpe" of the Latin American variety but rather a combination of governors, government officials and military leaders who had joined together to oust Goulart when they became convinced that he was leading Brazil to economic and political disaster. As to the current situation, the rebel government now has full control of the country. The military leaders in Brazil have long visualized themselves as guardians of the democratic process.

Secretary Rusk described the major problems which the new government in Brazil faces. First are the economic problems which involve renegotiation of large loans coming due shortly and revision of those economic policies of Goulart which had resulted in inflation and economic difficulty. The Goulart men will have to be removed, which

---

[1] Source: Johnson Library, National Security File, NSC Meetings File, Vol. I, Tab 7, 4/3/64. Top Secret. Drafted by Bromley Smith. McCone also drafted a record of the meeting. (Central Intelligence Agency, Job 80–B01285A, No. 2, Memos for the Record, 1 January–5 April 1964)

[2] Shortly before the NSC meeting, Rusk called Robert Adams in ARA: "Sec asked him to put together a dozen examples of appointments that Goulart was making that looked like extremism, and 3–4 good examples of kinds of proposals G was making which seemed to undermine constitutional situation down there. Sec needed them by 1:15 for 2 pm meeting." (National Archives and Records Administration, RG 59, Rusk Files: Lot 72 D 192, Telephone Calls 3/20/64–4/9/64)

[3] Goulart met President Kennedy during a visit to Washington, April 3–4, 1962. For documentation on the visit, including memoranda of conversation, see *Foreign Relations, 1961–1963*, vol. XII, Documents 223–225. Attorney General Kennedy met Goulart in Brasilia on December 17, 1962. A memorandum of conversation, transmitted in airgram A–710 from Rio de Janeiro, December 19, is in the National Archives and Records Administration, RG 59, Central Files 1961–63, 033.1100–KE/12–1962.

means a reorganization of the governmental structure. There is a reasonable prospect now that the new government will turn its attention to the major problems of Brazil. The U.S. did not engineer the revolt. It was an entirely indigenous effort. We now have fresh hope that Brazil can face up to its current problems.

Senator Dirksen asked how much money we had given in grants to Brazil. Director Bell reported that we had made very few grants but had made many large loans. Senator Dirksen then asked if there were any outstanding unpaid loans. Mr. Bell replied that we are now owed approximately $136 million in payments on loans which amount to between $500 and $700 million. Senator Dirksen asked whether Brazil had lived up to its agreement to the stabilization plan we had financed. Mr. Bell replied that we had put up $60 million when they began to implement parts of the stabilization plan. When the Brazilians did not follow through on the plan, we then stopped further assistance.

Senator Hayden asked whether it was not true that the Brazilians had an excellent record of loan repayment. Mr. Bell said no Brazilian loan was in default.

Senator Morse said he thoroughly approved of the way the President and the State Department had handled the situation in Brazil. He said we would have to provide new economic assistance to Brazil but he hoped that the time had come when we could get something for this new aid.

The President replied that we are hard at work with our allies to provide the economic help which the new Brazilian government will need. We are doing everything possible to get on top of the problem of helping the new government.

Senator Dirksen asked about the position the new government would take toward expropriation of U.S. private investments. Secretary Rusk said that we did not know, but that one of the first things we would talk to the new government about would be their attitude toward expropriating U.S. property.

Senator Fulbright asked what effect there would be in Latin America if the coffee legislation[4] now before the Senate were rejected, as appeared probable. Secretary Rusk replied that Senate rejection of the coffee plan would be very serious for us and for the Brazilians, as well as to the Latin Americans.

Senator Dirksen said he felt that if the legislation were called up now it would be defeated.

---

[4] Reference is to legislation allowing the United States to fulfill its obligations under the International Coffee Agreement of 1962. The bill, rejected by the House of Representatives in 1964, was eventually passed and signed into law in May 1965. (79 Stat. 112)

Under Secretary Ball said that we should look at the coffee agreement in the light of the new Brazilian situation. If the agreement were rejected by the Senate, the new Brazilian government would consider the action a "no confidence" vote. He said he could not stress too much the importance of Senate approval of the coffee agreement. A rejection would be no less than a disaster for the entire Alliance for Progress.

[Omitted here is discussion unrelated to Brazil.]

Bromley Smith[5]

---

[5] Printed from a copy that bears this typed signature.

---

209.   Telegram From the Embassy in Brazil to the Department of State[1]

Rio de Janeiro, April 7, 1964, 7 p.m.

2204. Ref: Deptels 1336[2] and 1342.[3]

1. We fully agree concerns expressed reftels. Fortunately, similar feelings are shared by many influential elements in leadership of revolution, including most of the governors concerned (with possible exception Adhemar), UDN leaders in Congress, and at least some of military.

2. I distinguish between two types of constitutional problem. Those concerning timing of congressional election of president and eligibility Castello Branco seem to me of secondary order, subject to juridical rationalization without undue distortion. Distinguished lawyers have already expressed view that Article 79[4] (2) reference to election

---

[1] Source: National Archives and Records Administration, RG 59, Central Files 1964–66, POL 23–9 BRAZ. Secret; Priority. Passed to the White House, CIA, JCS, OSD, CINCSO, CINCSTRIKE also for POLAD, and CINCLANT also for POLAD.

[2] In telegram 1336 to Rio de Janeiro, April 6, the Department stressed the importance of preserving the "color of legitimacy" and asked the Embassy to consider what the United States could "appropriately do to influence events in this direction." (Ibid.)

[3] In telegram 1342 to Rio de Janeiro, April 6, the Department reported that a *New York Times* representative had phoned to comment on recent developments, including allegations of censorship and a "rumored threat to close Congress if uncooperative on Presidential changes." The Department suggested that the Embassy use its influence to "check or slow down such developments." (Ibid.)

[4] Reference is to the Brazil constitution of 1946.

being held "thirty days after the last vacancy" can be construed as meaning "within thirty days," since constituent assembly would otherwise have said "on the thirtieth day".

Congress is now passing a law to establish the manner of the election, which will also cover this point. As to eligibility under article 139 (I) (C), there is plausible argument that in context of nearby articles this refers only to direct popular elections and not to indirect election by Congress. As a second line of retreat in case Castello Branco, chiefs of general staff may be construed as referring only to general staff of the armed forces, and not to chiefs of staff of individual services.

3. Atmospheric noises about shutting Congress down are, I believe, only from irresponsible sources and need not be taken seriously.

4. What seems to be more serious is question public liberties and cancellation mandates extreme left-wing deputies. In this respect, there is real problem of vigorous desire on part military leadership of revolution to make quick and effective purge of Communist and other subversive extremists in public services, trade unions, and Congress. There are ten or twelve congressmen such as Brizola, Neiva Moreira, Juliao, Marco Antonio Coelho, Max da Costa Santos, Benedito Cerqueira, and Sergeant Garcia, whose active participation in efforts at violent subversion is certainly beyond doubt and should be readily subject to objective proof. Unfortunately, articles 45 and 213 are very strong protections of congressional immunities. The harder-line military are talking about revoking the mandates of up to forty left-wing congressmen, which would be grossly excessive, but even the most moderate feel it essential to revoke those of some ten to twelve. The right way to do this would be under article 48 (2), but with the PTB solidly opposing, it would be very difficult to secure a two-thirds absolute majority for this purpose. The cases of Governors Arraes and Seixas Doria appear to have been cared for through impeachment by their respective legislative assemblies. The two related problems are press censorship and holding of suspected subversives without habeas corpus.

5. On press censorship, we have pointed out through both military and civilian channels importance of not creating hostility among foreign and especially US journalists. I got a strongly helpful reaction on this from Lacerda, who at six pm instructed an aide to determine who was responsible and say he would denounce it publicly if not called off forthwith. He was on way to see Castello Branco and promised make this point strongly.

6. The military leadership has prepared a so-called "institutional act" designed to revoke parliamentary immunities, life tenure for professors and judges, and stability of tenure for civil and military public employees, and there is under debate today the question whether this should be simply issued as an executive act of the high command of

the revolution or perhaps issued ad referendum by Congress. Putting a good juridical face on the former would be very difficult, but it may already be a fait accompli. We have tried to use our limited influence in the circumstances, and I stress that it is limited, to maintain the greatest possible color of legitimacy in the form of congressional sanction.

7. I took advantage of an almost accidental date with the new War Minister Monday[5] afternoon to point out that we are happy with the results of the revolution, that we want to support the new government in every possible way, but that our ability to support depends upon domestic congressional and public opinion which is very sensitive to anything which smacks of an old-fashioned reactionary Latin American military coup. For this reason, while recognizing the need for an effective purge of true subversives, juridical appearances are highly important. Tuesday morning, I arranged to convey a similar message to Castello Branco, doing it through Colonel Walters since I felt it unwise to see Castello personally at present stage. Walters also talked with Colonel Miranda of National Security Council. I made the same points in call on Lacerda Tuesday afternoon. War Minister Costa e Silva was not very responsive. Castello Branco, who is more sophisticated and civil minded, did appear to understand it and undertook to bear it in mind. Lacerda fully acknowledged the point, which fits with his own current campaign to dampen down excesses by police and army. He felt it unlikely, however, that some form of juridically questionable institutional act could be avoided, saying it was an inevitable bridge between the revolution and the full restoration of constitutional guarantees.

8. Department should bear in mind that Brazil had very narrow escape from Communist-dominated dictatorship and is only few days past what could have been civil war type confrontation. I see no way now of pushing this question further without over-straining our credit and producing counter-productive reactions. If other opportunities present themselves, we will make use of them.[6]

Gordon

---

[5] April 6.

[6] Gordon raised the question of "constitutional formalities" in a meeting with Mazzilli on April 8. After expressing similar concern, Mazzilli said that he was "using all resources to secure meeting of minds between military and political forces, with conservation of constitutional forms as 'point of honor for the country.'" (Telegram 2209 from Rio de Janeiro, April 8; National Archives and Records Administration, RG 59, Central Files 1964–66, POL 23–9 BRAZ)

210. Transcript of Telephone Conversation Between Director of Central Intelligence McCone and John J. McCloy

April 9, 1964, 11:10 a.m.

[Source: Central Intelligence Agency, Job 80–B01285A, DCI (Mc-Cone) Files, Telephone Calls, Eyes Only, 3/4/64–5/19/65. No classification marking. 4 pages of source text not declassified.]

211. Telegram From the Embassy in Brazil to the Department of State[1]

Rio de Janeiro, April 10, 1964, 2 p.m.

2235. References: Embtels 2230 and 2231.[2]

1. I must confess to considerable dismay at Thursday's[3] course of events, leading to the promulgation last night of the institutional act as a fait accompli on the exclusive authority of the military ministers. The juridical rationalization of the revolution as containing its own inherent constituent power is a wordy statement that might makes right (or makes law). Until yesterday morning, we had understood that congressional coverage and a plausible dress of legitimate continuity would be achieved, but apparently the congressional leaders would not accept certain of the demands insisted upon by the military leadership, who in turn were pressed by some of the more radical younger officers. The latter were concerned that maneuverings by Kubitschek and PTB might prevent the removal from key power centers of many active participants in Goulart's extreme left conspiracy. We should be

---

[1] Source: National Archives and Records Administration, RG 59, Central Files 1964–66, POL 15–3 BRAZ. Confidential; Immediate; Limdis. Repeated to the White House, OSD, JCS, CINCLANT, CINCSTRIKE, CIA, and CINCSO.

[2] Telegrams 2230 and 2231 from Rio de Janeiro, both April 10, forwarded the translated texts of the Institutional Act and its preamble. (Ibid.) The act was signed on April 9 by three military ministers: Artur Costa e Silva (Army), Francisco de Assis Correia de Melo (Air Force), and Augusto Hamann Rademaker Grünewald (Navy). Although the act "maintained" the constitution of 1946, it also suspended the legal guarantees of lifetime and job tenure for 6 months and allowed the signatories to suspend the political rights of any individual for 10 years, including legislators at the federal, state, and municipal level.

[3] April 9.

able secure more details on the failure of Wednesday's negotiation during the course of the day.

2. Mitigating aspects of the development are that: (a) Congress not being closed, although presidency much strengthened in relation to Congress; (b) six-month time limit on suspension of certain constitutional guarantees; (c) confirmation of next year's presidential election on dates provided by 1946 constitution; (d) limitation of application of whole institutional act to period ending January 31, 1966; and (e) conservation intact of federal system with state autonomy and constitutional arrangements.

3. Greatest hope for avoidance of undemocratic excesses rests in character and convictions of Castello Branco, who this morning appears almost certain of election, Dutra having withdrawn and Kruel possibly doing likewise. We are planning communicate to Castello by one means or another the signal importance from viewpoint foreign opinion and future collaboration of his reaffirmation devotion to democratic procedures, respect for individual liberties, and reestablishment of harmonious collaboration among the three constituted branches of government in the national interest.

4. Meanwhile we are faced with difficult problem USG public stance over coming few days. We take as basic premise the absolute necessity that the new government succeed both politically and economically. They will need our cordial and generous support to do so. At same time, we do not see how we can pretend to approve of way in which institutional act was issued. After reviewing various alternatives, I have concluded that our best stance until Castello's inauguration (which is now expected on Sunday) is the closest possible approximation to golden silence.

5. Specifically, we recommend that any USG spokesman say in response to questions substantially as follows: "The Brazilian Congress is scheduled to elect a president and a vice president on Saturday afternoon to serve for the remainder of the five-year presidential term ending January 31, 1966. They are expected to take office shortly thereafter. In these circumstances, we prefer to withhold any comment regarding the institutional act and its implications until the new president has taken office and made the policies of his government known."

6. As additional unattributed background for press, we suggest you point out that only since revolution has depth and breadth of subversive activity become clear, affecting many government agencies, both military and civilian, trade unions, journalism, teachers, transport and communications, etc., all systematically aided and abetted by Goulart regime. Accumulating evidence points to a Goulart plan to complete a left-wing coup d'état prior to May 1, which would have involved the closing of Congress and either a Peronista type or outright

Communist-dominated dictatorship with no respect for democratic forms or constitutional liberties and no mercy for opponents. Steps in this included planned violence against Rio April 2 democratic rally, to be followed by intervention in Guanabara, other announced Goulart left wing rallies throughout April, and CGT ultimatum to Congress to accept all reforms by April 20 under penalty general strike which Goulart had said publicly he would not oppose. It appears that May 1 was to have been a victory celebration under Communist sponsorship. Country was in process becoming armed camp, with grave danger massive bloodshed. Starting with March 13 rally, Communist backing of Goulart became open and total. Goulart's collaboration with Communists and associates had become so close in final weeks that he was becoming their virtual prisoner. Kruel and others tried almost desperately as late as March 31 to get Goulart to disavow the CGT and the Communists but without avail. As to the congressmen whose mandates were revoked this morning the majority were demonstrably implicated in direct subversive activities, such as instigating NCO and enlisted men rebellions, fomenting rural violence and land invasions, distributing arms and organizing guerrilla forces. Others were implicated in Goulart plans for abolishing constitutional order. Some half dozen were known CP members masquerading under other party labels. While we do not seek to justify extra-legal processes adopted by revolutionary leaders to carry out "operation clean-up", a substantial purge was clearly in order.

7. We are not making any announcements on aid projects during this interim, pending inauguration and policy declarations by new president.

Gordon

---

212. Telegram From the Embassy in Brazil to the Department of State[1]

Rio de Janeiro, April 20, 1964, 11 p.m.

2331. 1. Herewith highlights my first private talk with President Castello Branco in Brasilia Saturday morning,[2] lasting eighty minutes.

---

[1] Source: National Archives and Records Administration, RG 59, Central Files 1964–66, POL 15–1 BRAZ. Confidential; Priority.

[2] April 18.

After exchange courtesies, I congratulated him on inaugural address and remarked that we looked on April revolution as possible turning point in affairs Latin America and world as well as Brazil, provided proper use made of opportunity. Also spoke of convergence US and Brazilian interests on major issues, interest in seeing a strong and progressive Brazil, and desire approach possible divergences on any minor issues with good will on both sides. President concurred and expressed special appreciation for LBJ telegram.[3]

2. President then noted that American press reaction to his speech had been favorable, but concern clearly existed in US as to possible revolutionary excesses. He understood the withdrawal of political rights, Celso Furtado[4] had been especially badly received. I replied that there was indeed such concern, not because of disagreement with basic purposes of revolution, but because repressive measures could be arbitrary or excessive, state police in Sao Paulo seemed presently very extreme, and some judicial or other review procedure would have important favorable effect on free world opinion. Also said Furtado case especially sensitive in view his international renown, CIAP membership, and possible invitation by an American University as visiting professor. President said he understood Furtado had appointed many Communists to SUDENE, which I acknowledged, but I then explained in some detail reasons our own appraisal Furtado. President listened attentively to this exposition. (See separate wire on discussion Furtado case with Justice Minister Milton Campos.)[5]

3. We then turned to discussion economic and social problems. President inquired at some length about Alliance for Progress, Marshall Plan, and my earlier interest in Brazilian economic development. While expressing great confidence in medium and long-term Brazilian prospects, given effective policies and administration, I emphasized technically difficult problem of coping with inflation which had in January–February reached annual rate one hundred and fifty percent, an importance of well planned investment program to cushion shock of this inflation and spread austerity burdens as equitably as possible. Indicated our readiness to support both short and long-run efforts within general AFP framework and available resources. President asked me to review history of Brazilian planning and AFP coordinat-

---

[3] Reference is to Johnson's message congratulating Castello Branco after his election on April 11 to succeed Goulart as President of Brazil. (Telegram 1401 to Rio de Janeiro, April 14; Johnson Library, National Security File, Special Heads of State Correspondence, Brazil, Branco Correspondence, Vol. I)

[4] Former head of the Superintendency for the Development of the Northeast (SUDENE).

[5] Telegram 2330 from Rio de Janeiro, April 20. (National Archives and Records Administration, RG 59, Central Files 1964–66, POL 29 BRAZ)

ing efforts in recent years, and concluded this discussion by saying he placed highest importance on effective public investment planning and coordinating mechanism, this under active study, and he hoped arrive at decision by next Wednesday, April 22.

4. Following suggestion by Foreign Minister, I then explained AMFORP history and status to president, pointing to use Colombian precedent as possible means for early solution. Explained urgency solution from viewpoint avoiding further deterioration electric service and starting financing important new projects to avoid medium-term power shortage in center south. President undertook review promptly with Finance and Mines Ministers, as well as Foreign Minister.

5. President asked me about prospects additional PL 480 supplies and debt rescheduling, to which I replied with summary exposition present status.

6. Talk also touched on general international developments such as Sino-Soviet dispute and French policies under de Gaulle. President felt Russia relatively quiescent but ChiComs rashly and dangerously expansionist. He showed particular interest in France, remarking that de Gaulle had always seemed to him obsessed with concept of national greatness symbolized simply by military power, a concept Castello Branco regarded as obsolete and irrelevant to present world realities.

7. Contrast between tone this talk and that recent Goulart audiences was as day and night. Castello Branco was alert, attentive, intelligent, and responsive. He made no incautious predictions on future line of action, and I did not seek any. He obviously still feeling his way on many matters of organization, administration, and policy, but appeared to be doing it thoughtfully and conscientiously. I left the interview with the feeling that this was a most auspicious beginning.

Gordon

213.   Special National Intelligence Estimate[1]

SNIE 93–64   Washington, May 27, 1964.

THE POLITICAL SITUATION IN BRAZIL

The Problem

To assess the stability of the Castello Branco regime and the outlook in Brazil during his stated term in office.

Conclusions

A. President Castello Branco, whose term runs through January
1966, probably will provide reasonably effective political leadership
along moderate reformist lines.[2] It is unlikely that the supporters of
deposed President Goulart will be able to mount a serious challenge
to the stability of the new regime, although some leftist extremists may
attempt demonstrative acts of violence to discredit it. The principal
danger to the stability of the new regime is the possibility of a falling
out between Castello Branco and some groups within the military who
want a more thorough purge of the old political order. We believe that,
with some concessions to expediency, he will succeed in maintaining
general control of the situation. (Paras. 2–15)

B. Brazil's economic and social problems—worsened but not
caused by Goulart's disruptive rule—are not amenable to quick or pain-
less solutions. The new regime is likely to take constructive steps on
several fronts, but over the next years or so it probably will be unable
to do much more than to lay a basis for future progress. It probably
will enact a number of social reforms as an earnest of its concern for
Brazil's depressed classes, but will concentrate initially on combatting

---

[1] Source: Central Intelligence Agency, Job 79–R01012A, O/DDI Registry. Secret;
Controlled Dissem. According to a note on the cover sheet this estimate was prepared
in the Central Intelligence Agency with the participation of the intelligence organizations of the Departments of State and Defense and the National Security Agency. The
United States Intelligence Board concurred in this estimate on May 27.

[2] The Director of Intelligence and Research, Department of State, feels that the thrust
of this estimate is overly optimistic in several respects. He believes that it does not adequately take into account the enormous gravity and many-sided challenge of the political situation; the persisting confrontation of powerful forces on both the right and the left
which will hamstring necessary reformist action; the political inexperience of the President and most of his Cabinet and the absence of enough qualified second- and third-level
technical personnel; and the prospective destabilizing role of some of the revolution's military leaders who would emphasize continuing repressive action at the expense of meaningful social reforms. For these reasons, the Director believes that there is an even chance
that the regime will slip into increasing authoritarianism, thus precipitating another constitutional crisis within the period of the estimate. [Footnote in the source text.]

inflation and on other measures needed to get the economy rolling again. For political reasons, however, it probably will stop short of stringent austerity measures. It will need considerable foreign economic assistance to reschedule Brazil's huge short-term debt and to help cushion the shock of the economic stabilization measures it does undertake. (Paras. 16–21)

[Omitted here is the Discussion section of the estimate.]

214.   **Telegram From the Embassy in Brazil to the Department of State**[1]

Rio de Janeiro, June 10, 1964, noon.

2790. 1. President Castello Branco received me in Brasilia Tuesday afternoon[2] for one and one-quarter hours. At start, I presented him book on White House, recently published Portuguese translations of LBJ biography and collection of speeches, and Kennedy half dollar. All were graciously acknowledged.

2. I said purpose of visit was to review general situation prior to Washington consultations[3] and learn Castello's state of mind after two months in office. President asked if I had seen Juracy Magalhaes recently (I had done so late Tuesday morning) and then showed me staff report on areas of friction abroad, including chapters on AMFORP, Hanna, CTB, French contentious cases, and remittance of profits, saying that work on resolution of all was going forward rapidly. Then showed me separate mimeographed bill on profits remittance revision, which would receive final cabinet consideration Thursday and go to Congress promptly thereafter. President emphasized systematic staff

[1] Source: National Archives and Records Administration, RG 59, Central Files 1964–66, POL 17 US–BRAZ. Confidential; Priority; Limdis.

[2] June 9.

[3] Gordon was scheduled to arrive in Washington on June 13 to review the status of economic assistance to Brazil. (Telegram 2695 from Rio de Janeiro, May 29; National Archives and Records Administration, RG 59, Central Files 1964–66, AID(US) 9 BRAZ) He was one of six Ambassadors in Latin America to meet President Johnson on June 18; see Document 18. According to Rusk's Appointment Book Gordon also met Rusk on June 18; no substantive record of the meeting has been found. (Johnson Library) The next day the Department reported that AID had approved a $50 million loan to Brazil for balance of payments assistance. Although the agreement was to be signed immediately, the actual disbursement of funds was made contingent on settlement of the AMFORP dispute. (Telegrams 1776 and 1778 to Rio de Janeiro, June 19; National Archives and Records Administration, RG 59, Central Files 1964–66, AID(US) 9 BRAZ) The United States and Brazil signed the loan agreement on June 23.

work as basic feature his administration, saying he felt pleased with progress considering that neither he nor ministers had expected to be in office and therefore had lacked period of advance preparation. He mentioned main legislative items of housing, taxes (in two phases), bank reform, agrarian reform, the strike regulation law, all as indicating real progress in governmental process. He said threefold goals of inflation containment, development, and reform were no mere slogans, but genuine objectives which were being fleshed out in administrative and legislative measures. We had a little interchange on need for popular slogans to win broad support, which president acknowledged but said he approached with wariness, considering damage done the country by such past slogans as "petroleum is ours," and "reforms with or without the constitution."

3. President then said he had great interest in Alliance for Progress and its effective application in Brazil. Said he felt threefold program entirely in line with charter of Punta del Este, also actively interested in having social as well as economic side maintained, noting special importance of social side in northeast. He said investments in human beings essential even for effective economic development there, and he rejected argument that social benefits would come automatically from promotion of industrialization. President talked warmly of recent Recife meeting with Kubish.

4. I then turned conversation to political side, saying that cancellation Kubitschek political rights would raise serious questions abroad and asking how he would explain it if in my place.[4] President first traced formal steps in procedure, stating that charges and requests for cancellation came from three ministers, that evidence was carefully collected, National Security Council considered and recommended, and he then acted. As to reasons, he said they were both past and future. In past, despite Kubitschek's substantial contributions to development of country, these had been made without regard to financial responsibility and with large scale corruption, including personal enrichment Kubitschek and his friends. In addition, Kubitschek had wooed Communist support, and had paid price of letting them get into the gov-

---

[4] On June 5 the Department suggested that Gordon convey to Castello Branco the "seriousness" of international reaction to the suspension of Kubitschek's political rights. (Telegram 1697 to Rio de Janeiro; ibid., POL 29 BRAZ) In telegram 1716 to Rio de Janeiro, June 9, Mann also recommended that Gordon express to Castello Branco "the mounting concern which we feel here" regarding actions taken under the Institutional Act: "The failure on the part of the Brazilian Government to follow due processes of law and to proceed in a democratic manner will increase our difficulties in responding to Brazilian requests for economic assistance." (Ibid.) The Embassy reported that telegram 2790 had arrived after "Ambassador's call on Castello Branco in Brasilia and on eve his departure for U.S." (Telegram 2818 from Rio de Janeiro, June 11; ibid.) Mann reported on the "Kubitschek thing" in a telephone conversation with the President, June 11; see Document 16.

ernmental machine, where as previously they had been working on students and trade unions and others outside. He said that among other things, Kubitschek had dismissed Lucas Lopes, who now one of Kubitschek's leading defenders, as Finance Minister at insistence of Prestes. As to future, cancellation of mandate and therefore candidacy was essential to safeguard country against rebuilding of same phenomena of corruption and Communist infiltration from which country had suffered in last decade. Kubitschek had been intending to base his candidacy not merely on PSD, but on Goulart supporters in PTB and on Communist collaboration. President said he recognized that procedures had distasteful aspects, not meeting usual norms of right to defense or judicial review, but he felt that conditions of country initiated by Kubitschek himself and greatly intensified by Goulart had made exceptional procedures indispensable to effective clean-up and replacement of country on sound track of honest democratic government. June 15 would end this phase, any further clean-up actions taking place under normal National Security Law S. President noted that popular reaction to Kubitschek cancellation had been very small. The Congress was debating subject at that very moment, and he expected PSD speeches denouncing injustice and making some sort of manifesto, but he did not believe PSD would obstruct governmental program.

5. I then asked whether he planned to issue any sort of official declaration or justification of action on Kubitschek. President replied that something of sort was being projected, on basis partial rather than full dossier, since full revelation would be embarrassing to nation. I urged strongly desirability of issuance some form official justification, emphasizing importance of this to public opinion abroad. President appeared to be impressed by my emphasis on this point.

6. I then speculated on political effects, including likelihood that PSD might now turn to Kruel as candidate, and danger militarization of whole political process, noting concern in foreign press and public opinion of possible slide into military dictatorship. (This whole political discussion was conducted with caution, since I am still developing personal relationship with Castello Branco of type permitting candid treatment such matters.) President replied he well aware concern of excessive militarization but absolutely confident that action his government would dispel this concern. Pointed out that military candidates in Brazil had never gotten much enthusiasm, even from the armed forces noting such cases as those Monteiro, Lott, etc. Also said he would require any officers desiring to be candidates to take leave from jobs, said they could not use their offices as campaign headquarters in the way Lott had done. He said, incidentally, that Kruel had telephoned a few days ago to indicate his personal endorsement of cancellation Kubitschek political rights.

7. I then raised question of possible prolongation Castello's own mandate. On this, he was reticent, although indirectly indicating reluctance

consider anything which appeared to be of personal benefit to him. We discussed in this connection length of necessarily unpopular austerity phase of anti-inflation effort, which he said might be much longer than six months but he hoped would be over by first anniversary of revolution next April. Also said that essence of his government would be noninvolvement in campaign. Remarked with smile that Lacerda had had anti-Goulart issue as major campaign weapon, and might in future become anti-Castello, although he hoped that Lacerda's future political posture would become more positive than negative.

8. As conversation concluding we covered smaller points. President said had discussed C–130 project with Air Minister earlier same day, with negotiations to proceed. Details will go through JBUSMC.

9. In response to question on embarked aviation, President said he would settle this within few weeks. Issue could be settled only by President, and he intended to resolve it once for all. Then remarked that Kubitschek had bequeathed country two aircraft carriers, the *Minas Gerais* and *Brasilia*, one anchored uselessly in Guanabara Bay and the other anchored uselessly in the central plateau.

10. President inquired on relation timing my return and Juracy Magalhaes arrival in Washington. Said he placed highest hopes on Juracy's effectiveness as Ambassador. In addition to formal credentials, he is giving Juracy personal letter to LBJ.[5] He also mentioned Lacerda's mission to Europe and US to help explain revolution, and indicated hope President Johnson might be able receive Lacerda.

11. President then asked me about US political party convention prospects, Presidential elections, and other aspects current US scene. We also talked of common acquaintances, President speaking of Colonel Walters in terms of affection and respect. Conversation ended on most cordial note, leaving me impression real progress in melting reserve which is one of Castello's personal characteristics.

12. *Comment.* My general impression was extremely favorable. I did not encounter any nervousness or anxiety on Castello's part, despite fact that Kubitschek action obviously tough decision. On contrary, impression was rather one of calm resolve to get on with problems of clean-up, administrative rebuilding, and positive program. I also noted feeling of greater confidence on economic subjects, together with full backing policy lines recommended by Campos.[6]

Gordon

---

[5] Magalhaes evidently delivered the letter when he presented his credentials to President Johnson on July 9. (Johnson Library, President's Daily Diary)

[6] In a June 15 memorandum to Bundy, Sayre offered the following comment: "All reporting indicates Brazil is seriously proceeding on reform measures. Unfortunately there is an undercurrent that the U.S. owes Brazil assistance because it threw out the Communists." (Ibid., National Security File, Country File, Brazil, Vol. IV, 4/64–8/64)

215. Letter From the Ambassador to Brazil (Gordon) to the Assistant Secretary of State for Inter-American Affairs (Mann)[1]

Rio de Janeiro, August 10, 1964.

Dear Tom:

This is in reply to your letter of July 31,[2] carried here by Bill Rogers at the beginning of last week. Bill's trip was extremely helpful for all of us. In addition to some immediate problems, including the Rio–São Paulo highway question, it gave us the chance to review the broad strategy of our economic assistance relationships with Brazil in the light of the way in which the governmental program has been shaping up. It has also given Bill some most useful firsthand insights into the attitudes and problems of the Campos–Bulhões team and of the Castello Branco government in general in the economic field.

From our own talks in June,[3] I know that you and I are in accord that the coming months are a time of exceptional importance in determining the economic and political course of Brazil for perhaps a long period to come, with derived effects on the whole future of Latin America. In this respect, the revolution was decisive in creating new opportunities, but not necessarily in how those opportunities will be used. The Castello Branco government must make good use of this time, and our own efforts should be directed toward promoting and supporting that objective. It would be a disastrous error for us to relax in our relationships with Brazil on the mistaken theory that the revolution had eliminated the Communist or Peronist danger here and things could now simply take care of themselves. I know that this is not your view, but with the world so full of urgent crises, I occasionally have the feeling that some elements in the bureaucracy are all too ready to relax into a "business as usual" frame of mind.

Your letter of July 31 is concentrated mainly on the stabilization effort. The Castello Branco government, for its part, has constantly emphasized the three-fold goals of stabilization, development, and reform.

---

[1] Source: National Archives and Records Administration, RG 59, ARA/LA Files: Lot 66 D 65, Brazil, 1964. Confidential; Official–Informal.

[2] Attached but not printed. In his letter to Gordon, Mann reported that the Johnson administration had recently given "a considerable amount of thought to the problem of helping Brazil to get its house in order." According to Mann immediate action was necessary. "If Brazil fails to act responsibly in the months immediately ahead," he argued, "we will then be in a crisis situation again, perhaps of even larger proportions." Mann also reported, however, that IMF officials had expressed "great skepticism about the 'gradualist' approach to the problem of inflation," a concern shared by "those of us who are working on this problem in the Department."

[3] See footnote 3, Document 214.

I believe that this rather broader emphasis is correct, for both economic and political reasons. It is true that rampant inflation is the most acute of the economic problems facing the government. Yet it would be an error to concentrate policy-making entirely on anti-inflation measures, or to give stabilization an exclusive priority, even for a limited period of time.

In economic terms this is because Brazil is still a fairly poor country with a very rapidly growing population, which was suffering in the last year from stagnation along with accelerating inflation. It must continue the building of essential economic and social infrastructure and the stimulation of private investment in both industry and agriculture at the same time that it is fighting hard to reverse the inflationary forces. Even in the interests of stabilization itself, moreover, the acceleration of certain types of investments, such as those designed to finish up projects already begun, so as to get some goods and services out of investment already made, or those designed to improve agricultural output and a better flow to market, will contribute directly to supply and demand equilibrium. The problem cannot be tackled simply on the demand side. And in political terms, there must be a reasonably widespread conviction that burdens of austerity are being spread with equity and that beyond the tunnel of austerity there is the light of development and of progressive reform.

The alleged dichotomy between the "once for all" or "gradualist" attack on inflation, mentioned in your luncheon with the IMF people, seems to me an essentially false option. Inflation at the rate of 120 percent per year, which had been reached in Brazil in the first quarter of this year, is the economic counterpart of a heavy locomotive on a down slope or a heavy merry-go-round, with a tremendous amount of momentum built into it in the form of habits and expectations in all sectors of the community—businessmen, bankers and borrowers, workers and consumers. There is no way of stopping such a machine abruptly without producing an explosion or converting the energy of momentum into such intense heat that it will consume the whole institutional structure.

The realistic questions are: (a) Is the goal really stabilization or is it simply continuing inflation at a substantial even if lower rate, and (b) is the time period by which stabilization is to be achieved politically and economically a realistic one? Even the most orthodox monetarist would not expect to achieve stabilization in Brazil's present circumstances in less than six to twelve months. Whether it should be six to twelve, twelve to eighteen, or eighteen to twenty-four months does not seem to me a matter of fundamental doctrinal difference. The essential objective is that the goal be the right one, the direction of policy the right one, and the time be what is realistically feasible. An effort to bring about an excessively abrupt halt to inflation would either mean massive deflation, with wholesale bankruptcies and very heavy unemployment, or would require the kind of price-wage freeze and direct intervention in every phase of the economy which could only be enforced in a rigid dictatorship. Given Brazilian habits and attitudes, I doubt whether even a rigid dictatorship could enforce it.

With respect to the restoration of confidence and the change of expectations, I cannot agree that it makes little difference whether the rate of inflation is fifty percent or a hundred percent. In my mind, the direction of change is as important as the actual rate of inflation at any given moment. The change of expectations involved in shifting from a constant or accelerating rate of inflation to a decelerating rate of inflation is as significant as the change involved in shifting from some inflation to no inflation. I see two critical points of inflection in the inflationary curve: the change from concave upward to concave downward (which is the move from acceleration to deceleration), and the later change from concave downward to actual stability.

That much having been said, the problem before us is to judge whether the Brazilian government's policies are really bringing about this first point of inflection, whether the deceleration will be maintained, and whether its pace is sufficiently rapid. The cases cited by the IMF of "all-out campaigns for a limited period of time"—Greece, Formosa, and Bolivia—seem to me only partially relevant. They involved either beginning situations which were much less severe than the present one in Brazil or volumes of outside aid which constituted a far larger proportion of domestic gross product than can conceivably be envisaged in the Brazilian case. The world is not prepared to finance an import surplus in Brazil of one or two billion dollars a year. Such a surplus could not be absorbed here, even if financing were available, because industrialization has already proceeded to the point where such staggering competition from the outside world would be unacceptable.

I do not want to prejudge the new Brazilian economic plan, since we are just beginning our analysis of it. Ralph Korp's[4] preliminary indications, however, suggest that it is, in some respects at least, encouragingly tough considering the situation with which this government began in April. Castello Branco, Campos, and Bulhões show no fear of unpopularity as such for a limited period of time. They accept this as inevitable. The danger of those who would play personal politics with Brazil's profound problems lies at the present in other quarters.

---

[4] Financial Attaché in Rio de Janeiro.

Castello Branco's willingness to have his term extended was essentially a result of his conviction that there would be another year of unpopular measures, and that the active campaign period should wait until after the eventual up-turn rather than getting started in the midst of this unpopular phase. I even have doubts as to whether the government program may not be excessively austere on some points, notably the postponement of any further military or civilian civil service wage increases until after December 1965. I should like to leave a quantitative discussion of these matters, however, for analysis in the coming days and weeks when we have had a better chance to study the details of the program.

Although I was not personally involved in the mid-1950's, as you were, I know the history of the broken promises in connection with past aid package negotiations with Brazil. Since 1961 I have been painfully and intimately involved with them. Looking back at the 1953 and subsequent cases with some historical perspective, however, I am not persuaded that our Export-Import Bank loans were all to the bad. It is a misfortune that Kubitschek was not restrained from various inflationary follies, including the building of Brasilia. On the other hand, the positive things that were done as a result of the project-formulating work of the Joint Brazil–US Economic Commission in the early fifties, and the later help from some World Bank and much Export-Import Bank financing, did make possible the São Paulo development which in turn created the middle class which won the April revolution here in Brazil. And Brazil did enjoy a six to seven percent annual growth rate all through the 1950's, even though there were imbalances in some of this growth. So neither in economic nor in political terms was that money simply thrown down the drain. Quite the contrary. This is not an argument for aid now regardless of performance, but merely a caveat to the over-gloomy view of our actions a decade ago. Obviously we do want effective performance now, and there is good reason to believe that the Castello Branco government will provide it.

In arriving at judgments on the relation between the performance of the new Brazilian government and our own (and IMF's and others') support, we must bear in mind that these are not mutually independent phenomena. These questions always involve the will of the government concerned and the political capacity to make that will effective. On the former point, my judgment is that this government has a stronger will for the right policies than any other in Brazil's postwar history. On the latter point, our own support in adequate quantity and at the right time may itself make a decisive contribution. If we wait too long to observe performance we may by that very delay make the performance impossible. The only satisfactory arrangement is to have the performance and the outside support run in parallel, and with both related to realizable targets.

The government is already under heavy political fire from an unhealthy and unholy alliance. That alliance naturally includes the Communist, fellow travelling, and extreme negative nationalist forces who were in the Goulart camp. It includes conservative land owners who hate the thought of even the most minimal land reform. It includes the backward monopolistic nationalist business group which fears competition from foreign private investment and opposes any domestic democratization of capital or internal competition as well. And in recent weeks it has threatened to include the powerful voice of Carlos Lacerda for purely personalistic reasons; I hope that his basic intelligence will soon put these in their proper perspective, but I cannot yet be confident of this.

So far, Castello Branco has maintained a resolute tranquillity in pushing ahead with what he believes is right, but some positive economic and social gains along with the wage austerity and other negative aspects of the stabilization program may be crucial to the survival of the government's program—and conceivably in certain circumstances, to the survival of the government itself. It is especially important that sacrifices not all appear to be concentrated on wage-earners, or in any event that progress is in sight on housing and education as an offset to temporary wage level sacrifices.

We should also be careful to define performance requirements in terms which are within reasonable judgments of what is politically manageable by a relatively strong and good willed government, but one which does not possess dictatorial powers. As I see the postwar record, a chronic source of disillusionment with IMF stand-by agreements in Latin America has been the extraction of commitments from hard pressed finance ministers who did not themselves believe they were capable of being carried out when those commitments were signed. It is a sobering experience to review the history of these agreements and the brief periods within which many of their provisions were disregarded. These would not be good precedents for us to follow in present Brazilian circumstances.

It is against the above background that we should confront the question of the timing and nature of further economic support for the Brazilian program. We should of course continue processing projects as rapidly as the mechanics permit. As to the next phase of comprehensive negotiation, there emerged from a long discussion Thursday afternoon[5] among Bill Rogers, Jack Kubish, Ralph Korp, and myself the conclusion that the desirable timing would be in mid-October, related to the Campos presentation to CIAP now scheduled for about October 10. We believe that it would be most desirable to promote the

---

[5] August 6.

negotiation of an IMF stand-by agreement at the same time. We have already suggested to Campos the desirability of requesting the presence of at least one IMF Staff man here as soon as possible.

Ideally, IMF assistance should be used to liquidate commercial arrears and reduce the backlog of financial arrears (including payments to small suppliers who cannot be included in the rescheduling negotiations and cutting down the excessive volume of outstanding swaps, the renewal of which is itself an inflationary factor). It would be helpful to obtain corresponding action from the private banks, at least in reopening the $90 million in US bank credit lines and longer-term credits from both US and European banks along the lines of the 1961 arrangements. Our own assistance would include an estimate of the total project support through fiscal '65 at least, and a complementary program loan from AID. I would hope that at the same time the World Bank would be prepared to make further encouraging qualitative noises about its expectations in Brazil, and that the IDB might indicate some orders of magnitude of its expected assistance. I naturally also hope that Harold Linder[6] might by then be prepared to consider some modest new project loans for especially attractive projects within the Export-Import Bank's traditional fields of activity. Together with a forecast on PL 480, this could make a substantial showing of external support for the GOB efforts, with both good economic and good political results.

It would also be very desirable to give at least some preliminary indications in October of what might be done during the calendar year 1966. Exactly what and in what form, I would prefer to defer for recommendation after seeing how much of a basis the Brazilian program affords. Even with respect to 1965, there is the critical question of what portion of our commitments, if any, may be contingent upon Congressional action in the form of supplemental authorization and appropriation for the present fiscal year.

So far as broad magnitudes of development assistance are concerned, assuming that the stabilization effort is going in the right direction and that IMF resources are concentrated on short-term strengthening of the balance-of-payments position, I believe that Brazilian needs for total annual long-term capital inflow during the next few years are in the general range of six hundred to seven hundred million dollars per year. This is consistent with the "Gordon formula" of thirty percent for Brazil applied to the Punta del Este overall figure of more than two billion per year in annual outside resources. More important, it is consistent with a rough macro-economic analysis of the Brazilian

---

[6] President and Chairman, Export-Import Bank.

situation, and with rough estimates on sectoral requirements and sectoral lending opportunities and absorptive capacities.

As to the sources from which such a total might be made up, the following indicates reasonable orders of magnitude:

AID and Export-Import Bank	$250 million
PL 480	75
IDB	75
IBRD and IDA	100
European and Japanese Bilateral	50–100
Net private (gross would be larger)	100
Total	$650–700 million

This total is about three and one half percent of GNP. Since it is additional investment and takes the form of high return imports, it could make the critical difference between an unsatisfactory and a satisfactory growth rate.

The short-term problem of food supply, also mentioned in your letter, is one which has been greatly worrying me. It is a major contributory source to the growing unpopularity of the present government, although it arises now by coincidence and is not a result of the stabilization effort. I have reviewed the problem at length with Dick Newberg[7] and Jack Kubish. They advise that the main remedies, some of which cannot be effective rapidly, lie in domestic action here, but there are some contributions we can make through technical assistance and through certain elements of the AID program, such as rural credit and fertilizer imports, as well as through PL 480. We have helped Newberg to secure a strong position in the Agriculture Ministry to advise on improvement of relevant domestic policies, and we will have further specific recommendations for our action in the near future.

Let me conclude on a somewhat personal note. I have the impression—I hope erroneously—that some elements in Washington may look on me as a mere advocate for anything the Brazilian government may request, or a proponent of unlimited and unconditional aid to Brazil simply because I am Ambassador here. This is not a stance that I want to occupy or feel justly described as occupying. Many GOB proposals or requests are turned down here without Washington ever hearing of them. Like Castello Branco, the AID Mission and I are interested in successful policies and good results, not in ephemeral popularity.

---

[7] Director, Office of Agriculture and Rural Development (AID) in Rio de Janeiro.

At the same time, having helped guide United States strategy through the tortuous period of the Goulart regime, and also being vindicated (so far at least) with respect to the political moderation and progressive reformism of the Castello Branco regime (see recent issues of *Newsweek* compared with their June appraisals), I do feel entitled to some degree of credit and to reasonable promptness of response from Washington when I plead urgency. The bureaucratic machine in recent weeks has occasionally been exasperatingly slow or unresponsive. A good example is the absence of action on the declaration of US-use PL 480 cruzeiros as surplus, on which Ralph Burton will show you my recent letter to Kermit Gordon.[8] Another example is the very chilly first response to the proposal for including a Guanabara housing project in the AFL–CIO housing guarantee program. These two examples have a direct bearing on our influence with youth and labor groups, both of which we have been repeatedly (and rightly) enjoined to cultivate with all instruments at our disposal.

I have sometimes been reminded of the magnificent little book by F.M. Cornford, entitled *Microcosmographia Academica*—only fifty pages long and a valiant precursor of Parkinson—which is a masterpiece of exposition of bureaucratic obstructionism. Among other principles, Cornford points out that there is "generally only one reason for doing something, but many reasons for doing nothing". The present is not the time to apply this principle in Brazil!

I need hardly emphasize, after the recent Foreign Ministers' meeting on Cuba[9] and the prompt Brazilian response on Vietnam,[10] that in its international posture the new Brazilian government has now rejoined the free world. In addition to the economic issues discussed in this letter, this political consideration is a valid reason for resolving close cases in favor of support for Brazil. I do not have as long an experience in Latin American affairs as you, but my own has been very intensive in the past eight years. I believe that wise policies on our part may help to set this country, and with it much of the rest of the continent, on a long-lasting course of healthy development as a firmly-anchored member of the free world community and an assured ally of the United States. Such an objective warrants a strong effort on our part and a willingness to take some risks.

---

[8] Director, Bureau of the Budget. The "recent letter" from Lincoln Gordon to Kermit Gordon has not been found.

[9] See Documents 19–23.

[10] Reference is evidently to the Brazilian response to President Johnson's personal message on the Gulf of Tonkin incident; see *Foreign Relations*, 1964–1968, vol. I, Document 281.

Please forgive the length and rambling character of this letter. I hope it may be helpful in clarifying our frame of mind here in Rio on these fundamental issues.

With warm personal regards,

Sincerely,

Lincoln

---

216. **Memorandum From Robert M. Sayre of the National Security Council Staff to the President's Special Assistant for National Security Affairs (Bundy)**[1]

Washington, September 30, 1964.

I am reluctant to burden you with the rather lengthy memorandum and telegrams attached[2] but there is a "great debate" going on about our policy toward Brazil. I think you need to know about it. The success (or failure) of our Brazilian policy will determine the course of events in Brazil for years to come.

Essentially, Rostow is suggesting the shock treatment. Gordon is pressing for strong support of what might be called a moderate course, although bringing inflation down from 140% to 10% in less than two years may not be regarded as moderate by those people who get hit.

I believe everyone agrees with Rostow on the seriousness of the issue and the objective. The argument is over means. On that, I side with Gordon. But I think both make a mistake in trying to apply U.S. and Western European economic theories to Brazil. In homogenous commodities, price may respond fairly well to supply and demand theory. Even here, however, poor marketing makes this debatable. But on manufactured products, Latins are real monopolists. Any program that is based on the premise that increasing supply will result in an

---

[1] Source: Johnson Library, National Security File, Country File, Brazil, Vol. VII–a, 8/64–11/68. Confidential.

[2] Attached but not printed are a September 14 memorandum from Rostow to Mann; telegram 700 from Rio de Janeiro, September 24; and telegram 42 from Brasilia, September 28. In a September 7 memorandum to Mann, Rostow proposed a "broad strategy" for attacking inflation in Brazil: "The Situation in Brazil—now reinforced by the election of Frei in Chile—gives us a rare and perhaps transient interval of opportunity. We could not conceive of a government in Brazil more mature, more level-headed about relations with the U.S., and in its attitudes towards private enterprise." (National Archives and Records Administration, RG 59, Central Files 1964–66, POL 15–1 BRAZ)

automatic cut in prices in Latin America, fails to recognize this social attitude. Social and political rigidities in Latin America are strong. I think this is why Tom Mann views with some skepticism that even the "moderate" program pushed by Gordon will be carried out and he, therefore, wants to keep on maximum pressure by putting out our money generally after Brazil delivers the goods.[3]

RMS

---

[3] Bundy wrote his response on the memorandum: "I'm with Gordon. Rostow is very strong but not strong enough to remake Brazil one-handed." On November 2 AID Administrator Bell approved a proposal to provide Brazil with $100 million for project loans and $150 million for a program loan "on the most concessionary terms legally available." (Memorandum from Mann to Bell, October 29; ibid., ARA/LA Files: Lot 66 D 65, Brazil 1964) The United States and Brazil signed the agreement on December 14.

---

217. **Telegram From the Embassy Office in Brasilia to the Department of State**[1]

Brasilia, May 4, 1965, 2130Z.

153. For President and Secretary of State from Harriman.

1. Immediately upon arrival in Brasilia 1330 Tuesday, I was received by President Castello Branco for one and one-half hour working luncheon, together with FonMin Vasco Leitao da Cunha and Ambassador Gordon. Conversation was cordial, frank, and very much to the point.

2. In my opening exposition, I first reviewed reasons for President Johnson's emergency action last Wednesday,[2] collapse local authority

---

[1] Source: National Archives and Records Administration, RG 59, Central Files 1964–66, POL 7 US/HARRIMAN. Secret; Immediate. Repeated Immediate to Rio de Janeiro and Priority to Buenos Aires, Santiago, Lima, Quito, Bogota, Caracas, Mexico City, Panama, Guatemala, USCINCSO, and USUN. Passed to the White House, DOD, and CIA.

[2] On Tuesday, April 27, the President sent U.S. Marines to the Dominican Republic to protect American lives in the midst of civil war; he later claimed that action was necessary to prevent the establishment of a Communist dictatorship. In response to criticism that he had acted unilaterally, the President dispatched Ambassador at Large Harriman and a team of high-level officials to Latin America for consultation, i.e., to explain the decision and to seek support from other countries. Before Harriman arrived in Brasilia, Walters met Castello Branco to "prepare a favorable atmosphere." When Harriman landed at the airport, Walters gave him a note: "Don't push too hard. The door is open." (Vernon A. Walters, *Silent Missions*, pp. 399–401)

in Dominican Republic and increasing takeover of rebellion by foreign-trained Communist elements. Since we aware of GOB support for multilateral force resolution and indications of willingness contribute thereto, I concentrated on immediate problems how secure effective OAS action to authorize I–A force and work toward Dominican Republic conditions permitting people peacefully choose own government. I also expressed appreciation GOB public support President Johnson's actions.

3. Castello Branco replied that problem had two aspects. Substantive one was to avoid Communist seizure of another country, as well as saving innocent lives. Formal one was to legitimate actions through effective OAS measures. GOB subject to two constraints in sending troops: (a) must have OAS request and (b) must have congressional approval. It is vitally important secure two-thirds MFM vote on I–A force. To get this, most effective step is to galvanize OAS five-man commission on spot and get them to take three steps soonest: (a) secure effective cease-fire, (b) make clear to LA governments and publics the nature and extent of Communist threat, and (c) to insist on constitution of I–A force under its political guidance. He said commission so far acting too much like Red Cross body and not taking enough political leadership. He instructed FonMin to communicate forthwith to Penna Marinho in this sense.

4. We also discussed Brazilian approaches through Ambassadors here and in Washington to press Peru and Ecuador to favorable vote. They will also work on Chile, Uruguay and Mexico, although not expecting much from latter two.

5. Castello Branco stated failure secure two-thirds vote would create major rupture in OAS and also be signal for political violence in much of hemisphere. He felt sure that US would not withdraw any forces and made clear he would not want us to. On this point, I assured him President Johnson would stand firm until it was clear that Dominican people would have opportunity establish government of own choice. If MFM vote not secured, Castello Branco doubted possibility going through with May 20 Rio conference.

6. Castello Branco stated categorically that after favorable MFM vote he would request congressional authority to send force. We did not discuss size of force or command arrangements, but ARMA's contacts indicate Brazilian military thinking of one infantry battalion, one MP company, and possibly a tank company totalling up to one thousand men. Castello Branco had discussed Monday evening with congressional leaders and was seeing them again at 1500 when we adjourned. Their reaction was that OAS request was key, and that with such request favorable vote would be given although with some difficulties in chamber. Castello Branco also thought MFM might want to

decide specifically on which countries to invite to send forces, and they should if possible include one of the "shy maidens."

7. In discussing hostile attitude Chile and Venezuela, I mentioned personal friendship with Bosch as one element and reluctance believe that he had lost effective leadership of rebellion to Communist and allied elements. Castello Branco said he had received two telegrams from Bosch protesting US intervention, but shows no disposition to credit Bosch line.

8. After presidential meeting, we continued briefly with FonMin, who sending instructions to Penna Marinho through OAS. GOB has been without direct communications with Santo Domingo Embassy for three days. We offered ours if they have any trouble, but agree OAS politically preferable channel if working.

9. FonMin also gave us copy their Monday morning instructions to MFM representative, strongly opposing Mexico, supporting US actions and resolutions. Translation follows separately.

10. FonMin also gave preliminary views on how Dominican Republic crisis will require being taken into account at May 20 Rio Conference if held, specifically possibility acting on establishment permanent arrangements for emergency I–A peacekeeping force.

11. Castello Branco agreed to keep in closest touch with us here and in Washington to concert specific moves to achieve our mutual objectives on which there appears to be full agreement.[3]

Gordon

---

[3] On May 6 the OAS voted to form an Inter-American Peace Force, a unit that augmented U.S. forces with contingents from several member states led by Brazil. Six days later, the OAS voted to postpone the Second Special Inter-American Conference scheduled to start in Rio de Janeiro on May 20. For documentation on the Dominican crisis, see *Foreign Relations, 1964–1968*, volume XXXII.

218.   National Intelligence Estimate[1]

NIE 93–65   Washington, May 12, 1965.

PROSPECTS FOR BRAZIL

The Problem

To assess the character of the Castello Branco regime, and to estimate Brazil's political and economic prospects over the next year or two.

Conclusions

A. The Castello Branco government has provided responsible and effective leadership, reversing the movement toward chaos of the Goulart period and making an impressive start toward reasonable solutions of Brazil's many problems. President Castello Branco commands, largely on his own terms, the strong support of the military establishment and the cooperation of Congress. This has enabled him both to preserve the qualified constitutional system imposed by the military after Goulart's removal and to press ahead with his program of major reforms. (Paras. 1–11)

B. So serious and basic are the economic problems inherited by the Castello Branco government, however, that despite its determined efforts improvements can come only slowly. While attempting to bring Brazil's hyperinflation gradually under control, the administration is also trying to prepare the way for rapid economic growth and meaningful social reform. Its accomplishments so far have fallen short of its aims: it could not prevent a small decline in the economy in 1964, and its goals of relative price stability and vigorous economic expansion by 1966 are probably already beyond reach. Nevertheless, it has achieved much in correcting the worst imbalances and has set the stage for a significant reduction of inflation and a respectable rate of economic growth. (Paras. 17–27)

C. Popular discontent is likely to increase over the next year, primarily because all elements of the population are feeling the pinch of the regime's austerity program. Because the regime's integrity and authority are widely respected, however, this discontent is not likely to

---

[1] Source: Central Intelligence Agency, Job 79–R01012A, O/DDI Registry. Secret; Controlled Dissem. According to a note on the cover sheet this estimate was prepared in the Central Intelligence Agency with the participation of the intelligence organizations of the Departments of State and Defense and the National Security Agency. The United States Intelligence Board concurred in this estimate on May 12. The estimate superseded SNIE 93–64 (Document 213).

precipitate a major challenge to political stability. Over the next year, leftist extremists will probably try to carry out sporadic sabotage and terrorism, but their capabilities are limited and Brazil's security forces will almost certainly be able to handle any threat they may pose. The so-called hardline groups in the military are likely to attempt to coerce the President occasionally, as in the past, but such pressures will almost certainly not threaten his overthrow or even force him to reverse his essentially moderate political policies. (Paras. 12–16, 28–34)

D. There is, of course, a potential conflict between the regime's determination to ensure the continuation of its program and its desire to hold presidential elections as scheduled in November 1966. To ensure continuation of its policies through an electoral victory, the regime will probably seek to form a combination of political machines at the state level that can "deliver" the vote. Castello Branco would be the strongest pro-regime candidate. Although he has so far flatly refused to run, there will be considerable pressure on him to change his mind. In any case, we consider it likely that the election will be held. (Paras. 36–39)

[Omitted here is the Discussion section of the estimate.]

219. Memorandum From William G. Bowdler of the National Security Council Staff to the President's Special Assistant for National Security Affairs (Bundy)[1]

Washington, October 26, 1965.

SUBJECT

Storm Clouds in Brazil

In the past few days the political-military crisis in Brazil, resulting from the October 3 gubernatorial elections and the return of President Kubitschek on October 4, has become more serious. Former Ambassador Juracy Magalhaes, who recently returned to Brazil,[2] reportedly believes that the Castello Branco Government has lost considerable ground since October 3.

---

[1] Source: Johnson Library, National Security File, Country File, Brazil, Vol. V, 9/64–11/65. Secret.

[2] Magalhães was appointed Minister of Justice and the Interior on October 7.

The "hard line" supporters of the April 1964 Revolution interpreted the recent elections as a defeat for the Revolution. They fear a return to power of pre-revolutionary elements associated with subversion and corruption. Governor Carlos Lacerda is in the forefront of the "hard line" movement.

On October 13 President Castello Branco sent to the Congress special measures to forestall the anti-revolutionary implications of the election results and of Kubitschek's return. These measures were designed in large part to mollify the "hard-liners." The measures have run into trouble in the Congress. The Castello Branco Government, lacking the necessary votes to put them through, has been placing the heaviest possible pressure on the Congress and has indicated that the Congress must either vote with the Government or risk losing its right to participate in the nation's political decisions.

The Congressional vote was originally scheduled for today. As indicated in recent cable traffic,[3] there has been considerable speculation that the government, anticipating defeat, was prepared to declare a state of siege or to issue a new Institutional Act to counter anticipated coup action by the "hard-liners." Embassy Rio reports that the vote has been postponed until tomorrow.[4] This probably indicates that the government is hopeful of being able to put together enough votes by then to pass the legislation.

Ambassador Gordon left for Brazil this morning.[5] He will be in Rio by this evening.

ARA has recommended to Secretary Rusk that we take a position of complete neutrality in word and deed on this one.[6] I think this is the wisest course to follow for the time being.

WGB

---

[3] The principal cable is telegram 885 from Rio de Janeiro, October 25. (National Archives and Records Administration, RG 59, Central Files 1964–66, POL 23–5 BRAZ)

[4] In telegram 891 from Rio de Janeiro, October 26; ibid.

[5] Gordon was in Washington, October 11–26, for consultations on economic assistance to Brazil.

[6] The Department instructed the Embassy as follows: "During current crisis in Brazil, Department believes that best posture for US is one of complete neutrality both in word and deed. Given extreme sensitivity of issues involved, U.S. officials should refrain from making any public statements at this time." (Telegram 655 to Rio de Janeiro, October 26; National Archives and Records Administration, RG 59, Central Files 1964–66, POL 23–BRAZ)

220.   Telegram From the Embassy in Brazil to the Department of State[1]

Rio de Janeiro, October 27, 1965, 1851Z.

910. 1. It will be obvious to Department that second Institutional Act[2] represents severe setback in our own hopes, which I believe have been fully shared by Castello Branco himself, Juracy Magalhaes, and most key advisers of GOB, that Brazil could maintain uninterrupted march on road back to full constitutional normalcy. All the defects in law and principle contained in the first Institutional Act (see my Embtel 2235,[3] April 10, 1964) have been repeated in the second, amplified by fact that this no longer in first flush of successful revolution following near chaos.

2. My first impression, without opportunity since Tuesday[4] night return for any conversations outside Embassy staff, is that this measure reflects much greater than necessary concessions to hard line, engendered by unfortunate concomitance of Lacerda intemperance, Kubitschek return, provocative statements of Supreme Court president, and other adventitious factors generating emotional military reactions which have reduced the President's effective authority and weakened congressional support for government. In longer term perspective, it is the price paid by Castello Branco for failure to start months ago the systematic building of a political base and his reluctance to develop a strong domestic program of propaganda and public relations.

---

[1] Source: National Archives and Records Administration, RG 59, Central Files 1964–66, POL 23–5 BRAZ. Confidential; Immediate; Limdis. Repeated to Brasilia and passed to White House, DOD, and CIA.

[2] Castello Branco announced the second Institutional Act on the morning of October 27. The act revived several elements of its predecessor, including the authority to suspend the political rights of citizens and elected officials for 10 years. It also expanded membership on the Supreme Court, dissolved the existing political parties, and increased the government's power to intervene in the individual states, declare a state of siege, and recess the Congress. Presidential elections were scheduled for October 1966 with Castello Branco declared ineligible to succeed himself. On October 27 Bundy prepared a memorandum to the President on the crisis leading to the second Institutional Act. A handwritten notation on the memorandum indicates it was not sent. (Johnson Library, National Security File, Country File, Brazil, Vol. V, 9/64–11/65)

[3] Document 211.

[4] October 26.

3. As in previous case, act falls well short of outright dictatorship. Congress remains, although obviously subject even greater executive pressures, press remains free, and opposition political organizations will be recreated under terms July 1965 party statute. Governors elected October 3 are expected to be empowered. Nevertheless, reassertion at this late date of unqualified revolutionary constituent authority is very arbitrary law-making, with no bow either to Congress, plebiscite, or other device for popular legitimation, and we must expect US and foreign press and other reactions accordingly.

3. [*sic*] In face this fait accompli we confront several difficult problems. Some OARS may be tempted to react vigorously, even to point of cutting relations, or to refuse attendance November 17 LA conference. Domestically, today's action reflects a polarization of forces which in long run can only serve interests of extreme left or right and which it is in US interest to seek depolarize in any way we can.

4. I believe we neither can nor should avoid a formal public reaction to Institutional Act no. two. Suggested text in para 6 below, choice of spokesman obviously best determined by Department. Purpose is to express concern, strengthen President's hand in resisting hard line pressures for harsh application new powers, and at same time to indicate continuing broad support of economic policies and program.

5. In event Department spokesman queried re continuation aid to GOB, suggest reply on lines GOB program fits Punta del Este criteria, has just been reviewed and warmly endorsed by CIAP, and withdrawal support would not only undermine further economic and social progress but also reduce prospects early achievement full constitutional normalcy.

6. *Begin text:* The USG regrets that the Brazilian executive authorities have felt that, in order to safeguard the country from a recurrence of the chaotic political and economic conditions which made necessary the revolution of March 1964, it was necessary to adopt a new series of extra-ordinary measures. It feels confident, however, in view of the record of the Castello Branco government during the past 18 months, that these measures will be applied with moderation and restraint. It [also] hopes that the very substantial progress already made in the efforts toward economic stabilization, renewed development, and the reform and modernization of economic and social institutions will be carried forward to full realization, and that Brazil's precious heritage of constitutional government based on representative democracy will be consolidated as the institutional foundation for the further progress of this greater sister nation. *End text.*

7. Department may wish repeat this message in whole or part to other LA posts.[5]

Gordon

---

[5] Bowdler forwarded the telegram to Bundy as an attachment to an October 27 memorandum in which he argued: "I think that Gordon might be able to make his point with Castello Branco, Juracy Magalhaes, and others, in private talks and avoid running the serious adverse risks." Bundy concurred. (Johnson Library, National Security File, Country File, Brazil, Vol. V, 9/64–11/65) In telegram 670 to Rio de Janeiro, October 28, the Department informed Gordon that the Embassy was free to express concern to "selected Brazilians" in private, but the Department would continue to give "no comment." (National Archives and Records Administration, RG 59, Central Files 1964–66, POL 23–5 BRAZ) On October 29 Gordon reported raising the issue with Magalhães, who "naturally preferred silence to condemnation, but saw no harm and some real merit" in an official U.S. statement of "regret." Gordon recommended making a high-level statement as soon as possible, which he believed could be done "without undue inconsistency and to overall benefit." (Telegram 949 from Rio de Janeiro; ibid.) The Department, however, refused to change its position. (Telegram 688 to Rio de Janeiro, October 30; ibid.)

---

221.   Telegram From the Embassy in Brazil to the Department of State[1]

Rio de Janeiro, November 3, 1965, 1817Z.

993. Subject: Talk with President Castello Branco on Second Institutional Act.

1. Taking advantage of All Souls' holiday, President asked me to meet him Tuesday[2] morning for almost two-hour private conversation on above and related subjects. President started by inquiring about Mrs. Gordon's recent trip on Sao Francisco River, his own similar voyage forty years ago, problems of internal road and rail transport and coastal navigation in Brazil, comparisons with French transportation system as he saw it in 1936–38. Thence talk moved to disastrous United Front experience in France, perspicacity of de Gaulle in those days compared with now, refusal of old French generals to listen to him, etc. Castello then said that such topics were agreeable to discuss on a holiday morning, but were not reasons for which he had asked my call.

---

[1] Source: National Archives and Records Administration, RG 59, Central Files 1964–66, POL 23–5 BRAZ. Confidential; Priority; Limdis.

[2] November 2.

2. Turning to second Institutional Act, President said he had spent some time Monday afternoon reviewing foreign press comments. He mentioned *Washington Post* sympathetic attitude but also harsh condemnation by *New York Times* and *Herald Tribune*, several Paris papers, and comments elsewhere in Latin America. He said he was not surprised at sharpness of some foreign reaction, recognizing that close acquaintance with Brazilian history and contemporary reality was essential to understanding of what had happened.

3. He then made brief exposition of immediate background of the Institutional Act (partly overlapping Embtel 988)[3] saying that substantial portion of Congress and several Supreme Court justices had mistaken his desire to return to constitutional normality as willingness to return to the prerevolutionary past. Kubitschek's misunderstanding had been even greater. In eyes these groups, April revolution had not signified a serious change of direction for Brazil; it was rather a mere change of persons in power which could easily be reversed. As early as October 15, Castello had become convinced that this misunderstanding must be corrected, either through congressional acceptance of the government's proposed new legislation on federal-state relations and restriction of Cassados or through issuance of second Institutional Act. Strenuous endeavors were made to bring home to Congress the significance of the choice, but in considerable measure due to Kubitschek and Lacerda influence, an adequate number of congressmen had not been persuaded. He then requested my own observations.

4. Prefacing with request permission to speak personally and with complete candor, I replied at length. I said that he knew our official public position to be that these were internal political matters, but had some reason to suppose that my own reactions were widely shared by Washington authorities. I said the initial impact on me had been both shock and sorrow. I had been shocked at extent of arbitrary powers assumed through the act and sorrowful at fact that it symbolized a major setback in his own effort, which American authorities had followed with great sympathy, to bring about full constitutional normalization without jeopardizing basic purposes of revolution. I appreciated that in the immediate circumstances the alternative might have been even worse, and I understood the adventitious factors of Kubitschek's return and Lacerda's agitation, but I could not help regret that the situation had gotten to the point where such a choice was necessary. I

---

[3] Telegram 988 from Rio de Janeiro, November 2, reported on a discussion the previous evening between Castello Branco and Vernon Walters. (National Archives and Records Administration, RG 59, Central Files 1964–66, POL 23–5 BRAZ)

referred to missed opportunities during the last twelve months to begin building a serious political base for revolution and to develop adequate domestic propaganda and internal public relations designed to
give a broad sense of public participation and enlist the support of various influential groups. Where governors or candidates had done so, I
remarked, they had generally been successful in recent state elections,
as in cases Parana, Para, Maranahao, and Goias, but federal government had failed to take such measures on nation-wide basis.

5. Then quoting National Archives motto that "What is past is pro-
logue," I said I could summarize present view by saying this was a lost
battle but not necessarily a lost war. For future, I saw both constructive possibilities and also very serious dangers. I then specified a number of critical issues.

6. The first concerned the use that would be made of the extraordinary powers, which in themselves were obviously juridically
barbarous. It seemed to me clear that, despite the widespread acceptance in the country for the Institutional Act, ranging from enthusiasm to relief to passivity, tension between the hard line and the
moderate line of the revolution was certainly not ended. (A) It was
still visible in question whether governors-elect Negrao de Lima
and Israel Pinheiro would be installed in office. (B) It would also be
reflected in the extent of new cassations. (C) Then there was sensitive and important issue of restrictions of press freedom. On this point
(although I had not yet seen Deptel 696),[4] I said was well aware of
irresponsibility of much of Brazilian press, having myself frequently
been victim of distortions or misrepresentations, but President must
be aware that foreign opinion regarding Brazil was formed by reporting of newpapermen and nothing could antagonize them more
rapidly than restrictions on press freedom. Castello interrupted at this
point to indicate his concurrence.

7. Second important issue for future, I continued, was that of his
own tenure in office, referring to press reports his possible resignation
on January 31. Mildness of some of foreign reaction to Institutional Act,
I said, must be attributed to his own demonstrated record of moderation and personal confidence which he had inspired abroad.

8. Third critical issue concerned positive side of revolution, including success of Juracy's effort to build political base and development of effective internal public relations emphasizing positive goals
of modernization and constructive reform as well as opposition to
corruption and subversion. Here too Castello interrupted to express

---

[4] In telegram 696 to Rio de Janeiro, November 1, the Department suggested that
Gordon "make Juracy and others see heavy cost GOB would pay abroad for restricting
press freedom in Brazil." (Ibid., PPB 9 BRAZ)

concurrence, saying this required team effort and he was now reconstructing ministerial team with this as well as other points in mind.

9. Turning then to grounds for worry about future, I said that essential concern was that situation might slide into outright military dictatorship. Persons familiar with Brazilian history knew that historic political role of armed forces had been to intervene to place nation back on tracks of order and progress when it was threatened with being derailed, in effect exercising "moderating power" contained in the imperial constitution until 1889, but not themselves to govern. Now there seemed to be some indication of desire by armed forces to assume governmental responsibility itself. Men drawn from military career had of course played large part in Brazilian politics historically and at present, but I saw an important distinction between "civil military" types such as Juracy, Ney Braga, Jarbas Passarinho,[5] and Castello Branco himself, and others whose essential view was that all problems could be resolved by force alone, rather than by persuasion and enlisting of public support or a judicious mixture between persuasion and force. If this latter type won control, I could see no reason to expect Brazil to be exempt from universal rule that force breeds counterforce. I felt that radical left in Brazil, as illustrated in nomination of Marshal Lott,[6] had been deliberately trying to precipitate military dictatorship in hopes of securing power through long-run broadly based united front movement of protest and reaction.

10. President listened attentively to this long exposition, interrupting at several points but not dissenting. He remarked that few people outside Brazil had understood depth of corruption and subversion which had been tolerated under Kubitschek and then actively stimulated under Goulart. He cited a statement of Luis Carlos Prestes, Secretary of Brazilian Communist Party, in late 1963 to affect that "We already have the government but do not yet have the power." Thence effort to neutralize armed forces by subversive organization of NCO's. This led to digression in which we compared Goulart regime to recent Indonesian experience under Sukarno, perhaps only two historic examples of deliberate "superversion" of national institutions in mistaken view that Communists could always be controlled.

---

[5] Braga and Passarinho were the outgoing governors of Paraná and Pará, respectively.

[6] Henrique Batista Duffles Teixeira Lott, Minister of War under President Kubitschek, had been nominated for Governor of Guanabara as the candidate of the Brazilian Labor Party (PTB). His candidacy was subsequently voided by the Superior Electoral Tribunal.

11. I then asked President his general impression of my reactions to institutional act. He replied that they were reactions of a good and close observer, but he thought too pessimistic. I said that this was good news and asked why. He replied for two reasons: (a) My combination of American and university backgrounds may have made me too perfectionist on some points of juridical principle, and (b) he was convinced that a military dictatorship could be and would be avoided. He then proceeded to describe two types of military dictatorships, the classical Latin American type of simply ruling by force and enjoying fruits of power and more recent Nasserist type, with socialist overtones and drumming up of popular support through intense nationalism. He thought Brazil would resist implantation of either type. I raised question whether certain of Lacerda's writings and some thinking among younger officers might not be signs of incipient Nasserism in Brazil. President thought this was possible but unlikely, especially if effective work now done to build political base for revolution. He expressed confidence in success of Juracy's efforts in this regard. Although saying it would be work of months and not merely days or weeks. He thought November would be critical month in laying out basic guidelines of this effort and its success should be readily visible by about next March.

12. President then changed subject to University of Brasilia, saying that he was returning there early Wednesday in order to deal at firsthand with that crisis. Juracy had reported to him talk with Vice President Lowry of Ford Foundation which I had arranged last Saturday.[7] I repeated Lowry's concern that present crisis threatened major loss to Brazil of non-Communist professors, especially in sciences where talent scarce and jobs easily obtained elsewhere. This was in addition to adverse foreign reaction to mishandling an admittedly extremely difficult problem of faculty and student subversion at Brasilia.

13. In conclusion, President raised subject of forthcoming Rio Conference and visit of Secretary Rusk. He expressed keen desire for long private talk with Secretary, apart from protocol visits and any social affairs such as projected Roberto Campos dinner. He thought that perhaps Saturday afternoon or Sunday November 20 or 21 would be best indicated time.

14. Throughout this long talk, I was seeking to appraise President's general frame of mind in face of last week's critical developments. He was somewhat tired and still reflecting some of extreme tension to which he had been subjected but basically well composed

---

[7] October 30.

and apparently conscious of heavy responsibilities he still faces and prepared to come to grips with them. I did not request, and he did not offer, specific commitments on any of points outlined above, but I believe they may have some real weight in decisions of coming weeks.[8]

Gordon

---

[8] In telegram 1046 from Rio de Janeiro, November 7, Gordon reported having an "extremely encouraging" talk about the situation in Brazil with Juracy Magalhães on November 6. Since Castello Branco had described Gordon as "deeply worried but excessively pessimistic," Magalhães offered reassurance: the purpose of the Second Institutional Act was "to save Brazilian democracy, not to destroy it." Magalhães was confident that world opinion would recognize this once certain events transpired, including: "the installation of the recently elected state governors; the rebuilding of a political party structure; the direct election next year of other governors and congress; and the moderation with which the arbitrary powers of the IA–2 (Institutional Act No. 2) will be used." (National Archives and Records Administration, RG 59, Central Files 1964–66, POL 15–1 BRAZ)

---

222.   Telegram From the Department of State to the Embassy in Brazil[1]

Washington, November 7, 1965, 2:09 p.m.

744. For Ambassador from Secretary. Subject: Recent Developments in Brazil.

I have read your telegram 993[2] reporting your conversation with Castello Branco on Brazil's Second Institutional Act.

You have struck precisely correct note. Although we have been maintaining silence publicly on Second Institutional Act, Castello Branco and other Brazilian leaders should be made acutely aware our

---

[1] Source: National Archives and Records Administration, RG 59, Central Files 1964–66, POL 23–5 BRAZ. Confidential; Exdis. Drafted by Kubish and Sayre on November 6, cleared by Vaughn and U. Alexis Johnson, and approved by Rusk. In a November 6 memorandum to Rusk, Vaughn recommended approval of the telegram: "I am convinced that other crises may develop in which the Brazilian military will be tempted to become even more dominant and repressive, and I am concerned that perhaps some of our own U.S. officials, particularly in the military services, may not fully appreciate the serious damage to our interests which could result from such a development. This cable should make our basic policy view quite clear and strengthen Ambassador Gordon's hand, and ours in ARA, in executing that policy." (Ibid., POL 23–9 BRAZ)

[2] Document 221.

serious concern and deep disappointment over recent developments in Brazil. We had strongest hope that Brazil was moving toward effective exercise political democracy and was achieving substantial success in its economic reform and development programs. We sincerely regret backwards steps on the political side and earnestly hope that the arbitrary powers assumed in the Institutional Act will be employed with the greatest moderation and restraint.

Because of Brazil's great size and influence in hemisphere, events in Brazil have far-reaching consequences throughout the hemisphere. Important developments in Brazil inevitably affect the United States and the free world. The emergence of a repressive authoritarian regime would represent a serious reverse in an otherwise rather encouraging series of developments throughout the hemisphere under the Alliance for Progress. Unless the danger of a sharp movement to the extreme right is averted, the basis will be laid for vigorous reaction from the left and serious political instability in Brazil. We must do whatever we can to avoid such developments. The Alliance for Progress and many of our hemispheric policies and programs can only be effective with the cooperation of a Brazilian government that is following progressive policies and avoiding the extremes of both the right and the left.[3]

I am sure you have already been talking to your Country Team about the situation in Brazil and what influence the United States might be able to bring to bear. I also understand that you will soon be submitting recommendations on the specific short-term policies and lines of action we should follow with respect to the Brazilian government. In the meantime, I wanted to emphasize to you my concern about developments in Brazil and to urge that you and your Country Team consider very thoroughly how we can best bring our influence to bear, including economic and military assistance, to persuade Brazilian leaders—especially Brazilian military leaders—to pull back from their apparent commitment to increased authoritarianism.[4]

Rusk

---

[3] The following sentence was removed from the beginning of the last paragraph: "I have discussed Brazilian developments with the President who is apprehensive over this recent turn of events in Brazil."

[4] In his reply Gordon urged that the Department reconsider its decision against issuing a public statement: "By holding to line that Second Institutional Act is purely domestic political affair, we tend to give impression inside Brazil, in rest of LA, and in US itself that we condone or even applaud what has been done." (Telegram 1083 from Rio de Janeiro, November 9; National Archives and Records Administration, RG 59, Central Files 1964–66, POL 23–5 BRAZ) The Department declined Gordon's request, maintaining that the press saw nothing inconsistent or paradoxical in a public stance of "no comment." The Department was concerned, however, about press reports that the Embassy disagreed with official policy: "This is extremely unfortunate and we assume you are dealing with this matter in the manner you think best." (Telegram 802 to Rio de Janeiro, November 12; ibid.)

223.   Telegram From the Embassy in Brazil to the Department of State[1]

Rio de Janeiro, November 14, 1965, 2129Z.

1124. Ref. Embtel 967.[2]

1. Depressing and dangerous situation described in recent messages has brightened notably over past several days as result well-conceived and executed GOB campaign to expound positive aspects and purposes of revolution. This campaign has also given important psychological boost to President's prestige and image as being in command of situation, sorely lacking in weeks following October 3. Nevertheless it is not yet possible to have full confidence in continuation this prospect. In longer view, developments during past three months have obviously represented substantial retrogression in terms political objectives Castello Branco government (CBG). Institutional Act No. 2 (IA–2), however its powers may be used, stands not only as symbol of authoritarianism to outside world but also could tempt extremist political and military leaders to seize control of this ready-made dictatorial mechanism. Problem for United States policy is to assess to what extent and in what ways USG can use its resources and influence so that powers of government remain in moderate hands while danger of move toward extremism is reduced and constitutional legitimacy and the rule of law restored, in order to contribute to building of permanent political bases for stability plus progress.

2. At outset we should have no illusions regarding our ability greatly to influence course of political developments in Brazil, given its size and complexity and ease with which attempts to intervene in domestic politics could backfire.

3. Whenever opportunities are afforded (as in my recent conversations with President Castello Branco and Justice Minister Juracy Magalhaes)[3] I intend to say frankly to political and military leaders of country that USG not only regrets arbitrary assumption of discretionary powers by CBG, but sees serious danger of slippage into undisguised military dictatorship unless way is found to reassert unequivocally

---

[1] Source: National Archives and Records Administration, RG 59, Central Files 1964–66, POL 23–5 BRAZ. Secret; Priority; Limdis. Repeated to Brasilia.

[2] In telegram 967 from Rio de Janeiro, October 31, the Embassy described conditions leading to the Second Institutional Act, analyzed public reaction to its promulgation, and assessed political consequences for the "foreseeable future." According to this assessment, Costa e Silva had emerged from the crisis in a "greatly strengthened position," while Lacerda's ability to influence events had been "diminished considerably." (Ibid.)

[3] See Document 221 and footnote 8 thereto.

hierarchical authority of President, military ministers, and major troop commanders over radical elements among middle-rank officers. At same time, Defense Attaché, who enjoys respect and brotherly affection of almost every top figure in Brazilian army has been authorized, under my close direction, to convey similar thoughts to selected influential senior and middle-level military commanders whose discretion can be trusted. Other appropriate senior Country Team officers, both civilian and military, will privately and discretely make known USG position.

4. There is risk that one or another of our interlocutors may resent this kind of talk and may therefore attempt to build our action into public issue of interference in internal affairs. However, this risk is acceptable since the message as such is unobjectionable. Risk of not making clear our views is that it could lead to miscalculated assumption there is no limit to USG toleration of arbitrary abuse of power by GOB. (Brastel 62[4] shows this assumption already present to a degree.) Defense Attaché reports many officers now beginning to show interest in USG views on Brazilian developments about where IA–2 could lead them. Our encouragement needed to stimulate especially military to think hard before taking further rash initiatives in political area.

5. Reftel noted first real test of new situation is installation of Guanabara Governor-elect Negrao de Lima December 5. Although tension continues on this issue, with Negrao's testimony to IPM[5] on Communist Party Nov 15 or 16 being a delicate passage, odds now seem much better than ever after unequivocal stand taken by President, that this crisis point will be passed relatively calmly.

6. We may be able exercise some salutary influence in this situation. We are making clear that USG watching it closely as one test of GOB intentions, although this is clearly internal affair, we are reminding selected contacts that US Congress, which controls purse strings on foreign assistance, is responsive to negative US public opinion attitudes on issues such as this.

7. Additionally Embassy and USG should treat Negrao as any of other governors-elect, although without making contrived public issue of it. For instance, I intend to have program officer of AID mission seek appointment with Negrao for purpose of briefing him on Guanabara projects completed, under way and under discussion, and eliciting any ideas he may have on future areas of cooperative effort. Moreover, if Negrao should again express interest in going to US, as he did immediately following elections, we should respond by offering facilitative assistance, plus financial assistance if indicated.

---

[4] Dated November 5. (National Archives and Records Administration, RG 59, Central Files 1964–66, POL 15 BRAZ)

[5] Military Police Investigation.

8. Similar treatment should be provided to Governor-elect Pinheiro in Minas Gerais, although problem is less serious and immediate since President has already received Pinheiro and inauguration not due until January 31, 1966.

9. On longer-range problem of building permanent political base, CBG now seems to be headed in right direction of organizing new party to support revolution, getting political as well as technical talent in cabinet, and mounting sustained public relations campaign. Although abolition existing parties should theoretically facilitate task of building revolutionary party, other factors complicate task. Abrupt extinction of parties has left residue of confusion and ill feeling, parochial and personal differences and ambitions at state and municipal levels, which was one of reasons for proliferation of parties, will require time and patient effort to overcome. It is, however, noteworthy and encouraging sign of deep-seated Brazilian democratic orientation that while Mexican example of single-party institutionalized revolution is well known to Brazilians, no serious movement to follow this example has surfaced.

10. During past ten days, our early concern that Castello Branco might give up fight and precipitate succession prematurely has been resolved by his unequivocal declaration of intent to serve until March 15, 1967, and to use this time actively to pursue economic and political goals of revolution. One of these goals is ending of arbitrary powers of IA–2 at time of transmission of presidency, so that successor regime will be functioning on basis of a reformed and stabilized democratic political system. The Secretary should have the opportunity to stress importance of this point when he meets with Castello Branco during Rio Conference.[6] We should take advantage of all high-level visitors to Brazil in coming weeks and months to express similar viewpoint, especially to WarMin Costa e Silva and to other political and military leaders.

11. Where local and personal bitterness appear to be holding up progress toward establishment of an effective party structure, and opportunities are afforded in conversations with the political figures involved, we intend discreetly make clear the importance USG attaches to this element of CBG program.

---

[6] At the meeting in Rio de Janeiro on November 20, Rusk assured Castello Branco that the concern previously expressed by Gordon was "by no means limited to the Ambassador. A cold reading of the terms of the Institutional Act could not but leave a shocking effect, especially to Americans trained to regard the constitution and its limitations on all branches of the government as the fundamental basis of organized national life. The reader not familiar with Brazil and with the President's character and attitudes could easily be misled, since he had no way of knowing what the Institutional Act was not intended to be in practice." (Telegram Secto 51 from Rio de Janeiro, November 23; National Archives and Records Administration, RG 59, Central Files 1964–66, POL BRAZ–US)

12. To give technical support to development of party and popular support base, we should through covert channels renew our offer to provide assistance to CBG in scientific opinion sampling. In this same area, continued encouragement should also be given to the government's program, launched since his return by Juracy, to explain government's programs and objectives to people. Radio-TV appearances by cabinet officials, state governors, and congressional spokesmen for administration have already begun to have positive effect.

13. Our post-institutional act view of AID strategy is fully covered in redraft of Brazil annex paper,[7] prepared at White House request and sent Bundy via courier (copy pouched Kubish), supplemented by Embtel 1053.[8] Subsequent CBG actions, including strong policy declarations in President's Niteroi and Rio speeches of Nov 11 and 13, confirm our confidence in continuity CBG efforts for stabilization, development, and reform and make even more conclusive the choice of strategy and maintenance of aid negotiating timetable recommended in those documents.

14. We are also giving thought to alternative lines of action if situation takes sharp turn for worse in short or medium term future. These will be subject separate message.[9]

Gordon

---

[7] A copy of the revised draft, November 4, is in the Johnson Library, National Security File, Country File, Brazil, Vol. V, 9/64–11/65.

[8] Telegram 1053 from Rio de Janeiro, November 8, forwarded several revisions to the text of the Brazil annex paper. (National Archives and Records Administration, RG 59, Central Files 1964–66, AID(US) BRAZ)

[9] Not found.

224. Memorandum From Secretary of State Rusk to President Johnson in Texas[1]

Washington, December 3, 1965.

The Problem:

Your authorization is requested to proceed in early December with negotiations with the Government of Brazil for a program loan to cover Calendar Year 1966, and to conclude the loan if negotiations produce a Brazilian commitment to a satisfactory program. Concurrent negotiations are expected to be in process between the IMF and the Government of Brazil for an extension of Brazil's IMF standby agreement, and the United States and IMF expectations of Brazilian commitments have been coordinated.

Discussion:

Since coming to power in April 1964, the Castello Branco Administration has conducted an admirably tough economic program of stabilization, development, and reform. These self-help measures have been on the whole very effective in reducing the rate of inflation and commencing a broad-based and very promising process of economic development and social progress. We consider that Brazil has made excellent use of the support we have been providing and is today conducting the strongest program of economic self-help in the hemisphere.

AID provided a $50 million contingency loan to the new government in June 1964, and on the basis of formal self-help commitments made by Brazil to CIAP, a $150 million program loan was authorized last December. Other international assistance for 1965 included a $53.6 million U.S. Treasury exchange agreement and a $125 million IMF standby agreement, as well as project assistance from AID, the Inter-American Bank, and the World Bank, and a modest amount under PL–480.

The Brazilian performance this year has on most points exceeded the commitments for self-help undertaken a year ago. This record was warmly endorsed in a formal CIAP review last month.

Additional funds are required for 1966 to support an expanded level of import necessary to achieve Brazil's investment and growth

[1] Source: National Archives and Records Administration, RG 59, Central Files 1964–66, AID(US) 9 BRAZ. Confidential. No drafting information appears on the memorandum. According to the President's Daily Diary, Johnson was at his Ranch in Texas, November 19–December 12 and December 21–January 2, 1966. (Johnson Library)

objectives. Ambassador Gordon and his country team have strongly recommended an AID program loan of $150 million, plus a number of project loans (estimated to total around $75–$100 million) and a new PL–480 agreement (preliminary estimate: $35 million). The program loan decision needs to be taken now, in order to relate the timing and the content of our negotiations properly to those of IMF.

The country team's estimates are that Brazil's needs for net capital imports to support an adequate rate of economic and social development, supplementing intensive self-help measures to mobilize internal resources, are on the order of $600–$1000 million a year for the next several years. The country team considers that, allowing for imports from private investment, international institutions, PL–480, and AID project loans, the "resource gap" justifies a program loan of at least $200 million in 1966. The structure of Brazil's trade and balance-of-payments, however, makes it unlikely that more than $150 million of resources in the form of additional developmental imports from the U.S. can be effectively transferred and used. Even this figure implies a substantial increase in Brazilian imports from 1965 levels.

Administrator Bell and his staff in Washington, recognizing the uncertainty of any balance-of-payments projections and the greater familiarity of the country team with conditions in Brazil, nevertheless consider that the very substantial improvement in Brazil's balance-of-payments position over the last year, the doubts about the amount of increase in Brazilian imports in 1966, and the availability for emergency needs of additional sources of funding from the IMF, combine to suggest that $100 million might turn out to be enough to support the Brazilian self-help program.

The question has been raised whether a portion of the development import needs should be financed by drawings on the IMF over and above the amounts needed to repay IMF loans coming due in 1966. Such IMF resources, however, should be reserved for unforeseen short-term balance-of-payments difficulties arising from commodity price fluctuations or other factors beyond the country's control. (Note that a one cent per pound drop in coffee prices loses Brazil $25 million over a year.) What Brazil currently needs is long-term development capital rather than short or medium-term balance-of-payments support. Like many other less developed countries, Brazil's foreign indebtedness structure is already overweighted with short and medium-term debt, and we have been pressing them to avoid further such accumulations.

Both Ambassador Gordon and Administrator Bell agree that if Brazil continues its present strongly favorable economic progress it should be possible to reduce the level of the program loan for 1967 and to reduce AID assistance to Brazil progressively thereafter.

Ambassador Gordon and his country team believe that their recommendation for a $150 million program loan on economic grounds is strongly reinforced by political considerations. Their views are summarized in the following paragraphs.

From a situation of galloping inflation, growing stagnation, and imminent leftist, anti-American dictatorship less than two years ago, the Castello Branco government has brought Brazil halfway along the road to price stability. It has restarted development on a sound long-term basis. It has reversed the nationalist and statist trends to favor private enterprise and foreign investment. It has undertaken major modernizing reforms. It has adopted a strongly pro-Western foreign policy. It is fighting a life-and-death struggle against both right and left-wing extremists to preserve these policy lines, ensure a like-minded successor regime, and restore constitutional normality. It has enjoyed our vigorous political and economic support.

In October 1966, elections are scheduled for Congress, eleven State Governors and all State legislatures; as well as an indirect election of the successor President by the Congress. Castello Branco has only recently and belatedly begun the task of building a strong political base and popularizing the positive goals of the revolution. The local currency counterpart of our program loan, to be applied largely to private enterprise expansion, education, health, and agricultural development can make a major contribution to the success of this effort.

To reduce our program loan for 1966 from the $150 million level being provided in 1965 would appear to be a withdrawal of U.S. support at the most decisive moment in the Castello Branco effort.

Nor can we neglect the effect of reduced support for Brazil on our whole stance toward Latin America and the Alliance for Progress. The proposed loan, while large in dollars, is relatively small in relation to Brazil's size. It amounts to $1.77 per capita, compared with proposed program loans for 1966 of almost $10 per capita for Chile and $4 for Colombia. A reduction now would look like a penalty for effective self-help. It would be taken as a deliberate blow to the largest nation in Latin America, in face of the Castello Branco regime's wholehearted cooperation with us in hemispheric and world affairs, including the provision of a sizable military contingent in the Dominican Republic. Since Brazil by itself is 35 percent of Latin America, and the Alliance stands or falls by success or failure there more than anywhere else, reduced support for Brazil now would look like a retreat from our renewed commitments to sustain the Alliance, including your warmly welcomed pledge reported by me to the Inter-American Conference in Rio.

The risks to U.S. political and security interests if our policy should fail in Brazil are enormous and the costs of failure would be very large in relation to the sums under discussion. Such failure might take the form of an anti-American nationalist military dictatorship or of a Communist-controlled regime. Both are plausible hypotheses. Continued full support for Castello Branco and his policies is the best insurance available against these contingencies.

Use of U.S. Funds. The program loan will be used to finance basic imports from the United States. A major share of the counterpart funds will be used for loans to finance private sector development in agriculture, industry, and housing. Other amounts will be used to finance special programs in education, labor, and public health.

Effect on U.S. Balance of Payments will be minimal in view of the restriction on the use of the loan funds for imports from the United States. Disbursements will not occur until well into 1966. Measures introduced by the Central Bank will increase the attractiveness of United States exports and thereby result in additional follow-on exports from the United States. The expectations for 1966 are that there will be a net capital inflow into Brazil from Western Europe, Japan, and the international financial institutions.

Recommendation:

Weighing these factors together, it seems to me we have two alternative courses of action:

1. To authorize a program loan of $150 million, stating during the negotiations that we are not sure that the requirements of Brazil's recovery will in fact call for the full amount during 1966, that we expect to review requirements quarterly during the year, and if less than the full amount is needed, the remainder will be held back for disbursement in the following year and taken into account in negotiations for AID loans at that time.

2. To authorize a $100 million program loan, stating during the negotiations that requirements may in fact call for larger amounts if the actual pace of Brazilian recovery and growth so indicates, and we would be prepared to add to the loan up to a maximum of $150 million if it is needed during the year.

I consider that the minimal economic needs of the situation might be met by the second alternative, especially if there is some lag in the implementation of the Brazilian investment program. On the other hand, political considerations so strongly favor the first alternative that I believe it to be the clearly indicated course of action.

Accordingly, I recommend that you authorize us to proceed with negotiations for a $150 million program loan under the general framework outlined above, and in accordance with the detailed statement of proposed terms and conditions which is attached to this memorandum. Administrator Bell joins me in this recommendation.[2]

Dean Rusk

---

[2] A note on the memorandum indicates that the President approved the loan on December 11. In telegram 1014 to Rio de Janeiro, December 11, Harriman informed Gordon that, although the loan was not tied to Vietnam, the Department urgently sought his advice on how to approach Castello Branco for a suitable military contribution. (Ibid., National Security File, Country File, Brazil, Vol. VI, 12/65–3/67) In response Gordon suggested an informal approach without reference to the program loan. Any linkage between Vietnam and the program loan, he explained, "would be disastrous, and even private hint would arouse resentment from Castello Branco, who although good friend is also very dignified and proud Brazilian." (Telegram 1432 from Rio de Janeiro, December 12; ibid.) The Department agreed to treat Vietnam separately, but instructed Gordon to approach Castello Branco in an official capacity, i.e. on behalf of President Johnson. (Telegram 1018 to Rio de Janeiro, December 15; ibid.) The United States and Brazil signed the program loan on February 10, 1966.

---

225. **Memorandum From the President's Special Assistant for National Security Affairs (Bundy) to President Johnson in Texas**[1]

Washington, December 31, 1965, noon.

Averell Harriman and I owe you an interim report on the effort to get troops from Brazil to Vietnam. With your permission we separated the $150 million program loan from the issue of troops, but in the same meeting in which Gordon told Castello Branco about the loan, he made a very strong pitch on the troops and made it clear how much this matters to you.[2] Castello promised to give the matter his prayerful consideration. He pointed out that under the Brazilian Constitution Congressional approval is required before troops can be sent abroad and the Brazilian Congress does not reconvene before March. Gordon and our excellent military attaché General Walters (who are very close to Castello Branco) are following up on this and although it is clear that

---

[1] Source: Johnson Library, National Security File, Country File, Vietnam, Vol. XLIII, Memos (B), 12/13/65–12/31/65. Secret. The memorandum indicates that the President saw it. Bundy also attached a December 23 memorandum from Harriman to the President; see *Foreign Relations, 1964–1968*, vol. III, Document 240. Both were sent to the Ranch on December 31.

[2] An account of the meeting is in telegram 1456 from Rio de Janeiro, December 17. (Johnson Library, National Security File, Country File, Brazil, Vol. VI, 12/65–3/67)

Castello faces a bigger and harder political problem than Harriman and I thought possible, Gordon and Walters think that in time a Branco contribution in some form can be worked out.

Just before Christmas Harriman submitted to me a memorandum for you on this subject, but he asked me to hold it to see whether we would get something more from the Brazilians in the next few days. Nothing new and startling has come in and the above report is the essence as it now stands.[3]

McG.B.

----

[3] Although providing coffee and medical supplies, Brazil never sent troops or military supplies to Vietnam. (Department of the Army, *Allied Participation in the Vietnam*, p. 169)

----

226. National Intelligence Estimate[1]

NIE 93–66   Washington, August 18, 1966.

THE OUTLOOK FOR BRAZIL

The Problem

To estimate the situation in Brazil and the prospects for the next year or two.

Conclusions

A. Castello Branco has managed for the most part to preserve constitutional forms without endangering the objectives of the revolution and has retained solid military backing. His economic corrective measures are showing favorable results, but the results have come slowly and the measures have provoked widespread dissatisfaction.

B. The administration is determined to see that acceptable candidates are chosen in the series of elections scheduled for this fall. It is taking steps to ensure that no opponents will become governors in the

----

[1] Source: Central Intelligence Agency, Job 79R–01012A, O/DDI Registry. Secret; Controlled Dissem. According to a note on the cover sheet this estimate was prepared in the Central Intelligence Agency with the participation of the intelligence organizations of the Departments of State and Defense and the National Security Agency. The United States Intelligence Board concurred in this estimate on August 18. The estimate superseded SNIE 93–65 (Document 218).

indirect elections on 3 September in 12 states. But the touchiest election will be the direct popular one to be held on 15 November for federal congressmen and state legislators; Castello Branco may deem it necessary to interfere directly and obviously so as to retain a working majority in Congress.

C. Costa e Silva, who has been War Minister, is almost certain to be elected president by the present Congress on 3 October. He will probably not exert much influence in the "lame duck" period before his four-year term begins on 15 March. Castello Branco's policies will not change much in those months, though there will be some loss of momentum.

D. General dissatisfactions will persist, but the new government will probably succeed in keeping the opposition off balance and fragmented. At least to begin with, Costa e Silva's control over the military establishment will be firm, and we do not believe that a military coup against him is likely during the period of this estimate.

E. Costa e Silva's administration is likely to be a marked departure from Castello Branco's, not in its broad goals, but in style of governing, in choice of key advisors, and in certain lines of policy. In some ways he will probably perform better; for example, he will give higher priority to public relations and may reduce popular opposition to some extent. He is likely to try for better relations with students and labor organizations, but will take whatever measures seem necessary to prevent a resurgence of the extreme left.

F. In other matters, however, Costa e Silva will probably not do as well. In his efforts to "humanize" the economic program, he may weaken present checks on inflation. Because he is less judicious and more a man of action than Castello Branco, we see more chance that he might resort to harsh, authoritarian methods. Finally, we think that he will put more emphasis on Brazilian nationalism and that in time this could cause friction in US-Brazilian relations.

[Omitted here is the Discussion section of the estimate.]

227.   Memorandum From the President's Special Assistant (Rostow) to President Johnson[1]

Washington, December 6, 1966.

SUBJECT

Program Loan for Brazil

AID requests (Tab A),[2] under the new commitments procedure, your authorization to negotiate the following assistance package for Brazil for 1967:

—a $100 million program loan
—up to $90 million for project loans (fertilizer plant, power generating facilities, highway maintenance equipment, seed capital for a national savings and loan system, and agricultural diversification) without submitting each project for your approval.

AID also asks your approval to start discussions with the Brazilians on "sector" loans in agriculture, education and health for 1968 without making any specific dollar commitments. This lead time is necessary in order to influence the Brazilian 1968 budget preparations which begin in early 1967.

The $190 million loan level is $40 million less than you authorized for 1966.

BOB recommends approval of the AID request (Tab B).[3] Treasury objects to only one aspect. Joe Fowler is against the use of dollars for a $20 million savings and loan (home financing) project included in the $90 million project loan level. He argues that cruzeiro counterpart funds generated by the program loan should be used instead (Tab C).[4]

Joe Fowler consistently opposes the use of dollar loans for local cost financing because of their alleged adverse impact on our balance of payments position. To get at the facts, an inter-agency group under the direction of Charlie Schultze recently made a thorough study of this issue. State, CEA, AID and BOB—with only Treasury objecting—found that there was no inherent reason why project dollar loans for local costs should have any different effect on the balance of payments than other forms of aid.

---

[1] Source: Johnson Library, National Security File, Country File, Brazil, Vol. VI, 12/65–3/67. Confidential.

[2] Tab A was a memorandum from Gaud to the President, November 22; attached but not printed.

[3] Tab B was a memorandum from Schultze to the President, November 29; attached but not printed.

[4] Tab C was a note from Fowler; attached but not printed.

Other reasons why I do not go along with Joe Fowler's objection are:

—In Latin America in particular we find that our dollar assistance does not leak to any significant degree to other areas.
—The project loan in question is designed to stimulate institutional development in one area where Brazil is most deficient—home financing.
—The Brazilians agreed to our terms for the loan on the basis of dollar support and will probably scrap the project unless we carry through with it.
—Cruzeiro counterpart funds generated by the program loan are already largely earmarked for equally pressing local cost projects.

I am satisfied that the $190 million package has been carefully tailored to Brazil's needs and ability to use the money effectively. The safeguards on self-help, performance review and tied procurement will be adequately covered. Brazil's economic and political record in 1966 has not been all that we desired. But its over-all performance has been satisfactory and its collaboration with us on hemisphere and world issues continues to be close. The Costa e Silva administration is not expected to change this.

I recommend that you approve the package requested by AID.

Walt

1. Approve $100 million program loan:

Yes[5]
No
Speak to me

2. Approve $90 million project loan level (i.e. without subsequent individual project review):

Yes
Yes, but with $20 million savings and loan project covered by counterpart funds[6]
Prefer project-by-project review
Speak to me

3. Approve AID's request to start discussions on "sector" loans without specific dollar commitments:

Yes[7]
No
Speak to me

---

[5] The President checked this option.

[6] The President checked this option.

[7] The President checked this option and wrote: "Very confidential. Conditionally, provided I don't get boxed in as I have been by AID, Ag[riculture] and State on India." The United States and Brazil signed the program loan agreement on March 11, 1967.

228.   Memorandum of Conversation[1]

Washington, January 26, 1967, 12:31–12:55 p.m.

SUBJECT

Brazilian-U.S. Relations

PARTICIPANTS

Lyndon B. Johnson, President of the United States
Lincoln Gordon, Assistant Secretary of State for Inter-American Affairs[2]
John W. Tuthill, United States Ambassador to Brazil
José A. De Seabra, Interpreter

Arthur da Costa e Silva, President-elect of Brazil
Vasco Leitão da Cunha, Brazilian Ambassador to the United States
Edmundo Macedo Soares e Silva, President, National Confederation of Industries of Brazil

President-elect Costa e Silva expressed his appreciation for the opportunity to meet a man of the stature and leadership qualities of President Johnson, and stated emphatically that his country was, as it has always been, a staunch friend of the United States.

President Johnson said that he was well aware of the traditional friendship between the two countries, and was glad that the President-elect had been able to come to the United States before assuming his many important responsibilities. It is the intention of the United States to continue to cooperate with Brazil in all possible efforts towards achieving ever greater progress in that country.

Costa e Silva said that he hoped that the United States will continue to be favorably disposed toward Brazil while he endeavors to reestablish a totally democratic and legitimate regime in his country.

At this point, the two Presidents moved to the White House lawn and continued their conversation.

President Johnson expressed in warm and forceful terms his appreciation for Brazil's prompt and determined action during the Dominican crisis. Costa e Silva mentioned the part that he played at that time as Minister of War. He further stressed the need for continued vigilance and action against the danger of communism.

---

[1] Source: National Archives and Records Administration, RG 59, Central Files 1967–69, POL 7 BRAZ. Secret. Drafted by J.A. DeSeabra (OPR/LS) and S.C. Lyon (ARA/BR). Approved in the White House on February 2. The time of the meeting is taken from the President's Daily Diary. (Johnson Library) The conversation began in the Oval Office.

[2] A note on the memorandum indicates that Gordon, Tuthill, Leitão da Cunha, and Macedo Soares were present for part of the conversation only.

President Johnson said that the two countries should always stand together so as to resist effectively any totalitarianism, be it from the left or the right.

Then the conversation continued for a short time in the Cabinet Room in the presence of Assistant Secretary Gordon, Ambassador Leitão da Cunha, Ambassador Tuthill, and Governor Macedo Soares.

The Presidents exchanged complimentary remarks about their respective Ambassadors. President Johnson mentioned that he had granted very prompt recognition to the Brazilian revolutionary regime on the strong recommendation of Mr. Gordon. He added that even though such prompt action had created some difficulties for him at home, the subsequent turn of events had borne out the sound judgment of Mr. Gordon, who was to be considered a hero and not a "scapegoat."

---

229. Memorandum From the President's Special Assistant (Rostow) to President Johnson[1]

Washington, June 14, 1967.

SUBJECT

Brazilian Performance under the Program Loan

Costa e Silva has been in office for three months and it is apparent that his administration varies in style and substance from Castello Branco's. Performance in two areas are of particular concern to us: foreign policy and the domestic stabilization program.

Castello Branco carried out tough political and economic measures designed to consolidate the "revolution" with little regard to their impact on his public image. He kept a tight rein over policy making by his Cabinet. Cooperation with us on foreign policy matters could hardly have been closer.

Costa e Silva is much concerned with being "popular," restoring the "democratic" image of Brazil and "humanizing" the economic recovery program. At the same time, he personally does not want to depart too far from the objectives of the 1964 revolution. Costa e Silva appears to be leaving broad authority with his Cabinet Ministers without

---

[1] Source: Johnson Library, National Security File, Country File, Brazil, Vol. VII, 3/67–9/67. Confidential.

close coordination at the top. They have yet to hammer out an overall, consistent policy.

As a result, there is a puzzling ambivalence in the orientation of the Costa e Silva administration. For example, in foreign affairs Costa e Silva expresses close identification with our policies—and I believe he is sincere in this. But his Foreign Minister publicly advocates a "non-involvement" policy on Vietnam, insists on a nuclear-test-for-peaceful-uses exception in the Non-Proliferation Treaty, strikes a reluctant stance on Venezuela's complaint against Cuba and takes an equivocal position on our efforts to unscramble the Israel-Arab problem.

On the domestic front, Costa e Silva professed support for stabilization program and accepted the self-help terms of the $100 million program loan negotiated with Castello Branco. On that basis, we authorized the first $25 million tranche with the clear understanding that release of subsequent tranches would depend on performance.

Recent performance has been so poor that fiscal and monetary results deviate widely from CIAP targets which were conditions of the program loan agreement. These targets are no longer attainable. We are therefore being forced to revise our strategy and tactics regarding our economic assistance.

The failure of the Brazilians to meet the targets is illustrated by these key examples:

—At the end of May the budget deficit was 1.12 billion new cruzeiros, while the commitment for the full year was projected at 554 million new cruzeiros.
—The coffee price decision announced four days ago provides for a price increase to growers averaging 28% for the year, instead of the 10–15%, which we understood would be the target. (The increase will act as a strong disincentive to agricultural diversification.)
—The level of domestic credit appears to have expanded during the first five months of 1967 by 600 million new cruzeiros—the amount projected for the entire year.

It is not clear to what extent these policies are the result of catering to domestic political pressures, technical incompetence on the part of the new Ministers, or lack of coordination and control during the first months of the Costa e Silva administration.

What concerns us is that if Costa e Silva does not develop a responsible fiscal and financial program and stick to it, the stabilization program will be undermined and our assistance will be wasted.

State–AID, together with Treasury and BOB, have developed a strategy for trying to make the Brazilians face their problems and take corrective action. It has these elements:

—Tuthill will personally discuss the situation with Costa e Silva as soon as possible, making clear that we cannot make further disbursements of the program loan because of wide deviations from the loan agreement. He will also indicate that project and sector loans may be affected. At the same time, he will express our desire to continue to support Brazil's development and will propose that we renegotiate economic policy targets consistent with effective stabilization, development, and reform programs.

—The AID Mission Director will take similar action at the Ministerial level and Covey Oliver will talk to the Brazilian Ambassador here.

—AID/State will coordinate closely with the IMF and IBRD, both of whom will send review teams to Brazil in early July.

—If Costa e Silva is willing to develop a more adequate economic program, we will be prepared to negotiate a new agreement with him for release of the remaining $75 million of our FY 1967 program loan. The new agreement, of course, would be submitted to you before the final approval.

—If we cannot negotiate a satisfactory agreement in 1967, the $75 million will not be disbursed and we will try to negotiate a new program in 1968.[2]

Walt

---

[2] Rostow added the following handwritten postscript: "It may be wiser for you to pull him up short with a personal letter expressing your anxiety." No evidence has been found that Johnson sent the proposed letter to Costa e Silva.

---

230.   Telegram From the Embassy in Brazil to the Department of State[1]

Rio de Janeiro, August 4, 1967, 0110Z.

816. For the Secretary, pass White House for President Johnson, pass Defense Department for Secretary McNamara.

Subject: Conversation with President Costa e Silva re Supersonic Aircraft.

1. I saw Costa e Silva today, Foreign Minister Magalhaes Pinto and Counselor Herz [garble] were also present.

2. I told President Costa e Silva that I had returned to Washington last week under instructions from the USG in order that I could be fully informed on problems which existed for the American Government in connection with the economic and military aid programs and

---

[1] Source: National Archives and Records Administration, RG 59, Central Files 1967–69, AID(US) BRAZ. Confidential; Immediate; Exdis. Repeated to Brasilia.

the purchase by Brazil and other countries of supersonic aircraft.[2] Two days before seeing Costa e Silva I had discussed matter in full detail with Andreazza, who is Minister of Transport but who is quite clearly one of Costa e Silva's authorized channels for discussions with me. At that time Andreazza stated that he felt request for postponement of decision of supersonic aircraft for sixty days to be an acceptable request and stated that he would recommend such a position to Costa e Silva.

It was quite evident today that Andreazza had in fact done his duty. As soon as all of the basic points of the talking paper had been covered and after Costa e Silva had read President Johnson's letter, he said explicitly that he would agree to take no action until after October 1, 1967. He made it quite clear, however, that this was not an easy decision for him to make. He stressed the overall dangers of guerrilla activity in Latin America and the indications of an increased tempo in Brazil. He mentioned the bombing of the Peace Corps office two days ago as a symbol of this unrest. He stated that the government has arrested eleven men in the area where the states of Minas Gerais, Sao Paulo and Goias come together. These men had a supply of military equipment and bombs and were fabricating additional weapons. He said that every indication was that this was the same group that had attempted to assassinate him in Recife last July. He pointed out the relationship between this group and the Recife assassination attempt (which in fact did result in the killing of an admiral and two other persons) was not yet publicly known and asked that we hold this information close. He stated that he fully expects a stepping up of terrorist activity as a result of the LASO conference. [He indicated] that in a huge country like Brazil, Brazilian forces must have modern equipment and increased mobility. Speed could easily be of the essence in handling internal difficulties. Secondly, Costa e Silva stressed the question of morale in the Brazilian Air Force. He went over the well-known ground of the obsolescent nature of most of the equipment in the Brazilian Air Force. He stressed that the loss of morale was a constant worry to him.

3. Costa e Silva also repeated his well-known concern at the tendency of some people in the United States to think of Brazil as just an-

---

[2] On July 26 Tuthill met President Johnson "to discuss the Mirage airplanes that Brazil wants to buy from France." (Johnson Library, President's Daily Diary) In a July 25 memorandum to the President, Rostow explained that the meeting would allow Tuthill "to tell Costa e Silva that he personally discussed this problem with you." Although no substantive record of the meeting has been found, Johnson evidently gave Tuthill the letter for Costa e Silva. Rostow also recommended that Johnson review the talking points for the Ambassador's meeting with the Brazilian President. A draft letter and the talking points were attached to the memorandum. (Ibid., National Security File, Country File, Brazil, Vol. VII, 3/67–9/67) The final letter from Johnson to Costa e Silva, July 26, is in the National Archives and Records Administration, RG 59, Central Files 1967–69, POL 7 BRAZ.

other Latin American country. He asked for example how one could consider the security problems of Ecuador and Brazil on the same basis. He reverted to his war time experience when he said American equipment was shipped in such volume to the Brazilian forces that it couldn't be handled, at least temporarily. Since the war he and the Brazilian military have wished to strengthen bi-lateral relationship with the United States in the field of military equipment so that at a time of crisis, Brazilian military would be able to effectively use increased supplies of modern equipment. He stressed that only reluctantly would he go elsewhere for modern equipment, but he also once more repeated that if he couldn't get such modern equipment in the United States he had no choice but to go elsewhere. He also spoke scornfully of an armaments race as far as Brazil is concerned.

4. Despite these concerns, however, Costa e Silva stated that he recognized President Johnson's political problems at the moment and he wished to be helpful. He said that he would write a personal letter to President Johnson outlining his thoughts and describing in some detail the nature and timing of his needs re equipment.

5. I felt it would be useful for President Costa e Silva to be able to read and to ponder over the talking points as approved by President Johnson. Accordingly, we prepared a slightly modified version of the talking points in order to remove one or two minor points which we felt might be unnecessarily irritating to Costa e Silva. A copy of this modified version was left with Costa e Silva and is being air mailed to the Department.[3]

6. Costa e Silva noted particularly point three which states that USG is prepared "to authorize Northrop to begin contract talks after October 1." He stated that he was unhappy to see that the first planes could only be received after July 1, 1969. He felt that the first deliveries should be not more than 20 months after the commencement of talks. In fact, this would only move date back to June 1, 1969 but it was clear that he wants earliest possible deliveries. He indicated that French deliveries could be made much earlier.

7. Costa e Silva said several times that in any case the purchase of advanced equipment, including supersonic planes, did not represent a serious drain on Brazil's economy. In the case of French Mirages, he said that the French had indicated a willingness to accept payments over an eight to ten year time span. (*Comment:* William Sweet, who apparently represents Northrop on this deal in Rio, states that the Canadians can match the French in financing of the F–5s provided of course that the United States will authorize export.)

---

[3] Not found.

8. Throughout conversation which lasted more than an hour, Costa e Silva was serious but always friendly. It was quite clear that he recognized the seriousness of the political issue in the United States and he was anxious to avoid complicating problems for President Johnson. The seriousness with which he considers the question, however, and his determination to resolve it via modernization of the Brazilian forces was evident throughout. He wants to stick with the United States as his source of supply and training but he will go elsewhere if this cannot be done.

9. *Comment:* I feel that President Johnson's letter and talking points enabled us to pull this out of the fire at last possible moment, Costa e Silva clearly responded to what he felt was President Johnson's personal interest in matter and perceptive approach to it. It's now up to us after October 1.

Tuthill

231. Memorandum of Conversation[1]

Washington, August 29, 1967, 12:15 p.m.

SUBJECT

> Transmitting the Response of the President of Brazil to a Letter from the President of the United States

PARTICIPANTS

> *Foreign*
> Leitao da Cunha, Brazilian Ambassador to the United States
>
> *United States*
> The President
> Walt W. Rostow, Special Assistant to the President
> Covey T. Oliver, Assistant Secretary of State for Inter-American Affairs

Ambassador Leitao da Cunha took the occasion of his meeting with President Johnson to present a letter from Brazilian President Arthur da Costa e Silva[2] and to speak on the following subjects:

---

[1] Source: National Archives and Records Administration, RG 59, Central Files 1967–69, POL 7 BRAZ–US. Secret. Drafted by Oliver and approved by the White House on September 1.

[2] Dated August 24; attached but not printed.

1. The President of Brazil wishes the President of the United States to know that he has given the most careful and friendly attention to President Johnson's letter to him of July 26, 1967.[3] The President of Brazil assures the President of the United States that Brazil intends to continue its relations with the United States at the traditional level of close friendship. The President and Government of Brazil, moreover, have great confidence in President Johnson personally.

2. The President of Brazil understands the problems faced by the Executive Branch of the Government of the United States in the matter of supersonic military aircraft; and, as already communicated to President Johnson's Ambassador to Brazil, Brazil will abstain until October 1967 from further steps toward acquisition of such aircraft. The President of Brazil, however, must express his concern about the basic problem of aircraft modernization in Brazil. Brazil's Air Force equipment is today obsolete. In the period 1947–52, Brazil's Air Force equipment was equivalent in modernity, although much less numerous, to the equipment of the United States Air Force. But from 1952 on, Brazilian Air Force aircraft have become increasingly obsolescent. Today Brazil's military aircraft are approximately 20 years out of date, and Brazil's Air Force pilots are not able to receive training on modern equipment. It is essential that Brazilian pilots have opportunities to train on updated equipment in order that Brazil should be able to meet any national or international emergencies that might arise. With the obsolescent equipment now in use, the Brazilian Air Force encounters morale and recruiting difficulties.

3. The Ambassador then emphasized the essentiality to Brazil of the M–16 semiautomatic rifle.[4] The Ambassador stressed that modern small arms of this sort are essential for the defense of Brazil's Air Force bases. At the present time, he told President Johnson, these bases and other installations in Brazil are being defended by troops armed with 1909 bolt-action, Mauser rifles that themselves were only slight modifications of the 1898 model Mauser. Thus, Brazil's small arms are nearly 60 years behind the times.

4. The Ambassador alluded to the difficulties that Brazil is encountering in getting delivery of Hughes helicopters. His implication

---

[3] See footnote 2, Document 230.

[4] In telegram 392 from Rio de Janeiro, July 17, Tuthill maintained that "the sale of M–16 rifles is of critical importance to achievement of our overall policy objectives in Brazil." (National Archives and Records Administration, RG 59, Central Files 1967–69, DEF 19–8 US–BRAZ) In a memorandum to Rostow, July 26, Bowdler reviewed the difficulties involved in meeting the Brazilian request for the rifles, including supply requirements for the Vietnam war. Bowdler recommended that the United States supply the rifles over a 2-year period as long as delivery did not cause "domestic problems" or interfere with contracts with other foreign countries. (Johnson Library, National Security File, Country File, Brazil, Vol. VII, 3/67–9/67)

in this instance was that the difficulties lay with the supplier, and he acknowledged that the United States Government was having similar difficulties with the supplier as to helicopters needed for Viet Nam.

5. The Ambassador developed for President Johnson the concept of cyclical swings in national conduct as to nationalism. He stated that the swing in Brazil today, in a new administration following one that was not at all nationalistic, is toward "latent nationalism." This "latent nationalism" can be moderated by intelligent and understanding collaboration between the leaders of Brazil and friendly countries, especially the United States. If not moderated, this "latent nationalism" could lead to incidents or events not typical of the general history of relations between Brazil and the United States.

6. The Ambassador closed his presentation with a return to the problem of supersonic military aircraft. He stated: "Fundamentally, Brazil is not interested in acquiring supersonic military aircraft elsewhere; but, if there is no reasonable opportunity to acquire such aircraft from the United States, Brazil will have to look elsewhere, including France, from which country Brazil has even received a suggestion that a Mirage factory be set up in Brazil."

President Johnson said that the United States Government would certainly bear the President of Brazil's views very much in mind, in the first place because of President Johnson's very high regard for President Costa e Silva. (At this point, the President expressed to the Ambassador a degree of personal esteem for the President of Brazil that was obviously moving to President Johnson's listener.) President Johnson expressed his gratitude to the President of Brazil for his letter and for the additional message brought by the Ambassador of Brazil. As to aircraft, both the letter and the message show that Brazil is once again acting with reason and moderation. President Johnson said that he believes that the United States Government can find some answers to Brazil's needs. Although we are having great difficulties within the United States at the present time, the President of the United States is trying to find answers to the underlying problems so that policy may be stabilized. The President of the United States wishes to avoid, however, a chain reaction about military assistance matters involving supersonic aircraft.[5]

As to the M–16 semiautomatic rifle, the President of the United States very clearly understands Brazil's needs and regrets that the rifles could not have been supplied "yesterday." The President of the

---

[5] In a January 20, 1968, memorandum to the President, Rostow reported that Costa e Silva had decided to purchase F–5 aircraft instead of the French Mirage. Rostow commented: "No civilian president could have withstood the pressures he faced in the campaign to buy the French aircraft." (Ibid., Vol. VII–a, 8/64–11/68)

United States is hopeful that by working additional shifts and the like, the suppliers in the United States can meet both the needs of the United States and its allies in Viet Nam and some of the needs of Brazil.

232.   Memorandum From the President's Special Assistant (Rostow) to President Johnson[1]

Washington, December 5, 1967.

SUBJECT

Program Loan Assistance for Brazil

Herewith are *memos from Bill Gaud and Charlie Schultze (Tab A)*[2] *recommending action on further disbursements of the $100 million FY 1967 program loan* signed with Brazil last March. The Brazilian Finance Minister will be in town for talks tomorrow and Thursday.

In my memo to you of November 22 (Tab B),[3] I explained the poor self-help performance of Brazil which led to postponement of further disbursements after the initial $25 million tranche in July. Since then Brazil has not taken adequate fiscal and monetary corrective measures. As a result it has suffered a serious loss in reserves (some $250 million in five months) and faces a renewed inflationary surge next year.

The issue is whether we should make another disbursement now in anticipation of promised corrective action by next January or February or make it contingent on performance.

Ambassador Tuthill favors immediate release of $25 million to create a favorable political impact and because he is convinced that Costa e Silva is committed to stabilization.

Bill Gaud and Covey Oliver recommend tying the disbursement to prior satisfactory devaluation, credit tightening and budget trimming, leaving the timing up to the Brazilians. They would be willing to increase the tranche to $50 million if this would help the Minister take action now.

Charlie Schultze sides with Gaud and Oliver, except he questions increasing the release to $50 million in order to advance corrective action one month earlier. *Secretary Fowler shares this view.*

---

[1] Source: Johnson Library, National Security File, Country File, Brazil, Vol. VII-a, 8/64–11/68. Confidential.

[2] Dated November 30 and December 4, respectively; attached but not printed.

[3] Attached but not printed.

Given the importance of Brazil and your good relations with President Costa e Silva, I favor being as forthcoming as we can consistent with our overriding objectives of:

—keeping Brazil's momentum toward stabilization.
—maintaining a record on Brazil which will win continued Congressional support.

The Gaud–Oliver formula comes closest to satisfying all points. I recommend you approve it.

Gaud and Oliver also ask authorization to tell the Finance Minister that we are prepared *to negotiate a Program Loan agreement for 1968.* The exact amount and self-help conditions would be submitted to you for approval, probably in January. *I support this request.*

Walt

Approve Gaud–Oliver recommendation for $25 million *after performance,* with possible increase to $50 million for early action, and agree to negotiate 1968 program loan.

Approve BOB–Treasury variant of $25 million *after performance,* and agree to negotiate 1968 program loan.

Approve Tuthill recommendation for $25 million *now.*

Speak to me.[4]

---

[4] The President checked this option. In a memorandum to the President, December 13, Rostow explained that further discussion was unnecessary since the talks with Finance Minister Delfim Neto had resolved the matter: "$25 million will be disbursed early in January when Brazil takes the agreed exchange and credit actions" and the "remaining $50 million will be made part of the 1968 program loan." (Johnson Library, National Security File, Country File, Brazil, Vol. VII–a, 8/64–11/68)

233. Information Memorandum From the President's Special Assistant (Rostow) to President Johnson[1]

Washington, February 16, 1968, 1:30 p.m.

SUBJECT

Brazilian Political Scene Displays Danger Signals

I thought you would be interested in the following assessment on the Brazilian situation which Covey Oliver sent to Secretary Rusk yesterday:[2]

"As the Costa e Silva Government nears its first anniversary in office, it increasingly demonstrates authoritarian tendencies. The honeymoon Costa e Silva enjoyed during his first months in office has ended. Opposition attacks on the Government's lackluster performance, spearheaded by increasingly vituperative and telling thrusts from Carlos Lacerda, now seem to be severely stinging the Brazilian Military.

Although Costa e Silva can have no fear that his opposition has any chance of overturning his Government, his reactions to charges of weak leadership, corruption among some of his ministers, and 'military tyranny' may well be to clamp down unwisely on the Congress, the press, or opposition leaders themselves. He is being pressed by key military advisors to act more firmly against Carlos Lacerda and other gadflies in the civilian opposition. We have reports of a generalized unrest among military officers over the performance of the Costa e Silva Administration to date, and some evidence of a possible plot among extremist officers to assassinate Lacerda, should he continue his outspoken attacks on the Military as an institution. While we doubt that this will occur, some moves of a more authoritarian nature are distinctly possible in Brazil during coming weeks.

I have been in touch with Ambassador Tuthill about these reports and he is deeply concerned.[3] He fears that the Costa e Silva Administration, which has conspicuously failed to build a credible civilian political base, or to give any real role to its majority supporters in the Congress, will fall back all too readily on military means to deal with its civilian opposition. Should the Brazilian Military allow itself to be so provoked, the Ambassador foresees very serious consequences for

---

[1] Source: Johnson Library, National Security File, Country File, Brazil, Vol. VII–a, 8/64–11/68. Secret. The memorandum indicates the President saw it.

[2] Not found.

[3] Reference is to a February 2 letter from Tuthill to Oliver, and a February 6 letter from Oliver to Tuthill. (National Archives and Records Administration, RG 59, Central Files 1967–69, DEF 6 BRAZ)

U.S.-Brazilian relations in light of the violent press reactions in both Brazil and the U.S. which would occur, and the attitudes of key U.S. congressional leaders toward 'military governments' in Latin America.

Ironically, our bilateral relationship with Brazil has developed more favorably in recent weeks. The soluble coffee issue seems to be headed toward a satisfactory outcome; the climate for negotiating additional economic assistance this year is favorable; and the Brazilian Foreign Minister, Jose de Magalhaes Pinto, has recently been making obvious efforts to improve his relations with the U.S., probably reflecting his hope to build U.S. support for him as a successor to Costa e Silva. It is, therefore, possible that the next few months could see contradictory trends in the political and diplomatic scenes.

Although there are no immediate actions required, I thought you should be apprised of this new set of concerns."

Walt

---

234. Action Memorandum From the President's Special Assistant (Rostow) to President Johnson in Texas[1]

Washington, February 23, 1968.

SUBJECT

1968 Economic Assistance for Brazil

This package contains the unanimous recommendation of AID, State, Agriculture, and BOB, with Treasury concurrence, that you approve an economic assistance program for Brazil for 1968 of $255 million.[2] Of this amount, $170 million is FY 1968 money for program, sector and project loans, $50 million a carryover from the 1967 program loan, and $35 million of PL–480.

Brazilian performance last year was not as good as we would have liked. In large part, it was due to President Costa e Silva's new team getting its policies and priorities established. The soft spots were the large budget deficit, too rapid expansion of private credit and a sizeable depletion of foreign reserves. But inflation was reduced from 41%

---

[1] Source: Johnson Library, National Security File, Country File, Brazil, Vol. VII–a, 8/64–11/68. Confidential. Sent by pouch to the President at his Ranch in Texas.

[2] Attached but not printed are a memorandum from Zwick to the President, February 9, and two memoranda from Gaud to the President, both February 6.

in 1966 to 25% in 1967. The import liberalization program was maintained. And the January exchange rate and credit actions showed a renewed commitment to stabilization.

The negotiating strategy of our assistance package has been carefully coordinated with the IMF and World Bank. The self-help conditions are hard-headed but realistic. Gaud and Oliver find that the application of the Symington Amendment is not required. Applicability of the Conte–Long Amendment will depend on whether President Costa e Silva decides to buy supersonic aircraft or other sophisticated weapon systems. The aid package is structured to permit Conte–Long deductions if this becomes necessary.[3]

I recommend you approve the negotiating package as proposed by Bill Gaud and Covey Oliver.

Walt

Approve[4]

Disapprove

Call me

---

[3] For an assessment of the Conte–Long and Symington amendments, "Probable Consequences of a Refusal by the US to Sell F–5 Aircraft in Latin America," see Document 66.

[4] The President checked this option and added by hand: "ask Oliver to get maximum credit with all Brazilians on this." According to another copy of this memorandum, Assistant to the President Jim Jones relayed this message to Rostow by telephone on February 24. (Johnson Library, National Security File, Country File, Brazil, Vol. VII–a, 8/64–11/68) The United States and Brazil signed the program loan agreement on May 23.

235.   National Intelligence Estimate[1]

NIE 93–68   Washington, March 21, 1968.

BRAZIL

The Problem

To estimate the situation in Brazil and the prospects for the next year or two.

Conclusions

A. The Costa e Silva administration has many things in common with that of Castello Branco, but is relaxing some of the more stringent economic controls which the latter had imposed. It is also tolerating, and to some extent responding to, a greater expression of nationalistic feelings, which for the most part have long had an anti-US cast. Yet such policies will probably not bring Costa e Silva appreciable new popular support; instead, a troubled economy, plus political restraints which are not likely to slacken, will tend to diminish his popularity.

B. Civilian opposition will probably increase, but it is disorganized and unlikely to coalesce very effectively in the next two years. The military establishment probably will urge further restraints on civilian political dissidence, insist upon stronger leadership by the government, and press for the present moderate program of arms acquisition. The President will probably act strongly enough in these respects to satisfy most military opinion. Hence he is likely to stay in office until the end of his term in 1971, and his administration is likely to become somewhat more authoritarian.

C. Brazil's economy showed some progress in 1967, but its problems are too fundamental, too numerous, and too interrelated to permit any great gains in the next two years. Problems of inflation, the budget, and the balance of payments will be manageable, but will nevertheless remain serious. The restraints required to maintain a reasonable degree of financial stability will keep increases in production at modest figures. Thus economic improvement will not be sufficient to provide for much higher levels of living or to permit extensive social reforms or advances.

---

[1] Source: Central Intelligence Agency, Job 79R–01012A, O/DDI Registry. Secret; Controlled Dissem. According to a note on the cover sheet this estimate was prepared in the Central Intelligence Agency with the participation of the intelligence organizations of the Departments of State and Defense and the National Security Agency. The United States Intelligence Board concurred in this estimate on March 21.

D. Despite Brazil's increasing nationalism, the Costa e Silva government will maintain a much friendlier attitude toward the US than the Quadros or Goulart regimes did. It will not, however, follow the US lead in international matters as closely as Castello Branco's did, and we believe it will be less sympathetic toward the US role in Vietnam. It will probably continue to oppose ratification of the international treaty on nuclear nonproliferation in its present form.

[Omitted here is the Discussion section of the estimate.]

---

236. Telegram From the Embassy in Brazil to the Department of State[1]

Rio de Janeiro, December 14, 1968, 1625Z.

14310. Subject: Preliminary Assessment of Brazilian Political Situation in Light of 5th Institutional Act. Ref: Rio de Janeiro 14305.[2]

1. Institutional act decreed last night amounts to a self-issued license authorizing executive to govern without trappings or inconveniences of democracy. It signals bankruptcy of an effort by Brazilian military to demonstrate that they better able than civilian elements to move Brazil toward goals of development and political stability through democratic means. Failure of effort is not due to any demonstrated inability of Brazilian people to measure up to their role, but to incapability of military to understand what democracy is and how it works.

2. Present leaders of Brazilian military are patriotic, sincere, and proud. Historic military role of keeping country on the track by changing its government from time to time has produced an attitude of self-righteousness not easily permeated by opposing views, especially when advocated by persons or groups whose orientation is different from and perhaps suspect to disciplinarian minds.

---

[1] Source: National Archives and Records Administration, RG 59, Central Files 1967–69, POL 23–9 BRAZ. Confidential; Immediate. Repeated to Brasilia, Sao Paulo, Recife, and USCINCSO.

[2] Telegram 14305 from Rio de Janeiro, December 14, forwarded a free translation of the fifth Institutional Act (IA–5). (Ibid.) The act allowed the President to recess the congress, state assemblies, and municipal chambers; to intervene in the states and municipalities without constitutional restraint; to suspend the political rights of any citizen for ten years; to revoke legislative mandates at the federal, state, and municipal level; and to confiscate the property of anyone who may have "enriched themselves illicitly while exercising public office." Unlike previous acts, IA–5 did not have an automatic expiration date.

3. Current crisis had its precise beginnings in a speech by opposition deputy Moreira Alves on floor of Congress which was insulting to army. This incident, while injurious to pride of army, had no intrinsic significance and would have been ignored most places. When issue was blown out of proportion by military insistence on disciplinary action against Moreira Alves, it headed fatally for a constitutional confrontation which could only be resolved by defeat of Congress or of the military acting through weak and vacillating executive. When Congress won legal battle by refusing to remove Moreira Alves' immunity, military felt they could only recoup by extra-legal action clothed in pseudo-legality of an institutional act.

4. This confrontation occurred against a backdrop of problems generated by government's failure to understand Brazil's really fundamental needs in this era. GOB failure to take imaginative and convincing steps toward improvement of woeful educational situation and relief of depressed urban and rural laboring classes produced agitation for changing these conditions, especially within the church and among students. To a conservative group which does not accept inevitability of social revolution taking place in world, such activities appear unpatriotic and dangerous, and therefore are further justification for strong measures.

5. The institutional act and the arbitrary and repressive actions being based on it have produced as much of an about face in the direction the Brazilian Government claimed to be going as would an overthrow of the government. Indeed it is reasonable to believe that if Costa e Silva had held rigidly to the constitution, he would have been overthrown.

6. Within the United States Government, I believe we should understand the situation in this light. On the other hand, we are not faced with the problem of recognizing a new government nor with the need to announce suspensions of aid, military assistance, and other programs customary on overthrow occasions. As of this moment, it appears that our long-range interests might be better served if we were to avoid such overt actions. We should, however, without any announcement, for the moment quietly withhold any pending actions on disbursements or commitments.

7. There are going to be plenty of occasions in the future when divergent GOB and USG policies and attitudes will create friction between our governments, so we will do well to avoid now any that can be avoided.

A public statement at a high US Government level deploring the setback in development of Brazilian democracy is called for, and important to encourage friends of democracy in Brazil, but it should not point the finger too accurately at the persons or groups responsible. These people, while nationalistic and narrow, are fundamentally favorable to the US and can be counted on to side with us either sentimentally or overtly in any East-West confrontation. It is highly likely they will continue in control of Brazil for a number of years to come. It is from them we must obtain cooperation in enterprises of mutual interest and through them that we must work to help Brazil emerge from the underdevelopment of which their own attitudes are one manifestation.

Belton

237. Telegram From the Department of State to the Embassy in Brazil[1]

Washington, December 17, 1968, 0038Z.

288130. Subject: Developments in Brazil.

1) This message is first effort to assess serious impact of recent Brazilian developments on our current relations, gives initial policy guidance, and asks Embassy to focus on problems of deepest concern to us and on matters requiring decision over coming days and weeks.

2) For the moment, at least, Brazilian regime appears to have stripped itself of any disguise as military dictatorship, although possibly more akin to collegiate than one-strong-man type. Fifth Institutional Act and actions in immediate aftermath are harsh, not only in Brazilian context but also in comparison to some of hemisphere's other military regimes. We note that extra constitutional measures have no fixed expiration date and that measures against human rights are strong.

3) Would appreciate your looking for and commenting especially on following in your messages to come:

(a) Appearance of national leader or leaders who are both rational enough to understand serious problems in current situation and influential enough do something about them. Costa e Silva would obviously not seem qualify. Will he reassert himself? Will some other leader or group of leaders emerge? Or are we going to have to deal with likes of Gama e Silva, Portella, and Siseno Sarmento?[2]

---

[1] Source: National Archives and Records Administration, RG 59, Central Files 1967–69, POL 1 BRAZ–US. Secret; Priority; Limdis. Drafted by Proper and Kubisch on December 16 and approved by Vaky. Repeated to Brasilia, Sao Paulo, Recife, CINCSO, CINCLANT, and USUN.

[2] Reference is to Luís Antônio da Gama e Silva, Minister of Justice; Jaime Portela de Melo, Head of the Military Cabinet; and Siseno Sarmento, Commander of the First Army.

(b) Reappearance of moderation in handling of critics and press. We consider Brazil's press to be one of country's most important democratic institutions and believe it will provide one of the first signs of regime's relaxation, if such is to happen. The posture, comment, and continued independence of the church and its leading spokesmen also have highest importance.

(c) Clarification of regime's support—or lack thereof. We unable at this moment identify any major non-military group supporting recent actions. If this true, we must consider how long military will be able remain united and govern effectively.

4) We are clearly unhappy with events and do not intend sound happy. This is matter of basic policy which all members country team instructed observe. On other hand, following factors lead us to avoid expressing excessive unhappiness officially and publicly:

(a) Brazil is a big country of special importance to us on world scene, and there is no need to elaborate on range and significance of our interests there which have not changed materially as a result of last few days' developments although ways and means of serving them may have. Brazilians are aware of their role and not likely appreciate lectures from U.S.

(b) Despite current degree of repression, Brazilian traditions of moderation run deep, and we must allow that they will begin reassert themselves shortly. In addition, arrests and censorship may begin to stop in few days and may be uncoordinated acts of lower level officials and not established central Government policy.

(c) A major problem facing us is to avoid pushing Brazilian leaders into further irrational acts affecting our relations now and in future while, at same time, not leading Brazilian democrats and others in hemisphere to believe we complacent. There probably no way of fully achieving these irreconcilable goals, but we must endeavor strike best balance.

5) Current Brazilian actions can make it extremely difficult for us to initiate or maintain our cooperation on many fronts. This is a question of fact. We do not think it would be productive for us to remind Brazilians of this in terms that could be considered threatening. On other hand, neither would we wish lessening of U.S. assistance and cooperation to come as surprise. Delicate balance also needed to arrive at equilibrium between these extremes. Among programs and activities that need prompt consideration are such things as remaining 52,000 tons of PL 480 wheat for this calendar year, authorization and negotiation of AID and PL 480 assistance for 1969, deobligations on authorized but unsigned AID project loans, ongoing AID activities, A–4 aircraft request, destroyer escorts, submarines, press release on civil aviation agreement, soluble coffee mediation efforts, Peace Corps activities, Clear Sky, and Fernando de Noronha agreement. You will no doubt know of others. As you consider and recommend position we should take on these and similar matters, and obtain Washington ap-

proval, we will be giving expression in specific terms to over-all policy stance we want to assume.

6) In addition, you should consider desirability of mounting highly selective approaches on part of five or six top USG representatives in Brazil individually and privately to 20–30 influential Brazilians. These could be certain cabinet ministers, business leaders, key military figures, political leaders, plus labor, church, university and cultural leaders. On an unofficial basis, they could be told of our true feelings about developments, and the word would thus get around in Brazil without our publicly shaking our finger at the GOB. It has been suggested that USG official could make his points by referring to questions being asked in United States about what is really happening in Brazil and natural consequences thereof.

7) It would also be possible here for high ranking USG official to meet on a background basis with selected members of U.S. and foreign press giving our true reaction on a nonattribution basis. Thus word would get out in stories to Brazil and third countries that USG was distressed, without naming names or using quotes. U.S. Ambassadors in other LA countries could also be asked to present our views to their host governments and some governments in turn might possibly exert salutory influence on GOB. Embassy views requested on these thoughts.

8) Embassy should also consider how best to refer in Brazil to Ambassador's Washington consultation and how to use his farewell calls in Brazil to achieve desired results. He will be discussing this and other aspects this message on his return tomorrow.

Rusk

---

238. **Telegram From the Embassy in Brazil to the Department of State**[1]

Rio de Janeiro, December 19, 1968, 0220Z.

14464. Subject: Conversation with FonMin Magalhaes Pinto.

1. Had private meeting with FonMin Magalhaes Pinto and Secretary General Gibson Barboza tonight. As conversation proceeded

---

[1] Source: National Archives and Records Administration, RG 59, Central Files 1967–69, AID(US) BRAZ. Confidential; Immediate; Exdis. Repeated to Brasilia.

it became evident FonMin's primary interest was in how USG would handle aid programs. I told him that no recognition problem exists, and USG was not cutting aid. However reaction in Washington to recent events had been very strong. Although we did not wish aggravate situation by strong public statements, general feeling when I left was that A–4 issue and aid questions should be put in freezer until we had better indication of whether Brazil would revolve towards restitution of basic democratic rights (Minister readily agreed no such rights existed any longer). Told him USG would fulfill its contractual obligations but would take "wait and see" attitude on future AID programs and those presently under negotiation.

2. FonMin then gave lengthy exposition of events leading up to institutional act. Gist was that pressures had been building up for some time. Marcio Moreira Alves didn't represent more than ten or fifteen percent of problem, but his case was poorly handled and poorly resolved. Result was that it attracted all attention. After vote it became clear that military wanted President to take action.

3. FonMin stated (and other sources have confirmed) that President resisted. First night he told military there would be no solution that day. By second day it became clear that if he didn't act he would be "passed over" (ultrapassado). Thus he chose least bad course of action, which was issuance of fifth institutional act.

4. Minister said President's intention is to use massive powers he has firmly but moderately. Greatest fear of military was subversion, which would also affect economic development. Some of this was imaginary but some represented solid facts. President's intention is to resist radical groups and avoid image of military government.

5. FonMin stressed fact that neither institutional act nor complementary act closing Congress had termination date. Admitted "frankly" that absence of termination dates reflected desires of two groups: radicals who saw it as opening to continue harsh action for extended period, and liberals who saw it as opportunity to abandon extraordinary powers at first opportunity. FonMin could assure us President desired no dates in order be able terminate acts just as soon as he can neutralize radicals. He presently under pressure from military and unable make public statement to this effect but "USG should have confidence in him."

6. According FonMin, President hopeful Brazil can shortly present better image. It impossible make public announcement but he hopes convene Congress on normal constitutional date, which is March 1. Reconstitution of political sector not difficult task. Congress will function, but it will of course not have powers it previously had. Press presents much more difficult problem, but demands of censors will be reduced. President desires return full freedom of press as soon

as possible "but dust of institutional act has not yet settled." Biggest problem is that military hold press responsible for student agitation. It clear FonMin was at loss to explain just how press freedom can now be restored.

7. FonMin stressed that "President has taken situation in his hands." Asked that I tell Secretary Costa e Silva "will proceed on democratic road soonest but needs comprehension of USG." Specifically, FonMin said it would be useful if USG acts "with greatest prudence." Any condemnatory attitude in present excited atmosphere could permanently damage US–Brazil relations. Minister did not find it "useful to stop matters presently under consideration." Freezing them at this moment, he claimed, could lead to nationalistic reaction in army against US.

8. At this point I told FonMin yesterday's statement by Finance Minister Delfim Neto (Rio's 14456)[2] had been made without any consultation with us and was distinctly unhelpful. GOB was now pressing us for early action on AID programs on which it had previously dragged its feet. Attempts to use aid for political purposes could force a decision on USG which would not be in interest of either our countries.

9. FonMin claimed Delfim had spoken without consulting him. Said he believed Delfim had talked by telephone directly to Washington with "official of IDB or State Department official in charge of economic affairs." FonMin assured me he would speak to Delfim and other economic ministers tomorrow and urge them not to take precipitous action which could create political difficulties.

10. FonMin was clearly being good soldier and putting best light on bad situation. Will comment further in subsequent message.[3]

Tuthill

---

[2] In telegram 14456 from Rio de Janeiro, December 18, the Embassy reported that Delfim Neto had publicly stated that the United States would not restrict economic assistance to Brazil as a result of IA–5. (Ibid.)

[3] Not found.

239. Telegram From the Department of State to the Embassy in Brazil[1]

Washington, December 19, 1968, 2343Z.

289961. Ref.: State's 288130, Rio's 14464.[2]

1) Given the serious consequences for U.S.–Brazil relations that will inevitably follow if Costa e Silva and the military continue on path assumed over past few days, we are searching actively for some way or means to try and turn them back, even partially, from such a course. We recognize risk of a counterproductive result if we are too unskillful or untimely in our efforts. We also realize marginality of our influence and likely sensitivity of key figures in power, especially now.

2) Nonetheless, the stakes are high. A misguided and repressive military dictatorship would have grave consequences for Brazil and would set in motion a serious erosion in U.S.–Brazil relations which we must make every effort to avoid. We know that it may be necessary to endure such an erosion temporarily in order for us to remain free of identification with the Costa e Silva government and that our very long term interests in Brazil may best be served by working with what have become the disaffected groups in the country.

3) But we obviously must not resign ourselves too readily to such a regime as an inevitable consequence of what has happened in recent days. Almost all agree that Costa e Silva and the military overreacted in near cosmic terms to the provocation presented. Is it too late for them to redress the balance? Can a look by key Brazilians at U.S.–Brazil relations for the future play a part in turning the military juggernaut around, or at least in getting them to repair some of the damage already done? Is there still time to head off possibly worse acts yet to come?

4) These thoughts were behind para 6, reftel. We think following script is about right, subject to minor variations to accommodate to characteristics of person spoken to, and offer it for your urgent appraisal:

5) "Brazilians know that the United States thinks of its relationship with Brazil as a very special one, both as to the world as a whole and certainly within the hemispheric community. What Brazil does and how she does it is of very great significance. So far the changes made recently have not been taken in U.S. public opinion as marking a

---

[1] Source: National Archives and Records Administration, RG 59, Central Files 1967–69, POL BRAZ–US. Secret; Priority; Limdis. Drafted by Oliver, Vaky, and Kubisch and approved by Oliver.

[2] Documents 237 and 238.

definitive and irrevocable transition from democratic norms. There is still time and a good opportunity to avoid the congealing of public opinion in the U.S.A. along lines that would make it very difficult for any administration in this country to continue those degrees of cooperation and mutual assistance that the needs of the Brazilian people and our own deep friendship for them make desirable. Responsible people in both countries are surely aware of forces in the world that would like nothing better than to see relations between these two great countries of the Western Hemisphere decline to the merely correct, or even deteriorate farther, in a downward spiral. The one (script user) who speaks these words does not mean to threaten, intrude, or preach. As one personally committed to the transcendental cause of that unexpressed 'Alliance within an Alliance,' he feels he must say them in the hope that it is not too late for Brazilians to be able, as they always have before, to pull back from rigidities and to face their problems with elegance, compassion, wisdom and good spirit. North Americans do not suggest what might be done, not only because we do not so conduct ourselves with Brazilians, but also because we know that no one better than the Brazilians themselves can find hopeful and salutary ways out."

6) Style of approaches would be calm, friendly and frank—no histrionics, no threats and no tutelary or directive nuance. Uniformity of line by all U.S. officials that express it is highly important especially since also desirable use officials representing various U.S. agencies.

7) If you think some special person (such as General Walters, who is now in the United States) would be able to assist you in such an effort, let us know and we will try and make necessary arrangements. Your views requested on this point.[3]

Rusk

---

[3] In telegram 14524 from Rio de Janeiro, December 20, the Embassy concurred with the Department's assessment of the situation, but stressed the possible consequences of any precipitate action. In particular the Embassy recommended against sending a special emissary, which "would be viewed as interference Brazilian affairs and would be distinctly counterproductive. If emissary were a military figure would be interpreted by one & all as USG support for recent GOB moves and encouragement further movement to the right, no matter what he might say after arrival." (National Archives and Records Administration, RG 59, Central Files 1967–69, POL BRAZ–US)

240. **Telegram From the Embassy in Brazil to the Department of State**[1]

Rio de Janeiro, December 20, 1968, 1930Z.

14526. Joint Embassy/Defense Message. Subject: Developments in Brazil. Ref: State 288130.[2]

1. This telegram is first attempt to give our tentative views on matters raised para 3 reftel. Department will no doubt appreciate that in present fluid situation with various elements asserting their influence on a greatly altered power structure, precise answers are impossible.

2. Re paragraph 3(a), recent events have not essentially changed the names of those at the top of the GOB power structure. What has changed is the structure itself which in turn has altered the relationship of one leader vis-à-vis another. While we agree that Costa e Silva does not qualify as strong leader, he is probably as capable as anyone else who might take over in present circumstances. He clearly does not have the same autonomy he had before, nor is he likely to regain it. Moreover, his chances of finishing his term may have been reduced. Fact that he has publicly stated he in authority twice in as many days (Rio 14422 and 14435[3]) interpreted by many as evidence of his precarious position.

3. Nevertheless Costa e Silva still President of Brazil. His freedom of action has been limited by radical military elements but fact that he holds top position gives him an advantage in any struggle that others do not enjoy. Certainly USG will have to cope more and more with likes of Gama e Silva, Portella and Syseno Sarmento, but, hopefully, more moderate elements will hold the marginal balance of power.

4. In responding to paragraph 3(c), the Embassy believes that a tug of war presently going on between radicals and more moderate elements in military. On its outcome will depend regime's base of support. Principal issues being debated are how to deal with "subversion and corruption." Only significant military group which opposes act outright is idealistic "hardline" group led by Col. Boaventura Cavalcanti, but it not in position swing much weight. Radical element which has throughout crisis been led by Generals Syseno Sarmento, Commander of First Army; Moniz de Aragao, Chief of Veterinary Service;

---

[1] Source: National Archives and Records Administration, RG 59, Central Files 1967–69, POL 23–9 BRAZ. Confidential; Priority. Repeated to Brasilia, Recife, Sao Paulo, USCINCSO, USUN, CINCLANT, and Buenos Aires.

[2] Document 237.

[3] Dated December 17 and 18. (National Archives and Records Administration, RG 59, Central Files 1967–69, POL 15–1 BRAZ and POL 2 BRAZ, respectively)

Henrique Assumpcao, Syseno's chief of staff; and Portella of military household favors extended congressional recess and prolonged and thorough application of institutional act. More moderate element, which appears to be headed by Generals Lyra Tavares, Minister of Army; Reynaldo, Commander Command and General Staff School; Newton Reis and Bina Machado, both sub-chiefs of Staff of the Army, apparently favors early restoration of constitutional rights. Specifically, they reportedly respond sympathetically to pleas for reopening of Congress March 1. Costa e Silva portrayed by various sources as leaning toward moderation but unable to show his hand at present. His initial moves are simply directed towards re-establishing the credibility of his position. A key figure in this situation is General Castilho, Commander of the Vila Militar, who has been variously portrayed as a Syseno or Lyra Tavares man. Castilho was clearly one of those who transmitted the pressure from the banks, but his personal loyalties in the current struggle have not yet been defined. Basically he favors the "hard" approach and is a man of personal courage who enjoys popularity among junior officers.

5. Aside from small number of perennial pro-government politicians who have been falling into line, only major non-military group to support recent actions has been conservative-business class, particularly in Sao Paulo. Essentially, this group believes new regime will follow policies which will be more efficient and will benefit private enterprise. However, there are some influential businessmen who do oppose GOB actions and are worried about political trends. It should also be noted that a part of the educated population as always is basically apathetic and knows relatively little about recent events because of censorship.

6. It difficult to speculate at this point on signs of moderation in handling critics and press. Some prisoners have been released, some arrests are still being made and cassation lists are expected. There are those who think Congress can be reactivated on March 1 and that press censorship can be eased. We agree with Brasilia (Brasilia 3271)[4] that reopening Congress will be uphill battle. Yesterday, for example, Senate President Gilberto Marinho, Arena President Daniel Krieger, and hardline Senator Dinarte Mariz tried to see President but were unable to. In our view most that can be expected is that some sort of emasculated Congress may begin to operate within the next few months, but even this appears to us to be an optimistic prediction.

7. Question of press even more difficult. Various government sources tell us plan is to ease censorship gradually. Suggestions of self-censorship have already been made. Control will then be maintained

---

[4] Dated December 18. (Ibid., DEF 6 BRAZ)

by threats of renewed censorship and economic measures (most newspapers are in debt to GOB which has newsprint monopoly). This may meet with some success but it is hardly much of an improvement over current situation. Furthermore, we believe that there are still journalists in Brazil who would be courageous enough to speak out in the face of these threats, and we have no reason to believe military activists would be willing to accept any significant criticism of what they have done. Thus, we view restoration of press freedom as a long term process. Implicit recognition of this made in yesterday's press briefing when GOB spokesman said censorship will be maintained as long as necessary depending on cooperation of press (Rio 14500).[5]

8. Church has not yet assumed a formal position, but could be rallying point for opposition. Some prominent churchmen initially reacted with unequivocal opposition to recent developments. These include Secretary General National Conference Brazilian Bishops, Dom Aluisio Lorscheider, conservative Cardinal Jayme Camara of Guanabara and Archbishop Helder Camara of Recife, latter two of whom have issued strong public anti-government statements since December 13. Ultimate posture of church depends on future government conduct toward clergy and church prerogatives, but the prevailing tendency seems to be to speak out with greater unity in opposition to the act (Recife 1606).[6]

Tuthill

---

[5] Dated December 20. (Ibid., PPB 3)
[6] Dated December 19. (Ibid., SOC 12–1 BRAZ)

---

241.   Telegram From the Department of State to the Embassy in Brazil[1]

Washington, December 25, 1968, 0057Z.

292127. Subject: Developments in Brazil: Significance of Institutional Act (IA–5).

1) We are now proceeding on assumption that by early January situation in Brazil should have clarified sufficiently that USG will be

---

[1] Source: National Archives and Records Administration, RG 59, Central Files 1967–69, POL 23–9 BRAZ. Confidential; Limdis. Drafted by Kubisch on December 24 and approved by Vaky.

able to establish kinds of policy guidelines and make necessary operating decisions which will undoubtedly be required by then. In previous messages Country Team has been asked to provide its assessment and recommendations on these matters by first week in January and to consider whether DCM, who will become Chargé later in January, and AID Mission Director, and perhaps others, should come to Washington for short consultation.

2) While we have been furnishing you with highlights of reactions and thinking in United States, including in USG, we thought you might also find useful some preliminary comments as to how we perceive overall Brazil situation now, eleven days after promulgation of IA–5. We recognize that both you and we are by no means fully informed on details of what happened during first important hours following congressional vote of December 12, that we do not and may never know all of pressures that were exerted and by whom, nor what the realistic alternatives were. We also realize that new phase is only beginning to unfold and that it too early to say how exceptional powers will be used by Costa e Silva. Finally, we realize that Brazil's needs and performance cannot be measured against North American or northwest European standards of constitutional democracy, nor even easily expressed in Anglo-Saxon terms.

3) But, by whatever measuring standards one might be expected to apply, political development has been dealt a hard blow and human rights, as defined by minimum international standards, have already suffered to some extent and remain under serious threat. There is no arguing arbitrariness of IA–5 and powers it gives Costa e Silva. Looks to us that he can do almost anything he wishes to almost anyone in country with only a small handful of men having power to do much about it—and they are far from an appealing lot. Moreover, proximate circumstances which brought IA–5 into being would indicate an almost paranoiac overkill response to provocation presented. Seems almost incredible to us that threats to government or country's well being, or prevalence of subversion and corruption, were such as to warrant gross breaching of constitutional restraints and political and civil rights—or that, if so, there weren't wiser, more civilized and lawful ways of dealing with them.

4) It has become almost cliché to refer to Brazilian military establishment as being different from that of its hispanic neighbors. Undoubtedly this has been true for practically all of Brazil's modern history. Acting almost supra-Government, Brazilian military entered political arena infrequently and then only to save country when it appeared to be in last extremity. Under leadership of Castello Branco, armed forces provided backbone as impressive effort was made to establish a governmental system that would offer best blend of democratic,

popular participation in a free society and authoritarianism believed needed to ensure Brazil's order and progress. Clearly, constitution of 1946, modeled after U.S., had failed and permitted the near chaos of early 60's.

5) But, staying in power after '64, Brazilian military found themselves with responsibilities that go with governing. And in Brazil, like so many developing countries, there was certain to be widespread dissatisfaction with government's performance in many sectors, lacking as it did capital and human resources—and commitment of the society—to do all that needed doing, simultaneously. Natural consequence was criticism of military, and in Brazilian context, and in eyes of military itself, such criticism was to military like insult to flag or to nation's honor. Thus military reacted in name of patriotism and country against criticism, revealing that in this respect at least they have something in common with fellow professionals in other LA countries.

6) To us this appears to be important watershed in Brazil's political development. IA–5 of December 13 was throwback to its two predecessors of April 1964 and October 1965, but in our view has far more significance than either. Given near chaos and disorder which preceded and passion of moment that followed Goulart's ouster, April '64 Act could be understood. Even October '65 Act could be justified by Castello to some extent as he said to us morning after Act was promulgated—and later demonstrated in fact—that he only assumed powers not to use them. Moreover, neither of these Acts was as extreme as one of December 13, and both had clearly specified expiration dates. Even so, as you know, in retrospect we believe we erred after October '65 Act in not drawing back further from our close association and public identification with Castello Government.

7) Perhaps Brazil's misfortune has been that Costa e Silva became its president twenty-one months ago instead of one of others more favored by Castello Branco. With all laws, powers and constitutional provisions apparently needed to lead his country and govern effectively he has brought it to present state. Thus, the watershed: unable to succeed with kind of open democracy Brazil attempted from 1945 to 1964, country has now also lost its chance—at least for present—to move ahead even under strongly guided semi-authoritarian democracy.

8) In our view, therefore, prospects are not good. For foreseeable future military would appear be unwilling see Brazil buffeted by pressures resulting from free expression in even semi-open society. Nor, unless they change, can military accept criticism inherent to their role as government of developing country. Some Brazilian mutation of harsh authoritarian regime, therefore, and possibly some succession of such regimes, appears be in offing.

9) But, as stated in previous messages, and this of highest importance, U.S. interests and objectives in Brazil are virtually same now as they were eleven days ago. In the new circumstances we will undoubtedly have to adapt ourselves to revised ways of serving them. We await your further thoughts and recommendations as to how best to proceed and make foregoing available to you, not as representing full consensus in Washington nor to signal kind of analysis or recommendations we want. Rather, foregoing represents preliminary views of only small number of U.S. officials who have consulted on matter, and of several consultants outside Department who have had significant experience in Brazil, and does not reflect dissent of several who believe, stated at its most extreme, that we are greatly overemphasizing importance of recent developments in Brazil and that this episode will find its way into Brazilian history without greatly affecting period immediately ahead. We hope you will find these comments helpful and in your analysis and recommended policy lines will address more important questions raised.

10) Merry Christmas.

Rusk

---

242. Telegram From the Embassy in Brazil to the Department of State[1]

Rio de Janeiro, December 28, 1968, 1915Z.

14720. References: State 288130,[2] 291004,[3] 292127.[4] Joint State/AID Message.

1. In the absence of a clear view of what the Brazilian political future holds, the Embassy believes the basic premise on which the U.S. Government should operate is that we still want to see Brazil advance and develop, and therefore we continue to be willing to assist this

---

[1] Source: National Archives and Records Administration, RG 59, Central Files 1967–69, AID(US) BRAZ. Secret; Priority. Repeated to Recife and Sao Paulo.

[2] Document 237.

[3] In telegram 291004 to Rio de Janeiro, December 21, the Department suggested that the Embassy submit its recommendations on economic assistance and other bilateral matters within the next 2 weeks "if, as we expect, situation clarifies sufficiently for you to do so." (National Archives and Records Administration, RG 59, Central Files 1967–69, POL BRAZ–US)

[4] Document 241.

process wherever the prospects for accomplishment are reasonable. In adopting this premise we are recognizing that genuine political development can only be achieved as an extremely long-range result of other fundamental social and cultural improvements, which in turn can be assisted and accelerated with outside help of the sort we are able to offer. We assume that while in certain circumstances we would cut off aid, we would be reluctant to do so, thus we assume we are involved in a process of determining first how, under the new conditions existing in Brazil, we ought to tailor our programs for maximum results, and, secondly, how to use our preparedness to continue assistance as a stimulus to encourage the GOB to relax its political extremism. Another important consideration is the political image of the U.S. both here and throughout the Hemisphere. We are aware also that our posture must be adjusted to the need for continuing support for aid programs in Brazil among those U.S. public and Congressional elements who may favor aid in general but who have difficulty with the fact that it does not buy instant democracy.

2. We anticipate it will take some weeks or even months before the pattern of Brazilian Government and politics will become sufficiently clear to enable us to make final recommendations on the shape of our aid program to reflect fully the changed situation. Until the new norms of the IA–5 become spelled out in practice, e.g., in such areas as civil liberties, freedom of press and parliamentary and judicial processes, and until we know how the GOB will perform in the economic field under the changed circumstances, we feel a wait-and-see approach on new aid undertakings to be appropriate. Such an approach in the form outlined below would reduce (but not entirely avoid) the impression in Latin America and the U.S. that the USG uncritically accepts what has happened here. Moreover, if skillfully handled it might strengthen those elements in the military and the government who are counseling restraint in the use of IA–5 and an early restoration of civil liberties, although we must recognize that our influence on internal political events is marginal at best.

3. At the same time, we do not wish to breach existing commitments. To terminate or suspend activities which have been undertaken or authorized on the basis of good faith and with the investment of energies and financial resources on both sides could create an aftermath of distrust that could circumscribe our options for the future. Thus, for the initial wait-and-see period or first phase, and unless the situation deteriorates, we recommend a policy of (a) continuing activities covered by existing agreements and (b) proceeding, in an unhurried manner, with negotiations of outstanding loan authorizations, namely, health sector, southern states road maintenance, education sector, Passo Real, IBGE, agricultural research, to the extent practicable, or we would attempt to structure the completion of negotiations on these loans so

that the socially-oriented ones, such as health and education, would get signed first. If there is future political retrogression, we would once again suspend negotiations and further review the situation.

4. In all continuing activities we would seek to minimize and if possible avoid publicity. We must however expect pressures on GOB side to hurry negotiations and to generate publicity which we will be alert to combat.

5. During the wait-and-see phase we would not discuss further with the GOB the contemplated FY 1969 loan program (program loan, three education sector loans, and Manaus power). Of this package the most immediate significance for USG/GOB relations is the program loan, negotiation of which had been planned for January. These negotiations would have to be postponed sine die. The suspension of dialogue on new programs might well mean that we would not be able to authorize these loans, or at least some of them, before the end of the fiscal year. With this in mind, we may wish to reconsider fairly soon whether preparatory work on the education sector loans should not go forward as an exception to the "wait-and-see" approach, since these loans seem to us to be of high priority even under the changed political circumstances in Brazil.

6. In the meantime, we would convey the policy outlined above in broad terms to the top leadership of the GOB. We would say that, while we cannot anticipate the reaction of the new U.S. administration which will be taking office on January 20, we assume its attitude will be shaped by traditional U.S. concern for individual freedoms. Therefore, it is likely that the length of the "wait-and-see" period, particularly with respect to new FY69 assistance commitments, would be influenced by future Brazilian actions regarding civil liberties, press freedom, and the like. The Ambassador's farewell calls on the President and a number of cabinet officers would provide appropriate occasions to get this message across, and, possibly, to learn of the GOB's plans re IA–5.

7. In specific terms we thus envisage the following U.S. position, program by program:

A. FY68 Program Loan. Because of the undesirable impact payment of $50 million tranche now due under the FY68 program loan would have, we recommend protracted delay. We can expect considerable diplomatic pressure from the GOB to release these funds. No recommendation on the second tranche can be made at this time.

B. Development Loan Projects. In an attempt to avoid the impression that we were going back to "business as usual" our tactics would be different from those formerly employed in at least two respects: (1) we would not press the GOB to take action in order to move forward on pending matters, but instead would let the initiative come from the Brazilian side and (2) even with rapid movement on the part of the GOB to bring these pending matters to a head, we would reevaluate the political situation on one hand and the importance we attach to the particular loan on the other before any signings. Undue GOB delays or failures to meet conditions of the loans will lead to early termination and appropriate deobligations or de-authorizations. The deadlines which we had previously set for ourselves would have to be extended because of the current interruption and deliberate spacing of the signatures.

C. Development Grant Projects. Continuation of ongoing activities, with a special review of public safety program to determine whether modification of the current phaseout schedule would be appropriate in light of the changed situation.

D. Counterpart Releases. We advocate continuing releases of PL 480 and program loan counterpart generated from existing agreements. As indicated in Rio 14497,[5] further delays in a number of cases will be disruptive for projects in which we have had strong interest.

E. Housing Extended Risk Guarantees. Follow through with closing and signatures on already authorized guarantees. On December 2, USAID requested January 24 for execution of documents. BNH has not yet responded. Our information indicates that sponsors and BNH would be desirous of postponing until early March. USAID would concur on basis of current situation, but position of U.S. investors should be ascertained by AID/W. Further authorizations are not an immediate issue as GOB has not yet indicated interest.

F. Other AID Guarantees. Follow through on applications submitted where letters of intent already issued. Would also continue process new applications as these are essentially non-concessional, private sector to private sector activities.

G. Title II–PL 480. On humanitarian grounds, continuation of planned programs.

H. Title I–PL 480. Inasmuch as Title I sales are complementary to program assistance, negotiations on new agreement will also have to be delayed.

8. We have also considered our position concerning Exim-Bank financing and assistance from multilateral agencies. We recommend no change in Exim approach toward private sector projects. Such proposals should continue to be considered on their individual merits and within normal Exim financing policies. Pending projects for publicly-owned companies, such as Volta Redonda and Rio Doce, would be used by the GOB to create the impression that the U.S. has no qualms about new

---

[5] Not found.

economic assistance to Brazil: in general Exim should put a "slow man" on the job for the time being and final approval and announcement of each loan should be considered at the time in terms of its political impact.

9. On multilateral assistance, our recommendation is that projects being considered by the multilateral agencies be processed as per their usual policies and regulations. We should avoid actions that would lead to accusations that the U.S. is attempting to use multilateral agencies to accomplish unilateral political objectives. U.S. positions on specific projects should be taken on the merits of the individual projects.

Tuthill

---

243.   **Telegram From the Embassy in Brazil to the Department of State**[1]

Rio de Janeiro, January 9, 1969, 2340Z.

196. Subject: Call on President Costa e Silva. Accompanied by Pol Counselor I payed half hour farewell call today on President in presence of FonMin at President's summer palace in Petropolis.

President's greeting was effusive and following courtesies and rambling exchange on merits of contact lenses Costa e Silva himself broached subject of recent events by noting I would be leaving at a time when Latin America gives a confused impression: Colombia in state of siege, Peru, Bolivia, Argentina and now Brazil under "exceptional regimes." Uruguay didn't even have strength left to go into exceptional regime. It was good neighbor but has been "virtually turned over to Communists."

Costa e Silva showed considerable awareness and apparent comprehension of US criticism. Said US had "stratified life" and could not be expected understand problems of countries in development stage. Your democracy is the ideal, he noted, but we cannot pattern ourselves after your system. If US were in developing stage now it would be going through same problems we are experiencing. Even then, US had advantage of elite immigration whereas Portugal sent us its castoffs.

---

[1] Source: National Archives and Records Administration, RG 59, Central Files 1967–69, POL 17 US–BRAZ. Confidential; Priority; Limdis. Repeated to Brasilia, Sao Paulo, Recife, Montevideo, and CINCSO.

I assured him US did not wish to impose its pattern upon any country but I recalled that prior his election Costa e Silva had told me of three things I must bear in mind: 1) the military is the most political institution in Brazil, 2) the military want Costa e Silva to be President and 3) he, Costa e Silva would work for a return to a situation in which either a civilian or a military man could be chosen President. Told him I had used his statement in my reports to Washington, which was following present current developments with concern. Was there any message he wished me to convey?

President said that I as one who had lived here should explain "entire situation" to Washington, pointing out that there is "complete tranquility" in Brazil. (One of his favorite phrases which he used several times again today.) We have "maintained order." We had to sacrifice some of the "non fundamentals to preserve the fundamentals," but as soon as we can we will return to state of normality. This will be done "opportunely," but with the necessary caution.

President went on to castigate "political class" much along lines his New Year's eve speech. He had worked for an understanding between politicians and military but politicians didn't want understanding. If we only were acquainted with all facts we would know that politicians wanted to undo all the achievements of revolution. "No one worked harder with politicians than I but they refused to understand."

As example of difficulties he faced, Costa e Silva cited *Correio da Manha*. I wanted to ease press censorship, he said, but as soon as I did *Correio da Manha* printed a letter I was supposed to be sending to President elect Nixon (Rio's 149).[2] No such letter exists. This type of thing would not be permitted in US and *Correio* could be sued by you, but our laws are not strong enough to deal with irresponsible press ("yours in US is more responsible"). *Correio* even printed all the criticisms of the American and European press. For these reasons we had to seize yesterday's edition.

President noted military in Brazil have traditionally played political role. I have tried to break that tradition (he pointed to his civilian attire), but this can't be done from one hour to another. For the moment I have had to step back into my military role but as soon as possible I will resume forward progress in my civilian role.

Of one thing you can be sure, Costa e Silva said. There will be a presidential succession as provided for in constitution. Jokingly remarked that this would happen if for no other reason than that he doesn't like the job—it is too difficult.

---

[2] Dated January 6. (Ibid., POL 15–1 BRAZ)

President closed conversation by asking me to assure my government that Brazil is now a true friend of the US. This might not be the case under "the others" (presumably he was referring to the pre-1964 Goulart group).

Comment: Costa e Silva took on the attitude of a garrulous, kindly—and tolerant—grandfather worried about the wayward and disoriented members on the Brazilian political scene. He obviously wanted to give the impression that all was quiet and that he had only taken a slight—and temporary—detour from the democratic path. Following initial pleasantries, he launched into one of his long monologues and brought conversation to abrupt but cordial end after 1800 bugle sounded. It was hard to get word in edgewise.

It is difficult to know how much of this he believes himself. He is, of course, now aware of the restless forces within the Brazilian military but he may be convinced (or trying to convince himself) that he can contain them. The general impression that he gave us was that, despite his native shrewdness, he may well be underestimating the forces at work in this country.

Tuthill

---

244. Information Memorandum From the President's Special Assistant (Rostow) to President Johnson[1]

Washington, January 13, 1969, 3 p.m.

SUBJECT

Brazil

A political struggle within the army continues in Brazil—with the result in doubt, and the prize being de facto control of all levels of government. President Costa e Silva issued another "Institutional Act" on December 13 under extreme pressure from his fellow generals—he hopes to use its extraordinary powers sparingly, but he is being pressed hard to widen the political purge and to clamp down permanently on

---

[1] Source: Johnson Library, National Security File, Country File, Brazil, Vol. VIII, Filed by LBJ Library, 7/65–1/69. Confidential. The memorandum indicates the President saw it.

the Supreme Court, the press, and other opposition expression so that the "work of the Revolution" can be finished in peace. He *may* be unseated by his military colleagues if he continues to resist invoking more extreme repressive measures.

Meanwhile, the country stays quiet, helpless to affect the course of events. To varying degrees labor, church, students, journalists, "intellectuals", and most politicians are shaken and temporarily cowed. Most businessmen and some politicians applaud the tougher government line on "subversion and corruption". Censorship is now technically lifted—but newspapers must practice a form of rigid "self-restraint" or face confiscation.

Moderate civilian politicians urge the U.S. to wait quietly on the sidelines—not publicly denouncing the dictatorial trend—but holding back any new aid commitments until the struggle between moderates and radicals in the army is resolved. Our Embassy in Rio de Janeiro also advocates this course. State has followed this line since December 13—while maintaining normal diplomatic, aid, and military contacts, we have been "reviewing" our assistance programs, a polite way of saying "no new commitments."

So far, the Brazilian Government has *not* disputed our posture on aid. The Finance Minister *hopes* we will soon release $50 million from the 1968 program loan—an installment due in December for which Brazil's self-help performance fully qualifies. However, we are holding up this release until the political picture clears somewhat, in part in anticipation of strong negative reactions from the Congress, should we release quickly.

Unless Costa e Silva presses for the money—which he has *not* done to date, Secretary Rusk believes we should *hold* this important decision for the next Administration.

Walt

Chile

245. Memorandum From the Chief of the Western Hemisphere Division (King) to Director of Central Intelligence McCone[1]

Washington, January 3, 1964.

SUBJECT

Political Action Program in Chile

REFERENCES

A. WHD Memorandum to DCI on Same Subject Dated 24 December 1963[2]

B. Memorandum dated 30 December 1963 from E.H. Knoche requesting clarification on some points of the WHD Memorandum[3]

1. Our comments on the questions posed in Mr. Knoche's memorandum are listed below.

2. Support for the Democratic Front

On 19 December 1963 the Special Group approved a one-time payment [*less than 1 line of source text not declassified*] to the Democratic Front [*less than 1 line of source text not declassified*].[4] The suggestion for this payment originated with Ambassador Cole and was concurred in by Assistant Secretary Martin. Arrangements are now being made to transfer this money [*less than 1 line of source text not declassified*]. This Special Group paper did not request regular monthly payments to the Democratic Front.

During his December 1963 Washington visit, [*name not declassified*] mentioned that the Democratic Front required 1.5 million dollars for its election campaign—one million of which it could raise locally. The implication was a pitch for $500,000 from United States sources.

3. Present Assistance to the Christian Democratic Party

a. *Policy Approval*

In view of the ambiguous position of the Christian Democratic Party on a number of issues of interest to the United States, the subject

---

[1] Source: Central Intelligence Agency, Job 80–01690R, DDO Files, Western Hemisphere, Chile, [*file name not declassified*]. Secret. Drafted on January 2. Forwarded through the Deputy Director for Plans. Copies were sent to DDCI, DDP, and ADDP.

[2] Not found.

[3] Not found. Enno Henry Knoche was Executive Assistant to the Deputy Director of Central Intelligence.

[4] The minutes of the meeting are in Department of State, INR/IL Historical Files, Special Group Files, Meetings, January 2, 1964.

of assistance to this party was periodically coordinated at various levels, with the people responsible for policy. The idea of assisting the Christian Democrats was first broached to us on 22 March 1962 by Ambassador Cole and the then Special Assistant to the President, Richard Goodwin. The Special Group approved a program of assistance to the Christian Democrats on 19 April 1962 and again on 30 August 1963.[5] The Latin American Policy Committee approved the continuation of the assistance at meetings held on 10 January 1963 and 20 June 1963.[6] On 14 August 1963 Mr. Martin and Ambassador Cole agreed again that this assistance should continue. The Special Group paper on one-time assistance to the Democratic Front which was approved on 19 December 1963 refers explicitly to our assistance to the Christian Democrats.[7]

b. *Rationale for this Assistance*

The reasons for our non-attributable assistance to the Christian Democratic Party are:

(1) To Deprive the Chilean Communist Party of Votes

The Christian Democratic Party is the fastest growing party in Chile. Its social program and evangelical fervor has enabled it to compete successfully with the Communists for the votes of students and workers. The Christian Democratic Party is the only non-Communist party in Chile in a position to attack directly the Communist Party at its mass base. This has been demonstrated in the municipal elections of April of last year, in the student elections, and in the fight for control of labor unions, which, though still controlled by the Communists, are showing the signs of Christian Democratic Party inroads.

(2) To Achieve a Measure of Influence Over Christian Democratic Party Policy

This objective could not be realized effectively because of security restrictions under which we must operate in this case. The Special Group, in approving assistance to the Christian Democratic Party, insisted that this assistance be non-attributable. [*1½ lines of source text not declassified*] Since security has been tightly maintained, Eduardo Frei, the leader of the Christian Democratic Party, is unwitting of the fact that he is being aided by the United States Government and believes that this assistance is being provided by his [*less than 1 line of source text not declassified*] friends.

---

[5] The funding approved was [*text not declassified*] and [*text not declassified*], respectively. The minutes of the Special Group meetings are in the Department of State, INR/IL Historical Files, Special Group Files, Meetings, April 26, 1962 and September 6, 1962.

[6] The minutes for both meetings are ibid., LAPC Action Minutes, 1962–1963.

[7] Reference is to a CIA paper for the Special Group, December 13, 1963. (Ibid., Special Group Files, Meetings, December 19, 1963)

(3) To Foster a Non-Communist Coalition

One of the original objectives in March 1962 was to strengthen the Christian Democratic Party so that it would be more attractive to the Radical Party as a coalition partner. Up to April 1963 the Radicals had been the largest single party and the Christians the second largest in Chile. Hence a coalition of these parties with the greatest voter appeal was viewed as a viable non-Communist barrier. Since the Radical Party joined the Conservatives and Liberals in their own alliance, the Democratic Front, on 11 October 1962, this objective is not now feasible.

4. Parliament's Role in the Election of a President

In the event no candidate achieves a majority, the Chilean constitution does provide parliament with the right to select the president between the two leading candidates. The composition of the present parliament is such that it could select the runner-up over the Popular Front candidate. Historically, however, parliament has never passed over the candidate who received the largest popular vote, and we have no hard intelligence to the effect that any leading groups are planning to do this, if it should become necessary, nor do we have any indication that public opinion would approve such a move. Moreover, parliamentary elections are scheduled for March 1965, and it is unlikely that many parliamentarians will conclude that their reelection will be best assured by going against the will of the people by flouting Chile's proud democratic spirit and by assuming the responsibility for the civil unrest that would follow such a decision.

5. Military Intervention

Traditionally, the Chilean military establishment has not interfered with the political life of the country. The last military coup occurred in 1932. The Chilean military stood idly by and watched a Popular Front government assume power in 1938 and permitted it to govern until 1941 when it fell of its own weight and without military intervention. Although the military have the capabilities to intervene, we have no intelligence or other reports indicating they are planning or considering this.

6. How Business Circles View the 1964 Elections

The fact that the Socialist/Communist Front did not do as well as anticipated in the municipal elections of April 1963 has created some new optimism in regard to the 1964 election results. However, although we (and our counterparts in the State Department) do not view the election of the Popular Front candidate as a probability, we do feel it is a distinct possibility. Business circles of course have no illusion about what would happen should the Socialist/Communist Front win, but they believe this possibility to be less likely than we do.

Should a Christian Democratic victory occur, it might be noted that the Christian Democratic Party tends to favor selective nationalization and increased state planning. Undoubtedly, private industry would be in a better position with Duran as president and will probably suffer increased restrictions under a Christian Democratic administration.

7. Should we be Supporting the Christian Democratic Party

Although the Christian Democratic Party and the Democratic Front do not, in large measure, compete for the same votes and the Christian Democratic Party has demonstrated its ability to compete with the communists for worker votes, its position on a number of issues of interest to the United States makes it advisable to reexamine our aid to this party. [*2½ lines of source text not declassified*] In any event, we must face the fact that the Christian Democratic Party will be less favorable and responsive to United States Government policies than the Democratic Front, that it will try to establish relations with Iron Curtain countries, that within the limited capability of Chile it will endeavor to increase its trade with the Soviet Bloc and will not follow the United States lead in foreign policy with the same willingness as the present government.

8. Should we Alter our Chilean Program

Two aspects of our Chilean program should be exploited with Secretary Mann.

a. Depending on [*less than 1 line of source text not declassified*] our intelligence reports, and State Department findings, the entire subject of Chilean election subsidies, with particular emphasis on assistance to the Democratic Front, should be discussed with Secretary Mann.

b. If a decision is made to continue assistance to the Christian Democratic Party, an effort should be made to achieve greater influence over it by modifying the Special Group restriction on non-attributability. Funds could be provided in a fashion causing Frei to infer United States origin of funds and yet permitting plausible denial.

J. C. King[8]

---

[8] Printed from a copy that bears this typed signature.

246. Memorandum From the President's Special Assistant (Dungan) to the President's Special Assistant for National Security Affairs (Bundy)[1]

Washington, January 18, 1964.

It seems to me that the Special Group might, at an early date, give consideration to the interests of the United States in the Chilean election which occurs in December 1964.[2] No one familiar with Latin American affairs has any doubt as to the importance of the outcome of this election, not only in Chile but throughout the hemisphere.

I believe it is an opportune time for us to review what our posture should be toward the two major non-communist political groupings and whether we should be furnishing indirect assistance to either or both.

I would suggest that State and CIA be given the assignment to make an assessment of the situation—an updating of the recent NIE[3]—and make a recommendation with regard to support. This should be undertaken promptly, in my opinion.[4]

RAD

---

[1] Source: National Security Council, 303 Committee Files, Subject Files, Chile thru 1969. Top Secret.

[2] The presidential election in Chile was scheduled for September 4.

[3] Reference is to NIE 94–63, "The Chilean Situation and Prospects," October 3, 1963, an analysis "with particular reference to the September 1964 presidential elections." (*Foreign Relations*, 1961–1963, vol. XII, American Republics, Microfiche Supplement, Chile)

[4] At the end of the memorandum is the following typewritten note: "Mr. Jessup telephoned Mr. Dungan to advise him that Chilean proposals have been approved recently and another paper may be forthcoming in a few weeks. Mr. Dungan never returned the calls."

247.   Memorandum for the Record[1]

Washington, February 28, 1964.

SUBJECT

> Conversation between Chief and Deputy Chief, WHD with Assistant Secretary
> Mann, on 28 February 1964

1. On 28 February 1964 Chief, WHD advised the undersigned of his conversation with Mr. Mann in which Mr. Mann expressed a desire to have the Special Group approached for the purpose of obtaining its approval for election support of the Democratic Front [*less than 1 line of source text not declassified*] Mr. Mann's rationale was that Duran, being more pliable—from the American viewpoint—in economic matters than Frei: that American copper companies would conceivably be ready to invest five hundred million dollars in Chile as they were prepared to do in 1958, that Duran might draw further votes away from Allende, all this would point to the desirability of helping [*name not declassified*] at this time. Mr. Mann felt that the [*less than 1 line of source text not declassified*] injection recently given [*name not declassified*] when compared with the [*less than 1 line of source text not declassified*] a year given the CD's was out of balance; Mr. Mann felt that the support to the CD should be continued because they too offer strong competition to Allende.

2. Chief, WHD requested the undersigned to think about the best way to get a paper to the Special Group at the earliest possible date.[2]

[name not declassified][3]

---

[1] Source: Central Intelligence Agency, Job 90–347R, DDO Files, [*file name not declassified*]. Secret. Drafted in the Western Hemisphere Division.

[2] In telegram 04580 to Santiago, February 28, the CIA reported that a proposal to increase financial support to the Democratic Front would be submitted to the Special Group on March 5. The CIA also indicated that the administration intended to propose a cutback in the subsidy to the Christian Democratic Party. (Ibid.) The Special Group, however, did not meet on March 5 and failed to discuss Chile at its next meeting, March 12. (Department of State, INR/IL Historical Files, Special Group Files, Meetings)

[3] Printed from a copy that bears this typed signature.

248. Editorial Note

In a memorandum to Assistant Secretary Mann, March 6, 1964, Ralph W. Richardson, the officer-in-charge of Chilean affairs, assessed the significance of the upcoming congressional by-election in Curicó. Although the seat itself was not important, Richardson explained that the by-election would "serve to measure the relative strengths of the political parties," possibly determining "future realignments prior to the Presidential election." He pointed out that Julio Durán Neumann, the Democratic Front (DF) presidential candidate, had already declared the by-election a national "plebiscite," confident that the DF parties would repeat their share of the municipal elections in April 1963, when they received a combined 49% of the vote. The Popular Action Front (FRAP), however, also enjoyed a "special advantage" at Curicó: "its candidate is the son of the late Socialist Deputy." As for the presidential election, Richardson concluded that "the time is rapidly approaching when we should come to some basic decisions, whatever the outcome of the Curicó election. I think we need to weigh not only the probabilities of victory by the DF and the PDC, but also such issues as whether it is in the US interest to try to keep Durán and the Democratic Front in the race, even if we were to decide to do what we can to favor Frei's chances of winning." (Washington National Records Center, RG 84, Santiago Embassy Files: FRC 69 A 6507, 1964, POL 14 Elections (Presidential) 1964 (1))

On March 15 the FRAP candidate won the Curicó by-election with 39.5 percent of the vote; the next day, Durán resigned as the DF presidential candidate. McGeorge Bundy asked Ralph Dungan to comment on these events at a White House staff meeting, March 18: "Dungan said he was not really upset about the by-elections in Chile in which the communists gained, nor, he said, is the ambassador. There is a three to one chance that everything will turn out all right. Bundy reminded him that with those odds, we could lose five countries in Latin America." (Memorandum for the record by W.Y. Smith, March 18; National Defense University, Taylor Papers, Chairman's Staff Group) On March 25 Assistant Secretary Mann also discussed the political fallout from Curicó at a meeting with Central Intelligence Agency officials, including Desmond FitzGerald, J.C. King, and Cord Meyer. According to a record of the meeting: "FitzGerald said the most important thing is to keep people from panicking as a result of Curico. King proposed we give additional support [less than 1 line of source text not declassified], but through channels other than those now being used. [1 line of source text not declassified] He said the Agency is thinking in terms of [less than 1 line of source text not declassified]. Cord Meyer said this would of course have to go to the Special Group. King agreed." Mann wondered whether "a leftist Radical candidate in the race wouldn't help keep leftist Radicals from drifting to Allende." The participants agreed that "the matter will be pursued after Mann has talked with Cole." (Memorandum from Carter to Hughes, March 26; Department of State, INR/IL Historical Files, ARA–CIA Weekly Meetings, 1964–1965)

Richardson later commented on the impact Curicó had on the decision-making process: "While I agree that we certainly do have a situation to worry about, I still cannot repress a feeling of satisfaction in seeing how quickly and cleanly our 'decision' to swing behind Frei was made for us. I really had wondered before Durán's disaster whether we were going to get any definite decision from the front office on which group we should help." (Letter to Jova, April 3; Washington National Records Center, RG 84, Santiago Embassy Files: FRC 69 A 6507, 1964, POL 14 Elections (Presidential) 1964 (1))

---

249.   Memorandum From Gordon Chase of the National Security Council Staff to the President's Special Assistant for National Security Affairs (Bundy)[1]

Washington, March 19, 1964.

SUBJECT

Chiefs of Mission Conference—Brazil and Chile

I attended a few sessions of the Chiefs of Mission Conference. One of the more interesting included discussions by Ambassadors Gordon and Cole about the situations in Brazil and Chile.

[Omitted here is discussion on Brazil; see Document 185.]

Chile

1. In contrast to Brazil, the *economic* situation in Chile is remarkably good. Ambassador Cole said there is a growth rate of 5%, unemployment is at a low level, and savings are up. Progress has been made in land and tax reform. There are, of course, some problems—e.g. unfavorable balance of payments and inflation. These problems tend to be related to Chile's desire to push forward quickly in the field of economic development.

---

[1] Source: Johnson Library, National Security File, Country File, Latin America, Vol. I, 11/63–6/64. Secret.

One of the outstanding aspects of the Chilean economy is the extent of U.S. involvement. The U.S. has big stakes in copper and manufacturing of all kinds. The huge U.S. involvement in Chile leads the Chileans to an ambivalent attitude towards the U.S. For example, while they like us in many ways, there is plenty of latent hostility.

2. Chile's biggest problem is *political*—the election for the Presidency in September (it should be noted that in Chile the President has great power). It now appears that there may be only two primary candidates—Frei, the moderate, and Allende, the extreme leftist. If there is a two man race, Frei is very likely to win. If there is a three or four man race, Allende's chances will be improved. On balance, Ambassador Cole estimates that the odds are 3 to 1 against Allende winning in September. He noted, however, that a year ago he would have placed the odds at 10 to 1.

3. In effect, there are four possibilities vis-à-vis Allende and the election.

(a) Allende could get beaten at the polls.

(b) Allende could get the most votes but not get the Presidency. According to Chilean law, if no candidate gets a majority, the assembly chooses one of the two leading candidates. Normally, it chooses the candidate with the most votes; however, it does have constitutional power to pick the second biggest vote-getter.

(c) Allende could win but be overthrown by the armed forces or the "carbinieri"; this would have to be done before Allende gets a chance to consolidate his power. Normally, the armed forces are very non-political, but they might conceivably intervene if Allende won.

(d) Allende could win and stay in power.

4. If Allende wins and stays in power, we are in trouble. For example, he will probably nationalize the copper mines, which in turn, might end the aid program because of the Hickenlooper amendment;[2] this, in turn, could lead Chile to ask the Bloc for economic aid. There are very few significant short term things we can do between now and election time. Generally speaking, we should simply do what we can to get people to back Frei.

GC

---

[2] This amendment to the Foreign Assistance Act of 1961 was initially approved in August 1962, and subsequently revised in December 1963. Sponsored by Senators Bourke B. Hickenlooper (R–Iowa) and E. Ross Adair (R–Indiana), the amendment stipulated that the President suspend assistance to any country that expropriated the property of U.S. citizens or corporations without proper compensation. (76 Stat. 260)

250.   Memorandum Prepared for the Special Group[1]

Washington, April 1, 1964.

SUBJECT

    Support for the Chilean Presidential Elections of 4 September 1964

REFERENCES

    A. Memorandum for The Special Group, dated 13 December 1963, Subject: Financial Support to Chilean Democratic Front [*1 line of source text not declassified*][2]

    B. Memorandum for The Special Group, dated 27 August 1962, Subject: Support to the Christian Democratic Party of Chile (PDC)[3]

1. Summary

This is a proposal for political and propaganda action directed at the defeat of Salvador Allende, the Communist-supported candidate for the Chilean presidential elections of 4 September 1964. The sum of $750,000 is being requested for the implementation of courses of action that will contribute to this objective by increasing the organizational efficiency and campaigning ability of the Christian Democratic Party, by inducing as far as feasible, supporters of the former Democratic Front to cast their votes for Frei and deny their support to Allende, and by attempting to discourage third candidacies—such as Jorge Prat's. It should be noted that representatives of the Christian Democratic Party visited, on their own initiative, the U.S. Embassy in Santiago on 26 March and, after presenting their current and proposed budgets, asked for a one million dollar subsidy for Frei's campaign. The Embassy and our field representative recommended that this amount be provided for this purpose.

Funds for this activity have not been programmed for FY 1964 and are not available within the Agency; it is recommended that this amount be obtained from the Agency Reserve for Contingencies.

2. Problem

To provide financial support, as necessary, to the democratic forces of Chile in an effort to defeat Salvador Allende, the Communist-

---

[1] Source: National Security Council, 303 Committee Files, Subject Files, Chile thru 1969. Secret; Eyes Alone. Dungan forwarded the paper to Bundy as an attachment to an April 2 memorandum in which he commented: "As I told you this morning, I have no way of knowing whether $750,000 is the right amount, but I certainly would not balk at it. You might inquire, however, why the cost of campaigning in [*text not declassified*] Chile is always so much higher than it is in the United States. As I indicated, I will follow up with Des[mond FitzGerald] on the implementation of this program without getting in any further than is absolutely necessary." (Ibid.)

[2] Not printed. (Department of State, INR/IL Historical Files, Special Group Files, Meetings, December 19, 1963)

[3] Not printed. (Ibid., August 30, 1962)

sponsored candidate of FRAP. The objectives of this support are: (a) to minimize the number of democratic votes that may drift to FRAP as a result of the fractionalization of the Democratic Front; (b) to obtain the support of democratic parties and organizations for Eduardo Frei, the Christian Democratic candidate; (c) to strengthen the Christian Democratic organizational structure and campaigning ability so that it can appeal to the largest number of Chileans including FRAP voters, former Democratic Front supporters, and new voters; and (d) to induce "Independent" candidates, such as Jorge Prat, to withdraw from the campaign.

3. Factors Bearing on the Problem

a. The Curico by-elections of 15 March 1964 changed the Chilean political spectrum radically by forcing the withdrawal of the Democratic Front's presidential candidate, Julio Duran, and disrupting the Democratic Front coalition composed of the Liberal, Conservative, and Radical parties.

b. The dissolution of the Democratic Front has polarized the elections around the candidacies of Eduardo Frei of the Christian Democratic Party and Salvador Allende of FRAP. In this situation the preferences of the voters who had been committed to Duran become the key to the election and to the defeat of Allende. In turn, the attitudes of these voters will be heavily influenced by the official position of the Radical, Conservative, and Liberal parties. The parties of the Democratic Front coalition polled approximately 921,000 votes in the April 1963 municipal elections which amounted to 46% of the votes cast. (Out of this 46%, the Radicals got 21.6%, the Liberals got 13.1%, and the Conservatives got 11.3%.) As a basis of comparison it should be noted that the Christian Democratic Party obtained 453,000 (23%) votes and FRAP 583,000 (29%) votes at that time. Since the estimated electorate for the 1964 presidential elections is two and one quarter million, either candidate will have to poll roughly one million, one hundred, and fifty thousand votes to win. Thus, even if there is no precise correlation between the voting patterns of municipal as compared to presidential elections it is clear that neither candidate can hope to win the elections of 4 September without appealing to a substantial number of the Conservative, Liberal, Radical, and new voters.

c. It can be said, in general, that the majority of the Conservative vote will be for Frei in view of this party's Catholic tradition. The Liberal Party, which is staunchly anti-Communist, also can probably be depended upon to deliver a substantial segment of its vote to Frei. Historical factors, including the traditional anti-clericalism of the Radical Party and its past participation in a Popular Front Government, indicate that a substantial number of votes will probably shift from that party to FRAP.

d. The ability of the Christian Democratic Party to appeal openly for the vote of the former Democratic Front is seriously limited by Frei's need to maintain his image as an honest and dedicated leader of the underprivileged who is above political "deals." Conversely, the leaders of the former parties of the Democratic Front, especially the Radical Party which depends heavily on patronage to maintain its organization intact, would be hard pressed to throw their support to Frei in the absence of a PDC public appeal for their assistance. This dilemma poses the need for an external stimulus which will bring the Democratic Front parties and the PDC to a sophisticated agreement on the support of Frei for the presidential elections.

e. Apart from the problem noted above, there remains the persistent need to assist the PDC in the construction of an efficient capillary organization that will conduct an effective campaign, especially among peasants and women. A tentative analysis of the Curico election results indicate that the greatest FRAP gains and Democratic Front losses came from the category of peasants and women. Consequently, Frei must make a major organizational effort to counteract FRAP influence in these areas. The Curico campaign also demonstrated that the PDC organization is inadequately supplied with vehicles, party workers, loudspeakers, and the other accouterments of an effective campaign.

f. Thus, as a result of the situation outlined above, it becomes necessary to take all possible action to assist Frei in his campaign and to limit the number of former Democratic Front votes that might go to Allende. Some of the methods that will be used to achieve these objectives, insofar as feasible, are:

(1) Bring pressure to bear on the Radical Party to prevent it from formally endorsing Allende, or, failing in this, to remain neutral or to run its own candidate if it appears that he will not damage Frei. In the event the Radical Party declares for Allende, financial assistance will have to be provided to individual Radical leaders or groups capable of bringing Radical voters into the Frei camp.

(2) To influence the Conservative and Liberal parties to support Frei in a manner that will not damage his image as a reform candidate. To achieve this it will be necessary to provide financial assistance to the Liberal and Conservative parties or those of their leaders who will work to swing their votes behind Frei.

(3) Provide a substantial subsidy [less than 1 line of source text not declassified] for the purpose of strengthening his electoral machine and campaign capabilities. Efforts will also be made to influence Frei to reach a private agreement with the Radicals for their support in exchange for some patronage.

(4) Bring pressure to bear on Jorge Prat, partly through Conservative and Liberal leaders, to induce his withdrawal from the presidential contest.

(5) Provide financial assistance, as necessary, to ancillary organizations, such as youth and student groups, peasant organizations, slum dwellers' associations, labor unions, and women's clubs, to bring their votes to Frei.

(6) In the latter stages of the campaign to buy some votes outright if required.

(7) [3 *lines of source text not declassified*]

(8) Some funds will also be utilized for specialized propaganda operations, some of which will be black, to denigrate Allende.

4. *Coordination*

This proposal has been coordinated with the Assistant Secretary of State for Inter-American Affairs who believes that—should it appear necessary at a later date—additional funds should be sought.[4]

In this regard, it should be noted that on 26 March 1964 the Embassy was visited by Frei's [*less than 1 line of source text not declassified*] campaign managers who presented their current budget showing a rate of expenditure of $100,000 per month which they claim they are meeting with much difficulty. They also presented a proposed campaign budget for the next five months of $300,000 per month which they state would be required to mount an effective campaign. The Chileans suggested that the U.S. Government make up this difference which amounts to one million dollars for the period from now to election time. The Embassy and our field representative reviewed the budgets, felt they did not seem unreasonable, and subsequently recommended that the Chilean's request for one million dollars be granted as soon as possible.

At the same time, the Embassy strongly recommended that the mechanics of the operation insure that this assistance not seem to come from U.S. sources.

5. *Recommendation*

It is recommended that:

a. Action under paragraph 3 f above be approved for immediate implementation.

b. The U.S. Government provide $750,000 for this purpose.

c. Funds [*1½ lines of source text not declassified*], be passed covertly in a manner [*less than 1 line of source text not declassified*] to infer

---

[4] In a memorandum to U. Alexis Johnson, April 2, Mann approved the proposal with the following clarification: 1) that the money be divided, [*text not declassified*] going to support Frei and the remainder to other objectives; 2) that Frei be made "explicitly aware" that the U.S. Government was the source of the money; and 3) that the procedures for transferring the money be "closely coordinated with Mr. Mann." (Ibid., April 2, 1964)

U.S. Government origin of the funds yet permit us plausible denial if necessary. This will be done by attributing the funds, explicitly, to U.S. non-official sources. This approach is required in an effort to obtain some essential leverage [*less than 1 line of source text not declassified*]. It is realized that this recommendation does not reflect the Embassy's position.[5]

---

[5] The Special Group met on April 2 at 3:30 p.m. in the White House Situation Room. (National Archives and Records Administration, RG 59, U. Alexis Johnson Files: Lot 90 D 408, Date Books, 1964) The minutes of the meeting record the decision on Chile as follows: "The paper, 'Support for Chilean Presidential Elections,' was approved. Mr. FitzGerald announced that a solution to the slight difference of opinion between Ambassador Cole and the CAS in Santiago had been reached and that attribution of U.S. support would be inferred but there should be no evidence of proof. Mr. FitzGerald indicated that this was operationally feasible." (Department of State, INR/IL Historical Files, Special Group Files, April 9, 1964, 116)

---

251.   Telegram From the Embassy in Chile to the Department of State[1]

Santiago, April 22, 1964, 7:15 p.m.

939. Subject: Assessment Socialist-Communist Candidate Salvador Allende. Ref: Deptel 591;[2] Embassy A–703, 1/29/63;[3] A–755, 4/10/64.[4]

Allende is a chameleonic person who over years has appeared on occasion as idealistic socialist reformer who believes democracy and other times as military revolutionist striving bring revolution a la Cuba to Chile. His motivation and drive for more than twenty years have centered on his ambition become first Marxist president of Chile and be first to bring "popular democracy" to power in South America. The essential opportunism of man is evident but always within a leftist sphere or orientation. He does not possess unusual intelligence and his

---

[1] Source: National Archives and Records Administration, RG 59, Central Files 1964–66, POL 14 CHILE. Confidential; Priority. Repeated to POLADs at CINCLANT and CINCSO.

[2] Telegram 591 to Santiago, April 17, requested the Embassy's assessment of Salvador Allende: his personality, political objectives, and the short-term effect of his election, including the likelihood of a Communist takeover. (Ibid.)

[3] Airgram A–703 from Santiago, January 29, 1963, reported that the Popular Action Front (FRAP) had nominated Allende as its presidential candidate. (Ibid., Central Files 1961–63, 725.00/1–2963)

[4] In airgram A–755 from Santiago the Embassy transmitted and analyzed the FRAP campaign platform. (Ibid., Central Files, 1964–66, POL 12 CHILE)

ideas and program have changed little, if at all, over years. As politician he is good speaker and hard worker. Personally he is vain, quick tempered, easily offended, socially as well as politically ambitious, able turn on or off at will a considerable social charm. He is sensitive to charge he would be dominated by Communists or that he would institute anti-democratic measures. Nevertheless were he to achieve power we think he could be led by events into being harsh and ruthless with his opponents but more likely use exile than prison or pardon. It is probable that he thinks in terms Marxist regime similar Castro's Cuba in its free-wheeling, relatively independent line but more sophisticated, cultured, without emotional excesses of "tropical" country such as Cuba.

Domestically his major objectives appear be:

1) Nationalization copper, nitrate, iron, public utilities, banks, insurance, foreign commerce; 2) drastic land reform; 3) fully planned economy; 4) franchise to illiterates and military enlisted personnel.

Foreign policy objectives appear be:

1) Alignment with underdeveloped countries; 2) establish relations bloc countries and ChiComs; 3) drastic reduction US influence in Chile and Hemisphere including termination Military Assistance Pacts; 4) closer association with Cuba and pressure on OAS end Cuba's isolation and drastic but not clearly specified changes in OAS structure. As nearly as we can tell there is no visible disagreement on any above objectives between socialists and Communists. Presumably Allende as well as Ampuero socialists[5] desire greater degree independence from Moscow, are against Communist proposed "single party of left" and logical and emotional grounds exist to explain rivalry which now present between parties. Despite Allende's periodic statements (often to American press representatives) that he is not a Communist, and rather wide-spread belief among Chileans including many opposed to him that he basically democratic, mild socialist opposed to communism, record shows he has collaborated with Communists for more than 15 years with no apparent difficulty. We conclude shrewd Communist Secretary General Luis Corvalan has based his party's support for Allende on some sureness of expectation that serious disagreements with Communists on Allende's part will not arise. Probable that even should Allende be tempted to turn on Communist partners once in office he would be unable do so due perhaps as much to patterns and associations he has established over years as to any direct control by Communists.

---

[5] Followers of Raúl Ampuero Díaz, secretary general of the Socialist Party.

If Allende should win the Communists will be able rightfully to claim most of the credit and we would assume they will press for due recognition in the form of positions within Allende's government and will be granted them although socialists have told us and have been saying for years that these would not be key posts such as Interior or Defense. For Allende would be difficult say no to his principal supporting force which only one able effectively bring people into streets to support him should he desire it. We would expect many of Communists in various important but not top positions in ministries would come from those hundreds Chilean technicians and professionals now in Cuba who can be expected return immediately should Allende win. We would expect effective Commie control of several ministries could be achieved within few months after inauguration. We estimate bottom would drop out already shaky economy with Allende victory and beset by problems he likely turn naturally to Communists for support on more and more matters and in more and more areas. We think also Chilean middle-class will be rather easily intimidated by actual and threatened mob pressures which Communists can provide. Commie control likely become de facto in gradual manner not apparent most Chileans at least for many months.

Factors against takeover are first and most important armed forces including Carabineros, secondly Congress and thirdly strong Chilean democratic tradition which prevails in great majority presently politically aware Chileans. Communists are well aware obstacle armed forces present but they and Allende as well under existing system which calls for retirement of all officers senior to an officer promoted head service and promotion for all those below, at least have instrument which if played well offers possibility keeping armed forces neutral on sidelines political arena.

Among immediate effects Allende victory may be virtual panic among many upper and upper-middle class circles and certain paralization private investment. Our guess is Allende would try restore confidence by acting in reassuring manner fearing military and thinking of congressional elections in March 1965, but he would quickly have to take some nationalization step satisfy his supporters (most widely popular and least likely cause him trouble here would be telephone company). Should he gain control Congress through added socialist/Communist seats and possibly agreement with radicals and/or left-wing Christian Democrats he would press ahead more vigorously with his program. We would expect Communists to favor "respectable" democratic via pacifica course until such time as they have achieved control political apparatus and at least have neutralized armed forces. We think possible but not probable that should he win by very small plurality over Frei and Congress hesitate on naming him he will gamble on armed forces traditional non-interventionist role and bring mobs into streets pressure Congress and if successful might then continue with drastic measures in hope of gaining sufficient control to handle likely reaction from democratic forces.

Negative economic impact will be very great immediately and probably over short-term as well. Allende would probably try expand activities and efforts existing GOC institutions which directly involved in economy in effort compensate for lacks and lags in private sector. He will undoubtedly seek help from bloc and "unaligned" countries but conceivably might make unreasonable request of USG (e.g. low interest loan pay for expropriation copper companies and utilities) expecting turn down which he could use as ostensible justification Chilean public for turning [to] bloc. In general economic deterioration after Allende victory would tend stimulate and be used justify extreme internal measures toward full statist economic power as well as shift to excessive Chilean dependence Communist bloc aid and trade.

Jova

---

252. **Transcript of Telephone Conversation Between Director of Central Intelligence McCone and the Assistant Secretary of State for Inter-American Affairs (Mann)**[1]

Washington, April 28, 1964, 11:35 a.m.

DCI: Good morning, Tom.

M: Good morning, how are you?

DCI: I'm fine, how are you?

M: Fine. You sound like you are in a well.

DCI: I've got Pat Carter[2] here and we were talking over Chile. I wanted him to hear what we were talking about, so if it is agreeable with you, I'll continue to use this loud speaker.

M: O.K. sure.

DCI: Now, every place I go I get alarming reports on the intense effort of the Andes [?] backed probably by the Communists. I even got it from [3½ *lines of source text not declassified*] a frightening story of the

---

[1] Source: Central Intelligence Agency, Job 80–B01285A, DCI (McCone) Files, Telephone Calls, 3/4/64–5/19/64. Eyes Only. No classification marking. The text was prepared in the CIA from a tape recording.

[2] Marshall Carter, Deputy Director of Central Intelligence.

intensification of the Socialist Communists. He claimed they had 300 sound trucks and 3500 personnel, of which 3400 are members of the Communist Party, working on the Andes campaign at this time. I have no doubt that this is exaggerated . . .

M: Nevertheless, John, it is very serious. Are you familiar with the program we are working on?

DCI: Yes, I am thoroughly familiar with it.

M: Is there anything else we can do?

DCI: Yes there is. I do not think that your Embassy is set up to handle this problem properly. In the first place, Cole, the Ambassador, is not there and won't be there until the end of June. Secondly, this is an area, my people tell me, where he is lacking in experience and also lacking in courage. I think you ought to take a very good look at that. He is coming out of an academic life and this is something he doesn't know anything about you see. Second thing, your deputy chief of mission, fellow named Jova, I don't get a very good report on him either. I don't know him.

M: What we planned to do with Cole, psychologically mainly, was to get him to try to go back, fly down for 10 days in the middle of his vacation. He is a very hard man to handle. He wants to quit, you know.[3]

DCI: Yes, I know. He had his resignation . . .

M: And we thought it would be a mistake to send a new man down just on the eve of.

DCI: Yes, I think that is right, but I wondered whether you didn't have some political activist expert you could put down there on TDY.

M: Well, I think that is right. We'll do that.

DCI: What we have done—I have taken J.C. King and removed him of all responsibility. He is generating a lot of ideas [1½ lines of source text not declassified] and I am going to have the whole subject reviewed at the Special Group on Thursday[4] so that the White House and everybody will be in circuit on it. I would appreciate it very much if you could go over, if you are gong to be here Thursday, and sit in on it. Can you do that?

---

[3] In November 1963 Martin recommended that Rusk call the Ambassador; Jova had suggested that Cole might stay for the presidential election if his arm were "properly twisted." According to Martin, this tactic was successful. (Martin, *Kennedy and Latin America*, p. 322) The Department, however, informed Cole on February 5 that the White House would announce his resignation in 2 days. (Telegram 425 to Santiago, February 5; National Archives and Records Administration, RG 59, Central Files 1964–66, PER Cole, Charles W.) Two weeks later, President Johnson asked Cole to remain in Santiago until September; Cole agreed to do so. (Telegram 682 from Santiago, February 19; ibid.)

[4] April 30.

M: Yes, I can do that. I would like to. I have had the same idea that we should really wire in the White House on that.

DCI: All right. Well, let's do that on Thursday. I'll get Mac to put it on the calendar first thing and that would set it at 3:30 Thursday afternoon.[5]

M: I'll be there and in the meantime, is that the only thing that occurs to you that we are not already doing?

DCI: Well, I think we have to get in closer touch with this business group that [*name not declassified*] heads and see if they might . . . .

M: Well, we had a meeting on this the other day. J.C. was there. He can tell you all about it. On what they can do, I asked the small group of people not to tell me what they were going to do, but to tell J.C. Whatever had to be done to do it through him.

DCI: He has an idea that they might move in on this beef problem which you are familiar with, I guess.

M: I asked yesterday that somebody get [to] work on that. I was very discouraged. Tom Taylor[6] was talking about the beef thing which is important and I was unconvinced they were really going to get enough beef there. I asked the fellows yesterday to send a telegram out on this also, but . . .

DCI: Out to where?

M: I am going to work on it today to see what we can do about the beef. The trouble is that the passage to the Andes is going to be closed in about two weeks. If we don't get the cattle through on hoof then there isn't much storage facility there for frozen beef. We are going to have to fly it in almost by shuttle. And then there is the problem of price, of bringing the price down from the present level of 1750 pesos to 1350 pesos. That is a matter of money. But the first thing is to get the beef there or to get a secure way of making sure it will be there.

DCI: Well, we can go into that.

---

[5] At its meeting on April 30 the Special Group decided: "(a) that contact should be made with Ambassador Cole to urge his return for a visit in the coming weeks, (b) that talks with American business interests should proceed to determine the amount and method of their support, and (c) it was further decided that higher authority would be apprised of the closeness and importance of this Chilean election and that the Group itself would continue to review the problem in the coming weeks." (Memorandum for the Record, May 1; National Security Council, 303 Committee Files, Minutes, April 30, 1964) According to notes of the meeting taken by Hughes, "Mr. McCone said he had spoken twice to the Secretary about it [Chile] on the phone within the past 24 hours." Hughes also noted that "Mr. Mann asked how much money might be secured from American businessmen that McCone had been in contact with. McCone said about a million dollars." (Department of State, INR/IL Historical Files, Special Group Files, April 30, 1964)

[6] Reference is evidently to A. Thomas Taylor, president of International Packers, Ltd.

M: We are going ahead with a rather large PL 480 program and that is on the price of food again, but we are giving them all that they are asking for. The telegram we sent[7] was to ask them if this was really enough. We didn't want to treat this as a routine PL 480 type deal. We want to get enough food down there to bring prices down. I think your idea is a good one. We'll get the best guy we can down there on TDY.

DCI: Yes, that is what I would do, if I were you. We will keep J.C. in and we will give him all the support he needs.

M: Yes, I agree with that.

DCI: So that we will be . . . .

M: If you have any other concrete ideas, you'll let us know?

DCI: I'll get [name not declassified] on the telephone. He has called me once or twice on this and I might even go up and sit down and talk with him personally. I know him very well. I'll see if that can be arranged.

M: O.K. and if you get anything else concrete, let me know.

DCI: Will do.

M: I am worried about this. I think this is the biggest problem we have. O.K. John. Thank you.

DCI: Goodbye.[8]

---

[7] Telegram 613 to Santiago, April 27. (Johnson Library, National Security File, Country File, Chile, Vol. I, 1/64–8/64)

[8] McCone later attached a note entitled "Information on the Beef Requirements in Chile," in which he estimated that Chile would require "approximately 5,000 tons of cattle on the hoof per month."

---

253. Memorandum From the Assistant Secretary of State for Inter-American Affairs (Mann) to Secretary of State Rusk[1]

Washington, May 1, 1964.

SUBJECT

Presidential Election in Chile

---

[1] Source: Johnson Library, National Security File, Country File, Chile, Vol. I, 1/64–8/64. Top Secret. Drafted by Dentzer.

This memorandum will inform you of the status of the presidential race and indicate US Government activity concerning this important election.[2]

Situation

On September 4, two months before our own elections, a critical presidential election is scheduled in Chile. The two leading candidates are Salvador Allende, an avowed Marxist leader of a Communist-Socialist coalition, and Eduardo Frei. Frei heads the Christian Democratic Party, a somewhat left of center reform party close to the Catholic Church. In the 1958 election Allende came within 32,000 votes of winning a plurality and becoming president.

At this point in the campaign, most observers rate Frei slightly ahead, but the race will be extremely close and many things could happen in the four months before the election. The democratic forces are presently split, with Radical party candidate Julio Duran back in the race after the results of a congressional bi-election in March shattered his coalition of rightist parties and indicated he stood almost no chance of being elected. Also working against Frei is a Chilean tolerance for native Communists, who have long been on the public scene, and a long-standing anti-clerical feeling which hurts the Church-identified Christian Democrats.

Discussion of U.S. Action Program

Clearly, the September election will be determined by factors which are deeply rooted in the political, economic, and social fabric of the Chilean scene and by the campaign abilities of the major contenders. Given the consequences, however, if this major Latin American nation should become the first country in the hemisphere to freely choose an avowed Marxist as its elected president, the Department, CIA, and other agencies have embarked on a major campaign to prevent Allende's election and to support Frei, the only candidate who has a chance of beating him. Chief elements in this campaign are the following:

1) Providing covert assistance through secret CIA channels to Frei's campaign chest and for other anti-Allende campaign uses. [*less*

---

[2] Bundy forwarded this memorandum to the President under a May 13 covering memorandum that noted the importance of the upcoming Presidential election in Chile. "In essence, the problem we face is that a very popular and attractive candidate, named Allende, who has thrown in his lot with the Communists, has more than a fighting chance to win. We have a coordinated Government-wide program of action to strengthen his opponent and support actions in Chile which will work to the advantage of those now in power. It is a highly fluid situation and one in which there may have to be further action as we get into the summer. I have been very much encouraged by the determination and unity which all Departments of the Government are showing on this one, and we will be watching it very closely, but I do think you ought to know about it yourself." (Ibid., Memos to the President, McGeorge Bundy, Vol. IV)

than 1 line of source text not declassified] has been approved by the Special Group and earmarked for these purposes, and additional funds will be sought as necessary.

2) Providing AID loans in CY 64 amounting to approximately $70 million, principally in program budget loans to maintain the level of the government investment budget, thereby keeping the economy as a whole active and unemployment low. $60 million of this aid has already been extended.[3]

3) Examining means to alleviate the rising cost of living through efforts to increase the supply and lower the price of major foods. We are making available $20 million of PL 480, almost half of which is wheat. In addition, we are reviewing our on-going PL 480 Title III food distribution program through voluntary organizations to expand it wherever possible; the current FY 64 program costs $12.5 million and touches an estimated 2 million people, 1/4 of Chile's population.

4) Assisting U.S. business groups with information and advice through David Rockefeller's Business Group for Latin America—a blue ribbon group of American companies in Latin America—in their support of a Chilean business group helping Frei and attempting to hold down prices.

5) Organizing a political action and propaganda campaign through CIA contacts in coordination with or parallel to Frei's campaign. This includes voter registration drives, propaganda, person-to-person campaigning in the cities and rural areas, and arrangements to provide some Italian Christian Democratic organizers to Frei as advisers on campaign techniques.

6) Encouraging the GOC and IMF to avoid rupturing their standby stabilization agreement, a break which would have damaging financial and psychological consequences. An IMF team presently is completing a review in Chile, and a Chilean team sent by President Alessandri will arrive in Washington on May 4 for discussions with the Department.

7) Attempting discreetly through normal U.S. contacts with the non-political Chilean military and police to encourage their rising awareness of the subversion which would take place under an Allende government.

8) Continuing USIA placement in Chile of unattributed material, giving special care to low-keyed efforts which do not expose U.S. Government involvement.

---

[3] On April 3 the United States and Chile signed an agreement to provide $55 million in program loan assistance in CY 1964. For an account on how the funds were utilized, see United States Senate, Committee on Government Operations, Subcommittee on Foreign Aid Expenditures, *United States Foreign Aid in Action: A Case Study,* Washington, 1966, p. 31.

9) Encouraging, through covert ties and private U.S. organizations, effective anti-Allende efforts by Chilean organizations including the Roman Catholic Church, trade union groups, and other influential bodies, such as the anti-clerical Masons.

We are attempting to insure that extraordinary caution is observed in this action campaign to conceal official U.S. government interest, and we have rejected several ideas which have seemed to entail undue risks or excessive American involvement.

Personnel

I plan to strengthen our Embassy in Chile in the four months prior to the election by adding to the present staff there next week a top-ranking political officer with an excellent record on the Cuban desk, Robert Hurwitch.[4]

I also plan to raise with Ambassador Cole, who recently arrived in the U.S. by ship on two months' leave from post, the desirability of interrupting his vacation to return to Chile soon for a ten-day period. I am aware of the background concerning his two months' leave, but I am concerned about possible reactions in Chile and the U.S. to so long an absence in relation to this critical election.[5]

---

[4] Hurwitch was given the rank of first secretary in the Embassy's political section. Although he reported to Santiago in May, Hurwitch did not officially assume his position until July 5.

[5] Later that afternoon Mann told Rusk that "he would like to talk about Chile and a number of problems." A meeting was set for 6 p.m. (Rusk to Mann, May 1, 12:14 p.m., National Archives and Records Administration, RG 59, Rusk Files: Lot 72 D 192, Telephone Calls 4/20/64–5/22/64) According to Rusk's Appointment Book Rusk met Mann at 6:35 p.m. (Johnson Library) No substantive record of the conversation has been found.

254. Telegram From the Deputy Chief of Mission in Chile (Jova) to the Assistant Secretary of State for Inter-American Affairs (Mann)[1]

Santiago, May 5, 1964.

76320. Please pass to Mann and Dentzer from Jova.

1. Accompanied by Robinson[2] I had a two-hour conversation May 4 with Frei at latter's home. Also present was latter's top political advisor, Juan de Dios Carmona. At end of conversation[3] Frei asked to see me alone.

2. He started off this private conversation by expressing gravest concern activities and indiscretion of [name not declassified]. He said he had been horrified to hear that on at least two occasions [name not declassified] had spoken indiscriminately in regard to USG aid to the Frei campaign. On one occasion speaking to Salvador Pubill, PDC campaign finance manager, [name not declassified] told him he saw no emergency requirement in collecting funds from industrialists for campaign in view of fact that Frei was to receive one million dollars in assistance from USG. On another occasion he told Antonio Baeza of COPEC that the financial resources of the business community should be kept in reserve for the congressional elections in March as the Frei campaign was well supplied with funds amounting to approximately one million dollars from USG and private sources. On a third occasion he said (it was not clear to whom) that on his recent trip to the U.S. he had agreed arrange with [name not declassified] and his group that the technique to follow would be to feed funds raised by [name not declassified] to Frei to help him win campaign but with ultimate intention of using this as a noose with which to control him once he were elected president.

---

[1] Source: Department of State, INR/IL Historical Files, Chile, 1964–1967. Secret; Priority. Also addressed to Dentzer. The telegram was forwarded through CIA channels.

[2] John P. Robinson, AID mission director in Santiago.

[3] During the earlier discussion, Frei expressed "unusual optimism" concerning his electoral prospects—although he "jokingly observed that his selfish interests should lead him paint a bleaker picture to the US authorities for obvious reasons." (Telegram 999 from Santiago, May 5; National Archives and Records Administration, RG 59, Central Files 1964–66, POL 14 CHILE) Jova urged Frei to reconsider his position on a presidential election by congress should no candidate receive an absolute majority of the vote; Frei had publicly accepted the tradition of selecting the front-runner, even though the Chilean constitution formally allowed a choice between the two leading candidates. Jova reported that "this is obviously a course which does not appeal to him [Frei], but which he might be prepared to follow if the margin by which he trailed were small and providing the military as well as the congress were cooperative." (Telegram 1005 from Santiago, May 5; ibid.)

3. Frei said that he has only seen [*name not declassified*] three times in his life and on only one occasion, at a recent tea at his house, had serious campaign matters been discussed. He was concerned however at [*name not declassified*] thrashing around in a variety of political fields in which he was unfamiliar and in which he seemed to be enjoying "playing cops and robbers". He told me that he had impression [*name not declassified*] respected and paid attention to me and hoped that I would convey to him the message to be discreet. Statements such as those he had made above might already have done great damage to his campaign and moreover they were in large part untrue. He hoped that all concerned would be extremely careful on any loose talk on any matters connected with financial assistance. Much of this in any case was still undecided upon but any linking of him to USG or U.S. private sector financial assistance was fatal.

4. (FitzGerald and Gomez felt that their own conversation with [*name not declassified*] seems bear out some of above allegations. Hence we decided Belton[4] in view his close friendship might be best person admonish [*name not declassified*] and we asked him to do so prior his departure last night's plane.)

5. As will be reported in separate telegram[5] Frei said he thought that Duran should be kept in the race at any price. Although some members of his party disagreed with him he said he still was of firm opinion that a withdrawal by Duran might have as its consequence the endorsement of Allende by Radical Party or instances of individual Radical senators and deputies proclaiming Allende individually. Such actions would then enhance Allende's stature as "democratic", respectable candidate and would serve increase his independent votes.

6. He spoke with considerable cordiality in regard to Duran and expressed hope that some way might be found help him financially. While such support might be obtained from Radical bankers and business men, he doubted that enough would be forthcoming and felt that serious consideration should be given subsidizing him either from PDC campaign funds or from other (presumably USG) sources. He said subsidy required would add up to some escudos 450,000. From this campaign chest Radical deputies would in turn be subsidized at rote escudos 4,000 apiece. He said some "dignified" manner to channel this subsidy would have to be found, that it should not in any way be through PDC officials but might preferably be handled through some pro-Radical banker or business man.

---

[4] William Belton, then political advisor to the Commander in Chief, Southern Command, had been counselor at the Embassy in Santiago, 1956–1958.

[5] Telegram 1000 from Santiago, May 5. (National Archives and Records Administration, RG 59, Central Files 1964–66, POL 14 CHILE) On April 5 Durán reentered the race as the candidate of the Radical Party.

7. Frei said he would call on Duran personally in next few days in order try salve his feelings which have been hurt by other PDC activities and church attitudes. He would speak to [*name not declassified*] on latter and asked me to do same. (I intend to do this by merely reporting to [*name not declassified*] without comment some of Duran's complaints.)[6]

---

[6] Mann replied on May 18: "We informed [*name not declassified*] of [*name not declassified*] indiscretions and told him effort being made put gag on [*name not declassified*]. We have no reason to believe American business community will make contributions to campaign." (Mann to Jova, undated; Department of State, INR/IL Historical Files, ARA Country Files, Chile, 1964–1967)

---

255. Memorandum From the Deputy Director of Coordination for Intelligence and Research (Carter) to the Director of the Bureau of Intelligence and Research (Hughes)[1]

Washington, May 7, 1964.

SUBJECT

ARA–Agency Meeting of May 6, 1964

PARTICIPANTS

ARA—Mr. Mann, Mr. Adams, Mr. Pryce, Mr. Dentzer; Agency—Col. King, [*name not declassified*]; INR/DDC—Mr. Carter

Chile

Tom Mann referred to the attached communication[2] from our Chargé in Santiago indicating that [*less than 1 line of source text not declassified*] has been making indiscreet remarks about U.S. Government aid for Frei.

Mann said the people on the ground are apparently right, that we must have a low noise level.

[*name not declassified*] said he had always thought [*name not declassified*] "indiscreet", and added that what he didn't like was [*name not declassified*] trying to bleed us and not pay himself. (See attachment #2.)[3]

---

[1] Source: Department of State, INR/IL Historical Files, ARA/CIA Weekly Meetings, 1964–1965. Secret. Also addressed to Denney and Evans. Forwarded through Scott.

[2] Document 254.

[3] Not attached.

King said we should decide whether we will give money to the [*name not declassified*] group. Mann interjected that [*name not declassified*] was a blabbermouth. King agreed, but pointed out the influence [*name not declassified*] has [*less than 1 line of source text not declassified*]. Mann wanted to know how much money was involved and King thought roughly $300,000 from the private sector.

Mann said there was some question now of whether the private sector should give any support. He said he would see [*name not declassified*] the next day and that we owed it to him to tell him [*name not declassified*] is talking. Mann's inclination is to back away right now in view of what [*name not declassified*] has said. Mann then asked, "do you agree I advise him to lay off"?

The consensus of those present was in the affirmative.

[*name not declassified*] said the post had recommended [*less than 1 line of source text not declassified*] for [*name not declassified*], but that he himself thought [*less than 1 line of source text not declassified*] would be better.

King explained that the money could be passed in such a way that "[*name not declassified*] will know he is under obligation but will be unable to prove it."

Mann said he just wanted to be sure [*name not declassified*] stayed in the race. King and Dentzer wanted to lay on some conditions beyond just staying in the race, which they said [*name not declassified*] would do anyway.

Mann summed up by saying we had agreed on three things:

"1) We have decided to give [*name not declassified*] money.
"2) I will advise [*name not declassified*] to stay out and
"3) on Frei, go all out—give him whatever he needs."

King wanted to know if he could give [*less than 1 line of source text not declassified*] now. He thought this need not go to the Special Group. Mann agreed provided the Agency had the leeway to give it. But he said King should meantime look at the effect this has on the Frei position.

Mann remarked that Chargé Jova's reporting had become sharper in the past few days. He said he was getting more respect for Jova.

Mann also told J.C. King to check in with Jova when King returns to Chile. King, a bit unhappily, replied "if that's the way you want it."

Subsequent to the meeting Pryce informed King, [*name not declassified*] and me that Hurwitch will go to Chile immediately, but that Belton will not go at present, though he may go a month or so before the elections. Belton has just been in Chile in connection with his POLAD work at CINCSOUTH and this gave Jova a chance to consult with him.

256. Transcript of Telephone Conversation Between Director of Central Intelligence McCone and the Under Secretary of State (Ball)[1]

Washington, May 7, 1964, 11:45 a.m.

B: Yes, John, how are you.

DCI: Fine. Say, I have had J.C. King in New York on this Chilean problem and there was a plan worked out in a meeting with [*name not declassified*] and Geneen[2] of the IT&T [*less than 1 line of source text not declassified*] on how to handle this meat and food problem, inflation problem over the next 4 months. Now it can be handled through PL 480, AID, but it is going to require prompt and decisive action. I am calling you to have you jot it down on your pad to see that it doesn't get bogged down in the machinery of AID PL 480 and Alliance for Progress and all the rest.

B: I talked with Orville Freeman yesterday in the context of the beef problem and there is a way to kill a couple of birds with one stone. If we could get a lot of beef down there right now it would help relieve the (blot) here where the President is trying to find every possible way to buy beef. In the meantime, it is something they very much want.

DCI: Yes. Of course that involves quite a cost problem. The beef can be gotten in the Argentine and transported . . . .

B: Yes, but at the moment the President would be willing to go far out on using domestic beef for that.

DCI: Well, I talked to the President about it and I told him that was a possibility, if he wants to take the lumps on the cost, then it is perfectly all right. It means quite a subsidy and there may be some way to do that. That might be a sure way to get prompt action.

B: Well, that's the point. Now, the trouble is, all of this stuff isn't available. I mean, apparently there is some mottling on processing.

DCI: Well, I don't know . . . .

B: (. . . .) promised to look into it and he is supposed to call me this morning. Let me needle him on this whole thing.

---

[1] Source: Central Intelligence Agency, DCI (McCone) Files, Job 80–B01285A, DCI's Telephone Calls, 3/4/64–5/19/64. No classification marking. The text was prepared in the CIA from a tape recording.

[2] Reference is to Harold S. Geneen, president of the International Telegraph and Telephone Company.

DCI: They need 2700 tons of processed beef a month for the next 4 months. This is my own mathematics. Don't hold me to that figure. It may be up higher than that.

B: Well, they did make a contract with Uruguay, I think, or Argentina, I don't know, for part of it.

DCI: Well, now, unfortunately, I am going to be away for a couple of days, but I have got J.C. King on this Chile problem on a full-time basis. Now in addition to this, we have gotten the interested banking and industrial companies to come in and support political actions to the tune of million or million and one-half dollars and we will have to up our own ante in this thing, but the point I want to make is that this requires prompt action and this is one situation where we have to win the game. Tom is out of town. I don't know where he is. Tom Mann. But just keep this on the front burner and if there are any problems of procedure or approvals due to your machinery, why maybe we can use some of our machinery on a contingency basis, you see. In order to get immediate action.

B: I'll get a hold of Orville and Dave Bell and we will crank the thing right up.[3]

DCI: O.K. and I will be back here Sunday[4] or Monday and we'll talk about it. Good, fine, goodbye.

[3] In a May 8 memorandum to Bundy, Chase noted the importance of the PL–480 program in Chile, and urged the Department to "move fast on these programs and to let us know if there is any way we can help." Bundy approved. (Johnson Library, National Security File, Country File, Chile, Vol. I, 1/64–8/64) The United States and Chile signed a PL–480 agreement on June 30, which included a one-time provision to support beef imports (up to 3,000 metric tons for 1964), and doubled the previous amount of financial assistance allotted under Title IV for the export of agricultural commodities to Chile, i.e., from $21 to $42 million. (15 UST 1428)

[4] May 10.

257.   Memorandum for the Record[1]

Washington, May 12, 1964.

SUBJECT

Minutes of the Meeting of the Special Group, 12 May 1964

PRESENT

Mr. Bundy, Mr. Johnson, Mr. Vance, and Mr. McCone
Also present were Under Secretary Thomas C. Mann, Colonel J.C. King, and
Mr. Desmond FitzGerald

1. Chile

a. Mr. McCone referred to several meetings he had had in recent days with American industrialists with major interest in the Chilean economy. In one instance, David Rockefeller headed a group representing various companies. In another, he stated that he had been visited by Clyde E. Weed, Chairman of the Board, and Charles M. Brinckerhoff, President of Anaconda Copper Company. He had also received a visit from the Chilean copper magnate, Augustin Edwards. All were concerned with the closeness of the coming election, the amount of backing being funneled to Allende by outside interests, and the need to bolster candidate Frei with funds. Mr. FitzGerald, recently returned from Santiago, and Colonel J.C. King had also been in contact with business interests.

b. Mr. Mann had recently been in New York, he said, and he, too, had talked to some of these businessmen. He felt that there was already too much open talk in these circles which was filtering back to Chile. Even Frei had pointed out that publicized large-scale U.S. business support for his candidacy would be a kiss of death. On the basis of the risks and the apparent lack of security, he felt the U.S. "private sector" should not engage in political action in this Chilean election.

c. The concept of American commercial firms passing financial aid surreptiously to the U.S. government raised so many questions of ethics, financial and interrelationships that Mr. McCone said he felt the matter should be discussed in the Group. A lengthy exchange of views ensued, but the conclusion was that the legal aspects were too

---

[1] Source: Department of State, INR/IL Historical Files, Special Group Files, c. 120, May 14, 1964. Secret; Eyes Only. Drafted by Jessup. Copies were sent to Johnson, Vance, and McCone. The meeting was held at noon in the White House Situation Room. (National Archives and Records Administration, RG 59, U. Alexis Johnson Files: Lot 90 D 408, Date Books, 1964) No CIA action papers were prepared for the meeting. (Memorandum from Joseph W. Scott to U. Alexis Johnson, May 11; Department of State, INR/IL Historical Files, Special Group Files, May 14, 1964)

labyrinthine and the questions of tax benefits, conflicts of interest and corporation behavior were too murky to make any clear determinations. The risks of acting as an agent, in effect, of U.S. capital and the lack of assurance on security before, during, and after the election led to the agreement that McCone would convey to Mr. Weed the U.S. decision *not* to become a partner with business interests in covert political action but at the same time to assure him that the U.S. was making every effort, on a priority basis, to prevent the election of Allende.[2]

d. It was determined that Mr. FitzGerald would then come up with specific proposals for a large-scale covert political action program in support of Frei at an approximate cost of $2,000,000. It was anticipated that this paper would be ready for submission to the Special Group later this week.[3]

[Omitted here is discussion of Haiti.]

Peter Jessup

---

[2] President Johnson evidently approved this decision. At the weekly meeting between ARA and CIA representatives on May 21, FitzGerald referred to the President's "desire that U.S. private business not become involved in the Chilean election." Mann, alluding to Johnson's views on the subject, agreed to FitzGerald's proposal to meet Augustín Edwards in New York on the condition that the CIA bear "in mind the President's admonition." (Memorandum from Carter to Hughes, May 26; ibid., ARA–CIA Weekly Meetings, 1964–1965) No further evidence has been found on the substance or circumstances of this "admonition."

[3] The outcome of the Special Group meeting was discussed on May 13 at the weekly meeting between ARA and CIA representatives. FitzGerald reported that earlier "he had almost been thrown out of McCone's office" for characterizing the Special Group discussion on May 12 as "good." FitzGerald concluded, however, that "the amount of private sector money involved was 'too small' and the proposal 'too risky'." Mann agreed with this assessment, adding that "it is now up to us to come up with a meaningful USG program to defeat Allende." FitzGerald explained that the CIA had prepared a proposal to the Special Group "for an additional $1,250,000 for use in the Chilean election." "Mann commented that that was very well as far as it went, but that we shouldn't tie ourselves to that amount. FitzGerald said this was no problem, since we could get more if needed." (Memorandum from Carter to Hughes, May 14; ibid.)

---

258. Editorial Note

On May 14, 1964, the Special Group considered a proposal to increase the funds available for covert use in the Chilean presidential elections. In a May 13 memorandum for the Special Group the Central Intelligence Agency maintained that "recent political developments and additional information" indicated that an additional $1,250,000 was needed for the program to defeat Salvador Allende Gossens, the candidate of the Popular Action Front (FRAP). The proposal was designed primarily to increase financial support to Eduardo Frei Montalva, the Christian Democratic candidate, thereby allowing his party to "campaign at its full potential." The CIA also argued, however, that its assistance was "instrumental" in maintaining the Radical candidate, Julio Durán Neumann, who had recently avoided an attempt within his party to endorse Allende. (Department of State, INR/IL Historical Files, Special Group Files, May 14, 1964) The Special Group approved the proposal at its meeting on May 14, including a "tentative breakdown" for the additional funds. (Memorandum from the CIA, May 13; ibid.) According to the minutes of the meeting, the Special Group, while agreeing to the "overall amount" of the program, endorsed "the principle of financial flexibility," a principle which was explained as follows: "if, as the campaign develops, one segment needs additional support and another less, authority exists to shift the subsidy in the needed direction." Bundy informed the participants that "higher authority was aware of the seriousness of this election." (Memorandum for the Record, May 14; ibid., May 21, 1964)

---

259. Letter From the First Secretary of the Embassy in Chile (Hurwitch) to the President's Special Assistant for National Security Affairs (Bundy)[1]

Santiago, June 19, 1964.

Dear Mac:

I have had very much in mind your request for another opinion as to whether an Allende victory would be seriously detrimental to US national security interests. While a month in Chile hardly constitutes a valid basis in time for a definitive response, I am moved to write now before I become too deeply immersed in political detail, knowing that should the scene alter significantly I might write again.

I think that what is fundamentally happening in Chile is that political power has slipped from the hands of the upper classes and both the middle class (PDC) and the working class—or its spokesmen—(the FRAP) are making a determined bid to possess it. Traditionally, the middle class has looked upward and has been politically allied with

---

[1] Source: Washington National Records Center, RG 84, Santiago Embassy Files: FRC 69 A 6507, 1964, POL 14 Elections (Presidential) 1964 (2). Secret; Official–Informal.

the upper class. The comparatively recent emergence of the Christian Democratic party as an important political force, however, has brought a change. The PDC stems from and has in turn rallied to it the Chilean middle class, an agglomeration ranging in socio-economic terms from lower to upper middle class and in political terms from leftish to conservative orientations, and has attracted significant segments of the working class, as well. The upper class parties (Liberals and Conservatives) have in turn, somewhat reluctantly, come out in support of Frei, the candidate, but most find the PDC program too radical. The Socialists and Communists (now FRAP) have for decades struggled unsuccessfully to wrest political power from the upper classes through peaceful means via the ballot. Had not the PDC with its strong candidate attracted timely support, I think the FRAP with its good candidate would this time have had its best chance for victory to date. Whichever party wins, I believe, will effect social changes (diminishing the influence of the propertied classes) from which Chile probably will not be able to turn back. While under-estimating the resiliency of the upper classes would be foolhardy (they seem to have succeeded nicely in corrupting the Radicals), the ideology and spirit of the PDC seems to involve something deeper than mere political competition. The FRAP in power would recognize the upper classes only to the extent its purpose was served.

The Catholic Church has entered this game with a fair-sized stack of chips. The liberal wing of the Church, which is dominant here and ably represented by Cardinal Silva, is deeply attached to the Frei campaign and should derive considerable prestige and impetus from a Frei victory, within Church circles especially. Repercussions of a PDC victory in both Latin American political and Church circles should redound to our benefit. Conversely, an Allende victory in Chile would have discouraging effects throughout the Hemisphere.

On the other side, Radio Habana has been clamoring for an Allende victory. After his reverses in Venezuela and Brazil, Fidel must be desperate to demonstrate to his Soviet patrons through an Allende victory that they are indeed backing the right horse. The FRAP campaign appears well-financed and that Fidel among other outsiders has purchased a stack of chips would not be surprising. For the Soviets, an Allende victory should significantly strengthen their "peaceful coexistence" line to the discomfiture of the Chicoms, and encourage the USSR to allocate more resources elsewhere in LA to propagate similar victories. A Chilean base on the mainland would of course be very valuable to the USSR (cf. the long frontier with Argentina).

A Frei victory, on the other hand, could lead to greater adherence by Latin American left extremists to the Chicom line of violence. While in many senses a "violence" line might be easier for us to handle in

Latin America, it may not be amiss for our policy planners to take a look now at the implications for US policy toward the Hemisphere of a Frei victory as it relates to the Soviet/Chinese split.

To move from the broader dimensions of the significance of the Chilean elections, from which I really do not think the local situation can or should be divorced, assessments of the FRAP and Mr. Allende are of course critical. Ernst Halperin had done the best recent study of the Communists and Socialists in Chile that I have read (it is entitled *Sino-Cuban Trends: The Case of Chile*—Tom Hughes' people have it). One gains the impression in Chile that the Socialists are more intellectually inclined and not as tough-minded or as well organized as the Communists who constitute the dominant element in the FRAP. They are, incredibly enough, often more left than the local Communist Party, are less addicted to the via pacifica and are rather admiring of China.

Allende is a good vote getter, but does not seem to be a man of outstanding ability, courage or intelligence. Although many here maintain that once in power Allende would control or break with the Communists, the evidence is that he has made strong public and private commitments to them (nationalization of the copper mines, Cabinet membership, etc.) and has a long history of unmarred relations with them (dating from 1951). Given the stakes, it is really difficult to see how the outside as well as the local Communists would readily surrender their considerable financial and other investments in an Allende victory. Nor would Allende, given a thin margin of victory at best together with his personal qualities, be likely to be an independent— a la Castro. He might adorn his administration with as many respectable trappings as possible—pacts with the Radicals, and, less likely but still possible, with the left wing of the PDC. Beneath the dress, however, the heart of the matter should I think be regarded as heavily Communist-influenced, unless there were an accompanying open break with the Communists or similar clear evidence that Allende had chosen a course not hostile to us. I should be inclined to view ambivalence on his part negatively, for little in his past appears to warrant giving him the benefit of a doubt in view of his Communist alliance.

An Allende victory would constitute a defeat for US policy. It probably would be accompanied by alarms from the U.S. press and business interests, inevitably justified by Castro crowing and Soviet needling of the Chinese. As a practical matter, whatever our assessment of the significance of an Allende victory, we may find our maneuverability the day after the election (results are known rapidly here) severely circumscribed. (I have often thought that the real tragedy for us of Castro's having embraced the Marxist, rather than our, world lay in the limitations now placed upon the flexibility of US policy toward situations which superficially resemble that of Cuba.) Another

"Castro" in the Hemisphere, particularly one who achieved power through the democratic process in a country where we have invested the highest rate of per capita assistance, would be awfully tough to handle from both the international and domestic standpoints. This would clearly be a case where one and one totalled much more than two and the consequences throughout the Hemisphere of a second Castro would be serious. I would hope that we would, nevertheless, be able to avoid precipitate action and to retain enough flexibility to encompass the possibility that Allende unexpectedly might decide to steer his course in our direction either voluntarily or as a result of our margin of influence. The risks of a policy on our part which appears to accept Allende, however, could I think only be justified by expectations based on something much more concrete than a general notion that good-will on our part will engender a similar response.

You may imagine how pleased I am to be here and to have the opportunity to chew on this problem with very competent colleagues. I hope the foregoing has not needlessly taken too much time out of your busy day.

With warm regards.

Sincerely,

Robert A. Hurwitch[2]

---

[2] Printed from a copy that bears this typed signature.

---

260. Telegram From the Embassy in Chile to the Department of State[1]

Santiago, July 2, 1964, 11 a.m.

10. I saw President Alessandri for about one hour today accompanied by Jova. President said that while new $15 million credit helpful, he disappointed in that he expected $30 million along with a rise in copper prices. I reminded him that he could add the PL–480 proceeds to his $15 million but he maintained that little of this would

---

[1] Source: National Archives and Records Administration, RG 59, Central Files 1964–66, POL 14 CHILE. Confidential; Priority. Repeated to CINCSO and CINCLANT for POLADs.

arrive before election date and much not until after his mandate finished. Hence, he foresees deficit of as much as $45 million.

He said he profoundly disturbed by short-sighted political stance we seem to be taking in that he understands USG only concerned with period through September 5 with the implication being that an Allende victory might see shutting off of aid. He said that while he believes Frei will win we should not discount possibility of Allende victory and urged that we take longer, broader view of matter. Should Allende win, Alessandri would have two months during which to educate Allende and to "channel him into less poisonous paths." He did not think that Allende himself wanted "extreme solutions" and would do his utmost to hold down the Communists. In answer to my question, said he did not believe Allende is true Marxist but merely an opportunist whose campaign was considerably less violent than that of Gonzalez-Videla. When I expressed concern at Allende's links with Communists in today's circumstances, Alessandri observed that in many ways Communists easier deal with than Socialists and that his real fear was of Ampuero whom he considered real extremist. In any case, should Allende win, he hoped USG position would be one of reserved watchful waiting and readiness to move rapidly and with flexibility.

He maintained that if we closed all doors on Allende, we would push him further left and on path similar to Cuba. He compared cases of Cuba and Bolivia maintaining that latter had been saved by US flexibility but recognized that this flexibility easier for US due to minimum US investment as compared to Cuba and (Chile) he speculated whether Cuba might not have taken different route if US had been more prudent and then urged prudence in regard Chile even if Allende won.

In view of above, he felt it particularly necessary that during his last two months in office, Chile have an easier economic situation in order give Alessandri some room for economic maneuver during time when he will be "educating" the next president. Regardless of who wins, he said it would be necessary bring him down to earth after stratospheric euphoria of campaign and its many promises. If either candidate were to attempt to fulfill promises, would soon ruin Chile and would be thrown out in a short time. In many ways, he said Frei's lot will be more difficult than Allende's as he will be under greater pressure fulfill his promises.

In any case, regardless which is victor, Alessandri felt he himself would have important role to play during two month interim period and felt if he given the necessary assistance, his influence on next president might be decisive.

I told him that I would report his views to Washington and was certain that his opinion as to next administration would be useful. As regards his request for more aid, told him could make no commitment and while I would report his views to Department, still hopeful he would find that PL–480 would arrive soon enough to do the trick in conjunction with $15 million credit. The president said he wished he could believe this but is certain he would need more money.

Comment: I believe Alessandri's views important but think it by no means certain that Allende will be willing to work with Alessandri and be "educated" during interim period.

I see no immediate need give active consideration Alessandri request for additional $15 million. But it may become clear that further US aid required after IMF review Chilean situation scheduled later this month or, more likely, after September election. In either case, we should be prepared move fast if necessary.[2]

Cole

---

[2] The Chilean Ambassador to the United States, Sergio Gutiérrez-Olívos, reiterated much of Alessandri's argument in a meeting with Mann on July 6. According to a memorandum of the conversation, "Mann said that while he was not as optimistic as President Alessandri regarding Allende's susceptibility to influence, the Department intends to be realistic and flexible if Allende wins." (Ibid., AID(US) CHILE) In telegram 25 to Santiago, July 8, the Department reported that Alessandri should now feel reassured that the United States would not "cut his Administration adrift in final 60 days in event Allende wins." The Department, however, did not wish to negotiate the terms for additional economic assistance until September, "when our response can take into consideration Frei's views and/or situation then prevailing as well as incumbent GOC position." (Ibid., AID(US) 9 CHILE)

---

261. Information Memorandum From the President's Special Assistant for National Security Affairs (Bundy) to President Johnson[1]

Washington, July 8, 1964.

SUBJECT

Survey Poll on Chilean Presidential Candidates

You are right: [*less than 1 line of source text not declassified*] a poll in April and May of the three candidates for President in the Chilean

---

[1] Source: Johnson Library, National Security File, Country File, Chile, Vol. I, Memos 1/64–8/64. Secret.

election.[2] The poll showed that Frei (Christian Democrat) would receive 52% of the vote: Allende (Socialist-Communist) 36%; Duran (Radical) 7% and 5% undecided. [*less than 1 line of source text not declassified*] a poll in March before a by-election in which the Radicals lost badly. In that poll, Frei was also ahead. The second poll showed Duran lost badly and that Frei picked up slightly more of the voters who switched from Duran than did Allende.

The poll was taken by an experienced [*less than 1 line of source text not declassified*] firm which had previously conducted polls in Chile. Nevertheless, the poll was a small sample—only 2000. State regards it only as an indicator of how the situation lined up in May and not what it might be now or how it might end up on September 4.

Chilean President Alessandri thinks Frei is ahead but he also went to great lengths in a recent conversation with our Ambassador to urge that the United States keep an open mind on Allende and not cut off financial assistance should Allende win.[3]

The Chilean President race is a hard one. The Christian Democrats are coming from behind. They now have a good organization but they have to guard against over-confidence and fight all the way to the finish line if they hope to win.

[*1 paragraph (2 lines of source text) not declassified*]

McG. B.[4]

---

[2] Mann reported the results of the poll in a telephone conversation with the President on June 11; see Document 16.

[3] See Document 260.

[4] Printed from a copy that bears these typed initials.

---

262.   Editorial Note

On July 23, 1964, the 303 Committee considered a proposal to provide "supplementary support for the Chilean presidential elections." In a July 21 memorandum to the 303 Committee the Central Intelligence Agency reported that an additional $500,000 was needed for the program to defeat Salvador Allende Gossens, the candidate of the Popular Action Front (FRAP). The money would permit Eduardo Frei Montalva, the Christian Democratic candidate, to "maintain the pace and rhythm of his campaign effort"—and allow the CIA to meet any "last minute contingencies." The CIA explained that Frei had miscalculated his finances, an error "attributable to the PDC's inexperience in organizing a campaign of this magnitude." (National Security Council, 303 Committee Files, Subject Files, Chile thru 1969) In a July 23 memorandum to McGeorge Bundy, Peter Jessup recommended the proposal as follows: "We can't afford to lose this one, so I don't think there should be any economy shaving in this instance. We assume the Commies are pouring in dough; we have no proofs. They must assume we are pouring in dough; they have no proofs. Let's pour it on and in." (Ibid.) The 303 Committee approved the proposal for supplementary support at its meeting on July 23. (Memorandum for the Record from Jessup, July 24; ibid., Minutes, July 23, 1964)

---

263.   Telegram From the Embassy in Chile to the Department of State[1]

Santiago, July 29, 1964, 6 p.m.

167. Ref: Embtel 158.[2] Subj: Frei's Views on US Role in Final Days of Campaign.

Frei said he thought that the US and the Embassy in particular should continue to act with prudence and discretion in regard to his campaign. The last weeks of the campaign will be particularly bitter and great care should be exercised not to permit an extraneous matter to arise and possibly play a disruptive and possibly decisive role on the course of the campaign. He thought our own activities had been well handled in this regard and implied that he saw no reason why discreet contacts between Embassy and selected PDC leaders should not continue to be maintained.

When discussing financial resources he observed that PDC was adequately supplied and in any case it was desirable that the Chilean people themselves be made to feel an obligation to contribute and thus feel selves as personally involved in campaign. He hoped we could assist him, however, through furnishing information on FRAP

---

[1] Source: National Archives and Records Administration, RG 59, Central Files 1964–66, POL 14 CHILE. Confidential. Repeated to CINCSO and CINCLANT for POLADs.

[2] Telegram 158 from Santiago, July 29, reported on the circumstances that led to the meeting among Frei, Jova, and Stevenson. The Embassy also explained that the meeting was "the first time we had spoken with Frei for almost two months as due to FRAP attacks on Embassy and attempts link Embassy and PDC had thought it best maintain discreet distance." (Ibid.)

activities. He hoped that in our conversations with our liberal and conservative contacts we would stress to them the need to maintain the "national and popular character of the campaign" and that the face of the right not be shown too much. With our Radical friends he hoped we would urge them to keep Duran in the race.

He made the interesting observation that he felt that among the reasons that it was necessary for him to win by a really large majority was the reassuring effect that this would have on potential private investment from abroad. A win by a mere plurality or by a very narrow majority would keep alive the suspicion in the United States and Europe that communism was still just around the corner in Chile and this would discourage the massive investments that he felt Chile needed.

We told him that Ambassador very specially hoped he and his cohorts would keep in mind fact that US was also engaged in political campaign and that ill-considered statements or actions in Chile could also create complications there. "Understanding attitudes" were a two way street. Frei said he very much aware of this problem and sympathized with attitude of parts of American public which complained of lack of support and understanding for US policies in spite of extensive and long continuing assistance programs. A balance had to be struck between local and international considerations and this was often difficult.

Cole

264.   Memorandum From Robert M. Sayre of the National Security Council Staff to the President's Special Assistant for National Security Affairs (Bundy)[1]

Washington, July 31, 1964.

SUBJECT

Chilean Contingency Planning

The LAPC has held two meetings on a contingency plan for Chile. Although the first draft, and the revised draft which the LAPC considered July 30, cover contingencies should Frei win (a) handily or (b)

---

[1] Source: Johnson Library, National Security File, Country File, Chile, Vol. I, Memos, 1/64–8/64. Secret.

by a slim margin, all of the discussion has centered on the contingency of an Allende victory.[2]

As you are aware, the polls and recent reports indicate Frei is ahead. Frei himself is now plotting his strategy on winning big instead of just winning.

The consensus on contingency plans is shaping up as follows, based on current intelligence:

1. The revised draft of July 30 is too wordy (it runs to 31 double-spaced pages), attempts to cover too much ground, and proposes courses based on inadequate intelligence. It should be tightened up and shortened.

2. We should proceed on the assumption that Allende is bad medicine, but we should not slam the door because he might double-cross his Communist friends. President Alessandri, Felipe Herrera, and others, insist we can work with Allende.

3. The most likely possibility, should Allende win, is that he would try to establish a broadly based government, play for time to consolidate himself, and try to get the U.S. to finance his administration. We should, therefore, move promptly, but without provocation, to get him to define his position. We should do nothing that would let rumors start that we support him. (Current intelligence is that the Communist Central Committee is telling its people they cannot expect any important posts in an Allende Government at first.)

4. If Allende wins a bare majority, the key to keeping him out peacefully is Radical support for Frei in the Congress. The Chilean Congress has a tradition of confirming the candidate with the highest popular vote, but we could push for a Frei approval on the theory that the Chilean people gave a majority vote to policies espoused by Frei and Duran, and a minority to Communist-Socialist policies.

5. The Soviets will probably offer substantial financial assistance to Allende if we refuse, and may be even if we do not. But they would be inheriting an economy which is in serious difficulty as opposed to Cuba, where it was basically strong. In the Soviet-Chinese fight, Chile is extremely important to the Soviet thesis that communism can achieve power by peaceful means.

---

[2] The Latin American Policy Committee first met on July 9 to consider a draft of the contingency plan for Chile. The May 28 draft was forwarded on June 5 as an enclosure to airgram A–926 from Santiago. (National Archives and Records Administration, RG 59, Central Files 1964–66, POL 1–1 CHILE) The action minutes of the July 9 meeting are in the Johnson Library, National Security File, Country File, Latin America, Vol. II, Memos 6/64–8/64. The revised draft and the minutes of the LAPC meeting on July 30 have not been found.

6. We would have an extremely difficult time marshalling forces against letting a victorious Allende take office, or doing anything about getting him out. Chilean tradition is to let the victor take office. If the reluctance of Latin Americans on Cuba is any criterion, the Latins would not go along with a move against Allende. There would probably be a serious division of opinion in the U.S.

7. The armed forces in Chile are anti-Communist. It is possible that they might move as the Peruvian military did to keep out Haya de la Torre, but the odds are they would not. They would more likely play it as the armed forces did in Brazil, but divisions among the Chilean armed forces are less likely.

DOD is reviewing its supply situation in the Canal Zone, should additional riot control supplies be needed in a hurry. It is also identifying the location of additional supplies in the U.S., should these be needed. Riot control supplies already approved, are in place in Chile, and the feeling is that these are adequate for the foreseeable future, i.e., the next month or two.

State is having another try at a contingency paper and the LAPC will review it at an early meeting.[3]

RMS

---

[3] No evidence has been found that the LAPC met to discuss a subsequent draft of the contingency paper for Chile.

---

265.   Memorandum From the President's Special Assistant for National Security Affairs (Bundy) to President Johnson[1]

Washington, August 13, 1964.

This is merely an extra note of insurance, but you may want to know that we have been asked by our friends in Santiago not to make any public recognition of Chile's break with Cuba.[2] In response to this request, we are making no public statement at all, and when pressed

---

[1] Source: Johnson Library, National Security File, Memos to the President, McGeorge Bundy, Vol. VI. No classification marking. Copy to Reedy.

[2] Although it had recently voted against such action at the 9th Meeting of Foreign Ministers, Chile suspended diplomatic relations with Cuba on August 11.

by reporters we will say simply "This is a decision taken by a democratic government in the light of its own assessment of its international obligations, and that is all we need to say about it."

If we look as if we are interfering in any way, it will be bad for our friend Frei and good for the Communist-supported Allende.

The election prognosis continues favorable at the moment.[3]

McG. B.

---

[3] A handwritten notation at the end of the memorandum reads: "O.K. L".

---

266. **Memorandum From the Special Assistant to the Assistant Secretary of State for Inter-American Affairs (Barall) to the Assistant Secretary of State for Inter-American Affairs (Mann)**[1]

Washington, August 20, 1964.

SUBJECT

U.S. Identification with Frei in the Chilean Election

At your staff meeting, today, and in all conversations regarding the forthcoming election in Chile, both Chileans and Americans unquestioningly accept U.S. support of Frei. While the alternative of Allende is a horrible one, it is safe to predict that we will have many severe problems even with Frei, and that Chile's problems will not be solved automatically by the election results—at least this is what my Chilean friends tell me, and all support Frei.

Since we are identified as such ardent supporters, Frei is likely to ask for enormous sums of money on political rather than economic-development grounds. He is almost certain to urge us to finance some doctrinaire programs which will be unacceptable to the U.S.

Frei is not likely to have the political strength to cope with inflation and mount an effective stabilization program. Even if he obtains a majority of the popular vote, it is hard to believe that he will be able to coalesce a majority in the Congress, particularly since he cannot be sure of internal discipline on the part of the left wing in his own party.

---

[1] Source: National Archives and Records Administration, RG 59, ARA/LA Files: Lot 66 D 65, Chile 1964. Confidential. Copies were sent to Adams, Rogers, and Dentzer.

For the same reason, and in the light of his promises to workers and peasants, I don't see how he can tackle the problems of wage stabilization effectively.

Although I am sure we cannot change our over-identification with Frei before the election, I would recommend a much cooler, factual, "show-me" attitude as soon as the election results are known, so that he doesn't take for granted U.S. support for his programs on the theory that we consider him to be the only alternative to a Communist takeover. I am not suggesting that we should not be willing to provide massive aid to Chile if the conditions are right. But if we provide big sums without real assurance of permanent change for the better, the net result may be permanent change for the worse—and we'll get Allende next time around.

---

267.   Memorandum for the Record[1]

Washington, August 21, 1964.

SUBJECT

   Minutes of the Meeting of the 303 Committee, 20 August 1964

PRESENT

   Mr. Bundy, Ambassador Thompson, Mr. Vance, and Mr. McCone

1. A special meeting of the 303 Committee was called for 1600 on 20 August 1964 to discuss two papers concerning Chile: a CIA paper dated 20 August 1964, "Supplementary Support for the Chilean Presidential Elections of 4 September 1964,"[2] and an undated CIA memorandum, "Church Social and Political Projects in Chile."[3]

2. The first paper cited a cable of 19 August 1964 from the "Joint Embassy Election Team" in Santiago[4] seeking additional funds as the political race enters its last two and a half weeks. The sum requested was [*less than 1 line of source text not declassified*], and in view of the extreme long-range importance of the outcome of this political struggle, the Committee members felt that this late hour request was justified.

---

[1] Source: National Security Council, 303 Committee Files, Minutes, August 20, 1964. Secret; Eyes Only. Drafted by Jessup. Copies were sent to Thompson, Vance, and McCone.

[2] Not printed. (Ibid., Subject Files, Chile thru 1969)

[3] Dated August 20. (Department of State, INR/IL Historical Files, 303 Committee Files, c. 9, August 20, 1964)

[4] Not found.

3. The second paper dealt with the political action program undertaken by [*less than 1 line of source text not declassified*] in support of the CDP candidate. [*less than 1 line of source text not declassified*], apparently on the basis of conversations with various U.S. citizens, private and official, over the past year, assumed that he had a tacit commitment for financial support. Although no formal commitment to [*less than 1 line of source text not declassified*] was ever authorized, the Committee felt that [*less than 1 line of source text not declassified*], regardless of his erroneous impression, had made measurable contributions to the Frei campaign through his "front" organizations and that some allocation of funds should be made to defray his stated deficit of $395,000.

4. Accordingly, the Committee approved the sum of [*less than 1 line of source text not declassified*] as requested by the "Joint Embassy Election Team" with the stipulation that no more than [*less than 1 line of source text not declassified*] of this sum should be allocated to [*less than 1 line of source text not declassified*] political action program deficit.[5]

Peter Jessup

---

[5] According to his own notes of the meeting, "Ambassador Thompson commented that [*less than 1 line of source text not declassified*] seems a great deal, but he did not enter any caveat to that effect." (Department of State, INR/IL Historical Files, 303 Committee Files, C. 9, August 20, 1964)

---

268. Memorandum Prepared in the Central Intelligence Agency[1]

Washington, September 1, 1964.

SUBJECT

Chilean Election Forecast

1. The total of registered voters for the 4 September 1964 election is 2,915,000, 45.7% of whom are women. An estimated 83% turnout is expected amounting to approximately 2,400,000 voters going to the polls.

---

[1] Source: Johnson Library, National Security File, Country File, Chile, Vol. II, 9/64–11/64. Secret. Dungan forwarded the memorandum to Bundy and Moyers on September 4 and in a covering memorandum noted: "I know that both of you are interested in the Chilean election which is being held today. Therefore, I thought you would want to see a memorandum which I had prepared earlier this week by DDP giving their estimate of the outcome of the election. This analysis does not reflect the views of the Intelligence component of the Agency."

[Omitted here are the detailed results of several election predictions.]

b. An August 1964 sampling of the important areas of Santiago and Valparaiso shows Frei ahead by 20.2% over Allende in these cities:

Frei   54.4%

Allende   34.2%

Duran   6.9%

Undecided   4.5%[2]

(For an examination of details as well as regional polling data in five provinces, please see attachments 2 and 3.)[3]

6. *Divisional Estimate:*

a. We do not believe that it is possible to predict this election with any great degree of accuracy, that is to say, within one to two percent. For one thing, polling must be relatively inexact in view of the fact that expected voters this year exceed by more than one million the number of voters in the past presidential election. (This greatly increased expected vote is due mainly to laws passed during the Alessandri regime making voting mandatory.) As a consequence, pollsters do not have available the type of district bench marks which are used so extensively in polling in the United States. The enormously increased registration and expected vote can be assumed, however, to be of distinct advantage to the Christian Democrats in view of the fact that new registration will be heavily weighted among women who by and large favor Frei by more than two-thirds.

b. Some general regional observations are of interest. The northern provinces have traditionally been communist and radical strongholds. The PDC has worked hard to change this and Allende seems to have only a slightly favorable margin there. In the central urban area with its high number of women registrants Frei should win Santiago and Valparaiso by a substantial margin. In the central rural area Allende may carry Aconcagua and Talca with the vote being close all the way down to Malleco. The PDC seems to do not badly among the campesinos in Curico, Talca and Chillan. In the race in Concepcion, traditionally radical and marxist, Frei has a 50–50 chance.

c. From recent polls it would appear that the undecided vote as of the middle of August is about 5 percent. There is some indication that this undecided vote comes principally from Allende's semi-defectors; logically, one would expect it to be composed also of radicals who find it difficult to choose between a far leftist and a catholic candidate.

---

[2] Bundy forwarded these results to the President on August 25. (Memorandum from Jessup to Bundy, August 24; Johnson Library, National Security File, Country File, Chile, Vol. I, 1/64–8/64)

[3] None of the attachments was found.

d. We believe that Frei will win by a clear majority. From the point of view of U.S. interests a clear majority for Frei would be highly satisfactory and therefore we believe that this is the important point rather than trying to predict the exact percentage. Such a majority would mean that the election would not have to be thrown to congress and therefore that the uncertainties surrounding that process, including the possibility of rioting, would be eliminated. Furthermore, with a clear majority Frei would not have to make any political deals with other parties. Forced to predict, however, we would give the following: Frei—53 percent; Allende—41 percent; Duran—6 percent.[4]

---

[4] Rusk briefed the President on the Chilean election at a NSC meeting on September 1: "It looked as if a victory for the non-Communist forces in Chile would come up in the election 4 September, partly as a result of the good work of CIA; and this development would be a triumph for democracy and a blow to Communism in Latin America." (Memorandum for the record by Ray S. Cline, September 1; Central Intelligence Agency, Job 80–B01285A, DCI Files, Meetings with the President) The election was also discussed on September 2 at the weekly meeting between ARA and CIA representatives. While FitzGerald gave the DDP prediction cited above, Mann said that "his source had indicated that Frei would probably win by a plurality but not by a majority." Mann congratulated the Agency, saying that, "regardless of the outcome, he believes that we have done everything that is possible." (Memorandum for the record by FitzGerald, September 3; ibid., Job 78–03041R, DDO/IMS Files, US Government—State)

---

269. Editorial Note

On September 4, 1964, the Johnson administration closely monitored the official tabulation of votes for the presidential election in Chile. The Department of State received hourly updates from the Embassy in Santiago and forwarded the telegraphic reports to the White House. (Memorandum from Chase to Bundy, September 4; Johnson Library, National Security File, Country File, Latin America, Vol. II, 6/64–12/64; telegrams 366, 367, 368, 369, 370, and 371 from Santiago, September 4; National Archives and Records Administration, RG 59, Central Files 1964–66, POL 14 CHILE) Although the initial returns suggested the eventual outcome, the actual result was surprisingly decisive. With 87 percent of the electorate participating, Eduardo Frei Montalva, the candidate of the Christian Democratic Party, received 56 percent of the vote; Salvador Allende Gossens, the Popular Action Front (FRAP) candidate 39 percent; the Radical Party candidate, Julio Durán Neumann, finished third.

President Johnson addressed the importance of the Chilean election at a news conference on September 5. The election, he said, served as a reminder of the strength of democratic institutions throughout Latin America; it was a victory for democracy as well as a defeat for communism, i.e. "those who are hostile to freedom." The President suggested that some credit should go to the Alliance for Progress, whose ideals and programs Frei had endorsed during the campaign. Johnson was careful to point out, however, that the election "was an internal matter in which the people of Chile were the only judges of the issues." (*Public Papers of the Presidents of the United States: Lyndon B. Johnson, 1963–64*, Book II, page 1040) Frei expressed his appreciation for these remarks on September 7, when Ambassador Cole delivered an oral message of congratulations from President Johnson. Frei also praised the Embassy for its role during the campaign, citing "its discretion and cooperation." (Telegram 383 from Santiago, September 8; National Archives and Records Administration, RG 59, Central Files 1964–66, POL 14 CHILE)

In a September 2 memorandum the CIA argued that various elements of the covert political action program—the financial and organizational assistance given to Frei, the effort to keep Durán in the race, the propaganda campaign to denigrate Allende—were "indispensable ingredients of Frei's success." "Frei's chances of winning the election," the Agency concluded, "would have been considerably more tenuous, and it is doubtful if his campaign would have progressed as well as it did without this covert U.S. Government support." (Department of State, INR/IL Historical Files, Chile, 1964–1967) The day after the election Cole reported that the combined effort of U.S. agencies "contributed significantly to the very satisfactory Frei victory on September 4." (Telegram 372 from Santiago, September 5; National Archives and Records Administration, RG 59, Central Files 1964–66, POL 14 CHILE)

The 303 Committee also discussed the Chilean election at its meeting on September 10. The official minutes of the meeting record the discussion as follows:

"Mr. Bundy indicated that a vote of commendation should be extended to those responsible for the successful outcome of the Chilean election. Those present concurred wholeheartedly. Mr. McCone remarked that the voters, themselves, in Chile deserved some commendation for the high numbers of the electorate voting (86%) and the very few votes that were invalidated (six-tenths of 1%). Ambassador Thompson indicated that there were those who felt that President Frei could still prove a difficult personality. Mr. McCone commented that certain U.S. business leaders with direct interests were immensely pleased and felt that they could negotiate any problems arising during the Frei administration. Mr. McCone added that it was the present analysis of his area specialists that without the large scale covert support provided for the campaign, Frei would have gained, at most, a bare plurality. This was the first clear majority in a Chilean election in 22 years." (Memorandum for the Record by Jessup, September 11; Department of State, INR/IL Historical Files, 303 Committee Files, September 24, 1964)

270. Intelligence Note From the Director of the Bureau of
      Intelligence and Research (Hughes) to Secretary of State
      Rusk[1]

Washington, September 5, 1964.

SUBJECT

Frei's Victory in Chile has Broad Hemispheric Significance

A new dimension to democratic left. For the first time in Latin America, a Christian Democratic Party has achieved power. These parties, which are beginning to gain a foothold in several Latin American countries, are outspokenly pro-Western in foreign policy. In domestic policy, they advocate a middle road between capitalism and Marxism with strong emphasis on the role of the working man. The Communists and particularly the Castro regime have watched the Christian Democratic parties with concern, fearing that their advocacy of revolutionary changes with freedom might attract majority support. Frei's victory confirms their fears.

Smooth transfer of power foreseen. Frei will lose no time in designating the officials of his government. In staffing the ministries he will be able to call upon some of the most able technicians in the present Alessandri government who are members of his party. Outstanding among these is Sergio Molina, Director of the Budget and coordinator of Chile's 10-year development program, adopted in 1961. Foreign Office undersecretary, PDC member Enrique Bernstein seems likely to become the new Foreign Minister.[2] The PDC lacks enough top caliber technicians and administrators, however, to fill all the government's top posts and it will probably turn to political independents.

Congressional hurdle. Frei must now buttress his personal victory—the first majority obtained by any Chilean presidential candidate since 1942—with greater representation of his party in Congress where it has only 32 out of a 192-seat total. In August the PDC said that its most pressing goal is to increase its congressional strength in the March 1965 elections when all the Chamber and about half the Senate will be renewed. Although the party is almost 30 years old, its spectacular increase in strength has occurred only since the last congressional elections in 1961. While the present Congress may give Frei limited

---

[1] Source: Johnson Library, National Security File, Country File, Chile, Vol. II, 9/64–11/64. Confidential.

[2] Frei announced his cabinet on October 26: Gabriel Valdés Subercaseaux, a Christian Democrat, was named Minister of Foreign Affairs; Molina, a political independent, Minister of Finance.

emergency powers to help solve some of the country's immediate problems, Frei will need a much larger plurality over the long pull.

Even if his party doubled its strength in Congress next March, he would still need additional support in attacking Chile's longstanding problems. The two rightist parties (Liberal and Conservative), which helped to elect Frei as "the lesser of two evils", will probably desert him when he moves against their entrenched interests. He has repeatedly attempted to win the Socialists in the FRAP away from the Communists, but with virtually no success so far. His most likely source of new support seems to be the center Radical Party, which might cooperate with him in return for guarantees of security for the many Radicals holding government jobs.

Implications for US. Frei's victory is being hailed by stateside radio broadcasts as a victory both for Western democracy and the US. This is to some extent an over simplification, and the US will face problems as well as opportunities in Chile. While Frei has supported Western political objectives and the Alliance for Progress, he has at times been vigorous in his criticism of capitalism. His reform efforts will doubtless provoke propertied interests and lead to charges that he opposes free enterprise.[3] Meanwhile, Frei has scheduled an economic mission to the US. He has been holding conversations with US copper companies in an effort to achieve a mutually satisfactory relationship with them. The PDC goal is to double copper production by 1970 in order to generate the revenues needed to support the party's social program.

---

[3] The CIA assessed the outlook for the president-elect as follows: "Frei will be a less accommodating and a more nationalistic ally than Alessandri, because of his zeal for reform. Frei's favorable attributes more than offset this." "With some good fortune and tactful handling, Frei could become an outstanding leader and statesman in Latin America and an exceptionally valuable, if occasionally carping, friend of the United States." (Special Report prepared by the CIA, [*text not declassified*]; Johnson Library, National Security File, Country File, Chile, Vol. II, 9/64–11/64)

271. Memorandum From the President's Special Assistant for National Security Affairs (Bundy) to President Johnson[1]

Washington, September 20, 1964.

SUBJECT

Ralph Dungan and Chile

I have talked to both Dungan and Dean Rusk about this, and Rusk plans to talk to Tom Mann.[2] You may want to speak to Mann about it yourself on the El Paso trip.

Everyone agrees that the job of Ambassador in Chile is now highly important. Frei plans to embark on a course of anti-Communist reform which will involve important negotiations with major American copper interests. We need an Ambassador who is fundamentally sympathetic to the cause of democratic reform, but realistic on the need to meet the fair interests of our businessmen.

Tom Mann will do a very good job on protecting our interests, but he is a little insensitive to the Chilean need for reform. So Dean Rusk and I both believe that a progressive and imaginative Ambassador will be needed as a counterweight, and that Dungan would be an excellent choice. This situation is much like that in Panama, where Vaughn is doing an excellent job of producing new ideas, while Tom Mann keeps an eye on the brakes.

Ralph Dungan is a liberal Catholic with strong convictions on the need for progressive policies. He is also a realist. He is a good friend of Frei, with whom he has been in close touch for years. I am convinced that he wants to do this job because it engages all his own convictions, and not because he wants the empty pleasure of being called Ambassador.

---

[1] Source: Johnson Library, National Security File, Memos to the President, McGeorge Bundy, Vol. VI. No classification marking. A notation on the memorandum indicates the President saw it.

[2] Rusk raised the issue with Mann on September 3, the day before the presidential election. "The Sec asked if he [Mann] had a good man for Chile; we should have a name available soon. Mr. Mann said he had called [Deputy Assistant Secretary for Administration] Tom Beale and had pointed out the urgency. Mr. Mann said they had cleared through Ralph Dungan who had been mentioned as a chief candidate. Sec asked if Mann had any suggestions personally. Mann said we should take one of our better ambassadors out of the field—someone strong on economics. Assuming Frei wins, we will be faced with an economic problem. Mann said he did know someone else but had not yet had an answer. Mann suggested the Sec sound out the President. Mann thought the candidate should also know the language. Sec said let us give some thought to the matter; we should move fairly fast." (Rusk to Mann, September 3, 1964, 3:05 p.m., National Archives and Records Administration, RG 59, Rusk Files: Lot 72 D 192, Telephone Calls 8/25/64–9/13/64)

Ralph is not absolutely ideal for this job—it would be better if he had some business reputation, and better also if he spoke Spanish (although he is prepared to work on that passionately). But against any presently available businessman, Ralph has the great advantages of prestige in your Administration, proven sympathy for the progressive anti-Communist effort in Latin America, and a close personal relationship with Frei. He has the confidence of the Secretary of State, and he will be an energetic and loyal Ambassador for you personally.

Dean Rusk thinks we should send Cole's successor to Santiago very promptly. I myself do not believe that is very important. If you now make clear your intention to send Dungan at the right time, he could readily stay here until Thanksgiving or even New Year's. An able Chargé can easily keep house between now and then.

What is needed is a decision. It will not be good for the Frei administration to believe that we are unable to pick a man for this crucial job during the next six weeks. We have twice delayed Cole's resignation, and we have now run out of spare time.

If you do designate Dungan, I think we can get cordial and responsive notices from the *Times* and the *Post*, and also from other less doctrinaire observers of the Latin American scene.[3]

McG.B.

---

[3] The White House announced on October 2 that President Johnson had nominated Dungan as Ambassador to Chile. (Telegram 290 from Santiago, October 2, ibid., Central Files 1964–66, PER Dungan, Ralph) Dungan was officially appointed on November 24, confirmed by the Senate January 15 (Congress had been in recess at the time of his appointment), and recommissioned January 18. He presented his credentials in Santiago December 10.

272.   Memorandum From the Deputy Director of Coordination for Intelligence and Research (Carter) to the Director of Intelligence and Research (Hughes)[1]

Washington, October 1, 1964.

SUBJECT

ARA—Agency Meeting September 30, 1964

PARTICIPANTS

ARA—Mr. Mann, Mr. Adams, Mr. Pryce
CIA—Mr. FitzGerald, [name not declassified]
INR/DDC—Mr. Carter

Chile.

FitzGerald said the Station Chief in Chile had talked with Ambassador Cole shortly before the latter's departure from Santiago and that Cole said Secretary Rusk doesn't want us in our dealings with the Frei Government to use leverage acquired through support of the CD.[2] FitzGerald said this made him very unhappy. He wanted to know if Mann was aware of a directive of this nature.

Mann said he was not. In any case, he added, it depended on the way you use leverage. He doubted that the Secretary's directive was "as sweeping as it sounds." He thought the matter could easily be cleared up by talking with the Secretary.[3]

[name not declassified], who made a recent trip to Chile, said he found Jova (DCM) concerned about "our using our power position." Mann commented he was not worried about using it; only about our misusing it.

FitzGerald said "it's the atmosphere of mistrust that bothers me."

Said Mann: "Don't worry. I trust you."

Mann went on to reveal there will be a new Ambassador in Santiago soon and indicated it would be Ralph Dungan, though cautioned that this was to be held close since the agrement had not yet been requested.

---

[1] Source: Department of State, INR/IL Historical Files, ARA/CIA Weekly Meetings, 1964–1965. Secret. Also addressed to Denney and Evans.

[2] According to Rusk's Appointment Book, Rusk met with Cole on September 11. (Johnson Library) No substantive record of the meeting has been found.

[3] A handwritten note in the margin by this paragraph reads: "INR participation?"

Mann said a topflight economist is needed to replace the outgoing economic counselor.[4] In his view the political battle is over. The battle now will be in the economic field.

[*name not declassified*] reported that while in Chile he talked with [*less than 1 line of source text not declassified*] whom we assisted to the tune of [*less than 1 line of source text not declassified*] shortly before the September 4 election.[5] [*less than 1 line of source text not declassified*] told him that funds on hand would last only until December, clearly implying he expected more. [*name not declassified*] said he made it clear to [*less than 1 line of source text not declassified*] that no more funds would be forthcoming. Asked if [*less than 1 line of source text not declassified*] had clearly understood this [*name not declassified*] replied, "He didn't hear me."

[Omitted here is discussion of Cuba and Venezuela.]

---

[4] The outgoing chief of the economic section, Thomas R. Favell, did not report to his next assignment until August 1965. He was replaced 3 months later by Robert G. Walker.

[5] See Document 267.

---

273. Editorial Note

At a meeting with Central Intelligence Agency officials on October 12, 1964, Assistant Secretary Mann reported his approval of a proposal for additional covert assistance to the Christian Democratic Party. The proposal would provide [*text not declassified*] to maintain the grassroots organizations of the party—the slum-dweller and campesino departments—for the remainder of the calendar year. Ray Herbert, Deputy Chief of the Western Hemisphere Division, recommended extending the term of the program, arguing that the Christian Democrats were "the only effective force fighting Communists in these areas." Mann disagreed: the Christian Democrats might use U.S. support against the "other non-Marxist parties." He maintained that the current proposal was sufficient but agreed to reconsider the issue in several months. When Herbert raised the question of assistance for the congressional elections in March 1965, Mann was more adamant: "Tell them not to expect any help to beat other non-Commie groups. Tell them we helped them fight Marxists. This is different. This would be intervention." (Memorandum from Carter to Hughes, October 13; Department of State, INR/IL Historical Files, ARA–CIA Weekly Meetings, 1964–1965)

On October 13 the CIA drafted a memorandum to the 303 Committee detailing its program to support the Christian Democratic grass-roots organizations. Before the memorandum was submitted, however, Mann insisted on redrafting the proposal. The final memorandum stipulated that the CIA explain to Frei: a) the difference between assistance for a presidential election against a Marxist candidate and assistance for a congressional election against a field of democratic parties; and b) that the current program was intended for a "transitional period" only, to allow the Christian Democrats to combat Communist influence in the "campesino and slum sectors." (Ibid., 303 Committee Files, October 29, 1964) Ambassador-designate Dungan expressed similar concerns when asked to comment on the proposal:

"I would only add to the recommendation a caveat that support during this period does not mean a continuation of support for this or other PDC activities in the future. It seems to me that this should be made explicit so that no inference to the contrary might be drawn. It may well be that we will want to continue some support, but unless there are overriding considerations of which I am not aware at this time I believe it is a sound principle to permit popular democratic parties to go it alone. If the PDC or any other democratic party comes to power, part of assuming the responsibility that goes with power is finding ways and means of supporting the party structure."

The 303 Committee approved the CIA paper, as amended, by telephone on October 20. The official record of the decision notes that Dungan's statement set "the limitations under which any future proposals of this kind will be viewed in this Chilean post-election period." (Memorandum for the record from Jessup, October 22; ibid.)

274. Memorandum of Conversation[1]

Washington, October 12, 1964.

SUBJECT

Meeting of Mr. Mann with the Mission of President-Elect Frei of Chile

PARTICIPANTS

Mr. Mann, Assistant Secretary, ARA
Mr. Solomon, Deputy Assistant Secretary, ARA
Mr. Rogers, Deputy U.S. Coordinator, AA/LA
Senator Radomiro Tomic, Member, Chilean Delegation
Sergio Molina, Member, Chilean Delegation
Jorge Ahumada, Member, Chilean Delegation
José Piñera, Member, Chilean Delegation
Thomas R. Favell, Counselor Economic Affairs, Santiago
John P. Robinson, Director, USAID, Santiago
William T. Dentzer, Jr., Director, Bolivian-Chilean Affairs, ARA
Harry H. Lunn, Jr., Office of Bolivian-Chilean Affairs, ARA

Mr. Mann welcomed the special mission sent by President-elect Frei to begin economic discussions in Washington with the U.S. Government and international agencies. Senator Tomic, chairman of the mission, responded and noted the informal and unofficial nature of the team's visit since the Frei Government will not take power until November 3.

As an introduction to the economic program proposed by the new government, Senator Tomic described the political situation in Chile which had led to Frei's election on a program of "Revolution in Liberty". He noted that the March 15 by-election in Curico effectively had eliminated the candidate of the "status quo" government coalition and forced a choice between Frei's democratic reform program and the Marxist alternative offered by Allende. While Frei's decisive election showed the clear preference of Chileans for the democratic alternative, one could not ignore the nearly 40% vote for Allende. Chilean expectations for the Frei Government are high and immediate performance is necessary to consolidate the Government's position in the March 1965 Congressional elections.

Senator Tomic then commented on the basic contradiction of a country with rich resources and a facade of effective democracy which had failed to fulfill its economic and social promise to the people. For the future, one of the strongest assets of the country in fostering

---

[1] Source: National Archives and Records Administration, RG 59, Central Files 1964–66, POL 7 CHILE. Confidential. Drafted by Lunn.

democratic institutions would be the international solidarity enjoyed by Chile, especially within the Inter-American system inspired by Presidents Roosevelt, Kennedy and Johnson.

The Frei Government, Senator Tomic explained, would pursue parallel and inter-related economic and social programs. On the economic front, the government will attempt to spur development through doubling exports—primarily relying on increased copper production, but also emphasizing steel, paper, wood and fishmeal—and overcoming agricultural production and marketing problems. Priority social goals involve agrarian reform, education, housing and "promotion popular", a broad scheme of community social and economic action.

This program necessarily will be extremely expensive and Chile must rely on international solidarity to make possible the future pledged by Frei to the Chilean people; in particular, Chile looks to the United States for assistance. In economic discussions this week, Chile will seek renegotiation of debt falling due in the next few years held by agencies of the U.S. Government—especially the Export-Import Bank ($75 million) and the Treasury ($21 million)—and will make a case for further credits from these agencies, including program assistance from AID of $150 million.

Mr. Mann thanked Senator Tomic for his frank exposition and indicated the interest of the United States in President-elect Frei's objectives and the desire of the United States to provide significant assistance for a sound and realistic economic plan. He noted that we are far more prepared to give heavy assistance to a plan that will work than we are to contribute small amounts to a bad plan that merely increases a nation's debt and postpones the day of economic reckoning. The sole question was whether a program would work and be effective. Mr. Mann expected that discussions this week would focus on such basic technical issues as inflation and programs for productive and social investment, and that a program could be developed that we would find possible to support within the limits of our ability. In this connection, Mr. Rogers noted that FY 1965 funds for the Alliance are limited and subject to considerable competition as the result of favorable development opportunities elsewhere in the hemisphere.

Senator Tomic asked that an understanding on levels of U.S. assistance be reached as soon as possible because the new government needed to act quickly and decisively in the five months remaining before the Congressional elections. Senor Molina raised the particular problem he will face in assessing external resources for the budget message he must submit as Finance Minister on November 18. Mr. Mann indicated his expectation that the current week of discussions would make it possible to move ahead on arriving at subsequent assistance projections as the program and its requirements become clear.

275. Memorandum of Conversation[1]

Washington, October 17, 1964, 10 a.m.

SUBJECT

The Secretary's Second Meeting with the Mission of President-Elect Frei of Chile

PARTICIPANTS

The Secretary
Mr. Mann, Assistant Secretary, ARA
Mr. Solomon, Deputy Assistant Secretary, ARA
Senator Radomiro Tomic, Member, Chilean Delegation
Sergio Molina, Member, Chilean Delegation
Gabriel Valdes, Member, Chilean Delegation
Jose Pinera, Member, Chilean Delegation
Jose Zabala, Director, CORFO, New York
Mr. Dentzer, Director, Bolivian-Chilean Affairs, ARA

The Secretary asked whether the delegation was satisfied with its discussions in Washington.[2] Senator Tomic responded, expressing his satisfaction. Mr. Mann also expressed satisfaction with the talks.

In response to Secretary Rusk's question about the next step in negotiations, Mr. Solomon indicated that a mission would be sent to Santiago as soon as possible after Frei's inauguration to pursue these discussions further in conjunction with the Embassy and AID mission there.

The Secretary asked about the European portion of the delegation's trip. Mr. Valdes indicated the results of the trip were good, that the Europeans were interested in Chile, and that the Europeans were interested to know what the U.S. would do, especially on the question of debt rescheduling. Mr. Mann affirmed U.S. willingness to attempt to work out arrangements with the European creditor nations which would be in line with Chilean hopes.

Senator Tomic spoke of the importance of U.S. assistance to Chile in the spirit of inter-American solidarity, and emphasized that the Frei government wished to show achievement to the people before it

---

[1] Source: National Archives and Records Administration, RG 59, Central Files 1964–66, POL CHILE–US. Confidential. Drafted by Dentzer and approved in S on November 23. The time of the meeting is taken from Rusk's Appointment Book. (Johnson Library) The memorandum is part II of II; part I recorded Rusk's initial meeting with the Chilean delegation on October 14. (National Archives and Records Administration, RG 59, Central Files 1964–66, POL CHILE–US)

[2] In addition to meetings with Rusk and Mann, the delegation met with Dungan, AID Administrator Bell, EXIM Bank President Linder, and representatives of CIAP, IDB, IBRD, and IMF. (Telegram 331 to Santiago, October 17; ibid., POL 7 CHILE)

requested of them the full sacrifice that Chilean development would require. The Secretary assured him that the U.S. would keep in close touch with Senator Frei's advisers in the period leading up to the November 18 budget presentation to the Congress by the Chilean Minister of Finance, an event mentioned by the Chileans earlier as a date by which they hoped to have a clear picture of the amount of U.S. aid in 1965. Secretary Rusk also indicated his hope that efforts by the Chilean people would be called for at that time, and Senator Tomic assured him that this would be the case. Mr. Mann indicated he was willing to go along with the Frei government in postponing some of the sacrifices necessary so long as an earnest start was made now. He indicated to the Chilean mission that the Frei government would get at least what the Alessandri government received in terms of U.S. aid and added that he hoped circumstances would support even more aid. He stated the U.S. could not make any commitment now, however, and Tomic indicated he understood why this was the case.

Secretary Rusk inquired about agricultural imports into Chile, which he was informed ran about $125 million dollars a year. The Secretary stressed the importance of cutting back on this use of foreign exchange.

Senator Tomic asked for a special message from President Johnson to Frei on the occasion of the inauguration, and the Secretary indicated such a message would be sent.

The Secretary concluded the meeting by expressing his hope that the delegation has been satisfied with its mission to Washington. Senator Tomic indicated they were indeed satisfied and that they understood why the United States could not go further at this time, even though the Chileans might like to have a commitment. The Secretary assured Senator Tomic that the United States would move promptly in pursuing this subject and stressed again the two points mentioned in his previous interview with the delegation, the need for using foreign aid on a sound basis to build lasting achievements and the need to use funds committed on a timely and current basis. Senator Tomic assured the Secretary that Chile would do its part in carrying out the responsibilities of its partnership with the United States if the U.S. did likewise. He expressed the hope that Chile would be independent of U.S. assistance at the end of Frei's six years in office. Mr. Mann assured Senator Tomic that the U.S. was willing to help Chile or any friendly nation that sincerely tried to help its people and sought to put its own house in order.

276.   Telegram From the Embassy in Chile to the Department of State[1]

Santiago, November 13, 1964, 1 p.m.

126. For Mann and Bell from Solomon. I met with Frei for over two hours this morning, accompanied by Chargé, Dentzer and Robinson. Molina and Ahumada also present.

Frei opened meeting by expressing his great appreciation for substantially increased U.S. assistance and good will toward Chile shown in all levels of U.S.

He then took up the subject of U.S. assistance in CY 1965, explaining his approach to the first year of his government's life, that previous Chilean Governments had always asked the people to sacrifice for stabilization programs but that the programs never worked, that past governments had not cared about all the people, and that his people were mindful of this. For this reason, he wanted to achieve both a reduction in price inflation this year and show concrete benefits to the people, distinguishing his government thereby from its predecessors. He said that reaching the goal of only a 25 per cent price inflation in 1965 was his number one aim and that if he fell short of this, he would consider his first year a failure. If he attained this goal, he could go to the people with the political strength and moral right to demand greater sacrifice. He stated that he hoped, therefore, to sustain a heavy public investment program during this year, but he said that the information given him concerning proposed U.S. assistance for 1965 indicated it fell short by $40 million of his needs. I explained this was not so, and reviewed with him two budgets showing that 1965 U.S. assistance to the balance of payments including debt relief would be $135 million or 35 per cent greater than in 1964 and that 1965 assistance to the budget would be $102 million or 50 per cent greater than the actual 1964 level.

He was surprised and I believe impressed by these figures, which put U.S. aid in 1965 into the best—but fair and defensible—light, contrary to the figures presented on a different basis by his Minister of Finance. I further explained the changes we hoped to see in their investment program, exchange rate policy, etc. and believe was able to disabuse him somewhat of his belief U.S. conservative tradition underlay our position and rather that we were only concerned with workable achievement of targets.

---

[1] Source: National Archives and Records Administration, RG 59, Central Files 1964–66, AID(US) 8 CHILE. Confidential; Immediate. Passed to the White House.

Frei then turned conversation to the need for $20 million assist-ance for remainder of 1964. He said he had understood from reports to him prior to the Tomic mission to Washington and from subsequent conversations in Santiago with our Embassy that the U.S. would be willing to be of assistance for the final portion of 1964, that it was im-perative in terms of investor confidence that his government not be forced to break the IMF agreement, and that his government could not afford to begin its tenure by holding off unpaid creditors to an un-precedented extent. It then became clear that GOC would have 100 mil-lion escudos in unpaid bills as of December 31 in contrast to usual float of 50 million. Frei inquired whether it would be possible for the U.S. to give $20 million now, subtracting this sum from our announced pro-gram loan for 1965 for the time being, but with a "gentleman's agree-ment" that the same advance against 1966 assistance would be given toward end of 1965. After explaining impossibility of this, I offered to expedite as much as possible the processing of the aid program loan with the possibility if negotiations went quickly enough of signing the program loan agreement in mid December accompanied by initial tranche. However, this would still have to stretch over the full extent of CY 1965, and thus require adjustment in 1965 expenditures or rev-enues. Molina not enthusiastic about this and mentioned he might try New York banks and hoped we would give him support. I didn't an-swer and turned conversation to specific alternatives on finding local resources which we believe possible and preferable.

While this subject was left unresolved, it emphasized GOC need for wide access to escudos from the program loan to finance the in-vestment budget. I therefore agreed on Frei's request and as a gesture of cooperation to reduce the project component of our 1965 aid loan $10 million, increasing program loan to $80 million, as authorized by Washington.

Frei also asked that we jointly work out some kind of announce-ment concerning the nature of this week's talks. I told him we could not make any loan announcements or specify amounts of assistance but would be glad to work out some language of a generalized nature reporting on the work of the past week.

At conclusion of this general discussion, Frei asked me to stay on alone. Tenor of discussion was that he expected to come under attack in the coming months from certain sectors of the Chilean business community—not the industrial sector but the banking and commercial sectors—and he hoped to have U.S. understanding that these attacks would be based on reasonable curtailment by legitimate governmen-tal means of their power in society, as we would be able to judge for ourselves. I suggested as a friend that his best defense against such at-tacks was carrying out the financial discipline and other policies es-sential to both the private sector and overall Chilean development. He asked once again for our assistance in helping to resolve his financial problems of 1964, which he characterized as an infortunate inheritance from the previous government. In mentioning this, he acknowledged his confusion over previous reports that the U.S. would be willing to render such assistance, and he asked that U.S. officials never shrink from giving him any bad news about the future, whether it concerned aid or any other subject. In the course of agreeing I made clear what he had not realized before our discussions that any post election assistance would have had to come out of the same total Fiscal Year 1965 Chilean pot and really it boiled down to timing. He accepted this simplistic approach and conversation ended on warm note. We invited to tea today.[2]

Jova

_____

[2] An account of the "tea" meeting between Frei and Solomon is in airgram A–385 from Santiago, November 16. (Ibid., AID(US) 9 CHILE) The agreement to provide $80 million of program loan assistance in CY 1965 was signed on January 5. For an account of how the funds were utilized, see United States Senate, Committee on Government Operations, Subcommittee on Foreign Aid Expenditures, *United States Foreign Aid in Action: A Case Study* (Washington, 1966), p. 32.

_____

277.   Memorandum for the 303 Committee[1]

Washington, January 25, 1965.

SUBJECT

    Financial Support to Selected Candidates in the 7 March 1965 Congressional Elections in Chile

1. Summary

    This is a proposal to provide funds in the amount of [*less than 1 line of source text not declassified*] to approximately 35 selected candidates running for Senate and Chamber of Deputies (Lower House) seats in the 7 March 1965 congressional election in Chile. Selection of these candidates is being made jointly with the Ambassador. Each candidate is involved in a close race with a candidate of the Communist-Socialist

_____

[1] Source: Department of State, INR/IL Historical Files, 303 Committee Special Files, January–June 1965. Secret; Eyes Only.

FRAP coalition and in some cases against undesirable extremist candidates of his own or other parties as well. This action is primarily a denial operation against the FRAP [2 *lines of source text not declassified*]. Candidates to be supported represent all non-FRAP parties, and support is for specific individuals rather than for parties. Funds will be passed covertly through several channels to ensure maximum security. The net result of this operation should be an increase in the overall ability of the Chilean Christian Democratic Party (PDC) to promote those activities needed to bring about necessary reforms and to reduce the effectiveness of the FRAP opposition.

2. Problem

To defeat those FRAP candidates who are in close competition with candidates from other parties in the 7 March congressional election. Secondary advantages to be obtained from this denial operation will be: (a) the defeat of troublesome members of non-FRAP parties who are running on the same party ticket with the more moderate, pro-U.S. candidates who receive our support [2½ *lines of source text not declassified*].

3. Factors Bearing on the Problem

a. Significance of the Congressional Election

The March election will be the most important political event to take place in Chile in 1965 since its outcome will influence future political alignments and determine whether the Frei government can successfully carry out its reform program. Elective offices to be filled are all 147 seats in the Chamber of Deputies and 20 of the 45 Senate seats. The FRAP is trying to stage a comeback after its defeat in the September presidential elections, while the PDC, which is now a minority party with only four Senators and 28 Deputies, is hoping to obtain the congressional strength it will need to implement its reform program. Even if the Christian Democrats attain an election majority in the Chamber of Deputies they will still need the support of individuals in other parties to put through this program in the Senate. The Radical Party is badly split, and the moderate Radicals now in control of the party are being challenged by left-wing Radical candidates who are determined to swing the party into an alliance with the FRAP in opposition to the Frei government. A small dissident Socialist group which supported Frei in the presidential elections is running candidates under the label of the Democratic Party and is hoping to attract a portion of the electoral support of Socialists and other FRAP members who are dissatisfied with Communist domination of the FRAP coalition. The FRAP parties themselves were unable to reach a firm electoral agreement; in some districts there is an electoral pact whereby all FRAP coalition members are instructed to vote for one of the FRAP parties; in other districts the FRAP parties will be competing against each other.

b. Discussion

Since all political parties are participating in the March elections, we are not basing our support on a choice of one political faction, as was necessary in the presidential election where the campaign was clearly between the Christian Democrats and the Communists. The upcoming congressional races have been studied in great detail, electoral district by district, in order to select candidates of non-FRAP parties who need help in order to defeat their FRAP opponents and who have a good chance of success if they receive our support.

4. Coordination

This proposal has the approval of Ambassador Dungan, who has reviewed the list of proposed candidates and has agreed that covert support should be provided to most of them. The remaining candidates are under consideration and final selection will be made only with the approval of the Ambassador.

5. Recommendation

It is recommended that the amount of [*less than 1 line of source text not declassified*], which is available within the CIA, be used to provide covert support to selected candidates who are in close competition with FRAP contenders in the 7 March congressional elections in Chile.[2]

---

[2] Acting Deputy Under Secretary Thompson agreed to support the proposal on the understanding that Dungan would determine the amount of money actually spent. (Memorandum from Mann to Thompson, February 3; ibid.) The 303 Committee ratified this decision by telephonic vote on February 5. (Memorandum from Murat W. Williams to Mann, February 16; ibid.) On March 7 the Christian Democrats captured an absolute majority in the Chamber of Deputies and emerged as the strongest party in the Senate. In a March 11 memorandum, the CIA reported that Dungan had authorized [*text not declassified*] for 29 candidates, [*text not declassified*] of whom were subsequently elected. The Agency assessed the outcome as follows: "The landslide proportions of the Christian Democrats' congressional victory had not been expected by the Embassy or the CIA Station or, indeed, by President Frei himself. It is believed that Agency operations contributed modestly to the victory by insuring the defeat of some FRAP candidates who might otherwise have been elected and by helping to elect [*less than 1 line of source text not declassified*] Christian Democratic deputies which assured a working majority." (National Security Council, 303 Committee Files, Subject Files, Chile thru 1969)

278.   **Telegram From the Embassy in Ecuador to the Department of State**[1]

Quito, May 7, 1965, 2040Z.

842. For President and SecState from Harriman.[2]

During my brief visit to Santiago, GOC had made most thorough security arrangements through national police, lining streets where needed and protecting chancery and residence, as well as President's palace. We were greeted with some derogatory shouts and clenched fists, at the same time a certain number of friendly waves.

President Frei with Foreign Minister Valdes received Dungan and myself shortly after my arrival for over two hours and a half talk, mostly in English with little translation. Therefore we were able to cover a wide range of subjects. Frei listened attentively to my explanation of situation in Santo Domingo which required President Johnson's decision, with description of some vivid details of Communist take-over and atrocities. I emphasized that Communist subversion was now the dangerous aggression the hemisphere had to face and described Brazilian and Argentine ideas regarding necessity to expand permanent arrangements for rapid OAS peace keeping capability in order to avoid President being faced with necessity to take unilateral action in another crisis. I said that although he [Frei] appeared now to be out of sympathy with the President's decision, I believed he would reverse his opinion when all the facts were in and applaud the courage and decisiveness of President Johnson's action. In any event the immediate situation was being dealt with at USG's request through the OAS in both political and peace keeping fields. There appeared unanimous agreement in objective of creating stability which would permit Dominican people select government of their own choice. I asked for his full cooperation to this end.

Frei replied that he understood the President's dilemma and reasons his decision, but hoped that the President would understand the political scene in Chile. Chile has the largest Communist Party in the hemisphere. He believed he could reduce its influence through his

---

[1] Source: National Archives and Records Administration, RG 59, Central Files 1964–66, POL 7 US/HARRIMAN. Secret; Immediate. Repeated to Bogota, Santo Domingo, Caracas, Montevideo, Rio de Janeiro, Lima, Panama, Guatemala, Buenos Aires, USCINCSO, and USUN. Passed to the White House, DOD and CIA.

[2] On April 27 President Johnson sent U.S. Marines to intervene in the Dominican civil war. In response to criticism that he had acted unilaterally, the President sent Harriman to Latin America to explain the decision and seek support from other countries. Documentation on the Dominican crisis is in *Foreign Relations, 1964–1968*, volume XXXII.

policies. Communists had led in attacking former ruling class privilege. He was convinced the way to eliminate Communist influence was his social and economic revolution which would achieve more for the people and out-do them in appeal. He recognized importance of private investment and took pride in sensible new arrangements with Anaconda and Kennecott, and also with American Foreign Power and International Telephone and Telegraph. His policies were pro-American. He had won the election with that plank [in] his platform. He had great admiration for President Johnson's domestic program, but we had to understand Chile feared military dictatorship and military intervention as much as Communist subversion. Chile was getting along well today with civilian governments in Argentina and Peru whereas military dictatorship particularly in Argentina would reverse this situation and possible Argentine military intervention menace Chile's independence. He and his colleagues had worked hard to develop Christian Democratic Party. 20 years ago they only had 20 percent as many votes as the Communists whereas today Christian Democratic Party vote was five times as large as the Communists. American liberalism had given inspiration and courage to the CDP and he hoped that this liberal United States image would not now be blurred by military action or identification with and support of military regimes. The Communist issue was not as clear cut in Chile as in the United States and U.S. should be prepared to accept certain risks to maintain our liberal leadership. The Communists had helped awaken the people to oppose the status quo and had to be dealt with as part of the political scene in many L.A. countries. In Chile the Communists could be beaten through political action rather than military suppression. Frei expressed confidence that his program would succeed and thus Communist influence would fade. I interrupted to say that Communist danger was different in almost every country and the tactics in dealing with it had to be flexible.

After much discussion, he agreed. He pointed out that he could not jeopardize his own leadership and that of the CD Party by becoming involved in military intervention in D.R. He therefore could not support the OAS resolution and cannot send troops.[3] If he proposed it, he would be defeated in Congress and reduce his influence. In any event he obviously did not want to take this action. Dungan asked if he would send a medical unit. This he declined as any military unit, even medical, required congressional action. But when I pressed him to participate, mentioning Peruvian food shipment, he finally agreed to send relief supplies. I pressed him on the necessity for

---

[3] The OAS voted on May 6 to establish an Inter-American Peace Force, a unit that augmented U.S. forces in the Dominican Republic with contingents from several member states. Chile was one of five countries to vote against the proposal. (Department of State *Bulletin*, May 31, 1965, pp. 854–869)

Chile, as representing constructive liberal force in L.A., to take an active part in helping solve Dominican situation, and urged him to send a representative in whom he had confidence to Santo Domingo to keep him informed of the true situation during coming months. He admitted that he had no confidence in his present Chargé and turning to Valdes told him to select someone promptly. Neither man had any suggestions of concrete action to be taken except to state that some reasonably representative government must be established soonest with elections to follow as soon as practicable. He had expressed no choice of factions. He did however refer to Bosch as "a coward remaining securely under American protection in Puerto Rico." He had had communications from Colonel Caamano but had no judgement of his position. I explained rebel isolated position in a small part of Santo Domingo and lack of control of other parts of the country. I said we must avoid unilateral political action in the recognition of any group as this was almost as bad as unilateral military action. He agreed and commented that we must await more information from Santo Domingo particularly the commission's report.[4]

As I took my leave Frei expressed hope that even though we had differed on D.R. situation, and might again disagree on tactics for achieving mutual objectives this would not affect warm friendship that existed between our two countries and intimate personal relationship he had with Dungan in Santiago. He expressed great confidence in Tomic and hoped he could develop similar relationship in Washington.[5]

To Santiago for Dungan:

Since this written in Quito hope you will make such comments or additions you feel desirable.[6]

Coerr

---

[4] On May 1 the OAS voted to send a five-member committee to the Dominican Republic. The committee was instructed to seek a negotiated settlement and report its conclusions or recommendations. Chile abstained from the proposal. (Ibid., May 17, 1965, pp. 738–748)

[5] President Johnson and Mann reviewed Chile's role in the Dominican crisis on May 25: "Mr. Mann said that although the Mexicans voted against us, they did not lobby against us. The Chileans did, and they are the ones who hurt us. The President said he thought we should take a few siestas ourselves and go to sleep for a while on some of their requests. Mr. Mann said he could not agree more." The two men later discussed how to implement this policy: "Mr. Mann said that we would have to go slow but we should put a price tag on it without ever admitting this has anything to do with their actions. The President said that Mr. Mann should tell these people that he is doing his best, but people are upset and it is very, very difficult. Mr. Mann said he understood very well." (Johnson Library, Papers of Thomas C. Mann, Telephone Conversations with LBJ, May 2, 1965–June 2, 1966)

[6] Dungan's account of the meeting between Frei and Harriman was transmitted in telegrams 1722 and 1729 from Santiago, May 7 and 8, respectively. (Both in National Archives and Records Administration, RG 59, Central Files 1964–66, POL 7 US/HARRIMAN)

279. Telegram From the Embassy in Chile to the Department of State[1]

Santiago, June 14, 1965, 1540Z.

1920. Subject: Project Camelot.[2]

Communist newspaper Saturday morning, June 12, broke story Project Camelot under headline "Yankees Study Invasion of Chile," subheaded, "Project Camelot Financed by U.S. Army," etc.

Embassy recently became aware through university community of serious anxiety middle-of-the-road scholars with this project and specifically with the manner in which university people here were approached by SORO personnel.[3]

I consider, particularly under current conditions, this effort to be seriously detrimental to U.S. interests in Chile and urgently request full explanation of Department Army actions in this regard. Was this project approved by the Department?

On basis December 4 memorandum SORO concerning Project Camelot,[4] consider this whole effort not only politically dangerous, but a serious duplication of other U.S. Government efforts, and a waste of government funds. Urgently request guidance from Department and explanation from Army OSD this activity in Chile without prior notification.[5]

Dungan

---

[1] Source: National Archives and Records Administration, RG 59, Central Files 1964–66, DEF 11 US. Confidential; Priority. Passed to DOD.

[2] See Document 280.

[3] The Special Operations Research Office, a private research organization affiliated with the American University in Washington, D.C.

[4] A copy of the memorandum is in the National Archives and Records Administration, RG 59, Central Files 1964–66, DEF 11 US.

[5] The Department subsequently reported that it had expressed its concern in a letter to the Secretary of the Army. (Telegram 1238 to Santiago, June 17; ibid.) In the letter, the Department complained that the arrangements for Camelot fell "far short of the kind of coordination that such an ambitious project may require." In addition to telegram 1920 from Santiago, the Department had received other reports of the "unfavorable impression made by the Camelot project on Latin American scholars—a fact of considerable political importance." (Letter from Llewellyn Thompson to Stephen Ailes, June 19; ibid.) Joseph Califano, Special Assistant to the Secretary and Deputy Secretary of Defense, defended the project in a memorandum to Bundy, June 24: "No Camelot research activities have been authorized or conducted outside the continental United States, including Chile. The only known contact is a letter written by a U.S. scientist to a Swedish social scientist presently resident in Chile." (Johnson Library, National Security File, Country File, Chile, Vol. III, 12/64–9/65)

280.   Memorandum From Secretary of State Rusk to President Johnson[1]

Washington, June 30, 1965.

I understand that you wish a brief memorandum on the "Camelot" matter.[2]

I have discussed this with Secretary McNamara and he and I agreed that we personally would both review urgently the Army sponsored research activities on political and international problems outside the United States and try to prevent the kind of stir and misunderstanding which has arisen from Camelot.

Senator McCarthy's office is trying to locate him in order that he and I can be in touch by telephone in order to arrange a meeting to discuss it with him.[3]

Camelot is an Army sponsored project being carried out by the Special Operations Research Office. It is a large-scale unclassified project calling for an estimated 140 professional man hours of work and a budget of more than $4,000,000. The proposed study would attempt to make a scientific analysis of international tension and war and insurgency and counterinsurgency. Considerable case work abroad is envisaged, including intensive studies of Bolivia, Colombia, Paraguay, Peru and Venezuela.

Such studies made by private social scientists would probably elicit little attention, even though some of the "jargon" of the social scientists subjects them to quick public misunderstanding. The sponsorship of such studies in foreign countries by our own military services touches upon sensitive nerves and can cause problems. In Chile, for example, discussions among social scientists about the project was the basis for a sharp communist attack as well as criticisms from skeptical and more traditional social scientists themselves.

---

[1] Source: National Archives and Records Administration, RG 59, Central Files 1964–66, DEF 11 US. Confidential. No drafting information appears on the memorandum.

[2] The President had asked Mann for a memorandum, particularly in the wake of an upcoming investigation by the Senate Foreign Relations Committee: "I want a complete report from you on your best judgment sometime before the day's over on this Camelot project and Ralph Dungan and what he did about it, and who got this stuff out, the Army and the State Department fighting about it." "I don't know why Ralph Dungan's getting it out in the paper and why it's getting published, and what the story is, and give me a memo on it so I can understand it." (Johnson Library, Recordings and Transcripts, Recording of telephone conversation between President Johnson and Thomas Mann, June 30, 1965, 12:57 p.m., Tape F65.52, Side A, PNO 1)

[3] I did reach him; he is relaxed and will wait until Fulbright returns and can talk about it. This was a part of McCarthy's attitude toward CIA, etc. DR. [Footnote in the source text.]

It is my understanding that, inside the United States, there are important differences of opinion among social scientists about the utility of this type of quantitative research project.

Secretary McNamara and I will follow up on this here, and I will try to help Ralph Dungan cool tempers in Chile.

This will serve as the report which you requested from Tom Mann earlier today.[4]

Dean Rusk[5]

---

[4] The Department of Defense announced the cancellation of Project Camelot on July 8. The President subsequently directed the Secretary of State to "establish effective procedures which will enable you to assure the propriety of Government-sponsored social science research in the area of foreign policy." (Letter from the President to Rusk, August 2; *Public Papers of the Presidents of the United States: Lyndon B. Johnson, 1965*, Book II, p. 832)

[5] Printed from a copy that indicates Rusk signed the original.

---

281. Memorandum From William G. Bowdler of the National Security Council Staff to the President's Special Assistant for National Security Affairs (Bundy)[1]

Washington, November 10, 1965.

SUBJECT

   Chilean Program Loan

BOB will have back to you sometime today the Chilean loan paper with Schultze's recommendation.[2] I understand that BOB will recommend a reduction of $10 million in the $80 million recommended.

Our negotiating team has not left for Santiago and will not do so until the President's authorization is in hand. Dungan has been informed of the delay.[3]

---

[1] Source: Johnson Library, National Security File, Country File, Chile, Vol. IV, 10/65–7/67. Confidential.

[2] Attached but not printed are memoranda to the President from Bell (November 6) and Schultze (November 10).

[3] In telegram 431 to Santiago, November 9. (National Archives and Records Administration, RG 59, Central Files 1964–66, AID(US) 9 CHILE)

At staff meeting on Monday[4] you asked why the program loan had to be as high as $80 million. The AID memo to the President does not really address itself to this question. The Chileans wanted $100–$130 million for 1966. State, AID, and the Country Team scaled this down to $80 million, based on these considerations:

a) This amount is what *they think* Chile needs to cover its balance of payments deficit and to produce the local proceeds necessary for Frei to continue an *adequate* level of public investment to maintain the momentum of his "Revolution in Liberty".

b) An amount higher than $80 million would reduce the pressure on Chile to make needed self-help efforts.

c) An amount appreciably lower (say $60 million) would confront the Chilean Government with the need to cut its 1966 investment program even more drastically than we are proposing, or resort to inflationary financing. Frei would undoubtedly opt for the latter and thereby aggravate the problem which is Chile's most serious obstacle to a viable economy.[5]

BOB is recommending a reduction of $10 million. The BOB argument is that increased copper prices and better tax collections make a reduction of this magnitude possible without materially affecting either Chilean balance of payments or the public investment budget. As I mentioned in staff meeting this morning, BOB also has in mind demonstrating to Chile and other aid recipient countries that we follow a flexible approach in setting the limits of our assistance.

The state of play as I write this memo is that BOB is waiting to hear from Dave Bell whether he goes along with the BOB cut and will modify his memo accordingly.

I think that the cut can probably be justified. But we need to weigh the political impact from these standpoints:

1. If the project loan assistance for Chile (which was $16 million in FY 1965) is not continued in FY 1966 (as ARA says is the case, and they have agreed to that), the net reduction of our assistance will be *$26 million.*

2. The assistance to Brazil should also reflect a corresponding reduction if we are to avoid invidious comparisons.

---

[4] November 8.

[5] In a November 10 memorandum to Bundy, Mann reported taking another consideration into account: "the fact that the Chilean Government was most uncooperative in the Dominican crisis." Although he concurred in providing the $80 million program loan, Mann suggested a confidential mission to tell Frei "that we expect cooperation to be a two way street and that we are very disturbed about the Chilean Government's attitude towards the Dominican crisis." (Johnson Library, National Security File, Country File, Chile, Vol. IV, 10/65–7/67)

I suggest that in your memo to the President recommending approval of the loan, you make these points:

1. On the anniversary of his first year in office (November 3) President Frei addressed the nation. Regarding U.S. aid, he said:

"Without abandoning any of our fundamental positions, we have maintained loyal and frank friendship with the United States and have found in them understanding for our task and fundamental economic cooperation for the life of the country, which is a debt that we recognize".

2. Chile has told us that it will participate in the Rio Conference.[6]

3. We can hardly do less for a strong democracy like Chile than we do for shaky constitutional government in Colombia and a de facto government in Brazil.

4. In terms of the contest between democracy and communism to bring reform and prosperity to the people of Chile, and of the other Latin American countries, we have a big stake in the success of the Frei experiment.[7]

WGB

---

[6] Reference is to the Second Special Inter-American Conference which was held in Rio de Janeiro November 17–30.

[7] The memorandum to the President was apparently never sent. On November 15 the Department informed the Embassy that action on the program loan had been deferred pending the outcome of the Harriman–Solomon mission. (Telegram 454 to Santiago, November 15; National Archives and Records Administration, RG 59, Central Files 1964–66, FN 10 IMF)

---

282. **Telegram From the President's Special Assistant for National Security Affairs (Bundy) to the Ambassador to Chile (Dungan)[1]**

Washington, November 12, 1965, 8:48 p.m.

CAP 65695. Eyes Only for Ambassador from McGeorge Bundy.

1. October price rise in Chilean copper from 36 to 38 cents is asserted by companies to be a primary reason for identical U.S. copper

---

[1] Source: Johnson Library, National Security File, Situation Room File, Outgoing Traffic, 11/9/65–11/14/65. Secret; Eyes Only. A draft with Bundy's handwritten revisions is ibid., White House Central File, Confidential File, Oversized Attachments, December 1965.

price rise announced this week by Anaconda and Phelps Dodge. This creates most serious concern here and leads us to ask what combination of carrots and sticks might persuade the Chileans to reduce their price by 2 cents.

2. We fully recognize that export price of copper is a deeply sensitive question in Chile and that world copper market is tempting at present. But we also believe strongly that long-run price stability is deeply in interest of both U.S. and Chile, and CEA as well as some of the wisest heads in copper business tell us that high copper prices may simply lead to rapid substitution of aluminum in important sectors of the market, like automobile radiators and local electric transmission lines. High voltage lines have already been lost to aluminum.

3. We thus see a strong basis of common interest between Johnson and Frei administrations and sensible copper companies in preventing runaway copper prices.

4. We have our eye on the following possible sticks:

(1) Pending $80 million program loan.
(2) Hold-up on investment guarantees for $80 million Kennecott loan to Chile and $135 million new Anaconda investment with the result that there would be no expansion.
(3) Hold-up on pending Ex-Im Bank applications for $135 million of loans to companies operating in Chile.
(4) Use of 700-thousand-ton U.S. stockpile to break world copper market.
(5) Use of government incentives to promote substitution of aluminum for copper.

5. Among carrots available we are considering:

(1) Strengthening of program loan in return for price rollback. As we see it, two-cent increase brings only 38 million a year to Chilean Government, and we are ready to consider sympathetically any politically manageable deal which would cover cost of rollback.
(2) Continuing warm political support for Frei on all practicable issues.
(3) Personal appeal to Frei from highest level here.

6. We recognize difficulty of Chilean decision to reduce prices and are prepared to do our best to create a situation in which such a decision can be strongly defended by Frei. It occurs to us, for example, that a price rollback here might usefully set stage for later Chilean action, and there may be other things we can do which you would see more clearly than we can. In any event, your assessment should consider relative advantages of Chilean rollback before, with, or after a decision by American companies to rescind U.S. price increases.

7. We know this is a tough one, but effective rollback of copper price increases is at least equal in importance to earlier aluminum

rollback. Chilean rollback now looks like the key, so success with Frei is of first importance to us. We count on your political imagination to devise best possible tactics to achieve this result.

Please answer via same communications channel.

---

283. **Telegram From the Ambassador to Chile (Dungan) to the President's Special Assistant for National Security Affairs (Bundy)[1]**

Santiago, November 13, 1965, 1530Z.

131545Z. Eyes Only for McGeorge Bundy from Ambassador. Ref: CAP 65695.[2]

1. Understand generally impact copper price rise and effect on US economy and problems caused by increase following on heels aluminum roll-back. Request urgently some backup data on inflation effect in order make convincing case here if this course is directed. Taken as given the question of inflationary impact copper price rise, I wonder whether you have bought too easily the assertion that Phelps & Anaconda price increases necessitated by Chilean action. In other words, there are two ways in which US economy could be protected: (1) force roll-back in Chilean price increase as you suggest or (2) force American companies to absorb raw material price increase. Here are some factors which suggest course number two.

A. Pure copper bars put on board ship *Antofagasta* at cost of 14½ cents per pound—copper sold in US at 38 cents and on LME at 65 cents per pound. Somebody makes a hell of a profit.

B. Chilean copper represents only 13 percent American consumption. According 1963 Bureau Mines figures Chilean imports to US 228,000 tons out of consumption 1,744,000 tons. Therefore, theoretically Chilean price rise need have minor inflationary impact in US. Chileans believe that substantial amounts Chilean copper now being bought US companies 38 cents going into London market at 65 cents.

C. USG has held off antitrust suit US companies at our request pending outcome copper legislation. Suggest you consult findings Department of Justice regarding price and market control in copper be-

---

[1] Source: Johnson Library, White House Central File, Confidential File, Oversized Attachments, December 1965. Secret; Eyes Only. Repeated to the Department of State.
[2] Document 282.

fore we embark on what I consider to be a suicidal course in terms of American foreign policy.

2. I mention the above among other elements which should be considered before the decision is made to force Chile to back down on its recent price increase. I am not an expert on copper prices and marketing, but I know enough to lead me to question whether forcing Chile to back down is the only or best method to pursue in order to keep prices to US copper consumers within non-inflationary limits.

I am certain that you have already given thorough consideration to inevitable adverse political effects of course suggested reftel. Political effects not only in Chile but through the LDC's. Nevertheless, I feel I must state my own opinion before we embark on this course.

Carrot-stick combination listed might succeed in forcing GOC rollback. The cost to the Frei government and to the extent that it represents the hope of democracy and the Alliance for Progress in Latin America would be incalculable. Recent increase to 38 cents strongly supported by all political parties including the conservatives and public opinion. Lagarrigue[3] now struggling against increasing pressure to push price to 40 cents in view of tight market apparently continuing well into the future. In other words, to force Frei government to a rollback might very well bring the government down or so weaken it as to make it difficult or impossible to pursue the reform program on which it is embarked.

Substitution question is not paramount in Chilean minds. Their research shows very tight supply for immediate future and increase markets in developing countries as means of meeting long range marketing problems. Moreover Chileans believe that substantial sales in London market over relatively long period at high prices plus long term prospective tight supply has probably already caused whatever substitution is likely to occur. In other words, the substitution has or is occurring without any price benefits redounding to Chile.

However the overriding consideration in your suggestion is whether we are going to confirm in the minds, not only of Chileans, but all the world the Marxist propaganda line that our only interest is in protecting the profit situation of our American companies. I realize completely that there is a large and critical American self-interest involved here. I have no doubt that it is important to maintain stable prices in primary metal in the American market. The central political question is who will pay the piper. Reftel clearly says that in every case where a price is to be paid it will be paid by the producing country to the advantage of the American entrepreneur.

---

[3] Javier Lagarrigue, head of the Chilean Copper Department.

I respectfully suggest that most serious consideration be given to the very long-run adverse political effects that course suggested in reftel will have for the United States. I also respectfully suggest that the course suggested is political suicide for the US in the developing world and particularly Latin America.

If after your meeting today you conclude a Chilean roll-back is the only solution I will put together your imposing arsenal of sticks and not so imposing supply of carrots and make a deal. It can be done, I believe. But the price will be atrocious and I strongly recommend that every other course be explored before we resort to the one suggested reftel. There is also a very real possibility that Frei as a matter of principle and practical politics will consider this suggestion beyond the pale.

I shall stand by for instructions. If you decide that the pitch should be [made] I will try to do it today or tomorrow when I have lunch with Frei.

Incidentally, the copper veto has not yet been released.[4] I would not be at all surprised to see the whole Chileanization scheme scrapped in face of proposal in reftel and we would end up with marketing monopoly if not outright nationalization. It probably would be economic suicide for Chile but I think they might risk it.

Dungan

---

[4] Reference is to Frei's program to manage the copper industry, which was approved by the Chilean Congress on November 3. Frei subsequently modified the proposal by presidential veto.

284. Memorandum of Telephone Conversation Between President Johnson and the Under Secretary of State for Economic Affairs (Mann)[1]

November 13, 1965, 12:15 p.m.

The President said he wanted to talk about the Chilean copper thing. He said he guessed that Mr. Mann had seen all the traffic including Dungan's cable[2] saying the copper companies want to roll back. Mr. Mann said he had not seen the cable. The President asked Mr. Mann to get all of the communications and to read them and then they could see what could be worked out. The President said that Mc-Namara had talked with the President of Anaconda[3] and they don't want a higher price. They say that the trouble is that Frei only has 30% of the Senate and they forced him to raise the price to 38 and will force him to go to 40. The President said that the danger was that they would go up further.

The President said he had been advised to send a person down to convince Frei that he should roll the price back to 36¢. Ralph Dungan says that the copper companies ought to roll back, not Chile. The President said he thought we had to find some way to say we will both roll back. He thought we should explain that if our economy goes bad we will not be able to give any loans. Ask them to keep the price down and keep it out of the papers. Tell them we have not decided on an $80 million loan—probably will give them 60, but we will talk about that later.

The President said he had been informed that Mr. Mann was not the one to go down to Chile for this job. Mr. Mann said that was correct—he was too visible. The President said they were suggesting Clifford, but he did not like to use these private lawyers who had clients of their own.

Mr. Mann asked about Bob Anderson and the President said he thought he was a little too much Johnson. Mr. Mann said he thought he was a very convincing talker and that he can make a very good case. Mr. Mann said he thought perhaps we should send someone down outside of government.

---

[1] Source: Johnson Library, Papers of Thomas C. Mann, Telephone Conversations with LBJ, May 2, 1965–June 2, 1965. No classification marking. Drafted by Patricia A. Saunders. Mann was in Washington; the President was in Texas. According to the President's Daily Diary, Johnson placed the call. (Ibid.)

[2] Document 283.

[3] Charles Jay Parkinson.

Mr. Mann said that Mr. Bundy was suggesting a young fellow named Gensberg (?)[4] on his staff. Mr. Mann said he did not know him. The President said he was more of a price man in this country and he did not think he was the one to do it.

Mr. Mann said we needed a tough guy and that the best negotiator in this building was Tony Solomon. He negotiated the agreements with Brazil and the first one with Chile and Mr. Mann was convinced that he would do the job. He added that Mr. Solomon has no political image—he is just a very good economist. Mr. Mann said if the President wished to choose someone to go, Solomon could accompany that person. This would eliminate the need for the person chosen by the President to speak Spanish.

The President asked if Berle would be any good. Mr. Mann said he might. He said he knew the Latins and he has a liberal image.

Mr. Mann said he thought the trick would be to send somebody down to say the first objective is to get a roll back to 36¢. Mr. Mann said he would have to say that the American companies would go along with it. Even if this failed, at least we should get a commitment not to go any higher. Mr. Mann said he would hope that both things could be accomplished. He said he thought the substitution argument 36 to 38¢ makes aluminum competitive with copper, and the argument that Chile has a program to increase its production from 600,000 to 1 million tons by 1970, should show that the Chilean Government has every reason to keep the price down so that they do not lose the market. They should go into volume rather than price. Mr. Mann said it might also help if we could offer them something on our tariff. He said he did not know what the US attitude would be but we do produce 90% of our own consumption.

Mr. Mann said another arrangement would be the stockpile. And another would be the AID package.

Mr. Mann said the one thing we should not do is offer them any kind of political support. He said that Frei was o.k. but that his party has leftwingers and the opposition is leftwing and they may shift any day on Chicom representation in the UN or they could take all of Latin America away from support of keeping them out. They could also shift on the Dominican Republic.

The President asked if they had any communists in the government. Mr. Mann said no, but they are in the opposition. He said that in the party they have socialists who are even left of the communists—

---

[4] Reference is apparently to Edmund E. Getzin, chief of the Division of Industrial and Strategic Materials Division, Office of International Commodities, Bureau of Economic Affairs, Department of State.

who are for violent political action. He said that he felt, with these pressures, we could not depend on Frei's political moves. The President asked what political support Mr. Mann was talking about and Mr. Mann said that he was referring to the paragraph in the cable that went out last night from the W.H.[5] The President asked who sent it and whether Mr. Mann had seen it. Mr. Mann explained that Mr. Bundy had tried to reach him but he was at the Japanese [Embassy?] and they could not get to him.

Mr. Mann said that the President should not forget that Frei has a lot of leverage on us because of the US copper industry and the deal just through Congress. He said we should not push him too far.

Mr. Mann said the second thing was the cartel with Zambia and Congo. He said Zambia will be under great pressures to impose economic pressures against Southern Rhodesia[6] and if they do then there will be the problem of getting Zambian copper out. He said this copper goes through Rhodesia and the Rhodesians could retaliate. One-sixth of the world's copper is produced in Zambia and if this were taken off the market Mr. Mann did not think we could hold the price line. Mr. Mann said he thought we should get the UK to help us in urging the Zambians not to get into blows and counter-blows with the Rhodesians.

The President said that he thought Mr. Mann should try to pull this together. The President said that he is advised that an emissary should go to Chile right now. McNamara thinks that the price will go to 40¢.

The President said he would like to have a memo from Mr. Mann on the following items.

Points:

1. How do we increase our own production and the production of friendly countries—work around the clock, do it any way we can.

2. Find out what procurement the government has—not only Defense Department but each and every agency.

3. Forego, substitute, postpone or minimize the use of copper.

4. See what the principal civilian requirements are such as power companies, what suggestions they have on how they could minimize consumption—civilian as well as government.

5. Try to evolve some plan that could be sold to any leftist that would show it would be to his gain rather than loss.

---

[5] Document 282.

[6] On November 11 Prime Minister Ian D. Smith unilaterally declared Rhodesia's independence, prompting Zambia and Great Britain to press for economic sanctions.

a) Frei's expansion program
b) Substitution argument
c) Stock pile
d) Tariff
e) AID Package

Mr. Mann asked the President who was in touch with the companies and the President said McNamara and Califano.

[Omitted here is discussion of possible candidates for the mission to Chile.]

---

285. **Memorandum by the Under Secretary of State for Economic Affairs (Mann)**[1]

Washington, November 13, 1965.

Our views on the Chilean export of the copper problem follow:

You should know that we have a telegram from our embassy in Zambia[2] reporting that President Kaunda believes that the British measures against Southern Rhodesia are deficient; and that if the rebellion is not nipped in 3 months, the Rhodesian rebels can consolidate their positions and begin winning sufficient international support to make the unilateral declaration of independence irreversible. Kaunda believes that active participation by Zambia in the sanctions program is indispensable if the program is to succeed. He says Zambia cannot be the channel for sustaining the Smith regime. Kaunda, therefore, requests the British and us to provide contingency and economic assistance so as to permit Zambia to impose a total boycott on all Rhodesian imports, including coal.

George Ball and I believe this poses even more serious problems than last month's Chilean price increase. We are sending a cable,[3] copy of which will be repeated to you, which will in essence point out that Katanga and Rhodesia supply 25% of the world's supply of copper and if this were taken off the market, not only would a world shortage and sky-rocketing prices result, but the British would lose a large amount

---

[1] Source: Johnson Library, White House Central File, Subject File, Ex BE 4/Copper. No classification marking. Drafted by James D. Johnston, Mann's staff assistant. The memorandum was evidently sent to the President at the LBJ Ranch in Texas.

[2] Telegram 711 from Lusaka, November 12. (National Archives and Records Administration, RG 59, Central Files 1964–66, POL 16 RHOD)

[3] Not further identified.

of foreign exchange (British have spoken to George Ball about 200,000,000 pounds), which they have asked if we could replace. We have replied to the British in the negative, given our balance of payments situation. We are saying to Kaunda that Zambian sanctions against Southern Rhodesia would hurt Southern Rhodesia less than counter-sanctions against Zambia by Southern Rhodesia would hurt Zambia, since: (a) railroad through which Zambian copper now moves to sea passes through Southern Rhodesia and we are not certain of time it would take or the cost to ship Zambian copper by other means; (b) Zambia is dependent on Rhodesia for coal. Telegram presumably will say that we are not prepared to pick up large checks either for Zambia or for the British if Zambia engages in sanctions campaign against Southern Rhodesia. Also, Zambia may have in mind military and other actions in addition to economic sanctions.

On the Chile side of the copper problem, we think an effort should be made to get Frei to agree: (a) to rollback copper price from 38¢ to 36¢ *contingent* on U.S. industry taking the lead and, (b) regardless of Frei's willingness to do a rollback, to agree to resist pressures which Dungan reports already exist for additional price rises. Avoidance of additional price increases in view of the uncertain Zambian situation is even more important than the rollback.

In approaching Frei, we should not push our case to the breaking point since Chile's ability to reverse its position on the agreement reached with the copper companies and Chile's ability to expropriate the copper mines, gives Frei real leverage in the precise area which is of most concern to us at this time.

Ball, Solomon and I agree that the most effective way to approach Frei would be to emphasize the following point:

1. A 38¢ price level—and even more so if price levels increase—will result in substitution of aluminum for copper. This conflicts with the plans of the Chilean government already publicly announced to increase copper production from 600,000 to 1,000,000 metric tons by 1970. The United States is, itself, a large copper producer and we believe maximum revenue from industry will be gained by paying attention to volume as well as to price.

2. Not only in order to maximize the return from the copper mining industry but also in order to prevent inflationary price increases consistent with actions which the U.S. government has already taken with regard to aluminum, the U.S. government would be prepared to sell from its stockpile. We should not commit ourselves at this time to sell, or to sell at any particular price level, but should leave the impression in Frei's mind that we will probably sell from our strategic stockpile if the price remains at 38¢. The experts tell us that the President has the authority to sell from the 775,000-ton stockpile by mak-

ing a determination that the national security justifies such action. There would, however, almost certainly be sharp criticism of this action on the ground that a security stockpile was being used to support price policy.

3. Inflationary price rises in the U.S. set off by copper will have an adverse impact on the U.S. competitive position and hence on U.S. balance of payments position. This would, of course, affect the ability of the U.S. to finance its AID program. We, therefore, think that Frei should cooperate with us in maintaining a reasonable price level in copper. If the Chilean government can cooperate with us, we would be prepared to finance through the Exim Bank, the purchase of 2 jet aircraft valued around $15 million and to make a program loan at an $80 million level. This would help cushion the loss of $16 million which would result from a 2¢ rollback in the price of Chilean copper.

4. The U.S. will undertake at the earliest opportunity within the GATT framework to eliminate the present U.S. tariff of 1.7¢ a pound on imported copper (this has some, but only limited, attraction for Chile because Kennecott and Anaconda, under an agreement with the Chilean government, currently absorb this tax so that Chilean government revenues would not be currently affected. However, this has some attraction for Chile since it does remove one trade barrier and presumably increases their ability to extract additional concessions from the companies).

We have considered, but do not yet have final opinions, on the following additional aspects of the problem:

1. Increase of production. Our present information from industry sources is that it would take 12 to 18 months to increase production either here or abroad.

2. U.S. government procurement. We will try this afternoon to get some figures or information on this from other U.S. government agencies and will report later.

3. Possibility of postponement or substituting uses of copper. Our first information is that the substitution of aluminum for copper in underground cables and in some automobile parts, such as radiators, is not yet technically and economically feasible. It may be in the future. We need more time to report on this.

4. Suggestions from major users of copper as to ways of minimizing consumption. We will need more time to report on this. Consultation with industry will be required.

5. In addition to the points suggested above, arguments Frei could use to convince Leftists and Nationalists that copper rollback is in Chilean interest. We could suggest to Frei that Chile, Canada, the United Kingdom, Peru, Zambia, the U.S. and other copper producers consult together concerning measures for keeping prices at a level

which will not invite substitutions and be harmful to the copper industry and at the same time meet world demand during this period of shortage and uncertainty. Frei might find that participation in a committee of this kind would be useful to him from a domestic political standpoint.

On the separate question of who might be the most effective persons to approach Frei, George Ball and I believe that Governor Harriman and Tony Solomon, together, would be the best choice for this job.[4]

Thomas C. Mann[5]

---

[4] A handwritten note from Marvin Watson records the President's decision: "Califano—call Tom Mann notify Harriman and Solomon ask them to undertake this assign[ment] and proceed as your judgment dictates." (Johnson Library, White House Central File, Subject File, Ex BE 4/Copper) For another account of these instructions, see Joseph A. Califano, Jr., *The Triumph and Tragedy of Lyndon Johnson: The White House Years*, p. 102.

[5] Printed from a copy that bears this typed signature.

---

286.   Telegram From the Embassy in Chile to the Department of State[1]

Santiago, November 16, 1965, 0001Z.

629: Ref: Embtel 626.[2] For President from Harriman. Pass Ball, McNamara, Mann, Califano, Bundy.

1. At 3 p.m. Ambassador Dungan, Solomon and I met with President Frei alone at his private residence. I stressed President Johnson had personally sent mission to share with Frei some of his problems as U.S. President:

A. Inflation. Underlined serious concern that unless great care exercised inflation could jeopardize continued success of full employment economy policies beneficial not only U.S. but world economy. If we can hold prices, success possible without serious reduction overseas expenditures.

---

[1] Source: National Archives and Records Administration, RG 59, Central Files 1964–66, POL 7 US/HARRIMAN. Confidential; Immediate; Exdis. Passed to the White House.

[2] Telegram 626 from Santiago, November 15, reported that Harriman had arrived in Santiago without publicity. (Ibid., INCO COPPER 17)

B. Balance of Payments. Though situation somewhat improved, we have come to limits requiring great care be exercised.

C. Copper Prices. Reviewed steel and aluminum cases. Said President Johnson feels Chile the bellwether: If Chile brings price back to 36 cents price rise can be prevented. Said President Johnson asks Frei's cooperation to reverse this recent price increase knowing he is equally concerned with the health of the world's economy. Pointed to gain for Chile in discouraging substitution for copper. Noted that President Johnson feels that Frei and he have same material as well as political interest in this.

2. I then said we realize there are serious political difficulties for President Frei in considering this, and that we are prepared to discuss ways and means of helping him cooperate in bringing copper price back to 36 cents. We authorized to discuss ways of compensating Chile for short-term loss involved. Moreover, we would welcome any ideas on ways in which we can help Frei with political problems his cooperation would pose.

3. President Frei responded that "naturally" he must consider the question because President Johnson had sent a personal mission asking him to do so. "My disposition is to help, because the United States helps us. But the problem is not easy," he said, giving the following reasons:

A. It is not just a problem of the U.S. market, but also the London market which indirectly affects prices on more than one million tons of copper in the world market.

B. All political elements in Chile have attacked the GOC for not setting even higher copper prices. The conservatives, radicals and liberals have even been more strongly critical than the Communists. The most reasonable of congressmen have spoken of 45 cents, the radicals of 50 cents, and others even more.

C. Substitution problem very serious, Frei convinced, when London market goes over 60 to 62 cents. (Yesterday it was 67 cents.)

D. Some producers (not American companies) are purchasing copper at 38 cents, processing it, and selling in Europe at 67 cents. In view of this Frei has been criticized here for discouraging further price increase.

E. GOC cabinet members are unanimously in favor of increasing the Chilean selling price still further. Frei has stood alone in cabinet arguing for "rational" pricing policy. GOC has advised European consumers of intention (but not formal decision) to raise Chilean price to 40 cents in early January if the present conditions of the London market continue. All members of cabinet feel price should be over 40 cents.

4. President Frei then described his difficult struggle to reverse the serious inflation which existed when he came into office, and emphasized the "tremendous importance" to Chile for balance of payments and other reasons for a one cent change in the copper price. "For us copper is not just one problem; it is the problem," Frei said. He recognized he must have good will for President Johnson whom he described as extremely open and generous toward Chile.

5. Frei asked if U.S. could not keep U.S. price at 36 cents by removing 1.7 cent import duty. Solomon replied that though that should be part of the considerations, the price stability of the world copper market which we both desire requires the cooperation of our two countries. Unilateral U.S. action on tariff without GOC roll-back would promote undesirable multiplicity of price markets in various parts of the world.

6. Frei said he would consult with his advisers, and arranged for Solomon and Dungan to meet at 6 p.m. this evening with Saez, Lagarrigue and Tomic to explore in depth ramifications and possibilities. He agreed that this evening's meeting might be first of several. He has agreed to see us again possibly 10 o'clock this evening if other meeting makes sufficient progress.[3]

Comment: Difficult as yet to judge whether Frei's willingness to explore possibilities represents simply courtesy to President Johnson or a degree of substantive flexibility. Obviously he will be influenced by the advice of his experts as well as his political pressures. Strike still unsettled and copper bill must be returned to Congress shortly with both item vetoes and essential additional provisions requiring majority approval of both Houses.

Dungan

---

[3] An account of the meeting among Solomon, Sáez, and others is in telegram 630 from Santiago, November 16. The Embassy also reported that Frei had decided against meeting at 10 p.m. in order to confer with his advisers. (Ibid., POL 7 US/HARRIMAN)

---

287.   Telegram From the Embassy in Chile to the Department of State[1]

Santiago, November 17, 1965.

642. Fm Harriman to the President. Info Ball, Mann, McNamara, and Califano.

At a meeting with Ambassador Dungan, Solomon and me this evening, President Frei (Tomic, Saez, Lagarrigue also present), received

---

[1] Source: National Archives and Records Administration, RG 59, Central Files 1964–66, INCO COPPER 17. Secret; Immediate; Nodis. No time of transmission appears on the telegram; it was received in the Department at 4:42 a.m.

us in a grave mood. He began by stating simply and clearly that President Johnson's request for rollback of copper price poses the most difficult problem conceivable for his government at this time. However, referring to substantial assistance US provides Chile, Frei stated that it was not in his "hands" to say no to a request from President Johnson for cooperation. Frei said that the economic difficulties of the price rollback, although important, were not controlling and that the discussions between us had been "positive".

1) Political Problem for GOC: Before describing further the substance of his response, Frei elaborated political problem request poses. If GOC reduces copper price to 36 cents it will have to face a "political crisis of the highest magnitude." Although he personally can understand why it is desirable accede President's request, it is absolutely impossible to explain to the Chilean people [who] see US as so tremendous, powerful and rich that it is not possible for them to understand why such step necessary. No political party, nor the military nor the ordinary Chilean would understand. Opposition already maintains that GOC has given excessive benefits to American companies in copper agreements. Only today, he noted, important Chilean mining entrepreneurs called on him urging that time ripe to raise copper prices to 45 cents. Frei asked specifically that I inform President Johnson that he can count on GOC's cooperation but "If President Johnson can find another formula, another way, he will again render us a new service. But if he cannot find another way of handling this problem, we will cooperate even though this means for GOC the gravest risk in its history."

2) Timing of Chilean Response: Frei then turned to problem of timing proposed Chilean rollback. Two factors make present moment extremely unfavorable for rollback:

A) Copper strike, which hope to resolve within a week, resolved by drastic action. (President Frei this afternoon, exercising emergency powers, arrested several leaders of socialist-led copper workers union and took over operation mines.)

B) Copper legislation, which he hoped would be resolved in a month. To move price down now would probably kill legislation, Frei concluded.

3) Two alternatives proposed by Frei: First—Chile would roll back price in its world sales but only after other major producers take the initiative. Politically impossible for GOC to take initiative for rollback. Initiative would bring his government down. Chile would, however, follow lead by U.S. domestic and European producers, and we could inform the European producers of this agreement which GOC would confirm. I responded that our understanding had been that Chile was the bellwether, and I questioned whether USG has leverage to induce Europeans take lead.

Second—bilateral arrangement with U.S. to reduce price on copper for U.S. consumption to 36 cents. Frei turned to this second alternative by saying that if U.S. and Europeans cannot take initiative, let
us then restrict the problem to the U.S. market. Chile's real interest is
in cooperating with the U.S., not with Europe, which would benefit
from general reduction in Chilean price. Frei said there have been several instances in past when price to U.S. for Chilean copper was
below general Chilean world producers' price; the most noteworthy
example the agreement in 1951 with President Truman which was
dictated by Korean War circumstances.[2] Vietnam is similar situation,
Frei noted.

Frei made it clear that his preference is for the second alternative.
When Solomon explained U.S. faced with difficult problem if action
not taken within few days, Frei responded that under second alternative we could begin discussions immediately on informing U.S. domestic producers of impending Chilean rollback and in the meantime
Chile could suspend application of 38 cent price to exports for U.S.
consumption.

4) Importance to GOC of U.S. cooperation: Frei went to considerable lengths to stress his conviction that Chile's national interest lies in
promoting close and cooperative relationship with USG. If U.S. is truly
interested in Chile's "experiment" it will succeed, he said. Frei explained that "We are for free enterprise, not [Communist?] economy.
We must make agricultural and economic reforms made 30 years ago
in Europe and the United States, in spite of strong opposition from
vested interests." It is essential for GOC that Chilean people sense
clearly USG confidence in GOC.

5) I told President Frei we would advise Washington of his proposals and left open question of considering other alternatives.

Comment: Ambassador Dungan and Solomon concur with me that
compelling Frei, assuming that could be done, which we doubt, to take
the first open action to rescind the price increase would represent too
high a political cost to Chile and to the U.S. Also we believe there is
fair chance (based on our conversations with Brinckerhoff of Anaconda
and other copper experts), that given their past opposition to price increases, European producers would go along with U.S. domestic producers in rescinding price increase if they were assured that Chile
would follow as Frei has promised. However, Washington is in better
position to ascertain if this presumption correct under present world
circumstances. Certainly it is the unanimous view of all experts that

---

[2] Documentation on the agreement, which was concluded on May 7, 1951, is in *Foreign Relations, 1951*, vol. II, pp. 1239–1242, 1258–1273, and 1276–1279.

raising margin requirements in New York copper market and tightening trading practices on London Metal Exchange (with its consequent reduction in prices) would make this price reduction more feasible for all producers, both in Africa and the U.S., as well as for the GOC.

Question arises if Frei's second alternative—reducing prices to 36 cents on all sales to U.S. market—is not more advantageous from U.S. viewpoint since the cost of offsetting Chile's financial loss would be 1/6 or less of the cost under the first alternative. Also it then makes sense to apply export controls on copper to keep the U.S. economy on 36 cent copper which is certainly easier than trying to keep worldwide producer sales on 36 cents, particularly with possibility of Zambian difficulties.

If, however, decision is to opt for first alternative of worldwide price reduction, then we believe that economic package outlines previous cable 636[3] would probably suffice, bearing in mind Frei's caveat about U.S., Canadian and European producers reducing prices first with him following after strike and copper bill settled, estimated to take four weeks.

Although we are not recommending it, if it is difficult to reach decision quickly between alternatives, we could attempt to conclude now agreement with Frei based on alternative two, but leaving open to us option for reasonable time to explore feasibility of alternative one.

During conversation Frei was informed by Dungan of uncertain GOC position on ChiCom representation issue. Frei reacted immediately. Went to telephone and ordered GOC representative to vote against admission Communist China.

Dungan

---

[3] Telegram 636 from Santiago, November 16, reported on a second meeting among Solomon, Sáez, and others, in which the Chileans suggested elements of a tentative agreement. (National Archives and Records Administration, RG 59, Central Files 1964–66, INCO COPPER CHILE)

288.   Telegram From the Department of State to the Embassy in Chile[1]

Washington, November 17, 1965, 8:47 p.m.

469. For Harriman and Solomon. Please express to President Frei President Johnson's warm personal thanks for his offer of cooperation. We are gratified that he understands the reasons why the failure to hold the price line in the US economy would be detrimental not only to the US but to the hemisphere and the world.

In view of the need for urgent action here and Frei's political difficulties described in Embtel 642[2] we accept Frei's second alternative, i.e., a bilateral arrangement between Chile and the US.

We plan, as a first step, to make a public announcement[3] at 7:15 p.m. Washington time today November 17 which will refer to hostilities and disturbances on world scene and threatened disruptions and distortions of copper market which pose problem of inflationary pressures in copper and generally throughout our economy. (You may inform Chileans that because of press leaks today on copper problem it was necessary to move quickly in order to avoid risk that substantial quantities of copper would be attracted abroad by higher prices.) USG announcement will cover following specific points:

1. USG will promptly make available approximately 200,000 tons of copper from the stockpile and arrange for its orderly disposition to correct current imbalance between supply and demand. FYI. The mention of this amount of copper does not foreclose the possibility of additional releases in the future should this prove to be necessary. End FYI.

2. Special export licenses will henceforth be required for exports of copper produced in the US or imported for consumption in the US market. Export licensing procedure would apply to scrap. FYI. This would be necessary to prevent higher prices elsewhere draining copper from this economy. Licenses would of course be granted for Chilean copper imported into the US in blister form for processing and re-export. End FYI.

3. The President will recommend to Congress early in 1966 a suspension of import duties for a limited period of time. The exact nature

---

[1] Source: National Archives and Records Administration, RG 59, Central Files 1964–66, INCO COPPER 17. Secret; Nodis; Flash. Drafted by Mann, cleared at the White House and by Bell (paragraph on AID), and approved by Mann.

[2] Document 287.

[3] The text of the announcement made by Secretary of Defense McNamara is in telegram Tosec 42 to Rio de Janeiro, November 18. (National Archives and Records Administration, RG 59, Central Files 1964–66, INCO COPPER 17)

of the Executive's recommendation to the Congress will be determined after appropriate consultation with the Government of Chile, the US copper industry and the US Congress. FYI. An alternative formula would be the elimination of the 1.7¢ a pound tariff so long as the world price should remain above a certain level. The GOC should not be informed of this however unless Washington specifically so authorizes you. End FYI.

4. USG will discuss with Directors of New York Commodity Exchange solution of problem of excessive speculation in copper trading, perhaps by raising the margin requirements to a figure comparable to requirements for trading on the New York Stock Exchange. FYI. USG has no legislative authority to direct that this be done. End FYI.

Once this announcement is made we believe, on basis of our conversation with members of US copper industry today, that US producers will in the case of Kennecott maintain its current 36¢ price level and that other US producers will roll back to 36¢ a pound. We estimate the steps taken in the announcement will result in a 36¢ price level in our market.

As we understand, GOC, when US price level at 36¢ is established, would be willing to make available, through the usual commercial channels, copper in quantities currently being imported for consumption in the US at a price of 36¢. FYI. The current level of US imports of Chilean copper for domestic use is about 100,000 tons per annum. We would prefer not to specify the 100,000 tons, thus leaving open the possibility of being able, depending on future developments, to maintain some flexibility in level of Chilean copper imports into this market. Request your opinion however on whether failure to specify precise tonnage would create a substantial risk that GOC will attempt to reduce this amount in the future especially if world prices remain at a level higher than 36¢.

Continue FYI. Similarly, we are inclined to believe it would be advantageous to US to fail to fix precise term of bilateral arrangements with Chile since future is somewhat unsure, especially in view of uncertainties surrounding future relations between Southern Rhodesia on one hand and Zambia and Katanga on the other. We are hopeful that Zambia and Katanga copper can continue to be exported at current or increased levels but we cannot be sure that there will be no temporary interruptions in flow from these sources.

Continue FYI. In addition to current level of 100,000 tons imported from Chile, US is currently importing about 150,000 tons from Canada produced by International Nickel and Noranda and 50,000 tons from Peru produced by the Cerro Corporation. The industry estimates that since both Canada and Peru have free economies most of Canadian and Peruvian imports will continue to flow into this market and that it will adjust to 36¢ price level since it is in the interest of these producers to maintain their traditional customers in this market and also because a part of this fabrication of this copper is done in US. The 200,000 ton imports from Canada and Peru will presumably be partially offset by export controls on scrap which according to our latest information is now leaving US at rate of about 135,000 tons annually. Balance can presumably be made up from stockpile. We do not think it is necessary therefore to approach Canadian and Peruvian Governments at this time. End FYI.

The US, in cooperation with policy of Chilean Government to reduce inflationary pressures in Chilean economy and promote Chilean economic development and social progress and, in cooperation with programs of international institutions, will make available 90 million dollar program loan on terms and conditions to be agreed upon by Governments of US and Chile. Negotiations will commence immediately and will follow self-help principles already discussed between two governments. Ten million dollars was added to 80 million dollar figure previously under consideration in view of estimated four million dollar loss to Chilean economy from roll back to 36¢.

Report urgently whether this arrangement is satisfactory to Chilean Government.

FYI. Foregoing leaves unresolved question of worldwide roll back which, as we understand, GOC is in any case unable to accept until copper legislation is finally approved by Chilean Congress and until strike is settled. Depending on reaction of world market to steps described above we have in mind possibility of discussing with GOC later question of general roll back. We leave to your discretion question of whether this possibility should be mentioned to GOC at this time. Our immediate aim is to obtain roll back in Chilean copper exported to US and this is paramount for time being.

Likewise we leave to your judgment whether to inform Chilean of following: Industry members today expressed strong opposition to copper commodity agreement. It is possible that we will be able to bring them around on this point but we are not in a position now to make any commitments to GOC beyond statement that we are prepared to discuss this problem with them since a commodity agreement would presumably require Congressional approval and we are uncertain at this time of what Congressional attitude would be, especially if US industry is strongly opposed.

We did not reveal to industry today fact that Chileans had raised with you possibility of USG using its influence to get companies to agree to additional concessions in their negotiations with GOC. We estimate situation at moment here is such that this would be unwise since our program is dependent on cooperation of industry. We are not therefore in a position to make any commitments at this time concerning negotiations between GOC and copper companies beyond undertaking to permit floating of 20,000 dollar Chilean bond issue in this market and permitting financing of Chilean copper expansion program along lines already discussed.

For same reasons we did not discuss with industry representatives question of creation of revolving fund and have not had time to study effect on US economy of increased Chilean capacity to process copper. You should therefore make no commitments regarding this.

We are however as always ready to discuss with Chileans these and other problems in an effort to find a mutually beneficial solution.

Report soonest GOC reaction to foregoing.[4]

Ball

---

[4] Frei accepted the U.S. proposal in a meeting with Harriman on November 18. Harriman and Frei agreed that the understanding should be "essentially verbal," but that Solomon and Sáez would draft an unsigned memorandum for the record. (Telegram 661 from Santiago, November 18; ibid.) Califano forwarded a copy of the unsigned memorandum to President Johnson on November 20. (Johnson Library, White House Central File, Confidential File, Oversized Attachments, December 1965)

---

289. Memorandum From the President's Special Assistant (Rostow) to President Johnson[1]

Washington, December 10, 1966.

SUBJECT

Loans for Chile

AID requests (Tab B),[2] under the new commitments procedure, your approval of a $65 million assistance package for Chile divided as follows:

—$35 million *program* loan;
—$20 million *sector* loan for agriculture;
—$10 million *sector* loan for education.

---

[1] Source: Johnson Library, National Security File, Country File, Chile, Vol. IV, 10/65–7/67. Confidential.

[2] Tab B was a memorandum from Gaud to the President, November 16; attached but not printed.

The request is $25 million under what you approved for 1966, and $40 million less if the PL 480 reduction is included.

Joe Fowler concurs in the proposed program (Tab C).[3] AID knows about the understandings mentioned by Fowler in his note. Charlie Schultze recommends your approval (Tab A).[4]

One aspect in which you will be particularly interested is the relationship of continued high copper prices and the level of our assistance. Bill Gaud foresees the possibility that copper prices in 1967 may stay close to the present high level. Against this possibility, he plans to release the $35 million program loan in three tranches, the final $15 million subject to need in the light of copper prices and exchange reserve trends. From the windfall copper earnings this year, the Chilean Government has agreed to use, as the situation permits, $40 million for advance repayment of short term US debt: $7 million to the US Treasury and $33 million to US private banks.

Tony Solomon and Linc Gordon strongly recommend that we *not* try to get the type of copper arrangement with Chile that we had this year. Their reasons and alternative suggestion for handling—which they have discussed with Joe Califano and Gardner Ackley—are explained in the memorandum at Tab D.[5] They propose securing a Chilean commitment that Anaconda will supply the United States with 125,000 tons or more at market price during 1967 instead of extending this year's deal which would cost AID $25 million for the difference between 36 cents and present market price.

I join Gaud, Fowler and Schultze in recommending that you approve the Chilean aid package.[6]

Approve

Disapprove

Speak to me

---

[3] Tab C was a memorandum from Fowler to the President, undated; attached but not printed.

[4] Tab A was a memorandum from Schultze to the President, November 30; attached but not printed.

[5] Tab D was a memorandum from Gordon to the President, November 23; attached but not printed.

[6] None of the options below is checked. On December 20 the Embassy reported that Frei had decided to forego the program loan due to increased revenues from the high price of copper. (Telegram 2119 from Santiago, December 20; Johnson Library, National Security File, Country File, Chile, Vol. IV, 10/65–7/67) In a December 21 memorandum to Rostow, Bowdler called the report a "bombshell," although he noted that Frei still wanted $30 million of sector assistance. Bowdler also commented: "This demonstration of Chilean self-help is welcome, even if it makes AID's estimates of Chilean requirements look a little sick." (Ibid.)

Joe Califano and I recommend that you approve the Solomon–Gordon formula for meeting our copper requirements from Chile for 1967.

Approve[7]

Disapprove

Speak to me

Walt

---

[7] The President checked this option.

---

290. Intelligence Note From the Director of the Bureau of Intelligence and Research (Hughes) to Secretary of State Rusk[1]

No. 55   Washington, January 25, 1967.

SUBJECT

Frei Moves to Break Political Impasse in Chile

President Eduardo Frei has faced up squarely to the major political crisis which began on January 17 when the Chilean Senate denied him permission to leave the country for a visit to the US.[2] He has chosen to force what may be a political showdown with his opposition rather than to risk further erosion of his leadership and authority to execute foreign policy and to implement his domestic program. Although the outcome of Frei's struggle with the opposition is by no means assured, his prospects of success now seem reasonably good.

---

[1] Source: National Archives and Records Administration, RG 59, OPR/FAIM/IS Files: Lot 81 D 121, Chile (INR), Background Intelligence Notes and Memorandums, 1963–1974. Confidential.

[2] President Johnson announced on December 20, 1966, that Frei had accepted his invitation to make an official visit to Washington February 1–2, 1967. The statement included the following remark: "I am particularly interested in learning more from President Frei about the achievements of his great experiment of revolution in freedom." (*Public Papers of the Presidents of the United States: Lyndon B. Johnson, 1966*, Book II, pp. 1446–1447) Senators who opposed the visit cited this remark in refusing to grant permission for Frei to leave the country. (*New York Times*, January 18, 1967) Although both sides continued to discuss the possibility of a visit, Frei never visited the United States as President of Chile.

Frei will fight. Frei will be both aggressive and shrewd in combatting the presently united Senate opposition. He undoubtedly hopes to inflict sufficient damage within opposition ranks to ensure a viable course for his program during the remaining three years of his tenure in office. He will try to use to full advantage the sympathy for him and outrage toward the Senate opposition felt by many Chileans who Consider that their national prestige has been tarnished. His proposal for a constitutional amendment which would allow him to dissolve Congress and call new elections has apparently taken the initiative away from the opposition and frightened some sectors within it. In his battle to sustain his political leadership, Frei will probably rely heavily upon generating and channelling public opinion to support his cause and confound his enemies. At the same time, he will seek to divide the fragile and eventually untenable togetherness which at present unifies the right, the Radical center, and the extreme left. On the tactical level, Frei has already begun to oust officeholders belonging to the opposition parties—principally Radicals—from government jobs.

The escalating conflict. The spectacular success of Frei and his Christian Democratic Party (PDC) in the 1964 and 1965 elections badly shook the opposition parties. Instead of the traditional Chilean Government by coalition and compromise, the opposition was faced with a well-defined program backed by a party controlling a majority in the Chamber of Deputies and the largest single bloc (13 of 45 seats) in the Senate. Initially, the opposition sought to delay and compromise, but the President's resistance to any watering down of his program, reinforced by his continued popular support, brought about a hardening of opposition which finally came to a head on January 17 in the Senate veto of his US visit.

A blow where it hurts most. Frei has devoted much time and effort to developing a position of leadership in hemispheric affairs. As one of the outstanding Latin American advocates of social reform within a democratic framework, he has travelled widely to express his views to other leaders in the Hemisphere and in Europe. Frei hoped to use the occasion of his planned trip to the US to strengthen his prestige and to discuss with President Johnson topics which may appear on the agenda of the Summit meeting that is under consideration for April. The opposition parties not only bore a cumulative grudge against Frei over domestic issues but also strongly resented the boost to Frei's standing which the US visit would have represented. Their refusal to allow him to leave the country was a measure of this resentment and an attempt to undercut Frei's prestige by casting doubt on his authority in Chile.

The Senate's action arouses uncertainty as to whether Frei will attend the proposed Summit meeting, where he would be expected to play an influential role. For the moment, at least, Frei's attention has focused so sharply upon his domestic concerns that he undoubtedly has relegated the Summit meeting to second place in his order of priorities.

Constitutional reform proposal challenges opposition. The opposition-controlled Senate can maintain its bottleneck on Frei's legislative program and—as has been seen—can seriously hamper his conduct of foreign policy; at least until the next congressional elections in 1969. To overcome this stalemate is now the principal task facing Frei; to do so without either sacrificing vital aspects of his program or abandoning his democratic principles poses a major challenge to his ingenuity. Confident of his public support, Frei denounced his obstructionist opposition on January 19 in announcing the constitutional reform proposal to allow dissolution of Congress and holding of new elections. Rejecting both compromise and unconstitutional methods, he challenged the opposition parties to let the people decide who should speak for them.

Frei has stated his case in such terms that an outright rejection of the reform proposal by the opposition parties would be tantamount to an admission that they fear elections, and that Frei is right in calling the opposition "unrepresentative." Nevertheless, the proposed constitutional amendment is complicated, and Congress could well spend many months discussing and amending it. Moreover, the constitution requires that 60 days elapse between passage of an amendment by both houses and final approval by a joint session. Meanwhile, the municipal elections on April 2 will test the state of public opinion and thus each party's chances in national elections. A great victory by the PDC would adversely affect the prospects for passage of the constitutional amendment, so far as opposition party acquiescence is concerned; and a poor showing by the PDC would be likely to cause the administration to reconsider its position on the amendment; if neither extreme occurs, the amendment may well go through.

Can Frei win? Frei's personal commitment to his program and to the battle to establish presidential authority gives him an intangible but very real psychological advantage. He seems to have maintained very substantial popular support and the personal affront administered him by the opposition has almost certainly enhanced his popular appeal. His constitutional reform proposal obviously entails considerable risk to the PDC, but perhaps even more to the opposition. Certainly the risk to some Radical and National Party senators is so great that the very threat of the proposed amendment may provide useful opportunities for disarming some elements of the Senate opposition, and perhaps thus open the way for new working arrangements within the present Senate.[3]

---

[3] The proposal to amend the constitution was passed on December 30, 1969, and signed into law on January 21, 1970. In addition to a provision for national referenda, the amendment allowed the President to leave the country for 2 weeks without congressional approval. The amendment took effect on November 4, 1970—the day after Frei left office.

291.   Editorial Note

In early 1967 the Johnson administration considered a proposal to provide financial support to the Christian Democratic Party (PDC) for the municipal elections in April. When Deputy Assistant Secretary Sayre first raised the issue on February 17, Assistant Secretary Gordon replied: "On substance, you know my ground rule that we should engage in election funding only where there is a clear US national interest at stake. In Chile there was in the 1964 national elections but this is not at all self-evident in the 1967 municipals. It also seems to me extraordinary that PDC should still need funding on this scale after two years in national power." "Much as we admire Frei," Gordon concluded, "a very strong case would have to be made to justify this funding, and I have grave doubts that it can be made." (Memorandum from Gordon to Sayre, February 18; Department of State, INR/IL Historical Files, Chile, 1967–1968)

At a March 2 meeting with Sayre, William V. Broe, chief of the Western Hemisphere Division, Directorate for Plans, reported that Ambassador Dungan had forwarded a request from President Frei for funds to cover half of the PDC campaign budget of $1 million. Although he was against financial support for the party, Dungan suggested an alternative: a direct subsidy of $75,000 to Frei himself. Dungan also recommended that the Johnson administration "express interest" in giving the Christian Democrats assistance to "organize the party more rationally and put it on a self-sustaining basis." After presenting the Ambassador's views, Broe commented: "The $75,000 sop to Frei would accomplish little," he argued; "if we were to give any support at all, we would have to go all the way." In Broe's opinion, the United States should decline the request but do so in such a way as to "hold out hope for the future." Sayre maintained that the Christian Democrats were not as badly organized as was generally believed. Moreover, Gordon had already questioned the need for the program since there was no apparent threat to U.S. interests. Sayre, therefore, agreed to await the outcome of the municipal elections, i.e. to see how well the PDC could do "without outside help." Sayre thought the Department would instruct Dungan to "hold out some hope" to the Christian Democrats "but not do anything." Broe replied that, "in view of the time elapsed already, the Party has probably already gotten this message." (Memorandum for the record by Sliffman [Broe], March 6; ibid., Latin America, 1966, 1967, 1968)

292. Memorandum of Conversation[1]

Punta del Este, April 13, 1967, 2 p.m.

SUBJECT

Chilean Progress and American Assistance

PARTICIPANTS

For the U.S.
President Lyndon B. Johnson
Secretary of State Dean Rusk
Assistant Secretary Lincoln Gordon

Ambassador to OAS Sol M. Linowitz
Special Assistant to the President
 Walt W. Rostow

For Chile
President Eduardo Frei
Foreign Minister Gabriel Valdes
Ambassador Radomiro Tomic

Ambassador Pedro Daza (LAFTA)
Amb. to OAS Alejandro Magnet
Special Advisor Raul Saez

Both President Johnson and Secretary Rusk expressed their praise for the progress made in Chile under the Frei administration. Secretary Rusk said it was important for the entire hemisphere that Chile become a successful example of economic and social progress. President Frei said progress had been achieved in a number of fields, such as housing, education, health, and industrialization, but a great deal of work remained to be done in the field of agriculture. He said he faced opposition from two extremes: the right on the one hand, and the left, composed of the Socialists and Communists, on the other. The Socialists were now more extremist than the Communists. The left coalition was acting in a very aggressive fashion, realizing that if the Frei administration were successful, particularly in the field of agrarian reform, this success would have a far-reaching impact, not only in Chile, but throughout Latin America. It would spell the end of any hope for power in the hands of the extreme left.

When Secretary Rusk asked President Frei what his most pressing problem was, he replied that it was the whole problem of agriculture. Chile was going to have to spend $170 million on food imports this year. In addition, Chile's rural population was pressing for a betterment of their conditions. In the past, any attempts to increase the prices of agricultural products had been attacked as a boon to the wealthy land-owners. Now, however, with an increasing number of small farm-

---

[1] Source: National Archives and Records Administration, RG 59, Central Files 1967–69, POL 7 IA Summit. Confidential. Drafted by Barnes. Approved in S on April 19 and by the White House on April 22. The luncheon meeting was held at President Johnson's temporary residence. The memorandum is part II of II parts. Part I, "Conference of Chiefs of State," is ibid. The meeting of American chiefs of state was held at Punta del Este, April 12–14.

ers being created under agrarian reform, this problem is decreasing in magnitude. Chile needed fertilizer, seed, and credit for its agrarian reform and modernization problem.

In this connection, Chile would like American assistance in a pilot agricultural project. Chile would be able to finance compensation for land, but would appreciate assistance in the other aspects of this project.[2]

Finally, President Frei said that, in spite of what some others had said in the course of the conference,[3] he felt Chile had received the proper understanding and cooperation from the United States.

---

[2] Tomic raised the "pilot agricultural project" in a conversation with Gordon, April 27. Although he failed to offer any details, Tomic maintained that agrarian reform in Chile would fail without U.S. assistance. Gordon reiterated the "U.S. commitment to agrarian reform in Latin America and our interest in seeing it succeed in Chile." Gordon suggested, however, that further discussion of the issue take place in Santiago. (Telegram 184953 to Santiago, April 29; ibid., POL 7 CHILE)

[3] Reference is evidently to critical remarks made by President Arosemena of Ecuador; see Document 51.

---

293. Letter From the Ambassador to Chile (Dungan) to the Assistant Secretary of State for Inter-American Affairs (Gordon)[1]

Santiago, April 19, 1967.

Dear Linc:

Before getting into the main business of this letter, I want to offer my most sincere congratulations to you as the person most responsible for the success of the Punta del Este meeting. I know that in many ways it was the product of team effort, but I also know that without your persistent and wise leadership it could have been a fiasco. We are all in your debt.

It occurred to me that while you had the benefit of our various cabled analyses of the recent municipal elections,[2] you might like to have

---

[1] Source: National Archives and Records Administration, RG 59, ARA Files, 1967: Lot 70 D 150, Chile 1967. Confidential; Official–Informal. A notation on the letter indicates it was sent on April 24.

[2] The "cabled analyses" are telegrams 3420, 3468, and 3658 from Santiago, April 3, 5, and 14, respectively. (All ibid., Central Files 1967–69, POL 18–1 CHILE) The Christian Democratic Party received 36 percent of the vote; the Radical Party finished second with 16 percent; the Communist, National, and Socialist parties split the remainder.

an informal rundown of the situation as I see it. There is no doubt that the Frei government and the PDC took a drubbing in the eyes of the public and the world, despite the fact that they made substantial gains in the number of local officials whom they elected, and despite the fact that they held onto significant elements of the electorate. In my opinion the psychological defeat which they suffered was due in large measure to their political error of projecting the municipal election as a plebiscite. The situation is not dissimilar to that which we have in the United States. You know the reluctance of an incumbent President to commit his prestige in a Congressional election, but it would be virtually impossible to get a President to put his prestige on the line in a whole series of local contests. I'm really at a loss to know why this happened here, and the only reason that I can deduce is that, stung by the Senatorial rebuke in January, Frei felt that he had to strike back in a decisive way. Moreover, I think he was bemused by the prospect that the magic of Freismo could even pull him through an election in which local issues and candidates traditionally have dominated the picture.

If he had not made it a plebiscite he could have very well argued that this was simply a normal return of voters to their traditional political homes. If, on the other hand, the PDC had come out as everyone was predicting they would, he could have claimed it as a magnificent surge in support of his program despite the normal trend in municipal elections. There is no doubt that the plebiscite decision was a major political blunder which is now well recognized here in Chile.

But regardless of the psycho-political effect, do the election returns have any real significance in terms of indicating an ideological or political preference of the *electorate*? I am inclined to think not. I believe that the Chilean electorate is essentially a conservative electorate, but a large part of it is also unsophisticated and really not clued in to the real issues on a day-to-day basis. They tend to participate in elections every three or four years without any continuing involvement, through the press or otherwise, in what could be called "issue politics." Moreover, in each election there is a rather substantial group of new voters whose political allegiances are increasingly difficult to predict. My own belief is that local candidates and a certain discontent over PDC style (prepotencia), and the adverse effect of stabilization on upper and middle class voters combined to drive voters into their traditional political patterns.

If the election does not represent a significant shift in the socio-political opinions of the electorate, it does represent a reshaping of party political strength—the net effect of which is to shift the effective political spectrum left. This may sound somewhat involved, but let me describe what I mean. The Radical Party is in the control, and is likely to remain in the control, of a Marxist-oriented faction. As a minority and power-hungry party, the temptation to amalgamate with other elements will be overpowering, as we are now seeing in the Colchagua Senatorial election where the Radicals have joined in support of a Socialist candidate. I believe that the Communists will give tacit support to this kind of a coalition, and among the three of them, on the basis of the municipal percentages, they control more than 45% of the vote. If you add to this grouping some disaffected left-wing PDCers and some spiteful Nacionales, you have a majority of the Chilean electorate. The only coalition of forces (not necessarily of parties) is left leaning. There does not appear to me to be any attraction on the right. I would like to think that there is some possibility of the center left elements in the Radicals regaining control of their party and mobilizing their share of the electorate in support of some sort of a loose arrangement with the PDC, but I honestly do not see it. Surprising though it may seem, the anti-clerical basis of radicalism is present here, but even more important, is the rejection by the moderate elements of the Radicals, including Julio Duran, of the reformist policies and programs which the PDC and we have backed in Chile in recent years.

Looking ahead, the picture as I see it is as follows. First, there will be a two to two and a half year period of jockeying and flirtations between Radicals and Socialists, perhaps some elements of the PDC with the Communists, and probably continued friction between the Communists and the Socialists. In short, the political picture in the immediate future is likely to be very murky.

In the face of this, the Christian Democrats are faced with basically two choices. First, nailing their shirt to the mast and plowing ahead with their program, changing their rhythm to accord with economic reality, and I believe most importantly, abandoning their ideological penchant and attempting to build bridges to any respectable element in the community which will support a progressive program. I describe this political policy as pursuit of the politics of consensus, and abandoning the politics of ideology.[3] I believe that Frei can do this because he is by far the strongest political force within the PDC. If he puts himself forward as President of all the Chileans and makes clear in ways that he has not done heretofore that he is working for the welfare of the bulk of the Chileans, he may be able to pull it off. In other words, he must seek to build around a core of 30–35% of the electorate

---

[3] In a May 16 letter to Dungan, Gordon replied that he was "heartily in accord" with this conclusion: "In observing the Frei–Tomic dichotomy over the last year, I have been increasingly impressed with the absurdity of Tomic's notion that the PDC could be made into a kind of Chilean PRI (in Mexican terms), and concerned at various missed opportunities to seek the support of moderate Radicals and others outside the PDC fold. Is there anything that we might do to encourage your recommended trend, other than friendly conversations when the opportunity permits?" (Ibid., ARA Files, 1967: Lot 70 D 150, Chile 1967)

a sufficient number of people who believe in the soundness of his program to carry his party and his candidate to victory in 1970. This will take some doing because it involves very courageous acts on the economic side and a really completely new style of Chilean politics.

The alternative to Frei being able to pull this off, I think, is a return to the old system of three political forces, with the Presidency probably going to a so-called Popular Front candidate elected with the basic support of the Radicals and Socialists, and I believe, the tacit support of the Communists. In such a situation the PDC would come in with about 30% of the vote and the Nationals with about 15–20%. It is impossible to predict what kind of a program such a government would advance, but I cannot but think that it would be either a do-nothing government or one which would be oriented radically to the left.[4]

For the moment I really don't think there is very much for us to do except to keep our lines open to all elements, especially the Radicals and the Nationals, and wait for the situation to clarify somewhat. I think we should continue to support the bulk of the Frei program because it is the most sensible—indeed the only coherent program in Chile today. However, I think our support must be extended with a firmer hand than probably has characterized our effort here in the past. I do not mean by this to be self-accusatory, although undoubtedly we have made mistakes. I am simply reflecting my conviction that the situation is a good deal crunchier at the present time than it was before the April elections. It's an up-hill fight, politically and economically, and is going to require a higher degree of discipline on their part than they were willing to accept heretofore. Fortunately or unfortunately, we are part of the disciplinary side of the equation.

I hope these thoughts may serve to clarify rather than to confuse those of you who are trying to make something out of this complex situation. I assure you that we are not pessimistic but that we, as I think the present government does, recognize the need for change of style and a change of pace. I don't think there's much danger of a strong shift to the left within the PDC, but only the next few months will be able to give us a clear indication of that.

With every best wish.

Sincerely,

Ralph

---

[4] Sayre wrote the following comment in the margin: "This is puzzling since Socialists are farther to the left than Communists." Gordon also picked up on this point in his letter of May 16 cited above: "Given the extremely radical position of the Socialists, and your own description on page 2 of the controlling Radical faction as Marxist oriented, why should one be confident that a Popular Front Presidency would not 'be oriented radically to the left.' On the face of it, that would seem precisely the orientation to be expected." (Ibid.)

294. Memorandum From the Assistant Secretary of State for Inter-American Affairs (Gordon) to the Deputy Under Secretary of State for Political Affairs (Kohler)[1]

Washington, April 25, 1967.

SUBJECT

Proposal to Aid Moderate Elements in Radical Party of Chile

There is attached a memorandum for the 303 Committee[2] that proposes covert financial assistance of $20,000 to the moderate faction of the Radical Party (PR) of Chile to attempt to contain the drift of this Party, under its present pro-Marxist National Committee, toward an alliance with the Communist-Socialist Popular Action Front (FRAP). The memorandum points out that the PR holds the balance of power in the Chilean Senate between President Frei's Christian Democratic Party (PDC) and the FRAP, and notes that under the current leadership of the National Committee (CEN) the Party has tended increasingly to vote with FRAP to obstruct key legislation of President Frei's program, the success of which the US regards as of first importance. The memorandum also states that the Committee has recently enjoyed a considerable accrual to its prestige because of the relative success of the PR in the 2 April nationwide municipal elections.

Election of CEN members is to take place at the Party convention in June. It is argued in the memorandum of proposal that were the leftist control of the Committee eliminated or diluted in this election, sentiment in the PR to maintain the current voting alliance with FRAP would be weakened, and that the likelihood of effective collaboration between the two groups in the 1969 Congressional and the 1970 Presidential campaigns would also be reduced. The expenditure contemplated in the memorandum is directed toward this Committee election.

ARA agrees that the ends sought by the proposal are desirable.[3] We recognize that there is no guarantee that the action contemplated

---

[1] Source: Department of State, INR/IL Historical Files, 303 Committee Files, c. 49, April 28, 1967. Secret; Eyes Only. Sayre initialed the memorandum for Gordon.

[2] Dated April 8; attached but not printed.

[3] In a draft memorandum from Gordon to Kohler, April 19, this sentence continues: "but we have serious doubts that the action recommended would be successful." A handwritten note on the draft memorandum indicates that Sayre decided to withhold signature on the memorandum until the Embassy had the opportunity to clarify its "contradictory advice." (Department of State, INR/IL Historical Files, Chile, 1967–1968) In his reply on April 25 Dungan stated his case as follows: "I believe that this program is reasonably sure of accomplishing its modest purpose to deny an open field to the Marxist-oriented wing of the party. It is a one-shot operation which may or may not have future implications for the U.S. I believe that the risks are minimal and the prospects for success in the attainment of limited objectives are good. To take no action involves little risk but a high probability that the present leftist-oriented leadership of the CEN will be strengthened." (Ibid.)

will in fact achieve the ends sought, but we believe that on balance it represents the most practicable means immediately available to ensure that we can go into the 1969 and 1970 campaigns with some reasonable prospect of preventing the undesirable coalition.

ARA recommends that you support the proposal in the 303 Committee.[4]

---

[4] According to the minutes of the April 28 303 Committee meeting: "The proposal to help save the Radical Party from marriage with FRAP was approved by the committee with some members curious about whether $20,000 was sufficient to keep the prospective bride intact. It was explained that this was estimated to be about what the traffic could properly bear at this time." (Memorandum for the record, May 1; ibid.) On July 3 the Embassy reported that the election for the national committee of the Radical Party had resulted in a "resounding triumph" for the leftist faction. (Telegram 21 from Santiago; National Archives and Records Administration, RG 59, Central Files 1967–69, POL 12–3 CHILE)

---

295. Memorandum From the President's Special Assistant (Rostow) to President Johnson[1]

Washington, June 27, 1967.

Mr. President:

Last December you authorized Bill Gaud to negotiate with Chile a program loan ($35 million) and *sector loans in agriculture ($20 million) and education ($10 million). The sector loans were to be submitted to you for final approval.*

You will recall that because of the windfall from high copper prices, *President Frei decided last December to forego the program loan* as long as the price of copper remained high. He asked, however, that negotiations proceed on the sector loans.

Since then, the price of copper has dropped sharply. The Chileans are discussing with AID *the possibility* of a program loan covering the balance of 1967. Negotiations on the agricultural sector loan are proceeding. The education loan agreement has been completed.

---

[1] Source: Johnson Library, National Security File, Country File, Chile, Vol. IV, 10/65–7/67. Confidential.

Attached is a memorandum from Bill Gaud[2] *asking your approval of the educational sector loan. Charlie Schultze* and *Joe Fowler concur* in the request, as does *Covey Oliver.*[3]

The loan is justified because:

—Chilean self-help this year has been good.
—Chile has agreed to two major steps for improving its overall economic performance as conditions for this loan.
—Chilean performance in education has been impressive.
—The loan will accelerate Chile's own efforts.
—It is in line with the Punta del Este decisions to put increased emphasis on education.

I recommend approval.[4]

Walt

---

[2] Attached but not printed was a June 16 memorandum from Gaud to the President.

[3] Attached but not printed was a June 24 memorandum from Schultze to the President.

[4] The approve option is checked. A handwritten note on the memorandum reads: "Mr. Bowdler said he'd notify all concerned. RLN."

---

296. Information Memorandum From the President's Special Assistant (Rostow) to President Johnson[1]

Washington, July 20, 1967, 3 p.m.

Mr. President:

In the past few days, President Frei has suffered two body blows from his own Christian Democratic Party.

The Party's National Council on July 12 published an extraordinarily naive—and unhelpful—statement saying that:

—the Cuban-backed Latin American Solidarity Organization (Castro's vehicle for promoting "national liberation" movements) should be allowed to establish an office in Chile provided it does not stimulate violence.

---

[1] Source: Johnson Library, National Security File, Country File, Chile, Vol. IV, 10/65–7/67. Confidential. A notation on the memorandum indicates that the President saw it.

—guerrilla warfare is a phenomenon resulting from underdevelopment and exploitation by national oligarchies and foreign interests, and not always attributable to Cuba.

The statement reflects the ascendancy of "left-wing" elements of the Party and their desire to strike a "liberal" stance in the face of goading by the Socialist-Communist coalition which has picked up voting strength in recent municipal and by-elections. Frei responded with a strongly-worded, public denunciation of LASO. This statement also helped reassure President Leoni and the Christian Democrats in Venezuela who were furious over the Chilean PCD declaration.

The second set-back is the capture of the Party national leadership by the "left-wing" during last weekend's National Assembly. Ralph Dungan reports that Frei, who has remained aloof from Party politics, did not intervene in the Assembly and the "moderates" were not a match for the more aggressive "left-wingers".[2]

The new leadership will try to push Frei towards greater nationalization of important sectors of private enterprise. Anticipating this, Frei, in signing the new Agrarian Reform Law on July 16, made clear that he would not vary from his announced government program fostering the growth of the private sector.

Ralph Dungan concludes that Frei is so strong with the rank and file of his party that the new leadership will not be able to budge him from his policies if he is willing to take his case to the Party faithful.

Walt

---

[2] Reported in telegram 206 from Santiago, July 19. (National Archives and Records Administration, RG 59, Central Files 1967–69, POL 12 CHILE) Dungan left Chile on August 2 to assume his new responsibilities as the first Chancellor of Higher Education in New Jersey. On July 25 the White House announced that his replacement would be the Ambassador to Ethiopia, Edward M. Korry. Korry was confirmed by the Senate on August 23 and presented his credentials in Santiago on October 16.

297. Memorandum From William G. Bowdler of the National Security Council Staff to the President's Special Assistant (Rostow)[1]

Washington, December 18, 1967.

SUBJECT

Chile: Frei Suffers Another Setback

President Frei seems to have suffered another setback yesterday when the Christian Democratic candidate for a Senate by-election in the conservative, agricultural 8th District of southern Chile lost by 58 votes to the Communist-backed Radical nominee. Lavendero, a young dynamic, middle-of-the-road Christian Democrat who strongly supports Frei, waged a vigorous personal campaign. But the party machinery, now controlled by the more leftist elements of the PDC, sat on their hands. Baltra, an old-time Radical politician of extreme left bent and president of the Chilean-Soviet Friendship Institute, ran in combination with the FRAP coalition. The Communists, in a quiet, sophisticated way, campaigned hard for him.

The Baltra victory—if sustained[2]—is expected to consolidate the Radicals joining forces with FRAP in a move to beat the PDC in the 1970 Presidential elections.

It will also weaken Frei's hold over the PDC by giving the more radical elements—already unhappy over Frei's moderation—ammunition to swing the party further left.

Frei has had a rough year on the political front. It started off with the Senate denying him permission to visit the US. The PDC made a poor showing in the spring municipal elections. At the summer party convention, the radical young turks took over the party leadership. They embarrassed Frei with their sympathetic statement on the LASO conference.[3] More recently Frei has had a hard time getting his party to back him on his anti-inflationary wage readjustment program.

There are still three years to the next elections. If the Christian Democrats are to stay in power, they will have to show more cohesion and success than they have during the past 12 months.

WGB

---

[1] Source: Johnson Library, National Security File, Country File, Chile, Vol. V, 6/67–11/68. Confidential.

[2] Baltra was subsequently declared the winner in the Senate by-election.

[3] The first conference of the Latin American Solidarity Organization was held in Havana, July–August 1967.

298.   Information Memorandum From the President's Special Assistant (Rostow) to President Johnson[1]

Washington, January 18, 1968.

SUBJECT

Ed Korry Reports on Chile

When Ed Korry called on you before going to Chile,[2] you told him that he is an Ambassador with a built-in "self-starter" who did not need to be pushed from Washington. The attached report[3] demonstrates the accuracy of your remark.

After observing the Chilean scene for three months, he concluded that Frei was being out-maneuvered by the Chilean Communist Party, with potentially serious implications for Chilean democracy and for us. He decided to discuss the situation with Frei, which he did on January 3 with good results.

Ed's analysis runs like this: Since taking office, Frei knowingly played along with the "opening to the left" tactic (i.e., diplomatic and trade relations with Moscow and friendly dialogue with the Chilean Communist Party), of which his Foreign Minister and Ambassador Tomic are leading advocates. He did this to curry Communist support to put through his "Revolution in Liberty" program. In the process he shunned cooperation with democratic forces to the right of the PDC (i.e., the Radical Party) and increasingly blamed them for hindering passage of that program. This alienated the Radicals and blurred the sharp distinction between those who believe in democratic principles and those who do not which emerged so clearly in the 1964 elections and won Frei the presidency. In the ideological confusion, the Chilean Communist Party smartly out-maneuvered Frei by: making a formal alliance with the Radicals; maintaining their coalition relationship with the Socialists; and establishing a working intimacy with key members of Frei's own party. As a result, the Communists were pushing the government into an isolated position in which Frei seemed to be unable to control his party and was forced to lean more heavily on the discredited Right for survival.

---

[1] Source: Johnson Library, National Security File, Country File, Chile, Vol. V, 8/67–11/68. Secret. A notation on the memorandum indicates that the President saw it.

[2] According to the President's Daily Diary, Johnson met Korry for a brief "courtesy call" on October 4, 1967. (Johnson Library) No substantive record of the meeting has been found.

[3] Airgram A–327 from Santiago, January 10; attached but not printed. Another copy is in the National Archives and Records Administration, RG 59, Central Files 1967–69, POL CHILE–US.

Ed thinks our policy has been partially to blame for this state of affairs because we have over-emphasized economic support of Frei's program—which Ed fully supports—in the mistaken assumption that economic performance would produce the political results we seek. He thinks the US Ambassador should be providing more *political assistance.*

A chance trip with Frei on January 3—three days before the Christian Democratic National Convention—gave Korry the opportunity to express his concern to the President. Frei welcomed the discussion and apparently responded to Ed's counsel. At the Convention, Frei had a head-on collision with the wing of his party which wants a further shift to the left and which won control of the party leadership last July. Frei won and forced the radical directorate to resign. He also unequivocally attacked the Communists.

I think Ed's analysis is dead right. The "self-starter" came into play at a critical moment.[4] Time will tell whether Frei will be able to re-establish a clear-cut distinction between the Communists and anti-Communists and win back the confidence of the democratic forces which elected him in 1964. We are fortunate to have Ed in Chile as Frei moves toward the crucial national election of 1970.

Walt

---

[4] The CIA later claimed its share of credit: "We wish to point out that the Ambassador's awareness of the situation and the information he used in carefully stirring Frei to action were largely the result of our intelligence effort in Chile" and "the result of close briefings provided the Ambassador by Station personnel." (Memorandum from Broe to Helms, January 24; Central Intelligence Agency, DDO Files, [*file name not declassified*])

---

299. Information Memorandum From the President's Special Assistant (Rostow) to President Johnson[1]

Washington, February 15, 1968, 7:15 p.m.

SUBJECT

The Cabinet Resignation in Chile

---

[1] Source: Johnson Library, National Security File, Country File, Chile, Vol. V, 8/67–11/68. Confidential. A notation indicates that the President saw the memorandum.

Ambassador Korry reports that President Frei's Cabinet resigned last night.[2] He accepted the resignations and is expected to announce a new slate of Ministers by tomorrow.

This is the long-expected Cabinet reshuffle. It is designed to give Frei a free hand in shaping new policies for coping with mounting political and economic problems.

To continue his stabilization program, Frei needs new legislation regulating wage increases covering last year's inflation (about 22%) and some retrenching of his more ambitious programs. His wage readjustment proposal, which would have substituted bonds for most of the cash, was withdrawn after the Senate made clear it would not approve. Prospects for getting any non-inflationary proposal through are not encouraging.

The Senate opposition comes not only from the "outs" on the right and left, but from elements inside his own party. In his three years in office. Frei has not cultivated support from the non-communist parties. On the contrary, he has alienated them. He now finds he has less support in the Congress than he did when he started out.

Complicating matters further, a President in Chile begins suffering from "lame-duckitis" after he passes the half-way mark in his term. Ed Korry in a cable today[3] describes the situation in these terms.

"Chilean politics have descended into pre-electoral arena with all parties maneuvering for advantages prior to the 1969 Congressional elections. It is painfully clear that all opposition parties are putting partisan interests ahead of the country's; their determination is to discredit Frei as a governing force; their belief is that the PDC can be blocked from renewing its mandate in the 1970 presidential vote, if Frei is paralyzed or severely limited from executing his proposals."

Korry is working closely with those who will form the new economic team. How they will work out a sound economic program for 1968 within the existing framework is not clear. It is reassuring to have a smart operator on the scene.

Walt

---

[2] Telegram 2474 from Santiago, February 15. (National Archives and Records Administration, RG 59, Central Files 1967–69, POL 15–1 CHILE) The Embassy also reported that the key figure in the new cabinet was Raúl Sáez, the Minister of Finance. (Telegram 2494 from Santiago, February 15; ibid.)

[3] Not further identified.

300.   Briefing Memorandum From the Assistant Secretary of State for Inter-American Affairs (Oliver) to the Under Secretary of State (Katzenbach)[1]

Washington, March 5, 1968.

SUBJECT

Ambassador Tomic and Christian Democratic-Communist Popular Front in Chile

President Frei told Ambassador Korry that it would be valuable to him if we could take advantage of farewell meetings with Ambassador Tomic to emphasize the total US coldness to any possibility of a Christian Democratic Popular Front combination with the Communist Party in Chile.[2] You may wish to take advantage of the occasion of your March 7 luncheon with Ambassador Tomic to discuss this with him, possibly before or after the luncheon. If, given the ceremonial nature of the luncheon, it seems inopportune to do so, we can see that Ambassador Tomic receives our thoughts on this matter on some other occasion.

As you can see from the general briefing memorandum for the luncheon,[3] Ambassador Tomic has ideas about forming a political grouping of the left and left-center. He clearly includes the Communists in his thinking. President Frei believes that Ambassador Tomic has convinced himself that the US would be willing to provide the same degree of support to such a coalition government including Communists as it does to the present government. President Frei believes that Tomic should be disabused of this idea, and he hopes that we would make our opposition clear before Ambassador Tomic returns to Chile. President Frei said that Ambassador Tomic running on a straight PDC ticket would be the strongest presidential candidate in 1970, and that it would be within his character to decide to make a deal with the moderate forces in Chile in pursuit of the presidency if need be.

---

[1] Source: National Archives and Records Administration, RG 59, Central Files 1967–69, POL CHILE–US. Secret. Drafted by Shankle and cleared by Morris. Initialed for Oliver by Sayre.

[2] Reported in telegram 2547 from Santiago, February 21. (Ibid., POL 7 CHILE)

[3] In this March 5 memorandum from Oliver to Katzenbach, Oliver explained that Tomic had a "good chance" of winning the 1970 presidential election and that the purpose of the luncheon was to convince him that "he has made friends at the highest levels of the U.S. Government." (Ibid., POL 17 CHILE–US)

Ambassador Korry stresses that in discussing this matter with Tomic, there should be no indication of initiative from him or from President Frei.[4]

---

[4] Donald F. Herr, staff assistant to the Under Secretary, wrote the following note on the memorandum: "I have heard that Chilean Communists are less red than the Socialists. Tomic's idea of a coalition of the left may not be all that bad. At any rate, it is worth further investigation." The talking points for the meeting suggested that Katzenbach "privately" discuss the problems associated with a Popular Front in Chile, including the following argument: "The United States is a strong supporter of Christian democracy in Latin America. Any combination with communists, however, could only serve to bring this support into question." (National Archives and Records Administration, RG 59, Katzenbach Files: Lot 74 D 271, Luncheon—March 7, 1968, Host for Chile Ambassador Tomic) No substantive record of the luncheon has been found.

---

301.   Memorandum of Conversation[1]

Washington, March 19, 1968, 10:30 a.m.

SUBJECT

Farewell Call by Ambassador Tomic

PARTICIPANTS

Foreign
Ambassador Radomiro Tomic, Ambassador of Chile

United States
Secretary Rusk
Mr. Patrick F. Morris, Country Director, Office of Bolivian-Chilean Affairs

After an exchange of pleasantries with Ambassador Tomic on his sojourn in the U.S. and his pending departure for Chile, Secretary Rusk asked the Ambassador about the present economic difficulties in Chile and the prospects for the future. He said that he understood that there was a possibility of an alignment of democratic parties with non-democratic parties in Chile, and asked Ambassador Tomic to comment on it.

Ambassador Tomic answered that he wanted to be absolutely frank with the Secretary and therefore he had to admit that the gov-

---

[1] Source: National Archives and Records Administration, RG 59, Central Files 1967–69, POL 17 CHILE–US. Confidential. Drafted by Morris on March 20 and approved in S on March 21. The meeting was held in the Secretary's office. According to the Secretary's Appointment Book, Rusk briefly met Korry before meeting Tomic. (Johnson Library) No substantive record of that meeting has been found.

ernment of President Frei had reached the limit in its ability to carry forward its program of economic and social reform within a democratic framework. He explained that the government lacks the popular support primarily from organized labor to reach its stabilization goals as originally projected. The Christian Democratic party will have to accept the fact that it cannot get over 33% of the vote in the forthcoming congressional and presidential elections and therefore must look to working with other parties if it is to continue as an active promoter of social and economic change in Chile. There is the need for a new alignment of forces and a re-definition of social and economic goals to coincide with this realignment. Under these circumstances, it is possible that the Christian Democratic party will enter into some kind of arrangement with other parties on the left.

The Secretary commented that of course Chile would have to make its own decisions regarding its political future, but that any democratic party should make a very careful examination of the ultimate aims and objectives of the Communist party before entering a political arrangement with them. He said that he could not speak on Chile, but that the pattern of Communist party activities in Southeast Asia and the Middle East clearly indicates that they have not abandoned their goals of world domination. He said that the tradition of democratic institutions in Chile might make it strong enough to withstand the strains of a coalition government which included the communists but that in some of Chile's neighbors with less strong institutions such a coalition might have more serious results. He then asked why a coalition of democratic forces of the Center and Left could not be worked out.

Ambassador Tomic answered that the situation in Chile was very confused. He said that the moderates within the Radical party were not in control of the party machinery; that the Right was generally discredited and there were many divisions in the non-communist Left. It is necessary that a new combination of forces be brought into being which is not based upon the leadership of an individual, (caudillismo or personalismo) but which expresses the needs and aspirations of the Chilean people. The Christian Democratic party is a vital and modern party which is guided by the aspirations of a majority of the electorate, but it will not achieve its objectives within the narrow confines of its own structure. It can serve as a nucleus for a broader and more inclusive political expression. He said that he recognized that it would take a number of miracles to bring such things to pass.

The Secretary congratulated him on his ambassadorship of three years in Washington and wished him well on his return to Chile.[2]

---

[2] Tomic also made a farewell call on President Johnson, March 22. A brief account of the meeting is in a March 22 memorandum from Bowdler for the file. (Johnson Library, National Security File, Country File, Chile, Vol. V, 8/67–11/68)

302. Record of Discussion at the 32nd Meeting of the Senior Interdepartmental Group[1]

Washington, March 21, 1968.

PRESENT

Under Secretary of State, Chairman
Deputy Secretary of Defense
Chairman, Joint Chiefs of Staff
The Director of Central Intelligence
The Administrator, Agency for International Development
Mr. Akers for the Director, United States Information Agency
Special Assistant to the President
Under Secretary of Treasury
Deputy Under Secretary for Political Affairs
Counselor of the Department
SIG Staff Director

DOD
Mr. Lang
General Orwat
Mr. McGiffert

State
Mr. Oliver
Ambassador Korry

[Omitted here is discussion of future meetings.]

II. Chile

The Chairman said that he had asked Mr. Oliver to present several of the particularly difficult problems in Latin America to the SIG prior to SIG discussion of the Joint State/Defense Study.[2] He thought that this would be useful to SIG members in giving them a more detailed knowledge of particular country problems.

---

[1] Source: National Archives and Records Administration, RG 59, S/S–SIG Files: Lot 70 D 263, SIG/RA #34, 3/26/68, Future Meetings. Secret. Drafted by Hartman on March 26. ARA prepared a discussion paper for the meeting in which it reviewed the current political and economic situation and recommended that the United States support the anti-inflationary program of the Frei administration while encouraging "the development of a moderate political consensus in Chile of which the Christian Democrats would be the main element." (Ibid., SIG/Memo #57, 3/20/68, 32nd SIG Meeting)

[2] Reference is to a study entitled "Latin America: A Recommended U.S. National Strategy," prepared under the direction of Ambassador Edwin M. Martin. The SIG discussed the Martin study at its meetings on May 2 and June 13. At the latter meeting, Katzenbach directed that the country teams consider the study "in their policy/program planning and development." (Ibid., SIG/RA #41, 6/26/68, Chairman's Summary at Discussion and Decision)

Ambassador Korry then gave a presentation on the general situation in Chile and the problems faced by Frei as he approaches the coming elections. Ambassador Korry stressed his conclusion that Chile's long history of democratic evolution would continue. He felt that this might very well mean however, a more left-wing group coming to power, possibly with the active cooperation of the Communist Party. This would obviously present special problems in our relationship with Chile. He thought that the record of the Chilean Government in agricultural reform and anti-inflation measures was reasonably good but that the test, particularly on inflation controls, was only now coming. A major factor in Chilean elections, aside from the personality of the candidate in the presidential election, is the rate of inflation.

Ambassador Korry also described the copper situation and the windfall benefits that the copper companies have gained because of the strike in the United States and its effect on world copper prices. Ambassador Korry pictured the political party structure and mentioned the status of current aid discussions.

Mr. Katzenbach summed up the discussion by saying that our choices in terms of US actions were narrow. In essence, we were trying to take out insurance which would in some way strengthen the moderate forces in the coming 1969 congressional elections. We could do this through applying additional resources, particularly where they helped achieve economic stabilization. But we had to make a choice at some point about whether to apply pure IMF doctrine with the risk of seriously damaging moderate forces or taking a less rigid stand. The central problem remained, however, how to hold inflation in controllable limits. He agreed with Ambassador Korry that whatever we did in Chile, we should conduct ourselves in as unobtrusive a fashion as possible and not allow US prestige to be completely tied to one personality.

[Omitted here is discussion of Panama.]

AA Hartman
Staff Director

303.   Telegram From the Embassy in Chile to the Department of State[1]

Santiago, March 29, 1968, 2205Z.

3042. Subj: The End of the Revolution in Liberty.

1. However the current maneuverings among the Chilean parties may end, the inescapable fact is that we are witnessing the end of the noble and necessary Frei experiment in "Revolution in Liberty." Because the US has attached so much prestige and so many resources to the person of Frei and to his programs, it is essential in my view that we understand now the situation as it is and gear our actions as well as our policies to it.

2. The current congressional struggle over the GOC's wage readjustment bill is both an uproarious wake for the Frei administration and a licentious baptism for an unrecognizable bastard offspring. No one now has manageable control over events in Congress, least of all the President. Having reportedly decided that he erred in making a deal two weeks ago with the Communists, he is seeking to "balance" his opening to the left with one to the right—or to anyone.

3. I say the revolution in liberty has ended because, as Ambassador Tomic told the Secretary in his farewell call March 19,[2] the government of President Frei has reached the limit in its ability to carry forward its program of economic and social reform within a democratic framework. Tomic's judgement is beyond dispute. Neither the political nor economic situation provides meaningful opportunities for Frei to move forward. At best he can only "consolidate." For the remaining two years nine months of his term he can only fight for a semblance of personal dignity and an appearance of control over events.

4. At the time I left for Washington three weeks ago today, we were using our influence to seek a locus of interim stability. In our view, the one hope of consolidating the past gains of the Frei administration and of effecting a political equilibrium prior to the March 1969 congressional elections was the program which the new Minister of Finance Raul Saez had agreed to execute. While no one had any illusions about the defensive nature of the Saez budget, particularly since at best it involved a retreat to an inflationary rate of 25 to 30 pct, it did offer an opportunity to control economic forces, to achieve a defensible level of growth, to make a start on the reduction of a swollen bureaucracy,

---

[1] Source: National Archives and Records Administration, RG 59, Central Files 1967–69, POL 23–9 CHILE. Secret; Priority; Limdis. Repeated to USCINCSO.

[2] See Document 301.

to concentrate on production improvement, to create a climate of quasi confidence in the business and foreign sectors and above all to lay a base for improved performance prior to the 1969 congressional and 1970 presidential elections.

5. As Saez and we feared, the President caved at the first crunch. He fell into a trap laid by the Communist Party which astutely recognized that the Saez ministry would have the effect of stopping the slide of Chilean politics to the left. The Communists wanted Saez out and they maneuvered him to the sidelines.[3] Having sucked the President into a position of dependence on Communist goodwill, the Communists, true to their word are now seeking to gut the rest of the bill. Indeed they are having difficulties explaining their initial maneuver with Frei to their own militants in the labor field. Hence the President, having made dubious gain from his mismatch with the Communists is back at square one with nothing ahead but the adders and snakes of the other political parties. He now regrets his liaison with the Communists as does his Minister of Interior Perez Zujovic who was the midwife of this abortion. Frei must not know the axiom which governs the lives of surgeons and of statesmen—that you can never afford to say "oops."

6. There are those who believe that the only real option open to Frei is to operate temporarily outside the democratic framework. Exponents of this approach believe he could turn to the military to impose a program that would hold the inflationary line and establish some economic and political order. After taking into account (a) the posture adopted two weeks ago by the military chiefs in their interview with Frei in which they reportedly eschewed stronger options and pressed instead the military's wage claims (b) the absence of a potential man on a white horse and the generally unimpressive intellectual caliber of the leading officers (c) the proclivity among officers to join with the civilian claimants and to blame the GOC for the failure to manage Chile's economic affairs well, particularly their pay raises (d) the reluctance, to use the mildest adjective of Frei, to take extra-constitutional measures, I can only conclude that this possibility is an outside one. In any event I have no sympathy for it.

7. The structure and tradition of Chilean democratic politics has for many decades pushed parties into alliances. As I have reported almost from the time of my arrival here, three years of aloof operation above this historic pattern has (perhaps it was inevitable) led to the political isolation of Frei. Historic examination will also show the

---

[3] Sáez resigned on March 15 and was replaced by Andres Zaldivár. (Telegram 2844 from Santiago, March 15. (National Archives and Records Administration, RG 59, Central Files 1967–69, POL 15–1 CHILE)

dispassionate observer that almost every President has had three years in which to introduce reforms before being immoblized by the political system prior to the extended period of campaigning for one kind of election or another. Moreover, some of the reforms of the past (e.g. the first Alessandri's introduction decades ago of social security) were perhaps as "revolutionary" in Chile as anything attempted by the Frei government thus far. Finally, it has been the custom for Chilean Governments in the second half of presidential tenure to accept, however reluctantly and fatalistically, the inevitability of printing money as the only "democratic" way out of the political impasse. What we are hearing as a debate in Congress right now is the reversion to form. And it must be honestly stated that Frei is seeking to hold some kind of line. Thus far he has rejected such crackpot ideas as importing 4,000 cars to sell in this seller's market at profits of E 50,000 each to fill budgetary gaps and such potentially explosive proposals (from his own party) as breaking the copper agreements by taxing the companies' income or adding an export tax on copper. But to get a law he will probably have to yield some place. If there were no law, the odds are that we would then be in a situation of "revolution" or "liberty" since the cost of living the first two months has risen fast (8.4 percent) and since the official index increase of 21.9 percent for 1967 has not yet been compensated. Most Chileans prefer not to analyze long-term economic trends: rather they want cash to pay bills. In their overwhelming majority they will not blame the political parties: they will hold the GOC responsible for blocking increases.

7. [sic] Senator Ibanez, the leading light of the Nacional Party and former Finance Minister Lucho MacKenna (under Alessandri) called on me yesterday to enlist my consent for a scheme they wanted to negotiate with GOC. Their proposal called for division of wage readjustment bill into two separate bills: (a) one would be confined strictly to readjustment aspects including a 21.9 percent cash payment to one third of public sector workers now scheduled to get 12.5 percent through mechanism of cash bonus: the wage increases for all the public sector would be financed by higher consumption taxes (which is a part of GOC proposal) and by further cuts in GOC expenditures and (b) separate financing bill for rest of fiscal expenditures. In latter Nacionales would insist on heavy cutbacks in agrarian reform programs including firing of MinAgriculture Trivelli and INDAP head Chonchol, cancellation of planned increase in sales tax, reduction of wealth tax. The role they had given the U.S. was to use the program loan for housing and for CORFO's planned investment.

A. I rejected their proposal, pointing out inter alia that, as far as I was concerned, availability of program loan depends on meaningful anti-inflation program and other criteria. I seriously doubted Frei would accept their proposal. If they really interested in healthy economy it was essential that they help get sensible wage bill through Congress now so housing starts could begin without delay. I added that I did not want to get involved in Chilean party politics. They had collaborated with the Communists in getting rid of Saez. Their explanations for their actions were not convincing to me. Therefore since they were among the parties who had gotten themselves into this mess over wage readjustment they must extricate themselves.

B. Late today left-wing newsmen were spreading rumors that Nacionales were going to vote for Reajuste because I had called them in (sic) to denounce their politicking and to accuse them of accelerating Communist gains.

8. Senator Ibanez put forward the extraordinary argument that the U.S. owed Chile's pro-American private enterprise sector "damages" because of our support of Frei's programs. In support of this thesis he invoked the recent toast by the Vice-President of Ambassador Tomic and of the Frei government. In this connection, we are informed by AP's Lee Brady that today he asked Communist Senator Teitelboim his reaction to Vice-President's toast and that the reply Brady says he filed was that if Tomic ever had chance to be president it has disappeared. What Teitelboim presumably meant is that CP won't play ball with Tomic which was his view at this time in any case.

9. Thus far, I have made clear to all who have sought me out—and I have sought no one—that U.S. is leaving it to Chileans to decide their political and economic future. U.S. aid has nothing to do with parties or with personalities but with effective use of economic resources. I got this across to Foreign Minister Valdes who summoned me for unrelated business when he broached subject. I noted to him that GOC has not consulted U.S. about deal with Communists nor any other aspect of current political problem, that we had no complaints and I trusted he had none either. He did not. I also mentioned to him that GOC's total silence on anti-American terrorism contrasted with the immediate denunciation by Allende and Teitelboim and that I wondered if this reversal of roles taken together with Zuniga's eulogy of the guerrillas in Bolivia meant that the U.S. should deal in the future with the FRAP in such matters.

10. Once we have clearer idea of what kind of bill will emerge from Congress and its likely effects on U.S.-Chile relations as well as perspectives of Chilean politics, we will provide our views by cable.[4]

Korry

---

[4] The Embassy reported on April 4 that the Senate had narrowly approved a modified version of the wage readjustment bill. (Telegram 3107 from Santiago; ibid., LAB 11 CHILE) An analysis of the "budgetary effects" of the bill is in telegram 3149 from Santiago, April 9. (Ibid.)

304.   Memorandum From the Chief of the Western Hemisphere Division (Broe) to the Deputy Director for Plans, Central Intelligence Agency (Karamessines)[1]

Washington, April 26, 1968.

SUBJECT

Circumstances Leading up to CIA Participation in Electoral Operations in Chile

The second confrontation in Chile between the Christian Democratic Party and the Socialist–Communist Political Front (FRAP) will come in September 1970. In the first round in 1964, the Christian Democrats were victorious resulting in the election of President Frei. Since that time the Christian Democrats have encountered increasing difficulty in both the economic and political fields. As an indicator of their economic problems, inflation which was reduced in the first two years of the Frei administration from a level of about 39% to 17% a year has begun to climb again. In 1967 the rate was 21% and for the first three months of 1968 it was 10%. Since these are government figures the actual rate is undoubtedly higher. Perhaps even more important than a deteriorating economic situation has been the development of a leftist trend within the non-Communist political parties and a growing political isolation of the Frei administration. The Radical Party, a key left of center group, is now controlled by its more extreme faction which favors an electoral alliance with the FRAP. The National Party, a right of center group, which has borne the brunt of some of the reforms carried out by the Christian Democrats, such as in the agrarian sector, has been alienated from the Christian Democrats and is now in active opposition. Even within the Christian Democratic Party itself there is a strong extreme faction which would be amenable to collaboration with the FRAP and for a period was in control of the party leadership. The control of the Radical Party by its extreme faction is one of the more worrisome aspects of the situation since a Radical–FRAP electoral alliance could elect a president in 1970. As a recent example of the desperate situation confronting Frei, the administration felt it had to turn to the Communist Party to get Congressional approval of their wage readjustment bill. The Communists exacted their price by forcing the Christian Democrats to remove a no-strike provision from the bill. During further consideration of this bill the Christian Democrats then turned to the National Party for support; they in turn forced the Frei administration to agree to lower taxes. As a result of both of these deals the prospects for increased inflation are better than ever.

---

[1] Source: Central Intelligence Agency, DDO/IMS Files, Job 79–00207A, [*file name not declassified*] Political and Economic 1968. Secret.

Faced with this deteriorating situation and with the prospect that if left unchecked the present political trends could bring to power a popular front government in Chile in 1970 the Ambassador began to mobilize his Embassy. He brought together key officers, which included the Chief and Deputy Chief of Station, and began to map out his program. It was understood by all that the major response by the Embassy would have to be in the overt sector probably through providing additional program loan assistance to the Chilean Government in order to help it hold down inflation and to carry forward its essential programs. It was also recognized that a smaller, supplementing effort would be needed in the covert field through an election operation in connection with the Congressional elections of 1969. These elections are all important since their outcome will determine the nature of the party alliances that will be formed in connection with the presidential election of September 1970.

Using information and analyses provided by the Embassy's political section as well as from [*less than 1 line of source text not declassified*] the Station has begun to put together a political action program to be carried out within the context of the overt effort. The final political action proposal will be a joint Station/Embassy effort with the Ambassador playing the key role. This proposal is expected to arrive in Washington within the next 7–10 days and will be submitted to the 303 Committee for approval.[2] The basic concept is to undertake a district by district analysis of the voting patterns and electoral trends in each district so that we can determine where covert leverage can be most effectively applied. With this information the objective is to elect as many moderate candidates of the Radical, Christian Democratic, and National parties as possible at the expense of the FRAP. If this can be successfully accomplished and an overt program implemented, our prospects for heading off a FRAP victory in 1970 might be improved.

William V. Broe

---

[2] Korry subsequently forwarded a proposal for a "covert election operation of very limited scope," a [*text not declassified*] contingency fund including direct support to moderate candidates from the Christian Democratic, Radical, and National parties. According to an undated memorandum prepared by the CIA: "The Ambassador has no intention to channel support to candidates through the political parties themselves because of the danger that funds so channeled would be used to support individuals contrary to our interests; i.e. left-wing Radicals and left-wing Christian Democrats." (Department of State, INR/IL Historical Files, Chile, 1967–1968)

305.   **Information Memorandum From the Assistant Secretary of State for Inter-American Affairs (Oliver) to Secretary of State Rusk[1]**

Washington, May 15, 1968.

SUBJECT

Chilean Political Situation

Discontent within Chile's traditionally apolitical military forces has added new dimensions to President Frei's political difficulties. Recent events in Chile have aroused widespread public uneasiness accompanied by rumors and allegations that a military coup was possible or even imminent.

All branches of the military and the national police are dissatisfied with their pay and allowances. The military have been displeased by the weak authority of the GOC in dealing with political opposition and strikes. However, despite these and some professional grievances, there is no evidence of conspiracy or plotting within the military or police. In an attempt to placate the military, President Frei has appointed his personal friend, retired Army General Tulio Marambio, as Minister of Defense. He has also designated a personal friend as new CINC of the Army, and named a retired general to become new Director of the strike-plagued Postal Service. The appointment of General Marambio, the first military man to hold cabinet position in more than ten years, is not in itself sufficient to placate the military. On the contrary, he was considered a "political general" by his peers before his retirement. However, Marambio has already initiated discussions on substantial pay increases which should take some of the heat out of the military discontent. Also, the GOC now seems to be demonstrating a firmer hand in the face of strikes. This should improve the government's image in the eyes of the armed forces.

On the other hand, the appointment of a military man to the cabinet has exacerbated public tensions which have been steadily growing as President Frei becomes more and more a lameduck president, and as his authority and control appear to be weakening. The basic political struggle is taking place in congress, where President Frei's 1968 anti-inflationary wage policy proposals are being debated. The political attitudes towards these proposals, however, should be viewed in

---

[1] Source: National Archives and Records Administration, RG 59, Central Files 1967–69, POL CHILE. Confidential. Drafted by Shankle and Morris. Copies were sent to Korry and Bowdler. A notation on the memorandum indicates Rusk saw it.

the context of a situation where all political parties have found common cause in a campaign to discredit President Frei and the Christian Democratic Party. At stake are the 1969 congressional and 1970 presidential elections.

President Frei's wage proposals have already been emasculated. Indeed, it is questionable whether what remains of President Frei's initial proposal can even be considered anti-inflationary, or if in its present state it would only contribute further to the inflationary spiral.

The current level of political tensions can be expected to continue, if not increase. All the strikes are not over, and preferential treatment for the military could trigger strike activity on the part of other public employees. Prospects are that there will be continued agitation from wage earners as the rate of inflation accelerates. With the government unable to impose its will on the congress to approve an anti-inflationary wage policy, it will probably rely more and more heavily on the police and armed forces to contain labor pressures. Even though there is little evidence of a possible coup, there is a real possibility that the police and the military, by receiving special wage treatment and carrying out the government's dictates in containing labor pressures, will become more closely identified with and eventually more involved in the Frei Administration. The appointment of military officers who are personal friends of President Frei to key positions may indicate that the process has already begun. Although each move by Frei with the military has a logic of its own, the inexorable buildup of circumstances compelling the military and the government toward each other, if carried to extremes, could eventually compromise the military's traditional apolitical stance. This would come about more by accident than design. But the result would be that the military, caught up by circumstances, would find itself propelled into positions and activities which clearly extend into political and government spheres.

The spectre of military participation has frightened the Communist Party, the best organized of President Frei's opposition, into a counter-coup campaign. The communists justifiably fear that they would be the first victims of any extra-constitutional steps by the Frei Administration or the military. The communists charge that the US is plotting with the Chilean right to persuade the military to initiate a coup. On the other hand, in an attempt to establish its own credentials with the military, the communists are expressing their sympathy for the financial plight of military personnel.

Although there has been no significant evidence of military plotting or conspiracy, and although it is most unlikely that extra-constitutional means will be employed to deny President Frei the remainder of his presidential term; the entire process of cabinet changes, military appointments, coup scare and communist counterattack must be viewed as a manifestation and warning signal of the political and economic malaise gripping Chile. Its acknowledged successes notwithstanding, President Frei's Administration has not succeeded in solving Chile's ingrained economic problems, particularly inflation. Social discontent and political agitation are on the upswing. The political consensus with which President Frei assumed office, unless in retrospect it was in fact illusory, has disappeared. He faces political opposition on every front, including from within his own party.

Although the wage bill struggle, a festering sore that has been draining the country's energies since last October, is almost over, the more serious, deeply rooted problems are still unsolved. We expect that the political difficulties that plague the Frei Administration will continue and even possibly grow worse as the forthcoming elections draw nearer. However, in considering the current and projected crisis situation, we should not lose sight of the fact of Chile's jealously guarded tradition of constitutionalism and democratic processes. This is the foundation of the Chilean political and social structure, and all political parties and groups, except the most extremist, quasi-terrorist lunatic fringe, can be expected in the final analysis to behave in a manner consistent with this tradition, even though their tactics are so self-serving as to raise serious doubts.

---

306. Memorandum From the Assistant Secretary of State for Inter-American Affairs (Oliver) to the Deputy Under Secretary of State for Political Affairs (Bohlen)[1]

Washington, July 5, 1968.

SUBJECT

    Chile: Assistance to Congressional Candidates

The attached memorandum[2] asks 303 Committee approval of a proposal that we help elect, through covert financial assistance, moderate candidates in the 1969 elections in Chile. An initial contingency fund of $350,000 is requested, which would be used for this purpose

---

[1] Source: Department of State, INR/IL Historical Files, 303 Committee Files, c. 71, 7/12/68. Secret; Eyes Only. Initialed for Oliver by Sayre.

[2] Dated June 20; attached but not printed.

at the direction of the Ambassador on recommendation of an Embassy "election team" made up of State and CIA personnel.

The memorandum identifies a number of factors at work in Chile since early 1967 that have gravely eroded the position of President Frei and his moderate supporters and that have led to a situation in which all three of the likely important candidates in the 1970 presidential elections are actively seeking Communist Party support. These adverse influences include a renewed upsurge of inflation, a decline in the rate of increase of the GNP, a loss of momentum in the pace of social reform, and loss of important areas of support in Congress with an accompanying assumption of leadership of the Christian Democratic and Radical Parties by left-wing elements. The upshot of these developments is a real possibility that in 1969 Chile will elect a Congress dominated by the Communists and by the Socialists, who in Chile are a particularly doctrinaire and left-wing group. Such a development would in turn bring quite material prospects that in 1970 there will be elected as President either a pro-Communist President or—as in the case of former Ambassador Tomic—one who can be unduly dependent on Communist and Socialist support.

The objective of the attached proposal is therefore to promote the election in 1969 of the greatest possible number of moderate senators and deputies in order to maximize effective opposition to the popular front candidate in 1970 and to create a body of moderates who could act as a restraint on the policies of any popular front president, should one be elected.

The determination as to which candidates will be supported will be made by the Embassy election team. Support will go to the candidate as individuals rather than to party organizations, for these organizations will almost certainly nominate some men that the U.S. would not wish to assist. The money will be made available to those selected through a number of tested individual channels whose stature is such that their contributions will appear natural and appropriate. Risks of exposure, while of course present, are believed to be acceptable. As Embassy selections are made, and as the campaign procedes, the Agency will from time to time submit reports to the 303 Committee on the progress of the Embassy's efforts.

Of the $350,000 sought, $250,000 would be used in the manner described above. $100,000 would be spent for media operations (CIA has access to two of Chile's leading newspapers and to a national net of radio stations); for possible support to a new splinter socialist party in order to exacerbate socialist differences; and for support to farm, youth and urban organizations that are effective among particular sectors of the electorate.

ARA agrees with the objectives of the proposal program and believes that the methods and tactics described in the CIA memorandum are suited to their attainment. The forces led by Frei are by and large dedicated to reform through the democratic processes; they represent therefore an important alternative to the varieties of social extremism that trouble the politics of Chile and of much of the rest of Latin America. The survival and health of these forces is desirable and congenial to our interests. I therefore recommend that you support the proposed action program.[3]

---

[3] The 303 Committee considered the proposal at its meeting on July 12. Broe explained that the funds would act as a "reserve" to support individual moderates who would be "carefully selected in an effort to brake the leftward drift toward a popular front which threatens to engulf Frei." "By early planning, a country team setup, and personal direction of Ambassador Korry," Broe maintained, "significant results are possible." The Committee approved the proposal "with the proviso that monthly progress be indicated to the committee from this moment on." (Memorandum for the record by Jessup, July 15; Department of State, INR/IL Historical Files, 303 Committee Files, c. 71, 7/12/68) The 303 Committee received progress reports on the congressional elections on September 3 and December 27. (Ibid., c. 73, 9/3/68 and c. 74, 12/27/68)

---

307.   Action Memorandum From the President's Special Assistant (Rostow) to President Johnson[1]

Washington, July 24, 1968.

SUBJECT

$20 Million Program Loan for Chile

Herewith a recommendation from Bill Gaud, Covey Oliver and Ed Korry, endorsed by BOB and Treasury, that you authorize a $20 million program loan to Chile for the remainder of 1968 (Tab B).[2]

Charlie Zwick's lucid memorandum summarizing the loan proposal (Tab A)[3] has all the essential elements and I will not repeat them. You should understand, as Charlie points out in his recommendation, that the loan is primarily a political bailing out operation to help President Frei and the moderate Christian Democrats make the best possi-

---

[1] Source: Johnson Library, National Security File, Country File, Chile, Vol. V, 8/67–11/68. Confidential.

[2] Tab B was a memorandum from Gaud to the President, July 15; attached but not printed.

[3] Tab A was a memorandum from Zwick to the President, July 20; attached but not printed.

ble showing in the Congressional elections in March 1969. These elections set the stage for the Presidential elections in September 1970.

After a record of steady progress in reducing inflation and stimulating development and reform during 1964, 1965 and 1966, President Frei fell on hard times in 1967 and 1968 when the opposition on the left and right ganged up on his anti-inflation program. If we do not help him to the extent recommended, he will either have to slash his investment budget for Alliance programs or engage in highly inflationary Central Bank borrowing, either of which will have serious adverse political implications for him in the March 1969 elections.

I join Ed Korry and Covey Oliver in the political judgment that our interests in Chile are best served by helping Frei through this particularly hard period. Hopefully, our aid, combined with his own self-help measures, will enable him to reverse the economic trends and make a good showing in the Congressional elections. If it does not turn out that way, we will still be free to decide how we will gear future aid.

In recommending that you authorize negotiation of the loan, I suggest you do so on an ad referendum basis.

Walt

Approve[4]

Disapprove

Call me

---

[4] This option is checked, and a July 25 handwritten notation by Bowdler indicates that Rostow informed Bowdler and Dottie Fredley. On August 27 Rostow reported that the negotiations had been concluded, that Chile had agreed to the fiscal and monetary conditions, and that a severe drought in Chile "makes the program loan more important than ever in President Frei's economic planning." The President authorized the loan. (Telegram CAP 82188 from Rostow to the President, August 27; Johnson Library, National Security File, Country File, Chile, Vol. V, 8/67–11/68)

308. Action Memorandum From the President's Special Assistant (Rostow) to President Johnson[1]

Washington, October 17, 1968, 11:50 a.m.

SUBJECT

PL 480 Program for Chile

The attached memorandum (Tab B)[2] from Orville Freeman/Bill Gaud recommends your approval of a $3 million PL 480 sales agreement with Chile for corn/grain sorghum and rice. Chile would repay this amount in dollars over a 20-year period, with a 10 percent down payment.

This PL 480 assistance for Chile is urgently needed because of a severe drought which has caused an emergency shortage of livestock feed. Chile has done quite well in meeting the self-help conditions we set in an earlier agricultural sector loan and PL 480 agreement.

The Chilean Goverment is feeling particularly isolated after the recent military coup in Peru, as Chilean leaders see themselves completely surrounded by military regimes. President Frei would undoubtedly welcome a sign of US support for his democratic government at this moment.

Charlie Zwick supports the Freeman/Gaud recommendation (Tab A).[3] I also recommend that you approve the negotiation of this sales agreement with Chile.

Walt

Approve[4]

Disapprove

Call me

---

[1] Source: Johnson Library, National Security File, Country File, Chile, Vol. V, 8/67–11/68. Confidential.

[2] Tab B was a memorandum from Gaud and Freeman to the President, October 10; attached but not printed.

[3] Tab A was a memorandum from Zwick to the President, October 15; attached but not printed.

[4] This option is checked. Handwritten notations by Bowdler indicate that Dottie Fredley and Sam Lewis were informed on October 17 at 4:50 p.m. and 4:55 p.m., respectively, and a copy was sent to Fredley on October 18.

309.   Action Memorandum From the President's Special Assistant (Rostow) to President Johnson[1]

Washington, January 14, 1969, 4:55 p.m.

SUBJECT

FY 1969 Assistance Program for Chile

Bill Gaud and Covey Oliver have requested your authorization to negotiate a $68 million economic assistance package with Chile for 1969 (Tab C).[2] The package includes a $20 million program loan, a $10 million agricultural sector loan, a $36 million PL 480 agreement, and $2 million in project loans. Orville Freeman joins Gaud in recommending your approval of the PL 480 sale agreement—mainly for wheat, corn, and rice (Tab D).[3]

Charlie Zwick has some reservations about Chile's economic performance and prospects. On balance, however, he recommends your approval of the whole package (Tab A).[4]

Joe Barr is prepared to support all elements of the package except the program loan. He questions the need for balance of payments support of this magnitude, and raises other questions about the realism of AID's proposed negotiating instructions. He states that he can not weigh what he sees to be economic shortcomings in the program loan proposal against political considerations underlying our support for President Frei, and would have to leave that to your judgment. Barr is satisfied, moreover, that the arrangements governing AID lending in Chile provide reasonably satisfactory protection for the US balance of payments (Tab B).[5]

We provided a $20 million program loan for Chile in 1968. The final installment was released in December. Chile's performance on the self-help commitments under that loan and under an earlier agricultural

---

[1] Source: Johnson Library, National Security File, Country File, Chile, Filed by LBJ Library. Confidential.

[2] Tab C was a memorandum from Gaud to the President, December 23; attached but not printed.

[3] Tab D was a memorandum from Gaud and Freeman to the President, December 23; attached but not printed.

[4] Tab A was a memorandum from Zwick to the President, January 6; attached but not printed.

[5] Tab B was a memorandum from Barr to the President, January 10; attached but not printed.

sector loan of $23 million has been reasonably satisfactory—especially when Chile's economy is being buffeted by the worst drought in its history. As Zwick and Barr state, progress toward price stability has been slipping. The outlook is now for about 30 percent inflation in 1969—up from 28 percent last year. But without substantial continued foreign support, Frei's stabilization program could completely collapse. The drought has undermined both agricultural and industrial production and sent unemployment rates skyrocketing. To deal with this temporary social and political crisis, Frei is having to divert funds for temporary jobs and emergency farm credit. So far, Chile is managing its economic crisis with considerable skill. The outlook for 1969 is not as bleak as Zwick and Barr suggest.

This assistance package has been worked out in close cooperation with the IBRD and the IMF, both of whom have negotiating teams in Chile now to work out overall agreements to support Frei's 1969 program. Our negotiating objective in the fields of fiscal, exchange rate, and monetary policies are integral parts of this effort. For example, Chile is seeking an IMF standby, and the IMF team doubts that Chile will qualify without the prospect of the US assistance package outlined in this memorandum. It is very important to the future of Frei's economic program that we be able to negotiate our package this month in parallel with the other two international agencies. Our negotiating leverage is also augmented by simultaneous negotiations.

Critical congressional elections are scheduled for March in Chile. Frei's term runs until late 1970. His ability to continue those constructive programs in such fields as agrarian reform and education which have made Chile a leader in the Alliance for Progress depend heavily on the kind of showing his party makes in the March election. With the great strains placed on the economy by the drought, Frei needs both the assistance proposed and the strong moral support implied by a negotiating package of this type. Ambassador Korry urges your approval of the negotiations so that no time-lag can intervene in the rhythm of our support for Frei's program.

Chile has made outstanding achievements in the social and political fields under the Alliance for Progress—and Frei is currently reasserting a strong leadership position within the Christian Democratic Party to consolidate many of these gains during his two years in office. Although Chile's economic problems are worrisome, Frei has shown remarkable tenaciousness and courage in facing up to them in recent months. I have looked carefully into the reservations expressed by Barr and Zwick, and I think they are based to some extent on a misunderstanding of recent actions taken by the Chilean Government and Congress.

On balance, I think Chile is a good bet and that President Frei deserves our full support. I recommend that you authorize negotiation of the full assistance package as outlined in the Gaud memorandum at Tab C.

Walt

Approve[6]

Disapprove

Call me

---

[6] The first and last options are checked and the President wrote: "Let's pass until next week." In a January 16 memorandum to the President, Rostow reported: "Rusk is inclined to go with Ed Korry's view on the Chilean loan. If you approve, he will clear with [Secretary of State-designate William P.] Rogers—if it is the transitional problem that concerns you." In response, Johnson checked the "Talk to President" option. (Johnson Library, National Security File, Country File, Chile, Filed by LBJ Library) On January 17 Korry reacted angrily to a report that the Department of the Treasury had "rejected" the program loan: "If parochialists in Treasury are going to exercise veto power over US foreign policy, if they are to be both arrogant and powerful enough to assume such political responsibilities in defiance of the considered judgments of State, AID, and the President's personal representative, then it is the latter's responsibility to record for history the range of possible consequences of their action." (Telegram 215 from Santiago, January 17; National Archives and Records Administration, RG 59, Central Files 1967–69, POL CHILE–US) President Johnson subsequently approved the loan.

Colombia

310. Letter From the Ambassador to Colombia (Oliver) to the Assistant Secretary of State for Inter-American Affairs (Mann)[1]

Bogotá, November 18, 1964.

Dear Tom:

We are not yet reporting officially what I am going to sketch for you here, because we want to check on the principal source of information, Dr. Harold Dunkerly of the Harvard Advisory Group to the Ministry of Finance.

On Monday last[2] Dr. Dunkerly had a meeting with Fowler and got a general picture of the thinking that developed in Washington regarding the future of the AID program for Colombia. In generalized terms, Fowler left Dunkerly with the impression that the program for the future would be based on the success of the fiscal and budgetary program that at the time of our departure for Washington seemed well on its way through Congress as a result of the political consensus that Lleras Restrepo was supposed to have achieved.

Yesterday Dunkerly asked to see me (with Fowler). He said that he had had a long conversation Monday afternoon with Calle. Without linking his visit to any request from Calle, Dunkerly nonetheless managed to communicate the impression that he was speaking Calle's mind. Dunkerly said that the Government's program was "in jeopardy" and that the situation for the future was "highly dangerous." He explained that Carlos Lleras Restrepo had turned out, so far, to be a "damp squib" ("wet firecracker" in American English). The expected consensus had not been achieved. Calle, who has no political power of his own and had staked everything on Lleras' effectiveness, now foresaw not only a net loss of a half billion pesos in expected increased revenues but the fearful prospect of heavy political demands from the Coffee Federation on the present fisc. At maximum, the Federation could pressure for drain of another half billion from the Central Bank and have already asked for drawing rights for 150 billion for the current month. We are getting together a complete analysis on the details of the immediately foregoing. The details will come later and officially.

---

[1] Source: National Archives and Records Administration, RG 59, ARA/LA Files: Lot 66 D 65, Colombia 1964. Secret; Official–Informal. A copy was sent to ARA/CV.

[2] November 16.

The big point is that the economists on the GOC side, including Calle, foresee that, if an effective political turnaround does not take place, this country will be in galloping inflation by next March. This will present not only a severe economic setback but have very grave political repercussions.

What Dunkerly wants me to do is to get in touch with Lleras Restrepo and seek to induce him to take an active leadership role on the economic front. Dunkerly's idea is that I should use the lever of possible loss of program aid, which is running about one-fourth of the Colombian budget on present projections. My own feeling is that Lleras is too sophisticated for this gambit to be credible. My inclination is simply to go over with him the very serious consequences for Colombia and for the Alianza as a whole if this situation is not corrected. We have much more reflection to do here before the Country Team makes recommendations through official channels.

I have had a request in to see the President ever since my return from Washington, and I would like to get to talk to him before I see Lleras Restrepo. If the President does not give me an interview today, I cannot see him until next Monday, at the earliest, because of my official visit to Operations UNITAS at Barranquilla–Cartagena.[3]

I am very sorry to have to report this situation. Dunkerly is true to his profession, that is, he is somewhat of a crepe hanger, and that is one of the reasons we are checking out his conclusions before reporting officially.

Henry Dearborn tells me that in his whole time here he has never heard so many rumors about golpes and the like as during the three days I was in Cali on my official visit there. The Minister of Labor told me at lunch yesterday that he thought there was "a clear and present danger" of a golpe. *Time* is not helping. The Chinese Ambassador told me he thought the piece in the issue of November 13 was absolutely outrageous.[4] There has, to my way of thinking, been a continuous *Time* line building up Ruiz and turning down the legitimate Government of Colombia. I noticed the Ruiz build-up even before you rang me up about this assignment. It seems to go on steadily.

---

[3] In a meeting with Valencia on November 25 Oliver outlined the difficulties involved in completing the 1964 program loan, including marine insurance and forward procurement. Valencia suggested that Oliver discuss the details with Calle. (Telegram 530 from Bogotá, November 27; National Archives and Records Administration, RG 59, Central Files 1964–66, AID(US) 9 COL)

[4] Reference is to a brief report on the anti-guerrilla campaign in Colombia, which, according to *Time* magazine did not progress "until two years ago when Major General Alberto Ruiz Novoa became War Minister." (*Time*, November 13, 1964, p. 61)

Ambassador Stewart's telegram quoting the views of President Leoni is also very much in my mind.[5]

I am convinced that we have got to do everything we can to uphold constitutional government in Colombia. This may even require us to consider AID assistance on a bail-out basis, although I certainly hope it never comes to that. Be assured that I will do everything I can to help Colombia remain a country of law and a worth-while model of economic development.[6]

Sincerely yours,

Covey

---

[5] Leoni suggested that the United States "move cautiously" before recognizing the new regime in Bolivia. Any precipitate action by the United States, he argued, "might have direct bearing on Colombia and the political ambitions" of General Ruiz. (Telegram 712 from Caracas, November 16; National Archives and Records Administration, RG 59, Central Files 1964–66, POL 16 BOL)

[6] In his reply Mann instructed Oliver to disabuse anyone with "doubts about our full support constitutional government and fact that American public and official opinion would react adversely to a military movement in Colombia." (Telegram 356 to Bogotá, November 27; ibid., AID(US) 9 COL)

---

311. Telegram From the Embassy in Peru to the Department of State[1]

Lima, December 9, 1964, 5:05 p.m.

695. From Mann. Following are my first reactions to latest Colombian exchange crisis. Would appreciate views of Ambassador Oliver and Department. Costanzo[2] leaves tonight for Washington after first meeting with Minister Calle scheduled to take place this afternoon. He will bring to Department details our discussion here.

First, it seems to me first question we must ask ourselves is whether, if GOC makes no change in its exchange policy, disbursement of $45 million would stabilize the situation. On basis of info available to me I doubt very much that it would. It was, I am told, recognized

---

[1] Source: National Archives and Records Administration, RG 59, Central Files 1964–66, FN 1 COL. Confidential; Immediate. Repeated to Bogotá. Passed to the White House. Mann was in Lima to attend the third annual meeting of the Inter-American Economic and Social Council (ECOSOC).

[2] Henry J. Costanzo, director of the Office of Latin America, Department of the Treasury.

in 1963 that the maintenance of two exchange rate system was difficult at best and would require a high level of confidence in the peso to maintain. I understand that the then Minister of Finance, Carlos Sanz de Santamaria, refused at that time to move to a single rate, or some other more adequate system, but agreed to reconsider if exchange loss should exceed $30 million in 1964. It seems clear that the weak political position of President Valencia, the recent capital flights, and the relatively heavy recent foreign exchange losses present us with a very different situation from the one we faced in 1963 and when we signed the 1964 aid program.

Instead of confidence, there is an obvious lack of confidence in the ability of the government to avoid devaluation. Purchase and sales of exchange this week should tell us more. But I understand that outstanding import licenses total about $500 million which can be presented for payment at the nine-to-one rate at any time. All of this suggests that unless effective corrective action is taken first, the disbursements would be quickly wasted in a futile effort to maintain a nine-to-one import rate while price rises over past two years suggest it should be at least closer to thirteen-to-one. This kind of a futile exercise would presumably not promote either political stability or economic progress.

Second, there is the question of whether we are obligated by the loan agreement to make the disbursement, having in mind that Colombian performance has been relatively good on the self-help measures specified in the agreements and that there is no agreement on exchange rate. It would seem to me that marine insurance issue gives us an out. Perhaps the attitude of Congress re taxes gives us another peg but I assume this would be more relevant to 1965 performance. Do our program loan agreements contain a general escape clause which can be used where conditions have changed to such an extent to make it impossible to achieve its purpose? If not, it seems to me they should in the future.

Third, is the question of whether the U.S. should seek to avoid the political onus for the urgently needed exchange reforms. This is a luxury I don't think we can afford. However, I understand the IMF is willing to return a team to make suggestions about corrective action. The IMF rather than the U.S. should suggest the precise corrective action needed. I understand there are a number of possibilities, some of which might be more acceptable to Valencia than others. In this connection, is it correct that one of principal political problems is public promise of Valencia not to devalue plus belief that movement from nine-to-one rate would not only be a partial devaluation but would raise food costs as well? Would it be feasible to use PL 480 to help in food cost front?

Finally, it seems to me both Colombian and U.S. interests would be best served by urging that corrective action in exchange rate be taken forthwith and that disbursements of our aid be used to support GOC effort. For this we could stick on marine insurance issue as Ambassador Oliver suggests, perhaps with whatever adjustments are necessary on issue of forward procurement.

Will report on conversations with Calle today.[3] Would appreciate Ambassador and Department reactions this line of thought.[4]

Jones

----

[3] In the meeting with Mann on December 9, Calle acknowledged that resolute action was necessary not only to address the exchange rate but also to adjust much of the government's economic program. In return, Mann agreed to expedite the 1964 program loan by resolving the outstanding issues of marine insurance and forward procurement. Mann believed there was no alternative and step was "essential part of measures needed to keep Colombian economy viable." (Telegram 698 from Lima, December 10; National Archives and Records Administration, RG 59, Central Files 1964–66, FN 10 PERU/IMF) Although Valencia continued to resist devaluation, the two sides eventually agreed on a formula to resolve their legal differences, thereby freeing $35 million of the program loan by December 31. (Memorandum from Sayre to Bundy, December 21; Johnson Library, National Security File, Country File, Colombia, Vol. I, 12/63–7/65)

[4] No response has been found.

----

312.   **Paper Prepared in the Bureau of Intelligence and Research[1]**

Washington, May 5, 1965.

COLOMBIA: SITUATION AND PROSPECTS

The Basic Judgment

Political tensions in Colombia have once again built up to crisis point. There is, as on the many other occasions when the National Front government has been torn by deep partisan conflict, a chance that some

----

[1] Source: National Archives and Records Administration, RG 59, ARA/CV Files, 1965: Lot 67 D 622, POL 2 Sitreps. Secret. Drafted in INR/CA by Robert R. Hendon, Thomas C. Colwell, and Mary K. Manzoli. Forwarded to Mann as an attachment to a May 5 memorandum from Wolfe who noted that Sayre had requested the paper on Mann's behalf earlier in the day, thereby precluding its coordination within either the Department or the intelligence community. (Ibid.) Sayre forwarded the paper to Bundy on May 12. (Memorandum from Sayre to Bundy, May 12; Johnson Library, National Security File, Country File, Colombia, Vol. I, 12/63–7/65)

fundamental change in the governing authority will be made. That change could come by military coup or through some basic political rearrangement in the form and composition of the government. Colombian politicians of all stripes and the military establishment, however, have a way of coming together for mutual advantage in time of crisis and thereby averting a break up of the National Front and a return to civil strife or military dictatorship. We believe that the danger of a military coup or a breakdown in the Front is greater today than a year ago, or even several months ago, but we are still inclined to feel that the end is not at hand yet.

The Current Situation

The recently announced alliance of the majority Laureanista–Alzatista (L/A's) faction of the Conservative Party and two smaller opposition parties, the Liberal Revolutionary Movement (MRL) and the Popular National Alliance (ANP), has created the latest, serious problem for the Front government of Conservative President Valencia. The alliance formalizes the L/A's de facto opposition to the National Front government, which along with absenteeism in the Congress and lack of party discipline, has served to block passage of important legislation since mid-1964. The Liberal Party that shares the responsibility of government with the Conservative Party in the National Front and the Ospinista minority faction of the Conservative Party (still loyal to the National Front) are pressuring Valencia to remove the L/A's from the government or to exact a pledge of legislative support from them. Valencia is extremely reluctant to make any move that would further undermine his already shaky government.

What May Happen

Valencia probably will respond to the present crisis—as he has to other crisis situations in the past—by temporizing, in hopes that it will go away. If the Liberals force the issue and the L/A's remain intransigent, Valencia may be forced to remove the latter from their government posts. This measure would probably kill any chance for congressional action on a major fiscal package now under consideration and all but end hopes for any meaningful legislation before elections in March 1966 when a new congress is to be chosen. An outcome to the present crisis of this sort would probably not topple the Valencia government.

The National Front's problems are growing, however, and its political base for dealing with these problems is shrinking. The greatest danger that may emerge from the latest crisis is that it may lead Liberal Party leaders to believe that the National Front cannot survive the electoral test in 1966 when it is their turn to put a member of their party in the presidency. As a result, the Liberals may decide to conspire with the military with the idea of bringing about an extra-legal change of government through which they would gain the upper hand. The military, faced with a growing problem of subversive violence, may be receptive to the Liberals' overtures, thinking perhaps that the Liberal leaders might be able to help them establish effective government. At this time there is little indication that the Liberals are seriously considering an extra-legal change or, for that matter, that they have the military support they would need for such a move.

Economic Problems as a Factor

Colombia's financial condition is deteriorating and the economic frustrations of the masses contribute to political tensions. Inflationary pressures are not great at the moment but a push against prices is expected in coming months. A Special Session of the Congress, called to consider a package of revenue proposals, may reject some of the measures proposed by the Valencia government that could at least limit the size of a prospective large 1965 budget deficit. The spread between the official and the free rate of exchange is increasing and the government lacks the international reserves to protect the official rate against speculative raids and the rising demand for imports. Valencia's heavy commitment to avoid devaluation has prevented his administration from taking the remedial measures that are necessary to rectify the monetary and exchange situation.

The prospect is that Colombia will try during the balance of 1965 to obtain short-term commercial financing to relieve pressures on the exchange rate and impose additional indirect taxes on imports. With government attention devoted primarily to maneuvering its way through the country's political and financial difficulties, it does not seem likely that Colombia will make much headway on basic long-term social and economic reform in the near future.[2]

---

[2] Mann briefed President Johnson on Colombia during a telephone conversation the afternoon of May 5. He told the President "we have a problem in Colombia." Mann explained that Colombian President Valencia is very pro-U.S., but "does not know beans from bull about economics" and wants $60–100 million a year to maintain rates of exchange that are unrealistic. Valencia does not want to devalue or stop inflation because it will cost him popularity, but if he doesn't do something "it will cost us billions without giving us anything." Mann told Johnson that "we have this type of problem all over the world, but in Colombia it is a matter of leadership. He said if it blows it won't necessarily go Communist but he did not think this guy would last. He said he has been very anti-Communist and a good friend but does not know anything about running a country." (Johnson Library, Papers of Thomas C. Mann, Telephone Conversations with LBJ, May 2, 1965–June 2, 1966)

313.   Telegram From the Department of State to the Embassy in Colombia[1]

Washington, May 22, 1965, 2:18 p.m.

954. Our first objective in Colombia is to prevent overthrow of constitutional government especially if there is a chance that golpe may result which would bring to top undesirable extremist elements on either side.[2]

Our second objective is to get government to institute necessary reforms and adopt such other measures as necessary to assure its longer term stability.

As between these two objectives it is obvious we must choose the first if the situation requires it. We undersand from all of your reports however that the situation in Colombia does not require us to make such a choice at this time. On the contrary we understand that GOC has taken advantage of current demonstrations for the purpose of imposing a state of siege which will permit it to institute the measures necessary to achieve economic and political stability. We also understand from your messages that government is now in firm control of situation with support of police and military and that government is moving as swiftly as it can to adopt needed reform measures. We on our side are also prepared to move swiftly to complement Colombian action.

If there are any moves which the United States Government can make to assist the GOC in present political crisis, you should not hesitate to recommend them.[3] Moreover if for any reason you do not

---

[1] Source: National Archives and Records Administration, RG 59, Central Files 1964–66, POL COL. Secret; Immediate; Limdis. Drafted by Sayre, cleared by Palmer and Eaton, and approved by Sayre.

[2] On May 21 Valencia declared a state of siege in response to violent student demonstrations against U.S. intervention in the Dominican Republic. In a May 21 memorandum to Mann, Vaughn reported: "This action should place the GOC in a stronger position for taking effective action in maintaining public security and resolving its continuing economic problems." (Ibid., ARA Files, 1965–67: Lot 70 D 295, Colombia, 1965)

[3] Oliver forwarded a preliminary reply in which he reported that the Colombian Government was, in fact, reluctant to use the state of siege as a means to institute fiscal reforms. (Telegram 1473 from Bogotá, May 24; ibid., Central Files 1964–66, DEF 6 IA)

believe our position outlined Deptel 949 is adequate, you should not hesitate to say so.[4]

If pressure for furnishing military contribution to IAF in Dominican Republic substantially contributes to present political crisis, you may indicate to GOC US would hope contribution can be made but we will not press if this the case.

Rusk

---

[4] Telegram 949 to Bogotá, May 21, reported on international efforts to stabilize Colombia's finances, particularly as a result of the recent mission of Gerald M. Alter, director of the Western Hemisphere Department, World Bank. After two meetings with World Bank, International Monetary Fund, and Department of State officials, Alter was instructed to return to Bogotá with joint conditions for extending emergency financial assistance to Colombia. The conditions stipulated that the Valencia administration impose a 4.5 peso per dollar payment tax for the remainder of its term. (Ibid., FN 16 COL) The Embassy considered the overall strategy "excellent," although it advised against authorizing Alter to speak on behalf of the U.S. Government. (Telegram 1463 from Bogotá, May 22; ibid., E 1 BRAZ)

---

314.   **Memorandum From the Assistant Secretary of State for Inter-American Affairs (Vaughn) to Secretary of State Rusk**[1]

Washington, June 4, 1965.

SUBJECT

Situation in Colombia

1. As indicated in recent previous memoranda from Mr. Read to Mr. Bundy on this subject,[2] a serious political and economic situation is developing in Colombia and the United States has been trying to

---

[1] Source: Johnson Library, National Security File, Country File, Colombia, Vol. I, 12/63–7/65. Secret. Drafted by Hill and Eaton. Read forwarded this memorandum to Bundy on June 4.

[2] Memoranda from Read to Bundy, May 7, May 22, and May 24, are ibid.

obtain action which would shore up the National Front Government of President Valencia.[3]

2. The immediate situation is that President Valencia has been unable yet to follow through on his earlier decision to institute an economic program (including a de facto devaluation of the peso) which, together with substantial aid from the U.S. and international lending institutions, would tend to stabilize the economic and political situation. The economic program and de facto devaluation were worked out over the last few weeks in outline between the World Bank and the Minister of Finance, with the approval of President Valencia.

The United States made a positive response to these negotiations by indicating to the Government of Colombia through the Bank its readiness to support such a program with immediate release of $10 million from the 1964 program loan and, subject to negotiation, with $60 million in FY 1966 AID program funds, and additional support from PL 480, Export-Import Bank and Treasury for a total of about $100 million over the next twelve months if the devaluation was the 50 per cent believed by the Bank, the IMF and our economists to be the appropriate level for effectiveness. (This would have been effected by imposing a 4.5 peso "payments tax" on top of the import exchange rate of 9 pesos to the dollar; President Valencia approved first a 3 peso tax and then a 3.5 peso tax as negotiations continued.)

President Valencia's approval of effective devaluation was a major change in his previous position. His Government devalued just after he came to office in 1962, but the devaluation was a failure through mishandling. He did not want to try again and overruled a recommendation for a new devaluation from his previous Minister of Finance last December. The persuasion of circumstances over the last months, including the need to cut back imports sharply, changed his mind.

In addition, the U.S. readied a negotiating team and developed its negotiating position to be ready to go to Colombia instantly when the Colombian program was approved by the Cabinet and made arrangements for funds to be made immediately available to support the Colombian effort. The IMF also indicated to the Colombian Government its readiness to roll over Colombian indebtedness and provide

---

[3] Mann reviewed the Colombia crisis with President Johnson earlier that morning and told the President he was holding a meeting on Colombia and that the situation is very bad. Mann reported the "World Bank thing becoming unglued. The President said it looked as if we ought to pour all the money we can in—try to save the President [Valencia]. He said he thought this was better then trying to remake the government. Mr. Mann explained how difficult it would be to pour enough money in. He said they were going to kick around several alternatives and then planned to go over and talk with McGeorge Bundy so the President's staff would be clued in." (Ibid., Papers of Thomas C. Mann, Telephone Conversations with LBJ, May 2, 1965–June 2, 1966)

an additional standby of $20 million, and the IBRD was prepared to provide large project assistance. This outside official support, together with the return of normal private foreign credit lines which would have accompanied adequate monetary, fiscal and exchange rate measures, would have permitted higher imports. Higher imports, together with appropriate internal financial policies, would have led to increased production and employment rather than a stagnant economy.

3. The Colombian Minister of Finance first indicated that he expected to get the required unanimous Cabinet approval under the existing state of siege and take action by Presidential decree at the 3.5 if not 4.5 peso tax level over or just after the week end of May 30–31. This did not come about. In the intervening week, serious difficulties have arisen. Unanimous Cabinet approval has not been obtained. Leadership elements in the Liberal Party, which forms part of Valencia's coalition, have opposed the devaluation.

News of the proposed devaluation leaked to the Colombian press and set off a strong adverse reaction. In Congress, opposition elements were joined by some Liberals in denouncing the devaluation. President Valencia, today reported in Bogota's press as himself opposed to devaluation, has apparently done little to get the Cabinet, the national leadership, or public opinion behind the proposed program. Carlos Lleras Restrepo, the leading Liberal, has tried to stay in the background for political reasons, disassociating himself from the proposed devaluation. The Finance Minister indicated that he expected action by today, Friday, June 4, but there are no indications that he has yet enough votes for the needed unanimous Cabinet decision.

4. Indecisive leadership and the difficulties of acting through the coalition National Front system lie at the root of the present mishandled situation. Alberto Lleras, who was President prior to Valencia, governed through much of his administration with a state of siege for public order reasons. The state of siege also permitted him to act by decree when Congress did not act because it was hampered by the rule that unless otherwise decided by a two-thirds majority, all action must be by two-thirds majority. Lleras did not use his decree authority extensively. Valencia has attempted until now to govern without the state of siege. But the political base of the National Front has tended to fragment as time has passed. Consequently, Congressional action is continually more difficult to achieve. Therefore Valencia has turned to the state of siege device. But even with the state of siege he needs a political base of support because there are now mechanics for reversing his decree rulings. Thus leadership is needed and he has been lacking in this quality especially on economic issues.

5. Should the Colombians not approve an adequate economic program, including exchange reforms, the economic and political situa-

tion may be expected to erode further. Economically, intensified exchange controls would be tried, together with tight credit to the private sector. But imports, production and employment would be down and inflationary pressures high.

Politically, the prospects would be for impaired stability of the government rather than sudden or violent action to depose it, but this could change. At the least the National Front would lose ground at the March 1966 Congressional elections, probably primarily to the forces of former dictator Rojas Pinilla, and would have uncertain prospects in the May 1966 Presidential elections. Economic deterioration could lead to a decision by Valencia to resign or by the military, persuaded by the business elite, to take over.

The military under its present leadership is opposed to taking over civilian political power, but it might be persuaded to later if the situation deteriorated sufficiently. Lower level military leaders have not been active politically either, but they also might become restive later if the general situation deteriorated badly. They might then become responsive to former Minister of War Ruiz, who is presently quiet but has had political ambitions.[4] A united military takeover led from the top would probably be peaceful. A takeover incited from the lower ranks could be bloody. There is no indication that Communists would play a significant part in a takeover under either circumstance, but the situation could change.

6. De facto devaluation also entails political risks, especially if badly handled, but the benefits in terms of a sense of a positive forward movement of the economy and corresponding political gains would be high if well handled.

7. President Valencia may appeal for sizeable U.S. loans without a satisfactory economic program or devaluation but granting such aid would offer no solution.

One hundred million dollars from the United States, which is the extent to which we are prepared to support a good program, would not greatly change the economic situation without such a program because private bank and commercial credits would not be available for lack of confidence in financial policies, and the international financial institutions would not provide complementary support.

As much as three to four hundred million dollars from the United States Government would be needed for one year to provide the same amount of push to the economy without a good Colombian program as would be achieved with $100 million with a good program. And

---

[4] Ruiz, who was forced to resign the War Ministry in January, announced on May 9 that he would also discontinue his recent attempt to found a political movement.

even then the Colombian Government would have to undertake a larger devaluation and greater financial adjustments in 1966 after the next President came to office.

8. The U.S. is continuing actively to take steps to help stabilize the situation and shore up constitutional government in Colombia. In addition to readiness to quickly support an acceptable program with large scale loans (see paragraph 2), the following actions are now under way:

(a) Ambassador Oliver is being instructed to see President Valencia and certain other Colombian political leaders, after checking with the Minister of Finance, if the Colombian Government still seems to be wavering on undertaking a positive economic program.

(b) I have arranged to consult with Colombian Ambassador to the United States Uribe and Dr. Carlos Sanz de Santamaria, Chairman of the CIAP and a former Colombian Minister of Finance.

(c) Ambassador Bernbaum is returning to Venezuela to convey our assessment and position to the Venezuelans and obtain their thinking and possible assistance. President Leoni has previously conveyed to us his great concern about Colombia; many Venezuelan leaders believe that an overthrow of constitutional government in Colombia would sooner or later encourage one in Venezuela.

(d) The Ambassador of Brazil is likewise being called in to convey our position to Brazil.

We have considered sending someone to Bogota to reinforce Ambassador Oliver in his conversations with President Valencia and others there but have decided against it because Ambassador Oliver has close and effective relations with President Valencia, our doing so at this juncture might open us up too much for special appeals for assistance without a program, and to do so might also imply too much United States involvement in the delicate issue of devaluation.[5]

---

[5] On June 5 Mann told the President that his June 4 meeting on Colombia (see footnote 3 above) had included Sanz de Santamaría and Uribe, in addition to those in the administration who were either "concerned with" or "knew about" Colombia. After the meeting, Mann asked that Vaughn prepare a memorandum on the situation in Colombia for the Secretary, which is the source text. Mann also gave Johnson the following assessment: "If the government does not take the necessary steps then in the next two or three days we think there will be a change but we do not see any danger of a commie takeover if the Army stays united. We have no evidence of a split." The President asked Mann to set up a task force to develop plans for Colombia, as well as Guatemala and Bolivia. "We should have a special task force on top of it with the best names," Johnson said, "and be prepared in advance instead of waiting until they are shooting at us." (Memorandum of conversation, June 5, 12:10 p.m.; Johnson Library, Papers of Thomas C. Mann, Telephone Conversations with LBJ, May 2, 1965–June 2, 1966)

315.   Memorandum From the President's Special Assistant for National Security Affairs (Bundy) to President Johnson[1]

Washington, June 30, 1965, 6:25 p.m.

SUBJECT

Colombia

Since one of the stickiest areas in Latin America these days is Colombia, I thought you might be interested in having a brief report on the more immediate and major problems in that country as well as U.S. efforts and plans to cope with them.

1. The most serious immediate problems appear to be economic. Lack of political and economic confidence has caused the free rate of exchange to depreciate from 10 pesos to the dollar in October 1964 to 19 pesos to the dollar now. The official import rate is over-valued at 9 pesos to the dollar and is increasingly under pressure. Liquid reserves are dangerously low and business activity threatens to be curtailed by the lack of essential imports and of credit. There is a substantial inflationary potential because of the gap between budget expenditures planned for 1965 and anticipated revenues.

2. There is a difference of view on how to meet these problems. On the one hand, the Monetary Fund, the World Bank and the U.S., along with a number of high-level Colombians (e.g. the recently resigned Finance Minister), believe that Colombia must institute a comprehensive economic program, which should probably include such measures as budget balancing, wage-price restraint, an increase in imports and a de facto devaluation of about 50%; we would be prepared to support such a program with up to $90 million of new commitments.

On the other hand, President Valencia holds a different view. While, in May, he appeared ready to go along with the above comprehensive economic program, he has more recently said that such a program would be politically too risky, particularly the de facto devaluation (we don't agree).

What Valencia seems to prefer is that we provide substantial assistance (estimates vary from $200 million to $400 million), without taking the necessary self-help measures, on the grounds that this would enable him to avoid a revolution or at least an electoral defeat for the

---

[1] Source: Johnson Library, National Security File, Memos to the President, McGeorge Bundy, Vol. 11. Secret. A notation on the memorandum indicates that the President saw it. According to another copy, the memorandum was drafted by Bundy and Gordon Chase. (Ibid., Country File, Colombia, Memos, Vol. II, 6/65–9/66)

National Front in Colombia. We are not anxious to meet Valencia's desire, among other things, because it will cost us a lot more money and because we believe that a large loan to Colombia without adequate self-help measures, would severely undercut the credibility of an important Alliance for Progress dimension.

3. The situation, however, is not without hope. Largely as a result of our Embassy's efforts, there are indications that a number of influential Colombians are becoming more and more convinced of the need for a positive economic program. State's present estimate is that the odds are slightly in favor of Colombia attempting a comprehensive economic program of the type outlined above, although probably with some changes. State also estimates that the odds are somewhat better than even that the program, if attempted, will be reasonably successful.

4. If, in the last analysis, President Valencia refuses to undertake a comprehensive economic program a number of contingencies could develop. These are analyzed in the attached contingency plan,[2] which notes that the most likely contingency is continued drift and deterioration under the National Front and that the next most likely contingencies are (a) the withdrawal of Valencia, (b) a military takeover, and (c) a general uprising. State does not foresee the danger of a Communist take-over in Colombia in the short term, in view of the fact that the extreme left in Colombia is badly fractured, poorly led and not very popular.[3]

McG. B.

---

[2] Attached but not printed. The contingency plan was prepared in response to the President's request for a "task force" on Colombia. (Memorandum from Vaughn to Rusk, June 22; National Archives and Records Administration, RG 59, Central Files 1964–66, POL 23 GUAT) The Latin American Policy Committee drafted the plan, which was then forwarded to the White House on June 24. (Memorandum from Read to Bundy, June 24; ibid., ARA Country Files: Lot 68 D 385, LAPC—Colombia)

[3] Bundy wrote the following note at the end of the memorandum: "You may have seen Charles Bartlett's praise of this policy yesterday." Bartlett was a columnist with the *Chicago Sun Times*.

316.   National Intelligence Estimate[1]

NIE 88–65   Washington, July 9, 1965.

PROSPECTS FOR COLOMBIA

The Problem

To estimate Colombia's prospects over the next year, with particular reference to the viability of the National Front system of government.

Conclusions

A. The National Front system of government has not functioned effectively, particularly under the presidency of Valencia (since 1962). The recurrent crises of the past year have aggravated the country's basic economic problems and political tensions. (Paras. 4–17)

B. The Valencia administration is under strong pressure from organized labor, business interests, and military leaders to cope more effectively with the deteriorating situation, but so far has proved incapable of developing and carrying out a sustained program of remedial action. The National Front system contains so many built-in checks and balances that it allows the multiplicity of political factions embraced within it to prevent decisive political action. Moreover, the measures which we believe to be most urgent—e.g., a further devaluation, more effective price and wage controls, and increased taxes—would be unpopular and difficult for any government to carry out. (Paras. 10–17, 28, 30)

C. Despite widespread and rising dissatisfaction with its performance, the Valencia government may be able to continue in office, at least until the close approach of the congressional election scheduled for March 1966. But even if it should be able to bring itself to adopt and carry out a program likely to prove beneficial over the longer term, it is unlikely that such a program could produce sufficient improvements before the election to reverse the growing popular dissatisfaction. The Opposition will probably gain enough seats in Congress to deprive the Front of the two-thirds majority required to do business under the present system. (Paras. 28, 30–31)

---

[1] Source: Central Intelligence Agency, Job 79–R01012A, O/DDI Registry. Secret; Controlled Dissem. According to a note on the cover sheet this estimate was prepared in the Central Intelligence Agency with the participation of the intelligence organizations of the Departments of State and Defense and the National Security Agency. The United States Intelligence Board concurred in this estimate on July 9.

D. There is likely to be rising demand for a basic change in the system. This would be extremely difficult to accomplish by constitutional means and may therefore lead to a military coup with respectable civilian support. Such a move would entail considerable risk of precipitating various sorts of violence; it is unlikely that the military would undertake it unless they were convinced that a national crisis was inevitable in any case. But if there were to be a coup during the period of this estimate, the military would probably be able to control the situation. (Paras. 19–27, 29, 32–33)

E. A military coup would not in itself solve any of Colombia's basic problems. It might open the way to the establishment of a new system of civil government more capable of dealing with them, or it might lead to a period of unpopular authoritarian rule. On the other hand, the prolongation of the present ineffectual system of government tends to increase the severity of Colombia's problems and to enchance the appeal of those who favor radical social revolution, including the present relatively ineffective groups who advocate violence. (Para. 34)

F. The residual rural banditry is criminal rather than political in character. The Communists and other extremist groups are not now capable of overthrowing the government or even of sustaining insurgency in any considerable area. (Para. 21–26)

[Omitted here is the Discussion section of the estimate.]

---

317.   Memorandum From the Director of the Bureau of the Budget (Schultze) to President Johnson[1]

Washington, October 29, 1965.

SUBJECT

Loan for the Government of Colombia

In the attached memorandum[2] the AID Administrator has requested your approval to sign a loan of $65 million for the Government of Colombia by November 1, or as soon thereafter as negotiations are completed.

---

[1] Source: Johnson Library, National Security File, Memos to the President, McGeorge Bundy, Vol. 16. Confidential. Forwarded to the President as an attachment to a memorandum from Bundy, October 30, who commented: "Charlie Schultze's memorandum seems to me first-rate and I fully concur with it." (Ibid.)

[2] Attached but not printed.

This is the first such aid commitment submitted on an individual basis for your approval. We will shortly recommend to you procedures to provide for your review of the AID program at three critical points:

(a) The approval of a country program in the budget process;
(b) Approval of specific commitments ready for execution; and
(c) Regular reporting of progress on the country's self-help efforts and actions taken by AID in this process.

AID has spent almost a year convincing the Colombians that we are serious about self help:

• we have entered into no loan agreements with them so far this year,
• we even *withheld a payment last January* of $10 million under the previously approved 1964 loan,
• negotiating together with the IMF and the World Bank, AID now is getting *written commitments* from Colombia that promise some real progress.

Actions already taken

In fact, *some of the toughest measures have already been executed.* 1. In September, Colombia devalued its currency by a substantial percentage. The IMF, World Bank, and AID all think this devaluation will be successful in eliminating the biggest single drain on the Colombian economy, particularly in the private sector. All three agencies will be watching the results closely. 2. The Colombians have imposed a 20 percent surcharge on income tax, and 3. They have effectively more than doubled the export tax on coffee, to change a heavy government subsidy into a self-sustaining operation.

Commitments and controls on future action

The loan agreement *won't be simply for measures already taken.* AID *will only disburse the $65 million in quarterly segments,* $20 million on signing and $15 million each in February, May, and August. And each release will be made only if a review of performance indicates that Colombia is making good progress in a number of important areas, including:

—a flexible exchange rate policy and a liberalized trade policy
—a non-inflationary fiscal, monetary, and wage policy
—tax improvement measures which should help support a 10 percent increase in public investment
—new program for agricultural development and reform
—an expanded program of primary education financed at the local level.

The funds will be used to finance imports from the U.S. Secretary Fowler is satisfied with the provisions of the loan from a U.S. balance of payments point of view. *Special conditions* will be attached which have the effect of neutralizing the balance of payments impact in 1965.

Other contributors

In addition to AID, the World Bank and the IMF are contributing $130 million. Their commitments will also be tied to the same self-help efforts that the U.S. is insisting upon. The three agencies (AID, IMF, IBRD) have worked out a common approach and joint arrangements to make this work.

I recommend that you approve this loan request.[3]

Charles L. Schultze

---

[3] Before approving the loan the President asked for further comment from Oliver and Mann. Oliver replied: "A democratic, confident Colombia is of the greatest importance to our strategic and political national interests; and a new program, sound on development merits, is also the best guarantee we can supply that Colombia will achieve orderly, constitutional transfer of power in the 1966 elections." (Telegram 630 from Bogotá, November 2; Johnson Library, National Security File, Memos to the President, McGeorge Bundy, Vol. 16) Mann wrote: "If we fail to come through in a timely way with our end of the bargain, the progress which has been made could begin to come unraveled because of political pressures in Colombia." (Memorandum from Mann to the President, November 2; ibid.) Both reports were forwarded as enclosures to a memorandum from Bundy to the President, November 2. Johnson approved the loan "with reluctance, reservations and considerable misgivings—but with the understanding that it results in no loss in bal of pay this yr & that Oliver, Vaughn & Mann, Schultze, follow this day to day adm. & keep us informed." (Memorandum from Bundy to the President, November 2; ibid.)

---

318. Memorandum From William G. Bowdler of the National Security Council Staff to President Johnson[1]

Washington, March 24, 1966, 5:30 p.m.

SUBJECT

Colombian Congressional Elections

Last Sunday[2] Colombia held congressional elections. Going into the elections, the National Front Government (FTN)—a coalition of the Liberal and Conservative parties which have alternated in power since

---

[1] Source: Johnson Library, National Security File, Country File, Colombia, Vol. II 6/65–9/66. Confidential. A copy was sent to Bill Moyers.

[2] March 20.

1958—appeared to be in deep trouble.[3] An FTN defeat could have produced a fragmentation of the political party structure with very serious consequences for our interests in Colombia.

With 90% of the vote tabulated, the FTN—to everyone's surprise—has scored an impressive victory:

—It increased its margin of the popular vote to 57% and gained an equally large edge in congressional seats.

—It has left the opposition in disarray, with the non-communist left badly beaten and the far right under former dictator Rojas Pinilla, although somewhat strengthened, still far short of being able to challenge the FTN.

—It virtually assures the FTN candidate—Liberal Carlos Lleras—clear sailing in the May 1 presidential elections.

—It substantially improves the FTN chances of being able to get a 2/3 working majority in the Congress so that it can govern within the terms of the FTN agreement rather than under a state of siege decree, as it has so often had to do in past years.

The FTN victory *for us* means:

—improved prospects for more stable, efficient and progressive government in Colombia over the next four years.
—continued good performance on our Program Loan agreement.
—continued cooperation with us on major international issues.[4]

WGB

---

[3] In a March 18 memorandum to Rusk, Gordon concluded: "Although the final results could go either way, it appears that the opposition coalition will probably win about 51% of the votes cast, as well as a majority of the seats in the congress. Under these circumstances, a post-election coup by the military against the opposition is a possibility, although not a probability. Should the opposition win more than 55% of the votes cast, a military coup would become somewhat more likely." (National Archives and Records Administration, RG 59, ARA/CV/C Files: Lot 69 D 407, POL 14 Elections)

[4] Two handwritten notes on the memorandum by Komer and the President read: "Good news, contrary to early press reports. RWK" and "Congratulate Covey Oliver. L."

319. Letter From the Director of the Office of Colombian-Venezuelan Affairs (Hill) to the Ambassador to Colombia (Oliver)[1]

Washington, April 1, 1966.

Dear Covey:

1. The primary reason for our decision against your proposal [*1 line of source text not declassified*] was the general premise that we should not run the potential risks of such action unless U.S. national security is directly involved. This does not seem to be the case in Colombia at the present time.

2. Your proposal was discussed thoroughly in ARA/CV and with Bob Sayre, who also discussed it with Tom Mann. The general consensus, including the concurrence of CIA, was to decide against your proposal, although Tom would have liked to have discussed it with Mr. Gordon. This was not practical within the time frame because of Mr. Gordon's absence until next Monday.[2] Even so, Mr. Gordon's general views are known to coincide with what was decided.

3. I think that the purpose of your proposal was well taken, [*4 lines of source text not declassified*]. I agree entirely with the line of thought in this regard as expressed in paragraph 3 of your proposal message.[3] A poor showing by the opposition and a small vote for the Lleras candidacy might well put the Lleras administration at a psychological disadvantage subsequently and give opposition elements an advantage in their efforts to undermine his government. Nevertheless, the congressional elections of March 20 constitute in themselves a genuine mandate for the FTN and should provide an answer to any future criticism that Lleras was not the majority choice. Such a position could certainly be justified with the press and with the other countries in the Hemisphere. In view of the mandate provided by the congressional elections and in view of the fact that we have no assurance now that

---

[1] Source: National Archives and Records Administration, RG 59, ARA/NC Files: Lot 72 D 235, Eyes Only. Secret; Official–Informal; Eyes Only.

[2] April 4.

[3] In paragraph 3 Oliver argued: "As I see it, a determined, vigorous, plausible candidate of opposition within constitution would be a good thing for Colombia. It would mark beginnings of a new party alignment related to twentieth century issues. It would call attention to specific alternative lines of development-related action that could be asserted and debated on their merits. It would canalize protest into proposals for democratic action; and these would (1) help Lleras with less open-minded power groups in his entourage and (2) keep masses from buying dialectical shibboleths out of ignorance and dissatisfaction with their alternation from government processes." (National Archives and Records Administration, RG 59, ARA/NC Files: Lot 72 D 235, Eyes Only)

the present political system or U.S. interests in Colombia will be jeopardized, [5 lines of source text not declassified].

4. In analyzing further your proposal, I think it needs to be broken down into two parts: (1) Ruiz as an effective opposition presidential candidate during the next month, and (2) the related possibility of the development of a new opposition party with middle and lower class support within the democratic left. (I think Ruiz' insight that the failure of the MRL has left a vacuum on the democratic left in Colombia, as mentioned in paragraph 2 of Embtel 1258,[4] is certainly correct.)

5. With regard to part 1, I think the surest advantage of your proposal lies in the short range context. The advantage of providing legitimacy for the Lleras administration probably outweighs the disadvantage of possible troubles stirred up for the FTN in the short and perhaps the long range by a more effective opposition. Apart from the general premise mentioned in paragraph 1 above, your proposal would probably be a good idea simply in the short range context.

6. Part 2 of your proposal raises the question of whether a new opposition party is really desirable. In this regard, we are not yet prepared to accept fully the possible argument that the two traditional parties have lost their usefulness and must necessarily be replaced by a new party or parties in order that Colombia may have a democratic system capable of stability and progress. If the National Front system were discarded and if real competition between the Conservative and Liberal parties were once again possible, it is our hope that one or both of these parties (but more likely the Liberal party) might assume the role of a progressive reform party sufficiently to meet popular aspirations, keep the support of labor, and win new support from the middle and lower classes.

7. Consequently, it would seem that a major goal which we should try to pursue during the coming Lleras administration should be modification of the National Front to permit such competition, preferably a modification permitting the free participation and competition in the political system of all parties. Such a development should benefit the traditional parties more than the opposition, we think, if the traditional parties concentrate on reform and if the modification of the system were undertaken soon. Basically, traditional parties would have an advantage over the opposition because of tradition, existing organization,

---

[4] In telegram 1258 from Bogotá, March 25, the Embassy described a meeting between Ruiz and an Embassy officer, March 24; paragraph 2 concluded that Ruiz was "still undecided but seemed inclined run," while paragraph 3 reported that Ruiz had "discussed great vacuum extant on Colombian democratic left owing failure MRL." (Ibid., Central Files 1964–66, POL 14 COL)

capable leadership, and an apparent continuing appeal to a significant segment of the Colombian people. As long as the restrictive ground rules of the National Front prevail, the traditional parties will suffer from the lack of competition and the lack of meaningful alternatives.

8. Nevertheless, the idea of a new opposition party such as you suggest has several positive aspects. First, it would fill the void in the democratic left, if the traditional parties can't. Second, it would channel the existing opposition, particularly ANAPO, along more responsible lines and prevent a default to extremism. Third, it might help to pressure a modification of the National Front.

9. Possible negative aspects of such a party might include the following. First, such an opposition party led by Ruiz might be more likely to heighten discontent than to clarify issues and might well make it more difficult for Lleras to govern. This would be particularly unfortunate if there is a good chance that Lleras' economic and social program will be good. Second, it is not clear that Ruiz' ideas and programs would be all that good. Certainly it is highly doubtful that they are as good as those of Lleras at this stage. Third, there is some room for doubt whether an effective opposition party such as you envisage could really get very far at this time. It is quite likely that even with Ruiz such a party might not remain cohesive and effective for very long. A struggle for control between Ruiz and Rojas[5] might well take place. A presidential campaign of one month duration might be insufficient to strengthen Ruiz' position enough to effectively challenge Rojas. In addition, there is some question whether Colombia is really ready or much interested in a new party. The congressional elections seemed to support this argument to a certain extent. It would probably take a strong charismatic figure, like a Betancourt or a Frei or even a Gaitan,[6] to generate such a movement. At this point, there is not much on which to base such a party in Colombia except for ANAPO and possibly the UTC.

10. In sum, while your proposal has much merit [*2½ lines of source text not declassified*], the case is just not strong enough [*1½ lines of source text not declassified*]. I should add that my own view was influenced by knowledge of operations of this sort in the past which, despite being advertised as secure and effective, proved to be neither. Nevertheless, all agree that it is to your credit to have made such a proposal and shows your alertness to the situation as it is developing.

---

[5] General Gustavo Rojas Pinilla, former President of Colombia (1953–1957), was the founder and leader of ANAPO.

[6] Jorge Eliécer Gaitán, leader of the Liberal Party until his assassination in Bogotá on April 9, 1948.

11. Actually, it would be more appropriate for the FTN to finance Ruiz as an opposition candidate. If the FTN recognizes this as advantageous, and if the FTN is astute and Machiavellian enough, it may do so. I was glad to see from paragraph 6 of Embtel 1285[7] that this may be the case.

If you have any comment with regard to any of the above, please let us know.

With best regards,

John Calvin Hill, Jr.[8]

---

[7] According to paragraph 6 of telegram 1285 from Bogotá, March 30, there was speculation that the National Front was "asking for further contributions from followers in order finance opposition candidate if money proves only obstacle." (National Archives and Records Administration, RG 59, Central Files 1964–66, POL 14 COL)

[8] Printed from a copy that bears this typed signature.

---

320. Information Memorandum From the Assistant Secretary of State for Inter-American Affairs (Gordon) to Secretary of State Rusk[1]

Washington, April 30, 1966.

SUBJECT

Colombian Presidential Elections

Colombian presidential elections are scheduled for Sunday, May 1 (today). The candidate of the National Front, Carlos Lleras Restrepo, a Liberal, is expected to win handily with as much as 70% of the vote. The opposition candidate, Jose Jaramillo Giraldo, a political lightweight, is supported actively only by the followers of ex-dictator Gustavo Rojas Pinilla, and has no real chance of challenging Lleras.

The elections may be plagued by abstention and by public order disturbances. Because of the National Front's victory in the congressional elections on March 20 and the poor prospects of Jaramillo, voter apathy is likely to be widespread, with the result that Lleras may win with less than 2 million of 7 million possible votes. Dissident Liberal and

---

[1] Source: National Archives and Records Administration, RG 59, ARA/CV/C Files, 1966: Lot 69 D 407, POL 14, Elections. Confidential. Drafted by Lord. A notation on the memorandum indicates that Rusk saw it.

Conservative leadership has called for abstention by its adherents. Both Lleras and Rojas stand to be somewhat embarrassed by a small voter turn out. Voting could also be affected by the current student strike over university issues, if the students try to interfere with orderly elections. If elected, Lleras is scheduled to take office on August 7 for a four-year team. Lleras is a combination of politician, economist, and businessman, who is expected to provide capable administration and improved economic policies. He may be hampered in implementing his development and other legislative programs by the lack of the required two-thirds congressional majority. If so, he may have to either seek to amend the constitution or else continue to govern by decree under a state of siege, as the present Conservative administration of President Valencia has done since May 1965.[2]

---

[2] In telegram 1423 from Bogotá, May 2, the Embassy reported that Lleras won the election, and that voter turnout had been higher than expected. (Ibid., Central Files 1964–66, POL 14 COL)

---

321. Memorandum From the President's Special Assistant (Rostow) to President Johnson[1]

Washington, September 19, 1966.

SUBJECT

Colombia: What We Achieved With Our Program Loan

A year ago when Colombia faced a severe political-economic crisis, you authorized a $65 million program loan to Colombia on the basis of meaningful self-help measures. Today the situation in Colombia contrasts most favorably with that of last fall, thanks in considerable part to that loan.

The outlook then was grim:

—The budget was seriously in deficit.
—The inflationary threat was grave.
—Disposable foreign exchange reserves were badly depleted.
—Substantial payment arrears had accumulated.
—An over-valued exchange rate resulted in stifling controls.
—Public confidence was at a low ebb.

---

[1] Source: Johnson Library, National Security File, Country File, Colombia, Vol. II, 8/65–9/66. Confidential. A notation on the memorandum indicates that the President saw it. A copy was sent to Bill Moyers.

—The spring general elections and survival of the National Front were in doubt.

In September, 1965, the Consultative Group (IBRD, IMF, AID) helped the Colombians draw up a stabilization program buttressed by external financial support. After a year the program has removed the main causes of instability. This is the picture today:

—The current budgetary surplus has reached levels permitting an acceleration of investment expenditures.
—The inflationary spiral has been brought under control.
—Net exchange reserves have increased by some $41 million, with payments arrears eliminated.
—Trade liberalization has exceeded the IMF target.
—There has been a resurgence of confidence inside and outside Colombia.
—The elections were orderly and the democratic, progressive forces of the National Front emerged strengthened.

Much remains to be done, of course, but our investment in this important Latin American country during the past 12 months has paid off.

Walt

---

322. Memorandum From the President's Special Assistant (Rostow) to President Johnson[1]

Washington, November 15, 1966.

SUBJECT

Program Loan for Colombia for 1967

AID and BOB request, under the new commitment procedures, your authorization to negotiate a $100 million program loan for Colombia for the balance of CY 1966 and CY 1967. Joe Fowler raises no objections on balance of payments grounds although he maintains his reservations on *program* as against *project* lending.[2]

---

[1] Source: Johnson Library, National Security File, Country File, Colombia, Vol. III, 10/66–11/68. Confidential. Forwarded to the President under cover of a November 15 note in which Rostow reported: "Because of the urgency in getting on with loan negotiations with Colombia, Secretary Rusk will raise at the luncheon meeting today the attached authorization request."

[2] Attached, but not printed, are memoranda to the President from Schultze (November 5), Fowler (undated), and Gaud (October 31).

The amount is $35 million more than you approved for 1966:

—$20 million to support Lleras and his vigorous development program.
—$15 million to cover the balance of 1966 (our loan went only to October).

As last year, we will coordinate our loan negotiations with the IMF and the IBRD-led Consultative Group for maximum leverage on self-help commitments. They are expected to furnish $65 and $100 million respectively.

A loan of this magnitude is justified because:

—Lleras needs this amount to launch his development program while continuing stabilization measures.
—Colombia's self-help performance this year has for the most part been highly satisfactory, and should be better under Lleras, a sophisticated economist and more able political leader than his predecessor.
—The self-help requirements and tying procedures are well conceived to maximize our interests.
—Lleras belongs to the new generation of democratic, progressive Latin American leaders whom we wish to see succeed.
—Lleras has already taken the leadership in promoting accelerated Latin American economic integration—the cornerstone of our summit package.

I am satisfied with the soundness of the proposed loan and join in the recommendation that you approve it.

Later this month we will seek your approval of CY 1967 program loans to Brazil and Chile, both in considerably *lesser* amounts than you approved for this year.

Walt

Approve

Disapprove

Speak to Me[3]

---

[3] Although none of the options is checked, the issue was decided at the Tuesday luncheon on November 15. According to a record of the meeting Johnson cleared the negotiations, but asked "if we really want to blow that much on Colombia." (Johnson Library, National Security File, Files of Walt W. Rostow, Meetings with the President, April–December 1966) Rostow answered this question in telegram CAP 661074 to the President, November 27: "The Colombia loan was calculated within a plan to live with the FY 1967 appropriation for Latin America. The object was to give Colombia the kind of lift we have given at a critical stage to Brazil and Chile in the past two years. Now Brazil and Chile are moving, aid is on the way down." (Ibid., Country File, Colombia, Vol. III, 10/66–11/68) President Johnson subsequently approved signing the loan as negotiated. (Memorandum from Rostow to the President, April 26, 1967; ibid.)

323.   Telegram From the Embassy in Colombia to the Department of State[1]

Bogotá, April 27, 1967, 2325Z.

4414. 1. At President Lleras' invitation [*less than 1 line of source text not declassified*] I went to his private residence last night to brief him on security developments as we see them, especially related to recent upsurge guerrilla activities. [*2½ lines of source text not declassified*][2]

2. President conceded that memo confirmed his own fears for the immediate situation but appeared visibly sobered and perturbed by its implications, including the role of Cuba in professionally training and supplying guerrilla needs. He then reviewed need for new tactics by GOC armed forces. He feels present situation under control however precarious but apprehensive lest another three or four successful forays by guerrillas against the military will undermine army morale and perhaps cause loss of confidence in ability his government maintain law and order.

3. President cited military and police reports that rural populace attitude toward security forces has worsened in recent months while guerrilla bands woo tacit support local peasants by ample use of funds, paying generously for food and local supplies.

4. President has called meeting for April 28 his top military commanders for discussion new tactics to cope with deteriorating situation.[3]

Carlson

---

[1] Source: National Archives and Records Administration, RG 59, Central Files 1967–69, POL 23 COL. Secret; Limdis.

[2] Not found.

[3] On May 9 Lleras met Ambassador Carlson [*text not declassified*] for a "second round of discussions on insurgency activities." Lleras stated his belief that the counterinsurgency campaign must be waged as "a concerted coordinated effort," employing civic action programs as well as unconventional military tactics. The efforts of the previous administration, he maintained, had been hampered by deficiencies in such factors as funding, imagination, and coordination among the intelligence services. Lleras also asked the Americans for "suggestions on specific and concrete tactical measure that might be used." (Telegram 4580 from Bogotá, May 11; National Archives and Records Administration, RG 59, Central Files 1967–69, POL 23 COL)

324.   **Memorandum From the Assistant Secretary of State for Inter-American Affairs (Oliver) to the Deputy Under Secretary of State for Political Affairs (Kohler)**

Washington, August 16, 1967.

[Source: Department of State, INR/IL Historical Files, 303 Committee Files, c. 57, August 22, 1967. Secret; Eyes Only. 2 pages of source text not declassified.]

---

325.   **Memorandum From William G. Bowdler of the National Security Council Staff to the President's Special Assistant (Rostow)**[1]

Washington, April 19, 1968.

SUBJECT

Colombia

You asked for a memorandum covering Colombia's economic performance and the difficulties arising from current loan negotiations for 1968.

Colombia's Economic Performance

With a $100 million program loan from us and sound exchange, fiscal and budgetary policies laid down by President Lleras, Colombia had a good year in 1967:

—despite the sizeable drop in coffee revenues, 4.5% growth in GNP was achieved;

—careful budget management and improved tax collections (up 20% over 1966) made possible a 42% increase in public investment, primarily in agriculture and education;

—wise monetary measures held the cost of living increase to 8% compared with 13% in 1966;

—minor exports were up 20% over 1966;

—sound management of the exchange rate permitted a gradual depreciation of 16% without the usual strains;

—commercial arrears were eliminated by July 1967, although substantial arrears in the capital market remain;

---

[1] Source: Johnson Library, National Security File, Country File, Colombia, Vol. III, 10/66–12/68. Confidential.

—planning at the national level, especially in education and agriculture, greatly improved.

To the economic gains must be added Lleras' success on the political-security front. He achieved a good working majority in both houses to achieve passage of reform measures. Guerrilla activity fell to a new low under a two-pronged offensive of increased military pressure and economic assistance to heretofore neglected rural areas.

The Loan Negotiations

The principal components of the aid package for 1968 are a $58 million program loan and a $15 million agricultural sector loan. PL 480 sales of $14.5 million are also involved.[2]

When Lleras was over the economic barrel last year, he agreed to specific performance targets in writing, although it grated on him. This year, with a clear record of significant accomplishments, he dug in his heels and asked that the assistance package for 1968 be given on faith that he will maintain sound economic policies.

When negotiations began last month, AID was edgy about certain backsliding indicators:

—in January Lleras had stopped further adjustments in the certificate exchange rate;

—a promised additional 20% liberalization of imports had not materialized;

—the desired additionality had not been achieved and Treasury was pressing for sterner action.

This prompted AID to serve up the 1968 package with another set of conditions involving specific performance targets. Lleras balked. When he failed to liberalize imports 20% by March 31, as he had promised, AID withheld payments of the last $20 million tranche of the 1967 loan.

At the height of the impasse, Lleras broke off talks with World Bank representatives, the leaders of the negotiating group. And he let it be known to AID that he would not accept fixed targets on the key issues of devaluation, import liberalization and additionality.

Since then, both sides have maneuvered away from their rigid positions:

—Lleras wrote Schweitzer[3] that the dual exchange rates will be unified soon and, subsequently, the unified rate will be flexible "along the lines observed during 1967." AID now finds this satisfactory;

---

[2] President Johnson approved negotiation of the aid package to Colombia in late February. (Memorandum from Rostow to the President, February 24; ibid.)

[3] Pierre-Paul Schweitzer, managing director of the International Monetary Fund.

—The Colombians recently started strong efforts to safeguard the US share of the commercial market within its completely controlled import system;

—AID is willing to drop prior commitments on import liberalization during 1968 in favor of performance review in October which could affect the amount of the second tranche. AID would link the level of coffee receipts, aid disbursements and import targets so that greater than expected coffee receipts or failure to increase imports could result in reduced loan disbursements. Lleras says this is agreeable;

—AID will not insist on a 20% liberalization of imports *before* releasing the last tranche of the 1967 loan and will release the money as soon as the 1968 loan agreement is initialled. Lleras says once he has the money in hand, he will liberalize in the amount agreed.

So negotiations are back on the tracks and should be completed in the next two or three weeks.[4]

Lessons to be Learned

At the outset, AID was too demanding on specific written commitments. They should have known from last year's experience that Lleras, with a good record behind him, would not agree to terms which rubbed him the wrong way in 1967. AID should have been willing to settle for more general assurances.

Lleras was too swift in taking umbrage—but this is his nature.

With more firm direction from the top, this kind of thing could be avoided, but you are familiar with that situation.

WGB

---

[4] The United States and Colombia signed two agreements, the $58 million program loan and the $15 million agricultural sector loan, on July 15. The PL–480 agreement was signed on May 31.

Ecuador

326. Editorial Note

In telegram 923 from Quito, May 22, 1965, the Embassy assessed the internal threat to the junta in Ecuador. Although a change did not appear imminent, the Embassy recommended emphasizing "the imperative of unity" to all factions of the military, while warning opposition leaders that a revolutionary alliance with the Communists would attract the "deep distrust" of the United States. The Embassy also reported that it was encouraging the junta to form a counter-insurgency group "capable of snuffing out initial revolutionary attempts to establish insurgent forces." (National Archives and Records Administration, RG 59, Central Files 1964–66, POL 23–9 ECUADOR) On July 14 the Department noted that demonstrations had so weakened the junta that plans to hold elections in July 1966 appeared "unrealistic." To avoid a violent overthrow of the government, the Department suggested that the Embassy urge the junta to "shorten substantially scheduled transfer of power, modify composition significantly, or transfer power to provisional civilian government." (Telegram 26 to Quito; ibid., POL 15 ECUADOR) The Embassy replied that such interference would not "expedite the process," since the junta had just announced a new plan to restore constitutional order. Meanwhile, the Embassy reiterated its proposal to support the junta in forming a counter-insurgency group. (Telegram 59 from Quito, July 15; ibid.)

[*text not declassified*] (Department of INR/IL Historical Files, 303 Committee Files, c. 24, August 26, 1965) The Department countered by citing NSAM 177 (see *Foreign Relations*, 1961–1963, volume IX, Document 150), which assigned overall responsibility for police assistance programs, including counter-insurgency efforts, to the Agency for International Development. The Department argued that an overt program managed by AID and maintained under the Ecuadorean National Police stood a better chance of surviving the junta. (Memorandum from Vaughn to Thompson, August 16; Department of State, INR/IL Historical Files, 303 Committee Files, c. 24, August 26, 1965)

On August 26 the 303 Committee approved the proposal to support a counter-insurgency group in Ecuador, subject to further clarification of the organizational details. (Memorandum for the record by Jessup, August 27; ibid., c. 25, September 9, 1965) In telegram 221 from Quito, September 6, Coerr explained that, due to growing opposition within the military, "it would be impossible to establish special unit in DGI." Coerr recommended transferring the unit to the army, although this might pose "a problem in inter-agency relations within USG."

(Telegram 221 from Quito, September 6; National Archives and Records Administration, RG 59, Central Files 1964–66, POL 23–3 ECUADOR) On September 9 the 303 Committee decided that the Department of Defense [text not declassified] should "sort out these arrangements and keep the committee informed by phone." (Memorandum from Carter to Vaughn, September 13; Department of State, INR/IL Historical Files, 303 Committee Special Files, July–December 1965). [text not declassified] (Memorandum from Jessup to Vance, September 10; National Security Council, Special Group/303 Committee Files, Subject Files, Ecuador)

---

327. Memorandum From William G. Bowdler of the National Security Council Staff to President Johnson[1]

Washington, March 28, 1966, 6:30 p.m.

SUBJECT

    Situation in Ecuador

For the past week the Military Junta in Ecuador has been faced with mounting pressures to step down. It began with a commercial strike in Guayaquil last Tuesday and has gradually spread to other cities. The base of the movement has also broadened to include other anti-Junta groups—political parties, chauffeurs federation, students, etc. A deteriorating economic situation has added to the Junta's woes.

Last Friday the Junta, with the firm backing of the Armed Forces, seemed to be gaining the upper hand. Over the weekend, the picture changed as the strike continued and clashes between the Armed Forces and university students and other demonstrators increased.

Ambassador Coerr called State this afternoon to report that the Junta had announced that: (1) its members would "reintegrate" themselves into the Armed Forces and (2) there would be drastic changes in the plan for transition to constitutional government. Elections had been set for July 3. He did not know yet to whom the Junta would be turning over the government. The most likely possibility seemed to be a non-partisan civilian acceptable to the military and anti-Junta ele-

---

[1] Source: Johnson Library, National Security File, Country File, Ecuador, Memos, 12/63–11/68. Secret. A copy was sent to Bill Moyers. A notation on the memorandum indicates that the President saw it.

ments. A Guayaquil business-man—Clemente Yerovi—and former President Galo Plaza are rumored as likely candidates.[2]

So far the Armed Forces remain united and firmly in control of the security situation. This afternoon's announcement reflects their decision that the present Junta should step down because it has lost public confidence and can no longer maintain a political climate which will permit meaningful elections in July. For the Armed Forces the way out is to put in a new face and adjust the date for elections to allow tempers to cool and make fresh preparations for elections.

Ambassador Coerr is active in this very fluid situation, using his influence to bring about a government of conciliation as rapidly as possible, while continuing to press for a return to constitutional government without delay.

There is nothing further at the moment that we can do from here. The Inter-American Interdepartmental Regional Group meets tomorrow to review the situation.[3]

WGB

---

[2] In a March 29 memorandum for the President, Bowdler reported that Yerovi had been chosen as interim civilian President and was "known to be friendly towards the United States, which should ease our task in dealing with him." (Ibid.)

[3] The Interdepartmental Regional Group for Inter-American Affairs met on March 29 to consider a draft contingency plan on Ecuador. A record of the meeting is in IRG/ARA Action Memo #4, April 1; National Archives and Records Administration, RG 59, ARA/IG Files, 1966–68: Lot 70 D 122, IRG/ARA Action Memos, 1968.

---

328. Memorandum From William G. Bowdler of the National Security Council Staff to President Johnson[1]

Washington, March 30, 1966, 6 p.m.

SUBJECT

Ecuadorean Crisis

The situation in Ecuador moved back toward normalcy, although there still are a few trouble spots.

---

[1] Source: Johnson Library, National Security File, Country File, Ecuador, Vol. I, 12/63–11/68. Confidential. A copy was sent to Bill Moyers. A notation on the memorandum indicates that the President saw it.

The commercial strike has been called off. Interim President Clemente Yerovi took over at noon and announced a three-point program: prompt elections, austerity to solve the financial crisis, and protection of the "sucre" against devaluation. He has not named his cabinet, although he indicated that it would be broadly representative, including the political parties.

The trouble spots are where communist-led students have seized provincial government buildings in two provinces. Government security forces have cleared them out in one province but have not yet acted in the other. Our Peace Corps volunteers have been threatened by the communists in this province. Ambassador Coerr has personally called the Defense Minister and National Police Chief to request protection of the volunteers.

The question of recognition is pending. It is contingent on whether President Yerovi, in a diplomatic note to be delivered soon, presents his government as a continuation of the former regime or a new one. The lawyers in State say we can play it either way.[2]

Paradoxically, the change in leadership enhances the chances of having meaningful elections. The military junta had scheduled elections for July, but could not get the political parties to participate. President Yerovi may have to delay elections two or three months beyond July, but he is expected to get full participation.

WGB

---

[2] According to circular telegram 1935, April 4, the Embassy received a note in which the new government expressed its firm intention to return to constitutional rule. Although the note failed to address the legal question of continuity, the Department saw "no reason [why] we should not continue relations with Ecuador," pending consultation with other Latin American governments. (National Archives and Records Administration, RG 59, Central Files 1964–66, POL 15 ECUADOR) The Department authorized delivery of a note to the Ecuadorian Foreign Ministry on April 12, expressing the desire of the U.S. Government to continue cordial relations. (Circular telegram 1970, April 8; ibid.)

329. Memorandum From the President's Special Assistant (Rostow) to President Johnson[1]

Washington, June 23, 1966.

SUBJECT

Emergency Budget Support for Ecuador

Dave Bell, with the concurrence of Charlie Schultze and Joe Fowler, requests your authorization to negotiate a loan of up to $10 million to Ecuador to help meet its budgetary needs for the balance of this year. Their memoranda are attached.[2]

The background to this request is:

1. The two-month old interim civilian government of President Yerovi inherited a serious budget problem from the ousted military junta.

2. Despite its belt-tightening efforts, it still confronts a deficit estimated at $15 million. Any further belt-tightening would be at the expense of its badly needed development and reform program. This should be avoided.

3. Last month you authorized negotiation of a loan of $4 million. This authorization recognized that $4–6 million more might be necessary. The Yerovi Government declined the $4 million loan, considering the amount inadequate and the self-help conditions proportionately too stiff.

4. Since then the Government has taken several self-help measures on its own and worked out assistance arrangements with the IMF ($13 million standby) and some New York banks ($11 million to meet foreign exchange needs).

5. Our $10 million loan would be tied to additional self-help measures and released in installments based on performances.

I consider this a good loan from an economic and political standpoint. President Yerovi has established a realistic schedule for returning the country to constitutional government by the end of the year. He needs our support for constitutional, as well as economic, recovery.

Walt

Approve loan[3]

Disapprove loan

Speak to me

---

[1] Source: Johnson Library, National Security File, Country File, Ecuador, Vol. I, 12/63–11/68. Confidential.

[2] Attached but not printed are memoranda to the President from Schultze, June 14, and Bell, June 7.

[3] This option is checked.

330.   Telegram From the Department of State to the Embassy in Ecuador[1]

Washington, April 22, 1967, 2:55 p.m.

180672. Ref: Quito 5478.[2]

1. We concur line you took in Quito 5478.

2. Arosemena's activities have effect on three levels which are interrelated (a) hemispheric, (b) US–Ecuador, and (c) international financial agencies.

3. At present moment Ecuador in general and Arosemena in particular are regarded as being "off-base". Although Latins share some of underlying concerns of Ecuador, they repudiated his tactics and many of specific complaints. Arosemena misjudged Latin temperament on overall hemispheric problems. This is understandable because politically Ecuador has more in common with Bolivia (which was not present) and Haiti (which played no real part in OAS preparations or Summit meeting) than it has with most LA countries. It is in our interests to maintain general hemispheric view that Arosemena is attacking inter-American system, Alliance, etc. and not United States.

4. United States posture must be one of dignity and understanding in response to "shin kicking" by Arosemena. Our line will be that we are following principles of Alliance, that we have taken into account January CIAP review in cooperating with Ecuador and that we are working closely with IBRD and IDB. FYI. If Ecuador desires special CIAP review to deal with its specific complaints we will be glad participate. We are discussing this possibility with Sanz. End FYI.

5. If Arosemena carries his irresponsible conduct too far, i.e. he creates financial or other crisis, there is risk forces opposed to him will unite to oust him. It is therefore important that you a) discreetly set or keep record straight by letters to President, Minister of Finance, etc., after meetings in which Ecuadorean complaints are clarified (at opportune times you can find ways to make clarifications public), b) avoid any comments or suggestions that could be taken as implying Arose-

---

[1] Source: National Archives and Records Administration, RG 59, Central Files 1967–69, POL ECUADOR–US. Confidential; Immediate; Limdis. Drafted by Sayre and approved by Gordon.

[2] President Otto Arosemena Gomez, who was elected by a constituent assembly on October 16, 1966, publicly criticized the Alliance for Progress at the meeting of American Presidents in Punta del Este April 12–14. An account of his meeting with President Johnson on April 13 is in Document 51. Telegram 5478 from Quito, April 22, reported on a meeting with Defense Minister Febres Cordero, in which Coerr argued that Arosemena's criticism of the Alliance was jeopardizing "continued USG investment in AID program." (National Archives and Records Administration, RG 59, Central Files 1967–69, POL 15–1 ECUADOR)

mena has become obstacle to US-Ecuadorean relations and should be removed, and c) act promptly to discourage any change in constitutional order in Ecuador.

6. We should adhere guidelines of Alliance and CIAP. We should close ranks with other lending institutions and make certain we are in step. If there are programs or projects that are not working, we should correct them or terminate them. Watchword should be "patience."

7. We recognize that you have trying situation in Ecuador. Impact Arosemena's conduct now limited to Ecuador with rest of Hemisphere lined up with US. It is important that we avoid doing anything here or in Ecuador that would change this favorable situation.

Rusk

---

331. Telegram From the Embassy in Ecuador to the Department of State[1]

Quito, May 13, 1967, 2220Z.

5824. 1. I called yesterday at my initiative on President Arosemena for review of Ecuadorean–U.S. relations prior to my departure on home leave (mentioning that this leave coordinated with children's vacation and had been long planned).

2. After congratulating him on political gains he had made as result his performance Punta del Este,[2] I pointed out that these gains had been made largely at expense of aid program's reputation. I pointed out that the program's degree of success depends largely on its political support by the government and political acceptability to the people, both of which had suffered significantly through the attacks which he had been making, especially since his return from Punta del Este. I said I thought his public statements about the aid program were unbalanced, in that they mentioned nothing good about it, and in some cases erroneous, in that they disregarded pertinent facts.

---

[1] Source: National Archives and Records Administration, RG 59, Central Files 1967–69, POL ECUADOR–US. Secret; Limdis.

[2] According to an April 20 INR report Arosemena received an enthusiastic reception after Punta del Este as "the only Latin American president with the 'courage to put the US in its place'." Arosemena's performance "fed Ecuador's pride which—apart from Ecuador's coming in second in a basketball competition in Scranton, Pennsylvania—has had little sustenance in recent years." (Ibid., ARA/EP/E Files: Lot 70 D 247, POL 15 Arosemena Government)

3. During our discussion Arosemena stuck to his guns, reasserting his declarations about the aid program and giving ground, by tacitly accepting my point of view, in only two respects. When I told him I had been disappointed that he had publicly declared the U.S. was requiring "inadmissible" conditions on the malaria loan, despite the fact that I previously assured him I would take no position on requests until sub-ministerial negotiations had reached either agreement or clear disagreement, he obviously got the point but avoided comment. When I pointed out that he had urgently requested my assistance in signing the primary education loan and then expressed recognition only by publicly disputing whether his or the Yerovi government should get the credit for having eliminated from the loan twenty "humiliating" conditions, he laughed in hearty agreement.

4. He declared he would never accept conditions that we are negotiating in the proposed malaria loan designed to insure that the National Malaria Eradication Service (SNEM) be independent and employ an outside administrator, and he asked why we tried to impose these conditions on him when we had not imposed them on the military junta. He was surprised and interested to learn that these conditions had characterized the successful program that had been started before the military junta assumed power and terminated in 1965.

5. I assured him and he recognized that we are interested in carrying forward the program on Alliance for Progress criteria and with no thought of any period of coldness or retaliation in reaction to his criticisms. He commented that we had authorized two grant projects since his return from Punta del Este and called my attention to the very favorable publicity he had given to the signing of the public safety project agreement.

6. He continued to rant about the performance of the TAMS engineering company under the road construction agreement. When I called his attention to my previous suggestion that he meet personally with TAMS representatives in order to get from them information with which to form a balanced picture of the value of their operations, he said he would meet with them only to kick them physically out of his office.

7. Our conversation being interrupted by his need to meet with his cabinet and chiefs of staff in order to consider the Duran strike situation which had produced some dead and wounded, he suggested that we continue our talk early next week.[3]

Coerr

---

[3] Arosemena and Coerr held "two strenuous hour-long negotiating sessions" on May 16 and 17, reaching agreement on the wording of the proposed Malaria loan. (Telegram 5909 from Quito, May 17; ibid., Central Files 1967–69, AID(US) 8–5 ECUADOR)

332. Memorandum From the President's Special Assistant (Rostow) to President Johnson[1]

Washington, August 29, 1967.

Mr. President:

Herewith a recommendation from Agriculture and AID, concurred in by State, Treasury and BoB, that you authorize a $2.2 million P. L. 480 sale to Ecuador for small quantities of wheat and tobacco.[2]

Despite Arosemena's unhelpful performance at Punta del Este and doubts regarding the *economic* justification for P. L. 480 help, I favor this modest assistance:

—Arosemena has pulled back a considerable way from his Summit obstreperousness, joining with our Ambassador on August 17 in a public celebration of the 6th anniversary of the Alliance for Progress.

—The local currency proceeds will be used to encourage much-needed improvements in agriculture—a key Summit objective.

—Arosemena has made considerable progress during 1967 in getting Ecuador's budgetary and balance of payments situation straightened out.

—We have a stake in continued political stability in Ecuador which Arosemena has achieved while returning the country to constitutionality via elections scheduled for next June.

Walt

Approve

Disapprove[3]

See me

---

[1] Source: Johnson Library, National Security File, Country File, Ecuador, Vol. I, 12/63–11/68. Confidential.

[2] Attached but not printed are memoranda to the President from Schultze, August 24, and Gaud and Freeman, August 21.

[3] The last two options are checked. Rostow apparently did not raise the issue again until September 6, when he returned the memorandum to the President with a request for additional guidance. (Memorandum from Rostow to the President, September 6; Johnson Library, National Security File, Country File, Ecuador, Vol. I, 12/63–11/68) Johnson's response is recorded in a note dictated later that day aboard Air Force One: "I don't want to agree to that Ecuador thing. Hold up on it. They can argue with me about it, but I am not going to force this. I haven't forgotten Punta del Este." The note indicates that Jones informed Rostow of the President's decision on September 7. (Ibid.)

333. Telegram From the President's Special Assistant (Rostow) to President Johnson[1]

Washington, September 8, 1967.

CAP 67779. Ecuadorean PL–480 Loan: Special Factors Involved.

When we informed Covey Oliver of your decision on the PL 480 loan to Ecuador, he expressed deep concern.

I told him to prepare a memorandum to you giving his reasons why he considers it important to make the loan. This is his message to you:

I am working very hard on trying to turn the Ecuadorean President's attitude toward the Alliance for Progress around. I cannot promise success, but I have fair hopes. Your Ambassador there has been active and helpful, and I have spent about three hours with the AID Director there[2] on this topic while he was here.

The Ambassador, the Director and I believe that there is a reasonably good chance that if handled as a good teacher would handle a lagging and defensive pupil, we might bring President Arosemena up from the bottom of the Alliance class to the median level. (The Ambassador has written me (eyes only)[3] that if allowed to drift and sour even more, this man might do something foolish, such as declaring a prominent Embassy official persona non grata. This latter should not be taken as a threat but as an indication of the President's basic psychological problem: he was a late starter on what the Alliance is all about, and he has yet to catch up with the other presidents in understanding.)

Another factor, very important in Latin ways of looking at things, is that my able predecessor pretty well made what the Ecuadoreans consider a commitment about this PL–480 loan—at least it seems that he did not spell out to the Ecuadoreans all the steps involved in getting final approval.

A new Ecuadorean Ambassador will be presenting credentials to you on September 12. The denial of the loan will make it hard for me to carry on my special course for Ecuadoreans with him, as I had expected.[4]

---

[1] Source: Johnson Library, National Security File, Country File, Ecuador, Vol. I, 12/63–11/68. Secret. A notation on the telegram indicates that the President saw it. Oliver's original memorandum to the President, September 7, is ibid., Memos to the President, Walt W. Rostow, Vol. 40.

[2] L. Paul Oechsli.

[3] Not found.

[4] According to the President's Daily Diary, the new Ambassador, Carlos Mantilla Ortega, presented his credentials to the President in a brief meeting (12:23–12:28 p.m.) at the White House on September 12. (Johnson Library) Johnson met Oliver immediately following the reception (12:28–1:04 p.m). No substantive record of either conversation has been found.

334. Telegram From the Department of State to the Embassy in Ecuador[1]

Washington, September 18, 1967, 2024Z.

39022. Subject: PL–480 Sales Agreement. Ref: State's 33719.[2] Joint State/AID Message. For Coerr from Oliver.

1. PL–480 memorandum covering 15,000 MT wheat and 582 MT tobacco and tobacco products has been approved in principle but not yet formally. Delay in obtaining approval reflects continuing concern at highest level over GOE's criticisms of U.S. trade and AID policies expressed during Punta del Este Conference.[3]

2. Accordingly, I am requesting Ecuadorean Ambassador to call upon me afternoon September 19, for purpose not only disclose high level approval but also indicate to Ambassador difficulties posed for USG by irresponsible statements of government receiving assistance from USG.

3. I recognize this may eliminate some of impact which you hoped to gain by announcement there. However, I consider it essential disabuse Arosemena of assumption that he has special relationship with high level USG officials.

4. Negotiating authorization re PL–480 Agreement will be forthcoming ASAP following September 19 meeting.

5. Would appreciate any comments or suggestions you may have prior to September 19 meeting.[4]

Rusk

---

[1] Source: National Archives and Records Administration, RG 59, Central Files 1967–69, AID(US) 15–8 ECUADOR. Confidential; Immediate; Limdis. Drafted by J.F. Smith; cleared by Berlin, Sayre, and Fowler; and approved by Oliver.

[2] In telegram 33719 to Quito, September 7, Oliver reported: "Final decision on PL–480 sales agreement highly unlikely this week. I am working on matter but could not assure you response will be favorable." (Ibid.)

[3] According to Robert M. Phillips, chief of the Embassy's political section, Johnson was so displeased at the thought of rewarding Arosemena with the PL–480 loan that "it was only on the fourth try that the President relented and then solely on condition that Covey Oliver would call in Carlos Mantilla and let him know that we were getting tired of Ecuadorean griping about the conditions of aid." (Letter from Phillips to Coerr, September 26; ibid., ARA/EP/E Files: Lot 70 D 247, POL 15 Arosemena Government)

[4] Coerr's comments are in telegrams 1033 and 1034 from Quito, September 19. (Ibid., Central Files 1967–69, AID(US) 15–8 ECUADOR) After receiving a written report on the meeting with Mantilla, Johnson approved Oliver's recommendation "to inform Ambassador Coerr that he may proceed with negotiations." (Memorandum from Rostow to the President, September 19; Johnson Library, National Security File, Country File, Ecuador, Vol. I, 12/63–11/68)

335.   Memorandum From William G. Bowdler of the National Security Council Staff to the President's Special Assistant (Rostow)[1]

Washington, September 28, 1967.

Walt—

As Covey puts it: "Arosemena flunked his course".

From the attached cable you will see that last Tuesday he picked up where he left off at Punta del Este in attacking the Alliance for Progress.[2]

Covey has taken these actions:

—instructed Wym Coerr to go play golf and negotiate no aid agreements.

—delayed action on two pending loans in the IDB.

—asked Jim Fowler to background Ben Welles (*NY Times*) on the speech and refute each charge made.

Arosemena seems to be in the final stages of negotiating a $30 million loan with a consortium of European banks—at 8½% interest with "no strings attached"—and therefore thinks he can thumb his nose at us again.

I want to wait until next Monday[3] to see how this business shakes down before reporting to the President.[4]

WGB

---

[1] Source: Johnson Library, National Security File, Country File, Ecuador, Vol. I, 12/63–11/68. Confidential.

[2] Reference is to telegram 1154 from Quito, September 27; not attached. At a reception for Latin American journalists on September 26, Arosemena called the Alliance for Progress "a frustrated hope," a criticism that was widely reported in newspaper accounts the following day. (National Archives and Records Administration, RG 59, Central Files 1967–69, AID(AFP))

[3] October 2.

[4] Rostow relayed a brief report to the President on September 30. (Telegram CAP 67847 to the LBJ Ranch; Johnson Library, National Security File, Country File, Ecuador, Vol. I, 12/63–11/68)

336. Editorial Note

On October 3, 1967, Ambassador Coerr reported his view that economic assistance to Ecuador could no longer be justified in the wake of President Arosemena's renewed criticism of the Alliance for Progress. In response Coerr recommended: a) delivering a diplomatic note stating that, until "the two governments hold a full and frank exchange of views," all loans would be temporarily suspended; b) withdrawing authorization to negotiate the PL–480 agreement; c) offering an official reply in his speech at the American School in Guayaquil on October 6. (Telegram 1226 from Quito; National Archives and Records Administration, RG 59, Central Files 1967–69, AID (US) 9 ECUADOR) The Department indicated "general agreement" with Coerr's analysis, stating that, to continue economic assistance after Arosemena's attack, would only encourage the view that the "U.S. cow, when kicked, gives more milk." Negotiations for the PL–480 agreement, as well as development loans, were therefore suspended, in accordance with the Ambassador's recommendations. The Department declined, however, to authorize a written response, fearing the "effect of note would be to make matter bilateral issue between U.S. and Ecuador." (Telegram 50611 to Quito, October 7; ibid.) As an alternative, the Department approved Coerr's suggestion to respond orally "to correct the record" in the American School speech doing so "in non-personal and non-polemic terms, and in context of positive description of U.S. assistance." (Telegram 49689 to Quito, October 6; ibid., AID(AFP))

---

337. Memorandum From the President's Special Assistant (Rostow) to President Johnson[1]

Washington, October 7, 1967, 7:43 p.m.

Our ambassador in Ecuador gave what is described as a factual speech on the history of our aid relations with Ecuador. As a result of this speech they have asked for his withdrawal within forty-eight hours. We do not have the text yet of what he said but will have it tomorrow.[2]

---

[1] Source: Johnson Library, National Security File, Memos to the President, Walt W. Rostow, Vol. 44. No classification marking.

[2] The text of Coerr's speech was transmitted in telegram 1299 from Quito, October 8. (National Archives and Records Administration, RG 59, Central Files 1967–69, POL 17 US–ECUADOR)

I am told by Bob Sayre that Secretary Rusk thinks that we probably should not ask for the withdrawal of the Ecuadorean ambassador to Washington. I believe we should decide that tomorrow.

During the night Bob Sayre and Bill Bowdler will be studying the precedents and getting us more information from Ecuador.

I shall be in touch with Secretary Rusk tomorrow and will forward to you his recommendations plus all the materials we have bearing on the problem.

WWR[3]

---

[3] Printed from a copy that bears these typed initials.

---

338.   Memorandum From the President's Special Assistant (Rostow) to President Johnson[1]

Washington, October 8, 1967, 1:40 p.m.

SUBJECT

Recall of our Ambassador to Ecuador

Supplementing my note of 12:10 p.m. today,[2] these are the steps which Covey Oliver is recommending to Sec. Rusk:

1. Instruct Ambassador Coerr to leave Quito by 5:35 p.m., October 9, when the 48 hour period expires.

2. Call in the Ecuadorean Ambassador this afternoon to give him a note saying we will honor the request but expressing regret that

---

[1] Source: Johnson Library, National Security File, Country File, Ecuador, 12/63–11/68. Confidential. Another copy indicates that the memorandum was drafted by Bowdler. (Ibid., Memos to the President, Walt W. Rostow, Vol. 44)

[2] In an October 8 memorandum to the President, Rostow reported Rusk's decision that "we, as a great power, should not over-react to Arosemena's childishness," presumably in reference to a proposal to retaliate by requesting Mantilla's recall. In forwarding the text of Coerr's speech, Rostow also commented: "Although I can understand a government being annoyed with an Ambassador that takes up, point by point, arguments made by its President—and even making fun of one—his speech hardly justified being taken as a federal case." (Ibid., Country File, Ecuador, Vol. I, 12/63–11/68)

Arosemena has taken offense at the free discussion of the successes and failures of the Alliance. (Tab A)[3]

3. Release the two notes to the press, together with Coerr's speech.

4. Also tell the press that we had planned, before we were aware of the Ecuadorean note, to ask Coerr to come to Washington to work on a study of our long-range relations with Latin America. (This is in fact true. The study is to cover our military relations.)[4]

5. Not retaliate against Arosemena by asking for the recall of Ambassador Mantilla.

6. If asked about continued economic assistance to Ecuador, respond that Ecuador is a member of the Alliance for Progress and loans to Ecuador will continue to be judged by Alliance criteria. (From a practical standpoint this means no assistance because of Ecuadorean nonperformance, unless we decide otherwise.)

I understand that Covey is also recommending to Sec. Rusk that he call you to get your approval on these steps.[5]

By way of precedents, on two previous occasions Latin American governments have asked our Ambassadors to leave:

—by Brazil during the Eisenhower administration, for public criticism of Brazilian coffee policy; [6]
—by Haiti during the Kennedy administration, for alleged plotting against Duvalier.[7]

The text of the Ecuadorean note is at Tab B.[8]

Walt

---

[3] The note, Tab A, is attached but not printed. The exchange of notes is in Department of State *Bulletin*, November 6, 1967, p. 621. A brief account of the Oliver–Mantilla meeting is in telegram 50652 to Quito, October 8. (National Archives and Records Administration, RG 59, Central Files 1967–69, POL 17 US–ECUADOR)

[4] As instructed in telegram 50568 to Buenos Aires, October 7. (Ibid., AID(AFP))

[5] Rusk approved these recommendations "on his own responsibility," asking only that Rostow so inform the President. (Memorandum from Rostow to the President, October 8; Johnson Library, National Security File, Country File, Ecuador, Vol. I, 12/63–11/68)

[6] On December 3, 1954, the White House announced the resignation of James S. Kemper, U.S. Ambassador to Brazil; Kemper became the source of controversy by predicting an imminent fall in the price of coffee.

[7] On June 14, 1963, the Government of Haiti requested the recall of U.S. Ambassador Raymond L. Thurston.

[8] Attached but not printed.

339.   Action Memorandum From the Assistant Secretary of State for Inter-American Affairs (Oliver) to the Under Secretary of State (Katzenbach)[1]

Washington, October 12, 1967.

SUBJECT

U.S. Representation in Ecuador

Discussion:

The recall of Ambassador Coerr and the policy you approved on economic assistance will require some adjustments in our representation in Quito. I propose to proceed as follows:

1. Our Embassy will be headed by the Chargé, probably until the end of President Arosemena's term in September 1968.

2. We will consider assigning an additional officer to the Embassy if a definite need is established.

3. After the AID Mission Director completes the review of existing loans with the Ecuadorean Government, he will be transferred and not replaced, unless and until a situation develops in which we would foresee the need to develop a new and active aid strategy toward Ecuador. We expect the review would be completed within the next six to eight weeks and that the transfers would take place as soon as possible thereafter. We expect that there will be other AID personnel changes and reductions but these cannot be identified immediately.

Recommendation:

That you approve the foregoing line of action.[2]

---

[1] Source: National Archives and Records Administration, RG 59, ARA Files, 1967–69: Lot 72 D 33, Ecuador. Secret. Drafted by Sayre and cleared in draft by Gaud and Idar Rimestad, Deputy Under Secretary of State for Management. The memorandum was originally addressed to the Secretary; the word "Under" was subsequently inserted by hand.

[2] Katzenbach approved this recommendation on October 16.

340.   Telegram From the Embassy in Ecuador to the Department of State[1]

Quito, October 17, 1967, 0430Z.

1422. To be delivered 8:00 a.m. October 17, 1967. Subject: Meeting with FonMin Prado. Ref: State 51806.[2]

1. Chargé called on FonMin Prado at latter's request evening of Oct. 16. During hour-long interview variety of subjects discussed. This message covers recall Ambassador Coerr, GOE–USG relations, and U.S. assistance policy to Ecuador. Other topics (LA armaments developments, Plaza OAS candidacy, Ecuador–Peru relations) will be treated in septels.[3]

2. ForMin asserted GOE request for Ambassador Coerr's recall based on "undeniable fact" that he had become "obstacle" to continued friendly relations between GOE and USG. FonMin said President Arosemena could not be expected sit down and talk in frank and cooperative spirit with Ambassador who had ridiculed him in public speech (FonMin referred to humorous anecdote about $350 allowance and to analogies to football contained in speech as particularly offensive to President). In view this situation, FonMin said, President and he decided best way to put GOE–USG relations back on right track was to request "removal of obstacle as soon as possible". FonMin then stated at length that the GOE had always sought and would continue to seek only the closest and most cordial relations with USG.[4] (He then shifted to other matters treated in septels.)

---

[1] Source: National Archives and Records Administration, RG 59, Central Files 1967–69, AID(US) 9 ECUADOR. Confidential; Immediate. Repeated to Guayaquil and USCINCSO for POLAD.

[2] In telegram 51806 to Quito, October 10, the Department forwarded instructions for the meeting with Prado. If Prado raised the issue of AID in Ecuador, the Embassy should propose a joint review to determine whether any loans required termination. In this event, the Embassy should also "make clear that we are suggesting this action as a result of President Arosemena's statements of September 26 and that it is not in retaliation for Ambassador Coerr's recall." (Ibid.)

[3] Telegram 1444 from Quito, October 17, reported discussion on the candidacy of former President Galo Plaza as OAS Secretary General. (Ibid., OAS 8–3) No telegram has been found reporting discussion of "LA armaments developments" or "Ecuador–Peru relations."

[4] Phillips later contradicted Prado's account: "While we had some indications of a lack of personal rapport between Wym and Otto Arosemena, it seems likely that the evil genius behind the demand for Wym's recall was Foreign Minister Prado, who apparently took full advantage of Otto's vanity and his impetuousness." (Letter from Phillips to Lubensky, December 21; ibid., ARA/EP/E Files: Lot 70 D 247, POL 17 Persona Non Grata)

3. Chargé responded that USG position re recall Ambassador Coerr had been made amply clear in Department's note of October 8 to Ecuadorean Embassy, and that there was nothing further to add except to reiterate as stated in note, USG also desired maintain traditionally friendly relations with GOE.

4. Stating that USG sincerely wished USAID loan agreements with GOE to constitute basis for fruitful cooperation rather than discord, Chargé then proposed bilateral review of existing loans, and suggested that GOE designate reps to meet with USG reps to consider each loan in detail. Purpose of review would be to determine specific GOE objections to terms of any loans. After GOE objections specified, USG would attempt satisfy these objections, or, failing this, would propose that loan or loans be terminated by mutual accord.

5. Re new loan applications to AID, Chargé stated that in interest clarifying situation, USG believed review of existing loans should be completed prior to any consideration new applications. Chargé emphasized that new loans would then be examined from standpoint AFP criteria, but that none would be approved unless GOE gave prior assurances re their acceptability.

6. FonMin replied that in principle review seemed sound method to arrive at differences and to attempt solve them. He asked Chargé put proposal in writing, after which he would consult with President Arosemena, who he thought would agree with idea (Embassy recommendation on how to put proposal in writing to follow).[5] FonMin did not show concern about postponement new loan applications. He added that if review existing loans proved successful, same method could be applied to new loan applications thus ensuring beforehand their acceptability to GOE. Re meeting AFP criteria, FonMin said that GOE largely endorsed these, and recalled that President Arosemena had refused to sign Presidents' declaration at Punta del Este not because he disagreed with contents (which FonMin said GOE supports completely), but because declaration did not go far enough.

7. Chargé said Embassy understood GOE performance vis-à-vis AFP criteria would be subject of Oct 20 CIAP meeting. FonMin said he aware of meeting, but confessed he did not know who GOE rep would be since Intriago had resigned as FinMin. Chargé stressed importance of meeting and of GOE attendance. FonMin said he intended check to make sure GOE competently represented.

---

[5] In telegram 1443 to Quito, October 18, the Embassy forwarded its recommendations. (National Archives and Records Administration, RG 59, Central Files 1967–69, POL 17 US–ECUADOR) The Department instructed the Embassy to submit for approval any written communications to the Ecuadorian government regarding economic assistance. (Telegram 56494 to Quito, October 19; ibid., AID(US) 9 ECUADOR)

8. Re recent negotiations between GOE and European commercial lenders, Chargé mentioned dangers inherent such borrowings on short-term, high interest-rate conditions, and pointed out obvious contrast with concessional terms offered by AFP lending agencies. FonMin replied he first to admit AFP agency terms much more favorable, but asserted that urgency Ecuador's needs might oblige GOE to seek loans on harder terms. He said country could not always wait the "months and years" required to negotiate loans from AFP agencies. In reply to Chargé's question if GOE had projected its future debt-servicing burdens if it indulged in long-scale borrowing on hard terms, FonMin asserted that if proceeds wisely invested, loans could pay for themselves in increased productivity. Alluding to domestic political factors, FonMin said "government which expects some day to return must show results when first in office." He referred to President Arosemena's promise to build one school a day for rest of his term, and implied that promise had to be kept no matter where funds came from.

9. Status PL 480 authorization was not raised during meeting.

10. Comment follows.[6]

Crowley

---

[6] No further comment from the Embassy has been found.

---

341. **Information Memorandum From the Assistant Secretary of State for Inter-American Affairs (Oliver) to Secretary of State Rusk**[1]

Washington, December 22, 1967.

SUBJECT

President of Ecuador Hopes U.S. Will Appoint New Ambassador

On December 20, Ecuadorean Ambassador Carlos Mantilla told me that President Otto Arosemena is most anxious that a new U.S. Ambassador be appointed soon. According to Mantilla, Arosemena fears that extreme leftists and other political antagonists will seek to build

---

[1] Source: National Archives and Records Administration, RG 59, Central Files 1967–69, POL 15–1 ECUADOR. Confidential. Drafted by Kilday on December 21. A notation on the memorundum indicates that Rusk saw it.

pre-electoral confusion into a situation of disorder, hoping thereby to disrupt or prevent the elections. He believes that during this critical period the presence of a U.S. Ambassador would be a major stabilizing factor as it would signify the restoration of close U.S.-Ecuadorean relations as well as President Johnson's personal interest in the reestablishment of full constitutional government in Ecuador.

I told Ambassador Mantilla that President Johnson genuinely regards our Ambassadors as his personal representatives, and that he personally decides questions relating to ambassadorial appointments. I opined that Ambassador Coerr probably would have been replaced by now if President Arosemena had not chosen to express his dissatisfaction by formally and publicly requesting the Ambassador's recall. I said that I was not aware of President Johnson's plans regarding a successor to Ambassador Coerr nor would it be possible for me to make unsolicited recommendations to the President on this question. I did promise the Ambassador that I would inform you of President Arosemena's feelings in the matter.

It is clear that the absence of a U.S. Ambassador in Quito is the cause of considerable discomfort to President Arosemena and his political faction. However, there is no convincing evidence that the extreme left has the capability or even the intention of preventing elections, or that the absence of an Ambassador in any way favors the ambitions of this political grouping. The Bureau is watching this situation closely, but at this moment I am not persuaded that our over-all interests would be served by the early replacement of Ambassador Coerr. To the contrary, in view of the insulting manner in which Ambassador Coerr was ejected, I feel that the naming of his replacement in the near future would have a most undesirable effect on the U.S. image in Ecuador and elsewhere in Latin America.

---

342.   Action Memorandum From the President's Special Assistant (Rostow) to President Johnson[1]

Washington, January 25, 1968.

SUBJECT

　　IDB Loan to Ecuador

---

[1] Source: Johnson Library, National Security File, Country File, Ecuador, Vol. I, 12/63–11/68. Confidential.

Since Punta del Este no new AID loans have been given to the Arosemena Government in Ecuador. Disbursements on existing loans have been held up pending a review of which ones Ecuador wants badly enough to meet the self-help criteria. This process will be strung out for the remainder of Arosemena's tenure (until September 1, 1968).

The Inter-American Development Bank (IDB) will shortly have to decide on a $3 million loan to resettle small farmers under the agrarian reform program. The loan will be on concessional terms from the Fund for Special Operations to which we are the principal contributor and where our vote is decisive.

The question arises whether your injunction against lending to Arosemena applies to the IDB as well as AID.

I recommend that you not carry the freeze to the IDB where our opposition to a small loan to improve agriculture which meets all IBD criteria will be taken as vindictive on our part.

Walt

OK to approve IDB loan[2]

Freeze also applies to him

Call me

---

[2] This option is checked.

---

343. **Information Memorandum From the President's Special Assistant (Rostow) to President Johnson**[1]

Washington, March 6, 1968.

SUBJECT

Ecuador

Last Saturday President Arosemena reshuffled his cabinet. He dropped Foreign Minister Julio Prado, the architect of his Punta del

---

[1] Source: Johnson Library, National Security File, Country File, Ecuador, Vol. I, 12/63–11/68. Confidential. A notation on the memorandum indicates that the President saw it.

Este posture and the ouster of Ambassador Coerr. In his place he appointed Gustavo Larrea, until recently Ambassador in Washington.

Because Larrea is such a good friend of the United States, this is obviously intended as a conciliatory gesture toward us. In return, Arosemena hopes you will respond by appointing a new Ambassador. This was made clear when Larrea flew to Venezuela two weeks ago to talk to Covey Oliver about the impending cabinet changes.

Other indications of Arosemena's desire to kiss-and-make-up prior to elections (June 2) and transfer of power (September 1) are:

1. his reasonably cooperative and conciliatory attitude on the joint review of their complaints about the AID program;
2. no attacks on the Alliance since September 1967;
3. the prompt release without publicity of a US tuna boat seized by an Ecuadorean frigate last week.

Our Chargé in Quito recommends that we respond favorably to these conciliatory actions, short of sending a new Ambassador until after the June elections. Among the things he suggests are:

1. let it be known publicly around April 1 that appointment of a new Ambassador is under *active consideration;*
2. resume low-level technical talks on pending loan applications (in the understanding that negotiations would not be completed until termination of Arosemena's mandate).[2]

Covey Oliver will be sending you his recommendation on how we might proceed.[3] I will withhold judgment until I see what Covey advises. In any event, we should say nothing about *consideration* of a new Ambassador to Ecuador until you fill the vacancies at Buenos Aires and Montevideo. There are indications that the Argentines and Uruguayans are a little restive on this score. They would take amiss any indication that Ecuador is receiving prior attention

Walt

---

[2] In telegram 3295 from Quito, March 5. (National Archives and Records Administration, RG 59, Central Files 1967–69, POL 17 US–ECUADOR)

[3] Not further identified.

344. Discussion Memorandum From the Deputy Director of the Office of Ecuadorean-Peruvian Affairs (Berlin) to the Assistant Secretary of State for Inter-American Affairs (Oliver)[1]

Washington, August 6, 1968.

SUBJECT

Timing of the Arrival in Quito of Ambassador Sessions

Discussion:

You will recall that Embassy Quito recommended in June that the new Ambassador not present credentials to President Arosemena, but that he arrive in Quito and present his credentials at the time of or immediately following the inauguration.[2] This office disagreed with that recommendation and argued that the best interests of the United States would be served by the Ambassador's arrival in Quito before the end of the Arosemena administration.

These opposing recommendations originated in differing judgements over the political future of Arosemena and the relationship to that future of the arrival of a new U.S. Ambassador. Briefly, the Embassy argued that the reelection of Arosemena in 1972 would not be in the interests of the United States and, accordingly, the United States should take no action that would tend to improve Arosemena's chances for re-election. To send an Ambassador now would amount to reconciliation with Arosemena and, in the judgement of the Embassy, would rehabilitate his image and increase his potential for re-election in 1972 or later. Thus, the United States should not send an Ambassador to present credentials to Arosemena.

We agreed that the arrival of an Ambassador during the Arosemena administration would amount to a reconciliation with Arosemena and we maintained that this is precisely what the U.S. should seek. We judged that Arosemena stands a better than even chance of returning to the Presidency at some point in the future, and we doubted that these odds would be altered substantially by the refusal of the U.S. to effect a reconciliation with him. (Certainly the repeated election of Velasco indicates that the Ecuadorean electorate is not greatly

---

[1] Source: National Archives and Records Administration, RG 59, ARA/EP/E Files, 1968: Lot 70 D 478, Personal Mail. Confidential. A handwritten note reads: "For Your 3:30 pm Meeting Today." No substantive record of this meeting has been found.

[2] In telegram 4823 from Quito, June 10. (Ibid., Central Files 1967–69, POL 17 ECUADOR) José María Velasco Ibarra was elected on June 2 to serve a fifth term as President.

influenced by a candidate's past relationship with the U.S. or by fears that the U.S. might not find him acceptable.) Thus, in the possibility that Arosemena may well return to the Presidency anyway, we thought it would be wise to effect a reconciliation with him now and thereby to maximize chances of developing a better relationship with him the next time around.

The arguments pro and con that were fairly clear in June have become somewhat obscured with the passage of time and with new developments. Favoring presentation of credentials to President Arosemena are the following new considerations:

a) President Arosemena's cooperation with the U.S. on the IBRD fisheries loan question;

b) Our current efforts to persuade Foreign Minister Larrea to obtain agreement from Velasco Ibarra to meet with the U.S. in a fisheries conference. Our Chargé in Quito believes that Larrea would undertake this mission with greater enthusiasm if he knew the Ambassador were to present his credentials before September 1.

New considerations which tend to argue against presentation of credentials include the following:

a) The nomination and confirmation of Ambassador Sessions[3] already constitute something of a rapprochement with Arosemena and have been cited by Arosemena as evidence that U.S.-Ecuadorean relations are as good as ever.

b) The arrival of the Ambassador just before the inauguration, rather than a month or six weeks before the inauguration, would be so obviously designed to put the U.S. blessing on Arosemena that it could displease Velasco and add a minor but unnecessary irritation to the U.S. relationship with him. Our Chargé in Quito thinks it possible that the arrival of the Ambassador now could make Velasco less willing to commit himself to a fisheries conference before he takes office.

c) The arrival of the Ambassador after the inauguration might be taken by Velasco as a highly complimentary U.S. effort to make a qualitative distinction between him and Arosemena.

Conclusion:

The arguments for and against the arrival of Ambassador Sessions are relatively equal in weight and strength. His arrival would put us on an excellent footing with President Arosemena in the event Arose-

---

[3] According to the President's Daily Diary, the issue of an ambassadorship for Edson O. Sessions, a Chicago businessman and former Ambassador to Finland, was raised in a June 19 telephone conversation between the President and Senate Minority Leader Everett Dirksen (R–Illinois). (Johnson Library) Dirksen called the President to discuss a possible Latin American post for Sessions on July 3, the same day Crowley requested verbal agreement for Sessions as U.S. Ambassador to Ecuador. (Telegram 5222 from Quito, July 4; National Archives and Records Administration, RG 59, Central Files 1967–69, POL 17–1 US–ECUADOR) On July 26 the White House announced the nomination, which was confirmed by the Senate 3 days later.

mena returns to the Presidency, but his nomination and confirmation already have taken the sting out of our previous posture of no Ambassador for Arosemena. His arrival before September 1 might well be an irritant in the relationship with Velasco but this is likely to become insignificant as time passes. Arrival before September 1 might well induce Arosemena to try harder to please us on the fisheries issue, but it might also lead Velasco to a less accommodating position on the same problem.

Recommendation:

Although we no longer see a clear and strong advantage to the U.S. on either side of the issue, we incline to accommodation of President Arosemena and Foreign Minister Larrea. Therefore, we recommend that Ambassador Sessions proceed to Quito to present his credentials to President Arosemena and to attend the inauguration ceremony and that he then return to Washington to arrange his business and personal affairs before departing to take up his post on a permanent basis.[4]

---

[4] Sessions presented his credentials to President Velasco in a formal ceremony on September 26. (Telegram 6625 from Quito, September 30; ibid.)

Mexico

345. Telephone Conversation Between President Johnson and the Assistant Secretary of State for Inter-American Affairs (Mann)[1]

Washington, January 25, 1964, 12:20 p.m.

[Omitted here is discussion of the negotiations to resume diplomatic relations with Panama.]

President: Please, let's get it in shape so we can get some people named now. And let's find some good top men. I am not at all happy with my Ambassador to Mexico. I want to get the greatest man in America. I had the greatest and I pulled him up here. He got me in Panama right after he got here.[2] And now I want you to find me—I want a Marlin Sandlin. I want somebody that's forty-five years old. You reckon he could get out of his business interests and give them up and go down there?

Mann: Well, you said you didn't want another Texan there. Marlin would be. The trouble with Marlin is, he's chairman of the board of Pan American Sulphur.

President: Well, couldn't he get out of that and resign it and give up his interests?

Mann: He could, but he'd be attacked and so would you.

President: All right.

Mann: I think Marlin's a great guy—

President: Well, let's get—

Mann: —but it depends on your political judgment.

President: No, he would be. What else can we get?

Mann: Well, we can get him Colombia. You could move Freeman to Mexico.

President: I want to get some man I know in Mexico that's my friend, that's looking after me, that's my manager, that's damned able.

---

[1] Source: Johnson Library, Recordings and Transcripts, Recording of telephone conversation between President Johnson and Thomas Mann, Tape F64.07, Side B, PNO 3. No classification marking. This transcript was prepared in the Office of the Historian specifically for this volume. An informal memorandum of conversation, including discussion of Panama, is ibid., Papers of Thomas C. Mann, Telephone Conversations with LBJ, January 4, 1964–April 30, 1965. According to the President's Daily Diary (Johnson Library), Andrew Hatcher and George Reedy were in the Oval Office when Johnson called Mann.

[2] Mann was Ambassador to Mexico prior to his appointment in December 1963 as Assistant Secretary of State for Inter-American Affairs. He began his new assignment on January 3, 6 days before student demonstrations led to the crisis in Panama.

And I want him to understand business and I want him to be young and attractive. I want him to be a Sargent Shriver type.

Mann: Well, why don't you pick a good lawyer with good political sense? Somebody you know and have confidence in? We've got some Foreign Service people. I know that Friday,[3] the Secretary and Ball thought that they were going to—the Secretary said he was going to recommend Freeman, who is your, probably one of the two best you've got in Latin America. The other one being in Brazil.

President: OK.

Mann: Mexico. We could fill Colombia. But if you want somebody you know personally, and you don't know Freeman—

President: No, I don't.

Mann: —that would eliminate him. But he's good and he would be loyal to you.

President: Well, don't you know somebody that I know that's good?

Mann: I can get on the phone.

President: Like Marlin?

Mann: Well, I really hesitate for you—

President: I'm not talking about Marlin. I'm talking about somebody of his same qualifications, that's got his appearance.

Mann: Let me then try—I'll talk to Marlin and see if we can't cook up two or three names for you.

President: All right. Do that.

Mann: Probably be from Texas, but that wouldn't bother you?

President: No, but I'd rather get some other state. California might be good.

Mann: I think a young lawyer with good political instincts is what you want.

President: What about a Mexican?

Mann: Well, I wouldn't recommend that to you.

President: We got a helluva good Mexican out there that's head of finance department, California.

Mann: Well, if you know him. He has a couple of strikes on him. The Mexicans don't like what they call "pochos," that means people—

President: All right. OK. All right. The Mexicans won't take a white man. I don't—God-damned if I can understand that.

Mann: Well, it's a—

---

[3] January 24.

President: OK. That's all right. You go on and get me a good one. But get me one. I want to help them. We've been miserable to the Mexicans. I want you to get some in your Department. If you know any smart ones, you hire some. The Alliance for Progress. You don't have to go to Puerto Rico.

Mann: I think we could hire him up here and that would be easy. If you've got a fellow you want hired up here—

President: Well, but hell, he gets more than you do. He gets $23,000 a year.

Mann: Well, everybody gets more than we do, but—

President: You find some Cornelli, or—What's his name, George?

Reedy: Luevano

President: Cornevano? What?

Reedy: Luevano. Danny Luevano.

President: Luevano. Danny Luevano. He's the head of finance in the state of California and they say he's a damned-able citizen. He's coming in next week and I'll send him to see you.

Mann: All right. Fine.

President: OK.

Mann: Fine.[4]

---

[4] In a subsequent discussion with Mann on ambassadorial candidates, the President agreed to move Fulton "Tony" Freeman to Mexico, replacing him in Colombia with Covey Oliver. (Johnson Library, Recordings and Transcripts, Recording of telephone conversation between President Johnson and Thomas Mann, February 5, 1964, 10:35 a.m., Tape F64.10, Side B, PNO 4) On February 29 Johnson announced the appointment of Daniel M. Luevano to be Assistant Secretary of the Army.

346. Memorandum of Conversation[1]

Palm Springs, February 21, 1964, 4:30 p.m.

SUBJECT

Meeting between President Johnson and President Lopez Mateos

PARTICIPANTS

President Johnson
President Lopez Mateos

Mexican-American Relations

President Johnson said that relations between the United States and Mexico had never been better.[2] He said that this situation was due largely to the work of President Lopez Mateos. He said that he would like to meet with President Lopez Mateos at Chamizal some time before the latter leaves office and that the meeting should be the occasion for a tribute to President Lopez Mateos. The Mexican President replied that he too would like a meeting at Chamizal. He added that the Chamizal solution should not be credited to him personally but rather to the rule of law and the goodwill evidenced by the two countries. He said that Mexico planned to erect a monument to President Kennedy at Chamizal.[3]

President Johnson said that he had heard from American businessmen in Mexico that they were very pleased with the treatment they had received from the present Mexican Administration. He asked whether

---

[1] Source: National Archives and Records Administration, RG 59, Central Files 1964–66, POL 7 MEX. Secret. Drafted by Donald F. Barnes (LS) and Hawthorne Q. Mills (S/S–S). Approved by Bromley Smith on February 27. The meeting was held at the President's residence. According to the President's Daily Diary, Johnson stayed at the private home of Louis Taubman, a Texas oil and real estate developer, throughout his visit to Palm Springs. (Johnson Library) After the private meeting the two Presidents were joined by their respective advisers for further discussion. A memorandum of conversation is in the National Archives and Records Administration, RG 59, Central Files 1964–66, POL 7 MEX. Presidents Johnson and López Mateos were in Los Angeles to receive honorary degrees, Doctor of Laws, from the University of California.

[2] Johnson briefly discussed the state of U.S.–Mexican relations with Mann, February 19; see Document 2.

[3] The Convention Between the United States of America and United Mexican States for the Solution of the Problem of Chamizal transferred 630 acres of land along the Rio Grande to Mexico, thereby confirming the arbitration award of 1911. The convention was signed on August 29, 1963, ratified by the Senate on December 17, and entered into force on January 14, 1964. (Department of State *Bulletin*, February 3, 1964, p. 186) For documentation on the negotiation of the convention, see *Foreign Relations, 1961–1963*, vol. XII, Microfiche Supplement, Mexico. Johnson and López Mateos met at Chamizal on September 25, 1964, for a ceremony marking settlement of the dispute. For text of Johnson's remarks, see *Public Papers of the Presidents of the United States: Lyndon B. Johnson, 1963–64*, Book II, pp. 1117–1122.

equally good treatment would be received from the next Administration. President Lopez Mateos replied that the new Administration would extend even better treatment to American businessmen in Mexico.

President Lopez Mateos said that a number of recent events had led his country to adopt certain international policies which had been interpreted by some people as anti-American. President Johnson noted that Mexico had every right to exercise an independent foreign policy and he was sure that when the chips were down Mexico would be on the side of the United States. President Lopez Mateos affirmed that this was the case. He added that the U.S. Presidents he had dealt with invariably had shown great understanding of Mexican problems and that he had attempted to show an equal understanding of American problems. This approach had created the unprecedented goodwill that exists between the two countries.

Alliance for Progress

When President Johnson requested President Lopez Mateos' opinion of the Alliance for Progress, the latter replied that Mexico, unlike some countries in South America, believed that the program was sound. All projects which had been carried out in Mexico had been fruitful and effective, and his only criticism was that the Alliance often moved too slowly. Mexico had always understood that the Alliance was a cooperative effort, which was not the case with some South American countries that had been unwilling to effect the necessary internal reforms.

General de Gaulle

Asked for his opinion of General de Gaulle and French recognition of Red China, President Lopez Mateos replied that he believed de Gaulle had a Napoleonic complex and was moved by the idea that France, for historical reasons, had to make an effort to achieve standing as a major world power. He believed the retirement of Chancellor Adenauer who had formed such close ties with General de Gaulle had led the latter to feel that France would now be isolated within Europe. His reaction was to create a new center of attention in the Far East by recognizing Red China and in Latin America by visiting Mexico.

President Johnson asked whether Mexico would be influenced by France's recognition of Red China. President Lopez Mateos replied emphatically that it would not. He added that his country would always make its own foreign policy decisions.

Panama

In reply to President Johnson's request for his opinion on Panama, President Lopez Mateos replied that he felt the two countries had been boxed in by words. He believed the United States realized that the 61-year old treaty had to be brought up to date, while at the same time Panama did not want to administer the Canal. He believed that

Panama was incapable of running the Canal by itself. The positions of the two countries were not as far apart as they seemed and a solution could be found if they could break out of the vicious circle of words. President Lopez Mateos said that except for the loss of life the incidents that had taken place in Panama were unimportant in themselves. As long as the basic Panamanian grievances remained Castroites and Communists throughout Latin America would take advantage of the situation to add fuel to the flames. He said that most thinking Latin Americans believed that the time had come for the United States to revise the treaty.

President Johnson said that the United States was always ready to sit down and discuss the treaty with Panama, but that under no circumstances could this country agree in advance on the revisions.

Cuban Subversion

President Johnson said that he was very concerned over Cuban efforts to export its revolution, as evidenced by the arms cache that had been found in Venezuela. President Lopez Mateos replied that it was impossible to export revolutions. He said that if fertile soil for a revolution existed in a given country, that country would have a revolution of its own without the need of importing one. If fertile soil did not exist, no one could successfully create a revolution in that country. He gave Mexico as an example, saying he was sure that Mexico with almost forty million inhabitants had more Castro sympathizers than Venezuela, but that these people had had no success in spreading their ideas. As far as propaganda was concerned, Venezuela was spreading more anti-Castro propaganda than Cuba was spreading anti-Venezuela propaganda.

Braceros

President Johnson asked President Lopez Mateos for his opinion of the bracero question now that the U.S. Congress was going to let the agreement expire.[4] He said that he realized that the braceros represented a sizeable source of foreign exchange for Mexico.

President Lopez Mateos replied that he had always felt that the use of Mexican braceros in the United States was a matter of mutual convenience rather than an obligation on the part of the United States. As Mexican Secretary of Labor many years ago he had told representatives of American unions that as soon as Mexican braceros received wages equal to American workers, he knew that U.S. farmers would prefer to use American labor. He still recognized that fact. His main

---

[4] The "Bracero program" was passed in July 1951 as an amendment (PL 82–78) to the Agricultural Act of 1949. (65 Stat. 119) The program authorized the recruitment of migrant farm labor from Mexico for work in the United States. Although voting to extend the program in 1961 and 1963, Congress allowed the law to lapse at the end of 1964.

concern was that illegal border crossings be prevented. He said it was logical to expect more illegal crossing attempts both because many Mexicans would continue to want to work in the United States and many American farmers would seek continued cheap labor. The only ones to be hurt by these illegal crossings would be American workers whose wages would be depressed. The Mexican Government would have to undertake a public works program to provide employment for the braceros. This would undoubtedly be a priority matter for the next Administration. It might perhaps be possible to start a large settlement program in the southeastern part of Mexico, although the necessary financial resources were not available.

Salinity

President Johnson acknowledged that the problem of the salinity of Colorado River water was a source of concern to Mexico. He said that a solution to this problem should be legislative rather than judicial but that the United States would have to await the outcome of experiments conducted by the Bureau of Reclamation. He noted that authorizing legislation and appropriations would have to be obtained from Congress and that he did not believe he could present such a request before January 1965. He said that he was aware of Mexico's concern, since Texas farmers were also concerned over salinity of the lower Rio Grande.

President Lopez Mateos said he was aware of the problems that President Johnson faced with the Congress and that he did not want to give the impression that he was pressuring the United States, although he recalled that President Kennedy had told him that the Bureau of Reclamation experiments would be concluded in October of 1963.[5] He said that he was confident that a solution would be worked out, and asked whether the two governments might not set a date by which the salinity problems of both rivers might be settled. President Johnson replied that since Congressional action was involved it would be difficult to set a date.[6]

---

[5] Kennedy was in Mexico, June 29–July 1, 1962, for a state visit with López Mateos. For a memorandum of conversation on the salinity problem, see *Foreign Relations, 1961–1963*, vol. XII, Microfiche Supplement, Mexico. A joint statement also addressed the salinity of the water supply along the border. (*Public Papers of the Presidents of the United States: John F. Kennedy, 1962*, pp. 529–531)

[6] For text of the joint statement issued following the meeting in Palm Springs, see ibid.: *Lyndon B. Johnson, 1963–64*, Book II, pp. 305–308.

347.   Editorial Note

On May 11, 1964, President Johnson called Assistant Secretary Mann to discuss a recent incident involving the Ambassador to Mexico, Fulton "Tony" Freeman. Johnson asked: "What's this story about Freeman mixing up in politics down in Mexico?" He then described an article in which the Ambassador reportedly said that the Partido Revolucionario Institucional (PRI) candidate, Gustavo Díaz Ordaz, would win the presidential election on July 5, and spoke "approvingly" of the expected result. The opposition was already criticizing Freeman for interference in Mexican affairs. Although he had not seen the story, Mann doubted that Freeman could have made the statements attributed to him. He assured the President: "My advice to Tony was to stay away from the press in Mexico." The two men agreed that the story was "bad for the [Mexican] administration and bad for us." Johnson told Mann to call Freeman for a report on the incident. (Johnson Library, Recordings and Transcripts, Recording of telephone conversation between President Johnson and Thomas Mann, May 11, 1964, 12:17 p.m., Tape F64.26, Side B, PNO 2)

Mann reported back to the President within the hour:

Mann: I talked to Tony on the telephone.

President: Yeah.

Mann: He said what happened was: last Wednesday [May 6] he went over to make a speech at the University Club there and the press got a hold of it and asked him what he thought about who's going to win the election. He said that was none of his concern. They asked him then what the American press was saying about the Mexican election. He said he told them what the American press was saying.

President: He ought to have told them that he wasn't a reporter.

Mann: Exactly. And I told him—He knows he's goofed on it but apparently it's not a major issue down there yet. It was [unintelligible] the opposition PRI got a hold of it and made a statement. But this was just a one shot affair that happened last Thursday or Friday. There hasn't been any published it since or any editorials about it. And I reminded him again that the magic words were: "We don't intervene in Mexican internal affairs. They're perfectly capable of running their own government." And he agreed that was the line he would follow and not let the press push him off that line.

President: All right. (Ibid., Recording of telephone conversation between President Johnson and Thomas Mann, May 11, 1964, 12:50 p.m., Tape F64.26, Side B, PNO 3) The portions of the conversations printed here were prepared in the Office of the Historian specially for this volume.

348.   Memorandum From Secretary of State Rusk to President Johnson[1]

Washington, June 22, 1964.

SUBJECT

  Salinity Problem with Mexico

Over the last month, State and Interior carried on intensive discussions to find a solution to the salinity problem. A proposal was worked out which Mr. Dungan and I discussed with Senator Hayden.[2] I understand that the Senator found it acceptable, but that we are unable to proceed with negotiations until other problems on the Colorado, which the Senator regards as related, are also settled. I am not certain Mexico will accept the proposal but it gives us a negotiating position for the first time.

In the meantime, Mexico continues to receive what it regards as poor quality water. Mexicali farmers are agitated, and carrying on weekly demonstrations. They plan demonstrations throughout Mexico on July 12. Although they have been assured by Mexican officials that a solution is forthcoming momentarily, they are aware of none and fearful of receiving water beginning in October which they consider unusable for irrigation. They use U.S. Department of Agriculture handbooks to prove their case. The Mexican President has been told by his Senate Majority Leader (Senator Moreno Sanchez), that the United States would solve the problem before you meet with Lopez Mateos in October. The incoming Mexican President, Diaz Ordaz, has told the Mexicali farmers that if the problem is not solved by the time he takes office in December, he will present the dispute to the International Court. Emotions are running high in Mexico. Whereas the Mexican Government was trying to keep things quiet, demonstrations now are obviously being carried out with the approval of the Mexican Government. After three years of the best relations in our history with Mexico, we are clearly headed for trouble unless a solution is found quickly.

Although the effect on our relations with Mexico will be serious, the probable risk to the water rights of the seven Colorado Basin States

---

[1] Source: Johnson Library, National Security File, Country File, Mexico, Vol. I, Memos, 12/63–12/65. Confidential. Another copy indicates that the memorandum was drafted by Mann. (National Archives and Records Administration, RG 59, ARA/MEX Files: Lot 69 D 377, POL 33 Water, Boundaries, Inland Waters)

[2] Senator Carl T. Hayden (D–Arizona), chairman of the Senate Committee on Appropriations. Johnson reviewed the negotiations with Senator Hayden in a telephone conversation with Assistant Secretary Mann on June 11; see Document 16.

is equally disturbing. Over the two and one-half years that this dispute has dragged on, Mexico has insisted more and more that it is entitled to water of equal quality. Mexico argues that the Treaty[3] divided the waters of the Colorado, and that it is unjust for Mexico to receive all of the drainage and for U.S. irrigators on the opposite bank of the river to receive sweet water from storage. We can make a fairly persuasive case on the basis of the history of the Treaty, and the Treaty itself, against the Mexican contention for equal treatment. But I am rather uneasy about arguing before the International Court, where all but a few of the judges are from the less developed countries, that Mexico is not entitled to equal treatment. We estimate that we are now delivering to Mexico 600,000 acre feet of drainage water to fulfill our Treaty commitment. At ultimate development (about 1980), it is estimated that we will be delivering about 900,000 acre feet of drainage water. With run-offs averaging 10 million acre feet or less over the last several years, the danger of an adverse decision requiring us to deliver water from storage is uncomfortably evident.

Although neither Senator Hayden nor Reclamation have been willing to acknowledge the risks we are running, they are now acting as if they understood them.

It is essential that we begin negotiations with Mexico immediately if we are to have any hope of selling the proposal which has been worked out. More delay, accompanied by anti-American demonstrations in Mexico, may make it politically impossible for Mexico to agree to anything we would regard as reasonable. I hope that you can get Senator Hayden's agreement that we may proceed with negotiations.[4]

Dean Rusk

---

[3] Reference is to a treaty relating to the utilization of water from the Colorado and Tijuana Rivers and from the Rio Grande. The treaty was signed by the United States and Mexico on February 3, 1944. (59 Stat. (pt. 2) 1219)

[4] Hayden attended the weekly legislative leaders breakfast with President Johnson on June 23. (Johnson Library, President's Daily Diary) No substantive record of the meeting, or evidence that the salinity problem was discussed, has been found.

349. Memorandum From the Assistant Secretary of State for Inter-American Affairs (Mann) to Secretary of State Rusk[1]

Washington, July 2, 1964.

SUBJECT

Mexican Elections, July 5

The Mexican presidential campaign, ending with the July 5 elections, has been unusually active with minority parties, both left and right, having been encouraged by the dominant "official" party, the Institutional Revolutionary Party (PRI), to campaign forcefully in opposition to the Government. In early April, there was some fear that the PRI's policy of an open campaign might result in violence especially in outlying rural areas. This fear was heightened, on April 6, when PRI candidate Gustavo Diaz Ordaz found himself in the midst of an unfriendly demonstration mounted by leftists and communists in the northern city of Chihuahua. The PRI did not meaningfully curb the leftist opposition but it did greatly increase the security protection for Diaz Ordaz. This proved sufficient to deter demonstrators and the rest of the campaign was almost completely free of disturbances.

It is expected that Diaz Ordaz will win the kind of overwhelming victory that PRI presidential candidates are accustomed to.[2] Current Mexico City guesses are that he will get between 85 and 90 percent of the popular vote with most of the remainder going to the conservative National Action Party (PAN). Except for the marxist Popular Socialist Party (PPS), no communist or far leftist parties are registered for participation in the election. A communist party, the Peoples Electoral Front (FEP), is running a candidate, even though the party is unregistered, and he will probably get several thousand write-in votes.

Diaz Ordaz, the next President of Mexico, is 53 years old, a native of the state of Puebla, and a former Minister of Interior in the Government of the incumbent President, Adolfo Lopez Mateos. Diaz Ordaz has a reputation as a forceful personality and was considered to be the most moderate of all the aspirants to the PRI presidential nomination.

A specific conclusion that can be drawn from Diaz Ordaz' campaign speeches, traditionally general in their content, is that the candidate is determined realistically to attack the problem of rural poverty in Mexico. To effect the necessary changes, Diaz Ordaz will have to

---

[1] Source: National Archives and Records Administration, RG 59, ARA/MEX Files: Lot 71 D 188, POL 14 Diaz Ordaz Election—1964. Confidential. Drafted by Harry Bergold (ARA/MEX) and initialed for Mann by Adams. A notation on the memorandum indicates that Rusk saw it.

[2] Díaz Ordaz won the presidential election with approximately 88 percent of the vote.

force the Mexican bureaucracy to bring to bear on the agrarian problem a number of essential technical, financial and other institutional reforms. In foreign affairs, the Diaz Ordaz administration may from time to time take positions closer to ours than was the case under the Lopez Mateos Administration, but no major shifts in Mexican policy are expected in the short run.

---

350. Memorandum From the President's Special Assistant for National Security Affairs (Bundy) to President Johnson[1]

Washington, July 27, 1964.

SUBJECT

Salinity Problem with Mexico

The Mexican Ambassador will call on you at 6 PM, July 28, to deliver a letter from President Lopez Mateos on our proposal to resolve the salinity problem on the lower Colorado River. Secretary Udall, Tom Mann, and Mr. Sayre, from my staff, will attend.

The Mexican Ambassador will make three basic points:

1. Mexico appreciates the efforts the U.S. has made to achieve a solution to the salinity problem. The U.S. proposal being discussed in the International Boundary and Water Commission would reduce the amount of salt in water delivered to Mexico, but there would still be more salt than would result from normal irrigation operations. The proposal promises a further reduction in salt from Wellton-Mohawk, but gives no indication as to when. Moreover, it still contemplates the delivery of underground salt water and not "return flow," as defined by the Treaty.

2. Mexico regards a by-pass channel (either entirely separate, or within the present channel of the Colorado River) as the only way to achieve a prompt and satisfactory solution.

3. Mexico will continue to reserve its legal position on the interpretation of the 1944 Treaty and international law just as both countries did in the Chamizal settlement.

I recommend that you inform the Mexican Ambassador:

1. We share the Mexican desire for an early solution to this problem.

---

[1] Source: Johnson Library, National Security File, Country File, Mexico, Vol. I, Memos, 12/63–12/65. No classification marking.

2. We will review our proposals to see if there is any possible way to reduce further the amount of salt which would be delivered to Mexico this winter. We will also try to give Mexico an answer on when the Wellton-Mohawk district can achieve normal operation, i.e., when it will be in salt balance.

3. We have studied the by-pass channel alternative. We know that Mexico is interested in a result that would be satisfactory to both governments, and not necessarily in the alternatives the U.S. adopts to achieve that result. At the moment we cannot say whether a by-pass channel should be included in the combination of works to achieve that result.

4. We agree that we should seek a practical solution with no attempt to interpret or modify the 1944 Treaty. We have no problem with both sides reserving their legal positions.[2]

McGeorge Bundy[3]

[2] Although he delivered the letter as scheduled, Carrillo Flores reported that "the situation had changed since the letter had been written in that the Mexican Commissioner had given the views of the Mexican Government to the United States Commissioner." President Johnson asked Udall "to take action to resolve the salinity problem." Johnson also extended an invitation for Díaz Ordaz to visit his Texas ranch in October. (Memorandum of conversation, July 28; National Archives and Records Administration, RG 59, Central Files 1964–66, POL 33–1 MEX–US)

[3] Printed from a copy that bears this typed signature.

---

351.   Editorial Note

[text not declassified]

---

352.   Memorandum of Conversation[1]

LBJ Ranch, Texas, November 13, 1964, 10–11:45 a.m.

SUBJECT

President Johnson's Conversation with President-elect Diaz Ordaz

[1] Source: National Archives and Records Administration, RG 59, Central Files 1964–66, POL MEX–US. Confidential. Drafted by Sayre. Approved in the White House on December 10. The memorandum is part I of II. Part II recorded discussion on November 12 on Mexican-Cuban relations. (Johnson Library, National Security File, Country File, Mexico, Diaz Ordaz Visit, 11/12–11/13/64)

PARTICIPANTS

The President
President-elect Diaz Ordaz
Antonio Carrillo Flores, Ambassador of Mexico
Thomas C. Mann, Assistant Secretary
Angier B. Duke, Chief of Protocol
Robert M. Sayre, White House staff
Donald Barnes, Interpreter

The President outlined his economic philosophy. He emphasized especially the need to maintain the confidence of investors. He observed that investors have to feel secure and have no fear that their investments will not be destroyed or confiscated by the government. The United States was now in its 45th month of unbroken economic growth. The President felt that investors' confidence was a major factor in setting this record. He regarded a high level of investment as basic. Without it, plants would not be built, nor jobs created. He was not disturbed at a high level of profit. On the contrary, he welcomed it because the government got 52¢ out of each dollar of profit. The greater the profits of business, the more government received to carry on essential programs.

Diaz Ordaz expressed general agreement with this philosophy, but he said Mexico had a special problem which could not be resolved by guaranteeing the security of investment. This problem was the extent to which the Mexican economy was dependent on actions of the United States Government. He then discussed cotton (threat of variable subsidy); sugar (no assured quota); coffee (no U.S. legislation implementing the International Coffee Agreement); silver (U.S. stocks could upset the market); lead and zinc (stagnation in industry because of over supply); fluoride (tariff barriers), etc.

Diaz Ordaz said Mexico needed long term assurances on its primary products so it could do long term planning. He said that Mexico had always found great comprehension in the United States. But he regarded this as an "act of grace," by the United States.

(Mr. Sayre asked the Mexican Ambassador later if this did not amount to a suggestion for a trade agreement. The Ambassador said it probably did, but a bilateral agreement and not participation in GATT. Mexico found no merit in joining GATT.)

Diaz Ordaz said the President could expect any Mexican Ambassador to be persistent, because it needed cooperation on its primary products to avoid a very serious situation.

The President said he understood this problem. He was certain that the Mexican President-elect understood the political problems of the United States on importing primary products because they were not different from the problems the President-elect would face. The President said he would like to be helpful on, for example, sugar. But when he agreed on a foreign quota, he had to hold down the domestic quota.

The inevitable result was that farmers who could vote in the United States asked why Mexicans who do not even live in the United States got quotas and American farmers did not. Sugar is now grown in 22 states and the Senators from these states are, of course, pressing for increased domestic quotas.

The President said he knew that the Coffee Agreement was essential. He noted the problem of only having coffee consumers in the United States and no producers interested in market stability. But he assured the Mexican President-elect that he would seek action on coffee. He observed that it would be very difficult to get good legislation, but in doing so we would show our real friendship for Latin America.

Diaz Ordaz said he understood the situation perfectly. He regarded these problems as trade matters and hoped they would be dealt with as trade problems and not political problems. He thought that relations would be stronger if Mexico did not have to depend on loans or special legislation by the United States Congress.

The President said he could not agree that loans adversely affected relations. He recalled his own personal experience in borrowing money from a friend when his friend had reason to doubt that he would ever be repaid. The President considered the lender as one of his best friends and still did today. He thought that loans on special terms were helpful.

Diaz Ordaz said there were two urgent problems:

1. Colorado River Salinity

He said that he knew we had reached agreement in principle and that only a few details remained to be worked out.

Diaz Ordaz said he could not agree with the United States that it had no obligations as to quality merely because it is not mentioned in the Treaty. He thought the United States had an obligation to act responsibly. He was confident that the International Court would hold that the water users on the right bank of the river were entitled to the same quality of water as those on the left bank. He thought the problem could be settled in the near future if the Boundary Commission had instructions to do so.

The President said that the United States Boundary Commissioner had such instructions. He observed that Commissioner Friedkin was one of the most competent persons he had working for him and knew he would do a good job. He said he could not accept the legal viewpoint, which Diaz Ordaz had outlined, but that Diaz Ordaz could be assured that the United States would do the right thing.

The President referred to the salinity problem on the Rio Grande, which was so injurious to farmers in the United States. Diaz Ordaz said that Mexico is ready to do what is necessary to solve this problem on the basis of the same principle he proposed for solution of the Colorado River problem.

2. *Migratory Workers (Braceros)*

Diaz Ordaz said he understood the problems of the United States and why PL–78 had not been extended.[2] But he expressed concern that the situation which existed before the agreement would recur. He said Mexico would not ask for extensions of the agreement or the hiring of Mexican workers. He wanted the United States to prevent illegal entries and improper recruiting activities. He wanted to be assured that any Mexicans brought in on private contracts were properly treated.

The President said that both Mexican and United States labor unions had opposed PL–78. The Secretary of Labor was making a concerted effort to find workers in the United States. If this effort did not prove successful, then he thought the United States and Mexico should enter into a new agreement. He urged that such an agreement be simple and avoid the bureaucratic red tape which plagued the existing program.

At 11:45 a.m. the meeting ended and the President and President-elect departed for a tour of the Ranch.

---

[2] See footnote 4, Document 346.

---

353.   Memorandum From the President's Special Assistant for National Security Affairs (Bundy) to President Johnson[1]

Washington, March 12, 1965.

SUBJECT

Salinity Problem with Mexico

We agreed in late January on the text of a proposed five-year agreement with Mexico in an effort to reach a practical solution to the salinity problem. We have been checking it out since then with domestic interests to make certain it is acceptable before signature. The

---

[1] Source: Johnson Library, National Security File, Memos to the President, McGeorge Bundy, Vol. IX. No classification marking.

text of the agreement, in the form of a Boundary Commission Minute, is attached.[2]

We have also worked out a five-year truce under which both countries agree to negotiate remaining differences instead of going to the World Court. The chief remaining difference is Mexico's claim for damages which State is thinking of disposing of in a loan to help rehabilitate the Mexicali Valley.

State and Interior are working on a memorandum of understanding between them to define the responsibility of each agency for carrying out the proposed agreement.

Udall and Mann consider the proposed settlement as better than generally thought possible and recommend we accept it.

The seven Colorado Basin States were consulted at a meeting at Phoenix on January 26–27. The seven Governors have now written you accepting the agreement with some reservation, expressing their appreciation for the close consultation with them, and commending the negotiators. Interior believes it has satisfied the Governors on their reservations. It is recommended you reply in general terms to the Governors and leave the technical points for Secretary Udall to handle.

Senators Hayden and Anderson and Congressman Aspinall have accepted the agreement. However, Senator Hayden made his approval subject to the condition that you would send up a budget amendment for FY 1966 requesting the $2.2 million needed to complete the $5 million in works called for in the agreement (Interior has $2.8 million), and $3 million to start a $7 million 17-well ground water recovery project in the Yuma area.

Interior recommends that you accept Hayden's conditions. Budget concurs, but recommends that Hayden be informed that the 94-well ground water recovery program in the Yuma area, of which the 17-well project is a part, poses difficult problems in our relations with Mexico, which must be studied thoroughly. The Administration's commitment is, therefore, limited to the 17 wells. Mexico has protested the 94-well ground water recovery program, but State interposes no objections to the 17 wells. Budget will send separately the proposed budget amendment for your signature and transmission to the Congress.

We considered the possibility of a ceremony in connection with the signing of the agreement. Mexico is opposed. They regard the agreement as a hard bargain, and thus difficult to sell politically in Mexico. Simultaneous Presidential announcements of the settlement are planned at the time of signing. I will recommend the draft of such a statement after it has been worked out with Mexico.

---

[2] Attached but not printed.

Recommendations:[3]

1. That you sign the attached letters[4] to the Governors of the Basin States.

2. That you approve the Budget amendment.

3. That you authorize the signature of the proposed agreement with Mexico.

McG.B.

---

[3] The President approved all three recommendations. The agreement on the salinity of the lower Colorado River was signed on March 22. The text of the agreement, a statement by President Johnson and a joint State–Interior announcement are in Department of State *Bulletin,* April 12, 1965, pp. 555–557.

[4] Not attached.

---

354. Memorandum From the President's Special Assistant for National Security Affairs (Bundy) to Secretary of State Rusk and Secretary of the Interior Udall[1]

Washington, April 6, 1965.

The President has approved the proposed agreement with Mexico, which the Departments of State and Interior recommended, as the best attainable measures we could take now to settle the salinity problem. The Wellton–Mohawk problem is a special case, but it would be desirable to look at projected future operations on the Colorado River so that we will avoid the possibility of a future dispute with Mexico.

We should consider whether projected future operations will serve the basic interests of the United States. The basic interests here involved are, of course, protection of the water rights of the United States and the maintenance of friendly relations with our nearest southern neighbor. The example of excellent relations with Mexico also has a bearing on our world posture.

I know that some of the Basin States continue to be dissatisfied with the 1944 Water Treaty itself and believe that our policy should

---

[1] Source: Johnson Library, National Security File, Country File, Mexico, Vol. I, Cables, 12/63–12/65. Confidential.

be conditioned by the fact that Mexico was guaranteed a quantity of water larger than it should have been given. I should think our best interests are served by carrying out in good faith the bargain made in 1944. I gather that the Mexican response to comments that the 1944 Treaty was a bad bargain for the United States has been that Mexico made bad bargains in 1848 and 1853.

One of the conclusions that the two Departments have apparently reached, after more than three years of work on the Wellton–Mohawk problem, is that the United States has an obligation to act reasonably in conducting irrigation in the United States. In technical terms, this translates itself into a requirement that U.S. irrigation districts maintain approximate salt balance. This fairly well defines our legal view of the 1944 Water Treaty.

On the other hand, Mexico has from the first held to the view that the Treaty divided the waters of the Colorado and that it was, therefore, entitled to the same treatment as users in the United States. In short, it asserts that the United States has no right to deliver all of the drainage water to Mexico, but should divide it proportionally among all the users on the lower Colorado.

If, as is apparently generally expected, the overall quality of water in the lower Colorado continues to deteriorate, it would be to Mexico's interest to test its legal theory. On the other hand, it is in our interest to avoid such a test. But if we are to do so, we need complete data on projected developments as the basis for developing an agreed strategy.

The Department of the Interior should take the leadership in developing data on the following points and any others that the two Departments consider appropriate. I would hope we could have the study before the end of the year. The study should assume that the Department of the Interior will in the course of the next few years be able to limit flows to Mexico to its guaranteed annual allotment of 1,500,000 acre feet:

1. What will the quality of water delivered to Mexico be each year over the next twenty years? This should consider existing projects, those contemplated in the Pacific Southwest Water Plan, and others that might be developed over the next twenty years.

2. What will the quality of water delivered to U.S. irrigation projects below Imperial Dam be overall and by project for these same years?

3. What quantity and percentage of Mexico's guaranteed annual amount will be drainage return flow for these same years?

4. What U.S. irrigation districts in the lower Colorado River now use drainage return flow for irrigation? Is it contemplated

that these amounts will increase or decrease over the next twenty
years?[2]

Mcgeorge Bundy

---

[2] The proposed study has not been found. In a memorandum to Rusk, March 22,
1966, Sayre complained: "The Interior Department ought to have been able to furnish
us before now the results of studies on the salinity of water to be delivered to Mexico
that the White House requested in April 1965." (National Archives and Records Administration, RG 59, Central Files 1964–66, POL 33–1 MEX–US)

---

355. Memorandum From the President's Special Assistant for National Security Affairs (Bundy) to President Johnson[1]

Washington, December 21, 1965, 2 p.m.

SUBJECT

Lower Rio Grande Salinity Problem

The attached memo from State (Tab B)[2] explains that the US-
Mexico Boundary and Water Commission (IBWC) has come up with a
recommendation for solving the lower Rio Grande salinity problem. The
solution involves building a canal in Mexico to take the saline drainage
to the Gulf of Mexico. Cost of construction and of operation and maintenance (estimated $1.2 million) would be shared on an equal basis. State
proposes that announcement of the IBWC recommendation be in the
form of a joint press release by you and President Diaz Ordaz.

The IBWC recommendation has been staffed out. Bureau of the
Budget is on board. Congressman de la Garza wants to introduce the
enabling legislation. Senator Yarborough has been filled in and supports the project. The local Texas farmers, needless to say, are all for it.
Interior is not directly involved, but has been informed.

The project is a good one. It is beneficial to farmers on both sides
of the border. It is in line with your general effort to solve boundary
problems with Mexico. At a time when other Latin American countries
are denouncing—and shooting—each other over border disputes, it is

---

[1] Source: Johnson Library, National Security File, Country File, Mexico, Vol. I,
Memos, 12/63–12/65. No classification marking.
[2] Tab B is a memorandum from Read to Bundy, December 15; attached but not
printed.

a good example of how states with a common border can cooperate to mutual advantage. From a domestic and foreign standpoint, I think it would be advantageous for you to be associated personally with it.

I, therefore, recommend that you authorize us to negotiate with the Mexicans for a joint Presidential announcement along the lines of Tab A.[3] If you authorize the negotiations, we will, of course, check the text worked out with the Mexicans with you before giving it to Bill Moyers for release.

Mcg.B.

Authorize negotiations for a Presidential announcement[4]

Prefer not making it a Presidential announcement

---

[3] Attached but not printed.

[4] The President checked this option. For text of the press statement released by the White House on December 30, see Department of State *Bulletin*, January 24, 1966, p. 118. On February 10, 1967, the White House announced that the United States and Mexico had approved an agreement to solve the salinity problem of the Rio Grande. (Ibid., March 13, 1967, pp. 428–429; and *Public Papers of the Presidents of the United States: Lyndon B. Johnson, 1967*, Book I, p. 175)

---

356.   Memorandum of Conversation[1]

Mexico City, April 14, 1966.

SUBJECT

    Conversation between Presidents Johnson and Diaz Ordaz, Los Pinos, Mexico City

PARTICIPANTS

    President Lyndon B. Johnson, United States
    President Gustavo Diaz Ordaz, Mexico

---

[1] Source: Johnson Library, National Security File, Country File, Mexico, Vol. II, 1/66–2/67. Confidential. Drafted by Barnes on April 27 and approved by Walt Rostow on June 2. The meeting was held at Los Pinos on the "evening of April 14 and morning of April 15." According to the President's Daily Diary, Johnson met Díaz Ordaz in a private session on April 14 (9:30–10:15 p.m.); the two men met again the next morning (9:20–10:37 a.m.) with their key advisers. (Johnson Library) President Johnson was in Mexico City for an informal visit, including a ceremony to dedicate a statue of Abraham Lincoln. For his remarks at the dedication and other occasions during the visit, see *Public Papers of the Presidents of the United States: Lyndon B. Johnson, 1966*, Book I, pp. 416–422.

Cotton

President Diaz Ordaz said that Mexico had suffered considerable losses because of a drop in cotton prices. He complained that the Soviet Union was depressing the international cotton market by buying and then reselling cotton for export at low prices. He said that the United States, and Mexico, plus the other cotton-producing Latin American countries, supplied over half of the world market, and were therefore in a good position to affect world prices. He expressed his appreciation for the position adopted by the U.S., which could easily dump cotton, thereby getting rid of its surpluses and in the process ruining the economies of many countries, including Mexico. This, he said, would be like winning all of the chips in a poker game: the game would be over. He was encouraged by the establishment of the International Cotton Institute, headed by former Mexican Agriculture Secretary Rodriguez Adame, but believed that a world agreement would be useful to help in the stabilization of prices.

President Johnson replied that he was aware of the importance of cotton to so many countries, and that the U.S. would continue to study possible means of stabilizing prices. He said that an overly high price for cotton might lead to a loss of markets, because of competition by synthetic fibers.

Sulphur

President Diaz Ordaz said that the Pan American Sulphur Company and the Mexican Government differed over the amount of sulphur reserves in Mexico, and that the company estimated the reserves as being higher than did the Mexicans. This was an important difference of opinion, since the reserve estimates had a direct bearing on the amount of sulphur that Mexico would allow the company to export. President Johnson suggested a compromise between the two figures, and requested Mexico to do everything it could to permit increased exports to the U.S., to alleviate the strong pressures for an increase in sulphur prices in the U.S., which in turn contributed to inflationary trends. President Diaz Ordaz said that he would look into the matter, and that Mexico would do anything it could in this direction. He wanted to point out that the above-mentioned company had maligned Mexico in many other countries, saying that Mexico was not living up to its agreements, while the truth was that the company had not been able to export its allocated quota the previous year.

Cultural Exchange

President Johnson recalled that when he was a Senator, he had visited the then President-elect of Mexico, López Mateos, in Acapulco, and that at that time there were a number of issues pending between the two countries: The Chamizal, Colorado River salinity, for example.

Now, all of those problems had been settled, and he thought that this was a propitious time to launch a joint and positive effort, taking advantage of the absence of major differences. He suggested that the two Presidents each appoint a panel of imaginative men, to come up with suggestions for an exchange of persons; not of students or teachers, but in different fields. He proposed, for example, that the U.S. might send Secretary Freeman to advise Mexico on agricultural problems, much in the same line as the Secretary's trip to Vietnam. He also mentioned the possibility of Under Secretary Mann going to Mexico to consult with the Government on economic problems, including the cotton matter. He suggested that Mexico might send representative artists to tour the U.S., particularly in areas with a heavy concentration of Mexican-Americans. As an example, he mentioned Cantinflas.[2] He also said that thought might be given to having Mexico send persons to provide leadership to Mexican-American citizens in the U.S.

President Diaz Ordaz said that he thought that this proposal was a good one. Mexico had a number of artists it could send to the U.S. He would exclude painters, since in Mexico, because of a certain snobbish approach, many painters were Communists, and he would not want to send them to the U.S.

Future Visits

President Johnson suggested that the two Presidents and their families might meet at Big Bend National Park, and in the adjoining Mexican forest area, to emphasize recreation and conservation. President Diaz Ordaz said that he was all in favor of this, and suggested that the two Presidents also visit the Amistad Dam nearby. His only concern, a minor one, was that he would have to obtain permission from the Mexican Congress to cross the border, and he did not want to have to go to his legislature too often for this purpose. President Johnson said that this problem could be obviated by having the two Presidents meet on the Mexican side of the border.

Mexican Economy

Both Presidents agreed that the Mexican economy was doing very well; President Diaz Ordaz said that his country had reached the "take-off" point. They both also agreed that Mexico should increase its efforts to assist less developed countries, particularly in Central and South America. President Diaz Ordaz said that he intended to follow this course. It had been amusing, he said, during his recent visit to Central America, to see how Mexico is considered there, and especially in Guatemala, as the "Colossus of the North." He said that the best Am-

---

[2] "Cantinflas" was the stage name of the Mexican comedian Mario Moreno.

bassadors Mexico had in these countries were Central Americans who had studied in Mexico, many of whom had married Mexican girls. There were large numbers of Central Americans studying in Mexican institutions at the present time.

In-bond Warehouses

President Diaz Ordaz said that he was interested in settling the problem of in-bond warehouses on the border, since sales from these warehouses produced no revenue to either government. President Johnson said that he agreed that the matter should be studied.

Ex-Im Loan to PEMEX

President Diaz Ordaz effusively expressed his delight that we have broken a long taboo against Exim Bank loans to nationalized oil companies. He stated that Mexico probably could have obtained the loan elsewhere but was happy that our policy has changed. He also referred to the unhappiness that arose in the United States over the credit Mexico obtained about two years ago for the purchase of Soviet drilling equipment. He said that Mexico was extremely unhappy about the Soviet equipment which is far inferior to the latest U.S. equipment and even to some equipment that Mexico has.

President Diaz Ordaz' Central American Trip

At the luncheon at Los Pinos, President Johnson asked Diaz Ordaz to tell Mrs. Johnson about his trip to Central America. President Johnson indicated that he might wish to send Mrs. Johnson on a similar trip.

Cuba, Dominican Republic and OAS

The two Presidents, in their conversation, did not mention Cuba, the Dominican Republic, or the OAS.

President Johnson mentioned the Dominican Republic briefly to Foreign Secretary Carrillo Flores stating that he had to do something when Ambassador Bennett called while the Embassy was being fired upon. He also told the Foreign Secretary that Castro had told the British Ambassador in Havana that the Soviets had let Cuba down badly on two occasions, once over missiles and once over the Dominican Republic. The Foreign Secretary made no comment.[3]

---

[3] For text of the joint statement issued following discussions with Díaz Ordaz, see *Public Papers of the Presidents of the United States: Lyndon B. Johnson, 1966,* Book I, pp. 422–424.

357. Memorandum From the Under Secretary of State for Economic Affairs (Mann) to President Johnson[1]

Washington, August 30, 1966, 12:45 p.m.

Mr. President:

Carlos Trouyet and others in the Mexican private sector recently bought a number of Mexican cotton textile mills and invested capital in modernizing them. The pressure on Diaz Ordaz is almost certain to come principally from these owners. Measured in terms of millions of square yards, Mexican cotton textile exports to the U.S. have risen from virtually zero some 3 or 4 years ago to an estimated level of perhaps 60 to 70 million in 1966.

An increase of this magnitude in Mexico's traditional exports of cotton textiles to our market cannot continue because (a) this would be unfair to many other cotton textile exporting countries which, at our insistence, have agreed on voluntary restraints, and (b) because the long-term cotton textile agreement negotiated some years ago would unravel. The pressure in Congress for protective import quotas on cotton textiles would then be irresistible.

I therefore believe the U.S. has no alternative but to make clear to Mexico that it is necessary to work out with them a ceiling on the level of their cotton textile exports to this market and that, failing in this, we will have to impose the quota that the world agreement contemplates. This ceiling should be a generous one, but in any event Mexico will come out with a much higher level of exports than they are entitled to from an historic point of view.

The tactic is important. I suggest that Walt Rostow and Linc Gordon call in Margain and explain that you really had no choice in this matter for the reasons stated in the preceding paragraph, and you are under great pressure not only from the industry but from all the interested departments, as well as other cotton exporting countries. Walt and Linc should explain to the Ambassador that under the long-term agreement which Mexico is party to, notice is required, and that this notice will have to be given. They should add that this would still allow 60 days to negotiate a satisfactory level, and they should suggest that the Mexicans send their best team to Washington to talk about this at their earliest convenience. The U.S. negotiating team should be

---

[1] Source: Johnson Library, National Security File, Memos to the President, Walt W. Rostow, Vol. 11. No classification marking. Rostow forwarded the memorandum as an attachment to an August 30 note in which he recommended approval of "Tom's suggested strategy."

headed by Linc Gordon if he is here, and if not, by Bob Sayre. Commerce and the other interested departments should of course participate. The negotiations conducted through Freeman thus far have not prospered and, in my judgment, it is not likely that they will as long as we negotiate through the Embassy in Mexico City.

Some two or three days following this meeting, a more formal notice should be given the Mexican Embassy at working levels and in the most abbreviated and polite form possible. The lawyers may say that this must be done in writing. If so, this is O.K. provided care is taken with the text.

There will be some repercussions in Mexico simply because all Mexican Governments must continually demonstrate to their people that they are negotiating tough with the U.S. There may be some adverse publicity. However, it would be easy to overestimate the significance of any initial official government reaction to the conversation and notice, since the Mexicans know as well as we do that their whole economy depends on our cooperation. They will have to find a way to adjust just as soon as they are convinced that there is no more give in the U.S. position.[2]

Tom Mann[3]

---

[2] The President approved these recommendations at the Tuesday luncheon on August 30. (Memorandum from Rostow to the President, August 30; ibid.) According to the President's Daily Diary, luncheon participants included Rusk, McNamara, Moyers, and Rostow. (Johnson Library) No substantive record of the meeting has been found.

[3] Printed from a copy that bears this typed signature.

---

358. Memorandum From the President's Special Assistant (Rostow) to President Johnson[1]

Washington, September 29, 1966.

SUBJECT

Status Report on Your April 15 Agreements with President Diaz Ordaz

---

[1] Source: Johnson Library, National Security File, Memos to the President, Walt W. Rostow, Vol. 13. Confidential. A copy was sent to Moyers.

Secretary Rusk and Linc Gordon will be in Mexico this weekend for the inauguration of the new Mexican Foreign Office Building.[2]

I thought you would like to know where we stand on implementation of the decisions you reached with President Diaz Ordaz last April 15, some of which will be discussed by the Secretary and Linc during the visit.

Measures to Expand Border Trade

Ambassador Turkel[3] will make this study. He has for the past several weeks been briefing himself on a part-time basis. Next Monday, October 3, he starts full-time work on the project. Professor James Gander will be working with him. Professor Gander has developed a bibliography and collected information on border trade which will serve as the starting point for the project. After briefings and research in Washington, Ambassador Turkel will move his base to El Paso. He plans to have his study completed in about three months. The Mexicans have also named their man.

Consultation on Cotton

Secretary Freeman visited Mexico City June 6–7. He had a full and frank exchange of views with President Diaz Ordaz and other high officials on the cotton pricing problem. He reassured the Mexicans that the U.S. would: (1) not dump cotton, (2) not sell cotton below 22 cents a pound for the marketing year 1966–67, and (3) continue to support Mexico on an international cotton commodity agreement. This trip fulfilled your commitment to the Mexican President.

Since then, the problem of limiting cotton textile imports from Mexico has arisen with which you are familiar. Discussions with the Mexicans continue. Their latest response indicates movement in the direction of a negotiated settlement.

Expeditious Transfer of Chamizal

Commissioner Friedkin is close to completing acquisition of lands now in private hands to be transferred to Mexico under the Chamizal settlement. Federal agencies are also letting bids for the relocation of public utilities now on those lands. Once these tasks are completed, we will be in a position to set a date for the formal transfer. We would like to hold the ceremony on September 25, 1967. This is the anniversary

---

[2] Rusk was in Mexico City, September 30–October 1. Memoranda of his conversation with Díaz Ordaz on September 30 are in the National Archives and Records Administration, RG 59, ARA/MEX Files: Lot 69 D 377, POL 7 Visit—Secretary Rusk.

[3] Ambassador Harry Turkel had been appointed "to study problems and make recommendations regarding facilitating trade in the U.S.-Mexican border area." (Department of State *Bulletin,* January 9, 1967, pp. 70–71)

of your meeting with President Lopez Mateos in 1964 for the symbolic transfer. It also gives us time to get the Chamizal Memorial Park and Memorial Highway projects underway so that their dedication can be made part of the ceremony. We have informed the Mexicans of this time-table.

The House has passed a bill authorizing 100% federal financing of the Chamizal Memorial Highway. The Senate Foreign Relations Committee has reported out a bill requiring the State of Texas to pick up 50% of the tab. Senator Yarborough will try to have this amount reduced to 10% when the bill goes to conference.[4]

Commission to Raise Living Standards in Border Communities

State and OEO have developed a comprehensive plan for establishing the Joint Commission, including negotiations with the Mexicans (Stage I), an initial study of economic and social problems of the border communities (Stage II), and specific proposals for administering and financing our part of the program likely to emerge from the study (Stage III). You have authorized action on Stages I and II. State reviewed the proposals with the House and Senate Latin American Subcommittee and ran into no significant problems. Secretary Rusk and Linc Gordon will be discussing them with the Mexicans this weekend. On his return next week, Linc will call Ambassador Telles to express your wish that he take the chairmanship of the U.S. Section of the Commission.

Creation of Lincoln–Juarez Scholarship Funds

State has worked out a plan for funding our part of the program and selecting the scholars. It has also prepared detailed proposals for the creation of a Joint Commission to supervise the operations of the two funds and has asked Ambassador Freeman to discuss them with the Mexicans. Secretary Rusk and Linc will be following up on this matter.

Increase in Cultural Exchange

Charlie Frankel[5] has done an excellent job of stepping up the flow of U.S. cultural programs to Mexico. I sent you his first report last May. At Tab A[6] is his most recent account of what he has done. Getting the Mexicans to reciprocate looms as a problem.

---

[4] The final version of the bill (PL 89–795), which was signed into law on November 8, placed a ceiling of $8 million on the federal contribution to the Chamizal highway. (80 Stat. 1477)

[5] Assistant Secretary of State for Educational and Cultural Affairs.

[6] Attached but not printed.

Rio Colorado Salinity

The Mexicans have been concerned that (1) our ground water recovery program on the lower Colorado River would reduce the underground water flows to Mexico and (2) our substituting these recovered waters for surface waters in the river water delivered to them under the 1944 Water Treaty would leave Mexico with poor quality water.

State and Interior have reached agreement on the nature of the assurances to be given to Mexico on these points. Secretary Udall is going to Mexico in November to present the assurances.

This summer Mexico asked us for additional water to cover an acute shortage. Despite our tight situation, Interior agreed to lend them 40,535 acre feet to be repaid over a period of time depending on the adequacy of our runoffs next year.

Gulf of California Nuclear Desalinization Plant

The Joint Study Group is continuing its pre-feasibilities studies. The pace of their work has moved more slowly than we would like. Our members have virtually completed their assignments. But the Mexicans have not kept pace. At their request, a meeting of the Group scheduled for October has been postponed to January, or later.

W. W. Rostow[7]

---

[7] Printed from a copy that bears this typed signature.

---

359.   Memorandum From the President's Special Assistant (Rostow) to President Johnson[1]

Washington, October 24, 1967.

SUBJECT

Ford's Difficulties in Mexico

The attached memorandum from Tony Solomon[2] describes a serious problem the Ford Motor Company is having with its operations in

---

[1] Source: Johnson Library, National Security File, Country File, Mexico, Diaz Ordaz Visit, Background and Misc., 10/26–28/67. Confidential.

[2] Attached but not printed.

Mexico. He suggests that you mention the matter to President Diaz Ordaz.

The difficulty in a nutshell is this:

Ford built a plant in Mexico City to produce sophisticated assembly-line production tools. It exports about $5 million worth of these per year. Part of the deal was that in exchange for this investment the Mexicans would add 5000 units to Ford's basic quota of automobiles (20,000) produced in its car plant. The tool plant is a marginal operation. The car plant is profitable only with the additional quota.

The Mexicans, in a move to force Ford to allow Mexican capital to buy into the company, (i.e., Mexicanization program), has told Ford that it can no longer have its extra quota of cars. Ford has gained a temporary reprieve, but says that it will close down its tool plant operation unless it is allowed to retain its additional quota.

We feel that Ford is being unfairly treated. They built the tool plant in the understanding that they could produce more cars. This understanding is being withdrawn. We think it is bad for Mexico and our whole Alliance for Progress effort to have private enterprise in an attractive venture as tool-making squeezed out.

Consequently, Tony suggests that you propose to President Diaz Ordaz that he appoint someone from his personal staff to go into the problem quietly with your representative.[3] As Tony notes, it would not be productive to have Secretary Rusk raise this with Carrillo Flores, since he would have to turn it over to his Cabinet colleague who is behind the squeeze.

I concur in Tony's suggestion.

Walt

I'll make the proposal[4]

Prefer not to

See me

---

[3] Rostow added the following suggestion: "For example, Tony Solomon."

[4] This option is checked. According to a handwritten note on the memorandum, the President told Jim Jones: "Be sure I'm reminded of this." No evidence has been found that Johnson raised the issue with Díaz Ordaz during the state visit.

360. Editorial Note

On October 26, 1967, President Díaz Ordaz arrived in Washington for a 3-day state visit to the United States. Following the ceremonies, Díaz Ordaz met President Johnson for a broad discussion of U.S.-Mexican relations. The official memoranda of conversation record the following topics: Hemisfair, Chamizal, Vietnam, Latin American Common Market, Mexican Temporary Workers, U.S.-Mexican Border Development Commission, Friendship Parks, Screwworm Barrier, Possible Trade Restrictions, Latin American Nuclear Free Zone, Nuclear Desalinization Plant, and Mexican Scientific Development. (Johnson Library, National Security File, Country File, Mexico, Visit of President Diaz Ordaz, Chamizal Settlement, 10/26–28/67) On October 27 Johnson and Díaz Ordaz met for another discussion, addressing such issues as Peru, Brazil, and Military Equipment for Mexico. (National Archives and Records Administration, RG 59, Central Files 1967–69, POL 7 MEX) The two Presidents then attended a ceremony in the Rose Garden, where Secretary of State Rusk and Foreign Minister Carrillo Flores signed the formal agreement legalizing the transfer of Chamizal to Mexico. On October 28 the state visit concluded with a joint ceremony at El Paso and Ciudad Juárez to mark the Chamizal settlement. For remarks made by Johnson and Díaz Ordaz during the trip, see *Public Papers of the Presidents of the United States: Lyndon B. Johnson, 1967,* Book II, pages 945–962; and Department of State *Bulletin,* November 20, 1967, pages 673–685. Documentation on the visit is also in the Johnson Library, National Security File, Country File, Mexico, Visit of President Diaz Ordaz; and National Archives and Records Administration, RG 59, Official Visit Chronologies, 1967: Lot 68 D 475, V–49A and V–49B.

361. Information Memorandum From the President's Special Assistant (Rostow) to President Johnson[1]

Washington, March 9, 1968.

SUBJECT

Mexican Border Restrictions

---

[1] Source: Johnson Library, National Security File, Country File, Mexico, Vol. IV, 1/68–10/68. Confidential.

Prior to Christmas and Washington's birthday the Mexican Government instituted tough customs inspection against returning Mexican nationals resident outside the border zone travelling overland from shopping trips to Texas border cities. US merchants, particularly in Laredo, felt the pinch and made loud complaints at State, here and on the Hill. On both occasions strong representations to the Mexican Ambassador and the Foreign Office brought relaxation of the enforcement.

While we protested the Mexican action, our grounds were not strong because the Mexican Government was simply enforcing customs regulations on the books—even though not always applied. Mexico has a peculiar customs system under which nationals returning by air can bring back a long list of articles duty free, while overland returnees are restricted to just a few items. We understand the severe enforcement measures at Christmas and Washington's birthday were due to pressure of Monterrey merchants who anticipated heavy purchases in US border cities by Mexicans living in the interior.

The issue of eliminating the discrepancy of exemptions between air travellers and overland travellers was raised in the US–Mexico Trade Committee meeting last December. The Embassy has also taken it up with the Foreign Office. In view of the recent difficulty, State instructed Ambassador Freeman on March 1 to press for a resolution of the problem.[2] He is to point out that purchases along the border by our respective tourists is a two-way street. For years we have waived the Treasury requirement that US tourists must remain at least 48 hours outside the US before taking advantage of the duty-free exemptions for purchases abroad. In the new proposals governing US tourism, Mexico has a privileged position. We expect the Mexicans to reciprocate.

Specifically, Freeman is to seek:

—simplification and clarification of customs regulations.
—elimination of differences between air and overland travellers, hopefully making the overland treatment conform to the more liberal air treatment.
—assurances of consistent enforcement during holiday and non-holiday periods.

I will keep you posted on how these talks progress.[3]

Walt

---

[2] In telegram 123164 to Mexico City. (National Archives and Records Administration, RG 59, Central Files 1967–69, FT 23 MEX)

[3] An initial report on the Embassy's efforts is in telegram 3868 from Mexico City, March 15. (Ibid.)

362.   Information Memorandum From the Assistant Secretary of State for Inter-American Affairs (Oliver) to Secretary of State Rusk[1]

Washington, July 31, 1968.

SUBJECT

Student Disturbances in Mexico

After five days, the worst student disturbances in Mexico City in 20 years appeared to be abating on July 31 as federal troops were withdrawn from the city. The demonstrations and rioting primarily involved secondary students, protesting police brutality and grievances against the bus companies, who were subsequently incited by communist and pro-Castro groups. Police sources have reported four students dead, and over 200 persons injured.

When student demonstrators overwhelming riot police in the center of the city on July 29, army troops had to be called in to restore order and to expel students from the secondary schools they had occupied.

Following the initial disorders July 26 the Government arrested Communist Party (PCM) leaders and raised a communist paper. The press continues to stress communist and foreign involvement and the Government has indicated its intention to deport large numbers of foreigners including known communists even if they were not involved in the disorders. The daughter of U.S. folksinger Pete Seeger and one other American are among those who were arrested.

Embassy Mexico reports that while there is broad sympathy among students for the demonstrators and against police, there is little popular support, and even some resentment of the disruption caused.

The GOM may have used the disorders as a pretext to remove from circulation those communist leaders who it suspected might have led disturbances during the Olympics in October.

President Diaz Ordaz has not cut short a trip in the provinces in an apparent effort to minimize the importance of the riots. Protection of our Embassy has been excellent, and the American School, closed July 30 because of a bomb scare, reopened July 31, as did the National University.

---

[1] Source: National Archives and Records Administration, RG 59, Central Files 1967–69, POL 23–8 MEX. Confidential. Drafted by Maxwell Chaplin (ARA/MEX). A notation on the memorandum indicates that Rusk saw it.

The student grievances about police brutality, bus company failure to indemnify injured students and Government violation of university "autonomy" remain. When news of the four student deaths (currently suppressed) becomes public, further disorders are likely, though current estimates are that the worst of the violence has run its course.

363. Information Memorandum From the Assistant Secretary of State for Inter-American Affairs (Oliver) to Secretary of State Rusk[1]

Washington, September 20, 1968.

SUBJECT

Mexico—Prospects following Occupation of the National University

The Mexican Government, in occupying the National University, has now committed itself to coercion as its method of ending the two-month long student disorders. The next week should reveal whether or not the majority of students have the will to continue their opposition in the face of the Government's declared policy.

At this point, we see the following as likely developments flowing from the GOM decision:

1. The GOM will continue to take a hard line against the students and will occupy other educational facilities as necessary.

2. The Olympic Games will be held, although marred by sporadic violence.

3. Students are not likely to attract significant support from other important sectors and will not threaten the stability of the Government in the short run.

4. The prestige of Diaz Ordaz' regime has been damaged both because of its initial vacillation in handling the students and because of its violation of university autonomy.

---

[1] Source: National Archives and Records Administration, RG 59, Central Files 1967–69, POL 23–8 MEX. Confidential. Drafted by Michael Yohn and Maxwell Chaplin. A notation on the memorandum indicates that Rusk saw it.

364. Information Memorandum From the Assistant Secretary of State for Inter-American Affairs (Oliver) to Acting Secretary of State Katzenbach[1]

Washington, October 3, 1968.

SUBJECT

Mexican Situation

Last night's serious violence in Mexico City seems to have been the result of provocation by student extremists and gross over-reaction by the security forces. We see its significance as follows:

1. It was a sharp blow to President Diaz Ordaz and his Government, both because of the excessive force used and because it underscores the GOM failure, after 11 weeks, to eliminate violence.

2. It reopens the question of whether the Olympics can be held. An International Olympic Committee decision to postpone, or cancel, the games would have serious political consequences for the Diaz Ordaz regime.

Issues for U.S.

The continuing violence raises two concerns for the U.S.: 1) the safety of U.S. athletes and visitors to the games and 2) U.S. participation in scientific and cultural activities associated with the Olympics.

Thus far, the violence has been contained in certain areas of the city, has not been directed against the U.S., and has not threatened any visitors exercising reasonable caution. Therefore we do not feel a warning to our citizens is warranted at this time.

Our participation in the scientific and cultural activities is still going forward as planned, with the exception of the space and nuclear energy exhibits, whose installation at university sites has been delayed at GOM request.

We believe it important to avoid any indication that we lack confidence in the GOM's ability to control the situation. Accordingly, in responding to press questions today the Department's spokesman said that we believe the GOM will provide security to visitors and that we are not warning against visiting Mexico City during the Olympics.

---

[1] Source: National Archives and Records Administration, RG 59, Central Files 1967–69, POL 23–8 MEX. Confidential. Drafted by Michael Yohn.

365. Information Memorandum From the President's Special Assistant (Rostow) to President Johnson[1]

Washington, October 5, 1968.

SUBJECT

Mexican Riots—Extent of Communist Involvement

You asked about the extent to which the Cuban Communists or other foreign groups were involved in the Mexican riots this week.

The CIA analysis attached (Tab A)[2] concludes that the student demonstrations were sparked by domestic politics, not masterminded by Cubans or Soviets. Their primary role was restricted to supplying some money to student groups.

CIA believes the weapons employed by the students could have been obtained locally. Although they did not start the trouble, Mexican Communists, Trotskyists, and Castroites all capitalized on the disorders once they began and took active parts.

An FBI report (Tab B)[3] asserts that a Trotskyist group initiated the sniper fire at the police and army from prepared positions in various apartment buildings, and they were responsible for touching off the bloodshed. This so-called "Olympia Brigade" reportedly obtained automatic weapons from Cuban and Guatemalan extremist organizations and plans acts of sabotage during the Olympic games.

Walt

P.S. Bruno Pagliai called when he was in Washington for the Bank and Fund meetings. He had talked with President Diaz Ordaz. Diaz Ordaz vows that he will establish law and order and see the Olympics through. Diaz Ordaz says that the riots were carefully planned. A good many people came into the country. The guns used were new and had their numbers filed off. The Castro and Chinese Communist groups were at the center of the effort. The Soviet Communists had to come along to avoid the charge of being chicken.

Walt

---

[1] Source: Johnson Library, National Security File, Country File, Mexico, Vol. IV, 1/68–10/68. Secret. A notation on the memorandum indicates that the President saw it.

[2] Tab A is a memorandum prepared by CIA, October 5; attached but not printed.

[3] Tab B is a cable from FBI Director Hoover to the President, et al., October 5; attached but not printed.

366.   Memorandum From Secretary of State Rusk to President Johnson[1]

Washington, December 11, 1968.

SUBJECT

Your Meeting with President Gustavo Diaz Ordaz, Friday, December 13, 1968

The Visit

You last saw President Diaz Ordaz when he made a State Visit to the United States in October, 1967. At that time, you visited the Chamizal site and participated in a ceremony at the Mexican Chamizal Monument. This latest visit will be the final step in the historic Chamizal settlement—to inaugurate the President Adolfo Lopez Mateos Channel which will carry that portion of the Rio Grande which was relocated as a result of the Agreement. It will be your sixth meeting with President Diaz Ordaz and will give you the opportunity to stress the cordial relations which exist between our countries.

Mexico Today

The student conflict which erupted July 15 is drawing to an end. The Student Strike Committee has called for a return to classes and is being heeded by increasing numbers of students. The threat of violence has largely passed, although we expect the students will continue to pressure the Government for certain legal reforms and for the replacement of several unpopular police officials. The prolonged nature of the conflict, and the fact that the Government of Mexico resorted to heavy repression on several occasions, have somewhat marred President Diaz Ordaz' image. The President, however, remains in firm control of his Government and continues to enjoy broad support throughout Mexico. For the coming year he will give much of his attention to the decision on a candidate to succeed him in 1970. There are no clear favorites at this point.

Mexico's economic situation continues to be relatively favorable with real GNP growth averaging 3 percent per year, and a rate of inflation within acceptable bounds. Mexico continues to have an excellent international credit rating. Recently, however, several soft spots have become apparent for which remedial action will probably be necessary: 1) a trend towards excessive foreign borrowing to compensate for a sharply increased current account deficit; 2) an industrial sector

---

[1] Source: National Archives and Records Administration, RG 59, Central Files 1967–69, POL 7 MEX. Confidential.

which has difficulty in competing in world markets and; 3) a poverty stricken rural sector which encompasses 50 percent of their nation's population but accounts for only 16 percent of the GNP.

The Olympics, as you know, were held with outstanding success. The Games were a source of great national pride for all Mexicans.[2]

Dean Rusk

---

[2] Attached but not printed are: talking points, a tentative schedule, a status report on matters previously discussed by the Presidents, and biographic data. According to the President's Daily Diary, the two Presidents met on the Paso del Norte Bridge in El Paso, Texas, December 13, 11:33 a.m. CST. (Johnson Library) The schedule was largely ceremonial; no memorandum of conversation has been found. For text of Johnson's prepared remarks and luncheon toast, as well as the respective efforts of Díaz Ordaz, see *Public Papers of the Presidents of the United States: Lyndon B. Johnson, 1968–69*, Book II, pp. 1186–1192.

Panama

367. Memorandum of Telephone Conversation[1]

January 10, 1964, 0151Z.

SUBJECT

Conversation between General Taylor and General O'Meara

Gen O'Meara: Some Panamanian school kids came up into the area in the afternoon and tried to plant a Panamanian flag on the Balboa High School Flag Pole. The crowd built up but the Panamanian police were able to eject them from the Zone.

Gen Taylor: When did it all start?

Gen O'Meara: It started about 4 or 4:30 in the afternoon.

Gen Taylor: Was this carefully premeditated?

Gen O'Meara: It was spontaneous to begin with. I have no indication that this was a planned operation, however, during the evening when the kids went back to the school, the mob started forming. They got beyond the competence of the Canal Zone Police to handle it. Reports we have were that some of the police were physically attacked and used their weapons to defend themselves. Apparently, there were some wounded. At 1959 (local) the Acting Governor asked me to assume Command which I have done (Fleming, by the way, is on his way to the States). We immediately moved troops into position. The initial reports we get are that wherever troops have made contact, the mob has fallen back, without any difficulty. As far as I can determine now, there are not many Panamanians in the Canal Zone though some of them who are there have set some fires. That is the situation as of this moment.[2]

Gen Taylor: Have you any estimate of the size of the mob involved?

---

[1] Source: Johnson Library, National Security File, Country File, Panama II, Part B, January–February, 1964. No classification marking. Taylor was in Washington; O'Meara was in Panama.

[2] Background information on the riot and a report by Colonel David Parker, Acting Governor of the Canal Zone, is in "Panamanian Situation Report for the President of the United States," prepared by the NSC, January 10, 4:30 a.m. (Johnson Library, National Security File, NSC Histories, Panama Crisis, 1964) An initial report on the riot was transmitted in telegram 305 from Panama City, January 10, 5:53 a.m. (Ibid.) Director of the Office of Central American and Panamanian Affairs V. Lansing Collins' account of his actions during the evening of January 9 is in a January 10 memorandum for the record. (National Archives and Records Administration, RG 59, Central Files 1964–66, POL PAN–US)

Gen OMeara: Yes, there are varying estimates. They say Fourth of July Avenue is pretty well jammed. There are some estimates of 4000 people. A lot of these reports we are getting are rather exaggerated. Some of them have established to be false, once we got our own people on the ground to look the situation over. However, it is unquestionably a sizable mob. We got an intercept from the CZ police about 20 minutes ago and orders went out to the Guardia Nationale to clear the mob from Panama without using gunfire if possible. About 5 minutes ago we got a report that the Acting Governor had talked to Diarino?[3] (spelling) and asked him if he would break up the situation. Viariano as you know is the Commandant of the Guardia Nationale. He said it was much too large for him to handle and he was not moving on it. This is certainly a contradiction of what we heard over the radio but that doesn't mean that both things are not correct. Viarino is not a terribly courageous man. Some of his underlings are much stronger.

Gen Taylor: This is a picture of considerable disorder in Panama itself and all along the borders.

Gen OMeara: Probably some buildings have been set fire to but so far as we know everything is under control. Some fires have been set within the Zone. Some automobiles have been burned along Fourth of July Avenue. These were probably Panamanian automobiles.

Gen Taylor: Meanwhile your troops are being used simply to back up the —?

Gen OMeara: No, I have taken over completely. Wherever the troops appear on the scene, the CZ police fall back and come under the command of my troop commanders. I am in complete command.

Gen Taylor: You are in command of all forces now?

Gen OMeara: I am law and order now. I am in command of the Canal Zone.

Gen Taylor: Of course, you are keeping all your people out of Panama and defending only the Canal Zone.

Gen OMeara: That is correct. We will not move out of the Canal Zone boundaries. I made an announcement over the radio telling all people to return to their quarters and anyone not living in the Zone, working in the Zone, or going to school in the Zone to leave the Zone immediately.

Gen Taylor: Is there anything we can do up here?

Gen OMeara: No, I don't think so. I think we will have the situation well in hand in less than an hour. If not, I will certainly call you back.

---

[3] Commander Bolivar Vallarino, Commandant of the National Guard.

Gen Taylor: Your estimate is that this was spontaneous and gradually building up?

Gen OMeara: We have no evidence that it is other than spontaneous. This is very hard to assess at this time. There is no evidence that this was an organized affair. Though it is possible in view of the large numbers who developed between 1800 and 2000 local.

Gen Taylor: Has this flag affair been an issue before?

Gen OMeara: Yes. It started in the Zone with the school kids when the flags were taken down in front of the school the—US flag. US school kids made a big fuss about it and after about 3 days fussing in the papers, the Governor who is arriving in Miami now, has been handling this and I have not been involved at all—this is not my business. After about 3 days of furor in the local papers the Panamanian students today finally entered into the thing and started putting some Panamanian flags on the grounds of the American High School in Balboa. This is what really triggered the affair.

Gen Taylor: This is a question of whether they have a Panamanian flag flying in front of the High School in Balboa. Was that the start of it?

Gen OMeara: The Governor has 16 sites which by the agreements between the two governments, confirmed by the two Presidents, at which the Panamanian flag will be flown with the American Flag. The US schools were not included. The issue of whether the US flag would be pulled down was raised by the US students. Several of them raised flags where they had previously been taken down. That's been the fuss over the last three days. Today the Panamanians joined in the fun.

Gen Taylor: Are these Panamanian students who are attending American Schools?

Gen OMeara: No, these are Panamanians who came from Panama.

Gen Taylor: Let me know if I can be of any help.

Gen OMeara: I believe we will have it in hand in the next hour.

Gen Taylor: Has Secretary McNamara called you?

Gen OMeara: No one has called me except you.

Gen Taylor: I will block him off then.

368. Memorandum for the Record[1]

Washington, January 10, 1964.

SUBJECT

White House Meeting on Panama, 10 January 1964

PRESENT WERE

The President

For State
Messrs. Rusk, Ball, Mann, Martin, and Collins

For Defense
Messrs. McNamara, Vance, and Ailes

For USIA
Mr. Wilson

For the White House
Messrs. Bundy, Dungan, Salinger, and Moyers

For CIA
Messrs. McCone and Helms

1. The meeting opened at 0930 without the President who joined at 1015. The initial effort was to establish the facts which had caused the riots of the night before in Panama City and the Canal Zone. Mr. Mann briefed on the flag incident and the background of the flag controversy between the United States and Panama. Casualty figures up to that point were cited and agreed on at least as far as Americans were concerned (3 United States soldiers dead, 34 Americans injured). Mr. McCone pointed out that Panamanian Communists had taken advantage of the flag incident to kick off trouble of a kind which we had been predicting ever since last summer would occur the end of December or early in January.[2] [3 *lines of source text not declassified*] (Mr. McCone repeated this briefing later when the President had joined the meeting.) The undersigned spoke of the Panamanian student-organized demonstration which was scheduled to begin at 1100 today, also of the problems which might arise depending upon where it was decided to bury the students killed in the rioting the night before. There then followed a general discussion of the tactics to be used in dealing with

---

[1] Source: Central Intelligence Agency, DCI (McCone) Files, Job 80–B01285A, Meetings with the President. Secret. Copies were sent to the DCI and the Chief of the Western Hemisphere Division.

[2] In a telephone conversation with McCone, McGeorge Bundy stated that he was "most dissatisfied" that trouble in Panama had "been brewing for 3 days and nobody was informed of it. I think that is disgraceful." McCone responded: "Yes. I didn't know a thing about it." (Telephone conversation between DCI and McGeorge Bundy, January 10, 8:45 a.m.; ibid., DCI Telephone Calls, January 1–March 30, 1964)

these problems in the OAS, the United Nations Security Council, with President Chiari, etc. Attention was given to the handling of the Senate and House leadership in connection with the problem. It was also decided to destroy cryptographic and other sensitive material in the Embassy so that it could be evacuated if this seemed desirable.

2. After the President took over the meeting, he was brought up to date on the situation in Panama and on the actions which the Secretary of State was proposing. After considerable discussion of these proposals, the following were decided upon:

A) The President would speak on the telephone with President Chiari, provided that Mr. Salinger was able to ascertain through President Chiari's Press Secretary that President Chiari would receive the telephone call.

B) Mr. Mann would head a delegation representing President Johnson to leave for Panama immediately, this group to include Messrs. Vance, Martin, and Dungan. [1 line of source text not declassified]

C) The OAS Peace Committee would be encouraged to make an immediate investigation of the situation on the ground.

D) Mr. Ball would get in immediate touch with the congressional leadership to brief them on developments.

E) The White House would issue a statement to the press announcing the Mann mission and appealing for an end to violence in Panama.

3. There was considerable attention paid to the history of difficulties with Panama over the Canal Zone. Touched on were the legal problems, financial considerations, and the traditional attitudes of the "Zonies" who have always had strong support from certain congressional committees.

RH
Deputy Director for Plans

369. Telephone Conversation Between President Johnson and
      Senator Richard Russell[1]

Washington, January 10, 1964, 11:25 a.m.

President: Dick?

Russell: Yes sir.

President: I want to talk to you—off the record a minute—about
this Panama situation. What do you think about it?

Russell: Well, Mr. President, I predicted as far back as 1956 that
something like this was going to happen. I'm not at all surprised. I
don't know all the facts of it—Harry McPherson talked to Bill Dodd
on the phone and told him something about it, but I just don't know.
'Course, I know that nobody is going to agree with this except me, but
I think this is a pretty good time to take a strong stand; people in this
country, I think, are ready for it. I may be a fool, but if I had said anything, if I were the President, I'd just tell them—I'd say this is a most
regrettable incident and it will be thoroughly investigated, and—however the Panama Canal Zone is a property of the United States, the
Canal was built with American ingenuity and blood, sweat, and sacrifices, that it was of vital necessity for the economy and defense of every
nation of this hemisphere and that under no circumstances would you
permit the threat of interruption by any subversive group that may be
undertaking to establish itself in this hemisphere. I'd give a little lick
to Castro in there. I don't know what the State Department—I suppose
they have suggested you make an apology.

President: No, but it looks like—it doesn't look good from our
standpoint.

Russell: Well, it started with a bunch of school boys, from what I
hear about it, and those people down there—they've had a chip on
their shoulders for a long time.

President: Yeah, they have and we've known it.

Russell: And we've helped it on four different occasions, and if I
made a statement, I'd point that out. We have voluntarily increased
payments to them and they have that high standard of living there proportionally—not as compared with our country, but with the other
Latin American countries—because I think that some 40–50 thousand
of 'em worked on that Canal in conjunction with the operation, and

[1] Source: Johnson Library, Recordings and Transcripts, Recording of telephone conversation between the President and Richard Russell, Tape F64.04, Side B, PNO 1. No
classification marking. This transcript was prepared in the Office of the Historian specifically for this volume.

one thing I certainly would do is—if it were me—that man—if the fellow got up in the United Nations and went to attack us on account of anything that happened about the Canal, I'd have Adlai Stevenson ask them if they're willing to go back to the status quo. People that we did the injury [to in] connection with the Canal is not the Panamanians— we brought them out of the jungles, where they were hiding, thinkin' that old Cortez was still trying to get 'em for slaves—several hundred years after Cortez' death. People we did an injustice with was Colombia—took that isthmus away from 'em and set up that puppet government down in Panama. So anything that's happened out of the Canal is more of an injury to Colombia than it is to Panama, and if I wanted to be Machiavellian about it, I'd get that Colombia delegate to get up and just raise the devil about that. It's really injurious to Colombia to even have a Panama—that's part of Colombia. I don't know how the State Department is going to handle it—of course it does look like— but it all happened on American soil. That's one thing, primarily, that you can—and it grew out of this agreement about the flag down there that started with Eisenhower, and I think Kennedy fortified it when he went down there, and that was a mistake to start with—but it was done. He insisted to the State Department that it increase payments every two years. What does the State Department think you ought to do about it?

President: We've had a meetin' of the Secretary of Defense, the Secretary of State, Cy Vance, Bundy, and the group that we normally meet with. Tom Mann says that—I talked to him a couple of times during the night,[2] and he's a pretty solid fellow, pretty strong, pretty pro-American—he says that our students went out and put up our flag in violation of our understanding. They started to put up their flag and we refused it, and we made our people take down our flag, and their rioters increased—Communists we know there, we've been having some contact with—they had a lot of Molotov cocktails and they'd planned this thing apparently just usin' the flag as an excuse. But they would have kicked it off some other way some other time, but this was ideal. Then our damned fool police started shootin' into 'em, and they say—

Russell: I hear they killed 13–14 Americans.

President: Yeah, yeah, when they started doin' that, then snipers started pickin' off American troops a little later. But we fired into our civil guard, which are our employees and Panama Canal Zone employees. They started firin' into the crowd and shot off 4500 rounds of ammunition, and—

Russell: Well, if they'd stayed on American soil, and if there's any one thing that is essential to the economic life as well as the defense

---

[2] No record of the President's telephone conversations with Mann has been found.

of every nation in the hemisphere, it is the Panama Canal, and we can't risk having it sabotaged or taken over by any Communist group. And there's no question in my mind but what Castro's—that's his chief aim there.

President: That's what he tells—that's what he tells.

Russell: And I would certainly say that in any statement I made even if I had to be rather apologetic to the Panamanians in accordance with the State Department's idea—undoubtedly was inspired—right after Castro came into power, you know, he sent a group down there and like to have taken the damn country over—they landed on the coast there.

President: I thought I might do this: I thought I might call—if I could talk to him—he claims he's broken off diplomatic relationship— but I might call their President and say I regret it is a situation of violence that developed, and I thought we should do everything we could to restore quiet, and I appreciate his calling the Panamanian people last night to remain calm and hope he'll do everything possible to quiet the situation, and I'll do the same. And I'm going to send my trusted representatives, Tom Mann and other Panama Canal Board people in there today to assist in findin' a solution to the situation, and both of us are aware of the possibility that the elements unfriendly to both of our countries are tryin' to exploit the situation, and I want to keep in close personal touch with him. Then I thought I'd send Tom Mann and Ed Martin and the Assistant Secretaries, Cy Vance, on the Panama Canal Board, and probably this boy Dungan, who's handled it here at the White House and who is a pretty level-headed fellow—used to be on Kennedy's committee.

Russell: That's sensible, but I—

President: Don't know, I might ask Harry McPherson—he's been down there and been awful concerned about it. I might ask him to go with 'em.

Russell: Well, you couldn't get a better boy to come back and give you a clear report as an observer—he wouldn't be stampeded in any way. I certainly take a chunk out of the Communists; you're going to have trouble there all through your entire tenure as President—in that area down there. Castro is going to pick up the tempo of his activities down there, in his desperation, and that's goin' to be a trouble spot. I have held that opinion for several years, now, and especially when they extended—they increased the payments here the last time—in which I said that we were in danger there because if we [unintelligible] on the part of the Panamanians that we've done them some injustice. We've really done them a hell of a favor. They're a whole lot better off than the Colombians. They have better income, everything else. Not that that satisfies 'em; the only way you can satisfy 'em is to give 'em the

Canal and that wouldn't completely satisfy 'em. You'd have to operate it for 'em too.

[Here follows conversation unrelated to Panama]

President: They're going to get the President of Panama. I'll call
you back.[3]

Russell: All right.

President: Bye.

---

[3] The President called Russell again at 1:25 p.m. to inform him of the substance of
the conversation with Chiari. The President told Russell that he informed his advisers,
"I was damned tired of their attacking our flag and Embassy, and our USIA, every time
somebody got a little emotional outburst—so they had better watch out." Johnson informed Russell that Mann, Martin, and Vance were going to Panama and that, "Cy Vance
can be pretty tough." Russell responded that O'Meara was "a pretty good man." Johnson stated that O'Meara "has had to order his people to start shooting again" and that
it was "hot as a firecracker" in Panama. Johnson then told Russell that the "position we
ought to be on the Hill" is that the administration acted swiftly and properly and was
sending the right men there. Johnson remarked, "they tell me that everyone in Latin
America is scared of this fellow Mann. They highly regard him because he's a tough
guy." Russell responded that he hoped there was "iron" under Mann's "velvet gloves."
(Johnson Library, Recordings and Transcripts, Recording of telephone conversation between President Johnson and Richard Russell, Tape F64.04, Side B, PNO 3)

---

370. Transcript of Telephone Conversation Between President Johnson and Panamanian President Chiari[1]

January 10, 1964, 11:40 a.m.

President Johnson: Hello Mr. President.

Mr. President, I wanted to say to you that we deeply regret the situation of violence that has developed there.

We appreciate very much your call to the Panamanian people to
remain calm.

We recognize that you and I should do everything we can to restore quiet and I hope that you'll do everything possible to quieten the
situation and I will do the same.

---

[1] Source: Johnson Library, National Security File, NSC Histories, Panama Crisis,
1964. Secret; Eyes Only. President Johnson was in Washington; President Chiari in
Panama City.

You and I should be aware of the possibility and the likelihood that there are elements unfriendly to both of us who will exploit this situation.

I am sending immediately, my trusted representative, Secretary Thomas Mann and others associated with him and the White House to Panama to assist in finding a solution to the present situation and accurately finding the facts.

I think it's important that we keep in close personal touch with each other, and I will be ready to do that.

I hope you'll give Secretary Mann any suggestions he has that might result in the development of correcting the situation.

President Chiari: Would you please allow me a moment, Mr. President?

I am going to tell you now, President Johnson, the same that I plan to tell Mr. Thomas Mann when he arrives either later today or tomorrow. I feel, Mr. President, that what we need is a complete revision of all treaties which affect Panama–U.S. relations because that which we have at the present time is nothing but a source of dissatisfaction which has recently or just now exploded into violence which we are witnessing.

President Johnson: Tell him that first we must find out what caused the riot, get all the facts in this situation. Mr. Mann will be there for that purpose. We have got to see what all entered into this, and we will want to receive from Mr. Mann any suggestions he has.

President Chiari (interpreted): The President wishes to say, sir, that he wants President Johnson to be aware of the fact that President Chiari came to Washington in 1961 and at that time he spoke to President Kennedy and that since 1961 and those conversations, not a thing has been done to alleviate the situation which has provoked this violence, and Panama now has 8 to 10 dead and over 200 wounded in the hospitals.

President Johnson: Tell him there's nothing we can ever do that justifies violence, and we want to look forward and not backward, and what we must do is to review with responsible and able and trusted officials of this government the situation that he reviewed with President Eisenhower in 1960 and with President Kennedy in 1961, and Mr. Mann can do that with him on the ground, and then we will look at the facts and try to deal with the problem in this country. We have a problem here just as he has it there.

Tell him that violence is never any way to settle anything, and I know he and Secretary Mann can get together, and he can give him a viewpoint of his country, and we will give him the viewpoint of our country and we will carefully and judiciously and wisely consider both viewpoints and reach an area of agreement.

President Chiari (through interpreter): The President is in complete agreement with you, Mr. President, that violence leads nowhere, however, he feels that he must take cognizance of our intransigence and our indifference to Panama problems during the past two years, especially in recent months where things have been at a standstill, and it is urgent that men of goodwill, you in the United States and President Chiari in Panama, should attempt an urgent solution to these problems.

President Johnson: Tell him the people will be in the plane in 30 minutes—the most respected people I have to talk to him about it in detail, and in the meantime I am going to count on him to preserve order there as I'm going to preserve it here.

President Chiari: At what time will the airplane arrive in Panama?

President Johnson: Approximately five hours.

President Chiari (through interpreter): He's very grateful for your cooperation.

President Johnson: Tell him I don't know how to act more promptly than that.

President Chiari (interpreter): They say that's very fine, and they're very very grateful.

President Johnson: But say to the President that we're having a serious problem as we know he has one there, and it's going to take the wisdom and the strength of all of us to solve it.

President Chiari (interpreter): He said one of the things that President Chiari admires in President Johnson is the fact that he is a man of action and of few words, therefore, they have great confidence that this situation will finally be resolved.

President Johnson: Thank him very much—Goodbye.

---

371.   Memorandum From the President's Special Assistant for National Security Affairs (Bundy) to President Johnson[1]

Washington, January 10, 1964.

SUBJECT

Panama Situation Report, 7:00 p.m.

---

[1] Source: Johnson Library, National Security File, Memos to the President, McGeorge Bundy, Vol. I, November 1963–February 1964. No classification marking.

1. The OAS without debate is sending the peace committee to Panama at once. This committee as now set up includes Argentina, Colombia, Chile, Dominican Republic, and Venezuela.[2] Dean Rusk says it is friendly to us.

2. Panamanians have sent in a note definitely breaking relations,[3] and their political noise level remains high. We are not confirming break in relations, since after all we expect Mann to see Chiari.

3. The U.N. Security Council meets tonight and while there will be some noise, Rusk expects that the dispatch of the OAS peace mission will hold the line for tonight.[4]

4. On the central front of restoring peace and safety, the immediate prognosis is better. Rusk, McNamara, and I agree that tonight will be the test whether we have a turning point here.[5]

5. Mann has landed.

McG. B.[6]

---

[2] On January 10 the OAS issued a communiqué announcing the formulation of the Inter-American Peace Committee comprised of representatives of Chile, Venezuela, Colombia, the Dominican Republic, and Argentina. The committee was to travel to Panama to investigate the situation and recommend measures for a settlement of the dispute. The text of the communiqué is in Department of State *Bulletin,* February 3, 1964, p. 152.

[3] The message severing diplomatic relations was from Panamanian Foreign Minister Galileo Solis to Secretary Rusk, January 10, 3:10 p.m. (Johnson Library, National Security File, NSC Histories, Panama Crisis, 1964)

[4] Rusk had urged that the OAS Peace Commission take up the problem in a noon meeting with departing Panamanian Ambassador Augusto Arango. (Memorandum of conversation, January 10; National Archives and Records Administration, RG 59, Central Files 1964–66, POL PAN–US)

[5] On the night of January 10 Johnson told Senator Mike Mansfield: "I'm waiting on that Panama thing to see if they have another riot there." He added: "I think these damned Communists are goin' to cause trouble every place in this country they can, and I think we've got to get a little bit hard with 'em." Johnson continued: "I don't know— Dick Russell may be right. He says that they're goin' to do this in every damned nation they can." (Johnson Library, Recordings and Transcripts, Recording of telephone conversation between President Johnson and Mike Mansfield, January 10, 10:25 p.m., Tape F64.05, Side A, PNO 1)

[6] Printed from a copy that bears these typed initials.

372.   Telegram From the U.S. Southern Command to the Department of State[1]

Panama City, January 11, 1964, 0840Z.

SC1118A. For Secretary Rusk from Assistant Secretary Mann.

Secretary Vance and I met for an hour and a half with President Chiari, Foreign Minister Solis, and Mr. Morgan, Head of the US Section, Foreign Office.

We first said that in our opinion the most urgent question was to reestablish peace and law. President readily agreed. Vance made point that US would maintain order in the Canal Zone.

Chiari then referred to his telephone conversation with President Johnson[2] and in forceful tones said that more conversations would serve no useful purpose unless Washington group had authority to agree immediately to a "structural revision" of outdated 1903, 1936, and 1955 treaties. Chiari said that unless we had this authority he would proceed to break diplomatic relations and leave the whole problem to his successor. He said little had come of his talk two years ago with President Kennedy and that the Panamanian people were tired of excuses and delays and particularly tired of hearing the US say "this or that treaty provision is not negotiable."

I made it very clear that I had no authority to agree to discuss "structural revision" of the treaty, but said I would report his statement to the President and to the Secretary of State. I said that in my personal and unofficial opinion the answer would be automatically negative simply because there were certain things politically impossible in the US just as there are in Panama; that politics was the art of the possible; that there were a number of states we did not have relations with; and while we would regret having no relations with Panama, this was something we could live with even though this would create an impasse which would make it impossible for the two governments to deal with urgent problems; and finally, this would be contrary to the best interests of both governments.

While we were stuck on this point, I inquired what he meant by use of expression "structural revision." He said he simply meant an agreement under which representatives of the two countries would meet and start with a clean slate to negotiate a completely new treaty.

---

[1] Source: Johnson Library, National Security File, NSC Histories, Panama Crisis, 1964. Confidential. Repeated to OSD and JCS and passed to the White House.

[2] See Document 370.

He thought that specifics of the needed revisions could best be developed during the course of those negotiations.

I then inquired whether he thought it was worth while for the US and Panama to try to reach as large an area of agreement as possible on what had actually happened in the last two days. I said that Washington regretted this as much as Panama and I pointed out that American lives had also been lost. I said I hoped we could stipulate a good many facts. Chiari replied that he thought that this was the job of the Peace Committee and so there was no reason to try to reach an understanding on what had happened because "Our people will blame you and your people will blame us." To this I replied that there were a number of gaps in our information and I presumed a number of gaps in his, for example, was the Panamanian flag torn by American students or by Panamanian students? We have some pictures of this part of the incident that might be of interest to him. Who fired the first shot? What factors were responsible for the relatively heavy gunfire? Toward the end of this part of discussion, Chiari seemed to warm to this idea of a fact finding Panama-US group. It is not impossible that we will get to work with a Panamanian committee to determine the true facts.

I told Chiari that we had information which indicated that the Communists were involved in the disturbances. Chiari readily agreed that this was the case. I pointed out that Castro agents in Panama were as great a danger to Panama as they are to the US Government. We are both in the same boat.

I then pointed out to him that considerable progress had been made in cooperating with Panama since 1960. The Thatcher Bridge exists; the Zone honors Panamanian exequaturs; Panamanians have received wage increases; the number of security jobs for which Panamanians were not eligible has been reduced; agreement has been reached on withholding Panamanian income taxes for Panamanian employees; agreements have been reached on flying the Panamanian flag along with US flags in the Zone. Chiari agreed that this was progress but stated that the Thatcher Bridge had been agreed to in 1942 and that Governor Fleming unilaterally decided on wage increases without Washington's instructions.

Chiari then took off on the flag issue in very strong language and said the US had not lived up to its agreement. He said that after his conversation with President Kennedy in 1961 he believed that Panama and the US had reached a reasonable agreement. In the ensuing months, however, US restrictions were noted with respect to flying the Panamanian flag at military installations, the US schools, and on ships transitting the Canal, moreover, he pointed out that the US elected to lower the US flags at certain installations rather than fly the Panamanian flag at those agreed to places. He seemed to be impressed when we replied that Washington was not aware until last night that this was a serious issue. I said he should understand very clearly that the US lives up to its agreements. He agreed that flag issue should be discussed, stating that it was the "hot potato" of the moment.

We agreed to discuss the flag issue tomorrow evening at a time and place to be arranged after discussions with the Foreign Minister. I suggested that we might meet with the Foreign Minister and report back to him.

Chiari said that the US ought to withdraw its military forces from the Zone border area and replace them with police and firemen. I said that this illustrated the divergencies in our information since we understand that General O'Meara's troops fired only at individual snipers. It was police that were engaged in the heaviest fire. Chiari did not reply to this.

We both deplored the loss of life and I pointed out that American lives had been lost on the Atlantic side without any return shots being fired by US. Chiari said "All I know is that 16 Panamanians died and over 200 are wounded."

We were met at the airport and conducted to the palace in cloak and dagger fashion and much of the conversation was conducted with background of 600 Panamanians outside chanting "Out with the gringos." All of this could have been staged. Nevertheless, conversation which began in a cool and almost hostile atmosphere ended on warm note. In beginning Chiari's intention may have been to probe hard for a soft spot on issue of "structural revision" of treaty.

Recommend I be authorized to inform Chiari that US will not now agree to negotiations to bring about "structural" changes in treaty; and that I be authorized to say that this does not necessarily close the door for all time for discussions on treaty revisions, since it is possible that current studies on feasibility of sea level canal may eventually lead to a change in our attitude. Entire Washington group concurs in this recommendation.

Saturday morning we expect to send separate telegram on flag issue.[3]

---

[3] In telegram SC1125A to McNamara, January 11, Vance reported that he planned to inform the Panamanian Foreign Minister that U.S. and Panamanian flags would be flown outside public schools in the Canal Zone. (Johnson Library, National Security File, Country File, Panama, Riots, Part A, Vol. II, January–February, 1964)

373.   Editorial Note

On January 11, 1964, President Johnson considered instructions for Assistant Secretary of State for Inter-American Affairs Thomas Mann and his party for their discussions in Panama. In consultation with Mc-Namara and Bundy, the Department of State prepared instructions that were based on Mann's recommendation earlier that day as outlined in the last substantive paragraph of Document 372.

The President sought the advice of Senator Russell and read the draft instructions to him over the phone. According to their conversation, the draft instructions proposed that both sides agree on the facts surrounding the riots; that "we should be forthcoming on flag issues since our good faith is involved"; that, with regard to structural revision of the treaty, "we cannot agree to formal negotiation in which revision of fundamental relationships and responsibilities would be a pre-arranged and accepted objective," but "that does not mean that there might not be certain aspects of the treaty of importance to Panama which could, after informal discussion, be taken up between the two governments." The draft instructions urged Mann to "remind Chiari that considerable progress has been made on many points" as a result of his discussion with President Kennedy, and that after restoration of relations, if further progress is made in talks not earlier than February or March, and if "Chiari's mood improves, it might be well to suggest that highly discreet cooperation between us about the Communists and especially Castro plotting, both against Panama and the United States, be continued and strengthened." The instructions concluded that events taking place in Panama "have demonstrated clearly that the reality behind the reports pointed toward Panama as a special target of Communist conspiracy." The draft instructions were not found.

In reviewing the draft instructions with Russell, the President voiced his concerns: "I'm a little bit dubious. I'm afraid that we're going a little bit further than we ought to go, but it is pretty difficult to say to people that you just won't talk, I mean, it won't be courteous if you won't listen to 'em." In particular, with respect to the instruction concerning structural revision of the treaty, the President said: "It seems to me that we're kinda givin' in there and respondin' at the point of a pistol." Johnson then stated: "What I am doing here, if I approve these instructions— I am agreein' to discussion of the treaty." He reflected, "I know damned well one thing—I can take the position of discussion—we'll discuss it but we won't do anything. But I guess if you're goin' to discuss it you ought to discuss it in good faith, and that's what they want, and I don't know how that's goin' to be interpreted in the public eye—whether they've got to kill a few American soldiers to get us to discuss somethin'—I don't like that. On the other hand we've got to do somethin'."

Russell responded that the draft instruction to Mann was "a hell of a long thing you're sendin' down there. It would confuse me if I were down there with all the pressures that he must feel in that atmosphere down there." Johnson reported that Mann and Vance "had a good talk" with Chiari and "both of 'em were awfully tough with him." Johnson also pointed out the sensitive political aspects of the crisis: "Every damned one of 'em are runnin' against us for their re-election. Six hundred of 'em stood outside and said 'get out of here Gringos.'" Russell agreed: "They've been doin' that—the one that denounces the colossus of the north most vociferously is the one that wins, and that's been true the last three elections they've had. On the surface we haven't got a friend there, but if we weren't there they wouldn't have anything. They would be livin' out there half-naked in those swamps. . . . You can't close the door to any negotiations, but you can certainly [say] that we can't negotiate in this atmosphere, but we'll talk to you some time later."

In response to Johnson's inquiry if the draft instruction was "softening up" what Mann had recommended, Russell said: "One or two sentences seem to me like it's sort of puttin' him in a halter." "That's what it seems to me" the President responded. Russell suggested that the President simply tell Mann that he agrees with his recommendation and that he's "depending on your good judgment." (Johnson Library, Recordings and Transcripts, Recording of telephone conversation between President Johnson and Senator Richard Russell, January 11, 1964, 1:05 p.m., Tape F64.05, Side A, PNO 2)

Johnson then called Bundy and told him that he had "confidence in Mann's good judgment." The President said that he would tell Mann:

"Tom, you are a man on the ground with common sense and we trust you and Cy Vance or we wouldn't have sent you there, and we are prepared to support you, and we agree in essence with your recommendation. We—therefore—we're not goin' to discuss structural changes in the treaty at this point. However, you are at liberty to assure the President that under appropriate circumstances, we'll be very happy to discuss any troublesome problems with them, but we're not goin' to do it at the point of a gun. We've got the rest of the world to live with. People just can't take the law into their own hands and they didn't protest what these kids did—they just started shootin' and riotin'. And if we go in there and start opening up a treaty under those circumstances, we'd be the laughing stock of the world." (Ibid., Recording of telephone conversation between President Johnson and McGeorge Bundy, January 11; 1:25 p.m., Tape F64.05, Side A, PNO 3)

Bundy included these points, along with concurrence in Mann's proposed flag plan, in a revised instruction and told the President that he had been "up and down the question of all the other things that are at issue." Bundy also had a January 11 memorandum from Gordon Chase on these matters. (Johnson Library, National Security File, Country File, Panama, Riots, Part B, Vol. II, January–February, 1964) "Each and every one of them," he told the President, "in one way or another, has a political hooker attached to it" and that "every one of them has either a Congressional obstacle or a legal obstacle and it's a tricky business." He suggested that Mann take up these matters at a later time. (Ibid., Recordings and Transcripts, Recording of telephone conversation between President Johnson and McGeorge Bundy, January 11, 1964, 1:25 p.m.) The portions of the conversations printed here were prepared in the Office of the Historian specifically for this volume.

---

374. Telegram From President Johnson to the Assistant Secretary of State for Inter-American Affairs (Mann) in Panama[1]

Washington, January 11, 1964, 5:34 p.m.

CAP 64016. Reference your CINCSO 110840Z SC1118A.[2]

1. We have full confidence in you and in Vance, and fully concur in what you have done so far.

2. We agree in essence with your recommendation in last paragraph of reftel and also with you and Vance on flag issue.

3. You should tell President that we cannot negotiate under pressure of violence and breach of relations and that therefore his demand for agreement to structural revision of treaties is unacceptable.

4. You should also tell him that in the appropriate circumstances and when peace has been restored, we will give sympathetic welcome to discussion of all troubles and problems with our Panamanian friends.

---

[1] Source: Johnson Library, National Security File, NSC Histories, Panama Crisis, 1964. Confidential; Flash. Repeated to Rusk, McNamara, and McCone.

[2] Document 372.

375. Telegram From the Assistant Secretary of State for Inter-American Affairs (Mann) to Secretary of State Rusk[1]

Panama City, January 12, 1964, 0656Z.

SC1144A. Vance, Mann, Martin, Stuart and LtCol Moura met this afternoon with Panamanian Foreign Minister Solis, David Samudio, Director of Planning of the Presidency, Eloy Benedetti, Judiciary Advisor of the Foreign Office, William Arango, recalled Panamanian Ambassador to Washington, and Morgan Morales, Head of U.S. Section of the Foreign Office. The meeting was in two parts. Between the two meetings, all of the Panamanians, except Arango, went by car to the palace where they consulted with President Chiari and returned with the President's reply. Foreign Minister said at end of first conversation he could make no comment until he had consulted with Chiari. Five topics were discussed:

1. We informed the Panamanians of Secretary Vance's decision that American flags would be flown outside of schools in the Zone and, in compliance with U.S.-Panama agreement, Panamanian flags would be flown side by side with U.S. flags. I said this meant 18 new flag stations and would raise the total number of flag stations to about 35. He pointed out Vance's decision involved no new concession but only execution of prior agreement. We pointed out no concession possible under duress.

Panamanians pressed hard for display of Panamanian flag on ships transiting canal and in U.S. military installations in Zone. We replied we were disposed to study these two issues but could make no commitment. After return from Presidency, Panamanians stated that flying of flag at 18 schools should not in any sense be interpreted as settlement of question of whether U.S. was complying with Kennedy–Chiari communiqué during Presidential visit.[2] During conversation on this point, we offered to coordinate press release covering this with Panamanians. After returning from Presidency, Panamanians made clear Vance's decision was U.S. unilateral decision. We said we understood both sides reserved their position on remaining flag issues. We have reports that Panamanians in streets applauded radio announcements of Vance's press release.

2. We informed Panamanians that five known agitators were at that moment haranguing large and growing crowd in Shaler triangle and requested that Guardia Nacional be instructed to arrest these five men, all of who have received training in Cuba. The Foreign Minister

---

[1] Source: Johnson Library, National Security File, NSC Histories, Panama Crisis, 1964. Confidential; Immediate. Passed to the White House, CIA, OSD, and USUN.

[2] The text of the communiqué is in *Public Papers of the Presidents of the United States: John F. Kennedy, 1962,* pp. 481–482.

requested names of the five men and these were supplied him. We stated that situation was urgent and if there was further delay in authorizing Guardia Nacional to act, situation could become critical in terms of Panamanian ability to maintain law and order and could lead to bloodshed on a much greater scale than had taken place in the last few days. We also informed Panamanians that there have been four more U.S. military casualties today on the Atlantic side of Zone. Fire returned with shotgun today on only one sniper. Also snipers were firing regularly into the Tivoli Hotel from Panamanian territory. U.S. lieutenant was wounded by this fire after meeting. (Shortly before midnight, Mann telephoned Foreign Minister and told him four snipers on roof of legislative palace still firing into Tivoli Hotel.)

After returning from Presidency, Foreign Minister stated categorically and with considerable emphasis that the President had decided to order National Guard to restore order and that this would be accomplished forthwith.

While not certain, our estimate is that if Guardia Nacional acts with decisiveness and speed, it can probably still regain control of the situation. Further delay could be fatal. A few minutes ago, Vallarino, first commandant of the Nacional Guard, informed General Bogart that he was on way to the Presidency and after his return he expected to request us to supply him with tear gas. (A truck was immediately loaded with tear gas in anticipation of such a request.)

While Foreign Minister's statement regarding restoration of order was unconditional, we received word through chairman of Peace Committee that Nacional Guard would act only if U.S. military withdrew from Canal Zone boundary, a sufficient distance so as to be invisible from Panama side.

General O'Meara stated that on the Pacific side this condition already exists except when necessary to repel invaders and except for two military police at each Zone entry point stationed there to control entry of legitimate traffic. This has been conveyed to Tejera and condition has been withdrawn, though Chiari has asked and received authority to announce he is acting at request of Chairman, Peace Commission.

3. We informed Panamanians we had had a long and constructive discussion with Peace Committee which had requested us to designate U.S. official who could work with committee.[3] We replied immediately

---

[3] At a 4:30 p.m. meeting of the OAS Peace Commission in Panama City on January 11, Mann stated: "One, we cannot negotiate under pressure of violence or threats to break relations; therefore, any demand for structural revisions is not acceptable to the United States. Two, under appropriate circumstances, and after peace has been reestablished, we welcome the idea of discussing all problems with our Panamanian friends." (Memorandum for the record prepared by Lieutenant Colonel Arthur S. Moura, January 11; Johnson Library, National Security File, NSC Histories, Panama Crisis, 1964)

that Martin would represent U.S. Presumably the Peace Commission made the same request of Panamanians. After his return from Presidency, Foreign Minister stated that Ambassador Arango would be representative of GOP before commission.

Parenthetically, we report that Peace Committee impressed us as being objective and constructive. They correctly stated their first job was to bring an end to disorders. They said that they did not consider themselves to be a fact-finding committee but that their role was rather one of conciliation. In addition to our giving them an oral summary of developments since the beginning of violence, we informed committee of Vance's decision to fly U.S. and Panamanian flags in front of Zone schools and gave them candid statement of U.S. position on issue of treaty revision. Committee stated that it did not consider itself authorized to get into issue of possible "structural revisions" of treaty but thought committee could be useful in trying to identify issues which could contribute immediately to present crisis and to attempt to conciliate differences between the two governments on these issues. We expressed agreement in principle. In our opinion, commission's view realistic and constructive. We offered fullest cooperation, including facilities for inspecting Zone and detailed inspection of places in Zone where controversial events have taken place, including inspection of vehicles alleged to be tanks. We contradicted commission's information machine guns were used by U.S. police and military. We stressed factors of surprise, small size of Zone police, aggressive and violent attitude of Panamanians who invaded Zone, necessity of protecting women and children, and overwhelming superiority of Panamanians as compared with police available in earliest stages of rioting.

4. We next informed Panamanians of U.S. positions as described in numbered paragraphs 3 and 4 of White House message CAP 64016.[4] Essentially same position had been given Chiari night before. Panamanians asked for repetition. We carefully went over this ground twice. Upon their return from presidency, Panamanians stated President Chiari would discuss this and other substantive issues only after they had demonstrated their capability to restore order in Panama. We have unconfirmed reports Panamanians will continue to insist, as Chiari did in his first conversation, that U.S. agree in principle to "structural revisions" of treaty as a condition precedent to GOP agreeing to further discussions of outstanding issues, including resumption of relations. Department should understand clearly this is principal issue and not our willingness to engage in discussions. It is however still possible that Chiari will cave.

---

[4] Document 374.

5. We stated to Panamanians we were at a loss to reconcile Chiari's complaint to me that we had not promptly named an Ambassador to replace Farland with statements of GOP officials over radio and to our charge here that diplomatic relations already severed. We asked for clarification. Upon their return from presidency, Panamanians stated that this was also issue that would be discussed with us after GOP had restored order in Panama City. We expect, but cannot be sure, we will be told tomorrow that relations have been severed. If this proves to be the case, this is obviously irrational maneuver on Chiari's part to strengthen his pose before Panamanian people as the champion of Panamanian sovereignty and its claims to Canal Zone. As an out, Panama may intend to use Peace Committee as forum for discussions of outstanding issues.

At conclusion of meeting, Foreign Minister requested that we postpone our return to Washington. We said we had intended to return Sunday[5] but would stay over a while longer.[6]

---

[5] January 12.

[6] Rusk informed the President that the delegation planned to leave Panama City following the 3 p.m. meeting with Chiari on January 13, and Johnson approved. (Recording of telephone conversation between President Johnson and Rusk, January 13, 12:45 p.m.; Johnson Library, Recordings and Transcripts, Tape F64.05, Side A, PNO 5) The President called Bundy to arrange to meet Mann and the delegation upon their arrival in Washington. The President then asked Bundy, "How are we goin' to leave the impression with the country that we're not soft on Panama after Rusk tells the AP that we're goin' to negotiate." Bundy responded that Rusk swore he didn't say that. The President replied that the "AP quotes him all morning long. I heard it as sayin' that as soon as we get quieted down, we're goin' start negotiatin'." Bundy agreed to talk to Rusk. The President then stated, "I talked to him so damned much about it that I'm gettin' embarrassed for mentioning it." Both Bundy and the President agreed that most leaks came from the Department, not Rusk. Bundy suggested Rusk was "a clam presiding over a sieve." The President continued to complain about leaks and suggested that Bundy tell Ball, Harriman, "and the rest of them" that he was "getting damned sensitive about it." (Recording of telephone conversation between President Johnson and Bundy, January 13, 1:05 p.m.; ibid., Side B, PNO 2)

376. Memorandum of Conversation[1]

Panama City, January 13, 1964, 3:15 p.m.

SUBJECT

Panama

PARTICIPANTS

Panama
His Excellency Roberto F. Chiari, President
His Excellency Galileo Solís, Foreign Minister

United States
The Hon. Ralph Dungan, The White House
The Hon. Cyrus R. Vance, Secretary of the Army
The Hon. Thomas C. Mann, Assistant Secretary of State

Mr. Dungan, Mr. Vance and I called on President Chiari today in the Palace at about 3:15 in the afternoon. Foreign Minister Solis was present. Earlier in the day Solis had himself suggested that it would be appropriate for us to pay a courtesy call on the President.

I began the conversation by expressing our appreciation for the courtesies we had received and said we had come to pay our respects and to ask his leave to return to Washington now that progress had been made in restoring peace and order.

I said that I had already said to the Foreign Minister that there was no hurry in telling us whether Panama would be willing to resume diplomatic relations. Mr. Martin was staying behind to work with the Peace Committee and he could relay to Washington any message on the subject.

President Chiari said he had already decided to withdraw Panamanian diplomatic personnel from Washington and to remove the seal from the Embassy building. He requested that we do the same.

I said that we regretfully accepted his decision but that we wanted to make absolutely certain the President understood that we were ready to resume discussion of all problems, including those concerning the Panama Canal treaties, provided only there was no duress and no pre-condition about a prior agreement to "structurally revise" the treaties.

---

[1] Source: National Archives and Records Administration, RG 59, Central Files 1964–66, POL PAN–US. Confidential. Drafted by Mann on January 14. The meeting was held at the Presidential Palace.

The President said further discussions about the existing treaties were useless. The condition to resumption of relations was that we agree to make a fresh start, to consider the treaties abrogated and to sit down to negotiate a new one fair to Panama and fair to the United States.

The conversation to this point was largely in Spanish. I asked the President for permission to repeat in English to my colleagues what he had just said. I did this and the President, who speaks English fairly well, confirmed in English that my summary was accurate.

Mr. Dungan then said that he found it difficult to reconcile this position with the friendly conversations about United States-Panamanian relations which he and President Kennedy had had in 1962 in Washington.[2] Dungan said that emphasis in these meetings had been on reaching "practical solutions to practical problems."

President Chiari said that he and President Kennedy had indicated sympathy to a fresh start to discussions about the Zone which did not take into account the existing treaties. A Joint Commission was set up. Since then little had been accomplished, he said, because the Americans said this or that issue was ruled by existing treaties or for other reasons. So the Joint Commission accomplished nothing. It was no use to start this kind of thing again.

President Chiari, continuing to speak in English, then said that United States equipment at the Rio Hato base should be evacuated by sea instead of being taken overland where it would be seen by Panamanians. The evacuation could be done by sea, in landing craft already at the base, and it would be all right if this were done in three or four weeks. Meanwhile the Guardia would protect the base and after its evacuation the Government would use the base buildings as schools to protect them. Neither we nor the President mentioned base personnel or the agreement under which we occupy the base. We made no comment on the statements about the Rio Hato base save to say we would look into this matter.

At this point, I asked if the three of us might speak to the President and the Foreign Minister alone. The Assistant Chief of Protocol, the Chief of Protocol and Captain Boyd of the Guardia (really of the Presidential Guard), who were sitting down the drawing room were then asked to leave, and they did.

---

[2] A memorandum of this conversation, June 12, 1962, is printed in *Foreign Relations,* 1961–1963, vol. XII, Document 405.

I then said that, entirely unrelated to the topics we had discussed, and because we would not soon be talking directly to each other again, I wished him to know that, according to our intelligence:

a) The Castroites, the Communists, have penetrated high positions in his Government and among them were advisors to the President himself.[3]
b) Castro would soon be trying to introduce arms into Panama.
c) Most of the persons just arrested for leading the recent riots have been released.

The President only nodded. He made no comment. I said I thought the President should know about our conclusions, based on our intelligence, because, though we were interested in stability in and peace with Panama, communism was even a greater danger to Panama than it was to the United States.

Finally, I asked if I could speak frankly about one final point: Since we would have no relations, I wanted to make absolutely clear that it was up to us to maintain order in the Canal Zone and to prevent invasions from the Zone into Panamanian territory; and equally it was up to the Government of Panama to maintain order in Panamanian territory and prevent invasions of people from Panamanian territory into the Zone. There should be no mistake. We would have to defend ourselves, including the women and children in the Zone, if mobs should again force their way into the Zone. The casualties could be heavy. No one except the Government of Panama could prevent further intrusions into the Zone. The responsibility on both Governments to maintain peace during the break in relations was therefore a heavy one.

The President expressed his agreement and, after observing the amenities, we took our leave.

The conversations were carried out in an atmosphere which was rather solemn and official-like but everyone was polite at all times. There were no recriminations except perhaps that the President's statements about past failures to reach agreement could be called almost bitter.

---

[3] On January 13 Helms provided the Department of State with information linking Panamanian official Thelma King and the Arias Madrid family, including presidential hopeful Arnulfo Arias, with the Castro regime. (Memorandum from Helms to Hughes; Central Intelligence Agency, Job 78–03041R, DDO/IMS Files, [file name not declassified])

377. Memorandum of Conference With the President[1]

Washington, January 13, 1964, 9:45 p.m.

OTHERS PRESENT

Secretary Rusk, Secretary McNamara, Director McCone, Under Secretary Ball, Mr. Chayes, Mr. Lansing Collins (State), Mr. Jenkins (part time), Mr. Moyers, Mr. Bundy, Mr. Bromley Smith

There was no formal discussion between 9:45 PM and 10:00 PM when the Mann delegation[2] arrived in the Cabinet Room. The President informally commented on a State Department draft press statement to be issued at the conclusion of the meeting.[3]

Assistant Secretary Mann reported that there was a possibility of a revolution in Panama tonight. The delegation had learned that Arias might join with the Communists to overthrow Chiari. Several members of the delegation stated that Chiari was in trouble from both the right and the left and agreed that his overthrow was a possibility. Mr. Mann stated his view that the U.S. should not intervene with U.S. troops in a Panamanian coup unless it was clear that the revolutionists would be successful.

The members of the delegation paused to read a CIA report which had been [1 line of source text not declassified]. The report indicated there was some substance to a plan for a coup to be launched tonight.[4]

Secretary McNamara left the room to telephone General O'Meara,[5] Commander of the Southern Forces, to instruct him to get to Chiari the report of the coup plans. General O'Meara was to tell Chiari that our informing him of the coup plans was evidence of our support of him against a revolutionary group.

---

[1] Source: Johnson Library, National Security File, Files of McGeorge Bundy, Miscellaneous Meetings, Vol. I. Secret. Prepared by Bromley Smith.

[2] The Mann delegation, which had just returned from Panama were: Mann, Vance, Dungan, and Colonel J.C. King.

[3] For the statement as released on January 14, see Department of State *Bulletin*, February 3, 1964, p. 156.

[4] Not found. Similar reports are in a telegram from Martin and O'Meara to Mann and Vance, received January 13 at 10:10 p.m. (USCINCSO SG1186A, January 13; National Archives and Records Administration, RG 59, Central Files 1964–66, POL 23–8 PAN)

[5] At 9:45 p.m. in the first of two telephone calls McNamara made during this meeting to O'Meara, McNamara told him to "give the substance of the message that is there to President Chiari." (Johnson Library, President's Daily Diary) Also see footnote 7 below.

Mr. Mann reported on the delegation's conversation with Chiari this afternoon.[6] The Panama President returned to the position taken during the first talks, i.e., Panama will not discuss any problem with the U.S. until the U.S. agrees to revise the three existing treaties with Panama.

With respect to a possible coup in Panama, Mr. Mann recommended that if Chiari requested our assistance, we should intervene in the Panamanian Republic with U.S. troops. If Chiari appears to be losing to a coup led by Arias and the Communists, we should intervene after a request from Chiari. Mr. Mann's view was that Chiari appears to have the support of the people, and, therefore, the chances of Arias and the Communists overthrowing him is not great. He admitted that the loyalty of the Panamanian National Guard would be crucial in a revolutionary situation.

The President said that we cannot permit Arias and the Communists to take over Panama. We should immediately inform General O'Meara.

Mr. Mann said that General O'Meara could tell General Vallarino, the Commander of the Panamanian National Guard, that we will not let the Communists take over Panama. In case the Guard was thinking of defecting from Chiari, we could tell them that we would support the existing government against an Arias–Communist coup. Also, General O'Meara could tell General Vallarino that if the Guard needed help in preventing a Communist take-over, we would help the Guard. Chiari would also be told of our intentions.

Secretary Rusk wondered whether we should tell Arias. He was thinking of a pro-American, such as Robles, who may have the loyalty of the National Guard, with whom we could work more easily than Chiari. He thought that perhaps we should tell the Guard and Robles.

The President asked why we should not tell Arias that we have received reports that Communists are trying to take over. We could say that the U.S. will not accept a Communist take-over and anyone who goes with them we will oppose as well.

Secretary McNamara left the room with Secretary Rusk and the President to telephone General O'Meara.[7] The substance of the conversation is contained in a copy of the message attached to these minutes.[8] The President and Secretary Rusk were present and participated

---

[6] See Document 376.

[7] The instructions given O'Meara during the second telephone call at 10:30 p.m. were confirmed by telegram (see footnote 8 below) at the request of President Johnson. (Johnson Library, National Security File, Panama Riots, Vol. II, Part A, January–February 1964)

[8] Telegram CAP 64020, January 14, 12:37 p.m. (Ibid.)

in the discussion of each point as it was given by Secretary McNamara to General O'Meara.

In response to the President's request, Mr. Mann gave additional information on his talks with President Chiari, who is probably under heavy pressure from National Guard leaders and Panamanian businessmen because of his hostility toward the U.S. Mr. Mann believes that Chiari will eventually agree to talk with us even though he refuses to do so now. He recommended that we play our cards very carefully until such time as internal pressure in Panama forces him to accept our basis for discussions. In response to the President's question, Mr. Mann said Chiari advisers, several of whom are left-wing Communists, are telling Chiari to hold out because the U.S. will give in to his demands.

The President asked whether we could prove that arms had reached Panama from outside. He was told that we have considerable substantial evidence but no actual proof that Cuba or any other country has shipped arms to Panama.

Mr. Mann said that Chiari's actions were irrational and not in the interests of Panama. Secretary Rusk said that he believed Chiari's advisers could make a rational case in support of Chiari's refusal to negotiate with us now. Looking at it from the Panamanian side, Chiari's advisers could say that he should keep pushing against us, thereby building support for Panama's case among members of the OAS and the UN. Even if Panama did not win full support in these two organizations, the difficulties caused to us would prompt us to come closer to meeting the Panamanian demands. Thus, by refusing to talk now, Panama could expect to create a situation which they might think would force us to be more forthcoming on treaty negotiations.

Mr. Mann said that President Chiari had told us that we would have to leave our base at Rio Hato and remove the equipment now there.

In response to a question from the President as to what we should now do, Mr. Mann said we should play the entire problem in low key during the Presidential elections in Panama. A longer range plan should be developed involving negotiations with Colombia and Nicaragua for permission to build a sea-level canal in their territories. Once these two options were obtained, we could return to the Panamanians and tell them that we were going to build a sea-level canal either in Colombia or in Nicaragua which would greatly reduce the importance of the existing Panama Canal. The Panamanians would then be prepared to make a satisfactory deal with us. Mr. Mann stated that a sea-level canal could be built for approximately $300 million and was already required. Because it would be built at sea level, few people would be required to operate it since it would have no locks. The security problem would also be less.

Under Secretary Ball demurred with respect to the need for a sea-level canal and said it would cost billions and was not required on the basis of existing traffic for the year 2000.

Mr. Mann asked and received the President's permission to develop a long-range plan which would meet the serious situation in Panama. He said we could not solve the dangerous situation which now exists unless we came up with a long-range plan to satisfy Panamanian demands.

In response to Secretary Rusk's question, Secretary Vance said we could operate the Panama Canal independent of any help from Panama if we had to. Panamanians residing in the Canal Zone could operate it if necessary. Therefore, we can operate the Canal without Panamanian cooperation. This means that we are not obliged to find an immediate solution to the present problems because we face the prospect of not being able to keep the Canal open.

Secretary McNamara returned to the room following a second conversation with General O'Meara who reported that the coup information contained in the CIA message had been passed to Chiari in a meeting attended by one of Chiari's advisers who is a known Communist. General O'Meara believed that this Communist would relay our knowledge of the Communist coup to his party members. Therefore, General O'Meara concluded that any coup was stopped for tonight.

The President asked whether we had proof that Castro was involved in the Panama rioting. Mr. Mann said we had received reports of Cuban arms going to Panama, but we had no conclusive proof.[9] Not enough time had elapsed since the riots began for Castro to send armed support to Panama. Secretary Vance said we did, in his opinion, have evidence of Castro's support.

Director McCone said that one of our informants had told us last August that there would be trouble in Panama in January, that Panama was Castro's number one priority target, and that Castro had agreed to send arms to revolutionary elements in Panama.

The President asked whether there were any more reports of crisis situations in Latin American countries. He expressed his concern that the Administration would be accused of knowing exactly what was going to happen and not doing anything. He did not want to have a Pearl Harbor type situation on his hands. He asked what we had done on the basis of the report Mr. McCone referred to. Mr. Bundy replied that he believed it was fair to say that the intelligence community had not predicted that civil disorder would break out in Panama as it had. He knew of no other crisis situation, with the pos-

---

[9] [text not declassified] (Central Intelligence Agency, Job 80–B01285A, DCI (McCone) Files, Meetings with the President)

sible exception of Bolivia, where an effort may be made by the leftists to overthrow La Paz's government. In response to the question of what we had done, Secretary Rusk said we had exchanged information with the Latin American countries about Castro's activities.

The President asked Mr. Mann to give a detailed report on his trip to Panama. Mr. Mann began by calling attention to the exemplary way in which our military forces in the Canal Zone had handled a very difficult situation. Mr. Dungan and Secretary Vance fully agreed with this statement. Mr. Mann said that the group's final meeting with Chiari was as tough as the first and quite different from the friendly attitude which prevailed in meetings with other Panamanian officials between the first and final Chiari meeting. Mr. Mann said the Panamanians had broken relations with us before the delegation had even arrived in Panama and now refused to renew relations. He said it was possible that the OAS peace commission might bring about a restoration of relations. He predicted continuing and growing trouble in Panama in the days ahead.

Secretary Rusk made the following points:

(1) We cannot be pushed out of Panama because we have overwhelming force there. Some 8000 U.S. troops could easily handle the few thousand National Guardsmen in Panama. The President asked whether this was so, and Secretary McNamara said it was.

(2) U.S. presence in the Canal Zone is so beneficial to Panama that responsible Panamanians realize that the Republic's economic future depends on our remaining in the Zone.

(3) The members of the OAS peace commission have indicated that they are fed up with the Panamanian attitude and are not hostile to us. Their attitude will be reflected in the attitude of several Latin American governments.

(4) We will be supported in our insistence on conditions which permit us to continue operation of the Canal by those countries which are interested in the unhampered use of and in the security of the Canal.

On the other side, Secretary Rusk said that the Panamanians can make things very difficult for us in the OAS and in the UN. Additionally, there are many who will have sympathy for the Panamanians because they believe we have not been fair to the Panamanians. We must acknowledge that the heavy-handed way in which we have handled treaty matters in the past has led some to lose sympathy with us.

Secretary Vance said that while there are many problems, the crucial issue is U.S. sovereignty. If we lose our sovereignty in the Zone, he doubts we can protect the Canal.

Mr. Mann said we must face the fact that the Panamanian aim is full control of the Zone. If we agree to treaty revisions now, the Panamanians will demand more changes before the ink is even dry on the new treaty. The unsatisfactory situation cannot be solved without major changes in the future. He repeated his belief that we must consider building a sea-level canal.

Mr. Ball said one thing we could do promptly would be to reconstitute the Panama Canal Board which is now not attuned to the situation in Panama.

Secretary McNamara said an immediate requirement was the naming of a political chief who would speak for the U.S. Government and be above the Commander-in-Chief, Southern Forces, as well as the Governor of the Canal Zone. Mr. Dungan filled in details of the three sources of power now which exist under present U.S. organization arrangements. Secretary McNamara said in his view the U.S. Ambassador should be the chief and should boss the entire operation. Secretary Rusk had certain doubts that a U.S. Ambassador, based in the Republic of Panama, could operate the Canal, which is a huge business enterprise, employing thousands of people.

The meeting was interrupted while the President and others read a report of Foreign Minister Solis' press conference. It now appears that the Panamanians are willing to talk without prior commitments and without an agenda. This is our position also.

The remainder of the meeting was spent in redrafting the press statement made at the conclusion of the meeting (copy attached).

(Note: This is only a partial record because of my absence during part of the meeting.)[10]

Bromley Smith[11]

---

[10] Another account of this White House meeting was made by J.C. King whose account records three points not covered by Smith: (1) Mann had indicated that he believed "eventually we should negotiate with the Panamanians, but that there should be no fixed requirements levied upon us before sitting down to discuss demands"; (2) in response to the President's inquiry, Vance indicated that U.S. troops showed great restraint and did not provoke the Panamanians; and (3) the President said "we must be firm but not inflammatory." He also said "we have done nothing to be ashamed of," and that "in public statements we do not want to give any impression we are willing to consider revision of the Treaty." (Memorandum from King to McCone, January 15; ibid.)

[11] Printed from a copy that bears this typed signature.

378. Telephone Conversation Among President Johnson, the
       Assistant Secretary of State for Inter-American Affairs
       (Mann), and Ralph Dungan of the National Security Council
       Staff[1]

Washington, January 14, 1964, 1:03 p.m.

[Omitted here is the opening portion of the conversation which
was not recorded. According to Mann's record of the conversation,
which covers the opening portion of the discussion, Martin reported
that the OAS Peace Committee informed him that Chiari had agreed
to three things: (1) "The Panamanians will not withdraw their personnel from Washington and we will not need to withdraw our personnel
from Panama"; (2) "All conversations between us and the Panamanians will be conducted through the Committee and the Committee
wants it this way. Mr. Mann said he thought this was a good idea";
and (3) "According to Velarde (press secretary) Panamanians are now
agreeable to settling the bus strike on reasonable terms. Mr. Mann said
this was very important." (Johnson Library, Papers of Thomas C. Mann,
Telephone Conversations with LBJ, January 4, 1964–April 30, 1965)
Martin's report of the Peace Commission's 5:30 p.m. meeting, January
13, 1964, is in USCINCSO telegram SC1188A, January 14. (Ibid.,
National Security File, Country File, Panama, Riots, Vol. II, Part A,
January–February)]

Mann: Solis said—that's the Foreign Minister—he has told the
Committee that they are now willing to agree that if they have bilateral talks with us—new relations—and if we fail to reach an agreement,
Panama will recognize the old treaty—the 1903 treaty and the two
amendments still stand. In other words, this means they're not revoking the treaty, and that is, I think, very important. According to the
Foreign Minister, they estimate the talks will take 2 to 3 years before
they're concluded. That will give us plenty of time, and it will take

---

[1] Source: Johnson Library, Recordings and Transcripts, Recording of telephone conversation among President Johnson, Thomas Mann, and Ralph Dungan, Tape F64.05,
Side B, PNO 4. No classification marking. This transcript was prepared in the Office of
the Historian specifically for this volume. According to Mann's record of this conversation, he called the President to advise him of the latest information he had received from
Martin in Panama, and Dungan was in Mann's office during his telephone conversation
with the President. (Ibid., Papers of Thomas C. Mann, Telephone Conversations with
LBJ, January 4, 1964–April 30, 1965)

plenty of time to go into all these things in depth. Takes the heat off immediately, and this is also important.[2]

Now, the Panamanians, according to the Committee, always—they've been shifting so fast you can't be sure—are now willing to resume relations and begin talks on the whole range of problems between the U.S. and Panama, which would include treaties, and undoubtedly would include their demands for treaty revision. They would agree at the same time to continue law and order in the Zone and avoid violence, which is the main point. There would be no agenda to these talks and no pre-commitments on our part. We would not commit ourselves to anything; just begin to talk—negotiate. The question that the Committee asked Ed Martin is, how soon would he be prepared to begin talking. The Panamanians have said it may take them a couple or three months to get ready. We should answer that we would be ready in a month and sooner, if necessary. Just to keep the record straight on this.

Dungan: After O'Meara has satisfied himself that order has been restored—would be a couple of days.

Mann: Now, the Panamanians were, I think, unreasonably, but nevertheless—I am sure this is an important political factor—disturbed about our references to the soldiers. They don't know yet about Vance meeting with the press, on the record, which is still going on—or was a couple of minutes ago—and they don't know about the Secretary's television conference. I thought I would call Ed about those so he can get word to the Committee beforehand and prepare them on these in case there's something in there, and if we get this—if we can get this, Mr. President, I think we've achieved substantially everything that you asked us to. I think it's a good deal for us.

President: What do we get out of it besides a lot of talking with them and their raisin' hell about revisin' the treaties?

Mann: Well, the first thing you do is—that situation down there is so explosive that we avoid large-scale, major large-scale casualties—prevent it. Give us time to get tempers time to cool down there and sit down and look at the thing, and there may well be things that we can readily agree to, and try to find a basis for agreement between us and

---

[2] In his assessment of Martin's discussions with the Peace Committee on January 13, Bundy told the President that, "in sum, they show a substantial back-off by Solis from the position taken by Chiari with Mann." Bundy informed the President: "There is some evidence that the Panamanians are feeling for a way to get discussion going without sticking firmly to their talk of agreement to discuss revision of the treaties. This is clearly what the Peace Committee wants and is pressing them for. But when directly pressed on this point, Solis did not budge and the formal position is just as it has been—the Panamanians say that relations are broken and will remain broken until we agree to discuss revision of the treaties." (Memorandum from Bundy to the President, January 14; ibid., Memos to the President, McGeorge Bundy, Vol. I, November 1963–February 1964)

the Panamanians. That preserves all our vital interests and, I think this is something we should [unintelligible].

Dungan: You're not, Mr. President, if you move back exactly to the position that the United States was in prior to the time of this outbreak—and you have gained, it seems to me, for what it's worth, the approbation of all of Latin America. Position, I think, is much stronger in Latin America because we have stood up strongly, you haven't been oppressive, and you haven't lost a bloody thing. You're no different on the treaty revision part than you were before the outbreak began.

Mann: We're not conceding anything yet except that we're ready to talk. That's all we're—

President: You don't think there will be an interpretation placed on setting these conferences that we're implying that we're goin' into 'em with good faith to revise the treaty?

Mann: Well.

Dungan: As a matter of fact, Mr. President, it seems to me after you've had an opportunity—now I realize that there's a distinction between the substantive and political—but after you've had a chance to review a lot of these issues and after they've been talked through over a couple of years, it probably will be—you will come to the conclusion that you will want some treaty revision without substantially changing our sovereign right or your "as is" sovereign rights in the Canal Zone.

Mann: I agree with you that the way this was phrased is very important.

Dungan: Very.

Mann: What I suggest on that is that we, through the Committee with the Panamanians in both ways we will—discussion will include something like the whole range of U.S.-Panamanian relations. Try to avoid—

President: I sure don't want to imply that I'm goin' to sit down and talk to 'em about changes that I'll make in the treaties and revise the whole thing, and all they got to do is burn the USIS, Embassy, and then we come in—hat in hand—and say come on boys, we'll let you write your ticket.

Mann: We've agreed, as I said earlier, that there are no preconditions. We're not committing ourselves to any treaty revisions.

President: Well, just make that awfully clear in our statement—all right?

Dungan: And also, they're very insistent on not giving any of this publicity, is that right, Tom?

Mann: Right. I'm coming to that. The Committee, not the Panamanian Government, is putting the pressure on both us and the Panamanians to avoid official statements to the press until we can get time to talk and let tempers cool down. In the long run, Mr. President, we're going to be judged by our deeds and not our words.

President: But you may not be around to judge 'em if they think we're sittin' down to revise some treaties, Tom.

Mann: Well, that's true, and I think we have to go up on the Hill and explain very clearly what—

President: Did you go up there this mornin'?

Mann: Haven't been up yet, sir, but I'm waiting for Vance to get through.

President: Uh huh.

Dungan: I called Dan Flood this morning.

President: How did Vance get along? Anybody know?

Mann: We don't know yet.

Dungan: Not finished yet.

Mann: I think I will get up this afternoon and talk to Vance and work out a plan to get in touch with some key people on the Hill.

President: I think that's very good. Okay. Anything else?

Mann: That's all, sir, but is it all right to say that we will agree to—

President: I think we can always agree to talk and listen. I don't want to imply that we're—by so doin'—that we're making any commitment of any kind.

Mann: All right, sir.

President: I want to be fair and want to be reasonable and want to be just to these people, and if we've got problems with wage scales or arrogant military people or Zonites that cause these troubles, or any improvement or changes we can make, we're anxious to do it—wage scales, or whatever it is. But if they think that all they gotta do is to burn a USIS and shoot four or five soldiers and then we come runnin' in and—hat in hand—well, that's a different proposition.

Mann: No, I think this is clear. We've won our point. We're not going to negotiate under duress—that is, until law and order is restored.

President: What do you mean that they're upset about what we said about the soldiers? Do you mean about their behavin' admirably under extreme provocation?

Mann: Yes. [chuckle] They're the most unreasonable people, Mr. President, you can imagine, but we still have to live with them [unintelligible].

President: Well, you better go on and get started on your other Canal—

Mann: Well, that's what I think, too.

President: I do, too, and I thought so before you got back here. So, the quicker you get on it, the better off we'll—

Mann: I'll tell Ed that we will agree to tell the Committee we will agree to discuss the whole range of U.S.-Panamanian relations.

President: Have you talked to Secretary Rusk and McNamara?

Mann: I talked to Ball—Mr. Rusk is at dinner, but I think I will touch base with him . . .

President: Did you talk to McNamara?

Mann: Not yet.

President: Talk to McNamara and if it's agreeable to them, it's okay by me.

Mann: All right sir. Thank you very much.

President: Bye.

---

379. Editorial Note

On January 15, 1964, the Inter-American Peace Committee issued a communiqué noting its satisfaction with "the re-establishment of peace" between the United States and Panama, "which is an indispensable condition for understanding and negotiation between the parties." The English-language version of the communiqué reported that the parties have agreed to re-establish diplomatic relations and "have agreed to begin discussions which will be initiated thirty days after diplomatic relations are re-established by means of representatives who will have sufficient powers to discuss without limitations all existing matters of any nature which may affect the relations between the United States and Panama." (Department of State *Bulletin*, February 3, 1964, page 156)

Initial reaction to the communiqué in Washington indicated that the crisis may have passed. At the January 15 daily White House staff meeting, Bundy commented that "our success in Panama thus far is largely due to the first-rate personal performance of the President." (Memorandum for the record prepared by William Y. Smith, January 15; National Defense University, Taylor Papers, Chairman's Staff Group)

Following release of the communiqué in Panama, however, a dispute arose between the parties over interpretation of the text whether the Spanish word "negociar" meant "discuss," as it appeared in the English text, or "negotiate," as the Panamanians argued. According to a January 16 memorandum from Bundy to Johnson, President Chiari said in a public statement on January 15: "I promised the nation that diplomatic relations would not be re-established with the United States until that country consented to begin negotiations for the drafting of a new treaty, and this promise has been obtained through the mediation of the Inter-American Peace Committee.'" (Memorandum to the President from Bundy, January 16; Johnson Library, National Security File, Memos to the President, McGeorge Bundy, Vol. I, November 1963–February 1964) According to a report from Martin in Panama, Foreign Minister Solis had said to him: "Chiari had to say what he did because 'Communists are still agitating and the university students have not understood IPC communiqué.'" (Telegram SC12300A from Martin to Mann, January 15; ibid., NSC Histories, Panama Crisis, 1964)

President Johnson told Rusk on January 16: "I think we sit tight on the Peace Committee's statement. It's possible that some of the left-wingers will try to force Chiari's hand but I think we've gone about as far as we can go at this point, and I think he'll find a way to swing around and not cause too much trouble." (Recording of telephone conversation between President Johnson and Secretary Rusk, January 16, 1:15 p.m.; ibid., Recordings and Transcripts, Tape F64.06, Side A, PNO 4)

---

380.   Telegram From the Department of State to the Embassy in Panama[1]

Washington, January 16, 1964, 12:01 p.m.

7294. For Martin from Mann. In view of the agreement that all discussions between the United States and Panama should be through the Peace Committee and risk that Chiari will use meeting with you for his own political purposes, suggest that you postpone your meeting with Chiari and convey orally following message to Trucco with request that he orally deliver message to Chiari in our behalf:

1. From the beginning we have made it clear to all concerned that the United States is willing, in language of English text of Peace Committee report, "to discuss without limitation all existing matters of any nature which may affect the relations between the United States and Panama." As the minutes of the Peace Committee show, this clearly

---

[1] Source: Johnson Library, National Security File, NSC Histories, Panama Crisis, 1964. Confidential; Immediate; Limdis. Drafted by Mann and cleared by Rusk and the White House. A copy was passed to the White House.

means that the Government of Panama would be free to raise any questions it wished.

2. We will not negotiate under pressures whether these pressures be aggressions against the Canal Zone or threats of mob violence or the breaking of diplomatic relations or any other kinds of pressures. Nor will the United States accept Panamanian pre-conditions as Panama's price for being willing to discuss issues with the United States.

3. Our insistence on the word "discuss" rather than the word "negotiate" in the Peace Committee's English version of the communiqué was to avoid any possibility that the Government of Panama would interpret the phrase "negotiate without limitations" as any kind of a pre-commitment to replace the existing treaties with a new treaty. In this connection, the United States notes that according to a report appearing in *The New York Times* of January 16:

"President Chiari, in a ten minute broadcast, stated categorically that Panama regarded Washington's accord to 'negotiate without limitations' as a commitment to replace existing treaties with a new one."

4. The English text of the Peace Committee report therefore uses the word "discuss" instead of "negotiate". The United States acquiesced in translating the word "discuss" as "negociar" in the Spanish text only because the word "discutir" was thought by some to have a connotation of conflict. The minutes of the Peace Committee clearly show however that the consistent United States position was that stated in paragraphs 1 and 2 of this memorandum.

5. The issue therefore was and remains simply this: Is the Government of Panama agreeable to discussions with the United States covering the whole range of issues affecting United States and Panamanian relations? Or does the Government of Panama refuse to enter into discussions with the United States unless the United States first agrees to Panamanian preconditions about replacing or structurally revising existing treaties?

Rusk

381.   Memorandum From the Acting Deputy Secretary of Defense (Vance) to the Chairman of the Joint Chiefs of Staff (Taylor)[1]

Washington, January 22, 1964.

It is requested that you develop contingency plans for U.S. military intervention in the Republic of Panama[2] under the following circumstances:

1. The present Government of Panama requests U.S. military assistance to prevent its overthrow by Communist/Castro oriented political groupings.

2. A Communist/Castro oriented government has seized power in Panama and a decision is made by the U.S. to intervene for the purpose of replacing it with a government friendly to the interests of the U.S.

Under each of the assumptions listed above, planning should envision two separate responses by the Guardia Nacional.[3] These are:

1. Guardia opposes the Communist takeover.

2. Guardia supports the Communist takeover, is neutral, or is divided in its loyalties.

The purpose of the military action will be to establish sufficient control over selected territories in the Republic of Panama as to permit a non-Communist government to exercise power in the Republic. Minimum force will be utilized to achieve this objective. Further, the

---

[1] Source: Washington National Records Center, OSD/ISA Files, FRC 330 68 A 4023, Panama, 1964. Top Secret.

[2] An entry in the President's Daily Diary, dictated by Valenti, indicates that at 8:30 a.m. on January 22 the President "instructed Secretary of Defense McNamara to have plans ready for any contingency in Panama. If a coup is used, let us have detailed plans prepared for it." (Johnson Library)

[3] In a telephone conversation with Mann at 9:30 a.m. on January 22, the President expressed his concern about the capabilities of the Panamanian National Guard and reported that he had asked McNamara "to get ready for the worse if something happened down there." Although Mann told the President that "the relationship between the Army and the Guard is good," the President felt that it might be necessary to seal off the Canal Zone "for security reasons." (Memorandum of telephone conversation between Mann and President Johnson, January 22; ibid., Papers of Thomas C. Mann, Telephone Conversations with LBJ, January 14, 1964–April 30, 1965)

planning should envision the earliest possible withdrawal of U.S. forces after the objective is achieved.

These plans should be developed as a matter of priority.[4]

Cyrus R. Vance[5]

---

[4] The JCS informed USCINCSO the night of January 22 that Major General F.T. Unger of the Joint Staff, representing General Taylor, would arrive in Panama January 23 to consult with O'Meara and Martin and assist in the development of contingency plans that would be "for priority consideration by the Joint Chiefs of Staff." (JCS telegram 4506 to CINCSO, January 22; National Archives and Records Administration, RG 59, Central Files 1964–66, DEF 1–1 PAN) McNamara sent the President a summary of the JCS plan for military intervention in Panama on January 31. The concept of the plan was based on quick reaction, early seizure of centers of power within Panama City, securing the installations and borders of the Canal Zone, and secondarily sealing of Colon because it was a "Communist stronghold." (Johnson Library, National Security File, Panama Riots, Vol. II, Part F, January–February, 1964)

[5] Printed from a copy that bears this typed signature.

---

382. Telephone Conversation Between President Johnson and Senator Richard Russell[1]

Washington, January 22, 1964, 6:55 p.m.

[Omitted here is a brief conversation not related to Panama. The President then read Senator Russell a press statement on Panama he planned to make. Johnson subsequently issued the statement on Panama, slightly revised but with no substantive changes from the text as described to Russell, to news correspondents on January 23. (Department of State *Bulletin*, February 10, 1964, pages 195–196)]

Russell: Well, I guess that's all right, if you feel like you've got to issue a statement.

President: Well, I think we've got to get back to—

Russell: [Unintelligible] come in there and march across the Zone [unintelligible] across the Panama Canal Zone.

President: No, we're not. They're—

---

[1] Source: Johnson Library, Recordings and Transcripts, Recording of telephone conversation between President Johnson and Richard Russell, Tape F64.07, Side A, PNO 3. No classification marking. This transcript was prepared in the Office of the Historian specifically for this volume.

Russell: Come and walk across—go swimmin' in the locks if he wants to.

President: Yeah, but our people—no, we don't. We don't want 'em to leave. They think they can put that Canal out of commission—6 months mighty easy, and we got to be awfully careful about security. And they're not goin' to let any mobs come in there, and they're not goin' to let Castro set up a new government, although every night they think he's goin' to—and we're tryin' to get the thing back.

Russell: I wish to hell he'd—Castro'd seize it. Then, maybe, dammit, those people in the State Department and these weepin' sob sisters all over the country would let us go in there and protect our rights. I wish old Castro would seize it.

President: Well, now, this is pretty—don't you think this is a pretty good statement? This is not State Department talk.

Russell: I know it.

President: It's right out of my office here with Jack Valenti and Ted Sorensen.

Russell: [Unintelligible] you feel like you had to issue any statement.

President: Oh, I think I have to try it or do all I can to bring about an adjustment of some kind—

Russell: There's people who are hurting—we ain't hurting—we're not—

President: Yeah, but—yes, we are hurtin', Dick. We're hurtin' in the hemisphere and we're hurtin' in the world. That damn propaganda is all against us, and it's just everywhere, it just looks—

Russell: I read a piece in the *Manchester Guardian,* and one in this London paper, and they both said that we ought to have learned by one mistake in Cuba not to make another now by surrendering here in Panama.

President: Well, we're not surrendering. But I think that there are a good many chicken things that we can do and should do, and Vance thinks so, and thinks that we should have done 'em, and—for instance, we think that we've got a very archaic Board—Panama Canal—we think our governor is no good, he's an old ex-military fellow. That Board of Engineers—that's not up to it. Nobody thinks it is—Vance, General O'Meara.

Russell: Well, we've been retiring them off down there for a long time.

President: And we know our Ambassador wasn't worth a damn. He just sold out to the Panamanians a hundred percent. Came back and denounced everybody, and that's why he got fired—because he wanted to run for governor of West Virginia on the Republican ticket.

But he said that he wanted—he's one hundred percent Panamanian, and he was just raisin' hell about what the Zonists were doing. We've got a list of things that's two pages long[2] that we can do and we ought to do, and that don't sacrifice anything. But, there is some merit to their side—not in violence, not in shootin' people, but what I think is—I don't think I can get by with a press conference without this question comin' up. I just think it's as sure as the sea. I've got to see the Peace Commission in the mornin.'[3] I've got to follow some kind of a discussion with 'em, and this has been pretty much my line.

Russell: Yeah, you're not changing your position any. I just thought I'd let him sweat for a while there.

President: Well, I am. I'm lettin' him sweat.

Russell: Have you withdrawn your aid yet?

President: Yeah, we're not giving them a damn thing, and furthermore, just confidentially, I've moved all of our dependents—I'm movin' 'em out to South Carolina.

Russell: Well, if you've done that, you'll hear from Chiari before long and he'll be on his knees. I just wouldn't be too swift if I were you.

President: I'm not. I'm goin' to wait until day after tomorrow. I'm goin' to wait another day or two. But—

Russell: Hold it just as long as you can, Mr. President. You've got all the cards—and this damn yappin' over here about this OAS—it don't amount to a thing—just because they feel like they've got to stick together whenever one—you got to get down and really talk to 'em underneath the bed sheets, they say. Well, I don't blame you a damn bit.

President: I came back here last night from the Canadian Embassy and Rusk and the whole outfit met with me and I stayed up until 2:00. I was at the desk at 1:00, and I was the only man in the room that said, "No." I didn't have Vance and McNamara, but I told every one of 'em—

Russell: Rusk belongs to the *New York Times, Washington Post,* the *St. Louis Post-Dispatch.*

President: I said I am not about—not one goddamned bit—as long as I'm President, which is goin' to be for 11 months, gentlemen—I'm not about to get on my knees and go crawlin' to him and say I want

---

[2] The Department of State plan described 14 specific actions which could be taken in the Canal Zone to improve relations with Panama, 8 potential minor revisions to the Canal Treaty that would have the same effect, and discussed a potential sea level canal. (Attachment to a covering memorandum from Read to Bundy, January 21; National Archives and Records Administration, RG 59, Central Files 1964–66, POL PAN–US)

[3] The President received the Inter-American Peace Committee at the White House at 10:40 a.m.; the meeting lasted no later than 11:05 a.m. (Johnson Library, President's Daily Diary) No other record of the conversation has been found.

to apologize to you for you shootin' my soldiers; by God I ain't goin' to do it. I wasn't raised in that school, and they hushed up and didn't say anything. But I'm gettin' ready to have a press conference and I got to be prepared—and I'm goin' to be prepared on everything if I can, and this is one of the things to be prepared on. And I just want to check it with you before I—

Russell: Well, if you got to issue a statement, that's about as good as you can make.

President: All right. Okay. You know anything else?

Russell: I was hoping you might defer it.

President: Well, I'm goin' to defer it. I'm goin' to defer it.

Russell: I think you've got all the cards, and the little flurry here in the States—Rusk and that crowd, I imagine, Cousin Adlai—I haven't seen or heard from him, but I imagine Cousin Adlai is—

President: I haven't heard a word from him. I haven't heard a word from him.

Russell: But the people of this country are just one million percent back of your position.

President: Well, I don't know whether they know it or not, but I did get a poll in Pennsylvania today that shows—

Russell: I know it—you ask any Congressman or Senator about his mail.

President: Do you know what Pennsylvania—a fellow running up there for Senate took the most reputable poll in Pennsylvania today and you know it shows I get more Republicans than the Republicans get, and I beat Scranton 79 to 20. I beat Goldwater 82 to 17 in Pennsylvania.

Russell: You just go on and do what is in this country's interest, and tell Rusk and these other fellows to jump in the lake, and it'll stay that way. The American people have been crying for somebody that had some of the elements of "Old Hickory" Jackson in him. They thought they had him in old Ike, but Ike had to be a captive of those people because he didn't know what else to do. You know this government; you know the world. Ike—he was limited in his experience and afraid of himself, so he leaned completely on John Foster Dulles.

President: Well, everybody is when you get—

Russell: I know, but somebody down there just got to take the bull by the horns one of these days and play the part of old Andrew Jackson—say, "well gentlemen, this is it."

[Omitted here is discussion unrelated to Panama.]

383.   Editorial Note

On January 25, 1964, President Johnson telephoned Assistant Secretary Mann to inquire whether the Inter-American Peace Committee was making any progress on a draft agreement on resumption of diplomatic relations between the United States and Panama. Mann replied that "we do not have a solution," and "we don't want to agree on anything before checking with the President." Mann said that "he did not think the President should be too optimistic because when he sounded optimistic this encouraged the Panamanians to think that we were willing to agree to what they wanted." He told the President that he, Vance, and Dungan would be working some more on the draft and "thought it best not to bother the President until they had their homework done." Johnson asked Mann to get the draft into shape. (Memorandum of telephone conversation between Mann and President Johnson, January 25, 12:20 p.m.; Johnson Library, Papers of Thomas C. Mann, Telephone Conversations with LBJ, January 14, 1964–April 30, 1965)

The President received a copy of the draft the afternoon of January 25. Asked if he concurred by Acting Secretary of State George Ball, the President stated: "I don't want to be pinned to it for another 30 minutes." (Recording of telephone conversation between President Johnson and George Ball, January 25, 2:05 p.m.; ibid., Recordings and Transcripts, Tape F64.07, Side B, PNO 4) Johnson then called Senator Russell and told him he thought the draft was "all right, but I just didn't want to wrap it up and get it tied" without getting Russell's views. The President was concerned that "there's some sleeper in it" he couldn't see. He then read the text of the draft agreement:

"The governments of Panama and the United States have accepted the invitation made to them by the Peace Committee with a view to reestablishing diplomatic relations between the two countries as soon as possible, and to seek prompt elimination of the causes of tension between the two countries. The parties have agreed between themselves that 15 days after having reestablished the above mentioned relations, they will appoint special ambassadors with sufficient powers to negotiate—in other words to discuss—a good faith attempt to resolve all the problems without any limitations whatsoever that affect the relations between the countries." The draft concluded: "Each of the governments shall be absolutely free to present for discussion any matter and take any position they deem necessary. All agreements reached will be promptly implemented in accordance with the constitutional processes of each government."

Russell indicated that the draft "sounds all right" but "the State Department will use that as a basis to—just to try to negotiate that treaty away." The President pointed out that Tom Mann was the key official on this matter and "he's the strongest guy over there." Russell then noted: "I see you've got that word 'negotiate' in there, and that was what the breach was over before, wasn't it?" He thought the issue was over "the difference between 'discuss' and 'negotiate'." Johnson said that "one was 'discuss' the problems and the other was 'negotiate' a treaty. I didn't want to agree before I sat down to 'negotiate' a new treaty. I agreed to sit down and talk and discuss any problems but discussing a problem and negotiating a treaty is a different thing." Johnson continued, "I don't mind negotiatin' on the problems—that's what I'm anxious to do—but I'm not willin' to negotiate a treaty in advance." Russell then indicated that he thought that was "all right." (Recording of telephone conversation between President Johnson and Richard Russell, January 25, 2:30 p.m.; ibid., Tape F64.07, Side B, PNO 5) The portion of the conversation printed here was prepared in the Office of the Historian specifically for this volume.

The President then called Mann and said that "he did not want the word 'negotiate' to appear. He said 'agree' or 'discuss' are all right. He said it could read 'with sufficient powers to enter into a good faith agreement to resolve all the problems'" between the countries. Johnson told Mann he was ready to approve the draft with that modification. Mann said he didn't think the Panamanians "were going to buy" the modified draft. He said he "thought their whole idea in the wording was to make it appear that we were going to scrap the old treaty and start negotiating a new one." He said he thought "we could live with the draft we had given the President." (Memorandum of telephone conversation between Mann and Johnson, January 25, 3:05 p.m.; ibid., Papers of Thomas C. Mann, Telephone Conversations with LBJ, January 14, 1964–April 30, 1965) There is a recording of the Mann–Johnson conversation which amplified their discussion. In this recording, President Johnson said, "Well, we don't have to live with anything they give us." He continued, "Now, remember this: I think we've got the cards. I don't give a damn what you say about Latin America—they're goin' to have to depend on us and they're not goin' to take over there. We're goin' to take over if anybody does, and the more they wait, the more they suffer and the more trouble they're in, and they've got to come to us. We don't have to come to them." He asked Mann if there was anything in the modified draft that indicated the U.S. was "caving," and Mann responded "no," not in the modified draft. (Recording of telephone conversation between President Johnson and Thomas Mann, January 25, 2:50 p.m.; ibid., Recordings and Transcripts, Tape F64.07, Side B, PNO 7) The portion of the conversation printed here was prepared in the Office of the Historian specifically for this volume.

On January 27 Mann called Johnson to inform him that "as we anticipated," the Panamanians had not bought the new draft agreement and that "an impasse had been reached." He also informed the President that the Peace Committee had "read the riot act" to Miguel Moreno, the Panamanian contact with the Peace Committee. (Memorandum of telephone conversation between Mann and President Johnson, January 27, 7:20 p.m.; ibid., Papers of Thomas C. Mann, Telephone Conversations with LBJ, January 14, 1964–April 30, 1965) Mann also told Johnson that "we don't like the language" being proposed by the Panamanians, and that they would continue their efforts to work out an acceptable agreement. (Recording of telephone conversation between President Johnson and Thomas Mann, January 27, 7:20 p.m.; ibid., Recordings and Transcripts, Tape F64.08, Side A, PNO 5)

On January 29 President Johnson discussed the Panamanian revisions with Russell who felt, "this is utterly unreasonable. I thought we'd already gone too far, but when they come in and make us admit—make us agree in advance—to rewrite the treaty in some unknown way that we don't even know, I just don't believe any reasonable person would support that." (Recording of telephone conversation between the President and Russell, January 29, 10:30 a.m.; ibid., Side B, PNO 4) In a conversation with Senator Mansfield later that morning Johnson told him that the Peace Committee was about to break off negotiations because the Panamanians insist that the United States "revise these treaties in advance without knowing how they want them revised, and unless we agree to that, they want to take it to the OAS." Johnson stated, "I'm going to tell 'em that we just can't do that." Mansfield agreed: "That's right. You can't do it and you can't give them a blank check before you sit down." (Recording of telephone conversation between the President and Mansfield, January 29, 11:11 a.m., ibid., Tape 64.09, Side A, PNO 1) The portions of the conversations printed here were prepared in the Office of the Historian specifically for this volume.

---

384. Memorandum of Conversation[1]

Washington, January 29, 1964.

SUBJECT

Panamanian Complaints concerning the Canal Zone

PARTICIPANTS

Ambassador Tejera Paris, Chairman, Inter-American Peace Committee
Ambassador Miguel J. Moreno, Jr., of Panama
Ambassador Ellsworth Bunker of the United States[2]

---

[1] Source: National Archives and Records Administration, RG 59, Central Files 1964–66, POL PAN–US. Confidential. Drafted by Bunker.

[2] Bunker was confirmed by the Senate as U.S. Representative to the Council of the Organization of American States on January 23.

I suggested to Ambassador Tejera that it might be helpful if he, Ambassador Moreno and I could have an informal talk to see whether we could find any alternative formula which might bring the two sides closer together. Accordingly, we had lunch together, and in the course of our conversation I said to Ambassador Moreno that I thought it might be helpful if he could tell me the major issues with which Panama was concerned.

Ambassador Moreno replied that, in the first place, he wanted to make it clear that the nationalization, security, or demilitarization of the Canal was not an issue. Panama recognized that the security of the Canal was an obligation of the United States which it could not and should not give up.

The points, however, with which Panama was concerned were the following:

1. *Perpetuity*

The Ambassador said that he did not want to specify what might seem a reasonable period, but that some time limit should be written into the Treaty, and that there was a strong feeling among all Panamanians that the perpetuity clause was outdated and unnecessary today. He doubted that if a treaty were to be negotiated today anywhere, a perpetuity clause would be acceptable.

2. *Re-examination of Panama's Sovereign Rights in the Zone*

Flying the flag, he said, is one way of achieving this. There has been a feeling, however, among Panamanians that whenever the question of sovereign rights is raised by Panama, the United States is prone to fall back on Article III of the 1903 Treaty.

3. *Larger Benefits from Operation of the Canal*

Ambassador Moreno felt that Panama should have a greater share in revenue from the Canal. Panama also felt that it suffered from unfair competition from U.S. commissaries, which sold luxury goods at very low prices.

4. *The Position of Panamanian Workers*

While the principle of equal pay applied, the fact was that most of the higher-paying jobs are occupied by Americans and the lower-paying ones, by Panamanians. The provision that security positions should be occupied only by Americans had been used to pre-empt positions for U.S. citizens. The number of security positions, he said, had been increased to some 3000 in order, it was felt, to eliminate Panamanians.

Ambassador Moreno went on to say that Panama was not intransigent, that President Roosevelt had agreed to negotiations in 1934, with the result that a treaty had been agreed to in 1936. President Eisenhower had also agreed to negotiate in 1953, and a treaty had been agreed to in 1955. It was difficult for him to understand, therefore, why the United States was so fearful of an agreement to negotiate. I explained to him again that the interpretation which President Chiari had put on the word had made agreement to negotiate a revision a precondition for entering negotiations. As I had explained in the meetings of the IAPC, this we could not and would not do. I did not believe that any country would be willing to enter negotiations on the basis of prior conditions.

Ambassador Moreno went on to say that because of past experience in negotiating with the United States, precise language in the communiqué to be issued by the IAPC was important. I asked whether he could suggest language and whether we could attempt to work out language which would be mutually acceptable. He then suggested the following as a substitute for paragraph 3:

"Within the thirty days following the re-establishment of said relations, the parties will designate Special Ambassadors with sufficient powers to reconsider, without limitation, the relations between the two countries, including the review (revisión) of the Treaties and other agreements regarding the Canal, with sufficient powers to enter into new pacts (pactos) which may result from said review."

I said that I would consult my government to see whether some such wording would be acceptable, and that I would meet with him and Ambassador Tejera after a meeting which was scheduled for the White House at 3:45 p.m.[3]

Ambassador Tejera remarked that he felt it would be unfortunate to have the dispute go to the Council. It would result in stirring up old hatreds and playing into the hands of the communists, who would resort to the demagogic appeal of anti-imperialism. This could be dangerous for his own country as well as for other Latin American nations.

After the White House meeting, I met with Ambassador Tejera and Ambassador Moreno at 6:00 p.m., and informed them that the language proposed by Ambassador Moreno was not acceptable. Ambassador Moreno said that he would have no alternative then but to present his

---

[3] Bunker, Mann, Ball, Vance, and Dungan met with the President at 3:50 p.m., and then they were joined in the Cabinet Room by the Congressional leadership to discuss Panama. This meeting lasted until 5:15 p.m., when the Congressional leadership departed. At 5:25 p.m. the remaining group convened with the President in the Oval Office until 6 p.m. (Johnson Library, President's Daily Diary) No other record of these meetings has been found.

government's note to the Chairman of the Council, requesting that a meeting be convened. He telephoned me later at 10:00 p.m. to say that this was then being done.[4]

---

[4] On January 29 Panama broke off talks with the Inter-American Peace Committee and formally requested a meeting of the OAS Council in order to invoke the Rio Treaty on the grounds of United States aggression. The Panamanian request is in OAS doc, OEA/SerG./V/C–d–1189. Bunker's statement to the OAS Council rejecting all charges of U.S. aggression against Panama, January 31, is in Department of State *Bulletin*, February 24, 1964, pp. 300–302. In circular telegram 1390 to all ARA posts and CINCSO for Martin, January 30, the Department of State presented the basic U.S. position in the OAS Council, pointing out that "informal soundings" among other COAS representatives indicated "considerable doubt" that the Panamanians could obtain the necessary 11 votes to invoke the Rio Treaty. (National Archives and Records Administration, RG 59, Central Files 1964–66, POL PAN–US)

---

385.   Memorandum From Senator Mike Mansfield to President Johnson[1]

Washington, January 31, 1964.

SUBJECT

The Panama Situation

I. In response to your request, this memorandum contains observations and suggestions relative to the Panamanian situation. They are based on limited access to the facts and on history. As such, they are, at best, additional yardsticks which may have some use in weighing the difficult decisions which fall within your heavy responsibilities.

II. The following *assumptions* underlie the observations and suggestions in this memorandum.

A. We have only one fundamental national interest to protect in the present situation. We have got to insure untroubled and adequate water-passage through Central America. It is desirable to seek to secure this interest at a minimum total cost to this nation and, if possible, by ways which do not undermine our capacity to exercise a constructive influence elsewhere in Latin America.

---

[1] Source: Johnson Library, National Security File, Country File, Panama, Vol. I, December 1963 to January 1964. No classification marking. The memorandum is unsigned.

B. The pressure for social change is just short of violent revolution in Panama and in much of the rest of Latin America. The pressure comes primarily from the inside, from the decay and antiquation of the social structures of various Latin American countries.

Even if we desired to do so, we could not, as a practical matter, stop the pressure for change. But we may have something constructive to contribute to the form and pace of the change if we play our cards carefully and wisely.

C. Change in Panama is part of the whole problem of change in Latin America. Our actions with respect to the part will have a significant effect on our ability to act constructively with respect to the whole.

D. Our actions in Panama will produce respect, rather than fear and suspicious hostility in Latin America, provided that our unquestionable power is used only with restraint and with justice and in accord with the decent opinion of Latin America.

III. If the above assumptions are accurate and are at the heart of our national interest in the present situation, the following general observations on United States policy will be derived from them:

A. Those United States policies (words and actions) which preserve untroubled water-passage through Central America but also tend to permit reasonable and peaceful adjustments in our relationship to the changing situation in that region make sense in terms of our national interests.

B. Conversely, those policies (words and actions) which enable us to preserve the water-passage only by a large increase in the costs of military and police protection and at the price of intensified suspicion and antagonism towards the United States throughout Latin America are to be minimized or avoided entirely if at all possible.

IV. Specific suggestions on policy (words and actions):

In the light of these assumptions and general observations the following specific suggestions may be worth considering:

A. Welcome, wholeheartedly, consideration by the OAS of the difficulties in Panama and urge that body's help in finding a solution; offer every facility for on-the-spot study in the Zone.

B. Reject firmly but without fanfare the charges of aggression and also make it clear that we will not accept unilateral dictation from any nation, large or small.

C. Make clear that the President of the United States does not quibble over words such as "discussion or negotiations"; that, if changes are desirable, as well they may be, we are prepared at all times to sit down to discuss, to negotiate and to agree on a mutually acceptable basis.

D. Avoid boxing ourselves in at home against change through the fanning of our own emotions by crediting Castro and Communism too

heavily for a difficulty which existed long before either had any significance in this Hemisphere and which will undoubtedly continue to
plague us after both cease to have much meaning.

E. Stress with our own involved bureaucracy that our national interest is trouble-free water-passage, not the safeguarding of an outdated position of privilege (Zonists, understandably, might have difficulty differentiating between the maintenance of their special interests
and the national interests). To this end, at an appropriate time:

1. Act to limit continuous service in the Zone for all U.S. military
and civilian personnel to a maximum period of four years and seek a
sharp reduction particularly in civilian personnel.
2. Cut the commissaries or so alter and limit their character that
they will handle only those few unique items of U.S. merchandise
which may not be readily available locally.
3. Fully integrate all schools and colleges in the Zone.
4. Tighten up on all salaries and emoluments to Zone employees
to bring them in line with general U.S. personnel practices applicable
elsewhere to overseas personnel.

F. Indicate a readiness, at an appropriate time and when not under duress, to consider:

a. Steps to give additional recognition to Panamanian titular sovereignty in the Zone.
b. Revision of the rental agreement.
c. An increase of Panamanian participation in the operation of the
Canal up to and including some Panamanian representation on the
Board of the Canal Company, always, however, contingent upon the
need for a trouble-free operation of the waterway.

G. Begin to give serious consideration in diplomacy to marshalling international support for a Mexican-owned and operated canal
through Mexico, with a view to sobering the Panamanians in their demands and, also, in recognition of the growing need for additional
water-passage through Central America.

Some or none of the above specifics may have applicability in the
light of your understanding of all the facts. They are merely sugges-
tive of the kinds of words and actions which, it would seem, might be
helpful in the present difficulty. And to ease those difficulties may be
the best that can be hoped for until it is crystal clear that another canal
will be built and our dependence on this outdated monopoly will have
thereby been reduced.

386.   Memorandum From the Assistant Secretary of State for Inter-American Affairs (Mann) to Secretary of State Rusk[1]

Washington, February 1, 1964.

SUBJECT

The Panama Problem

It seems to me that the "line" we take from here on out in our talks with Panamanians and with other Latin Americans is very important.

Chiari decided to put pressure on the United States to force us to agree, in advance of discussions, to negotiate a new treaty to replace, or at least substantially alter, existing treaties. As Moreno has confirmed to Bunker, this means language which can be interpreted as United States pre-commitments to open up the sovereignty and perpetuity issues to re-negotiation.

Breaking of relations was part of the tactic of pressure. The demagogic press, television and radio campaigns by Panamanian media, controlled for a time from the Presidencia itself, was part of the tactic. So was the complicity of Panamanian Government officials in the 36 hours of violence. The demagogic appeals to Latin American governments for support, intransigence in the Peace Committee and the invocation of the Rio Treaty on false charges of United States "aggression" were part of the tactic. Chiari's "painting himself into a corner" by unnecessary public statements was part of the tactic.

In launching the campaign, Chiari was gambling that the United States would yield. The gamble turned out to be a bad one. We have already gone as far as we can in making concessions. Chiari has not really moved an inch.

All of these facts are, or will be, known to knowledgeable people in Latin America. There are signs that at least some Latin Americans are beginning to realize the dimensions of Panamanian irresponsibility and understand that the validity of their treaties and their interests, as well as ours, are involved.[2]

---

[1] Source: National Archives and Records Administration, RG 59, Central Files 1964–66, POL PAN–US. Confidential. A handwritten note on the memorandum reads "Secretary saw."

[2] On January 30 Lansing Collins provided Mann with an analysis of Latin American official opinion on the Panama situation, which indicated that Latin American officials deplored any attempt by Panama to take the issue to the United Nations and "have expressed understanding of our firm position in Panama." (Memorandum from Collins to Mann, January 30; ibid.)

It is doubtful that Chiari can yield. If the impasse continues, it seems equally doubtful that Chiari can "hang on" until the May elections. He may decide voluntarily to turn the office over to someone else. He may be overthrown. Nevertheless, anti-communist political leaders of the country continue their active or tacit support of Chiari because this is "good politics" as long as there is a chance that the United States will yield to Chiari's pre-conditions.

As long as the anti-communist political leaders continue their support of Chiari's tactic, only the communists or Arnulfo Arias, perhaps in combination with each other, will have an organization and a plan— in short, the capacity—to fill the vacuum which Chiari's departure will leave.

If this estimate is correct, then it would make good sense to disabuse all Panamanians, and indeed all Latin Americans, of any ideas that, in the end, we are going to save Chiari by agreeing to his pre-conditions. Only then will anti-communists adjust to reality and begin to organize and plan. When they adjust to reality Chiari will lose support. But we gain by giving anti-communist elements the time and the opportunity to organize an alternative to a communist-infiltrated or communist-controlled government.

By being candid and decisive we would also minimize the risk that other Latin Americans will miscalculate in the current OAS proceedings.

---

387.   Telephone Conversation Between President Johnson and the Assistant Secretary of State for Inter-American Affairs (Mann)[1]

Washington, February 3, 1964, 7:10 p.m.

[Omitted here is discussion unrelated to Panama.]

Mann: Now, the other thing is more important. On Sunday morning,[2] I had a long talk with Sanchez Gavito—the Mexican—and he's worked up an idea which he's put on paper. It says that in case the Rio

---

[1] Source: Johnson Library, Recordings and Transcripts, Recording of telephone conversation between President Johnson and Thomas Mann, Tape F64.10, Side A, PNO 5. No classification marking. This transcript was prepared in the Office of the Historian specifically for this volume.

[2] February 2.

Treaty is—the Council votes to invoke the Rio Treaty as Panama has requested and there will be a commission—a five man, five nation commission set up which will act as a mediating body between the U.S. and Panama [unintelligible]. Secondly, that there would be a U.S.-Panama—plus one other—a three man commission to investigate the facts, what happened. Now he sent over this morning to Ralph Dungan a copy of this draft. I've suggested several changes, after talking with the Secretary, and most of these have been bought, subject to your approval, by us. I think that this resolution, if it goes through, would be satisfactory from our point of view—just as satisfactory as we can expect at this time in the meeting in the OAS. Tonight this draft will probably be circulated, and I just wanted to be sure you had—or Ralph, or somebody, I haven't been able to get him this afternoon—had an opportunity to—

President: Ralph's here now, but he's talkin' about appointments. He hadn't talked about the Mexico draft.

Mann: All right. Well, he's got the papers, and—

President: Well, he keeps them on deep freeze up there. He never does let me see what he gets—

Mann: And if I could talk to him one minute, I could get him the latest information I have on these drafts.

President: Now, I'll tell you what I think. I think the Secretary ought to make a full scale speech outlining what happened in Panama, and just saying we're ready to talk, willing to talk, eager to talk, but we're not gonna negotiate a treaty in advance. But he ought to say that our flag went up by our kids; they made a mistake; they came in and shot our soldiers; we gave them birdshot; we tried to defend ourselves the best we could, but they burned our USIA office; and just outline what horrible things they did without sayin' they're horrible. But let the world know it. John McCone told me that every country he went to—Spain was just up in arms, France couldn't understand it, Great Britain thought it was terrible; Germany thought—couldn't understand why we had started shooting in Panama, because we've been—

Mann: We'll start drafting a speech right away.

President: I've just been beggin' you all to do it, and I know damn well my Johnson City instinct tells me that you oughtn't to sit on your can and do nothin', and I've made one or two statements myself. But the *New York Times* says that we've said nothin', and I just think it's awful that we just sit here like a bunch of mummies and run under the ground, and I think you ought to have a full—

Mann: We'll do a draft and I'll tell you about the—

President: John McCone talked to the head of every government in Europe, and every one of 'em think we're terribly wrong, and our side has never been given, and when he explained it to 'em they said, "well where in the hell has your Secretary of State been."[3]

Mann: All right, we'll start drafting away on that and get it out.[4] Now, should I talk to Ralph about these latest changes?

President: Yeah.

[Omitted here is discussion unrelated to Panama.]

---

[3] During a February 6 luncheon meeting with Rusk, McCone restated that "world opinion was thoroughly convinced that the United States actually invaded Panama, killing Panamanians," and that he "could not understand the reluctance on the part of the President and Rusk to admit participation of Castro Communists in the Panama situation." (Memorandum for the record by McCone, February 6; Central Intelligence Agency, DCI (McCone) Files, Job 80–B01285A, Memos for the Record, January 1–April 5, 1964)

[4] In a telephone conversation with the President on February 5 Mann reported that Secretary Rusk was planning to make a statement on February 7 that would correct a number of misconceptions in the press on the events in Panama. He also reported that work was continuing on the Gavito plan, and that the meetings in the OAS were proceeding well. "I thought Bunker handled himself extremely well," he said. "The Latins are—nearly all of them expressed, when they voted for the Rio Treaty, said they were not passing on who was guilty and who was innocent. They made that very clear, and I think that was very helpful." (Recording of telephone conversation between President Johnson and Thomas Mann, February 5, 10:35 a.m.; Johnson Library, Recordings and Transcripts, Tape F64.10, Side B, PNO 3) Rusk addressed the dispute with Panama at his press conference on February 7; for text, see Department of State Bulletin, February 24, 1964, pp. 274–275.

---

388.   Telegram From the Department of State to the U.S. Southern Command[1]

Washington, February 8, 1964, 1 p.m.

USCINCSO 17. For Martin from Mann. Re Your SC1666A.[2] Appreciate your helpful analysis of current situation in Panama.

I am sure you understand that we would prefer to see Chiari continue in office because of inevitable risks for us inherent in any political upheaval and probability that United States will be blamed for causing Chiari's downfall. At same time I do not believe we should alienate

---

[1] Source: National Archives and Records Administration, RG 59, Central Files 1964–66, POL PAN–US. Confidential; Immediate. Drafted by Mann and cleared by Bunker.

[2] In telegram SC1666A, February 7, Martin provided Mann with a long analysis of political developments and possibilities. (Ibid.)

Arnulfo Arias or any other non-communist political group for the reason that they may come to power no matter what we do or say. If they do we will have to deal with them. It seems to me, therefore, that as between non-communist groups our attitude should be one of strict nonintervention and that we should take special care to avoid the appearance of having intervened against Chiari.[3]

You are correct in saying that our main concern at moment is to prevent growth of commie influence and especially any commie takeover. In this connection, we will, as you suggest, review all evidence available to us regarding Arnulfo Arias and his group and their connections with leftists and extremists, especially communists. I think it is obviously important for us to have as clear an idea as we can get of the role and influence which the communists would have should Arnulfo Arias take over.

I learned this morning that the General Committee acting under the Rio Treaty has appointed a five man committee consisting of representatives of Mexico, Paraguay, Uruguay, Brazil and Costa Rica to do both the mediation and the investigation job.[4]

Sanchez Gavito says the strategy is to go slow on the investigation and to push hard on mediation with the aim of getting relations restored and United States-Panamanian bilateral talks started.

At the same time, Sanchez Gavito stated that there is an OAS consensus that the OAS should have a presence in Panama City and that the plan is for the five man committee to depart for Panama soon. Sanchez Gavito estimated that the five man committee might stay in Panama a week or ten days and then return.

---

[3] In a meeting between representatives of ARA and CIA on February 5, Mann had inquired what the Communists would do should Chiara fall. He said "if the commies take over we are ready to send in troops, but we want to know in advance." Mann was told that there was no evidence the Communists were working with Arnulfo Arias and that it would not be "the end of the world" if Arias took over, since "Arnulfo was probably the only one that could control the streets." (Memorandum from Carter to Hughes, Denney, and Evans, February 6; Department of State, INR/IL Historical Files, ARA/CIA Weekly Meetings, 1964–1965)

[4] On February 4 Bunker defended the U.S. record in Panama concerning the events of January 9 and 10 before the Organization of American States Council. (Department of State *Bulletin*, February 24, 1964, pp. 302–304) On February 7 the Council met and adopted a resolution calling upon both sides not to take steps that might endanger the peace and creating a general committee of all members of the Organ of Consultation, except Panama and the United States, to investigate the events of January 9 and 10, to submit a report on efforts of the Governments of Panama and the United States to find a solution, to assist in finding a "just solution," and to create special subcommittees as needed. The resolution was adopted by a vote of 15–0–2 (Chile and Colombia). The text of the resolution is ibid., p. 304.

Even though Cottrell is arriving in Balboa today, I think you should stay on in Panama long enough to be sure that the committee is not going to plunge immediately into an investigation of the facts or take other important action during its stay there. When had you planned to return to Washington?

Rusk

---

389.   **Telephone Conversation Between President Johnson and the President's Special Assistant for National Security Affairs (Bundy)[1]**

Washington, February 20, 1964, 5:05 p.m.

President: Adlai has got a new formula that starts us out where we were the first day to negotiate a treaty—a new treaty—with the Panamanians.[2]

Bundy: Oh, I don't believe it.

President: And he doesn't see anything wrong with it, and if he were Secretary of State and the President both he would negotiate it. And, so I thanked him and told him to put it in the mail and send it down. You watch for it.

Bundy: (Laughter) What am I supposed to do with it, make him burn it, or answer?

President: Oh, he was kind of sniffy. He said that I hope that you won't reject it out of hand; I hope you'll carefully consider it.

Bundy: Well, we'll do that.

---

[1] Source: Johnson Library, Recordings and Transcripts, Recording of telephone conversation between President Johnson and McGeorge Bundy; Tape F64.13, Side B, PNO 7. No classification marking. This transcript was prepared in the Office of the Historian specifically for this volume.

[2] During a conversation a few minutes earlier with Johnson, Stevenson suggested that Chiari was interested in the following formula to resolve the impasse with the United States: "the two parties agree to appoint negotiators to discuss and review all aspects of U.S.-Panama relations, including the Canal Zone. The President responded that, "we could've agreed on that, Governor, the first day." Johnson stated that this language would give the impression that the United States would re-negotiate the treaty, or at least that is the way the Panamanians would view it. Stevenson suggested that the language did not include a pre-commitment to re-negotiate the treaty, and he asked Johnson to consider it seriously rather than rejecting it immediately. The President was not convinced. (Recording of telephone conversation between President Johnson and Adlai Stevenson, February 20, 5 p.m.; ibid., Tape 64.13, Side B, PNO 6)

President: 'Cause the quicker you settle this one the better off you'll be, and so forth. And the truth of it is I think Mr. Chiari wants to settle it.

Bundy: Uh huh. Uh huh. Has he had anything from the Panamanians or is this out of his own head?

President: Oh, I think he's just gettin' into a field where—he's been down talking to the State Department about it and they added to it, "without any prior commitments." Now, were you in here the other day when we had the Senators here?

Bundy: No sir, I was still on that short holiday (laughter).

President: I wish you'd been here and heard the hell I caused by just mentioning it.

Bundy: Yeah.

President: And I'm not—well, anyway, we just want to carefully consider it, weigh it and everything, and then do nothing about it.

Bundy: Right.

President: I'm not going to use—the two words I'm not going to use are "negotiate" and "revising the treaty."

Bundy: Yep.

President: I told them that to begin with, and the quicker they find that out, the better off they'll be.

Bundy: Right.

President: And, if we can get any other language—I think that we say that when we say we'll talk to 'em about anything, anywhere any time.

Bundy: We've got a good sentence in tomorrow's speech on that. It says we'll talk about all problems, and we'll, you know, we can do it any time and any place. There's no problem. And I think, Mr. President, that there's a new formula that ought to be looked at, which is that we ought to get some third party to say what they think they want to sit down and talk about, and we say what we think we ought to talk about, and then we just agree to talk about it. We don't care what Chiari says he's going to do. He can say, "I'm going in to revise the treaties," and we say "we're going to discuss." That wouldn't bother you, would it? He can propose anything he wants.

President: Well, I'd let him cool off for awhile.

Bundy: That's what I—you know, my honest judgment, I'm sorry to say, is that I think there's not a five percent chance of settling this before their elections.

President: I think that's right.

Bundy: I think it's easier just to play it along. Now, there are some hazards down there, and Panama is not in the best of condition, and there's some losses in moving this direction, but the losses—we've taken an exceedingly clear position—the losses in moving away from that are very much greater. I've seen the polls on this subject, and I'm sure you have—the position of the U.S. Government—

President: Well, I just brought over a picture of Ted Sorensen and his girl, and Walter Winchell is on the same column, and he's got the damnedest diatribe about how we've been mistreated you ever saw.

[Omitted here is a brief discussion unrelated to Panama.]

390.   Memorandum From the President's Special Assistant for National Security Affairs (Bundy) to President Johnson[1]

Washington, February 25, 1964.

SUBJECT

Panama

I want to tell you quite privately that I agree with Dean Rusk that it would be good to get Panama off the stage for the present, if we can do so without retreat.[2] The two basic elements which you have established and defended without a break since January 9 are that we will not agree in advance to revision of the treaties, and that we will not agree to "negotiate." I believe that any form of language which leads to a resumption of relations and a beginning of talks is a victory for the United States and for you, if these two conditions are met.

There are rumors of deterioration in Panama, and we could well have trouble of various sorts between now and May. Of course these same rumors are helping to move Chiari—if he *is* moving. As long as the monkey is clearly on Chiari's back, we can stand any trouble, but if we should have a chance to get language which meets our essential conditions and let it go, I think we could come under some attack. It is not yet clear that we have such language, and there is one word that

---

[1] Source: Johnson Library, National Security File, Country File, Panama Riots. Vol. II, Part G, January–February, 1964. Bundy wrote the following note at the top of the page: "P[resident] read but doesn't really agree."

[2] Rusk, McNamara, Mann, and Bundy met with the President from 5:45 to 6:05 p.m. on February 25. (Ibid.; President's Daily Diary) No written record of their conversation has been found, but it was at this meeting that Rusk presumably made this suggestion.

I would change in the Costa Rican draft,[3] the last word "negotiators." But we are getting close.

I have always supposed that if we did get into talks with the Panamanians we would find ourselves able to agree to significant changes in our existing relations without giving way on gut issues like the perpetuity clause or our own ultimate responsibility for the security and effectiveness of the Canal. Your choice of Vaughan as your prospective Ambassador shows your own readiness to pick a man who has much more basic sympathy for the Panamanians than for the conservative Americans in the Canal Zone (almost too much so, in my judgment).

The talks can go on for a long time, and there should be a clear understanding on both sides that they will. But I myself think they can lead to a new level of understanding, provided we get past election year emotions on both sides.

We have been right so far, and there is nothing cosmic about this issue yet, but I do think it would be good to take talks with no retreat if we can get them.

McG. B.

---

[3] The draft language reads: "The parties agree to appoint negotiators with sufficient powers to discuss and reconsider all aspects of United States of America-Panamanian relations, including the canal treaties, to seek the prompt elimination of the causes of the dispute with a view to harmonizing the just interests of both parties and their responsibilities to the Hemisphere and world trade. Both parties agree to discuss the differences existing between them without preconditions as to the positions they may consider necessary to adopt as a final result of the meetings that will take place between the negotiators." (Telegram 3195 from USUN, February 26; National Archives and Records Administration, RG 59, Central Files 1964–66, POL PAN–US)

---

391. Telephone Conversation Between President Johnson and Senator Richard Russell[1]

Washington, February 26, 1964, 12:10 p.m.

President: Dick?

Russell: Yes sir.

---

[1] Source: Johnson Library, Recordings and Transcripts, Recording of telephone conversation between President Johnson and Richard Russell, Tape F64.14, Side B, PNO 1. No classification marking. This transcript was prepared in the Office of the Historian specifically for this volume.

President: Getting a lot of power and pressure here on Panama, now, and I've got this thing down to about where it says practically what I've been saying all the time. I don't know how I can resist it much longer when the Secretary of State, Defense, and Bundy, and all my advisers, think that we're going to cause an explosion if we don't sit down at the table with them. They've come in now with a Costa Rican proposal that is two paragraphs, and I want to read it to you. I think if you'll take one moment I'll read you what Bundy says to me. It is kind of a summary:

[The President read the text of Document 390.]

Now, he feels rather deeply there because I overrode all of them last night—in fact, this morning with this combined language:

[Omitted here is the language from footnote 3, Document 390.]

Russell: Well, of course, Panamanians are going to accept that as an assurance that we will make some substantial changes in the provisions of the treaty. I know you're under a bit of pressure down there, Mr. President.

President: Well, I know, but as I see this, I don't say I'm going to do a damned thing but discuss it, and that is what I've said the first moment I talked to him. And now maybe I read it wrong, but I've got it down to where that's about what I say. I'm not going to have any pre-conditions whatever.

Russell: What's the word after "pre-conditions"?

President: "Without pre-conditions as to the positions they may consider necessary to adopt as a final result of the meetings that will take place between the negotiators."

Russell: The trouble is that this pressure is going to be relentless, and those negotiators will go down there and want to give something and then Bundy and Rusk and *New York Times* school of thought will put relentless pressure on you.

President: That's right—there's no question—they've been doin' that for 2 months.

Russell: And they will not give the American people even a part of their view. It has never been mentioned here that the last time we had to settle with them we gave them about $40 million worth of property down there—just gave it to them out of hand. I don't know what they've done with it. I reckon Chiari and these other Presidents have stolen it. You can steal it and get your hands on it once you're in there. But we gave them a tremendous amount of property there and they're going to expect something equally big or bigger out of this, and I don't know how we're just gonna get it. Of course, it could get it through a treaty or be taken out of the Alliance for Progress funds, but there's never going to be a time that that group's not going to be urging you to give in to Panama [unintelligible].

President: We know that. We know that. Well, I'll say Bundy has supported me on this all the way through. I've just taken it on and Mann has supported me—Tom Mann. Tom thinks it's brought us a good deal of respect in the Hemisphere. Tom Mann thinks this has helped us. Tom Mann thinks we're stronger in the Hemisphere today than we were 90 days ago because of what we've done in Panama and what we've done in Cuba. He thinks we're in worse shape than we've been in 20 years, and that the Hemisphere is in a very dangerous position, but he thinks that these two little insignificant moves have let them know that—"don't tread on me." And he thought they needed to know that pretty much.

Russell: I can't help but feel that it has helped us.

[Omitted here is discussion relating to Cuba and other parts of the Hemisphere.]

President: Now, let me go back again. I've got to sit down and talk to 'em, and I don't know how I can get by saying any less.

Russell: There's just one thing in there that shook me a little bit. Go ahead and read it again.

President: "The parties agree to appoint negotiators"—I named Tom Mann—"with sufficient powers to discuss and reconsider"—they've got to say that they've got to have the power to discuss—"all aspects of U.S. and Panamanian relations"—I told them that from the first day I'll discuss anything, anywhere, any time, but I wouldn't agree on any pre-conditions before I sit down—they didn't make me do that with the Russians in Berlin—"including the Canal Zone treaties with a view to"—doing what?—"to harmonizing the just interest of both parties"—I assume our men will look after our interests—we'll just have to fight that—"seeking the prompt elimination of the causes of dispute—"

Russell: We being in there is the cause of it.

President: "and fulfill their responsibilities to the Hemisphere and world trade. Both parties agree to discuss the differences existing between them without pre-conditions as to positions they may consider necessary to adopt as a final result of the meetings that will take place between the negotiators." Now, that adds up in one word—and I may not be—if I can read and understand—now, I'm not a lawyer, and I may not be—but I have not implied or said that I would do anything except discuss any problem they had.

Russell: It is all very clear to me except that word "reconsider." I don't exactly understand what you're going to reconsider.

Johnson: Well, the first thing, we've got no diplomatic relations. We've got to start out—talk. They want so many employees. They say the Canal Zone has got all our people. They've got different wage rates. They've thought up a good many of these things and our people tell me that maybe we ought to have a civilian governor instead of some retired military man that knows nothing about it, that maybe we—Cy Vance says that he can take a list of 15–20 minor things that could create some of this friction with the workers.

Russell: They don't know what they want, Mr. President. We pay them almost the same thing now. There's little difference for the overseas. A Panamanian working for the Canal gets the same thing as a canal worker on a lock on the Savannah River in Augusta.

President: But some of them get a pack of cigarettes for 15 cents in the Zone and 50 cents some other places—got commissaries and all kinds of different cut-rates. Anyway, they think—the Army thinks—Vance thinks—and I think he's pretty able about it—that we can find a good many things that would improve conditions, if we'd been alert to it. We ought to have a new Board and able Board with good men on it—Gene Black type of man, instead of some just honorary [unintelligible] deal, and they all understand that this is a real problem and we've got real interests to protect. Tom Mann thinks we ought to start taking some borings in Nicaragua for a sea-level canal, and he thinks that will put them in place a little bit. We've got a good many things that we think we can do that will help, but we're just refusing to agree on any language now, and I have said I'll discuss anything, any time.

Russell: Well, I think that's all right, except when you get together, then the price is going to be—

President: Oh, hell, yes, that's right. But I can't fail to get together without hurting myself, can't I?

Russell: Well, I don't think you're hurt up to now.

President: No [unintelligible]. Well, thank you my friend.

Russell: Yes sir.

---

392.   Editorial Note

On February 26, 1964, at 12:31 p.m., President Johnson spoke on the phone with Adlai Stevenson, who was in Washington to testify at a hearing of the Senate Foreign Relations Committee. Stevenson urged the President to approve the language of a proposed agreement between the United States and Panama that had been worked out by President Orlich of Costa Rica (see footnote 3, Document 390.) Johnson said to Stevenson: "I think when you say you're gonna reconsider the treaties that the implication is you're gonna rewrite the treaties, and that you're gonna rewrite the substance of 'em, and that you're gonna get rid of the perpetuity clause, which they're claiming, and I think that they'll think that. And then the heat that's gonna be on me when they—*The New York Times*—and my negotiator sits down with 'em— they come back in—it's gonna be something terrific." Johnson then complained about Panama's actions and expressed his willingness to discuss anything, but reiterated his opposition to having "to say in a written document that I am going to reconsider a treaty." Johnson continued: "I've talked to the leading people who would have to consider a treaty and I couldn't find one vote anywhere. And I think that we're just toying with somethin' that we couldn't have the United States Senate—my honest judgment is I couldn't get 20 votes for any treaty that substantially rewrote the present one."

Stevenson presented the case for resolving the issue as soon as possible by accepting the current language, which he told Johnson he had drafted in part:

"I do think that it's awfully important from your point of view to clear away this little mess, because it's affecting the attitude of Latin Americans way beyond the boundaries of Panama, as you know. I feel as though we're stuck on this dime, and that this controversy between this miniscule country and the United States is totally avoidable and unnecessary—it's a diversion of attention from the major problems in Latin America. I just think that from the State Department point of view it's much better to get this one out of the way with language as good as this, which is so far from where we started, we'd be well advised to do it."

Johnson told Stevenson that he preferred to use the term "representatives" rather than "negotiators." (Recording of telephone conversation between President Johnson and Adlai Stevenson; Johnson Library, Recordings and Transcripts, Tape F64.14, Side B, PNO 2)

The President then spoke to Rusk about the proposed language of the agreement with Panama. "There's no use in our debating it; we'd better just let it ride for a day or two." The President agreed to allow Rusk to come to the White House to discuss the draft language, but told him: "I'm not going to buy what I got on my desk." (Recording of telephone conversation between President Johnson and Dean Rusk, February 26, 1:10 p.m.; ibid., Tape F64.15, Side A, PNO 1)

Johnson talked to Senator William Fulbright later that afternoon: "Adlai came down and started a heat wave on Panama. He got into negotiations up there without anybody knowing it and he came up with a proposal that we turned down in the first hour when we talked to the President of Panama, and we have made positive proposals to 'em and we think that in due time they will come around and get them, but I had to see Tom Mann and I had to see Rusk and I had to talk to Adlai for an hour . . ." (Recording of telephone conversation between President Johnson and William Fulbright, February 26, 3:06 p.m.; ibid., Tape F64.15, Side A, PNO 2) The portions of the conversations printed here were prepared in the Office of the Historian specifically for this volume.

The afternoon of February 26 Thomas Mann sent the mission at the United Nations a variation on the Orlich text that the President would accept provided that Panama "resumes relations with the United States prior to commencement of discussions." The revised text reads:

"The parties agree to appoint authorized representatives with sufficient powers to discuss and consider all aspects of United States and Panama relations, without any limitation whatever, to seek the prompt elimination of the causes of dispute with a view to harmonizing the just interest of both parties and their responsibilities to the Hemisphere and world trade. Both parties agree to discuss the differences existing between them without preconditions as to the positions they may consider necessary to adopt as a final result of the meetings that will take place between the authorized representatives." (Telegram 2284 to USUN, February 26; National Archives and Records Administration, RG 59, Central Files 1964–66, POL PAN–US)

Although there were indications from some Panamanians that the dispute would soon be resolved, by February 29 there was no official response from Panama on the revised text of the proposal set forth by President Orlich. Mann informed the White House he had been told that Sanchez Gavito, the Mexican Ambassador to the OAS, was prepared to put forth a proposal to the OAS Peace Committee that would perhaps break the deadlock between the United States and Panama on the language of an agreement. Mann wrote to Bundy that "this approach has possibilities because it gets us off the hook of being unable to agree on the pre-conditions." (Memorandum from Mann to McGeorge Bundy, February 29; Johnson Library, National Security File, Country File, Panama, Vol. III, March 1964) After consulting with Bundy that afternoon, the President approved the proposal "as a basis for negotiations to be conducted by Ambassador Sanchez Gavito, acting entirely on his own initiative. The fact of prior consultation with the United States Government will not be revealed." (Memorandum for the record by Bundy, March 29; ibid.)

393. Telephone Conversation Between President Johnson and Secretary of State Rusk[1]

Washington, March 2, 1964, 11:35 a.m.

President: What's the news on your front today?

Rusk: Well, I think that maybe your press conference helped ease things—the tension—a bit on this Panama business.[2] I think we may find a way to get some progress there. Cyprus: we're expecting word from the Turks about—

President: On Panama, what are we going to do? Is Tom Mann getting Mexico to say that we are anxious to talk any time, anywhere about anything, period?

Rusk: That is the present ploy. That is the present move so that the two governments would not have to say anything, but the OAS would simply recommend that they establish relations and get to the conference table. But you'll have a chance to see any text before any agreement is given on it. Have you had any reactions to your press conference from the Hill today?

President: No.[3]

[Omitted here is discussion unrelated to Panama.]

President: Now, on Panama I think if the Mexican thing doesn't work today, we ought to come in some other place, and somebody ought to say tomorrow, we want to talk any time, anywhere, about anything. We're ready. Let's press them; let's shove them a little bit.

---

[1] Source: Johnson Library, Recordings and Transcripts, Recording of telephone conversation between President Johnson and Dean Rusk, Tape F64.15, Side B, PNO 1. No classification marking. This transcript was prepared in the Office of the Historian specifically for this volume.

[2] In a press conference on February 29 President Johnson stated he realized that the treaty with Panama had been written in 1903 and modified from time to time, that "problems are involved that need to be dealt with and perhaps would require adjustment in the treaty." He also said that "Just because Panama happens to be a small nation, maybe no larger than the city of St. Louis, is no reason why we shouldn't try in every way to be equitable and fair and just. We are going to insist on that. But we are going to be equally insistent on no preconditions." (*Public Papers of the Presidents of the United States: Lyndon B. Johnson, 1963–64*, Book I, p. 325)

[3] In a telephone conversation with the President that evening, Senator Fulbright, reacting to the President's press conference statement on Panama, told Johnson: "I thought you put it very well." The President responded: "All right. You just stay with me and we'll do all right." (Recording of telephone conversation between President Johnson and William Fulbright, March 2, 8:50 p.m.; Johnson Library, Recordings and Transcripts, Tape F64.16, Side A, PNO 2) Earlier that day George Ball had told the President: "I thought you did splendidly, and I thought you advanced the possibility of working something out." (Recording of telephone conversation between President Johnson and George Ball, March 2, 11:50 a.m.; ibid., Tape F64.15, Side B, PNO 2)

Rusk: Right.

President: If we need to call Chiari again, maybe we ought to get in direct communication with him and say, "why don't we resume diplomatic relations and sit down. We got a number of plans for improving this thing if you'll do it, and we may not have an agreement for a year or two, but there's no reason why we ought to stand off and bark. It's not helping your economy and it's not helping ours."

Rusk: Right.

President: I'd let them be squeezed a little more down there. I think that before they go Communist, that they'll go American. That's my judgment. If you squeeze their nuts just a little bit—I think we've been too generous, *The New York Times* and *Washington Post* with them—and now we've showed we're a little reluctant. I think that maybe they're more willing to come along if we shove it up to them.

[Omitted here is discussion unrelated to Panama.]

---

394. Memorandum From the Joint Chiefs of Staff to Secretary of Defense McNamara[1]

JCSM–157–64   Washington, March 2, 1964.

SUBJECT

US Policy Toward Panama (U)

1. In consequence of the present difficulties in US-Panamanian relations, the Joint Chiefs of Staff have undertaken an appraisal of US military requirements in Panama for consideration in the development of a national position toward that nation. The salient features of this appraisal, amplified in the Appendix and Annexes hereto,[2] are summarized below.

2. Access to a canal remains vital to the economic, political, and military interests of the United States. If denied access to such a canal, the United States could defend its interests in limited or general war,

---

[1] Source: Washington National Records Center, FRC 330 69 A 7425, PAN 381, Panama Crisis, January–March, 1964. Secret. A note on the memorandum reads: "Sec Def has seen."

[2] Attached but not printed.

but its ability to do so would be impaired. Without the availability of such a canal, transportation costs would be increased with adverse economic effects on the United States and certain Latin American countries, whose political stability, in consequence, would be adversely affected.

3. As long as the Panama Canal remains the sole water route across Central America, security of these vital interests of the United States dictates the continued employment of a substantial number of US citizens for an indefinite period and a buffer zone for its protection. The former places affluent American communities next to Panamanian slums. The latter results in unused land over which Panama is denied the exercise of sovereignty. Given this situation, it is difficult to devise any arrangement permanently satisfactory to both the United States and Panama.

4. The present Panama Canal is, in some respects, already inadequate and, during the last quarter of this century, will reach the point at which it will not be able to handle the volume of traffic demanding its services. The construction of a wider, deeper, sea-level canal would be advantageous to the military, economic, and political interests of the United States. It would be less vulnerable to sabotage, fewer forces would be required for its protection, and the largest naval ships could be accommodated. Over the long range, its construction would permit modification of the basic factors which are presently the source of continuing US-Panamanian friction. Over the short range, early decision and active manifestation of a US intent to construct such a canal might facilitate US discussion with Panama. Of various plans for a new sea-level canal, one which reduces vulnerability to disruption of the existing and proposed canal by a single military attack, or by the action of a single political group, is preferred militarily.

5. In addition to the protection of the canal, the US military presence in Panama is associated with hemispheric security. The importance of this latter mission is increasing with the growing threat of Castro-communist subversion. Panama is valuable in this connection because US forces and facilities are already there. The United States could acquire, but only at a substantial price, comparable facilities elsewhere. Nevertheless, no substitute presently exists, and the United States should seek to maintain the military base complex in Panama considered essential for the purpose of hemispheric security.

6. To provide a basis for the determination of a US position and the development of detailed positions necessary to support national policy, the Joint Chiefs of Staff recommend that the Secretary of Defense:

a. Support:

(1) An early decision for the construction of a sea-level interoceanic canal at a location which reduces vulnerability to disruption

of both the existing and proposed canals by a single military attack, or by the action of a single political group.

(2) Action which will clearly indicate that the early construction of such a canal is a firm US intention.

(3) The concept that discussion with Panama be premised on the firm US intent to construct such a canal.

(4) The view that the United States should insist on maintaining military areas and facilities related to the operation, maintenance, sanitation, and protection of the Panama Canal and to hemispheric security. However, nonessential areas and facilities in the Canal Zone, including acreage not required for a minimum buffer zone, should be identified by US agencies for possible transfer to Panama in the event further concessions are deemed necessary. In return for any US concessions, the United States should insist on Panamanian recognition that at present, and for the foreseeable future:

(a) The US military presence in Panama is important to and in furtherance of hemispheric security.

(b) The conclusion of an agreement pertaining to base rights and the status of military forces outside the Canal Zone is an important and appropriate contribution Panama can and should make to the inter-American system.

b. In implementation of subparagraph 6 a (4) above, request the Secretary of the Army, in his capacity as personal representative of the President and as the stockholder of the Panama Canal Company, to:

(1) Provide appropriate guidance to the Governor of the Canal Zone/President of the Panama Canal Company for a joint study, with the Commander in Chief, US Southern Command, of areas and facilities which might be transferred to US military jurisdiction.

(2) Determine whether the Canal Zone Government will agree to transfer to US military jurisdiction that part of the Coco Solo complex, with attendant housing, which is presently under Canal Zone Government control.

c. In implementation of subparagraph 6 a (4) (b) above, direct the preparation of a proposed base rights and status of forces agreement for eventual use in discussions with the Republic of Panama.

For the Joint Chiefs of Staff:

Maxwell D. Taylor
Chairman
Joint Chiefs of Staff

**395.   Telegram From the U.S. Southern Command to the
Department of State**[1]

Canal Zone, March 5, 1964, 0740Z.

SC2024A. For Mann from Cottrell. Following is the way I add up the situation at the present moment:

1. Heavy pressures on Chiari are increasing daily from business men and publishers to restore relations and arrest the economic decline. Support from this group for standing on principles has vanished in direct proportion to the threat to their pocket books. Their former support is turning rapidly to criticism of Chiari having handled the situation very badly.

2. Workers in Panama are very concerned as notices of layoffs are received, and their former support for the government is vanishing.

3. Arnulfo's star is rising among the workers as a magician who will restore the situation. Thus, Chiari must see that a continued stalemate is working against his administration and against the chances of Robles in the May elections. The oligarchy's fear of Arnulfo is providing additional political pressure on Chiari for an early settlement.

4. The forces exerting pressure on Chiari to stand firm are his hard line left advisors, student leaders and Communists, plus possibly Moreno and Boyd with political axes to grind who have nothing to lose and much to gain if they can induce the US to cave on the negotiate point.

5. I believe the National Guard is capable of controlling any violence instigated by the left and would do so if Chiari moved towards accommodation.

6. The formula of rioting to attract US attention and extract concessions is an old ploy used successfully in the past. The killing in the January 9–16 affair was an unexpected result brought about by the trained Communist additive to the old recipe. The killings produced a real shock causing Chiari to over react and paint himself into a corner.

7. I believe Moreno and Boyd were turned loose by Chiari to see how far they could go in pushing the US to accept the Chiari position. This probing ran into a stone wall and I think the realization is now sinking in here that the stalemate can only be broken by a Chiari retreat from his position.

8. The former violent feelings against Americans, the zone and the US armed forces are receding rapidly in my opinion. Visiting

---

[1] Source: National Archives and Records Administration, RG 59, Central Files 1964–66, POL PAN–US. Confidential.

Americans, consular officers and Americans living in Panama City now move freely about the city without molestation or evidence of any apparent hostility on the part of the general population.

9. In my opinion the Communists made great headway in promoting the riots and during the present stalemate, particularly in strengthening and broadening the base of their organization. However, in the present climate I do not think they yet have the capability of matching or neutralizing the National Guard.

Conclusion: Despite the hazards of political predictions, in my best judgment at this moment, I think the shifting of the balance of forces here indicates a Chiari accommodation and restoration of relations at any time within this month. I do not believe he will sit tight until the May elections much less October. If he were to make this mistake I think he will be removed. Based on my previous experience in Panama during similar but less serious riots I believe that this last tantrum is nearing its end. There may be a coup if Chiari does not move but I do not believe there will be any further rioting against the zone this year. Amen.

---

396.   Telephone Conversation Between President Johnson and Senator Richard Russell[1]

Washington, March 9, 1964, 9:45 p.m.

President: I think this is pretty much our formula and I've got to let them know in the morning, and it looked all right to me but there might be a catch in it and I just want to check it.

"The governments of the Republic of Panama and the United States of America have agreed to re-establish diplomatic relations as soon as possible to seek the prompt elimination of the causes of conflict relative to the Panama Canal and to attempt to resolve other problems existing between them without limitations or any pre-conditions of any kind. As a result, within 30 days following re-establishment of diplomatic relations, both governments will designate special am-

---

[1] Source: Johnson Library, Recordings and Transcripts, Recording of telephone conversation between President Johnson and Richard Russell, Tape F64.16, Side B, PNO 3. No classification marking. This transcript was prepared in the Office of the Historian specifically for this volume.

bassadors with sufficient powers to carry out discussions and negotiations with the objective of reaching a just and fair international agreement which will eliminate the above mentioned causes of conflict and resolve the other problems referred to above. Any agreements that may result would be subject to the constitutional processes of each country."

Russell: [Laughter] Well, that's one of the most skillfully worded statements I ever read, Mr. President.

President: Well, it's ours. We've had to be negotiatin' and we've had new treaties and everything, and I said I'm willin' to say I'll meet 'em any time, anywhere, any place, and do what's fair and just and right, but I will not agree to negotiate a new treaty unless I think that one is required and I'm not going to agree to any precondition. I'm going to say that I don't so they don't get misled.

[Omitted here are several minutes of word-by-word analysis of the statement, discussion of haggling over language, and conversation related to Cuba.]

President: He [Mann] came in the other day and asked me to sign this agreement and said we're close to it and we need to sign it now, and we attached appendix A and B, your conversation, the press—and Chiari's, and I said, "No I won't sign that; I just won't do it." He had Rusk with him; he had Bundy with him; and he had McNamara with him. All of them had recommended it and I said I'm not going to do that and he said, "Why?" And I said because Chiari says he's going to have a new treaty and I'm not going to admit to it. I may have one— may agree to it—but I'm not going to say I'm going to have it. I said that from the first day. Now, the second thing I'm not going to say—I am not going to say in your formal statement here, you say "negotiate." I'm not going to say I am going to negotiate a new treaty. Now, that's in the formal statement, and that's in Chiari's statement, so those two things go out. So he said, we'll do what you say. So I cut it back and sent it back to 'em. Now they're coming in here tonight at 8 o'clock with this statement. Now Chiari hasn't approved it but the OAS has urged this be done.

Russell: Well, he's gettin' weak.

President: Well, I told them to squeeze his nuts a little more [unintelligible].

Russell: Has got him by the balls and he has to come in a little later 'cause you've got his water cut off—he can't move.

President: Now, I notified Cy Vance 5 o'clock this afternoon. They think they're going to have a big demonstration if this happens, and that they're gonna try and take over—the Communists are—and I just said we're not going to have any Cuba there. They say it will be from the Communists who've got a foothold there and they're going to be raising hell about it and are going to try to have a Communist coup when this takes place.[2]

Russell: Well, half of the police he's got there can beat the socks off of 'em.

President: Well, this General O'Meara can. They tell me he's smart. He's on the job and I trust him.

Russell: O'Meara's tough as hell. You give him the reins.

President: I've done given him the reins; I've done given him the reins. I told Cy Vance at 5 o'clock this afternoon to tell O'Meara that we would not have another Cuba in this hemisphere, if he had enough men; if he didn't, I'd send him some more.

Russell: Don't need the men, just a little freedom of movement. O'Meara is a pretty tough fellow.

President: Well, he's got his orders. Okay, now if you don't see anything wrong with this I'm going to go on.

Russell: Well, it's all right, not near as bad as I thought you'd be driven to.

President: No, you didn't think I'd be driven to it. Now don't go needlin' me, Dick. What are you tryin' to do, I'm still at work. I haven't even had dinner and you just needle me, my friend—now don't.

Russell: I wouldn't be your friend if I didn't tell you what I thought.

President: Well, now you do think it is wonderful. You didn't think I'd run, did you?

Russell: No. No, you haven't.

President: So help me, I'm not runnin' yet.

Russell: No. You left the door open to get out. You haven't run a foot yet.

President: Well, we've always—you've never said you wouldn't sign a new—you'd do what is fair, don't you?

Russell: Absolutely.

President: That's all I'm going to do.

Russell: I hope so.

President: If it's not fair and just, I'm not going to do it.

[Omitted here is discussion of Vietnam.]

---

[2] In that telephone conversation, Vance warned President Johnson that Chiari "is going to recognize us now and therefore we're tightening up our shoe laces in case there should be any violence associated with that." (Recording of telephone conversation between President Johnson and Cyrus Vance, March 9, 5:05 p.m.; ibid., Tape F64.16, Side B, PNO 2)

397.   Editorial Note

On March 10, 1964, the President talked on the telephone with Mc-
George Bundy about the latest proposed language for an agreement on
Panama. The President was concerned about reports from Panama and
in the press that an agreement with Panama leading to resumption of
relations and the prospect of negotiations for a new treaty was imminent. Johnson told Bundy: "We're not goin' to have prima facie evidence that we're agreeing to a new treaty." He did not want to be put
in the position of being bullied by *The New York Times* and *Washington
Post* into accepting an agreement that could be interpreted as U.S. acceptance of the Panamanian demand to negotiate a new treaty. Referring to some of their journalists, the President told Bundy: "I think
they're very dangerous characters, and I don't think that we can allow
them to get us boxed in here." He continued: "Let's don't have Nixon
and the rest of them saying we're negotiatin' a treaty." (Recording of
telephone conversation between President Johnson and McGeorge
Bundy, March 10, 10:57 a.m.; Johnson Library, Recordings and Transcripts, Tape F64.17, Side A, PNO 1)

The President then called Mann and told him that he had spoken
to Bundy and there were three things he opposed in the draft: the mention of "negotiations," "Panama Canal," and "international." "Now, if
I have to give," he said, "I'd leave 'Panama Canal' in up in the first
paragraph, although it's desirable to take out, and I might even take
'international.' I'm not going to take 'negotiations', though." He added:

"And I'd squeeze their nuts a little down there, anyway, if I were
you. I'd tighten it a little bit and let them worry a little bit. I don't think
we need to come hat in hand. We've been fair, and we're going to continue to be fair, but let's don't—just—I'm tired of these people that recede and concur every time the U.S. is attacked. I want to resist somebody somewhere, some time. I'm not a warmonger, and don't want to
go to war. But I don't think we're goin'."

Mann said that he had "some other ideas that would protect us
some." The President then told Mann:

"You were just as right as you could be, my friend, on negotiations
the first day—not that it means anything other than discussion, but to
them it means a new treaty, and we might as well face this thing now.
If we agree and get along then when we don't have a new treaty, they're
going to say we made a commitment and couldn't live up to it, and I
don't want to be in that position. I'd rather take the heat now." (Recording of telephone conversation between President Johnson and Thomas
Mann, March 10, 11:11 a.m.; ibid., Tape F64.17, Side A, PNO 2) The portions of the conversations printed here were prepared in the Office of
the Historian specifically for this volume. Another record of this conversation is in a March 10 memorandum of conversation; ibid., Papers
of Thomas C. Mann, Telephone Conversations with LBJ, January 14,

1964–April 30, 1965. The Mann record of the conversation indicates that it took place at 11:40 a.m.

According the President's Daily Diary, Johnson met for lunch with Rusk, Mann, and McGeorge Bundy at 1:12 p.m., March 10, during which Panama was no doubt discussed. (Johnson Library) No other record of this meeting has been found.

---

398.   Special National Intelligence Estimate[1]

SNIE 84–64   Washington, March 11, 1964.

THE SHORT RUN OUTLOOK IN PANAMA

The Problem

To examine the situation and short run prospects in Panama, with particular emphasis on the Castro-Communist threat.

Conclusions

A. The process of political change in Panama, where the uneasy rule of the elite was being challenged by a variety of extreme nationalists, has been accelerated by the canal crisis. With general elections scheduled for 10 May, political maneuvering is in full swing. All the candidates are virtually compelled to take a strong nationalistic stand. Candidates and party alignments are still likely to be changed. The power struggle may not be resolved at the ballot box; any of the principal candidates might resort to a coup rather than accept defeat. A new government might feel more able to compromise on the canal issue, although it would first try to consolidate its control of the government apparatus.

B. The Communists and Castroists, riding the current wave of rabid nationalism, have made substantial gains. They have established effective cooperation with each other, have expanded and improved their organizations, and have increased their influence with nationalists both in and out of government. We do not believe that they are strong enough at this stage to carry out a coup by themselves. We be-

---

[1] Source: Central Intelligence Agency, Job 79R 01012A, DDI Files, O/DDI Registry. Secret; Controlled Dissem. According to a note on the cover sheet, this estimate was prepared in the Central Intelligence Agency with the participation of the intelligence organizations of the Departments of State and Defense and the National Security Agency. The U.S. Intelligence Board concurred in this estimate on March 11.

lieve that in the immediate future they will concentrate on working with radical nationalist elements to undermine the already weakened rule of the traditional oligarchy. They will also seek to keep the canal issue alive and unresolved.

C. One durable result of the crisis is this: from a negligible factor in Panamanian life, the Communists and the Castroists have become a significant one. Their short run prospects have been sharply improved, and the longer the treaty issue remains agitated, the more lasting their gains are likely to be. Even if their strength and influence should diminish, the heightened level of nationalism will persist, and will confront the US with a succession of difficulties.

[Omitted here are sections I. "The Political Framework," II. "The Canal Issue," and III. "Riots and Their Aftermath."]

IV. The May Elections

14. The approach of the presidential election makes it extraordinarily difficult for the Chiari government, or any political group, to take a moderate stand on the canal issue. With extreme nationalism in the ascendant, each candidate will be judged by his position on this issue, and the campaign will have a high content of Yankee-phobia.

15. *The Contenders.* There are, at this stage, seven presidential candidates.[2] (Chiari cannot succeed himself.) There is strong pressure within the oligarchy to have the two conservative coalitions agree on a single unity candidate, but thus far neither candidate has been willing to withdraw. Of these currently running only four are of consequence.

a. *Marco Robles* is a member of the conservative National Liberal Party and the candidate of the parties in Chiari's governing coalition. [*2 lines of source text not declassified*] In effect, he will be largely judged by Chiari's success or failure.

b. *Juan de Arco Galindo* is a member of the conservative National Patriotic Coalition and candidate of the Opposition Alliance (OA). [*1 line of source text not declassified*] The OA, like most Panamanian coalitions, is an amalgam of personalistic parties, and some of its leaders are unsavory opportunists. Galindo's main problem will be to keep the OA together.

c. *Arnulfo Arias* is leader and candidate of the nationalistic Panamenista Party. [*7 lines of source text not declassified*] Some opinion holds that Arnulfo may have come to the conclusion that accommodation with the US is a necessity. [*2 lines of source text not declassified*]

---

[2] See Annex for a complete list of Panama's political parties and coalitions. [Footnote in the source text. The Annex is attached but not printed.]

d. *Miguel Moreno,* the candidate of the small ultranationalist National Reformist Party, is also supported by a diversity of other elements. He himself has frequently expressed violently anti-US views, and the vigor with which he has recently presented Panama's case before the OAS has made him a national figure. He still has little chance of election as the nominee of a minor party, but key members of the oligarchy may decide that his current popularity would make him a strong unity candidate. In this capacity, he would probably have the backing of Colonel Bolivar Vallarino, commander of the National Guard, with whom he has long had close personal ties. Moreover, some of the Communist leaders see in him a way to supplant the oligarchy by a transition government which could pave the way for a "socialist revolution." [*less than 1 line of source text not declassified*] Moreno also happens to be the only important candidate that the PdP has much hope of influencing.

16. *The Election Outlook.* Political forces in the country are still shifting and are likely to keep on doing so throughout the campaign. If an honest election were held with the present party line-up, Arnulfo would probably win against the divided oligarchy. We believe the chances are better than even, however, that the oligarchy will close ranks around a unity candidate, perhaps Moreno or Robles. In this event, the election would probably be close. The oligarchy controls the National Electoral Board which supervises the counting of votes and arbitrates voting disputes, and this could be decisive in a close election.

V. The Possibility of a Coup

17. With Panama in a state of acute tension there is some chance of a coup. It could come from any one of several directions. The oligarchy might seek to forestall an election victory, or a coup, by Arnulfo. Arnulfo might mount a coup himself, fearing that the oligarchy meant by chicanery or violence to keep him from the Presidency. The Communists and Castroists might come to believe that they could use the masses in the streets to nullify the government's police power and thus seize control with a small number of resolute activists. Such an attempt would, however, mean risking their present assets and their increasing influence. We do not regard the likelihood of a coup as very great at present; it will probably increase, especially in the event of continued economic deterioration. The period between the elections in May and the new President's assumption of office in October will be a delicate one.

18. If a coup attempt were launched, the attitude of the Guardia Nacional (GN) would be crucial; indeed, any coup plotters would almost certainly seek to enlist the GN's support, or to neutralize it. The GN is Panama's only security force and numbers about 3,500 men. It

is a disciplined and fairly competent body, believed to be loyal to its commander, Colonel Bolivar Vallarino. It could probably control minor civil disorders, but in the event of widespread and sustained disturbances it would probably not be capable of maintaining control without substantial outside assistance.

19. Vallarino has in the past shown himself reluctant to undertake decisive action on his own initiative, except when the interests of the GN were involved. He is bitterly opposed both to Arnulfo and to the Communists, and realizes that he would almost certainly lose his job if either took over. Hence, we believe that Vallarino would oppose a coup attempt by either. He would probably support a coup launched by the oligarchy to prevent Arnulfo's election; he might even act to prevent Arnulfo from taking office if he were elected.

VI. The Outlook

20. *The Government.* The intense and conflicting pressures on Chiari will almost certainly increase. The economic consequences of the impasse will be felt more and more by the Panamanians. To some, especially the oligarchy, this argues for attempts at a settlement with the US. In the minds of most, however, it probably increases anti-US sentiment. The situation is further complicated by the May elections; if Chiari appeared to be settling for something less than a US commitment to write a new canal treaty, the government coalition would almost certainly be defeated in the election—and large-scale rioting might be renewed.

21. A new Panamanian Government might have stronger mass support and thus more room for maneuver on the canal issue. Its leaders, even if rabidly nationalistic, would no longer be under election pressures, and presumably would have to concern themselves with reversing the process of economic deterioration. However, a new government would be likely to go slow, seeking first to consolidate its control of the governmental apparatus.

22. *The Castroists and the Communists.* Although both the Castroists and Communists have made significant gains since the crisis, we do not believe that, at this stage, they are strong enough by themselves to seize power. Nor do we believe that they intend in the immediate future to risk their gains and assets in such an attempt; PdP leaders have expressed concern that the US might directly intervene to prevent or redress a Communist takeover. However, if it appeared that radical nationalists were about to seize power, the Castroists and Communists would probably join them in the hope of securing positions of major influence.

23. Barring such an opportunity, the short run tactics of the PdP and its sympathizers are to extend their influence, to build up their assets, and to consolidate their gains. They will continue to support the

government's intransigent stand, and they will attempt to exert pressure on the administration to stand firm. At the same time, they will try to undermine the oligarchy, perhaps charging it with plans to betray Panama to the US. They will capitalize on any opportunity to exploit economic dissatisfactions and chronic social inequities. Even the more militant VAN can be expected to adopt similar tactics, at least for the near future.

24. The crisis has made many Panamanians more receptive to the ultranationalist line advanced by the Castroists and Communists. For some, especially among the lower classes, the oft-repeated charges of Yankee aggression have been proved. Especially during the election period, the Castroists and Communists will continue to profit from the strong nationalistic and anti-US sentiments rampant in Panama, whatever their origin. If and when this chauvinistic fervor diminishes, some reduction of their influence is likely. But it will not vanish away. One durable result of the crisis is this: from a negligible factor in Panamanian life, the Communists and the Castroists have become a significant one. Their short run prospects have been sharply improved, and the longer the treaty issue remains agitated, the more lasting their gains are likely to be. Even if their strength and influence should diminish, the heightened level of nationalism will persist, and will confront the US with a succession of difficulties.

399.   Editorial Note

On March 12, 1964, McGeorge Bundy informed President Johnson that the delegation of five Organization of America States Ambassadors was prepared to work out with Panama the new language of an agreement that would include the most recent changes reflecting the President's requirements, and that Mann was "very eager" to have the President's concurrence. Johnson insisted on another look to make sure the language was right. "I know that it's awfully important that we settle some of these things," he told Bundy, "and they're mounting and pickin' up, but I'm not that anxious to settle it, and I'd just rather ride 'em out and take the consequences than to capitulate." He added: "Tom capitulates easier than I thought. He was the strongest guy you ever saw when he started. Are there some forces that have got him worried?" Bundy responded: "I honestly believe that he feels that he has won this one, and you're looking for the third touchdown instead of the second." (Recording of telephone conversation between President Johnson and McGeorge Bundy, March 12, 10:31 a.m.; Johnson Library,

Recordings and Transcripts, Tape F64.17, Side A, PNO 4) The text of the OAS language is in telegram 462 to Panama City, March 12; National Archives and Records Administration, RG 59, Central Files 1964–66, POL PAN–US)

Secretary Rusk, Assistant Secretary Mann, and McGeorge Bundy joined President Johnson at 1:26 p.m. in the Oval Office to discuss the situation. William J. Jorden in *Panama Odyssey,* includes an account of the meeting in which the President's anger and disappointment with Mann, as expressed to Bundy in the telephone conversation cited above, had not subsided. According to Jorden's account, Mann threatened to resign and Johnson threatened to fire him, but the moment passed and the two agreed to work together. Mann also agreed to inform Ambassador Sanchez Gavito that the President would not accept the language. (University of Texas Press, Austin, 1984, pages 79–80)

On March 16, the third anniversary of the establishment of the Alliance for Progress, the OAS released the proposed language. At 12:10 p.m. that day the President addressed the Inter-American Committee on the Alliance for Progress on the dispute with Panama:

". . . The United States will meet with Panama any time, anywhere, to discuss anything, to work together, to cooperate with each other, to reason with one another, to review and to consider all of our problems together, to tell each other our opinions, all our desires and all our concerns, and to aim at solutions and answers that are fair and just and equitable, without regard to size or the strength or the wealth of either nation.

"We don't ask Panama to make any precommitments before we meet, and we intend to make none. Of course, we cannot begin on this work until diplomatic relations are resumed. But the United States is ready today, if Panama is ready. As of this moment I do not believe that there has been a genuine meeting of the minds between the two Presidents of the two countries involved.

"Press reports indicate that the Government of Panama feels that the language which has been under consideration for many days commits the United States to a rewriting of the 1903 treaty. We have made no such commitment and we will not think of doing so before diplomatic relations are resumed and unless a fair and satisfactory adjustment is agreed upon." The text of the President's remarks is printed in *Public Papers of the Presidents of the United States: Lyndon B. Johnson, 1963–64,* Book I, pages 383–384.

On March 16 at 4:40 p.m., Bundy reported to President Johnson that Mann had spoken to the OAS Ambassadors, who wanted to know whether, in the continued absence of an agreement between Panama and the United States, more mediation would be helpful. The ambassadors also inquired about a response to Panama if it asked for an agreement on the basis of the two paragraphs presented earlier in the week, and how to respond if Panama requested a U.S. Ambassador. Bundy consulted with Mann on these two points and told the President that he and Mann were in agreement that with respect to the offer for further mediation, "We're inclined to say, 'no, thank you very much, you've done your best, but we think that the problem is one of a meeting of minds between the two governments.'" He added: "to the first question we would say, 'no, there is no meeting of the minds between the two parties, and we just have to recognize that there isn't.'" As to a possible Panamanian request for the resumption of diplomatic relations with the United States, Bundy proposed that they reply, "why certainly, if it is understood that there is no agreement between the United States to revise the treaty." Bundy also suggested that the United States "reopen the question of what these paragraphs say," to ensure that Panama cannot justify that the United States has agreed to negotiate a new treaty. Johnson told Bundy that the OAS Ambassadors should "continue to play" with the two paragraphs and go back to the Panamanians "to get them straightened out and make them quit lying and saying that we've agreed to negotiate a treaty." (Recording of telephone conversation between President Johnson and McGeorge Bundy, March 16, 4:40 p.m.; Johnson Library, Recordings and Transcripts, Tape F64.17, Side B, PNO 2) The portions of the conversations printed here were prepared in the Office of the Historian specifically for this volume.

---

400. Memorandum From the President's Special Assistant for National Security Affairs (Bundy) to President Johnson[1]

Washington, March 18, 1964.

SUBJECT

  Panama

Ralph Dungan tells me that he spoke to you about a proposal which Sterling Cottrell has made for the next step on Panama. Cottrell's proposal was made to Tom Mann, and I have not yet had a chance to get Tom's comment on it, but here it is:[2]

---

[1] Source: Johnson Library, National Security File, Country File, Panama, Vol. III, March 1964. Secret.

[2] The President and Bundy discussed the proposal on March 18. The President told Bundy "it appeals to me; I'm ready to do that—be glad to—go on, tell 'em to do it." Johnson also stated, "We're anxious to resume relations, one; talk, two." (Memorandum of telephone conversation between President Johnson and McGeorge Bundy, March 18, time undetermined; Johnson Library, Recordings and Transcripts, Tape F64.18, Side A, PNO 2)

We should announce our readiness to resume normal relations in the following language—or alternatively, and to me less effectively—we could have the OAS urge this course on both countries in closely parallel language:

"The Government of the United States proposes that normal relations with the Government of Panama be restored through the reestablishment of diplomatic relations. It also proposes that Special Ambassadors from each country be appointed to ascertain and examine all outstanding issues between the two countries and to prepare a joint recommendation to both governments as to how these issues can be resolved in fair and satisfactory manner.

"If the Government of Panama agrees, relations will be restored immediately and the Special Ambassadors will be appointed within 30 days thereafter."

If you should wish to do this, it could be announced by Pierre[3] after your OAS meeting this afternoon. My own instinct is still to wait a few days, but you may wish to turn discussion to a new proposal and away from the difficulties of recent days.

McG. B.

---

[3] Pierre Salinger.

---

401.   Editorial Note

On March 21, 1964, President Johnson informed Secretary Rusk that he had decided to make a public and background statement on Panama. The President wanted to clear the air and put the issue in perspective by focusing on the positive aspects of U.S.-Panamanian relations throughout history. He told Rusk that he intended "to invite the press in and spend 10 to 15 minutes with me, just talking with me, off the record." He read a draft of the public statement to Rusk, who thought it was "very constructive." The text of the statement released on March 21 is printed in *Public Papers of the Presidents of the United States: Lyndon B. Johnson, 1963–64*, Book I, pages 404–405. Johnson then told Rusk he thought he would say to the press on background:

"I've seen a lot about this Panamanian situation—I've seen a lot of speculation and discussion, back and forth. This is a very important problem for both countries and I've given a lot of thought to it. Our situation has never changed since Secretary Rusk and McNamara and I met the first morning, and I called the President of Panama. And I said, then, in effect this and I have repeated it ever since. But somehow or other, I'm not sure that everybody understands it, and this is our position then and this is our position now." (Recording of telephone conversation between President Johnson and Dean Rusk, March 21, 12:16 p.m.; Johnson Library, Recordings and Transcripts, Tape F64.18, Side B, PNO 2)

Mann agreed with Rusk that the President's proposed statement was all right to be presented to the press as background. Mann reported that Rusk had just met with Ambassador de Lavalle, Chairman of the OAS, who had asked for suggestions on how relations between Panama and the United States could be restored and suggested going back to the two paragraphs on which the OAS Committee had almost succeeded in obtaining an agreement earlier in the month. "We can't do that after we've broken up, and after they leaked everything to everybody," Johnson told Mann in a telephone conversation. "We can't ever agree on those two paragraphs. They ought to know that—or we would have agreed to 'em the other day." Mann suggested getting the OAS to work with them on alternatives. Johnson indicated that his preferred alternative was "one, to resume relations; two, discuss everything—review everything." (Recording of telephone conversation between President Johnson and Thomas Mann, March 21, 1:25 p.m.; ibid., Tape F64.19, Side A, PNO 3)

After his conversation with Mann, the President consulted Senator Russell, who asked why Johnson felt it was important to issue a statement. "It's made only, Dick, to try to get off of dead center." Johnson continued: "The Secretary of State has really had no authority in this thing—and Assistant Secretary of State either—because I told 'em that I'm not goin' to agree to negotiate a new treaty, and so it's been more or less taken out of their hands, and the ball's in my court." The President indicated that the OAS should go back to Chiari. He told Russell: "What I'm going to do when I make this statement—I'm going to give it to the head of the OAS and I'm going to say to the OAS, 'now goddammit, I've gone as far as a human bein' can go. You got to make this fellow go.' I'm gonna put the ball back in his court." Russell assured Johnson that if he felt compelled to make a statement, "I think it's all right." (Recording of telephone conversation between President Johnson and Richard Russell, March 21, 1:32 p.m.; ibid., Tape F64.19, Side A, PNO 4) The portions of the conversations printed here were prepared in the Office of the Historian specifically for this volume.

The President issued his statement at a press conference held at 1:45 that afternoon at the White House. Later that afternoon, he told Mann that "he had a hell of a good press conference," and read the complete transcript of the press conference over the phone. Mann said that the statement "may help to clarify things over there." He told the President: "I don't mind fighting the Panamanians—rather enjoy it, but I don't want to fight this whole OAS." He indicated that if the United

States had to negotiate an agreement with the Panamanians, "we'll go carefully." (Memorandum of conversation, March 21, 3:35 p.m.; ibid., Papers of Thomas C. Mann, Telephone Conversations with LBJ, January 14, 1964–April 30, 1965) A portion of the conversation was recorded and is ibid., Recordings and Transcripts, Tape F64.19, Side B, PNO 2.

---

402. Memorandum of Conversation[1]

Washington, March 23, 1964, 3:30 p.m.

PARTICIPANTS

Ambassador Moreno of Panama
Ambassador Bunker of the U.S.

SUBJECT

Panama–U.S. Relations

I met Ambassador Moreno at the 1925 F Street Club for a private, off-the-record talk. I made it clear to him that I was doing this on my own responsibility and that it was important that the subject of our discussion should be kept confidential and not divulged to the press.

I said that it seemed to me President Johnson's statement of March 21[2] had been most constructive. In some ways it was broader and went beyond the OAS communiqué of March 15.[3] It indicated to me that there was now a genuine meeting of the minds between the two presidents. Furthermore, we had struggled over words and semantics for

---

[1] Source: National Archives and Records Administration, RG 59, ARA/Panamanian Affairs Files: Lot File 66 D 329. Confidential. Drafted by Bunker. Copies were sent to Mann and Allen (RPA). A copy was also sent to Rusk under cover of a memorandum by Bunker on March 24.

[2] See Document 401.

[3] Released on March 16, it reads: "The Governments of the Republic of Panama and of the United States of America have agreed to reestablish diplomatic relations as soon as possible to seek the prompt elimination of the causes of the conflict relative to the Panama Canal and to attempt to resolve other problems existing between them, without limitations or preconditions of any kind.

"Consequently, within 30 days following the reestablishment of diplomatic relations, both Governments will designate special ambassadors to carry out discussions and negotiations with the objective of reaching a fair and just agreement which will eliminate the above-mentioned causes of the conflict and resolve the other problems referred to above. Any agreements that may result would be subject to the constitutional processes of each country."

two and one-half months, to date without results, and it seemed to me that the time had come to substitute action for words. I suggested that one of several procedures might be followed.

1. President Chiari might issue a statement welcoming President Johnson's statement, indicating that as a result of the statement there was a genuine meeting of the minds, that it was obvious that both sides wished to resolve their difficulties and that therefore, the Government of Panama was prepared to resume diplomatic relations with the United States.

2. The Government of Panama might authorize Ambassador Moreno to state that in view of President Johnson's statement of March 21 that the United States is prepared to review every issue that now divides the two countries and every problem which the Panamanian Government wishes to raise, the Government of Panama is prepared to resume diplomatic relations to be followed by the appointment by both countries of special representatives with full authority to discuss all problems and with the responsibility for seeking solutions.

3. We might deliver joint or simultaneously separate notes to the OAS saying that both governments are resuming diplomatic relations and expressing appreciation to the OAS for its efforts to bring about an understanding between the two governments.

Ambassador Moreno said he felt that in some ways, the "agreement" of March 15 was more specific than the wording of the President's statement. I pointed out to him that there had been no "agreement", that in the course of negotiations here we had agreed to several texts which Panama had not accepted and they had agreed to a text finally which we had not accepted. It seemed to me that having gone through 28 texts we had about exhausted the possibility of finding mutually acceptable wording and that the time had come to act. I thought that now it must be evident to both sides that our procedural objectives were really identical; i.e., we both wanted to resume diplomatic relations, we were both ready to discuss, consider, review—whatever words one wished to use for the process—all of the problems existing between us in an effort in good faith to find fair, reasonable and just solutions. That being so, let us get on with the job.

Ambassador Moreno said that there had been a good reaction in Panama to President Johnson's statement and that President Chiari would make a statement this afternoon regarding it. He would try to get the text as soon as possible. He commented that he felt there might be criticism in Panama on the procedure I had suggested on the ground that the Government was backing down still further from its original position and acting on the basis of wording less precise than that in the March 15 communiqué. I replied that it seemed to me that President Johnson's statement was no less precise and, in fact, was more comprehensive, and therefore in a way more favorable to Panama. Ambassador Moreno then said that he would want to talk with his Government and would keep our conversation on a strictly confidential basis.

---

403. Memorandum From the President's Special Assistant for National Security Affairs (Bundy) to President Johnson[1]

Washington, March 24, 1964.

SUBJECT

Chiari statement: our next move

I. If you find the Chiari statement[2] unhelpful and wish to back away from any resumption of relations, I think we should quietly but promptly let it be known that the Chiari statement has not increased our hopes. We could point quietly to his references to the contractual clauses of the treaty and his desire to solve all differences and all problems "once and for all." We could also note his reference to "the necessary constitutional procedures," which means a treaty. On this course, we should simply be back where we were, and you would be standing pat on your statement of last Saturday.[3]

II. A second course would be to say that you find the Chiari statement interesting but that we need to examine more closely the two OAS paragraphs before we come to a final agreement. On this course, we could put to the OAS language which does not mention the Panama Canal directly and which replaces the words "discussions and negotiations" by less fought-over phrases. Tom Mann thinks there is a fair chance of success in this course and that with luck he could win the OAS representatives back on to our side. I think Bill Moyers has language to propose on this course.

---

[1] Source: Johnson Library, National Security File, Memos to the President, McGeorge Bundy, Vol. II. No classification marking.

[2] On March 24 Chiari issued a statement responding to Johnson's public statement of March 21, agreeing in principle with the proposal to resume relations and begin talks, but reiterating his support for the OAS formula—see footnote 3, Document 402. A Department of State translation of Chiari's statement, forwarded to the White House on March 25, is in the National Archives and Records Administration, RG 59, Central Files 1964–66, POL 15–1 PAN.

[3] March 21; see Document 401.

III. The third course is to decide that a prompt de facto resumption of relations is more important than the fact that any Panamanian politician will have to speak in terms somewhat like those which Chiari uses. If we make this view, then I would advise an immediate announcement along the lines of the draft statement attached.[4]

I think these choices are quite clear-cut, and I doubt if we need a long discussion of it.[5]

Mc.G. B.

---

[4] Not found attached.

[5] In a handwritten note at the end of the memorandum Bundy added: "P took still another course, a sort of III in which we try to resume *without* agreeing to 2-para formula." In a telephone conversation with Bundy that evening, Johnson inquired whether Rusk was prepared to accept Chiari's statement. Bundy responded: "I think—no sir, I don't think that. I think he did not want to have us back away, and we're not doing that, and I think I've talked to Tom [Mann] more recently than I have the Secretary, and he's thought about it more. Tom, I think, will be very pleased with this thing—finding out what the hell they mean—and then going the course of trying to amend the two paragraphs in the light—in the general line that you approved tonight. I don't think we're going to have any trouble with the Secretary on this." (Recording of telephone conversation between President Johnson and McGeorge Bundy, March 25, 7:32 p.m.; Johnson Library, Recordings and Transcripts, Tape F64.20, Side A, PNO 8)

---

404.   Memorandum From the President's Special Assistant for National Security Affairs (Bundy) to President Johnson[1]

Washington, March 25, 1964.

SUBJECT

Panama

I have spoken with Tom Mann and set in train the negotiating process you authorized last night.[2]

Ambassador Bunker will be going to Moreno today and will make the following presentation:

1. We have made our statement;
2. You have made your statement;

---

[1] Source: Johnson Library, National Security File, NSC Histories, Panama Crisis, 1964. Secret. Copies were sent to Mann and Dungan.

[2] See footnote 5, Document 403.

3. Why don't you resume relations at once?
4. If you resume, of course we will resume and send an Ambassador forthwith.

If the Panamanians accept this démarche, we are in. If they come back and ask questions about our view of the OAS two paragraph formula, then Bunker will come back to Mann, and Mann will instruct him to say that if the Panamanians wish to go this more complicated route, we would have to insist on minor modifications in the formula. Tom would then negotiate to get the Panama Canal and the word "negotiations" out of the two paragraphs. This second phase is not being discussed even with Bunker until we see how the first phase works.

In all this we are keeping the number of those informed as small as possible, and we are pointing out to the Panamanians that we can negotiate quietly to resume relations, or make our case to the newspapers, but we can hardly do both at once. But we do not kid ourselves that Moreno or his compatriots will be as quiet as we would like.

McG. B.[3]

---

[3] Printed from a copy that bears these typed initials.

---

405. Telephone Conversation Between President Johnson and the President's Special Assistant for National Security Affairs (Bundy)[1]

Washington, March 25, 1964, 5:30 p.m.

Bundy: [Tape begins mid-conversation] from Moreno who says that they just don't think that they can sell—and keep the peace—a straight resumption of relations on these two statements.[2] Ambassador Bunker would now like to go back to Moreno and suggest that there be a resumption of relations on the basis of a letter that we would send

---

[1] Source: Johnson Library, Recordings and Transcripts, Recording of telephone conversation between President Johnson and McGeorge Bundy, Tape F64.20, Side B, PNO 2. No classification marking. This transcript was prepared in the Office of the Historian specifically for this volume.

[2] Reference is to Johnson's statement of March 21 and Chiari's communiqué of March 24; see Document 401 and footnote 2, Document 403.

to the head of the OAS, which I'd like to read to you, because I think it's a good play:

"I have the honor to advise Your Excellency that the Governments of Panama and the United States of America have agreed to resume diplomatic relations as of today's date, exchange of Ambassadors forthwith. My government will appoint without delay a special representative together with a representative of government of Panama—will be empowered to review all the issues between the two countries and to seek a fair and just resolution of these issues."

Then there's a paragraph thanking the OAS for its constructive and untiring and invaluable work, etc. This would be just a way of letting them off the hook of the fact that we're not going to buy those two paragraphs. The question of whether we would go back and renegotiate the two paragraphs could be left down the pike and we wouldn't have to cross it. As I say, Ambassador Bunker, who's close to this, thinks there's—you know—a fighting chance that this would work, and I see no pain in it. Is that all right with you?

President: Now what do we do when we write 'em that? Do we embrace the two paragraphs?

Bundy: No, we do not. We do not refer to the two paragraphs, and we're simply standing on your statement in this letter. Yeah. No, we do not, Mr. President, and we've made it clear to Moreno that those two paragraphs are not agreed and that we have not accepted them, and we cannot at this stage accept them. That's been made very clear to him today, and what we'd like to do is to let that sink in overnight and then go back to him tomorrow and say, now we've got another idea which is that we could write the OAS and say we're going ahead that we're going to review all these issues and seek a fair and just resolution—doesn't refer to the Panama Canal, doesn't mention negotiations, and it doesn't mention the two paragraphs.

President: What makes you think that they would take this if they wouldn't take anything—

Bundy: Gives him something to say, that we have given one more statement of our intent to seek a fair and just resolution and that—what I think—I think the reason Ambassador Bunker wants to do it is not so much that the expectation of agreement is necessarily very high, but that we're quite sure that this will be regarded as a forthcoming act from Lavalle's point of view—the head of the OAS Council—and that that would give us pressure against Panamanians from other Latin Americans, instead of having the position in which they say they seem to be the ones who are being forthcoming with respect to the OAS recommendation. I myself think, Mr. President, to be honest with you, I'm not quite as optimistic as Ambassador Bunker, but I can't see that we lose anything by trying this one more, and I think we gain to the degree that the OAS people begin to think we're the ones who put the ball back in their court. If it doesn't work, then at least it's their play, and we aren't being asked what our next step is.

President: Well, I don't understand it. It doesn't have any appeal to me, but if you and Rusk think it's all right, and think it's the thing to do, I'd go ahead.

Bundy: Well, the real question is whether it has any negative to you, Mr. President.

President: No, no.

Bundy: And I don't see anything in that—it's a perfect—it's a diplomatic play.

President: No, it doesn't have any negative. The reason it doesn't is because I can't see what purpose it serves.

Bundy: [unintelligible] any positive in it either [laughter].

President: That's right, but I don't want—I don't quite understand it, and I don't want to be obstinate. If you and Rusk think it's all right, it's all right with me.

Bundy: We do, yes sir, and so does Tom.

President: All right.

Bundy: Aye, aye, sir.

---

406.   Telegram From the President's Special Assistant for National Security Affairs (Bundy) to President Johnson in Texas[1]

Washington, March 30, 1964, 2257Z.

CAP 64105. On Panama, Secretary Rusk, Mann, and I would now like your authority for Bunker to propose the following letter to Moreno for possible delivery by both governments in identical notes to the Chairman of the OAS Council. We do not believe the Panamanians will accept this solution, but we do believe it is useful to offer it as a means of getting basic responsibility fixed back on Panama.[2]

---

[1] Source: Johnson Library, National Security File, Country File, Panama, Vol. III, March 1964. Secret. The telegram bears a handwritten note by Jack Valenti that reads: "LBJ approved by phone to Secy Rusk, 3/30/64."

[2] The Consul in Panama (Taylor) reported on March 28 that, with the Panamanian elections scheduled for early May, "Chiari's present seemingly rigid stand motivated by political considerations." He also indicated that "Senator Fulbright's remarks have bolstered Chiari's belief that if he stands firm he will eventually obtain close to what he originally stipulated." (Telegram 514 from Panama City, March 28; National Archives and Records Administration, RG 59, Central Files 1964–66, POL PAN–US) Regarding Fulbright's remarks, see footnote 3 below.

The operative paragraph is paragraph 2, and you will want to check it word for word.

The word "re-examine" is safe, and I think we should stick with it at this stage. We could also use nearly any other word except "negotiate," but I think we should allow the Panamanians to make further suggestions if they have enough interest.

If you approve this move by word to Valenti or Connell, Bunker would present this proposal to Moreno tomorrow, along with a clear statement that this is the best we can do and that he should not expect any softening of the U.S. position because of the Fulbright speech. FBI reports make it clear that Moreno and Chiari have put undue weight on Fulbright's remarks,[3] thinking that they indicate public pressure in the U.S. for an early settlement on terms more favorable to Panama than those we are proposing.

Bunker believes that this offer of identical notes will regain support for us in the OAS Committee.

Draft letter follows:

Note: In second paragraph in place of re-examine, we might use deal with.

Draft Note—United States

Your Excellency:

1. I have the honor to advise Your Excellency that the Governments of the Republic of Panama and the United States of America have agreed to resume diplomatic relations as of today's date.

2. In order to seek the prompt elimination of the causes of conflict existing between them, my government will also appoint without delay a special Ambassador with sufficient powers to re-examine all the issues between the two countries, without limitation or preconditions of any kind, with the objective of reaching a fair and just agreement, subject to the constitutional processes of each country.

---

[3] On March 25 Fulbright made a speech advocating that the United States renegotiate the Panama Canal Treaty. Johnson complained: "I'm just within an inch of gettin' an agreement with them and every time I do, *The New York Times*, *The Washington Post*, or some damn fool Senator gets up and knocks it off." (Recording of telephone conversation between President Johnson and Spessard Holland, March 25, 4:40 p.m.; Johnson Library, Recordings and Transcripts, Tape 64.20, Side A, PNO 10) The President also complained to Bundy that "they all assume Fulbright speaks for the administration." Bundy responded that it was "extraordinary that Fulbright would take such a stance." The President replied, "Fulbright's that way, though. He is very unpredictable." Johnson also recalled Truman's onetime quip that Fulbright was only "half-bright." (Recording of telephone conversation between President Johnson and McGeorge Bundy, March 25, 4:35 p.m.; ibid., PNO 11)

3. The Government of the United States of America desires to express its gratitude for the untiring and invaluable efforts of the members of the Inter-American Peace Committee, the Council of the Organization of American States, the General Committee and the Special Delegation, without which this constructive result would not have been possible.

4. Accept, Excellency, the renewed assurances of my highest consideration.

Ellsworth Bunker

Ambassador

Representative of the United States of America on the Council of the Organization of American States

His Excellency
Dr. Juan Bautista de Lavalle,
Chairman of the General Committee of the Council
of the Organization of American States,
Acting Provisionally as Organ of Consultation.

---

407. Memorandum From the President's Special Assistant for National Security Affairs (Bundy) to President Johnson[1]

Washington, April 1, 1964.

SUBJECT

Ambassador Bunker's meeting with Moreno

Bunker reports that he had a quite satisfactory talk with Moreno this afternoon.[2] He presented to Moreno the attached redraft, from which the direct reference to the Panama Canal has been removed.[3] He told Moreno that he had your personal backing in making this proposal and that what you were aiming at was the simplest, clearest understanding that was possible. He told Moreno further that you did not want complicated language which might stand in the way of

---

[1] Source: Johnson Library, National Security File, Memos to the President, McGeorge Bundy, Vol. III. No classification marking.

[2] In a telephone conversation earlier that afternoon, Bundy told the President that "we're again sort of within a very few inches of an agreement" with Panama. (Recording of telephone conversation between President Johnson and McGeorge Bundy, April 1, 2:23 p.m.; ibid., Transcripts and Recordings, Tape F64.22, Side A, PNO 2)

[3] Not attached; the language as approved is printed in Department of State *Bulletin*, April 27, 1964, p. 656, and *American Foreign Policy: Current Documents, 1964*, pp. 365–366.

getting an agreement through the Senate at some later time. He told Moreno that we had no fall-back position and that if this did not work we thought it would be best to wait until the elections.

All in all, he sounds as if he had acted like the excellent Ambassador that he is, and I wish we had used the technique of sending him in with your direct instructions before now.

Moreno did not seem to be terribly distressed at the omission of the Panama Canal reference, but he did argue strongly for the inclusion of the footnote saying that the word "agreement" is used "in the broadest sense that the word has in international law." Bunker told him that we did not want that clause in the statement of agreement, but when Moreno said that it would be only a repetition of what the Chairman of the Council has said before, Bunker indicated that we would not object to having Chairman Lavalle repeat it on his own. He took this position because Dean Rusk had told him earlier that phrase was really no bother to us, and that in fact it protects us. Dean's reasoning is that "the broadest sense" covers everything from an informal oral understanding to a treaty. It remains true that some Panamanians will read this note as meaning that the agreement which is being sought will be a new treaty.

But as long as we are not pinned to this understanding directly, and as long as we are protected by the fundamental clause of the whole arrangement—"without limitations or preconditions of any kind"—I think we can endure to have the Chairman interpret the agreement in this way. Do you agree? If not, we should tell Bunker at once.

Moreno left Bunker saying that he would do his best to button up an agreement on this basis. My own guess is that we may get one more bit of pressure from Panama, but Bunker is optimistic.[4]

McG. B.[5]

---

[4] On April 2 the NSC met to review a number of issues including Panama. According to Bromley Smith's account of the meeting, Rusk stated that "there may be developments later today with respect to wording of an announcement which would be acceptable to us." (Summary Record of NSC Meeting No. 525, April 2, noon; Johnson Library, National Security File, NSC Meetings File, Vol. I, Tab 6, 4/2/64) According to McCone's account of the meeting, Rusk reported that "there was a possibility that today or tomorrow there would be a break which would permit us to move to the conference table" with Panama. McCone noted in his record of this NSC meeting that "on April 1st, the President asked me personally if I thought we were acting correctly on this Panama issue. I replied that I felt his position was defendable and would not recommend any changes." (Memorandum for the record by McCone, April 2; Central Intelligence Agency, DCI (McCone) Files, Job 80–B01285A, Meetings with the President) Prior to the NSC meeting on April 2, Johnson queried McNamara about the pending agreement. He responded that having an agreement would be helpful and the timing, in spite of the Fulbright speech, was all right. "I think if it drifts on too long, there'll be criticism mounting in our own press, so I would conclude it." (Recording of telephone conversation between President Johnson and Robert McNamara, April 2, 11:15 a.m.; Johnson Library, Recordings and Transcripts, Tape F64.22, Side A, PNO 5)

[5] Printed from a copy that bears these typed initials.

408. Telephone Conversation Between President Johnson and Robert Anderson[1]

Washington, April 3, 1964, 12:55 p.m.

Anderson: Hello, Mr. President.

President: Say, looks like we are going to get this Panama agreement worked out.

Anderson: Yes.

President: And then we are going to have to negotiate—uh, resolve some problems we have between the two of us.

Anderson: Yes.

President: And we'll have a full time ambassador and all the staff we need but we want you to be the top lawyer on negotiatin' with them.

Anderson: I'll do whatever you say, Mr. President.

President: Well, that's what I want, and I'll give you everything you need and I just want to—if we have to rewrite a treaty—well, we want to look at it carefully and I just want some fella that I have absolute confidence in. And I want to be measured by only one standard, and that's what is right and just and fair. And I think if you do that, you could be very helpful. You could start 'em off and then come in from time to time, but just be kinda my advisor on it, and let me name you as my man.[2]

Anderson: All right, sir. Now, you know, of course, that I don't really know much about—

President: I don't care about that. Good thing you don't.

Anderson: All right, sir.

President: You still got your law license, haven't you?

Anderson: That is correct.

President: Good-bye. Bye.

Anderson: Okay, my friend.

---

[1] Source: Johnson Library, Recordings and Transcripts, Recording of telephone conversation between President Johnson and Robert Anderson, Tape F64.22, Side B, PNO 2. No classification marking. This transcript was prepared in the Office of the Historian specifically for this volume. Robert Anderson was a lawyer and former Secretary of the Treasury under President Eisenhower.

[2] Shortly before this conversation, the President consulted Mann, who urged that Anderson be designated to head the team: "We need a tough guy now to get down to the hard negotiating and I would try to talk Bob into it." (Telephone conversation between President Johnson and Thomas Mann, April 3, 12:06 p.m.; ibid., PNO 1)

409.   Summary Record of the 526th Meeting of the National Security Council With the Congressional Leaders[1]

Washington, April 3, 1964, 2 p.m.

Various Subjects

The President opened the meeting with the Congressional Leaders by saying that his purpose was to bring them up to date on recent developments. Various Council members would report on current situations. He first called on Secretary Rusk for a summary of developments in Brazil.

[Omitted here is discussion of Brazil (Document 208) and Vietnam (*Foreign Relations*, 1964–1968, Volume I, Document 107).]

The President then turned to Panama and read the declaration which he said he would make this afternoon if the Council approved.[2] He summarized the U.S. position on the Panama negotiations, i.e., that we would not accept preconditions but we were prepared to review with the Panamanians all problems. He characterized the declaration as containing nothing offensive to either side and as stating the same position he had taken during his first telephone conversation with President Chiari of Panama[3] which took place immediately after the incident in Panama. He informed the group that he had chosen former Secretary of the Treasury Robert Anderson as his Special Ambassador to conduct the negotiations with the Panamanians.

Senator Mansfield and Senator Fulbright interrupted to state their belief that the agreement proposed by the President was an excellent one.

The President then announced that he was seeking Panamanian agreement for Jack Vaughn as U.S. Ambassador. He summarized in detail the career of Mr. Vaughn.

The President asked whether the Council approved the declaration, and hearing no objection, the President said we would proceed to give our statement to the OAS group. He then praised Ambassador Bunker for his contribution to reaching an agreement.

Secretary Rusk explained that we could not accept any precommitment with respect to negotiation with the Panamanians because, if we did not reach any agreement, we could be accused of bad faith. If the

---

[1] Source: Johnson Library, National Security File, NSC Meetings File, Vol. 1, Tab 7, 4/3/64. Top Secret. Drafted by Bromley Smith. The meeting lasted no later than 3:35 p.m. (Ibid., President's Daily Diary) McCone has a much briefer account of the Panama discussion in his record of this meeting. (Central Intelligence Agency, DCI (McCone) Files, Job 80–B01285A, Memoranda for the Record)

[2] See footnote 3, Document 407.

[3] Document 370.

Panamanians denounced the existing treaty they could use a charge of our bad faith in arguing before the International Court that the treaty was no longer valid. There is no reference to the Panama Canal in the agreement. We are not calling attention to this because if we did we would create a problem for President Chiari. Chiari's opponents could say he had retreated from his position that he would not renew relations with the U.S. until we had agreed to renegotiate the treaty. Secretary Rusk said that the solution of the current phase of the Panama problem would clear the atmosphere for OAS action on the Cuban arms cache in Venezuela.

The President said that our insistence on talking without preconditions was our first and last position. We may be prepared to accept changes in the treaty but we could not do so until the Panamanians had agreed to talk without preconditions.

There followed a brief procedural discussion as to how Special Ambassador Anderson would be formally empowered to proceed. Confirmation by the Senate is not required because he will have the personal rank of Ambassador.

Senator Hickenlooper said the Panamanians had denounced the treaties. What would we do if in the first discussion the Panamanians took the position that no treaty existed? Secretary Rusk replied that as far as he knew the Panamanians had not denounced the treaties. They recognized the existence of the treaties and their language attacking them had not gone so far as to claim that they had no validity.

Senator Morse said that the Panamanian agreement was a great agreement and he congratulated the President and the Secretary of State. He said, however, he felt obliged to say that he disagrees entirely with the program for South Vietnam.

[Omitted here is further discussion of Vietnam.]

Turning to Panama, Senator Saltonstall said that in his view the problem there arose because of the attitude of U.S. citizens in the Canal Zone. He asked what we were doing to improve this situation. The President replied that Deputy Secretary of Defense Vance had gone down to Panama, had reviewed the situation, and had recommended certain changes which have already taken place. In addition, General O'Meara, Commander-in-Chief, U.S. Southern Command, is to make additional recommendations on this subject.

[Omitted here is discussion of Africa.]

The President then read a draft press statement which would be issued following the conclusion of the meeting (copy attached).[4] The statement was approved by those present.

---

[4] Not attached but an apparent reference to a statement made to the White House correspondents by Press Secretary George Reedy, at 3:40 p.m. (Johnson Library, National Security File, NSC Meetings, Vol. I)

The President then read a statement which he is going to make to the OAS Ambassadors at 4:00 PM covering the Panama agreement (copy attached).[5]

Senator Humphrey stated that the President's statement on Panama was excellent. He said our forbearance and patience had paid off.

[Omitted here is discussion of Vietnam, Cuba, and Cyprus.]

The President then explained to the group that he had put in a call to President Chiari of Panama on the assumption that the meeting would be finished. President Chiari was now on the line and he said he would now talk to him. (The photographers entered to take pictures.) The record of the conversation is attached.[6] Only one side of the conversation was audible to those present. At the conclusion of the conversation the President commented that President Chiari had broken into English at the end to say, "That's the way to do it," then returning to Spanish.

[Omitted here is discussion of Zanzibar and Indonesia.]

The President asked all those present to go with him to the Fish Room to meet the OAS Ambassadors gathered there to hear the President's statement on Panama. The Cabinet Room had to be vacated so that the television cameras could be put in place.

Bromley Smith[7]

---

[5] Not attached; printed in Department of State *Bulletin*, April 27, 1964, pp. 655 and 656, and *American Foreign Policy: Current Documents, 1964*, pp. 366–367.

[6] Not attached; for the transcript of this telephone conversation, see Document 410.

[7] Printed from a copy that bears this typed signature.

410.   Telephone Conversation Between President Johnson and
Panamanian President Chiari[1]

April 3, 1964, 3:35 p.m.

President: Hello, Mr. President, this is Lyndon Johnson. I wanted
to express our great pleasure at the agreement that has been reached.

President Chiari: He is delighted, Mr. President, that both nations
have been able to find a formula in order to re-establish diplomatic relations. He wishes to thank you for that and he is delighted that the
two nations now will be able to discuss the problems that for so long
have been between them.

President: We appreciate your desire to move on to a lasting agreement, Mr. President, that will resolve these difficulties, and I am today
appointing the ablest and strongest man that I know, former Secretary
of Treasury Mr. Robert Anderson, to be our Special Ambassador.

President Chiari: Has he been named as Special Ambassador?

President: Yes, sir, he will be named as Special Ambassador to do
the negotiating. He was Secretary of the Treasury under President
Eisenhower and is a man that enjoys my unlimited confidence.

President Chiari: He is delighted, Mr. President, and he wishes to
thank you very much. He wishes to assure you that sometime during
tomorrow they will nominate a very capable Panamanian to represent
Panama in Washington as Ambassador.

President: Thank him very much, and we look forward to hearing about his nomination. Tell him that Mr. Anderson is a first-rate
lawyer, having been a Professor of Law. He's—his instructions will be
to secure a fair and just agreement that will be satisfactory to the people of both nations.

President Chiari: He is delighted, Mr. President, and he is certain
that as long as there is good will and good faith on both sides that we
will be able to resolve these long standing problems that have existed
between the two nations, and that he looks forward to a future of the
friendliest possible relations between the two nations, since they have
the same common objectives.

President: Well, tell him as we stated in the very first conversation we had together that we cannot have any pre-commitments. But

[1] Source: Johnson Library, Recordings and Transcripts, Recording of telephone conversation between President Johnson and President Chiari, Tape F64.22, Side B, PNO 4.
No classification marking. This transcript was prepared in the Office of the Historian
specifically for this volume. President Johnson was in Washington; President Chiari in
Panama City. Except where noted, President Chiari spoke through a translator.

Mr. Anderson will listen to all the differences that exist between the two nations and we will try to find an agreement that will be satisfactory.

President Chiari: Fine, Mr. President. That's very fine.

President: Tell him we expect to name a Mr. Jack Vaughn who has lived in Panama a goodly part of his time and who is now head of the Peace Corps for Latin America, to be our regular Ambassador there.

President Chiari: Fine, and I'm delighted, Mr. President.

President: He has had a decade of service in Latin America and he's been on the faculty of Johns Hopkins School of International Studies here.

President Chiari: Fine. Thank you very much, Mr. President.

President: He spent from 1952 to 1960 in and out of Panama and some of his friends no doubt will know him.

President Chiari: He is certain that that will be the case, Mr. President.

President: And tell him that we would like to have clearance on him just as quickly as we can, and we'll submit it through channels shortly.

President Chiari: Fine, with a great deal of pleasure, Mr. President. And we will do the same with you, Mr. President, as soon as possible.

President: All right. So tell him that the two countries can now sit down together without limitations or pre-conditions of any kind and as friends try to find the proper and fair answers.

President Chiari: [in English] That is the right way to do it and I hope we get success on that. [through translator] That is the right way to do it and I hope we get together on that.

President: [Chuckle] Thank you, Mr. President. I'm lookin' forward to seein' ya.

President Chiari: [in English] Okay. Good-bye.

---

411.   Editorial Note

[*text not declassified*]

412. Memorandum From Albert E. Carter in the Bureau of Intelligence and Research to the Director (Hughes)

Washington, April 10, 1964.

[Source: Department of State, INR/IL Historical Files, ARA/CIA Weekly Meetings, 1964–1965. Secret. 2 pages of source text not declassified.]

413. Memorandum for the Record

Washington, April 17, 1964.

[Source: Central Intelligence Agency, DCI (McCone) Files, Job 80–B012785A, 303 Committee, 1964. Secret; Eyes Only. 3 pages of source text not declassified.]

414. National Security Action Memorandum No. 296[1]

Washington, April 25, 1964.

TO

Secretary of State
Secretary of Defense

SUBJECT

Interdepartmental organization for Panamanian affairs

The President has approved the following organizational arrangements relating to the formulation and execution of U.S. policy in Panama.

---

[1] Source: Johnson Library, National Security File, Country File, Panama, Vol. V, May–June 1964. Secret.

1. Panama Review Group

a. The Panama Review Group, composed of the Secretary of the Army, the Assistant Secretary of State for Inter-American Affairs, the Special Representative, a White House representative, and chaired by the Assistant Secretary of State for Inter-American Affairs, will be the principal point of focus below the President for the formulation and execution of policy with regard to Panama. The Executive Secretary of the Panama Review Group will be designated by the Department of State.

b. The Panama Review Group will work closely with the officers supporting the Special Representative in exercising control over actions which might affect the treaty discussions, publicity, and security.

2. Panama Review Committee

A Committee composed of the Ambassador to Panama, CINCSO, and the Governor of the Panama Canal Zone, and chaired by the Ambassador, will be established and will meet periodically at the call of any member to discuss conditions in Panama and the Zone and exchange reports and proposals on actions to be undertaken in the interests of the United States and better U.S./Panamanian relations. The President expects that the members of this Committee will share their concern fully and frankly with each other, and will work together closely in discharging their respective responsibilities. Any differences which may arise will be referred to the Panama Review Group located in Washington. Any action agreed upon by the Panama Review Committee will be reported to Washington by the Ambassador *before* this action is taken, whenever such action could affect the work of the Special Representative. The Special Representative will be notified through Washington of such proposed action.

McGeorge Bundy

415. Memorandum From the President's Special Assistant for National Security Affairs (Bundy) to President Johnson[1]

Washington, May 8, 1964.

SUBJECT

Panamanian Elections

1. A meeting of the Panama Review Group was held today to discuss the Panamanian elections, scheduled for Sunday.[2]

2. The group agreed that the general shape of the problem is as follows: *First,* we can expect to see attempts at vote-fixing by all three candidates—Robles, Arnulfo, and Galindo. *Second,* while it is not a certainty, there probably will be some violence during the elections, particularly on Monday and Tuesday when the votes will be counted. Such violence will be primarily and initially between Panamanians. But we cannot discount the possibility that Communist and student elements will take the opportunity to make attacks against American targets, in and out of the Zone.[3]

3. We have no favorites in the election and our posture throughout this period will be strictly "hands-off." Generally speaking, there are only two exceptions to this policy. We will take appropriate steps to protect American lives and property, if it becomes necessary to do so. And we will act if there is a clear danger of a Communist take-over, which is not likely.

4. The following U.S. Government actions have been taken or are in train.

(a) U.S. military forces have been readied to take prompt action in the event they are needed. 2000 airborne troops will be available to

---

[1] Source: Johnson Library, National Security File, Country File, Panama, Vol. V, May–June 1964. Secret.

[2] May 10. The memorandum for the record of this meeting, held at the White House and drafted by FitzGerald on May 12, is in the Central Intelligence Agency, Job 78–03041, Directorate of Operations, [*file name not declassified*].

[3] The CIA warned of this possibility in [*document number not declassified*], May 7. (Johnson Library, National Security File, Country File, Panama, Vol. V, May–June 1964) In a May 8 telegram from the Canal Zone, USCINCSO indicated the CIA conclusions were "entirely reasonable." (Telegram SC3415DA for JCS; National Archives and Records Administration, RG 59, Central Files 1964–66, POL PAN–US) According to Gordon Chase of the NSC staff, "State and Ambassador Vaughn seem to feel that CIA has overstated the dangers of a serious explosion." (Memorandum from Chase to Bundy, May 8; Johnson Library, National Security File, Country File, Panama, Vol. V, May–June 1964) Lansing Collins reported that Vaughn had indicated that "he agreed with the tone" of the CIA report, although he thought the conclusions "slightly exaggerated." (Memorandum of conversation, May 8; ibid.)

arrive in the Canal Zone in 10 hours. About 1300 Marines will be 20 miles off Panama shores (but out of sight) by Sunday morning. All this is *most* privately done and Cy Vance assures me there will be no leak.

(b) Appropriate Government departments and agencies will be alerted to watch the Panama situation closely on a 24 hour basis.

(c) To minimize the possibility that the press will blame us for whatever happens in the elections, State plans to make it clear, on a background basis, that we have no favorites in this election; as a matter of fact, none of the candidates are shining lights.

(d) Long-standing emergency instructions to Americans in Panama are in effect (e.g. stay off the streets). In the event of attacks on the Zone, the Zone police will minimize shooting and will rely, insofar as possible, on such devices as tear gas, which they now have in plentiful supply.[4]

5. The White House Situation Room has been alerted to watch the elections closely; for spot status reports over the weekend, you may want to call the Situation Room directly. For "deeper" analysis, I will, of course, be available. But we probably won't know much before Monday.

McG. B.

---

[4] A Contingency Plan for Panama, prepared on May 1 and approved by the Departments of State and Defense, and the CIA, was forwarded to Bundy at the White House on May 7. (Washington National Records Center, OSD Files: FRC 330 69A 4023, Panama, 1964)

---

416.   Telegram From the Embassy in Panama to the Department of State[1]

Panama City, June 1, 1964, 2 p.m.

672. Drama of May 10 Panamanian presidential election will formally close June 6 when Marco Robles scheduled receive credentials

---

[1] Source: National Archives and Records Administration, RG 59, Central Files 1964–66, POL 14 PAN. Confidential. Repeated to CINCSO, CINCLANT, Governor of the Canal Zone, and DIA.

as President-elect in formal ceremony at Los Santos.[2] Following is Embassy's preliminary assessment of aftermath of election:

Possibility of widespread violence in protest against Robles victory now seems slight because: government's political organization was skillful enough and sufficiently well-heeled to keep its backstage manipulations fairly well hidden; Arnulfo Arias apparently has no stomach for an effort at violent rebellion, at least at this time; and National Guard remains alert and capable and is backing Robles.

Robles is widely regarded as honest man who, while no great statesman or intellect, will nevertheless be more forceful President than Chiari has been. It is generally thought he will be less tolerant than Chiari was of Communist and crypto-Communist elements. He describes himself as simple country boy from the interior who won honest election, who is compromised by no political debts, and who will run his government with firm hand.[3]

Trouble with this portrait is that political organization which engineered his victory was just as crooked as any other in living memory in Panama, he or his close associates have already shown disconcerting readiness to cooperate with certain leftists, and his victory was heavily financed by number of people who will certainly present him with political bill he will probably not be able refuse even if he wants to.

This is not to say however, that Robles is not, from our point of view, an improvement over Chiari, but how much of one is problematical. He is probably somewhat stronger character; he is perhaps educable; he doubtless realizes it is good politics, at least in short-term, to seek improved relations with US; and he has cooperated with US in past.

Not clear yet what kind of National Assembly Robles will have to work with since official count not yet finished and all kinds of frantic deals are being made. Prospects are he will command narrow majority but will be confronted with very active opposition. Assembly will probably also contain one or two able and energetic Commies or near-Commies.

---

[2] On May 29 the Embassy has reported on the results of the election in Panama, in which Robles received 130,154 votes; Arnulfo Arias 119,786 votes; Galindo 47,629 votes; Molino 9,714; and three other candidates shared just over 10,000 votes. (Telegram 667 from Panama, May 29; ibid.)

[3] CIA and ARA representatives met on May 15 to review the election. CIA reported that after Galindo refused to withdraw, Robles was "under no illusion that he is running ahead of Arnulfo Arias." Robles believed that he would "ostensibly win the election due to National Guard support and its control of balloting." (Memorandum from Carter to Hughes, May 15; Department of State, INR/IL Historical Files, ARA–CIA Weekly Meetings, 1964–1965)

Chiari government is undoubtedly in difficult financial straits which will be worse by October when new administration takes over. We will almost certainly be importuned to bail them out.

In short, prospects are: (1) next four months will be difficult going for Chiari government which encountering severe financial problems (2) economic conditions may so deteriorate that Panamenistas and Communists may find pretext to undertake, perhaps jointly, major protest efforts such as mass demonstrations, general strike, etc. (3) Chiari government will weather interim period and (4) in October Robles will take over government facing economic and financial problems with which unable cope without external financial assistance. Present indications are Robles government will follow much along same pattern as that of Chiari and other recent Panamanian governments and will be largely representative of same pressure groups, but it does not appear that in immediate future we will face another crisis like last January. Time is running out, however, and we shall have to work harder to get Panamanians begin face up to their fundamental social and economic problems.

Vaughn

---

417.   Memorandum From Secretary of Defense McNamara to President Johnson[1]

Washington, August 27, 1964.

SUBJECT

Actions Taken in the Canal Zone to Improve Relations with Panama Since the Riots of January 1964

Under the supervision of the Secretary of the Army, as a part of a continuing program to improve relations with Panama, the following specific actions have been taken since January by the Canal Zone Government and the Panama Canal Company.

---

[1] Source: Johnson Library, National Security File, Country File, Panama, Vol. VI, August 1964–January 1965. Confidential. A note on the first page reads: "Classified confidential only because of the references to the hiring of Panamanians for the Canal Zone police force (Item 4), and the proposed reduction in the 25% tropical differential pay (Item 7). These are sensitive matters with our U.S. citizen employees."

1. *Flying Panamanian flags in the Canal Zone.*

Action. During the January riots, the decision was made to adhere meticulously to the agreement to fly the Panamanian flag wherever the U.S. flag is flown on land by the civilian authorities in the Canal Zone. Dual flag poles and dual flags have been installed at all schools in the Canal Zone. A formal agreement with the Republic for the half-masting of flags on national days of mourning is under discussion. Pending such agreement, the flags of both nations are half-masted for either nation's days of mourning.

2. *Disciplinary action against U.S. citizen employees.*

Action. Two employees whose opposition to the Administration's policies exceeded normally acceptable standards have been discharged, and a third has been demoted. These employees' acts included publication of libelous material and other acts of rank insubordination. The discharged employees' appeals are currently under consideration in the U.S. Civil Service Commission. These discharges will have a salutary effect on any employee who may be inclined to make inflamatory public statements in opposition to conciliatory moves toward Panama.

3. *Wage increases to Panamanian employees.*

Action. A series of wage increases was initiated in 1962, designed to eliminate the marked gap between wage levels in categories of jobs held for the most part by Panamanian citizens and the categories held mostly by U.S. citizens. The third and final increase under this program was put into effect in July 1964. The program will increase annual labor costs in Canal Zone agencies by approximately seven and one-half million dollars.

4. *Hiring of Panamanian citizens for the Panama police force.*

Action. In the past all police positions in the Canal Zone have been designated as Security Positions, reserved for U.S. citizens only. Thus, law enforcement in the all-negro non-U.S. citizen communities within the Canal Zone and along the Canal Zone border has been carried out by white U.S. citizen policemen, creating both national and racial conflicts in police actions involving Panamanians. On August 21, 1964, by an amendment to Army regulations made possible by Executive Order 11171, authority was granted to the Governor of the Canal Zone to employ 25 Panamanian citizens for the police force outside the Security Position category. This action was not taken in response to any Panamanian demand, but it gives promise of better relations between the Canal Zone police and the Panamanian citizens in the Zone. It also opens a new category of jobs formerly closed to Panamanian citizens.

5. *Review of security positions.*

Action. At the time of the establishment of the Canal Zone Merit System in 1959 some 4,000 jobs in the Canal Zone were classified as Security Positions, reserved for U.S. citizens. Periodic reviews since that time reduced the number to approximately 2,500. The Governor of the Canal Zone has been directed to restudy the Security Positions in the Canal organization with a view to further reducing the total.

6. *Desegregation of public accommodations.*

Action. Traditionally, Canal Zone communities and public accommodations have been segregated along national lines, which amounted to racial segregation in that most Panamanian citizen employees are negro. With the passage of the Civil Rights Act in the U.S., the Governor of the Canal Zone issued orders eliminating the last vestiges of racial segregation by desegregating all swimming pools and Government housing within the Zone.

7. *Reduction of the tropical differential.*

Action. While again, not in response to any Panamanian demand, the Secretary of the Army has formally proposed to the employee organization in the Zone a prospective reduction in the tropical differential paid to U.S. citizen employees from 25% to 15%. Although not done for this purpose, such a reduction would have a beneficial effect on relations with Panama. When carried out, it would help eliminate accusations of inequality of treatment and will create some additional job opportunities for Panamanians. This action derives from a three-year study and is now in the final stages of discussion with employee representatives. The Secretary of the Army will visit the Canal Zone on 28 August to participate in these discussions. A final decision on implementing details of the reduction is expected soon afterward.

8. *Establishment of a Labor Advisory Committee.*

Action. For approximately two years, the Governor of the Canal Zone has been discussing with representatives of the Government of Panama the establishment of a bi-national Labor Advisory Committee to advise him on labor matters involving Panamanian employees of the Canal enterprise. General agreement has been reached with Panama on the terms of reference for the Committee, and its early establishment is anticipated.

9. *Panamanian Consultants to the Board of Directors of the Panama Canal Company.*

Action. Panama has long aspired to some participation in the management of the Panama Canal Company. The President recently approved the recommendation of the Secretary of the Army that two prominent residents of Panama, one Panamanian citizen and one U.S. citizen businessman, be appointed as consultants to the Board of Directors of the Panama Canal Company. The U.S. Ambassador and the Governor of the Canal Zone have nominated appropriate individuals and invitations will be extended to them at an early date.

10. *Scholarships in the Canal Zone College.*

Action. In early June, the Governor of the Canal Zone announced a scholarship program for ten Panamanians to attend the Canal Zone College. Forty-seven applicants took examinations, and final selection of the winners was made on August 15.

11. *50th Anniversary of the Panama Canal.*

Action. The 50th Anniversary of the opening of the Canal occurred on August 15th of this year. The Anniversary was commemorated by quiet and restrained ceremonies which were not offensive to Panama.

12. *Resumption of community relations programs.*

Action. The Governor of the Canal Zone and the U.S. Ambassador have discussed with the Foreign Minister of Panama the resumption of various Canal Zone-Republic of Panama community relations programs. Canal Zone support of rural medical clinics has been resumed, and the city officials of Colon joined in Canal Zone 4th of July celebrations. Other similar activities are being encouraged.

13. *Electric power and water for Panamanian border communities.*

Action. Prior to the January riots, action was under way to provide Canal Zone water and electric power to several Panamanian border communities remote from Panamanian sources. The lines required within the Canal Zone have been installed, and initiation of service awaits only the completion of installations required on the Panamanian side.

14. *Coordination of public information activities.*

Action. Steps have been initiated to improve coordination of the public information activities of the Canal organization, the military commands, and the U.S. Embassy, both in normal times and during emergencies.

15. *Sea level canal proposal.*

Action. At the invitation of Ambassador Anderson, the Secretary of the Army explained the status of the sea level canal project to

Ambassador Illueca of Panama on 7 July. The scope of the engineering problems, the economic advantages to Panama of such an arrangement, and the possibilities of a canal in Colombia were covered. Subsequent statements by Panamanian officials indicate their recognition that the U.S. must eventually build a sea level canal and could possibly build it outside Panama.

The numbered actions above are confined to those primarily within the authority of the Secretary of the Army and the Governor of the Canal Zone. They do not include actions such as AID activities, loans, and grants, wholly within the authority of the U.S. Ambassador and the Department of State or actions within the Canal Zone in support of State Department discussions. The latter are being handled by the Department of State through Ambassador Anderson and Ambassador Vaughn and are still in the preliminary discussion stages. They include proposals such as the extension of Panama's commercial activity in the Canal Zone, release of unneeded lands and installations, a corridor under Panama's jurisdiction across the Zone, enforcement of certain Panamanian laws in the Canal Zone, and many other Panamanian aspirations requiring inter-agency action of Congressional approval to accomplish. Progress on these broader matters has been delayed pending the installation of the new President in Panama. They will also be affected by Panama's reaction to a formal U.S. proposal for site surveys including the required option for operating rights in a sea level canal.

The best prospect for a major improvement in U.S.-Panamanian relations is that offered by the sea level canal project. If the United States and the Republic of Panama can agree on the nature of the operating rights which the United States must have if a sea level canal is to be constructed in Panama, this agreement would put to rest many of the emotional issues which now plague our relations. It would also clear the air of many of the uncertainties with respect to United States policy which are the source of most of the unrest among the U.S. citizens in the Zone. Initially, this agreement would be operative only with respect to survey rights but would also include a detailed option for further arrangements for U.S. operating rights in a sea level canal. It would not commit the U.S. in any way to the construction of such a canal. The Department of State and the Department of the Army are actively engaged drafting a proposal along these lines which will be ready for clearance with appropriate Congressional committees and discussion with Panama in the near future.

S. 2701, the site survey authorization bill, has passed the Senate and is scheduled for House action in early September. A hearing was held on 17 August 1964 before the Senate Appropriations Committee on the proposed FY 1965 funds for the site surveys which are the first step in the sea level canal project.[2]

Robert S. McNamara

---

[2] This bill became Public Law 88–609 on September 22, and created the Atlantic-Pacific Interoceanic Canal Study Commission to determine the best means of construction, and estimated cost of such canal.

---

418.   Telegram From the Embassy in Panama to the Department of State[1]

Panama City, October 8, 1964, noon.

251. Subject: Current Assessment of US–Panama Relations.

With advent Robles government we find our position here greatly improved in several respects:

1. We are now dealing with a more responsible Panamanian Government which is determined tackle number Panama's chronic problems with courage and vigor. For example, it is already moving forward with realistic plan for development of country's interior, something US has long advocated. It has pledged itself to thorough tax and budgetary reform in accordance with Alliance for Progress precepts and Robles has so committed himself to US in detail and in writing. More importantly, he has already undertaken some measures along these lines with sufficient signs of meaning business that he has raised real crisis of anguish from traditional vested interests, including some of his own political supporters.

2. We can communicate sensibly and candidly with Robles government.

3. Robles has pledged himself to firm stand against Communist agitation, in welcome contrast to his predecessor, and his past conduct as Minister of Government and Justice gives credence to his present statements of intent.

4. Both publicly and privately Robles has indicated willingness negotiate sea-level canal treaty with US and his FonMin has indicated willingness negotiate military base rights.

---

[1] Source: National Archives and Records Administration, RG 59, Central Files 1964–66, POL PAN–US. Secret. Repeated to Governor of the Canal Zone, USCINCSO, and CIA.

Thus on whole we have in Robles and his government something far better, from point of view US interests, than might have been hoped for under circumstances—stagnant state of Panamanian economy; four years of drifting and corruption under Chiari; acute, universal, and long-standing Panamanian dissatisfaction with arrangements governing Panama Canal; and still fresh memory of events of January 1964 which saw our bilateral relations plummet to their lowest point in history and caused US to be charged with aggression before UN and OAS.

All this looks good and I believe there is much on plus side of ledger, much more perhaps than we had any right to expect. I am persuaded, however, that these circumstances do no more than provide us with brief breathing spell and do not in any way eliminate severe problems which face us as result profound and continuing Panamanian dissatisfaction with existing treaty arrangements governing present canal. They provide us time to find solutions to our present problems, although they perhaps provide us time to find solutions.

We cannot realistically expect Robles to be satisfied with mere talk about future canal or even with negotiation of liberal arrangements providing for new canal. Pressures are increasing for changes, here and now, with regard to present canal. Robles will not be able to ignore them. Neither will we.

I share Governor Fleming's great concern, as reflected in minutes of Panama Review Committee meetings and in his own reporting to Washington, over adverse image which Panama Canal (and therefore US) enjoys here. I am constrained to add, however, that I do not believe it can be improved without actual changes in practice, most probably including changes in law and treaty structure, we are not going to solve our problems by better or more accurate or more extensive public relations measures.

I submit following propositions as guides to policy formulation for next few weeks and months:

1. Whatever we propose do about sea-level canal, we must prepare ourselves for substantial early adjustments in present arrangements. In my judgment these should include (a) increased annuity (b) greater direct Panamanian participation in commercial activities in Canal Zone (c) agreement to further symbols of Panamanian sovereignty such as issue of Panamanian stamps in Canal Zone and requirements for merchant vessels to fly Panamanian flag as well as US flag during transit of canal and (d) some formula which would put terminus (10 years? 15 years? Opening of sea-level canal?) on our present perpetual rights in Canal Zone.

Elusive problem of sovereignty, which is what sticks most in Panamanian craw, would not be eliminated by any of above and might, in long run, be increased. I think we would however alleviate problem for short run which is presumably all we need.

2. Panama remains small, immature, backward country trying to deal with world's most powerful nation. Fact that Panamanians have not yet, so far as I am aware, produced coherent bill of particulars in forum of special ambassadors will not relieve US of burden of producing sensible proposal. We are not thereby relieved of our basic problem of engendering healthful political atmosphere of partnership, in absence of which we will have only unpersuasive legalisms and physical force to protect our vital interests.

3. Next January 9 is date of crucial importance. If Robles is unable by then to point to substantial concrete progress in negotiations with US he will be faced with severe internal pressures which will put great strain on his ability to control situation, could result in fall of his government, and could lead to assumption of power by extremist regime of either right or left and in any event will sorely tempt him deflect these internal pressures onto US. Neither alternative appears helpful to say the least. (One possible device to relieve situation might be state visit by Robles to Washington in, say, December, but here again there would have to be more than eyewash.)

I recognize there are two fundamental questions which my argument raises and which deserve answer. First is why should we give away quids without, apparently, exacting equivalent quos? Answer lies, I believe, in fact that only real quo of lasting value to us here is responsible stable Panamanian Government and society which can and will work with US in enduring partnership solidly based in political reality. Robles has it in his power to give us such quo provided we protect him by actions which make clear that we are sympathetic to Panamanian aspirations and are prepared to go long way to meet them, in short that to cooperate with US is compatible with Panamanian pride. I am convinced that if we are forthcoming Panama will also be forthcoming, at least to far greater degree than if, as in the past, we hold back and force Panama to wring reluctant conessions from us in atmosphere of acrimonious and niggardly bargaining.

Secondly, why should we give anything away until we have nailed down all future guarantees we need? Answer is that we do not have luxury of time and Panama simply will not play this game anyway. One sure way to prevent our getting arrangements we want for future canal is totally to resist Panamanian efforts to modernize present arrangements. We should not underestimate Panama's capacity to cut off its nose to spite our face.

Vaughn

419.   Memorandum of Telephone Conversation[1]

Washington, November 18, 1964, 2:35 p.m.

PARTICIPANTS

The President
Mr. Mann

The President called and asked Mr. Mann what was happening in Panama. Mr. Mann explained about the change in Ambassadors and asked if that was what the President was referring to. The President said he wanted to know how Anderson's negotiations were coming and mentioned the up-coming anniversary of the riots of last year.

Mr. Mann said this situation was charged with dynamite.[2] He said he was leaving in 15 minutes to talk to Secretary Ailes. Mr. Mann said that he was working on a sea level canal treaty on which the Department agrees and to which they hope to get Defense's agreement.[3] Mr. Mann said that they are going to have to talk to the President about calling in the Leadership and going over it with them, if the President is satisfied with the text of the sea level canal. Mr. Mann said we are getting ready to negotiate with Colombia, Panama and Nicaragua and then crank up some publicity to improve our image. Mr. Mann said what we wanted is reasonable but the Panamanians won't like it. He said what they wanted essentially is for us to dig the ditch and turn it over to them after we get our money back.

Mr. Mann said that we have kept Bob Anderson informed about all these things, that he has a copy and knows what we are doing. Mr. Mann said the Panamanians themselves have not done much negotiating because they have not been able to agree on a position among themselves and they have used our elections as an excuse. The Presi-

---

[1] Source: Johnson Library, Papers of Thomas C. Mann, Telephone Conversations with LBJ, January 14, 1964–April 30, 1964. No classification marking.

[2] On October 13 Robert M. Sayre of the NSC staff wrote Bundy that Vaughn suggested "the United States must make meaningful concessions to Panama, or anti-U.S. elements in Panama will use the anniversary of January 9, 1965 for another blowup." (Ibid., National Security File, Country File, Panama, VI, August 1964–January 1965) On November 12 Mann told a meeting of officials from ARA and CIA that he "considered it likely that 'all hell will break loose' in Panama January 9." (Memorandum from Carter (INR) to Hughes; Department of State, INR/IL Historical Files, ARA–CIA Weekly Meetings, 1964–1965)

[3] Documentation on U.S.-Panama negotiations on the Canal treaty, from 1964 through the Johnson administration is in the National Archives and Records Administration, RG 59, ARA/SR/PAN Files: Lots 73 D 286 and 73 D 216, and ARA/LA/PAN Files: Lot 75 D 457.

dent said that we should push Mr. Anderson to push them and say that he is ready to go.

Mr. Mann said that the record is very clear that we have pushed them, not once but many times.

The President said to add it again today. To tell them he is ready to talk. He told Mr. Mann to instruct Anderson to proceed and contact them and say that the President is waiting on them. The President said perhaps it would help if we could make some adjustment in wages and show a little social consciousness. Mr. Mann said he thought we could. He said so far Defense, the Governor and O'Meara are all opposed to recommendations made by the Ambassador. The President asked what some of these recommendations were and Mr. Mann mentioned the following:

Flying flags all over the place, including on ships that pass through the canal.
Making Spanish an official language, a second language.
Collecting Panamanian income taxes inside the Zone for the Government of Panama.
Use of Panamanian postage stamps in Canal Zone.
Appointment of consultant to the Board of Directors.
Establishment of labor advisory committee.
Supplying them with free potable water to increase annuity.

Mr. Mann said he thought we are going to be able to do some of these and we have to do it before Christmas. The President said even before that. The President said that the students were not as well disciplined as he. He mentioned that a year later we were right where we started.

The President asked Mr. Mann if he should tell McNamara to review this thing again and see what he can do. Mr. Mann said this sounded good and said he would tell Steve Ailes and they would go over it.

The President asked Mr. Mann if he had spoken to Adlai Stevenson after his visit and Mr. Mann said he had not seen him, but that he had received a letter and a memo from Stevenson and had written him a letter.[4]

The President asked who had turned down these recommendations and Mr. Mann said Steve Ailes, the Chairman of the Board of the Panama Canal Company. He said he thought [garble] stockholder.

The President said he thought that McNamara had more social consciousness than that and that he would rather make adjustments in time than to plant his feet in concrete.

---

[4] None found.

Mr. Mann told the President that the thing that is going to help us the most is to get out in front with a lot of publicity on this new canal. He said then we can get this whole thing in perspective, we can tell everyone here and in Panama and the whole world that the present canal is limited and that we are going to build a new one and therefore we are dealing with a wasting asset. Mr. Mann said what we were not going to be able to do, unless the President thought it was politically possible, is to make the sweeping concessions on sovereignty and perpetuity that they want.

The President said that he would talk to McNamara[5] and told Mr. Mann to put a red flag on two things; one the conference with Leadership—to notify them plenty ahead of time so that he did not have to call them in on Christmas Day on a crisis basis—to move it up, and secondly see if we can't get the Ambassador's recommendations re-worked.

---

[5] Apparently having just spoken to the President, McNamara called Mann to say that "he was very anxious to see us make changes" in Panama and required a list of things Mann would like done sent "over immediately." (Memorandum of telephone conversation between Mann and McNamara, November 18, 2:45 p.m.; Johnson Library, Papers of Thomas C. Mann, Telephone Conversations with LBJ, January 14, 1964–April 30, 1965)

---

420. Memorandum From the President's Special Assistant for National Security Affairs (Bundy) to President Johnson[1]

Washington, undated.

SUBJECT

Relations with Panama and Sea-Level Canal Negotiations

A briefing for you on relations with Panama and proposals for negotiations with Panama on canal problems has been arranged for December 2 at 5:45 PM.

Relations with Panama

The Robles Administration passed a test of strength during the week of November 23–27 against Communist and anti-American

---

[1] Source: Johnson Library, National Security Security File, Country File, Panama, Vol. VI, August 1964–January 1965. Confidential.

elements. The demonstrations which occurred were not primarily directed at the United States, but were intended to protest what these elements regarded as a weakening of the Panamanian position in its negotiations with the United States. Although the National Assembly sustained the Government, it did so in a resolution which called for abrogation of the 1903 Treaty. Before these events, it was hoped that a satisfactory interim program, until a sea-level canal were opened, might be the nine-points agreed to between State and Defense (Tab A).[2] It is doubtful now that such an interim program would be adequate. State suggests the following program, on which McNamara has not yet had a chance to decide his position.

Possible Package Program

1. *A general policy statement* which discusses relations with Panama and negotiations on a sea-level canal (draft attached Tab B).[3] Such a statement, if made this month, would permit us to seize the initiative and dampen current efforts by anti-American elements in Panama to stage large anti-American demonstrations on January 9; avoid any appearance of responding to pressure generated by demonstrations; and provide the terms of reference for the conduct of negotiations with Panama and other countries on a sea-level canal.

Such a statement would restate our major objectives in operating the present or any future canal; recognize that the existing canal and treaty arrangements are becoming obsolete; note the Congressional authorization for a sea-level canal study, and give some ideas on how the surveys would be conducted, and how a sea-level canal would be financed, constructed, operated, maintained and defended; discuss what we propose to do about the present canal during the interim period until a new one is opened, including the protection of the interest of American and Panamanian employees; and request the cooperation of all in this forward-looking program.

2. *A sea-level canal treaty* which would give us the right to conduct necessary surveys and construct a new canal at our option. (Draft of

---

[2] Tab A, atttached but not printed, is a November 19 memorandum from Mann to McNamara, that contains nine interim steps that would demonstrate to Panama progress in the negotiations and reduce the possibility of violence. These were: (1) flying Panamanian flags in addition to the American flag and flag of registry; (2) Spanish as an official language in the Zone; (3) use of Panamanian postage stamps with Canal authority overprinting in the Zone; (4) a Panamanian and an American citizen resident in Panama to join the Canal Board of Directors; (5) negotiations for a Labor Advisory Committee; (6) negotiations for an agreement for purchase of gasoline for use in the Zone; (7) negotiations for withholding and remittance to Panama of income taxes of Panamanian employees of private companies in the Zone; (8) negotiations to permit private Panamanian companies to establish businesses in the Zone; and (9) free treated water to Panama.

[3] Tab B, attached but not printed, is a draft outline of a policy statement prepared by Mann on November 28.

November 18 is attached at Tab C.[4] There are still some disagreements between State and Defense on this draft which they hope to reconcile before the December 2 meeting.) The treaty would separate the security aspects from the business of operating a canal. The canal would be operated and maintained by an international commission on a self-sustaining basis. Defense of the sea-level canal would be the responsibility of the United States and Panama (Colombia or Nicaragua–Costa Rica) with almost the entire burden falling on the United States.[5]

The country in which the canal is located would retain sovereignty, but would grant to the Commission specific rights which would enable the Commission to control, operate, maintain and protect the canal. The suggested composition of the Commission is such that we would have a majority.

This treaty, and the base rights treaty under 3 below, would be negotiated with Panama, Colombia, and Nicaragua-Costa Rica before we begin surveys or other works. Such simultaneous negotiations in advance would put us in the best bargaining position with these countries. Panamanian oligarchs will not like the international approach on operating the canal, but this offers the best basis for selling it to world opinion and puts us in a favorable position.

3. *A base rights treaty* to accompany a sea-level canal treaty which covers the continued stationing of our forces in Panama (Colombia or Nicaragua-Costa Rica). Present treaties permit such forces only for defense of the canal, and we need to broaden this to cover hemisphere defense. Such a treaty would be similar to the NATO status of forces agreements, but it cannot be drafted until Defense determines what areas of lands it needs for bases.

4. *A new treaty with Panama* which would replace all existing treaties and would remain in force until two years after a sea-level canal opens. The Panamanian Foreign Minister has informed us that the Robles Administration must obtain agreement to negotiate a new treaty if it is to remain in office. Ambassador Vaughn agrees with this assessment. In drafting it, we would follow the same technique as on the sea-level canal—recognize Panamanian sovereignty but then provide specific

---

[4] Tab C, attached but not printed, is a draft of the treaty prepared November 18.

[5] The Joint Chiefs addressed the issue of a proposed sea-level canal in two memoranda to McNamara on December 2, JCSM–1012–64 and CM–285–64. (Washington National Records Center, OSD Files: FRC 330 70 A 1266, Pan 800 (4 January, 1965), Sea Level Canal, and Johnson Library, National Security File, Country File, Panama, VI, August 1964–January 1965, respectively) The JCS generally concurred in the proposed treaty provided "joint defense" included the right of the United States to defend the host country against Communist domination as well as to defend the canal. The JCS also noted that the draft treaty should be submitted to careful analysis and interagency coordination before it was adopted as policy.

grants of rights to the United States. Some 80% of the provisions could be the same as in the three existing treaties. (State has prepared a rough draft, which is attached Tab D.)[6]

The purpose of such a treaty would be in great part psychological—to remove those emotional issues (sovereignty, etc.) which provide grist for agitators in Panama, and at the same time, preserve our essential rights and requirements for operation, maintenance and protection of the canal (operation of courts, police jurisdiction, stationing of military forces, etc.). It would include those items from the nine-point interim program (Tab A above) that are appropriate. At the same time we must expect the Panamanians to insist that many of the peripheral privileges we have hitherto enjoyed, which cannot reasonably be justified as *necessary* for the operation, maintenance and protection of the canal, will probably have to be eliminated (operation of commissaries, movie houses, bowling alleys, use of Canal Zone stamps, use of unneeded land and facilities, and so forth). We should be able to soften the blow on civilian employees by cost-of-living allowances or agreement by Panama that the employees may run cooperative stores, or both.

5. *An undertaking on our part* to help Panama to adjust economically to the construction of a sea-level canal elsewhere in Panama or in another country.

For the meeting on December 2, it is proposed that we concentrate primarily on the proposed policy statement. If you approve the statement, you could then review it with the leadership on December 18, and any others you thought appropriate, such as General Eisenhower. It is hoped that the statement could be issued before Christmas.

It is intended that all the proposed treaties be negotiated with Panama at the same time, and the package then presented to the Senate for ratification. Only the sea-level canal and base rights treaties would be negotiated with Colombia and Nicaragua-Costa Rica.

Secretary McNamara plans to bring Cyrus Vance and Steve Ailes to the briefing.

Tom Mann would be accompanied by Robert Anderson, Leonard Meeker (State's Acting Legal Adviser), Ambassador Vaughn and Edward Clark (Director of Panamanian Affairs). Secretary Rusk is meeting with Foreign Ministers who will be in New York for the meeting of the U.N. General Assembly. He has reviewed the general features of the program outlined above and concurs in them. But he does not

---

[6] Tab D, attached but not printed, is the Department of State draft prepared on November 26.

believe we should at this time raise the possibility of using nuclear detonations to build the canal.

Bob Sayre and I would also attend the briefing.

McGeorge Bundy[7]

---

[7] Printed from a copy that bears this typed signature.

---

421. Draft Record of Meeting[1]

Washington, December 2, 1964, 6:30 p.m.

PARTICIPANTS

White House
The President
McGeorge Bundy
Robert M. Sayre

State
W. Averell Harriman, Acting Secretary
Robert Anderson, Special Ambassador
Thomas C. Mann, Assistant Secretary
Leonard Meeker, Acting Legal Adviser
Jack Vaughn, Ambassador to Panama
Edward Clark, Director of Panamanian Affairs

Defense
Cyrus Vance, Deputy Secretary
Steven Ailes, Secretary of the Army

The President inquired as to the status of the nine points which had been discussed as a possible interim program on the Panama Canal.[2]

Mr. Ailes said that the points had been studied by State and Defense and had been agreed upon, but that action had not been taken because of new suggestions which were to be discussed at the meeting.

---

[1] Source: Johnson Library, National Security File, Files of McGeorge Bundy, Miscellaneous Meetings, Vol. I. Confidential. Drafted by Sayre on December 4. The meeting was held in the Cabinet Room at the White House. No other record of this meeting was found.

[2] The nine points were contained in a November 19 memorandum from Mann to McNamara; see footnote 2, Document 420.

Mr. Anderson said that the nine points had originated in a memorandum from Foreign Minister Eleta. Eleta presented them to Mr. Anderson in a meeting in New York City, and asked for a response within three or four days. Eleta said that he needed U.S. agreement on these points in his feud with Ambassador Illueca. Mr. Anderson told him that this was an internal Panamanian problem in which the United States did not want to become involved. The United States would consider the points only in the context of US-Panamanian relations.

Mr. Anderson then turned to the general problem of negotiations with Panama. He said the 1903 Treaty was an emotional problem with Panama. Panama would not be happy with any patchwork on it. He did not believe there could be any lasting settlement with Panama on such a basis. On the other hand, he was fully aware that the United States could not give up any of its essential rights. He said a draft proposal had been prepared which the President might consider, but he himself was not ready to recommend the specific draft he had in his hand.

The President asked what he was specifically expected to do. The President said he did not think a large meeting was the proper forum for a decision by him on the matter. He said such decisions invariably leaked before he was ready to make them because some of the participants felt a compulsion to talk to newsmen, or to people who leaked the decision to newsmen. He emphasized strongly that decisions affecting the national security had to be protected. Premature release of information could adversely affect our negotiating position and, therefore, the security and defense posture of the United States. He took the gravest view of the improper release of information obtained in conversations with him.

Mr. Bundy said that the purpose of the meeting was a briefing. He thought that the whole problem should be laid out so that the President would be aware of it. He saw no need for any specific decision at this point, and the President was not being asked for that. All that was desired at this time was an indication, on the basis of the briefing, whether Mr. Anderson, State and Defense, should proceed to draw up specific recommendations which the President could consider.

The President suggested Mr. Anderson proceed with his presentation.

Mr. Anderson said that there were four principles on which he thought we should proceed:

1. There had to be a new instrument. Mr. Anderson was aware of a difference in opinion between State and Defense on the tactical approach, i.e., whether you say there will be a new treaty and then negotiate with the Panamanians on what goes into that treaty, or whether you say you will negotiate with the Panamanians on what concessions you will give up and then put the remainder in a new treaty. He thought this was largely a matter of semantics. The important point was whether we

agreed that there will be a new treaty. The words could be worked out for any proposed statement. In any case, everyone agreed that we had to insist that the existing treaties are binding and must be observed until a new treaty enters into force.

2. The new treaty would have a time limit, defined as a specified length of time after the new sea-level canal opens for operations. He thought that the "perpetuity clause" had to go, and the idea of limiting the new treaty in duration on the basis of opening a new canal seemed a reasonable and feasible approach.

3. The United States would recognize that Panama has sovereignty. There should be no debate about whether it is titular sovereignty, or whether the United States has rights as if it were sovereign.

4. The United States must have those rights which are essential to the operation of the canal during the life of the new agreement. He thought it entirely possible to define what those essential rights are.

Mr. Anderson thought if everyone agreed on these general principles, then he, State and Defense could draft a proposed policy statement[3] which the President could review with the Congressional leadership on December 18, and such other persons as the President thought necessary.[4] The objective would be to announce such a policy statement immediately after a discussion with the leadership. He thought that the general approach with the leadership should be that the policy statement represents what the Administration has decided must be done.

Mr. Mann associated himself with the four principles as outlined by Mr. Anderson. He said State had already drafted a proposed new treaty. The draft included all of the rights which Army and State considered essential. He regarded it as a tough document and was not certain it could be sold to Panama. He emphasized that it should be negotiated at the same time as the sea-level canal treaty and a base rights agreement. He viewed them—with respect to Panama—as one package. Mr. Vance agreed with this point.

---

[3] President Johnson issued a statement concerning a decision by the United States to build a sea-level canal and to negotiate a new treaty with Panama on December 18. For text, see *Public Papers of the Presidents of the United States: Lyndon B. Johnson, 1963–64,* Book II, pp. 1663–1665, and *American Foreign Policy: Current Documents, 1964,* pp. 370–372.

[4] In JCSM–1052–64, December 17, the JCS informed McNamara that they agreed in principle with a draft of the President's statement on Panama, provided the draft incorporated some proposed changes. The JCS also indicated that a "policy directive delineating a specific course of action is urgently required" and recommended its development "as a matter of priority." (Washington National Records Center, OSD Files; FRC 330 69A 7425, Pan 381 (18 January, 1964), Panama Crisis, August–December 1964) Former President Eisenhower was consulted on December 16 and according to the record of this briefing said "that 'by and large' the draft statement on Panama is 'all right' and that he doesn't see anything wrong with it." (Memorandum prepared in the CIA, December 17; Johnson Library, National Security File, Country File, Panama, Vol. VI, August 1964–January 1965) The record of meeting with the Congressional leadership on December 18 is ibid., Bundy Files.

Mr. Mann said we should negotiate with Panama, Colombia and Nicaragua–Costa Rica simultaneously.

The President inquired why these negotiations were necessary and why a new treaty was necessary. Would it not be possible to do what was proposed by executive action?

Mr. Mann said there were several sites for a canal. He thought we should look at them. He did not think the decision could be made on the basis of cost alone. It might be cheaper to build a canal in Panama, but not get a treaty there that is politically acceptable.

Mr. Anderson said that there are matters which cannot be settled except by treaty. The nine points could probably be carried out by executive decision. But return to Panama of unnecessary lands required Congressional approval. He referred to a triangle of land (Shaler Triangle) that is of absolutely no use to the United States, but without a treaty we cannot return it to Panama.

Mr. Ailes said estimates on digging a new canal in Panama are about $750,000,000. Digging one in Colombia would cost about $1.1 billion. He said digging it by conventional means, or using atomic detonations, would make a difference in the cost. He had no estimate on the route through Nicaragua-Costa Rica.

Mr. Anderson thought that the "how" of digging a canal should not be a consideration now. Nor did he think that the cost should be the basis for a determination. Mr. Mann agreed. He thought we should consider the technical aspects and the cost, but we also had to consider the political situation.

Mr. Harriman said we should avoid any discussion of "how," especially any discussion of the use of atomic power. With the test ban treaty we could not use atomic detonations. In 10 or 15 years, when we get ready to build a canal, the whole state of the art might be different.

The President asked for Ambassador Vaughn's comments.

Ambassador Vaughn said he agreed with the views expressed by Ambassador Anderson. He viewed the anniversary date of the riots in 1964—January 9—as a crucial date. He expected riots of even more serious proportions unless some action were taken before that time which would remove the Canal Zone as a popular issue.[5]

---

[5] According to a December 9 memorandum from Jessup to Bundy, "Mr. McCone has been riding the Panama horse quite hard lately." Jessup continued, "He feels strongly that time is running out unless the U.S. is prepared to make substantial concessions here and that anything short of a bilateral agreement which meets the issue head on will result in the fall of Robles." (National Security Council, Files of the 5412 Special Group/303 Committee, Panama)

The President inquired whether the United States had failed to live up to its commitments taken in April 1964, to appoint special Ambassadors and to begin discussions immediately and in good faith.

Ambassador Vaughn said that it was fulfilling its commitments. He did not regard this as the problem. He noted that the January 1964 riots were carried out without any effort by the Chiari Government to control them, and some reason to believe the Government supported them. The situation was different now. The Robles Government had responded effectively to demonstrations in November. He did not expect it to be behind demonstrations this January. The leaders now would be the communists, hyper-nationalists and the Castroites. They would have an issue—no apparent progress in a year. Unless we could effectively deflate this issue, he saw these anti-American elements uniting into an FALN-type operation. (The FALN is a Castroite-Communist terrorist organization operating in Venezuela.) He expected this would lead to bombings, including an effort to bomb the canal. He did not want to "cry wolf," but he honestly believed we were in for real trouble unless we acted.

Ambassador Vaughn regarded the Canal Zone as the classic colony. In our national interest he thought it had to be eliminated or else we were in for the same kind of trouble we see in Africa. In response to a question, he said he did not expect it to go the way of Africa because he thought we were smarter than de Gaulle.

Mr. Bundy interjected that the dietary habits were different in Panama also.

Mr. Anderson said there was no suggestion that we had been derelict. Ambassador Illueca (Panama's special Ambassador for discussions on Panama) was engaged in a personal feud with Foreign Minister Eleta. He wanted to be the spokesman. He did not want to respond to instructions from the Foreign Office. Eleta decided to remove him. Panama has now named five Ambassadors to conduct discussions with the United States. De la Rosa had been elected the spokesman. If Panama had its way, Ambassador Anderson said it wanted us to get out of the Canal entirely and let Panama run it. Then it would try to profit from what it considers its monopoly position. He said he had made it completely clear to the Panamanians that the United States would not agree. The canal was essential to our security. It was essential to world commerce. We had obligations which we could not ignore.

Ambassador Anderson said that the Panamanian negotiating group told him they had 52 points which they wanted to discuss. He offered to discuss them. But he said it should be done informally. No papers would be passed. While they were talking, if they said one day that they accepted a point and the next day that they had to reject it, he would understand. At the same time, he would have the same options. He said there should be nothing in writing until the discussions had progressed to a point where it was obvious there was an area of agreement. Second, he said he wanted it clear that what he said today would not be in the paper tomorrow. He said the Panamanians accepted this approach.

Ambassador Anderson said that the Panamanians then proposed a joint declaration. It gave the Panamanians the best of both worlds. He offered to discuss it with them on Friday, December 4. They wanted agreement immediately because they had to leave next week and would not be back until January 2 or 3. When Ambassador Anderson inquired why, they said they had to go back and consult to get approval on the 52 points. At the same time, they insisted that they had to have something before January 9. Ambassador Anderson said that this led him to conclude that the United States would have to act unilaterally so that it could be said this month.

Mr. Ailes said a sea-level canal could be built at its present location. He said Congress had appropriated $400,000 to initiate the work of an Interoceanic Canal Commission, but wanted site surveys first before it appropriated any money for a canal.

Mr. Anderson said that he was thinking of December 18 as the date for a meeting with the leadership to review the Administration's plans. In the proposed sea-level canal, he said we were thinking of an international commission to run the canal. We knew Panama opposed this. Maybe they would come around. Mr. Mann interjected that simultaneous negotiations with Colombia and Nicaragua–Costa Rica should help. We favored an international commission because it gets us away from the big-little country controversy.

In response to a question, Ambassador Vaughn said there were probably 600 card-carrying Communists in Panama. He estimated there were 300 Cuban trained terrorists. The Communists have cells in the rural areas. They claim they can bring 20,000 demonstrators from there into Panama within a day. He thought they could. At the moment, they have no issue. He thought there were 20,000 sympathizers. The Communist stronghold is in the University. The danger is not the Communists alone. It arises when the Communists and the nationalists (and on the Canal issue every Panamanian is a nationalist) combine over an issue. January 9 provided such an issue.

The President inquired why things had quieted down in April. Ambassador Vaughn said he thought that the agreement which had been reached at that time gave the Panamanians hope that their aspirations would be realized. Mr. Bundy thought a major reason was also that the Panamanians had grown weary. Mr. Mann observed that the economic pinch which resulted from the unrest, lack of tourists, fall of business activity, etc., was certainly a major reason.

Ambassador Vaughn thought that a policy statement, based on the four principles Ambassador Anderson had outlined, would keep things reasonably quiet.

Mr. Mann said that the nine points which had been discussed were no longer considered to be an adequate interim program.

Mr. Ailes thought this might be true, but an announcement of a new treaty would stir up old attitudes on the Hill. He recognized that the January 1964 riots had shaken those old attitudes and that there was more understanding of the problem now.

Mr. Vance added that there has also been changes in the composition of the Congress, which had helped.

Mr. Mann said he thought a statement was necessary domestically to put the problem in prospective, and to get the people to look to the future instead of to the past.

The President said he would consider a statement after it had been prepared by Ambassador Anderson, State and Defense.[6] Thereupon the meeting ended 7:20 PM.

_____

[6] According to the President's Daily Diary, Anderson and the President met alone in the Oval Office from 7:16 to 8:18 p.m. (Ibid.) In *Panama Odyssey*, William Jordan briefly recounts this meeting. (p. 100)

---

422. Memorandum From the Assistant Secretary of State for Inter-American Affairs (Mann) to the President's Special Assistant for National Security Affairs (Bundy)[1]

Washington, undated.

SUBJECT

Panama

This is in response to your query whether (1) we should be taking any further action to prevent trouble in Panama on January 9 or in the near future, and (2) whether there is anything we should do, overtly or covertly, to prevent Panamanian public opinion from swinging against the presence of our military forces there.

_____

[1] Source: Johnson Library, National Security File, Country File, Panama, Vol. VI, August 1964–January 1965. Secret.

As regards the possibility of disturbances on January 9, the Communists have been thrown off balance by the President's statement, President Robles has assured Ambassador Vaughn that no trouble will be tolerated, and what appears to be a very satisfactory solution to the half-masting of flags on that date has been worked out between the Canal Zone and the Panamanian Government. Ambassador Arias has likewise informed the Department that the Panamanian Government anticipates no difficulty in handling any attempts at disorders on January 9. Embassy Panama's telegram 427, December 31,[2] indicates belief that prospects are good of getting through this period without major difficulty.

In view of the above, we agree that there is nothing further now that we can effectively do to minimize the possibility of disturbances on January 9, but we are launching a longer-term program to capitalize on the initiative the President's statement has given us. A telegram outlining our views is already in draft, and we shall be in touch with the White House and other agencies on this program in the next few days.

With regard to the problem of influencing Panamanian public opinion on the question of our military forces and bases, we have considered the possibility of inducing an official Panamanian statement disowning the recent statement by Castillero Pimentel in which he called for the withdrawal of U.S. forces. Foreign Minister Eleta discussed this statement with Ambassador Vaughn, indicating that Castillero had been reprimanded and soliciting Vaughn's advice regards the advisability of the Panamanian Government issuing a statement that Castillero was not speaking for the Government. Ambassador Vaughn expressed his judgment to Eleta that it would be preferable not to make such a statement at this time.

We are inclined to agree with Ambassador Vaughn's on-the-spot judgment on this point, although we believe that such a statement might be appropriate a little later after the ground has been prepared. To this end, [less than 1 line of source text not declassified] through the Panamanian press, radio and TV which will have the objective of educating the Panamanian public regarding the important part the United States military presence plays in the Panamanian economy, pointing up the disastrous consequences for Panama if the United States bases

---

[2] Not printed. (National Archives and Records Administration, RG 59, Central Files 1964–66, POL 23–8 PAN)

should ever be closed and pointing the finger at the Communists as those who are pushing this line for their own ends.[3]

TCM

---

[3] At a meeting with CIA and ARA representatives on December 30, Mann reported that the President had phoned him and asked "for guarantees that there would be no trouble in Panama on January 9." FitzGerald assured Mann that Robles had been "strengthened greatly by President Johnson's statement on the canal." Mann asked what CIA had done to ensure that there would be no trouble. FitzGerald told Mann that "Robles had been assured of all the support he asked for" and "any demonstrations would be easily controlled by the Panamanian Government." (Memorandum from Stuart to Hughes, Denney, and Evans, December 31; Department of State, INR/IL Historical Files, ARA–CIA Weekly Meetings, 1964–1965) Another record of this meeting was prepared by FitzGerald. (Memorandum for the record, December 31; Central Intelligence Agency, Job 78–03041R, DDO/IMS Files, [file name not declassified])

---

423.   National Security Action Memorandum No. 323[1]

Washington, January 8, 1965.

SUBJECT

   Policy toward the present and future of the Panama Canal

TO

   The Secretary of State
   The Secretary of Defense
   The Director, Central Intelligence Agency
   The Chairman, Atomic Energy Commission
   The Director, Bureau of the Budget
   The Director, U.S. Information Agency

   1. Basic policy toward the present and future of the Panama Canal has been set forth by the President in a statement on December 18, 1964, of which an authentic copy is attached.[2] This statement makes it U.S. policy to work toward a new sea level canal and to propose renegotiation with Panama of the existing Panama Canal Treaties.

   2. The Secretary of State is requested to begin discussions as appropriate with the Governments of Panama, Colombia, Nicaragua, and

---

[1] Source: Johnson Library, National Security File, Country File, Panama, Vol. VI, Memoranda, September 1964–January 1964. Secret.

[2] Attached but not printed; see footnote 3, Document 421.

Costa Rica, with respect to the possibilities of a sea level canal. The Secretary is requested to determine which of these governments would be interested in the possible construction of a sea level canal through its territory. The United States is prepared to begin negotiations with interested governments on the terms and conditions for the construction and operation of a sea level canal. Depending on the results of these negotiations, it is expected that we would proceed with selected site surveys.

3. We have in mind a treaty for a sea level canal in which sovereignty over the canal area would remain in the country or countries through which the canal would pass. The United States would be authorized, at its option, alone or with others, to undertake construction. Financing would be the primary responsibility of the United States Government, but the door could be left open for it to accept contributions from other sources, both public and private.

4. The United States Government has no final position on the exact form by which interested governments might join in operation of a sea level canal. There are advantages and disadvantages in an international commission which might include representatives of users or of financing groups or of the Organization of American States. There are equally advantages and disadvantages in bilateral operation by the United States and the country through which the canal might run. Moreover, it is possible to think in terms of two layers of responsibility, one bilateral and the other broadly international. Final decisions on these matters will be made by the President in the light of further advice and recommendations from the Secretary of State and the Secretary of Defense.

5. It is expected that the defense of the new canal would be the responsibility of the United States and the country or countries through which the canal runs. We should seek treaty terms which give to the United States the necessary rights and freedom of action to ensure the effective security of the canal regardless of the actions of the other country or countries.

6. The tolls for a sea level canal would be fixed in such a way as to put the canal on a self-sustaining basis, to pay an annuity to the host government, to amortize this investment and to serve the interests of world commerce. Like the present canal, the new interoceanic canal would be open to the vessels of all countries on the basis of equality.

7. Whatever treaties are agreed upon would, of course, be subject to approval and ratification in accordance with the constitutional procedures of the United States and the other country or countries involved.

8. With respect to the negotiation with Panama, the following principles will guide our negotiators:

(1) We are glad to join with the Government of Panama in searching for solutions which are compatible with the dignity, responsibility

and sovereignty of both nations. It is clear that we must make provision for the continued protection and operation of the existing canal by the United States until it is replaced.

(2) We are prepared to negotiate a new treaty with Panama governing the present lock canal, based on the retention by the United States of all rights necessary to the effective operation and protection of the canal, including administration of the areas required for these purposes. This treaty would replace the 1903 Treaty and its amendments. It should recognize Panama's sovereignty. It should provide for a termination date for rights retained by the United States based on the operational date of a sea level canal wherever it might be constructed. It should provide for the effective discharge by the United States of its responsibilities for hemispheric defense. The present treaties would, of course, remain in effect until a new agreement is reached.

(3) The new treaty for the existing canal should include adequate provisions to ensure continuation of our military bases and activities in the Canal Zone until the closing of the existing canal, without loss of necessary rights or freedom of action. The treaty should make no distinction between the use of bases for purposes of protection of the canal or for hemispheric security. The agreement should contain appropriate acknowledgment of Panama's contribution to hemispheric security under these arrangements. In addition, arrangements should be included to continue existing U.S. military base rights in the Republic of Panama outside the Canal Zone and to create appropriate status of forces provisions for U.S. servicemen when outside the Zone.

(4) Upon the closing of the existing canal, our military rights under the new treaty as discussed in the preceding paragraph will terminate. Therefore, negotiations should also be started for a base rights and status of forces agreement with Panama, related to hemispheric security, to come into effect upon the closing of the present canal. This new agreement should provide for continuation of U.S. military bases and facilities in the present Zone and outside the Zone in the Republic of Panama, with such changes as are needed. The agreement should also cover whatever new arrangements are needed in connection with the security and defense of the new canal wherever it is located.

(5) Wherever the new canal is built it will create new opportunities. To be sure, closing of the present canal would cause economic problems for Panama, but these would be offset to a great extent by those new opportunities which would be created if the sea level canal were built there. Panama would benefit not only from the actual construction of such a canal, but would also continue to enjoy the benefits of the present canal until the new one were completed. We are prepared to consider now with Panama a program of how best to take advantage of these opportunities and to meet these problems. The ef-

ficient employment of Panamanian workers employed in the present canal whose services would not be needed in the operation and maintenance of the sea level canal will form a major topic of our discussions with Panama.

(6) We will also take every possible step to protect the employment rights and economic security during the transition period of United States citizens now employed in connection with the operation, maintenance, and defense of the present canal. We shall do what is necessary to find them employment fitting their skills and experience and by providing retraining where this is called for.

9. In summary, the President's new policy sets three principal tasks before the United States Government, in order to satisfy the requirements of the present and the future:

(1) Working out satisfactory arrangements for the construction and operation of a new sea level canal;

(2) Providing a new treaty framework for the interim period to govern the operation and administration of the present lock canal; and

(3) Agreement on the terms of arrangements for facilities for defense of the existing and sea level canals and for the security of the Hemisphere.

These three problems are intimately interrelated and, to the maximum degree practicable, should be addressed simultaneously.

10. NSAM 152 dated April 30, 1962, and NSAM 164 dated June 15, 1962,[3] are rescinded; except paragraph 6 b and c (2) of NSAM 152.

McGeorge Bundy

---

[3] For texts, see *Foreign Relations, 1961–1963*, vol. XII, Documents 402 and 406.

424. **Information Memorandum From the Assistant Secretary of State for Inter-American Affairs (Mann) to Acting Secretary of State Ball[1]**

Washington, February 1965.

SUBJECT

Sea-Level Canal Discussions with Central American Countries

Secretary Ailes and I visited Panama and Colombia on February 1 and 2. Secretary Ailes was unable to accompany me on visits to Nicaragua and Costa Rica (January 28 and 29) because of other commitments. Attached is the list of persons who accompanied us.[2]

In Nicaragua and Costa Rica, I met with the Presidents and Foreign Ministers, as well as members of the Administration and opposition parties. In Costa Rica, I also talked to all of the former Presidents since 1944.

In Panama, Secretary Ailes and I talked only to the Foreign Minister. Although we met with President Robles and other Panamanian officials, we did not engage in any extensive discussions with him on a sea-level canal, or other matters, because it was clear Robles wanted his Foreign Minister to handle the discussions.

In Colombia, we talked to the President, the Foreign Minister, and the Cabinet in separate meetings. Because Colombia has a National Front Government, this included the country's important leaders, but it did not include as broad a spectrum of the opposition as we talked to in Costa Rica.

The atmosphere was favorable in Nicaragua, Costa Rica and Colombia—especially in Colombia. We found a general willingness to authorize preliminary reconnaissance of proposed routes and to enter into negotiations looking toward the construction of a sea-level canal. We found a general concern about the future of Panama, if the canal were constructed other than in Panama. Especially in Costa Rica and Colombia, Government leaders offered to be of assistance in bringing Panama around to a favorable attitude. In all three countries we heard

---

[1] Source: National Archives and Records Administration, RG 59, ARA Assistant Secretary Files: Lot 70 D 295, Panama. Confidential. The date is stamped on the memorandum but is too faint to determine a day; Rusk was not in the Department February 1–14. (Johnson Library, Rusk Appointment Book) The memorandum indicates that the Acting Secretary saw it.

[2] Attached but not printed.

suggestions of a multi-lateral arrangement designed to be most helpful to Panama in making the transition from the present lock canal to a sea-level canal.

We found a general misunderstanding in all of the countries about the earnings from the canal; the role which the canal plays in the Panamanian economy; the economic benefits of the canal to the US; the fact that the present canal had not been amortized; and the difference between the rights needed for the present canal and those that might be required for a sea-level canal. I believe we cleared up much of this misunderstanding, but much more needs to be done.

In Panama, we found the Foreign Minister very unhappy that we were discussing a sea-level canal with other countries. He regarded it as blackmail. He insisted that we have a legal and moral obligation to operate the present canal until Panama agrees that we might cease operation. I told him that we would be as helpful as we could to Panama, but we did not consider that existing treaties imposed such a legal or moral obligation. Panama believes that further violence in the Canal Zone would be detrimental to the world position of the US, and it therefore regards violence as a bargaining weapon. It also considers that it has a trump card, with respect to US military bases in the Canal Zone.

Panama regards a canal as its primary natural resource, and gives little evidence of a willingness to consider seriously an economic development program in which a canal is only one industry. The Foreign Minister expressed willingness to consider international control of a sea level canal during the period of amortization. But afterwards, he said the canal would be under the exclusive control of Panama. Panama would be willing to consider some restrictions on its authority to set tolls, but it was clear that Panama regarded itself as one of the world's main toll roads, and that its present intention is to exact a tribute as high as the traffic will bear. The Foreign Minister seemed unwilling to accept our view that a canal should be thought of as a service to world commerce, with the primary benefits for Panama to be derived from secondary developments, such as new ports, industries, and other economic activity.

I will be talking to Robert Anderson in the next few days about additional personnel he may need to continue the necessary negotiations. I believe we should now move forward as rapidly as possible with the objective of concluding the necessary treaties with the interested countries by the end of this year.

425. Memorandum From the President's Special Assistant for National Security Affairs (Bundy) to President Johnson[1]

Washington, May 10, 1965.

SUBJECT

Panama Canal Treaty Negotiations

Agreement has been reached by Tom Mann, Jack Vaughn, Steve Ailes and Bob Anderson on a new and forthcoming approach to the Panama Canal treaty negotiations. On the basis of the new instructions, Anderson hopes to be able to hold rapid and fruitful discussions with the Panamanians.

The core of the new approach is to tell the Panamanians that:

(1) Our aim is to negotiate with them promptly a sea level canal treaty acceptable to both countries;

(2) U.S. base rights and a status of forces agreement will be negotiated along with but separate from the canal treaty;

(3) if agreement on a sea level canal is reached and U.S. base rights are obtained, we will alter our existing rights under the 1903 treaty and work out an interim treaty or a transitional agreement covering the period from the present to the coming into effect of the sea level canal treaty; and

(4) we will attempt to finish our negotiations with the Panamanians before talking further about site surveys or a sea level canal with Colombia, Costa Rica or Nicaragua.

Bob Anderson will be talking with Congressmen tomorrow about the new approach in keeping with our commitment to tell certain Congressmen informally about any new proposals before informing the Panamanians.[2]

---

[1] Source: Johnson Library, National Security File, Bundy Files, Memos to the President, Vol. X. No classification marking.

[2] In a May 7 memorandum to Bundy, Mann emphasized the need to keep Congress informed: "We should be very sure that Congress is going along with us at all stages of the negotiations." (Ibid., NSC Histories, Panama Crisis, 1964)

If all goes well, the new approach will be explained to the Panamanians at a meeting in the State Department this Wednesday.[3]

Mcg. B.

OK[4]

Speak to me

---

[3] May 12.

[4] This option is checked. In a telephone conversation with Anderson on May 17, the President told him: "God almighty, you watch Panama any way you can." Johnson continued, "Where you can really talk to 'em and—gonna work out all right—do it so they can't say that we messed around for a year and wouldn't talk to 'em." (Recording of telephone conversation between President Johnson and Robert Anderson, May 17, 9:07 a.m.; Johnson Library, Recordings and Transcripts, Tape F 65.29, Side A, PNO 1 and 2)

---

426. Memorandum From Secretary of State Rusk to President Johnson[1]

Washington, June 22, 1965.

SUBJECT

Panama—Canal Negotiations

Secretary McNamara, Ambassador Anderson and I are scheduled to meet with you at twelve noon Wednesday June 23 to discuss the status of Canal negotiations with Panama.[2] The principal subject for discussion and decision will be a proposed new arrangement for joint United States-Panamanian operation of the present Canal.

Discussion:

Agreement has now been reached by the United States and Panamanian Special Representatives to negotiate, separately but concurrently, (1) base rights and status of forces agreements, (2) a new treaty to replace the 1903 Treaty and (3) a sea level canal treaty and to submit

---

[1] Source: Johnson Library, National Security File, Country File, Panama, Inter-Oceanic/Panama Canal Negotiations, Vol. I. Confidential.

[2] According to the President's Daily Diary, the meeting with the President was held between 12:30 and 1 p.m. on June 23. (Johnson Library) William Jordan briefly covers this meeting in *Panama Odyssey.* (p. 109)

them as a package to the legislative authorities of both countries. I am informed that the Panamanian negotiators accept willingly that the United States should have responsibility for protection of the Canal and the ultimate say in the operation and maintenance of the Canal; they have, however, taken a firm position that Panama should share in the activities of the Canal Zone Government as well as the Panama Canal Company. A decision is therefore required whether the United States can agree to joint management and, if so, what form such an arrangement should take.

State and Army have studied this question and believe that a formula for joint management which will protect the United States objective of retaining ultimate, unimpaired control can be devised. There is enclosed a paper entitled "Possible Elements of a Joint Panama Canal Authority" drawn up by State, Army and Ambassador John N. Irwin II, which sets forth the outlines of such a formula.[3] This paper is limited to the concept for a joint authority. It is also contemplated that the treaty will contain a separate provision empowering the President of the United States to take such action as he deems necessary to assure continued effective operation of the Canal under adverse conditions.

Consideration has been given to providing for participation by Panama on the Board of Directors of the present Panama Canal Company. This course, which also accepts the concept of joint administration, would be difficult to negotiate, would probably never be entirely acceptable to Panama, and would not offer the political advantages of a clean break with the past and a fresh new start with Panama. I believe an entirely new approach might also be easier to take to Congress.

Recommendation:

That decision in this matter be deferred pending full discussion with Ambassador Anderson on Wednesday.

Dean Rusk

---

[3] Attached but not printed.

427.   Memorandum From the President's Special Assistant for
National Security Affairs (Bundy) to President Johnson[1]

Washington, August 30, 1965, 1:30 p.m.

SUBJECT

The Panama Canal Negotiations

1. I have just talked at length with Bob Anderson and he tells me
that the political problems of the Panama negotiations are now getting
ripe for a brief report to you. I agree with him. There are decisions in
the offing which only you can make and which I think you will want
to make directly with Bob.

2. The essence of the situation is that Anderson and his team are
very clear now on the need for a Joint US–Panama Authority to run
the present Canal under the new treaties with Panama. You have approved this idea in principle, and for discussion, but there is no final
Presidential decision, and still less any public White House position.

3. In discussing this idea on the Hill, in a preliminary way, Anderson's colleagues, Jack Irwin and Bob Woodward, have found substantial preliminary resistance from the House Subcommittee led by
Mrs. Sullivan, and also from Senator Hickenlooper.

4. Anderson himself has stayed away from the House Subcommittee so far. He does not want to be in the position of giving them a
fat target before there is a definite US Government position. He fears
that if he were to advocate the Joint US–Panama Authority before you
have made your own decision, he would be inviting public and definite opposition from Mrs. Sullivan and others.

5. Anderson is convinced that the Joint Authority will be indis-
pensible to a successful negotiation. He is also convinced that real US
interests can be protected, essentially by giving both Presidents a veto
of changes in the existing code which covers the existing Canal. Anderson & Company therefore plan to make a flat recommendation to
you in favor of a Joint Authority.

6. The next question is that Bob needs to know whether you want
him to be the spokesman or whether you wish to announce your decision yourself, perhaps to an appropriate group of bipartisan leaders. He
and I are inclined to think that if the President and Commander-in-Chief
were spokesman on an issue of this sort, the chances of effective

---

[1] Source: Johnson Library, National Security File, Memos to the President, Mc-
George Bundy, Vol. 13. Confidential.

support would be greatly increased. This is, of course, what happened when you announced that you planned to negotiate these new treaties last December.

7. Anderson is now preparing a definite and clear recommendation on the Joint Authority for submission to you.[2] He can come in and get your decision either in the latter part of this week or after Labor Day. We think our tactics should be decided fairly soon because the Panamanian Congress is in October, and our own Congress should know our position before it goes home. On this basis, may I make an appointment through Marvin Watson for Anderson:

Later this week[3]

Early next week

Speak to me

8. I have talked to Larry O'Brien about the problem of Mrs. Sullivan—and probably Dan Flood—and he thinks we have a lot of ways of handling this sort of opposition, and that on the Hill in general it is well understood that it is time for change in US–Panama relations. I will plan to ask him to join in the Anderson meeting (if he hasn't gone off to deliver the mail).

McG. B.

---

[2] Document 428.

[3] None of the options is checked, but Bundy wrote at the top of this memorandum: "Hold for Panama meeting Thurs." The President met with Anderson and Irwin in the Oval Office at 1:55 p.m. on September 2. (Johnson Library, President's Daily Diary) No other record of this meeting has been found, although a September 14 memorandum from Assistant Secretary for Inter-American Affairs Jack Vaughn to Rusk indicated that "The President approved" the Anderson and Irwin recommendations "and directed Ambassador Anderson to canvass the Congress to ensure that there would be sufficient Congressional support." (National Archives and Records Administration, RG 59, Central Files 1964–66, POL 33–3 PAN)

428.   Memorandum From the President's Special Representatives
(Anderson and Irwin) to President Johnson[1]

Washington, September 2, 1965.

SUBJECT

Panama Canal Treaty Negotiations

Since May, the United States negotiators have been discussing with the Panamanians three treaties, an Interim Treaty (regarding the existing Canal), a Sea Level Canal Treaty and a Base Rights and Status of Forces Agreement. All aspects of the discussions have been carefully coordinated with the Departments of State and Defense on a continuing basis. We have reached a point in the negotiations at which we wish to bring to your attention the far-reaching nature of the proposals which have been discussed, and alternatives, and to recommend courses of action for your decision.

We have informed key Senators and Representatives about the general progress of the negotiations and are meeting with varying degrees of concern, in some cases deep concern, because of the prospect that the United States may actually relinquish practical aspects of sovereignty, and because there might be delegated to a new Joint Authority the important functions which the Congress has heretofore controlled directly, such as: formulation of new laws for the Canal Areas, approval of the budget and expenditures, and decisions with respect to tolls, commercial enterprises and employment conditions.

Based upon your decisions resulting from this meeting, we recommend that you advise the leaders of Congress (including the majority and minority leaders of the Foreign Relations, Armed Services, Appropriations and Commerce Committees of both Houses and the House Merchant Marine and Fisheries Committee and its Panama Canal Subcommittee) of your policy goals with respect to the Panama Canal and of the guidelines you have given to the United States negotiators. In view of the extent to which the suggested new participation by Panama in the practical application of sovereignty will depart from tradition, it is doubtful that anyone but you can persuade the leaders of Congress to accept these changes.

---

[1] Source: Johnson Library, National Security File, NSC Histories, Panama. Confidential. The memorandum was unsigned, but a handwritten line at the top of the first page indicates it was from Anderson and Irwin.

I. INTERIM TREATY

1. Form of Administration of Existing Canal

Following the guidance of your December 18, 1964, statement,[2] we have sought a treaty which will recognize the sovereignty of Panama while retaining such rights as are necessary to provide effective operation and defense of the Canal and to enable us to treat fairly and helpfully the Canal employees, both United States and non-United States. We are seeking a treaty which will be recognized as a sincere and generous effort on the part of the United States to meet Panama's aspirations; so that, if it should be rejected by Panama or if accepted and later events require the use of military force to ensure the operation or defense of the Canal against hostile Panamanians, the United States will be in a more favorable position, and especially in Latin America, than under the 1903 Treaty or a new treaty in which Panama does not participate as a real partner.

We have been discussing with the Panamanians two formulas for Panamanian participation in the administration and operation of the Canal:

(1) a proposal (suggested by us) that Panama be given a minority participation on the Board of Directors of the existing Panama Canal Company, the authority and responsibility of the Board to be expanded to include functions now exercised by the Governor, and

(2) a proposal (suggested by Panama but also considered independently by us to be a possible solution) to create by the Interim Treaty a Joint Authority in which the United States and Panama would share as partners full authority and responsibility to operate the Canal and administer the Canal Areas.

We recommend proposal (2), the Joint Authority, because:

(a) While meeting the principal aspirations of Panama, we believe we can retain for the United States (i) the ultimate control of the administration and operation of the Canal through majority control of the Board of Members or by having a "casting vote," and (ii) the unilateral right for the President of the United States to defend and secure the Canal under any circumstances in which he believes such action necessary.

(b) It is an overt expression of Panamanian sovereignty and will be a major step in eliminating the "foreign colony" stigma with which Panamanians view the Canal Zone.

(c) It seems to offer the best hope of concluding a mutually satisfactory bilateral arrangement with Panama which will both ensure the

---

[2] See footnote 3, Document 421.

continued effective operation and defense of the Canal and reduce the likelihood of violent United States-Panamanian confrontations.

(d) It is doubtful that we could negotiate successfully Panamanian membership on the Board of Directors of the existing Panama Canal Company. The Panamanian negotiators state that the Panamanian Government has never officially recognized the Panama Canal Company, that its existence has been a continued source of irritation to Panama, and that it is not compatible with a recognition of Panama's sovereignty.

(e) United States agreement to participation by Panama on the Canal Company's Board of Directors would, in effect, be accepting the idea of joint administration without receiving the political benefit which would flow from an offer of a new and real form of partnership with Panama, as under the Joint Authority proposal.

(f) The United States can include in the Treaty provisions which will ensure fair treatment to the employees (both United States and non-United States) in the light of the changed circumstances, and the United States Government can take action independent of the Treaty to provide for the United States employees.

The principal disadvantages of the proposed Joint Authority are:

(a) It removes the United States, and particularly the United States Congress, from direct control over the Canal. Ultimate control would be exercised through a Board of Members the majority of whom would be appointed by the President of the United States.

(b) A significant number of Senators and Representatives will oppose strongly a real partnership with Panama. They will consider it a "giveaway" and a weakening of our historic position of strength in Central America, a position they believe is needed to ensure the defense of the Western Hemisphere and to retain reasonable tolls for the benefit of both world commerce and United States shipping and those who ship the cargoes, particularly those ships and cargoes involved in trade between the east and west coasts of the United States. Their principal concern, however, might be said to be the instability of Panama and its Government, the seeming lack of capacity of its people, the lack of concern of the controlling "oligarchy" for the masses, and the activity of Communist elements.

In addition to the above two proposals, Panamanian representation on the Board of the Canal Company and creation of a Joint Authority, there are several possible alternate concepts of administration. Among these are:

(a) Maintain the existing Panama Canal Company and Canal Zone Government while granting significant concessions to Panama.

(b) Abolish the Panama Canal Company/Canal Zone Government and reestablish an independent United States Government agency similar to that existing before the establishment in 1950 of the Panama Canal Company; grant significant concessions to Panama, perhaps including some form of Panamanian participation in the functions of the United States Government agency.

(c) Create by treaty a multinational agency composed of representatives of the United States, Panama and the principal users of the Canal, or perhaps others selected by any variety of ways.

(d) A plan, known as the Machado Plan, under which the World Bank would be authorized to organize an international corporation to purchase the interests of the United States in the Panama Canal Company and the Canal Zone Government and obtain from Panama a long-term franchise to operate the Canal as an international waterway on a self-sustaining and self-liquidation basis. This plan might provide a quick and practical business solution of the problem and avoid many of the political differences which have arisen in the past.

Alternatives (a) and (b), maintenance of the existing organization or establishment of a new independent Government agency, would be much more acceptable to Congress than the proposed Joint Authority, but neither would meet the Panamanian aspiration for sovereignty. We believe Panama would refuse Alternative (a) but might be induced to accept Alternative (b) for a specified and fairly short term of years if convinced there was no hope for some form of real participation.

Alternatives (c) and (d), multinational operation and the Machado Plan, would be difficult to sell both to Panama and to Congress, but we believe it possible to do so to the Panamanians if they are convinced they cannot negotiate a satisfactory bilateral arrangement.

2. *Tolls and Unamortized United States Investment*

These two subjects present primarily internal United States political problems.

(a) Tolls

One of the traditional purposes of the Canal has been its contribution to world commerce. The United States never raised tolls since the Canal was opened, and inflation has had the effect of reducing tolls to approximately one-third of the 1914 toll. Strong voices in Congress have opposed any increase in tolls, even though many Canal Governors have recommended increasing them.

It would probably be possible to establish a new tolls system, based party on value of cargo, which would be more equitable while more profitable. We recommand that the Joint Authority be empowered to hold toll hearings and fix tolls, possibly subject to the Presidents of the United States and Panama each having a unilateral power to veto increases.

(b) Unrecovered United States Investment

The unrecovered United States investment in the existing Canal enterprise is fixed variously at from $329,000,000 (net direct investment) to $463,000,000 (equity of the United States Government). There are two schools of thought: (i) those who believe that the United States has been more than repaid through the use of the Canal for commercial and defense purposes for a period of over 60 years, including two world wars, the Korean war and the current world situation, and (ii) those, including many in Congress, who believe the unrecovered investment should be recovered.

The Panamanians dispute the amount of our unrecovered investment and argue that the United States has adopted intentionally the policy that has resulted in no amortization. They point out that the United States can afford to subsidize world commerce but that Panama cannot, so either the tolls should be raised to bring an optimum income to Panama or the United States should pay Panama an equivalent sum.

A related factor is that the Panama Canal Company now pays interest to the United States Treasury (approximately $11,000,000 in 1964) on the interest bearing investment of $329,000,000 computed on the basis of statutory criteria established by Congress. After payment of the interest, the Panama Canal Company now is not able to establish adequate reserves for capital improvements.

If you approve the Joint Authority proposal, we shall try to achieve some formula which will permit recovery of the unrecovered investment in the 1903 Canal, either by agreeing on a figure to be amortized under the new arrangement or by obtaining a new equity when the sea level canal financing is arranged. Acceptance of the Joint Authority proposal would have the effect of discontinuing present interest payments to the United States Treasury.

Other Issues

Among other difficult and sensitive issues in the negotiations of the Interim Treaty are the law to be applied in the new "Canal Areas," the system of courts, the financial solvency of an independent Joint Authority, the commercial enterprises of the Panama Canal Company, the welfare of the employees, and the question of defense and security of the existing Canal. We believe that reasonable solutions can be achieved under the Joint Authority proposal.

With respect to the duration of the Interim Treaty, Panama opposes strongly tying the duration to the effective date of a sea level canal because of the United States position that we may build the sea level canal in Colombia or elsewhere. However, we believe we can obtain an Interim Treaty with a duration of between 35 to 60 years.

Public Announcement of Progress in Negotiations

The President of Panama wishes to make a public announcement of progress in the negotiations before the opening of the Panamanian National Assembly on October 1. It may be advisable to have a joint announcement of the President of the United States and the President of Panama in order to assist the President of Panama and to have more control over the exact wording. What can be said will depend on the progress made not only on the Interim Treaty but also on the Sea Level Canal Treaty and the Base Rights and Status of Forces Agreement. The primary interest of the Panamanians is the Interim Treaty.

II. SEA LEVEL CANAL TREATY

1. Option

In the Sea Level Canal Treaty we are seeking essentially an option to construct a sea level canal in Panama at a time and place and by a means of our own choosing. Panama wishes to have a sea level canal if one is constructed, but the concept of the option causes difficulty to Panama because of our announced intention to seek similar options from Colombia and from Nicaragua and Costa Rica. If we are successful in signing three satisfactory treaties with Panama it may be advisable to reconsider present plans to proceed with site surveys in Colombia, Costa Rica and Nicaragua.

We anticipate difficulty, particularly in obtaining an open-ended option to construct a sea level canal by nuclear methods. Consequently, it may be necessary to agree to share with the host countries the decision with respect to construction of a canal by nuclear means.

2. Form of Control

No decision has yet been made with respect to the agency to control a sea level canal. Should it be multinational, binational, or possibly a combination of the two?

We recommend that the treaty provide for a multinational agency composed of representatives of the United States, the host country, the financiers and the principal users of the Canal but include a provision to permit the United States and the host country to decide on a bilateral agency rather than a multinational agency if the United States and the host country, before the financing arrangements are made, each determines that it prefers a bilateral arrangement.

3. Other Issues

Although there are numerous other complicated problems, such as the method of financing, defense of the canal, tolls, compensation of the host country, question of provision for repayment to the United States of the unrecovered investment in the 1903 Canal, and the duration of the controlling agency and of the treaty (including Panama's desire to own the sea level canal outright after the cost has been amortized), we refer to these only for your general information and do not seek decisions at this time.

4. Congress

Congressional criticism is most likely to be reflected in concern over multinational control of a sea level canal, and over control of tolls. Some have expressed the view that a new canal should be built outside of Panama.

III. BASE RIGHTS AND STATUS OF FORCES AGREEMENT

The Base Rights and Status of Forces Agreement has been prepared by the Department of Defense and is based on similar agreements with other countries. The present draft provides that the bases will be made available by Panama free of charge, in keeping with a worldwide Department of Defense policy. The Panamanians may expect payment.

The prosposed Base Rights and Status of Forces Agreement will be opposed by some in Congress on the grounds that we are giving up areas in which we are now "sovereign," turning them over to Panamanian sovereignty, and taking them back under a treaty which gives us less control than we now possess.

IV. GENERAL

1. Compensation to Panama

In the Sea Level Canal Treaty draft, we have provided for an annual payment of a fair and reasonable return to Panama, without specifying the amount. In the Interim Treaty we provide for a payment to Panama in the proportion of Panama's interest in the Joint Authority. There is no provision in the Base Rights and Status of Forces Agreement for any payment to Panama. We have included in the Sea Level Canal Treaty draft a general undertaking to assist Panama in meeting the adverse economic impact of a sea level canal which will be caused by a sharp decrease in employment and similar changes in the existing economy.

The Panamanians have indicated that they will put a price on the use of their land and water areas (their "greatest natural resouce") and either expect to receive it from the canal revenues, or for the United States to pay the difference. As stated earlier, there is a possibility Panama may demand rent for use of the military bases. They will ask United States assistance in meeting their economic problems when the sea level canal is opened.

2. Possible Special Trade Relationship with Panama

The Panamanian President, Foreign Minister and special negotiators have expressed, at various times, a pointed hope that the United

States might be willing, because of the unique relationship with Panama, to grant Panama trade preferences or even a complete exemption from customs duties in the United States market. The most active negotiator, Ambassador Aleman, has said that this would result in new investments in small industries in Panama—on the order of those that have been developed in Puerto Rico—which would have markets in the United States, and that this business would become so important to Panama eventually that Panama would beseech the United States to remain in partnership in canal operations in order to retain the trade preference that would be made dependent upon the Canal partnership. Such a trade relationship would be logical, would cost the United States virtually nothing (since there are now few Panamanian products that would compete more effectively in a duty-free United States market), and would assure the United States an increasing reciprocal market in Panama while promoting a longer Canal partnership.

We have been told informally in the State Department that special legislation for this purpose possibly could be justified upon the basis of the unique Canal relationship, and we recommend that you direct the Executive Branch to seek to devise a plan for such a special trade relationship and, if found feasible in the light of all other United States trade relationships, to formulate such legislative proposals as it may be desirable to submit to the Congress.[3]

---

[3] Attached but not printed is Annex A, a list of 31 members of Congress briefed by Irwin and Woodward.

429. Memorandum From the President's Special Assistant for National Security Affairs (Bundy) to President Johnson[1]

Washington, September 11, 1965, 11 a.m.

RE

Panama

Bob Anderson spent this last week working on the Hill for the Panama proposals that you approved in principle, subject to such consultation. Yesterday he gave us a report which is generally encouraging. A detailed write-up is being prepared and should be available to you before Monday.[2] In essence, Anderson reports understanding and support from about 9/10ths of the 36 Senators and Representatives he saw, running the spectrum from Mansfield to Mendel Rivers. The only negative notes of significance were struck by Hickenlooper, Russell and Mrs. Sullivan.

Hickenlooper said that while he would have done it differently, he would not actively oppose your judgment. Russell said he was against the proposals and would vote against them, and would make a brief statement for history against them, but he knew that if you were for them, they would carry, and he wanted you to know specifically that he was not going to make a general fight against you on this issue. He disagreed, and he wanted history to know of his disagreement, but that was all.

Mrs. Sullivan was the one person who gave indications that she might wish to make a fight on the issue. She couched her argument in terms of the failure of American policy to meet the needs of the simple people of Panama. She claimed that we were merely giving further aid and comfort to the "oligarchy." Henry Wilson and others who know her think this is merely a screen for her real concern, which is with the Americans in the Zone and the powers of her committee. Tom Mann and Henry Wilson are going to try to find ways of talking further with her.

Bob Anderson presented his report with his usual modest precision, but those who heard him were enormously impressed by the job he has done. He himself is wholly confident that there is now a solid basis for a firm approach to the Panamanians, and precise language is

---

[1] Source: Johnson Library, National Security File, Country File, Panama, Inter-Oceanic/Panama Canal Negotiations. No classification marking. A note on the memorandum indicates the President saw it.

[2] September 13. The "write-up" has not been found.

being drafted for his use in this approach next week. If all goes well, there should be enough of an understanding with the Panamanians for an important joint statement by the two Governments safely ahead of the October 1 meeting of the Legislature in Panama. Our assumption is that this statement should be made by the two Presidents together, and the papers are being prepared with this object.[3]

I have the impression that Bob Anderson has been determined to show that anything Goldberg can do, he can do better.

McG. B.

---

[3] On September 24 President Johnson read an approved joint statement on areas of agreement on a potential treaty that was simulataneously released in Panama by President Robles. The statement and Johnson's prefatory remarks are printed in *Public Papers of the Presidents of the United States: Lyndon B. Johnson, 1965*, Book II, pp. 1020–1021.

---

430.   Special National Intelligence Estimate[1]

SNIE 84–66   Washington, July 14, 1966.

PROSPECTS FOR STABILITY IN PANAMA

The Problem

To estimate the situation in Panama and the prospects for stability over the next six to twelve months.

Conclusions

A. Discontent with social and economic conditions, particularly with the high level of unemployment and the poor and inadequate housing in the cities, is continuing to grow among the Panamanian population. Criticism of the Robles government's handling of the Canal negotiations will probably become more intense after the National Assembly reconvenes on 1 October. Students and urban slum dwellers

---

[1] Source: Central Intelligence Agency, Job 79–R01012A, O/DDI Registry. Secret; Controlled Dissem. According to a note on the cover sheet this estimate was prepared in the Central Intelligence Agency with the participation of the intelligence organizations of the Departments of State and Defense and the National Security Agency. The United States Intelligence Board concurred in this estimate on July 14.

will probably be in the forefront of any violent manifestations against the Panamanian elite or against the US.

B. New civil disturbances are probable over the next six to twelve months; more likely than not they will be precipitated by sudden, unpredictable incidents. We believe that the Communists in Panama have the capability to intensify and broaden such disturbances to some extent, but that the Robles government and the Guardia Nacional would still be able to restore control. Even if no disorder or upheaval takes place during the period of this estimate, the Panamanian political situation is likely to become somewhat more fragile than it is at present.

C. Arnulfo Arias and his Panamenista party have the strength—which the Communists lack—to transform a civil disturbance into a popular rising against the Robles government. In the event of prolonged and widespread disturbances, the Guardia probably could not maintain control without outside assistance—presumably from US forces in the Canal Zone. However, Arnulfo seems inclined to bide his time, hoping that rising discontent over the Canal issue will bring him to power in the presidential elections of May 1968, if not sooner. In the event that both the Panamenistas and the Communists should take part in a successful effort to overthrow Robles, we think that Arnulfo would dominate the successor regime without allowing the Communists to gain major influence.

[Omitted here is the 5-page Discussion section of the estimate.]

431. Memorandum From Secretary of State Rusk to President Johnson[1]

Washington, July 25, 1966.

SUBJECT

Panama

You are scheduled to meet on Tuesday, July 26, 1966 at 6:00 p.m. with the principal officials concerned to discuss Panama.[2]

---

[1] Source: National Archives and Records Administration, RG 59, Central Files 1964–66, POL PAN–US. Secret. Drafted by Clark and cleared by Gordon.

[2] The meeting was held in the Cabinet Room at the White House. Johnson participated in the meeting between 6:43 and 7:35 p.m. (Johnson Library, President's Daily Diary)

Background

The IRG/ARA met on July 21, 1966 to review United States policy toward Panama in the light of the status of the treaty negotiations and the current political situation in Panama.[3] The Special National Intelligence Estimate (Enclosure 5) was also considered. Specific subjects discussed were: (1) prospects for the successful conclusion of new treaties with Panama (Enclosure 1), (2) the possible need for a contingency plan for use if the treaty negotiations reach an impasse, (3) short-range actions in the economic and social field which might be taken by the United States to improve the atmosphere in Panama for the treaty negotiations (Enclosure 2), (4) actions which might be taken to assist Panama to develop and carry out a program of long-range economic and social development (Enclosure 3), and (5) Panama's request for expanded United States direct assistance to its National Guard to improve its capability to maintain internal order (Enclosure 4).[4]

IRG/ARA Conclusions

The following conclusions were reached by the IRG/ARA:

1. That we continue our present policy of endeavoring to negotiate expeditiously new canal treaties with the Robles Government.

2. That a special Inter-Departmental Working Group be formed to develop by September 6, 1966 a contingency plan for use should treaty negotiations reach an impasse within the next six months.

3. That we press forward with the GOP to develop and carry out an urban impact program.

4. That we impress upon the GOP the urgent need to draw up a long-term economic development plan to fit into the anticipated new treaty arrangements; that we seek the establishment by Panama of a Development Authority for this purpose; and that we offer our assistance and cooperation in this undertaking.

5. That we meet the GOP's request for grant aid to expand the National Guard.

---

[3] A summary record of the IRG/ARA meeting is in the National Archives and Records Administration, RG 59, ARA/IG Files: Lot 70 D 122, IRG/ARA Action Memos, 1968.

[4] Enclosure 1, Status of Treaty Negotiations; enclosure 2, Urban Impact and Development Loan Program for Panama, FY 1967; enclosure 3, New Development Authority for Panama; and enclosure 4, Grant Aid for National Guard, are attached but not printed. Enclosure 5, SNIE 84–66, is Document 430.

Issues for Decision

1. Urban Impact Program

A decision is needed regarding the priority this program should receive, considering the FY 1967 AID funds available and the competing demands of other areas.

2. Long-Range Economic Development Plan

Assuming that the GOP will be receptive to United States proposals for formulating a long-range economic development plan and establishing a Development Authority, a decision is needed on whether specific assurances can be given to the GOP that expanded financial and technical resources will be made available to the Development Authority to implement the plan.

3. Darien Gap

The proposal to complete the Darien portion of the Pan American Highway which you mentioned in your April 15, 1966 speech in Mexico has relevance to Panama's long-range development. A decision on this matter which is being requested separately would assist in formulating a long-range development plan for Panama.

4. Assistance to National Guard

The IRG/ARA has agreed that in spite of the political risks involved the United States should finance the new 500 man addition to the Guard and the salaries of the 500 men added in 1965. This assistance would be made through a general budgetary support grant which would be made in such a way as to involve the least possible political risk. Your approval is requested of the course of action agreed upon by the IRG/ARA.

Dean Rusk

432.   Memorandum From the President's Special Assistant (Rostow)[1]

Washington, July 27, 1966.

MEMORANDUM FOR

The Secretary of State
Administrator Gaud
Director Helms
Secretary Resor
Assistant Secretary Gordon
Ambassador Anderson

SUBJECT

Presidential Directives on Panama

In order that we all have a clear understanding of the directives given by the President at the conclusion of our Panama review meeting on Tuesday, July 26, I thought it useful to recapitulate them as follows:

1. Director Helms is to review the [*less than 1 line of source text not declassified*] to assure that it is in a position to furnish ample and timely intelligence on developments.[2]

2. Assistant Secretary Gordon is to establish a Contingency Planning Group and immediately to proceed to develop alternative courses of action should the treaty negotiations reach an impasse.[3] Ambassador Irwin will give special attention to determining maximum concessions which we might make to the Panamanians, taking into consideration the requirements to retain United States control of operation and defense of the Canal and what the Congress is likely to accept. Assistant Secretary Gordon and Ambassador Irwin will work closely together in carrying out their respective assignments and both keep Ambassador Anderson fully informed.

---

[1] Source: National Archives and Records Administration, RG 59, Central Files 1964–66, POL PAN–US. Secret; Sensitive.

[2] In a July 27 memorandum to the CIA's Deputy Director for Plans setting forth the President's directive for the Agency, Helms noted that "the President wants us to watch the situation in Panama most closely and to do everything we can to guard against being caught by surprise in terms of riots, attempts to overthrow the government, and other possible troubles in the area." (Central Intelligence Agency, Job 80–B01285A, DCI (Helms) Chronological Files, July 1, 1966–December 31, 1966)

[3] A draft of a Department of State contingency study on Panama, based on the President's directive, was prepared on September 16. (Johnson Library, National Security File, Memos to the President, Walt W. Rostow, Vol. 15)

3. Assistant Secretary Gordon, in consultation with Administrator Gaud, is to:

a. establish a group to review actual and planned assistance to Panama with a view to developing and putting into effect as rapidly as feasible sound projects for economic and social development, with special emphasis on those having more immediate human impact.[4]
b. develop a plan for a Panama Development Authority, which Mr. Gordon will try to persuade the Panamanians to accept.
c. assist United States businessmen interested in private investment in Panama.

4. Secretary Gordon is to proceed with arrangements for further grant assistance to strengthen the National Guard.

5. In order to assure full coordination within the government, Secretary Gordon is to pass on all public statements and new initiatives relating to Panama. He is to coordinate these closely with Ambassador Anderson for their possible effect on the canal negotiations.

W. W. Rostow

---

[4] Department of State and AID proposals for dealing with economic and political issues in Panama were presented to the President under cover of a July 25 memorandum from Rusk to Johnson. (National Archives and Records Administration, RG 59, Central Files 1964–66, POL PAN–US)

---

433. Memorandum From the President's Special Assistant (Rostow) to President Johnson[1]

Washington, September 22, 1966.

SUBJECT

Status of Panama Account

This is where we stand on implementation of the directives which you gave at the Panama Review Meeting on July 26.

---

[1] Source: Johnson Library, National Security File, Country File, Panama, Vol. VIII (part 2 of 2), September 1966–May 1967. Secret. A note on the memorandum indicates that the President saw it. Copies were sent to Moyers and Henry Rowen of the Bureau of the Budget.

1. *Review of [less than 1 line of source text not declassified]*

Dick Helms has completed the review. As a result, changes in [*less than 1 line of source text not declassified*] have been made. [*1½ lines of source text not declassified*]

2. *Contingency Plans Against Negotiation Impasse*

Linc Gordon has prepared a paper (Tab A).[2] It is being reviewed by the Country Team, our negotiators and the Latin American IRG. The deadline for completion is September 27.

Jack Irwin was not able to make an estimate of the prospects for successful negotiations by our target date of September 15 for the reasons discussed in the last paragraph of this memorandum.

3. *List of Possible Concessions*

Jack Irwin was charged with determining maximum concessions which we might make to the Panamanians, taking into consideration our requirements for control and defense of the Canal and what Congress is likely to accept. A paper listing possible concessions (Tab B)[3] is being reviewed in State and DOD. Ambassador Anderson, who is in town today, will also be going over it.

4. *Economic Study Group*

A team under the leadership of Philip Klutznick recently completed a survey of Panama's short-term and longer-term needs. A summary of the contents of the report is at Tab C.[4]

The short term recommendations call for an immediate impact program of $16 million covering urban renewal and rehabilitation projects. As indicated in George Ball's memo at Tab D,[5] these recommendations have been accepted and Ambassador Adair instructed to begin negotiations immediately.

5. *Plan for a Panama Development Authority*

Ambassador Adair has discussed the desirability of setting up an Authority with President Robles and Foreign Minister Eleta. He got a non-committal, lukewarm response.

The Klutznick team looked into the matter and concluded that the better part of wisdom was to work through the existing Planning Board

---

[2] See footnote 3, Document 432.

[3] Tab B, attached but not printed, is a draft report, "Possible Unilateral United States Activities," September 8.

[4] Tab C, attached but not printed, is an undated report prepared by Klutznick on Panama aid program.

[5] Tab D, attached but not printed, is a September 9 memorandum from Ball to President Johnson.

and try to strengthen it. They found that the Board as an institution is equipped to handle budget, economic and social planning as well as physical planning and evaluation. The main problem is an incompetent Director. State/AID are trying to get him replaced and the staff augmented with capable people.

6. Stimulate Private Investment in Panama

We are not doing well on this. Bill Gaud is making a survey of investment guarantee applications which AID has received. Beyond that State and AID have done nothing. I will have another go at Linc and Bill. I recommend the next time you talk to them, you press hard for immediate action. Our private sector can play an important role in Panamanian development and we must take advantage of this asset.[6]

7. Assistance to the National Guard

We have told the Panamanians that we are willing to subsidize (indirectly) an increment of 500 men for the balance of this fiscal year if they will put the increase in their budget. (We are already paying for 500 men added to the force last year.) They want us to pay for 1000 men without it showing in the budget in the mistaken idea that this is the best way to hide our subsidy.

A 500 increment is as much as they can successfully handle. President Robles' opposition is already starting to make political hay of the fact that the government is carrying 500 more men on the force than appears in the current budget and that the U.S. is footing the bill.

8. Status of the Negotiations

Negotiations advanced at a steady clip during July and August. The first round on the draft treaties served to identify areas of difference. The second round focused on analysis of the differences and means for resolving them.

Half way through this round (September 1) the Panamanians asked for suspension of talks while they returned to Panama to help work out their government's position on economic compensation. This has caused a delay in our timetable of September 15 for Jack Irwin's estimate of the prospects for reaching a settlement.

Negotiations are tentatively scheduled to be resumed on September 27. Jack expects that it will be several more weeks before he can give you a valid judgment on the prospects. Jack is understandably cautious. But the record of the negotiating sessions show a good spirit and flexibility on the part of the Panamanians. At this point, there is more reason for optimism than pessimism.

---

[6] A handwritten note by Rostow next to this paragraph reads: "I'm going to dig into this personally."

9. Congressional Consultations

On August 24 Jack Irwin briefed the Senate Foreign Relations Committee on the status of the negotiations. Fulbright, Hickenlooper, Gore, Lausche, Carlson and McGee were present. The Senators were interested, full of questions and appreciative. There were no surprises beyond Fulbright's comment that he would vote against a sea-level canal treaty that did not provide for multilateral operation.

Walt

---

434.   Memorandum From the Representative to the Organization of American States (Linowitz) to President Johnson[1]

Washington, March 14, 1967.

SUBJECT

Panama Canal Negotiations

Bob Anderson called me today from New York in order to pass on this word:

At the Summit Meeting in Punta del Este, President Robles of Panama plans to talk to you about the progress in negotiations with reference to the Panama Canal matter. Bob Anderson feels that Robles will want to put pressure on you to speed up the discussions and negotiations.[2] He suggests that you might want to take the play away from Robles by telling him at once that you have been pushing for carrying on the negotiations as speedily as possible and that your understanding is that good progress is being made.[3]

---

[1] Source: Johnson Library, National Security File, Country File, Panama, Vol. VIII, September 1966–May 1967. Confidential. A notation on the memorandum indicates Johnson saw it.

[2] Panamanian Foreign Minister Eleta made a similar request to Rusk when he visited Washington in January. (Memorandum of conversation between Rusk and Eleta, January 18; National Archives and Records Administration, RG 59, Central Files 1967–69, POL 33–3 PAN–US)

[3] According to a memorandum of conversation of a meeting between Gordon and Panamanian Ambassador Ricardo Arias, April 2, the Ambassador told President Johnson that President Robles hoped that all outstanding questions concerning the treaty negotiations "might be settled through direct presidential discussions" at the upcoming meeting in Punta del Este. Johnson replied that "both sides had good negotiating teams and there was no reason to 'pass the buck' to the Presidents at this time. He understood the importance of the time element, but thought that the negotiations could be pushed ahead rapidly by the negotiating teams themselves." (Ibid., POL 33–3 CZ)

Bob says that three points still remain unsettled in connection with the negotiations: (1) compensation, (2) how long the treaty should last, and (3) jurisdiction over personnel. He proposes that when Robles raises the question of compensation with you, you might want to point out to him that it would be difficult to have Congress accept a guaranteed revenue figure substantially in excess of the present $2 million per year, and that therefore it would be mutually advantageous to explore other ways of providing added revenue to Panama. (Bob proposed, for example, some tariff arrangements which might be favorable to Panama.)

The Panamanian Foreign Minister, Fernando Eleta, spoke to me about this situation a couple of times in Buenos Aires. I am not, however, close enough to the negotiations to comment on Bob Anderson's suggestions, but I know he would be pleased to discuss them with you personally if you had a few minutes to do so before the Summit.

Sol M. Linowitz

---

435.   Memorandum of Conversation[1]

US/MC–9   Punta del Este, April 13, 1967, 8:45 a.m.

SUBJECT

U.S. Panamanian Canal Treaty Negotiation

PARTICIPANTS

United States	Panama
President Johnson	President Marco A. Robles
Secretary Rusk	Foreign Minister Fernando Eleta
Mr. Rostow	Ambassador Ricardo Arias
Secretary Gordon	Ambassador Diogenes de la Rosa
Ambassador Irwin	Mr. Hernan Porras, Special Advisor
Mr. Neil Seidenman, Interpreter	

President Robles said he wished to take up two points in particular with President Johnson, and in the matter of "one farmer to another." The first was the matter of arrangements under the new treaty governing the administration of justice in the Canal Area Panama

---

[1] Source: National Archives and Records Administration, RG 59, Central Files 1967–69, POL 7 IA–SUMMIT. Confidential. Drafted by Neil A. Seidenman (OPR/LS) and approved in the White House on April 28. The discussion was held during a "working breakfast."

wishes to uphold its sovereignty over the Area, but considers that such sovereignty cannot be successfully exercised without the ability to administer justice in the criminal, civil and administrative fields. Panama recognizes that the effective functioning of the Joint Authority will require certain preconditions. Panama considers joint administration of justice acceptable, however, with reference only to cases directly related to the operation of the Canal. He appealed to President Johnson to help to bring about agreement between the two countries on this score. He stated that from the Panamanian standpoint, criminal acts not related to the operation of the Canal should not be prosecuted by any but Panamanian authorities, as provided by the Constitution and laws of Panama.

The second point President Robles wished to bring up concerned revenue to Panama accruing from the Canal. Every country receives benefit from the utilization of its own natural resources. Panama's principal resource is its geographic position and the interoceanic canal made possible by that position. President Robles stated that Panama has never received fair compensation for its contribution and role making possible the building and operation of the canal. The rate survey carried out by the American firm, Arthur D. Little,[2] indicates that Panama could be receiving much more from the Canal than its present revenue. Panama is working to enhance the social and economic development of its country, consistent with the goals of hemispheric growth and progress adopted at Punta del Este in 1961. By now Panama has contracted foreign loans to the extent that it is approaching the saturation point in its external credit position. A continuation of present policies in this area could lead to "asphyxiation".

President Robles went on to say that Panama wants no more than a fair return from the Canal, so as to be able to secure the financial resources needed for economic and social development programs. Those programs are now proceeding well, but they would stand to suffer in the absence of sufficient funds to feed them. An important source of such funds should be Panama's share in Canal revenues, by virtue of its geographic and human contribution to the Canal.

President Robles said the negotiation of these problems can proceed in the climate of tranquility that his administration has maintained. It is of great political importance for President Robles to be able to sign the treaty as soon as possible, so as to eliminate the nationalistic passions and emotional effects surrounding this issue, which otherwise could give rise to agitation and set up a prolonged chain of disturbances in Panama.

---

[2] Arthur D. Little Company studied the issue of tolls and concluded that they could be raised 125 percent without affecting Canal traffic.

President Robles said that the key elements of timing include the fact that the ordinary session of the Panamanian Legislative Assembly begins in October 1. During that session, according to the rules of procedure, a whole range of issues may be taken up, with all the attendant opportunities for prolonged and politically biased debate. If the agreement can be concluded well before the ordinary session, President Robles would be able to call a special session, in which debate would be limited exclusively to the Treaty.

President Robles said that the other key date is that of forthcoming elections in Panama. He has been able to create a climate of tranquility for the signing and ratification of the Treaty. However, if the process drags on too long, he would hardly be able to contain the situation throughout the weeks and months of political campaigning, which is already in its initial stages. The presidential elections are to take place on May 1, 1968.

President Johnson expressed understanding of the wishes of President Robles, and said that we, too, want to conclude the agreements at the earliest possible date. We share Panama's sense of urgency, and are anxious to do all possible to speed up the negotiations. He will speak with Ambassador Anderson promptly on his return and issue appropriate instructions to our negotiators to this effect. The President told Robles that he would personally follow the progress of the negotiations. He agreed with him in his desire to avoid dragging on too long, which could make trouble for both countries, and he would be prepared to meet again with Robles if this should be useful.

With regard to Panama's share of benefits from the Canal, President Johnson stated that he assumed the amounts to be received by Panama would be determined, based on the revenue sharing concept, upon traffic volume through the Canal and Canal earnings derived from the volume. The President assured Robles of his awareness of Panama's needs for development programs. There are problems of mutual concern in all our countries, and we appreciate their importance to Panama.

With reference to the issue of justice, President Johnson said the United States would be happy to review the question of civil justice. There are some problems involved, but he would ask that the civil issue be reviewed again, in order to discover some solution that would be mutually satisfactory.

The President agreed with President Robles on the importance of the earliest possible conclusion of the agreement. He reiterated that the Canal earnings would rise according to the volume of the traffic. Also, we would ask our negotiators to give sympathetic review to the matter of justice. The President went on to say that he had spoken with Ambassador Anderson on several occasions in the past about the negotiations. The latter has been out of the country for several weeks, and there has been no recent opportunity to discuss these matters further with him. The President told Robles that as a result of this meeting he would again take these things up with him so that he (Ambassador Anderson) and Ambassador Irwin could bring about a speed-up in our work.[3] The President expressed the hope that this approach would meet with the satisfaction of President Robles, and assumed that Robles' people would be available for rapid pursuit of the negotiations. He praised President Robles for the wisdom of his view that he should get these matters behind him well before the elections.

President Robles brought up the subject of land return to Panama. He explained that as things now stand, Panama City and Colon, at their present stage of growth, are hemmed in, with no further space available in which to expand. He stated that these lands are not needed for the operation or defense of the Canal. If they could be returned to Panama, this would provide for further development of these two cities. He noted that this matter is also politically sensitive, and could lead to irritations and resentment. Secretary Rusk commented that he had spoken recently to Secretary McNamara on the subject of return of land areas to Panama and that Secretary McNamara said he would review sympathetically Panama's requests. President Johnson said he, too, would review this issue.

The interview closed with a discussion of the statements[4] to be made to the press, which have been separately reported.

---

[3] On April 22 Rostow reported to President Johnson that "all concerned are operating with the sense of urgency you promised Robles." He outlined progress in the areas discussed between the Presidents at Punta del Este, indicating that "Anderson and the Panama Review Group will want to discuss the deal with you prior to sounding out key Senators and presentation to the Panamanians." (Memorandum from Rostow to President Johnson, April 22; Johnson Library, National Security File, Country File, Panama, Vol. VIII (part 1 of 2), September 1966–May 1967)

[4] Johnson's statements at Punte del Este are in *Public Papers of the Presidents of the United States: Lyndon B. Johnson, 1967,* Book I, pp. 444–451.

436.   Special National Intelligence Estimate[1]

SNIE 84–67   Washington, May 4, 1967.

PANAMA

The Problem

To consider the prospect for political stability and for the Canal treaties between now and the scheduled inauguration of a new president in October 1968.

Conclusions

A. Increased tension and political turbulence are likely as the presidential campaign and the issue of new Canal treaties impinge on a situation none too stable in the first place.

B. The small number of elite families, long in political and economic control, may be hard pressed in the elections of May 1968 to keep one of their own in the presidency and to retain dominance of the National Assembly. The challenge will come from Arnulfo Arias, whose anti-elite Panameñista Party is the country's only mass movement. The danger of serious disorders will probably become somewhat greater than at present, and could become much greater.

C. Although there are a great many important political variables in Panama, the timing of the completion of the treaty negotiations will be a crucial factor in determining the extent of political unrest as well as the chances for ratification and implementation of the treaties.

D. In view of such uncertainties on the political scene, there will clearly be major problems in getting the Canal treaties completed, ratified, and then held to by the government succeeding that of President Robles. Unless the treaties are ratified before October 1967, there is small chance of getting satisfactory treaties completed until after a new administration takes office in October 1968.

[Here follows the 8-page Discussion section of the estimate.]

---

[1] Source: Central Intelligence Agency, Job 79–R01012A, O/DDI Registry. Secret; Controlled Dissem. According to a note on the cover sheet this estimate was prepared in the Central Intelligence Agency with the participation of the intelligence organizations of the Departments of State and Defense and the National Security Agency. The United States Intelligence Board concurred in this estimate on May 4.

437.   Memorandum From the President's Special Assistant (Rostow) to President Johnson[1]

Washington, June 9, 1967, 8:25 p.m.

Mr. President:

Bob Anderson called me this afternoon to tell me the following:

—The negotiation is now at the wire.[2] He hopes to wind it up at a meeting starting at 10:00 a.m. tomorrow with Panamanian negotiators.

—On the gut issue of financing, they will keep the 90¢ toll, which leaves 25¢ left over above costs. He would first propose a division of 17¢ for Panama; 8¢ for the U.S. His fallback is 20¢ for Panama, 5¢ for the U.S. This means that Panamanians might fetch up with between $15 and $20 million a year, depending on traffic. This compares with the $80 million a year they sought.

—We would permit Panamanian jurisdiction over certain criminal cases in the Zone for personnel not associated with the Canal; tourists, etc.

—The lock canal treaty would terminate in the year 2000 except if we were actually in the process of building a new sea-level canal at that time, in which case the treaty would run on to the year 2010.

—The treaty governing the sea-level canal would run 60 years from the time it became operational.

—Compensation to be paid Panama under a sea-level canal treaty would be decided at the time of the financing and in the light of the financing method. (Bob Anderson cleared this position, which varied from his initial instructions, with Bob McNamara and Covey Oliver.)

—We will give up to the Panamanians certain territories which we have agreed with the JCS; but two antenna fields would have to be moved at some future time, involving an estimated cost of $6 million.

—We would also surrender an area in which we have military quarters, which are desirable but not necessary to the defense arrangements.

---

[1] Source: Johnson Library, National Security File, Country File, Panama, Vol. IX, Memoranda and Miscellaneous. No classification marking. There is an indication on the memorandum that Johnson saw it.

[2] On May 31 Rusk sent the President a memorandum on the status of the negotiations. Rostow transmitted it to the President with the observation: "The remaining hurdle is the price tag—but that's not exactly trivial!" (Both ibid.)

—We would surrender some piers for which they would be able to earn some money.

—We would surrender one area containing houses now occupied by Panamanians, on the stipulation that the occupants would keep their present houses.

—The Panamanians will accept without change a standard status forces agreement, approved by the JCS.

As noted, the only variation from instructions which have been cleared with you and on the Hill, is the question of a compensation formula for the sea-level canal. Although Bob McNamara gave his assent, there appears to be some concern among the military that ambiguity about the compensation formula will weaken our option on the sea-level canal and might leave us at the turn of the century without military base rights.[3] I am now checking into the seriousness of this point. You may wish to talk directly tonight with Bob Anderson about it.

Finally, Bob Anderson notes that we have come to a strategic psychological moment. He thinks he can clinch the deal tomorrow; and that the deal is viable on the Hill. He cannot vouch for its viability in Panamanian politics.

If he gets your go ahead, they will make a firm decision tomorrow morning that they have a treaty and then take a few days getting the details on paper.

I recommend that you talk to Bob Anderson this evening, directly.[4]

Walt

---

[3] A June 10 memorandum from Sayre to Rusk reported on this problem: "Anderson talked twice to General Wheeler and with Secretary Resor on the JCS and Army problems on the sea level canal compensation provisions. Wheeler's preoccupations relate to the period after the lock canal terminates. They are (1) continued neutrality of the canal, (2) access and transit for U.S. warships, etc., and (3) defense of the canal." (National Archives and Records Administration, RG 59, ARA Files: Lot File 72 D 33, Entry 5396, Panama)

[4] The President's Daily Diary indicates that Johnson commented on Rostow's recommendation that the President speak to Anderson: "I'll have to do that tonight—which I'll do." There is no indication in the Daily Diary that the President spoke to Anderson, nor has any other record of such a conversation been found. (Johnson Library)

438. Memorandum From the President's Special Assistant (Rostow) to President Johnson[1]

Washington, June 16, 1967, 7 p.m.

Mr. President:

Bob Anderson called in to report the present state of the Panama negotiations. He will be meeting again on Monday[2] afternoon. He will use his own judgment in dealing with the two positions set out below unless you wish to give him instructions which he would, of course, welcome.

I. Our position

We have offered:

—17¢ per ton for the Panamanians; we would keep 8¢;
—the lock canal treaty ends in the year 2000, but will continue to 2010 if construction on the sea level canal is under way;
—the sea level canal treaty would run 60 years from the time it became operational;
—we would maintain the right to defend the lock canal for 10 years past the expiration of the treaty (the Panamanians argued for 5 years);
—payments under the sea canal would be negotiated at the time that financing was arranged; but guidelines are written into the present treaty.

II. Panamanian position

They ask:

—20¢ per ton for Panama in the first year; 5¢ for the U.S.;
—an increase of 1¢ up to 25¢ per year in the subsequent five years (at this time that would absorb the calculated amount available after costs without raising tolls; but in the future, that may not be the case since other aspects of the treaty are likely to reduce canal costs.);
—a guarantee for the value of the dollar over the whole period of the life of the lock canal in terms of the purchasing power of the dollar in 1967;
—a guarantee of $1.9 million a year (the present annuity) in addition to the sums to be derived from the new split of profits from tolls;
—a 60–40 division in favor of Panama if tolls should increase (we are calling for a 50–50 split);
—an exchange of letters in which we agree to look into their request for preference in U.S. markets for Panamanian goods;
—a U.S. commitment to build a 4-lane highway 10–12 miles in length from our military base in Rio Hato to La Chorreda;

---

[1] Source: Johnson Library, National Security File, Country File, Panama, Vol. IX, Memoranda and Miscellaneous. Confidential.

[2] June 19.

—the U.S. should build an underpass between the beach and Rio Hato to avoid our military vehicles from crossing the highways;

—that we build an all-weather road from Vera Cruz to Arrajan—about 8–10 miles.

III. Bob Anderson's thinking

Up to this point he has made no concessions to the Panamanian position. His thought is that he move his offer up from 17¢ a ton to 20¢, leaving us 5¢. As an alternative he is considering letting 20¢ be the base, letting the Panamanian take rise 1¢ a year for 5 years, but reserving 10¢ for ourselves (this reservation would not be real unless tolls were raised over this period or operating costs declined).

Without any commitment he would be prepared to give a letter indicating our willingness to consider the problem of Panamanian preference in the U.S. market.

He is hesitant about the roads, underpass, etc., because he doesn't know the price tag and they would be subject to Congressional appropriation.

The atmosphere has gotten increasingly emotional as the climax of the negotiation comes near. De La Rosa has stated that he would probably have to resign if the Panamanian proposal is not accepted. They have almost certainly been in informal communication with their President. They have suggested Presidential communications. Bob Anderson has tried to discourage this by saying that's not the way we operate.

As he approaches this final stage, having narrowed the issues, his general attitude is to be mildly generous about the financial terms—and prepared to take the heat in the Congress for that—rather than to risk for the President and the country a Panamanian explosion.

He concluded, as I indicated, by saying that he didn't wish to burden you at this time. He wished you to know how things were proceeding and that he would welcome any guidance you might wish to give him before his meeting on Monday afternoon.[3]

Walt

---

[3] In a June 17 note to Rostow, the President wrote: "Walt, call and thank him very much and tell him we follow his general judgment." Rostow annotated this note: "done." (Johnson Library, National Security File, Country File, Panama, Vol. IX, Memoranda and Miscellaneous)

439. Information Memorandum From the Acting Assistant Secretary of State for Inter-American Affairs (Sayre) to Secretary of State Rusk[1]

Washington, June 27, 1967.

SUBJECT

Panama Canal Treaties

President Johnson and President Robles announced June 26 that the negotiating teams of the United States and Panama had reached agreement on the details of three new treaties relating to (a) the present Lock Canal, (b) a possible Sea Level Canal in Panama, and (c) the Defense of the Panama Canal and its Neutrality. The announcement, copy attached,[2] states that the Treaties are being submitted to the representative Governments, that arrangements will be made for signature after approval by the two Presidents, and that the Treaties will then be presented to the two countries legislative body for consideration in accordance with their constitutional processes. Neither the texts nor details of the Treaties are being made available to the press or public at this time.

The following are the major points in the three treaties:

1. The Lock Canal Treaty

(a) *The Treaties of 1903, 1936, and 1955* with Panama are terminated as are all other agreements or treaties which are inconsistent with the Lock Canal Treaty.

(b) *The Administration.* A United States–Panama binational entity, called the "Joint Administration of the Panama Canal", would be established and would operate the Panama Canal and administer the "Canal Area". The Administration would assume control of the Canal and Canal Area not sooner than six months nor later than twenty-four months after the Treaty enters into force. The Administration would be governed by a Board of nine members, five appointed by the President of the United States and four appointed by the President of Panama. The Board acts by a majority vote unless otherwise provided in the Treaty. The Chairmanship of the Board would alternate annually between a United States and a Panamanian member. In order to carry out

---

[1] Source: National Archives and Records Administration, RG 59, Central Files 1967–69, POL 33–3 CZ. Confidential. Drafted by Clark and R.A. Frank (L/ARA).

[2] The statement that Johnson and Robles announced on June 26 was attached, but is not printed. For text, see Department of State *Bulletin*, July 17, 1967, p. 65, or *American Foreign Policy: Current Documents, 1967*, p. 660.

its responsibilities and functions, the Administration would have numerous express rights and powers, including the right and power to promulgate a statute of laws, to establish a court system, and to establish a police force. Some Panamanian civil laws would apply in the Canal Area and some Panamanian criminal laws may apply in the Canal Area. The Panamanian courts would have some jurisdiction in the Canal Area.

(c) *The Canal Area.* The "Canal Area" is delimited in the Treaty and includes land and water areas which comprise the present Canal Zone. Land and water areas in the present Zone which are no longer necessary for the operation of the Canal would be returned to Panama.

(d) *Employees.* The Administration would have all rights and powers relating to employment policies and labor relations with its employees. Persons presently employed by the Panama Canal Company and the Canal Zone Government would be transferred to employment of the Administration under conditions established in the Treaty. Such persons would receive the same compensation they presently receive; would be guaranteed increases in minimum wages; would receive salary increases to offset any possible increase in the cost of living or other net financial disadvantage through their transfer; and would continue to receive the benefits of the United States Civil Service retirement law and all other protections and benefits equivalent to those in effect prior to the transfer.

(e) *Taxation.* The Administration would be exempt from all Panamanian taxes, with the exception that the Administration would pay Panamanian taxes on certain retail or other commercial enterprises it may continue to operate.

(f) *Tolls.* The Treaty provides that the Administration will operate the Canal to provide to Panama and the United States a fair return "in the light of their contributions to the creation and maintenance of the Canal and in the interest of world commerce". The Administration, in its first year of operation, would pay to Panama seventeen cents per long ton of commercial cargo transiting the Canal, and that annual payment would increase by one cent for five succeeding years, the annual payment to Panama thereafter being twenty-two cents per long ton. In fiscal 1969, seventeen cents per long ton would, according to present predictions, be approximately sixteen million dollars. The Administration would, in its first year of operation, pay to the United States eight cents per long ton of commercial cargo, and that annual amount would increase by one cent for two years, the annual payment to the United States thereafter being ten cents per long ton.

(g) *Neutrality and Non-Discrimination.* The Panama Canal would remain neutral and would be open to vessels of commerce and of war of all nations on terms of entire equality and non-discrimination.

(h) *Termination.* The Treaty would remain in force until December 31, 1999; however, it would be superseded by the Sea Level Canal Treaty if the United States constructs a sea level canal.

2. *Sea Level Canal Treaty*

The Sea Level Canal Treaty in effect provides that the United States has an option, which it must exercise within twenty years, to construct a Sea Level Canal on the site of the present Lock Canal or in the Darien region of Panama. The Sea Level Canal would be operated by an "Inter-Oceanic Canal Commission". The Commission would be governed by a Board consisting of nine members, five appointed by the President of the United States and four by the President of Panama. The United States, after consultation with Panama, may offer others the right to participate in the financing of the Canal, and, in this case, those who participate in the financing might be represented on the Board. The Board would have numerous express powers to operate and maintain the Sea Level Canal; however, the "Canal Area" would be abolished and the Commission therefore would have no powers with respect to court, laws, and law enforcement. The Treaty would terminate sixty years from the date the Sea Level Canal is opened, but not beyond 2067.

3. *Defense Treaty*

Both the Lock Canal Treaty and the Sea Level Canal Treaty provide that Panama and the United States shall provide for the defense, security, neutrality, and continuity of operation of the Canal in a Defense Treaty signed on the same date. Under the Defense Treaty, the United States retains certain defense areas in which it may maintain its Armed Forces. The Treaty provides that "In case of an international conflagration or the existence of any threat of aggression or any armed conflict or other emergency endangering Canal defenses," Panama and the United States "would take such preventive and defensive measures necessary for the protection of and common interests in effectuating purposes of the Defense Treaty." The United States may act unilaterally in the Defense Areas or in the Canal Area. The United States would be able to use the Defense Areas for "related security purposes" and would consequently continue other military activities, such as training. The Defense Treaty contains extensive provisions relating to the status of our forces similar to other status of forces agreements.

440.   **Memorandum From the President's Special Assistant
(Rostow) to President Johnson**[1]

Washington, August 8, 1967, 7 p.m.

SUBJECT

Robles Delays Signing of Panama Canal Treaties

Panamanian President Robles has assured Ambassador Adair that the Panama Canal Treaties will be signed but not without further delay.

Robles hopes to be able to sign before the end of August but the State Department believes a more realistic date would be the middle or end of September.

In the attached copy of a cable from Panama,[2] Adair reports that Robles says he needs additional time for discussions with Panamanian leaders. He believes, and Adair agrees, that the delay in signing is working in favor of eventual approval. Adair believes Robles will not press for ratification of the treaty before his 1968 elections.

State officials agree with Adair that we should not pressure Robles into an early signing.

Secretary Rusk will be making recommendations shortly. He is expected to suggest that key members of Congress be informed of the current situation at an early date. Consideration is also being given to releasing to the press the texts of the treaties accompanied by an explanation of the delay in signing.[3]

Walt

---

[1] Source: Johnson Library, National Security File, Country File, Panama, Vol. IX, June 1967–April 1968. Secret. There is an indication on this memorandum that Johnson saw it.

[2] Telegram 368 from Panama, August 8, is attached but not printed.

[3] Memorandum from Rusk to President Johnson, August 8. (Johnson Library, National Security File, Memos to the President, Walt W. Rostow, Vol. 37, August 1–10, 1967) On August 10 Sayre informed Rusk that the President had approved the official release of the draft treaties, but only after consultation with Panama. On August 11 Anderson stated he "saw no positive advantage to releasing the draft treaties." Eleta and Panama's chief negotiator both thought release at this time "undesirable." (Memorandum from Sayre to Rusk, August 16; National Archives and Records Administration, RG 59, Central Files 1967–69, POL PAN–US) Leaked texts of the treaties had already appeared in the *Chicago Tribune* and were printed in the *Congressional Record* of July 17, 21, and 27, 1967.

441.   Memorandum From the President's Special Assistant (Rostow) to President Johnson[1]

Washington, October 6, 1967, noon.

SUBJECT

Panamanian Developments

Encouraging Economic Outlook

A year ago we were concerned about public unrest in Panama arising from sluggish economic conditions. You will recall that you authorized a high impact economic assistance program.

We are a long way from solving Panama's basic problems of unemployment and maldistribution of income, but the short term gains are encouraging. Our Embassy reports that Panama has achieved a remarkable annual growth rate of 8%, which is expected to continue. Business is booming. Growth in the manufacturing sector is higher than the overall average. Exports are up, but so are imports. The deficit is made manageable by higher earnings from the Zone. The Embassy says that much of the growth stems from confidence by the business community that satisfactory treaties will be negotiated which will bring larger income to Panama.

Further Slippage on the Treaties

With respect to the treaties, we have more slippage in the Panamanian timetable. Robles is still consulting key persons on the drafts. This process will not be completed until the end of October. During November, Robles and Eleta expect to consolidate all the changes recommended by the Council, Cabinet and ex-Presidents. The Panamanian negotiating team would return to Washington around mid-November. Talks on the changes they want—Eleta says about 70—are expected to last until the end of January. According to their schedule, signature would take place in late January or February, with ratification to follow in a special session of the National Assembly after their May Presidential elections.

All of this hinges, in the first place, on the nature of the treaty changes they propose. Eleta says most of them are "drafting" changes. Assuming this hurdle is passed, there remains the question of who the Presidential candidates will be and who wins the elections. Beyond

---

[1] Source: Johnson Library, National Security File, Country File, Panama, Vol. IX, June 1967–April 1968. Confidential. A handwritten L on the memorandum indicates the President saw it.

that arises the question of whether we want to seek ratification in the middle of our presidential campaign. The prospects for the treaties continue to be "iffy".

Walt

---

442. **Information Memorandum From the President's Special Assistant (Rostow) to President Johnson**[1]

Washington, December 28, 1967.

SUBJECT

Panama: Politics and the Treaties

Five months ago we were ready to sign the new Canal treaties. Today it is clear that the lameduck Robles Government will not be able to follow through on signature.[2] The treaties will pass to the successor administration which assumes office on October 1, 1968. It is a safe bet that this administration will want to put its stamp on the treaties. So renegotiation to some degree early in 1969 is a virtual certainty.

This turn of events has worked out well for us:

—we will have gained 5 years of relative stability following the 1964 riots.

—the generous treaties which Bob Anderson negotiated have disarmed our critics.

—the delay in signature is not due to us but to failure of Robles to prepare the way for action in Panama—this is well understood.

—the delay removes the treaties from the Panamanian electoral campaign (elections are on May 12, 1968) as well as our own, which is to our advantage.

---

[1] Source: Johnson Library, National Security File, Country File, Panama, Vol. IX, June 1967–April 1968. Confidential. A handwritten notation on the memorandum indicates the President saw it.

[2] In a November 13 memorandum to Helms, Director of the Office of National Estimates Sherman Kent stated, "the political maneuvering now underway in Panama in preparation for the presidential election of 1 May 1968 is increasing the chances of civil disorder and has virtually eliminated any chance of progress on the draft Canal treaties—at least until after a new Panamanian president takes office in October 1968." Kent indicated that Arnulfo Arias was "the odds on favorite" to be the next president if elections were free and fair. He would be "sticky" to deal with. The Robles government, according to the memorandum, was in no position to press approval of the treaties, especially because popular, nationalistic opinion was increasingly opposed to them. (Washington National Records Center, OSD Files: FRC 330 72 A 2468, Panama 000.1, 1967)

At Punta del Este Robles urged you to ask the US negotiators to step up the pace of the negotiations so that he could sign and obtain National Assembly ratification before the 1968 political campaign got underway. You obliged him. But he had not done his homework with his congress. He ran into trouble, temporized, and ended up unable to muster sufficient support to put the treaties through.

The electoral campaign caught up with him. What little chance he had at least to sign the treaties vanished when he mishandled the selection of his successor by his loosely-knit coalition. As a result, four of the parties bolted and joined his arch-rival Arnulfo Arias. If the elections are anywhere near honest, the charismatic Arias is bound to win.

Arias—who was twice elected President and both times deposed by the National Guard—is a flamboyant and erratic leader. His problems with staying in power have been with his own people rather than with us. Whether he has mellowed with the years, we don't know. We have followed carefully his attitude toward the treaty negotiations. In this he has been most prudent. He has aimed his criticism at Robles as a president who had no right to negotiate the treaties because of his fraudulent election in 1963 [1964]. But he has carefully avoided attacking us or the contents of the treaties.

A year from now when the treaties are looked at again, there may be substantial reasons for a major overhaul. Assuming Arias wins and is allowed to take office, he may seek substantial changes. But we may also want to reconsider the approach in the light of what the Plowshare experiments demonstrate and the Canal Study Commission may have concluded by then on the best route to follow.

Walt

443.   Action Memorandum From the President's Special Assistant (Rostow) to President Johnson[1]

Washington, March 19, 1968.

SUBJECT

Panama Situation

The Panamanian electoral crisis is coming to a head[2] with the impeachment trial of President Robles now slated to begin on Monday, March 25.[3] I recommend you devote a few minutes of today's luncheon meeting to a review of this problem.[4]

The Present Situation

Neither President Robles nor Opposition Candidate Arias give any sign of backing off from their intransigent positions. Robles keeps putting pressure on National Guard Commander Vallarino to side with him, but so far Vallarino has kept strictly neutral.

The trial may force Vallarino's hand. Arias will expect him to carry out the National Assembly's verdict and whatever orders the new President gives him. Robles will not step down. He hopes the Supreme Court will invalidate the Assembly's action and Vallarino will close the Assembly.

Under these circumstances, the pressure on Vallarino will be to say plague on both houses and take over the government. There are some unconfirmed indications he is planning such action if the politicians do not compose their differences.

What We Have Done

We do not want to take sides, nor become too heavily engaged in any mediation effort. We believe a face-saving formula for all parties would be to have the OAS send electoral technicians and observers to

---

[1] Source: Johnson Library, National Security File, Agency File, SIG, 32nd Meeting, March 21, 1968, Vol. 4. Secret.

[2] In telegram 125046 to Bogota, San José, and Panama City, March 5, the Department pointed out that "while a physical clash between the opposing Arias and Samudio [Robles' successor candidate for President] factions has been averted, the underlying issue of control of the electoral machinery—and hence the outcome of the May 12 elections—has not been resolved. Therefore, it is only a matter of time before the political cycle produces another crisis." (National Archives and Records Administration, RG 59, Central Files 1967–69, POL 14 PAN)

[3] Telegram 128456 to Mexico City, Rio de Janeiro, and San José, March 12, provides background on the onset of the impeachment crisis. (Ibid.)

[4] Tom Johnson's notes of this luncheon meeting do not include discussion of Panama. (Johnson Library, Tom Johnson Meeting Notes)

help in arranging honest elections. The OAS has done this in several Caribbean countries.

At our urging, the Colombians and Costa Ricans have proposed electoral specialists, but gotten nowhere. We have encouraged Archbishop Clavel and his "third-force" group of civic and business leaders to advance the idea, but they have had no success. There are indications that Arias would probably accept outside observers if Robles and his candidate, Samudio, would. Anything that promotes fair elections favors Arias' election. But Robles last weekend publicly stated that observers were not necessary because the elections would be "free and pure".

What We Might Do

State has so far approached the problem with extreme caution.[5] While I think prudence is called for, I also believe some modest risk-taking might spare us from a military coup in Panama and possible bloodshed.

The key is Vallarino and his National Guard. Only he has the power to enforce a settlement on both sides or take over the government.

So far we have not dealt directly with Vallarino. Last week he expressed a desire to see CINCSO Commander General Porter, but word was sent back that he should deal with Ambassador Adair on political matters. Ambassador Adair has instructions to urge Vallarino—if he comes calling—to push both sides into accepting outside observers.

What I would like to have Secretary Rusk explore with his advisers is for us to take the initiative with Vallarino and press him to use the OAS observers formula as the way out of the impasse. If he is agreeable and asks for our help, we should be prepared to support his efforts with Robles, Samudio, Arias and the Archbishop.

Should it become public that we have taken this initiative, I do not see that we have lost anything. For, we are not taking sides, we are supporting constitutional government, we are encouraging free and honest elections using a method already employed by four other Caribbean countries, and we are trying to head off either a bloody clash between the contending parties or a military coup.

W. W. Rostow[6]

---

[5] In a March 19 note for Rostow, Bowdler pointed out: "I have not gotten very far in persuading ARA to take more initiative in the Panamanian situation." Bowdler continued, "I am not a wild-eyed interventionist. But remembering what neutral inactivity cost us in the DR, I would like to try an additional low-risk initiative." (Ibid., National Security File, Agency File, SIG, 32nd Meeting, March 21, 1968, Vol. 4)

[6] Printed from a copy that bears this typed signature.

444.   Information Memorandum From the President's Special
        Assistant (Rostow) to President Johnson[1]

Washington, March 26, 1968, 8 p.m.

SUBJECT

Panama Situation

There is a marked deterioration in the situation in Panama in the wake of the National Assembly's impeachment of Robles on Sunday[2] and the increasingly repressive actions taken by the National Guard against the rival government of "President" Del Valle and Opposition Candidate Arias.

National Guard Commander Vallarino has not formally abandoned his neutral stance of maintaining law and order until the Supreme Court rules on the Assembly action.[3] But under this guise, he has ransacked the headquarters of opposition candidate Arias and cordoned off the National Assembly Building—the seat of the Del Valle Government.

There was a showdown at 5:00 p.m. today when "President" Del Valle, his Cabinet and the majority of the National Assembly members tried to enter the Assembly Building. Ambassador Adair has just reported the National Guard drove them off with barrages of tear gas.

So far, we have not been dragged into the dispute. But the danger signals are up. The heavy-handed action by the National Guard against the Arias–Del Valle group could bring a sharp public reaction.[4] This reaction could be turned against us out of frustration or hostility by

---

[1] Source: Johnson Library, National Security File, Country File, Panama, Vol. IX, June 1967–April 1968. Secret. A note on the memorandum indicates the President saw it.

[2] The United States was notified on March 27 that, by virtue of a judgment issued by the Panamanian National Legislative Assembly, Robles had been deposed and First Vice President Maz Del Valle had been sworn in as President on March 24. (Telegram 139993 to all Latin American posts, April 1; National Archives and Records Administration, RG 59, Central Files 1967–69, POL 15 PAN)

[3] The Supreme Court of Panama, with one dissenting vote, ruled the Robles impeachment proceedings unconstitutional, and Robles, with the support of the National Guard, retained the Presidency. Additional information is in circular telegram 136251 to all Latin American posts, March 26 (ibid., POL 15–1 PAN), and in a memorandum from Rostow to President Johnson, April 1. (Johnson Library, National Security File, Country File, Panama, Vol. IX, June 1967–April 1968)

[4] In a March 25 memorandum to Rusk, Oliver noted that "the position taken by the Guard has aroused considerable resentment in opposition circles, who interpret it as evidence of Guard partiality to Robles." (National Archives and Records Administration, RG 59, Central Files 1967–69, POL–PAN)

playing on the fact that the tear gas (being used rather indiscriminately) is from the US and we have heavily subsidized increases in the strength of the National Guard during the past two years. References to this are beginning to appear in the anti-Robles propaganda.

So far, the general public—and even the students—have been apathetic and aloof from the political maneuvering. Even the communists and their allies have not taken sides. Whether the action by the Guard this evening will bring the people into the streets in support of Arias and Del Valle remains to be seen.

Ambassador Adair continues to monitor the situation closely. He believes there is little we can do to influence events in this domestic squabble which would not drag us into the middle.

Walt

---

445.   Information Memorandum From the President's Special Assistant (Rostow) to President Johnson[1]

Washington, May 11, 1968, 11:55 a.m.

SUBJECT

Panama Elections: Sunday, May 12, 1968

Tomorrow Panama holds national elections. The outlook is for peaceful balloting. If there is trouble, it is most likely to come after the results are announced.[2]

The assumption is that the official candidate, David Samudio, will win. President Robles controls the electoral machinery. The National Guard is actively backing Samudio. So the stage is set for Samudio to emerge the victor—by foul means if fair ones do not work. The CIA reporting shows that the Robles government is ready to engage in massive manipulation of the ballot boxes if necessary.

---

[1] Source: Johnson Library, National Security File, Country File, Panama, Vol. X (part 3 of 3), May–December 1968. Secret. A note on the memorandum indicates the President saw it.

[2] On April 26 Helms warned the President: "in view of the Panamanian election two weeks hence, I think you may be interested to note our concern that it may not go off as smoothly as one is inclined now to think." (Memorandum from Helms to Johnson; Central Intelligence Agency, Job 80–B01285A, DCI (Helms) Chronological Files, January 1, 1968–July 31, 1968)

Opposition candidate Arnulfo Arias has campaigned actively despite his loss of face in the unsuccessful impeachment struggle against President Robles last month. Prior to this setback, most observers believed Arias would win a clear majority. How voters will react to Arias' lack of muscle in the impeachment showdown and the government's apparent intention to insure Samudio's victory, we do not know.

The intensity of any public reaction to manipulation of election results will hinge on the degree to which the ballot boxes are stuffed and how blatant Robles and Samudio are about it. The showdown should come on Monday or Tuesday.[3]

Bromley Smith[4]

---

[3] May 13 or 14.
[4] Smith signed for Rostow above Rostow's typed signature.

---

446. Editorial Note

On May 30, 1968, the Panamanian Board of Election announced that Arnulfo Arias had defeated David Samudio by approximately 175,000 to 134,000 votes. In an assessment of the prospects of the Arias government, Director of the Bureau of Intelligence and Research Hughes informed Secretary Rusk that "When it was obvious that despite extensive irregularities committed by Samudio partisans and the Guard, Arias and the NU had received an overwhelming majority of the votes in the May 12 elections, the Guard, perhaps fearing violence, moved to a neutral position assuring a relatively fair vote count and an Arias victory. It seems unlikely that Samudio can block Arias' accession to the Presidency by October 1. The period prior to the inauguration will be one of horse trading between Arias, the other NU leaders, Samudio supporters, the National Guard, and anyone else who desires influence in the incoming government." (Research Memorandum RAR–16 from Hughes to Rusk, July 22; National Archives and Records Administration, RG 59, Central Files 1967–69, POL PAN–US)

447.   Telegram From the Embassy in Panama to the Department of State[1]

Panama City, May 20, 1968, 2250Z.

3434. Subject: Minotto[2]–Vallarino Conversation.

1. Minotto met privately with Vallarino at noon today for approximately half an hour. His report on meeting follows:

2. Having met General Vallarino twice before in 1965 and 1967 there was no problem in immediately resuming our previous cordial relationship.

3. I advised the General that I was on a business trip to Panama and points south and that prior to leaving my hometown of Phoenix, Arizona, the superintendent of the Arizona Highway Patrol had given me a personal letter for the General and also a large gold star appointing him a Colonel in the AHP (the highest rank this organization had to confer). Vallarino was very pleased and said he would thank Superintendent James Hegarty of the AHP in a personal letter for the honor conferred on him. Having successfully disposed of the "cover," I then asked the General if he would be good enough and give me 10–15 minutes of his time for a private and confidential discussion. His answer was, "I will be very happy to talk to you."

4. I started our conversation by making it very clear that I was not connected with the U.S. Government at this time, not like a year ago and other times when I was a staff member of the United States Senate, Committee on Appropriations.

5. I also made it very clear that the Ambassador, or any person connected with our Embassy in Panama, was not aware of what I would discuss with him, nor had I seen the Ambassador prior to my visit to him today.

6. I informed the General that on my way from Arizona to Panama I had further discussions with people of authority and particularly in Washington with Members of Congress, people with a long record of service (such as Senator Hayden) and who had over the years gone by shown a warm interest and a friendly feeling towards Panama and its people.

7. These people, whose names I did not elaborate on (except Senator Hayden) were all quite concerned about the newspaper reports emanating from Panama and gave a rather detailed and vivid account

---

[1] Source: National Archives and Records Administration, RG 59, Central Files 1967–69, POL PAN–US. Secret; Exdis; No Distribution Outside the Department.

[2] James Minotto, former staff member of the Senate Appropriations Committee.

of the presidential elections and the present status of uncertainty and unrest.

8. I told the General that I as a private citizen and being fairly familiar with Latin America was equally concerned with the people above referred to, that Panama's image was in grave danger as not being a democratic republic that adhered to the democratic principles of the people electing their president, but that unscrupulous forces were, according to many newspaper reports, and I emphasized that my knowledge was solely obtained from newspaper sources, trying to manipulate the election of their candidate, even though he had been defeated by a substantial majority at the polls.[3] I did not mention the name of this candidate. I continued to explain to the General the seriousness of this situation in our relations with Panama, because the American people get their information about what is going on in the world from newspapers, TV and radio, and that the large volume of critical reports about the honesty of the Panamanian election could have very damaging repercussions in the political and economic field as well.

9. Congress has its ears tuned to public opinion, and if the thought were to prevail that Panama had a government that did not represent the choice of the Panamanian people, such programs as aid, military assistance, and the pending Panama Canal negotiations could be seriously impaired.

10. I said to General Vallarino: "General, I am speaking solely in a private capacity, but let me tell you that people of great prominence in the United States feel that the future of Panama lies in your hands. You have had over many years an unblemished record, you yourself told me a year ago that you had no ambitions to be President, that you were dedicated to your job as head of the National Guard of Panama, the only armed forces of your republic, to maintain law and order and to protect the constitution and the rights of the people.

11. I have assured my friends at home that you would never tolerate any crooked practices and that you would stand firm for an honest election. I also understand that at present the National Election

---

[3] On May 17 Hughes informed Secretary Rusk that "Arnulfo Arias apparently received such large majority in the May 12 election that the government cannot impose its presidential candidate, David Samudio, without resorting to extensive and blatant fraud. Nevertheless, the Samudio forces seem determined to arrange their victory. Once again the National Guard is caught in the middle, but this time internal dissension is threatening the unity of the Guard. Commandant Vallarino, who is wavering in his support for Samudio, must contend with a powerful clique of officers so deeply committed to Samudio that they fear a NU victory would cost them their jobs." (Memorandum from Hughes to Rusk, Intelligence Note 360, May 17; National Archives and Records Administration, RG 59, Central Files 1967–69, POL 14 PAN)

Board is checking the presidential elections returns and rejecting any irregularities. May I ask you the one and only question that I would like to have your views on?" His answer was, "Yes, go ahead." Then, sir, please tell me if you would stand by the decision of the National Election Board and if necessary enforce it. His answer was, "I will enforce the decision of the constitutionally created National Election Board, and I will not tolerate any act that would void the will of the people." I added, regardless who the presidential candidate is, who would get the majority of the popular vote? His answer was, "Yes".

12. Finally I mentioned the National Tribunal, which I understand is composed of three men, to whom complaints about irregularities are submitted. I also mentioned that there was a rumor that such a small group of men could be swayed by material promises, thus nullifying the will of the people.

13. He smiled and said: "My actions will be guided by the decision of the National Election Board, and I will not go beyond the decision of the NEB.

14. As I bade the General goodbye, I told him that I would pass on to my friends at home what he had told me and that I felt sure they would be very happy to hear this and that he (General Vallarino) was doing a great service to his country, to the cause of democracy, and to the continuance of amicable and useful relations between his country and the United States.

15. In conclusion, I wish to state that our conversation was at all times an extremely friendly and open discussion, and I very definitely gathered that impression that the General was sincere in what he told me and that his statements honestly reflected his stand in this matter.

Adair

448. Telegram From the Embassy in Panama to the Department of State[1]

Panama City, October 9, 1968, 2105Z.

4872. For Asst Secretary Oliver and Sanders ARA/Panel. Subject: Possible New Crisis in National Guard.

1. New GN crisis is presently in the making. Dept has by now received reports submitted this morning through intelligence channels.[2]

2. At noontime Col Urrutia asked MLGP CMDR Seddon to come to his office where he explained that President Arias was not keeping his earlier promises relative to the GN and that the GN officers feared the President was eventually going to destroy the GN organization. As examples of broken promises he mentioned (1) Arias' latest intent not formally to name Pinilla as first commandant because of shortage of funds and (2) Arias' statement to Urrutia (which Urrutia says he did not pass on to the officers concerned) that Torrijos and Boris Martinez would have to go. Urrutia did not mention to Seddon anything about a coup.

2. Urrutia said he wanted to be sure that Ambassador Adair was aware of the current situation and that he would like an opportunity to talk with me. He did not specifically ask Seddon to make an appointment for him. Seddon promised to convey Urrutia's explanation to me. Seddon, having talked with me before meeting Urrutia, told the latter that the Ambassador could not involve himself in changes of personnel in the GN. Seddon also commented that as CMDR in chief the president had right to assign GN officers as he deemed fit. Urrutia acknowledged this but added that the officers "were not fools and could see the handwriting on the wall."

3. A few minutes after talking to Urrutia this noon, Seddon talked with Vallarino who told him the outlook was not good and that he should watch developments closely. He expected trouble—not now—but in about six months time.

---

[1] Source: Johnson Library, National Security File, Memos to the President, Walt W. Rostow, Vol. 98, October 5–9, 1968. Secret; Exdis; Immediate. Repeated to Pancanal Govt and USCINCSO. Rostow sent a copy of this telegram to President Johnson at 7 p.m. October 9 and commented: "The attached indicates that there are now again thoughts within the National Guard in Panama of a coup against Arias." (Ibid.) On September 26 the CIA had sent the White House a memorandum alerting them to "coup talk" among members of the National Guard likely to be affected by Arias' proposed changes in the leadership of the Guard. (Ibid., Vol. 96, September 26–30, 1968)

[2] The White House received information indicating that a group of National Guard officers reached a decision to stage a military coup and take over the government within the next 48 hours. (Ibid., Country File, Panama, Vol. X (2 of 3), May to December 1968)

4. The question is whether I should speak with Urrutia and if so what to tell him. My door has always been open to anyone wanting to see me. If Urrutia calls on me, Arias will know it soon thereafter. I feel it would be almost imperative for me to tell Arias of Urrutia's call. Urrutia probably would not object. By such action I and the USG would be in the middle. Other GN officers as well as political supporters of both Arias and Samudio would soon know of my involvement.

5. If Arias and the GN should become reconciled thereafter, we might gain good will. If the GN should reluctantly abandon the reported but still unverified plans for a coup on grounds of an inferred disapproval on part of US after my talk with Urrutia, the opposition press would probably charge interference and claim this was proof of US support of Arias in the recent elections.

6. If a coup occurs and Urrutia should claim he asked for an appointment beforehand with the US Ambassador and was refused, we may come in for criticism from other sources.

7. In the event Urrutia should come to my office, I could make the following points:

(1) The USG has made clear its stand on respect for constitutional processes. (2) USG has maintained strictly neutral attitude in Panama's recent elections and does not intend to interfere in Panama's domestic politics. Relationship between President of Republic and GN is domestic matter. (3) Panama has established reputation in recent years for law and order. Panama has completed three 4-year terms of office without an unconstitutional change. These are important facts to bear in mind relative to GOP's image both at home and abroad. (4) I trust that whatever GN does, it will have good of country at heart rather than individual personal advantage. (5) Suggest that GN make every effort resolve its problems through peaceful discussions.

8. I propose (but will await Dept reply) to send Seddon back to Urrutia to say he has given me Urrutia's message, that I appreciate the information and that I hope differences can be resolved through friendly reason and discussion. If Urrutia again raises point of meeting with Ambassador, Seddon would tell him the door of my office was always open and if he wanted to make an appointment Seddon would arrange it. If Urrutia asks for the appointment, Seddon will tell Urrutia that I would probably feel compelled to inform Pres Arias of the discussion.

9. If Urrutia comes to my office, I would subsequently seek an appointment with Arias. Failure to do the latter would almost inevitably lead to greater criticism of US involvement if a coup were to follow my talk with Urrutia.

10. Embassy has no hard evidence which would support claim of some GN officers that Arias is planning to destroy the GN although intelligence reports do indicate that Arias is planning further changes

to consolidate his control over the GN. On the contrary, the statement issued by Arias immediately prior to the inauguration bespake respect for GN and intent not only to preserve promotion system but to raise salaries. Torrijos and Boris Martinez are both strong-minded officers and being the most vulnerable may well be the force behind the present crisis.[3]

Adair

[3] On October 9 Samuel Lewis of the NSC staff sent a memorandum to Rostow stating that "there is substantial danger that a coup is in fact being contemplated." Lewis wrote that there was "nothing more on this situation than contained in the two messages [see footnotes 1 and 2 above]. I have talked to State and stressed the importance of doing everything we can to avoid the demise of another constitutional government on the heels of the Peru affair. Oliver will get guidance to Adair tonight. [*less than 1 line of source text not declassified*] of what is in the wind, in case he has not already sniffed it out." (Ibid., (3 of 3), May–December 1968) The guidance telegrams have not been found.

449.   Memorandum for Record[1]

Washington, October 12, 1968, 6:50 a.m.

SUBJECT

Coup in Panama

1. At about 2200 EDT on 11 October, Guardia Nationale (GN) elements began taking over the National Government in Panama City and the City Governments of Colon and David. USCINCSO Duty Officer confirmed the fact that the Tocumen Airport had been closed to traffic by the GN. He also reported that USSOUTHCOM forces were in Readiness Condition 2, that Major General Dany was present in the Joint Operations Center and that battle staffs were being manned.

2. Within several hours, the GN took over the Presidential Palace and appeared to be in general control of the provinces. Meanwhile, President Arias, with several members of his cabinet, took refuge in

[1] Source: Johnson Library, National Security File, Country File, Panama, Vol. X (part 3 of 3), May–December 1968. Secret.

the Canal Zone and requested to see the US Ambassador or the Canal Zone Governor.[2]

3. The coup appears to be headed by Lt Col Omar Torrijos and supported by Major Boris Martinez and Major Federico Boyd. Lt Col Urrutia, the newly appointed commandant of the GN, is under arrest. Guardia Nationale troops are arresting the political followers of President Arias (Panamanistas) in both Panama City and Colon.

4. Former GN First Commandant Vallarino, who reportedly was fishing on an off-shore island, expressed surprise at the coup and GN troops reportedly have been ordered to prevent him from entering the Commandancia. The Tocumen Airport was reopened early on the morning of 12 October and although sporadic acts of violence have been reported, the GN continues to maintain public order.

5. Ambassador Adair and Canal Zone Governor Major General Leber, who were in Washington, D.C. on 11 October, are returning by USAF aircraft to Panama, with an ETA of 0838 EDT 12 October.

M. W. Kendall
Brigadier General, USA
Deputy Director for Operations (NMCC)

---

[2] In telegram CAP 82541, sent to President Johnson at the LBJ Ranch at 12:12 a.m. EST and received at 1:15 a.m. CST, October 11, Rostow informed the President: "A military coup has taken place against President Arias after 11 days in office. The National Guard is evidently following orders from General Vallarino who went through the motion of resigning as Guard Chief earlier yesterday, along with other disgruntled officers." The telegram continued, "troops control the Presidential Palace but Arias had escaped to the Canal Zone and has requested asylum." The telegram concluded that while Arias' large popular following could be expected to resist, the coup had some civilian support and was "well organized and planned." (Ibid.)

---

450. Telegram From the President's Special Assistant (Rostow) to President Johnson in Texas[1]

Washington, October 12, 1968, 2103Z.

CAP 82561. Herewith the line Secretary Rusk is taking on Panama. State 254600 to Panama.

---

[1] Source: Johnson Library, National Security File, Memos to the President, Walt W. Rostow, Vol. 99, October 10–15, 1968. Secret.

1. At present seems to us we have three immediate objectives:

(A) Prevent civil strife and bloodshed;

(B) Seek some solution to political crisis that will preserve as much constitutionality as possible; and

(C) Avoid to the extent we can having US be target enmity of significant elements of Panamanian nation.

What happens in Panama on heels of Peru will also be relevant in terms encouraging or discouraging similar acts other countries.

2. We believe following is appropriate scenario for immediate future:

(A) We should not facilitate any attempts by Arias overturn junta by violence. All your reports thus far and intelligence assessment here indicate he cannot now be successful and any effort would only lead to bloodshed without satisfactory solution. It may in fact be necessary at some future point to actively discourage Arias from all political activity, and we may have to return to our original posture of asking him again to refrain from political activity while in the zone.

(B) We believe that we should now approach junta and guardia through appropriate informal channels and tell them compromise with Arias coalition and utilization some formula of constitutional government is critical to nature of our future relationships, and that US attitude toward new governments will be guided thereby. We understand this may eventually mean giving up on Arias, but critical now to see if his government can be utilized to form new civilian or part-civilian government. For example, we note CIA sitrep here indicates coup leaders have asked First VP Arango to assume presidency but he has thus far refused.

(C) Per telcon,[2] approach to Aleman will be made along following lines.

"You know that a complete break with constitutional government is much more difficult for other countries to deal with than is some variation on the original constitutional arrangement. First preference would be to see if something can't be worked out for Arias to return. If this proves impossible, how about a government headed by Arango? The worst situation would be for a military junta to set itself up completely apart from the constitution."

(D) In addition you are now authorized have Seddon make similar discreet and quiet approach to Guardia officers making same points and pointing out in appropriate tone how difficult it will be for us to continue be of assistance to Guardia in long-run future.

---

[2] Not further identified.

(E) All such approaches are, of course, to be quiet, unofficial and undertaken with utmost discretion.[3]

Rusk

---

[3] On October 12 the IRG Group discussed appropriate U.S. action in response to the coup in Panama. In reporting results of this meeting to Adair, Oliver noted: "key question is as to manageable and desirable extent to which U.S. should seek to influence formation of new 'respectable' government by Junta." (Telegram 254640 to Panama, October 13; National Archives and Records Administration, RG 59, Central Files 1967–69, POL 2 PAN) A report on these discussions is in the minutes to the IRG meeting, held 8:40–10:40 p.m. October 13. (National Archives and Records Administration, RG 59, ARA/IG Files: Lot 70 D 122, 5451, IRG/ARA Minutes)

---

451.   Information Memorandum From the President's Special Assistant (Rostow) to President Johnson[1]

Washington, October 14, 1968, 5:30 p.m.

SUBJECT

   Panama Coup

I am attaching the latest situation report on Panama, drafted by Covey Oliver's inter-agency working group. Its tenor is encouraging.[2]

   Avoidance of major bloodshed or violence which could threaten the canal has been the top priority governing US actions toward President Arias. We have denied him access to radio facilities in the Zone with which he might have fomented mob action against the Junta, and have, of course, refused to help him militarily. Time is now rapidly running out for him.

   Although we have no formal relations with the Junta, key US moves in the last 36 hours have included:

—discreet efforts to persuade the Junta to take Arias back peacefully, or to install the Vice President in his place. (Unsuccessful.)

—stressing the importance of a civilian character for the government—and promptly calling new elections. (Junta agrees.)

---

[1] Source: Johnson Library, National Security File, Country File, Panama, Vol. X (Part 3 of 3), May–December 1968. Confidential. A separate copy of this memorandum indicates that it was drafted by Samuel W. Lewis. A note on the memorandum indicates the President saw it.

[2] Dated October 14; attached but not printed.

—allowing Arias to remain in the Zone, but insisting that he stop his political operations so long as he stays there. (Political activity apparently reduced or suspended since the warning was given last night.)

—trying to engage the OAS with some mediation role (Galo Plaza won't call the OAS Council into action unless any violence erupts; however, informal OAS consultation is now going on among eight key country representatives).

—avoiding making public statements on the bankruptcy of Arias's situation as long as possible so as not to increase the possibility of his attempting to turn his followers' ire against the US. (Pressure from the US press now is enormous, however—and distorted news stories are appearing widely here. State will provide a full background briefing tomorrow.)[3]

Multilateral consultations about recognition of the Junta will begin tomorrow—after it is obvious to all that Arias's bid for forceful return has failed, and that the Junta's provisional government is indisputably in control.

Walt

---

[3] The press background briefing has not been found.

---

452. **Information Memorandum From the President's Special Assistant (Rostow) to President Johnson**[1]

Washington, October 21, 1968.

SUBJECT

Panama

Two issues will very soon require your decision:

1. What to do about President Arias, still a refugee in the Canal Zone.

2. Recognition of the new provisional government.

---

[1] Source: Johnson Library, National Security File, Country File, Panama, Vol. X (Part 3 of 3), May–December 1968. Secret. A note on the memorandum indicates the President saw it. Another copy of this memorandum records Lewis as the drafter. (Ibid., Memos to the President, Walt W. Rostow, Vol. 100, October 16–22, 1968)

Arias' Future

Ten days after taking refuge in the Zone, Arias still refuses to leave the Zone voluntarily, either to seek asylum in other countries (several have offered it) or in the US. The OAS refuses to become involved. Bob Anderson is trying today to persuade him to come to the US. There is some chance he may succeed.[2]

We have progressively tightened control on his visitors and communications. Yet despite his repeated assurances of "good behavior" to Governor Leber, he continues political activity which threatens to incite violence. Recent examples include:

—telegrams to you, other American Presidents, the UN, and the OAS Council; (Tab A)[3]
—a press conference Saturday by his principal advisor;
—supply of money and encouragement to supporters in Panama;
—calls via clandestine media for violent resistance to the Guard.

Initially stunned and disorganized by the National Guard's coup, Arias' supporters are regrouping. A general strike today is eighty percent effective in Panama City; some skirmishes with the Guard have occurred; tension is rising, and a spark could ignite serious bloodshed. Arias now has no chance to return to office except through violence. Should it erupt while he is in the Zone, the National Guard will blame the US and might well stand aside from protecting US installations.

According to Governor Leber, Ambassador Adair and General Porter at CINCSOUTH, Arias' presence in the Zone can be tolerated only 2 or 3 more days at most.[4] If persuasion fails, forcible expulsion would raise the spectre of a western hemisphere "Dubcek case." Army and State are working on "scenarios" in which we would expel him using plausible legal procedures to minimize the "kidnapping" appearance. Nonetheless, involuntary removal would undoubtedly be widely condemned, no matter how justified.

---

[2] Rostow reported that evening that Arias "will leave voluntarily for the U.S. tonight by U.S. military aircraft." He added: "Bob Anderson's telephone call apparently did the trick." (Memorandum from Rostow to President Johnson, October 21, 8:10 p.m.; ibid.)

[3] Attached but not printed.

[4] In a meeting between U.S. military authorities in the Canal Zone and General Torrijos on October 19, Torrijos pressed for "help of U.S. military and other U.S. Government agencies" to "get Arias out of Canal Zone promptly." Torrijos argued that Arias' presence in the Canal Zone was a "threat to political stability in Panama," a threat to regularizing commerce and the Panamanian economy, a threat to U.S.-Panamanian relations, and a threat to Junta plans for returning the government to civilian constitutional control. ([*text not declassified*]; Central Intelligence Agency, Directorate of Operations, [*file name not declassified*])

Recognition

Several factors bear on the timing of diplomatic recognition:

—no other governments have yet recognized and they are moving slowly so long as Arias is in the Canal Zone.[5]

—rapid recognition by the US will imply to many Latins US support for the military coup and probable connivance.

—prompt recognition would reassure the new government that we are not favoring Arias and would calm their nerves (they are getting extremely nervous and unpredictable).

—early recognition might make expulsion of Arias easier to justify, since he would no longer be a President still technically in his own country.

In light of the conflicting arguments, Secretary Rusk has not yet decided to recommend early resumption of relations.[6]

Walt

---

[5] In an October 19 memorandum to Rusk, Oliver noted: "I have managed fairly wide communication through the Latin Americans of the dilemma, and I am now beginning to get some promise of results as to resumption of relations by Latin American countries. I should like to see Japan, the U.K., and the EEC countries act fairly soon." (National Archives and Records Administration, RG 59, Central Files 1967–69, POL PAN–US)

[6] At the Tuesday luncheon meeting on October 22, Rusk reported: "Arias left the Canal Zone. We can now hold up on recognition of the government." Later in the meeting, President Johnson responded: "Okay on that, holding off for a while." (Notes on President's Tuesday Luncheon, October 22; Johnson Library, Tom Johnson Meeting Notes)

---

453.   Memorandum From Samuel W. Lewis of the National Security Council Staff to the President's Special Assistant (Rostow)[1]

Washington, October 29, 1968.

Walt—

Tom Mann talked with Bill Bowdler yesterday about Arias. At Arias' request, Mann spent an hour with him on Sunday morning. Mann's record of the meeting is attached.[2]

---

[1] Source: Johnson Library, National Security File, Country File, Panama, Vol. X (part 3 of 3), May–December 1968. Confidential; Limdis.

[2] Attached was an October 28 memorandum prepared by Mann of his meeting with Arias on October 26.

Mann feels that we should do our best to continue being nice to Arias, to the extent possible, because he and his followers will continue to be important in Panamanian politics. Mann thinks we will have to retain Arias' goodwill if we are ever to get a canal treaty which can be ratified by Panama.

So far, no US officials except Bob Anderson have talked with Arias, although Covey Oliver has been prepared to see him if he asked. Mann is suggesting some kind of "hand-holding" by State may be in order. I've discussed this with Oliver's Deputy, Pete Vaky, in Oliver's absence, and they are thinking it over. There are obvious risks because of Arias' unpredictability and the way in which he may distort any such contacts.

Incidentally, an FBI report suggests Arias is attempting to arrange for air and sea transportation back to Panama.

Sam

454.   Special National Intelligence Estimate[1]

SNIE 84–1–68   Washington, November 1, 1968.

THE SITUATION IN PANAMA

The Problem

To assess the character and the short-term prospects of the military regime.

Conclusions

A. Military rule of Panama is likely to continue for some time, perhaps a year. The provisional government, headed by two former colonels, is mainly a front for the leaders of the coup, who are now in

---

[1] Source: Central Intelligence Agency, Job 79–R01012A, O/DDI Registry. Secret; Controlled Dissem. According to a note on the cover sheet the Central Intelligence Agency and the Departments of State and Defense and the NSA participated in the preparation of the estimate, which was submitted by the Director of Central Intelligence and concurred in by all members of the United States Intelligence Board except for the AEC and FBI representatives who abstained because the subject was outside their jurisdiction.

command of the Guardia Nacional.[2] But the situation is fluid, and relationships among the new leaders of the Guardia and between the Guardia and the provisional government are subject to a variety of strains.

B. The Guardia staged the coup of 11 October in order to protect its own position rather than to carry out any specific program for Panama. The new regime has pledged a return to constitutional government via elections, but has not specified any time-table and the procedures it has outlined could cause a considerable delay.

C. It is unlikely that any effective opposition to the new regime will develop over the short term from supporters of Arnulfo Arias, extreme leftists, or the oligarchy. We expect the regime and most of the oligarchs to adjust gradually to each other.

D. Although it is eager to secure recognition by the US, we doubt that the regime would be very responsive to pressure from the US, particularly with respect to a time-table for elections. A prolonged delay in recognition would bruise the feelings of the leaders of the new regime, but they would not be likely, in any case, to encourage blatant anti-Americanism.

E. We doubt that the military regime will act upon the draft Canal treaties which were widely criticized in Panama. The regime, however, might move to open discussions looking toward revised agreements which would be signed and ratified only after constitutional government had been restored.

[Omitted here is the 12-page Discussion section of the estimate.]

---

[2] In a November 1 memorandum to Rostow, Lewis reported that "CIA confirms that there is no communist influence visible in the Panamanian Junta or Provisional Government." Concerns about Colonel Omar Torrijos, one of the principals in the coup, were primarily about his brother, but "Torrijos himself, however, has shown no sympathy for the Party in the past." Lewis added: "All indications are that the problem with the Panamanian Junta is that it may succumb to the temptation to impose rightist authoritarian solutions, not that it is under leftist influence." (Johnson Library, National Security File, Country File, Panama, Vol. X (part 1 of 3), May–December 1968)

455.   Action Memorandum From the President's Special Assistant
       (Rostow) to President Johnson[1]

Washington, November 9, 1968.

SUBJECT

Panama

State is very anxious to obtain your approval to resume diplomatic
relations with Panama on Monday, November 11. (Tab A)[2]

By delaying until now, we have obtained important concessions
from the Provisional Government.

—restoration of some of the constitutional guarantees which had
been suspended by the junta;
—dismissal of two pro-Communist newspaper editors who had
received their jobs as a favor to the brother of a key member of the military junta;
—formal public commitment to hold new elections, restore all constitutional guarantees, and return government to full civilian control—
within a reasonable period of time;
—relaxation of press censorship, and reopening of opposition
newspapers.

Further delay, however, will probably be self-defeating.

We have FBI and CIA reports showing that Arias is planning to
try to regain power by violent means.[3] He is trying to arrange to re-
enter Panama clandestinely and is encouraging supporters in Costa
Rica to initiate guerrilla warfare from across the border. Failure by the
U.S. to recognize is encouraging these efforts.

Ambassador Adair believes that we should resume relations on
Monday, November 11, so that our announcement will follow closely
the action yesterday restoring some of the constitutional guarantees.
State's proposed press release highlights our concern for continued
movement toward full restoration. (Tab B)[4]

-----

[1] Source: Johnson Library, National Security File, Country File, Panama, Vol. X (part
3 of 3), May–December 1968. Secret.

[2] Tab A, attached but not printed, is a November 1 memorandum from Rusk to the
President requesting authorization for resumption of diplomatic relations with the new
Government of Panama.

[3] Information from the FBI report on Arias' plans is in a November 11 memoran-
dum from Vaky to Rusk's Special Assistant, Harry Shlaudeman. (National Archives and
Records Administration, ARA Files: Lot 72 D 33, Entry 5396, Panama) Information from
the CIA report is in an Agency memorandum of November 21 entitled "Activities of
Arias Supporters in Costa Rica." (Johnson Library, National Security File, Country File,
Panama, Vol. X (part 3 of 3), May–December 1968)

[4] Attached draft dated November 9; see footnote 5 below.

Eighteen countries have now recognized. The thirteen in Latin America include all the major nations of the hemisphere except Canada and the United States.

CIA has looked carefully at Arias' public charges that the military junta is Communist-dominated. All available evidence shows that leftist influence is slight—less than was present in Arias' own government.

I recommend that you authorize resumption of diplomatic relations with Panama on Monday, November 11.

Walt

Approve recognition[5]

Disapprove

Call me

Approve press statement

Disapprove

Call me

---

[5] This option is checked and two handwritten notes on the memorandum, both dated November 12, indicate the President's approval and Rostow's notification of Reed, Lewis and Bunker. The Department requested the Embassy in Panama to inform the Panamanian Government of this decision in telegram 270098 to Panama, November 12. (National Archives and Records Administration, RG 59, Central Files 1964–66, POL PAN–US) On November 13 the Embassy in Panama City advised the Panamanian Foreign Ministry of the resumption of relations. The Department statement released that day is in Department of State *Bulletin,* December 2, 1968, p. 573.

---

456.   Telegram From the Department of State to the Embassy in Panama[1]

Washington, December 6, 1968, 9:41 p.m.

283324. For Ambassador. Subject: Arias' Plan for Reestablishment of Democracy in Panama: Arias–Oliver Conversation.

---

[1] Source: National Archives and Records Administration, RG 59, Central Files 1967–69, POL 15 PAN. Secret. Drafted and approved by Oliver. Also sent to San José and USUN for Anderson.

1. Arias and Oliver met alone, December 6, at Department. Conversation was based on Arias' Nov 19 letter to President.[2] Arias agreed that conversation was to be held under "strict rules of confidential state security", as his letter to President had suggested. Oliver said he was going to listen, as President would have, pointing to a wall photo of President listening to Oliver.

2. Conversation was cordial. Oliver found Arias in good control of himself and seemingly objective about his problems. At four points in conversation, Oliver was able to warn and advise against adventurism on Costa Rican-Panamanian frontier,[3] thanks to way in which conversation was steered. Arias agreed throughout that he did not want bloodshed and that he sought ways of keeping groups on frontier from engaging in use of force.

3. In letter to President Johnson, Arias had said he wished to present a "simple pragmatic plan" to restore Constitutional Government. In conversation with Oliver, Arias outlined plan as follows:

(a) USG to continue policy of keeping all types of assistance relations with present Junta at minimum and seek all opportunities to indicate moral displeasure and concern at continuation military regime in Panama.

(b) Arias to continue and intensify his efforts to work out a united front of civilian politicians. Front would include all elements of Panamanian traditional politics that could be brought together, including Samudio and practically everybody else, except Eletas, who are only civilians playing ball with Junta. (Arias insisted that Junta had shown disrespect and distaste for all civilian politicians except Eletas and a few of their hangers-on.) Arias intimated that he might be willing to deal with other civilian politicians on question of who would lead in first reinstallation civilian government.

(c) Build up of pressures under lines of action (a) and (b) should be directed toward displacement top command of present Junta and its replacement by wiser and more moderate National Guard leaders. After this transitional change in Junta had been made, in due course

---

[2] Not printed. (Johnson Library, National Security File, Special Heads of State Correspondence, Panama, Presidential Correspondence) In informing the President of the Arias letter on November 23, Lewis indicated that Arias had said that "such a meeting could head off unspecified dangerous problems in Panama." Lewis also reported that although the Department did not recommend that the President meet with Arias, Lewis thought that he should be seen by "a responsible U.S. Government official" and suggested Covey Oliver. (Memorandum from Lewis to Johnson, November 23; ibid.)

[3] In a December 3 memorandum to the President, Rostow reported that, "ex-President Arias' followers have started some guerrilla efforts along the Costa Rican frontier. Only one encounter with the Panamanian National Guard has been confirmed, but the prospect is for continuing skirmishes." (Ibid., Country File, Panama, Vol. X (part 1 of 3), May–December 1968)

Panama could go back to some form of civilian government, either on basis of past election, de facto shift from military to civilian Junta, or some new electoral basis. Arias insisted present Junta leaders would not permit this evolution to take place; hence they have to be displaced;

(d) To make (a) effective, according to Arias, Seddon and Angueiras should be replaced on U.S. MilMission by new men, loyal to prospect of shift back to civilian rule. These men must be very able and astute. Arias explained that regardless of their personal attitudes and viewpoints, Seddon and Angueiras are popularly thought to be in cahoots with present Junta leaders. Their replacement now would be signal to people that USG not in fact overly friendly to Junta.

(e) Probably best man to replace top of present Junta under (c) would be Col. Abel Quintero, presently on duty at Inter-American Defense Board here. Arias seemed to dismiss Vallarino and Urrutia.

4. In conversation Arias complained mildly at outset about attitude U.S. Embassy in San Jose as being opposed to needs of Panamanian refugees in Costa Rica. This led to first of several Oliver tacks on dangers of border adventurism. In synthesis Arias came to these positions:

(a) He is opposed to violence and does not want to see operations from Costa Rica;

(b) He recognizes that violence may bring other leaders to top, using his name, and that present Junta might be strengthened by a frontier challenge;

(c) He cannot be sure he can control the frontier groups unless he has something to give them in the way of hope, such as by evolution of proposal in para 3. (At this point Oliver made it clear that he did not think Arias ought to try to "bargain" his dissuasion of frontier elements against USG "acceptance" of Arias Plan. Arias then recast his position, saying that main thing was to see what could be done to take care of refugees who could not safely return to Panama. Arias insisted there were far more unarmed and homeless refugees than potential guerrilla fighters along Costa Rican border and expressed belief that proper refugee care would reduce danger armed conflict.)

5. Arias tried throughout to establish environment for further discussions on basis "Arias Plan". Oliver made no such commitments but said he would transmit Arias' views.

6. Department will now begin study of situation and shortly will instruct as to further passing of this information and as to possible lines of action. Meanwhile Amb's comments on basis this report are invited.[4]

Rusk

---

[4] During a December 10 meeting Anderson "strongly advised Arias to withdraw from public view, stay out of Panamanian affairs, go where he can be comfortable and unnoticed, and sit and wait." Arias "expressed warm appreciation for this advice and assured Anderson that he will follow it." (Telegram 285234 to Panama City, December 11; National Archives and Records Administration, RG 59, Central Files 1967–69, POL 15 PAN)

---

457.   Memorandum for the File[1]

Washington, December 9, 1968.

SUBJECT

    Panama

Walt Rostow told me today that the President does not want to "provide any military assistance" to the Panamanian junta during the remainder of his Administration, unless it were a case involving vital US national security. Rostow agreed that such a situation does not currently exist.[2]

Rostow authorized me to talk discreetly with Covey Oliver, without putting anything on paper, to see that all decisions on MAP or public safety assistance are stalled through January 20. Rostow indicated the President's concern covered even innocuous MAP assistance items such as spare parts, tools, field canteens, etc. on a straight sales basis.

---

[1] Source: Johnson Library, National Security File, Country File, Panama, Vol. X (part 1 of 3), May–December 1968. Secret. Prepared by Lewis of the NSC staff.

[2] On December 3 Rostow informed the President that the National Guard Commander had asked to purchase from U.S. Army stocks, $20,000 worth of field equipment and combat rations for counter-insurgency operations. Adair recommended approving the sale, which did not include weapons or ammunition. The Department authorized Defense to make the sale, but Rostow noted that Arias and his followers would create adverse publicity if they learned of the transaction. The President wrote on the memorandum: "I question this, call me. L." (Ibid.) On December 5 a representative of the Junta approached U.S. officials requesting military assistance, particularly two helicopters, "for use by the National Guard to contain insurgency in Panama." (Undated CIA report under cover of a memorandum from William V. Broe to Assistant Secretary of Defense Lang, December 9; National Archives and Records Administration, RG 59, ARA Files: Lot 72 D 33, Entry 5396, Panama)

If State insists on the necessity for some sort of military aid, whether it involves hardware or training, the issue should be presented to the President by Secretary Rusk for decision.

I discussed this matter orally with Ben Read (S/S), Art Hartman (U), and Pete Vaky (ARA) in Covey Oliver's absence, making the President's wishes clear to each of them. They all affirmed that no *affirmative* decisions would be made on any MAP or Public Safety items without prior consideration by the President.

Samuel W. Lewis

---

458.   Action Memorandum From the President's Special Assistant (Rostow) to President Johnson[1]

Washington, December 30, 1968, 6:30 p.m.

SUBJECT

Military Assistance for the Panamanian National Guard

Since the Panamanian coup in October all U.S. assistance to Panama's National Guard has been suspended. Secretaries Rusk and Clifford have now concluded we should resume assistance on a very limited scale in order to safeguard our working relationship with the Guard necessary for security of the Canal Zone. Rusk states:

—We have turned down Guard requests for training, repair and maintenance services, and routine "soft goods" items. Guard officers are already showing some resentment against the U.S.

—We may have to ask for the Guard's help during January, should anti-U.S. agitation occur as in past years on the anniversary of the 1964 student invasion of the Zone.

—The Panamanian Government has been taking steps toward the restoration of constitutional government; new elections are publicly planned for early 1970; Panama also is seeking our advice on badly needed reforms in public administration and education.

—We cannot indefinitely suspend assistance to the Guard and continue to count on Guard assistance in protecting the Zone.

---

[1] Source: Johnson Library, National Security File, Country File, Panama, Filed by LBJ Library. Secret. A handwritten note on the memorandum reads: "Jones told Walt."

Rusk believes that some renewed training plus about $15,000 worth of spare parts, shop and maintenance equipment, and automobile tools—all previously programmed—will safeguard our relationship with the Guard for the time being. Deliveries of arms, tear gas, ammunition, or heavy equipment would remain suspended—along with training for combat operations. Adverse publicity should be minimal.

The Canal Zone Governor, the Joint Chiefs of Staff, and Secretary Clifford all concur in Rusk's recommendation.

Former President Arias' efforts to stir up guerilla operations against Panama show no real results to date.

I believe you should approve resumption of very limited military assistance to Panama, as detailed in Rusk's memorandum.

Attached is the memorandum from Secretary Rusk.[2]

Walt

Approve[3]

Disapprove

Call me

---

[2] Dated December 26; attached but not printed.
[3] This option is checked.

Paraguay and Uruguay

459. Telegram From the Department of State to the Embassy in Uruguay[1]

Washington, June 12, 1964, 12:47 p.m.

480. From Mann. We note that Embtel 829[2] reports your belief that if a golpe was in fact seriously contemplated it has been frustrated or effectively deferred and we approve of your decision to have Embassy officers quietly pass word around that United States is opposed to the violent overthrow of constitutional government. Hoyt will carry message from me to Yriart to same effect.

It seems to us here the real course of rumors about golpes stems from basic dissatisfaction on the part of the Uruguayan people with inept way in which Uruguayan government has managed its affairs. Even before we received your telegram we had commenced study of suggestions United States might make to Uruguay re their unsatisfactory economic situation, but we wonder whether political reform is not also an essential ingredient of political stability.

Do you agree that there is need for single executive and if so what are Colorado and Blanco groups prepared to do so that country can move in an orderly fashion in this direction? What other political reforms should be taken by the Uruguayans while there is perhaps still time?

I recall that in case of Cuba posture of U.S. Government was one of unqualified opposition to dictatorship even to the point of denying Batista arms. Cuba enjoyed a privileged position in trade. Communist takeover nevertheless followed due, in my opinion, partly to disenchantment of Cuban people with a series of inefficient, ineffective and corrupt governments which had failed to fairly distribute wealth and were oblivious to needs of poor.

Maybe the best service we can make towards preservation of democracy in Uruguay is to make it work. How can we do this?

Rusk

---

[1] Source: National Archives and Records Administration, RG 59, Central Files 1964–66, POL 23–9 UR. Confidential. Drafted and approved by Mann. Mann briefed President Johnson on the situation in Uruguay, June 11; see Document 16.

[2] In telegram 829 from Montevideo, June 11, the Embassy provided details of an "alleged golpe." (National Archives and Records Administration, RG 59, Central Files 1964–66, POL 23–9 UR)

460. Letter From the Assistant Secretary of State for Inter-American Affairs (Mann) to the Ambassador to Uruguay (Coerr)[1]

Washington, June 23, 1964.

Dear Wym:

As you will have gathered from our telegram 480 of June 12,[2] I am concerned by the present lack of leadership and drift in Uruguay. All of the danger flags seem to me to be flying high and I wonder whether there is anything that we can do to help the Uruguayans get things back on the track before we are faced with the prospect of a coup. I take it we still have some time.

Specifically, I have been wondering whether it would be productive or counter-productive for you, quietly and on a personal rather than an official basis, to plant the idea with your close personal friends that maybe the democratic elements in Uruguay might like, on their own initiative, to begin thinking in terms of amending the constitution so as to do away with the plural executive and restore the single executive. I understand from Hank [*Hoyt*] that one way to do this would be to obtain a two-thirds majority in both houses of congress, followed by a majority plebiscite vote in favor, as was done in 1951.

This is, of course, all very delicate and your judgment will be better than mine. It depends to a large extent on your judgment as to whether we would stir up any hornets nests by making such a suggestion, that is to say, whether any great body of opinion in Uruguay is still wedded to the side of a plural executive and whether out of such discussions this could emerge as a Uruguayan rather than U.S. idea. All of this is, of course, none of our business, but it does seem to me that it is difficult to think in terms of meaningful reforms and dynamic leadership which will be needed to get things going again in Uruguay unless it is constitutionally possible to have leadership. This would be only a first step to be sure, but it might be an indispensable step to make democracy work in Uruguay.

This was really the question behind my telegram 480. I don't know whether the idea is any good at all but would appreciate having your views on this or any other thing we can do to help. If you think it would be wise, given the propensity for all Embassy messages to leak through the Foreign Office in Montevideo, for me to talk with Juan

---

[1] Source: National Archives and Records Administration, RG 59, ARA/APU/U Files: Lot 67 D 468, Letters (Official–Informal) from and to Embassy Montevideo. Secret; Official–Informal. Drafted by Mann.

[2] Document 459.

Yriart, I could undertake to do so. Another problem is that I don't know whether Yriart has any political influence in Uruguay.

Hank reminds me that we have four congressional leaders who are coming up to look at our electoral processes in the fall. I don't know whether it would be wise for me to ask questions, for example, of a group of this kind who are relative strangers. In any case, I would not wish to do anything without your concurrence.

Meanwhile, we are going to do everything we can to keep the dike of democracy up in Uruguay. But if the general situation continues to deteriorate, I suspect we will find ourselves in the same position as the little Dutch boy who was looking at more holes than he had fingers.

With best wishes,

Sincerely,

Thomas C. Mann[3]

---

[3] Printed from a copy that bears this typed signature.

---

461. Telegram From the Embassy in Uruguay to the Department of State[1]

Montevideo, July 8, 1964, 6 p.m.

21. For Mann. Deptel 480.[2] I heartily agree that last month's golpe scare stemmed chiefly from dissatisfaction with GOU's inability act constructively on increasingly obvious economic problems, and that we must continue our intense and difficult efforts to help Uruguayan democracy to work in order our basic objective of maintaining Uruguayan independence. I also agree that Uruguay's greatest weakness is political. We therefore tend naturally to think of political reform and specifically of the possible advantages, from viewpoint of USG objectives, of having Uruguayan reform their constitution to replace present collegiate executive with single executive. Our analysis must consider (1) constitutional basis of reform, (2) its political chances, (3) its theoretical comparative advantages, (4) its practical comparative advantages, (5) conclusion, (6) recommended U.S. action.

---

[1] Source: National Archives and Records Administration, RG 59, Central Files 1964–66, POL 15 UR. Confidential.

[2] Document 459.

(1) Uruguayan constitution, section XIX chapter III, provides for amendment on initiative (a) of 10 percent of citizens inscribed in National Civic Register, (b) by proposal approved by two-fifths full membership General Assembly; either (a) or (b) then requiring approval by "absolute majority of citizens participating next national elections" and "this majority must represent at least 35 percent of all persons inscribed in National Civic Register", (c) approval of proposed amendment by absolute majority general assembly, subsequent approval by national constituent constitution called for purpose, and approved by electoral majority as above in special election.

(2) (A) Given comparative strength of Blanco and Colorado parties in relation to each other, and their internal fractionalization, it is very unlikely that either party could put through constitutional amendment against opposition of the other.

(B) Substantial elements of Blancos and Colorado would have to combine to achieve constitutional amendment, but this unlikely. At present Blancos expect to lose and Colorados to win 1966 elections. Blancos would expect to have greater power in collegiate than single executive system and in past have favored collegiate executive when they expected to lose. Although many Blancos now favor single executive in principle it appears at present they would refuse cooperation in seeking constitutional reform. Colorados traditionally have favored collegiate system and at present appear reluctant move toward single executive because they fear such move would increase their internal divisions. Probable Blanco opposition and Colorado reluctance gives reform little political chance.

(3) (A) Theoretical comparative advantages of collegiate versus single executive from U.S. viewpoint difficult to estimate. Weakness of collegiate system in which majority party is now fractionalized and lacks leadership are obvious. Question is whether single executive under conditions we assume will prevail after next general elections would be more advantageous to U.S. First and basic of these conditions would be continuation of law of "lemas." This system permits many different factions within each of two major parties participate in national elections and gives these elections character of simultaneous primaries and general elections. Within each party this system has effect of institutionalizing political cohabitation without agreement and gains electoral cooperation without promoting subsequent unity. (See A–356, December 14, 1963.)[3] Post-election fractionalization in both parties is reflected not only in NCG but parliament.

---

[3] In airgram A–356 from Montevideo, the Embassy analyzed the "Political Structure of Uruguay's Traditional Parties." (National Archives and Records Administration, RG 59, Central Files 1964–66, POL 12 UR)

(B) Law of "lemas" is Uruguayan device (a) to preserve two major parties against otherwise probable danger they would split formally into multiplicity of minor parties as in other parliamentary systems, and (b) to avert civil strife between two major parties. It has served at least these two purposes with moderate success for many years. However, presumably it will also continue to facilitate fractionalization within parties regardless of whether executive is collegiate or single. Theoretically, single executive might be able to supply more leadership than collegiate, but on other hand it could also stimulate more opposition. Collegiate system worked with comparative efficiency when majority united under party boss in 1954–1958. (This boss was Luis Batlle whose policies left much to be desired from U.S. viewpoint.) Theoretical advantages and disadvantages about even or possibly shaded on side of single executive.

(4) So our immediate practical question must be to estimate nature of likely winner should there be single executive in 1966. Blancos at present appear unlikely to win. Among Colorados, most likely candidates would be:

Luis Batlle (age 67), long-time leader of list 15; General Oscar Gestido (age 62), present member NCG and acknowledged leader list 14; Zelmar Michelini (age 40) leader list 99. Among these three, Batlle and Gestido almost hopeless beyond repair as economic thinkers. Michelini intellectually able to think in economic terms, and politically promising, but reliability from U.S. point of view untried, and his competence as political boss dubious. Doubtful that present selection of candidates would produce single executive through whom we could pursue U.S. objectives as effectively as through collegiate system. Comparative practical advantage lies with collegiate system.

(5) Since theoretical comparative advantage of single executive at present appears slight and unsure, and immediate practical comparative advantage lies with continuative collegiate system, we do not recommend USG attempt work in favor of constitutional reform.

(6) (A) One set of conditions could change above estimate and recommendation. Although highly improbable, it is conceivable that the growing economic and political pressures may lead major factions within both Colorados and Blancos to agree on constitutional reform in 1966 elections. Should we see this process developing well among both parties we might discreetly attempt to help it along. However, for us to speak in favor of constitutional reform before such development would probably incur the heavy liabilities of U.S. involvement in a prime domestic political dispute and would be counterproductive in that it would enable the opponents of constitutional reform to attack it as U.S.-inspired.

(B) Under these conditions our basic courses of action must be to continue attempt identify and strengthen economically and politically constructive elements in Uruguay along lines LAPC. We are submitting specific course of action with revised LAPC, airpouching 10th.[4]

Coerr

---

[4] The Embassy forwarded its proposed revisions to the LAPC paper in airgram A–14 from Montevideo, July 12. (Ibid., POL 1 UR–US)

---

462.   Memorandum From Robert M. Sayre of the National Security Council Staff to the President's Special Assistant for National Security Affairs (Bundy)[1]

Washington, August 7, 1964.

The LAPC discussed Paraguay on August 6.[2]

Ambassador Snow reported a noticeable political liberalization in Paraguay. Public criticism of the regime is permitted in the press and otherwise, but it is cautious and not extensive. The general public is reasonably content with the political situation, and there is no serious agitation against Stroessner. Ambassador Snow said he had devoted considerable effort to determining the number of political prisoners, and found them highly exaggerated. He has concluded that there are no more than a dozen, give or take a few. He considers figures alleging that there are thousands of political exiles as fiction. He would put the figure at 600–700 at most, and of these he has been told by the Paraguayan Foreign Minister,[3] that all but about 25 would be permitted to return to Paraguay unmolested. He reports police brutality as minimal, probably no more than in Mexico, or other Latin American countries in which he has served. He is concentrating his efforts on emphasizing respect for human rights, etc. None of this changes the fact that Stroessner is a dictator of the Odria or Somoza type. He is definitely not of the Trujillo, or Duvalier stripe, however.

There was general agreement on the line that we should treat the Paraguayan Government and its officials with respect, but that we should carefully avoid becoming identified with Stroessner, or lay our-

---

[1] Source: Johnson Library, National Security File, Country File, Paraguay, Vol. I, 1/64–8/68. Confidential.

[2] The minutes of the meeting have not been found.

[3] Raúl Sapena Pastor.

selves open to the assertion that we "support" the Stroessner Government. Our line should be to the Government, and to opposition leaders, that our interests is in working with the Paraguayan people, and helping to improve their well-being.

On the economic side, Paraguay is doing reasonably well, and the economic situation is improving. We have a modest technical assistance program. We have made one small loan. The discussion was about expanding it. There was general agreement that we had an obligation to improve the Asuncion airport. An American firm did the engineering, the Eximbank loaned the money to build it, and an American firm did the construction. The airport is breaking up because of poor drainage. There was also general agreement that we might consider one or two other projects.

As a side light, Mr. Mann reported on his conversations with Senators Morse and Gruening on Haiti. He said he had laid out the possibility to them of being pushed out of Haiti by Duvalier unless we were a little more forthcoming. He inquired as to their attitude on approval of investment guarantees. Senator Morse thought we should go further and approve project loans. Senator Gruening agreed on investment guarantees, but asked that we keep it quiet. In sum, up against the hard realities, they come out about where we do.

As a result of the LAPC discussion, Ambassador Snow will submit a new paper on Paraguay, which as he put it, would "open the throttle a little" on AID assistance.[4]

RMS

---

[4] Not further identified.

463. Memorandum From the Assistant Secretary of State for Inter-American Affairs (Mann) to Secretary of State Rusk[1]

Washington, December 1, 1964.

SUBJECT

Uruguayan Situation Report

Last June we called Ambassador Coerr on consultation because we were becoming increasingly concerned as to what might be done to make the Uruguayan economy and Uruguayan democracy work. Since then we have become even more concerned because the situation has deteriorated further and there have been for the first time in many years rumors of serious unrest in the Uruguayan military and the possible threat of a military coup. We hear that both Argentina and Brazil are also concerned over the situation in Uruguay and in fact that certain of the Brazilian military might be in favor of a coup should Uruguay fail to restrict the activities of Brazilian exiles (including former President Goulart and his brother-in-law, ex-Governor Brizola) now in Uruguay.

Factors leading to this serious situation are: the growth rate in recent years has been almost zero; the inflation rate has reached between 40 and 50% and the budget deficit is large and growing; Uruguay's foreign exchange position is becoming precarious and wool exporters are pricing themselves out of the market. At the same time the nine-man collegium Executive is having great difficulty in reaching decisions and implementing them and the parties which elected them to power are fragmented and virtually leaderless after the death or absence from the scene of four of the leading politicians. Although the Uruguayan Development Council has come up with an excellent diagnosis of the country's problems and what should be done about them, the government has not as yet taken the corrective action. Both our Ambassador and the Uruguayan Ambassador here believe that the measures necessary to improve the situation can only be taken by the Uruguayans themselves.

As a result of our concern, we telegraphed to Ambassador Coerr on November 25[2] and his reply is contained in Tab A.[3] In effect he confirms the deteriorating situation and points out that there seemed to

---

[1] Source: National Archives and Records Administration, RG 59, Central Files 1964–66, POL 23–9 UR. Secret. Drafted by Hoyt on November 30. A notation on the memorandum indicates that Rusk saw it.

[2] Telegram 278 to Uruguay. (Ibid.)

[3] Telegram 519 from Uruguay, November 29; attached but not printed.

be two alternatives: (1) either a change by a coup or (2) a constitutional change on a basis which would provide an opportunity for the two traditional political parties to work more closely together on the country's problems.

We agree with the Ambassador that a constitutional solution is the one which we should hope for and support. The military who have been mentioned as possible leaders of a coup are not qualified and probably would not have any significant civilian support. They would be opposed strongly by the well-organized Communists and a takeover by incompetent military could degenerate into further chaos and advantages for the Communists. On the other hand, constitutional reform will be slow and the situation may become so bad that those favoring constitutional reforms will not have time to bring them about. The Embassy points out, however, that the increasing political and economic pressures on the government and the increased rumors of a coup are bringing the politicians closer together on the need for constitutional reform, and that a solution along these lines is now more probable than heretofore.

The Embassy estimates that a coup is not imminent despite rumors and increased military preoccupation with the country's problems. The military apparently have decided to meet with the nine-man Executive to impress on that body the need of getting on with the business of government. But, apparently most military do not favor a coup. Unfortunately, we have not seen much to indicate that the government is prepared to take the necessary action and an IMF representative who visited Uruguay last week states that there seems to be no competence nor understanding of economic problems within the upper echelons of government.

A series of strikes, inflation, and the worsening economic situation are increasing disillusionment within all sectors of Uruguay. Despite Uruguay's reputation as a model democracy, and the general antipathy to a coup within the country, a spark from any of these incidents might touch off a wave of more popular support for a coup.

Our Ambassador has recommended that we start to give more attention to the movements for constitutional reform and judiciously support such movements without identifying ourselves with any particular plan. He also has recommended that he take this line with the new Brazilian Ambassador, and we concur, believing this might be the best channel to get word of our views back to the Brazilian Government and help forestall any move which the Brazilian military might be inclined to make towards supporting a Uruguayan military coup.

I wish you to be informed of this situation because while it might drag on for a long while (and the Uruguayans do have remarkable recuperative power), it also might degenerate fast and we might find a coup taking place. A coup in "model" Uruguay would have many repercussions throughout the hemisphere. Our main problem is that we can do little to help the Uruguayans. They are failing to make democracy work and the remedies lie almost exclusively in their own hands.

I attach as Tab B my reply to Embassy Montevideo's telegram no. 519.[4]

---

[4] Telegram 284 to Uruguay, November 30; attached but not printed.

---

464. Special National Intelligence Estimate[1]

SNIE 98–65   Washington, June 17, 1965.

THE SITUATION IN URUGUAY

The Problem

To assess the economic and political situation in Uruguay, the potentialities for extremist subversion, and the involvement of Brazil and Argentina, over the next year or so.

Conclusions

A. There is growing dissatisfaction with Uruguay's present governmental system, particularly with its nine-man executive, the National Council of Government (NCG). This device, designed to prevent one-man or one-party rule, has also prevented effective governmental action to halt a steady economic deterioration marked by growing budgetary deficits, an accelerating inflation, a decline in real wages, and a banking crisis. (Paras. 3–9)

B. Within the period of this estimate, the NCG may be reformed by constitutional amendment, or there may be a credible prospect of the adoption of such an amendment in the general election to be held in November 1966. However, the political and legal obstacles to such

---

[1] Source: Central Intelligence Agency, Job 79–R01012A, O/DDI Registry. Secret; Controlled Dissem. According to a note on the cover sheet this estimate was prepared in the Central Intelligence Agency with the participation of the intelligence organizations of the Departments of State and Defense, the National Security Agency, and the Federal Bureau of Investigation. The United States Intelligence Board concurred in this estimate on June 17.

a reform are great. Moreover, reform of the NCG would not, in itself, end the factionalism which characterizes Uruguayan politics or ensure effective action to cope with the economic situation. (Paras. 17–18)

C. In Uruguay there is already some apprehension of a military coup to alter the political system. We consider it almost certain that no such move is now imminent. If, however, the situation continues to deteriorate without effective remedial action by the NCG or a credible prospect of constitutional amendment, the odds in favor of a coup attempt will mount. If there should be a coup, it would almost certainly be initiated by non-Communists. If initiated by a President who had full military support, the actual takeover would almost certainly be quick and effective. Any other coup attempt would almost certainly encounter both military and popular resistance and might result in prolonged and widespread violence and disorder. (Paras. 19–21)

D. The Communists have no illusion that they could seize power in Uruguay in present circumstances. They are apprehensive of a rightist coup, however, and are preparing to stimulate popular resistance to one. In a confused and disorderly situation, their labor leadership and paramilitary capabilities could be an important factor. It is unlikely that they could gain a dominant influence, but, if they were to make a substantial contribution to the defeat of a coup attempt or to a democratic counter-coup, they would gain respectability and further political opportunities. (Paras. 10–14, 22)

E. Brazil is seriously concerned about the subversive threat which would result if Communists or extreme leftists were to gain power or important influence in Montevideo. Brazil would be reluctant to intervene militarily in Uruguay without US and Argentine concurrence and OAS approval, but would almost certainly do so if convinced that the situation there required it. (Paras. 22–25)

F. If Brazil were to intervene in Uruguay, the Argentine military would wish to intervene also. An incidental consequence might be the overthrow of the constitutional government in Argentina, if it did not sanction Argentine military intervention. If Argentina did intervene, it would almost certainly be in collaboration (rather than conflict) with Brazil. (Paras. 26–28)

[Omitted here is the 10-page Discussion section of the estimate.]

465.   Memorandum of Conversation[1]

Sec/MC/12   Asunción, November 24, 1965, 10:25 a.m.

SUBJECT

   U.S.-Paraguayan Relations and Hemisphere Problems

PARTICIPANTS

U.S.   *Paraguay*
The Secretary   President Stroessner
Ambassador Snow   Foreign Minister Sapena Pastor
                                      Acting Foreign Minister Gonzalez Torres

During the Secretary's visit to Paraguay he was received by President Stroessner at the National Palace. At the beginning there were photographers and reporters in the President's office as well as certain members of his staff, but as soon as the initial amenities had been exchanged, all present departed except the President, Secretary Rusk, the Foreign Minister (Raúl Sapena Pastor), the Acting Foreign Minister (Dionisio Gonzalez Torres) and Ambassador Snow.

Recalling his daughter Graciela's visit to Washington in President Kennedy's time, the President observed that she had told him of meeting the Secretary and of finding him to be a warm, gracious and unpretentious person. The Secretary was most welcome here, the President's only regret being that the visit was of such short duration.

Secretary Rusk said that President Johnson would undoubtedly wish him first of all to convey to President Stroessner his appreciation for the sending of Paraguayan troops to the Dominican Republic. President Stroessner said that the Paraguayan people were true friends of the United States. Paraguay's foreign policy, which had been consistent and unequivocal, was based on the same broad objectives as that of the United States. President Stroessner had from the outset favored the entry of U.S. troops into the Dominican Republic and his intention throughout had been to cooperate with the United States. Referring to Cuba as an example, he said that the Paraguayans realized the need of timely intervention on the part of other free countries against communist takeovers in the hemisphere.

Secretary Rusk said that at times we found it necessary, as in the Dominican case, to act without being able publicly to explain in full the reasons for our action. This was because of the sensitivity of intel-

---

[1] Source: National Archives and Records Administration, RG 59, Central Files 1964–66, POL PAR–US. Secret. Drafted by Snow and approved in S on December 16. Rusk stopped in Paraguay after attending the Second Special Inter-American Conference in Rio de Janeiro November 16–24.

ligence information. The communists, in their insistent campaign to dominate the world, were constantly engaged in subversive plotting. In the Dominican Republic, Vietnam and the Congo they had had concrete plans of that nature.

President Stroessner, with further reference to the troops in the Dominican Republic, reported having received a special message from General Palmer, the American commander, to the effect that the Paraguayan troops were superb and that the President and the Paraguayan nation had every reason to be proud of them. The President said he understood and applauded the U.S. action in Vietnam, which was worthy of a great people like the Americans. Secretary Rusk informed him that since 1945 the U.S. had sustained 160,000 casualties worldwide in the cause of peace and freedom. As for Vietnam, we were faced with two essential alternatives: either we could withdraw and in so doing leave all of Southeast Asia open to conquest by the Red Chinese, or we could stand firm. The President could rest assured that we would stand firm.

The Secretary then commented on the encouraging degree of economic and social developments he understood had occurred in Paraguay and asked the President if he wished to comment on the subject. The President instead spoke for several minutes on political issues including certain leaders in the hemisphere whom he distrusted. The Brazilian general commanding the OAS forces in the DR had sent him word that the situation there was chaotic, that the provisional President was a communist and that the Minister of Justice was likewise. As for Juan Bosch, the President continued, he was a thoroughly contradictory man. Instead of thanking the U.S. and other OAS countries for having sent troops to preserve his country from communism, Bosch was actually advocating the seeking of an indemnity from the United States, Brazil and Paraguay. The President also believed it was a mistake to have caused the removal of General Wessin y Wessin from his command and political position in the DR. Wessin was a staunch anti-communist. It was likewise erroneous, the President continued, to assert as some did that Fidel Castro had "betrayed" the Cuban revolution. Castro had always been a communist and the Cuban revolution was strictly a communist affair from the start. People like Betancourt, who had given much aid and comfort to Castro in the early days, were the kind who now supported Bosch and misrepresented the Cuban revolution. The President also criticized "Pepe" Figueres on similar grounds, suggesting that he and these other Caribbean political figures were and had been unduly influential in Washington, and that in consequence the U.S. was being misled with regard to the Dominican Republic. Secretary Rusk doubted that the Figueres–Betancourt–Muñoz Marín group were currently asserting unusual influence. When they had offered their services earlier this year to the OAS as a sort of interim commission to administer the DR, the offer had not been accepted.[2]

The President returned to the subject of the Paraguayan people. He described them as a homogeneous race, instinctively and thoroughly anti-communist. A while ago a delegation of Uruguayan leftists had come to Asunción to petition for the release of several communist prisoners being held by the Paraguayan Government. A group of Paraguayan citizens spontaneously staged an *anti*-communist demonstration in front of the hotel where the delegation was staying. Demonstrations in other Latin American countries were almost invariably pro-communist and anti-U.S., he reminded those present. According to FAO statistics, the people of Argentina, Uruguay and Paraguay were among the best fed in the world. Considering all children of primary school age, Paraguay had the highest percentage attending school of any country in Latin America. A hundred years ago, according to the Almanach de Gotha, Paraguay was the most developed country in South America. It was a great country then, a great country now and he felt deeply honored to be a Paraguayan. When the time came for dispatching troops to the DR, the only problem was of restricting the number because the troops all wanted to participate. One amusing incident had resulted in his allowing a young soldier to go with the contingent extra-complement.

The President next took up the question of the sugar quota, setting forth the Paraguayan position, pointing out that Bolivia for some reason had not only received a quota but had been given the prospect of an increase in the initial figure, whereas Paraguay had been entirely deprived of its previous quota. The Secretary frankly explained that the sugar quotas were worked out by the legislative branch of the U.S. Government[3] in a complicated manner. By the time State Department officials and others had learned of what was happening to the Paraguayan quota, it was too late to influence the result because Congress was at that moment hastening to adjourn. President Stroessner requested that the U.S. examine the possibility of restoring a quota to Paraguay a year from now, the Secretary assured him that his request would receive careful attention.

The President's next topic was the need for more agricultural credit. This was not a rich country, he said, but it could be if its agri-

---

[2] The final version of the memorandum eliminated the following sentence at this point: "Moreover, a Texas President in the White House was not likely to sit idly by while the communists took over the DR."

[3] The final version of the memorandum eliminated the following clause at this point: "—in what could be described as a confused atmosphere and—."

cultural and human resources were developed properly. Such could only be done with an adequate volume of foreign credit. More money was needed now for the small Paraguayan farmer. By contrast, a rich country like Venezuela shouldn't need outside help, although it appeared to be getting it. The Paraguayans did much with little; there was no misery here, even if there were many with very few material possessions. One should contrast conditions here with the slums in Caracas and elsewhere.

The Secretary stated that he had discussed the level of aid with Foreign Minister Sapena and Ambassador Snow. The U.S. would always be interested in knowing the President's view of priorities in aid matters. President Johnson also was convinced, he said, that rural development was indeed of the utmost importance. If the combined efforts of all in this regard should prove inadequate, the world might possibly be facing a food crisis one of these days. The tendency in the developing countries had been to neglect the rural people in favor of industrial development.

Stressing the theme that inadequate attention had hitherto been paid to his views and his requests for U.S. aid, both military and economic, the President informed the Secretary that he had spoken many times about these matters to Ambassador Snow, but he was not certain that whatever the Ambassador had reported was reaching the top of the U.S. Government. He believed we were far more attentive to the pleas of such countries as Chile and Bolivia for example, both of which countries possessed very unstable political structures. The late President Kennedy, however, had seen fit to state publicly that the Government of Paz Estenssoro was a "model for the hemisphere". He (President Stroessner) had been told by Paz Estenssoro himself that Paraguay had the model government. President De Gaulle, President Castello Branco, General Ongania, an ex-Foreign Minister of Uruguay and others had assured him that he was a great president presiding over an exemplary government.

The Secretary assured the President that the U.S. Government intended always to give thoughtful attention to its relations with Paraguay.

The President took up the topic of arms assistance. "We Paraguayans," he said, "do not play our anti-communism for U.S. dollars. We will be anti-communist with the United States, anti-communist without the United States, or even anti-communist against the United States, if that ever should be necessary." The President then gave details regarding U.S. arms he had heard were being supplied to Uruguay and Bolivia, two countries which were receiving considerable military aid, whereas Paraguay was receiving very little indeed. All of the American military officers of the Southern Command in the Canal Zone assured him that the one and only obstacle was the State

Department. The military officers referred to were in favor of much more generous treatment for Paraguay, but it was always the State Department which blocked their way. He could not understand this because Paraguay was just about the only country in the hemisphere which had remained consistently in support of U.S. policies, had not wavered from its anti-communist stand, had maintained a period of internal peace and growing prosperity for eleven years, had held its currency stable and had aroused the admiration of various other countries. In view of how things really were in Paraguay and of such testimony as he had previously quoted, he was curious to know just how the mind of the State Department really worked. He realized that people like President Johnson and Secretary Rusk were extremely busy people, but he thought that Paraguay should receive more attention at the top and more favorable treatment in general.

The Secretary said that if President Johnson were sitting where he was in President Stroessner's office, the latter would quickly discover that President Johnson knew a good deal about Paraguay and the two chiefs of state would be talking like neighboring ranchers within a few minutes.

Before departing, the Secretary took occasion to express to the President his admiration for Foreign Minister Sapena Pastor as a highly competent colleague with whom it had always been a pleasure to work.[4]

W.P.S.

---

[4] The final version of the memorandum eliminated the following sentence at this point: "The interview lasted approximately an hour and five minutes."

---

466. Memorandum From the President's Special Assistant (Rostow) to President Johnson[1]

Washington, June 28, 1967.

Mr. President:

In the attached memoranda[2] Bill Gaud requests your approval to negotiate a $15 million agriculture sector loan with Uruguay.

---

[1] Source: Johnson Library, National Security File, Country File, Uruguay, Vol. I, 1/64–12/68. Confidential.

[2] Attached but not printed are memoranda to the President from Schultze, June 24, and Gaud, June 15.

Our ability to negotiate such a loan now comes at a critically important time:

—President Gestido under the new constitutional system has the authority and purpose to resolve Uruguay's serious economic problems.[3]
—These problems were brought on by a decade of drift and unwise policies by weak collegiate governments which built up the income of the urban sector at the expense of the rural sector.
—Uruguay's productive capacity is in agriculture and the solution to the problems must begin with modernization of policies and practices in this sector.

The conditions accompanying the loan require specific actions by the Uruguayan Government to remove the major disincentives to investment and production in agriculture. President Gestido has indicated willingness to take hard self-help measures. We have every reason to think that our conditions will be acceptable to his economic team and to him. In addition to the conditions, our negotiating position calls for release of loan funds in four tranches, each based on a prior review of performance.

Covey Oliver, Joe Fowler and Charlie Schultze have reviewed the loan package and recommend approval. I concur.

Walt

Approve[4]

Disapprove

See me

---

[3] On November 27, 1966, the Uruguayan electorate voted to replace the National Council of Government with a one-man presidential system. President Gestido assumed office on March 1, 1967.

[4] The President checked this option.

467.   Information Memorandum From the Assistant Secretary of State for Inter-American Affairs (Oliver) to Secretary of State Rusk[1]

Washington, August 18, 1967.

SUBJECT

Uruguayan Situation Report

The economic-political crisis in Uruguay is deepening. The situation might be described as a "crisis of confidence" which has affected members of the government, the two main political parties and the people. The crisis arises principally from the inability of the government to grapple effectively with the serious economic-financial situation confronting the country; spiraling inflation, budget imbalance, balance of payments problems, and the added burden of repairing the serious damage to the economy caused by inclement weather of the last six months. These problems in turn have given rise to social problems; i.e., strikes, work slowdowns, and communist agitation.

The ineffectiveness of the government is due to the indecisive nature of President Gestido's leadership. Despite the hopes of Uruguayans and the USG, Gestido has been unable to rise above "politics as usual", and not being very clever politically, he has managed to alienate the largest part of his own Colorado Party. The political crisis of June 1967 illustrates this situation: Gestido's reaction to an attack on his managing of the economic situation by the leader of the largest faction of the Colorado Party was to exclude that faction from his government, form a new government representing only a minority (one-third) of the Party and completely reverse his administration's economic policy from one seeking an IMF-type solution to one of rigid controls.

We, however, share the Country Team's doubts that a coup will be attempted in the short term. Gestido still has several options open to him both on political and economic fronts. Politically, he could broaden the base of his administration by coming to agreement with the leaders of other factions of the Colorado Party or alternatively he could form a coalition government with selected factions of the opposition Blanco Party. The Embassy continues to urge the administration to adopt a sound stabilization and economic growth as a basis for US and IMF support. If Gestido could bring himself to heed this advice, which he receives not only from us but from the majority of the mem-

[1] Source: National Archives and Records Administration, RG 59, ARA Files, 1967–1969: Lot 72 D 33, Uruguay. Confidential. Drafted by Sayre and Sanders. A notation on the memorandum indicates Rusk saw it.

bers of his own political party, he could perhaps restore confidence in himself and his government.

Foreign Minister Luisi, Ambassador Yriart, other high Uruguayan officials, and we expected the present crisis when Gestido decided against a sound economic program and opted for controls and other economic measures that have previously been so ineffective. At the moment we see no other course open to us but to await sound Uruguayan policies which we can support. We have rejected the alternative of supplying US dollars to support an unrealistic exchange rate and inadequate economic policies.

---

468. Action Memorandum From the President's Special Assistant (Rostow) to President Johnson[1]

Washington, December 12, 1967.

SUBJECT

    PL 480 Agreement with Uruguay

Herewith a unanimous recommendation that you authorize negotiating a $19.3 million PL 480 agreement with Uruguay.[2]

Uruguay needs this assistance. The loan has been carefully coordinated with the Agricultural Sector Loan you authorized last June. The new Uruguayan President[3] has pledged to support the economic recovery program launched by President Gestido which the PL 480 and Sector loans are designed to support.

I recommend approval.

Walt

Approve[4]

Disaprove

See me

---

[1] Source: Johnson Library, National Security File, Country File, Uruguay, Vol. I, 1/64–12/68. No classification marking.

[2] Attached but not printed are memoranda to the President from Schultze, December 7, and Gaud and Acting Secretary of Agriculture Schnittker, December 1.

[3] President Gestido died on December 6; he was succeeded by Vice President Jorge Pacheco Areco.

[4] The President checked this option.

469. Action Memorandum From the President's Special Assistant (Rostow) to President Johnson[1]

Washington, March 19, 1968.

SUBJECT

Visit of Paraguayan President Stroessner

Tomorrow President Stroessner comes to Washington for a two-day official visit. Your participation is limited to:

11:30 a.m.—Welcoming Ceremony at the South Lawn.
12:00 noon—Office meeting with President Stroessner.
8:00 p.m.—State dinner.

A reception is being offered by the Paraguayan Ambassador at the Pan American Union on Thursday evening, but I advise against your attending.

President Stroessner is coming armed with a "shopping list" as he did at Punta del Este. Nick Katzenbach's briefing memorandum (Tab A)[2] describes what the items are. Most of them are for economic assistance, but there also may be a request for artillery. He may support the requests by possibly offering a Paraguayan army unit for Vietnam.

Nick counsels that you be non-committal on the offer of troops and handle the request for aid and military equipment by saying your advisers will study the requests and be in touch with him later. This is how his Punta del Este shopping list was handled—with good results.

The principal problem with this visit is President Stroessner's image in certain circles as an old-style Latin American dictator and criticism of you for inviting him.[3] So far, we have had only one newspa-

---

[1] Source: Johnson Library, National Security File, Country File, Paraguay, Visit of President Stroessner, 3/20–21, 1968. Confidential.

[2] Tab A was a March 18 memorandum from Katzenbach to the President; attached but not printed. President Johnson met Stroessner at Punta del Este on April 13. In addition to presenting his "shopping list," Stroessner received an invitation to visit Washington after complaining that he was "developing a complex about it." Memoranda of conversation are in the National Archives and Records Administration, RG 59, Conference Files, 1966–1972: Lot 67 D 586, CF 151. A CIA assessment on "Stroessner's Paraguay," March 1, is in the Johnson Library, National Security File, Country File, Paraguay, Vol. I, 1/64–8/68.

[3] In a memorandum to Rostow, March 18, Harry C. McPherson, Jr., Special Counsel to the President, anticipated the criticism: "I wish we weren't entertaining Stroessner so soon after Bobby's announcement. For better or worse, he has the militarist-oligarchist image that liberal Democrats have complained about for years; I imagine Bobby will attack his presence here as symbolic of what's wrong with the Alianza, etc. 'If Jack were in office, the White House would be entertaining Eduardo Frei.'" (Ibid., Visit of President Stroessner, 3/20–21, 1968) On March 16 Senator Robert F. Kennedy announced his candidacy for President of the United States.

per article striking this theme—in the *Washington Post*. The characterization is unfair to him and your purpose in having him up here.

Stroessner has granted considerable political liberalization in recent years and is making steady headway with economic and social reform and development. The charts at Tab B illustrate this.[4] We want to encourage this trend. The suggested welcoming statement and toast (Tab C) are designed to put the visit in this context.[5] The press backgrounder will do likewise.

The points we would have you stress in your talks with the Paraguayan President are:

1. that he continue political liberalization so that the principal opposition can function freely;
2. that he press forward with reform of budget and tax structures which CIAP has recommended as being of primary importance;
3. that we appreciate Paraguay's help in the OAS and UN, where Paraguay is now a member of the Security Council.[6]

W. W. Rostow[7]

---

[4] Attached but not printed.

[5] Attached but not printed. For Johnson's welcoming remarks and toast to Stroessner, see *Public Papers of the Presidents of the United States: Lyndon B. Johnson, 1968–69*, Book I, pp. 419–424.

[6] According to the President's Daily Diary Johnson met Stroessner in the Cabinet Room on March 20, 12:14–12:50 p.m. (Johnson Library) When Stroessner mentioned several requests for economic assistance, Johnson "expressed sympathetic interest and suggested that these be taken up with Secretary Rusk." (Memorandum of conversation, March 20; National Archives and Records Administration, RG 59, Central Files 1967–69, POL 7 PAR) Memoranda of his conversation with Rusk, March 21, are ibid.

[7] Printed from a copy that bears this typed signature.

Peru

470. Telegram From the Embassy in Peru to the Department of State[1]

Lima, January 15, 1964, 1 p.m.

829. For: Mann. IPC Case. Embtel 822.[2]

Reference contains our recommendations for action immediate future subject case and related effect aid program. As you doubtless informed, since GOP broke off negotiations with IPC on October 28 and submitted an unsatisfactory draft bill to Congress we have been dragging our feet on implementing aid program and endeavoring by this means to influence GOP toward more sound and sober attitude this case.

Peculiarity situation is that in effect we have been applying Hickenlooper amendment[3] without Peru as yet having taken specific acts which would legally warrant such course. This in part came about, ironically, through President Belaunde's asking Moscoso last September if USG through AID might not facilitate solution with IPC.[4] What he actually had in mind was USG help for IPC to pay $50 million bonus GOP sought. While we of course could not do this, we were on the point of announcing a rather large AID package totaling some $64 million and I was instructed on the last critical weekend of October 28 to inform Belaunde that this amount was ready for announcement. The idea was that such an announcement might help to deflect any Peruvian public or congressional criticism from Belaunde administration-proposed settlement with the IPC.

---

[1] Source: National Archives and Records Administration, RG 59, Central Files 1964–66, PET 6 PERU. Confidential; Limit Distribution.

[2] In telegram 822 from Lima, January 14, the Embassy advocated a flexible "policy of restraint," i.e., linking the level of economic assistance to progress in the negotiations for an IPC settlement. (Ibid.) In approving the Embassy's recommendations, the Department also provided the following guidance: "Peruvians can make own deductions to this effect, but link must not be obvious and must be denied if they ask. You will simply have to give bland explanation of further delays (i.e. on projects still frozen) by stating programs 'being processed' and that this taking longer than originally expected; part of blame could be placed on reorganization here." (Telegram 549 to Lima, January 22; ibid.)

[3] Amendment to the Foreign Assistance Act of 1961 initially approved in August 1962 and subsequently revised in December 1963. Sponsored by Senators Bourke B. Hickenlooper (R–Iowa) and E. Ross Adair (R–Indiana), the amendment stipulated that the President suspend assistance to any country that expropriated the property of U.S. citizens or corporations without proper compensation. (76 Stat. 260)

[4] Moscoso raised the issue with Belaúnde on August 28, 1963. For background information on the IPC case, see Document 478, and *Foreign Relations*, 1961–1963, vol XII, Document 432.

Since GOP took course it did notwithstanding this gesture, and there ensued press campaign here, principally through *El Comercio,* to demonstrate that Peru could do what it wanted with IPC without penalty, we took decision to hold back on these new programs in hopes of using this asset to influence a better course. In my opinion this was proper thing to do. It has had effect of sobering GOP attitude and, I hope, of increasing chances for satisfactory solution. Nevertheless, to use AID program at such a stage to influence the outcome of a particular problem is of course to tread on dangerous ground for obvious reasons. I earnestly hope, therefore, that we can resume a normal pace of operations at earliest possible moment consistent US interests. I believe this moment will have arrived when and if the executive branch is once again in negotiating contact with the IPC.

Once this has happened, we will have gone full circle and nothing concrete will have been changed with single exception of GOP's laws nullifying arbitration awards which formed tax base for IPC operations. As to these acts, however, we have officially stated our reservations; IPC has declared its view that awards remain in full force and effect; and UK has now formally protested and, for its part, declared awards still to be valid.

As you are doubtless aware, this case, plus that of Peru telephone company which now seems to have a more hopeful aspect,[5] constitute the only dark clouds on a rather encouraging situation here. A respectable, democratic and progressive regime is in office and it gives every evidence of a desire for close collaboration and warm friendship with US. The economy is sound, growing and diversified. While Peru has severe problems, it also has many elements of strength which should make it possible to achieve real progress here under Alliance for Progress. I hope you will agree with us as to the tactics to follow at this stage, and that you will be able promptly to impress on Peru's new Ambassador, Celso Pastor,[6] as we have tried to do, the importance of renewing actual negotiations as soon as possible and, eventually, of achieving bilateral solution of this problem.[7]

Jones

---

[5] The Peruvian Telephone Company, a subsidiary of the International Telegraph and Telephone Company, was engaged in negotiations to maintain its position in Peru. Documentation on these negotiations is in the National Archives and Records Administration, RG 59, Central Files 1964–66, TEL PERU; ibid., ARA/EP/P Files, 1955–1964: Lot 67 D 566, Perutelco—TEL 11; ibid., ARA/EP/P Files, 1963–1967: Lot 70 D 139, Telecommunications, IT & T Working File.

[6] Mann met Ambassador Pastor and Peruvian Vice President Seone on January 30. (Telegram 575 to Lima, January 31; ibid., Central Files 1964–66, POL PERU–US)

[7] President Johnson asked Mann about Peru on February 12. Mann replied: "I don't think Peru is my main concern at the moment. I have a report that President Belaunde has a plan of a takeover [of IPC] in 30 years. There is a claim for back taxes of $50 million. I'm going to have to warn about expropriation and the Hickenlooper Amendment applies to this." (Memorandum of telephone conversation; Johnson Library, Papers of Thomas C. Mann, Telephone Conversations with LBJ, Jan. 14, 1964–April 30, 1965)

471. Editorial Note

In a June 27, 1964, letter to Ambassador Jones, the Peruvian Minister of Government and Police requested U.S. assistance to equip and maintain a Special Police Emergency Unit (SPEU). (Airgram A–020 from Lima, July 8; National Archives and Records Administration, RG 59, Central Files 1964–66, DEF 19 US–PERU) After considerable debate in Washington, the U.S. Government informed the Peruvian Government of its tentative support, citing the prospective role of the SPEU in dealing "with a variety of threats including riots, subversion, terrorism, demonstrations, land invasions, civil disobedience, and uprisings up to and including small-scale guerrilla activities." (Airgram A–294 from Lima, October 29; ibid., POL 23 PERU) The formal negotiations to establish the SPEU were conducted primarily through the Agency for International Development and complicated by competing interests of the Department of Defense and the Central Intelligence Agency. In a December 10 letter to Jones, Nicholas McCausland, the officer-in-charge of Peruvian affairs, reported that the JCS feared the SPEU was "a pilot project by which CIA plans to get its oar into operational activities in Latin America." (Ibid., Lima Embassy Files, Classified Personal Papers of Ambassador J. Wesley Jones: Lot 73 F 100, McCausland, Nicholas V.)

On April 8, 1965, the Special Group (CI) met to consider the counter-insurgency situation in Latin America, particularly in view of the SPEU proposal. According to the minutes of the meeting (Document 28), the participants "endorsed the CIA/AID proposal for a special airborne police unit to be tried on an experimental basis in Peru." The provisional agreement stipulating U.S. assistance for the SPEU was signed in Lima on June 26. In a memorandum to Secretary Rusk, August 18, Assistant Secretary Vaughn reiterated the importance of supporting the program: "the insurgency situation in Peru has shaken the Peruvian Government and we are now hearing reports of a possible military coup if President Belaunde does not deal with it effectively." "We believe that the correct way to deal with insurgency is first with civilian police forces [i.e. the SPEU]. When it escalates to the point where civilian police forces can no longer handle it, then it becomes a problem for the army." (National Archives and Records Administration, RG 59, ARA Files, 1967–1969: Lot 72 D 33, Special Group CI (1964–1966))

472.   Letter From the Deputy Director of the Office of Ecuadorean-
Peruvian Affairs (Barnebey) to the Ambassador to Peru
(Jones)[1]

Washington, September 30, 1965.

Dear Mr. Ambassador:

I want to report to you on the results of a meeting Jack Vaughn
had last Friday[2] with Tom Mann, with Rostow, Sayre, Johnston, and
myself in attendance. The meeting covered Jack's approach to date and
proposed increased flexibility in our policy on the IPC negotiations.

Let me stress at the outset that this is merely an advance notification of how Jack is thinking of handling the problem, and is subject to modification depending on the outcome of certain key conversations he will hold in coming days. Jack reviewed for Mann the
results of his conversations with President Belaunde,[3] concluding by
saying that there seems to be little prospect for solution of the IPC
case in the next year or so. Moreover, Jack is inclined toward the view
that Belaunde may prefer to keep the IPC case around for resort to
possible expropriation as and when the political going gets particularly rough.

Based upon Jack's report, he and Mann discussed what would
be the next appropriate step. Their conclusions were essentially as
follows:

1. An assurance would be sought from Belaunde that he
would not expropriate IPC during the remainder of his presidential
term.

2. Subject to getting this assurance from Belaunde and further con-
versations as Jack deems necessary with Congressional leaders (notably
Senator Hickenlooper) and the company, IDB soft loans to Peru would
be resumed. The first such loan would be the $18 million Comunidades
Indígenas loan to be approved in the course of the next few weeks.
(Activity under this loan, to be administered by several ministries and
Cooperación Popular, would be directed toward strengthening the

---

[1] Source: National Archives and Records Administration, RG 59, ARA/EP/P Files,
1959–1968: Lot 72 D 101, PET 6 (IPC) 1965. Confidential.

[2] September 24.

[3] Vaughn visited Lima in early-September as part of a 2-week trip to Latin America. An account of his meeting with Belaúnde is in telegram 347 from Lima, September
2. (National Archives and Records Administration, RG 59, Central Files 1964–66, ORG 7
VAUGHN)

legally recognized indigenous communities of the highlands; proceeds of the loan would be re-lent to the communities for agricultural improvement and community development projects.)

3. Until a satisfactory solution is achieved in the GOP–IPC negotiations, we would continue the policy of denying AID loans to Peru. Belaunde would be told that we recognize his political difficulties in settling the IPC case, but he would have to come to recognize U.S. domestic political considerations as a limitation on AID lending decisions.

During the conversation a great deal was said about Belaunde's apparent weakness as a President and as a politician, as illustrated by his lack of determination to settle the IPC case. Mann called attention to the country's economic problems, such as a potential inflationary spiral, the Government's failure to put its fiscal house in order, and its failure to adopt progressive taxation which would work toward eliminating some of the greatest disparities in Peru's income distribution. Mention was made, too, of the counter-insurgency campaign, with Ambassador Pastor having told Jack how seriously he views the problem and the new Foreign Minister apparently having told Reuters that communism is no problem in Peru. Dr. Rostow reiterated his view that we should approve specific development loans as a counter-insurgency move (a position not regarded as persuasive, particularly as to combatting insurgency on a short-term basis). On the other hand, Dr. Rostow's statement in support of Belaunde's efforts toward rural modernization and national integration was received rather better.

There was general agreement as to the disenchantment Mann, Vaughn and others have come to have regarding Ambassador Pastor's contribution toward improving U.S.-Peruvian relations. The consensus seemed to be that Pastor has not been able to look beyond Peru's boundaries during his service as Ambassador here, and apparently cannot see, let alone convey to his Government, a larger view of U.S. or free world interest in many of the issues confronting his and our Government.

In this regard Jack called attention to Ambassador Pastor's latest offer to take a leading role in the IPC negotiations. During the September 22 conversation, Pastor mentioned seeking "plenipotentiary powers" from Belaunde to negotiate this dispute. Pastor also said he might ask that two or three Peruvian experts concerned with these negotiations come to Washington to join him in working out this matter. During the conversation Jack did not comment upon this possibility, but I would be interested in your views as to whether such a course of action would be useful.

I will keep you informed as to the progress of the impending policy change.[4]

Sincerely,

M. R. Barnebey[5]

---

[4] In a December 23 letter to Jones, Barnebey reported that Vaughn was seriously considering whether to modify the soft loan freeze policy, possibly as early as the end of January 1966. In reference to the possibility that APRA might obstruct a settlement in the IPC case, Barnebey also offered the following suggestion: "It occurs to me that given the excellent relations that another agency has with Aprista leaders in Lima, you might want to explore how some of these contacts can be used effectively in the event that an overt approach to Aprista leaders does not yield beneficial results." (Johnson Library, Papers of John Wesley Jones, Classified [Correspondence])

[5] Printed from a copy that bears this typed signature.

---

473. Memorandum of Conversation[1]

Sec/MC/21   Rio de Janeiro, November 17, 1965, 3 p.m.

SUBJECT

 Relationship of International Petroleum Company and U.S. Loan Policy

PARTICIPANTS

 U.S.
 The Secretary
 Walt W. Rostow, Counselor, Dept. of State, and Chairman Policy Planning Council
 Jack Hood Vaughn (Coordinator), Assistant Secretary of State for Inter-American Affairs
 Neil A. Seidenman, OPR/LS, Reporting Officer
 H. W. Baker, American Embassy Rio de Janeiro

 Peru
 Jorge Vasquez Salas, Foreign Minister of Peru

The Secretary said that this was a problem that was making our lives very complex, and Presidents Kennedy and Johnson had made

---

[1] Source: National Archives and Records Administration, RG 59, Central Files 1964–66, PET 6 PERU. Confidential. Drafted by Neil A. Seidenman in LS and H. W. Baker, labor attaché at the Embassy in Brazil, on November 19 and approved in S on January 20, 1966. The meeting was held at the Hotel Gloria. The memorandum is part III of III. A draft memorandum of the entire conversation is ibid., ARA/EP/P Files, 1967: Lot 70 D 139, POL 3 OAS—General. Rusk was in Rio de Janeiro November 16–24 for the Second Special Inter-American Conference.

special efforts to move resources into Latin America and specifically into Peru in support of the Belaunde Government. However, legislation on foreign investments has been passed by the United States Congress.[2] Specifically, foreign assistance legislation has provisions limiting appropriation of funds for countries whose governments confiscate investments or property of American enterprises.[3] The Secretary said he was not here to negotiate on the IPC problem and reiterated our commitment to support the prosperity and independence of Peru.

The Foreign Minister expressed his appreciation for the Secretary's concern over this problem. "My government," he said, "shares this concern." This was a matter that has been the subject of serious, earnest, concentrated study by the Peruvian Government. He said the Peruvian Government has never expected and does not expect or intend to confiscate or seize any property or infringe on the rights of any individual or company within the territorial bounds of its country. Peru simply desires to be in a position where it can control and manage the natural wealth of the country. In the process of implementing the laws and regulations applicable to this area in Peru, he said, Peruvian authorities have no intention of subjecting any party to discrimination but rather adhere to the principle that non-national interests certainly should not be allowed to enjoy greater benefits than Peruvian nationals; that all should have equal status under the laws of the country. To proceed otherwise would be tantamount to going back to the practices of extraterritoriality. The Foreign Minister said he hoped the United States would realize a country must be in a position to dispose of its own wealth and resources, not with a view to punishing any one, but in a way that parties concerned will be justly compensated. Peru has undertaken a program of land distribution. To carry out this reform it is necessary to expropriate to progress toward an equitable redistribution of the national landed estate. However, Peru lacks adequate financial resources to pay for all of this property and must compensate former owners with long-term bonds which the GOP intends to make fully redeemable within the prescribed period. If it is legal to make compensation for expropriated property in the form of bonds, certainly this should be acceptable to foreign property owners as well. This is not a plan for confiscating property.

The Secretary said that he would like to have some time to review the Minister's remarks and talk again while they are still here together. The Secretary said that perhaps it would be desirable to have further

---

[2] The phrase, "which is the source of [the] problem," concluded the sentence in the draft memorandum, but was subsequently removed in S.

[3] The final version of the memorandum also eliminated the following sentence at this point: "The Secretary said he had testified against this legislation but it was passed, and we have it."

discussions between the governments, since previously there had only been contacts of the company involved with the Peruvian Government.

The Foreign Minister said he believed the problem was a matter of national jurisdiction, not subject to handling on a government-to-government basis. In the view of the GOP it would be a great mistake to transfer this problem to the realm of diplomacy which would simply mean repeating an historic error committed by Peru at a time when it allowed important property within its territory to remain under the ownership of British interests.

The Secretary stated that this was a decision to be made by the Peruvian Government; the Peruvian Government makes its decisions and the American Government makes its decisions, so these decisions should be balanced. The Secretary said we are only asking that due consideration be given to the factors involved in the hope that both parties can adjust their respective interests. On our side, the Secretary said, it is a matter of our being able to tell the American taxpayers what we are doing with their tax money and that it is worthwhile.

---

474. Editorial Note

In early January 1966 Ambassador Jones suggested a plan for "political action" to resolve the status of the International Petroleum Company (IPC) in Peru. In a January 4 message, Jones explained that President Belaúnde could not submit an IPC settlement to Congress without the tacit support of the American Popular Revolutionary Alliance (APRA). There was, however, a problem: "A decision of such importance to APRA can only be made by party leader [Victor] Haya De La Torre who is at present in Europe." Jones, therefore, recommended that a U.S. official approach Haya in Europe in an attempt "to persuade him to send assurances to President Belaunde that the Apristas will make no trouble over the issue and urge him [Belaunde] to act now." (Memorandum from Broe to Vaughn, January 4; Department of State, INR/IL Historical Files, Latin America Country File, Peru, 1961–1964) [*text not declassified*]

At a meeting with a U.S. official in Hamburg, January 16, Haya agreed to support a fair settlement of the IPC case and acknowledged that Belaúnde's latest proposal, as outlined by the officer, was, in fact, reasonable. According to a subsequent report: "No financial or other commitments were made, nor were any requested by Haya." (Memorandum to the 303 Committee, January 17; ibid., 303 Committee Special Files, January–June 1966)

475.   Memorandum From the Ambassador to Brazil (Gordon) to President Johnson[1]

Washington, January 29, 1966.

SUBJECT

    Letter to Peruvian President Belaunde

In a recent conversation with Ambassador Jones, President Belaunde expressed deep frustration over Peru's failure to obtain major concessional assistance from the U.S. which he attributes to the fact that he has not yet reached an agreement with the ESSO-owned International Petroleum Company (IPC) on the basis for its continued operations.[2] Belaunde is under strong political pressure to expropriate the IPC holdings, which he does not want to do. On the other hand, he has not been able to accept a satisfactory settlement with the Company because he assesses the political risks to himself and his party as too high. The Company has made several reasonable proposals during the past two years. A fuller description of the issues involved in the IPC case is at Tab C.[3]

Walt Rostow, Tom Mann and I have been reexamining our position on the IPC case in the light of the Belaunde–Jones conversation. We have reached the conclusion that the conversation opens the door for a new effort to work out a basis for more effective cooperation with Peru's development plans and a simultaneous understanding on the IPC case. We have decided that Walt Rostow, under the cover of a CIAP mission to discuss multinational projects for opening the South American heartland, should go to Lima next week to discuss with Belaunde:

1. Peru's economic, financial and reform performance and prospects, including their relation to possible increased USG and multilateral assistance to Peru.

---

[1] Source: Johnson Library, National Security File, Special Head of State Correspondence, Peru—Belaunde Correspondence. Confidential. Another copy indicates that Bowdler drafted the memorandum. (Ibid., Memos to the President, McGeorge Bundy, Vol. 19) Gordon was in Washington for his Senate confirmation as Assistant Secretary of State for Inter-American Affairs; he did not formally assume his new responsibilities until March 9. In a memorandum to the President, January 27, Bundy explained that Gordon "will bring cool good sense" to the IPC case—a case on which, he admitted, "we have been a shade rigid." (Ibid.)

[2] Belaúnde summoned Jones on January 20, declaring that "he would never sign an agreement [with IPC] under pressure, that US aid policy must first return to normal before he could conclude an agreement." In reporting the conversation, Jones suggested that "a promise of additional aid now might be an important element in support of those other factors which the Department is aware now working toward a settlement." (Telegram 1036 from Lima, January 21; National Archives and Records Administration, RG 59, Central Files 1964–66, PET 6 PERU)

[3] Dated January 29; attached but not printed.

2. His willingness and ability either to reach a mutually satisfactory settlement with the Company or, at least, to give assurances that the status of IPC will not be changed for the duration of his term (3 years) except as mutually agreed by Peru and the Company. The present operating conditions are not unsatisfactory to the Company.

Tentative guidelines for Rostow's talks with Belaunde are at Tab B.[4]

Walt Rostow's hand would be greatly strengthened if he were to carry a personal letter from you to Belaunde. Based on previous conversations with Belaunde, we believe that having the letter may well spell the difference between success and failure of his mission. The thrust of the letter would be your interest in seeing Belaunde carry forward his economic and social development plans on the basis of a strong self-help program backed by well-organized and sustained external support and in clearing the path of misunderstandings and obstacles which impede full cooperation between our two governments. The obstacles refer not only to the IPC case, but also to Belaunde's public criticism of the Alliance and the need for better management of the Peruvian economy and greater effort in basic reforms. The text of a suggested letter is at Tab A.[5]

The way this letter is phrased and the CIAP cover which Rostow would use in making the trip (one of many he has made to Peru in recent years) reduces the risk of disclosure of the purpose of the visit and places us in a good position publicly to refute charges, should they be made, that the Rostow visit is a pressure move on the IPC case.

I think we should take advantage of this opportunity to seek a solution to this knotty problem which, if left unsettled, poses a serious threat to US–Peruvian relations and to our Alliance image. Another consideration is that aspects of the Belaunde program are designed to bring the long neglected Indian population into the mainstream of national life, thereby countering communist efforts to use Indian discontent to launch a guerrilla movement. Much stands to be gained by the Rostow trip, and the risks are minimal.

I recommend that you send the suggested letter.[6]

Lincoln Gordon

---

[4] Dated January 28; attached but not printed.

[5] Dated January 29; attached but not printed. The final version of the letter is in the Johnson Library, National Security File, Country File, Peru, Vol. II, 1/66–10/67.

[6] Bundy forwarded the proposal under the cover of a memorandum to the President, January 29, on which he wrote the following parenthetical comment: "a good bargain with Belaunde will help us on all fronts & Walt is a good bargainer." Johnson indicated that he would "prefer not to send the letter," but "let's discuss [the issue] further." (Ibid., Special Head of State Correspondence, Peru—Belaunde Correspondence) The President discussed the letter, as well as the "overt and covert purposes" of Rostow's trip to Peru, at a February 3 meeting in the Oval Office. (Johnson Library, President's Daily Diary) After minor revisions, Johnson signed the letter and directed Rostow to deliver it to Belaúnde. (Note from Marie Fehmer to Juanita Roberts, February 3; ibid.)

476.   Memorandum From the Counselor and Chairman of the Policy Planning Council (Rostow) to President Johnson[1]

Washington, February 10, 1966.

You have the cabled reports of my mission to Peru plus the Washington instructions I followed.[2]

The facts are:

1. Belaunde fully met the condition we laid down; namely, that he give to you personally his assurance that the status of IPC would not be impaired in the lifetime of his administration.

2. He subsequently confirmed his verbal message to me in a conversation with Ambassador Jones. He knows I reported in writing; he knows you have that report; and he has confirmed its accuracy.[3]

3. What he permitted me to communicate to you, he has often said to some of our officials. But this time he knew he was making a most solemn and personal political deal. It could be explosive for him if it is known. He has put his political life in your hands. That is why I asked my cables to be handled with such special care.

4. Before I left, Linc Gordon cleared the deal with Senator Hickenlooper. As you know, I was recruited for this job by all three of my Latino pals: Tom Mann, Jack Vaughn, and Gordon.

5. As the attached cable[4] indicates, there is some irony in all this: Belaunde is the most pro-U.S. business President in Latin America. IPC is simply an inherited political problem peculiarly difficult for his rickety coalition. His campaign speeches and subsequent dilatory tactics have not helped. But basically he wants a settlement if he can swing it: he doesn't want to nationalize: if he breaks his word to you, the Hickenlooper Amendment is there, and he knows it.

6. I recommend that we proceed promptly with the $15–20 million A.I.D. package as promised.

---

[1] Source: Johnson Library, National Security File, Country File, Peru, Vol. II, 1/66–10/67. Secret; Eyes Only. The President also received an advance report on the Rostow mission from Bromley Smith on February 9. (Ibid., Memos to the President, McGeorge Bundy, Vol. 20)

[2] Rostow's instructions were attached as Tab B to Document 475. Bowdler forwarded the "cabled reports" to the President under the cover of a February 10 memorandum. (Johnson Library, National Security File, Country File, Peru, Vol. II, 1/66–10/67) These were telegrams 1107 and 1114 from Lima, both February 5. (Also in National Archives and Records Administration, RG 59, Central Files 1964–66, PET 6 PERU and POL 29 PERU, respectively) Rostow delivered the letter in a meeting with Belaúnde on February 4. A detailed account of the meeting is in airgram A–450 from Lima, February 9. (Ibid., POL PERU–US)

[3] In telegram 1124 from Lima, February 8. (Ibid., POL PERU–US)

[4] Telegram 1138 from Lima, February 10; attached but not printed.

7. Sometime at your leisure and convenience, I'd like to tell you what the east slopes of the Andes look like. The last real frontier. Real nice place to bring up kids.

Walt

---

477. Memorandum From the President's Deputy Special Assistant for National Security Affairs (Komer) to President Johnson[1]

Washington, February 15, 1966, 5:30 p.m.

SUBJECT

Peruvian President's Reply to Your Letter

I received the Peruvian Ambassador this afternoon who wanted to deliver President Belaunde's reply to the letter which you sent to him via Walt Rostow.[2]

The reply is in Spanish and I have sent it to State for translation. The principal points are:

1. He is profoundly grateful for your letter.

2. The conversations with Walt Rostow permitted a fruitful exchange of constructive ideas. Before replying to you, he wanted to talk first with Ambassador Jones.

3. The opening of the eastern slopes of the Andes offers a new frontier for colonization which will help win the battle over hunger and poverty. U.S. help in the initial phase of feasibility studies, as well as the new phase of actual work, will be of inestimable importance.

4. The cordial relations between our two countries is reflected in the growing participation of U.S. private capital in Peru. The contribution of these companies is much appreciated.

5. The only point that causes "certain preoccupation" is the "notorious difference" between the loan assistance given by "Official Institutions" to Peru in comparison to other countries. From his conversations with Rostow he gathers that there is the intention to "balance the flow of assistance" under the Alliance.

6. There is no reason for concern over the activities of U.S. businesses in Peru, which throughout the history of the country have never

---

[1] Source: Johnson Library, National Security File, Country File, Peru, Vol. II, 1/66–10/67. Confidential.

[2] The letter from Belaúnde to Johnson, dated February 10, included an English translation. (Ibid., Special Head of State Correspondence, Peru—Belaunde Correspondence)

been the victims of arbitrariness or unjust treatment. Where problems have arisen, they have been discussed with a high sense of responsibility and without precipitous action. He is confident that the few cases pending solution will be resolved by harmonious agreement.

7. He greatly appreciates your personal support for his "Cooperacion Popular" program designed to bring the Indian communities into the mainstream of Peruvian life.

8. He has sent through Ambassador Jones his pledge of support for the Pope's peace efforts in Vietnam.

The letter in tone and content is friendly and forthcoming. Point 2 is his way of referring to his understanding with Walt Rostow on the IPC case (Tab A). His reference to wanting to talk to Ambassador Jones before replying to you refers to his desire to review the memorandum of understanding which Walt prepared. Points 4, 6 and 7 are designed to provide additional reassurance.[3]

RWK

Tab A

Memorandum of Understanding Prepared by Walt Rostow and Shown to President Belaunde by Ambassador Jones

The following memorandum will be the basis of my report to President Johnson:

(1) President Belaunde wishes President Johnson to understand that he will try to settle within the next year the IPC case.

(2) Under no circumstances does President Belaunde intend to confiscate IPC. (Ambassador Jones will say that he presumes that this is in response to the formula which we reiterated three times yesterday that the status of IPC "would in no way be further impaired.")

(3) It is President Belaunde's judgment that his political possibilities for settling the IPC case would be improved by a resumption of normal aid relations with the U.S. along the lines of the sequence presented to him on Friday afternoon.

(4) With respect to Viet-Nam President Belaunde wishes President Johnson to know that he will continue to support the peace initiatives of the Vatican.

---

[3] The President wrote the following instruction at the end of the memorandum: "Bob see me." For an explanation of what Johnson may have had on his mind, see footnotes 2 and 3, Document 479.

478. **Memorandum From the Under Secretary of State for Economic Affairs (Mann) to President Johnson**[1]

Washington, February 19, 1966.

AID TO PERU AND THE IPC PROBLEM

The La Brea y Parinas oil field in Peru (which is only part of the IPC's holdings) was the subject of a dispute between the United Kingdom and Peru in the early part of this century. In 1918 the Peruvian Congress authorized its Foreign Minister to arbitrate. An arbitration award was handed down in 1922 which established a tax regime for this particular oil field. In 1924 the IPC, now but not then a subsidiary of Standard Oil of New Jersey, bought this oil field from the British owners. As far as I know, it is undisputed that the American company bought in good faith reliance on the award.

The Miro Quesada family, which owns the largest Lima newspaper, El Comercio, has conducted for many years a newspaper campaign for nationalization of the entire oil industry in Peru. In addition, this newspaper asserts that the award was not valid and hence, under its tax calculations, IPC owes Peru more than the approximately $70 million dollars at which the company values its assets in La Brea y Parinas.

Like Illia in Argentina, Belaunde, who depended on El Comercio's support in his campaign, promised to settle the IPC problem. In his inaugural address on July 28, 1963 Belaunde stated that he would settle it within 90 days.

In August 1963 Mr. Moscoso went to Lima and discussed with Belaunde the possibility of announcing a large aid package in order to provide a better atmosphere in Peru for a settlement. Active negotiations between Peru and IPC were going on at that time and when it appeared, near the end of the 90-day period, that a solution was imminent, our Ambassador was instructed to offer a $64 million dollar aid package to Belaunde. Two days after this offer was officially made, Belaunde broke off negotiations with the company and submitted two options to the Peruvian Congress. One was nationalization. The other was a contract under which, according to the company, IPC would have

---

[1] Source: National Archives and Records Administration, RG 59, Central Files 1964–66, PET 6 PERU. Confidential; Nodis. In an attached transmittal note to the President, Mann explained that the IPC problem was a "case study on the difficulties of (a) using aid as a lever to further the national interests and (b), without going into detail, getting the Inter-American Bank to play an effective role in promoting self-help." The memorandum was forwarded under the cover of a February 21 memorandum from Komer to the President. (Johnson Library, White House Central Files, Confidential File, Co 234)

been obliged to pay more than 100% of its net earnings and which it therefore considered confiscatory.

The Peruvian Congress did not follow either option recommended by Belaunde. Instead, it passed two other laws; one nullifying the 1918 Act which had authorized the arbitration and the other declaring the arbitration award null and void.

At this point, in the first week of November 1963, it was decided not to go ahead with the $64 million dollar aid package previously promised with the aim of encouraging the Peruvian government to resume negotiations with IPC. The Peruvian government was not officially informed of this decision.

In February 1964 the Peruvian Congress passed another law, in essence authorizing the President to negotiate with IPC and to submit the negotiated solution to Congress for approval. This was part of the "buck-passing" between Belaunde and the opposition-controlled Congress which has recently complicated the problem.

In 1964 and 1965 I and various Department officers talked with Belaunde, urging him to reach agreement with the company or, in the alternative, to agree to submit the legal issue of the validity of the award, which underlies the problem, to the International Court or to arbitration. Belaunde says in essence that domestic political pressures are too great to permit agreement on what the company regards as fair terms. He refuses to go to the World Court or to arbitration because he knows he will almost certainly lose.

He talks, instead, of the dangers of communism if we do not increase aid levels. He has made several public statements criticizing the sluggish AID procedures; and his Ambassador to Washington (and his brother-in-law) and others conducted a campaign consisting of complaints about our alleged attempts to influence internal Peruvian policy. Meanwhile, El Comercio has stepped up its attacks against IPC. Its line was to urge the President to nationalize, arguing that the U.S. would not react.

Certain elements in our Congress and press have spoken about my "hard line" policy and about the big U.S. jumping on poor, defenseless, democratic Peru in order to increase the profits of oil companies. These sources do not mention the United States' stake in opposing widespread disregard of contracts in the contract society in which we live. Nor do they mention the importance to the success of the Alliance of the private sector, whose participation on an adequate scale depends on observance of contracts.

In spite of these criticisms, I believe the policy has been successful in achieving its principal objective, i.e., deterring confiscatory action by Belaunde.

The tactic has been not to cut off, but to cut back, aid without specifically admitting to Belaunde that we were doing so. Our premise was that our relations with Peru would in the long run be better if we deterred confiscation than if Belaunde were lulled into a sense of security leading to confiscatory action which would then oblige us to apply rigidly the Hickenlooper-Adair Amendment. During calendar year 1964 we authorized road loans of $39 million dollars through AID and Eximbank; agricultural credit of $8 million dollars, and a labor housing cooperative loan of $6 million dollars. These were made on Ambassador Pastor's oral assurances to me on three separate occasions that the IPC case would soon be settled.

In 1965 we made a $2 million dollar project loan for an agricultural university and continued our Peace Corps, technical assistance and military aid programs which total about $26 million dollars a year. In addition, Peru continued to receive substantial loans from the Inter-American Bank and other international institutions. In 1966 the Inter-American Bank made a $20 million dollar soft loan which, like its loans in 1965, were almost wholly from U.S. funds.

During 1964 the company, incidentally, offered to give up its title to the oil and gas in place and to accept in lieu thereof an operating contract to terminate in twenty-five years. In September 1964 the company thought it had reached an understanding, which had been reduced to writing and orally agreed upon by two representatives of Belaunde, only to have it rejected by the President a few months later who claimed throughout that he was under irresistible domestic pressures. One principal issue remaining is whether the total "tax take" of Peru will be 85% or a smaller figure in the range of 65–75% which the company wants. The company considers this precedent important to its efforts to hold the present world tax split. They tell me they would prefer nationalization and loss of this investment to agreeing to a bad tax split precedent.

Mr. Gordon proposed the recent Rostow Mission to Peru. As near as I can make out, Mr. Belaunde has committed himself not to "confiscate" the IPC property during his term of office. In his letter to you, President Belaunde states:

"The misinformed and irresponsible statements made in recent years by certain organs of the foreign press about the intended confiscation of foreign companies established in this country are completely groundless and are disproven by facts in a nation whose acts conform faithfully to its constitution and laws."

The question is whether, despite the undertaking not to confiscate, Belaunde may take other action such as increasing taxes which might be tantamount to confiscation. On this I understand we have Belaunde's oral assurances to Rostow and Jones that he will take no action which will further impair the company's position. The majority opinion here is that Belaunde will probably not take any precipitate action during his term of office against the company but will leave the problem for his successor. Belaunde is not a decisive person and if he is not misled into thinking that the United States will continue a large aid program regardless of his actions, I think we could afford to take this chance. Belaunde is a weak man, but he has his good points. I concurred in the Rostow Mission and in view of Mr. Gordon's feeling on the matter, I concur in the following recommendations:[2]

1. We make additional project loans to Peru as follows:

$9 million dollars agricultural credit loan, part of which would be funded with P.L. 480 local currency; $2 million dollar loan for community development (Cooperacion Popular); $3 million dollars for feasibility studies of new projects; $1½ million dollars for civic action training and $4 million for road construction.

2. That no additional project or program loans be made from AID funds without your approval until we have negotiated with Peru a realistic self-help program comparable to those already negotiated with Brazil, Chile and Colombia. The self-help negotiations can best be conducted under the leadership of the World Bank, which is interested in playing this role, and with the cooperation of the International Monetary Fund.

Inflation in Peru was at a 15% rate in 1965 as compared with 10% in 1964 and 6% in prior years. The inflation is in part due to budgetary deficits and the inadequacy of Belaunde's agricultural policies.

3. Belaunde should be told orally, when the project loans are signed, that self-help is essential; that we will be obliged under the Hickenlooper–Adair Amendment to stop disbursements on all outstanding loans if confiscatory action is taken; that our ability to extend large scale loans on soft, concessional terms is limited both by our own balance of payments and budgetary problems and by the relatively strong position of the Peruvian economy; and that we expect Peru to be more forthcoming and consistent in dealing with the threat of communism to the hemisphere.

Finally, I should add that our tactics in dealing with Belaunde have been influenced by large U.S. private investments in Peru, particularly in mining.

Thomas C. Mann[3]

---

[2] According to a letter from Barnebey to Jones, March 4, the White House informed the Department on February 26 that the President approved these recommendations. Barnebey remarked: "In view of all the current interest in assistance to Peru on the 5th, 6th, and 7th floors of this building, not to exclude that of the White House, we should strike while the iron is hot." (National Archives and Records Administration, RG 59, Lima Embassy Files, 1966: Lot 69 F 191, PER Jones)

[3] Printed from a copy that bears this typed signature.

479. Memorandum From the Under Secretary of State for
Economic Affairs (Mann) to President Johnson[1]

Washington, February 22, 1966.

SUBJECT

Allegations About Change in Our Aid Policy for Peru

Mr. Komer has a summary of the facts regarding the IPC problem
as it affected our aid program in Peru. I hope you will have a chance
to read it.[2]

From the beginning, *our objective has been to prevent a confiscatory-
type action.* The record does not show any difference of objective or tactic between the Kennedy Policy in late 1963 and our policy in 1964–66.

This policy has been successful. We will have our maximum chance
of ultimate success if we follow the three recommendations made in
my memorandum of February 19. However, if the Peruvian press were
to report Belaunde's promise not to confiscate, Belaunde would be
charged with having "sold out" the national patrimony. The danger is
that Belaunde would then feel obliged to prove his "patriotism" by
moving against the IPC property. This could, in turn, bring into operation the Hickenlooper–Adair Amendment, relations between the U.S.
and Peru would then be in open crisis. And we would have failed to
obtain our objective.

The proposed AID loans to Peru *do not represent a change in policy
or tactic.* From the beginning we have been granting or withholding
soft loans depending on whether we thought it would help us achieve
our objective. In 1964, for example, we made larger loans than those
now proposed.

The investor agrees with our tactic. Yesterday the highest officials of
the IPC volunteered to me their appreciation. They expressed agreement with the tactics which have been recommended. Their hope is
that they can go quietly to work and reach some kind of a modus
vivendi which will postpone the problem of this particular oil field

---

[1] Source: Johnson Library, National Security File, Country File, Peru, Vol. II,
1/66–10/67. Secret. A notation on the memorandum indicates that the President saw it.

[2] At 11 a.m., Mann called the President to ask if he had seen the memorandum on
the "IPC–Peruvian matter." (Document 478) Johnson admitted he had not, but instructed
his staff to "get him an announcement that balanced this thing." He told Mann "to get
it on paper but to make sure that the President was not announcing that we have back-
tracked and made a bad mistake and Bobby Kennedy had forced him to change it." The
President further stated that "he did not object to the deal made" but "does object to announcing both deals which says that the Mann–Johnson policy has been abandoned and
we are going to sit back and let them confiscate." (Johnson Library, Papers of Thomas
C. Mann, Telephone Conversations with LBJ, May 2, 1965–June 2, 1966)

while enabling them to get on with improvements they wish to make in other properties. I do not, therefore, expect any dissent from Senator Hickenlooper or from the private sector.

The *Eder article is therefore incorrect in its major premise.*[3] But I do not think it follows from this that we help ourselves by debating details of delicate foreign policy issues in the press because, given Latin American realities, this would make it impossible to achieve our foreign policy objectives.

The difficulty we are having with press treatment of our Latin American policy stems from the fact that the other side has preempted the field. No knowledgeable person outside of government is willing and able to take them on and to counterattack by dealing with the real, and not the phony, issues. I have already spoken with you about my suggestions on how to deal with this. I expect to have something concrete on this soon.

Thomas C. Mann

---

[3] In an article attributed to Richard G. Eder, February 10, *The New York Times* disclosed that the United States had quietly reversed its policy of restricting economic assistance to Peru as a means to force a favorable settlement in the IPC case. President Johnson's reaction was twofold: he demanded an investigation of the leak and instructed that "no new loans are to be made to Peru without [his] prior approval." (Memorandum from Bowdler to the President, February 10; ibid., National Security File, Country File, Peru, Vol. II, 1/66–10/67) In a February 21 letter to Jones, Cutter explained: "The spate of newspaper articles concerning our AID policy in Peru caused considerable worry here coming as it did with the Viet Nam debates and other Senate criticism of our policies and the President became personally involved. In view of this high level interest, no decision could be made until fully cleared with the White House. The receipt of Belaunde's letter has now made it possible to move ahead with recommendations to the White House." (National Archives and Records Administration, RG 59, Lima Embassy Files: Lot 73 F 100, Cutter, Curtis C.)

---

480.   Memorandum From the President's Deputy Special Assistant for National Security Affairs (Komer) to President Johnson[1]

Washington, February 23, 1966, 5 p.m.

The Peru Matter. After further checking, I feel obligated to report back honestly my private feeling that countering the unfortunate news

---

[1] Source: Johnson Library, National Security File, Memos to the President, McGeorge Bundy, Vol. 19. Secret. A notation on the memorandum indicates the President saw it.

leak runs too much risk of stirring up even more trouble—and of a set-back to the promising course set in train by Rostow's successful visit:

1. Disturbing as such leaks are, this one was a two-day wonder unnoticed in the country at large. But if we leak a counter-story, even as mild a one as Walt Rostow reluctantly suggests, we may open the whole issue up again. Will smart-aleck reporters like Kurzman[2] and Eder settle for the Rostow line or start digging again? Our quiet deal with Belaunde also undermined Bobby Kennedy and others, who were planning to speak out on Peru—we might stir them up again.

2. On the merits, we got the maximum politically possible from Belaunde on the IPC case. Moreover, things are going our way in Peru. Stirring up the IPC case again might put us right back in an impasse again.

3. Should we penalize Belaunde, who acted in good faith? We still want to be tough with Peru, but (as Tom Mann proposes) it's better to shift the argument to the much firmer ground of needed self-help and anti-inflation measures. If we press hard on these lines, no one can le-gitimately complain.

4. We could keep Peru on a short rein by stretching out the four small loans (actually totalling only $15 million, since the rest is local currency), and saying that any help beyond this would depend on ad-equate self-help. Putting out *this* story 4–5 weeks from now when the first loan was ready for signature would create no problems.

5. Then in six months or so, if all goes well, we'll have ample op-portunity to correct the record by demonstrating how the hard line on aid has paid off in such countries as Pakistan, India, Turkey, Colom-bia, Brazil, *and Peru.*

I have no special axe to grind on this Peruvian affair, and I fully realize the problems created by loose talk. It doesn't come from over here. But in this case correcting the record may hit the wrong culprits.[3]

R. W. Komer

---

[2] Dan Kurzman, foreign correspondent for *The Washington Post.*

[3] The President wrote the following note at the end of the memorandum: "I agree—go ahead." In telegram 854 to Lima, March 9, the Department instructed Jones to tell Belaúnde his assurances that IPC would not be "further impaired" were satisfactory; and the U.S. Government would consider individual AID project loans "on their mer-its," including the Cooperación Popular community development loan of $2.1 million. (Johnson Library, National Security File, Country File, Peru, Vol. II, 1/66–10/67) Jones relayed this message to Belaúnde on March 17. (Telegram 1303 from Lima, March 10; ibid.)

481. Memorandum From the President's Special Assistant (Rostow) to President Johnson[1]

Washington, May 27, 1966, 8 p.m.

SUBJECT

Loan to Peru for COOPOP[2]

Last February you authorized resumption of significant concessional lending to Peru, provided President Belaunde agreed to solve, or maintain the status quo on, the International Petroleum Company (IPC) case and take effective self-help measures. You told Bill Bowdler that you did not want the loans to be authorized without your prior approval.

The first loan is now ready. It is a good loan—$2.1 million for community development programs in Indian villages. Belaunde has kept his word on IPC and is working out in a highly satisfactory manner with us and the World Bank a development program based on sound self-help measures. All interested agencies, including Treasury, have approved the loan.

I recommend that you authorize us to go ahead.

Walt

Approve[3]

Disapprove

See me

---

[1] Source: Johnson Library, National Security File, Country File, Peru, Vol. II, 1/66–10/67. Confidential. Earlier in the day Rostow received a memorandum from Read which, "in view of the President's interest in this particular problem," requested White House concurrence for the loan. (Ibid.)

[2] Cooperación Popular.

[3] This option is checked. A notation by Bromley Smith indicates that S/S and Bowdler were informed on May 28.

482.   Memorandum for the Record

Washington, May 8, 1967.

[Source: Department of State, INR/IL Historical Files, 303 Committee Files, c. 51, May 5, 1967. Secret. 3 pages of source text not declassified.]

483.   Memorandum From the President's Special Assistant (Rostow) to President Johnson[1]

Washington, May 19, 1967.

SUBJECT

Program Loan for Peru

The attached memoranda contain a request by Bill Gaud for authorization to negotiate a $40 million program loan with Peru, and concurrences by Charlie Schultze and Joe Fowler.[2]

Need for the Loan. Since he took office in 1963, President Belaunde has pressed a development program targeted largely toward opening the interior of Peru. Public investment has outstripped revenues and led to inflationary pressures and a foreign exchange drain which now threaten financial stability. The program loan—part of a joint program worked out with the IBRD and the IMF totalling $175 million—is designed to permit Belaunde to correct his financial difficulties while continuing a reasonable development effort.

Conditions for the Loan. Belaunde's budgetary deficit for the year starting July 1, 1967 is expected to run up to $186 million if remedial action is not taken. Exchange reserves dropped nearly $30 million during the first quarter of 1967.

The proposed loan would be negotiated if:

—The Peruvian Congress authorizes new revenue measures which will net $116 million.
—The government cuts back expenditures by $15 million.

---

[1] Source: Johnson Library, National Security File, Country File, Peru, Vol. II, 1/66–10/67. Confidential.

[2] Attached but none printed.

—Belaunde turns down the military's bid to spend some $30 million on supersonic jet aircraft.

—Peru negotiates a satisfactory standby agreement with the IMF.

These conditions involve tough decisions from which Belaunde has until recently shied away. But on May 8 he asked the Congress for authority to raise revenues and cut expenditures in the amounts indicated above. The loan will be contingent on his getting this authority and accepting the other conditions.

The loan would be disbursed in three installments, each contingent on compliance with the terms agreed upon.

Funding the Loan. Funds are presently available from the FY 1967 appropriation to cover the loan. If there is a long delay in the negotiations it will have to be funded in FY 1968.

Other related considerations. Together with Frei, Lleras and Leoni, Belaunde represents a new generation of political leaders of democratic bent, deeply interested in modernizing their countries. We have a stake in seeing Belaunde and his program succeed.

Belaunde has stuck faithfully to his promise not to impair the position of the International Petroleum Company. IPC continues to operate under the same conditions that existed when Belaunde took office. Negotiations between IPC and government continue. Differences have been narrowed, but a final settlement has not been reached.

In the past we have had trouble with Peru over seizure of our tuna boats. There have been no recent incidents. We have proposed negotiations on a conservation agreement and are awaiting Peru's response.[3]

Recommendation

I joined Fowler and Schultze in recommending authorization to negotiate the loan subject to the conditions stated and to further consultation with you prior to signature of the loan agreement.

Walt

Approve

Disapprove

See me[4]

---

[3] On October 2, 1966, three U.S.-owned tuna clippers were detained for operating within the 200-mile fisheries jurisdiction claimed by Peru. The boats were released on October 6. Memoranda on the tuna boat incident from Rostow to the President, October 4, 6, and 7, are in the Johnson Library, National Security File, Country File, Peru, 1/66–10/67. Documentation on the incident and the controversy over the legal limit of Peru's territorial waters is in the National Archives and Records Administration, RG 59, Central Files 1967–69, POL 33–4 PERU.

[4] The President checked this option and wrote: "What does [Lincoln] Gordon & [Sol] Linowitz do or say on these loans? They should be in on them. L."

484. Telegram From the President's Special Assistant (Rostow) to President Johnson in Texas[1]

Washington, May 29, 1967, 1648Z.

CAP 67481. Peru Program Loan.

On May 19 I sent you a memorandum transmitting a request from Bill Gaud for authorization to negotiate a $40 million program loan with Peru.[2] The loan is designed to help Belaunde correct inflationary and balance of payments problems while continuing his development efforts. Joe Fowler, Charlie Schultze and I concurred in the request.

The loan was to be tied to four self-help conditions. These conditions represent tough political decisions for Belaunde, but are essential to any stabilization program. I noted that we did not know whether Belaunde would be willing to make these decisions and get Congress to act on additional revenue measures.

You sent the memo back to me inquiring whether Secretary Rusk and Linc Gordon had endorsed Gaud's request. It has the full endorsement of Gordon who originated the authorization request. Since Bill Gaud acts as Secretary Rusk's agent in these matters, the loan authorization was not submitted to him. I am confident, however, that he would go along with the Gaud–Gordon recommendation.

Since I forwarded the memorandum to you, President Belaunde has acted—successfully—on one of the four conditions: a cutback in government expenditures. He has had partial success in a second: substantial additional revenues via new import duties and internal taxes.

It is important that we be in a position to tell Belaunde that we are prepared to help him if he is willing to take strong self-help action. He may be unwilling to meet all our conditions or, accepting them, unable to get the Congress to enact new taxes. In either case, the responsibility would be his and not our unwillingness to help as we have in the case of his principal neighbors: Brazil, Chile and Colombia.

---

[1] Source: Johnson Library, National Security File, Country File, Peru, Vol. II, 1/66–10/67. Confidential.

[2] Document 483.

With the clarification on Linc Gordon's endorsement of the loan, may we proceed with the negotiations subject to the stipulated conditions?

Yes[3]

No

See me

---

[3] The President dictated the following instructions: "Walt: I don't want Gaud making loans to South America without consulting with our Latin America men. You might talk to Oliver about this when he gets back." (Note from the President to Rostow, May 29; Johnson Library, National Security File, Country File, Peru, Vol. II, 1/66–10/67) Jim Jones, Assistant to the President, subsequently reported: "Walt Rostow said Covey Oliver has now reviewed the Peru loan and agrees with the necessity of going ahead. Does the President approve?" Jones informed Rostow of the President's approval on May 30. (Note from Jones to the President, undated; ibid.) According to a memorandum from Rostow to Gaud, May 31, President Johnson authorized the negotiations "in the understanding that the agreement reached with Peru will be submitted to him for review prior to signature." (Ibid.)

---

485. Telegram From the Department of State to the Embassy in Peru[1]

Washington, June 17, 1967, 8:01 p.m.

212297. Ref: Embtel 5814.[2] For Ambassador.

1. You should seek immediate interview with President Belaunde regarding program loan and Peruvian plans purchase Mirage aircraft.

2. You should inform President you will receive instructions within a few days which will authorize you to discuss Peruvian Air

---

[1] Source: National Archives and Records Administration, RG 59, Central Files 1967–69, DEF 12–5, PERU. Confidential; Immediate. Drafted by Sayre, cleared by Vance, and approved by the Secretary.

[2] Telegram 5814 from Lima, June 14, reported that Peru was considering the purchase of Mirage fighter aircraft from France. (Ibid.) In a June 15 memorandum to the Secretary, Oliver explained that "a contract between Peru and France on the Mirage seems imminent." He recommended that Rusk raise with McNamara a proposal to begin delivery of supersonic fighters to "the major South American countries" in 1969. In an attached note Rusk wrote that he would "like to speak to Covey Oliver on this." (Ibid., ARA Files, 1967–1969: Lot 72 D 33, Military Assistance Program) According to the Secretary's Appointment Book Rusk met Oliver and Sayre on June 17 at 5:28 p.m. (Johnson Library) No substantive record of the meeting has been found.

Force requirements for F–5 aircraft. These instructions will define as specifically as possible at this time how we would propose to carry out our commitment to assist Latin Air Forces in obtaining suitable replacement jet fighter aircraft beginning in 1970. It should be made clear that financing would be on commercial basis outside MAP.

3. At the same time you should make clear that you cannot make specific commitment that this means delivery of F–5 aircraft to Peru could begin in 1969. This would depend on overall performance of Peruvian economy as set out in program loan negotiation paper.

4. We could not agree to be party to transaction which diverted substantial Peruvian resources from economic to military purposes when the latter purposes are of low priority.

5. You should also make clear that your instructions on the program loan specifically provide that diversion by Peru of substantial resources to low priority military requirements (read jet fighters from France) would preclude the negotiation of program loan.

6. We cannot of course tell Peru how to utilize its resources. We assume Peru is committed goals of Alliance as we are and that it wants to give highest priority to economic and social development. If Peru decides otherwise then U.S. must make its decision consistent with Charter of Punta del Este and Declaration of Presidents. We would regret our inability to help Peru in such circumstances but we would be left with no other alternative.[3]

Rusk

---

[3] In a meeting with Jones on June 20 Belaúnde maintained that Peru needed supersonic fighters due to the "unsettled condition" of the world. Jones explained that the United States was reviewing its policy on supersonic aircraft in Latin America, but warned: "If GOP decided use its resources buy plane like Mirage, USG would feel it inappropriate use its resources for program loan." After arguing that the "two things should not be tied together," Belaúnde blamed the Department for its "uncompromising attitude toward Peruvian armed forces and suggested we adopt more understanding position of Pentagon." Jones reported: "I restrained myself." (Telegram 5881 from Lima, June 20; National Archives and Records Administration, RG 59, Central Files 1967–69, AID(US) 9 PERU)

486. Editorial Note

On July 6, 1967, the Department instructed the Embassy to discuss the status of economic assistance with President Belaúnde, particularly in view of legislation before the Peruvian Congress to expropriate holdings of the International Petroleum Company. (Telegram 2229 to Lima; National Archives and Records Administration, RG 59, Central Files 1967–69, PET 6 PERU) In a meeting on July 10 Ambassador Jones recalled Belaúnde's assurance to Walt Rostow in February 1966 that the IPC would not be "further impaired" during his administration. (Telegram 211 from Lima, July 12; ibid., DEF 19–8 US–PERU) Jones also warned of the "adverse effect this law would have, once promulgated, on US–Peruvian relations," referring to the penalties set by the Hickenlooper amendment. (Telegram 190 from Lima, July 11, ibid., PET 6 PERU) Belaúnde replied that he needed more time to resolve the IPC case and pleaded for action "this week" on the program loan. After a heated exchange concerning Peruvian efforts to purchase French aircraft, Belaúnde complained "with strong words about local forces conspiring against him to defeat his program of government and force devaluation." "I have seldom seen the President so distraught," Jones observed. "It was a stormy session." (Telegram 192 from Lima, July 11; ibid., DEF 19–8 US–PERU) Telegrams 190 and 192 from Lima were retyped and forwarded to President Johnson, with a note from Rostow on July 13. Marvin Watson recorded the President's response: "Walt get this over to C[ovey] Oliver. Ask him to talk with T[ony] Solomon and Tom Mann about it. Oliver give the President a memo of recommendations." (Johnson Library, National Security File, Country File, Peru, Vol. II, 6/65–9/66)

---

487. Memorandum From the Assistant Secretary of State for Inter-American Affairs (Oliver) to President Johnson[1]

Washington, July 15, 1967.

SUBJECT

International Petroleum Company Case in Peru

---

[1] Source: Johnson Library, National Security File, Country File, Peru, Vol. II, 1/66–10/67. Secret.

The Peruvian Congress has adopted and sent to President Belaunde a law purporting to expropriate a portion of the properties of the International Petroleum Company (IPC). Belaunde must now decide (1) either to sign or act otherwise on this legislation, and (2) once the law is promulgated to take one of several alternative actions to carry out its terms. Our latest information indicates that Belaunde is trying to postpone signing the measure until late this month, in the hope that meanwhile he can work out an acceptable solution to this problem. We believe that the best such solution would be for Belaunde to conclude the long-pending negotiations with the company for a 25-year service contract—in return for the company's ceding its claim to surface or sub-surface rights on its oil property in northern Peru.

We have had Ambassador Jones set out our views on this problem to President Belaunde and Foreign Minister Vasquez.[2] We have sent our Deputy Chief of Mission in Lima to London to talk with Haya de la Torre, leader of Belaunde's political opposition, to urge him to take some of the pressure off Belaunde on the IPC issue.[3] We have also suggested following up your exchange of letters with Belaunde of February of last year by sending a letter to him from Walt Rostow urging a reasonable settlement.[4]

We are considering still further steps. Depending on developments, we could send a high-level emissary to Lima to urge Belaunde to reach a settlement with IPC. We are also trying to use our other assets to help Belaunde reach a reasonable decision, and our best means for this purpose would be the immediate approval and announcement of the pending $15 million program loan to his country. Our objectives are to convince Belaunde that the IPC decision is up to him, and him alone, and to use all the means available to us to persuade him to reach the right decision.

C.T.O.

---

[2] Jones met the Foreign Minister on July 13 to discuss the issues raised in his meeting with Belaúnde, July 10. (Telegram 251 from Lima, July 13, National Archives and Records Administration, RG 59, Central Files 1967–69, PET 15–2 PERU)

[3] Haya was visiting Oxford University. At the instigation of IPC representatives, Jones recommended Siracusa for an "urgent" mission to secure Haya's support in the IPC case. (Telegram 231 from Lima, July 13; ibid., PET 6 PERU) The Department authorized Siracusa's trip to London after consultation in Washington. (Telegram 6379 to Lima, July 13; ibid.)

[4] Bowdler wrote the following note on the memorandum: "Walt Rostow has asked your views on whether to do this." Rostow also sought guidance in a July 15 memorandum to the President. The President decided that Rusk should write the letter; Read was so informed on July 17. (Ibid.) No evidence has been found that Rusk sent the letter to Belaúnde.

488. Memorandum From the President's Special Assistant (Rostow) to President Johnson[1]

Washington, July 15, 1967, 5 p.m.

Mr. President:

President Belaunde faces probably the toughest situation of his three-year administration. He is engaged in three hard, interrelated fights:

—with his military on the acquisition of French supersonics and higher military expenditures.
—with his Congress on the IPC expropriation.
—with his Congress and business interests on higher import duties and taxes.

At the end of May, with your authorization, we offered to negotiate a $40 million program loan contingent on four conditions:

—an IMF standby agreement.
—$157 million in new revenue measures.
—$15 million cutback in expenditures.
—no French supersonic aircraft.

Belaunde made a good try to meet these conditions. He *succeeded* in:

—negotiating the IMF standby.
—raising at least $90 million of the $157 million of new revenue.
—making the expenditure cutback.

Because of his military and Congress, *he fell short in:*

—putting through new taxes.
—getting a commitment from the military not to buy French supersonics, although he has so far staved off their closing a deal.

Bill Gaud and Covey Oliver ask your approval (Tab A)[2] for their negotiating a $15 million program loan—an amount equivalent to the first tranche of the $40 million package, with the balance to come later if he delivers on the original conditions. This would:

—acknowledge his self-help efforts to date.
—encourage him to press forward with the other tax measures.
—strengthen his hand with the Congress on IPC and the military on supersonics.
—ultimately, perhaps, save him from a political crisis in which he would quit or be toppled.

---

[1] Source: Johnson Library, National Security File, Country File, Peru, Vol. II, 1/66–10/67. Secret.

[2] Tab A was memoranda to the President from Gaud and Schultze, July 12 and July 15; attached but not printed.

The $15 million would be conditioned on:

—drawing at least $21 million of the IMF standby.
—submitting new tax legislation to the Congress in August.
—holding the 1968 military budget to the 1967 level.
—agreeing not to buy supersonics until 1969–70 when we plan to make available F–5's in Latin America.
—working out a satisfactory arrangement on IPC.

On the IPC problem, Covey Oliver describes the current situation and steps he has taken, and proposes to take, in the memo at Tab B.[3]

In recommending approval of the $15 million program loan, Charlie Schultze includes a personal note on the F–5 issue (Tab C).[4] The background to this problem is that in 1965, when the Latin Americans were pressing to acquire supersonic aircraft, Bob McNamara agreed to program F–5's for delivery in 1969–70 to delay purchases. The military in Peru, and now in Brazil, impatient to acquire supersonics, have started negotiations with the French. If we are to head off these deals, we must:

—renew our willingness to provide F–5's.
—begin purchase talks with the interested countries toward the end of this year, with delivery date in late 1969 or 1970 (lead time is 20 months).
—use our economic assistance as a lever in getting these countries not to go supersonic until then.

I recommend that you approve the $15 million program loan with the five stipulated conditions.

Walt

Approve[5]

Disapprove

See me

---

[3] Document 487.

[4] Tab C was a memorandum from Schultze to the President, July 15; attached but not printed.

[5] None of the options is checked but the President wrote the following instructions for Rostow at the top of the first page of the memorandum: "get Bob Mc[Namara's] opinion on plane deal & his judgment as well as Rusk on effect this will have in Congress on Hickenlooper et al. & call me."

489.   Memorandum From the President's Special Assistant (Rostow) to President Johnson[1]

Washington, July 18, 1967.

Mr. President:

I suggest we consider under the "Other" item of our "Tuesday Lunch"[2] agenda the Peruvian program loan and the related issues of IPC and supersonic aircraft. Rusk and McNamara will come prepared to give you their views.

Prospects on IPC

Belaunde told the IPC representative yesterday that he had four options for handling the IPC bill:

1. Form a dummy corporation with majority Peruvian capital and enter into an operating contract with it. (IPC won't buy this formula.)
2. Veto the bill. (Politically Belaunde can't afford to do this.)
3. Sign the bill and drag out implementation indefinitely.
4. Promulgate the law and send it back to Congress for clarification as to whether it permits him to enter into an operating contract with a foreign company.

He did not commit himself to which option he would follow. What scant evidence we have indicates that he would go for the fourth option if Haya de la Torre (head of the opposition APRA Party) will give assurances that APRA will not attack him if he makes an operating contract with IPC.

We have a man in London now talking to Haya de la Torre.[3] Haya returns to Peru this Thursday[4] and, if he is so inclined, could reach an understanding with Belaunde in time for Belaunde to follow the fourth option. If Haya won't play ball, the betting is that Belaunde will start

---

[1] Source: Johnson Library, National Security File, Country File, Peru, Vol. II, 1/66–10/67. Confidential.

[2] See Document 490.

[3] In a meeting at Oxford on July 18 Siracusa told Haya that the "highest levels of the United States Government" were closely monitoring the IPC case; the Department thought the case had reached a "critical and climactic moment" that could have "far reaching effects for better or for worse on US–Peruvian relations." Haya replied with the following "unequivocal" assurances: he was opposed to "petroleum exploitation by the state"; he would clarify his position in a public speech upon his return to Lima; and he would privately assure Belaúnde that APRA would not attack the government if it sought a negotiated contract with IPC. (Telegram 496 from London, July 19; National Archives and Records Administration, RG 59, Central Files 1967–69, PET 15 PERU) Rostow forwarded a copy of this telegram to the President under the cover of a memorandum dated July 20. (Johnson Library, National Security File, Memos to the President, Walt W. Rostow, Vol. 35)

[4] July 20.

with the fourth option and then slip into the third so as to maintain the "no impairment" agreement he has with you.

One related favorable development is that the Peruvian Government yesterday announced that agreement had been reached with ITT over the telephone system. Over a three-year period:

—ITT will make an immediate modest expansion of telephone facilities.
—Peruvian users will be able to "buy out" the company.
—A much larger expansion of service will follow, open to international bidding in which ITT can take part.

The Background on Supersonics

Beginning in 1963, the larger South American countries indicated their interest to go supersonic. To hold them off, McNamara agreed then to sell them F–5's in 1969–70 if their economic position permitted.

Since 1965, Argentina, Chile and Venezuela have bought planes from us, the U.K. and West Germany, respectively—but they were all subsonic.

Peru, and recently Brazil, have shown impatience over waiting until 1969–70 for F–5's and have started negotiations with the French for Mirages.

The situation we now face is:

—We can't make F–5's available, or enter into negotiations, right away because of the adverse impact it would have in Congress on the Alliance and MAP.
—Unless we have an attractive alternative, Peru and Brazil will buy Mirages and the Congressional reaction will be just as severe.
—Our best strategy is to reiterate the McNamara pledge and tell them to be patient until later in the year on implementation.

Behind this strategy lie these considerations:

—Northrop could start talks in October or November after the Congress adjourns.
—The lead time for F–5's is 20 months, which would place delivery in the time frame of 1969–70.

Walt

P.S.—I have just learned that the House Foreign Relations Committee has approved an amendment to the AID bill (Ross Adair introduced it) banning aid of any kind to any Alliance country that acquires supersonic military jet aircraft from any source or by any means.

This amendment is mischievous in the extreme, since some countries will obtain such aircraft whether we like it or not. To the proud Latins, sanctions of this nature produce the opposite effect of what they are intended to achieve.

I can see much of the good work of the Summit going down the drain if this amendment is maintained.

490. Notes of Meeting[1]

Washington, July 18, 1967, 6:06–7:30 p.m.

NOTES OF THE PRESIDENT'S MEETING
WITH
SECRETARY RUSK
SECRETARY McNAMARA
WALT ROSTOW
McGEORGE BUNDY
GEORGE CHRISTIAN

[Omitted here is discussion of other matters.]

On the subject of supplying supersonic fighters to Peru, it was agreed that the Peruvian government wanted these planes primarily for prestige value and not for any practical defense purposes. The President cited a ticker item which said Congress had proposed that the U.S. would not provide aid to any country with supersonic planes.

Secretary Rusk pointed out that the proportion of aid funds committed to defense has been steadily dropping in Latin American countries. The President said a briefing should be arranged on the subject, especially with the Congress in mind.

Secretary McNamara pointed out that the total number of tanks in Latin America is less than the number in Bulgaria alone. The Secretary said the number of aircraft in the 21 Latin American countries is less than the number operated by Sweden alone.

Secretary McNamara said that the politicians do, however, depend on the Army.

The President asked, "Isn't there some way we can show the Congress what happened in Venezuela?" Secretary Rusk said that he and Secretary McNamara had talked to the Congress many times about this. Secretary Rusk said there is a very real guerrilla problem there.

The President said it seemed to him as though it would be a wise course to get out some of those old Cuba speeches and show the Congress what could happen if we aren't able to help these countries. The President said there will be many other Cubas in Latin America unless we do. The President said Assistant Secretary Oliver thinks we should give the $15 million in aid to Peru.

---

[1] Source: Johnson Library, Tom Johnson Meeting Notes. Literally Eyes Only. Drafted by Tom Johnson. The meeting was scheduled as a substitute for the Tuesday luncheon meeting. (Rostow to Rusk, July 18, 11:25 a.m.; National Archives and Records Administration, RG 59, Rusk Files: Lot 72 D 192, Telephone Calls 7/1/67–7/24/67)

Secretary McNamara said he would give the $15 million in aid if they met the conditions which have been set forth. Secretary Rusk said Peru would not buy the conditions.

The President said that Rusk and McNamara and Rostow should get together and clear up this matter and come back to him with a recommendation.[2]

[Omitted here is discussion of other matters.]

[2] No evidence has been found that Rusk and McNamara submitted a written recommendation to the President.

---

491.   Telegram From the Embassy in Peru to the Department of State[1]

Lima, July 25, 1967, 2300Z.

432. Subject: Program Loan Negotiations and Military Spending. Ref: State 9115.[2]

1. Stedman, Acting AID Mission Director, and I called on President this morning. Said we had come in response to his request made to Dentzer and me earlier this month (Lima 192)[3] for emergency financial assistance; that we were instructed to leave a memorandum with him embodying offer and requirements accompanying it. However before going over memorandum I said I would like to make a few observations orally. Belaunde agreed and I proceeded as follows:

(A) Program loan offered in memorandum was additional to regular program of project lending.

(B) All negotiations for program loan would be terminated if position of IPC was permitted to deteriorate. In view of pending legislation on expropriation and nationalization La Brea y Parinas and its anticipated promulgation into law USG could not continue negotiations on program loan or later conclude loan agreement or later disperse funds under it if position of IPC were impaired.

[1] Source: Johnson Library, National Security File, Country File, Peru, Vol. II, 1/66–10/67. Confidential; Priority. Forwarded to the President under the cover of a July 27 memorandum from Rostow. (Ibid.) Additional documentation on the meeting is in telegram 443 and airgram A–44 from Lima, both July 27. (National Archives and Records Administration, RG 59, Central Files 1967–69, PET 15–2 PERU and POL PERU–US, respectively)

[2] Telegram 9115 from Lima, July 19, contained the Department's instructions on the program loan negotiations and military spending. (Ibid., AID(US) 9 PERU)

[3] See Document 486.

2. President interrupted me to explain that position of IPC would not be altered even with promulgation of new law which he said he was going to sign last possible moment (we assume July 26 or 27); otherwise Congress would promulgate law for him which was politically undesirable in light all his other problems with legislative body. He intends issue supreme decree at time of signing law providing for status quo at La Brea y Parinas until final solution its future operation can be worked out. While status of IPC would thus he said not be impaired, he expressed irritation at what he considered constant interference over the years of this company with his development program. He complained that company was stubborn and had refused to make concessions necessary for him politically to reach agreement. He referred again to formation of dummy corporation with majority Peruvian shareholders which he said would make it easy for him to sign operating contract immediately. Otherwise he implied negotiations would have to continue beyond 30-day period granted by pending bill.

3. My third observation on program loan, I continued, related to level of military expenditures. I explained that domestic political facts of life in US were such that it was not possible for US to provide program loan assistance to countries whose military expenditures were substantial. For example purchase of supersonic aircraft by Peru now would endanger Foreign Assistance Appropriation for this year not only for Peru but for all LA. To negotiate program loan we would require understanding with GOP that budget of armed forces next year would be no greater than this and of course that there be no purchase of supersonic fighters. President reacted violently to this point saying he could not limit Peruvian military in their defense requirements nor could he admit of any interferences in internal affairs of Peru for $15 million or $50 million or $100 million. Said he must make it absolutely clear that he would sign no document which limited sovereign powers of Peru. If this were our requirements he would forget about assistance from US and "seek other routes."

4. I explained again problems of administration in Washington with Congress over this sensitive issue and showed President copy of draft Congressional amendment to Foreign Aid act introduced into lower House committee making mandatory suspension of aid to countries that purchase supersonic aircraft. Said I understood similar amendment had also been introduced in US Senate. While administration was opposed to this kind of limitation and amendment to Foreign Aid bill it was reflective of attitude of Congress and of political problem which Department and White House had at moment in relation to our overall foreign aid program.

5. I handed President memorandum (section b of reftel with informal Spanish translation). He went through first paragraphs hurriedly until he came to $15 million figure where he expressed some dis-

appointment that it was not $40 million figure originally discussed with him. I said lower figure might be considered "first tranche" and then if various steps outlined in memorandum were successfully completed we could begin next year discussion of remaining $25 million. I urged President to study memorandum carefully, discuss it with his advisors and, if he decided to proceed along these lines, to inform us when Stedman could begin negotiations with FinanceMin and President Central Reserve Bank. I said USG had no desire to limit Peruvian sovereignty as he had suggested but rather we hoped that with understanding of political problems in Washington, President would be willing in spirit of collaboration to work out with us various understandings necessary to proceed promptly with program loan. We spoke of relationship of this offer to IMF standby, to Peru's self-help efforts and to our desire help Peru not only with its development but with its immediate financial problem. Because Belaunde had said earlier he would never put his signature to any agreement that mentioned military or limited their activities Stedman and I assured him that understanding on level of military expenditures would not need be reduced to written agreement.

6. Belaunde was obviously upset by various conditions regarding program loan offer, particularly those relating to limitations on military. He spoke of his happy relations with military which so essential to any regime in Peru and with some bitterness over what he felt USG was doing to weaken its relations with Peruvian military who were bulwark against Communist infiltration in this continent. We were together one hour and 10 minutes and I believe at end, although we left him somewhat dejected, he had decided to make effort to meet conditions surrounding program loan offer.[4]

Jones

---

[4] On August 3 the Peruvian Government informed the Embassy that the terms of the program loan were unacceptable; the amount of the loan was too small in relation to the severity of its conditions. The government also had "great problems" in discussing the aircraft issue, since military matters were secret and "not subject to negotiations with foreign governments." (Telegram 542 from Lima, August 4; National Archives and Records Administration, RG 59, Central Files 1967–69, AID(US) 9 PERU) The Embassy recommended shelving the program loan until developments allowed a more favorable opportunity for negotiation. The Embassy admitted, however, that a policy of withholding financial assistance could lead to "further cooling in US–Peru relations," which, by its own assessment, "have not been at such low ebb for several years." (Telegram 602 from Lima, August 8; ibid.) The Department concurred. (Telegram 18729 to Lima, August 10; ibid.)

492. Telegram From the Department of State to the Embassy in the United Kingdom[1]

Washington, July 28, 1967, 2113Z.

13904. For Ambassador Only. Following message, dated July 28, 1967, from the President to the Prime Minister, sent by WH Private Channel, is for Embassy FYI only:

Begin Text

I have reviewed your request on the sale of Canberras to Peru with the greatest care.[2] I appreciate your consulting with us on this matter and the cooperation we have had from your Government on military sales to Latin America.

Congressional feeling on the acquisition of unnecessary military equipment by under-developed countries receiving economic assistance from us has reached such a point that the whole foreign aid program is threatened.

Peru is at present seeking substantial economic assistance. Were they to use scarce foreign exchange on military procurement at a time when we are furnishing dollars to tide them over financial difficulties, the Congressional and public reaction would be so strong that our ability to continue supporting the Alliance for Progress would be seriously endangered. Earlier this week our Ambassador in Lima informed President Belaunde of our willingness to conclude a sizeable loan provided we could agree, among other things, on a total level of military spending, with special attention to costs of major equipment purchases such as aircraft.

---

[1] Source: National Archives and Records Administration, RG 59, Central Files 1967–69, DEF 12–5 PERU. Secret; Immediate; Nodis. Text received from the White House and approved by Francis Meehan (S/S). A draft message to Prime Minister Wilson that was nearly identical to the final version, was enclosed in a July 27 memorandum from Rusk to the President. (Ibid.) Rostow forwarded the draft to the President under the cover of a July 27 memorandum. A handwritten note indicates that Johnson returned this memorandum on July 28, evidently implying his approval of the message. (Johnson Library, National Security File, Memos to the President, Walt W. Rostow, Vol. 26)

[2] Rostow forwarded Wilson's request under the cover of a memorandum to the President, July 26. Wilson acknowledged the "right of the U.S. government to withhold permission in this case, since these aircraft are partly M.D.A.P.-funded." The Prime Minister maintained, however, that the sale should be approved; Peru already had Canberra aircraft and could acquire "less suitable aircraft" from other sources, e.g. the French. "Indeed, in his present mood," Wilson argued, "De Gaulle might regard this as an excellent opportunity to make trouble for and between us; and, of course, between yourselves and the Peruvians." (Ibid.) Additional documentation on the Canberra issue is in the National Archives and Records Administration, RG 59, Central Files 1967–69, DEF 12–5 PERU.

President Belaunde understands that the purchase of French Mirage aircraft would make it impossible for us to go forward with the loan. Unfortunately the Canberras also fall within our general conditions to Peru about levels of military spending, and we could not successfully explain to Congress why under such circumstances we have given consent to sell Canberras to Peru.

I feel that I must do all that I can at this time to meet widely and deeply held Congressional objections to unnecessary arms expenditures by countries such as Peru. This includes equipment of United States origin. Certain influential Congressmen have for the moment expressed their concern about supersonic military aircraft, because it is the supersonic Mirage that has been the major problem. But I am sure that if I did consent to the sale of the sub-sonic but medium-range Canberra, Congressional reactions would be equally strong.

For these reasons, and with full understanding of the embarrassing position in which the British aircraft representatives in Lima will find themselves, I must conclude that we cannot alter the negative decision on the proposed sale.

I realize that the United Kingdom group will have to tell the Peruvians why the Canberra sale cannot go forward, and I have no objection to their doing so. While there is some added risk that the denial of Canberras might of itself trigger a Peruvian decision to spurn American assistance and buy Mirages, I have some doubt that this would occur. It seems to me that it is a risk which we will have to take, given our major problems with the Congress with our foreign aid programs. *End text.*

Rusk

---

493.   Telegram From the Embassy in Peru to the Department of State[1]

Lima, September 27, 1967, 2246Z.

1469. For Oliver from Ambassador. Subj: Supersonic Aircraft and Peruvian Stability.

---

[1] Source: National Archives and Records Administration, RG 59, Central Files 1967–69, DEF 12–5 PERU. Secret; Limdis; No Distribution Outside Department.

1. [*less than 1 line of source text not declassified*] of 24 and 26 September,[2] cites parallel information from several good sources to effect that Peru has signed contract for twelve Mirage jets costing $28 million. While this is not documentary evidence of a purchase, we have long believed that some commitment to French company has been made and consider the sources good enough to constitute confirmation of purchase short of documentary evidence or official announcement.[3]

2. We have made abundantly clear in reporting recent developments our belief that a prompt negotiating of US program loan assistance will be an imperative element for the restoration of confidence so sorely needed if Peruvian situation is to be stabilized and economic recovery and continued progress thereafter initiated.[4] If this is not done, and unless there is a restoration of confidence in the next few months, it is our judgment that authoritarian intervention in one form or another is highly likely. Yesterday we reported General Doig's remark that unless situation improved there would be no elections in 1969.[5]

3. Since we assume the single most inflexible impediment to our providing program loan assistance is the reported purchase of Mirages, I urge that every force be used at this time to achieve a decision permitting us promptly to make a firm and specific counter-offer of F–5's. I cannot assure that such a counter-offer would be sufficient to undo what has probably already been done to acquire Mirages, since it is likely that a substantial down-payment has been made. However, unless we have authority to counter the French deal with a firm offer now and then go ahead with a program loan, it is our considered opinion that Peru's fine democratic experience under President Belaunde is not likely to survive to end of his term. A military intervention in Peru

---

[2] Not found.

[3] In telegram 1508 from Lima, September 29, the Embassy reported that Peru had agreed to purchase 14 Mirage fighters from France, including the delivery of two training aircraft, before the end of 1967. (National Archives and Records Administration, RG 59, Central Files 1967–69, DEF 12–5 PERU)

[4] On July 27 the parliamentary coalition supporting the Belaúnde administration refused to attend sessions of Congress, citing the controversial election of an opposition candidate to the presidency of the Senate. The resulting constitutional crisis was further aggravated by a crisis in the government's finances; a run on the foreign exchange reserve eventually forced the administration to devalue the currency on September 1. The immediate political effect of devaluation included: (a) the installation of the new Congress on September 4; and (b) the formation of a new Cabinet on September 7. An INR analysis of the crisis is in a memorandum from Denney to the Secretary, September 14; an Embassy assessment is in telegram 1359 from Lima, September 20. (Ibid., FN 17 PERU and POL 15–2 PERU, respectively)

[5] As reported in telegram 1444 from Lima, September 26. (Ibid., POL 15–1 PERU) General Julio Doig Sanchez was the new Peruvian Minister of Defense.

would be such a blow to our general policies under the Alliance for Progress that an all-out effort to save the situation is now imperative.

4. I know you will do everything possible to obtain the kind of authority we request with regard to F–5's and thus give us a chance to resume our constructive policies of support for Belaunde administration and Peru's other democratic institutions.

Jones

---

494.   Memorandum From the President's Special Assistant (Rostow) to President Johnson[1]

Washington, October 5, 1967.

SUBJECT

Latin American Purchase of Supersonic Aircraft

The Peruvians have contracted to buy French Mirages despite our repeated warnings of the consequences. The story broke publicly in the *New York Times* yesterday morning.[2]

Peru's action—unless we can turn it around—threatens a supersonic aircraft race among the larger South American countries. It also means serious trouble for us with Congress on MAP and Alliance for Progress appropriations. For Peru it will result in no program assistance at a time when Belaunde is in critical need of help for his stabilization and development programs.

Belaunde finds himself in this bind because of his weak political position. The military looms large in the political structure and they have been pressing hard for modernization of old equipment. The opposition-controlled Congress has played politics by authorizing, on its own initiative, a substantial amount for military purchases. Belaunde was unable to block Congressional action, and he has not felt strong enough to order his military to drop the Mirage deal.

---

[1] Source: Johnson Library, National Security File, Country File, Peru, Vol. III, 10/67–1/69. Secret.

[2] According to the article, written by Neil Sheehan, French aircraft industry sources confirmed that "Peru had signed a contract about two months ago to purchase approximately 12 Mirage V's from Marcel Dassault General Aerodynamics, the French aircraft manufacturer."

There is a possibility that we can turn this situation around if we do two things:

—renew our offer to negotiate a $40 million program loan which you authorized last May (Belaunde was then unable to meet our conditions. Now, with increased taxes, spending limitations, IMF standby and devaluation, he is close to doing so, provided he stops the Mirage deal.).

—tell Belaunde what we told Costa e Silva last July—that we would allow Northrop to sell them F–5's for delivery in 1969–70.

Covey Oliver and Bill Gaud recommend that you approve negotiation of the program loan based on the substantial economic self-help measures taken by Belaunde since May (Tab A).[3] On the basis of previous reviews of the loan package, BOB and Treasury have no problem with the substance of the proposal.

A condition for the loan would continue to be no Mirages. I believe there is a chance of Belaunde making the military backtrack if he can:

—demonstrate that their action is depriving the nation of vital economic assistance.
—offer them the alternative of F–5's by 1969/70.

Before proceeding further in our offer of F–5's in Latin America, the SIG[4] believes that *we should touch base with Congress.* SIG proposes:

—a frank discussion of our military policy toward Latin America.
—a detailed explanation of how little of Latin American military expenditures goes into hardware (most goes for salaries and allowances).
—the serious consequences for the Alliance for Progress if we do not provide a reasonable alternative to limited modernization of military equipment, specifically F–5's.

SIG (Katzenbach, Nitze, Gaud and myself) has approved the scenario and talking points paper at Tab B for the handling of the F–5 issue.[5] Secretary McNamara and Secretary Rusk concur. Everyone recognizes that consultation on selling F–5's may adversely affect foreign aid legislation while the bill is pending in Congress. However, the consequences of doing nothing about the Peruvian purchase, or offering our own supersonics behind Congress's back are far more severe.

---

[3] Tab A was a memorandum from Gaud to the President, October 4; attached but not printed.

[4] Senior Interdepartment Group, Nick Katzenbach is chairman. [Footnote in the source text.]

[5] Both dated October 3; attached but not printed. The SIG discussed U.S. policy toward Latin American security forces, including F–5 aircraft, at its meeting on September 28; see Document 65.

I am convinced that unless we help Belaunde reverse the action taken by his military, we will be in deep trouble in Peru, and our ability to support for Alliance for Progress seriously weakened.

I strongly recommend that you authorize consultations with Congress along the lines of the scenario paper and that subject to the results of these talks, you approve renegotiation of the program loan on the basis of the conditions in the Gaud memo.

Walt

1. Approve consultation with Congress[6]

Disapprove

See me

2. Approve program loan renegotiation, subject to Congressional talks[6]

Disapprove

See me

---

[6] The President checked this option.

---

495. Telegram From the Department of State to the Embassy in Peru[1]

Washington, October 17, 1967, 2323Z.

55490. Subject: Authority to Negotiate Program Loan; Offer of F–5's. Ref: State 55492.[2] For Ambassador and AID Mission Director.

1. You are authorized to open negotiations with GOP for $40 million program loan on terms and conditions set forth in AID Adminis-

---

[1] Source: National Archives and Records Administration, RG 59, Central Files 1967–69, AID(US) 9 PERU. Secret; Immediate; Limdis. Repeated to USCINCSO, Sao Paulo, and Brasilia. Drafted by Bloomfield; cleared by Bowdler, Glaessner, Sharp, and Hartman; cleared in draft by Gaud, Lang, Fowler, Palmer, Sayre, Breen, and E. Jay Finkel at Treasury; and approved by Oliver.

[2] In telegram 55492 to Buenos Aires, Caracas, Lima, Rio de Janeiro, Santiago, Sao Paulo, and Brasilia, October 17, the Department reviewed U.S. policy toward the sale of F–5 aircraft to Latin America as "guidance for further discussions by addressee posts with host countries." (Ibid., DEF 19–8 US–LA)

trator's Memorandum for the President of October 4, 1967.[3] You should keep Department informed of progress of negotiations. Agreements reached are subject to normal approval procedures in Washington. You should also inform Belaunde that USG has authorized Northrop to begin direct negotiations immediately with GOP for sale F–5 aircraft.

2. In making your presentation to President Belaunde, you should inform him that President Johnson has approved loan offer and sale of F–5's because of great importance he attaches to resolution of Peru's current difficulties in a manner which will not jeopardize the United States' ability to continue supporting Peru's public investment program. President Johnson understands the expanded role which President Belaunde has charted for the Peruvian Government in creating the basis for a more diversified and equitable development of the economy and is anxious that USG be able to share in that effort through financial and technical assistance.

3. Because of the high priority which USG gives to development task in Peru, we are deeply concerned how military spending situation in Peru will affect US assistance program. You should point out that the purchase of Mirage aircraft, and indeed the sharp increase in military expenditure authorizations in general over the past year, not only affect the possibility of a program loan but could jeopardize our ability to provide Peru with economic assistance in other forms as well. Long-standing USG concern in both Executive and Legislative branches that scarce resources needed for economic development not be diverted into unnecessary military expenditures has lately been heightened by reports of planned acquisitions by Latin military of expensive armaments. Seriousness with which Congress views these developments is reflected in proposed amendment to Senate version of FAA bill (the so-called "Symington Amendment")[4] now being considered by House-Senate Conference. This amendment (text of which pouched to Mission Director on October 10) would instruct President take into account the percentage of an aid-recipient's budget devoted to military purposes and degree to which country is devoting foreign exchange to military purchases, and would require him to suspend economic assist-

---

[3] Not printed. (Johnson Library, National Security File, Country File, Peru, Vol. III, 10/67–1/69)

[4] Reference is to an amendment to the Foreign Assistance Act of 1961, sponsored by Senator Stuart Symington (D–Missouri), which was approved on November 14. (81 Stat. 459) On January 8, 1968, Congress passed a related amendment to the FAA, sponsored by Representatives Silvio O. Conte (R–Massachusetts) and Clarence D. Long (D–Maryland), requiring the President to withhold economic assistance to any "underdeveloped country" that used military assistance to acquire sophisticated weapons systems. The provision did not apply to Greece, Turkey, Iran, Israel, Taiwan, the Philippines, Korea, or any country that the President exempted on national security grounds. (81 Stat. 937; 81 Stat. 940)

ance including PL 480 sales when such assistance is "permitting the diversion of other resources to military expenditures to a degree which interferes with economic development." You should also draw Belaunde's attention to similar provision aimed specifically at "sophisticated or heavy military equipment" in law already approved by Congress replenishing Fund for Special Operations of IDB.[5] It was because of this provision and its possible interpretations, for example, that USG has been uncertain as to what its reaction should be to proposed $10 million loan from IDB for Peru's Industrial Bank.

4. It is for foregoing reasons, and none other, that a condition of the loan is assurance by President Belaunde that Peru will not acquire supersonic aircraft from France or third countries.[6] This means that Peru must cancel any arrangements it may have already made for acquisition of Mirage or similar aircraft.

5. You should tell Belaunde that we are aware of his difficulties in convincing Peruvian military that they should forego all modernization, as illustrated particularly by Air Force's desire to replace aging pre-Korean War aircraft, which becoming increasingly difficult to maintain in safe flying condition. For this reason, USG as long as two years ago promised to make F–5 aircraft available to certain LA countries in 1969–70 time frame. F–5 is relatively unsophisticated, light aircraft with much cheaper initial purchase price and maintenance cost than Mirage and more suited to Latin American Air Forces' mission.

6. Financing of F–5's will have to be through commercial (non-U.S. Government) sources. Acquisition at present will be limited to one squadron (12–18 aircraft). Sale of F–5's will also be conditioned on non-acquisition of Mirage or of similar aircraft elsewhere. You should also inform Belaunde in confidence that, in keeping with our commitments to supply these aircraft to certain other South American countries in 1969–1970 time frame, in addition to Peru we are authorizing Northrop to open negotiations with Brazil, and we are prepared to permit manufacturer to sell F–5's to Argentina, Chile, and Venezuela.

7. Report Belaunde's reaction soonest.

Rusk

---

[5] Reference is to an amendment to the Inter-American Development Bank Act, approved September 22, 1967. (81 Stat. 227)

[6] In telegram 55520 to Lima, October 18, the Department corrected this sentence to read: "It is for foregoing reasons, and none other, that a condition of the loan is assurance by President Belaunde that Peru will not acquire Mirage aircraft from France or similar aircraft from third countries." (National Archives and Records Administration, RG 59, Central Files 1967–69, AID(US) 9 PERU)

496.   Telegram From the Embassy in Peru to the Department of State[1]

Lima, October 24, 1967, 2254Z.

1949. Subject: Program Loan and F–5's. Ref: Lima 1886.[2]

1. President received me this morning. I thanked him for having seen Siracusa during my absence in Trujillo last week to discuss new offer of program loan and sale of F–5's.[3] I had received full account of their conversation and of President's reaction to terms and conditions of our two offers. Nevertheless, Washington had instructed me to follow up Siracusa's presentation and to seek with President solution to present impasse.[4] I admitted that our offer of F–5's had arrived late and that if it had come earlier we might have avoided present situation. Unhappily this had not been possible for reasons which Belaunde was aware and I referred to harsh press and Congressional criticism directed at Department since announcement of its decision to make F–5's available to Peru and Brazil. I referred to desire of President Johnson and his government in Washington to assist Belaunde administration, particularly in its present financial difficulties but reaffirmed that purchase of French fighters would make this impossible. USG could not be put in position of appearing to finance with large program loan Peruvian purchase of expensive supersonic aircraft in third country such as France.

2. Belaunde interrupted about this point to say emphatically that what had been done was done and could not be changed. He said was waste of time to discuss Mirage deal further—that it was closed issue. If he were not absolutely frank with me [we] could pretend there were possibilities of reversing GOP position but this is not case and USG had best accept this as basis for future relations with Peru. If, Belaunde continued, this means end of economic relations between Peru and US, sooner he knew this the better.

3. I said I hoped that over past few days he had given consideration to serious problem which had arisen between us and might have some suggestions to offer for mutually agreeable solution. I said I had

---

[1] Source: National Archives and Records Administration, RG 59, Central Files 1967–69, AID(US) 9 PERU. Secret; Priority; Limdis. Repeated to USCINCSO for POLAD.

[2] In telegram 1886 from Lima, October 20, Jones reported waiting for confirmation of his appointment with Belaúnde. (Ibid.)

[3] Judging it important to move "with greatest speed if Mirage purchase to be forestalled," Siracusa requested and received an appointment with Belaúnde on October 19. (Telegram 1852 from Lima, October 19; ibid.)

[4] The Department instructed Jones to return to Lima immediately and "follow up with Belaunde in order to emphasize great importance USG at highest level attaches to our proposal." (Telegram 56485 to Lima, October 19; ibid.)

come as old friend and personal admirer of Belaunde to see if there were not some way of circumventing or avoiding Mirage problem and of getting his government and mine off this particular hook. I suggested that General Porter, CINCSO, might come to Lima to discuss possible solution directly with Peruvian military. Belaunde said this would be waste of time. I then suggested that French military might use Peruvian commitment and downpayment, if any, as credit against other military purchases in France, such as Allouette helicopters, as means of withdrawing from Mirage deal. Belaunde rejected this too as impossible, saying such action would only replace one problem with another, this time in ranks of the military. He said it would create "national scandal" if GOP should now cancel Mirage deal and not one Peruvian could be counted upon to approve such reversal of policy which would be made to appear as undermining of national defense.

4. There then ensued long discourse on Peruvian armed forces' responsibility to nation; to Peru's disastrous experience in last century when she cancelled some arms purchases in England and subsequently lost war to Chile and rich potassium nitrate possessions in south. Peru is rich in natural resources and will defend them; he said and even referred to proximity of Toquepala (Southern Peru Copper Corporation) to Chilean border. He lamented fact that so many US Senators were ignorant of Peruvian history and public sentiment.

5. I asked President for his suggestions as way out. He replied we should divorce French Mirage from program loan and go ahead with latter "quietly and without publicity" or that we might extend amount of some of our present loans such as one to CORPAC (Exim Bank loan for airports) for which GOP is having difficulty financing its counterpart.

6. Belaunde seemed harassed by countless urgent problems arising from generally tense situation in country and specifically from yesterday's disturbances Lima–Callao and to general strike in Arequipa which he fears might proceed to Puno and Cuzco. He complained of sleepless nights, of wrestling with salary tables when he should be working on new road projects, and of Communist agitators taking advantage of situation. He told me again that his refusal to appear on national television to explain present crisis to people was because, if he did, he would have to implicate US Government which had failed to support him in time of need. (He referred directly to program loan which he believes would have averted present financial crises.)

7. On this second try I believe we must accept Belaunde's rejection of Mirage cancellation as final within limits his capability and authority. I still think worthwhile Northrop representative come Lima and make direct contact with PAF in effort persuade them of superiority Northrop product and terms.

Jones

497.   Memorandum From the President's Special Assistant (Rostow) to President Johnson[1]

Washington, October 31, 1967, 12:30 p.m.

SUBJECT

Tuesday Luncheon: Peru

At today's luncheon Secretary Rusk may raise the problem of the deteriorating political and economic situation in Peru and what we can do about it. Both State's Intelligence Bureau and CIA see the possibility of a military takeover in the next few weeks if Belaunde continues his do-nothing attitude and public confidence in him keeps on slipping.[2]

How Peru got into this Situation

During the past 18 months, increasing Government budget deficits and excessive use of foreign credits by both the public and private sectors accelerated the underlying inflationary tendencies and triggered mounting speculation against the Peruvian currency. These economic difficulties were intensified by a breakdown in the tenuous political relationship between the opposition-controlled Congress and the Executive, leading to an impasse that prevented Congress from meeting for 39 days in August and September.

The Government finally was forced to allow a devaluation on September 1. This devaluation of nearly 50% could provide a basis for certain beneficial adjustments to take place in the economy. However, because of the Government's inability to put into effect necessary economic and financial measures to complement the devaluation and cope with its effects, a general atmosphere of drift in national leadership has developed. This has produced a crisis of confidence between the Government and the Peruvian people which is aggravated by a sudden rise in the cost of living.

---

[1] Source: Johnson Library, National Security File, Country File, Peru, Vol. III, 10/67–1/69. Secret. Apparently drafted by Bowdler and based on an October 27 memorandum from Oliver to Rusk. (National Archives and Records Administration, RG 59, ARA/EP/P Files, 1967: Lot 70 D 139, POL 1 Plans) Bowdler forwarded the Oliver memorandum, and two intelligence reports (see footnote 2 below), to Rostow under the cover of an October 31 note. Bowdler remarked that Oliver had apparently recovered from the "passive attitude" reflected in his memorandum, i.e., that "the U.S. can probably do little to influence the situation." (Johnson Library, National Security File, Country File, Peru, Vol. III, 10/67–1/69)

[2] The INR assessment is Intelligence Note No. 857, October 27. (National Archives and Records Administration, RG 59, Central Files 1967–69, POL PERU) The CIA estimate is Special Memorandum No. 8–67, October 28. (Johnson Library, National Security File, Country File, Peru, Vol. III, 10/67–1/69)

The military is increasingly nervous over this drift and deterioration. We are getting more frequent reports that the military is ready to oust Belaunde in order to introduce a strong economic recovery program and prevent public unrest from snowballing.

What We Have Tried to Do

We have been urging Belaunde to take corrective fiscal and budgetary measures for the past 18 months. You will recall that we offered him a $40 million program loan last May, conditioned on certain self-help actions. At that time, the Mirage question was only a cloud on the horizon, but we warned him about it. He found our conditions too stiff; in fact they were not any more onerous than those accepted by Chile, Colombia and Brazil for program assistance.

Belaunde by July had taken sufficient self-help measures for us to offer him $15 million, with the remaining $25 million of our original offer to come after he had met the pending conditions. In the meantime, our information on Peru's Mirage acquisition had hardened, so we were more precise in making this a condition. Belaunde's reaction to this offer was that the conditions were too steep for the amount of money involved.

Early this month we made a third offer to Belaunde: $40 million based on virtually the same economic conditions and *no* Mirages. This time Belaunde said that the Mirage deal was a fact and not subject to change. If we made it a condition, then Peru would forego the program loan.

Where We Go From Here

If we allow matters to drift, we can expect a military coup in Peru. This would trigger a series of reactions—e.g., holding up aid to Peru, Peruvian military intransigence on Mirages, Brazilian military pressure to acquire Mirages, and sharp Congressional reaction—which could seriously undermine your Alliance for Progress effort.

The key issue at this stage is the Mirages. If we can devise some way for Peru to cancel the contract or resell the aircraft to a third country, the road is open to give Belaunde the aid he needs. This kind of support from us translates itself into public confidence which can enable Belaunde to climb out of the present quagmire.

What I find disturbing is that neither our Embassy nor State are applying imagination and energy to finding a formula for heading off the catastrophe. We need to be doing two things:

—contact key political and military leaders in Peru to urge patience and flexibility and asking them for their views on how to get around the impasse.
—develop formulas to offer the Peruvians to get them to cancel the Mirage contract or resell the Mirages to a third country.

We have urged Covey Oliver to work along these lines (Bill Bowdler has given him two possible formulas).[3]

Walt

---

[3] The President wrote the following instruction on the memorandum: "Walt—Let's meet on this." A note on the memorandum indicates that Johnson did not receive it until 7:35 p.m. on October 31. According to the President's Daily Diary the Tuesday luncheon group met on October 31 from 1:57 to 4:10 p.m. (Johnson Library) A handwritten note by Rostow explains that the subject was "important, but not discussed at lunch." Another note on the memorandum indicates Bowdler was notified on November 1.

---

498.   Memorandum From the President's Special Assistant (Rostow) to President Johnson[1]

Washington, November 6, 1967.

SUBJECT

Your 11:30 Meeting Today on Peru

The *purpose of the meeting* is to review the modalities of the proposal (Tab A) for persuading Peru to drop the Mirage deal.[2]
Those attending will be:

State: Secretary Rusk, Covey Oliver
DOD: Paul Nitze, Paul Warnke
CIA: Dick Helms
WH: Rostow, Bowdler

---

[1] Source: Johnson Library, National Security File, Memos to the President, Walt W. Rostow, Vol. 49. Secret. According to the President's Daily Diary the "off record" meeting was held in the Cabinet Room, 11:35–11:55 a.m. (Johnson Library) Sayre was added to Rostow's list of attendees. No other record of the meeting has been found.

[2] Not attached. Reference is probably to a paper drafted by Bowdler and forwarded to the President under the cover of a November 2 memorandum from Rostow. Rostow presented Johnson with two alternatives: (a) send a high-level representative to Lima—a man "who would carry more punch"—to determine whether Belaúnde and the Peruvian military were willing to negotiate; or (b) send a lower-level official "who could make the same soundings with less risk of publicity." The President indicated he would "prefer to have [a] meeting first" with representatives from DOD, State and CIA. (Ibid., National Security File, Country File, Peru, Vol. III, 10/67–1/69)

I suggest you follow this agenda:

1. *Workability of the Proposal.*

Comment: Covey Oliver has been checking with Northrop on the availability of F–5's, commercial credit for their financing and the training of Peruvian pilots. You might ask him to report on his findings.

2. *Your Emissary to Peru.*

Comment: Dr. Eisenhower told Covey Oliver last Friday[3] that he could not undertake the assignment until after Friday. Covey was getting in touch with him again to establish how soon after Friday he would be available.

Others who might do the job are listed at Tab B.[4]

An essential element of the approach to Peru is to make it as free from publicity as possible.

3. *Advisability of Using Brazil to Help with Peru.*

Comment: I sent you a CIA report on Saturday from a reliable source that President Costa e Silva had decided not to purchase Mirages.[5] *We have not been officially informed of this decision.* You might ask Secretary Rusk and Dick Helms how we might get the Brazilians to so notify us so that we in turn could ask President Costa e Silva if he would help in persuading President Belaunde not to go through with the Mirage deal.

W. W. Rostow[6]

----

[3] November 3. Johnson also raised the idea with former President Eisenhower: "[Belaúnde] is insisting on buying all these French planes, and we're in a hell of a mess, his country is in bad shape, and I thought he [Milton Eisenhower] could go down there" and give them "a fair evaluation of the problem." Eisenhower thought his brother "might be susceptive" to the idea. (Ibid., Recordings and Transcripts, Recording of telephone conversation between President Johnson and Eisenhower, November 4, 1967, 10 a.m., Tape F67.14, Side B, PNO 3) An informal transcript of the conversation is ibid., Chron Series.

[4] Not attached. Reference is probably to a memorandum from Rostow to the President, November 4, which contains a list of possible high-level envoys, including: Cyrus Vance, George Ball, Henry Cabot Lodge, William Scranton, Clark Clifford, and Lincoln Gordon. Johnson approved the recommendation to schedule a meeting at 11:30 a.m., November 6, without indicating his preference as emissary. (Ibid., National Security File, Country File, Peru, Vol. III, 10/67–1/69)

[5] *[text not declassified]* (Ibid., Brazil, Vol. VII, 3/67–11/68)

[6] Printed from a copy that bears this typed signature.

499.   Memorandum of Conversation[1]

Washington, November 8, 1967, 5:15 p.m.

PARTICIPANTS

The President
Assistant Secretary of State Covey T. Oliver
William Bowdler—White House
American Ambassador to Peru J. Wesley Jones

The President asked Ambassador Jones about the situation in Peru and the chances of survival of the Belaunde Administration. Ambassador Jones replied that Peru was going through a severe financial crisis caused by balance of payment difficulties and devaluation. The crisis however was primarily fiscal and not economic, since Peru is basically sound with its free enterprise system, its natural resources and its diversification of exports. The recent devaluation of the sol had been a shock to all Peruvians, including President Belaunde. Unfortunately, he had not prepared the Peruvian people for a devaluation, but rather had assured them it would never happen. He thus had painted himself into a corner and found it difficult now to explain and rationalize to the Peruvian people the sudden drop in the value of their currency.

The President asked about the Mirage deal and whether the Peruvians would cancel their contract with the French. Ambassador Jones replied that on his last of many conversations he had with President Belaunde on this subject Belaunde had told him categorically, "No"; that what had been done could not be undone, and that the United States must accept this as a fact in its future relationship with his country. Nevertheless, on previous occasions President Belaunde indicated that our F–5s would be an acceptable substitute. Ambassador Jones told the President that he would like therefore to have the Northrop representative authorized to make a firm offer in writing to the Peruvian Air Force as soon as possible to include training of Peruvian pilots next year plus the delivery of some aircraft in the latter part of 1968. Once this offer had been made, Ambassador Jones would like to

---

[1] Source: Johnson Library, National Security File, Country File, Peru, Vol. III, 10/67–1/69. Secret. Drafted by Jones and Bowdler. Copies were sent to Rostow and Oliver. The meeting was held in the President's office and according to the President's Daily Diary the meeting was from 5:26 to 5:36 p.m. (Johnson Library) Rostow had recommended that President Johnson meet Jones since "it would strengthen his [Jones'] hand considerably if he could say to President Belaunde that he had discussed Peruvian developments with you." (Memorandum from Rostow to the President, November 8; ibid., National Security File, Country File, Peru, Vol. III)

be authorized to go back to President Belaunde with a copy in hand and a $40 million program loan to make another try. The conditions for the $40 million would be F–5s for Mirages and improved performance in the fiscal field. Ambassador Jones confessed to the President that he was not sanguine that it would work, but he thought it was worth a try.

Ambassador Jones referred to the danger of a Peruvian military intervention in the Government of Peru if another devaluation, followed by increased cost of living, followed by strikes and violence were to occur. That, Jones said, was the sort of condition in which the Peruvian Military traditionally moved to take over the government.

The President said he had not been impressed at Punta del Este with President Belaunde. In rating him with all the other Latin Chiefs of State, he put him just above Arosemena. However, the President noted that Ambassador Jones seemed to have a good opinion of the Peruvian President. Ambassador Jones replied that he saw no alternative to the Belaunde Administration. It was important for Peru's democratic and constitutional progress that Belaunde finish his term of office (July 1969). He was the first President in a long line of military and aristocrats to have any interest in the development of all of Peru. He was not interested just in the coast, but in developing the high sierra and the jungle as well. If Belaunde completed his term in office, he would be only the fifth President in this century to do so. Finally, a military take-over of the government was no solution to Peru's problems. The military could not make the deficit or balance of payments problems disappear any more than a civilian government.

At one point in the conversation, Ambassador Jones said he would like authorization to sign some project loans on his return to Lima— loans which had been authorized in Washington but never signed. One particularly was for commercialization of agriculture which would be not only useful to the agricultural sector, but would be an evidence of United States interest for Belaunde's administration.

The President asked what the next step would be if the F–5 ploy were unsuccessful. Ambassador Jones confessed that we had not yet reached that point in our thinking. Mr. Oliver said that depending upon the interpretation given the Symington amendment and the final outcome on the Conte amendment, he hoped we could continue sector and project lending, although program assistance would be out.

The President indicated that he thought our offer involving substitution of F–5s for Mirages did not have much chance for success but wished us luck if we wished to try.

Finally, as the meeting was breaking up, the President again expressed his doubts about President Belaunde and his ability and political convictions.

500.   Action Memorandum From the President's Special Assistant
(Rostow) to President Johnson[1]

Washington, November 13, 1967.

SUBJECT

Peru

At Tab A is a memorandum from Nick Katzenbach recommending approval of talking points for Ambassador Jones on the Mirage–
F–5 question.[2] The talking points have been approved by DOD (Nitze)
and AID (Poats).

Over the weekend three developments in Peru both improve and
complicate the prospects for Peruvian acceptance of our F–5 offer:

1. *Flexibility in War Minister Doig's Attitude on Mirages.*

Jerry O'Leary and our Chargé talked to General Doig (Reports are
at Tab B).[3] Both detected certain flexibility in his attitude toward the
Mirages. Doig noted the difficulty of making a change now, but he also
volunteered the precedent of the Peruvian switch from French to US
helicopters in 1965. The Chargé thinks we have a fighting chance if we
give the Peruvians a firm offer on F–5s.

General Doig spoke warmly of General Harold Johnson to O'Leary
and our Chargé. Our Chargé recommends a confidential message from
General Johnson to Doig to stimulate him to reverse the Mirage deci-

---

[1] Source: Johnson Library, National Security File, Country File, Peru, Vol. III,
10/67–1/69. Secret. An attached note to the President states: "Mr. Rostow asked if you
could give your attention to this memo at your earliest convenience." Another note indicates that "the President called Mr. Rostow about this and talked at 2:47 p[.m.]
11–16–67." Although the President's Daily Diary confirms that the conversation took
place, no substantive record has been found. (Johnson Library)

[2] Tab A was a November 13 memorandum from Katzenbach to the President; attached but not printed. The talking points, drafted by Bowdler on November 10, presented the latest proposal to replace the existing Mirage contract with a similar agreement for F–5 fighter aircraft, including early pilot training and delivery beginning in
December 1968. (Ibid., Johnson Library, National Security File, Country File, Peru, Vol.
III, 10/67–1/69) In telegram 2347 from Lima, November 20, Jones proposed to avoid the
aircraft issue in his conversation with Belaúnde, "as means help us evaluate future IPC
impact on our overall interests here." (National Archives and Records Administration,
RG 59, Central Files 1967–69, PET 6 PERU) The Department replied that discussion of
the issue was left to Jones' discretion; the program loan, however, was not to be raised
without further instructions. (Telegram 73160 to Lima, November 22; ibid.)

[3] Telegrams 2213 and 2215 from Lima, November 11 and 12. (Both ibid., DEF 12–5
Peru) The telegrams were retyped and forwarded to the President. (Johnson Library, National Security File, Country File, Peru, Vol. III, 10/67–1/69) Jerry O'Leary, a *Washington Star* correspondent, was in Lima to interview General Doig.

sion. I am leery of any written messages, but I think Ambassador Jones could talk to General Johnson and carry an oral message. We have so suggested to Covey Oliver.

2. Trouble on the International Petroleum Case.

For the past two years, President Belaunde has skillfully wended his way through the difficult IPC case to keep his pledge to me not to impair the Company. Last summer when the opposition-controlled Congress forced his hand with a law nationalizing IPC's oil properties, Belaunde came up with what seemed like a wise solution. He signed the law nationalizing the oil fields which IPC was willing to give up in exchange for an operating contract, but he also worked out a formula allowing IPC to continue operating and referred to the Fiscal Tribunal the controversial question of IPC past taxes.

This past Friday[4]—on the eve of senatorial bye-elections—Belaunde published the Fiscal Tribunal's finding that IPC has "unjustly enriched itself" and issued two resolutions instituting judicial proceedings against IPC to recover IPC profits over the past 15 years and back taxes over the past 8 years. It is hard to see how Belaunde will be able to continue delivering on his "no impairment" pledge. But before making a final judgment, we should await Ambassador Jones' talk with him. Belaunde understands that there is no program loan if his bargain with me is not kept.

Politics seems to have dictated Belaunde's action.

3. Belaunde Suffers Reverse in By-elections

An important senatorial by-election was held yesterday. Despite the grandstand play on IPC, Belaunde's candidate is running far behind the opposition candidate. To compound Belaunde's difficulties, the Christian Democrats announced on the eve of the elections that they were withdrawing from their alliance with Belaunde's party. These reverses are not likely to improve Belaunde's capacity for decision and leadership.

Despite the gloomy outlook, I think it is still in our interest to proceed with the F–5 offer—if Belaunde is willing to cancel the Mirage contract—and with the $40 million program loan offer—if he takes the self-help measures and finds the formula for undoing what he appears to have done to IPC. Belaunde is a weak reed to lean on but better than a de facto military junta. We should try to prop him up if he is willing to do those things which are indispensable for our support. The record

---

[4] November 10.

should show we did everything possible, within reason, to preserve constitutional government in Peru.

I recommend that you approve the talking points.

Walt

Approve talking points[5]

See me

---

[5] Neither option is checked, but a note on a copy of the Katzenbach memorandum indicates that the talking points were approved by the White House on November 17. (National Archives and Records Administration, RG 59, Central Files 1967–69, DEF 12–5 PERU)

---

501.   Telegram From the Embassy in Peru to the Department of State[1]

Lima, November 22, 1967, 2251Z.

2397. Ref: Lima's 2347.[2]

1. President received me at noon today and was with him almost an hour. I reminded him I had been in Washington for week's consultation since we had last met and felt he would be interested in report of my activities there. Said I had found in Washington great interest in Peru and sincere desire to help Belaunde administration in these present difficult moments. I was received by President Johnson same day I arrived and during subsequent days my Washington sojourn I had interviews with Secretary of State,[3] Under Secretary Katzenbach and of course Assistant Secretary Oliver. All I had found very preoccupied by situation in Peru and especially concerned that Belaunde administration continue until end its term in July 1969 and that there be no interruption of constitutional government in Peru. As President Belaunde was aware from conversations over past nine months principal obstacle to US financial assistance had been acquisition of supersonic fighter

---

[1] Source: National Archives and Records Administration, RG 59, Central Files 1967–69, PET 6 PERU. Confidential; Immediate; Limdis.

[2] See footnote 2, Document 500.

[3] According to the Secretary's Appointment Book Jones met Rusk at 11:45 a.m. on November 13; the Secretary's next appointment was scheduled for 12:30 p.m. (Johnson Library) No substantive record of the meeting has been found.

aircraft. While I was in Washington there had been serious effort to find way to overcome this obstacle and I had been encouraged by progress made. Unfortunately almost at end of my consultations news had arrived of Peruvian government's action on November 10 against IPC. This news was so unexpected and for me inexplicable that I had asked permission return to Peru to investigate new situation thereby created. To me it seemed I concluded that position of company had drastically worsened and that government had taken new tack in its policy La Brea y Parinas.

2. Belaunde replied that recent actions involving IPC had been taken as result of moves made by opposition back in July to force his hand on this issue. He recalled that law 16674 which expropriated the La Brea y Parinas reserves, (Lima's 133)[4] had cancelled previous law giving him carte blanche to settle petroleum issue in any way he thought best. This law sponsored by opposition had for first time mentioned debts owed by company. Since these had to be determined he had referred matter to fiscal tribunal which was appropriate authority to determine what if any debts were owed state. From tribunal would go to courts where it would undoubtedly result in long drawn-out legal case. Issue is now in courts where it belongs and IPC can defend its position there. Company claims no back debts owed while tribunal has estimated sum to be collected. Courts will have to decide. Action of tribunal is not final verdict. This can only be made by courts, he explained.

3. As further explanation government's action against company November 10 Belaunde referred to recent by-elections Lima and Trujillo and said that while elections had been clean and accepted verdict of voters in electing opposition candidate, they had nevertheless dragged petroleum issue into elections. On November 9 Andres Townsend, Aprista congressman, had in electoral speech on TV charged Belaunde administration with having done nothing to resolve IPC problem (finding of tribunal against IPC was actually dated November 2 although not published until November 11). Finally, President said, IPC mixed too much in local politics; that it had some kind of relationship with Pedro Beltran, publisher of opposition newspaper *La Prensa*, and that it also was among those along with Marcona Mining Company that supported Ravines weekly television program which had consistently attacked Belaunde administration and had done so much damage to country. These people would probably like to see someone else in palace to resolve IPC issue in hurry, Belaunde said with some bitterness, adding that perhaps they should bring back General Odria to do it. I expressed surprise at these charges against

[4] Dated July 8. (National Archives and Records Administration, RG 59, Central Files 1967–69, PET 6 PERU)

IPC and said my knowledge of its extra-commercial activities in country in support of Peruvian culture had been favorable. Belaunde admitted that company worked efficiently and had excellent labor relations. Nevertheless during first 20 years of exploitation of La Brea y Parinas Peru had been badly cheated. I also remonstrated over Belaunde's inference that IPC and perhaps even we would prefer military dictatorship to resolve La Brea y Parinas. I assured him again of deep interest in Washington in democratic constitutional government throughout hemisphere and particularly of genuine concern that his administration survive to end its term as one of principal objectives of our policies. Belaunde said if anything happened to interrupt his tenure of office before July 1969 he would, unless they shot him, never give a moment's peace to interloper in palace since he would consider himself until mid-1969 Peru's legally elected chief of state. Should he be exiled he would station himself as near Peruvian border as possible to make life difficult for incumbent until next elections.

4. In response my repeated request for assurances that IPC's position had not been impaired by this recent action, Belaunde replied that he did not feel company's position had changed; that it had always been bad, and that he did not see that it had worsened. In response my reference to constant unfavorable publicity since government action November 10, including $150 million worth of so-called debts and almost daily speeches in Congress against company as evidence that its position had indeed deteriorated, President said people already knew that IPC had been reason for hold-up on aid to Peru which he estimated had cost country $100 million.

5. In response my question President said reference of tax and debt matter to tribunal had not shut door to continued negotiations with company. He felt settlement could still be found through direct talks even while case is in courts. Should additional debts eventually be confirmed by court verdict company could add some of its installations or other fixed assets over years to make up difference. He did not anticipate much change in company's position either through early conclusion to negotiations or through court action. Since company had its authority to continue operating under petroleum director's resolution (Lima's 647)[5] he felt things would continue as they were and that whole issue would continue to remain unresolved and "somewhat on the shelf." There would certainly be no conclusion by end of year as opposition congressman had suggested last night (Lima's 2390).[6]

6. In response another question Belaunde said he was of course willing continue negotiations with company and to resume conversa-

[5] Dated August 10. (Ibid.)

[6] Dated November 22. (Ibid.)

tion with Espinosa, adding he would telephone to invite him to palace when company manager had returned from States. He explained had not seen him before his departure because had been very busy in those days and because he had new Min of Development (Carriquiri) whom he wished to introduce into and make familiar with this old problem. (When Espinosa tried see Belaunde following decrees of November 10 he passed him off on Carriquiri.)

7. Supersonic issue came into conversation incidentally on several occasions during our long meeting. At one point Belaunde said laughingly he kept hoping Dessault Manufacturing Company might fail so Mirage would never arrive. In next breath he said whole issue was so unimportant in relation to Peru's needs and our assistance program. (I took some time to explain temper of US Congress on this issue which I had been able observe first-hand during my recent consultations.) I said of course supersonic issue had been thoroughly discussed in Washington and that I would hope sometime within next few weeks to go see him again to discuss its relationship with our desire to help Belaunde administration. I repeated again evident concern and willingness to help his government survive through its constitutional period which I had found at all levels in Washington. President replied with laugh that what he needed was "supersonic program assistance" or aid at supersonic speed.

8. In general I found Belaunde in good humor; even made few jokes and our personal relationship seemed unimpaired by recent events. However on occasion he spoke of "many, many problems" besetting him, of his many enemies in country and somewhat wistfully of final months of his term of office as period preparing to leave things in good order for his successor.

9. While assurances on IPC not very satisfactory I interpreted President's explanation of recent events as motivated by domestic political objectives and that continued negotiations are still possible. I believe it clear President has no intention of resolving La Brea y Parinas problem during his tenure in office and that he will accept any tactic that drags issue out over next 20 months. If, as he says, IPC can continue to operate as usual and take all legal steps to defend itself in courts, company's position may well continue to be tenable during rest of Belaunde administration. It then certain, however, to be hot issue in 1969 campaign. Consequently I believe press campaign by company either in US or in Lima at this time not advisable although no objection certainly to company restating its position regarding validity its titles and lack of debt GOP in press releases or advertisements and taking whatever vigorous action is open to it in local courts or eventually through British government in International Court of Justice.

Jones

502. Telegram From the Embassy in Peru to the Department of State[1]

Lima, February 27, 1968, 1826Z.

3720. Ref: Under Secretary's Memorandum of Feb 16 to me and Tabs.[2] Subj: Conversation with President Belaunde on Military Expenditures and IPC Case. From Oliver.

1. With Ambassador and Fowler, had talk with President Peru on above subject over period ninety-five minutes afternoon February 26. Conversation with President based on reference and tabs, especially talking points in Spanish to which I had added introductory paragraphs designed to highlight (I) genuineness wish USG to be of development assistance to Peru (II) my interest in "opening interior" programs, and (III) explanation that theme my presentation was to be "Obstacles To Beginning New Aid Negotiations." President met us alone; was cordial throughout; showed some physical tension during periods I was trying to read out or paraphrase talking points; intervened repeatedly during my presentation, speaking more in sorrow than in anger about USG incomprehension Peru's military needs and casual effects past failures aid to assist Peru effectively.

2. Symington and Conte–Long amendments.

(A) Military Budget.

I explained fully to President that Executive Branch USG was under legal obligation apply these amendments effectively and fully proposed do so. Sketched upcoming legislative session. Tendency of President (as Ambassador had predicted) was to interrupt in defense of importance of military to Peru and to blame policies of "State Department" for denying Peru assistance. With persistence I eventually got President to focus on point that US Executive has law to enforce; this was done by getting him to read Symington amendment in Spanish.

---

[1] Source: National Archives and Records Administration, RG 59, Central Files 1967–69, DEF 1 Peru. Confidential; Immediate; Limdis. Repeated to USCINCSO and La Paz. Retyped and sent to the White House as an attachment to a memorandum from Oliver to the President, March 4; Rostow forwarded the memorandum to Johnson the next day. Oliver recommended that the President postpone any decision as to whether the Symington or Conte–Long amendments would apply to Peru. "An official finding," he argued, "could well provoke a crisis of confidence in the Belaunde Government leading to a military takeover." (Johnson Library, National Security File, Country File, Latin America, Vol. VI, 10/67–4/68) Oliver also gave a brief account of his trip, including his conversation with Belaúnde, at a meeting of the NSC on March 6; see Document 69.

[2] The February 16 memorandum from Katzenbach to Oliver contained instructions for Oliver's trip to Peru, including talking points for his discussion with Belaúnde. An unsigned copy of the memorandum is in the National Archives and Records Administration, RG 59, ARA Files, 1967–69: Lot 74 D 467, Peru 1968. See also Document 66, and footnote 5 thereto.

In summary (see detail below) President promised us a memorandum tending to show that for Peruvian FY 1968 (begins April 1, 1968) budget just now being voted under leadership PM will present reduction over-all budget from dollars 1.3 billion to 1 billion ("... a superhuman effort whose repercussions may be far reaching..."); total military portion Peruvian FY 1968 budget will be down slightly from 1967; additions to new military budget being made in Congress not only do not reverse downward trend but represent mainly allowance increases designed to keep up with price rises following devaluation; identification portions military budgets going into civic action, pay, uniforms, food, training, and "services to public."

(B) Unnecessary Military Equipment.

President was not forthcoming with assurances. While not objecting on "intervention" grounds, he firmly denied validity foreign opinion on subject. (At one point I offered to prepare for his personal consideration a list of what I would consider tentatively to be "unnecessary" and/or "sophisticated." He did not take me up.) I did get it out that missiles, supersonics, certain naval vessels in these categories. (*Comment:* CT will be following very closely and reporting developments as to weapons categories, especially with regard to extent to which we might be able to hold Peru off from certain naval acquisitions during immediately critical year ahead.)

President said a number of things related to this subheading. Most worthy of reflection is this: United States unfortunately sees South America through twin veils of Mexico and Caribbean countries. Therefore does not see it clearly. United States does not stop to think that Mexico has enviable low military expenditures, because "... as Diaz Ordaz told me, Mexico is the primary defense orbit of the United States and knows it." USG would inevitably and immediately respond if international aggression or aggressive subversion should threaten the security of Mexico. Would US surely and under all circumstances respond if Peru were similarly threatened? Even during a Vietnam? Could the US response come soon enough? The President said that no Peruvian chief of state could take the risks that these questions imply.

3. Other presidential observations: as to "jet aircraft" (he did not use "Mirage"); "they are just a few to experiment with. Flying is like making love, one does not learn how to do it from a manual."

As to Canberras: "You (USG) also said they had no internal security effectiveness, but they do; and they fly slower than even the passenger airplanes subversives could fly in on. Is it not illogical to expect that the military aircraft of Peru should be slower than the commercial planes that come into our airports?"

"*The Washington Post* called the aircraft our air force wants 'playthings'; well, when someone is in the market for a new automobile, he does not buy a 1960 model in 1968."

"De Gaulle and Lubke while visiting here got nothing from Peru. Peru buys more from the US than it sells to her. When Vietnam is over you will be looking to your markets even more seriously than now."

4. Belaunde on USAID: (He never used "Alliance"; I always did.) For one reason or another AID has never given Peru the capital assistance it gives to Brazil, Chile, Colombia, all in the hundreds of millions of dollars. Peru has had to finance its own development by going to the commercial banks. It is this that caused Peru's foreign exchange reserves to go down and forced devaluation. AID assistance has now become urgent, because AID can soften the burden of Peru's development debt. We have spent what we borrowed on commercial terms wisely; we did not waste it. After 4-1/2 years as President, he had come to have more faith in Peruvians with pickaxes and shovels than in international lending agencies. What Peru cannot do for itself, AID should do with soft loans. (Paraphrased.)

In response to my comment that while Fowler and I were in Colombia, with lending program absolutely stopped for 15 months, I had envied Ambassador Jones and had looked with longing at Peru's flourishing export trade, Belaunde said: In those days when things were going well financially in Peru, you (USG) told us we were too prosperous to qualify for aid and now when our reserves are running out, you say we do not qualify because of poor fiscal performance.

5. Belaunde on Chile: "Peru has lost its national territorial treasure in considerable part to this neighbor. My own family suffered greatly (his ancestors came from Arica) and Peru was set back financially until only recently by the loss of territory to Chile. But we are not revanchists. We have our military system for domestic protection. We would never move against another country. We respect our international obligations. But if out of this country there should come further aggression or subversion against Peru, we must be able to defend ourselves." (Paraphrase of three statements, each substantially along above lines.)

6. Belaunde on development and public services by military: The President's first interruption of my presentation was to sound this theme. He ranged from civic action to disaster relief and dealing with urban disorder. (*Comment:* At no time did Belaunde allude to his political situation in relationship to armed forces. He did roundly castigate Odriista group in Congress for irresponsible obstructionism and stressed the accomplishments of his administration in establishing democracy.)

7. IPC Case: In closing minutes I finally got to IPC case as "second obstacle," stating that I had had a good lawyer-to-lawyer talk with his Prime Minister about case (septel).[3] Belaunde began complaining that company did not want to negotiate, that it was continuing to be

---

[3] Telegram 3716 from Lima, February 27. (National Archives and Records Administration, RG 59, Central Files 1967–69, DEF 1 LA)

intransigent. Went on to say that only two ways to handle this case: either do nothing ("company has not had one can of gasoline taken from it") or settle it completely with a "good situation". Ambassador and I both weighed in on side definitive settlement now, I saying that seemed to me all elements needed for a complete and fair solution now at hand. Ambassador pointed out that conversations between company and EPF most encouraging and asked President to support actively director of EPF in these negotiations. President said he would.

8. Toward end of conversation Belaunde said he had only 18 more months to serve. On whole he was pessimistic. He had not had the US support that would have permitted him to lead Peru where it ought to go. Later at dinner in honor our traveling group he seemed tense at first but mellowed as we talked of University of Texas days we had shared (without knowing each other), mildly insulted Texas A&M and Rice, exchanged warm toasts to President Johnson and host. Despite my expectation based on my suggestion at afternoon meeting, Belaunde did not initiate further substantive talks after the dinner. Both at dinner and in earlier meeting Belaunde spoke warmly of President Johnson: said he realizes President Johnson has problems of world to cope with and that Congressional situation sometimes did not permit a US President to do what he wanted or knew was desirable.

9. Ambassador's comment: The President had obviously been briefed on subjects to be broached by Assistant Secretary and at first mention of "military" interrupted Oliver's presentation to expound on virtues and constructive role of armed forces in Peru. (Using authority Deptel 115825 we had already informed Quintanilla, President's private secretary, of nature of Oliver's mission.)[4] While President continued to interrupt in defense of military, of his democratic administration and of Peru's position in hemisphere, Assistant Secretary patiently persisted in making full presentation his case based on instructions referred to above. At end of one hour and 35 minutes I am satisfied Belaunde understood our problem and issues involved despite his reluctance to discuss military expenditures and particularly military equipment items. President maintained his composure throughout though there were signs of emotion when defending role of military or complaining of lack US support for his development programs. Although evasive in his replies throughout President did not cut us short—as he might have done—on grounds of "national dignity" or unwarranted interference in Peruvian internal affairs. On balance conversations went well considering President's position vis-à-vis military here and delicate nature of subject discussed.

Jones

---

[4] Dated February 15. (Ibid., AID(US) 5)

503.   Memorandum From the Assistant Secretary of State for Inter-
American Affairs (Oliver) to the Deputy Under Secretary of
State for Political Affairs (Bohlen)

Washington, May 13, 1968.

[Source: Department of State, INR/IL Historical Files, 303 Committee Files, c. 69, May 22, 1968. Secret; Eyes Only. 2 pages of source
text not declassified.]

504.   Information Memorandum From William G. Bowdler of the
National Security Council Staff to President Johnson[1]

Washington, July 30, 1968, 5 p.m.

SUBJECT

President Belaunde Announces International Petroleum Company Settlement

On Sunday, July 28, in his annual message to the Peruvian Congress, President Belaunde announced settlement of the long-standing
dispute with the International Petroleum Company (ESSO-N.J.) over
the La Brea-Parinas (LB–P) oil fields.

The settlement is based on a formula proposed to Belaunde by
IPC. Agreement so far is only *in principle*. The detailed agreement remains to be negotiated.

The essential elements of the deal are:

—IPC hands over to the government all subsurface rights in the
LB–P oil fields and all surface installations.

—The government gives IPC a quit-claim on past taxes on LB–P
operations, agrees to sell at a mutually acceptable price all crude, natural gasoline and gas from LB–P fields to IPC for processing at its Talara refinery, and grants IPC the right to explore and produce petroleum in an area outside LB–P.

—IPC will expand its Talara refinery.

—The government will grant storage, distribution and marketing
concessions to IPC in Peru.

---

[1] Source: Johnson Library, National Security File, Country File, Peru, Vol. III,
10/67–11/68. Confidential. A notation on the memorandum indicates the President saw
it.

The deal is a statesman-like way out of a difficult problem. I hope it does not founder in the negotiation of the specifics. Until these are completed, and the agreement signed, it would be premature to consider the dispute closed.[2]

WGB

---

[2] On August 13 Rostow informed the President that the IPC problem had been finally settled, thereby removing "this dangerous matter from U.S.-Peruvian relations once and for all." (Telegram CAP 81956 to the LBJ Ranch; ibid.)

---

505. Editorial Note

In a meeting with Ambassador Jones on September 18, 1968, President Belaúnde requested U.S. assistance for five transportation projects. Belaúnde expected that the United States would support the projects "as evidence of its appreciation of government's courage in finally resolving this explosive problem [IPC case] and as a token of its support for government's fiscal policies and democratic constitutional character." (Telegram 7386 from Lima, September 18; National Archives and Records Administration, RG 59, Central Files 1967–69, POL 2 PERU) While citing several factors that would delay approval of the request, the Department indicated that "in light of strong GOP self-help program we have positive attitude." (Telegram 245358 to Lima, September 26; ibid., AID(US) 9 PERU) In a September 21 letter to Director of the Office of Ecuadorean-Peruvian Affairs William P. Stedman, Jr., Jones made a personal appeal for swift action: "I cannot over-emphasize the urgency of a favorable response to the Belaunde Administration in what is perhaps the most precarious period of his entire six years." (Johnson Library, Papers of John Wesley Jones, Classified [Correspondence]) Stedman replied by describing the bureaucratic difficulties involved in processing the loans: "The memorandum to get Peru off the Symington black list has been approved by Mr. Gaud and the White House has been notified. That opens up the way for the PL 480 for rice for which a memorandum approved by Secretary Freeman and Mr. Gaud was sent last week to the Bureau of the Budget for transmittal to the President. We ought to have word soon." Stedman insisted, however, that the Department fully appreciated "the urgency of getting the rice and the loans." (Letter from Stedman to Jones, September 30; ibid.)

506.   Information Memorandum From the Assistant Secretary of State for Inter-American Affairs (Oliver) to Secretary of State Rusk[1]

Washington, September 20, 1968.

SUBJECT

> Peru—Delicate Political Situation Threatens Upset of Recent Economic Advances and Possibly Constitutional Government

The decisive action of the Hercelles Cabinet to remedy the deteriorating economic situation in Peru and to solve the long-standing IPC problem has brought about a reaction from the right and the left which now threatens the stability of the Cabinet, its economic recovery programs, and quite possibly the constitutional process.

Background

After a steadily deteriorating economic situation had continued for ten months, the Peruvian Congress granted the executive branch sixty days of extraordinary powers to cope with the situation. The Cabinet of Premier Oswaldo Hercelles acted quickly to remedy the economic deterioration. New taxes such as a large gasoline tax increase, however, were bound to elicit adverse reaction.

The package of measures taken by the Finance Minister, Manuel Ullos, re-established confidence on the part of the IMF, foreign banks, and foreign investors, and they are cooperating with the Government on stand-by arrangements and foreign debt rescheduling.

The Government also arrived at a settlement of the long-standing dispute with the American-owned International Petroleum Company. A complicated arrangement was devised in which the Company turned over the disputed oil lands in return for an exoneration from all alleged past debts and the right to continue its other operations in Peru.

The good effect of the Peruvian Government's actions of the past three months and its capacity to continue its recovery program are now in jeopardy because of domestic political considerations.

In addition to the public reaction against the new taxes, the IPC settlement is under strong attack. Die-hard elements on the extreme right and the extreme left have joined together to attack the solution as being unfavorable to Peru and a "give-away." The Peruvian mili-

---

[1] Source: National Archives and Records Administration, RG 59, ARA Files, 1967–69: Lot 74 D 467, September 1968—CTO Chron. Confidential. Drafted by Shumate on September 20 and cleared by Vaky and Stedman. The memorandum is an uninitialed copy.

tary has been reported as being quite concerned about the reaction to the IPC solution and there are even rumors of certain elements considering this as a pretext for a coup.

Present Situation

At the present moment, according to our Embassy, [*less than 1 line of source text not declassified*], and even the Peruvian Embassy here, the situation is delicate. President Belaunde is in his sixth and final year, with elections scheduled for June, 1969. The apparent probable winners of next year's elections, APRA, hold one of the keys in the situation. Its majority congressional bloc supported the President in granting extraordinary powers and on settling the IPC dispute. Nevertheless, APRA does not wish to be tied to the program if it becomes unpopular, especially with regard to taxes or the oil dispute. More importantly, it desperately wants elections to be held and realizes it must give Belaunde at least enough support to ward off coup-minded elements. However, influential elements in the military still fear APRA, and would prefer a coup to a democratic Aprista victory.

The Peruvian military thus holds another key in the situation. They can, of course, intervene at a moment's notice and often have in the past. During the last year of crises, however, despite the numerous opportunities at hand, the military has refrained from taking action. As the presidential elections draw closer, this crisis is a greater danger to constitutional government.

President Belaunde is the third key element. He is a skilled politician, and on many occasions has fashioned solutions from apparently irreconcilable political problems. His will to finish his term in office and preside over an orderly and democratic transition is an important element in the equation.

Since the President is not directly threatened by a Cabinet crisis, one of the safety valves in moments of extreme stress is the resignation of the Cabinet. In the past year, there have been four Cabinets in Peru. The present Cabinet is by far the strongest Peru has had in years. Its demise would be a body blow to the economic recuperation of the country and would inflict a staggering set-back to confidence both within and outside of Peru. Further, the fact is there are practically no competent individuals left who would accept Cabinet positions in this lame duck Government. Therefore, the military might feel compelled to take over or to install military officers in key civilian ministeries.

The United States is largely on the sidelines in this situation. Our aid involvement has varied from minimal to naught (in 1968) and our relationship has been beset by serious and emotional problems—IPC, the Mirage purchase, tuna boat seizures, etc. Unfortunately, at almost any moment these U.S.-Peruvian bilateral issues can create problems of great importance in Peruvian politics. This is especially true when the problem involves possible application of legislation such as the Symington, Conte–Long, Hickenlooper, Pelly and Ship Loan Recall Amendments.

We expect Mr. Hercelles (who holds both Prime and Foreign Minister portfolios) to attend the UNGA—probably after October 5—if the political situation is sufficiently calm. We will provide you with current briefing material when an appointment with you is arranged.

---

507.   Telegram From the Embassy in Peru to the Department of State[1]

Lima, September 28, 1968, 0007Z.

7578. For Oliver from Ambassador. Subj: Political Atmosphere.

1. As you have seen from our recent cables reporting the political battle which erupted out of criticism of the IPC settlement, and the related subsequent split in the Belaunde Accion Popular Party, there has been a drastic change in the political atmosphere in recent weeks. Heretofore, considerable optimism had been engendered as a result of the Hercelles' cabinet acting effectively and capably for ninety days in use of the special powers granted by the Congress. The fact that the Congress was out of session during that period also assisted by bringing about a sort of moratorium on politics. Unfortunately, the feeling of optimism has been seriously eroded as a result of the spectacle of the President and Vice President, through their adherants, engaging in demeaning battle over the party machinery and facilities and the bitter nightly debate of the issues in the Congress. This together with widespread mistrust of the government's handling of the IPC settlement has clearly reduced confidence in the democratic machinery and has doubtless encouraged many Peruvians to think along traditional lines of an authoritarian solution. As a result there is a great deal of talk about golpe and some air of expectancy.

2. We have not been able to pinpoint anything specific and have reason to believe that there is considerable lack of unity within the military itself. However, if a pretext were provided, as for example by serious public disorders, the military might move institutionally.

---

[1] Source: National Archives and Records Administration, RG 59, Central Files 1967–69, POL 15–1 PERU. Confidential; Limdis. Repeated to USCINCSO for POLAD.

3. Last night a rightist demagogue, Leon Velarde, who manipulates some Barriada dwellers for his own purposes spoke seriously to a political officer of the Embassy in terms of the imminence of a golpe in which he planned to be involved. The Embassy officer, in response to his query as to our attitude, told him in no uncertain terms that the US Government and this Embassy is dedicated to the fulfillment by the Belaunde administration of its term of office and the democratic selection of a successor. You may be sure we will lose no opportunity to make this policy crystal clear wherever we think it should be stated.

4. I don't intend that this be an alarmist telegram but believe you should know that there has now been created an atmosphere of tension and confusion. Up to this moment, however, all [*less than 1 line of source text not declassified*] and service attaché sources are negative on specific military plans for golpe.[2]

Jones

---

[2] Rostow repeated this assessment in a note to the President, October 1: "There is some talk of a military coup, but it does not appear imminent." (Johnson Library, National Security File, Country File, Peru, Vol. III, 10/67–11/68) A CIA information report on the possibility of a coup is [*text not declassified*]; ibid.

---

508.   Action Memorandum From the President's Special Assistant (Rostow) to President Johnson[1]

Washington, October 2, 1968, 4:40 p.m.

SUBJECT

Peru—PL 480 Agreement for Rice

The attached memorandum from Bill Gaud and Orville Freeman (Tab A)[2] recommends that you authorize a $10.7 million PL 480 sales agreement with Peru for 60,000 tons of rice. Charlie Zwick concurs (Tab B).[3]

---

[1] Source: Johnson Library, National Security File, Country File, Peru, Vol. III, 10/67–11/68. Confidential. Received in the President's office at 4:55 p.m. Another copy indicates the memorandum was drafted by Lewis. (Ibid., Memos to the President, Walt W. Rostow, Vol. 97)

[2] Tab A was a memorandum from Gaud and Freeman to the President, September 20; attached but not printed.

[3] Tab B was a memorandum from Schultze to the President, September 30; attached but not printed.

This agreement will be the first major new aid for Peru in over a year. A proposed AID loan package of about $25 million will also be ready for your approval in the near future. This proposal serves three important purposes:

—to provide much needed food supplies after a severe drought struck Peru this year;
—to provide tangible political support for President Belaunde at a key point in his administration, after he has taken several difficult development decisions;
—to help increase US commercial sales of rice and counter Communist Chinese competition.

In recent months, Belaunde has shown real courage in tackling Peru's economic problems, including putting through a major tax reform. He has also resolved the old and vexing dispute with the International Petroleum Company to IPC's satisfaction, thereby removing it as an irritant from US-Peruvian relations. These acts have produced expected political turmoil, and a Cabinet shake-up has just occurred. However, the new Cabinet, headed by a respected close friend of Belaunde, includes the key Ministers from his predecessor's Cabinet. It should continue the encouraging direction the Peruvian Government has recently followed.

Ambassador Jones has appealed for quick action on this request to help demonstrate our support for Belaunde's position.[4] I agree that a show of support at this moment is both warranted and needed.

As outlined in Charlie Zwick's memorandum, there was a question last year as to whether Peruvian military expenditures would not warrant application of the Symington Amendment. Belaunde has held down the level of military spending since that time, however, and State/AID have now determined that Peru is not diverting any US assistance to military expenditures, nor investing its own resources unnecessarily to a degree that interferes with its development.

All interested parties agree in recommending that you approve the PL 480 program for Peru at this time. The only difference in view concerns whether some notice should be given to Congress that you are proposing new aid to Peru after a hiatus. Katzenbach and Zwick think it might be advisable to inform key members of the Congress, particularly Senators Symington and Morse, that Peru does not fall within the purview of the Symington Amendment. Gaud and Oliver prefer

---

[4] In telegram 7619 from Lima, October 1, Jones reiterated the importance of U.S. assistance: "It is urgent that I be authorized as soon as possible to make favorable response to Belaunde's appeal for help as mark of confidence and support for him as constitutional President. I had hoped both PL–480 negotiating instructions and approval of Pucallpa–Aguaytia road project would have been in our hands by now. Belaunde needs help and needs it now. Swift approval of either or both these programs could be significant." (National Archives and Records Administration, RG 59, Central Files 1967–69, POL 15–1 PERU)

not to take any initiative towards the Congress, but are fully prepared to defend the determination should any question be raised. Mike Manatos agrees with Gaud and Oliver that the less said the better at this moment. I also share this view.

Walt

Approve loan

Disapprove loan

Call me

Inform key members of Congress, particularly Senators Symington and Morse

Do not inform Congress

Call me[5]

---

[5] The President checked this option. When Rostow learned that the President had read the memorandum without taking positive action, he urged Larry Temple, Special Counsel to the President, to ask that Johnson read the "marked passages" again. Temple returned the memorandum to the President. (Memorandum from Temple to the President, October 2, 5:10 p.m.; Johnson Library, National Security File, Country File, Peru, Vol. III, 10/67–11/68) According to the President's Daily Diary Rostow did not call Johnson until 11:45 p.m. (Johnson Library) No substantive record of this conversation, or evidence that it concerned Peru, has been found.

---

509.   Information Memorandum From the President's Special Assistant (Rostow) to President Johnson[1]

Washington, October 3, 1968, 10:50 a.m.

SUBJECT

Peru Coup

Contrary to our latest intelligence assessments, the Peruvian Army moved early this morning to oust President Belaunde and install a

---

[1] Source: Johnson Library, National Security File, Country File, Peru, Vol. III, 10/67–11/68. Confidential. A copy was sent to George Christian. A notation on the memorandum indicates the President saw it. Another copy indicates that the memorandum was drafted by Lewis. (Ibid., Memos to the President, Walt W. Rostow, Vol. 97)

"Revolutionary Junta".[2] Unhappiness over the IPC settlement was one obvious motive.

No violence or active resistance has yet occurred, but some could develop during the day. Early reports suggest the Navy and Air Force were not fully supporting the Army.

President Belaunde was arrested by the Army at his palace and flown to exile in Buenos Aires by the military.

We will soon have to face the question of recognition of the Junta, but should not do so until the dust settles.[3] Full consultation with the other OAS governments will be required. Meanwhile, our AID Mission Director—now here on consultation—will remain here and AID will suspend plans for new aid to Peru.

The last coup in Latin America occurred June 1966 in Argentina.

Walt

---

[2] President Johnson was informed of the coup d'etat at 6:30 a.m., when a briefing officer in the White House Situation Room forwarded a cable from the Embassy. The officer noted that he had briefed Rostow. (Note from Wotring to the President; ibid.) The cable in question, flash telegram 7639 from Lima, 030859Z, stated: "Apparent golpe in process, but have no details." Embassy reports on the progress of the coup are in the National Archives and Records Administration, RG 59, Central Files 1967–69, POL 23–9 PERU.

[3] In telegram 249329 to Lima, October 3, the Department reported: "Although we have not said so publicly, overthrow of Peruvian Government has effect of suspending diplomatic relations with GOP. We are assessing details of this general problem and in meantime know you will observe the cautions about contact with revolutionary forces." (Ibid.)

---

510.   Telegram From the Embassy in Peru to the Department of State[1]

Lima, October 3, 1968, 2045Z.

7661. Subject: Preliminary Analysis of Coup Motives.

1. Embassy telegram 7578 of September 27 [28][2] reported drastic deterioration in political atmosphere which reduced confidence in democratic machinery and produced air of expectancy on possible coup.

---

[1] Source: National Archives and Records Administration, RG 59, Central Files 1967–69, POL 23–7 PERU. Confidential; Immediate. Repeated to Buenos Aires, La Paz, Quito, Santiago, USCINCSO for POLAD, DOD for DIA, and USUN. Rostow forwarded a copy of the telegram to the President on October 3; a notation on his transmittal memorandum indicates that Johnson saw the telegram. (Johnson Library, National Security File, Country File, Peru, Vol. III, 10/67–11/68)

[2] Document 507.

It also contained one clear report of a coup threat. It is our preliminary view that military move was basically motivated by a determination to prevent an APRA victory in the election scheduled for next June. The total disarray of all other political parties which split along factional lines, culminating in the division of Belaunde's Accion Popular Party into warring factions, one headed by him and one headed by Vice President Seoane, served to dramatize the fact that the single, unified and disciplined party remaining was APRA. The fact that APRA leaders were increasingly confident of victory and insisted that Haya de la Torre would be their candidate served to ignite the fears of those in the military determined that Haya would never become President of Peru.

2. In the above conditions, military golpistas could take preventive action now, utilizing a pretext, or they could wait to see what happened. Apparently their preference was to execute a preventive coup rather than risk nullifying the results of an election which probably, as viewed at this time, would have resulted in an APRA victory.[3]

3. The political confusion and divisions which erupted out of criticism of the La Brea y Parinas settlement, and general public believe that the government had not been fully honest in what it revealed about this settlement, provided a pretext which was seized by the golpistas.

4. Factors which helped create the atmosphere in which the military golpistas could find pretext to move were such things as the unrelenting, bitter attack on the government and its financial and economic policies made by Pedro Beltran and his *La Prensa* newspaper, as well as by *El Comercio* newspaper, once a staunch supporter of Belaunde, which was bitter in its attack on the government over the La Brea y Parinas issue. The ineptness of APRA leadership which forced resignation of the Hercelles cabinet and thus contributed to the atmosphere of political crisis also helped bring on the coup which APRA did not want.

5. There are undoubtedly many conservative Peruvians who will welcome this move and some may have been involved in it. Such people have been increasingly hostile to the general trend of the Belaunde government and to many of the measures taken by the Hercelles cabinet under its special powers such as the imposition of a land tax, the tax on profits, the abolishment of bearer shares, and the reform of the tax collection system.

Jones

---

[3] In telegram 7651 from Lima, October 3, the Embassy reported that Juan Velasco Alvarado, commanding general of the army and chairman of the Joint Command, had emerged as the leader of the coup d'état. The Embassy considered Velasco "highly nationalistic and suspicious of U.S. policies," "ambitious, self-confident, not easily influenced, highly respected, extremely competent and intelligent," a "strong anti-Communist" and "firmly anti-APRA." (National Archives and Records Administration, RG 59, Central Files 1967–69, POL 23–9 PERU) In telegram 7705 from Lima, October 4, the Embassy offered a "preliminary evaluation" of the new military government. (Ibid.)

511.   Information Memorandum From the President's Special Assistant (Rostow) to President Johnson[1]

Washington, October 4, 1968.

SUBJECT

Peru Coup

The Military Junta appears firmly in control in Peru, supported by a united military establishment and some conservative civilians. Scattered violent protest acts by students are being quickly suppressed.[2] Labor has not heeded an effort to mount a general strike. Leaders of the majority APRA party strongly oppose the coup, but are apparently lacking weapons or capability for active resistance.

Detailed contingency plans for the coup were drawn up by the Peruvian Army many months ago which accounts for the smoothness of the operation. We don't know exactly what triggered their final decision, but the main motives apparently included:

—the growing conviction that a much hated APRA leader would succeed Belaunde as President if elections were held next year;
—unhappiness with political instability and economic doldrums;
—lack of confidence in Belaunde's choice of military ministers and his disregard of "military interest" in such matters as budgets and sophisticated weapons;
—resentment at the terms of the IPC oil settlement;
—personal ambition of General Velasco, Army Chief of Staff, soon to be retired.

State is carrying on consultations with other OAS governments prior to making any recommendation about recognition of the new regime. This process could go on for an extended period, perhaps as long as a month.

Unlike the case of the Argentine coup in 1966, we have made no official statement condemning the action of the military leaders, although State officials have made our unhappiness clear on a background basis. Oliver believes it better to allow the weight of Latin

---

[1] Source: Johnson Library, National Security File, Country File, Peru, Vol. III, 10/67–11/68. Confidential. A copy was sent to George Christian. A notation on the memorandum indicates the President saw it. Another copy indicates the memorandum was drafted by Lewis. (Ibid., Memos to the President, Walt W. Rostow, Vol. 97)

[2] On October 5 the Embassy received a note, dated October 3, which officially announced the formation of a new government under Division General Juan Velasco Alvarado. The note declared that the government had decided to respect its international obligations and intended to maintain cordial relations with the United States. (Telegram 7726, October 6; National Archives and Records Administration, RG 59, Central Files 1967–69, POL 23–9 PERU)

American sentiment to register first. So far, only Venezuela has officially deplored the coup.

Secretary Rusk appears Sunday morning on "Issues and Answers" and may, of course, be questioned about these events.[3]

Walt

---

[3] Rusk was interviewed, but did not receive any questions on Peru. For a transcript of the interview, see Department of State *Bulletin*, November 4, 1968, pp. 471–480.

---

512. Telegram From the Department of State to the Embassy in Peru[1]

Washington, October 6, 1968, 2001Z.

250839. For Ambassador from Oliver. Subject: Recognition Doctrine and the Peruvian Crisis.

1. My reply to you Saturday night was approved above me in Department as to general line.[2] This message relays for your consideration some so far entirely individual thoughts of mine as to possible courses for "post dust-settling" future. Herein I shall seek to open dialogue on relative desirability in Peruvian case of moving U.S. recognition doctrine and practice toward a variant of Estrada Doctrine[3] with-

---

[1] Source: National Archives and Records Administration, RG 59, Central Files 1967–69, POL 16 PERU. Secret; Priority. Drafted and approved by Oliver. Repeated as Tosec 83 to USUN for Rusk, who was attending the 23rd session of the United Nations General Assembly.

[2] The Embassy had requested instructions on overtures from individuals claiming to represent the new government in telegram 7725 from Lima, October 5. (Ibid., POL 23–9 PERU) The Department's response, drafted by Oliver and cleared in substance by Acting Secretary Katzenbach, stated: "Your reception of overtures should be cool and you should make it clear to intermediaries that you are only receiving suggestions for transmittal to Washington. You may add that USG especially interested in Junta's plans as to timing return to elected government." (Telegram 250828 to Lima, October 5; ibid.)

[3] Doctrine espoused in September 1930 by Mexican Foreign Minister Genero Estrada held that recognition of another government does not necessarily imply acceptance of its legitimacy. See Marjorie M. Whiteman, ed., *Digest of International Law*, Vol. 2, pp. 85–89.

out losing positive elements of Rio Resolution 26[4] as pressure points in favor of early return to elected government and assured respect for basic human freedoms.

2. Your preliminary characterization of Junta[5] coincides exactly with my feelings about it. There was no justification for this heavy-handed move; and it is very much in doubt whether Junta will be able to pick up quickly and ably enough the complicated strands of Peru's critical fiscal, foreign exchange, credit, and development needs. Junta officers probably do not have the savvy—and they may not be able easily to mobilize it outside their uniformed circle—that is essential if Peru is not to slip into a real economic and financial tailspin. For example, I wonder today and shall try to find out early in the week what IMF's thinking is about future of standby.

3. On recognition, it is apparent to me that our developing practices as to responses to coups no longer fits exactly within the text-book doctrinal pattern, i.e., one that assumes that the constitutional discontinuity caused by a coup automatically bars all standard inter-governmental relationships pending a new act of recognition of a golpista regime as the government of a State. (Hereinafter, "traditional doctrine.") Analytically, the main disadvantages of the traditional doctrine center on (i) historically-based general Latin-American distrust of USG use of power to withhold recognition; (ii) inhibition of any substantive relations, including diplomatic protection, during period of non-recognition; (iii) vast uncertainties about status of contractual relations (below international agreements level) between USG and the other state. Advantages of traditional view are (i) provident utilization of pressures arising from extra-constitutional regime's needs for our recognition; (ii) symbolization of our dislike of "bad" extra-constitutional changes, such as Peruvian one is.

4. Rio Resolution 26 may be based on assumption that traditional doctrine as to recognition will continue. (I have not been able to research this.) However, it does not seem to me that Rio 26 absolutely requires use of traditional doctrine. And as we know from Argentine case and current editorial comment about Peru, formal recognition fol-

---

[4] Resolution XXVI of the Final Act of the Second Special Inter-American Conference, signed on November 30, 1965, in Rio de Janeiro, recommended that OAS members consult before recognizing a de facto government, giving due consideration to: a) whether a foreign country was involved in the overthrow of the old regime; and b) whether the new regime promised to hold free elections, to honor its international obligations, and to respect human rights. After consultation, each country was free to decide whether to maintain diplomatic relations. (*The OAS Chronicle,* February 1966, p. 27)

[5] See Document 510 and footnote 3 thereto.

lowing consultations under 26 does "ring hollow", as October 6 *New York Times* editorial says.[6]

5. At some appropriate time, I think USG ought to shift toward the notion that a coup affects the intensity, intimacy and levels of our relations but does not automatically cut them off. I do not speak for anyone but myself on this. The question I raise with you in context of this message is whether the Peruvian coup might be the occasion for announcing and following a new doctrine. It does not require an immediate response from you, of course. Moreover, it may be that my personal views will not be acceptable. You will be kept informed.

6. Another alternative would be to follow in practice, but not announce, a new doctrine on this occasion. So far our responses (press briefings and your authorizations) fit within traditional doctrine, albeit somewhat imperfectly as some uncertainties already expressed by the involved American public show.

7. Related to para 6 is the problem of divergent attitudes in our business community arising from conflicting interests as to continuity or discontinuity in our formal relations. Moreover, if I may refer to legal matters outside present responsibilities, there are problems arising from tendency judiciary here to follow Department's views as to recognition or not in litigation involving a revolutionary regime's authority or lack of it to deal with state assets and other interests localized in this country or to make laws and rules that our Courts will treat as having governmental authority.

8. I want you to know that my personal feeling is one of revulsion and that if it were otherwise feasible and in our interest, I would not want to deal with Junta at all. Here I think I only reflect general feeling in this country. But I know that indefinite "suspension" is not going to be possible; and I am seeking the best way, not only to minimize losses, in the public affairs field and otherwise, but to help develop a more adequate approach to the coup problem in today's world.

9. I have cancelled a Southwestern speaking trip under Council for Foreign Relations auspices and shall tend store here during period immediately ahead. We are working closely with Cates and Poole (on TDY) at USUN, and I think that Vaky ought to go up to New York during week. The Latin Americans are meeting at UN on morning October 7. We are in close touch as to lines of inquiry and expect to have rather full readbacks.

---

[6] *The New York Times* editorial reads: "The State Department has properly withheld diplomatic recognition of the military junta that has unconstitutionally seized power. But the announcement that the United States is consulting with Latin American Governments on how to deal with the situation rings hollow."

10. Nearer to immediate operations, we need to get as clear a view as we can of circumstances surrounding IPC settlement. Junta's perjorative statements are receiving uncritical acceptance here. I do not propose we get into act, certainly not before IPC itself; but we do need to know all there is to know.[7]

Katzenbach

[7] In telegram 7797 from Lima, October 9, Jones agreed with the "pragmatic approach" of Oliver's recognition policy: "a prolonged suspension of several months or more would place intolerable stain on traditional ties between U.S. and Peru, seriously endanger private U.S. interests and probably prove counter productive in end." (National Archives and Records Administration, RG 59, Central Files 1967–69, POL 16 PERU)

---

513. Telegram From the Department of State to the Embassy in Peru[1]

Washington, October 10, 1968, 1701Z.

253028. For Ambassador from Oliver. Reference: Prior Traffic on Recognition Doctrine.

1. "Pragmatic" is a term I never use in relationship to our foreign policy. It simply has too much lustre and anyway it is an incorrect reference to the philosophies of James, Royce, and Peirce.

2. ARA/LA had a good talk out with U, M and L, Wednesday[2] forenoon. Naturally, the doctrinal point was not central. I very much doubt that the Peruvian situation, as it is beginning to shape up (IPC expropriation), will be the occasion for announcing any new recognition doctrine.[3]

3. But, and this is quite important: it was agreed that we can communicate with Junta on a wide range of matters, provided we assert that the act of communication is not "implied" recognition. This includes activities as to diplomatic protection and of warning about possible Sugar Act consequences of expropriation. Hereafter our suggestions and instructions on above and other matters will take this

[1] Source: National Archives and Records Administration, RG 59, Central Files 1967–69, POL 23–9 PERU. Confidential; Limdis. Drafted and approved by Oliver.

[2] October 9.

[3] On October 9 the Velasco regime issued a decree expropriating IPC property in Peru, including La Brea y Pariñas oil fields and the industrial complex at Talara.

evaluation into account. (What has been done, you see, is to free ourselves from tyranny of concept that a coup automatically cuts permissible communications during "suspension" down to those rather narrowly related to the resumption of relations.)

4. As we go forward, there is one thing we have to watch with
great care: our public deprecation of coup has for various reasons been
limited to working levels. (Personally I think it wiser not to advise public lamentations at very high levels, only to resume relations, as in 1962,
within month. This is not to be taken as a time estimate this occasion.)
But not having rended our garments and torn our hair in public heretofore, it would be bad in Latin America and here if we should go very
suddenly (even though happenstantially) into great public outcry after IPC nationalization. Fortunately, IPC's parent does not want us to.
We shall not comment on IPC at press briefing Thursday unless asked;
and if we are, response is a careful one that I drafted.[4]

5. I am sure you agree that CT and you have to keep an almost
psycho-ward watch on Junta leaders. Balance between firmness and
therapeutic permissiveness is very critical. As in the World War II story
about national character (as told by the Spanish), we do not want to
goad Peru into jumping out of airplane without a parachute! It is going to be hard, I very well know, to square what is professionally wise
with wide public expectations based on this or that simplistic notion.
But I still have faith that if we do it right and express ourselves adequately, results will not be adversely viewed by public here and elsewhere in Hemisphere.

Rusk

---

[4] In the press briefing on Thursday, October 10, the Secretary fielded several questions, including a query into the expropriation of IPC holdings in Peru. Rusk admitted
that "we were concerned and disappointed about the developments in Peru." "We don't
know yet what this announced move against the IPC will involve," he explained. "Presumably, the company will be the first to discover that and see what the issues are. But
we shall be following that closely at the appropriate time." (Department of State *Bulletin*, November 4, 1968, p. 481)

514.   Telegram From the Embassy in Peru to the Department of State[1]

Lima, October 11, 1968, 1602Z.

7870. Ref: (A) State 252730;[2] (B) Lima 7850;[3] (C) State 253684.[4]

1. DCM met privately last night with FonOff SecGen Ambassador Javier Perez de Cuellar and delivered letter as directed ref. (A). In doing so DCM called attention to fact that communication was a letter and not a note and that it addressed to General Mercado without further title. DCM said USG considered it important informally to establish dialogue for development of essential information without in any way implying recognition. Perez de Cuellar expressed understanding and agreement.

2. SecGen noted he career officer devoted without political inclination to serving his country and therefore continuing with revolutionary regime. He noted unhappily that General Mercado was his fifth Foreign Minister in about two years. He expressed opinion that President General Velasco and cabinet were patriotic Peruvians; nationalistic but not leftists. He hoped there could soon be constructive relations with the US so that the government would not become so frustrated as to find it necessary to deal with Communist regimes and which was not its desire.

3. SecGen said that he had received alarming information from Carlos Gibson in Washington about Hickenlooper and Sugar Act implications but in telex conversation with the Peruvian Chargé had been reassured on basis that USG had made no drastic public condemnations either of the golpe or of the expropriation.

---

[1] Source: National Archives and Records Administration, RG 59, Central Files 1967–69, POL 23–9 PERU. Confidential; Immediate. Repeated to USCINCSO and USUN.

[2] In telegram 252730 to Lima, October 9, the Department instructed Jones to deliver an "ordinary business letter" to General Edgardo Mercado Jarrin, addressing the new Foreign Minister by military title only, in response to the revolutionary government's note of October 3. "There is no danger," the Department explained, "that such a response will itself be taken as marking official resumption of relations." The letter asked: (a) when the government intended to return to constitutional rule; and (b) whether it would observe the property rights of foreign nationals in accordance with international law. (Ibid.)

[3] In telegram 7850 from Lima, October 10, the Embassy doubted that the new government would offer assurances about property rights "in light of developments yesterday regarding certain assets of IPC." (Ibid.)

[4] In telegram 253684 to Lima, October 11, the Department replied: "Your points carefully considered when sending letter decided and conclusion reached that essential ask questions." (Ibid.)

4. DCM said the lack of condemnatory statements by the USG should not be interpreted as in any way approving either act. DCM said it should be clear to the new government that the US deplored the interruption of constitutionalism and hoped for its prompt resumption. As for IPC, the United States recognizes the right of expropriation but also expects fulfillment of the obligation under international law to make just compensation. DCM noted then that it was precisely these concerns which motivated the letter at this time to General Mercado and that the questions posed therein were on these two subjects. As for the IPC matter, DCM said, an important earnest of the new regime's good intentions would be for it to put itself in contact with the company for the purpose of discussing compensations. Since this obviously is an issue in dispute, willingness of the regime to submit it to established procedures for negotiation, mediation or adjudicating of such disputes would be important.

5. Perez de Cuellar welcomed opportunity for informal contact and said GOP had already established such contacts through its missions in Washington and USUN. DCM said for time being it would probably be inadvisable for any direct meetings between Ambassador and General Mercado and asked to be advised whether the latter would wish to communicate informally with DCM via the SecGen or name another intermediary without official position in the GOP. SecGen expressed opinion that he would be intermediary as he had been, as Chief of Protocol, during the 1962 golpe.

6. General Mercado's reply will be communicated as soon as received. Assume Dept will instruct other ARA posts as to content this message as needed.

Jones

515. Memorandum From Secretary of State Rusk to President Johnson[1]

Washington, October 11, 1968.

SUBJECT

The Peruvian Situation

A Military Junta headed by Juan Velasco, Commanding General of the Army, deposed Peru's President Belaunde October 3, sending him into exile, installing an all-military Cabinet. As a result of the coup, diplomatic relations are in a state of suspension and U.S. assistance programs are under review. The Revolutionary Government, which appears to be highly nationalistic, justified its action on grounds of general unrest and loss of public confidence in the Government. The new regime particularly stressed the pretext that the August 13 agreement with the Government and the International Petroleum Company (IPC) over the La Brea y Pariñas oil fields was a sell-out. One of the Junta's first acts was to declare null the Act of Talara, which formed the basis of the IPC settlement, and on October 9 the President announced the expropriation of IPC's oil fields, refinery, and other assets. In other statements the regime has given no indication of plans for scheduling of elections, but it has stated that all international obligations will be met.

The United States has initiated bilateral consultations through its Embassies with other Latin American Governments on the situation in Peru and the question of recognition, in accordance with procedures established at the Second Inter-American Conference of 1965. Public comment by Department of State spokesmen has been limited to factual answers to questions about the situation and expressions of concern about the coup.

Preliminary indications are that, in addition to those countries which follow the practice of automatically recognizing new regimes on continuing relations, most Latin American countries will resume rela-

---

[1] Source: Johnson Library, National Security File, Country File, Peru, Vol. III, 10/67–1/69. Confidential. Another copy indicates the memorandum was drafted by Shumate on October 10. (National Archives and Records Administration, RG 59, Central Files 1967–69, POL 23–9 PERU) Forwarded to the President as an attachment to a memorandum from Rostow, October 14, in which Rostow explained: "Since Rusk's memorandum was drafted, the Junta has announced its intention to hold a national 'referendum' on the question of whether a new constitution is required before any elections are to be held. None of the Latin governments, except Venezuela, is disposed to insist on a commitment to hold elections as a pre-condition for recognition." (Johnson Library, National Security File, Country File, Peru, Vol. III, 10/67–1/69)

tions relatively soon. This would also be true of Western European and other trading nations. Only Venezuela has announced it is severing relations.

The implications of the IPC expropriation are being explored, including all relevant U.S. legislative provisions. These include the FAA and Sugar Act which can require a cutoff of U.S. assistance and of the sugar quota when property owned by U.S. citizens is taken without compensation. Standard Oil of New Jersey, the parent company of IPC, has asked that we take a reserved public position of the IPC take-over pending their own exploration of the possibilities of reaching some acceptable solution with the Peruvian regime.

In the period of "suspended" relations, we are making a realistic attempt to obtain from the military regime indications of its intentions to return to constitutional government within a reasonable time. We are also seeking its views as to international obligations to foreign citizens and property in Peru. While seeking clarification of these points, we are maintaining a flexible attitude to lower level administrative contact with the Military Government so that selectively we can do what we determine to be in our own interest, such as protecting American citizens, obtaining clearance for aircraft, and disbursing on loans to private parties. It is too early to judge when we will make a recommendation to you on resumption of relations.

Dean Rusk

---

516.   Telegram From the Embassy in Peru to the Department of State[1]

Lima, October 16, 1968, 2042Z.

7963. Department for Oliver. Subject: Meeting With GOP Officials. Ref: A) State 252730;[2] B) Lima 7923;[3] C) Lima 7888.[4]

[1] Source: National Archives and Records Administration, RG 59, Central Files 1967–69, POL PERU–US. Confidential; Immediate; Limdis. Repeated to USCINCSO for POLAD and USUN.

[2] See footnote 2, Document 514.

[3] Dated October 14. (National Archives and Records Administration, RG 59, Central Files 1967–69, POL PERU–US)

[4] Dated October 12. (Ibid., POL 15–1 PERU)

Summary: Ambassador and DCM met last night with revolutionary government Foreign Minister General Mercado and Foreign Office
Secretary General in private home.[5] Re questions transmitted in letter
authorized by ref. (A) General Mercado indicated the following:

(A) Revolutionary government referendum reported ref (C),
which will put to people question whether they wish future elections
under the present constitution, the present constitution amended or a
new constitution, will take place during calendar year 1969. This is first
step in electoral process but date for actual elections thereafter is
indefinite;

(B) The revolutionary government's undertaking to carry out international obligations does include those under general international
law as to the rights and property of foreign nationals. The question of
compensation for IPC expropriation will be decided in Peruvian courts.
[End summary.]

1. I met last night for about an hour and ten minutes in a private
home with General Mercado. I was accompanied by the Deputy Chief
of Mission and the General by the Secretary General of the Foreign
Ministry, Javier Perez de Cuellar. The atmosphere of the meeting was
businesslike and cool although not unfriendly as we have been closely
associated for many years with Perez de Cuellar, a professional diplo-
mat, and have also had some previous association with General Mercado on a friendly social basis. At the outset I referred to my informal
letter of October 10 and said the USG was interested in knowing the
revolutionary government's position on the questions posed therein.
General Mercado, in responding, spoke first about the second question
regarding undertakings under international law.

2. With some passion he asserted that the IPC expropriation was
a special case and that the government's action was necessary to correct a long standing problem. He said the action had met with the unanimous approval of the Peruvian people and was completely irreversible. I replied that it was not my purpose to discuss expropriation
since the United States recognized the right of a sovereign nation to
take territory within its jurisdiction for public purposes. I said, however, that the US also expected fulfillment of the corresponding obligation under international law to make prompt, adequate and effective compensation. In this regard I referred to the notes no.'s 116 and
152 of August 8 and 21, 1967 which we had given the Foreign Ministry

---

[5] On October 11 Perez de Cuellar called Siracusa to propose a meeting between
Mercado and Jones. Siracusa agreed to the meeting, subject to further instructions from
the Ambassador and the Department. (Telegram 7896 from Lima, October 12; ibid., POL
PERU–US) The Department gave its assent, suggesting, however, that Jones "merely listen and say only that you will transmit replies or views to Washington." (Telegram 254614
to Lima, October 12; ibid.)

making clear the US position on expropriation and compensation in specific case of La Brea y Parinas.[6] I suggested General read them. General Mercado replied that as provided in the Expropriation Act, decree law number 4, the question of compensation would be established in the Peruvian courts. He said it would be up to the courts to place a value on the property expropriated and also to determine the amount of the debts which IPC owed the GOP. The question of compensation would be solved by the balance of these accounts. When it was pointed out that the company does not acknowledge any debts, General Mercado replied that the Peruvian people nevertheless unanimously believe the debt existed. The DCM then suggested that opinion and fact might not be the same thing and asked whether, if the courts found the debts not to be real, the GOP would be prepared to make direct compensation to IPC. General Mercado seemed shocked by such a concept, said he could not imagine any court making such finding, but finally said that the decision of the courts would be respected. To illustrate he mentioned a recent decision by the Supreme Court which found in favor of the Conchan Oil Company (Calif. Standard) in a habeas corpus suit against the government on a tax dispute. I then suggested that it was the responsibility of the GOP, having themselves initiated the expropriation, also to take the initiative with respect to compensation which is its obligation and not leave it to the dispossessed to seek redress.

3. In connection with the foregoing discussion on IPC, General Mercado sought repeatedly to give assurance as to the "special" nature of IPC case. He said the revolutionary government, while it is nationalistic, is neither statist nor leftist and that it recognizes the need to protect and encourage private capital and to attract foreign private investment. He said Peru did not have the resources for development in any other way. At the end of the conversation, in response to a direct question by the DCM, he vehemently denied that the revolutionary government was influenced by a group of "Nasserist" colonels. He asserted that the armed forces were unified as a single man in determination to carry out their obligations to their country as they saw them under the constitution and to bring about necessary revolutionary reforms, before return to constitutional government. In this connection, he said the era of "old liberalism" was gone and the state must interest itself in the development of the nation. It must therefore take a promotional interest and that it must establish the channels in which private enterprise could operate freely.

---

[6] The texts of the notes are in telegrams 15548 and 22415 to Lima, August 3 and 17, 1967, respectively. (Ibid., PET 6 PERU)

4. In turning conversation to question number 1 of my letter regarding human rights and return to constitutionalism I said it was perhaps more important fundamentally than the other question we had just discussed. I felt I should make clear, I continued, how deeply the USG regretted the interruption of constitutional government in Peru and how concerned it was to have assurances of an early return to constitutionalism. General Mercado nodded his understanding of US attitude but asserted that the revolution had been necessary and that in carrying it out the armed forces had been fulfilling their obligation under the constitution. He said the politicians had prevented the constitution from working (had made a joke of it) and thus had defrauded the people from achieving their aspirations and blocked progress. While the legislature was supposed to be the primary power of the state in representation of the people, it had not functioned as foreseen in the constitution and the politicians had prevented fulfillment of Article 89 of the constitution which called for a "functional" Senate. This had never been fulfilled, he said, and the Senate, in being politically based, was simply a duplication of the Chamber of Deputies. The revolution had been carried out, he said, in order to give the people a chance to restructure their political organization and to correct its weaknesses. The only way this could be done, including rewriting constitution, he said, (and in this he was strongly supported by the Secretary General) was through the armed forces as the politicians would never set politics aside long enough to make the changes. He implied that the trend in recent years had been toward chaos and if not checked would have led Peru into communism. He said the only bulwarks for stability in a society such as Peru's were the church and the armed forces. In making these observations he asserted that we must understand that Peru is different from the United States and different from other L.A. countries and having its own character, it also has its own manner of resolving its problems. Referring to Chile and Venezuela, he expressed fear that failure of the democratic regimes there would open gates to communism.

5. On the specific question of a return to constitutionalism, General Mercado referred to the announcement of a referendum by the Prime Minister, General Montagne, on October 12. He said this was the first step and that the people would be asked in it whether they wanted to hold elections under the present constitution, under the present constitution amended or under an entirely new constitution. He said the referendum would be held during 1969, and that political parties would have full freedom of action in connection with it. He said the revolutionary government believes the people want to change the constitution, but that if the referendum should prove otherwise, it would be considered a rebuff (vote of no-confidence) and the armed forces would "go home". Presumably he meant turn the reins of government back

to civilians although he did not specify. He said no other de facto government "had the courage" to consult the people through plebiscite. Assuming the people opt for a new constitution or a modification of the present one, General Mercado said a "broadly based" commission would be established to do the draft. Asked whether there would then be a constituent assembly he admitted possibility but did not consider it necessary. He was quite vague as to any plans beyond the referendum and the constitutional change, but asserted that the whole process was designed to move toward eventual elections. As an analogy he said the elections were like D Day in Normandy and that "even Eisenhower" did not know exactly when D Day would occur.

6. In response to my question, Secretary General said this informal "non-official" meeting constituted answer to my letter of October 10.[7]

Jones

---

[7] In telegram 7994 from Lima, October 17, the Embassy judged that the assurances given by Mercado were sufficient to recommend prompt recognition of the new government. "Further delay in resuming relations," the Embassy maintained, "could only damage our interests, and would deny us the opportunity to have contacts which might have a beneficial influence on the future action of the revolutionary government." (Ibid., POL 16 PERU)

---

517. Telegram From the Embassy in Peru to the Department of State[1]

Lima, October 18, 1968, 2252Z.

8032. For Oliver. Ref: State 257311.[2] Subj: IPC.

1. Reftel discussed at length within Embassy this morning. We under no illusions as to grave repercussions on US relations with Peru for years to come, and in hemisphere if amendments invoked. We

---

[1] Source: National Archives and Records Administration, RG 59, Central Files 1967–69, PET 15–2 PERU. Confidential; Priority; Limdis.

[2] In telegram 257311 to Lima, October 17, the Department reported a formal request from officials of IPC and Jersey Standard to invoke the Hickenlooper amendment. The Department also issued the following instructions: "You are authorized in your discretion pass word to military government that matter now in hands our lawyers; that we cognizant as we trust they are too of consequences of application of Hickenlooper; but proceedings are required by law and so we are bound to act accordingly." (Ibid.)

nevertheless decided best course was to advise revolutionary government informally that possible application of Hickenlooper amendment
and Sugar Act as a result of 1967 expropriation is under active consideration in the Department. In doing so we felt it best not to reveal
that IPC and Jersey Standard have asked USG invoke these provisions.
We therefore presented current study by lawyers as a natural requirement of the law itself which binding on executive.

2. DCM informed FonOff SecGen privately in latter's home this
afternoon. Siracusa was careful to reiterate that no decision has been
made and that USG respects the right of expropriation so long as there
is compensation. He presented to the SecGen for ready reference copies
in English and Spanish of our Notes numbers 116 and 152 of August
8 and 21, 1967, which were presented in reaction to the expropriation
at that time.[3] He also presented copies of the two amendments in question as well as of our aide-mémoire of Nov. 7, 1963 presented in reaction to the nullification in that year of the arbitration award which is
basic to IPC case.[4]

3. Ambassador Perez de Cuellar's reaction was grave. He said this
was not the kind of a government likely to respond to pressure. He felt
invocation of these acts by the USG would unify Peruvians against US
and that Peru would receive solid support of other countries in the
hemisphere. He thought such acts would prejudge the legal determination of compensation now in the courts. (See Lima 7982.)[5] He promised to inform the Foreign Minister, General Mercado, with great care
so they would not jump to premature conclusions. He and the DCM
agreed on the imperative necessity of keeping this matter out of the
public domain until the two governments had had a chance to try to
deal with it.

4. *Comment:* We assure IPC and Jersey Standard's decision to request invocation of the amendments represents a willingness on their
part to accept the possible total expropriation of their interests in Peru
and a termination of all their activities here. Their attitude as expressed
in para. 3 of reftel seems clearly to suggest this. If we interpret para. 3
correctly it would seem almost a challenge to the GOP to intervene or
in someway take over, possibly by expropriation, IPC marketing system to avoid the exhaustion of stocks implied by the company's unwillingness to purchase from the expropriated refinery. We believe that

---

[3] See footnote 6, Document 516.

[4] A copy of the aide-mémoire is in the National Archives and Records Administration, RG 59, Lima Embassy Files, Subject Case File on the International Petroleum
Company: Lot 71 F 154, Sep–Dec 1963.

[5] Telegram 7982 from Lima, October 17, reported that the IPC had filed a "habeas
corpus action" in an attempt to nullify expropriation of its property. (Ibid., Central Files
1967–69, PET 6 PERU)

if matters come to this the military government will be more unified than ever and, at the outset at least, will be enthusiastically supported by Peruvians on a patriotic basis. The reaction would be not only against IPC but US-Peruvian relations would suffer an historic setback. A wave of anti-Americanism, which might endanger American lives and property, would result. We hope therefore that the Department in making its study will do so with fullest appreciation of potential consequences. Also urge make every effort to avoid publicity so long as the matter is under study and the vital decisions have not been taken.

5. With reference to the Embassy telegram no. 7994[6] recommending a prompt resumption of relations with the revolutionary GOP, we suggest that this is now more desirable than before. We have already said the GOP meets the normal requirements and should be recognized. Because of the seriousness of the subject of this telegram it is important that the avenues of normal intercourse be opened immediately so that we can deal with the matter. It is essential that the GOP not get the impression that recognition is being delayed as a pressure tactic in favor of IPC.

Jones

---

[6] See footnote 7, Document 516.

---

518.   Action Memorandum From the President's Special Assistant (Rostow) to President Johnson[1]

Washington, October 19, 1968, 3 p.m.

Mr. President:

Sec. Rusk requests your authorization to resume diplomatic relations with the new Peruvian Government which took power on October 3. (Tab A)[2] His memorandum projects this action on or about Wednesday, October 23. I understand, however, that State may now wish to recognize as early as Monday, October 21.

---

[1] Source: Johnson Library, National Security File, Country File, Peru, Vol. III, 10/67–1/69. Secret.

[2] Tab A was a memorandum from Rusk to the President, October 19; attached but not printed.

—The Military Government is in full control, and no significant opposition has materialized. It has met all the traditional tests for recognition.

—We have carried out full consultations with other OAS members. Argentina, Brazil, Mexico, and several others have already recognized. Most of the others will have recognized by Monday.[3]

—The new government has assured it will honor its international obligations and that it will hold a referendum to decide whether a new constitution shall be drafted before holding new elections. However, it may be many months, or even years, before freely elected government returns to Peru.

—The IPC expropriation will gravely complicate our future relations, but should be kept separate from the diplomatic recognition question. Prompt recognition may help us protect IPC's interest in obtaining a reasonable settlement.

—Resumption of relations does not imply resumption of all assistance programs.

Events in Panama are also moving toward early recognition by most countries. State may recommend that we follow suit next week. The Peru case should be resolved first.

I recommend that you authorize the resumption of diplomatic relations with Peru whenever Sec. Rusk wishes to move.[4]

Walt

Approved

Disapproved

Call Me

---

[3] October 21.
[4] No option is checked, but see Document 519.

519. Notes of Meeting[1]

Washington, October 22, 1968, 1:20–2:24 p.m.

THOSE ATTENDING THE MEETING WERE

The President
Secretary Rusk
Secretary Clifford
General Wheeler
CIA Director Helms
Walt Rostow
George Christian
Tom Johnson

[Omitted here is discussion of other subjects.]

Secretary Rusk: . . . We recommend that the USA now recognize Peru, if you approve.

The President: What does that do?

Secretary Rusk: Colonels have it in Brazil and Argentina.

The President: What if we didn't recognize Peru?

Secretary Rusk: It would complicate ourselves. But we have recognized 50 countries where coup d'etats have taken place.

Secretary Rusk: We are denied AID for Peru.

CIA Director Helms: Sugar quota would fall off once the Hickenlooper Amendment takes over.

Secretary Rusk: We don't get anywhere by not recognizing them. This is the 62nd coup I've lived through since I've been Secretary of State and Dick Helms did not cause a one of them—contrary to popular belief.

We can't impose our will over other countries. They will conduct elections in Peru.

We went two years without a coup in Latin America.[2]

[Omitted here is discussion of other subjects.]

---

[1] Source: Johnson Library, Tom Johnson Meeting Notes. No classification marking. Drafted by Tom Johnson. The meeting was held during lunch.

[2] At the end of his notes, Tom Johnson recorded the President's decision on Peru as follows: "Recognize him [Velasco] as soon as you want to." Rostow later told Benjamin Read that the President had given Rusk a "reluctant go-ahead to recognize, if that's what he [Rusk] wants to do." (Note from Bromley K. Smith to Lois Nivens, October 22; ibid., National Security File, Rostow Files, Meetings with the President, January–December 1968 [1])

520. **Information Memorandum From the President's Special Assistant (Rostow) to President Johnson**[1]

Washington, October 25, 1968.

SUBJECT

Resumption of Diplomatic Relations with Peru

At the Tuesday lunch[2] you authorized Secretary Rusk to resume diplomatic relations with Peru as soon as multilateral and Congressional consultations were completed.

All countries outside this hemisphere with whom Peru traditionally maintains relations have now recognized. All major Latin American countries except Venezuela have also resumed relations.

State has consulted with Senator Hickenlooper (the only Senator accessible) and the staffs of the Senate Foreign Relations Committee and House Foreign Affairs Committee, as well as staffs of Representatives Mailliard and Purcell.[3] No objection to our resumption of relations was voiced.

Secretary Rusk authorized our Embassy in Lima to answer the Peruvian Government's note at noon today (text of our note is attached at Tab A),[4] thereby signalling the resumption of diplomatic relations.

A brief low-key announcement will be made by State's press spokesman at the noon briefing today (a copy is attached at Tab B of this announcement).[5]

Walt

---

[1] Source: Johnson Library, National Security File, Country File, Peru, Vol. III, 10/67–1/69. Confidential. A copy was sent to George Christian. Another copy indicates the memorandum was drafted by Samuel W. Lewis. (Ibid.)

[2] See Document 519 and footnote 2 thereto.

[3] Representatives William S. Mailliard (R–California) and Graham Purcell (D–Texas).

[4] Attached but not printed. The text of the note is also in telegram 261223 to Lima, October 24. (National Archives and Records Administration, RG 59, Central Files 1967–69, POL 15–1 PERU)

[5] Attached but not printed. The text of the announcement is in Department of State *Bulletin*, November 11, 1968, p. 497.

521. **Telegram From the Embassy in Peru to the Department of State**[1]

Lima, November 6, 1968, 2340Z.

8336. Subj: Call on New President, General Velasco.

1. General Velasco received me very cordially on my first official visit since reestablishment diplomatic relations. He had press photographer present to record event. I told President I was happy to assure him that my government wished to continue the close and happy relations which had always existed between our two countries; that as Ambassador I was happy to have this opportunity to greet him personally as well as in the name of my government. I added that I hoped to continue working with his government as I had with past Governments of Peru in the best interests of Peruvian-American relations.

2. I informed the President that I had already had the opportunity to call on the Minister of Foreign Affairs and on the Prime Minister[2] and that I hoped to call on the other members of his cabinet within the next days and weeks. I told him that we had some urgent and important bilateral problems such as IPC, Cerro de Pasco, fisheries conference, Investment Guarantee Agreement, etc. I added that I had discussed the IPC case at some length with both the Prime and Foreign Ministers and assumed they would be informing him of our conversations on this subject. I expressed the hope that, if at any time in the future I needed to discuss these matters directly with him, he would be good enough to receive me. He assured me that this was the case and that his "door was always open to me".

3. President Velasco then spoke about the revolution and the reasons why he and the military had felt it necessary to move. He said the country had gotten into a mess, that the people were desperate, particularly those in the highlands. He mentioned particularly the area around Puno where there was near starvation. He referred to the desperate condition of Indian population and said "something must be done" for them. This was not one of those military coups in which the country was prosperous and the participants would benefit. On the contrary, the position of Peru had been desperate and he and his "team" had felt it necessary to save Peru from disaster. They did need help

---

[1] Source: National Archives and Records Administration, RG 59, Central Files 1967–69, POL 15–1 PERU. Confidential.

[2] A report on Jones' meeting with Mercado is in telegram 8201 from Lima, October 30, and a report on his meeting with the Peruvian Prime Minister, General Ernesto Montagne Sanchez, is in telegram 8337 from Lima, November 6. (Ibid., PET 6 PERU and POL 15–1 PERU, respectively)

and understanding from the United States and he hoped that some assistance would eventually be forthcoming. He said if they failed they would not only be hanged but the country would fall into either chaos or a Castro-type of government. The President said his government had an overall plan of general improvement but that it could not be revealed all at once since it was more prudent to proceed one step at a time. He referred to the chaotic situation of Peruvian universities which he said were centers of subversion and political agitation rather than of higher education. He also referred to what he considered were unsatisfactory conditions within Peruvian labor unions but did not elaborate. Finally, he referred to the press and insisted that he had said from the beginning and sincerely felt that freedom of press was essential. However, two periodicals *Caretas* and *Expreso* had exceeded bounds of correct behavior by insulting and attacking personally members of the junta. This, he said, could not be tolerated and that they must learn respect for the uniform. Hence the paper and magazine have been closed down and will not be permitted to reopen until November 15, which would require *Caretas* to miss one of its fortnightly issues. He expressed appreciation for attitude of daily newspaper *El Comercio* which supported the junta (he assured me without their having requested it to do so) and even for *La Prensa* which although it had criticized the government on many issues he felt was the kind of constructive criticism which the junta could accept. When the various reforms have been accomplished, the military junta would look forward to holding elections and turning the government back to a civilian administration. At that time he and his comrades in arms would very happily go back to their homes. In response to my question, he said he could not fix even an approximate date for this event.

4. Finally he mentioned that the last and decisive meeting of his group which led to the coup had been held at 7:00 p.m. on the night of October 1. He said the decision had been very tightly held and that this group consisted of "only six officers". He said the commanders of the five military regions had been informed except for the date and the hour when the coup would commence. With obvious relish he recalled he had seen me, the Mayor of Lima, Luis Bedoya Reyes, and the publisher of *La Prensa*, Pedro Beltran, at a dinner party the night of October 1 shortly after the decisive meeting on the coup. It seemed to please him that none of us suspected what he had just decided to do.

5. At end of interview I informed President of agrement, of Fernando Berckemeyer as Peruvian Ambassador in Washington, saying that I had handed written communication to this effect to Chief of Protocol that same morning. Velasco expressed his pleasure at this news and his confidence that Berckemeyer would serve Peru well in this important post.

Jones

Venezuela

522. National Intelligence Estimate[1]

NIE 89–64   Washington, February 19, 1964.

PROSPECTS FOR POLITICAL STABILITY IN VENEZUELA

The Problem

To estimate the outlook for political stability in Venezuela over the next two years.

Summary

President-elect Leoni will almost certainly take office without serious challenge, and will probably enjoy an initial period of relative political calm. Nonetheless, the problems of creating and maintaining a viable administration and of coping with underlying social and economic tensions—together with the likelihood of further terrorist activities—will almost certainly produce a series of political crises during the period of this estimate. The Leoni government probably will survive these crises.

Conclusions

A. Leoni is an experienced, generally capable political leader; but his ability to supply vital national leadership during a crisis is as yet untested. (Para. 15)

B. Leoni's relations with Congress are likely to start out relatively peacefully. His political opposition will almost certainly turn more belligerent over time, but we believe he will be able to maintain control of Congress on key issues through 1965. (Paras. 16–20)

C. The Communist and Castroist insurgents almost certainly will be unable to force their way to power during the period of this estimate, although they will retain a high capability for hit and run terrorism, including attacks against US personnel and property. Leoni probably will have to resort at times to extraordinary measures such as suspension of constitutional guarantees to contain the insurgency

---

[1] Source: Central Intelligence Agency, Job 79–R01012A, O/DDI Registry. Secret; Controlled Dissem. According to a note on the cover sheet this estimate was prepared in the Central Intelligence Agency with the participation of the intelligence organizations of the Departments of State and Defense, the National Security Agency and the Federal Bureau of Investigation. The United States Intelligence Board concurred in this estimate on February 19.

threat within tolerable limits (by Venezuelan standards), and his timing in initiating these measures may involve him in difficulties with either Congress or the military. (Paras. 22–28)

D. The armed forces, the ultimate arbiters of political power in Venezuela, are generally disposed to support constitutional government for as long as it proves reasonably effective in dealing with national problems. In any event, the military is anxious to avoid an arbitrary move against the government which might alienate a large segment of the population. Thus a military coup is not likely unless Leoni becomes generally discredited with the population. Under such circumstances, a military coup would probably follow a relatively moderate course and offer the leftist insurgents little opportunity for substantial gains. (Paras. 29–31)

Discussion

I. Introduction: The Importance of Venezuela

1. Raul Leoni is scheduled to succeed Romulo Betancourt as President of Venezuela in March 1964. Leoni's success or failure in office will be of great importance to the US. Venezuela is of strategic importance as the world's largest exporter of oil. US capital investment in Venezuela totals about $3 billion, exceeded only by our investments in Canada and in the UK. Venezuela, moreover, holds great symbolic value for our policy in Latin America as a country attempting rapid social and economic progress through constitutional democracy. Venezuela remains a priority target in Communist efforts to promote violent revolution in Latin America, primarily because Fidel Castro cannot afford to allow such an important democratic reformist regime to succeed. Venezuela is also the only Latin American country in which leftist extremists, with moral and material support from Cuba, have been able to sustain an impressive level of insurgency.

II. Leoni's Inheritance: Betancourt's Problems and Achievements

2. President Betancourt's political legacy to his successor is a mixed one. On the one hand, Betancourt has moved constitutional democracy an important step forward by the very fact of surviving his legal term and successfully holding free elections. He also initiated an extensive program of social and economic reform. Finally, the last few months have been marked by a subsiding of political tensions, leading to a relatively auspicious environment for the transfer of power. On the other hand, Leoni will inherit, to one degree or another, the problems which have created recurrent crises for Betancourt from 1959 to the present: acute social tensions, limited national experience with representative government, Communist and Castroist insurgency, and the threat of a military takeover.

Political and Social Heritage

3. In addition to the direct assaults of leftist extremists and military dissidents, the Betancourt government has had to withstand harassment by opposition parties, obstruction of its program in Congress, and widespread popular indifference to the fate of constitutional democracy. These latter problems are rooted in Venezuela's lack of experience and confidence in representative government and in the acute social tensions prevailing in urban areas.

4. Venezuela has traditionally been ruled by military dictators; its only previous experience with democratic reformist government (1945–1948) was terminated by a military coup which led to the repressive dictatorship of General Marcos Perez Jimenez (1948–1958). Following his election in December 1958, Betancourt was able to form a strong multi-party coalition, because of widespread concern over the threat of another military intervention. By 1962, however, this coalition had splintered, and the opposition parties had gained control of the lower house of Congress. Various opposition parties joined with Communists and Castroists in a systematic obstruction of government programs, particularly of measures to control terrorism. The primary objective was to discredit Betancourt's Democratic Action party (AD). The political opposition apparently had come to fear AD's domination of the 1963 elections as much as it did the consequences of a military coup. From time to time the opposition parties threatened to boycott the elections.

5. Thanks largely to its petroleum, Venezuela has the highest per capita income in Latin America (over $700), and its government is assured of substantial revenues, much of which the Betancourt administration has directed into programs to promote the welfare of the poorest classes. Nonetheless, one-half of the country's eight million people lives under severely depressed conditions. Moreover, because of a large rural-to-urban migration in recent years, much of the country's economically depressed population now lives pressed together in urban slums, without steady employment or other conventional social ties, and without much concern for Venezuela and the maintenance of orderly government. Particularly in Caracas, where lawlessness is prevalent among the 300,000 slum dwellers, much of the population has regarded the government and the police—not the terrorists—as its main antagonists.

Military Dissidence

6. Betancourt has had to contend with rightist military plotting throughout much of his term. Moreover, of the five garrison rebellions during 1960–1962, the last two, Carupano and Puerto Cabello, involved dissident military officers collaborating with leftist extremist civilians. Betancourt has survived these plots and assaults largely because the chief

military commanders, and through them the bulk of the armed forces,[2] have remained loyal to the government. Betancourt, recognizing the military to be the ultimate arbiters of political power in Venezuela, assiduously cultivated this loyalty. He maintained military perquisites at a high level, flattered the military with frequent presidential attention and praise, and courted the personal friendship of key officers and garrisons. Most importantly, he maintained exceptionally good channels of communication between his office and all sectors of the armed forces as a means of explaining his policies and of monitoring the moods and anticipating the demands of the military. His efforts were favored by a growing political moderation among the military, stemming in part from an increasing professionalism among top officers and their fear that another military dictatorship would encounter stiff civilian opposition. At the same time, the military, keenly aware of Castro's extermination of the prerevolutionary military establishment in Cuba, regarded nervously Betancourt's politically motivated reluctance to crack down on leftist subversive agitation and violence. At times during 1963 a considerable restiveness spread throughout the military establishment.

Communist and Castroist Insurgency

7. Leftist extremists, led by the Venezuelan Communist Party (PCV), were the major disruptive force during the final years of the Betancourt administration. The PCV participated in the 1958 election, gaining 160,000 votes and nine seats in Congress. The party was propelled toward "armed struggle" against the government by its impatience with its limited opportunities to make gains through "political struggle," by the example of Castro's success in Cuba, and by the opportunities for violent action existing in Venezuela. The Communists found ready allies for insurgency in other extremist groups, most notably the Movement of the Revolutionary Left (MIR), a pro-Castro faction which split off from the AD party. They also found allies of convenience among rightist military dissidents.

8. The leftist extremists work through an organization called the Armed Forces of National Liberation (FALN). The PCV generally dominates FALN affairs, but undisciplined activists sometimes initiate terrorist activities on their own. The FALN is well organized and trained, aggressive and resourceful, but limited in numbers. Although the PCV and MIR combined probably can count on a political following in the tens of thousands, we estimate that the FALN has only some 600 to 800 active trained members, including those deployed in rural-based guer-

---

[2] The Venezuelan armed forces consist of four separate services with the following numbers of officers and men: Army—17,800; National Guard (a militarized constabulary)— 12,000; Navy (including Marines)—5,600; Air Force—2,500. [Footnote in the source text.]

rilla bands. Most members are recruited from among urban youth, traditionally defiant of authority and extremist in politics.

9. The FALN has been able to obtain most of its funds, small arms, and explosives in Venezuela, primarily through robberies. Almost certainly, however, it has received material and financial assistance from Cuba. Most notably, government forces last November discovered a cache of small and medium weapons on the Paraguana Peninsula.[3] In addition, more than a hundred FALN members have received paramilitary training in Cuba and elsewhere in the Communist Bloc. Cuban broadcasts to Venezuela endorsing the FALN cause and heralding its exploits have been an important boost to the insurgents' morale. Castro's moral and material assistance was an important factor in the early stages of the development of the FALN. Although Castro probably can call upon some elements in Venezuela to step up terrorism whenever it suits his purposes, at least over the past year the FALN has become an aggressive and effective terrorist organization that does not appear to need outside prodding.

10. The leftist extremists have used a variety of tactics in attacking the Betancourt government. During 1960–1962 they tried to force their way to power directly, first by means of a series of urban riots and then by a combination of guerrilla warfare in rural areas and the two garrison rebellions. These attempts only proved that they lacked sufficient popular and military support for the purpose. By late 1962, therefore, they turned to terrorism and sabotage as operations which could be conducted by a relatively few dedicated militants, but which would serve to discredit and weaken the Betancourt government while building up their own image and strength. In August 1963, they launched a major terrorist offensive to disrupt the December elections and provoke a military coup, hoping to profit from the resultant disorder and discord.

11. During most of 1963 the FALN was able to strike at a wide variety of targets, with a good chance of success, and very little risk of casualties or losses through capture. The police,[4] handicapped by poor

---

[3] Located in northwest Venezuela, the major area of FALN guerrilla activity (see map). [Footnote in source text. The map is not reproduced. On November 28, 1963, the Venezuelan Government announced that it had discovered a large arms cache on the coast of the Paraguaná Peninsula; that an internal investigation had determined that the arms were of Cuban origin, intended for use in a guerrilla operation to seize power in Caracas before the Presidential elections of December 1; and that evidence against Cuba would be presented to the Organization of American States thereby justifying retaliatory measures under the Inter-American Treaty of Reciprocal Assistance, the so-called "Rio Treaty" of 1947. Documentation on the subsequent campaign to indict and sanction Cuba before the OAS is in Documents 1 ff., and *Foreign Relations, 1961–1963,* vol. XII, Documents 169–171.]

[4] Civilian police forces in Venezuela number nearly 19,000 men. In the Caracas area, there are five separate civilian forces with a total of over 10,000 men and a National Guard contingent of 700 men engaged in police duties. [Footnote in the source text.]

organization, inadequate training, low morale, and legal restrictions established or enforced in reaction to the Perez Jimenez dictatorship, were no match for the terrorists. The political leaders of the FALN were protected from arrest by congressional immunity; rank and file members were able to take advantage of the legal sanctuaries provided by the autonomous universities and the de facto asylums of the slum districts. Moreover, even when arrested, terrorists often were able to regain their freedom through legal technicalities, bribery, or escapes.

12. FALN efforts to disrupt the election through terrorism were thwarted, however, by the combination of a well-timed government crackdown, a notable improvement in police performance, and a show of determination by the population not to be intimidated by the terrorists. Betancourt, using some measures of doubtful constitutionality, moved to reduce FALN's disruptive capability, before military restiveness got out of hand, and after five anti-government candidates had committed themselves to the presidential race. On 30 September the military was called upon to assist in a roundup of known extremists and suspected terrorists, including those hiding out in slum districts. In all, some 300 to 400 were jailed, including several PCV and MIR congressmen. In October, in response to pressure from the government, school officials closed Caracas' Central University, which further reduced the maneuverability of the terrorists. Starting in October, moreover, the police in Caracas, political nerve center of the country, proved to be a better match for the terrorists, inflicting more casualties and taking more prisoners than previously.[5] The FALN still was able to undertake a large number of hit-and-run raids, especially outside of Caracas. But because of accumulated losses in manpower and morale, it was either unable or unwilling to mount an impressive last-minute attack. Its repeated threats against the voters probably proved counterproductive. On election day (1 December) the population went to the polls in overwhelming numbers; FALN attacks were few and ineffectual. Since the election, the terrorists have been relatively inactive, which is in large part responsible for the political calm of the final Betancourt months.

[Omitted here is the final section of the estimate, "The Outlook for the Leoni Administration," which includes a detailed discussion of the Inauguration, President Leoni, Political Prospects, Social and Economic Issues, Leftist Insurgency, Leoni and the Military.]

---

[5] US advice and assistance contributed in large part to the improved performance of the police. Among other things, we were primarily responsible for the introduction of training in marksmanship and other practical subjects and the establishment of improved coordination among Caracas' many and often competing police agencies. [Footnote in the source text.]

523.   Action Memorandum From the Assistant Secretary of State for European and Canadian Affairs (Tyler) to Secretary of State Rusk[1]

Washington, July 10, 1964.

SUBJECT

Venezuela's Interest in British Guiana

A reliable controlled American source reports that Venezuela's Foreign Minister Ignacio Irribaren Borges wishes to talk with you privately during the Latin American Foreign Ministers Conference about British Guiana. He is expected to tell you that Venezuela is prepared to support the overthrow of Cheddi Jagan, and to seek our support for this venture.

Our Ambassador in Caracas has learned from the Minister of the Interior that Venezuela is ready to provide financial support for Forbes Burnham when the time is ripe for Jagan's overthrow.

A report from Georgetown advises that a person with good contacts in Venezuela is urging Burnham and D'Aguiar to form a "Revolutionary Government"; attempt a coup with the assistance of 100 trained men who will have had 30 days special training in Venezuela, and at the same time Cheddi and Janet Jagan will be kidnapped and taken to Venezuela.

You may wish to urge restraint on the Venezuelans, pointing out that plans are underway to seek a political resolution in BG through the democratic process of a Proportional Representation election. We hope that nothing will happen to impede this plan and we cannot support the Venezuelans even though we share their hope that someone other than Jagan will reach the top in British Guiana.[2]

---

[1] Source: National Archives and Records Administration, RG 59, Central Files 1964–66, POL 3 IA. Secret. Drafted by William B. Cobb, Jr. (EUR/BNA), on July 8. A copy was sent to Ball. A notation on the memorandum indicates Rusk saw it.

[2] According to the Secretary's Appointment Book Rusk met Iribarren on July 16 and 20. (Johnson Library) Memoranda of conversation, confined to discussion of the OAS resolution on Cuba, are in the National Archives and Records Administration, RG 59, Central Files 1964–66, POL 3 IA. No evidence has been found to indicate whether Iribarren raised the Venezuelan proposal to intervene in British Guiana.

524. Memorandum From the Director of the Office of Colombian-Venezuelan Affairs (Margolies) to the Assistant Secretary of State for Inter-American Affairs (Mann)[1]

Washington, January 13, 1965.

SUBJECT

Venezuela Asks U.S. Intercession in Settling Guiana Boundary Dispute

The Problem

On December 15, 1964, the Venezuelan Foreign Minister called on Mr. Ball (then Acting Secretary), and requested that the U.S. Government use its good offices to help bring the current negotiations between Venezuela and Great Britain on the British Guiana boundary dispute to a conclusion favorable to Venezuela. Mr. Ball told the Foreign Minister that he could not comment on the problem because he was not familiar with it, but said he would look into it.[2]

Background

In presenting his views to Mr. Ball, the Foreign Minister handed over a memorandum[3] that stated that the Venezuelan Government has obtained evidence which allegedly casts some doubt on the integrity of the American citizen members of the 1899 arbitration tribunal. The memorandum states that this information has not yet been made public, but offers to furnish the evidence to the Department in confidence for our study.

Another noteworthy development in this situation is the number of recent confidential reports indicating that the Venezuelan military are very sensitive to the boundary problem. They view the possibility that British Guiana may become independent under a pro-Communist government as opening the way for a Castro beach-head on the continent. They are also apprehensive because of the proximity of British Guiana to Venezuela's developing iron and steel and hydro-electric complex in Guayana State. There are indications that the military have already prepared a contingency plan for the seizure of the area by force should this seem to them necessary at some future time.

---

[1] Source: National Archives and Records Administration, RG 59, Central Files 1964–66, POL 32–1 BR GU–VEN. Confidential. Drafted by Crowley; cleared by Cobb, Whiteman, and Randolph. A copy was sent to Adams.

[2] According to a memorandum of this conversation Iribarren said "he hoped that the United States would lend support to the Venezuelan position." (Ibid.)

[3] Attached but not printed.

A further complicating factor is that Forbes Burnham, the new Premier of British Guiana, is reliably reported to believe that the U.S. Government has sufficient influence with Venezuela to cause the latter to drop its claim.

ARA/CV's Views

Our continuing attitude (with which EUR agrees) toward this boundary dispute is that we hope to see the problem satisfactorily settled between the two interested governments through quiet and friendly negotiations without our becoming involved.

We believe that Britain would be most reluctant to modify the 1899 arbitration award, and the head of the UK Foreign Office desk for Latin America, Mr. John Slater told us recently that the British experts have found no evidence in the material submitted to them by the Venezuelans which would in the British view vindicate the Venezuelan claim.

We believe that Britain in any event will not wish to impose a boundary change on the present inhabitants of British Guiana against their will. The Venezuelans are aware of this problem, but nevertheless seek to have the boundary rectified before independence so as to avoid the awkwardness of having to demand territory from an independent neighbor. Responsible leaders in British Guiana also hope that the problem will be solved before independence, since some of them fear that Venezuela might actually seize the disputed area from a weak and newly-independent neighbor.

Recommendations:[4]

Even though Venezuela regards this problem as a very real one, we believe that our present position of non-intervention should remain unchanged. However, since Mr. Ball said that we would look into it, we propose from a precautionary standpoint the following:

1. When the documentary evidence is received from the Venezuelan Government, it should be translated and furnished to L for a review of the alleged proofs submitted as to any fraud on the part of members of the arbitration tribunal, and of any possible implications regarding the U.S. members. Further action, if any, would depend upon

---

[4] There is no indication on the memorandum that Mann approved these recommendations. In a January 28 memorandum to Margolies, Adams dismissed any serious consideration of "evidence." "I think it is ridiculous on the part of the Venezuelan Foreign Minister to seek our 'good offices' with the U.K., and at the same time threaten to blackmail us on the allegedly fraudulent findings of an American 66 years ago." Adams suggested that the United States refuse to accept the evidence if Venezuela submitted it "in any formal way," e.g. by diplomatic note. Otherwise, Adams agreed that the United States should avoid involvement in the dispute unless it appeared that Castro might establish a "beach-head" in British Guiana. (National Archives and Records Administration, RG 59, Central Files 1964–66, POL 32–1 BR GU–VEN)

the authenticity of the evidence submitted by Venezuela as it might implicate American citizen members of the tribunal.

2. Apart from whatever conclusions the Department might draw from the evidence provided by Venezuela, it would, of course, be possible for Venezuela and the United Kingdom, should they so agree, to submit the question of the existence of any fraud and any consequent invalidity of the award either to an ad hoc arbitral tribunal, or to the International Court of Justice. For the present, however, we do not believe that the U.S. Government should try to urge this line of action upon the interested governments.

3. In order to allay the understandable fears of Venezuela that British Guiana might become a Castro beach-head on the continent after independence, the U.S. Government should give assurances to the Government of Venezuela, either through our Ambassador, or high-level officers of the Department, that we do not intend to stand idly by and allow such a course of events to take place, and that on the contrary we would use every resource to prevent such a development.

Note:

On January 15, Embassy Caracas reported that the visit of Prime Minister Burnham to Caracas was well received and that the subject of the boundary dispute was merely mentioned, and was neither discussed nor debated. (Emb Caracas 962.)[5]

----

[5] Dated January 15. (Ibid.)

----

525.   Telegram From the Embassy in Venezuela to the Department of State[1]

Caracas, March 22, 1965, 8 a.m.

1255. In my first substantive interview with President Leoni late last week,[2] I found him very in command of situation and fully in-

----

[1] Source: National Archives and Records Administration, RG 59, Central Files 1964–66, POL 1 VEN. Confidential; Immediate. Repeated to USCINCSO.

[2] March 18. Bernbaum first met Leoni on March 4 to present his credentials. The Embassy reported that "Leoni instead of limiting himself to the diplomatic pleasantries normal to such occasions lost no time in making a lengthy statement concerning US petroleum restrictions and the forthcoming US–Venezuelan petroleum discussions." (Airgram A–591 from Caracas, March 10; ibid., PET 17 US–VEN)

formed on such varying subjects as Venezuela's counterinsurgency efforts, its military equipment procurement program, its requirements for foreign loans for housing and other social development projects, and its aspirations for better treatment in US oil import policy. President was remarkably forthright and outgoing for first interview and obviously at present intends, within limits his domestic political situation, cooperate with us on give and take basis to improve US–Ven relations.

In response to my expression of our concern about possibility of increased Castro Communist emphasis on and support to guerilla movement, President expressed realistic assessment of situation, saying he had no allusions about sustained character of Communist subversion program so long as Castro in control of Cuba. He said he was being kept informed of developments and his info agreed substantially with ours.[3] He was familiar with attempted arms smuggling from Colombia but interested in possible smuggling from Algeria. He described continuing measures being taken against guerillas to keep them off balance and efforts to control border and maritime provinces. He further acknowledged he had been criticized for releasing a few unimportant prisoners but said this done to sow dissension among Communists and he had no intention at present of releasing important and dangerous prisoners. He welcomed my assurance that he could continue to count on US collaboration in meeting Communist insurgency threat and specifically expressed appreciation for prompt delivery HU 1B helicopters.

I questioned President about aircraft procurement program, pointing out that while Venezuela military was indicating interest in stepping up credit sales purchases from $10 to $20 million annually from US it was also purchasing Canberras from UK causing US some problems. President was fully familiar with Canberra purchase, underscoring it was necessary purchase for replacement, but was less sure about other negotiations (presumably for Hawker Hunters) although he knew question was one of price and availability as between US and UK. He appeared fully to accept that Venezuela needed improve aircraft inventory for coastal surveillance and for defense against Cuba.

---

[3] Reference is to a U.S. Government memorandum on Cuban subversion. Bernbaum told Leoni "that prior to leaving Washington, I had had a productive talk with President Johnson regarding United States-Venezuelan problems. I had found him greatly interested in the Venezuelan situation and in the solution to these problems. He had just read a memorandum covering the likelihood of a new Communist drive through Cuba against Venezuela and other Latin American countries and asked that I give a copy of this memorandum to President Leoni." (Airgram A–627 from Caracas, March 24; ibid., POL 23 VEN) President Johnson met Bernbaum and four other U.S. Ambassadors in Latin America February 8, 5:31–6:25 p.m. (Johnson Library, President's Daily Diary) No substantive record of the meeting has been found.

As conversation turned to economic subjects, President welcomed my statement to American Chamber of Commerce that Venezuela (like other less developed countries) would not be prejudiced by US balance of payments measures and, while recognizing reasons why aid concessional loans would no longer be available, he gave great importance to having continued access to long term IDB loans especially for housing. With respect to US investment, President acknowledged difficult position in which oil companies and Orinoco Mining had been put as result uncertainties about taxes and expressed hope that compromise could be reached by mutual concessions.

Leoni hit question of "discrimination" in our oil import policy hard (it is favorite theme of his) emphasizing it was political as well as economic question. He said he had sent President Johnson letter on subject through Minister of Mines Perez Guerrero and thought it essential that some progress be made at least on some aspects of problem.[4] He also urged revision of trade agreement, which he believed archaic, through quiet negotiations.

Range of subjects covered, some at my initiative and some at his, impressed me that Leoni is pretty well on top of his job, knows what he wants, and has a practical politician's rather than a theoretician's approach. It is, of course, too early to form a firm judgment but, this first interview gives basis for hope this is someone we can work with.

More detailed memcon follows.[5]

Bernbaum

---

[4] Leoni claimed that "he had attempted in this letter to make President Johnson aware of the necessary relationship between a satisfactory solution [of the petroleum problem] and Venezuela's ability to reach a successful conclusion against the Communist threat emanating from Cuba." (Airgram A–635 from Caracas, March 24; National Archives and Records Administration, RG 59, Central Files 1964–66, PET 17 US–VEN) Leoni's letter to Johnson, however, deals exclusively with petroleum; it does not refer to Cuba or communism. A copy of the letter, dated March 13 and delivered to the Department of State on March 19, is ibid., PET 1 US–VEN.

[5] Memoranda of conversation are attached to airgram A–627 from Caracas, March 24 (ibid., POL 23 VEN); airgram A–632 from Caracas, March 24 (ibid., DEF 19–3 US–VEN); and airgram A–635 from Caracas, March 24 (ibid., PET 17 US–VEN).

526. Letter From the Director of the Office of Colombian-Venezuelan Affairs (Margolies) to the Ambassador to Venezuela (Bernbaum)[1]

Washington, March 22, 1965.

Dear Mr. Ambassador:

SUBJECT

Oil Talks

The oil talks ended up relatively well under the circumstances due to the intervention of Tom Mann.

As I wrote to you before the talks opened,[2] our positions had frozen into a basically negative stance and I was very worried that the US would have no position other than a generally negative one.

Fortunately your telegram[3] arrived just at the right time and alerted Tom Mann to the serious political implications that were involved. He later said that when he saw your reference to the "black spot" in President Leoni's speech, his antennae quivered and he felt that it was necessary for him to take an active interest in the talks.

His intervention introduced a degree of movement in our position, and at the luncheon on Thursday[4] with Secretary Udall, the Secretary told the Venezuelan delegation that we were giving active consideration to the possibility of some preferential treatment for Venezuelan oil in our market as against oil from the Middle East. It turned out, however, that the Venezuelans insisted on receiving not merely better treatment than the Middle East but equal treatment with Canada. We then had rather sticky negotiations on the afternoon of Thursday and all day Friday in which the Venezuelans adopted a rather obdurate position in which they insisted that all discrimination between Venezuela and Canada had to be removed and furthermore that they wished to have a written assurance that the US Government agreed in principle with this position, even though we might not be clear as to how we might work it out technically. They stated that they were prepared to

---

[1] Source: National Archives and Records Administration, RG 59, Central Files 1964–66, PET 17–2 US–VEN. Confidential; Official–Informal.

[2] Letter from Margolies to Bernbaum, March 9. (Ibid.)

[3] In telegram 1219 from Caracas, March 12, the Embassy reported on a speech before the Venezuelan Congress, March 11, in which Leoni criticized U.S. policy on oil imports: "The maintenance of this discriminatory regime is a black blot on existing relations between Venezuela and the United States." (Ibid., POL 15–1 VEN)

[4] March 18.

remain indefinitely until we were in a position to give them such an assurance in writing.

The situation as I say looked rather grim with Interior and the E area both expressing the view that in asking too much the Venezuelans were likely to lose the opportunity to gain what appeared to us to be a substantial advantage in the situation.

This was the way the position rested until we met in Tom Mann's office late Friday afternoon. Tom with his customary frankness and directness explained to them that the issues involved required extensive consultations on our part with the President, the Congress and with our domestic industry and with other countries involved. Therefore, it was not practicable to give them the type of written assurance they required. He would, however, give them his personal undertaking to see that the issue was fully explored, although he made it clear that he could not guarantee any satisfactory results. They were satisfied, therefore, with the minute which was drafted by Mr. Mann and the Minister of Mines which was sent to you under cover of Deptel 975.[5]

As Tom outlined the situation there appeared to be only two methods of fully satisfying the Venezuelan complaint that overland exemption[6] was discriminatory.

One method, which the Venezuelans favored, was to award Venezuela a country quota. He said that this would in effect allow Venezuela to determine the amount of oil that we would receive and the price at which we would receive it. He said that it was politically impossible to work out a solution along these lines. He said that he had become involved in this type of question in connection with the coffee agreement and he was quite clear in his own mind that Congress would never tolerate an arrangement under which another country could dictate to the United States the price which it must pay for its imports of a specific commodity.

The Venezuelans demurred, sought to give assurances that any such power would be exercised by the Venezuelans with restraint, understanding, etc. Mr. Mann insisted, however, that it was hopeless to consider pursuing such a solution in the context of our political situation.

He said that the other possibility, and it seemed to him the only alternative, if the Venezuelans demands were to be met in full, was to set up some sort of Western Hemisphere licensing arrangement under

---

[5] Dated March 19. (National Archives and Records Administration, RG 59, Central Files 1964–66, PET 17–2 VEN)

[6] On April 30, 1959, the Eisenhower administration proclaimed an "overland exemption" to the Mandatory Oil Import Program, thereby allowing Canada and Mexico to avoid restrictions that applied to other oil exporting countries. (24 *Federal Register* 3527)

which oil imported from Canada would be subjected to a licensing arrangement comparable to that imposed on oil of Venezuelan origin with a preference to Western Hemisphere oil as against Middle East oil.

He said that this course of action was politically difficult for the United States and also, in his opinion, involved political risks for Venezuela. He noted that the Canadians were highly emotional on the subject of their oil exports to the United States. He said that he hoped that the Venezuelans would make it clear to the Canadians that they were the ones that insisted on our exploring such a solution, since he could well believe that the Canadians would not be pleased by this development. He noted that the arrangement would also involve a departure from our traditional policy of avoiding trade preferences which would stir up opposition at home and also might create problems with the Middle Eastern oil producing countries who also tended to become emotional about such issues. He asked whether the Venezuelan Government would make clear to the Middle East governments concerned that they had initiated this matter with us and would help to reconcile the Middle Eastern countries to this policy were it to be adopted by us.

Mr. Mann said that he had not, quite frankly, been fully informed of the Venezuelan feeling on the subject and President Johnson had not been informed of the matter at all up to the present. He said that he would take steps to see that the President was informed.

Mr. Mann said that in advancing the best solution he would not recommend it but would point out that it was apparently the only feasible answer to the Venezuelan complaint. He was unable to see how the matter would come out, depending on the consultations that were involved. The main thrust of his statement to the Venezuelans, however, was that this issue would be given serious and urgent consideration. It was on this basis that the Venezuelans left in a reasonably content frame of mind.

Speaking personally, I believe that it will be very difficult to put Venezuela and Canada on a completely equal footing. As a matter of fact the Venezuelans themselves recognize this and therefore suggested that the word "similar" rather than "equal" be used as identifying their position.

The new approach will of course require imposing licensing arrangements on Canadian oil and thereby introducing a form of frontier control between ourselves and Canada. As you know, we have been working over the past decades in efforts to limit such border controls and this will be a retrogressive step. It will undoubtedly give rise to considerable opposition both within this government and within Canada.

A favorable feature for anticipating some satisfactory solution lies in the fact that the domestic oil industry and the Department of Interior have not been satisfied with the rapid growth of Canadian oil imports to our market, and indeed the Canadian Government itself has been uneasy at the rate of growth which has been developing over the past year or so. At any rate we are starting this week to explore this subject in the Department on an urgent basis and talks with Canada should be held in the near future which should throw some light on how far we can get.

One of the subjects that arose from time to time during the talks was the possibility of a multilateral conference before our policy was finally firmed up. The Venezuelans thought it would be useful to have themselves, ourselves, and the Canadians around the table at the same time. It might be that the Mexicans, who also enjoy an overland exemption (which to be sure is of little economic importance) might have to be invited as well. The Interior Department seems for some reason very reluctant to arrange for multilateral talks. Mr. Mann left the question open for the time being.

I was encouraged by the fact that President Leoni in the message you sent up (Embtel 1255)[7] indicated that he expected progress to be made "at least on some aspects of the problem" and would be satisfied with a solution which improved the Venezuelan position in our market and augmenting the amount of money realized by Venezuela for the sale of its oil, without insisting that the position of Venezuela should be placed on an exact parallel with that of Canada. I hope the Venezuelans will take a realistic view of the situation because I believe that the possibilities are that something quite favorable to them can be worked out provided they do not adopt as rigid position as they took prior to our meeting in Mr. Mann's office.

With best regards,

Sincerely,

Daniel F. Margolies[8]

---

[7] Dated March 22. (National Archives and Records Administration, RG 59, Central Files 1964–66, POL 1 VEN)

[8] Printed from a copy that bears this typed signature.

527. Memorandum From the Acting Assistant Secretary of State for Economic Affairs (Solomon) to the President's Special Assistant for National Security Affairs (Bundy)[1]

Washington, May 26, 1965.

SUBJECT

Oil Import Controls and U.S. Relations With Venezuela and Canada

Since Tom Mann is in New York this afternoon he has asked me to take up this urgent matter with you.

1. The fundamental issue is that the Government of Venezuela is demanding that the new oil import control program covering the next five years which is to be announced by Presidential Proclamation the end of next month should provide "equal treatment" for Venezuela with that given to Canada. This has become a major political issue within the Venezuelan Government, the opposition parties to the Government and the Venezuelan public. Ideally they would like to receive an "over land exemption" like that enjoyed by Canada (that is no U.S. imposed limitation on oil imports leaving it up to the Government of Venezuela to control the exports of its oil companies to the U.S.). Both Interior and State agree that we cannot agree to this for many reasons. The other method of giving fully "equal treatment" to Venezuela would be to abolish formally the Canadian over land exemption (Mexico's is unimportant) as well as limiting in fact the rate of increase of Canadian oil exports to the U.S. The Canadian Government and our own people believe that to do so would possibly, and perhaps probably, result in the downfall of the Pearson Government and jeopardization of the bilateral defense and increasing free trade arrangements between Canada and the U.S. In brief this can become the hottest political issue in both Canada and Venezuela vis-à-vis the U.S.

2. Interior and State believe that the most practical and appropriate solution—although by definition not fully satisfactory to either side—is that contained in the attached position paper.[2] Presidential Proclamation before the end of June require that the content of this package be advised to the Canadian technical people in the next day or two and the Venezuelans shortly thereafter. We probably will need during the following week a Ministerial level meeting with the Canadians and we will insist on a Venezuelan meeting at the Ministerial

---

[1] Source: National Archives and Records Administration, RG 59, Office of Fuels and Energy, Petroleum Files: Lot 69 D 76, Petroleum 17–2, Oil Imports, 1965 May. A note on the memorandum indicates it was hand-carried to the White House on May 27.

[2] Not attached.

level to extract an acceptance by them of our proposals which could be issued publicly after the Presidential Proclamation.

In brief the package consists of:

a. The press release accompanying the Presidential Proclamation and future public references by us would talk of "planned coordinated pipeline movements" instead of "over land exemption".

b. A private formal commitment to us from the Canadian Government that it would confine its annual rate of increase in its oil exports to the U.S. to an over all of five percent. In addition the Government in Canada would be advised privately that if it were unsuccessful in meeting this annual commitment, the United States would take measures to enforce it.

c. The Government of Venezuela would be informed of the Canadian commitment, and would be assured that we would review with Venezuela each year Canadian performance, and that if it were not satisfactory the United States would consider the measures required to ensure this result.

d. A Western Hemisphere preference formula which would in fact make it slightly more attractive for U.S. refineries to import Venezuelan oil as compared to Near Eastern oil. In practice the Venezuelans could get some modest price increase as well as modest tonnage increase from this formula.[3]

Anthony M. Solomon[4]

---

[3] On May 27 Bundy asked the President if the memorandum required White House action. Johnson responded he would not be able to consider the issue until June 1. (Johnson Library, Recordings and Transcripts, Recording of telephone conversation between President Johnson and Bundy, May 27, 1965, 7:29 p.m., Tape F65.42, Side B, PNO 3) The President called Mann on June 4 to discuss "a memo on Venezuela and Canadian oil", an apparent reference to Solomon's May 26 memorandum. Johnson asked Mann "to go over this carefully from the President's standpoint and the national standpoint and see if there isn't something that can be done to ride it out for sixty to ninety days." Johnson said the proposal had been represented as "the best solution even though it will make both countries angry and also our industry." "It seemed to him," however, "the best way out is more of the same. No change, but we are studying it. Get rid of the Congress and then do what we need to do." (Ibid., Papers of Thomas C. Mann, Telephone Conversations with LBJ, May 2, 1965–June 2, 1966) Solomon met Perez Guerrero in New York to explain the President's decision. A memorandum of the conversation, June 14, is in the National Archives and Records Administration, RG 59, Central Files 1964–66, PET 17–2 US–VEN.

[4] Printed from a copy that bears this typed signature.

528. Telegram From the Embassy in Venezuela to the Department of State[1]

Caracas, November 15, 1965, 0215Z.

542. Following summary conversation between Secretary Rusk, President Leoni and others Nov 14 is based on uncleared memcom is FYI Noforn and subject to revision upon review:

Part I: U.S. Petroleum Restrictions

President Leoni said petroleum income central to Venezuela's economy and Venezuela would not be concerned if U.S. import restrictions were just and non-discriminatory. He recalled when matter arose during President Eisenhower's administration latter had agreed necessity of just solution to problem on basis hemisphere preference.[2] Subsequently President Kennedy had acknowledged agreement called for along hemisphere preference lines.[3] To date no progress has taken place. Meantime Venezuela's income from petroleum has been decreasing at same time balance of trade with U.S. turning disadvantageously against Venezuela and now is at unfavorable rate of over $300 million annually. President said further drain taking place through reliance on Venezuelan credits by American firms rather than through use dollar funds or credits. He said U.S. announcement continuation existing oil import policy without solution Venezuela problem could create serious difficulties.

Secretary responded that he hoped GOV understands U.S. faces many problems with its many trading partners in all parts free world. U.S. desires see Venezuela maximize its income but our producers also have income problems. Difficulties arise from close trading relations rather than from ignorance respective problems. The Secretary added that U.S. would consider what could be done to help Venezuela but he did not know whether what we could do would be acceptable. The

[1] Source: National Archives and Records Administration, RG 59, Central Files 1964–66, PET 15 US. Confidential; Immediate. Repeated to Rio de Janeiro. Passed to the White House.

[2] On March 10, 1959, President Eisenhower signed Proclamation 3279 instituting the Mandatory Oil Import Program. (24 *Federal Register* 1781) The same day Eisenhower released the following statement: "The United States recognizes, of course, that within the larger sphere of free world security, we, in common with Canada and with the other American Republics, have a joint interest in hemisphere defense. Informal conversations with Canada and Venezuela looking toward a coordinated approach to the problem of oil as it relates to this matter of common concern have already begun." (*Public Papers of the Presidents of the United States: Dwight D. Eisenhower, 1959*, pp. 240–241)

[3] On February 20, 1963, after 2 days of discussion in Washington, Presidents Kennedy and Betancourt issued a joint statement, including an agreement "that a strong and healthy petroleum industry is essential to Venezuela's prosperity, to the achievement of the goals set by the Alliance for Progress and for the security of the Hemisphere as a whole." (Ibid., *John F. Kennedy, 1963*, pp. 187–188)

important thing was that efforts to find a reasonably acceptable solution will be continued. Minister Mines Perez Guerrero expounded on petroleum restriction along lines already well known in Washington. He described negotiations and impasse due Venezuela's inability after considerable study to accept "Solomon" proposal[4] and U.S. inability go along with compromise solution of two ticket system which represented a considerable watering down of Venezuela's counter proposal. He also complained against suits instituted by U.S. Treasury against U.S. petroleum firms attempting to comply with Venezuelan pricing policies. I explained this due practice of some firms in paying Venezuelan taxes on basis prices higher than these actually realized to prevent later tax recovery suits by the GOV thereby reducing taxes due to USG.

President Leoni then invited former Minister Mines Dr. Juan Pablo Perez Alfonso to discuss subject. Perez Alfonso said last year's trade deficit with U.S. totalled $344 million figure which represented 5 percent gross national product. He referred also to fact that U.S. direct investment in Venezuela is 70 percent of total foreign investment in country and that U.S. interests derive 23 percent return on investment. He admitted surplus in all-over trade balance but emphasized declining markets in other areas and difficulties with countries with which GOV has favorable trade balances.

Secretary then asked Minister Perez Guerrero given difficulties that solution he had in mind. Dr. Perez said that at one time in talks with Secretary Udall two-ticket proposal had been made and hemisphere preference system also suggested. Now U.S. had decided neither approach to problem is feasible. Venezuela he said has no clean-cut answer but takes view that since oil import restrictions are authored by U.S. an adjustment should be offered by U.S. He confirmed in later talk with me that revival Solomon proposal would not be satisfactory. Secretary responded by saying U.S. and GOV should keep in close touch. Although not expert in this field, Secretary said he would take matter up with President Johnson and Secretary Udall. He said he could not guarantee an acceptable solution but would report on matter and perhaps in end something could be worked out.

Comment:

Secretary requests one more review of problem be made to see if something can be done to break impasse, even though such review will probably involve postponement proclamation. Results review should then be communicated to GOV prior issuance proclamation. This will fulfill his commitment to President Leoni to look at the problem again.

Bernbaum

---

[4] Reference is evidently to the proposal outlined in Document 527.

529. Telegram From the Department of State to the Embassy in Brazil[1]

Washington, November 19, 1965, 7:20 p.m.

Tosec 59. Udall has informed Mann that time for issuance of proclamation covering period January–June 1966 is fast running out and is pressing for issuance of proclamation which would not meet Venezuela's position. Puerto Ricans also urging prompt action for different reasons.

Udall states if proclamation is not issued soon we will have to postpone issuance until some time prior to July 1, 1966. I understand he is personally committed to domestic industry to make some minor changes in present proclamation.

Would appreciate knowing whether your conversation with Leoni reported in Caracas 542[2] contemplated personal conversation with President and Udall before final decision reached. Problem has as you know been under review for several months and even Solomon proposal which is unacceptable to the Venezuelans was opposed by the industry. We know of no compromise proposal which would meet Venezuela's demand which essentially is that we take away from domestic refiners of Venezuelan oil approximately 1.25 a barrel and pass on this difference between price of U.S. and Venezuelan crude to Venezuelan government. In course of last of several conversations we have had with Perez-Guerrero on this subject he indicated he would accept for time being passing on a fraction (say 10 to 20%) of the total involved but indicated that Venezuelan aim would be to increase this to a full 100% that is to say "de-ticketing" all Venezuelan crude. As you know this would require a country quota for Venezuela and in addition to objections of domestic refiners we would have to face strong opposition of US oil investors in Venezuela who, with some justification, are convinced Venezuela would use country quota as a basis for controlling sales of Venezuelan crude in this market. Since receiving your instructions we have reviewed once again our position both internally and with the Venezuelans and we have no new proposal to make. Perez-Guerrero has also sent us word that he has nothing new to offer other than this "de-ticketing."

---

[1] Source: National Archives and Records Administration, RG 59, Central Files 1964–66, PET 17 US–VEN. Confidential; Priority; Limdis. Drafted by Mann, cleared by Solomon, and approved by Mann. Rusk was in Rio de Janeiro November 16–24 for the Second Special Inter-American Conference.

[2] Document 528.

Some of the largest oil investors have been frankly told of the danger of a nationalistic reaction in Venezuela and they have informed us they prefer this risk to the risks inherent in the "de-ticketing" and country quota arrangement.

Would appreciate your instructions.[3]

Ball

---

[3] In telegram Secto 31 from Rio de Janeiro, November 20, Rusk replied: "It seemed obvious from my talks in Caracas that no formula is in sight which offers a solution regarding Venezuelan oil. Simply as a matter of courtesy, I would hope we could have some kind of consultation with the Venezuelan Government following my visit to indicate that we have been unable to find a necessary solution beyond those already suggested and it will be necessary now to proceed with the issuance of a proclamation. I look upon this as a diplomatic courtesy to let them know that their discussion with me had not been ignored. Probably Department's 431 to Caracas fully meets this requirement. Do not believe this issue will affect Rio Conference significantly." (National Archives and Records Administration, RG 59, Central Files 1964–66, ORG 7 S) According to telegram 431 to Caracas, State and Interior representatives informed the Venezuelan Embassy on November 17 that, although the U.S. Government "did not exclude possibility finding new approach," the "likelihood of discovering brand new scheme quite slim." (Ibid., PET 12 VEN)

---

530.   Editorial Note

On December 10, 1965, President Johnson signed Proclamation 3693, "Modifying Proclamation 3279 Adjusting Imports of Petroleum and Petroleum Products." (30 *Federal Register* 15459) The proclamation met the concerns of the petrochemical industry in Puerto Rico, but Venezuelan concerns for equal treatment under the oil import program were not addressed. At the press conference announcing the proclamation, Secretary of Interior Udall admitted that the negotiations with Canada and Venezuela had not produced "the type of ultimate consensus that could have resulted in changes." (Proceedings, December 10; National Archives and Records Administration, RG 59, Office of Fuels and Energy, Petroleum Files: Lot 69 D 76, Petroleum 17–2, Oil Imports, 1965 December) In an accompanying press statement, however, Udall proposed continuing discussions with Venezuela and recognized "that the oil industry in Venezuela has a special position in the contribution it makes to Western Hemisphere security." (Circular telegram CA–6451, December 22; ibid., Central Files 1964–66, PET 17–2 US)

On December 21 the Department of Interior issued several amendments to the oil import regulation, including an increase in the allocation for imports to the eastern United States and Puerto Rico, two markets traditionally dominated by the oil industry in Venezuela. (30 *Federal Register* 16080) Although the amended regulations did not specify a system of country quotas, the Department of State estimated that Venezuela could reasonably expect to increase its oil imports by 35,000 barrels per day. (Telegram 512 to Caracas, December 22; National Archives and Records Administration, RG 59, Central Files 1964–66, PET 17–2 US) The Department was encouraged by the initial reaction in Venezuela to the proclamation, thereby justifying "the efforts which Ambassador Bernbaum and the Department made to have references to the Venezuelan problem included in Secretary Udall's press statement." (Memorandum from Hill to Vaughn, December 15; ibid., ARA/NC/V Files: Lot 66 D 469, PET 17–2 U.S. Import Program, July–September 1965)

On December 31 the Leoni government informed the oil companies of a new regulation governing discounts on its residual fuel oil, a measure designed to raise revenue by raising the price of exports to the United States. (Washington National Records Center, E/CBA/REP Files: FRC 72 A 6248, Current Economic Developments, No. 745, January 18, 1966)

---

531. National Intelligence Estimate[1]

NIE 89–65   Washington, December 16, 1965.

VENEZUELA

The Problem

To estimate the situation in Venezuela and the prospects under the Leoni administration (until general elections in 1968).

Conclusions

A. Venezuela will probably continue to experience political stability and a favorable rate of economic growth over the next few years. However, it will still face deep-seated social problems. Most economic

---

[1] Source: Central Intelligence Agency, Job 79–R01012A, O/DDI Registry. Secret; Controlled Dissem. According to a note on the cover sheet this estimate was prepared in the Central Intelligence Agency with the participation of the intelligence organizations of the Departments of State and Defense and the National Security Agency. The United States Intelligence Board concurred in this estimate on December 16.

and social reform programs will be pushed vigorously through 1966. Thereafter budgetary restraints are likely to lead to some loss of momentum. This slowdown will almost certainly become a major issue in the December 1968 elections.

B. The government and security forces have dealt reasonably effectively with the leftist insurgency; the capabilities of the guerrillas and terrorists will probably decline further. The insurgents are not likely to pose a major threat to the government during the period of this estimate.

C. Some misgivings regarding the Leoni administration still persist among the military, but the military establishment is generally disposed to support the constitutional government. We believe that there is little chance of a successful military coup within the period of this estimate.

D. Leoni's governing coalition will probably hold together at least until the near approach of the elections scheduled for December 1968. The contest is then likely to be between two center-left parties, AD and COPEI, each claiming to be the more effective means of achieving social reform. If, in anticipation of this contest, Leoni should initiate a more radical reform program, he might thereby antagonize the military and increase the chances of a military coup.

E. The administration will make some attempts to increase Venezuelan influence in Latin American affairs, while holding to the Betancourt Doctrine of denying recognition to governments which come to power by overthrowing constitutionally-elected ones. Manifestations of economic nationalism—and in particular resentment over US restrictions on the importation of Venezuelan oil—will probably produce frictions in relations with the US.[2]

[Omitted here is the Discussion section of the estimate.]

---

[2] Bowdler forwarded an advance copy of the estimate with a December 17 memorandum to Bundy in which he noted that "the picture may not be as rosy as described." Citing telegram 648 from Caracas, December 16, Bowdler explained that "Bernbaum is sufficiently concerned to speak to Leoni about it and, subsequently, to selected military leaders. I have asked ARA to make sure Bernbaum does not tarry in letting military leaders know how strongly opposed we are to a coup against Leoni." (Johnson Library, National Security File, Country File, Venezuela, Vol. II, 8/64–8/66) Leoni told Bernbaum that he was not concerned by the rumors, since "there is no real basis for coup" and not "enough support within the military to stage one." Bernbaum reported that the Embassy would "continue to follow situation closely and take advantage any opportunities to discourage plotters." (Telegrams 648 and 653 from Caracas, December 16 and 17, respectively; National Archives and Records Administration, RG 59, Central Files 1964–66, POL 23–9 VEN)

532.   Memorandum From the Under Secretary of State for Economic Affairs (Mann) to the President's Special Assistant (Califano)[1]

Washington, January 6, 1966.

The conclusions expressed here supplement the two background memoranda on Venezuela residual oil, copies of which you have.[2]

Our best guess is that Venezuela seeks about 28¢ a barrel increase in the price of its residual oil.

This would mean a net loss to us balance of payments wise of about 50 million dollars. On the assumption that Interior continues to carry out its plans to liberalize the import of residual oil, we would expect that the price increase would be partially off-set by more competition, by a decline in the value of the "tickets" for imported resid, by the probable desire of residual oil importers to stay competitive with coal, and by the continuance of discounts to large users. Moreover, the price increase would probably be delayed for a while due to existing contracts but prices would probably gradually rise by almost 10¢ a barrel, if current ticket premiums are eliminated. There are about 300 million barrels of residual oil consumed annually in the United States.

If the Venezuelans after further discussion with the companies do not insist on the companies increasing prices but use the new price as the basis for tax calculation, it is Interior's judgment that the companies for competitive reasons may pass on only the 15 cent cost increase which will wipe out the ticket value and may result in very little price increase to the consumer.

On the other hand, efficient oil industries no longer produce resid in large quantities and we would probably have to admit that the Venezuelan price of resid is lower than it should be—principally because the private companies have deliberately kept it low in order to maximize their sales.

---

[1] Source: National Archives and Records Administration, RG 59, Central Files 1964–66, PET 17–2 US. Confidential. Drafted by Mann. President Johnson called Mann on January 6 to discuss "the resid matter," asking if Mann "was going to be able to work it out." Mann told Johnson that "it looked pretty tough for us to do anything because we do not have leverage. He asked the President to read the memo sent over today." (Memorandum of conversation, January 6; Johnson Library, Papers of Thomas C. Mann, Telephone Conversations with LBJ, May 2, 1965–June 2, 1966)

[2] Neither found. The memorandum of conversation cited in footnote 1 above notes that the President saw the two memoranda sent over on January 6. (Ibid.) Johnson may have seen a paper entitled "Consequences of Proposed Action of Venezuela re Residual Fuel Oil," January 4. (National Archives and Records Administration, RG 59, E/ORF FSE Files: Lot 70 D 54, PET 17–2, U.S. Imports, January 1966) No evidence has been found, however, that the paper was forwarded to the White House.

I do not believe the Venezuelan action was the result of our liberalizing our imports of residual oil since the Venezuelan motivation has been to capture the ticket premium. More probably it was something that the Venezuelans have been thinking about doing for some time and which they were loath to do while they still had hopes of getting us to change our policy so as to permit Venezuela to realize more on its sale of crude to the United States.

The oil companies will be negotiating with the Venezuelan Government and they have some hope of getting the Venezuelans to modify this price increase. I do not expect, however, that they will allow this to reach a breaking point with the Venezuelan Government.

We should instruct our Ambassador to support the companies' effort by making the following points at a high level:

1. There was no advance consultation with the United States.

2. The United States is doing everything possible to hold the line on balance of payments and price problems while carrying a very heavy load in Viet-Nam and around the world. Venezuela has both an economic and a security stake in our efforts. The recent action on residual oil makes it much more difficult for us.

3. If the purpose of the resid order was to use government action to force increased prices, this is bad in principle and violates the terms of the oil concessions. If the purpose of the order is to modify existing tax arrangements without advance notice and discussion with the companies, this is also bad in principle.

4. The price action if carried through rigidly may adversely affect in the long run the investment decisions of the oil companies.

5. While Venezuela and the United States have not agreed on the Venezuelan proposal to de-ticket Venezuelan crude, the United States is nevertheless the principal market for both Venezuela's crude and residual oil. It has been a safe and reliable market in which Venezuela is earning annually only slightly under a billion dollars. One of the reasons for this is the attitude of the United States to encourage preferences for Venezuelan crude. For example, Canada continues to import large amounts of Venezuelan crude and has refrained from exporting to the United States market some 50,000 barrels of crude a day which is readily available. In Puerto Rico the United States has required the two refineries and petro-chemical complexes to import feed stock from the Western Hemisphere, i.e., Venezuela. In spite of its balance of payments difficulties, the United States has maintained a requirement that the Defense Department continue to purchase foreign crude at the 1962 level of 120 million dollars a year, most of which is supplied by Venezuela. The action of the Venezuelan Government is inconsistent with these acts of cooperation.

II

Turning now to the question of leverage, I would be less than candid if I did not point out that these arguments may have no effect whatever on Venezuela for the following reasons:

A. Venezuela has a long established policy of trying to raise the price of its crude and residual oils while discouraging increased production on the ground that Venezuela is using up its irreplaceable natural resources too fast. They are not likely to be impressed with the argument about reducing the volume of their exports so long as they believe their revenues will not decline especially in the short term. They can carry through their new price policy flexibly, so as to preserve their European market.

B. What GOV wants from us in essence is an exemption of Venezuelan crude oil imports from our controls. This would pass to Venezuela the more than a dollar a barrel which our refineries now make on the "tickets" and, from their point of view, might result in price increases in the future in both crude and resid to say nothing of giving them a stranglehold on U.S. oil companies in Venezuela.

C. Venezuela technicians know that our leverage is very limited in the short term. While Venezuelan oil prices are somewhat higher FOB they are competitive in our market because of lower shipping costs as compared with Near Eastern and North African oils. And, insofar as resid is concerned, there is no alternate source to which we could readily turn for comparably priced residual oils. It is doubtful that the Defense Department could buy elsewhere more than a fraction of the heavier fuels we now buy from Venezuela, and to the extent they could buy in the United States, our balance-of-payments savings would be more than offset by the loss to our budget. Such measures as this and the freeing of the refineries and petro-chemical plants in Puerto Rico to buy elsewhere could be irritants rather than deterrents but as events develop, it might become advisable to try them.

D. Opinions of the experts are that the sheer inconvenience and cost of handling coal as compared with fuel oil make coal noncompetitive with most users of oil even at the price which Venezuela has in mind. Further, a sudden demand on the coal industry for substantial additional amounts of coal for the east coast would, it is estimated, result in a price increase in coal.

E. In addition, Venezuela has very considerable leverage on the United States because of our large investments there—more than 3 billion dollars. In the nationalistic climate which prevails there, steady pressures on investors in the form of increased taxes and otherwise is an ever-present danger. Also, it should be noted that Venezuela holds about $400 million in dollars and treasury obligations in its reserves and has been resisting pressures to follow the European pattern of increasing its gold holdings. There is nothing to prevent them from turning in dollars for gold.

III

If holding the price line is the decisive consideration, probably the most effective action—in addition to approaching the Venezuelans as suggested above—would be to de-control residual oil or so administer it so as to eliminate the ticket premiums. This would probably have the effect of eliminating the value of the tickets, currently estimated at 15¢ a barrel, from the resid price. Tighter restrictions on U.S. imports of Venezuelan residual oil would perpetuate the additional 15¢ a barrel ticket cost and would put pressure on resid prices in this market. It would not give us any leverage with Venezuela.

While de-control of residual imports would make economic sense from the standpoint of holding the price line—especially since the coal industry is said to be operating at a near capacity level and is experiencing a scarcity of coal miners—de-control would be strongly opposed by the coal industry and by those users of resid in this country who would lose the value of their "tickets."

Thus, this recommendation involves domestic political questions more than international ones.

Thomas C. Mann[3]

---

[3] Printed from a copy that indicates Mann signed the original.

---

533.   Telegram From the Embassy in Venezuela to the Department of State[1]

Caracas, January 12, 1966, 2131Z.

700. 1. All but last paragraph Deptel 554[2] read in translation to MinMines Perez Guerrero this morning.

---

[1] Source: National Archives and Records Administration, RG 59, Central Files 1964–66, FN 10 VEN. Secret; Priority.

[2] In telegram 554 to Caracas, January 11, the Department instructed the Embassy to "convey at high level USG concern with recent action taken by GOV concerning residual fuel oil," following the recommendations outlined in Document 532. (National Archives and Records Administration, RG 59, Central Files 1964–66, PET 17–1 VEN)

2. Perez clearly not impressed by balance of payments argument, pointing out that Venezuela also has its own budgetary problems which created by steady decline prices petroleum and products. He was sympathetic, however, to the argument regarding internal price stability. While admitting that the new program would inevitably involve price increases, he repeated previous assurances of flexibility in application designed not only to meet problem of competition but also to avoid excessive consumer impact. He again expressed belief that this could be facilitated by elimination excessive and unnecessary intermediary discounts and profit margins.

3. Perez conceded that many American consumers, particularly in New York area, were considering changeover to alternate fuel sources and that present measure might accelerate this process, but felt that this disadvantage far from adequate to outweigh numerous other advantages to Venezuela of program. One important factor in decision was anticipation of price decline due to enhanced competition resulting from first easing and then elimination of fuel oil import quotas. Since companies themselves could not prevent such a decline due to U.S. anti-trust laws, felt necessary for GOV to establish new discount procedure and thereby prevent price deterioration. Second and perhaps even more important, was the need to demonstrate to the Venezuelan people that the GOV had a clear policy to protect Venezuela's interests and knew how to apply it. Failure to take this or similar "reasonable" measure would have inevitably given clear field to proponents of more radical solutions to the petroleum problem, such as currently proposed increased taxes on "excessive petroleum profits" and even limitation of fuel oil exports to the U.S. While the measure taken was emphatically not in retaliation for the failure of petroleum negotiations, it was considered the most reasonable manner of facing up to the problem created by failure of the negotiations. He repeated this political argument a number of times.

4. With respect to our complaint regarding lack of prior consultation, Perez pointed out that we had not been distinguished for our prior consultations with Venezuela and inquired what would have been our position if Venezuela had consulted. He answered this by saying that we would undoubtedly have opposed the projected measure and that Venezuela would have been forced to go forward in the face of such opposition. He conceded my point that we might have been able to work out a solution with which both parties could live, but emphasized the impracticability of such talks in view of the danger of leaks and the limited time available.

5. It was made quite clear by Perez, in view of the foregoing, that there was no chance of reconsideration of the new discount policy but he did give assurances that all possible, consistent with Venezuela's

"legitimate" aspirations to protect its own interests, would be done to ensure reasonable, intelligent and moderate application of variations from the 10 percent discount which was termed only as a point of departure, depending on conditions in the various consuming markets. In this regard, Perez argued that the Venezuelan aspiration for a price increase in fuel oil, with 1958 prices as the point of departure, was not unreasonable. Although the dols 2.00 price that year followed the Suez crisis, prices of manufactured products purchased by Venezuela have risen considerably since that date, whereas non-U.S. crude and fuel oil prices have steadily declined. Taking into consideration price inflation during the past seven years, it seemed to him that the Venezuelan program was quite reasonable and just. He emphasized that Venezuela has steadily been suffering from price increases arising from the increased prices of U.S. products attributable to wage increases as well as U.S. inflation, and did not see why the U.S. could not accept Venezuela's attempt to protect its own position.

6. Perez said that he expected to be in New York City January 18 and 19, and in Washington January 20 and 21 on business involving the World Bank and the International Monetary Fund in connection with a study on Libya. He was instructing Perez de la Cova to suggest a luncheon or other meeting with USG officials at which time this problem could be discussed further.

Comment:

7. What Perez told me today was essentially similar to what he had told me January 4 and reported in this Embassy's A–530[3] of January 8 which was presumably received in Washington on January 10. I did not believe then and I do not believe now that it would be practical to expect any reconsideration of the GOV action. I do, however, feel that our talk today and talks to be held in Washington next week should make more likely implementation of the announced intention of the GOV to apply the program with minimum danger to the competitive position of fuel oil and to the price structure.

8. Having in mind the politically sensitive position of the GOV on petroleum, increased jockeying within and between the various political groups in anticipation of the '68 elections and gov preoccupation over the inadequacy of government revenues to finance its politically important social and economic programs, it does not seem realistic to expect any more. Our strongest cards today are the Venezuelan hope, however remote, of an eventual breakthrough on restrictions and the special position accorded Venezuela among petroleum producers on capital movements from the U.S. Our vulnerabilities are illustrated by

---

[3] Not printed. (Ibid., FN 10 VEN)

the new policy on fuel oil prices, large U.S. investments and sizeable Venezuelan Central Bank dollar deposits.

9. Although Perez Guerrero intimated that his government's action on residual fuel oil and claims for back taxes attributable to inadequate export prices would forestall more radical measures, I am not optimistic regarding the future. It seems to me and also to petroleum producers here that efforts toward increased taxation are most likely, if only because of the government's budgetary problem, and that the petroleum industry will be one of the prime targets.[4]

Bernbaum

---

[4] In a January 14 letter to Hill, Bernbaum emphasized that "retaliation by US would aggravate the Venezuelans—certainly this would be the case with an open kind of retaliation. And, I am afraid that the political importance of this issue is so great in Venezuela as to make it more likely that irritation here will be accompanied by further retaliation than by back-tracking on positions already taken." (Ibid., FN 11 VEN)

---

534. Memorandum of Conversation[1]

Washington, January 14, 1966, 10:15 a.m.

The President said that Marlin Sandlin[2] had raised the price of sulphur $5 a ton. Mr. Mann said this was the first he had heard of it. The President said that was the trouble, we were not on top of it. He said he thought Mr. Mann should call Mr. Sandlin and tell him that we certainly hope that he does not press this and remind him that if they keep the price up we will have to go to controls. The President said he thought this was awful. Mr. Mann said perhaps he should ask Mr. Sandlin to put a freeze on it and then come up here for a talk. The President said he thought this would be too late.

The President asked Mr. Mann if we had any leverage on Venezuela and Mr. Mann said we did not. The President said he thought it was foolish to raise the quota when we did. He said it seems almost

---

[1] Source: Johnson Library, Papers of Thomas C. Mann, Telephone Conversations with LBJ, May 2, 1965–June 2, 1966. No classification marking. Drafted by Patricia A. Saunders. According to the President's Daily Diary Johnson called Mann at 10:10 a.m. (Johnson Library)

[2] Marlin E. Sandlin, chairman of the Pan American Sulphur Company in Houston, Texas.

idiotic for us to take public funds to feed hungry children while we import extra oil from Venezuela. He said he thought that we ought to use coal and keep this oil out and put these people to work in the coal mines.

Mr. Mann said that would be great if it would work but went on to explain that only about 10% of the big users—mostly utilities— would be likely to convert to coal soon. Therefore, the conclusion was that coal could not replace the oil.

Mr. Mann said that the difficulty in his opinion really stems from the fact that the Venezuelans want the $1.25 that every refiner gets in this country as a result of his ticket taken away from the refiners and passed on to Venezuela.

Mr. Mann said that he would talk to Marlin Sandlin about the sulphur thing and would also let the President know after he had talked to the Venezuelan Minister of Mines Perez Guerrero who was coming to town. Mr. Mann told the President he hoped that Venezuela could administer this order in such a way as not to hurt us.

The President said if Mr. Mann was unable to reach him, he should give the info to Mr. Valenti.[3]

---

[3] Immediately following this conversation, Johnson called Udall to discuss the problem of Venezuelan oil. The President urged the Secretary to "find some way to really bring in a good load of this stuff that we can protect ourselves a little bit, and then say to Venezuela: 'When we try to increase your quota, give you a little relief, why then you stick a price to us. Now, we're not going to do that, we're just not going to have it. We want a lower price with a bigger quantity rather than a higher price.'" Johnson suggested a barter deal, possibly in the Middle East, but was otherwise emphatic: "I want somebody that's smarter than Venezuela." Udall admitted "maybe our people haven't looked hard enough at some move that would have the effect of shaking these Venezuelans." (Johnson Library, Recordings and Transcripts, Recording of telephone conversation between President Johnson and Udall, January 14, 1966, 10:15 a.m., Tape F66.01, Side B, PNO 5)

---

535. Editorial Note

On January 14, 1966, the Venezuelan Embassy informed the Department that Minister of the Interior Gonzalo Barrios was planning to visit Washington for 1 week starting January 18. The Embassy requested that Barrios receive an appointment with President Johnson, possibly in connection with the Minister of Mines and Hydrocarbons, Manuel Perez Guerrero, who was coming to Washington for oil consultations. (Telegram 569 to Caracas, January 14; National Archives and

Records Administration, RG 59, Central Files 1964–66, POL 7 VEN) In a meeting with Ambassador Bernbaum on January 15, President Leoni made a separate appeal for the appointment, explaining that its main purpose would be to allow "first direct contact with President Johnson through Barrios, who is most trusted aid." Barrios would deliver a personal letter to Johnson addressing several issues of mutual concern, including recent petroleum developments, the Venezuela–British Guiana border dispute, and the Vietnam war. (Telegram 709 from Caracas, January 15; ibid.)

Under Secretary of State Mann raised the Venezuelan request with President Johnson on January 15. According to a memorandum of the conversation: "The President said that was the last thing he wanted to do, negotiate on oil. Mr. Mann said that was right but Venezuela is so important that if the President could see him and then refer him to Udall and State, he thought it would be a good political move. He said he did not think the President should discuss details. He said he thought it would be good if the President could receive him because when the President sends people down to Leoni they are received by him and if his people could not get through to the President, it might hurt feelings. The President said for Mr. Mann to bring him in for five minutes then, and to be sure that was all he stayed." (Johnson Library, Papers of Thomas C. Mann, Telephone Conversations with LBJ, May 2, 1965–June 2, 1966) A January 19 memorandum from Mann to the President requesting the appointment for Barrios is in the National Archives and Records Administration, RG 59, Central Files 1964–66, POL 7 VEN.

---

536.   Telegram From the Department of State to the Embassy in Venezuela[1]

Washington, January 24, 1966, 3:35 p.m.

585. Following summary FYI only and Noforn. It is based on uncleared MemCon and subject to amendment upon review MemCon.

---

[1] Source: National Archives and Records Administration, RG 59, Central Files 1964–66, AID(VEN) VIET S. Confidential; Limdis. Drafted by Hill on January 21, cleared by Sayre and Bowdler, and approved by Mann. Repeated to London and Georgetown. According to the President's Daily Diary the meeting was held from 12:56 until 1:14 p.m. (Johnson Library)

President Johnson this noon received President Leoni's special emissaries Gonzalo Barrios and Manuel Perez Guerrero who delivered letter from Leoni and, as expected, brought up Vietnam, British Guiana border dispute, and petroleum.[2]

Barrios opened by expressing President Leoni's solidarity with President Johnson's policy of peace and said Venezuela wished express that solidarity by sending food and medicine to South Vietnam. President Johnson said we would welcome any help in resisting aggression and keeping Communism from enveloping free countries.

Barrios then turned to British Guiana border dispute, stating President Leoni had charged him to say Venezuela wanted peaceful solution and desired to keep British Guiana out of hands of Communist demagogues as that would be not only threat to hemisphere but direct threat to Venezuela. Barrios did not advance any particular solution but suggested President Johnson seek to obtain greater understanding of problem by all parties especially British. President Johnson said it was U.S. policy avoid getting involved in boundary disputes and doubted whether such involvement would be useful or acceptable to parties.

When petroleum came up, Perez Guerrero made presentation of importance petroleum to Venezuela's economy and political stability. He underscored Venezuela did not object to restrictions on imports of crude to U.S. but did object to discrimination in favor other countries. Described past conversations with U.S. as conducted with frankness and mutual understanding but said President Leoni disappointed no solution had been found. Leoni had, however, welcomed indication that U.S. recognized special position Venezuelan petroleum and was hopeful something could be worked out in near future. President Johnson replied that Venezuela was wise in continuing discussions with Departments State and Interior, as he had not personally dealt with details oil program since taking office. He expressed hope mutually satisfactory solution could be worked out.

---

[2] As the Venezuelan emissaries waited outside his office, Johnson returned a telephone call from Senator Clinton P. Anderson (D–New Mexico). Anderson explained the reason for his earlier call: "I know the boys from Venezuela are up in town. I've got friends in the petroleum industry that are worried about that situation." After a general discussion of Venezuelan oil, the President asked: "Now, what are we going to do ultimately, Clint, on this price thing? Now here is an illustration. These people are happy with what they are getting, they're doing well. Then we come along and say 'we are going to give you a great opportunity to bring in a lot more' and they answer us with a hell of a good price increase." The Senator suggested: "I think you ought to threaten them someday with a Price Control Act, have them start exploring it, hold some hearings on it, they might behave themselves." (Johnson Library, Recordings and Transcripts, Recording of telephone conversation between President Johnson and Anderson, January 21, 1966, 12:40 p.m., Tape F66.02, Side B, PNO 1) An uncorrected transcript of the conversation is also ibid., Chron Series.

At close interview, President indicated that, while he personally not involved in these matters, he would direct officials to work with Venezuelans here and Caracas towards eventually satisfactory solutions. Venezuelan delegates expressed themselves as pleased with interview. Barrios said President Leoni hoped two Presidents could meet and President Johnson said he hoped this would be possible within their respective terms of office.

Ambassador Tejera Paris also attended as did Mann, Sayre and Hill for Department. Copy letter being pouched Caracas.[3]

Rusk

---

[3] A copy of Leoni's letter to Johnson is in the National Archives and Records Administration, RG 59, Central Files 1964–66, POL 7 VEN.

---

537.   Telegram From the Embassy in Venezuela to the Department of State[1]

Caracas, September 29, 1966, 1955Z.

1840. 1. President Leoni's confident announcement that basis for solution of problems between petroleum companies and GOV has now been found and final agreement and discussion of bright economic prospects has pulled rug out from under those political elements who have been seeking discredit and undermine stability government. At same time, it is most positive step in last several months toward restoration economic confidence. Details speech reported separate tel.[2] While die-hard opposition sectors will undoubtedly continue their efforts, without substantive base of crisis between petroleum sector and government their cries of gloom, doom and communism will be ineffective. Thus, inspired anxiety (Embtel 1449)[3] which has existed past two months should taper off rapidly.

---

[1] Source: National Archives and Records Administration, RG 59, Central Files 1964–66, PET 6 VEN. Confidential; Priority. Repeated to USCINCSO, Bogota, Georgetown, and Mexico for Assistant Secretary Gordon.

[2] Telegram 1846 from Caracas, September 30. (Ibid., POL 2 VEN) Although Leoni did not announce the details of the settlement, the government allowed the companies to sell oil at competitive prices in return for payment of taxes on the basis of predetermined "reference prices." The companies also agreed to pay $155 million in back taxes through 1965.

[3] In telegram 1449 from Caracas, September 9, the Embassy explained that "uncertainty in financial community in past month resulted in contraction credit available and in last week a limited run on dollars. These developments in turn stimulated concern within the business community and now within the public at large." (Ibid., POL 15 VEN)

2. Political effects of particular importance include:

A. Opposition groups at ordinary session Congress which opens October 1 unlikely mount meaningful opposition to government on pending basic legislation, including tax reform bill.
B. Position of main opposition parties, COPEI, FDP, and FND, are at tactical disadvantage and will have hard choices to make when tax reform bill finally comes to vote.
C. With revenue base assured for remaining two years and several months of administration, government can move ahead confidently with social-economic program. AD party, particularly in states receiving substantial assistance in public works and alliance for progress projects, will be assured resources for building a record of accomplishment.
D. Opposition groups may now concentrate on charges of government mismanagement and press for investigation of public expenditures.
E. URD party which had considered withdrawal from coalition and expressed particular concern re petroleum policy may now be considerably more reluctant leave government.

3. Question of attitude Venezuelan military toward government and their role in nation's stability (which is always key ingredient) had again arisen last week as result number top level transfers which purportedly included replacing two top respected army officers with generals who are widely considered AD favorites. However consensus Country Team is that while number of top level changes have developed, the controversial changes have not yet occurred. Regardless whether they now do occur or not, government, having removed fundamental petroleum question from contention, has at same time significantly reduced possibility that military malcontents could count on national economic crisis as foundation for Golpe aspirations.

4. In addition, it should be noted that AD party at its national convention last week emphatically confounded irresponsible critics and press speculation by unanimously selecting highly respected Minister of Interior, Gonzalo Barrios, as party's secretary general. AD sources confirm to us that President intervened forcefully with party leaders to insure party unity would not be undermined by personal ambition by various potential presidential candidates.

5. In short, government agreement in principle with petroleum companies constitutes fundamental contribution national stability, and outlook today considerably brighter than it has been for several months.

Cottrell

538.   Telegram From the Embassy in Venezuela to the Department of State[1]

Caracas, January 31, 1967, 2000Z.

4034. 1. Ever sensitive military-government relationship in Venezuela has come under particular scrutiny in past month in wake of dramatic government use of military to intervene in Central University following Communist efforts to assassinate Army Chief of Staff.[2] The Communist effort to generate friction between government and military establishment has clearly backfired in terms of welfare of the Communist movement in Venezuela. At this point however, some speculation is extant re long-range effect on relations between the civilian government and military officers. On basis government's determination to carry through reforms which terminate once and for all inviolability of university campus (which enabled Communist exploitation of the campus) our assessment is that these doubts and irritations are in the process of being resolved.

2. Following Embassy comments are also designed to provide the context for DAO message no. 0051, January 1967 and [1 line of source text not declassified][3] which reported on existence military distrust and impatience with government in connection with university crisis.

3. Possibility that ever present irritations between military and civilian government could flare up into a significant crisis of stability is heavily influenced by general state of nation's economic and political situation. In a period of political crisis in which law and order are threatened, such as that which was manifested in Carupano and Puerto Cabello uprising, that which existed prior to the 1963 elections and on a lesser degree a year ago (see A–537 of January 11, 1966),[4] and briefly prior to the government's intervention in the university this past December, military unrest and dissatisfaction with government inefficiency inevitably increases. Same holds true, although to a lesser degree, in periods of economic deterioration. There is little doubt, for example, that many military officers were watching the crisis between

---

[1] Source: National Archives and Records Administration, RG 59, Central Files 1967–69, POL 23–8 VEN. Secret. Repeated to USCINCSO, Rio de Janeiro, Bogota, Santo Domingo, Santiago, Buenos Aires, Georgetown, and Moscow.

[2] On December 13 General Roberto Morean Soto, Chief of the General Staff of the Army, was wounded in a terrorist attack. The next day the Leoni administration suspended certain rights guaranteed by the constitution and occupied the Central University in Caracas.

[3] Neither found.

[4] Airgram A–537 is not printed. (National Archives and Records Administration, RG 59, Central Files 1967–69, POL 23–9 VEN)

the government and the petroleum companies which the government finally resolved last summer. In all of these periods of strain, when showdown came, military stood behind government. Both the political and economic situations have now improved over the past year and there are no fundamental pressures for the military to consider moving against the government.

4. Although some military officers have expressed serious reservations about the government's determination to carry through university reforms, there is no reason to doubt record to date indicating that government fully intends to carry through these reforms.

5. University residences which were long a virtual fortress of Communist activities have been closed and converted into classrooms. University Hospital which was a particular target for Communist activities is being fenced out of the campus and incorporated directly into the city. Government's draft university regulation which has now been publicly presented goes further than anyone would have expected and reserves for the government the responsibility for maintaining law and order within the campus. Although government spokesmen have indicated that there is flexibility in some of the more unexpected and sweeping effects of new regulations, have consistently and publicly reiterated that there is no flexibility in their determination that government police will patrol the campus just as though it were part of the city and thus inviolability of Communist campus haven is terminated once and for all. This was most recently stated to the Embassy by former Minister of Interior and present Secretary General of the AD party, Gonzalo Barrios, on January 27 and in press interview January 28 by present Minister of Interior Leandro.

6. Military officers with particular political interests naturally view university situation and government's performance from their own vantage point. It must, of course, be recognized that government has a much broader responsibility and it thereby seeks to construct a solution to national problems which reflects the national interest, which is not necessarily always exactly the same as the interpretation of national interest held by some military officers. Thus, some of chronic military critics are now denouncing government on these grounds.

7. Finally, it is essential in weighing military attitudes to recognize that Venezuelan military establishment is complex, varied and far from monolithic as to political attitudes. There are many officers, particularly at upper levels who are close to AD party or the opposition COPEI party which is also dedicated to constitutional government. Perhaps a majority of officers are largely apathetic about political issues and unlikely to actively play a role in such questions. There are some officers who are devoted to a "golpe" and military dictatorship regardless of which political party is in power. This means, of course, that we are not dealing with a solid bloc of military opinion.

8. In summary, we consider military government relationship has passed a number of tough tests since 1958 and present politico-economic situation in general, and government objectives and performances on university in particular, give ample basis for hope these relations will improve rather than deteriorate.

Bernbaum

---

539.   Telegram From the Embassy in Venezuela to the Department of State[1]

Caracas, March 15, 1967, 0030Z.

4778. Subj: Insurgency Problem.

1. In conversation with Leoni today, he drew parallel between present insurgency problem[2] and that faced by President Betancourt in 1962 prior to electoral period. He said it was important to build up extra forces for protection of cities and particularly communities near guerrilla zones so that main body of armed forces could function normally and provide essential security for electoral process.

2. Accordingly, Leoni said his government would require additional arms for special forces which will be created. He anticipates these arms will come from Western European countries (he mentioned Belgian guns) and from the U.S. He emphasized importance of more armament for helicopters so that they could better attack targets of opportunity, although he stated he believed for time being armed forces had sufficient numbers helicopters.

3. Leoni commented that Colombian insurgency a complicating factor and an even greater problem than it appears to be on surface. He said he confident GOV and armed forces can manage situation in Venezuela.

---

[1] Source: National Archives and Records Administration, RG 59, Central Files 1967–69, POL 23 VEN. Confidential; Priority. Repeated to Bogota, Rio de Janeiro, and USCINCSO.

[2] Reference is to the assassination on March 3 of Dr. Julio Iribarren Borges, former Director of Social Security and brother of the Venezuelan Foreign Minister. On March 4 the Leoni administration reinstated its suspension of constitutional rights, 2 days after those rights had been fully restored. Venezuela subsequently blamed Cuba for the assassination, thereby justifying further retaliatory measures from the OAS. Leoni raised this issue with President Johnson at Punta del Este; see Document 50.

4. Military credits and MilGrp agreement also discussed but are subjects of other message.[3]

Bernbaum

---

[3] Telegram SCVE 034–67 from the Commander of the U.S. Military Group in Venezuela to USCINCSO, March 15. (National Archives and Records Administration, RG 59, Central Files 1967–69, FN 6–1 VEN)

---

540.   Memorandum of Conversation[1]

US/MC–14   Punta del Este, Uruguay, April 11, 1967, 6 p.m.

SUBJECT

Petroleum Problems

PARTICIPANTS

United States
President Johnson
Mr. Walt Rostow
Assistant Secretary Gordon
Assistant Secretary Solomon
Mr. Neil A. Seidenman, Interpreter

Venezuela
President Leoni
Sr. Ignacio Iribarren Borges,
  Foreign Minister of Venezuela

President Leoni said that it was very gratifying for him to receive President Johnson and to have the opportunity on this occasion to discuss with him a very serious problem affecting Venezuela that had already been mentioned through correspondence on two previous occasions.[2] This was the problem that had been posed by President Leoni's personal envoys in the past, namely former Minister of Mines Guerrero and former Minister of Interior Barrios, who had discussed the fundamentals of the matter with the President at the White House.[3]

---

[1] Source: National Archives and Records Administration, RG 59, Central Files 1967–69, POL 7 IA–Summit. Confidential. Drafted by Seidenman and approved in the White House on April 28. The memorandum is part 1 of 3; parts 2 and 3 are Documents 541 and 50, respectively. According to George Christian, the meeting was held at Leoni's residence in Punta del Este. (Press statement, April 11; Johnson Library, President's Daily Diary) President Johnson attended the meeting of American Chiefs of State at Punta del Este, April 12–14.

[2] Leoni raised the oil issue in two letters to Johnson, March 13, 1965, and January 17, 1966. (National Archives and Records Administration, RG 59, Central Files 1964–66, PET 1 US–VEN and POL 7 VEN, respectively)

[3] For an account of Johnson's meeting with Barrios and Perez Guerrero, January 21, 1966, see Document 536.

President Johnson replied that he was happy to have the opportunity to visit with President Leoni. He expressed the desire of the Administration to be of help to Venezuela and said that he had read the letter[4] from the Venezuelan Government that had been received the week before. The President added that in the event that President Leoni got tired of having those fellows around, he, President Johnson, would not mind having their very able services to help him develop our trade relations with many countries in the world.

President Leoni stated that he could appreciate the workload being shouldered by the President. At the same time Venezuela has problems that must be grappled with and to which solutions must be found. At this particular time the most serious problem for Venezuela is oil. Today this problem is being compounded and Venezuela's prospects are being rendered increasingly obscure by the new restrictions that have gone into effect relating to the sulphur content of Venezuelan oil.

President Johnson stated that very careful consideration is being given to this problem. We realize what oil means to the Venezuelan economy, so that what we want to do is to try to roll with the punches and help Venezuela as much as possible. In this respect what we are aiming at is: 1) to solve the sulphur problem; and 2) to be able to use more oil from Venezuela. The President added that President Leoni and his associates have done such a good job in this area that the United States buys more oil from Venezuela than from any other country. The percentage involved here is 60 percent of our imports, and Venezuela has at least 30 percent more of our oil import market than any other country. We want to keep Venezuela's oil sales high, and therefore one thing we are doing at this time is to initiate talks with Canada to see whether or not we can get Canada to reduce its share (i.e. share of the growth rate, as Solomon explained to Mayobre the next day).

The President indicated that he had just signed a very important amendment to the proclamation on the oil import program that was going into effect relating to our imports of asphalt.[5] By this means certification could be issued by the Secretary of Interior for additional imports of asphalt based on the situation as evaluated by the Secretary. Such additional imports of asphalt would appear to be beneficial to Venezuela and would help us to meet our national requirements. We

---

[4] Dated April 4. The Department forwarded the text of the letter to Punta del Este on April 10. (Telegram 1172104/Tosec 64 to USDEL Punta del Este; National Archives and Records Administration, RG 59, Central Files 1967–69, POL 7 IA SUMMIT) In an April 7 memorandum to Bowdler, Sayre summarized the letter, outlined the U.S. position, and suggested points for the President to make in his meeting with Leoni. (Ibid., ARA/NC/V Files: Lot 69 D 19, PET 17–2, U.S. Import Program 1967, January–April)

[5] Proclamation 3779, April 10. (32 *Federal Register* 5919)

are studying the asphalt situation, and various members of the Cabinet have examined the issue of import controls. We are convinced that with additional imports of asphalt Venezuela would stand to benefit, and this would be useful to our people. The Secretary of Interior will have the authority to issue new allocations and documentation for such imports.

The President pointed out that this new paragraph means that the Secretary will carry out a continuing study of the supply and demand situation, and based on his judgment, consistent with our needs and objectives, will have additional authority to recommend maximum levels of asphalt importation outside of the present MOIP. This means that he can authorize additional imports of asphalt on this basis for consumption in our country without additional allocations or licensing procedures. President Johnson told President Leoni that if he had no objection to sending us this additional asphalt at a low price, he would issue the order the following day.

President Johnson went on to say that he took pride in, and wished to maintain, the record dollar volume of imports into this country, from Venezuela, of crude oil, residual oil, and asphalt, of any period in history. He noted that as he was signing this proclamation he had noticed some of the figures involved: in the period of his predecessor's administration—1961–63—the volume of imports was at 1,394 million barrels; during this administration, from 1964 to 1966, the volume was 1,604 million barrels. We went from $3.1 billion to $3.5 billion. Those were the three highest years for imports and revenues. In 1964 the figure was $1.127 billion; in 1965, $1.208 billion; and in 1966, $1.314 billion. The President summed up that we want to do three things: 1) to see what we can do to get the sulphur out of Venezuelan oil so that we can use it for our cities in a way that will not aggravate our air-pollution problems; 2) we want to try and see if we can get Canada to reduce its exports (i.e., its growth rate of exports) to this country, and the President said, "If I lose friends on the Canadian side, I hope that you will make them up to me on the Venezuelan side"; and 3) we would like to increase our purchases of asphalt at low prices so that we can put in roads for some of our poor farmers. This, concluded President Johnson, was just about all he could do at this time. This may make the Canadians mad at him.

President Leoni stated that he could recognize that we are now importing more volume from Venezuela than in the past; however, there has been a trend recently in Venezuelan exports that is not considered good. At present, these exports to the United States consist of cheaper grades of oil, which bring in smaller returns. There has been an increasing trend away from the crude oils toward the residual oils, which of course sell at lower prices, and each time the price per barrel goes down by five cents there is a huge loss involved for Venezuela. This trend has been noticeable and growing since 1959, and there has been a drop in the price each year. For this reason, the Venezuelan Government, together with the companies, is grappling with this problem and an arrangement has been reached by which to curb the downward trend of the price.

With regard to the sulphur, the Venezuelan Government endorses compliance with the regulations that have been put into effect by the health and municipal authorities. The government is working with the companies to encourage them to adopt the necessary techniques and processing that will enable them to comply with these standards. The largest American company operating in this area in Venezuela is, of course, Creole, which as things now stand will have to invest between $110 million and $118 million in order to be able to meet the new requirements.

President Leoni went on to say that the problem of the Venezuelan oil market in the United States is considered not merely from the standpoint of Venezuela's self-seeking interests, but also in the light of what Venezuela represents as a country in the Latin American area. Venezuela is a nation that is building a democracy with strong foundations. Its policy has reflected the principles that were endorsed in this very place (Punta del Este) at the time the Alliance for Progress was launched a few years ago. Venezuela has brought about a transformation in the lives of its people in the rural as well as in the urban areas. This has involved considerable expenditure on the part of the Venezuelan Government. This, of course, is something that the Venezuelan Government desires, and a part of this is the wish to promote industry in the country. But Venezuela in the past has been fertile soil to the natural enemies of democracy in Venezuela, and of the United States.

President Johnson said in answer to this that he was in agreement with what President Leoni was saying. He reiterated that we want to buy more oil from Venezuela so as to raise these purchases in volume and in dollar value. At present the totals for both of these items stand at their highest mark in our history, and we want to increase them. We are now trying to get Canada to reduce their participation in our market, to help us to do this. The President said that, in the second place, he wished to lift restrictions on residual oil imports, which from his political experience he knew would make a lot of miners mad at him. He added his hope that this would make the Venezuelans love him. The President explained that by using more residual we are cutting more and more into the coal market. Number three, we are requiring the Defense Department to supply its oil needs from Caribbean sources, which would mean that we would use large amounts of oil from

Venezuela for defense purposes. Fourth, an increase in refining capacity will open up greater opportunities for Puerto Rico, where Venezuelan oil is used. Finally, the President pointed out that his own state of Texas produced more oil than all of the other oil-producing states in the United States. At the present time the production quota is down to eight or nine days per month. The pumps are idle during the other twenty-two days of the month. Many people have gone away as a result—many operators have folded. The President said that we are doing all of this to help Venezuela sustain a sound economy. We are aware of the problems that Venezuela has to face and we are aware of the activities of our natural enemies in Venezuela and in the Hemisphere.

The President stressed that he hoped President Leoni understood that we were taking an unprecedented step in these talks with Canada, which involve an attempt to get Canada to change its trade relations with our country by limiting Canadian access to the U.S. oil market. As these talks progress, there is bound to be a strain on relations between the United States and Canada, but we are doing this in order to insure that the MOIP will not work to the detriment of Venezuela. This means a change in our treatment of Canada, but we consider it to be the best way to assure Venezuelan access to the U.S. market on a high level of sales.

President Leoni stated that the Venezuelan Government has recognized and appreciated the receptive approach on the part of the United States authorities toward the problem faced by Venezuela involving unequal treatment of Venezuelan oil. The measures that the President mentioned seemed to constitute one more step in the direction in which Venezuela was striving; namely, to attain equal treatment of Venezuelan oil vis-à-vis Canadian oil. What the President said about the talks with Canada would be helpful but the ideal solution would be to give Venezuela the same treatment as Canada. The solution to these problems admittedly is no easy undertaking, but with perseverance Leoni said he was confident that a way could be found to devise a formula satisfactory to the interests of both countries.

Going back to a previous point, President Leoni said he wished to call the President's attention to the fact that Venezuela, despite guerrilla activities, has developed a solid and stable political situation. It is sufficient to witness that labor unrest is no more to be found in Venezuela, whereas if we look over at the situation in the United States we find that there are frequent labor-management disputes, and a serious strike seems to be in the offing at present.

President Johnson interrupted President Leoni to report that a bill he had proposed in connection with the strike mentioned had just been passed in the Senate by a vote of 82 to 1, and in the House by a majority of 400 to 8, putting off the strike for a 20-day grace period.[6] He explained that at the end of these twenty days something else would very likely have to be done, but we were not going to have a major railroad strike in the country. The President explained to Leoni that he thought he would be interested in this, as the leader of a democracy.

President Leoni went on to say that several years had gone by without major strikes in Venezuela and industrial peace in his country now seemed to be on a solid footing. If, however, Venezuela were unable to maintain budgetary stability and thus were to run into difficulties in financing programs now underway for national development and social progress, there was no doubt that Venezuela would be subject to social upheaval. Our natural enemies have not been able to gain a foothold in Venezuela heretofore, but if this were to happen—if Venezuela were to be rocked by social imbalance—this could provide a welcome opening to them. This is why the oil problem appeared to be of significance to hemispheric security.

President Leoni said that it would perhaps be desirable for his Minister of Mines to be in touch with Assistant Secretary Solomon in connection with the dispositions that were mentioned by the President.

President Johnson heartily agreed, adding that if the President of Venezuela had no objection he would hold off issuing the asphalt order until the following morning just so that it would not appear that he had come here to "lose his trousers".

President Leoni said that this was encouraging to him, in view of the fact that he had hoped to be able to take something concrete back to Venezuela with him as a result of the encounter in Punta del Este. He was glad to receive information of the forthcoming talks with Canada and hoped that these would lead to the desired solution.

The President warned President Leoni that he would possibly have to pry him away from chasing communists in his country in order to get some angry Texans off his back. President Leoni replied that he was confident Texans would always be his friends. President Johnson said that Texans had always been his friends until he came to Punta del Este and spoke with the Venezuelan President. He went on to say that if a man is working only eight days a month, he will get very angry at anyone who tries to take one of those days away from him, and when they get angry these people sometimes lose their judgment. President Leoni reiterated his confidence that Texans would continue to be their friends, since they had once been "Latin Americans" themselves. He added the expression of his understanding of the heavy burden the President had

---

[6] On April 11 the U.S. Congress passed the President's proposal for an additional 20 day "cooling-off" period in the nationwide railroad labor dispute. The bill was delivered to Punta del Este where it was signed into law on April 12. (81 Stat. 12)

to carry, and that this problem was not nearly as grave as the struggle the President had to face in Vietnam, which he does in solitude and with admirable strength and wisdom.

The President reiterated his desire to cooperate with the Venezuelans in the work of facing the trials they are going through. The President once again said that we will try to find a solution to the oil problem through talks with Canada. The President concluded the conversation by telling President Leoni that the latter was fortunate to enjoy the services of one of the most popular and capable of all the Ambassadors to our country—that he and his wife were among the best liked members of the Diplomatic Corps.[7]

---

[7] Enrique Tejera-Paris.

---

541.   Memorandum of Conversation[1]

US/MC–14   Punta del Este, Uruguay, April 11, 1967, 6 p.m.

SUBJECT

  Venezuelan Requirements for Additional Military Equipment

PARTICIPANTS

United States	*Venezuela*
President Johnson	President Leoni
Mr. Walt Rostow	Sr. Ignacio Iribarren Borges,
Assistant Secretary Gordon	Foreign Minister of Venezuela
Assistant Secretary Solomon	
Mr. Neil A. Seidenman, Interpreter	

President Leoni said that the Venezuelan Government had reason to believe that there would be an intensification of communist aggression in the northern region of Latin America, meaning, he said, Guatemala, Colombia and Venezuela. Besides the need to combat in Venezuela any step-up in guerrilla activities, there was also a need to guaranty peaceful elections. This posed a need for Venezuela to strengthen its military forces in order to provide for the safety of peaceful, democratic processes. Therefore, Venezuela will have to undertake

---

[1] Source: National Archives and Records Administration, RG 59, Central Files 1967–69, POL 7 IA SUMMIT. Confidential. Drafted by Seidenman and approved in the White House on April 28. The memorandum is part 2 of 3; parts 1 and 3 are Documents 540 and 50, respectively.

additional outlays from its Treasury to meet defense needs. Ambassador Tejera-Paris has recently approached U. S. authorities, including the Defense Department, in order to present Venezuela's requirements in military equipment for these purposes. President Leoni stressed that what he was talking about would be outside of presently existing agreements with us. The principal interest involved here is a foreshortening of the period of delivery of military equipment. Failure to obtain the necessary equipment in a brief period of time would necessitate obtaining this equipment elsewhere. This was something that the President of Venezuela believed could not be postponed inasmuch as it was of vital importance to the country. He suggested that the President might use his good offices to help Venezuelan authorities solve the problem. Venezuela would make payment as soon as it could, but again he stressed that this was to be outside of present arrangements. President Leoni noted that Venezuela's present dollar commitment for arms and equipment being purchased from the United States and Europe amounted to approximately $12 million.

President Johnson asked precisely what kind of equipment he wanted. President Leoni said that there was no need for rockets or supersonic aircraft, of course, but only equipment and matériel necessary for maintaining internal security: ammunition, transportation vehicles, communications equipment, etc. He stressed, however, that the principal need here is for a brief delivery time, and not the 18 to 24 months normally required under present arrangements. The desirable delivery time would be three months.

President Johnson stated that our problem is: first, we do not want to be the arms merchants of the world; second, that Congress has forced us to reduce our program for financing military programs in Latin America to 85 million, including sales and grant;[2] thirdly, we do not want the communists to take over Venezuela. Therefore, we want to help if Venezuela wants to buy equipment. Fourthly, the problem that we are grappling with in Vietnam is causing a great drain on our military supplies. The enemy there is building up to try to overrun us in one area and to keep them from doing this we are pouring everything over there; this means ammunition, helicopters and other types of equipment, but if we have an available surplus in any of the items that Venezuela needs, we can sell them to her. This is why we would have to know exactly what items Venezuela would need.

---

[2] Reference is to an amendment, sponsored by Senator J. William Fulbright (D–Arkansas), to the Foreign Assistance Act of 1966, which set a ceiling of $85 million per fiscal year for military assistance and sales to Latin America, not including support for military training or the Inter-American Peace Force in the Dominican Republic. (80 Stat. 803)

President Johnson noted that he knew Ambassador Tejera-Paris very well. He had even been at the President's ranch the week before, together with his charming wife.[3] He said that he would go over this with the Ambassador. If we have the equipment available to sell, and if Venezuela wants it, they can have it, and we will do everything we can to help. The President said that if there was a problem of slowness in deliveries he would find a way to clear this up upon his return to the United States.

The President reiterated his desire to cooperate with the Venezuelans in the work of facing the trials they are going through. He reiterated our support for Venezuela's cause in the OAS against Cuba, which he said he hoped they would pursue with aggressiveness; we want to be of help in the matter of military equipment if we can—because we don't want Venezuela to have to wait one minute to chase the communists.[4]

---

[3] President Johnson entertained most of the Latin American diplomatic corps at his Texas ranch on April 1. (Johnson Library, President's Daily Diary)

[4] On May 12 Venezuela announced the capture of a guerrilla landing party led by officers of the Cuban army near the village of Machurucuto, 130 miles east of Caracas. Documentation of U.S.-Venezuelan efforts to seek retaliatory measures against Cuba under the OAS charter is in the regional compilation. In telegram 6106 from Caracas, May 17, the Embassy reported that a "US-Venezuelan agreement to provide equipment for 10 new anti-guerrilla battalions, pursuant to President Johnson–Leoni agreement at Punta del Este is in jeopardy," due to DOD concern for the limitations set by the Fulbright amendment. (National Archives and Records Administration, RG 59, Central Files 1967–69, DEF 19–4 US–VEN) The agreement was signed on May 18. In a May 19 memorandum to the President, Rostow commented: "This is a nice end to a move initiated by you at the Latin American Summit." (Johnson Library, National Security File, Country File, Venezuela, Vol. III, 12/66–12/68)

---

542.   Telegram From the Embassy in Venezuela to the Department of State[1]

Caracas, June 7, 1967, 1805Z.

6491. 1. I was called this morning to FonOff at request of FonMin, who received me in presence Minister Mines Mayobre. They told me they were under instructions President Leoni (a) to pledge Venezuelan

---

[1] Source: National Archives and Records Administration, RG 59, Central Files 1967–69, PET 15 VEN. Confidential; Immediate. Passed to the White House and USIA.

petroleum to needs of free world in current crisis,[2] but (b) also to convey request GOV be included in planning now going on in Washington for distribution this natural resource.

2. Mayobre said wire service stories report Emergency Committee on Petroleum is now being convened in Washington and GOV desires to be consulted. FonMin asked this request be telegraphed at once. He added Tejera Paris will be informed.

3. Mayobre stated events convince GOV that Venezuela is an essential part of "security zone" and should be accorded corresponding privileges. He said GOV concerned that great demands might now be made on its petroleum and, after crisis, market would again be limited. GOV wants to avoid this situation and therefore believes status in U.S. market should be improved.

4. I pointed out at this juncture that dislocation petroleum supply situation, if crisis continues, would be mainly in Western Europe. Mayobre agreed. He then said GOV realized on normal basis Middle Eastern and African oil more competitive in Europe. Venezuela, on other hand, from economic, political and hemisphere security point of view has a natural and complementary relationship with U.S.

Comment:

5. Would appear from foregoing that GOV believes Middle East crisis supports their contention that Ven oil vital to U.S. national security and therefore that Ven should receive better treatment under MOIP.

6. Although Emb of opinion that GOV has perhaps overestimated U.S. need for additional Venezuelan oil in present situation it nevertheless believes would be desirable for Dept give consideration to GOV participation, as appropriate, in meetings to consider effect present situation on petroleum supply and distribution, and that GOV be kept informed regarding plans involving increased use Ven petroleum.

7. GOV position re consultation consistent with text Kennedy–Betancourt communiqué of Feb 20, 1963.[3]

---

[2] Reference is to the outbreak on June 5 of the 1967 Arab-Israeli war. In response to Egyptian charges of Western support for Israeli air strikes, most Arab oil-producing states agreed by June 7 to suspend oil shipments to the United States and Great Britain.

[3] See footnote 3, Document 528.

8. I would appreciate Department's response soonest to considerations raised in foregoing conversation with two ministers.[4]

Herron

---

[4] In telegram 209131 to Caracas, June 7, the Department replied that Solomon and
Tejera Paris had discussed the impact of the Arab oil embargo on Western Europe, agreeing to "consult closely together during the present crisis." The Department added: "We
are reluctant to go further than bilateral consultations since we see considerable problems in inviting GOV to participate even as observer in US Foreign Petroleum Supply
Committee." (National Archives and Records Administration, RG 59, Central Files
1967–69, POL ARAB–ISR) Bernbaum later reported that the Leoni administration had
decided to increase production by 300,000 barrels per day, but that "production beyond
that amount will be subject new conditions." (Telegram 6586 from Caracas, June 14; ibid.,
PET 17–2 VEN)

---

543.   **Memorandum From the President's Special Assistant
(Rostow) to President Johnson**[1]

Washington, July 28, 1967.

Mr. President:

Venezuelan Ambassador Tejera-Paris called me yesterday to ask
for an appointment with you to deliver a letter from President Leoni.
He said he was under instructions to deliver it to you and make some
oral remarks. I gave him no encouragement but did not close the door.
An advanced copy of the English translation is at Tab A.[2]

What Leoni wants is revision of our Mandatory Oil Import Program (MOIP) to put Venezuela on a par with Canada and Mexico and
permit higher imports of Venezuelan oil. He looks upon increased demand on Venezuelan production resulting from the Middle East crisis
as further justification for this request.

We are not in a position to do what Leoni wants on the MOIP. You
told him this at the Summit when you outlined the steps you were prepared to take:

—talks with Canada to restrict their deliveries.
—additional imports of asphalt.
—assistance in desulphurization technology.

---

[1] Source: Johnson Library, National Security File, Country File, Venezuela, Vol. III,
Memos, 12/66–12/68. Confidential.
[2] Dated July 25; attached but not printed.

We are moving forward on all three of these commitments as described in the report at Tab B. Tony Solomon tells us that Stu Udall has not moved faster toward carrying out the pledge on asphalt because of opposition of his staff and Congressman Mahon.[3]

Because you can't oblige Leoni on what he is after, it is inadvisable for you to receive Tejera-Paris. Were you to see him, it would become known and expectations in Venezuela aroused. The government might even encourage such hopes. The resulting let-down of an unforthcoming reply would then be increased. Covey Oliver and Tony Solomon agree with this assessment.

I recommend that I tell Tejera-Paris that I have consulted you on an appointment and because of the pressure of business you asked that I receive him on your behalf.

Walt

You want to receive him

I should receive him[4]

Speak to me

Tab B

Memorandum From the Director of the Office of North Coast Affairs (Hill) to William G. Bowdler of the National Security Council Staff

Washington, July 27, 1967.

SUBJECT

Venezuelan Petroleum Problems

In the course of the President's April 11 conversation with President Leoni at Punta del Este a number of commitments to actions were made by the President within the overall context of our desire to help Venezuela as much as possible by using more oil from Venezuela. These undertakings, and the current status of the related U.S. actions, are summarized hereunder:

---

[3] Congressman George H. Mahon (D–Texas), chairman of the House Appropriations Committee.

[4] Johnson checked this option.

1. To initiate talks with Canada to see whether or not we can get Canada to reduce its share in the growth rate of the United States market (thereby giving Venezuela an opportunity to share in such growth).

Action taken:

A series of meetings has been held with Canada, the most recent being to present a U.S. revision of an informal Canadian proposal. This latest U.S. revision was presented by Assistant Secretary Solomon to Canadian Ambassador Ritchie on July 26. We feel that our position and degree of flexibility is fully outlined to the Canadians. At the moment we are not able to anticipate their willingness to agree to voluntary limitations of exports at a suitable level. We must await their response.

The Canadians have been insistent in their desire to expand petroleum exports to the U.S., and the most that we can expect by limiting the Canadians is only a small increase in offshore imports rather than the decline which would otherwise occur. The Venezuelans, while understanding our strong efforts to keep the Canadians from forcing a cutback in imports from overseas, will not get significantly more imports as a result of our negotiations with Canada.

2. The President indicated that he had just signed an important proclamation relating to U.S. imports of asphalt, enabling the Secretary of Interior to certify to the need of additional imports thereof outside the MOIP. The President indicated that the U.S. would like to increase its purchase of asphalt and that the matter would be kept under continuing review.

Action taken:

Following issuance of the proclamation, the Office of Emergency Planning has progressed with a detailed study of the U.S. asphalt requirements. Interior has under consideration implementation of the asphalt authority, and is awaiting the recommendations of the OEP study.

3. An undertaking to "see what we could do to get the sulphur out of Venezuelan oil".

Action taken:

a. The White House has established a Committee to coordinate technical economic research on the impact of air pollution problems under the chairmanship of HEW and CEA.

b. HEW to make available $2.7 million from FY 1968 contingency funds for research, including desulphurization. Findings as developed will be made available to Venezuela. President Leoni recently called the attention of Ambassador Linowitz to the latter understanding, indicating that he was awaiting news.[5]

c. Although not specifically discussed at Punta del Este, residual fuel oil was redefined by a Presidential Proclamation issued July 17 to include #4 fuel oil as a step toward air pollution abatement.[6] The redefinition had been supported by the GOV. This redefinition, which has been welcomed by the GOV, could allow Venezuela to maintain substantially the same level of earnings it has been receiving by supplying the great bulk of imported residual and thus offset the potential loss caused by the fact that the residual Venezuela has been supplying can no longer be sold under anti-pollution regulations. It will not, however, result in the use of more oil by the U.S. Moreover, the GOV, in a statement welcoming this U.S. action, has expressed serious concern with regard to a discretionary provision of the Proclamation which gives the Secretary of the Interior authority to reimburse with import allocations U.S. refiners who produce low sulphur residual. Venezuela fears this could redound to the benefit of non-Venezuelan crudes. Interior has told Venezuelan representatives that the implementation of this authority would provide the mechanism for utilizing traditional Western Hemisphere, low gravity, high sulphur crude to produce the required low sulphur residual. Interior is preparing regulations which will be open to public comment prior to implementation.

4. Passing mention was also made by the President to an increase of refining capacity in Puerto Rico, where Venezuelan oil is used.

Action taken:

Import applications for supplies to these refineries are still under study by Interior.

5. The President was categoric in asserting to President Leoni that 1 to 3 above was just about all he could do at this time. A more fundamental revision of the MOIP to remove "discrimination" in favor of overland imports by extending equal treatment to Venezuela remains a major Venezuelan aspiration. President Leoni in a conversation with Ambassador Linowitz on June 26 asserted that the Middle East crisis had shown the vital importance of Venezuela's oil resources to the United States and hoped this would be taken into account in the continuing discussions and negotiations between Venezuela and the U.S. regarding petroleum. The Venezuelan Ambassador has inquired at the Department of State about the possibility of revising the MOIP in

---

[5] Leoni met Linowitz in Caracas on June 26. An account of their discussion on petroleum was transmitted in telegram 6824 from Caracas, June 28. (National Archives and Records Administration, RG 59, Central Files 1967–69, PET 15 VEN)

[6] Proclamation 3794. (32 *Federal Register* 10547)

Venezuela's favor (he was given discouragement) and the Venezuelan press has also played up this theme. Venezuela has increased production by 300,000 barrels a day (about 9%) and President Leoni has stated that increases beyond that amount must be covered by long-term contract. Venezuela has no intention of increasing production on a crash basis only to find itself in economic difficulties after the crisis ends, as in 1956. President Leoni has used the current crisis to point out that Venezuelan production is just as strategically important to the U.S. as that of Canada and Mexico. We can therefore expect greatly increased pressure from Venezuela as and when the current crisis subsides, precisely at a time when domestic producers will also be resisting cutbacks.[7]

---

[7] In a letter to Leoni on August 8, President Johnson outlined the action taken to support Venezuelan oil, but discounted any hope of further improvement: "To go beyond these measures would involve a fundamental and drastic change in our entire petroleum policy and would bring into question the whole structure of our oil policy. Indeed, since we last spoke, the crisis in the Middle East has made it even more difficult to envisage changes in our oil import program." (National Archives and Records Administration, RG 59, Central Files 1967–69, POL 23–7 VEN) Bernbaum later warned that relations would deteriorate if Venezuela's share in the U.S. oil market declined due to events in the Middle East and clean-air requirements. (Telegram 1219 from Caracas, August 25; ibid., PET 17–1 VEN)

---

544.   Telegram From the Department of State to the Embassy in Venezuela[1]

Caracas, July 13, 1968, 2159Z.

202053. Following is uncleared memcon:

Under Secretary Katzenbach called in Venezuelan Ambassador Tejera Paris to discuss July 9 Venezuelan decree asserting sovereignty over territorial seas from 3 to 12 miles off of part of Guyana claimed by Venezuela. In cordial but serious discussion, Under Secretary made following points:

(1) Meaning of decree was unclear to us and we would appreciate explanation, as it was potentially serious both from point of view international law and point of view internal Guyanese politics.

---

[1] Source: National Archives and Records Administration, RG 59, Central Files 1967–69, POL 33–4 VEN. Confidential; Immediate. Drafted and approved by Hill. Also sent to Georgetown and London and repeated to USUN, USCINCSO, Recife, and Sao Paulo for Oliver.

(2) If intent decree were merely to put world on notice that when and if Venezuela attained sovereignty over territory it claimed, Venezuelan law with respect territorial waters would obtain, we would have no problem with it although it was difficult to see what advantage there was to Venezuela in issuing it at this time.

(3) If, however, as accompanying explanatory note seemed to suggest, Venezuela intended immediately to exercise rights of sovereignty in 3–12 mile zone we would take "most serious" view of situation. As international lawyer, he himself could not see how such claim could be asserted and doubted that Ambassador Tejera would, in his capacity as lawyer, defend it. International law was clear that maritime rights and rights to continental shelf (which Guyana always claimed) attached to coastal state and at present Guyana was clearly the coastal state. The U.S., therefore, did not accept decree's validity if it implied actual exercise of sovereignty and, if matter came up in international forum, we could not support Venezuela. While we would not make public statement unless we had to, we would have to advise U.S. shipping and other private interests if they asked that we did not accept validity of decree.

(4) We also viewed decree as serious in terms Guyanese electoral situation. It was, we thought, of more immediate interest to Venezuela than to us and hemisphere that Burnham win elections which would probably take place in December and that Jagan be excluded. Moves such as this claim were not helpful as they eroded Burnham electoral strength in difficult elections and diverted his attention during critical remaining six month campaign period. It also made it difficult for us to counsel Burnham to use moderation as he felt obligated to defend his position.

(5) We viewed explanatory note, with allusions such as "physical act of possession", as more disturbing than decree itself and wondered what intent of Venezuela was in light of assurances President of Venezuela and country's highest officials had given that Venezuela would not resort to force. Under Secretary again emphasized seriousness of our concern if Venezuela intended exercise sovereignty.

Tejera replied that he knew nothing of decree and explanatory note, having only received their texts, but he would immediately report to Caracas and ask for instructions. Speaking personally, he at first attributed decree to Guyanese intransigence in Mixed Commission and especially their refusal to accept Venezuelan proposals for joint development. He recited history of Venezuela's frustrations in attempt to get Guyana to discuss settlement of issue in Mixed Commission and claimed Venezuela, which desired settlement by peaceful means had used great restraint in contrast to Burnham's inflammatory actions such as his recent speech in Birmingham, U.K. With regard to claim to territorial sea, he was certain that disputed territory would some-day return to Venezuela and it was only natural and right Venezuela should have territorial waters which she would have under her Constitution and which are not claimed by party which wrongfully occupied disputed territory through inheritance from U.K. He would, however, query Caracas and let Under Secretary know as soon as he received reply.

For Caracas: You should convey above to President Leoni as soon as possible after clearance of memcon, hopefully early Monday.[2]

For London: You should convey substance to FonOff.

For Georgetown: You may convey general line of conversation to Burnham in strictest confidence but should avoid giving him any encouragement to take matter to international organizations.

Rusk

---

[2] July 15. In telegram 6896 from Caracas, July 16, the Embassy reported that Venezuelan officials were "piqued over US position on decree as stated Saturday by Katzenbach." In a meeting with Bernbaum on July 16, Iribarren declared that Venezuela's "territorial claims must take precedence over any consideration their effect on Guyana's domestic political situation." The same day Minister of Interior Leandro Mora told an Embassy officer that the Department did not appreciate "Venezuela's 'feelings' on this matter." (Telegram 6898 from Caracas, July 16; ibid.)

---

545.   Telegram From the Embassy in Venezuela to the Department of State[1]

Caracas, November 20, 1968, 2002Z.

8970. 1. President Leoni called me to Miraflores shortly after noon today to discuss Venezuelan seizure of 575 ton Cuban fishing vessel *Alecrin*. Although the President did not indicate the location, he said that the vessel, when seized, was in Venezuelan territorial waters.

2. He then reviewed the belief of the GOV, based on hard intelligence, that Castro Cuba was supporting and activating the launching of guerrilla elements along the coast and Trinidad and probably hoped to stage a dramatic incident before the Venezuelan elections December 1.

---

[1] Source: National Archives and Records Administration, RG 59, Central Files 1967–69, POL 33–4 VEN–CUBA. Confidential; Immediate.

3. As a result of information obtained by the GOV that several Cuban fishing vessels were near Venezuelan waters, the navy, in the past few days, had intensified patrols and the seizure of the *Alecrin* resulted.

4. I asked the President what the facts were with regard to news reports from Havana that the fishing boat was machine-gunned and perhaps the target of cannon fire. The President said that he could not answer this question yet since he did not have all the facts, but that as the facts came in he would have the Foreign Minister, who was present at the meeting, let me know.

5. The President said that the seizure of the *Alecrin* would have to be accepted by Castro in the same way that the U.S. has had to accept the seizure of the *Pueblo* by the North Koreans. He made it quite clear that Venezuela's patience is exhausted over Castro Cuba's continued efforts to intervene subversively in its affairs. He added that the Communist Party in Venezuela at the present time is playing a double game. On the one hand it has sought temporary respectability so that it can participate in the Venezuelan electoral process while at the same time preparing to resume subversive and possibly terrorist activities after the election.

6. The President seemed somewhat tense as he discussed this matter and apparently was seeking through me the moral support of the U.S. It is also my impression that GOV action in this case is to give an unequivocal [garbled text] to Cuba to stop its support of the armed struggle in Venezuela.

Bernbaum

---

546. Telegram From the Department of State to the Embassy in Venezuela[1]

Washington, November 21, 1968, 0149Z.

275231. Ref: Embtel 8970.[2] Subj: Venezuelan Seizure of Cuban Fishing Vessel.

---

[1] Source: National Archives and Records Administration, RG 59, Central Files 1967–69, POL 33–4 VEN–CUBA. Secret; Immediate; Limdis. Drafted by Vaky; cleared by Petersen; cleared in substance by Fitzgerald, Meeker, and Henry Bardach (EA); and approved by Oliver.

[2] Document 545.

1. Cuba has circulated note at U.N. violently protesting firing upon and seizure of Cuban vessel 100 miles from Venezuelan coast and accusing U.S. of complicity. Cuban Ambassador has appointment with U.N. SecGen tonight.

2. FYI. As you aware there strong reasons believe Cuban vessel seized in international waters and that Venezuelans themselves know it. End FYI.

3. *For Ambassador:* Possibility additional incidents as result of continued Venezuelan naval patrols obviously of great concern. There is no reason to assume that Havana will permit future incidents, if indeed it permits this one, to pass without retaliation, and as GOV aware Cuban air and naval forces have sophisticated equipment. Moreover there is some outside possibility that repeat incident may provoke some Cuban act against U.S. Serious confrontation between Venezuela and Cuba of this nature, or risk of Cuban military action, is obviously undesirable in terms of U.S., Venezuelan or hemisphere interests.

4. President Leoni's comparison of *Alecrin* seizure with *Pueblo* incident was not felicitous one. USG has maintained North Korea action in firing upon and seizure *Pueblo,* even if *Pueblo* was not in international waters as we believe it was violation of established international law. North Korea singularly unfortunate nation for Venezuela to imitate. Any case we do not wish encourage or stimulate seizures of vessels especially on high seas.

5. Recognizing provocation which GOV subject to and noting from reftel that Leoni probably seeking U.S. moral support, we think it important cool down Venezuelans and seek dissuade them from taking this kind of action. We especially think it important to avoid repetition of vessel seizure.

6. Accordingly you are asked to convey to GOV at appropriate level and in most appropriate way you think advisable, above concerns and advise them to cool it. Recognize that you are under constraints re revealing to Venezuelans that we aware seizure took place in international waters especially since Leoni told you it took place in territorial waters. Recognize also that we cannot abandon GOV in face of insurgency threat or seem convey unconcern. Hence will take tact to center Venezuelan attention on tactics used to combat Cuban threat and international repercussions of incidents such as this one which may not help Venezuelans. Obviously if there clear evidence *Alecrin* engaged in subversive mission and this provable Venezuelan position would be stronger. Our main concern this point is to dissuade them from seizure in international waters simply on suspicion which may later prove unwarranted and to avoid risk of confrontation and retaliation mentioned above.

Rusk

547. Telegram From the Embassy in Venezuela to the Department of State[1]

Caracas, November 21, 1968, 2325Z.

9001. Ref: Caracas 8987.[2]

1. President Leoni's reaction to my conversation this morning with Mantilla was prompt and vigorous. I saw him at his request late this afternoon. The President said he had been greatly concerned by Mantilla's description of his conversation with me. Our position implied to him a US tendency to wash its hands of the situation because of preoccupation with serious problems in other parts of the world. He was able to understand this but felt that it left Venezuela in the position of fending for itself on matters of vital importance to its security. He asked rhetorically whether it would not be necessary for Venezuela to turn to France for military equipment to defend itself now that there was the implication that the US would not assume responsibility and did not, in any case, want to furnish Venezuela with equipment at least equal in quality to that secured by the Cubans from the Soviet Union. He said that Venezuela might even find itself in the position of being forced to come to terms with the Soviet Union for its own protection. The President spoke in this vein for some time and I listened patiently, knowing from experience that he was blowing off steam.

2. After he finished, I read suitable excerpt from Deptel 275231[3] to give him the flavor of the Department's position as I had previously

---

[1] Source: National Archives and Records Administration, RG 59, Central Files 1967–69, POL US–VEN. Secret; Priority; Limdis.

[2] In telegram 8987 from Caracas, November 21, Bernbaum reported: "Due unavailability FonMin until tomorrow morning, I conveyed substance reftel [Document 546] to Manuel Mantilla SecGen Presidency. He said would immediately inform President Leoni. He showed understanding our position but emphasized importance of not giving Cubans idea US so worried over danger any problem with Cuba as to give Castro idea he could operate with impunity. He hoped Cubans would not get this impression from our position in UN debate. I said this obviously delicate problem and assured him that what I just said strictly between US and Venezuelan Government." (National Archives and Records Administration, RG 59, Central Files 1967–69, POL US–VEN)

[3] Document 546.

described it to Mantilla. This then produced another monologue along the same lines.[4]

3. [I] then told the President that in my opinion he was misinterpreting the Department's position. We were most definitely not washing our hands of Venezuela's problem. We understood and appreciated Venezuela's position at this critical electoral period with respect to very clear efforts by the Cubans to cause trouble. We had access to the same intelligence information he did. The Department's reaction, I said, was that of a friend and ally offering advice. We were counseling caution and the importance of playing the game according to the rules to avoid giving our common enemy an argument against Venezuela which could be used effectively in the UN and other international forums and as an excuse for reprisal. This was the tactic followed by us in our dealings with Cuba, the Soviet Union and the Communist world as a whole in the face of provocation. We felt it important for Venezuela to act only when sure of its position. In effect, I said, we were asking the President to "cool it." This apparently struck his fancy since he smiled broadly and visibly relaxed.

4. The President said that there was no question that the Cubans would allege that the vessel was seized outside of Venezuelan territorial waters. Venezuela's position was that the vessel was seized within Venezuela's territorial waters. There was no reason to believe the Cubans more than the Venezuelans. In the case of the *Pueblo*, the North Koreans claimed that it was seized within North Korean territorial waters while we claimed it was seized outside of territorial waters. As far as the President was concerned, Venezuela has acted in accordance with the rules and very definitely intended to do so in the future—that is, exercise its sovereignty over suspicious vessels when they were in Venezuelan territorial waters. He said Venezuela had no desire to impede the right of innocent passage. The important thing was that the passage had to be innocent. If foreign vessels wanted to transmit Venezuelan waters, there was nothing to prevent them from doing so by notifying the Venezuelan authorities of their intention. If, however,

---

[4] In a November 29 letter to Vaky, Bernbaum expressed fear that emphasizing Cuban access to "highly sophisticated equipment" may have backfired, noting "the emotional reactions of both Leoni and Leandro Mora to our admonition as an indication that they could not count on U.S. support." Although Leoni only hinted at the consequence, Leandro Mora was more explicit: if the Venezuelans "did not get the necessary equipment from us they would turn to Europe." Bernbaum admitted: "I have been kicking myself for having conveyed that portion of the Department's telegram to Leoni. We are now, unfortunately, in the position of having stimulated a desire, even demand, by the Venezuelans for the kind of equipment we don't want to furnish them and probably cannot furnish them in view of the temper of our Congress. I am afraid that both ARA and I fell down on this one." (National Archives and Records Administration, RG 59, Central Files 1967–69, POL 33–4 VEN–CUBA)

foreign vessels were found in Venezuelan waters, particularly vessels of countries to be considered hostile, it was incumbent upon the GOV to make certain of their bona fides. In this case, the Cuban fishing vessel was called upon to stop. Instead of acceding to this legitimate request, it ignored it, therefore rendering itself suspect. The President said that as far as he was concerned, any Cuban vessel found in Venezuelan territorial waters was going to be looked upon as suspicious. Fidel Castro was now on notice to that effect.

5. The conversation then turned to the domestic situation. The President said that the Communists presumably with Cuban assistance were planning to stage disturbances in Caracas with the allegation of electoral fraud. Subversive elements were infiltrating Caracas for that purpose. Recent assistance from Cuba was substantial and was continuing. A UPA announcement published in *Ultimas Noticias* on November 18 for all practical purposes represented a declaration of war. The GOV did not look upon this threat as dangerous but it was required to take all precautionary measures. The investigation of the Cuban vessel had to be appraised in the light of this situation.

6. Although I do not think that the President's ire and preoccupation over our position has been eliminated, I do believe that I left him in a considerably more relaxed state of mind and conscious of the need for caution in the future. I think it important that we have his problem in mind during any UN debate which may ensure and avoid statements which might tend to exacerbate GOV suspicions and concern without necessarily supporting this specific Venezuelan action, in the debate which may take place, reference by us to historically demonstrated Cuban subversive intervention in Venezuela and to its continuation would be in order and well received in Venezuela and other parts of LA. The Communists would do no less for their allies.[5]

Bernbaum

---

[5] The *Alecrin* was allowed to return to Cuba on December 20, nearly 3 weeks after the Presidential elections on December 1. The Venezuelan Foreign Ministry released a statement admitting that, "although vessel's way of proceeding was suspicious, no proof was found to confirm that ship was being used for transport of guerrillas or weapons." (Telegram 9396 from Caracas, December 21; ibid., POL 33–4 CUBA–VEN)

548.   Information Memorandum From the President's Special Assistant (Rostow) to President Johnson[1]

Washington, December 9, 1968, 6:35 p.m.

SUBJECT

Venezuelan Elections

The Christian Democratic candidate, Rafael Caldera, has finally been declared winner in Venezuela by the narrowest of margins.[2] He won by about 30,000 votes, or a margin of approximately 29 percent to 28.4 percent for his nearest rival. The election was held in remarkably good order, and there is every indication that power will pass peacefully to the opposition next March for the first time in Venezuela's recent history.

President-elect Caldera is founder of Venezuela's Christian Democratic Party, and has run unsuccessfully several times before for the presidency. He is able, responsible, and a moderate leftist—an expert in the field of labor law—and a strong anti-communist. He knows the United States well, and has supported the Alliance for Progress in general while criticizing "errors of operation".

Caldera's Party will be the second largest in the Congress and will have to form a coalition to put through a program. He may be somewhat more nationalistic in his dealings with American oil companies in Venezuela, but the general lines of Venezuelan policy toward the United States should continue after he takes office.[3]

Walt

---

[1] Source: Johnson Library, National Security File, Country File, Venezuela, Filed by LBJ Library. Confidential. A notation on the memorandum indicates the President saw it.

[2] In a December 3 memorandum to the President, Rostow reported that the election was "still too close to call," with Caldera clinging to a narrow lead over Barrios, the AD candidate. Rostow noted: "Either man would be satisfactory from our viewpoint, although Caldera would probably take a somewhat more nationalistic position on economic matters." (Ibid.)

[3] In telegram 9245 from Caracas, December 10, the Embassy analyzed the election results. (National Archives and Records Administration, RG 59, Central Files, 1967–69, POL 14 VEN) In airgram A–1366 from Caracas, December 13, the Embassy assessed the implications of the election for the United States. (Ibid., POL VEN)

Index

Note: All references are to document numbers

Ackley, H. Gardner, 289
Acosta Bonilla, Manuel, 104, 106, 108, 118
Adair, Charles W., Jr., 433, 440, 443, 444, 447, 448, 449, 450, 452, 455
Adair, E. Ross, 249, 489
Adams, Robert W., 18, 26, 28, 74, 149, 151, 188, 190, 193, 198, 200, 201, 203, 208, 255, 266, 272, 349, 524
Adenauer, Konrad, 346
Adhemar Pereira de Barros, 182, 184, 186, 187, 201, 209 AFL-CIO, 81, 117, 152
Agüero Rocha, Fernando, 90, 91, 92, 93, 94, 95, 96
Ahumada, Jorge, 274, 276
Aiken, George, 39
Ailes, Stephen, 279, 368, 419, 421, 424, 425
Akers, Robert Wood, 302
Alejos, Roberto, 75
Alemán, Roberto, 450
Alessandri Rodríguez, Jorge, 260, 261, 264
Alexander, Archibald S. 65
Allen, Ward P., 4, 5, 7, 14, 58
Allende Gossens, Salvador, 16, 173, 303
   Chilean Presidential election of 1964, 247, 249, 250, 251, 253, 254, 259, 260, 261, 264, 268, 269
   U.S. assessment of, 251
Alliance for Progress:
   Central American Export Development Program, 119
   Coordinator for, proposed, 43
   Counterinsurgency program, 3, 4, 6, 28, 61, 63
   Democracy and dictators, approach to (Mann Doctrine), 10
   Economic program, 41, 42, 44, 45, 46, 48, 49, 51, 52, 62, 69, 71
   Fourth Anniversary celebration of, 30
   Frontier development in South America, 40
   Funding for, 15
   Gordon appointment as Assistant Secretary of State, 37
   Inter-American Committee on the Alliance for Progress (CIAP), 1, 2, 10, 12, 13, 40, 67, 330

Alliance for Progress—*Continued*
   Johnson visit to Central American, 111, 112
   Johnson meeting with Latin American Ambassadors, 13
   Johnson meeting with Latin American Foreign Ministers, 21
   Johnson meeting with U.S. Ambassadors to Latin America, 18
   Johnson speech (*1964*), 10
   Kennedy visit to Latin American, 31, 32, 33
   Military program, 11, 25, 29, 65, 66, 67
   Oliver appointment as Assistant Secretary of State, 43
   Oliver visit to Latin American, 68, 69
   Presidents' meeting in *1965*, proposed, 26
   Press coverage, 2, 10, 12, 17, 49, 52
   Public relations efforts, 31, 43
   Rusk visit to Latin American, 33
Alsogaray, Alvaro C., 136, 138, 143
Alsogaray, Gen. Julio R., 128, 136
Alter, Gerald M., 313
Alves, Osvino, 205
Alves Bastos, Comdr. Justino, 192, 201
American and Foreign Power Company (AMFORP), 183, 212, 214
Ampuero Díaz, Raúl, 251, 260
Anaconda Copper Company, 257, 278, 282, 284, 285, 287, 289
Âncora, Gen. Armando de Morais, 203
Anderson, Clinton P., 353, 536
Anderson, Robert B., 1, 284, 452, 456
   Panama Canal treaty negotiations, 408, 409, 410, 417, 419, 421, 425, 427, 428, 429, 432, 434, 435, 437, 438, 440
Andrade, Victor, 159
Andreazza, Mario David, 230
Angueiras, 456
Anthis, Gen., 28
Aragão, Adm. Cândida, 191, 205
Aragão, Gen. Moniz de, 240
Arango, Augusto, 371, 450
Arango, William, 375
Arco Galindo, Juan de, 398
Arenales Catalán, Emilio, 103, 113

1143

All references are to document numbers

Index

Note: All references are to document numbers

All references are to document numbers

All references are to document numbers

All references are to document numbers

Johnson, Lyndon B.—*Continued*
 Paraguay, 469
 Peru, 470
  Attitude toward Belaunde, 499
  Communications with Belaunde,
   475, 477
  Coup of *1968*, 497, 499, 507, 509,
   510, 511, 515
  Military aircraft purchases and U.S.
   economic assistance, 488, 489,
   490, 492, 494, 495, 497, 498,
   499, 500
  Oil expropriations and U.S.
   economic assistance, 16, 475,
   476, 477, 478, 479, 480, 481,
   483, 484, 486, 487, 488, 489,
   500, 504, 515
  U.S. economic/development
   assistance, 508
  U.S. recognition of military junta,
   509, 511, 515, 518, 519, 520
 Sayre appointment to NSC staff, 17
 Uruguay, 16, 459, 466, 468
 Vaughn appointment as Assistant
  Secretary of State, 27
 Venezuela:
  British Guiana border dispute,
   536
  Communications with Leoni, 525,
   543
  Cuban arms cache in Venezuela,
   OAS resolution on, 8, 9, 14, 16,
   19, 21, 22
  Cuban infiltration of Venezuela,
   OAS action on, 50, 53, 55, 57,
   59, 60, 64
  Meeting with Barrios, 535, 536
  Meeting with Leoni, 50, 540, 541
  Oil exports to United States, 525,
   526, 527, 530, 532, 534, 536,
   540, 543
  Presidential election of *1968*, 548
  U.S. military/security assistance,
   61, 541
Johnson, U. Alexis, 3, 4, 5, 188, 193, 196,
 201, 202, 203, 205, 207, 222, 250,
 257
Johnson, W. Thomas, 42, 69, 490, 519
Johnston, James D., 285, 472
Johnston, James R., 91
Joint Chiefs of Staff (JCS), 25, 29, 65,
 192, 196, 198, 206, 381, 471
 Panama Canal treaty negotiations,
  394, 420, 421, 437

Jones, J. Wesley, 33, 311, 478
Peru:
 Constitutional government,
  proposed return to, 516
 Coup of *1968*, 499, 501, 507, 510,
  516, 521
 Military aircraft purchases and U.S.
  economic assistance, 485, 491,
  493, 495, 496, 499, 500, 501, 502
 Oil expropriations and U.S.
  economic assistance, 470, 472,
  474, 475, 477, 479, 480, 486,
  491, 501, 514, 516, 517
 U.S. economic/development
  assistance, 505, 508
 U.S. recognition of military junta,
  512, 513, 514, 516, 517
Jones, James R., 59, 63, 234, 332, 359, 484
Jorden, William J., 399
Jova, Joseph John, 74, 104, 107, 108, 117,
 118, 251, 252, 254, 255, 260, 263,
 272, 276
Jurema, Abelardo, 205

Kampelman, Max, 79
Karamessines, Thomas H., 171, 172, 304
Katzenbach, Nicholas deB., 65, 66, 67,
 71, 103, 105, 109, 110, 144, 300, 302,
 339, 364, 469, 494, 500, 502, 508,
 512, 544
Kaunda, Kenneth, 285
Kemper, James S., 338
Kendall, Brig. Gen. M.W., 449
Kennecott Company, 278, 282, 285, 288
Kennedy, Jacqueline, 183
Kennedy, John F., 3, 73, 208, 346, 369,
 370, 372, 376, 465, 528
Kennedy, Robert F., 37, 94, 162, 208,
 469, 479, 480
 Latin American visit, 31, 32, 33
 U.S. counterinsurgency program in
  Latin America, 3
Kent, Sherman, 441
Khrushchev, Nikita S., 16
Kilday, Lowell C., 341
Killoran, Thomas F., 98, 113, 117
King, Col. J. C., 148, 187, 188, 191, 202,
 203, 206, 245, 248, 252, 255, 256,
 257, 377
King, Thelma, 376
Kitchen, Jeffrey C., 196
Klein, Dave, 17
Klutznick, Philip, 433
Knoche, Enno Henry, 245

All references are to document numbers

All references are to document numbers

All references are to document numbers

All references are to document numbers

All references are to document numbers